TO THE INSTRUCTOR

WileyPLUS is built around the activities you perform

Prepare & Present

Create outstanding class presentations using a wealth of resources, such as PowerPoint™ slides, image galleries, interactive simulations, and more. Plus you can easily upload any materials you have created into your course, and combine them with the resources Wiley provides you with.

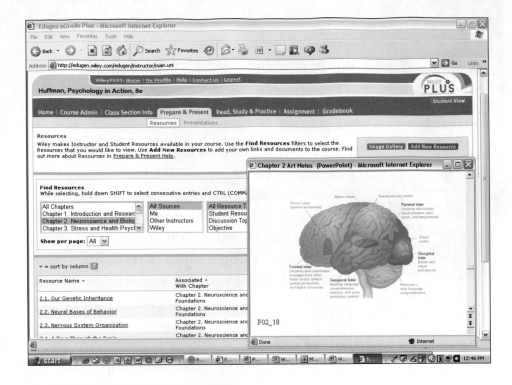

Create Assignments

Automate the assigning and grading of homework or quizzes by using the provided question banks, or by writing your own. Student results will be automatically graded and recorded in your gradebook. WileyPLUS also links homework problems to relevant sections of the online text, hints, or solutions— context-sensitive help where students need it most!

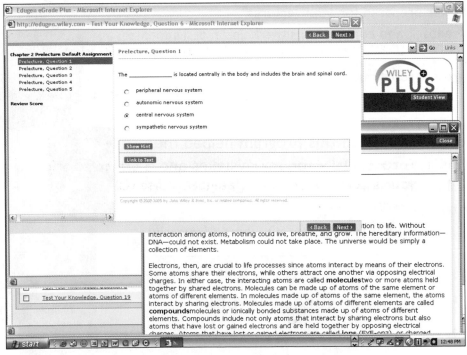

*Based on a spring 2005 survey of 972 student users of WileyPLUS

Track Student Progress

Keep track of your students' progress via an instructor's gradebook, which allows you to analyze individual and overall class results. This gives you an accurate and realistic assessment of your students' progress and level of understanding.

Now Available with WebCT and Blackboard!

Now you can seamlessly integrate all of the rich content and resources available with *WileyPLUS* with the power and convenience of your WebCT or BlackBoard course. You and your students get the best of both worlds with single sign-on, an integrated gradebook, list of assignments and roster, and more. If your campus is using another course management system, contact your local Wiley Representative.

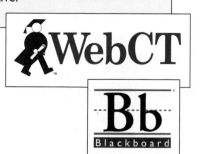

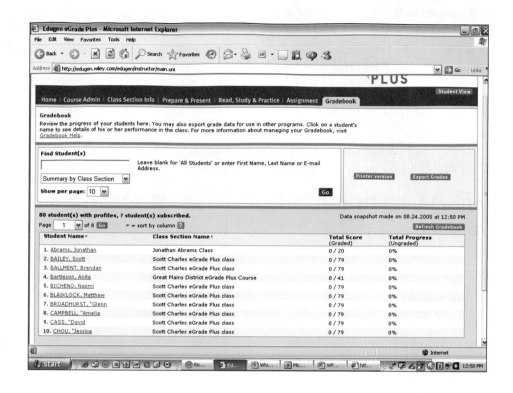

"I studied more for this class than I would have without *WileyPLUS*."

Melissa Lawler, *Western Washington Univ.*

For more information on what *WileyPLUS* can do to help your students reach their potential, please visit

www.wiley.com/college/wileyplus

76% of students surveyed said it made them better prepared for tests. *

TO THE STUDENT

You have the potential to make a difference!

Will you be the first person to land on Mars? Will you invent a car that runs on water? But, first and foremost, will you get through this course?

WileyPLUS is a powerful online system packed with features to help you make the most of your potential, and get the best grade you can!

With Wiley**PLUS** you get:

A complete online version of your text and other study resources

Study more effectively and get instant feedback when you practice on your own. Resources like self-assessment quizzes, tutorials, and animations bring the subject matter to life, and help you master the material.

Problem-solving help, instant grading, and feedback on your homework and quizzes

You can keep all of your assigned work in one location, making it easy for you to stay on task. Plus, many homework problems contain direct links to the relevant portion of your text to help you deal with problem-solving obstacles at the moment they come up.

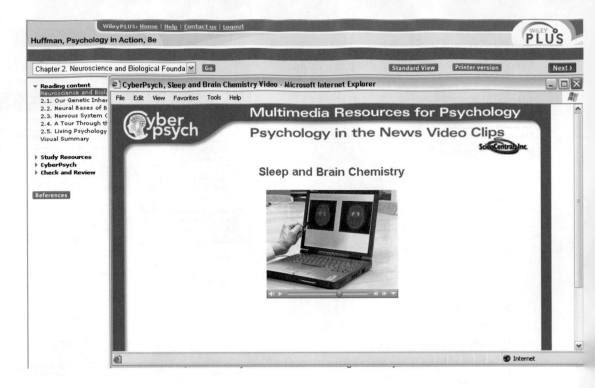

The ability to track your progress and grades throughout the term.

A personal gradebook allows you to monitor your results from past assignments at any time. You'll always know exactly where you stand.

If your instructor uses *WileyPLUS*, you will receive a URL for your class. If not, your instructor can get more information about *WileyPLUS* by visiting www.wiley.com/college/wileyplus

---

"It has been a great help, and I believe it has helped me to achieve a better grade."

Michael Morris, *Columbia Basin College*

69% of students surveyed said it helped them get a better grade.*

PSYCHOLOGY IN ACTION

EIGHTH EDITION

KAREN HUFFMAN

PALOMAR COLLEGE

WILEY

John Wiley & Sons, Inc.

VICE PRESIDENT & PUBLISHER	Jay O'Callaghan
EXECUTIVE EDITOR	Christopher T. Johnson
ASSOCIATE EDITOR	Jessica Bartelt
EXECUTIVE MARKETING MANAGER	Jeffrey Rucker
EDITORIAL ASSISTANT	Katie Melega
SENIOR PRODUCTION EDITOR	Sandra Dumas
CREATIVE DIRECTOR	Harry Nolan
SENIOR DESIGNER	Kevin Murphy
SENIOR ILLUSTRATION EDITOR	Anna Melhorn
PHOTO DEPARTMENT MANAGER	Hilary Newman
SENIOR PHOTO EDITOR	Jennifer MacMillan
PHOTO RESEARCHER	Elyse Rieder
MEDIA EDITOR	Lynn Pearlman
PRODUCTION MANAGEMENT SERVICES	Hermitage Publishing Services
COVER PHOTO	©2005 Lois Greenfield
INTERIOR DESIGN	Michael Jung
COVER DESIGN	David Levy

This book was typeset in 10/12 Janson by Hermitage Publishing Services and printed and bound by Von Hoffmann Corporation. The cover was printed by Lehigh Press.

This book is printed on acid-free paper. ∞

Huffman, Karen.
Psychology In Action, Eighth Edition

ISBN-13   978- 0-471-74724-6
ISBN-10   0-471-74724-6

Printed in the United States of America

10   9   8   7   6   5   4   3   2

CONTENTS IN BRIEF

CONTENTS

• • • •

Note: Chapters 17 and 18 available separately upon request.

PREFACE

> Dancing is the loftiest, the most moving, the most beautiful of the arts, because it is no mere translation or abstraction from life; it is life itself.
>
> HAVELOCK ELLIS, 1859–1939

Like *dance* is to the *arts*, *psychology* is the loftiest, the most moving, and the most beautiful of all sciences—at least to this author! Did you notice the beautiful and inspiring dancer on the cover of this book? Have you ever wondered why authors, editors, or publishers choose certain paintings or photos for their books? In our case, we chose a dancer for our cover to capture the theme or essence of this text: *Dance as an inspiration and metaphor for teaching and learning psychology.*

Ellis believes dance is life itself, but so too is psychology. Psychology can enlighten, entertain, and lift all of us to great heights. Unfortunately, studies find that introductory or general psychology is the only formal course in psychology that most students will ever encounter. Can one text and one course cover all the major concepts and theories, while still presenting the exciting and practical applications of psychology?

As the author of this text and a full-time teacher of psychology, I take this as an intimidating, but provocative, challenge. To meet it, I must be a "master choreographer." I must lead my readers and students step-by-step through the basic foundations of psychology. At the same time, I must provide time and space for "dance practice" in order to set the stage for a well-choreographed learning experience. In this psychology text, I present concise, straight-forward concepts, key terms, and theories, followed by quick activities (self-tests, check & review), examples (case studies/personal stories), and demonstrations (Try This Yourself, Visual Quizzes). Beginning with the first edition in 1987, this text has always emphasized active learning—hence the title "Psychology in *Action.*" Each edition has continued and improved upon this foundation.

WHAT'S NEW IN THE EIGHTH EDITION?

The latest edition of *Psychology in Action* takes active learning to an even higher level. To help insure student success, I have added several new pedagogical features and integrated them with the previous aids into three distinct, but overlapping "A's"— *Application*, *Achievement*, and *Assessment* (Figure 1).

Application

The first "A," **Application**, is essential to learning. As most instructors (and students) know, true understanding is much more than a simple memorization of terms and concepts to be retrieved during exams — and then quickly forgotten. To truly master psychology you must question, debate, experiment, and *apply* psychological principles to your everyday life.

As you can see in the left hand side of Figure 1, *Psychology in Action (8e)* includes numerous pedagogical aids dedicated to practical *applications* of psychology. Students often ask, "Why do I need to know this?" and "How does this help me in my everyday life?" Using specific terms and concepts found within that chapter, each of these aids clearly demonstrates the immediate relevance and application of psychology to everyday life.

My newest application pedagogical aid is the small introductory motivational boxes that open each chapter. These *Why Study Psychology?* boxes contain 4 to 6 bulleted highlights focusing on *what psychology can do for you*, which help stimulate interest and involvement in the upcoming material.

My second new feature, *Case Study/Personal Story*, provides background details of a person's life or experience related to the psychological topic discussed in the chapter. For

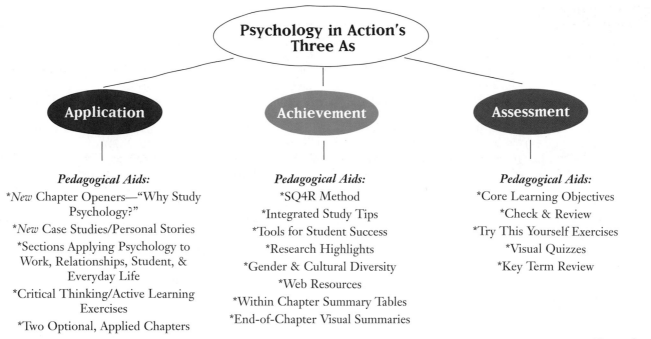

Psychology in Action's Three As

Application

Pedagogical Aids:
*New Chapter Openers—"Why Study Psychology?"
*New Case Studies/Personal Stories
*Sections Applying Psychology to Work, Relationships, Student, & Everyday Life
*Critical Thinking/Active Learning Exercises
*Two Optional, Applied Chapters

Achievement

Pedagogical Aids:
*SQ4R Method
*Integrated Study Tips
*Tools for Student Success
*Research Highlights
*Gender & Cultural Diversity
*Web Resources
*Within Chapter Summary Tables
*End-of-Chapter Visual Summaries

Assessment

Pedagogical Aids:
*Core Learning Objectives
*Check & Review
*Try This Yourself Exercises
*Visual Quizzes
*Key Term Review

Figure 1

example, Chapter 12 discusses research on emotional intelligence and the Case Study/Personal Story describes the emotional intelligence of Abraham Lincoln.

In addition to these two new pedagogical aids, I also continue the previous sections called *Applying Psychology to Work, Relationships, Student, and Everyday Life*. These expanded applications are closely related to chapter content. For example, Chapter 1 includes a special section, "Applying Psychology to Work: Careers in the Field," which provides job descriptions and opportunities within the field of psychology. Chapter 3's, "Applying Psychology to Student Life: Why You Shouldn't Procrastinate," provides research information and tips for overcoming this all-too-common problem. Table 1 presents a complete list of all applying psychology special topics, along with other highlights from *Psychology in Action* (8e)

TABLE 1 SAMPLE APPLICATION HIGHLIGHTS FROM *PSYCHOLOGY IN ACTION* 8E

Application of Psychology (in addition to the shorter discussions and examples throughout the text):

- Applying Psychology to Work: Careers in the Field (pp. 7–9)
- Applying Psychology to Everyday Life: Becoming a Better Consumer of Scientific Research (pp. 39–40)
- Applying Psychology to Everyday Life: How Neurotransmitters and Hormones Affect Us (pp. 59–63)
- Applying Psychology to Everyday Life: Overcoming Genetic Misconceptions (pp. 87–88)
- Applying Psychology to Student Life: Why You Shouldn't Procrastinate (pp. 105–106)
- Applying Psychology to Work: Would You Like to Be a Health Psychologist? (p. 112)
- Applying Psychology to Work: Is My Job Too Stressful? (pp. 118–119)
- Applying Psychology to Everyday Life: Problems with Believing in Extrasensory Perception (p. 164)
- Applying Psychology to Everyday Life: Self-Help for Sleep Problems (pp. 187–188)
- Applying Psychology to Everyday Life: Club Drug Alert! (pp. 195–196)
- Applying Psychology to Everyday Life: Classical Conditioning (pp. 236–238)
- Applying Psychology to Everyday Life: Operant Conditioning (pp. 239–241)
- Applying Psychology to Everyday Life: Cognitive-Social Learning (pp. 241–242)
- Applying Psychology to Student Life: Improving Long-Term Memory (pp. 258–261)

(table continues)

TABLE 1 (CONTINUED)

- Applying Psychology to Student Life: Overcoming Problems with Forgetting (pp. 265–266)
- Applying Psychology to Everyday Life: Recognizing Barriers to Problem Solving (pp. 293–295)
- Applying Psychology to Everyday Life: Are Your Marital Expectations Unrealistic? (pp. 373–374)
- Applying Psychology to Everyday Life: Dealing with Your Own Death Anxiety (p. 384)
- Applying Psychology to Relationships: Protection Against STIs (pp. 413–415)

- Applying Psychology to Student Life: Overcoming Test Anxiety (p. 425)
- Applying Psychology to Student Life: Testing Your Knowledge of Abnormal Behavior (p. 530)
- Applying Psychology at Work: Careers in Mental Health (p. 561)
- Applying Psychology to Everyday Life: What's Wrong with Movie Portrayals of Therapy? (p. 567)
- Applying Psychology to Relationships: The Art and Science of Flirting (pp. 585–586)

Select Samples of Psychological Science (in addition to the shorter discussions and examples found throughout the text):

Psychological Science Research Methods

- Basic versus applied research (p. 17)
- The scientific method (pp. 17–21)
- Ethical guidelines for research with human and nonhuman animals (pp. 21–23)
- Experimental, descriptive, correlational, and biological research (pp. 24–40)
- Methods for studying behavioral genetics (pp. 85–87)
- Split-brain research (pp. 78–83)
- Is there scientific evidence for subliminal perception and ESP? (pp. 162–163)
- How scientists study sleep (pp. 176–180)
- Discovering classical conditioning (pp. 209–213)
- Studying language development in human and nonhuman animals (pp. 303–305)
- Scientific measures of intelligence (pp. 309–312)
- Research methods for life span development (pp. 327–331)
- Scientific measures of personality (pp. 482–487)

Neuroscience

- Biological methods of research (pp. 36–39)
- How neurotransmitters and hormones affect us (pp. 59–63)
- Rewiring, repairing, and transplanting brains and spinal cords (pp. 90–91)
- Neuroplasticity, neurogenesis, and stem cell research (pp. 90–91)
- Psychoneuroimmunology (p. 104)
- Phantom pain and phantom limbs (p. 135)
- Biology of sleep and dreams (pp. 179–182)
- Biology and psychoactive drugs (pp. 196–197)
- Neuroscience and learning (p. 233)
- Neuronal and synaptic changes in memory (p. 269)
- Hormonal changes and memory (pp. 269–270)
- Where are memories stored? (pp. 270–271)
- Biology and memory loss (pp. 272–273)
- Biological influences on intelligence, including brain size, speed, and efficiency (pp. 317–319)
- Brain changes during development (pp. 335–336)
- Brain's role in gender differences and sexual behavior (pp. 395–397, 409–411)
- Biological processes and motivation (pp. 423–436)
- Brain and emotion (pp. 437–438)
- Biological aspects of personality (pp. 480–482)

- Biological contributors to mental disorders (pp. 510, 514, 521–522, 528–529)
- Biomedical psychotherapy (pp. 555–559)
- Biology of aggression (pp. 601–602)

Behavioral Genetics

- Basic principles and recent research (pp. 84–85)
- Methods for studying (pp. 85–87)
- Genetic influences on intelligence and the Bell Curve debate (pp. 317–319)
- Nature versus nurture controversy (pp. 327–328)
- Attachment and imprinting (pp. 349–352)
- Genetics and aging (p. 340)
- Genetic influences on eating disorders (pp. 430–433)
- Genetic contributions to personality (pp. 481)
- The role of genetics in mental disorders (pp. 510, 514, 521)
- Genetic contributors to aggression (p. 602)

Evolutionary Psychology

- Genetics and evolution (pp. 87–88)
- Basic principles such as natural selection (p. 87)
- Evolution of sex differences (pp. 88–90)
- Evolutionary/circadian theory of sleep (p. 181)
- Evolution and learning (pp. 233–235)
- Classical conditioning, taste aversions, and biological preparedness (pp. 233–234)
- Operant conditioning and instinctive drift (pp. 234–235)
- Evolution and language development (pp. 301–302)
- Evolution and emotions (pp. 450–452)
- Evolution and personality (pp. 463–464)
- Evolution and aggression (pp. 601–602)
- Evolution and altruism (pp. 605–606)

Cognitive Psychology

- Bottom-up and top-down processing (p. 160)
- Cognitive view of dreams (pp. 182–183)
- Cognitive-social learning (pp. 228–232)
- Memory processes and problems (pp. 248–273)
- Thinking, creativity, language, and intelligence (pp. 286–320)
- Cognitive development over the life span (pp. 341–349)
- Cognitive theories of motivation and emotion (pp. 425–427)
- Social-cognitive approaches to personality (pp. 478–479)
- Cognitive processes in mental disorders (pp. 509, 514–516, 522–523)

TABLE 1 (CONTINUED)

- Cognitive therapy (pp. 541–544)
- Cognitive processes in attitudes and prejudice (pp. 577–583)

Positive Psychology
- Dealing with pseudopsychology (pp. 5–6)
- Ethical research (pp. 21–23)
- Overcoming genetic misconceptions (pp. 87–88)
- Better living through neuroscience (pp. 90–91)
- Wellness (pp. 98–124)
- Hardiness (pp. 108–109)
- Biofeedback and behavior modificaiton for improved health (p. 117)
- Health and stress management (pp. 119–124)
- Preventing hearing loss (pp. 142–143)
- Understanding and overcoming sleep disorders (pp. 185–188)
- Healthier routes to alternate states (pp. 199–202)
- Attaining the benefits of meditation (p. 200)
- Therapeutic uses of hypnosis (p. 201)
- Successful use of reinforcement and punishment (pp. 224–225)
- Overcoming prejudice and discrimination (pp. 236–242)

- Understanding and overcoming superstition (pp. 240–241)
- Improving and understanding memory (pp. 248–280)
- Improved problem-solving (pp. 291–296)
- Creativity and multiple intelligences (pp. 297–299, 306–308)
- Promoting secure attachment and positive parenting (pp. 349–354)
- Romantic love and attachment (pp. 352–353)
- Marriage and family health and improvement (pp. 372–377)
- Positive careers and retirement (pp. 377–380)
- Positive aspects of aging and dying (pp. 381–385)
- Moral behavior (pp. 362–367)
- Benefits of androgyny (pp. 397–398)
- High achievers (pp. 434–435)
- Emotional intelligence (pp. 448–450)
- Suicide and its prevention (p. 515)
- How your thoughts can make you depressed (p. 516)
- Love and interpersonal attraction (pp. 583–594)
- Aggression understanding and reducing (pp. 601–604)
- Altruism and helping behaviors (pp. 604–606)
- Reducing prejudice and discrimination (pp. 608–609)
- Reducing destructive obedience (pp. 609–610)

Further applications are provided with each chapter's in-depth *Critical Thinking/Active Learning Exercises* located at the appropriate place in each chapter. These exercises are based on specific chapter content and devoted to developing various critical thinking skills. For example, the Critical Thinking/Active Learning Exercise in Chapter 16 asks readers, "Would you have obeyed Milgram's directions?" and helps develop independent thinking as a critical thinking skill.

Perhaps the most comprehensive and detailed applications are the two optional chapters. In response to increasing demand for more coverage of how psychology applies to business and work in the 21st century, we provide *Industrial/Organizational Psychology* (Chapter 17) and *Human Performance in a Global Economy* (Chapter 18). These chapters are available as a shrink-wrapped option to interested professors and their students. These chapters were co-authored by Gary Piggrem, a professor of psychology at DeVry University, and they provide a general overview of industrial/organizational psychology, along with an extended discussion of communication, conflict management, leadership, and persuasion techniques.

▣ Achievement

The second "A" is for Achievement. To fully master and understand information, you must employ a form of *metacognition*, which requires watching and evaluating your own thought processes. In other words, you must "think about your thinking and learning."

To help insure metacognition, and this type of achievement, *Psychology in Action* (8e) helps students examine and refine their personal studying and learning style. For example, this text incorporates one of the most respected study techniques, the *SQ4R Method (Survey, Question, Read, Recite, Review, and "wRite")*:

Survey and Question
Each chapter begins with four *survey* and *question* techniques: core learning outcomes, a chapter outline, a vignette that introduces essential concepts, and an introductory paragraph that previews content and organization.

Read

Each chapter has been carefully crafted for clarity, conciseness, and student *reading* level.

Recite and Review

To encourage *recitation* and *review*, the text offers a short *Check & Review* section that summarizes the previous material and offers four or five multiple-choice, fill-in, and short answer questions. An additional aid, the *Visual Summaries* at the end of each chapter, helps visually organize and connect essential chapter concepts. Each chapter also concludes with a review activity for the key terms that is topically organized with page references.

wRite

As part of the fourth R in the SQ4R method, this book is designed to incorporate *writing* as a way of improving student retention. In addition to the writing students do in the survey, question, and review sections, note taking is encouraged in the margin of each page, which have been kept as clear as possible. The Instructor's Manual, which accompanies this text, also describes a special "marginal marking" technique that can be easily taught to students. The accompanying *Student Study and Review Guide* discusses the SQ4R method in more detail.

In addition to the SQ4R method, this text also includes *Integrated Study Tips* (which appear throughout the text) offering specific techniques to improve learning and retention. For example, the study tip in Chapter 8 (p. 302) helps clarify overgeneralization and overextension. The study tip on positive and negative symptoms of schizophrenia in Chapter 14 (p. 520) incorporates earlier concepts of positive and negative as applied to reinforcement found in Chapter 6.

To help students become more efficient and successful, this text also includes a special feature called *Tools for Student Success*. Beginning in Chapter 1, there is a special end-of-chapter module that includes tips for active reading, time management, and improving course grades, as well as important resources for college success. In addition, several student success sections identified with a special icon are sprinkled throughout the text. For example, Chapters 6, 7, 8, 10, and 13 all include strategies for improving learning strategies, memory, test performance, and overall achievement.

To further increase metacognition and achievement, the Eighth Edition also offers the following special features:

• *Research Highlights* — Promotes understanding of the intricacies of scientific research.

• *Gender and Cultural Diversity Sections* — Encourages appreciation of similarities and differences between men and women and various cultures.

• *Web Resources* — Suggests Web sites that further Internet exploration of important psychological topics.

• *Within Chapter Summary Tables* — To increase student insight and "aha" experiences, I include numerous *Summary Tables*, some containing important illustrations, such as the table on drug actions and neurotransmitters in Chapter 5. The tables that compare classical and operant conditioning in Chapter 6 and contrasting theories of memory in Chapter 7 also serve as important educational tools.

• *End-of-Chapter Visual Summaries* — Each chapter of the text ends with a unique study tool that visually summarizes and organizes the main concepts. This *Visual Summary* is a two-page spread that can be used both as an overview to get the big picture before reading the chapter, and as a quick review after completing the reading. Students, faculty, and reviewers are all very excited by this feature. They report finding it "extremely helpful" and "the best study tool ever invented!"

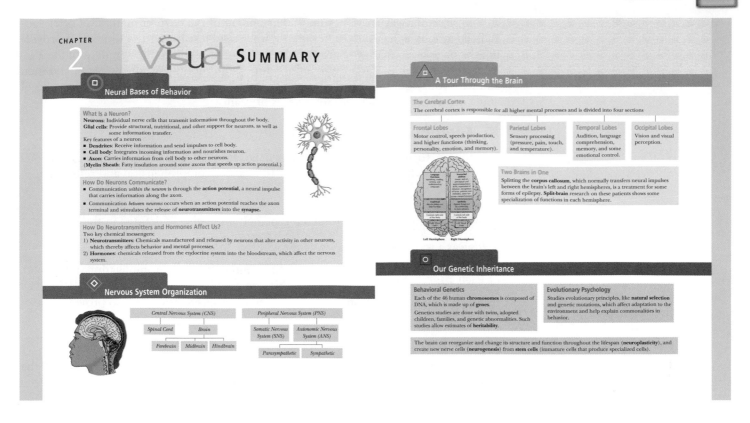

Assessment

The third A, **Assessment**, requires you to demonstrate your learning — to yourself and others. To do this, each chapter opens with 4 to 6 *Core Learning Outcomes* that model the type of questions you should ask and answer as you read the chapter. These objectives are repeated as a reminder and guidepost in the margin next to the section where the topic is discussed.

In addition to the core learning outcomes, numerous *Check and Review* sections are sprinkled throughout each chapter. This pedagogical aid provides a brief review of the preceding material, followed by a self-scoring quiz with 4 to 5 multiple choice, fill-in, or short-answer questions. I've also invented and included two unique pedagogical aids—*Try This Yourself* and *Visual Quizzes*. The widely copied Try This Yourself feature provides an opportunity to actively apply your knowledge with brief, hands-on exercises and demonstrations, high-interest and simple-to-do experiments, and self-scoring personal inventories. For example, many people do not know that each of their eyes has a tiny "blind spot" at the center of the retina in which no visual information is received or transmitted. The *Try This Yourself* exercise on page 139 shows how you can test this for yourself.

The second unique feature is what I call *Visual Quizzes*. After watching many students open their books and turn immediately to the photos and cartoons, I wondered how I could use this natural interest to foster greater mastery and appreciation of important psychological concepts and terms. My answer? Turn these photos and cartoons into a form of assessment. Like the *Try This Yourself* exercises, the *Visual Quizzes* require active participation and provide a form of self-testing and assessment. As a reader, you are asked to answer a specific question about a photo, cartoon, or figure which requires a mastery of key terms or concepts. To assess your understanding, the correct answer is printed upside down directly below the photo or cartoon (see Figure 2).

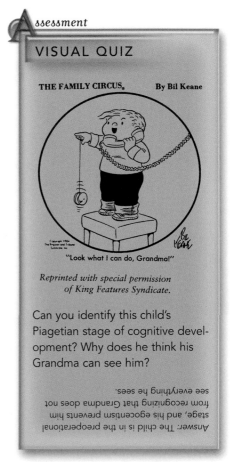

Figure 2

As a further way to asses your understanding of the chapter material, I offer special end-of-chapter *Key Term Reviews*. Rather than just listing the terms and providing the page references, you are reminded: "To assess your understanding of the Key Terms in Chapter ___, write a definition for each term (in your own words), and then compare your definitions with those in the text." This is an important assessment tool and a great way to review before quizzes or exams.

Additional Learning Aids

In addition to the previously mentioned pedagogical aids, *Psychology in Action (8e)* incorporates other learning aids known to increase comprehension and retention:

Key terms

Important terms are put in **boldface type** and immediately defined in the text.

Running glossary

Key terms also appear with their definitions and a phonetic pronunciation in the margin of each page near where they are first introduced. Calling out and defining key terms in the margin not only increases overall comprehension, it also provides a useful review tool.

End-of-text glossary

All key terms are also gathered in a complete, cumulative glossary at the end of the text.

Historical timeline

A grouping of famous contributors to psychology on the text's back endpapers provides a visual organizer and overview of the history of psychology.

ADDITIONAL CHANGES

In addition to the increased focus on the 3 A's (*application*, *achievement*, and *assessment*), the new edition of *Psychology in Action* includes other important changes described below. *(Please note that the following list includes only a sample of the most important new changes and additions. A full, detailed list, including material that was deleted from the previous edition, is available on our Web site [http://www.wiley.com/college/huffman]. I also invite all instructors and their students to contact me directly if you have questions about these changes. I sincerely appreciate your choice of* Psychology in Action (8e) *as your text, and I want to make your teaching and learning experience as smooth and enjoyable as possible.)*

New Research Updates

To keep pace with the rapid progress in neuroscience, behavioral genetics, evolutionary psychology, cognitive psychology, sociocultural research, and positive psychology, I have added more than 900 new references from 2000 to 2006. We also have several new "Research Highlight" sections, such as "Love at First Fright?" (Chapter 1), "The Theory Heard Round the World" (Chapter 6), "Memory and the Criminal Justice System," (Chapter 7), and "Obesity—Weighing the Evidence" (Chapter 12).

New Critical Thinking/Active Learning Exercises

A friend and colleague who specializes in critical thinking, Thomas Frangicetto at Northampton Community College, contributed several new exercises including "Applying Critical Thinking to Psychological Science" (Chapter 1), "The Biology of Critical Thinking" (Chapter 2), "The Development of Suicide Bombers" (Chapter 9),

"Morality and Academic Cheating" (Chapter 10), and "Hunting for Good Therapy Films" (Chapter 15).

New Case Studies/Personal Stories

Students often enjoy and seem to learn more if they have a "personal face or story" to attach to important psychological concepts. To accommodate this need, I have included several new case studies/personal stories, such as "A Life Without Fear?" (Chapter 1), "Phineas Gage" (Chapter 2), "Surviving 9/11" (Chapter 3), "Helen Keller's Personal Triumph" (Chapter 4), "The Tragic Tale of John/Joan" (Chapter 11), and "The Emotional Intelligence of Abraham Lincoln" (Chapter 12).

Expanded and Innovative Technology

Exciting new online resources can be used by the student who wants to improve skills or enrich his or her study of psychology, or by instructors who teach online courses or as a resource for their traditional lecture courses. These resources include practice quizzes, graded quizzes, demonstrations, simulations, Critical Thinking/Active Learning exercises, and links to psychology-related topics, Internet activities, as well as other valuable features and activities. As a user of *Psychology in Action*, you are guaranteed access to John Wiley & Sons student and instructor resource web sites at http://www.wiley.com/college/huffman. Check us out!

New Organizational Changes from 7e to 8e

- **Chapter 1**. To improve the flow of the material, the history of psychology was moved from the end of the chapter to the beginning. The previous *Doing Research in Psychology* section was also divided into two new sections—*The Science of Psychology* and *Research Methods*.

- **Chapter 2**. Also to improve the flow of the topics, I reorganized the first half of Chapter 2 to begin with the neuron, and then go on to the overall nervous system organization.

- **Chapter 3**. The previous *Coping with Stress* section has been expanded and reorganized, and it now appears at the end of the chapter with the title *Health and Stress Management*.

- **Chapter 6**. Previous application sections that appeared after each of the classical conditioning, operant conditioning, and cognitive-social learning sections now appear as a unit at the end of the chapter. This rearrangement was in response to reviewers who suggested that they could more easily ask students to read or delete these grouped applications depending on what they planned for classroom coverage and activities.

- **Chapter 7**. This chapter has been extensively revised, updated, and reorganized. Reviewers have applauded the brief beginning presentation of all four major theories of memory, followed by the focus on the traditional three-stage memory model. They also appreciated the redesigned sections on *Forgetting*, the *Biological Bases of Memory*, and the *Using Psychology to Improve Our Memory*. One reviewer stated that this was the clearest arrangement he had ever found in a memory chapter.

- **Chapter 8**. The *Intelligence* section has been significantly reorganized for increased clarity and expanded to include the latest research.

- **Chapter 9**. In response to reviewer suggestions, the section on *Cognitive Development* was slightly revised and moved ahead of *Social-Emotional Development*.

- **Chapter 10.** The previous section on *Additional Influences on Development* has been reorganized and expanded under the title *Meeting the Challenges of Adulthood.*

- **Chapter 12.** The four previous headings have been significantly revised and reorganized to improve the flow and clarity of the chapter.

- **Chapter 13**. Due to reviewer suggestions, the section on *Personality Assessment* now appears at the end of the chapter.

- **Chapter 14**. The *Other Disorders* section now includes coverage of *Substance-Related Disorders.*

- **Chapter 15.** The four previous headings have been significantly revised and reorganized into *Insight Therapies, Behavior Therapies,* and *Biomedical Therapies,* with a closing section on *Therapy and Critical Thinking.*

- **Chapter 16.** The chapter now includes a closing section, *Applying Social Psychology to Social Problems,* which has received very positive comments from reviewers.

 # SUPPLEMENTS

Psychology in Action (8e) is accompanied by a host of ancillary materials designed to facilitate the mastery of psychology. Ordering information and policies may be obtained by contacting your local Wiley sales representative.

Instructor Supplements

Videos
Visit our Instructor Web site to view and download a full assortment of short, lecture-enhancing videos designed for in-class or online courses to introduce new topics, enliven your classroom presentations, and stimulate student discussion. To help integrate these video clips into your course syllabus, we also provide a comprehensive library of teaching resources, study questions, and assignments.

Wiley also has a long-established partnership with the *Films for the Humanities,* which allows us to offer a selection of videos, such as Roger Bingham's series on the brain, to further increase your department's library of video resources. Please contact your Wiley sales representative for further information on specific titles.

PowerPoint Presentations and Image Gallery
Whether you are looking for a complete set of specific, text-related PowerPoints, or new images to enhance your current presentations, we have what you need. On the *Instructor Resource Web site,* we provide a full set of dynamic and colorful PowerPoints for each chapter highlighting the major terms and concepts. We also created online electronic files for most figures and tables in the text, which allow you to easily incorporate them into your PowerPoint presentations or to create your own overhead transparencies and handouts.

Wiley Faculty Network
Are you frustrated with complicated instruction manuals and computer trained technicians who can't respond to your specific psychology-related technology needs? The *Wiley Faculty Network* is your answer. These highly trained computer specialists are also college psychology teachers who offer one-on-one, peer-to-peer technical advice and teaching support to adopters of *Psychology in Action.* They guide you through a wide array of online course management tools and discipline-specific software/learning systems for your classroom. In addition, they help you apply innovative classroom techniques, implement specific software packages, and will tailor the technology expe-

rience to the needs of each individual class. Get connected with the *Wiley Faculty Network* at www.wherefacultyconnect.com.

Instructor Resource Web Site

Psychology in Action is accompanied by a comprehensive Web site with numerous resources to help you prepare for class, enhance your presentations, and assess your students' progress. All of the assets created for the Test Bank and Instructor's Resource Guide can be accessed directly from the Web site. Multi-media elements created for classroom presentation and student assignments are also available.

Web-Based Learning Modules

Psychology in Action offers a robust suite of multi-media learning resources, designed and developed to enrich classroom presentations and engage visual learners during study sessions. Delivered via the web, the content is organized in the following categories:

- **Animations** developed around key concepts and themes in psychology. Animations go beyond the content presented in the book, providing additional visual examples and descriptive narration.

- **Interactive Exercises** engage learners in activities that reinforce understanding of key concepts and themes. Through simple choice-making experiences, accompanied by immediate feedback, these exercises encourage learners to apply the knowledge gained by reading and viewing animations.

- **News You Can View from ScienCentral** represents a collection of 80 brief video clips, applying psychology concepts and themes to issues in the news today.

All these assets are available to adopters via password-protected book companion sites, and through our eGrade Plus e-learning courses.

Test Bank (available in WileyPlus and electronic format—Microsoft Word files)

Dr. Lynda Federoff, Indiana University of Pennsylvania, prepared both the hard copy and electronic versions of the test bank. The *Computerized Test Bank*, a multi-platform CD-ROM, which fully supports graphics, printed tests, student answer sheets, and answer keys. The software's advanced features allow you to create an exam to your exact specifications, within an easy-to-use interface. The test generation program has nearly 2,000 test items, including approximately 10 essay questions for each chapter (with suggested answers) and a variety of multiple choice and true/false questions. Each multiple choice question has been linked to a specific, student learning outcome, coded as "Factual" or "Applied," and the correct answer provided with page references to its source in the text. Also included are several "humorous questions" that can be inserted in tests to reduce test anxiety. In addition, the *Computerized Test Bank* includes questions from the *Student Study and Review Guide* and the main text's *Check and Review* questions, which allows you to easily insert these questions into quizzes and exams as reinforcers for student study and preparation.

Instructor's Resource Guide (available in hard copy and electronic format — Microsoft Word files)

Prepared by Kathleen Weatherford, Trident Technical College, this comprehensive resource includes for each text chapter: an *outline, student learning outcomes, outline/lecture organizer* (with page references to text), *lecture lead-ins, supplemental lectures* ("hot" topics), *key terms* (with page references), *a chapter summary/lecture organizer, discussion questions, suggested films and videos, activities section, three active learning/critical thinking exercises*, and a *writing project*. This *Instructor's Resource Guide* also includes numerous *Active Learning Exercises* specifically created for use with any size class.

WebCT

In addition to the Web site, we also offer a WebCT course management system in the highly customizable WebCT format. Ready for use in your online or traditional class, the course includes: chapter overviews, chapter reviews for each section, assignments, Web links, discussion questions, self-tests, quiz questions and test questions, as well as all standard features of WebCT, such as bulletin board, calendar, e-mail and chat room. A brief Instructor's Manual is available (in electronic format only) to assist you in your use of this course.

Blackboard

Due to its popularity, we also offer a Web course management system in the popular Blackboard format. The course includes: chapter overviews, chapter reviews for each section, homework assignments, Web links, discussion questions, self-tests, quiz questions, and test questions, as well as all standard features of Blackboard.

Assignment Questions

Numerous multiple choice, true/false, and essay questions are available for use in content management systems, for online homework, or for use in classroom response systems.

WileyPlus

Psychology in Action is available with **WileyPlus**, a powerful online tool that provides instructors and students with an integrated suite of teaching and learning resources in one easy-to-use Web site.

For Instructors:

- **Prepare and Present.** WileyPlus offers a wealth of Wiley-provided resources to help you prepare dynamic class presentations, such as student interactive simulations and engaging text-specific PowerPoint slides.

- **Custom Assignments.** Professors may create, assign, and grade homework or quizzes by using the Wiley-provided question/assignment bank or by writing your own.

- **Automatic Monitoring of Student Progress.** An instructor's grade book allows you to carefully track and analyze individual and overall class results.

- **Flexible Course Administration.** WileyPlus can easily be integrated with another course management system, grade book, or other resources you are using in your class, providing flexibility to build your course, your way.

For Students:

- **Feedback and Support**. WileyPlus provides immediate feedback on student assignments and a wealth of support materials that will help students develop their conceptual understanding of the class material and increase their ability to solve problems.

- **Study and Practice.** This feature links directly to text content, allowing students to immediately review the text while studying and completing homework assignments.

- **Assignment Locator**. This area allows students to store all tasks and assignments for their psychology course in one convenient location, making it easy for them to stay "on task."

- **Student Grade Book**. Grades are automatically recorded and students can access these results at any time.

(For more information, please view our online demo at www.wileyplus.com. You will find additional information about the features and benefits of WileyPlus, how to request a "test drive" of WileyPlus for *Psychology in Action*, and how to adopt it for class use.)

▣ Student Supplements

WileyPlus Web-Based Modules (see previous Instructor Supplements)

Student Companion Web Site

This Web site provides additional resources that compliment and support the textbook. Enhance your understanding of psychology and improve your grade using the following resources:

- *Interactive Key Term Flash Cards* that allow "drill and practice" in mastering key terms and concepts. You may also take self-tests on these vocabulary terms to monitor your progress.

- *Chapter Review Quizzes* provide immediate feedback for true/false, multiple choice, and short answer questions.

- *Online Guide* offers helpful guidelines about how to use the Web for research, and how to best find your desired information.

- *Annotated Web Links* put useful electronic resources into context.

Student Study and Review Guide

Prepared by Karen Huffman and Richard Hosey, this valuable resource offers you, as a student, an easy way to review the text and ensure that you know the material before your in-class quizzes and exams. For each textbook chapter, the study guide offers numerous tools designed to save you time, while also helping you master the core information. These tools include chapter outlines, core learning outcomes, key terms, key term crossword puzzles, matching exercises, fill-in exercises, an active learning exercise, and two sample tests (20 items each) with text-referenced correct answers. Each chapter of the *Student Study and Review Guide* also includes a copy of the *Visual Summaries* that appear at the end of each chapter in the text. Students in the past have copied these summaries to use during class lecture or text reading, so we've made your studying easier by including them in this study guide.

•
•
•

ACKNOWLEDGMENTS

The writing of this text has been a group effort involving the input and support of my family, friends, and colleagues. To each person I offer my sincere thanks. A special note of appreciation goes to Jay Alperson, Bill Barnard, Dan Bellack, Haydn Davis, Tom Frangicetto, Ann Haney, Herb Harari, Sandy Harvey, Richard Hosey, Terry Humphrey, Teresa Jacob, Kandis Mutter, Bob Miller, Roger Morrissette, Harriett Prentiss, Jeanne Riddell, Sabine Schoen, and Katie Townsend-Merino.

To the reviewers, focus group, and telesession participants who gave their time and constructive criticism, I offer my sincere appreciation. I am deeply indebted to the following individuals and trust that they will recognize their contributions throughout the text.

Student Feedback

To help us verify that our book successfully addressed the needs of today's college students, we asked current introductory psychology students to provide feedback about each chapter of the text. Their reactions confirmed our belief that the book is an effective (and some even said "entertaining") learning tool. We are grateful to the following students who took the time to share their honest opinions with us: Erin Decker, *San Diego State University*; Laura Decker, *University of California at Davis*; Amanda Nichols, *Palomar College*; Idalia S. Carrillo, *University of Texas at San Antonio*; Sarah Dedford, *Delta College (Michigan)*; Laural Didham, *Cleveland State University*; Danyce French, *Northampton Community College (Pennsylvania)*; Stephanie Renae Reid, *Purdue University–Calumet*; Betsy Schoenbeck, *University of Missouri at Columbia*; and Sabrina Walkup, *Trident Technical College (South Carolina)*.

Professional Feedback

The following professionals have helped us test and refine the critical thinking/active learning pedagogy that is found in this book: Thomas Alley, *Clemson University*; David R. Barkmeier, *Northeastern University*; Steven Barnhart, *Rutgers University*; Dan Bellack, *Trident Technical College*; JoAnn Brannock, *Fullerton College*; Michael Caruso, *University of Toledo*; Nicole Judice Campbell, *University of Oklahoma*; Sandy Deabler, *North Harris College*; Diane K. Feibel, *Raymond Walters College*; Richard Griggs, *University of Florida*; Richard Harris, *Kansas State University*; John Haworth, *Florida Community College at Jacksonville*; Guadalupe King, *Milwaukee Area Technical College*; Roger Morrissette, *Palomar College*; Barbara Nash, *Bentley College*; Maureen O'Brien, *Bentley*

College; Jan Pascal, *DeVry University*; John Pennachio, *Adirondack Community College*; Gary E. Rolikowki, *SUNY, Geneseo*; Ronnie Rothschild, *Broward Community College*; Ludo Scheffer, *Drexel University*; Kathy Sexton-Radek, *Elmhurst College*; Matthew Sharps, *California State University–Fresno*; Richard Topolski, *Augusta State University*; Katie Townsend-Merino, *Palomar College*; Elizabeth Young, *Bentley College*.

Focus Group and Telesession Participants

Brian Bate, *Cuyahoga Community College*; Hugh Bateman, *Jones Junior College*; Ronald Boykin, *Salisbury State University*; Jack Brennecke, *Mount San Antonio College*; Ethel Canty, *University of Texas–Brownsville*; Joseph Ferrari, *Cazenovia College*; Allan Fingaret, *Rhode Island College*; Richard Fry, *Youngstown State University*; Roger Harnish, *Rochester Institute of Technology*; Richard Harris, *Kansas State University*; Tracy B. Henley, *Mississippi State University*; Roger Hock, *New England College*; Melvyn King, *State University of New York at Cortland*; Jack Kirschenbaum, *Fullerton College*; Cynthia McDaniel, *Northern Kentucky University*; Deborah McDonald, *New Mexico State University*; Henry Morlock, *State University of New York at Plattsburgh*; Kenneth Murdoff, *Lane Community College*; William Overman, *University of North Carolina at Wilmington*; Steve Platt, *Northern Michigan University*; Janet Proctor, *Purdue University*; Dean Schroeder, *Laramie Community College*; Michael Schuller, *Fresno City College*; Alan Schultz, *Prince George Community College*; Peggy Skinner, *South Plains College*; Charles Slem, *California Polytechnic State University–San Luis Obispo*; Eugene Smith, *Western Illinois University*; David Thomas, *Oklahoma State University*; Cynthia Viera, *Phoenix College*; and Matthew Westra, *Longview Community College*.

Additional Reviewers

L. Joseph Achor, *Baylor University*; M. June Allard, *Worcester State College*; Joyce Allen, *Lakeland College*; Worthon Allen, *Utah State University*; Jeffrey S. Anastasi, *Francis Marion University*; Susan Anderson, *University of South Alabama*; Emir Andrews, *Memorial University of Newfoundland*; Marilyn Andrews, *Hartnell College*; Richard Anglin, *Oklahoma City Community College*; Susan Anzivino, *University of Maine at Farmington*; Peter Bankart, *Wabash College*; Susan Barnett, *Northwestern State University (Louisiana)*; Patricia Barker, *Schenectady County Community College*; Daniel Bellack, *College of Charleston*; Daniel Bitran, *College of Holy Cross*; Terry Blumenthal, *Wake Forest University*; Theodore N. Bosack, *Providence College*; Linda Bosmajian, *Hood College*; John Bouseman, *Hillsborough Community College*; John P. Broida, *University of Southern Maine*; Lawrence Burns, *Grand Valley State University*; Bernado J. Carducci, *Indiana University Southeast*; Charles S. Carver, *University of Miami*; Marion Cheney, *Brevard Community College*; Meg Clark, *California State Polytechnic University–Pomona*; Dennis Cogan, *Texas Tech University*; David Cohen, *California State University, Bakersfield*; Anne E. Cook, *University of Massachessetts*; Kathryn Jennings Cooper, *Salt Lake Community College*; Steve S. Cooper, *Glendale Community College*; Amy Cota-McKinley, *The University of Tennessee, Knoxville*; Mark Covey, *University of Idaho*; Robert E. DeLong, *Liberty University*; Linda Scott DeRosier, *Rocky Mountain College*; Grace Dyrud, *Augsburg College*; Thomas Eckle, *Modesto Junior College*; Tami Eggleston, *McKendree College*; James A. Eison, *Southeast Missouri State University*; A. Jeanette Engles, *Southeastern Oklahoma State University*; Eric Fiazi, *Los Angeles City College*; Sandra Fiske, *Onondaga Community College*; Kathleen A. Flannery, *Saint Anselm College*; Pamela Flynn, *Community College of Philadelphia*; William F. Ford, *Bucks City Community College*; Harris Friedman, *Edison Community College*; Paul Fuller, *Muskegon Community College*; Frederick Gault, *Western Michigan University*; Russell G. Geen, *University of Missouri, Columbia*; Joseph Giacobbe, *Adirondack Community College*; Robert Glassman, *Lake Forest College*; Patricia Marks Greenfield, *University of California–Los Angeles*; David A. Griese, *SUNY Farmingdale*; Sam Hagan, *Edison County Community College*; Sylvia Haith,

Forsyth Technical College; Frederick Halper, *Essex County Community College*; George Hampton, *University of Houston–Downtown*; Joseph Hardy, *Harrisburg Area Community College*; Algea Harrison, *Oakland University*; Mike Hawkins, *Louisiana State University*; Linda Heath, *Loyola University of Chicago*; Sidney Hochman, *Nassau Community College*; Richard D. Honey, *Transylvania University*; John J. Hummel, *Valdosta State University*; Nancy Jackson, *Johnson & Wales University*; Kathryn Jennings, *College of the Redwoods*; Charles Johnston, *William Rainey Harper College*; Dennis Jowaisis, *Oklahoma City Community College*; Seth Kalichman, *University of South Carolina*; Paul Kaplan, *Suffolk County Community College*; Bruno Kappes, *University of Alaska*; Kevin Keating, *Broward Community College*; Guadalupe Vasquez King, *Milwaukee Area Technical College*; Norman E. Kinney, *Southeast Missouri State University*; Richard A. Lambe, *Providence College*; Sherri B. Lantinga, *Dordt College*; Marsha Laswell, *California State Polytechnic University–Pomona*; Elise Lindenmuth, *York College*; Allan A. Lippert, *Manatee Community College*; Thomas Linton, *Coppin State College*; Virginia Otis Locke, *University of Idaho*; Maria Lopez-Trevino, *Mount San Jacinto College*; Tom Marsh, *Pitt Community College*; Edward McCrary III, *El Camino Community College*; David G. McDonald, *University of Missouri, Columbia*; Yancy McDougal, *University of South Carolina–Spartanburg*; Nancy Meck, *University of Kansas Medical Center*; Juan S. Mercado, *McLennan Community College*; Michelle Merwin, *University of Tennessee, Martin*; Mitchell Metzger, *Penn State University*; David Miller, *Daytona Beach Community College*; Michael Miller, *College of St. Scholastica*; Phil Mohan, *University of Idaho*; Ron Mossler, *LA Valley College*; Kathleen Navarre, *Delta College*; John Near, *Elgin Community College*; Steve Neighbors, *Santa Barbara City College*; Leslie Neumann, *Forsyth Technical Community College*; Susan Nolan, *Seton Hall University*; Sarah O'Dowd, *Community College of Rhode Island*; Joseph J. Palladino, *University of Southern Indiana*; Linda Palm, *Edison Community College*; Richard S. Perroto, *Queensborough Community College*; Larry Pervin, *Rutgers University, New Brunswick*; Valerie Pinhas, *Nassau Community College*; Leslee Pollina, *Southeast Missouri State University*; Howard R. Pollio, *University of Tennessee–Knoxville*; Christopher Potter, *Harrisburg Community College*; Derrick Proctor, *Andrews University*; Antonio Puete, *University of North Carolina–Wilmington*; Joan S. Rabin, *Towson State University*; Lillian Range, *University of Southern Mississippi*; George A. Raymond, *Providence College*; Celia Reaves, *Monroe Community College*; Michael J. Reich, *University of Wisconsin–River Falls*; Edward Rinalducci, *University of Central Florida*; Kathleen R. Rogers, *Purdue University North Central*; Leonard S. Romney, *Rockland Community College*; Thomas E. Rudy, *University of Pittsburgh*; Carol D. Ryff, *University of Wisconsin–Madison*; Neil Salkind, *University of Kansas–Lawrence*; Richard J. Sanders, *University of North Carolina –Wilmington*; Harvey Richard Schiffman, *Rutgers University*; Steve Schneider, *Pima College*; Michael Scozzaro, *State University of New York at Buffalo*; Tizrah Schutzengel, *Bergen Community College*; Lawrence Scott, *Bunker Hill Community College*; Michael B. Sewall, *Mohawk Valley Community College*; Fred Shima, *California State University–Dominquez Hills*; Royce Simpson, *Campbellsville University*; Art Skibbe, *Appalachian State University*; Larry Smith, *Daytona Beach Junior College*; Emily G. Soltano, *Worcester State College*; Debra Steckler, *Mary Washington College*; Michael J. Strube, *Washington University*; Kevin Sumrall, *Montgomery College*; Ronald Testa, *Plymouth State College*; Cynthia Viera, *Phoenix College*; John T. Vogel, *Baldwin Wallace College*; Benjamin Wallace, *Cleveland State University*; Mary Wellman, *Rhode Island College*; Paul J. Wellman, *Texas A & M University*; I. Eugene White, *Salisbury State College*; Delos D. Wickens, *Colorado State University–Fort Collins*; Fred Whitford, *Montana State University*; Charles Wiechert, *San Antonio College*; Jeff Walper, *Delaware Technical and Community College*; Bonnie S. Wright, *St. Olaf College*; Brian T. Yates, *American University*; Todd Zakrajsek, *Southern Oregon University*; and Mary Lou Zanich, *Indiana University of Pennsylvania*.

■ Special Thanks

Special thanks also go to the superb editorial and production teams at John Wiley and Sons. This project benefited from the wisdom and insight of Sandra Dumas, Anna Melhorn, Jennifer MacMillan, Mary Ann Price, Karyn Drews, Kevin Murphy, Marisol Persaud, and many others. Like any cooperative effort, writing a book requires an immense support team, and I am deeply grateful to this remarkable group of people.

I would also like to express my gratitude to Chris Johnson, Executive Editor. Chris came aboard during the production of this revision and was quickly and aptly "up-to-speed," and offering invaluable feedback and suggestions. I am very grateful for his guidance and support.

In addition, I am also deeply indebted to Jeffrey Rucker, Executive Marketing Manager, Lynn Pearlman, Media Editor, Jessica Bartelt, Associate Editor, Bria Duane, Marketing Assistant, and a host of others — all of whom helped enormously in the initial launch and ongoing production. Without them, this book and its wide assortment of ancillaries would not have been possible.

Next, I would like to offer my sincere thanks to *Hermitage Publishing Services* and *Radiant Illustration and Design*. Their careful and professional approach was critical to the successful production of this book. I especially thank Larry Meyer for his thoughtfulness and dedication to producing a "perfect book."

I also would like to express my continuing appreciation to my students. They taught me what students want to know and inspired me to write the book. In addition, these individuals deserve special recognition: John Bryant, Sandy Harvey, Michelle Hernandez, Jordan Hertzog-Merino, Richard Hosey, Christine McLean, and Kandis Mutter. They provided careful editing of this text, library research, and a unique sense of what should and should not go into an introduction to psychology text. I sincerely appreciate their contributions. If you have suggestions or comments, please feel free to contact me at my e-mail address: Karen Huffman (khuffman@palomar.edu).

Last, and definitely *not least*, I dedicate this book to my beloved husband, Bill Barnard, who has provided countless hours of careful editing, advice, and unwavering support for all 8 editions of this book.

PROLOGUE
CRITICAL THINKING/ACTIVE LEARNING
(Co-authored with Thomas Frangicetto along with contributions from his students at Northampton Community College)

Critical thinking has many meanings and some books dedicate entire chapters to defining the term. The word *critical* comes from the Greek word *kritikos*, which means to question, makes sense of, and be able to analyze. Thinking is the cognitive activity involved in making sense of the world around us. Critical thinking, therefore, can be defined as *thinking about and evaluating thoughts, feelings, and behavior so that we can clarify and improve them* (adapted from Chaffee, 1988, p. 29).

This text's focus on active learning naturally contributes to the development of critical thinking. I believe that an active learner is by definition also a critical thinker. Critical thinking is also a process. As a process — something you do — you can do it better. You can develop your critical thinking skills. Each chapter of *Psychology in Action* (and corresponding chapters in the *Student Study and Review Guide* and *Instructor's Resource Guide*) includes a specific *Critical Thinking/Active Learning Exercise* devoted to improving one or more of the components of critical thinking. To learn more about each of these components, study the following three lists. They present the *affective* (emotional), *cognitive* (thinking), and *behavioral* (action) components of critical thinking. You will find that you already employ some of these skills. But you will also discover areas you could strengthen through practice.

▧ Affective Components

The *emotional* foundation that either enables or limits critical thinking.

1. ***Valuing truth above self-interest.*** Critical thinkers hold themselves and those they agree with to the same intellectual standards to which they hold their opponents. This is one of the most difficult components to employ on a regular basis. We all have a tendency to cater to our own needs (see "self-serving bias" p. 576), and to ignore information that conflicts with our desires. Critical thinkers recognize that, even when it appears otherwise, the "truth" is always in our self-interest.

   "Psychic John Edward makes a lot of money off his supposed power to communicate with people's dead relatives...his "customers" should <u>value the truth over self-interest.</u> This means accepting the truth, even when it is not what they want to believe. We learned from the text that one reason people believe in psychics like Edward is because they "want to"—they willingly suspend disbelief" and put their self-interest above the truth." —LISA SHANK

2. ***Accepting change.*** Critical thinkers remain open to the need for adjustment and adaptation throughout the life cycle. Resisting change is one of the most common characteristics that human beings share. Because critical thinkers fully trust the processes of reasoned inquiry, they are willing to use these skills to examine even their most deeply held values and beliefs, and to modify these beliefs when evidence and experience contradict them.

   "As one becomes a parent for the first time, that individual must face the fact that accepting change plays a very big role. A new parent can no longer drop everything and do whatever they please, such as going to a club or bar to socialize or even just going out to dinner. They now have more responsibilities and different priorities." — JAMES CAVANAUGH

3. ***Empathizing.*** Critical thinkers appreciate and try to understand others' thoughts, feelings, and behaviors. Noncritical thinkers view everything and everyone in relation to themselves, which is known as "egocentrism." The ability to consider the perspective of another person—to empathize with them—is the most effective antidote to egocentric thinking.

> *"I think that one thing that everyone should do when they've lost a loved one is <u>empathizing.</u> Empathy is a great way to help each other in a time of need. Many times there is someone who just needs to talk and express his or her feelings. Being able to listen and understand what they are going through, helps make your response to them more effective and helpful."* — CHRISTOPHER FEGLEY

4. ***Welcoming divergent views.*** Critical thinkers value examining issues from every angle and know that it is especially important to explore and understand positions with which they disagree. This quality would be especially valuable to groups in the process of decision making. Welcoming divergent views would effectively inoculate the decision making process from "groupthink"—"faulty decision making that occurs when a highly cohesive group strives for agreement and avoids inconsistent information."

> *"Most Americans don't even try to understand the sociocultural influences that affect suicide bombers...but this issue has influenced me to welcome divergent views and try to understand that people in different cultures have different beliefs. Most Americans believe that martyrs are crazy, while Palestinians believe that martyrdom is something to be idolized. My decision to believe that martyrdom is a form of self-expression may clash with the views of many Americans but I grew up in a country where I have the right to believe what I want."* – SOPHIA BLANCHET

5. ***Tolerating ambiguity.*** Although formal education often trains us to look for a single "right" answer ("convergent thinking"), critical thinkers recognize that many issues are complex and subtle, and that complex issues may not have a "right" answer. They recognize and value qualifiers such as "probably," "highly likely," and "not very likely." Creative artists, in particular, must be willing to deal with uncertainty and be willing to consider many possible solutions ("divergent thinking").

6. ***Recognizing personal biases.*** This involves using your highest intellectual skills to detect personal biases and self-deceptive reasoning so you can design realistic plans for self-correction. Being an effective critical thinker does not mean the total absence of bias, but rather the willingness to admit, recognize, and correct bias.

> *"Because America is such a huge country of immigrants, many people—including me as a foreigner from Japan—become sensitive about discrimination and prejudice. I have had some difficult times. Once one of my American friends described some Asian people as "foxes," because of the way they look. She was joking, but I was not laughing. I felt very sad because she didn't even notice that I felt disrespected. She definitely needs to begin recognizing personal biases if she wants to have friends from different cultures."* — SAEMI SUZUKI

Cognitive Components

The *thought* processes actually involved in critical thinking.

7. ***Thinking independently.*** Critical thinking is independent thinking. Critical thinkers do not passively accept the beliefs of others and are not easily manipulated. They maintain a healthy amount of skepticism, especially about unusual or remarkable claims or reports. They are also able to differentiate being "skeptical" from just being stubborn and unyielding. They are, for example, willing to "welcome divergent views" and 1) weigh the substance of those views, and 2) adjust their own thinking if warranted ("accept change").

8. ***Defining problems accurately.*** To the extent possible, a critical thinker identifies the issues in clear and concrete terms, to prevent confusion and lay the foundation for gathering relevant information. At first glance, this component appears to contradict "tolerating ambiguity," but that is not so. Critical thinkers are able to tolerate ambiguity until it is possible to "define problems accurately."

9. ***Analyzing data for value and content.*** By carefully evaluating the nature of evidence and the credibility of the source, critical thinkers recognize illegitimate appeals to emotion, unsupported assumptions, and faulty logic. This enables them to discount sources of information that lack a record of honesty, contradict themselves on key questions, or have a vested interest in selling a product, idea, or viewpoint that are only partially accurate (a "half truth").

   "While it may be true that the majority of black people score lower than white people on IQ tests, it is important to ask: Why? To learn the answer it is indispensable to <u>analyze data for value and content.</u> To do so you must carefully identify the credibility of sources and evaluate all information from a multicultural perspective; for example, we must consider the daily battle against prejudice in our society and how minority students feel isolated from the rest of the white majority... So the environment has a lot of influence and the effect can be lower self-esteem which can result in lower scores." – ARANZAZU GARCIA

10. ***Employing a variety of thinking processes in problem solving.*** Among these thinking processes are (a) *inductive logic* — reasoning that moves from the specific to the general; (b) *deductive logic* — reasoning that moves from the general to the specific; (c) *dialogical thinking* — thinking that involves an extended verbal exchange between differing points of view or frames of reference; and (d) *dialectical thinking* — thinking that tests the strengths and weaknesses of opposing points of view.

11. ***Synthesizing.*** Critical thinkers recognize that comprehension and understanding result from combining various elements into meaningful patterns. Blending the affective, cognitive, and behavioral components of critical thinking into a deeper understanding of your world involves synthesizing. For example, feeling depressed because "nobody likes you" might lead to asking other people for feedback (welcoming divergent views), their views might help you realize that you do have good qualities that people like and that it isn't as bad as you thought (resisting overgeneralization), which could inspire you to try new behaviors (applying knowledge to new situations).

12. ***Resisting overgeneralization.*** Overgeneralization is the temptation to apply a fact or experience to situations that are only superficially similar. For example, having a bad experience with and forming a negative judgment of a person from a particular ethnic heritage and then applying that same judgment to all members of the same ethnic group. The failure to resist overgeneralization is often at the core of "prejudice."

13. ***Employing metacognition.*** Metacognition, also known as reflective or recursive thinking, involves reviewing and analyzing your own mental processes — thinking about your own thinking. Critical thinkers who are motivated to trace the origin of their beliefs put their thinking under intense scrutiny and can often be heard saying things like "What was I thinking?" or "I don't know why I believe that, I'll have to think about it."

▥ Behavioral Components

The *actions* necessary for critical thinking.

14. ***Delaying judgment until adequate data are available.*** A critical thinker does not make snap judgments. Impulsivity is one of the surest obstacles to good critical

thinking. Rash judgments about other people, "impulse" purchases of a new car or home, uninformed choices for political candidates, or "falling in love at first sight" can all be costly mistakes that we regret for many years.

"When it comes to debating the Iraqi war people are often misinformed and I believe it is my responsibility to inform them of the truth since I am in the U.S. Army Reserves. At first I did not agree with the war, but as a soldier I am supposed to do what I am told. I have worked with people who were part of the unit responsible for the Abu Ghraib prison scandal, and I have friends who are over in Iraq, some who support the war and others who do not... [but] some people judge the situation before they get all the information they need. This is why I try to convince them to delay judgment until adequate data in available.*"*
– LONGSU CHENG

15. ***Employing precise terms.*** Precise terms help critical thinkers identify issues clearly and concretely so they can be objectively defined and empirically tested. In the everyday realm, when two people argue about an issue they are often defining it differently without even knowing it. For example, in a romantic relationship two individuals can have very different definitions of words such as "love" and "commitment." Open communication that explores and identifies the precise shades of meaning is an important key to successful relationships.

16. ***Gathering data.*** Collecting up-to-date, relevant information on all sides of an issue is a priority before making decisions. Too often noncritical thinkers collect only information that confirms their point-of-view. For example, researchers can unintentionally skew a study in the direction of a desired outcome by only collecting data that will support it.

17. ***Distinguishing fact from opinion.*** Facts are statements that can be proven true. Opinions are statements that express how a person feels about an issue or what someone thinks is true. It is easy to have an uninformed opinion about any subject, but critical thinkers seek out facts before forming their opinions.

"I like that this text teaches us to distinguish fact from opinion, for example, to 'recognize statements that can be proven true' versus statements that merely reveal the way we feel about something. We must learn to tell the difference between the 'truth' and popular opinions we have learned from our parents and society." — WENDY MOREN

18. ***Encouraging critical dialogue.*** Critical thinkers are active questioners who challenge existing facts and opinions and welcome questions in return. Socratic questioning is an important type of critical dialogue in which the questioner deeply probes the meaning, justification, or logical strength of a claim, position, or line of reasoning. In everyday communication it is often easier to avoid the type of dialogue that would help solve problems and strengthen relationships, but it is an essential part of living an emotionally healthy life.

"My mother has been calling me for the last year and I know she is only talking to me because she is dying. It has taken me a long time to warm up to her because of the past ... I currently find myself encouraging critical dialogue *with her ... after many years we have finally started to express our feelings with each other. This dialogue has been most gratifying because now we have learned to become friends and enjoy each other's company. My hope is that when the end comes we will know that despite our faults we really loved each other."*
– TIM WALKER

19. ***Listening actively.*** Critical thinkers fully engage their thinking skills when listening to another. This may sound like the easiest or most obvious of all components, but it is one of the most difficult. Test this yourself the next time you are in a conversation with someone. After you've talked for a while ask the other person to summarize what you were saying. Or monitor your own listening prowess when the other person is speaking. How often does your attention wander? Crit-

ical thinkers "actively" engage in the conversation by "encouraging critical dialogue." They ask questions, nonverbally affirm what they hear, request clarification or elaboration, and so on.

20. ***Modifying judgments in light of new information.*** Critical thinkers are willing to abandon or modify their judgments if later evidence or experience contradicts them. Noncritical thinkers stubbornly stick to their beliefs and often "value self-interest above the truth."

"For much of my high school years, I procrastinated on almost every assignment. The process of change has been a slow one...however, I procrastinate less now that I am in college. In addition to prioritizing my work, and finishing the more important assignments sooner ... I have modified my judgment in light of new information. I know now that these assignments are primarily for my own benefit and that a certain level of self-motivation is required in order to succeed in life. I also realized that I am paying for my education so I may as well get as much out of it as I can." – TOM SHIMER

21. ***Applying knowledge to new situations.*** When critical thinkers master a new skill or experience an insight, they transfer this information to new contexts. Noncritical thinkers can often provide correct answers, repeat definitions, and carry out calculations, yet be unable to transfer their knowledge to new situations because of a basic lack of understanding or an inability to "synthesize" seemingly unrelated content."

A great many people think they are thinking when they are merely rearranging their prejudices.

WILLIAM JAMES

Dear Reader and Student of Psychology:

Welcome to the eighth edition of *Psychology in Action*. I believe that studying psychology can change your life. I think I've always loved psychology—long before I knew there was an entire science devoted to its study. But once I took my first college course in psychology, I was really "hooked." I discovered a scientific way of looking at behavior that I never fully understood in the past. I found psychology so uniquely intriguing and exciting because it studies you and me, and because it holds the key to so much understanding of our personal and social life.

My goals as a college instructor and author of this text are to introduce you to the incredible wealth of information in our field, and to show you how this information can be usefully applied to your own life and the world around you. Please consider this book as a long letter from me to you. I will guide you through a fascinating world that can transform your relationships with others and with yourself.

But I cannot do this alone. I've done all that I could imagine to make this text as engaging and worthwhile as possible. In order to truly understand and appreciate psychology (or any other discipline), however, you must become an active participant. As a lifelong advocate of active learning, I am firmly convinced that this is the very best method for mastering any important task—or for maintaining any important relationship. To encourage you to read and study actively, I've included a wide variety of active learning tools, including: **Tools for Student Success, Integrated Study Tips, Visual Summaries, Chapter Summary Tables, Visual Quizzes, Check and Review sections**, **Try This Yourself activities, Critical Thinking/Active Learning Exercises, Applying Psychology to Work, Relationships, and Everyday Life, Case Studies/Personal Stories,** and other additional techniques.

As you can see, this book can be part of an exciting intellectual adventure. If you use these tools to become an active participant, the study of psychology can lead you to an entirely new way of looking at the social world around you. I wish you the very best in college and in your life afterward. It is my fondest hope that *Psychology in Action* will contribute to your lifelong success.

Warmest regards,

Karen Huffman

Karen Huffman

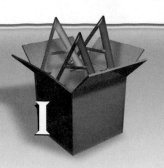

INTRODUCTION AND RESEARCH METHODS

Achievement

Core Learning Outcomes

As you read Chapter 1, keep the following questions in mind and answer them in your own words:

▷ What is psychology? What are its goals and main career specialties?

▷ Who are the important contributors to psychology, and what are the seven primary perspectives that guide modern psychology?

▷ What is the scientific method, and what are the key ethical issues in psychological research?

▷ What are the four major methods of psychological research?

▷ How can I use psychology to study and learn psychology?

Study **T**ip 💡

Core Learning Outcomes

These questions are an important part of the SQ4R method described in the Preface and the Student Study and Review Guide, which accompanies this text. You should attempt to answer these questions as you read the chapter. For reinforcement, they are repeated in the margins at the place where they are discussed.

Study **T**ip 💡

Chapter Outline

Each chapter begins with an outline of all major topics and subtopics. This pattern of headings is repeated within the chapter itself. The outline and corresponding headings provide mental scaffolds to help you organize and master information as you read.

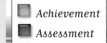

🔲 *Achievement*
🔲 *Assessment*
🔲 *Application*

*A*pplication

WHY STUDY PSYCHOLOGY?

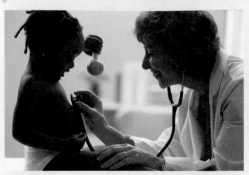

Jim Cummins/Taxi/Getty Images

Chapter 1 (and all other chapters in this text) will:

▷ *Increase your understanding of your-self and others.* The Greek philosopher Socrates admonished long ago, "Know thyself." Psychology is about you, me, and all the peoples of the world. Studying it will greatly contribute to your understanding (and appreciation) of yourself and others.

▷ *Better your social relations.* Thanks to years of scientific research and application, psychology has developed numerous guidelines and techniques that will improve your relationships with friends, family, and coworkers.

▷ *Enhance your career.* Whether or not you decide to work directly in the field, psychology can enrich your profes-sional life. Because all jobs require working with others, an improvement in your "people skills" can lead to direct career "profits."

▷ *Broaden your general education.* Why are you in college? Is becoming a more educated person one of your goals? Psychology is an integral part of today's political, social, and economic world, and understanding its principles and concepts is essential to becoming well informed.

▷ *Improve your critical thinking.* Would you like to become a more independ-ent thinker and better decision maker and problem solver? These are only a few of the many critical thinking skills that are enhanced through a study of psychology.

Welcome to the exciting world of *Psychology in Action*. As the cover of this text and its name imply, psychology is a *living*, dynamic field that affects every part of our lives—our relationships at home, college, and work, as well as politics, television, movies, newspapers, radio, and the Internet. I did not understand or appreciate the personal applications and incredible range of psychology when I began my first introductory course. I thought all psychologists were therapists, and I expected to study mostly abnormal behavior. Today, as a college psychology professor, I find that most of my students still share similar expectations— and misconceptions. Although psychologists do study and treat abnormal behavior, we also study sleep, dreaming, stress, health, drugs, personality, sexuality, motivation, emotion, learning, memory, childhood, aging, death, love, conformity, intelligence, creativity, and so much more.

To help you understand psychology's great diversity, this opening chapter pro-vides a wide-ranging, overall introduction to this text and the entire field. The first section, "Introducing Psychology," begins with a formal definition of psychology and an exploration of its four major goals. "Origins of Psychology" helps you understand how the field developed and where it is today. "The Science of Psychology" and "Research Methods" explore the scientific nature of psychology and the various meth-ods used to collect the data that make up the foundation of psychology. The chapter concludes with a special feature, "Tools for Student Success." This section offers numerous tips and techniques guaranteed to improve your grades and overall per-formance in all your college courses. Be sure to read it carefully.

INTRODUCING PSYCHOLOGY

What Is Psychology? Science Versus Pseudopsychology

The term *psychology* derives from the roots *psyche*, meaning "mind," and *logos*, meaning "word." Early psychologists focused primarily on the study of mind and mental life. By the 1920s, however, many psychologists believed the mind was not a suitable subject for scientific study. They initiated a movement to restrict psychology to observable behavior alone. Today we recognize the importance of both areas. Accordingly, **psychology** is now defined as the *scientific study of behavior and mental processes. Behavior* is anything we do—talking, sleeping, blinking, or reading. And *mental processes* are our private, internal experiences—thoughts, perceptions, feelings, memories, or dreams.

For many psychologists, the most important part of the definition of psychology is its emphasis on the word *scientific.* Psychology places high value on empirical evidence, or information acquired by direct observation and measurement using systematic scientific methods. As part of this emphasis on science, psychologists also focus on **critical thinking**, the *process of objectively evaluating, comparing, analyzing, and synthesizing information.* The study of psychology will greatly improve your critical thinking abilities. And this text includes several unique features designed to build and expand these skills. For example, each chapter contains numerous "Visual Quizzes" and "Try This Yourself" activities. If you would like to exercise your critical thinking skills, and test how much you already know about psychology, try the following "Try This Yourself" exercise.

Achievement

What is psychology? What are its goals and main career specialties?

Psychology *Scientific study of behavior and mental processes*

Critical Thinking *Process of objectively evaluating, comparing, analyzing, and synthesizing information*

Study Tip

Key Terms and Running Glossary
All key terms and concepts are boldfaced in the text the first time they appear. They also are printed and defined again in the margin as a running glossary. This boldfacing and running glossary provide a helpful way of reviewing key ideas before tests. If you want to check the meaning of a term from another chapter, use the glossary at the end of this text.

TRY THIS YOURSELF Application

Testing Your Knowledge of Psychology

Answer True or False to the following:

___1. In general, we only use about 10 percent of our brain.

___2. Most brain activity stops during sleep.

___3. Police departments often use psychics to help solve crimes.

___4. Punishment is the most effective way to permanently change behavior.

___5. Eyewitness testimony is often unreliable.

___6. Polygraph ("lie detector") tests can accurately and reliably reveal whether a person is lying.

___7. People who threaten suicide seldom follow through with it.

___8. People with schizophrenia have two or more distinct personalities.

___9. Similarity is one of the best predictors of long-term relationships.

___10. As the number of bystanders increases, your chances of getting help decreases.

Answers: 1. False (Chapter 2). 2. False (Chapter 5). 3. False (Chapter 4). 4. False (Chapter 6). 5. True (Chapter 7). 6. False (Chapter 12). 7. False (Chapter 14). 8. False (Chapter 14). 9. True (Chapter 16). 10. True (Chapter 16).

Study Tip

Try This Yourself
In each chapter, you will find several opportunities to apply what you are learning. These "Try This Yourself" sections are clearly identified with a special heading shown above. These activities are brief and fun to do. Research shows that actively involving yourself in learning greatly increases comprehension and retention.

Study Tip

Website Icons
A website icon appears at the bottom of every right-hand page for easy reference. This handy website, http://www.wiley.com/college/huffman, includes online tutorial quizzes, practice tests, active learning exercises, Internet links to psychology-related topics, additional "Check & Review" questions, and other valuable features that will be updated regularly. Visit this site often. It will help ensure success in this course.

How did you do? Students in my classes often miss several questions because this is their first psychology course. Errors also happen when we fail to examine critically "pop psychology" beliefs like the one about only using 10 percent of our brains. (Think about it. Would anyone believe that we could lose 90 percent of our brain and it would not matter?)

Interestingly, most college students mistakenly assume that psychologists are among the most likely to believe in psychics, palmistry, astrology, and other paranormal phenomena. This may be because students (and the public) often confuse scientific psychology with *pseudopsychologies*, which give the appearance of science but are actually false. (*Pseudo* means "false.") Pseudopsychologies include:

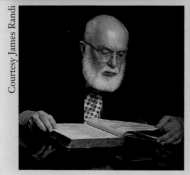

Capricorn: Today is a good day to make important decisions about your life based on arbitrary nonsense written by an anonymous stranger in a newspaper.

- *Psychics*—individuals who are supposedly sensitive to nonphysical or supernatural forces.

- *Mediums*—individuals who serve as a channel of communication between the earthly world and a world of spirits.

- *Palmistry*—reading a person's future or character from the lines on the palms.

- *Psychometry*—determining facts about an object by merely handling it.

- *Psychokinesis*—moving objects by purely mental means.

- *Astrology*—the study of how the positions of the stars and planets supposedly influence people's personalities and affairs.

For some, pseudopsychologies are mere entertainment. But studies around the world reveal widespread public belief in the paranormal (Peltzer, 2003; Rice, 2003; Spinelli, Reid, & Norvilitis, 2001–2002). Furthermore, many of us know people who spend hundreds, or even thousands, of dollars and many hours on calls to psychic hotlines and horoscope readings.

Psychology's Goals: Describe, Explain, Predict, and Change

In contrast to pseudopsychologies, which rely on testimonials and opinions, scientific psychology bases its findings on systematic research methodology and critical thinking. Psychology has four basic goals: to describe, explain, predict, and change behavior and mental processes.

1. **Description.** Description tells "what" occurred. In some studies, psychologists attempt to *describe*, or name and classify, particular behaviors by making careful scientific observations. Description is usually the first step in understanding behavior.

Courtesy James Randi

Do you know why this magician is so widely respected?

Answer: James Randi ("The Amazing Randi!") is a famous magician who dedicates his life to educating the public about fraudulent pseudopsychologists. Along with the prestigious MacArthur Foundation, Randi has offered $1 million to "anyone who proves a genuine psychic power under proper observing conditions" (About James Randi, 2002; Randi, 1997). Although some have tried, the money has never been collected. The offer still stands! If you would like more information about James Randi (and his million-dollar offer), visit his website at http://www.randi.org.

For example, if someone says, "Boy are more aggressive than girls," what does that mean? The speaker's definition of aggression may differ from yours. Science requires specificity.

2. **Explanation.** An explanation tells "why" a behavior or mental process occurred. In other words, *explaining* a behavior or mental process depends on discovering and understanding its causes. One of the most enduring debates in science has been the **nature–nurture controversy** (Gardiner & Kosmitski, 2005; McCrae, 2004). Are we controlled by biological and genetic factors (the nature side)? Or by environment and learning (the nurture side)? As you will see throughout the text, psychology (like all sciences) generally avoids "either-or" positions and focuses instead on **interactions**. Today, almost all scientists agree that nature and nurture interact to produce most psychological traits and even most physical traits. For example, research on aggression reports numerous interacting causes, including culture, learning, genes, brain damage, and higher levels of testosterone (Anderson, 2004; Burns & Katovich, 2003; Trainor, Bird, & Marler, 2004; Uhlmann & Swanson, 2004).

3. **Prediction.** Psychologists generally begin with description and explanation (answering the "whats" and "whys"). Then they move on to the higher-level goal of *prediction*, identifying the conditions under which a future behavior or mental process is likely to occur. For instance, knowing that alcohol leads to increased aggression (Buddie & Parks, 2003), we can predict that more fights will erupt when alcohol is sold at sports matches than when it is not sold.

4. **Change.** For some people, having "change" as a goal of psychology brings to mind evil politicians or cult leaders "brainwashing" unknowing victims. However, to psychologists, *change* means applying psychological knowledge to prevent unwanted outcomes or bring about desired goals. In almost all cases, change as a goal of psychology is positive. Psychologists help people improve their work environment, stop addictive behaviors, become less depressed, improve their family relationships, and so on. Furthermore, as you know from personal experience, it is very difficult (if not impossible) to change someone against her or his will. (*Joke question:* Do you know how many psychologists it takes to change a light bulb? *Answer:* None. The light bulb has to want to change itself!)

APPLYING PSYCHOLOGY TO WORK

Careers in the Field

Knowing what psychology is, and understanding its four major goals, would you consider a career in the field? Many students think of psychologists only as therapists. However, many psychologists work as researchers, teachers, and consultants in academic, business, industry, and government settings (Table 1.1). Many psychologists also work in a combination of settings. Your college psychology instructor may be an experimental psychologist who teaches, conducts research, and works as a paid business or government consultant—all at the same time. Similarly, a clinical psychologist might be a full-time therapist, while also teaching college courses.

What is the difference between a psychiatrist and a clinical or counseling psychologist? The joke answer would be "about $100 an hour." The serious answer is that psychiatrists are medical doctors. They have M.D. degrees with a specialization in psychiatry and a license to prescribe medications and drugs. In contrast, most counseling and clinical psychologists have advanced degrees in human behavior and methods of therapy (e.g., Ph.D., Psy.D., or Ed.D.). Many clinical and counseling psychologists also work as a team with psychiatrists.

Nature—Nurture Controversy *Ongoing dispute over the relative contributions of nature (heredity) and nurture (environment)*

Interaction *Process in which multiple factors mutually influence one another and the outcome—as in the interaction between heredity and environment*

Applications
Throughout the text, you will find many ways to use and apply your increasing knowledge of psychology. Some "Application" sections are related to work, whereas others involve relationships and everyday life.

Narrative Questions
These boldfaced narrative questions are part of the SQ4R method described in the Preface. They help focus your reading and increase your comprehension.

www.wiley.com/college/huffman

TABLE 1.1 SAMPLE SPECIALTIES IN PSYCHOLOGY

Biopsychology/neuroscience. *Neuroscientist Candace Pert (and others) discovered the body's natural painkillers called endorphins (Chapter 2).*

Clinical and counseling psychology. *For most people, this is the role they commonly associate with psychology — that of clinical or counseling psychologist.*

Experimental psychology. *Dr. Louis Herman's research with dolphins has provided important insight into both human and nonhuman behavior and mental processes.*

Psychologists often wear many hats. *Dan Bellack teaches full-time at Trident Technical College, serves as Department Chair, and also works with faculty on teaching improvement.*

Biopsychology/ neuroscience	Investigates the relationship between biology, behavior, and mental processes, including how physical and chemical processes affect the structure and function of the brain and nervous system.
Clinical psychology	Specializes in the evaluation, diagnosis, and treatment of mental and behavioral disorders.
Cognitive psychology	Examines "higher" mental processes, including thought, memory, intelligence, creativity, and language.
Counseling psychology	Overlaps with clinical psychology but practitioners tend to work with less seriously disturbed individuals and conduct more career and vocational assessment.
Developmental psychology	Studies the course of human growth and development from conception until death.
Educational and school psychology	Studies the process of education and works to promote the intellectual, social, and emotional development of children in the school environment.
Experimental psychology	Examines processes such as learning, conditioning, motivation, emotion, sensation, and perception in humans and other animals. (The term experimental psychologist is somewhat misleading because psychologists working in almost all areas of specialization also conduct research.)
Forensic psychology	Applies principles of psychology to the legal system, including jury selection, psychological profiling, and so on.
Gender and/or cultural psychology	Investigates how men and women and different cultures differ from one another and how they are similar.
Health psychology	Studies how biological, psychological, and social factors affect health and illness.
Industrial/organizational psychology	Applies the principles of psychology to the workplace, including personnel selection and evaluation, leadership, job satisfaction, employee motivation, and group processes within the organization.
Social psychology	Investigates the role of social forces and interpersonal behavior, including aggression, prejudice, love, helping, conformity, and attitudes.

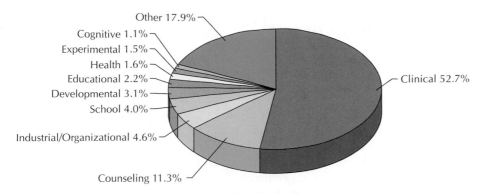

Other 17.9%
Cognitive 1.1%
Experimental 1.5%
Health 1.6%
Educational 2.2%
Developmental 3.1%
School 4.0%
Industrial/Organizational 4.6%
Counseling 11.3%
Clinical 52.7%

Figure 1.1 *Percentage of psychology degrees awarded by subfield.* Note that this is a small sampling of the numerous specialty areas in psychology. The percentages shown here are based on data from the American Psychological Association (APA), the largest professional psychological organization. The other major organization is the American Psychological Society (APS). Source: American Psychological Association, 2004.

Study Tip

Illustrations
Do not skip over the photos, figures, and tables. They visually reinforce important concepts and often contain material that may appear on exams.

To get an idea of the relative number of psychologists working in different fields of psychology, see Figure 1.1. If you are considering a career in psychology, this text will also present a rich variety of career options that may interest you. For example, Chapter 2 looks at the world of neuroscience. After studying it, you may decide you would like a career as a neuroscientist/biopsychologist. Chapter 3 explores health psychology and the work of health psychologists. And Chapters 14 and 15 examine problems in mental health and how therapists treat them. If you find a particular area of interest, ask your instructor and campus career counselors for further career guidance. It's also a good idea to check out the American Psychological Association's (APA) home page (http://www.apa.org/) and the American Psychological Society's (APS) website (http://www.psychologicalscience.org). Psychology is always looking "for a few good men"—and women.

Study Tip

Check & Review
As a form of assessment, each major topic concludes with an interim summary and four to six self-test questions that allow you to stop and check your understanding of the important concepts just discussed. Use these questions to review for exams, too. Answers appear in Appendix B at the back of the text.

Assessment

CHECK & REVIEW

Introducing Psychology

Psychology is the scientific study of behavior and mental processes. It emphasizes the empirical approach and the value of **critical thinking.** Psychology is not the same as common sense, "pop psychology," or pseudopsychology. The goals of psychology are to describe, explain, predict, and change behavior and mental processes.

Many avenues exist for those who want to pursue a career in psychology. These include biopsychology or neuroscience, experimental, cognitive, developmental, clinical, counseling, industrial/organizational, educational, and school psychology.

Questions

1. Psychology is the _____ study of _____ and _____.
2. What is the definition of critical thinking?
3. List and describe the four goals of psychology.
4. Name the subfield of psychology that studies each of the following topics:
   a. The brain and nervous system
   b. Growth and development from conception to death
   c. Thinking, memory, and intelligence
   d. Evaluation, diagnosis, and treatment of mental and behavioral disorders
   e. Application of psychological principles to the workplace

Check your answers in Appendix B.

CLICK & REVIEW
for additional assessment options:
www.wiley.com/college/huffman

Achievement

Who are the important contributors to psychology, and what are the seven primary perspectives that guide modern psychology?

ORIGINS OF PSYCHOLOGY

People have always been interested in human nature. Most of the great historical scholars, from Socrates and Aristotle to Bacon and Descartes, asked questions that we would today call psychological. What motivates people? How do we think and problem solve? Where do our emotions and reason reside? Do our emotions control us or are they something we can control? Interest in such topics remained largely among philosophers, theologians, and writers for several thousand years. Beginning in the late nineteenth century, psychological science began to emerge as a separate scientific discipline.

As you can see, psychology is a relatively young science and our discussion of its history will be brief. Throughout its short history, psychologists have adopted several perspectives on the "appropriate" topics for psychological research and the "proper" research methods. As a student, you may find these multiple (and sometimes contradictory) approaches frustrating and confusing. However, diversity and debate have always been the lifeblood of psychology and scientific progress.

Early Psychological Science: A Brief History

Wihelm Wundt (Vill-helm Voont) is generally credited with the "birth of psychology." As the acknowledged "father of psychology," Wundt established the first psychological laboratory in 1879 in Leipzig, Germany, and helped train the first generation of scientific psychologists. He also wrote *Principles* of *Physiological Psychology*, which is often considered the most important book in the history of psychology.

Wundt and his followers were interested primarily in studying conscious experience—how we form sensations, images, and feelings. Their chief methodology was termed *introspection*, monitoring and reporting on the contents of consciousness (Goodwin, 2005). If you were one of Wundt's participants trained in introspection, you might be presented with the sound of a clicking metronome. You would be told to focus solely on the clicks and report only your immediate reactions to them—your basic sensations and feelings.

Structuralism

Edward Titchener brought Wundt's ideas to the United States and established a psychological laboratory at Cornell University. Titchener was a kind of mental chemist who sought to identify the basic building blocks, or *structures*, of the mind. Wundt and Titchener's approach later came to be known as *structuralism*, which dealt with the *structure* of mental life. Just as the elements hydrogen and oxygen combine to form the compound water, Wundt believed the "elements" of conscious experience combined to form the "compounds" of the mind. Structuralists sought to identify the elements of thought through introspection and then to determine how these elements combined to form the whole of experience.

Unfortunately, it soon became clear that structuralism was doomed to failure. When different observers introspected and then disagreed on their experiences, no scientific way existed to settle the dispute. Furthermore, introspection could not be used to study nonhuman animals, children, or complex topics like mental disorders or personality. Although structuralism died out after a few decades, it made a lasting contribution by establishing a model for the scientific study of mental processes.

Functionalism

The decline of structuralism led to the development of a new school of psychology known as *functionalism*. This group of early psychologists studied how the mind *functions* to adapt human and nonhuman animals to their environment. Earlier structuralists might have studied "anger" by asking people to introspect and report on their

How would you describe this object?

Photodisc Green/Getty

If you were a participant in Titchener's laboratory, you would describe not what it is, but your subjective experience—the intensity and clarity of color, texture, shape, and smell. Structuralists called this research method *introspection*. The fact that your reported experience might differ from others, or that Titchener had no way to check the accuracy of your report, created significant problems for the structuralists.

individual experiences. In comparison, functionalists would have asked, "Why do we have the emotion of anger? What function does it serve? How does it help us adapt to our environment?" As you can see, functionalism was strongly influenced by Darwin's *theory of evolution* and his emphasis on *natural selection* (Segerstrale, 2000).

William James, an American scholar, was a leading force in the functionalist school. He also broadened psychology to include nonhuman animal behavior, various biological processes, and behaviors. In addition, his book *Principles of Psychology* (1890) became the leading psychology text—despite its length of more than 1400 pages!

Like structuralism, functionalism eventually declined. But it made a great impact on the development of psychology. It expanded the scope of psychology to include research on emotions and observable behaviors, initiated the psychological testing movement, changed the course of modern education, and extended psychology's influence to diverse areas in industry.

Psychoanalytic/Psychodynamic Perspective

During the late 1800s and early 1900s, while functionalism was prominent in the United States, the **psychoanalytic/psychodynamic perspective** was forming in Europe (Gay, 2000). Its founder, Sigmund Freud, was an Austrian physician who was fascinated with the mind's influence on behavior and the physical body. After encountering several patients with ongoing physical complaints that seemed to have no physiological basis, Freud assumed that their complaints must be psychological. Further studies of these patients convinced Freud that such problems are caused by conflicts between what people believe to be acceptable behavior and their unacceptable motives, which he believed were primarily of a sexual or aggressive nature.

These conflicts and motives were the driving forces behind behavior. But they are hidden in the *unconscious*, a part of the mind outside our awareness (Goodwin, 2005). In other words, we may develop physical complaints or do and say things without recognizing our true underlying motives. Freud also believed that early childhood experiences help shape our adult personalities and behavior—"The child is father to the man." To deal with these unconscious conflicts and early childhood influences, Freud developed a form of psychotherapy, or "talk therapy," called *psychoanalysis*.

Why is there such criticism of Freud? Freud's nonscientific approach and emphasis on sexual and aggressive impulses have caused a great deal of controversy over the years. Even some of Freud's most ardent followers—for example, Carl Jung, Alfred Adler, Karen Horney, and Erik Erikson—later broke away from their mentor. They did so largely because they wanted less emphasis on sex and aggression and more on social motives and relationships. Some also objected to possible sexist bias in his writings and theories. These early followers and their theories are called *neo-Freudians* (*neo*-means "new" or "recent").

Bettmann/Corbis Images

William James *(1842–1910). James was a leading force in the functionalist school of psychology, which stressed the adaptive and practical functions of human behavior.*

Psychoanalytic/Psychodynamic Perspective *Focuses on unconscious processes and unresolved past conflicts*

Keystone/The Image Works

Sigmund Freud *(1856–1939). Freud founded the psychoanalytic perspective, an influential theory of personality, and a type of therapy known as psychoanalysis.*

Behavior Perspective *Emphasizes objective, observable environmental influences on overt behavior*

John B. Watson *(1878–1958). Watson founded the school of behaviorism, which advocated that observable stimuli and responses should be the focus of psychology— not mental processes.*

Bettmann/Corbis Images

Ivan Pavlov *(1849–1936). Pavlov earned Russia's first Nobel Prize in 1904 for his study of digestion. But his lasting contribution to psychology was his accidental discovery of classical conditioning.*

Bettmann/Corbis Images

B. F. Skinner *(1904–1990). Skinner was a prominent figure in behaviorism and one of the most influential psychologists of the twentieth century.*

Nina Leen/Time Life Pictures/ Getty Images

Today, there are few strictly Freudian psychoanalysts left. But the broad features of his theory remain in the modern *psychodynamic* approach. Although psychodynamic psychologists are making increasing use of experimental methods, their primary method is the analysis of case studies. Their primary goal is to interpret complex meanings hypothesized to underlie people's actions.

Behavior Perspective

In the early 1900s, another major school of thought appeared that dramatically shaped the course of psychology. Whereas structuralism, functionalism, and the psychoanalytic school looked at nonobservable mental forces, the **behavior perspective** emphasizes objective, observable environmental influences on overt behavior.

John B. Watson (1913), the acknowledged founder of behaviorism, strongly objected to the practice of introspection, the study of mental processes, and the influence of unconscious forces. He believed these practices and topics were unscientific and too obscure to be studied empirically. Watson adopted Russian physiologist Ivan Pavlov's concept of conditioning to explain how behavior results from observable *stimuli* (in the environment) and observable *responses* (behavioral actions). In Pavlov's famous experiment teaching a dog to salivate in response to the sound of a bell, the bell is the stimulus and the salivation is the response.

Because nonhuman animals are ideal subjects for studying objective, overt behaviors, the majority of early behavior research was done with them or with techniques developed through nonhuman research. Using dogs, rats, pigeons, and other nonhuman animals, behaviorists such as John Watson in the early 1900s and, more recently, B. F. Skinner focused primarily on learning and how behaviors are acquired. They formulated a number of basic principles about learning that are explained in Chapter 6.

It sounds like behaviorists are interested only in nonhuman animals. Aren't any of them interested in humans? Yes, behaviorists are interested in people. One of the most well-known behaviorists, B. F. Skinner, was convinced that we could use behavior approaches to actually "shape" human behavior. This shaping could thereby change the present negative course (as he perceived it) of humankind. He did considerable writing and lecturing to convince others of this position. Behaviorists have been most successful in treating people with overt (observable, behavioral) problems, such as phobias (irrational fears) and alcoholism (Chapters 14 and 15).

Humanist Perspective

The psychoanalytic and behavior perspectives dominated the thinking American psychologists for some time. However, in the 1950s a new approach emerged—the **humanist perspective**, which stressed *free will*, self-actualization, and human nature as naturally positive and growth seeking.

Rejecting psychoanalysts' emphasis on unconscious forces and behaviorists' focus on stimulus, response, and the environment, humanists emphasized our unique ability to make voluntary choices about our own behavior and life. This is a sharp contrast to psychoanalysts and behaviorists who saw human behavior as shaped and determined by external causes beyond personal control.

According to Carl Rogers and Abraham Maslow, two central figures in the development of humanism, all individuals naturally strive to grow, develop, and move toward *self-actualization* (a state of self-fulfillment in which we realize our highest potential). Like psychoanalysis, humanistic psychology developed both an influential theory of personality and a form of psychotherapy, which will be explored in depth in upcoming chapters.

Cognitive Perspective

Some of psychology's earliest contributors were interested in consciousness and the elements of thought. Ironically, one of the most influential modern approaches, the

Humanist Perspective *Emphasizes free will, self-actualization, and human nature as naturally positive and growth-seeking*

Roger Ressmeyer/ Corbis Images

Two key figures in humanistic psychology. *Carl Rogers (1902–1987, left photo) and Abraham Maslow (1908–1970, right photo) both played significant roles in the development of psychology.*

cognitive perspective, harkens back to this time with its emphasis on thought, perception, and information processing.

Modern-day cognitive psychologists, however, study how we gather, encode, and store information from our environment using a vast array of mental processes. These processes include perception, memory, imagery, concept formation, problem solving, reasoning, decision making, and language. If you were listening to a friend describe her whitewater rafting trip, a cognitive psychologist would be interested in how you decipher the meaning of her words, how you form mental images of the turbulent water, how you incorporate your impressions of her experience into your previous concepts and experience of rafting, and so on.

Many cognitive psychologists use an *information-processing* approach in their studies (Goodwin, 2005). According to this approach, we gather information from the environment and then process it in a series of stages. Like computers, we first take in information, then process it, and then produce a response. Cognitive psychology plays a dominant theme in modern psychology.

Neuroscience/Biopsychology Perspective

During the last few decades, scientists have explored the role of genetics and other biological factors in almost every area of psychology, including sensation, perception, learning, memory, language, sexuality, and abnormal behavior. This exploration has given rise to an increasingly important trend in psychology, known as the **neuroscience/biopsychology perspective**.

As you will see in the upcoming discussion of psychological research in this chapter, neuroscientists/biopsychologists have developed sophisticated "tools" and technologies to conduct their research. They use these tools to study the structure and function of individual nerve cells, the roles of various parts of the brain, and how genetics and other biological processes contribute to our behavior and mental processes. We will return to the neuroscience/biopsychology perspective throughout Chapter 2 and other chapters.

Evolutionary Perspective

The **evolutionary perspective** derives from a focus on natural selection, adaptation, and evolution of behavior and mental processes (Buss, 2005; Rossano, 2003). Its proponents argue that natural selection favors behaviors that enhance an organism's reproductive success. That is, human and nonhuman animals exhibiting behaviors that contribute to survival will pass them on through their genes to the next generation.

Consider aggression. Behaviorists would argue that we learn aggressiveness at an early age. "Hitting another child stops him or her from taking your toys." Cognitive psychologists would emphasize how thoughts contribute to aggression. "He intended to hurt me. Therefore, I should hit him back!" Neuroscience/biopsychologists might say aggressiveness results primarily from neurotransmitters, hormones, and structures in the brain. In comparison, evolutionary psychologists would argue that human and nonhuman animals behave aggressively because aggression conveys a survival or reproductive advantage. They believe aggression evolved over many generations because it successfully met the adaptive pressures faced by our ancestors.

Sociocultural Perspective

The **sociocultural perspective** emphasizes social interactions and cultural determinants of behavior and mental processes. Sociocultural psychologists have shown how factors such as ethnicity, religion, occupation, and socioeconomic class all have an enormous psychological impact.

Unless someone points it out, however, few of us recognize the importance of these factors. As Segall and his colleagues (1990) suggest, when you go to school, you probably walk into a classroom at the same time on the same days, sit in the same chair, and

Cognitive Perspective *Focuses on thought, perception, and information processing*

Neuroscience/Biopsychology Perspective *Emphasizes genetics and other biological processes in the brain and other parts of the nervous system*

Evolutionary Perspective *Focuses on natural selection, adaptation, and evolution of behavior and mental processes*

Sociocultural Perspective *Emphasizes social interaction and cultural determinants of behavior and mental processes*

www.wiley.com/college/huffman

AP/Wide World Photos

Psychology in a global economy. *Technological advances allow instant communication for people who not long ago were isolated from events in the rest of the world. How do you think these changes affect these men from the Enaotai Island in West Papua New Guinea?*

Psychology Archives-The University of Akron

Mary Calkins *(1863–1930). Calkins was the first woman president of the American Psychological Association. She also established a psychology laboratory at Wellesley College and conducted important research on memory.*

Library of Congress Prints and Photographs Division

Kenneth Clark *(1914–2005). Clark was the first African American president of the American Psychological Association. He and his wife, Mamie, also conducted research on prejudice that was cited in 1964 by the U.S. Supreme Court.*

either listen to a trained teacher or participate in an activity designed and directed by that teacher. This is because it is the schooling system of your social world and culture. In another society or culture, such as a remote region of East Africa, you and your friends might gather informally around a respected elder, some of you sitting and others standing, all of you listening to the elder tell stories of the history of the tribe.

Just as a fish doesn't know it is in water, most of us are similarly unaware of the social and cultural forces that shape our lives. This is one of many reasons why we include such heavy coverage of socio-cultural psychology throughout this text.

Women and Minorities

Before leaving this brief history of psychology, we want to include the important contributions of women and minorities. During the late 1800s and early 1900s, most colleges and universities provided little opportunity for women and minorities, as either students or faculty. Despite these early limitations, both women and minorities have made important contributions to psychology.

Mary Calkins was among the first women to be recognized in the field. She performed valuable research on memory and in 1905 served as the first female president of the American Psychological Association (APA). Calkins' achievements are particularly noteworthy, considering the significant discrimination against women in those times. Even after completing all the requirements for a Ph.D. at Harvard and being described by William James as his brightest student, the university refused to grant the degree to a woman. The first woman to receive a Ph.D. in psychology was Margaret Floy Washburn (in 1894), who wrote several influential books and served as the second female president of APA.

Francis Cecil Sumner, without benefit of a formal high school education, became the first African American to earn a Ph.D. in psychology from Clark University in 1920. He also translated over 3000 articles from German, French, and Spanish and founded one of the country's leading psychology departments. One of Sumner's students at Clark University, Kenneth B. Clark, later (in 1971) became the first African American to be elected APA president. Along with his wife, Mamie, Kenneth Clark documented the harmful effects of prejudice (see Chapters 6 and 16). Their research had a direct effect on the Supreme Court's ultimate ruling against racial segregation in schools.

Sumner and Clark, Calkins and Washburn, along with other important minorities and women, made significant and lasting contributions to the developing science of psychology. In recent years, people of color and women are being actively encouraged to pursue graduate degrees in psychology. But as you can see in Figure 1.2, white (non-Hispanic) people still make up the majority of new doctorate recipients in psychology.

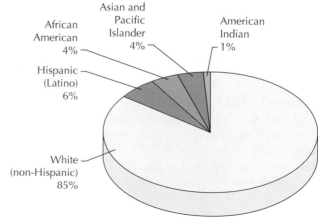

Figure 1.2 ***Ethnicities of doctorate recipients in psychology.***

African American 4%

Asian and Pacific Islander 4%

American Indian 1%

Hispanic (Latino) 6%

White (non-Hispanic) 85%

Modern Perspectives: Seven Approaches and One Unifying Theme

Early schools like structuralism and functionalism have almost entirely disappeared or blended into newer, broader perspectives. As you can see in Table 1.2, there are seven major perspectives in contemporary psychology: *psychoanalytic/psychodynamic, behavior, humanist, cognitive, neuroscience/biopsychology, evolutionary,* and *sociocultural.*

In discussing the seven modern perspectives in psychology, I have presented them separately and made distinctions between their philosophies and practices. Most psychologists recognize the value of each orientation, while recognizing that no one view has all the answers. Complex behaviors and mental processes require complex explanations. Thus, most psychologists recognize the value of using several perspectives.

TABLE 1.2 PSYCHOLOGY'S PRESENT—SEVEN MAJOR PERSPECTIVES

Perspectives	Prominent Figures	Major Emphases	
Psychoanalytic/ psychodynamic (1895–present)	Sigmund Freud Carl Jung Alfred Adler Karen Horney	Unconscious processes and unresolved past conflicts; the "mind" is like an iceberg with the largest, "unconscious," section hidden beneath the surface	
Behavior (1906–present)	Ivan Pavlov Edward Thorndike John B. Watson B. F. Skinner	Objective, observable environmental influences on overt behavior; the "mind" is like a "black box" that is unobservable and unmeasurable	Environment
Humanist (1950s–present)	Carl Rogers Abraham Maslow	Free-will, self-actualization, and human nature as naturally positive and growth-seeking	
Cognitive (1950s–present)	Jean Piaget Albert Ellis Albert Bandura Robert Sternberg Howard Gardner Clark Hull	Thoughts, perception, and information processing	
Neuroscience/ biopsychology (1950s–present)	Johannes Müller Karl Lashley David Hubel James Olds Roger Sperry Candace Pert Torsten Wiesel	Genetics and biological processes in the brain and other parts of the nervous system	
Evolutionary (1980s–present)	Charles Darwin Konrad Lorenz E. O. Wilson David Buss Margo Wilson	Natural selection, adaptation, and evolution of behavior and mental processes	
Sociocultural (1980s–present)	John Berry Patricia Greenfield Richard Brislin	Social interaction and the cultural determinants of behavior and mental processes	

Why do we need multiple and competing perspectives?

What do you see in the drawing to the right? Do you see two profiles facing each other or a white vase? Your ability to see both figures is similar to a psychologist's ability to study behavior and mental processes from a number of different perspectives.

Kaiser-Porcelain Limited

Biopsychosocial Model *Unifying theme of modern psychology that considers biological, psychological, and social processes*

One of the most widely accepted, and unifying, themes of modern psychology is the **biopsychosocial model**. This approach views *biological* processes (e.g., genetics, brain functions, neurotransmitters, and evolution), *psychological* factors (e.g., learning, thinking, emotion, personality, and motivation), and *social forces* (e.g., family, culture, ethnicity, social class, and politics) as interrelated influences.

Figure 1.3 *The biopsychosocial model combines and interacts with the seven major perspectives.*

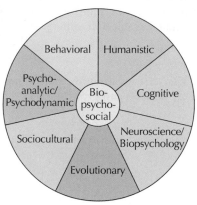

This new, integrative model proposes that all three forces *affect* and *are affected by* one another. They are inseparable. For example, feelings of depression are often influenced by genetics and neurotransmitters (biology). They are also affected by our learned responses and patterns of thinking (psychology) and by our socioeconomic status and cultural views of emotion (social). In the coming chapters, I frequently refer to one or more of the seven major perspectives shown in Table 1.2. However, the common theme of modern psychology, and this text, is an integrative, *biopsychosocial* approach (Figure 1.3).

Assessment

VISUAL QUIZ

Nina Leen/Time Life Pictures/Getty Images

Research has shown that some non-human animals, such as newly hatched ducks or geese, follow and become attached to (or imprinted on) the first large moving object they see or hear. Konrad Lorenz, an influential figure in early psychology, hatched these geese in an incubator. Because he was the first large moving object they saw at birth, they now closely follow him everywhere—as if he were their mother. When Lorenz was asleep on the ground with his mouth open, a goose even tried to feed him a live worm.

Using the information in Table 1.2, can you identify which perspective of psychology would most likely study and explain these behaviors?

Answer: Evolutionary

CHECK & REVIEW

Origins of Psychology

Among the early contributors to psychology, the *structuralists* sought to identify elements of consciousness and how those elements formed the structure of the mind. They relied primarily on the method of introspection. *Functionalists* studied how mental processes help the individual adapt to the environment. Seven major perspectives guide modern psychology: **psychoanalytic/psychodynamic, behavior, humanist, cognitive, neuroscience/biopsychology, evolution-**ary, and **sociocultural.** Today, the **biopsychosocial model** draws from all seven major perspectives. These modern perspectives and the biopsychosocial model permeate the field of psychology and will be discussed in detail throughout this text.

Questions

1. The _____ school of psychology originated the method of introspection to examine thoughts and feelings.
2. _____ investigated the function of mental processes in adapting to the environment.
3. Why are Freud's theories so controversial?
4. Which of the following terms do not belong together? (a) structuralism, observable behavior; (b) behaviorism, stimulus-response; (c) psychoanalytic, unconscious conflict; (d) humanism, free will

Check your answers in Appendix B.

CLICK & REVIEW
for additional assessment options:
www.wiley.com/college/huffman

THE SCIENCE OF PSYCHOLOGY

As mentioned in the beginning of this chapter, psychology is all around us, and its research findings are widely reported by television, radio, and newspapers. You will understand this research (and the studies cited in this text) better if we briefly discuss how psychologists collect, interpret, and evaluate data.

To begin, you should know that research strategies are generally categorized as either *basic* or *applied*. **Basic research** is typically conducted in universities or research laboratories by researchers interested in exploring new theories and advancing general scientific understanding—knowledge for its own sake without known real-world uses. Basic research meets the first three goals of psychology (*description, explanation,* and *prediction*). In contrast, **applied research** is generally conducted outside the laboratory. And it meets the fourth goal of psychology—to *change* existing real-world problems. Discoveries linking aggression to testosterone, genes, learning, and other factors came primarily from basic research. In contrast, applied research has designed programs for conflict resolution and counseling for perpetrators and victims of violence. It also has generated important safety and design improvements in automobiles, airplanes, and even stovetop burner arrangements (Figure 1.4).

Basic and applied research also frequently interact—one leading to or building on the other. For example, after basic research documented a strong relationship between alcohol consumption and increased aggression, applied research led some sports stadium owners to limit the sale of alcohol during the final quarter of football games and the last two innings of baseball games.

Now that you understand the distinction between basic and applied research, we can explore two additional topics in psychological research: the scientific method and research ethics.

The Scientific Method: A Way of Discovering

Like scientists in biology, chemistry, or any other scientific field, psychologists follow strict, standardized scientific procedures so that others—laypeople as well as scientists—can understand, interpret, and repeat or test their findings. Most scientific investigations generally involve six basic steps (Figure 1.5).

Achievement

What is the scientific method, and what are the key ethical issues in psychological research?

Basic Research *Research conducted to advance scientific knowledge*

Applied Research *Research designed to solve practical problems*

Figure 1.4 *Human factors and the real world.* Note how psychological research has helped design safer and more reliable appliances, machinery, and instrument controls. For example: (a) Controls for stovetops should be arranged in a pattern that corresponds to the placement of the burners. (b) Automobile gauges for fuel, oil, and speed should be easily visible to the driver. (c) Airplane controls and knobs are easier and safer to use if their shape corresponds to their function. (d) Airplane control panels should be arranged so pilots can safely operate and quickly respond to any emergency.

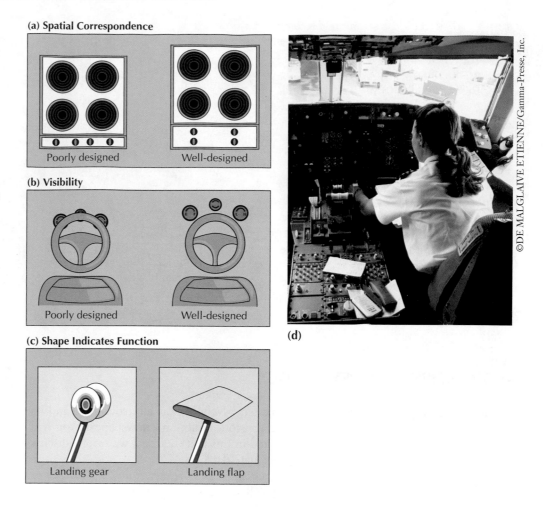

(a) Spatial Correspondence

Poorly designed   Well-designed

(b) Visibility

Poorly designed   Well-designed

(c) Shape Indicates Function

Landing gear   Landing flap

(d)

©DE MALGLAIVE ETIENNE/Gamma-Presse, Inc.

Figure 1.5 *Scientific method's six steps.* Science is a dynamic field where new ideas are continually being tested and revised. Most investigations involve six carefully planned steps, beginning with an identification of questions of interest and a review of the existing literature. They "end" with a return to theory building. Note that the steps are arranged in a circle, which symbolizes the circular, cumulative nature of science. One scientific study generally leads to additional and refined hypotheses, further studies, clarification of the results, and improvement in the overall scientific knowledge base, known as theories.

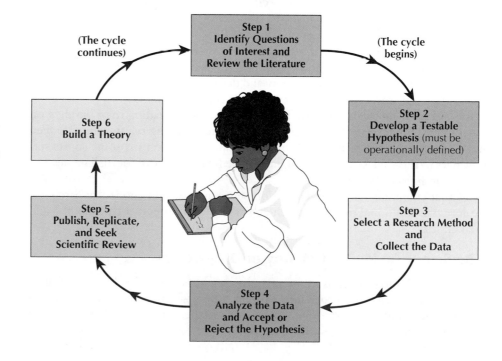

(The cycle continues)

(The cycle begins)

Step 1
Identify Questions of Interest and Review the Literature

Step 2
Develop a Testable Hypothesis (must be operationally defined)

Step 3
Select a Research Method and Collect the Data

Step 4
Analyze the Data and Accept or Reject the Hypothesis

Step 5
Publish, Replicate, and Seek Scientific Review

Step 6
Build a Theory

Step 1: Identify Questions of Interest and Review the Literature

Psychological research generally begins with informal questions. Students ask about the best study methods for tests. Dating couples want to know what factors are important for a happy marriage. And parents may want advice about their small child who begs to sleep with them in their bed.

What do you think about this last question? Should parents allow their children to sleep with them? According to most parents in Western, industrialized societies, "Children should sleep alone. Otherwise, they will become overly attached and never leave their parents' bed." Rather than simply accepting this popular opinion, let's imagine ourselves as psychologists. How can we scientifically test this notion?

Using the scientific method, our first official step would be *to review the literature*. We would carefully review what other professionals have to say about sleeping arrangements by searching and reading what has been published in major professional scientific journals, such as *Psychological Science* or the *Journal of Cross Cultural Psychology*. (Keep in mind that these journals are not popular media sources like newspapers or unofficial Internet reports.)

If you did conduct an actual literature review on children's sleeping arrangements, you would find several interesting discoveries. For example, cross-cultural studies generally report that the "family bed," where the entire family sleeps in one bed, is one of the most common arrangements in many parts of the world. And in these cultures, most people consider shared sleeping beds vital to a child's social and emotional well-being (see Abel et al., 2001; Javo, Ronning, & Heyerdahl, 2004; Rothrauff, Middlemiss, & Jacobsen, 2004).

Step 2: Develop a Testable Hypothesis

Once the review of literature is completed, our next step would be to develop a testable **hypothesis**: a specific prediction about how one variable relates to another. (*Variables* are simply factors that can *vary* or change.) A hypothesis may or may not be correct. It only provides a possible explanation for a behavior or mental process that can be scientifically investigated. To explore our original question about sleeping arrangements, our hypothesis might be: "Family bed sleeping arrangements lead to overly attached children." (In this hypothesis, sleeping arrangement is one variable and attachment is another.)

To be fully testable, a hypothesis must be formulated precisely (as opposed to vaguely or loosely). And the variables under study must be **operationally defined**, or stated in observable, measurable terms. How can we operationally define *sleeping arrangements*? What could we measure?

Hypothesis *Specific prediction about how one variable relates to another*

Operational Definition *A precise description of how the variables in a study will be observed and measured (For example, drug abuse might be operationally defined as "the number of missed work days due to excessive use of an addictive substance.")*

Step 3: Select a Research Method and Collect the Data

The third step in the scientific method is to choose the best research design to test our hypothesis and collect our data. We could choose naturalistic observation, case studies, surveys, experiments, and other methods discussed in the next section of this chapter.

Given our hypothesis about sleeping arrangements and attachment, we might choose the survey method. We would then need to design the survey, decide when and where to conduct it, and determine how to get the appropriate number of subjects, or *participants*. We might decide to mail 500 questionnaires to parents asking about their child's sleeping habits and attachment behaviors. Questions might include the following: "How many hours a day does your child sleep alone or with one or both parents?" "Does your child cry when you leave him or her in the care of another trusted adult?" "How does your child respond when you return after a brief (30-minute) separation?"

Step 4: Analyze the Data and Accept or Reject the Hypothesis

After we have designed the study and collected the survey results, the "raw data" must be analyzed to determine whether the findings support or reject our initial hypothe-

Throughout this text, you will see citations (authors' names and publication dates) at the end of many sentences, such as (Matlin, 2005). This tells you that the material comes from reputable sources and is as up to date as possible. Complete publication information (title of article or chapter, author, journal name or book title, date, and page numbers) is provided in the References section at the back of this book. You can use these references as a starting point for research projects, for additional information on a topic of interest, and to double-check any research cited in this text. As a critical thinker, never take the word of any one author or authors. Check their sources.

sis. To do such an analysis, psychologists use mathematical methods called *statistics* to organize, summarize, and interpret numerical data.

Step 5: Publish, Replicate, and Seek Scientific Review

To advance in any scientific discipline, researchers must share their work with one another and with the public. Thus, the fifth step in the scientific method begins when a researcher writes up the study and submits it to *peer-reviewed* scientific journals for publication. (Peer-reviewed journals require other psychologists to evaluate all material submitted for publication.) Based on these peer reviews, editors may accept or reject the study. Once a study is accepted and published, other scientists attempt to *replicate*, or repeat, the study. *Replication* increases scientific confidence if the findings are the same. If not, researchers look for explanations and conduct further studies. As responsible scientists, psychologists almost never accept a theory based on a single study. They wait for replication.

What if some replications find contradictory results? In this case, both the original and follow-up studies are publicly questioned and criticized in academic journal articles. When different studies report contradictory findings, researchers can also average or combine the results of all such studies and reach conclusions about the overall weight of the evidence. This method of averaging is called **meta-analysis**. For example, researchers Daniel Voyer, Susan Voyer, and M. P. Bryden (1995) did a meta-analysis of almost 50 years of research on gender differences in spatial abilities. They found that males do better than females on some, but not all, tests of spatial ability. This meta-analysis also found that the differences have decreased in recent years, possibly owing to changes in educational practices. As you can see, with time, the process of *scientific review* gradually discloses flaws. It also fine-tunes research and helps eliminate erroneous findings.

Meta-analysis *Statistical procedure for combining and analyzing data from many studies*

Step 6: Build a Theory—And Then the Cycle Continues

Steps 1 through 5 involved reviewing the literature, formulating a hypothesis, conducting the research, analyzing the data, and publishing the findings so they can be replicated and reviewed. Now, the fun begins. After one or more studies on a given topic, researchers may advance a theory to explain their results. Please note that psychologists generally define **theory** as *an interrelated set of concepts that explain a body of data*. Contrary to common usage, where the term *theory* refers to personal opinion and unproven assumptions, psychological theories are developed from careful research, empirical observation, and extensive reviews of existing scientific literature.

Can you see how and why scientific research continually changes? As Figure 1.5 shows, the scientific method is *circular* and *cumulative*. Scientific progress comes from repeatedly challenging, revising existing theories, and building new ones.

Ethical Guidelines: Protecting the Rights of Others

The two largest professional organizations of psychologists, the American Psychological Society (APS) and the American Psychological Association (APA), both recognize the importance of maintaining high ethical standards in research, therapy, and all other areas of professional psychology. The preamble to the APA's publication *Ethical Principles of Psychologists and Code of Conduct* (1992) admonishes psychologists to retain objectivity in applying their skills. It also requires them to maintain their competence and to preserve the dignity and best interests of their clients, colleagues, students, research participants, and society. In this section, we will explore three important areas of ethical concern: human participants, nonhuman animal rights, and clients in therapy.

Respecting the Rights of Human Participants

The APA has developed rigorous guidelines regulating research with human participants, including:

- *Informed consent.* One of the first research principles is obtaining an **informed consent** from all participants before initiating an experiment. Participants should be aware of the nature of the study and significant factors that might influence their willingness to participate. This includes all physical risks, discomfort, or unpleasant emotional experiences.

- *Voluntary participation.* Participants should be told they are free to decline to participate or to withdraw from the research at any time.

- *Restricted use of deception and debriefing.* If participants know the true purpose behind some studies, they will almost certainly not respond naturally. Therefore, the APA acknowledges the need for some *deception* in certain research areas. But when it is used, important guidelines and restrictions apply, including debriefing participants at the end of the experiment. **Debriefing** involves explaining the reasons for conducting the research and clearing up any misconceptions or concerns on the part of the participant.

- *Confidentiality.* All information acquired about people during a study must be kept private and not published in such a way that individual rights to privacy are compromised.

- *Alternative activities.* If research participation is a course requirement or an opportunity for extra credit for college students, all students must be given the choice of an alternative activity of equal value.

Respecting the Rights of Nonhuman Animal Participants

Research in psychology usually involves human participants. Only about 7 to 8 percent of research is done on nonhuman animals, and 90 percent of that is done with rats and mice (American Psychological Association, 1984).

Theory *Interrelated set of concepts that explain a body of data*

Study **T**ip

This ongoing, circular nature of theory building often frustrates students. In most chapters you will encounter numerous and sometimes conflicting hypotheses and theories. You will be tempted to ask, "Which theory is right?" But remember that theories are never absolute. As mentioned in the earlier discussion of the nature–nurture controversy, the "correct" answer is usually interactionism. In most cases, multiple theories contribute to the full understanding of complex concepts.

Informed Consent *Participant's agreement to take part in a study after being told what to expect*

Debriefing *Informing participants after the research about the purpose of the study, the nature of the anticipated results, and any deceptions used*

Joe Raedle/Newsmakers/Getty Images

Is nonhuman animal research ethical?
Opinions are sharply divided on this question, but when research is carefully conducted within ethical guidelines, the research can yield significant benefits for both human and nonhuman animals.

There are important reasons for using nonhuman animals in psychological research. For example, the field of *comparative psychology* is dedicated to the study of behavior of different species. In other cases, nonhuman animals are used because researchers need to study participants continuously over months or years (longer than people are willing to participate). Occasionally they also want to control aspects of life that people will not let them control and that would be unethical to control (such as who mates with whom or the effects of serious food restrictions). The relative simplicity of some nonhuman animals' nervous systems also provides important advantages for research.

Most psychologists recognize the tremendous scientific contributions that laboratory nonhuman animals have made—and continue to make. Without nonhuman animals in *medical research*, how would we test new drugs, surgical procedures, and methods for relieving pain? *Psychological research* with nonhuman animals has led to significant advances in virtually every area of psychology, including the brain and nervous system, health and stress, sensation and perception, sleep, learning, memory, stress, emotion, and so on.

Nonhuman animal research also has produced significant gains for animals themselves. Effective training techniques and natural environments have been created for pets and wild animals in captivity. Also, successful breeding techniques have been developed for endangered species.

Despite the advantages, using nonhuman animals in psychological research continues to be a controversial and ethical problem (Guidelines for the Treatment, 2005). Opponents argue that, unlike humans, other animals cannot give *informed consent*. They also question the so-called benefits of nonhuman animal research, especially considering the animals' suffering and loss of freedom. Proponents counter by saying that most nonhuman animal research involves naturalistic observation or learning experiments using rewards rather than punishments. Furthermore, most research does not involve pain, suffering, or deprivation (Burgdorf, Knutson, & Panksepp, 2000; Neuringer, Deiss, & Olson, 2000; Shapiro, 1997). As in most controversies, numerous questions remain unresolved—with no easy answers. How do we balance costs and benefits? To what extent do the costs to nonhuman animals justify the benefits? Is human life intrinsically more valuable than other animal life?

While the debate continues, psychologists take great care in the handling of nonhuman research animals. They also actively search for new and better ways to protect them (Atkins, Panicker, & Cunningham, 2005; Guidelines for the Treatment, 2005; Sherwin et al., 2003). In all institutions where nonhuman animal research is conducted, animal care committees are established to ensure proper treatment of research animals, to review projects, and to set guidelines that are in accordance with the APA standards for the care and treatment of nonhuman (and human) research animals.

Respecting the Rights of Psychotherapy Clients

Ethics are important in therapy as well as in research. Successful psychotherapy requires that clients reveal their innermost thoughts and feelings during the course of treatment. It follows, then, that clients must trust their therapists.

This places a burden of responsibility on therapists to maintain the highest of ethical standards and uphold this trust. Therapists are expected to conduct themselves in a moral and professional manner. They should remain objective, while at the same time becoming sufficiently involved with the clients' problems to know how best to help them. They also should encourage their clients to become involved and committed to a mutually agreeable treatment plan. In addition, therapists are expected to evaluate their clients' progress and report that progress to them.

Like the guidelines for confidentiality in research, all personal information and therapy records must be kept confidential. Records are only available to authorized persons and with the client's permission. Such confidentiality can become an ethical issue when a client reveals something that might affect or possibly injure another person. For example, if you were a therapist, what would you do if a client revealed plans to commit murder? Should you alert the police, or should you uphold your client's trust?

In cases of serious threat to others, the public's right to safety ethically outweighs the client's right to privacy. In fact, a therapist is legally required to break confidentiality if a client threatens violence to self or others, in cases involving suspected or actual child or elder abuse, and in some other limited situations. In general, however, a counselor's primary obligation is to protect client disclosures (Corey, 2005).

A Final Note on Ethical Issues

After this discussion of research ethics, you may be unnecessarily concerned. Remember that guidelines exist to protect the rights of humans, nonhuman animals, and therapy clients. Most importantly, a human subjects committee or institutional review board must first approve all research using human participants conducted at a college, university, or any other reputable institution. This group ensures that every proposed study provides for informed consent, participants' confidentiality, and safe procedures. Similar committees also exist to oversee and protect the rights of nonhuman animal participants.

The APA may officially censure or expel any member who disregards these principles. In addition, both researchers and clinicians are held professionally and legally responsible for their actions, and clinicians can permanently lose their license to practice.

What about ethics and beginning psychology students? Once friends and acquaintances know you're taking a course in psychology, they may ask you to interpret their dreams, help them discipline their children, or even ask your opinion on whether they should end their relationships. Although you will learn a great deal about psychological functioning in this text and in your psychology class, take care that you do not overestimate your expertise. Remember that the theories and findings of psychological science are circular and cumulative—and continually being revised.

David L. Cole (1982), a recipient of the APA Distinguished Teaching in Psychology Award, reminds us that "Undergraduate psychology can, and I believe should, seek to liberate the student from ignorance, but also the arrogance of believing we know more about ourselves and others than we really do."

At the same time, psychological findings and ideas developed through careful research and study can make important contributions to our lives. As Albert Einstein once said, "One thing I have learned in a long life: that all our science, measured against reality, is primitive and childlike—and yet, it is the most precious thing we have."

Assessment

CHECK & REVIEW

The Science of Psychology

Basic research studies theoretical issues. **Applied research** seeks to solve specific problems.

The scientific method consists of six carefully planned steps: (1) identifying questions of interest and reviewing the literature, (2) formulating a testable **hypothesis,** (3) choosing a research method and collecting the data, (4) analyzing the data and accepting or rejecting the hypothesis, (5) publishing followed by replication and scientific review, and (6) building further **theory.**

Psychologists must maintain high standards in their relations with human and nonhuman research participants, as well as in their therapeutic relationships with clients. The APA has published specific guidelines detailing these ethical standards.

www.wiley.com/college/huffman

RESEARCH METHODS

What is research, but a blind date with knowledge.

WILLIAM HENRY

Achievement

What are the four major methods of psychological research?

Now that you have a good basic understanding of the scientific method, we can examine four major types of psychological research—*experimental, descriptive, correlational,* and *biological*. As Figure 1.6 shows, all four types of research have advantages and disadvantages. We will explore each approach separately. But keep in mind that most psychologists use several methods to study a single problem. In fact, when multiple methods are used and the findings are mutually supportive, scientists have an especially strong foundation for concluding that one variable does affect another in a particular way.

Figure 1.6 *Four major methods of psychological research.*

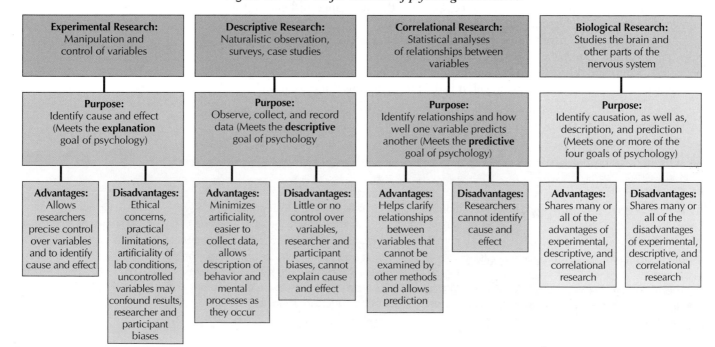

Experimental Research: A Search for Cause and Effect

Let's begin our discussion of types of psychological research with the single most powerful research method, the **experiment**, in which an experimenter manipulates and controls the chosen variables to determine cause and effect. Only through an experiment can researchers isolate a single factor and examine the effect of that factor alone on a particular behavior (Ray, 2003). For example, in studying for an upcoming test, you probably use several methods—reading lecture notes, rereading highlighted sections of your textbook, and repeating key terms with their definitions. Using multiple methods, however, makes it impossible to determine which study methods are effective or ineffective. The only way to discover which method is most effective is to isolate each one in an experiment. In fact, several experiments have been conducted to determine effective learning and study techniques (Son & Metcalfe, 2000). If you are interested in the results of this research or want to develop better study habits, you can jump ahead now and read the upcoming "Tools for Student Success" at the end of this chapter. There are also additional special "Study Tips" sections throughout the text identified with this icon

Experiment *Carefully controlled scientific procedure that involves manipulation of variables to determine cause and effect*

Key Features of an Experiment

An experiment has several key components: *independent* and *dependent variables*, and *experimental* versus *control groups*.

Independent and Dependent Variables If researchers choose to use an experiment to test a hypothesis, they must then decide which variables to manipulate and which to examine for possible changes. (A *variable* is simply anything that can *vary*.) The variables in an experiment are either *independent* or *dependent*. An **independent variable (IV)** is a factor that is selected and *manipulated* by the experimenter. In contrast, a **dependent variable (DV)** is a *measurable* behavior (or outcome) exhibited by the participant in the experiment. Because the IV is free to be selected and varied by the experimenter, it is called *independent*. The DV is called dependent because it is assumed to *depend* (at least in part) on manipulations of the IV. Keep in mind that the goal of any experiment is to learn how the dependent variable is affected by (depends on) the independent variable.

Independent Variable (IV) *Experimental factor manipulated to determine its causal effect on the dependent variable*

Dependent Variable (DV) *Experimental factor that is measured; it is affected by (or dependent on) the independent variable*

Imagine you are designing an experiment to discover whether watching violence on television causes aggressiveness in viewers. You begin by randomly assigning groups of children to watch three violent or three nonviolent television programs (the IV). After the viewing, you place a large plastic Bobo doll in front of each child and record for one hour the number of times the child hits, kicks, or punches the plastic doll (the DV). If you wanted to know whether a new medication was as effective as a currently used medication for social phobia (excessive, debilitating shyness), you could give different levels of the two drugs (IVs). Then you could measure the participants' anxiety and heart rate (DVs) in a social situation.

Note how the experimenter in the television viewing experiment (you), manipulated the IV (violent or nonviolent TV) and measured the DV (aggression). Once again, IVs are manipulated and DVs are measured.

Experimental Versus Control Groups In addition to IVs and DVs, each experiment must have one control group and one or more *experimental conditions*, or ways of treating the subjects/participants. Having at least two groups allows the performance of one group to be compared with that of another.

In the simplest experimental design, researchers *randomly* assign one group of participants to the **experimental group** and the other participants to the **control group**. In the violence-on-TV and aggression example, the experimental group would be exposed to the IV—in this case violent TV programs. The control group members would be treated exactly the same way as those in the experimental group, except that they would be assigned to a zero, or control, condition. This means they

Experimental Group *Group receiving treatment in an experiment*

Control Group *Group receiving no treatment in an experiment*

Figure 1.7 *Does TV increase aggression?* If experimenters wanted to test the hypothesis that watching violent TV increases aggression, they might begin by randomly assigning participants into one of two groups: *experimental group* participants who watch a prearranged number of violent TV programs, or *control group* participants who watch the same number of nonviolent TV programs. Then they would observe and measure the subsequent level of aggression. Note that the *manipulated variable* (IV) was violent TV or nonviolent TV. The *measured variable* (DV) was the number of times the child hit the plastic Bobo doll.

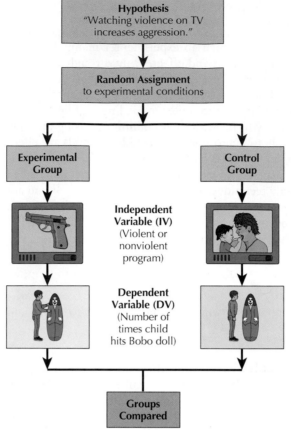

CONTROL GROUP   OUT OF CONTROL GROUP

Peter S. Mueller

would not be exposed to any amount of the IV. Instead, they would watch a nonviolent TV program for the same amount of time (Figure 1.7).

We also could design the experiment with more than one independent variable (IV). In the television viewing example, we would use different levels (or amounts) of TV viewing. If one group watches six hours of violent TV, the second variable might be a group that watches two hours of violent TV. These two groups would then be compared to the control group that watches no violent TV. Then we would measure and compare the aggressiveness of all three groups. Then we would attribute any significant differences in aggressive behavior (DV) to the amount of violent TV that was viewed (IV).

For both control and comparison groups, experimenters must ensure that all *extraneous variables* (those that are not being directly manipulated or measured) are held constant (the same). For example, the amount of time children were exposed to the plastic Bobo doll, the time of day, heating, and lighting would need to be kept constant for all participants so that they do not affect participants' responses.

Experimental Safeguards

Every experiment is designed to answer essentially the same question: Does the IV *cause* the predicted change in the DV? To answer this question, the experimenter must establish several safeguards. In addition to the previously mentioned controls within the experiment itself (e.g., operational definitions, having a control group, and holding extraneous variables constant), a good scientific experiment also protects against potential sources of error from both the researcher and the participant. As we discuss these potential problems (and their possible solutions), you may want to refer several times to the summary in Figure 1.8.

Researcher Problems and Solutions Researchers must guard against two particular problems—*experimenter bias* and *ethnocentrism*.

1. *Experimenter bias.* Experimenters, like everyone else, have their own personal beliefs and expectations. The danger in research, however, is that these personal biases may produce flawed results if the experimenter gives subtle cues or treats participants differently in accordance with his or her expectations.

   Consider the case of Clever Hans, the famous mathematical "wonder horse" (Rosenthal, 1965). When asked to multiply 6 times 8, minus 42, Hans would tap his hoof 6 times. Or if asked to divide 48 by 12, add 6, and take away 6, he would tap 4 times. Even when Hans's owner was out of the room and others asked the question, he was still able to answer correctly. How did he do it? Researchers even-

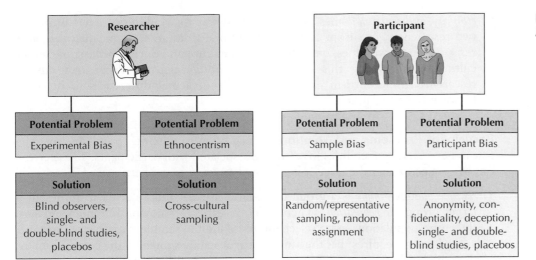

Figure 1.8 *Potential research problems and solutions.*

tually discovered that all questioners naturally lowered their heads to look at Hans's hoof at the end of their question. And Hans had learned that this was a signal to start tapping. When the correct answer was approaching, the questioners also naturally looked up, which in turn signaled Hans to stop.

When conducting research, this tendency of experimenters to influence the results in the expected direction is called **experimenter bias**. Just as Hans's questioners unintentionally signaled the correct answer by lowering or raising their heads, an experimenter might breathe a sigh of relief when a participant gives a response that supports the researcher's hypothesis.

Martha Lazar/The Image Bank/Getty Images

Can a horse add, multiply, and divide? Clever Hans and his owner, Mr. Von Osten, convinced many people that this was indeed the case. Can you see how this is an early example of experimenter bias? See the text for an explanation.

Experimenter Bias *Occurs when researcher influences research results in the expected direction*

You can see how experimenter bias might destroy the validity of the participant's response. But how can we prevent it? One technique is to set up objective methods for collecting and recording data, such as audiotape recordings to present the stimuli and computers to record the responses. Another option is to use "blind observers" (neutral people other than the researcher) to collect and record the data without knowing what the researcher has predicted. In addition, researchers can arrange a **double-blind study**, in which *neither* the observer nor the participant knows which group received the experimental treatment.

In a typical double-blind experiment testing a new drug, both the experimenters administering the drug and the participants taking the drug are unaware (or "blind") as to who is receiving a placebo, a fake pill or injection, and who is receiving the drug itself. Researchers use **placebos** because they have found that the mere act of taking a pill or receiving an injection can change the condition of a participant. (The term *placebo* comes from the Latin verb *placere*, "to please.") Thus, to ensure that a particular effect is indeed due to the drug being tested, and not to the *placebo effect*, control participants must be treated exactly like the experimental participants, even if this means faking the motions of giving them drugs or medications.

2. *Ethnocentrism.* When we assume that behaviors typical in our culture are typical in all cultures, we are committing a bias known as **ethnocentrism**. (*Ethno* refers to

Double-Blind Study *Procedure in which both the researcher and the participants are unaware (blind) of who is in the experimental or control group*

Placebo *(pluh-SEE-boh) Inactive substance or fake treatment used as a control technique, usually in drug research, or given by a medical practitioner to a patient*

Ethnocentrism *Believing that one's culture is typical of all cultures; also, viewing one's own ethnic group (or culture) as central and "correct" and judging others according to this standard*

www.wiley.com/college/huffman

ethnicity, and *centrism* comes from *center*.) One way to avoid this problem is to have two researchers, one from one culture and one from another, conduct the same research study two times, once in their own culture and once in at least one other culture. When using this kind of *cross-cultural sampling*, differences due to researcher ethnocentrism can be isolated from actual differences in behavior between the two cultures.

Participant Problems and Solutions   In addition to potential problems from the researcher, several possibilities for error are associated with participants. These errors can be grouped under the larger categories of *sample bias* and *participant bias*.

1. *Sample bias.* A *sample* is a group of research participants selected to represent a larger group, or *population*. When we do research, we obviously cannot measure the entire population, so we select and test a limited sample. However, using such a small group requires that the sample be reasonably similar to the composition of the population at large. If **sample bias**—systematic differences among the groups being studied—exists, experimental results may not truly reflect the influence of the independent variable.

   > **Sample Bias** *Occurs when research participants are not representative of the larger population*

   For example, much research has been done on the increased safety of having air bags in automobiles. Unfortunately, however, the research has been conducted almost exclusively with men. When car manufacturers apply findings from this research, with no regard for the sample bias, they create air bags sized for men. Tragically, these male sized bags may seriously damage (or even decapitate) small adults (mostly women) and kids. Because the purpose of conducting experiments is to apply, or generalize, the results to a wide population, it is extremely important that the sample represent the general population.

   To safeguard against sample bias, research psychologists generally use random/representative sampling and random assignment:

   - *Random/representative sampling.* Obviously, psychologists want their research findings to be applicable to more people than just those who took part in the study. For instance, critics have suggested that much psychological literature is biased because it is based primarily on white participants (see Robert Guthrie's 2004 book, *Even the Rat Was White*). One way to ensure less bias and more relevance is to select participants who constitute a representative sample of the entire population of interest. Proper *random sampling* will likely produce a representative, unbiased sample.

   - *Random assignment.* To ensure the validity of the results, participants must also be assigned to experimental groups using a chance, or *random*, system, such as tossing a coin or drawing numbers out of a hat. This procedure of **random assignment** ensures that each participant is equally likely to be assigned to any particular group and that differences among the participants will be spread out across all experimental conditions.

   > **Random Assignment** *Using chance methods to assign participants to experimental or control conditions, thus minimizing the possibility of biases or preexisting differences in the groups*

2. *Participant bias.* In addition to problems with sample bias, **participant bias** can occur when experimental conditions influence participants' behavior or mental processes. For example, participants may try to present themselves in a good light (the *social desirability response*) or may deliberately attempt to mislead the researcher. They also may be less than truthful when asked embarrassing questions or placed in awkward experimental conditions.

   > **Participant Bias** *Occurs when experimental conditions influence the participant's behavior or mental processes*

   Researchers attempt to control for this type of participant bias by offering anonymous participation and other guarantees for privacy and confidentiality. Also, as mentioned earlier, single- and double-blind studies and placebos offer additional safeguards. If participants do not know whether they are receiving the real drug or the "fake one," they will not try to overly please or deliberately mislead the experimenter.

Would you like to volunteer as a participant in psychological research?

The American Psychological Society (APS) has a website with links to ongoing studies that need participants. A recent visit to this site revealed several exciting studies, including:

- What Should Be Done with Child Abusers?
- Reactions to September 11 Terrorist Attacks
- Leadership Styles and Emotional Intelligence

- Bem Sex Role Inventory
- Internet Usage, Personality, and Behavior
- Adult Attention Deficit Hyperactivity Disorder (ADHD/ADD)
- Sensation and Perception Laboratory
- Web of Loneliness
- Sexual Behavior and Alcohol Consumption
- Marriage Inventory
- Are You a Logical Thinker?
- Web Experimental Psychology Lab

If you'd like to participate, go to http://psych.hanover.edu/research/exponnet.html.

Finally, one of the most effective, but controversial, ways to prevent participant bias is *deception*. Just like unsuspecting subjects on popular TV programs, like the old *Candid Camera* show or the newer *Jamie Kennedy's Experiment* or *Spy TV*, research participants will behave more naturally when they do not know they are part of a research project. However, many researchers consider the use of deception unethical—as we discussed in the previous section.

Misattribution of Arousal
Physiologically aroused individuals make mistaken inferences about what is causing the arousal

pplication

RESEARCH HIGHLIGHT

Love at First Fright?

Suppose you are watching a scary movie with a very attractive date. You notice that your heart is pounding, your palms are sweating, and you are short of breath. Is it love? Or is it fear? As you will discover in Chapter 12, a wide variety of emotions are accompanied by the same physiological states. Because of this similarity, we frequently misidentify our emotions. How can we experimentally prove this?

To answer this question, Donald Dutton and Arthur Aron (1974) asked an attractive female or male experimenter (confederates) to approach 85 male passersby either on a fear-arousing or on a non-fear-arousing bridge. They asked all participants to fill out questionnaires, and then gave them a phone number to call if they wanted more information.

Imagine yourself as one of the participants in this experiment. You arrive at the Capilano Canyon suspension bridge in North Vancouver, British Columbia. It is a 5-foot wide, 450-foot long wooden bridge attached by cables spanning the Capilano Canyon. When you walk across the bridge, it tends to tilt, sway, and wobble, and you have to stoop down to hold on to the low railings. If you happen to look down, you see nothing but rapids and exposed rocks in the river 230 feet below.

While standing at the middle of this swaying bridge, the experimenter approaches and asks you to fill out a questionnaire. Would you be attracted to this person? What if this person instead approached you on a firm wooden bridge with only a 10-foot drop to a shallow rivulet? Compared to men on the low, non-fear-arousing bridge, Dutton and

Aron found that a large proportion of the men on the fear-arousing bridge not only called the female researcher, but also revealed a much higher level of sexual imagery in their questionnaires.

At first glance, this may sound strange. Why would men who are in a state of fear be more attracted to a woman than men who are relaxed? According to what is now called **misattribution of arousal,** the men mistakenly attributed some of their arousal to their attraction to the female experimenter.

Although Dutton and Aron conducted this experiment in 1974, dozens of follow-up studies have generally confirmed their original findings. For example, Cindy Meston and Penny Frohlich (2003) conducted a similar experiment with individuals at amusement parks who were either waiting to begin or had just gotten off a roller-coaster ride. Participants were shown a photograph of an averagely attractive person of the opposite-sex. They were then asked to rate the individual on attractiveness and dating desirability. Consistent with the earlier findings of Dutton and Aron, ratings were higher among those who were exiting than entering the ride. Interestingly, this effect was only found with participants riding with a nonromantic partner. When romantic couples were riding together, there were no significant differences in ratings of attractiveness or dating desirability.

Can you see how Meston and Frohlich's research illustrates steps 5 and 6 in the scientific method? As mentioned on page 20, experimenters often replicate or extend the work of previous researchers. And, in this case, the differing results between romantic and nonromantic partners help fine-tune the original theory, which may in turn lead to new and better future theories. Both experiments also demonstrate how *basic research* can sometimes be *applied* to our everyday lives. In this case, the take home message is: Be careful of "Love at first fright!"

CRITICAL THINKING

Applying Critical Thinking to Psychological Science
(Contributed by Thomas Frangicetto)

Scientists in all fields must be good critical thinkers, and researchers (and students) in psychology are no exception. This first critical thinking exercise will help you in many ways, including:

- Insight into the interconnectivity of critical thinking and psychological science.
- Practice applying numerous critical thinking components.
- Review of important text content your professor may include on exams.

   Part I. In the space beside each "Text Key Concept," enter the number of the appropriate "Suggested Critical Thinking Component." Expanded discussions of each component can be found in the Prologue of this text (pp. xxx–xxxiv). Although you may find several possible matches, list only your top one or two choices. For example, for the first item, "Literature Review," if you decide that "Gathering Data" is the best critical thinking component, enter the number "16" in the blank space.

   Part II. On a separate sheet of paper, use specific text wording and critical thinking descriptions to fully explain your choices. Using the same example as above, you might say:

   In order for researchers to do a successful review of the literature, they would have to "carefully check what has been published in major professional or scientific journals," and they would do so by employing critical thinking component #16, gathering data.

   This means they would "collect up-to-date, relevant information on all sides of the issue" before proceeding with their research.

ACTIVE LEARNING

Text Key Concepts	Suggested Critical Thinking Components
Scientific Method	* Valuing Truth Above Self-Interest (#1)
_____Literature Review	* Welcoming Divergent Views (#4)
_____Develop a Testable Hypothesis	* Tolerating Ambiguity (#5)
_____Select a Research Method and Collect the Data	* Recognizing Personal Biases (#6)
_____Analyze the Data and Accept or Reject the Hypothesis	* Empathizing (#7)
_____Publish, Replicate, and Seek Scientific Review	* Thinking Independently (#7)
_____Build a Theory	* Defining Problems Accurately (#8)
	* Analyzing Data for Value and Content (#9)
Research Problems	* Synthesizing (#11)
_____Experimenter Bias	* Resisting Overgeneralization (#12)
_____Ethnocentrism	* Delaying Judgment Until Adequate Data are Available (#14)
_____Sample Bias	* Employing Precise Terms (#15)
_____Participant Bias	* Gathering Data (#16)
	* Distinguishing Fact from Opinion (#17)
	* Modifying Judgments in Light of New Information (#20)
	* Applying Knowledge to New Situations (#21)

Application

Experimental Research

An **experiment** is the only research method that can be used to identify cause-and-effect relationships. **Independent variables (IVs)** are the factors the experimenter manipulates, and **dependent variables (DVs)** are measurable behaviors of the participants. Experimental controls include having one **control group** and one or more **experimental groups,** and holding extraneous variables constant.

To safeguard against the researcher problem of **experimenter bias,** researchers employ blind observers, single- and **double-blind studies,** and **placebos.** To control for **ethnocentrism,** they use cross-cultural sampling. In addition, to offset participant problems with **sample bias,** researchers use random/representative sampling and **random assignment.** To control for **participant bias,** they rely on many of the same controls in place to prevent experimenter bias, such as double-blind studies. They also attempt to ensure anonymity and confidentiality and sometimes use deception.

Questions

1. Why is an experiment the only way we can determine the cause of behavior?
2. In experiments, researchers measure the _____ variables. (a) independent; (b) feature; (c) extraneous; (d) dependent
3. If researchers gave participants varying amounts of a new "memory" drug and then gave them a story to read and measured their scores on a quiz, the _____ would be the IV, and the _____ would be the DV. (a) response to the drug, amount of the drug; (b) experimental group, control group; (c) amount of the drug, quiz scores; (d) researcher variables, extraneous variables
4. What are the two primary sources of problems for both researchers and participants? What are the solutions?

Check your answers in Appendix B.

CLICK & REVIEW
for additional assessment options:
www.wiley.com/college/huffman

Descriptive Research: Naturalistic Observation, Surveys, and Case Studies

The second major type of research, **descriptive research**, observes and describes behavior without manipulating variables. Almost everyone observes and describes other people in an attempt to understand them. But psychologists do it systematically and scientifically. In this section, we will examine three key types of descriptive research: *naturalistic observation*, *surveys*, and *case studies*. As you explore each of these methods, keep in mind that most of the problems and safeguards discussed with the experimental method also apply to the nonexperimental methods.

Descriptive Research *Research methods that observe and record behavior without producing causal explanations*

Naturalistic Observation

When using **naturalistic observation**, researchers systematically measure and record the observable behavior of participants as it occurs in the real world, without interfering in any way. The purpose of most naturalistic observation is to gather descriptive information. Because of the popularity of researchers like Jane Goodall, who studied chimpanzees in the jungle, most people picture naturalistic observation occurring in wild, remote areas. But supermarkets, libraries, subways, airports, museums, classrooms, assembly lines, and other settings also lend themselves to naturalistic observation.

Consider the popular debate, "Do smaller classes result in greater student achievement? If so, for what type of student?" A researcher who wanted to study these questions might prefer not to use a controlled experimental laboratory setting. Instead, he or she might go to several classrooms and observe how children and teachers perform in their natural setting. In this type of naturalistic observation, the researcher does not manipulate or control anything in the situation. The observer tries to be as unobtrusive as possible, to become, as they say, "like a fly on the wall." The researcher might even conceal him- or herself in the background, standing

Naturalistic Observation *Observation and recording of behavior in the participant's natural state or habitat*

"Just pretend we're not here, Ms. Robinson..."

behind a one-way mirror. They could also observe from a distance while the participants are (hopefully) unaware that they are being observed.

Why do the researchers try to hide? If participants know someone is watching, their behavior becomes unnatural. Have you ever been driving down the street, singing along with the radio, and quickly stopped when you noticed that the person in the next car was watching you? A similar reaction occurs when participants in scientific studies realize they are being observed.

The chief advantage of naturalistic observation is that researchers can obtain data about a truly natural behavior versus possibly artificial behavior created in laboratory. Studies like those of Jane Goodall have shown us how forest chimps and gorillas adapt their behaviors to various zoo habitats. They have also improved zoo habitats to support more "natural" chimp and gorilla behavior.

On the downside, naturalistic observation can be difficult and time consuming. Furthermore, the lack of control by the researcher makes it difficult to conduct observations for behaviors that occur infrequently.

Surveys

Survey *Research technique that questions a large sample of people to assess their behaviors and attitudes*

Most of us are familiar with Gallup and Harris Polls, which sample voting preferences before important state or national elections. Psychologists use similar polls (or **surveys**) to measure a wide variety of psychological behaviors and attitudes. (The psychological survey technique also includes tests, questionnaires, and interviews.)

For example, in a survey of 11 cultures, Levine and his colleagues (1995) found that psychologist Scott Plous and his colleagues used the survey method to assess the attitudes and beliefs of animal rights activists. Plous and his colleagues approached hundreds of people who were attending an animal rights rally in Washington, D.C., and asked them to complete a detailed questionnaire (Plous, 1991). Plous also conducted a follow-up survey of activists attending a similar event six years later. Interestingly, he found several remarkable attitudinal changes over this relatively short period of time—particularly in what participants believed should be the highest priorities of the animal rights movement.

As you can see in Table 1.3, in 1990 a majority of activists saw animal research as the most important issue. Activists in 1996 considered nonhuman animals used for

TABLE 1.3 WHAT SHOULD THE ANIMAL RIGHTS MOVEMENT FOCUS ON MOST?

Issue	Year of survey	
	1990 (N = 346)	1996 (N = 327)
Animals used in research	54	38
Animals used for food	24	48
Animals used for clothing or fashion	12	5
Animals in the wild	5	3
Animals used in sports or entertainment	4	5
Animals used in education	1	2

Note. Figures indicate the percentage of respondents giving each answer.

TRY THIS

YOURSELF

Application

Would you like to try an informal replication of Plous's research?

Station yourself at a conspicuous spot on campus, in your dorm, or some other place. Ask random passersby whether they con-sider themselves animal rights activists or nonactivists. If they are activists, read them the question in Table 1.3 and record their responses next to the appropriate item. How do your survey results compare with those of Plous?

food as the most important. The 1996 survey also found a modest decline among activists in their support for laboratory break-ins. A majority also supported a proposal designed to reduce tensions between activists and researchers. Plous suggests that these responses might help encourage dialogue and a possible "cease-fire" in the ongoing animal rights debate (Plous, 1998). What do you think?

One key advantage to surveys is that they can gather data from a much larger sample of people than is possible with other research methods. Unfortunately, most surveys rely on self-reported data, and not all participants are completely honest. In addition, survey techniques cannot, of course, be used to explain *causes* of behavior.

The major advantage of surveys is their role in *predicting* behavior. Plous, for example, could not pinpoint the causes of the activists' beliefs. But the results of his survey might be used to predict the attitudes and goals of some animal rights activists in the United States. (As a critical thinker, can you see why his results are limited? Because he administered his survey only to participants at an animal rights rally, he lacked a random/representative sample.)

Case Studies

What if a researcher wants to investigate *photophobia*—fear of light? Because most people are not afraid of light, it would be difficult to find enough participants to conduct an experiment or to use surveys or naturalistic observation. In the case of such rare disorders, researchers try to find someone who has the problem and study him or her intensively. Such an in-depth study of a single research participant is called a **case study**.

Case Study *In-depth study of a single research participant*

Throughout this text, we will be presenting an expanded "Case Study/Personal Story" for most chapters, which adds a "human interest" touch to the research and core concepts. In this beginning chapter, the following example also helps illustrate the case study as a research method. Keep in mind, however, that case studies have their own research limits, including lack of generalizability and inaccurate or biased recall among participants.

Application
CASE STUDY / PERSONAL STORY

A Life Without Fear?

For a "first-hand" look at the case study method, imagine yourself as Dr. Antonio Damasio, distinguished professor and head of the Department of Neurology at the University of Iowa College of Medicine in Iowa City. You are introduced to a tall, slender, and extremely pleasant young female patient, referred to as "S." Tests show that she has normal, healthy sensory perceptions, language abilities, and intelli-

www.wiley.com/college/huffman

gence. Shortly after being introduced, S hugs and touches you repeatedly. You discover that this same cheerful, touching behavior pervades all areas of her life. She makes friends and romantic attachments easily and is eager to interact with almost anyone. By all reports, S lives in an extremely pleasant world dominated by positive emotions.

So, what is "wrong" with S? Can you diagnose her? Damasio and his colleagues began with comprehensive evaluations of the patient's physical and mental health, intelligence, and personality. Results showed that S was in good health with normal sensory perception, language ability, and intelligence. She also had remarkable artistic and drafting skills. Her one problem was that she could not identify facial expressions of fear. She easily recognized other emotions and could mimic them with her own facial muscles. And, interestingly, she could draw finely detailed faces showing all emotions—except fear.

After extensive neurological tests and extensive interviews, Damasio and his staff discovered that S's inability to recognize fear in someone's face resulted from damage to a very small part of her brain—the *amygdala*. As a result, "she has not learned the telltale signs that announce possible danger and possible unpleasantness, especially as they show up in the face of another person" (Damasio, 1999, p. 66).

They also found that S does not experience fear in the same way as others do. She intellectually knows "what fear is supposed to be, what should cause it, and even what one may do in situations of fear, but little or none of that intellectual baggage, so to speak, is of any use to her in the real world" (Damasio, 1999, p. 66). Her inability to recognize fear in herself and others causes her to be overly trusting of strangers and romantic partners. Can you see how this might create serious problems in social interactions?

At this time, there is no "happy ending" for S and others with similar damage. But case studies like this may eventually provide valuable clues that will lead to successful treatment.

■ Correlational Research: Looking for Relationships

Correlational Research *Scientific study in which the researcher observes or measures (without directly manipulating) two or more variables to find the relationships between them*

When nonexperimental researchers want to determine the degree of relationship, or *correlation*, between two variables, they turn to **correlational research**. As the name implies, when any two variables are *correlated*, they are "co-related." A change in one variable is accompanied by a concurrent change in the other.

Using the correlational method, researchers begin with their topic of interest, such as alcohol consumption during pregnancy. Then they select a group for study—in this case, pregnant women. After selecting the group, the researchers might survey or interview the selected group of women about the amount and timing of any alcohol use during their pregnancies.

After the data are collected, the researchers analyze their results using a statistical formula that results in a correlation coefficient, a numerical value that indicates the degree and direction of the relationship between the two variables. (Note that there is an important distinction between correlational studies and correlation as a mathematical procedure. *Correlational studies* are a type of research methodology in which researchers set out to identify relationships between variables. In contrast, **correlation coefficients** are statistical measures used in correlational studies, as well as with surveys and other research designs.)

Correlation Coefficient *A number that indicates the degree and direction of the relationship between two variables*

Correlation coefficients are calculated by a formula (described in Appendix A) that produces a number ranging from +1.00 to –1.00. The sign (+ or –) indicates the direction of the correlation, positive (+) or negative (–). The number (0 to +1.00 or 0 to –1.00) indicates the strength of the relationship. Note that both +1.00 and a –1.00 are the strongest possible relationship. As the number decreases and gets closer to 0.00, the relationship weakens.

A positive correlation is one in which the two variables move (or vary) in the same direction—the two factors increase or decrease together. As you know, for most

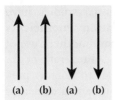

students a positive correlation exits between hours of study and scores on exams. When studying *increases*, exam scores *increase*. Or we can state it the other way. When studying *decreases*, exam scores also *decrease*. Can you see why both examples are positive correlations? The factors vary in the same direction—upward or downward.

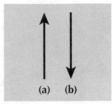

In contrast, a negative correlation is one in which the two factors vary in opposite directions. As one factor *increases*, the other factor *decreases*. Have you noticed that the more hours you work (or party) outside of college, the lower your exam scores? This is an example of a negative correlation—working and partying both vary in opposite directions to exam scores.

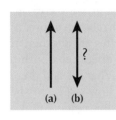

On some occasions, researchers will discover that there is no relationship between two variables—a zero correlation. Obviously, no relation (zero correlation) exists between your birthday and exam scores. And, despite popular belief, repeated scientific investigations of astrology have found no relationship between personality and the position of the stars (a zero correlation). Figure 1.9 provides a visual depiction and additional examples of positive, negative, and zero correlations.

Now that you understand the direction of correlations, consider the number itself (0 to +1.00 or 0 to –1.00). It represents the strength of the relationship. The closer the number is to 1.00, either positive or negative, the stronger the correlation between the variables. Thus, if you had a correlation of +.92 or –.92, you would have a high (or strong) correlation. On the other hand, a correlation of +.15 or –.15 would represent a low (or weak) correlation.

Pregnancy and smoking. Research shows that cigarette smoking is highly correlated with serious fetal damage. The more the mother smokes the more the fetus is damaged. Is this a positive or negative correlation?

The Value of Correlations

Correlational research is an important research method for psychologists. It also plays a critical role in your personal and everyday life. As you will see in upcoming chapters, numerous questions may be asked about how two things relate. How is stress related to susceptibility to colds? Does marijuana decrease motivation? How is intelligence related to achievement? When you read that "there is a strong correlation between … and…," you will now understand the significance. This also is true when you read news reports of the latest findings showing a strong (or weak) relationship between oatmeal and heart disease, or cellular phones and brain cancer.

In addition to providing greater knowledge of psychological data and news reports, understanding correlations also may help you live a safer and more produc-

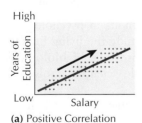
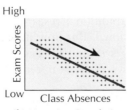
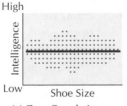

(a) Positive Correlation   **(b)** Negative Correlation   **(c)** Zero Correlation

Figure 1.9 *Three types of correlation.* The strength and direction of the correlation between two variables can be seen in these graphs (called scatterplots), with each dot representing an individual participant's score on the two variables. In the positive correlation (a), each dot corresponds to one person's salary and years of education. Because salary and education are positively and highly correlated, the dots are closely aligned around the line and point in an upward direction. Scatter plots (b) and (c) show a negative and zero correlation.

www.wiley.com/college/huffman

Correlation is NOT causation. Research shows that in the United States, ice cream consumption and drowning are highly correlated. Does this mean that eating ice cream causes people to drown? Of course not! A third factor, such as time of year, affects both ice cream consumption and swimming or boating. All of these can be related to increased chances of drowning.

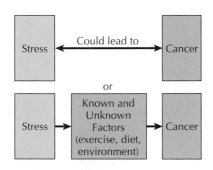

Figure 1.10 *Correlation versus causation.* Research has found a strong correlation between stress and cancer (Chapter 3). However, this correlation does not tell us whether stress causes cancer, cancer causes stress, or whether other known and unknown factors, such as the eating, drinking, and smoking, could contribute to both stress and cancer. Can you think of a way to study the effects of stress on cancer that is not correlational?

Biological Research *Scientific studies of the brain and other parts of the nervous system*

tive life. For example, correlational studies have repeatedly found high correlation coefficients between birth defects and a pregnant mother's use of alcohol (Bearer et al., 2004–2005; Gunzerath et al., 2004). This information enables us to reliably predict our relative risks and make informed decisions about our lives and behavior. If you would like additional information about correlations, see Appendix A at the back of the book.

Potential Problems with Correlations

Before we leave this topic, it is important to note that *correlation does not imply causation.* This is an error in logic commonly associated with correlational studies. Although a high correlation allows us to predict how one variable relates to another, it does not tell us whether a cause–effect relationship exists between the two variables. What if I said there was a high correlation between the size of a young child's feet and how fast he or she reads? Would this mean that having small feet *causes* a child to be a slow reader? Obviously not! Nor do increases in reading speed cause increases in foot size. Instead, both are caused by a third variable—an increase in children's age. Although we can safely *predict* that as a child's foot size increases, his or her reading speed will also increase, this *correlation does not imply causation.*

I use this extreme example to make an important point about an all too common public reaction to research findings. People read media reports about *relationships* between stress and cancer or between family dynamics and homosexuality. They then jump to the conclusion that "stress causes cancer" or that "withdrawn fathers and overly protective mothers cause their sons' homosexuality." Unfortunately, they fail to realize that a third factor, perhaps genetics, may cause greater susceptibility to both cancer and increased rates of homosexuality.

Once again, as Figure 1.10 shows, a correlation between two variables does not mean that one variable *causes* another. Correlational studies do sometimes point to *possible* causes, like the correlation between alcohol and birth defects. However, only the experimental method manipulates the IV under controlled conditions and therefore allows one to draw conclusions about cause and effect. If you compared psychological research to a criminal investigation, finding a correlation is like finding a person at the scene of the crime. Results from an experiment would be equivalent to finding the "smoking gun."

▣ Biological Research: Tools for Exploring the Nervous System

In the previous section, we explored traditional research methods in psychology—experimental, descriptive, and correlational. But how do we study the living human brain and other parts of the nervous system? This is the province of **biological research**, which develops and employs their own remarkable scientific tools and research methods (Table 1.4).

For most of history, examination of the human brain was possible only after an individual died. The earliest explorers dissected the brains of deceased humans and conducted experiments on nonhuman animals using *lesioning techniques.* (Lesioning in brain research involves systematically destroying brain tissue to study the effects on behavior and mental processes.) By the mid-1800s, this early research had produced a basic map of the nervous system, including some areas of the brain. Early researchers also relied on clinical observations and case studies of living people. Tragic accidents and diseases or other brain disorders offered additional insights into brain functioning.

TABLE 1.4 TOOLS FOR BIOLOGICAL RESEARCH

Method	Description	Sample Results
Brain dissection Science Pictures Limited/SPL	Careful cutting and study of a cadaver brain to reveal structural details. ***Brain dissection.*** *Structures of the brain can be examined by dissecting the brains of deceased people who donated their bodies for scientific study.*	Brain dissections of Alzheimer's disease victims often show identifiable changes in various parts of the brain (Chapter 7).
Ablation/lesions	Surgically removing parts of the brain (ablation), or destroying specific areas of the brain (lesioning), is followed by observation for changes in behavior or mental processes.	Lesioning specific parts of the rat's hypothalamus greatly affects its eating behavior (Chapter 10).
Clinical observations/ case studies	Observing and recording changes in personality, behavior, or sensory capacity associated with brain disease or injuries.	Damage to one side of the brain often causes numbness or paralysis on the body's opposite side.
Electrical recordings Phanie/Photo Researchers, Inc. ***Electroencephalogram (EEG).*** *Electrodes are attached to the patient's scalp, and the brain's electrical activity is displayed on a computer monitor or recorded on a paper chart.*	Using electrodes attached to a person's or animal's skin or scalp, brain activity is recorded to produce an electroencephalogram.	Reveals areas of the brain most active during a particular task or changes in mental states, like sleeping and meditation (Chapter 5); also traces abnormal brain waves caused by brain malfunctions, like epilepsy or tumors.
Electrical stimulation of the brain (ESB)	Using an electrode, a weak electric current stimulates specific areas or structures of the brain.	Penfield (1958) mapped the surface of the brain and found that different areas have different functions.

(Table continues)

www.wiley.com/college/huffman

TABLE 1.4 (CONTINUED)

Method	Description	Sample Results
CT (computed tomography) scan 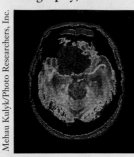 *Mehau Kulyk/Photo Researchers, Inc.*	Computer created cross-sectional X-rays of the brain; least expensive type of imaging and widely used in research. *CT scans.* *This CT scan used X-rays to locate a brain tumor. The tumor is the deep purple mass at the top left.*	Reveals the effects of strokes, injuries, tumors, and other brain disorders.
PET (positron emission tomography) scan 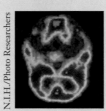 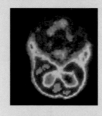 *N.I.H./Photo Researchers*	Radioactive form of glucose is injected into the bloodstream; scanner records amount of glucose used in particularly active areas of the brain and produces computer-constructed picture of the brain. *PET scans and brain functions.* *The top scan shows brain activity when the eyes are open, whereas the one at the bottom is with the eyes closed. Note the increased activity, red and yellow, in the top photo when the eyes are open.*	Originally designed to detect abnormalities, also used to identify brain areas active during ordinary activities (reading, singing, etc.).
MRI (magnetic resonance imaging) scan 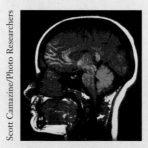 *Scott Camazine/Photo Researchers*	A high-frequency magnetic field is passed through the brain by means of electromagnets. *Magnetic resonance imaging (MRI).* *Note the fissures and internal structures of the brain. The throat, nasal airways, and fluid surrounding the brain are dark.*	Produces high-resolution three-dimensional pictures of the brain useful for identifying abnormalities and mapping brain structures and function.
fMRI (functional magnetic resonance imaging) scan	A newer, faster version of the MRI that detects blood flow by picking up magnetic signals from blood that has given up its oxygen to activate brain cells.	Indicates which areas of the brain are active or inactive during ordinary activities or responses (like reading or talking); also shows changes associated with disorders.

Modern researchers still use *dissection, lesioning, clinical observation,* and *case studies.* However, they also employ other techniques, such as electrical recordings of the brain's activity. To make these electrical recordings, scientists paste *electrodes* (tiny electricity-conducting disks or wires) to the skin of the skull. These electrodes collect electrical energy from the brain (brain waves), and the equipment to which they are attached depict them as wavy lines on a moving strip of paper. The recording of these brain waves is called an *electroencephalogram (EEG). (Electro* means "electrical," *encephalon* means "brain," and *gram* means "record".) The instrument itself, called an *electroencephalograph,* is a major research tool for studying changes in brain waves during sleep and dreaming (Chapter 5).

In addition to electrical recordings, researchers also use *electrical stimulation of the brain (ESB).* In this case, electrodes are inserted directly into the brain to stimulate certain areas with weak electrical currents.

Other new windows into the brain include several *brain-imaging scans* (see Table 1.4). Most of these methods are relatively *noninvasive.* That is, they are performed without breaking the skin or entering the body. They can be used in clinical settings to examine suspected brain damage and disease. They are also used in laboratory settings to study brain function during ordinary activities like sleeping, eating, reading, and speaking (Benazzi, 2004; Haller et al., 2005).

Computed tomography (CT) scans (a computer-enhanced series of X-rays of the brain) and *magnetic resonance imaging (MRI) scans* have been used to look for abnormalities in brain structures among people suffering from mental illness. *Positron emission tomography (PET)* and *functional magnetic resonance imaging (fMRI) scans* map actual activity in the brain. Such scans can be used to pinpoint brain areas that handle various activities, such as reading, hearing, singing, fist clenching, mental calculations, and even areas responsible for different emotions (Eslinger & Tranel, 2005; Friston, 2005; Reuter et al., 2004).

Each biological method has its particular strengths and weaknesses. But all provide invaluable insights and information. We will discuss findings from these research tools in upcoming chapters on sleep and dreaming (Chapter 5), memory (Chapter 7), thinking and intelligence (Chapter 8), and abnormal behavior and its treatment (Chapters 14 and 16).

©John Chase

One way to remember the difference between these four scans is to keep in mind that CT and MRI scans produce static visual slices of the brain (like a photo). PET and fMRI create ongoing images (like a video).

Application

APPLYING PSYCHOLOGY TO EVERYDAY LIFE

Becoming a Better Consumer of Scientific Research

The news media, advertisers, politicians, teachers, close friends, and other individuals frequently use research findings in their attempts to change your attitudes and behavior. How can you tell whether their information is accurate and worthwhile?

The following exercise will improve your ability to critically evaluate sources of information. Using concepts from the previous discussion of psychological research techniques, read each "research" report and identify the primary problem or research limitation. In the space provided, use one of the following to characterize the report.

CC = Report is misleading because correlation data are used to suggest causation.

CG = Report is inconclusive because there was no control group.

EB = Results of the research were unfairly influenced by experimenter bias.

SB = Results of the research are questionable because of sample bias.

_____1. A clinical psychologist strongly believes that touching is an important adjunct to successful therapy. For two months, he touches half his patients (group A) and refrains from touching the other half (group B). He then reports a noticeable improvement in group A.

_____2. A newspaper reports that violent crime corresponds to phases of the moon. The reporter concludes that the gravitational pull of the moon controls human behavior.

_____3. A researcher interested in women's attitudes toward premarital sex sends out a lengthy survey to subscribers of *Vogue* and *Cosmopolitan* magazines.

_____4. An experimenter is interested in studying the effects of alcohol on driving ability. Before being tested on an experimental driving course, group A consumes 2 ounces of alcohol, group B consumes 4 ounces of alcohol, and group C consumes 6 ounces of alcohol. After the test drive, the researcher reports that alcohol consumption adversely affects driving ability.

_____5. After reading a scientific journal that reports higher divorce rates among couples living together before marriage, a college student decides to move out of the apartment she shares with her boyfriend.

_____6. A theater owner reports increased beverage sales following the brief flashing of a subliminal message to "Drink Coca-Cola" during the film showing.

Answers: 1. EB; 2. CC; 3. SB; 4. CG; 5. CC; 6. CG and EB

Assessment

CHECK & REVIEW

Descriptive, Correlational, and Biological Research

Unlike experiments, **descriptive research** cannot determine the causes of behavior. But it can describe specifics. **Naturalistic observation** is used to study and describe behavior in its natural habitat without altering it. **Surveys** use interviews or questionnaires to obtain information on a sample of participants. Individual **case studies** are in-depth studies of a participant.

Correlational research examines how strongly two variables are related (0 to +1.00 or 0 to −1.00). It also identifies whether the relationship is positively, negatively, or not at all (zero) correlated. Correlational studies and **correlation coefficients** provide important research findings and valuable predictions. However, it is also important to remember that *correlation does not imply causation*.

Biological research studies the brain and other parts of the nervous system through dissection of brains of cadavers, lesion techniques, and direct observation or case studies. Electrical recording techniques involve attaching electrodes to the skin or scalp to study the brain's electrical activity. Computed tomography (CT), positron emission tomography (PET), magnetic resonance imaging (MRI), and functional magnetic resonance imaging (fMRI) scans are noninvasive techniques that provide visual images of intact, living brains.

Questions

1. _____ research observes and records behavior without producing causal explanations. (a) Experimental; (b) Survey; (c) Descriptive; (d) Correlational

2. Maria is thinking of running for student body president. She wonders whether her campaign should emphasize campus security, improved parking facilities, or increased health services. Which scientific method of research would you recommend? (a) a case study; (b) naturalistic observation; (c) an experiment; (d) a survey

3. Which of the following correlation coefficients indicates the strongest relationship? (a) +.43; (b) −.64; (c) −.72; (d) 0.00

4. The four major techniques used for scanning the brain are the _____, _____, _____, and _____.

Check your answers in Appendix B.

CLICK & REVIEW
for additional assessment options:
www.wiley.com/college/huffman

Achievement

Gender & Cultural Diversity

Are There Cultural Universals?

Psychology is a broad field with numerous subdisciplines and professions. Until recently, most psychologists worked and conducted research primarily in Europe and North America. Given this "one-sided" research, psychology's findings may not apply equally to people in other countries—or to minorities and women in Europe and North America, for that matter (Matsumoto & Juang, 2004; Shiraev & Levy, 2004). However, modern psychology, in particular *cultural psychology*, is working to correct this imbalance. Key research from cross-cultural and multiethnic studies is integrated throughout this text. Each chapter also includes a "Gender and Cultural Diversity" section with a special icon in the margin that looks like this: ✳

In this first gender and cultural diversity discussion, we explore a central question in cultural psychology: Are there *cultural universals?* That is, are there aspects of human behavior and mental processes that are true and *pancultural* or *universal* for all people of all cultures?

For many "universalists," emotions and facial recognition of emotions provide the clearest example of a possible cultural universal. Numerous studies conducted over many years with people from very different cultures suggest that everyone can easily identify facial expressions for at least six basic emotions: happiness, surprise, anger, sadness, fear, and disgust. All humans supposedly have this capacity whether they are shown the face of a child or an adult, a Western or non-Western person (Ekman, 1993; Ekman & Friesen, 1971; Hejmadi, Davidson, & Rozin, 2000; Matsumoto & Juang, 2004). Moreover, nonhuman primates and congenitally blind infants also display similarly recognizable facial signals. In other words, across cultures (and some species), a frown is recognized as a sign of displeasure, and a smile, as a sign of pleasure (Figure 1.11).

Critics of the universalist position emphasize problems with these studies. For example, how do you label and study the emotion described by Japanese as *hagaii* (feeling helpless anguish mixed with frustration). How can Western psychologists study *hagaii* if they have no experience with these emotions and no equivalent English words? Other critics argue that *if* cultural universals exist, it is because they are biological and innate—and they should be labeled as such. However, equating biology with universality has its own problem. Behaviors or mental processes that are universal may be so because of culture-constant learning rather than biological destiny (Matsumoto & Juang, 2004). For example, *if* we found that certain gender roles were

Study Tip

Gender and Cultural Diversity
These sections embedded in the narrative are identified with a separate heading and a special icon, as seen here. To succeed in today's world, it is important to be aware of other cultures and important gender issues.

Figure 1.11 *Do you recognize these emotions?* The recognition and display of basic facial expressions may be true "cultural universals."

expressed the same in all cultures, it might reflect shared cultural training beginning at birth, not an "anatomy is destiny" position. As we discussed earlier, scientists avoid the tendency to compartmentalize behaviors into either/or categories. Like the nature–nurture controversy, the answer once again is an *interaction*. Emotions and their recognition may be both biological and culturally universal. As a beginning student in psychology, you will encounter numerous areas of conflict, with well-respected arguments and opponents on each side. Your job is to adopt an open-minded, critically thinking approach to each of these debates.

In addition to building your critical thinking skills, hearing arguments from both sides also will develop your understanding of and appreciation for diversity, both intellectual and cultural. It might even improve your personal and business interactions. Richard Brislin (1993) told the story of a Japanese executive who gave a speech to a *Fortune* 500 company in New York. He was aware that Americans typically begin speeches by telling an amusing story or a couple of jokes. However, Japanese typically begin speeches by apologizing for the "inadequate" talk they are about to give. This savvy executive began his speech: "I realize that Americans often begin by making a joke. In Japan, we frequently begin with an apology. I'll compromise by apologizing for not having a joke" (p. 9). By appreciating cultural diversity, we can, like the Japanese executive, learn to interact successfully in other cultures.

TOOLS FOR STUDENT SUCCESS

Congratulations! At this very moment, you are demonstrating one of the most important traits of a critical thinker and successful college student—your willingness to accept *suggestions for improvement*. Many students think that they already know how to be a student and that student success skills are only for "nerds" or "problem students." But would these same individuals assume they could become top-notch musicians, athletes, or plumbers without mastering the tools of those trades? Trying to compete in a college environment with minimal, or even average, study skills is like trying to ride a bicycle on a high-speed freeway. *All students* (even those who seem to get A's without much effort) can improve their "student tools."

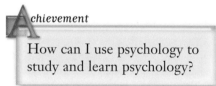

Achievement

How can I use psychology to study and learn psychology?

In this section, you will find several important tools—specific, well-documented study tips and techniques—guaranteed to make you a more efficient and successful college student (Figure 1.12). Mastering these tools may require extra initial time. But they save hundreds of hours later on. Research clearly shows that good students tend to work smarter—not longer or harder (Dickinson, O'Connell, & Dunn, 1996).

Figure 1.12 *Tools for student success.*

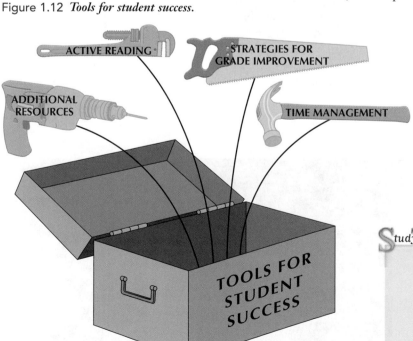

Study**T**ip

Tools for Student Success
This special feature in Chapter 1 includes tips for overall college success as well as success in this course. In addition, the Study Tip icon identifies additional sections in other chapters that address strategies for dealing with test anxiety and improving memory, performance, and overall achievement.

*A*ssessment

VISUAL QUIZ

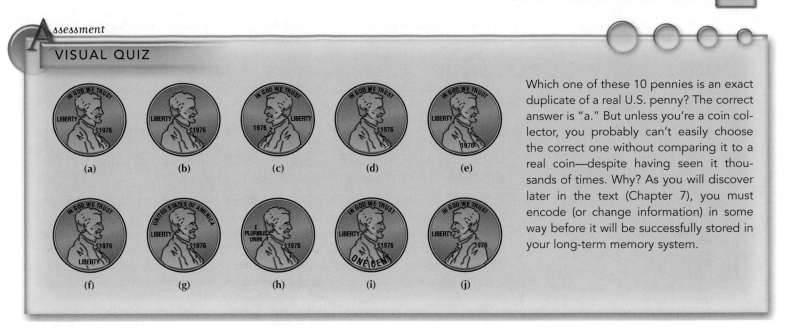

(a) (b) (c) (d) (e)

(f) (g) (h) (i) (j)

Which one of these 10 pennies is an exact duplicate of a real U.S. penny? The correct answer is "a." But unless you're a coin collector, you probably can't easily choose the correct one without comparing it to a real coin—despite having seen it thousands of times. Why? As you will discover later in the text (Chapter 7), you must encode (or change information) in some way before it will be successfully stored in your long-term memory system.

ACTIVE READING: How to Study (and Master) This Text

Have you ever read several pages of a text and then found you could not recall a single detail? Or have you read the chapters (possibly many times) and still performed poorly on an exam? Do you want to know why? Try the "Visual Quiz" on this page.

Can you see why I added this visual quiz to begin this section? I wanted to demonstrate how even a simple task of coin recognition requires *active study*. Most Americans cannot select a real penny among fake pennies even after years of using them to make purchases. Similarly, students can read and reread chapters yet still fail to recognize the correct answers on a test. To learn and remember, you must make a conscious effort. You must "intend to learn."

Admittedly, some learning (like remembering the lyrics to your favorite song) occurs somewhat automatically and effortlessly. However, most complex information (like textbook reading) requires effort and deliberate attention. There are a number of ways to *actively read*, remember, and master a college text.

STEP ONE: Familiarizing Yourself with the General Text

Your textbook is the major tool for success in any course. Most instructors rely on it to present basic course material, reserving class time for clarifying and elaborating on important topics. How can you be a more successful student (and test taker) and take full advantage of all the special features in this text? Consider the following suggestions:

- *Preface*. If you have not already read the preface, do it now. It is a road map for the rest of the text.

- *Table of contents*. Scan the table of contents for a bird's-eye view of what you will study in this course. Get the big picture from the chapter titles and the major topics within each chapter.

- *Individual chapters*. Each chapter of *Psychology in Action* contains numerous learning aids to help you master the material. There are chapter outlines, learning outcomes, running glossaries, "Check & Review" (summaries and self-test questions), "Visual Summaries," and more. These learning aids are highlighted and explained in the margin of this chapter.

www.wiley.com/college/huffman

- *Appendixes.* Appendix A (Statistics) and Appendix B (Answers to Check & Review Questions and Activities) present important information. The statistics appendix further discusses some of the concepts introduced in Chapter 1. It also explains how to read and interpret the graphs and tables found throughout the text. Appendix B contains answers to the "Check & Review" questions, "Try This Yourself" activities, and other exercises found in the chapters.

- *Glossary.* This text presents two glossaries. A running glossary appears in the margins of each chapter alongside key terms and concepts. A cumulative glossary, which gathers all key terms from each chapter, appears at the end of this text. Use this end-of-book glossary to review terms from other chapters.

- *References.* As you read each chapter, you will see references cited in parentheses, not in footnotes, as is common in other disciplines. For example, (Ventner et al., 2001) refers to an article written by Craig Ventner and his colleagues announcing the first successful mapping of the full human genome, which was published in 2001. All the references cited in the text are listed in alphabetical order (by the author's last name) in the References section at the back of the book.

- *Name index and subject index.* If you are interested in learning more about a particular individual, look for his or her name in the Name Index. The page numbers refer you to every place in the text where the individual is mentioned. If you are interested in a specific subject (e.g., anorexia nervosa or stress), check the Subject Index for page references.

STEP TWO: How to Read a Chapter

Once you have a sense of the book as a whole, your next step to success is improving your general reading skills. The most important tool for college success is the ability to read and master the assigned class text. Many colleges offer instruction in reading efficiency, and I highly recommend that you take the course. All students can become faster and more efficient readers, and this section can offer only the highlights of a full-length course.

One of the best ways to read *actively* is to use the SQ4R method, developed by Francis Robinson (1970). The initials stand for six steps in effective reading: *Survey, Question, Read, Recite, Review,* and *wRite.* Robinson's technique helps you better understand and remember what you read. As you might have guessed, *Psychology in Action* was designed to incorporate each of these six steps.

- *Survey.* Each chapter of the text opens with an outline and core learning outcomes in question format. Together, they provide an overview, or *survey,* of the chapter. Imagine trying to assemble a jigsaw puzzle without looking at the puzzle box cover to see what the overall picture should be. Similarly, knowing what to expect from a chapter can help you organize the main points when you read.

- *Question.* To maintain your attention and increase comprehension as you read, turn the heading of each section into a *question.* The "Core Learning Outcomes" listed at the beginning of each chapter and repeated in the margins already do this for the main sections. Use them as models for turning the second- and third-level headings into questions. Also, try to anticipate the questions your instructor might ask on an exam.

- *Read.* The first R in SQ4R refers to *reading.* Try to answer the questions you formed in the previous step as you read the chapter. Read carefully—in short, concentrated periods.

- *Recite.* After you have read one small section, stop and *recite* (summarize what you've just read—either silently to yourself or as written notes). Also, think of personal examples of major concepts and how you might apply a certain concept to real-life situations. This will greatly increase your retention of the material.

Study Tip

Most instructors rarely (if ever) expect you to memorize these parenthetical citations. They are provided so that you can look up the source of a study if you would like more information. At the same time, keep in mind that it is important to know who the authors of certain key studies and famous psychologists are. Therefore, their names are emphasized in the text's discussion.

- *Review.* To fulfill the third R in the SQ4R method *(review)*, carefully study the "Check & Review" sections that conclude each major section. When you finish the entire chapter, review your lecture and reading notes, and closely study the end-of-chapter "Visual Summaries." Before each class quiz or exam, repeat this review process, and your grades will dramatically improve.

- *wRite.* In addition to the *writing* you do in the above steps, take brief notes in the text margins or on a separate sheet of paper. This helps keep you focused during your reading. (The *Student Study Guide* that accompanies this text teaches a special "marginal marking" technique that my students find extremely helpful.)

The SQ4R method may sound time consuming and difficult. Recall, however, that once you have mastered the technique, it actually saves time! More important, it also greatly improves your reading comprehension—and exam grades.

TIME MANAGEMENT: How to Succeed in College and Still Have a Life

Time management is not only desirable; it is also essential to college success. If you answer yes to each of the following, congratulate yourself and move on to the next section.

1. I have a good balance among work, college, and social activities.

2. I set specific, written goals and deadlines for achieving them.

3. I complete my assignments and papers on time and seldom stay up late to cram the night before an exam.

4. I am generally on time for classes, appointments, and work.

5. I am good at estimating how much time it will take to complete a task.

6. I recognize that I am less productive at certain times of the day (e.g., right after lunch), and I plan activities accordingly.

7. I am good at identifying and eliminating nonessential tasks from my schedule and delegate work whenever possible.

8. I prioritize my responsibilities and assign time accordingly.

9. I arrange my life to avoid unnecessary interruptions (visitors, meetings, telephone calls during study hours).

10. I am able to say no to unnecessary or unreasonable requests for my time.

If you cannot answer yes to each of these statements and need help with time management, here are four basic strategies:

1. *Establish a baseline.* To break any bad habit (poor time management, excessive TV watching, overeating), you must first establish a *baseline*—a characteristic level of performance for assessing changes in behavior. Before attempting any changes, simply record your day-to-day activities for one to two weeks (see the sample in Figure 1.13). Like most dieters who are shocked at their daily eating habits, most students are unpleasantly surprised when they recognize how poorly they manage their time.

2. *Set up a realistic activity schedule.* Once you realize how you typically spend your time each day, you can begin to manage it. Start by making a daily and weekly "to do" list. Be sure to include all required activities (class attendance, study time, work, etc.), as well as basic maintenance tasks like laundry, cooking, cleaning, and eating. Using this list, create a daily schedule of activities that includes time for each of these required activities and maintenance tasks. Also, be sure to schedule a

www.wiley.com/college/huffman

	Sunday	Monday	Tuesday	Wednesday	Thursday	Friday	Saturday
7:00		Breakfast		Breakfast		Breakfast	
8:00		History	Breakfast	History	Breakfast	History	
9:00		Psychology	Statistics	Psychology	Statistics	Psychology	
10:00		Review History & Psychology	Campus Job	Review History & Psychology	Statistics Lab	Review History & Psychology	
11:00		Biology		Biology		Biology	
12:00		Lunch / Study		Exercise	Lunch	Exercise	
1:00		Bio Lab	Lunch	Lunch	Study	Lunch	
2:00			Study	Study			

Figure 1.13 *Sample record of daily activities.* To help manage your time, draw a grid similar to this and record your daily activities in appropriate boxes. Then fill in other necessities, such as extra study time and "downtime."

reasonable amount of "downtime" for sports, movies, TV watching, and social activities with friends and family.

Try to be realistic. Some students try to replace all the hours they previously "wasted" watching TV or visiting friends with studying. Obviously, this approach inevitably fails. To make permanent time management changes, you must shape your behavior (see Chapter 6). That is, start small and build. For example, schedule 15 minutes increased study time for the first few days, then move to 30 minutes, 60 minutes, and so on.

3. *Reward yourself for good behavior.* The most efficient way to maintain good behavior is to reward it—the sooner, the better (Chapter 6). Unfortunately, the rewards of college (a degree and/or job advancement) are generally years away. To get around this problem and improve your time management skills, give yourself immediate, tangible rewards for sticking with your daily schedule. Allow yourself a guilt-free call to a friend, for example, or time for a favorite TV program after studying for your set period.

4. *Maximize your time.* Time management experts, such as Alan Lakein (1998), suggest you should "work harder, not longer." Many students report that they are studying all the time. Ironically, they may be confusing "fret time" (worrying and complaining) and useless prep time (fiddling around getting ready to study) with real, *concentrated* study time.

Time experts also point out that people generally overlook important "time opportunities." For example, if you ride the bus to class, you can use this time to review notes or read a textbook. If you drive yourself and waste time looking for parking spaces, go earlier and spend the extra time studying in your car or classroom. While waiting for doctor or dental appointments or to pick up your kids after school, take out your text and study for 10 to 20 minutes. These hidden moments count!

STRATEGIES FOR GRADE IMPROVEMENT: Note Taking, Study Habits, and General Test-Taking Tips

- **Note taking.** Effective note taking depends on *active listening*. Find a seat in the front of the class and look directly at the instructor while he or she is talking. Focus your attention on what is being said by asking yourself, "What is the main idea?" Write down key ideas and supporting details and examples, including important names, dates, and new terms. Do not try to write down everything the instructor says, word for word. This is passive, rote copying—not active listening. Also, be sure to take extra notes if your professor says, "This is an important concept," or if he or she writes notes on the board. Finally, arrive in class on time and do not leave early—you may miss important notes and assignments.

- **Distributed study time.** The single most important key to improved grades may be distributed study time. Although it does help to intensively review before a quiz or exam, if this is your major method of studying, you are not likely to do well in any college course. One of the clearest findings in psychology is that spaced practice is a much more efficient way to study and learn than massed practice (Chapter 7). Just as you would not wait until the night before a big basketball game to begin practicing your free throws, you should not wait until the night before an exam to begin studying.

- **Overlearning.** Many students study just to the point where they can recite the immediate information. For best results, you should be able to apply key terms and concepts to examples other than the ones in the text. You also should repeatedly review the material (using visualization and rehearsal) until it is firmly locked in place. This is particularly important if you suffer from test anxiety. For additional help on test anxiety and improving memory in general, see Chapter 7.

- **Understand your professor.** Pay close attention to the lecture time spent on various topics. This is generally a good indication of what your instructor considers important (and what may appear on exams). Also, try to understand the perspective (and personality) of your instructor. Recognize that most professors went into education because they love the academic life. They were probably model students who attended class regularly, submitted work on time, and seldom missed an exam. Remember that professors also have many students and hear many excuses for missing class and exams. Finally, note that most professors enjoyed lectures during college and were trained under this system. Never say, "I missed last week's classes. Did I miss anything important?" This is guaranteed to upset the most even-tempered instructor!

- **General test taking.** Here are several strategies to improve your performance on multiple-choice exams:

  1. *Take your time.* Carefully read each question and each of the alternative answers. Do not choose the first answer that looks correct. There may be a better alternative farther down the list.

  2. *Be test smart.* If you are unsure of an answer, make a logical guess. Begin by eliminating any answer that you know is incorrect. If two answers both seem reasonable, try to recall specific information from the text or professor's lecture. Be sure to choose "all of the above" if you know that at least two of the options are correct. Similarly, if you are confident that one of the options is incorrect, *never* choose "all of the above."

  3. *Review your answers.* After you finish a test, go back and check your answers. Make sure you have responded to all the questions and recorded your answers correctly. Also, bear in mind that information relevant to one question is often found in another test question. Do not hesitate to change an answer if you get more information—or even if you simply have a hunch about a better answer. Although many students (and faculty) believe "your first hunch is your best guess," research suggests this may be bad advice (Benjamin, Cavell, & Shallenberger, 1984; Johnston, 1978). Changing answers is far more likely to result in a higher score (Figure 1.14). The popular myth of not changing answers probably persists because we tend to pay more attention to failures than successes. Think about what happens when you get a test back. Most students pay attention to only the items they got wrong and fail to note the number of times they changed from an incorrect to a correct answer.

  4. *Practice your test taking.* Complete the Check & Review sections found throughout each chapter and then check your answers in Appendix B. Make up questions from your lectures and text notes. Also, try the interactive quizzes on our website http://www.wiley.com/college/huffman. Each chapter of the text has numerous quizzes, most with individualized feedback. If you answer a question incorrectly, you get immediate feedback and further explanations that help you master the material.

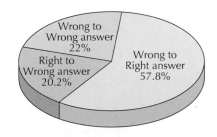

Figure 1.14 *Should you change your answers?* Yes! According to research, answer changes that go from a wrong to a right answer (57.8 percent) greatly outnumber those that go from a right to a wrong answer (20.2 percent). *Source:* Benjamin, L. T., Cavell, T. A., & Shallenberger, W. R. (1984). Staying with initial answers on objective tests: Is it a myth? *Teaching Psychology*, 11, 133–141.

www.wiley.com/college/huffman

ADDITIONAL RESOURCES: Frequently Overlooked Helpers

In addition to college counselors and financial aid officers, students often overlook these resources in their search for success:

1. *Instructors.* Get to know your instructors. They can provide useful tips for succeeding in their course. However, it is up to you to discover their office hours and office location. If their office hours conflict with your schedule, ask for an alternative appointment, try to stop by right before or after class, or e-mail them.

2. *College courses.* College instructors often assign two or three books per course and numerous papers that must be typed. *All students* can improve their reading speed and comprehension, and their word-processing/typing skills, by taking additional college courses designed to develop these specific abilities.

3. *Friends and family.* Ask friends or family members to serve as your conscience/coach for improved time management and study skills. After completing your daily activity schedule (page 00), set up weekly (or biweekly) appointments with a friend or family member to check your progress and act as your "conscience." You may think it would be easy to lie to your conscience/coach. But most people find it much harder to lie to another person than to lie to themselves (about calories, study time, TV watching, etc.). Encourage your conscience/coach to ask pointed questions about your actual study time versus your *fretting* and *prepping* time.

4. *Roommates, classmates, and study groups.* Although college roommates and friendly classmates can sometimes be a distraction, you can enlist their help as your conscience/coach or study partner. Also, ask your classmates and roommates what tricks/techniques they use to maintain their attention and interest during lectures or while reading texts.

If you would like more information on student success skills, consult the *Psychology in Action* website http://www.wiley.com/college/huffman. In addition to the interactive tutorials and quizzes mentioned earlier, we also offer specific Internet links for student success and recommend books and articles on time management and the other topics discussed here.

A FINAL WORD: Your Attitude

Imagine for a moment that the toilet in your bathroom is overflowing and creating a horrible, smelly mess. Whom should you reward? The plumber who quickly and efficiently solves the problem? Or someone who "tries very hard"?

Some students may believe they can pass college courses by simply attending class and doing the assignments. This might have worked for *some* students in *some* classes in high school. But it probably will not work in college. Most college professors seldom assign homework and may not notice if you skip class. They assume students are independent, self-motivated adult learners.

Professors also generally consider college a last stop on the way to the real world. They believe grades should reflect knowledge and performance—not effort. Points may be given in some classes for attendance, participation, and effort. However, the heaviest weight will usually come from exams, papers, and projects. Did you fix the toilet or not?

KEY TERMS
Assessment

*To assess your understanding of the **Key Terms** in Chapter 1, write a definition for each (in your own words), and then compare your definitions with those in the text.*

Introducing Psychology
critical thinking (p. 5)
interactions (p. 7)
nature–nurture controversy (p. 7)
psychology (p. 5)

Origins of Psychology
behavior perspective (p. 12)
biopsychosocial model (p. 16)
cognitive perspective (p. 13)
evolutionary perspective (p. 13)
humanist perspective (p. 12)
neuroscience/biopsychology
  perspective (p. 13)
psychoanalytic/psychodynamic
  perspective (p. 11)
sociocultural perspective (p. 13)

The Science of Psychology
applied research (p. 17)
basic research (p. 17)
debriefing (p. 21)
hypothesis (p. 19)
informed consent (p. 21)
meta-analysis (p. 20)
operational definition (p. 19)
theory (p. 21)

Research Methods
biological research (p. 36)
case study (p. 33)
control group (p. 25)
correlation coefficient (p. 34)
correlational research (p. 34)
dependent variable (DV) (p. 25)

descriptive research (p. 31)
double-blind study (p. 27)
ethnocentrism (p. 27)
experiment (p. 25)
experimental group (p. 25)
experimenter bias (p. 27)
independent variable (IV) (p. 25)
misattribution of arousal (p. 29)
naturalistic observation (p. 31)
participant bias (p. 28)
placebo [pluh-SEE-bo] (p. 27)
random assignment (p. 28)
sample bias (p. 28)
survey (p. 32)

Study Tip
Key Terms
The list of key terms at the end of each chapter is helpful to your mastery of the most important concepts. Try to recite aloud, or write a brief definition for, each term. Then, turn to the relevant pages in the chapter and check your understanding.

WEB RESOURCES
Achievement

Huffman Book Companion Site
http://www.wiley.com/college/huffman
  This site is loaded with free Interactive Self-Tests, Internet Exercises, Glossary and Flashcards for key terms, web links, Handbook for Non-Native Speakers, and other activities designed to improve your mastery of the material in this chapter.

American Psychological Association (APA)
http://www/apa.org/
  Richly layered home page of the APA with links to Internet resources, services, careers in psychology, membership information, and more.

American Psychological Society (APS)
http://www.psychologicalscience.org
  Official website of the American Psychological Society and a great place to start your search of psychology related websites.

Cyberpsychlink
http://cctr.umkc.edu/~dmartin/_psych2.html
  An index of psychology sites, including list servers, electronic journals, self-help, newsgroups, and software for psychologists.

Today in the history of psychology
http://www.cwu.edu/~warren/today.html
  Site that lets you pick a date (any date) from the history of psychology calendar and see what happened.

Want to be a research participant?
http://psych.hanover.edu/research/exponnet.html and
http://www.oklahoma.net/~jnichols/research.html
  Sites that offer great opportunities to participate in psychological research online.

Want to be an experimenter?
http://www.uwm.edu/~johnchay/index.htm
  Two sets of programs that allow you to explore classic experiments in psychology.

Psychweb
http://www.psychwww.com
  Links to classic works in psychology, scholarly resources, psychology journals, and career information for psychology majors.

Ethical principles of psychologists
http://www.apa.org/ethics/code.html
  Provides the full text of the ethical guidelines for professional psychologists.

Study Tip
Web Resources
Each chapter ends with a short list of suggested web links to further your achievement in psychology, including both your grade in the course and your personal interest in the field.

Visual SUMMARY

Introducing Psychology

What is Psychology?
Scientific study of behavior and mental processes that values empirical evidence and **critical thinking**.

Psychology's Goals
Describe, explain, predict, and change behavior and mental processes.

Careers in the Field
Occupational examples include experimental, biopsychology, cognitive, developmental, clinical, and counseling.

Origins of Psychology

- *Structuralism:* Focused on consciousness and the structure of the mind using introspection.
- *Functionalism:* Emphasized function of mental processes in adapting to the environment and practical applications of psychology.

Modern Perspectives

1. **Psychoanalytic/Psychodynamic:** Emphasizes unconscious processes and unresolved past conflicts.
2. **Behavior:** Studies objective, observable, environmental influences on overt behavior.
3. **Humanist:** Focuses on free will, self-actualization, and human nature as positive and growth seeking.
4. **Cognitive:** Emphasizes thinking, perception, and information processing.
5. **Neuroscience/Biopsychology:** Studies genetics and biological processes in the brain and other parts of the nervous system.
6. **Evolutionary:** Studies natural selection, adaptation, and evolution of behavior and mental processes.
7. **Sociocultural:** Focuses on social interaction and cultural determinants of behavior and mental processes.
- **Women and Minorities:** Sumner, Clark, Calkins, and Washburn made important contributions.

The Science of Psychology

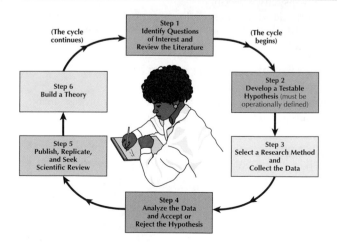

(The cycle continues) → Step 1 Identify Questions of Interest and Review the Literature ← (The cycle begins)

Step 6 Build a Theory

Step 2 Develop a Testable Hypothesis (must be operationally defined)

Step 5 Publish, Replicate, and Seek Scientific Review

Step 3 Select a Research Method and Collect the Data

Step 4 Analyze the Data and Accept or Reject the Hypothesis

Ethical Guidelines
Human research participants have rights, including **informed consent,** voluntary participation, limited and careful use of deception, **debriefing**, and **confidentiality**. Psychologists are expected to maintain high ethical standards in their relations with human and nonhuman animal research participants, as well as with clients in therapy. The APA has published guidelines detailing these ethical standards.

Research Methods

Four Major Research Methods

1. Experimental Research

Distinguishing feature: Establishes cause and effect.
Components:

■ **Independent variables** (what the experimenter manipulates)

■ **Dependent variables** (what the experimenter measures)

■ Experimental controls (including **control group, experimental group,** extraneous variables)

Experimental Safeguards

Researcher Problems

Experimenter bias prevented through blind observers, single- and **double-blind** studies, and **placebos.** Cross-cultural sampling prevents **ethnocentrism.**

Participant Problems

Sample bias prevented through random representative sampling and **random assignment. Participant bias** prevented through anonymity, confidentiality, single- and double-blind methods, placebos and deception.

2. Descriptive Research

Distinguishing feature: Unlike experiments, cannot determine causes of behavior, but can describe specifics.
Types of descriptive research:

■ **Naturalistic observation** describes behavior in its natural habitat without altering it.

■ **Surveys** use interviews or questionnaires on a sample of participants.

■ **Case studies** are in-depth investigations.

3. Correlational Research

Distinguishing feature: Provides important research findings and predictions by examining how strongly two variables are related, and if the relationship is positively, negatively, or not at all (zero) correlated.

4. Biological Research

Methods include brain dissection, lesioning, direct observation, case studies, electrical recording (EEG), and brain imaging (such as CT, PET, MRI, fMRI).

Tools for Student Success

1. Use Active Reading to Study this Text

■ Familiarize yourself with the general text

■ Use SQ4R to read each chapter: Survey/Question/Read/Recite/Review/wRite

2. Use Time Management to Succeed in College

■ Establish a baseline, set up a realistic activity schedule, reward yourself for good behavior, maximize your time

3. Strategies for Grade Improvement

■ Focus on note taking, distributed study time, overlearning, understanding your instructor, and general test-taking skills

4. Additional Resources

■ Instructors, typing and speed-reading courses, friends and family, roommates, classmates, and study groups

www.wiley.com/college/huffman

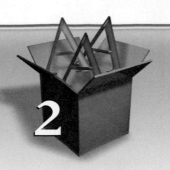

NEUROSCIENCE AND BIOLOGICAL FOUNDATIONS

Achievement

Core Learning Outcomes

As you read Chapter 2, keep the following questions in mind and answer them in your own words:

▷ What are neurons, and how do they communicate information throughout the body?

▷ How is the nervous system organized?

▷ What are the lower-level brain structures, and what are their roles in behavior and mental processes?

▷ How does the cerebral cortex control behavior and mental processes?

▷ How are heredity and evolution linked to human behavior?

Achievement
Assessment
Application

pplication

WHY STUDY PSYCHOLOGY?

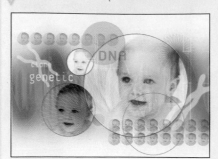

Digital Vision/Getty Images

Chapter 2 helps explain these fascinating facts:

▷ René Descartes, a seventeenth-century French philosopher and mathematician, believed that fluid in your brain was under pressure. If you decided to perform an action, this fluid would flow into the appropriate set of nerves and muscles, thus allowing the movement to happen.

▷ The reappearance of certain infant reflexes in adults may be a sign of serious brain damage.

▷ Even when reared apart, identical twins resemble each other more closely than fraternal twins in their IQ scores, numerous personality traits, and even their age at first sexual intercourse.

▷ A physician can declare you legally dead if your brain stops functioning—even though your heart and lungs are still working.

▷ Strong emotions, such as fear or anger, can stop digestion and sexual arousal.

▷ Cells in our brains die and regenerate throughout our lifetime. They are also physically shaped and changed by learning and from experiences we have with our environment.

▷ Scientists have created human embryos through cloning. The extracted stem cells from these embryos will be used for research and possible treatment for diseases like cancer, Parkinson's disease, and diabetes.

Sources: Abbott, 2004; Bouchard, 2004; Plomin, 1999.

Neuroscience *Interdisciplinary field studying how biological processes relate to behavioral and mental processes*

What are you doing at this very moment? Obviously, your eyes are busily translating squiggly little black symbols called "letters" into meaningful patterns called "words." But what part of your body does the translation? If you put this book down and walk away to get a snack or talk to a friend, what moves your legs and enables you to speak? You've heard the saying, "I think; therefore I am." What if you were no longer capable of thought or feeling? Would "you" still exist?

Although ancient cultures, including the Egyptian, Indian, and Chinese, believed the heart was the center of all thoughts and emotions, we now know that the brain and the rest of the nervous system are the power behind our psychological life and much of our physical being. This chapter introduces you to the important and exciting field of **neuroscience** and *biopsychology*, the scientific study of the *biology* of behavior and mental processes. It also provides a foundation for understanding several fascinating discoveries and facts, as well as important biological processes discussed throughout the text.

The first section of this chapter, "Neural Bases of Behavior," explores the *neuron*, or nerve cell, and the way neurons communicate with one another. "Nervous System Organization" provides a quick overview of the two major divisions of the nervous system—central and peripheral. "A Tour Through the Brain" explores the complex structures and functions of the major parts of the brain. The final section, "Our Genetic Inheritance," offers a brief discussion of the role of evolution and heredity in our modern psychological lives, and how neuroscience research can be applied to everyday life.

NEURAL BASES OF BEHAVIOR

What Is a Neuron? Psychology at the Micro Level

Your brain and the rest of your nervous system essentially consist of **neurons,** cells of the nervous system that communicate electrochemical information throughout the brain and the rest of the body. Each neuron is a tiny information processing system with thousands of connections for receiving and sending signals to other neurons. Although no one knows for sure, one well-educated guess is that each human body has as many as one *trillion* neurons.

These neurons are held in place and supported by **glial cells** (from the Greek word for "glue"). Glial cells surround neurons, perform cleanup tasks, and insulate one neuron from another so that their neural messages are not scrambled. Research also shows that glial cells play a direct role in nervous system communication (Rose & Konnerth, 2002; Wieseler-Frank, Maier, & Watkins, 2005). However, the "star" of the communication show is still the neuron.

Basic Parts of a Neuron

Just as no two people are alike, no two neurons are the same. However, most neurons do share three basic features: dendrites, cell body, and axon (Figure 2.1). **Dendrites** look like leafless branches of a tree. In fact, the word *dendrite* means "little tree" in Greek. Dendrites act like antennas, receiving electrochemical information from other neurons and transmitting it to the cell body. Each neuron may have hundreds or thousands of dendrites and their branches. From the many dendrites, information flows into the **cell body,** or soma (Greek for "body"), which accepts the incoming messages. If the cell body receives enough stimulation from its dendrites, it will pass the message on to the **axon** (from the Greek word for "axle"). Like a miniature cable, this long, tubelike structure then carries information away from the cell body.

Neuron *Cell of the nervous system responsible for receiving and transmitting electrochemical information*

Glial Cells *Cells that provide structural, nutritional, and other support for the neurons, as well as communication within the nervous system; also called glia or neuroglia*

Dendrites *Branching neuron structures that receive neural impulses from other neurons and convey impulses toward the cell body*

Cell Body *The part of the neuron that contains the cell nucleus, as well as other structures that help the neuron carry out its functions; also known as the soma*

Axon *A long, tubelike structure that conveys impulses away from the neuron's cell body toward other neurons or to muscles or glands*

Study **T**ip

Be careful not to confuse the term neuron with the term nerve. Nerves are large bundles of axons that carry impulses to and from the brain and spinal cord.

Figure 2.1 *The structure of a neuron.* Information enters the neuron through the dendrites, is integrated in the cell body, and is then transmitted to other neurons via the axon.

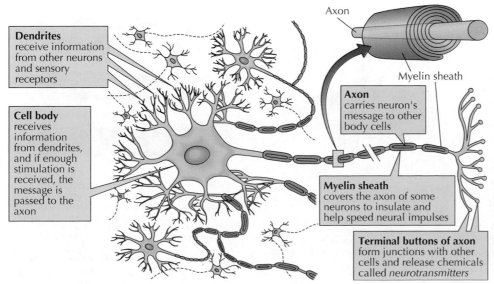

Dendrites receive information from other neurons and sensory receptors

Cell body receives information from dendrites, and if enough stimulation is received, the message is passed to the axon

Axon carries neuron's message to other body cells

Myelin sheath covers the axon of some neurons to insulate and help speed neural impulses

Terminal buttons of axon form junctions with other cells and release chemicals called *neurotransmitters*

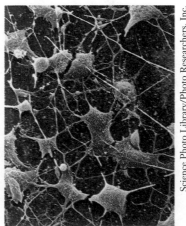

Science Photo Library/Photo Researchers, Inc.

www.wiley.com/college/huffman

Myelin [MY-uh-lin] Sheath *Layer of fatty insulation wrapped around the axon of some neurons, which increases the rate at which nerve impulses travel along the axon*

Study **T**ip

To remember how information travels through the neuron, think of the three key parts in reverse alphabetical order: Dendrite → Cell Body → Axon.

The **myelin sheath,** a white, fatty coating around the axons of some neurons, is not considered one of the three key features of a neuron. However, it is important because it helps insulate and speed neural impulses (Figure 2.2). Its importance becomes readily apparent in certain diseases, such as multiple sclerosis, where the myelin progressively deteriorates. This loss of insulation around the axons leads to disruptions in the flow of information between the brain and muscles, and the person gradually loses muscular coordination. For reasons that are not well understood, the disease often goes into remission. However, multiple sclerosis can be fatal if it strikes the neurons that control basic life-support processes, such as breathing or the beating of the heart.

Near each axon's end, the axon branches out, and at the tip of each branch are *terminal buttons,* which release chemicals (called *neurotransmitters*). These chemicals move the message from the end of the axon to the dendrites or cell body of the next neuron, and the message continues. Neurotransmitters will be studied in depth in the upcoming sections.

Figure 2.2 *Communication within the neuron—the action potential.*

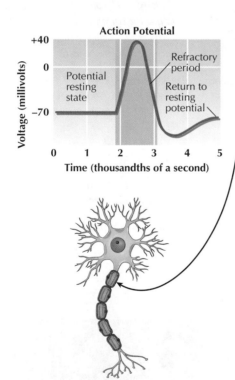

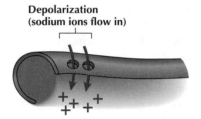

Resting, Polarized Membrane

Step 1: When the neuron is active, or *resting,* it is in a *polarized state.* The fluid outside the axon has more positively charged ions than the fluid inside, yielding a net negative charge inside. This is somewhat analogous to a car or flashlight battery. Batteries have positive and negative poles that are also "polarized." And, just as a battery has an electrical potential difference between the poles (1.5 volts for a flashlight battery), the axon membrane has a potential difference of about –70m Volts across it. (The inside is more negative by 70/1000 of a volt.)

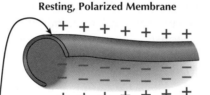

(potassium ions flow out)

Depolarization

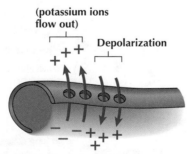

Step 3: This depolarization produces an imbalance of ions in the adjacent section on the axon membrane. Pores in this neighboring area now open, and more positively charged sodium ions flow in. Meanwhile, potassium channels in the previously depolarized section open. Once these channels open, the positive potassium ions move out to balance the electrical charge. Thus the resting potential is restored.

Depolarization (sodium ions flow in)

Step 2: When the cell body of the neuron receives sufficient stimulation via the dendrites from adjacent neurons, the electrical potential of the axon membrane near the cell body changes. When this potential change reaches a specific level, special voltage-controlled channels open, allowing a rapid inflow of positive sodium (NA) ions. This changes the previously negative charge inside the axon to positive—*depolarizing* the membrane.

Flow of depolarization

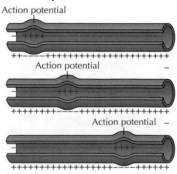

Summary: Through the sequential process of depolarization, followed by repolarization, the action potential moves continuously down the axon. This is like a line of dominoes falling, each one toppling the next. Or, like a fire burning in the forest, the neural impulse travels down the axon igniting one "tree" that then ignites the next, and the next. This neural message is called an *action potential.*

How Do Neurons Communicate? An Electrical and Chemical Language

The basic function of neurons is to transmit information throughout the nervous system. Neurons "speak" to each other or, in some cases, to muscles or glands, in a type of electrical and chemical language. We begin our discussion by looking at communication *within* the neuron itself. Then we explore how communication occurs *between* neurons.

Communication Within the Neuron—The Action Potential

The process of neural communication begins within the neuron itself, when electrical "messages" are received by the dendrites and cell body. These messages are passed along the axon in the form of a neural impulse or **action potential** (Figure 2.3). Because the neural impulse that travels down the axon is chemical, the axon does not transmit it in the same way that a wire conducts an electrical current. The movement down the axon actually results from a change in the permeability of the cell membrane. Picture the axon as a tube filled with chemicals. This tube is floating in a sea of still more chemicals. The chemicals both inside and outside the tube are *ions*, molecules that carry an electrical charge, either positive or negative.

Keep in mind that once the action potential has started, it continues. There is no such thing as a "partial" action potential. Similar to the firing of a bullet from a gun, the action potential either fires completely or not at all. This is referred to as the *all-or-none law*. Immediately after a neuron fires, it enters a brief *refractory period* where it cannot fire again. During the refractory period, the neuron *repolarizes*. The resting balance is restored with negative ions inside and positive ions outside. Now the neuron is ready to fire again.

How fast does a neural impulse travel? Actually, a nerve impulse moves slowly, much more slowly than electricity through a wire. Because electricity travels by a purely physical process, it can move through a wire at 97 percent of the speed of light, approximately 300 million meters per second. A neural impulse, on the other hand, travels along a bare axon at only about 10 meters per second.

Some axons, however, are enveloped in fatty insulation, the myelin sheath, which greatly increases the speed of an action potential. The myelin blankets the axon, with the exception of periodic *nodes*, points at which the myelin is very thin or absent (see again Figure 2.1). In a myelinated axon, the speed of the nerve impulse increases because the action potential jumps from node to node rather than traveling point by point along the entire axon. An action potential in a myelinated axon moves about 10 times faster than in a bare axon, at over 100 meters per second. As we discovered earlier, the importance of the myelin sheath becomes apparent when it is destroyed in certain diseases such as multiple sclerosis. The greatly slowed rate of action potential conduction affects the person's movement and coordination.

Communication Between Neurons—Neurotransmitter Action at the Synapse

Communication *between* neurons is *not* the same as communication *within* the neuron itself. As we have just seen, messages travel *electrically* from one point to another

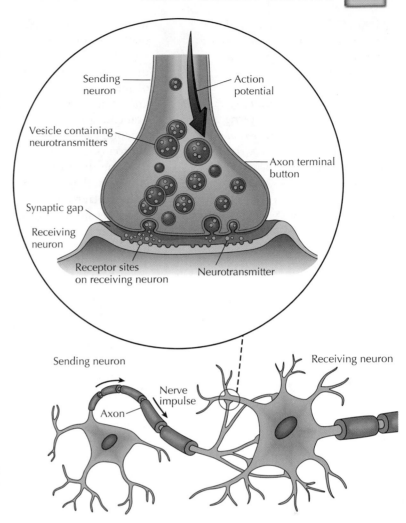

Figure 2.3 *Neurotransmitters—How neurons "talk" to one another.* In this schematic view of a synapse, neurotransmitter chemicals are stored in vesicles at the end of the axon. When action potentials reach the axon terminal, they stimulate the release of neurotransmitter molecules into the synaptic gap. The neurotransmitter chemicals then travel across the synaptic gap and bind to receptor sites on the dendrites or cell body of the receiving neurons. Neurotransmitters that do not "fit" into the adjacent receptor sites are decomposed in the synaptic gap or reabsorbed by the sending neuron.

Action Potential *Neural impulse that carries information along the axon of a neuron. The action potential is generated when positively charged ions move in and out through channels in the axon's membrane*

within the neuron. Now, watch how the same message is transmitted *chemically* from one neuron to the next.

Once the action potential reaches the end of the axon, it continues traveling down the branching axon terminals until it reaches the axon terminal buttons. The transfer of information from one neuron to the next occurs at the junction between them, known as the **synapse.** This synaptic juncture includes the tips of the terminal branches of the axon (the terminal buttons), the tiny space between neurons (the synaptic gap), and the ends of the dendritic branches or the cell body of the receiving neuron (see Figure 2.3).

The electrical energy delivered by the action potential causes the knoblike terminal buttons at the axon's end to open and release a few thousand chemical molecules, known as **neurotransmitters.** These chemicals (or neurotransmitters) then move across the synaptic gap carrying the message from the sending neuron to the receiving neuron.

After a neurotransmitter molecule travels across the tiny space of the synapse and attaches to the membrane of the receiving neuron, it delivers either an *excitatory* or *inhibitory* message. Note, however, that most receiving neurons also receive *both* excitatory and inhibitory messages from other nearby neurons (Figure 2.4). Because of these multiple and competing messages, the receiving neuron only produces an action potential when the total amount of excitatory messages received from various neurons outweighs the total number of inhibitory messages.

Can you see how this process is somewhat analogous to everyday decisions? Before deciding to move to a new apartment or home, we generally review and compare the relative costs and benefits of moving or not moving. If we have more reasons ("excitatory messages") to move, we move. If not, we stay put (inhibitory messages).

Although differentiating between excitatory and inhibitory messages may complicate your study of this chapter, the presence of competing messages is critical to your survival. Just as driving a car requires using both an accelerator and brake, your body needs both "on" and "off" neural switches. Your nervous system manages an amazing balancing act between *over*excitation, leading to seizures, and *under*excitation, leading to coma and death. Interestingly, poisons, such as strychnine, work by disabling many inhibitory messages. This disabling typically leads to overexcitation and uncontrollable, possibly fatal convulsions.

Synapse [SIN-aps] *Junction between the axon tip of the sending neuron and the dendrite or cell body of the receiving neuron. During an action potential, chemicals called neurotransmitters are released and flow across the synaptic gap*

Neurotransmitters *Chemicals released by neurons that affect other neurons*

Figure 2.4 *Multiple messages.* (a) In the central nervous system, the cell bodies and dendrites receive input from many synapses, some excitatory and some inhibitory. If enough excitatory messages are received, the neuron will fire. (b) Note in this close-up photo how the axon terminals from thousands of other neurons almost completely cover the cell body of the receiving neuron. (In this photo, dendrites are not visible.)

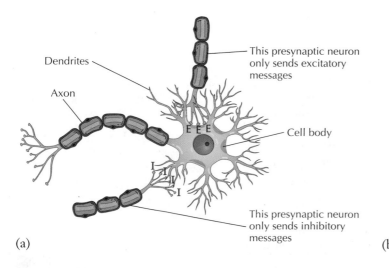

Dendrites

Axon

This presynaptic neuron only sends excitatory messages

Cell body

This presynaptic neuron only sends inhibitory messages

(a)

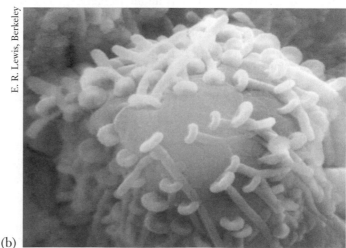

E. R. Lewis, Berkeley

(b)

Application

APPLYING PSYCHOLOGY TO EVERYDAY LIFE

How Neurotransmitters and Hormones Affect Us

We have seen how communication within a neuron is the result of changes in the electrical charges along its membrane. And we have seen how communication between neurons occurs at the synapse and can excite or inhibit the receiving neuron's action potential. But do you know how the major chemical messengers responsible for communication affect your everyday life? If not, let's briefly review the important role of *neurotransmitters* and *hormones*.

Neurotransmitters

Each neuron produces its neurotransmitters from materials in the blood, which are originally derived from foods. Researchers have discovered hundreds of substances known (or suspected) to function as neurotransmitters. Some neurotransmitters regulate the actions of glands and muscles; others promote sleep or stimulate mental and physical alertness; others affect learning and memory; and still others affect motivation, emotions, and psychological disorders, including schizophrenia and depression. Table 2.1 lists a few of the better-understood neurotransmitters and their known or suspected effects.

Endorphins Perhaps the best-known neurotransmitters are the *endogenous opioid peptides*, more commonly known as **endorphins.** These chemicals produce effects

Endorphins [en-DOR-fins] *Chemical substances in the nervous system that are similar in structure and action to opiates and are involved in pain control, pleasure, and memory*

SUMMARY TABLE 2.1 HOW NEUROTRANSMITTERS AFFECT US

Neurotransmitter	Known or Suspected Effects
Serotonin	Mood, sleep, appetite, sensory perception, temperature regulation, pain suppression, and impulsivity. Low levels associated with depression (Chapter 14).
Acetylcholine (ACh)	Muscle action, cognitive functioning, memory, REM (rapid-eye-movement) sleep, emotion. Suspected role in Alzheimer's disease.
Dopamine (DA)	Movement, attention, memory, learning, and emotion. Excess DA associated with schizophrenia, too little with Parkinson's disease (Chapter 14). Also plays a role in addiction and the reward system (Chapters 5 and 6).
Norepinephrine (NE) (or noradrenaline)	Learning, memory, dreaming, emotion, waking from sleep, eating, alertness, wakefulness, reactions to stress. Low levels of NE associated with depression, high levels with agitated, manic states (Chapter 14).
Epinephrine (or adrenaline)	Emotional arousal, memory storage, and metabolism of glucose necessary for energy release.
GABA (gamma aminobutyric acid)	Neural inhibition in the central nervous system. Tranquilizing drugs, like Valium, increase GABA's inhibitory effects and thereby decrease anxiety.
Endorphins	Mood, pain, memory, and learning.

similar to those of opium-based drugs such as morphine—they reduce pain and promote pleasure.

Endorphins were discovered in the early 1970s, when Candace Pert and Solomon Snyder (1973) were doing research on morphine, a pain-relieving and mood-elevating opiate derived from opium, which is made from poppies. They found that the morphine was taken up by specialized receptors in areas of the brain linked with mood and pain sensations.

But why would the brain have special receptors for morphine—a powerfully addicting drug? Pert and Snyder reasoned that the brain must have its own internally produced, or *endogenous*, morphine-like chemicals. They later confirmed that such chemicals do exist and named them *endorphins* (a contraction of *endogenous* ["self-produced"] and *morphine*). The brain evidently produces its own naturally occurring chemical messengers that elevate mood and reduce pain, as well as affect memory, learning, blood pressure, appetite, and sexual activity (Chapters 3, 4, and 11). Endorphins also help explain why soldiers and athletes continue to fight or play the game despite horrific injuries.

Neurotransmitters and Disease   One of the many benefits of studying your brain and its neurotransmitters is an increased understanding of your own or others' medical problems and their treatment. For example, do you remember why actor Michael J. Fox retired from his popular TV sitcom, *Spin City?* It was because of muscle tremors and movement problems related to a poorly understood condition called *Parkinson's disease (PD)*. As Table 2.1 shows, the neurotransmitter *dopamine* is a suspected factor in PD, and its symptoms are reduced with L-dopa (levodopa), a drug that increases dopamine levels in the brain (Negrotti, Secchi, & Gentilucci, 2005; Obeso et al., 2004).

Interestingly, when some Parkinson's patients are adjusting to L-dopa and higher levels of dopamine, they may experience symptoms that mimic schizophrenia, a serious psychological disorder that disrupts thought processes and produces delusions and hallucinations. As you will see in Chapter 14, excessively high levels of *dopamine* are a suspected contributor to some forms of *schizophrenia*. When patients with schizophrenia take antipsychotic drugs that suppress dopamine, their psychotic symptoms are often reduced or eliminated (Ikemoto, 2004; Paquet et al., 2004). However, the drugs may also create symptoms of Parkinson's. Can you explain why? The answer is found in the levels of dopamine released in their brains—*decreased* levels of dopamine are associated with Parkinson's disease, whereas *increased* levels are related to some forms of schizophrenia.

Another neurotransmitter, *serotonin* (see Table 2.1), may also be involved in the depression that often accompanies Parkinson's disease. Although some researchers believe Parkinson's patients become depressed in reaction to the motor disabilities of the disorder, others think the depression is directly related to lower levels of serotonin. As Chapter 14 discusses, antidepressant drugs, like *Prozac* and *Zoloft*, work by boosting levels of available serotonin (Delgado, 2004; Wada et al., 2004).

Neurotransmitters, Poisons, and Mind-Altering Drugs   An understanding of neurotransmitters explains not only the origin of certain diseases and their pharmaceutical drug treatments, but also how poisons, such as snake venom, and mind-altering drugs, such as nicotine, alcohol, caffeine, and cocaine, affect the brain (see also Chapter 5).

Most poisons and drugs act at the synapse by replacing, decreasing, or enhancing the amount of neurotransmitter. Given that transmission of messages *between* neurons is chemical, it is not surprising that many chemicals we ingest from food, drugs, and other sources can significantly affect neurotransmission. They can do so because their molecules have shapes similar to various neurotransmitters.

Alex Wong/Liaison Agency, Inc./Getty Images

Why study neurotransmitters? *Actor Michael J. Fox has been diagnosed with Parkinson's disease, which involves a decrease in cells that produce dopamine. In this photo, he is testifying before a U.S. congressional subcommittee to urge increased funding for research on Parkinson's and other medical conditions. For more information on his foundation for Parkinson's research, see www.michaeljfox.org.*

Jack Field/Corbis Images

Reuters New Media Inc./Corbis Images

Endocrine [EN-doh-krin] System
Collection of glands located throughout the body that manufacture and secrete hormones into the bloodstream

Hormones *Chemicals manufactured by endocrine glands and circulated in the bloodstream to produce bodily changes or maintain normal bodily functions*

Neurotransmitters, poisons, and drugs. Most poisons and psychoactive drugs work by replacing, decreasing, or increasing the amount of certain neurotransmitters. The neurotransmitter acetylcholine (ACh) is responsible for muscular contractions, including the muscles responsible for breathing. The poison curare blocks the action of ACh. This is why South American hunters sometimes apply it to the tips of their blowgun darts or arrows to paralyze their prey. Similarly, the botox poison also blocks ACh, and it is used cosmetically to paralyze facial muscles. In contrast, nicotine in cigarettes increases the effects of ACh, which increases the smoker's heart and respiration rates.

Neurotransmitters communicate with other neurons by binding to receptor sites in much the same way that a key fits into a lock. Just as different keys have distinct three-dimensional shapes, various chemical molecules, including neurotransmitters, have distinguishing three-dimensional characteristics. If a neurotransmitter—or a drug molecule—has the proper shape, it will bind to the receptor site (Figure 2.5a and 2.5b). This binding then influences the firing of the receiving cell.

Some drugs, called *agonists* (from the Greek *agon*, meaning "contest, struggle"), mimic or enhance the action of neurotransmitters (Figure 2.5c). For example, both the poison in the black widow spider and the nicotine in cigarettes have a molecular shape similar enough to the neurotransmitter *acetylcholine (ACh)* that they can mimic its effect, including increasing the heart rate. Amphetamines produce a similar excitatory effect by mimicking the neurotransmitter *norepinephrine*.

In contrast, *antagonist* drugs (from the Greek word meaning "a member of the opposing team") work by opposing or blocking neurotransmitters (Figure 2.5d). Most snake venom and some poisons, like the *curare* that South American hunters use, act as antagonists to ACh. Because ACh is vital in muscle action, blocking it paralyzes muscles, including those involved in breathing, which can be fatal.

Hormones

Did you know that the human body actually has two communication systems? We have just seen how the nervous system uses neurons and neurotransmitters to transmit messages throughout the body. But a second type of communication system also exists, which is made up of a network of glands, called the **endocrine system** (Figure 2.6). Instead of neurotransmitters, the endocrine system uses **hormones** (from the Greek *horman*, meaning to "stimulate" or "excite") to carry its messages.

Why do we need two communication systems? Imagine you are having a party and want to send out invitations. If you want a small party and only certain friends, you could make individual phone calls. Neurotransmission at the synapse is similar to

Normal Neurotransmitter Activation

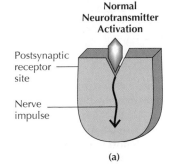

Postsynaptic receptor site

Nerve impulse

(a)

Blocked Neurotransmitter Activation

(b)

Agonistic Drug "Mimics" Neurotransmitter

(c)

Antagonistic Drug Fills Receptor Space and Blocks Neurotransmitter

(d)

Figure 2.5 *Receptor sites.* (a) Receptor sites on dendrites recognize neurotransmitters by their three-dimensional shape. (b) Molecules without the correct shape will not fit the receptors and therefore will not stimulate the dendrite. (c) Some agonist drugs, like nicotine, are similar enough in structure to a certain neurotransmitter (in this case, acetylcholine) that they mimic its effects on the receiving neuron. (d) Some antagonist drugs, like curare, block the action of neurotransmitters (again, acetylcholine) by filling a receptor site and thus not allowing the neurotransmitter to stimulate the receptor.

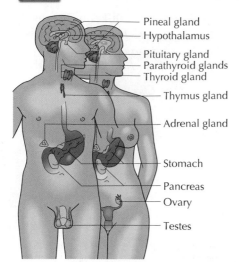

- Pineal gland
- Hypothalamus
- Pituitary gland
- Parathyroid glands
- Thyroid gland
- Thymus gland
- Adrenal gland
- Stomach
- Pancreas
- Ovary
- Testes

Figure 2.6 *The endocrine system.*
Hormones secreted by the endocrine glands are as essential as neurotransmitters to the regulation of our bodily functions. Both hormones and neurotransmitters perform one "simple" function—carrying messages between cells.

these individual calls. Messages are delivered to nearby specific receptors. What if you wanted a large party with thousands of people? You obviously could not phone everyone. Instead, you could send out a global e-mail message to all your friends asking them to invite all their friends. If those friends then invited all their friends, you would quickly have a very big (and expensive) party!

Hormones act like this global e-mail system. They are released directly into the bloodstream and travel throughout the body carrying messages to any cell that will listen. Hormones also function like your global e-mail friends who send along your message to other friends. A small part of the brain, the *hypothalamus*, releases hormones that signal the *pituitary* (another small brain structure), which in turn stimulates or inhibits the release of other hormones. (We will discuss these brain structures in detail in the upcoming section.)

What does the endocrine system have to do with you and your everyday life? Without the hypothalamus and pituitary, the testes in men would not produce *testosterone* and the ovaries in women would not produce *estrogen*. As you may know, these hormones are of critical importance to sexual behavior and reproduction. In addition, the pituitary produces its own hormone that controls body growth. Too much of this hormone results in *gigantism*; too little will make a person far smaller than average, a *hypopituitary dwarf.*

Other hormones released by the endocrine system play important roles in maintaining your body's normal functioning. For example, hormones released by the kidneys help regulate blood pressure. The pancreatic hormone (insulin) allows cells to use sugar from the blood. Stomach and intestinal hormones help control digestion and elimination.

An additional function of the endocrine system is its control of our body's response to emergencies. In times of crisis, the hypothalamus sends messages through two pathways—the neural system and endocrine system (primarily the pituitary). The pituitary sends hormonal messages to the adrenal glands (located right above the kidneys). The adrenal glands then release *cortisol*, a "stress hormone" that boosts energy and blood sugar levels, *epinephrine* (commonly called adrenaline), and *norepinephrine*. (Remember that these same chemicals also serve as neurotransmitters when released by neurons.)

In sum, the major functions of the endocrine system, including the pituitary, thyroid, adrenals, and pancreas, are to help with regulation of long-term bodily processes (such as growth and sex characteristics), maintain ongoing bodily processes, and assist in regulating the emergency response to crises. This brief discussion has covered only a few of the endocrine glands' most important functions. Nevertheless, even this limited coverage provides a foundation for understanding the brain, genetics, and evolution—topics found throughout this text.

A*ssessment*

CHECK & REVIEW

Neural Bases of Behavior

Neurons are cells that transmit information throughout the body. They have three main parts: **dendrites,** which receive information from other neurons; the **cell body,** which provides nourishment and "decides" whether the axon should fire; and the **axon,** which sends along the neural information. **Glial cells** support and provide nutrients for neurons in the central nervous system (CNS).

The axon is specialized for transmitting neural impulses, or **action potentials.** During times when no action potential is moving down the axon, the axon is at rest. The neuron is activated, and an action potential occurs when positively charged ions move in and out through channels in the axon's membrane. Action potentials travel more quickly down myelinated axons because the **myelin sheath** serves as insulation.

Information is transferred from one neuron to another at synapses by chemicals called **neurotransmitters.** Neuro-transmitters bind to receptor sites much as a key fits into a lock, and their effects can be excitatory or inhibitory. Most psychoactive drugs affect the nervous system by acting directly on receptor sites for specific neurotransmitters or by increasing or decreasing the amount of neurotransmitter that crosses the **synapse.**

Hormones are released from glands in the **endocrine system** directly into the bloodstream. They act at a distance on other glands, on muscles, and in the brain.

NERVOUS SYSTEM ORGANIZATION

Have you heard the expression "Information is power?" Nowhere is this truer than in the human body. Without information, we could not survive. Neurons within our nervous system must take in sensory information from the outside world through our eyes, ears, and other sensory receptors, and then decide what to do with it. Just as the circulatory system handles *blood*, which conveys chemicals and oxygen, our nervous system uses chemicals and electrical processes that convey *information*.

To fully comprehend the complex intricacies of the nervous system, it helps to start with an overall map or "big picture." Look at Figure 2.7. Note the organization of the nervous system as a whole, and how it is divided and subdivided into several branches. Now, look at the drawing of the body in the middle of Figure 2.7, and imagine it as your own. Visualize your entire nervous system as two separate, but interrelated, parts—the **central nervous system (CNS)** and the **peripheral nervous system (PNS).** The first part, the CNS, consists of your brain and a bundle of nerves (your spinal cord) that runs through your spinal column. Because it is located in the *center* of your body (within your skull and spine), it is called the *central* nervous system (CNS). Your CNS is primarily responsible for processing and organizing information.

Now, picture the many nerves that lie outside your skull and spine. This is the second major part of your nervous system—the PNS. Because it carries messages (action potentials) between the central nervous system and the *periphery* of the body, it is known as the *peripheral* nervous system (PNS).

Having completed our quick overview of the complete nervous system, we can go inside each of these two divisions for a closer look. We will begin with the central nervous system (CNS).

Central Nervous System (CNS): The Brain and Spinal Cord

Although we seldom think about it, our central nervous system (CNS) is what makes us unique and special. Most other animals can smell, run, see, and hear far better than we can. But thanks to our CNS, we can process information and adapt to our environment in ways that no other animal can. Unfortunately, our CNS is also incredibly fragile. Unlike neurons in the PNS, which require less protection because they can regenerate, damage to neurons in the CNS is usually serious, permanent, and sometimes fatal.

On the other hand, the brain may not be as "hard wired" as we once believed. As you'll see in the next section, the brain can reorganize its functions, rewire itself with new connections, possibly reroute neurons around damaged areas, and even generate new brain cells (Kim, 2005; Neumann et al., 2005; Song, Stevens, & Gage, 2002; Taub, 2002, 2004). In later chapters of the text, you will also discover that our brains change and remodel after new learning and experiences. Because of its central importance for psychology and behavior, the brain is the major subject of this chapter. We will discuss it in detail in the next section.

Achievement

How is the nervous system organized?

Central Nervous System (CNS) *The brain and spinal cord*

Peripheral Nervous System (PNS) *All nerves and neurons connecting the central nervous system to the rest of the body*

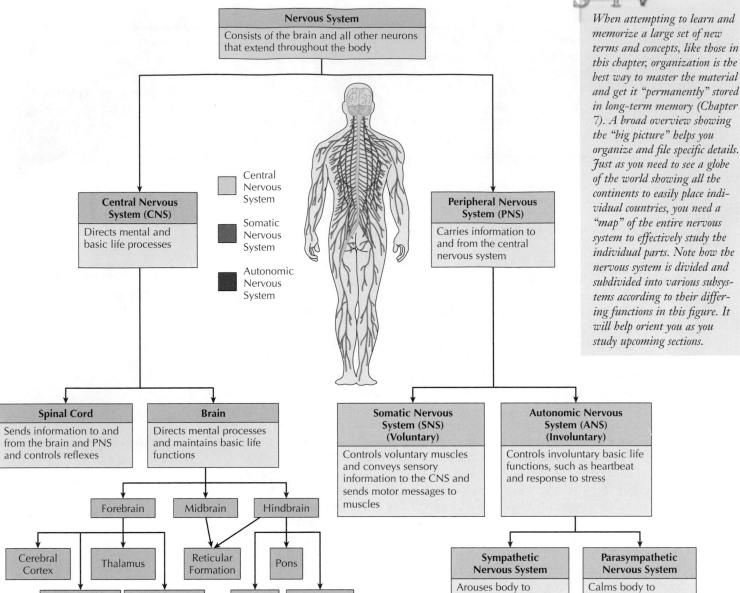

Nervous System
Consists of the brain and all other neurons that extend throughout the body

Central Nervous System

Somatic Nervous System

Autonomic Nervous System

Central Nervous System (CNS)
Directs mental and basic life processes

Peripheral Nervous System (PNS)
Carries information to and from the central nervous system

Spinal Cord
Sends information to and from the brain and PNS and controls reflexes

Brain
Directs mental processes and maintains basic life functions

Somatic Nervous System (SNS) (Voluntary)
Controls voluntary muscles and conveys sensory information to the CNS and sends motor messages to muscles

Autonomic Nervous System (ANS) (Involuntary)
Controls involuntary basic life functions, such as heartbeat and response to stress

Forebrain   Midbrain   Hindbrain

Cerebral Cortex   Thalamus   Reticular Formation   Pons

Limbic System   Hypothalamus   Medulla   Cerebellum

Sympathetic Nervous System
Arouses body to expend energy and respond to threat

Parasympathetic Nervous System
Calms body to conserve energy and restore the status quo

Summary Figure 2.7 *Organizational and functional divisions of the nervous system.*

Reflex *Innate, automatic response to a stimulus, such as the knee-jerk reflex*

The spinal cord is also important. It is a great highway of information into and out of the brain. But it is much more than a simple set of cables relaying messages. The spinal cord can initiate some automatic behaviors on its own. These involuntary, automatic behaviors are called **reflexes,** or *reflex arcs.* The response to the incoming stimuli is "reflected" back—automatically.

Think back to your most recent physical exam. Did your physician tap your knee with a special hammer to check your reflexes? Did your lower leg automatically kick out following this tap? This *knee-jerk reflex,* like the one that pulls your hand away from a painful fire, occurs within the spinal cord, without any help from the brain (Figure 2.8). Your brain later "knows" what happened a fraction of a second after the tap on the knee because neural messages are also sent along to the brain. The immediate, automatic response of the spinal cord, however, provides a faster reaction time.

We are all born with numerous reflexes (see Figure 2.9), many of which fade over time. But as adults we still blink in response to a puff of air in our eyes, gag when the

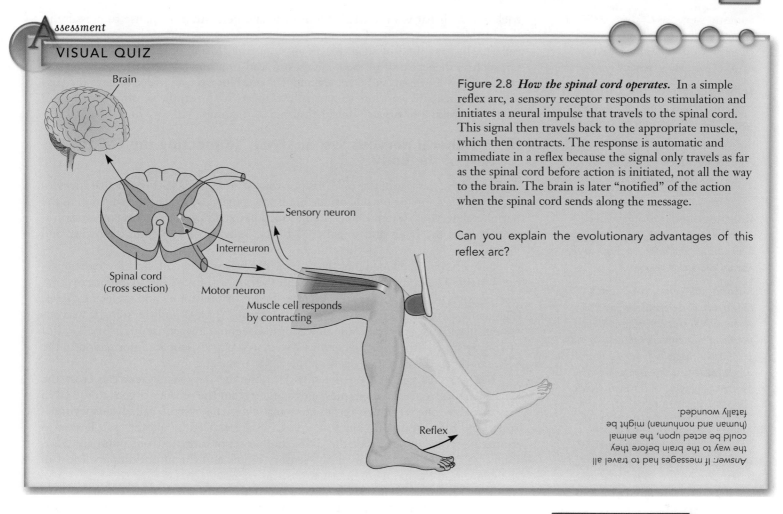

Brain

Sensory neuron

Interneuron

Spinal cord
(cross section)

Motor neuron

Muscle cell responds
by contracting

Reflex

Figure 2.8 *How the spinal cord operates.* In a simple reflex arc, a sensory receptor responds to stimulation and initiates a neural impulse that travels to the spinal cord. This signal then travels back to the appropriate muscle, which then contracts. The response is automatic and immediate in a reflex because the signal only travels as far as the spinal cord before action is initiated, not all the way to the brain. The brain is later "notified" of the action when the spinal cord sends along the message.

Can you explain the evolutionary advantages of this reflex arc?

Answer: If messages had to travel all the way to the brain before they could be acted upon, the animal (human and nonhuman) might be fatally wounded.

Testing for Reflexes

If you have a newborn or young infant in your home, you can easily (and safely) test for these simple reflexes. (Note: Most infant reflexes disappear within the first year of life. If they reappear in later life, it generally indicates damage to the central nervous system.)

(a) **Rooting reflex.** Lightly stroke the infant's cheek or side of the mouth, and watch how he or she will automatically (reflexively) turn his or her head toward the stimulation and attempt to suck.

(b) **Grasp reflex.** Place your finger in the palm of the infant's hand, and note the automatic closing of the infant's fingers around your finger.

(c) **Babinski reflex.** When you lightly stroke the sole of the infant's foot, the toes will fan out and the foot will twist inward.

Rooting Reflex
(a)

Grasp Reflex
(b)

Babinski Reflex
(c)

Figure 2.9 *Infant reflexes.*

www.wiley.com/college/huffman

Somatic Nervous System (SNS) *A subdivision of the peripheral nervous system (PNS) that connects to sensory receptors and controls skeletal muscles*

Sensory Neurons *Transmit messages from sense organs to the central nervous system; also known as afferent neurons*

Motor Neurons *Transmit messages from the central nervous system to organs, muscles, and glands; also known as efferent neurons*

Interneurons *Neurons within the central nervous system that internally communicate and intervene between the sensory and motor neurons*

Autonomic Nervous System (ANS) *Subdivision of the peripheral nervous system (PNS) that controls involuntary functions, such as heart rate and digestion. It is further subdivided into the sympathetic nervous system, which arouses, and the parasympathetic nervous system, which calms*

Sympathetic Nervous System *Subdivision of the autonomic nervous system (ANS) responsible for arousing the body and mobilizing its energy during times of stress; also called the "fight-or-flight" system*

Parasympathetic Nervous System *Subdivision of the autonomic nervous system (ANS) responsible for calming the body and conserving energy*

PictureQuest

The sympathetic nervous system in action. *The fight-or-flight response of the sympathetic nervous system mobilizes the body for action in the face of perceived danger.*

back of our throat is stimulated, and urinate and defecate in response to pressure in the bladder and rectum. Even our sexual responses are somewhat controlled by reflexes. Just as a puff of air produces an automatic closing of the eyes, certain stimuli, such as the stroking of the genitals, can lead to arousal and the reflexive muscle contractions of orgasm in both men and women. However, in order to have the passion, thoughts, and emotion we normally associate with sex, the sensory information from the stroking or orgasm must be carried to the brain.

◼ Peripheral Nervous System (PNS): Connecting the CNS to the Rest of the Body

The *peripheral nervous system (PNS)* is just what it sounds like—the part that involves nerves *peripheral* to (or outside of) the brain and spinal cord. The chief function of the peripheral nervous system is to carry information to and from the central nervous system. It links the brain and spinal cord to the body's sense receptors, muscles, and glands.

The PNS is subdivided into the somatic nervous system and the autonomic nervous system. The **somatic nervous system (SNS)** (also called the *skeletal nervous system*) consists of all the nerves that connect to sensory receptors and skeletal muscles. The name comes from the term *soma*, which means "body," and the somatic nervous system plays a key role in communication throughout the entire *body*. In a kind of "two-way street," the somatic nervous system first carries sensory information to the CNS and then carries messages from the CNS to skeletal muscles.

Because messages (action potentials) within the nervous system can cross the synapse in only one direction, messages coming from the sensory organs to the CNS are carried by one set of neurons in the somatic nervous system, called **sensory neurons.** And messages going out from the CNS are carried by another set, known as **motor neurons.** (Once inside the CNS, another set of **interneurons** internally communicate and intervene between the sensory inputs and the motor outputs. Most of the neurons in the brain are interneurons.)

When you hear a question from your instructor and want to raise your hand, your *somatic nervous system* will report to your brain the current state of your skeletal muscles. It then carries instructions back to your muscles, allowing you to lift your arm and hand. But the somatic nervous system does not make your pupils dilate or your heartbeat respond if a dangerous snake comes sliding into the classroom. For this, you need the other subdivision of the PNS—the **autonomic nervous system (ANS).** The ANS is responsible for *involuntary* tasks, such as heart rate, digestion, pupil dilation, and breathing. Like an automatic pilot, the ANS can sometimes be consciously overridden. But as its name implies, the autonomic system normally operates independently (*autonomic* means "autonomous").

The autonomic nervous system is itself further divided into two branches, the **sympathetic** and **parasympathetic,** to regulate the functioning of target organs like the heart, intestines, and lungs (Figure 2.10). These two subsystems tend to work in opposition to each other. A convenient, if somewhat oversimplified, distinction is that the *sympathetic branch* of the autonomic nervous system arouses the body and mobilized it for action—the "fight-or-flight" response. In contrast, the *parasympathetic branch* calms the body and conserves energy—the relaxation response. Keep in mind that these two systems are not an "on/off" or either/or arrangement. Like two children on a playground teeter-totter, one will be up while the other is down. But they essentially balance each other out. In everyday situations, the sympathetic and parasympathetic nervous systems work happily together to maintain a steady, balanced, internal state.

Returning to our previous example of the dangerous snake, do you see how these two branches of the autonomic nervous system also allow you to respond to dangerous or stressful situations? If you noticed a snake coiled and ready to strike, your *sympathetic nervous system* would increase your heart rate, respiration, and blood pressure.

Figure 2.10 *Actions of the autonomic nervous system (ANS).* The ANS is responsible for a variety of independent (autonomous) activities, such as salivation and digestion. It exercises this control through its two divisions—the *sympathetic* and *parasympathetic* branches.

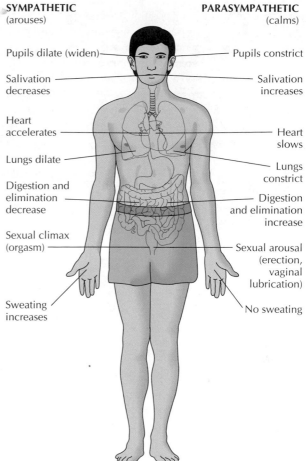

SYMPATHETIC
(arouses)

PARASYMPATHETIC
(calms)

Pupils dilate (widen)   Pupils constrict

Salivation decreases   Salivation increases

Heart accelerates   Heart slows

Lungs dilate   Lungs constrict

Digestion and elimination decrease   Digestion and elimination increase

Sexual climax (orgasm)   Sexual arousal (erection, vaginal lubrication)

Sweating increases   No sweating

It would simultaneously shut down your digestive and eliminative processes, and cause hormones, such as *cortisol,* to be released into the bloodstream. The net result of sympathetic activation is to get more oxygenated blood and energy to the skeletal muscles, thus allowing us to "fight or flee."

In contrast to the sympathetic nervous system, which arouses the body, the *parasympathetic nervous system* calms and returns your body to its normal functioning. It slows your heart rate, lowers your blood pressure, and increases your digestive and eliminative processes. Now, we understand why arguments during meals often cause stomachaches! Strong emotions, like anger, fear, or even joy, put the sympathetic system in dominance and prevent digestion and elimination.

Strong emotions and sympathetic dominance also explain many sexual problems. In order to have an orgasm, the body must go through several stages of arousal (Chapter 11). And, during sexual arousal, the body must be in parasympathetic dominance and relaxed enough to allow blood to flow to the genitals. If someone is excessively concerned about his or her performance, unwanted pregnancy, or sexually transmitted diseases, he or she will be in sympathetic dominance—thus preventing further sexual arousal and orgasm. A fearful, anxious body automatically sends most blood to the large muscles in preparation for "fight or flight"—not sex.

It is important to remember, however, that the sympathetic nervous system does provide adaptive, evolutionary advantages. At the beginning of human evolution, when we faced a dangerous bear or aggressive human intruder, there were only two reasonable responses—fight or flight. This automatic mobilization of bodily resources still has significant survival value in our modern life. But today our sympathetic nervous system is often activated by less life-threatening events. Instead of bears and intruders, we have chronic stressors like full-time college classes mixed with part- or full-time jobs, dual-career marriages, daily traffic jams, and rude drivers on high-speed freeways—not to mention terrorist attacks and global pollution. Unfortunately, our body responds to these sources of stress with full sympathetic arousal. And, as you will see in Chapter 3, chronic arousal to stress can be very detrimental to our health.

S*tudy* T*ip*

One way to differentiate the two subdivisions of the ANS is to imagine skydiving out of an airplane. When you initially jump, your sympathetic nervous system has "sympathy" for your stressful situation. It alerts and prepares you for immediate action. Once your "para" chute opens, your "para" sympathetic nervous system takes over, and you can relax as you float safely to earth.

A*ssessment*

CHECK & REVIEW

Nervous System Organization

The **central nervous system** is composed of the brain and the spinal cord. The spinal cord is the communications link between the brain and the rest of the body and is involved in all voluntary and reflex responses of the body. The **peripheral nervous system** includes all nerves linking sense receptors, muscles, and glands to and from the brain and spinal cord. Its two major subdivisions are the somatic nervous system and the autonomic nervous system.

The **somatic nervous system** includes all nerves carrying incoming sensory information and outgoing motor information to and from the sense organs and skeletal muscles. The **autonomic nervous system** includes the nerves outside the brain and spinal cord that maintain normal functioning of glands, heart muscle, and the smooth muscle of blood vessels and internal organs.

The autonomic nervous system is further divided into two branches, the parasympathetic and the sympathetic, which tend to work in opposition to one another. The **parasympathetic nervous system** normally dominates when a person is relaxed. The **sympathetic nervous system** dominates when a person is under physical or mental stress. It mobilizes the body for fight or flight by increasing heart rate and blood pressure and slowing digestive processes.

Questions

1. The nervous system is separated into two major divisions: the _____ nerv-ous system, which consists of the brain and spinal cord, and the _____ nerv-ous system, which consists of all the nerves going to and from the brain and spinal cord.
2. The autonomic nervous system is sub-divided into two branches called the _____ and _____ systems. (a) auto-matic, semiautomatic; (b) somatic, peripheral; (c) afferent, efferent; (d) sympathetic, parasympathetic
3. If you are startled by the sound of a loud explosion, the _____ nervous system will become dominant. (a) peripheral; (b) somatic; (c) parasympa-thetic; (d) sympathetic
4. What is the major difference between the sympathetic and parasympathetic nervous systems?

Check your answers in Appendix B.

CLICK & REVIEW
for additional assessment options:
www.wiley.com/college/huffman

A TOUR THROUGH THE BRAIN

We begin our exploration of the brain at the lower end, where the spinal cord joins the base of the brain, and then continue upward toward the forehead. You'll note that as we move from the bottom to the top, the functions of the individual brain structures generally change from "lower," basic processes like breathing to "higher," more complex processes such as thinking.

As you can see in Figure 2.11, the brain can be divided into three major sections: the *hindbrain, midbrain,* and *forebrain.* Also note the large section labeled as the **brainstem,** which includes parts of all three of these sections and helps regulate reflex activities important to survival (such as heartbeat and respiration). The distinctive shape of the brainstem provides a handy geographical landmark to keep us oriented.

Lower-Level Brain Structures: The Hindbrain, Midbrain, and Parts of the Forebrain

Brain size and complexity vary significantly from species to species. Lower species such as fish and reptiles have smaller, less complex brains than do higher species such as cats and dogs. The most complex brains belong to whales, dolphins, and higher primates such as chimps, gorillas, and humans. The billions of neurons that make up the human brain control much of what we think, feel, and do. Throughout our tour of the brain, keep in mind that certain brain structures are specialized to perform certain tasks, a process known as **localization of function.** But keep in mind that most parts of both the human and nonhuman brain are not so specialized—they perform integrating, overlapping functions.

The Hindbrain

Have you ever stood up quickly and felt so lightheaded that you almost fainted? Or have you wondered what allows you to automatically breathe and your heart to keep pumping despite being sound asleep? Automatic behaviors and survival responses like these are either controlled by or influenced by parts of your **hindbrain.** Three structures generally associated with the hindbrain are the *medulla, pons,* and *cerebellum.*

The **medulla** is the section of the hindbrain located near the base of the brain. It forms the marrow, or core, of the *brainstem. Medulla* is Latin for "marrow," and the brainstem is the "stalk" or stem that connects the spinal cord to higher regions in the brain.

Because the hindbrain and medulla are essentially an extension of the spinal cord, many nerve fibers pass through this region carrying information to and from the

Achievement

What are the lower-level structures of the brain, and what are their roles in behavior and mental processes?

Brainstem *Area of the brain that houses parts of the hindbrain, midbrain, and forebrain, and helps regulate reflex activities critical for survival (such as heartbeat and respiration)*

Localization of Function *Specialization of various parts of the brain for particular functions*

Hindbrain *Collection of brain structures including the medulla, pons, and cerebellum*

Medulla [muh-DUL-uh] *Hindbrain structure responsible for automatic body functions such as breathing and heartbeat*

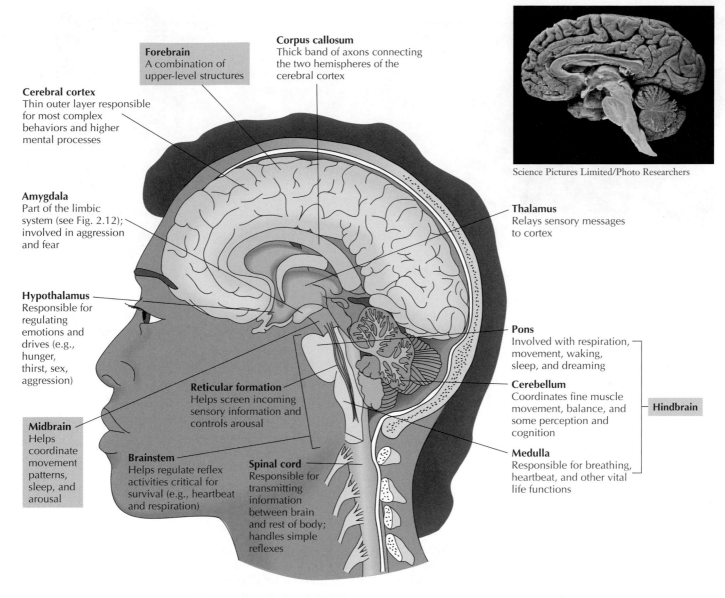

Forebrain
A combination of upper-level structures

Corpus callosum
Thick band of axons connecting the two hemispheres of the cerebral cortex

Cerebral cortex
Thin outer layer responsible for most complex behaviors and higher mental processes

Amygdala
Part of the limbic system (see Fig. 2.12); involved in aggression and fear

Hypothalamus
Responsible for regulating emotions and drives (e.g., hunger, thirst, sex, aggression)

Midbrain
Helps coordinate movement patterns, sleep, and arousal

Reticular formation
Helps screen incoming sensory information and controls arousal

Brainstem
Helps regulate reflex activities critical for survival (e.g., heartbeat and respiration)

Spinal cord
Responsible for transmitting information between brain and rest of body; handles simple reflexes

Thalamus
Relays sensory messages to cortex

Pons
Involved with respiration, movement, waking, sleep, and dreaming

Cerebellum
Coordinates fine muscle movement, balance, and some perception and cognition

Medulla
Responsible for breathing, heartbeat, and other vital life functions

Hindbrain

Science Pictures Limited/Photo Researchers

Summary Figure 2.11 *The human brain.* When a human brain is sliced down the center, splitting it into right and left halves, the right half looks like the top right photo. The drawing above highlights key structures and functions of the right half of the brain. As you read about each of these structures, keep this drawing in mind and refer back to it as necessary.

brain. The medulla also contains many nerve fibers that control automatic bodily functions, such as respiration and heartbeat. Therefore, damage to the medulla can be life-threatening. As we tragically discovered in 1968, when Senator Robert Kennedy was shot in this area of the brain, neither humans nor other animals can survive destruction of the medulla.

The **pons,** located above the medulla, is involved in respiration, movement, sleeping, waking, and dreaming (among other things). It also contains many axons that cross from one side of the brain to the other, which is why it is called the *pons,* Latin for "bridge."

The **cerebellum** ("little brain" in Latin) is located at the base of the brain behind the medulla and pons. (Some say it looks like a cauliflower.) In evolutionary terms, it is a very old structure responsible for coordinating fine muscle movement and bal-

Pons *Hindbrain structure involved in respiration, movement, waking, sleep, and dreaming*

Cerebellum [sehr-uh-BELL-um] *Hindbrain structure responsible for coordinating fine muscle movement, balance, and some perception and cognition*

www.wiley.com/college/huffman

VISUAL QUIZ

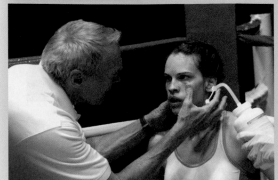

KPA/Omni-Photo Communications

Can you explain why professional boxing may cause coordination problems, partial or full paralysis, and even death?

Answer: When the boxer's head is repeatedly punched and snapped back, it damages the cerebellum and may lead to lack of motor coordination, stumbling, and loss of muscle tone. If the damage is severe enough, or if it involves the brain stem or spinal cord, paralysis and death may occur.

ance. Although the actual commands for movement come from higher brain centers in the cortex, the cerebellum coordinates the muscles so that movement is smooth and precise. The cerebellum is also critical to our sense of equilibrium or physical balance. Have you noticed how people stagger and slur their speech after a few too many drinks? Because the cerebellum is one of the first areas of the brain depressed by alcohol, roadside tests for drunk driving are essentially a measure of cerebellar functioning.

Research suggests that the cerebellum does much more than just coordinate movement and maintain physical balance. Using functional magnetic resonance imaging (fMRI), researchers have documented that parts of the cerebellum are also important for basic memory and sensory, perceptual, cognitive, and language tasks (Paquier & Mariën, 2005; Rönnberg et al., 2004; Thompson, 2005; Wild et al., 2004).

The Midbrain

Midbrain *Collection of brain structures in the middle of the brain responsible for coordinating movement patterns, sleep, and arousal*

The **midbrain** contains neural centers that help us orient our eye and body movements to visual and auditory stimuli, and works with the pons to help control sleep and level of arousal. It also contains a small structure involved with the neurotransmitter dopamine, which deteriorates in Parkinson's disease.

Reticular Formation (RF) *Diffuse set of neurons that screens incoming information and controls arousal*

Running through the core of the hindbrain, midbrain, and brainstem is the **reticular** (netlike) **formation (RF).** This diffuse, finger-shaped network of neurons filters incoming sensory information and arouses other areas of the brain when something happens that demands their attention. Abnormalities in the reticular formation are associated with attention deficit hyperactivity disorder, posttraumatic stress disorder, and other problems of arousal. Basically, without your reticular formation, you would not be alert or even conscious. In fact, if your reticular formation were cut off from the rest of your brain, you would move into a permanent coma.

The Forebrain

Forebrain *Collection of upper-level brain structures including the thalamus, hypothalamus, limbic system, and cerebral cortex*

The **forebrain** is the largest and most prominent part of the human brain. It includes several structures, including the *thalamus, hypothalamus, limbic system,* and *cerebral cortex.* The first three structures are located near the top of the brainstem. Wrapped above and around them is the cerebral cortex. (*Cerebrum* is Latin for "brain," and *cortex* is Latin for "covering" or "bark.") In this section, we will discuss only the first three structures. Because of its vital role in all complex mental activities, the cerebral cortex will have its own separate discussion following this one.

The Thalamus   Resembling two little footballs joined side by side, the **thalamus** serves as the major sensory relay center for the brain. Like an air traffic control center that receives information from all aircraft and then directs them to the appropriate landing or takeoff areas, the thalamus receives input from nearly all the sensory systems and then directs this information to the appropriate cortical areas. For example, while you are reading this page, your thalamus sends incoming visual signals to the visual area of your cortex. When your ears receive sound, the information is transferred to the auditory (or hearing) area of your cortex.

The thalamus also plays an active role in integrating information from various senses and may be involved in learning and memory (Bailey & Mair, 2005; Ridley et al., 2005). Injury to the thalamus can cause deafness, blindness, or loss of any other sense (except smell). This suggests that some analysis of sensory messages may occur here. Because the thalamus is the major sensory relay area to the cerebral cortex, damage or abnormalities also might cause the cortex to misinterpret or not receive vital sensory information. For example, research using brain-imaging techniques links abnormalities in the thalamus to schizophrenia (Clinton & Meador-Woodruff, 2004; Preuss et al., 2005). Schizophrenia is a serious psychological disorder characterized by problems with sensory filtering and perception (Chapter 14). Can you see how a defective thalamus might produce characteristics of schizophrenia, such as hallucinations and delusion?

The Hypothalamus   Beneath the thalamus lies the **hypothalamus** (*hypo-* means "under"). Although no larger than a kidney bean, it has been called the "master control center" for emotions and many basic drives such as hunger, thirst, sex, and aggression (Hinton et al., 2004; Williams et al., 2004). Its general function is regulation of the body's internal environment, including temperature control, which it accomplishes by regulating the endocrine system. Hanging down from the hypothalamus, the *pituitary gland* is usually considered the master endocrine gland because it releases hormones that activate the other endocrine glands. The hypothalamus influences the pituitary through direct neural connections and by releasing its own hormones into the blood supply of the pituitary.

Despite its relatively small size, the hypothalamus influences important aspects of behavior. It does this either *directly,* by generating some behaviors itself, or *indirectly,* by controlling parts of the autonomic nervous system (ANS) and endocrine system. An example of its direct effects are found when animals exhibit increased or decreased eating and drinking patterns depending on what area of the hypothalamus is affected (Chapter 12). The indirect effects of the hypothalamus are seen in the interaction of stress and the ANS (Chapter 3).

The Limbic System   An interconnected group of structures, known as the **limbic system,** is located roughly along the border between the cerebral cortex and the lower-level brain structures (hence the term *limbic,* which means "edge" or "border"). The limbic system includes the *fornix, hippocampus, amygdala, hypothalamus,* and *septum* (Figure 2.12). Scientists disagree about which structures should be included in the limbic system, and many include parts of the thalamus and cerebral cortex.

The limbic system is generally responsible for emotions, drives, and memory. However, the major focus of research interest in the limbic system, and particularly the *amygdala,* has been its production and regulation of aggression and fear (Blair, 2004; Pontius, 2005; Rumpel et al., 2005).

Another well-known function of the limbic system is its role in pleasure or reward. James Olds and Peter Milner (1954) were the first to note that electrically stimulating certain areas of the limbic system caused a "pleasure" response in rats. The feeling was apparently so rewarding that the rats would cross electrified grids, swim through water (which they normally avoid), and press a lever thousands of times until they collapsed from exhaustion—just to have this area of their brains stimulated. Follow-up studies found somewhat similar responses in other animals

Thalamus [THAL-uh-muss] *Forebrain structure at the top of the brainstem that relays sensory messages to the cerebral cortex*

Hypothalamus [hi-poh-THAL-uh-muss] *Small brain structure beneath the thalamus responsible for emotions and drives (hunger, thirst, sex, and aggression), and regulating the body's internal environment*

Limbic System *Interconnected group of forebrain structures involved with emotions, drives, and memory*

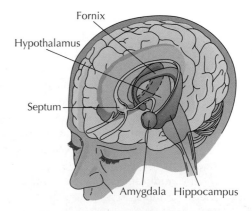

Figure 2.12 *Major brain structures commonly associated with the limbic system.*

www.wiley.com/college/huffman

Assessment

VISUAL QUIZ

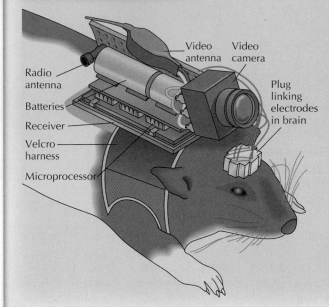

Radio antenna
Batteries
Receiver
Velcro harness
Microprocessor
Video antenna
Video camera
Plug linking electrodes in brain

Roborats in Action

In May 2002, a Brooklyn-based research team (Talwar et al., 2002) announced an ingenious technical breakthrough—"roborats." These live animals navigate complex terrain at the will of controllers at laptop computers more than 500 yards away (Dorfman, 2002). These "roborats" are important because researchers believe they may someday be sent into collapsed buildings to find survivors or detect land mines. The research itself also might lead to methods for artificial stimulation of brain regions that could bypass damaged nerves in paralyzed people.

Why do these rats respond to remote control? As you can see in the diagram, researchers implanted electrodes in the rat's brain that were connected to radio transmitters and miniature TV cameras. The researchers then sent electrical signals to the rat's brain to encourage them to turn right, left, or go straight ahead. When the rats responded correctly, they were rewarded with stimulation of their pleasure centers. Can you identify what area of the brain contains these pleasure centers?

Answer: The limbic system.

and even among human volunteers (e.g., Dackis & O'Brien, 2001). Modern research suggests that brain stimulation may activate neurotransmitters rather than discrete "pleasure centers."

Keep in mind that even though limbic system structures and neurotransmitters are instrumental in emotional behavior, emotion in humans is also tempered by higher brain centers in the cerebral cortex. Damage to the front part of the cortex, which connects to the amygdala and other parts of the limbic system, can permanently impair social and emotional behavior. This is yet another example of the inseparable interconnectivity of the entire brain.

Assessment

CHECK & REVIEW

Lower-Level Brain Structures

The brain is generally divided into three major sections: the hindbrain, midbrain, and forebrain. Parts of the **hindbrain**, the **pons** and **medulla**, are involved in sleeping, waking, dreaming, and control of automatic bodily functions; another part, the **cerebellum**, coordinates fine muscle movement, balance, and some perception and cognition.

The **midbrain** helps coordinate movement patterns, sleep, and arousal. The **reticular formation** runs through the midbrain, hindbrain, and **brainstem**, and is responsible for arousal and screening incoming information.

The **forebrain** includes several structures, including the thalamus, hypothalamus, limbic system, and cerebral cortex. The **thalamus** relays sensory messages to the cerebral cortex. The **hypothalamus** is involved in emotion and in drives associated with survival, such as thirst, hunger, sex, and aggression. The **limbic system** is a group of forebrain structures (including the amygdala) involved with emotions, drives, and memory. Because the cerebral cortex controls most complex mental activities, it is discussed separately in the next section.

Questions

1. What are the three major structures within the hindbrain?
2. Roadside tests for drunk driving primarily test responses of the _____.
3. What is the major sensory relay area for the brain? (a) hypothalamus; (b) thalamus; (c) cortex; (d) hindbrain?
4. Why is the amygdala a major focus of interest for researchers?

Check your answers in Appendix B.

CLICK & REVIEW
for additional assessment options:
www.wiley.com/college/huffman

The Cerebral Cortex: The Center of "Higher" Processing

Have you watched brain surgeries in movies and on television? After the skull is opened, the first thing you see is a mass of wrinkled, grayish tissue, aptly called *gray matter*. (The grayish color comes from billions of nerve cell bodies and their dendrites and some supportive tissue.) Directly beneath is the *white matter*, named for the whitish myelinated axons that connect the outer covering to lower sections of the brain.

The wrinkled, outer layer is called the **cerebral cortex,** which is responsible for most complex behaviors and our higher mental processes. Your cerebral cortex enables you to read this page and to think deeply about the information. It also allows you to decide whether you agree or disagree with what is presented and then discuss it with others. The cerebral cortex is the crowning glory of the brain. It plays such a vital role in human life that many consider it the essence of life itself. Without a functioning cortex, we would be almost completely unaware of ourselves and our surroundings. If this condition lasted for a month without signs of improvement, it would be known as a *persistent vegetative state (PVS)*. As we saw with the case of Terri Schiavo in 2005, the diagnosis and legal consequences of PVS are highly controversial (Figure 2.13).

Although the cerebral cortex is only about one-eighth of an inch thick, it is made up of approximately 30 billion neurons and nine times as many supporting glial cells. When spread out, the cortex would cover an area almost the size of a standard newspaper page. How does your cortex, along with all your other brain structures, fit inside your skull? Imagine crumpling and rolling the newspaper sheet into a ball. You would retain the same surface area but in a much smaller space. The cortex contains numerous "wrinkles" (called *convolutions*), allowing it to hold billions of neurons in the restricted space of the skull.

The full cerebral cortex, along with the two hemispheres beneath it, closely resemble an oversized walnut. They even share a very similar division down the center. This "dividing line" (or fissure) marks the *left* and *right hemispheres* of the brain, which make up about 80 percent of the brain's weight. In addition to specific functions discussed in a later section, the right hemisphere is responsible for control of the left side of the body, whereas the left hemisphere controls the right side of the body (Figure 2.14).

Cerebral Cortex *Thin surface layer on the cerebral hemispheres that regulates most complex behavior, including sensations, motor control, and higher mental processes*

Achievement

How does the cerebral cortex control behavior and mental processes?

Figure 2.13 *Terri Schiavo and the importance of the cerebral cortex.* (a) The 2005 debate over Terry Schiavo was largely about whether her husband should be allowed to remove her feeding tube because she was still able to move and breathe on her own and showed some reflexive responses. Terri's parents and others believed that these lower level brain functions were sufficient proof of life. Advocates on the other side felt that once the cerebral cortex ceases functioning, the "person" is dead and there is no ethical reason to keep the body alive. What do you think? (b) This 2002 CT scan of Terri's brain shows a significant shrinkage (or atrophy) of her brain tissue, which has been replaced by the dark cerebrospinal fluid and some connective tissue. (c) This is a CT scan of a normal brain.

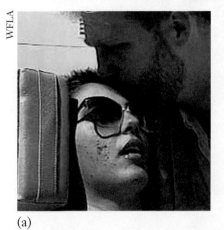
(a)

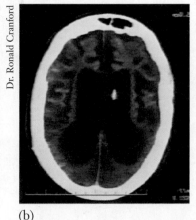
(b)

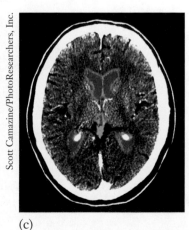
(c)

Figure 2.14 *Information crossover.* Information from the left side of your body crosses over to the right half of your brain.

Frontal Lobes *Two lobes at the front of the brain governing motor control, speech production, and higher functions, such as thinking, personality, emotion, and memory*

The two cerebral hemispheres are divided into eight distinct areas, or *lobes* (four on the left and four on the right). There are two *frontal lobes* (behind your forehead), two *parietal lobes* (at the top and to the rear of your skull), two *temporal lobes* (in the "temple" region above your ears), and two *occipital lobes* (at the back of your head). Divisions of these lobes are marked by visibly prominent folds, which provide convenient geographic landmarks (Figure 2.15). Like the lower-level brain parts discussed earlier, each lobe specializes in somewhat different tasks—another example of *localization of function*. At the same time, some functions overlap between lobes. As we describe each lobe and its functions, you may want to refer to Figure 2.15.

The Frontal Lobes

By far the largest of the cortical lobes, the two **frontal lobes** are located at the top front portion of the two brain hemispheres—right behind your forehead. The frontal lobes receive and coordinate messages from the other six lobes of the cortex. They also are responsible for at least three additional major functions:

1. *Motor control.* At the very back of the frontal lobes lies the *motor cortex*, which sends messages to the various muscles and glands in the body. All neural signals that instigate voluntary movement originate here. When you reach out to choose a

Figure 2.15 *Lobes of the brain.* This is a view of the brain's left hemisphere with its four lobes—frontal, parietal, temporal, and occipital—along with their major functions.

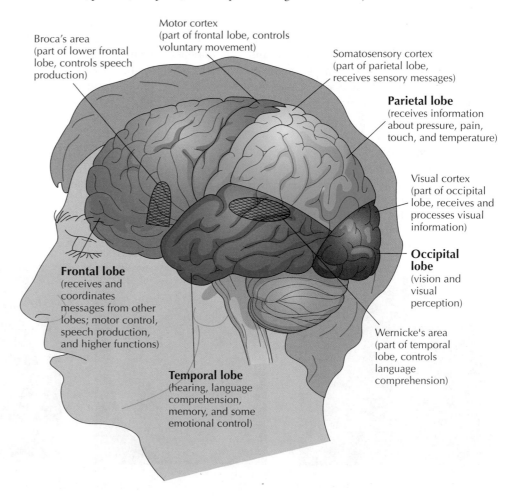

Broca's area (part of lower frontal lobe, controls speech production)

Motor cortex (part of frontal lobe, controls voluntary movement)

Somatosensory cortex (part of parietal lobe, receives sensory messages)

Parietal lobe (receives information about pressure, pain, touch, and temperature)

Visual cortex (part of occipital lobe, receives and processes visual information)

Occipital lobe (vision and visual perception)

Wernicke's area (part of temporal lobe, controls language comprehension)

Frontal lobe (receives and coordinates messages from other lobes; motor control, speech production, and higher functions)

Temporal lobe (hearing, language comprehension, memory, and some emotional control)

candy bar from a vending machine, the motor control area of the frontal lobes guides your hand to pull the proper lever.

2. *Speech production.* In the *left* frontal lobe, on the surface of the cortex near the bottom of the motor control area, lies *Broca's area*, which is known to play a crucial role in speech production. In 1865, French physician Paul Broca was the first to discover that patients with damage to this area had great difficulty speaking but could comprehend written or spoken language. This type of aphasia (or impaired language ability) has come to be known as *Broca's aphasia.*

3. *Higher functions.* Most functions that distinguish humans from other animals, such as thinking, personality, emotion, and memory, are controlled primarily by the frontal lobes. Abnormalities in the frontal lobes are often observed in patients with schizophrenia (Chapter 14). Damage to the frontal lobe affects motivation, drives, creativity, self-awareness, initiative, reasoning, and emotional behavior.

Application
CASE STUDY / PERSONAL STORY

Phineas Gage

In 1848, a 25-year-old railroad supervisor named Phineas Gage had a metal rod (13 pounds, 1¼ inches in diameter, and 3½ feet long) blown through the front of his face and brain (Figure 2.16). Amazingly, the blow was not fatal. Gage was stunned and his extremities shook convulsively. But in just a few minutes, he was able to talk to his men, and he even walked with little or no assistance up a flight of stairs before receiving medical treatment 1½ hours later.

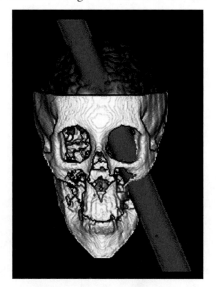

Although Gage did survive physically, he did not fare well psychologically. A serious personality transformation had occurred because of the accident. Before the explosion, Gage was "the most efficient and capable foreman," "a shrewd, smart businessman," and very energetic and persistent in executing all his plans. After the accident, Gage "frequently changed what he proposed doing, and was, among other things, fitful, capricious, impatient of advice, obstinate, and lacking in deference to his fellows" (Macmillan, 2000, p. 13). In the words of his friends and acquaintances, "Gage was no longer Gage" (Harlow, 1868). Following months of recuperation, Gage attempted to return to work but was refused his old job. The damage to his brain had changed him too profoundly.

According to historical records kept by his physician, Gage never again held a job equal to that of foreman. He supported himself with odd jobs and traveled around New England, exhibiting himself and the tamping iron, and for a time he did the same at the Barnum Museum. He even lived in Chile for seven years before ill health forced a return to the United States. Near the end of his life, Gage experienced numerous epileptic seizures of increasing severity and frequency. Despite the massive damage to his frontal lobes caused by the tamping iron, Phineas Gage lived on for another 11½ years, eventually dying from the epileptic seizures.

How did Gage physically survive? What accounts for his radical change in personality? If the tamping iron had traveled through the brain at a slightly different angle, Gage would have died immediately. But as you can see in the above photo, the

Figure 2.16 *Phineas Gage's injury.* An accidental explosion sent a 13-pound tamping iron through the brain of a young railroad supervisor Phineas Gage. The careful record keeping and in-depth reporting of his behavior after the accident provided valuable information on the short- and long-term effects of damage to the frontal lobes.

rod entered and exited the front part of the brain, a section unnecessary for physical survival. Gage's personality changes resulted from the damage to his frontal lobes. As this case study and other research show, the frontal lobes are intimately involved in motivation, emotion, and a host of other cognitive activities (Evans, 2003; Hill, 2004; Neubauer et al., 2004).

The Parietal Lobes

At the top of the brain, just behind the frontal lobes, are the two **parietal lobes,** which interpret bodily sensations including pressure, pain, touch, temperature, and location of body parts. When you step on a sharp nail, you quickly (and reflexively) withdraw your foot because the messages travel directly to and from your spinal cord. However, you do not experience "pain" until the neural messages reach the parietal lobes of the brain.

Let's talk briefly about two special sections—the *motor cortex* and the *somatosensory cortex.* Recall that the motor cortex lies at the back of the frontal lobe and controls voluntary movement. A similar band of tissue on the front of the parietal lobe, called the *somatosensory cortex,* receives information about touch in different body areas. As you can see in Figure 2.17, each part of the body is represented on the motor cortex and somatosensory cortex. However, the more important a body part is, the

Parietal [puh-RYE-uh-tuhl] Lobes
Two lobes at the top of the brain where bodily sensations are interpreted

Figure 2.17 *Body representation on the motor cortex and somatosensory cortex.* This drawing represents a vertical cross section taken from the left hemisphere's motor cortex and right hemisphere's somatosensory cortex. If body areas were truly proportional to the amount of tissue on the motor and somatosensory cortices, our bodies would look like the oddly shaped human figures draped around the outside edge of the cortex.

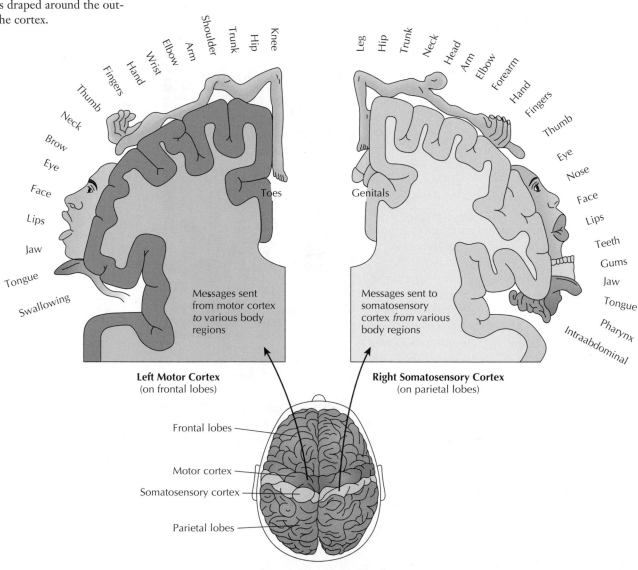

Would you like a quick way to understand your motor cortex and somatosensory cortex?

1. **Motor cortex.** Try wiggling each of your fingers one at a time. Now try wiggling each of your toes. Note on Figure 2.17 how the area of your motor cortex is much larger for your fingers than for your toes, thus explaining your greater sensitivity and precise control in your fingers.

2. **Somatosensory cortex.** Ask a friend to close his or her eyes. Using a random number of fingers (one to four), press down on the skin of your friend's back for one or two seconds. Then ask, "How many fingers am I using?"

Repeat the same procedure on the palm or back of his or her hand. You will find much more accuracy when you are pressing on the hand than on the back. Again, note in Figure 2.17 how the area of the somatosensory cortex is much larger for the hands than for the back, which explains the greater sensitivity in our hands versus our backs.

---

greater the area of cortex devoted to it. Note how the face and hands receive the largest share of cortical tissue. These areas are much more sensitive than the rest of the body and require more precise control. Note also that the greater the area of motor cortex, the finer the motor control.

The Temporal Lobes

The two **temporal lobes** (Latin for "pertaining to the temples") are found on the sides of the brain right above your ears. Their major functions are auditory perception (hearing), language comprehension, memory, and some emotional control. An area called the *auditory cortex* (which processes sound) is located at the top front of each temporal lobe. Incoming sensory information from the ears is processed in this area and then sent to the parietal lobes, where it is combined with visual and other body sensation information.

A section of the *left* temporal lobe, *Wernicke's area*, is involved in language comprehension. About a decade after Broca's discovery, German neurologist Carl Wernicke noted that patients with damage in this area could not understand what they read or heard. But they could speak quickly and easily. Unfortunately, their speech was often unintelligible. It contained made-up words, like *chipecke*, sound substitutions (*girl* became *curl*), and word substitutions (*bread* became *cake*). This syndrome is now referred to as *Wernicke's aphasia*.

The Occipital Lobes

As the name implies, the two **occipital lobes** (Latin *oh*, "in back of," and *caput*, "head") are located at the lower back of the brain. Among other things, the occipital lobes are responsible

©AP/Wide World Photos

Music and your brain. *Have you ever wondered if great musicians' brains are different from yours and mine? The answer is yes! Our brains are physically shaped and changed by learning and from experiences we have with our environment (e.g., Schmidt-Hieber et al., 2004; Shahin et al., 2003). This musician, Carlos Santana, has trained (and shaped) the auditory cortex of his brain to detect even the smallest gradations of sound.*

Temporal Lobes *Two lobes on each side of the brain above the ears involved in audition (hearing), language comprehension, memory, and some emotional control*

*S*tudy *T*ip

Remember that Broca's area in the left frontal lobes is responsible for speech production. Wernicke's area in the left temporal lobe is involved in language comprehension.

Occipital [ahk-SIP-ih-tal] Lobes *Two lobes at the back of the brain responsible for vision and visual perception*

for vision and visual perception. Damage to the occipital lobe can produce blindness, even though the eyes and their neural connection to the brain are perfectly healthy. The occipital lobes are also involved in shape, color, and motion perception.

The Association Areas

Thus far, we have focused on relatively small areas of the eight lobes that have specific functions. If a surgeon electrically stimulated the parietal lobes, you would most likely report physical sensations, such as feeling touch, pressure, and so on. On the other hand, if the surgeon stimulated your occipital lobe, you would see flashes of light or color.

Surprisingly, most areas of your cortex, if stimulated, produce nothing at all. These so-called quiet sections are not dormant, however. They are clearly involved in interpreting, integrating, and acting on information processed by other parts of the brain. Thus, these collective "quiet areas" are aptly called **association areas** because they *associate* various areas and functions of the brain. The association areas in the frontal lobe, for example, help in decision making and planning. Similarly, the association area right in front of the motor cortex is involved in the planning of voluntary movement.

As you recall from Chapter 1, one of the most popular myths in psychology is that we use only 10 percent of our brain. This myth might have begun with early research on association areas of the brain. Given that approximately three-fourths of the cortex is "uncommitted" (with no precise, specific function responsive to electrical brain stimulation), researchers might have mistakenly assumed that these areas were nonfunctional.

Association Areas *So-called quiet areas in the cerebral cortex involved in interpreting, integrating, and acting on information processed by other parts of the brain*

◼ Two Brains in One? A House Divided

We mentioned earlier that the brain's left and right cerebral hemispheres control opposite sides of the body. Each hemisphere also has separate areas of specialization. (This is another example of *localization of function*, yet it is technically referred to as **lateralization.**)

By the mid-1800s, early researchers had discovered that the left and right hemispheres carry out different tasks. In addition to mapping the brain and nervous system, they also noted that injury to one side of the brain produced paralysis or loss of

Lateralization *Specialization of the left and right hemispheres of the brain for particular operations*

sensation on the opposite side of the body. Also around this same time, case studies like Phineas Gage's documented that accidents, strokes, and tumors in the left hemisphere generally led to problems with language, reading, writing, speaking, arithmetic reasoning, and other higher mental processes. The "silent" right hemisphere came to be viewed as the "subordinate" or "nondominant" half, lacking special functions or abilities.

Split-Brain Research
In the 1960s, this portrayal of the left and right hemispheres as dominant and subordinate players began to change because of landmark research with **split-brain** patients.

The two cerebral hemispheres are normally connected at several places. But the primary connection between the left and right halves is a thick, ribbonlike band of nerve fibers under the cortex called the **corpus callosum** (Figure 2.18a).

In some cases of *severe* epilepsy, surgeons cut the corpus callosum to stop the spread of epileptic seizures from one hemisphere to the other. Given that brain surgery is a radical and permanent procedure, such an operation is always a last resort. It is performed only when patients' conditions have not responded to other forms of treatment. Fortunately, the results are generally successful—epileptic seizures are reduced and sometimes disappear entirely.

Split-brain patients also provide an unintended, dramatic side benefit to scientific research. Because this operation cuts the only direct communication link between the two hemispheres, it reveals what each half of the brain can do when it is quite literally cut off from the other. Although relatively few split-brain operations have been conducted since 1961, the resulting research has profoundly improved our understanding of how the two halves of the brain function. In 1981, Roger Sperry received a Nobel Prize in physiology/medicine for his split-brain research.

How do these patients function after the split-brain surgery? The surgery does create a few unusual responses. For example, one split-brain patient reported that when he dressed himself, he sometimes pulled his pants down with his left hand and up with his right (Gazzaniga, 2000). However, most patients generally show very few outward changes in their behavior, other than fewer epileptic seizures. In fact, one famous psychologist, Karl Lashley, joked that the corpus callosum's only function is to keep the two hemispheres from sagging (Gazzaniga, 1995).

The subtle changes in split-brain patients normally appear only with specialized testing. When a split-brain patient is asked to stare straight ahead while a photo of a fork is flashed to his left visual field, he cannot name it. But he can point to a photo of a fork with his left hand. Can you explain why?

To answer this question, you need to understand two major points about the brain. First, as you know, the left hemisphere receives and sends messages from and to the right side of the body, and vice versa. However, vision is different. Your eyes connect to your brain in such a way that, when you look straight ahead, the left half of your field of vision sends an image through both eyes to your right hemisphere. Similarly, the right side of your visual field is transmitted only to your left hemisphere (Figure 2.18b, c).

Assuming you do not have a split brain, if information were presented only to your right hemisphere, it would be quickly sent to your left hemisphere—where the speech center could name it. When the corpus callosum is split and experimenters present an image to only the left visual field, information cannot be transferred from the right hemisphere to the left. Thus, the patient cannot say what he saw. But he can point to a photo of the same object with his left hand (Figure 2.18d, e, f).

Split Brain *Surgical separation of the brain's two hemispheres used medically to treat severe epilepsy; split-brain patients provide data on the functions of the two hemispheres*

Corpus Callosum [CORE-pus] [cah-LOH-suhm] *Bundle of nerve fibers connecting the brain's left and right hemispheres*

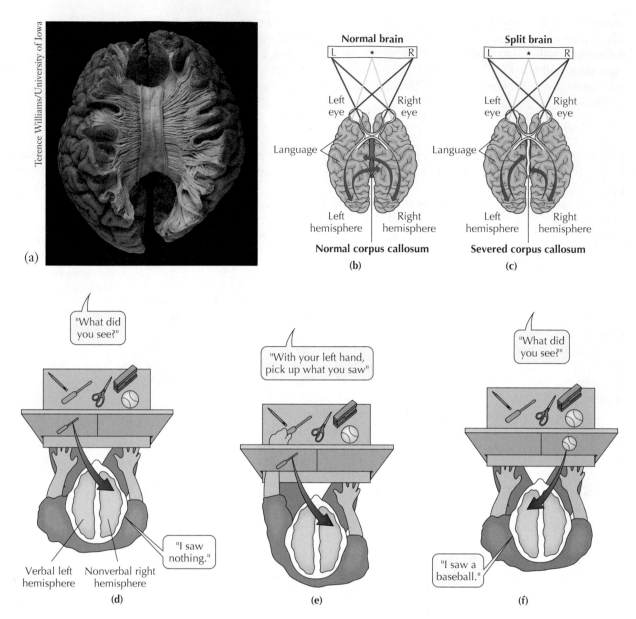

Figure 2.18 *Split-brain research.* (a) In this photo of an actual human brain, tissue from the top of the brain has been removed to expose the fibers of the corpus callosum, which connects the two hemispheres. (b) Imagine that this is a drawing of your brain and that you are being asked to stare straight ahead. Note how visual images from the left half of each of your two eyes connect only to the right half of your brain. Images from the right half of each eye connect to the left half. The information received by either hemisphere is transmitted across your corpus callosum to the other side. (c) However, when the corpus callosum is cut, the split-brain patient does not receive the information that is normally shared across the two hemispheres. (Note: Because the optic nerves are not part of the corpus callosum, when it is cut the optic nerves are not affected.) (d) When a split-brain patient stares straight ahead and a picture of a screwdriver is flashed only to the left visual field, information is restricted to the nonverbal right hemisphere. Therefore, the patient cannot name what he saw. (e) When asked to "pick up what you saw," the patient's left hand can touch the items hidden behind the screen and easily identify the screwdriver. This shows that the right hemisphere received the photo image of the screwdriver. But the patient could not name it because the information did not travel across the severed corpus callosum to the left hemisphere, where language is normally processed. (f) Note that when the image of a baseball is presented to the left hemisphere, the patient easily names it. Can you see why split-brain research is so important to brain researchers interested in studying the various functions of the two hemispheres?

Hemispheric Specialization

Dozens of studies on split-brain patients, as well as newer research on people whose brains are intact, have documented several differences between the two brain hemispheres (summarized in Figure 2.19). In general, for roughly 95 percent of all adults, the left hemisphere is specialized not only for language functions (speaking, reading, writing, and understanding language) but also for analytical functions, such as mathematics. In contrast, the right hemisphere is specialized primarily for nonverbal abilities. This includes art and musical abilities and perceptual and spatiomanipulative skills, such as maneuvering through space, drawing or building geometric designs, working jigsaw puzzles, building model cars, painting pictures, and recognizing faces and facial expressions (e.g., Bjornaes et al., 2005; Gazzaniga, 1970, 1995, 2000; Lambert et al., 2004; Sabbagh, 2004). Research also suggests that the right hemisphere may contribute to complex word and language comprehension (Coulson & Wu, 2005; Deason & Marsolek, 2005).

In another study, a team of researchers led by Fredric Schiffer (1998) at McLean Hospital in Massachusetts reported that different aspects of personality appear in the different hemispheres. In one patient, the right hemisphere seemed more disturbed by childhood memories of being bullied than did the left. In another patient, the right hemisphere experienced more negative emotions, such as loneliness and sadness, than did the left (Schiffer, Zaidel, Bogen, & Chasan-Taber, 1998).

Is this left- and right-brain specialization reversed in left-handed people? Not necessarily. About 68 percent of left-handers (people who use their left hands to write, hammer a nail, and throw a ball) and 97 percent of right-handers have their major language areas on the left hemisphere. This suggests that even though the right side of

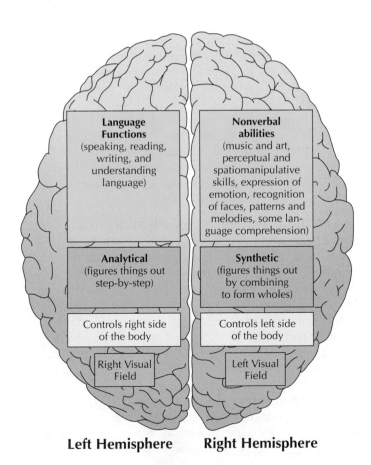

Left Hemisphere　　**Right Hemisphere**

Figure 2.19 *Functions of the left and right hemispheres.* The left hemisphere specializes in verbal and analytical functions. The right hemisphere focuses on nonverbal abilities, such as spatiomanipulative skills, art and musical abilities, and visual recognition tasks. Keep in mind that both hemispheres are activated when we perform almost any task or respond to any stimuli.

Would you like a demonstration of the specialized functions of your own two hemispheres?

Some research suggests that the eyes tend to move to the right when a mental task involves the left hemisphere and to the left when the task involves the right hemisphere (see Kinsbourne, 1972). Read the following questions to a friend and record whether his or her eyes move to the right or to the left as he or she ponders the answers. Try to keep the monitoring of your friend's eye movements as natural as possible.

1. Define the word heredity.
2. What is a function of punctuation marks?
3. Which arm is raised on the Statue of Liberty?

4. On a keyboard, where is the "enter" key.

The first two questions involve language skills and the left hemisphere. Answering them should produce more eye movement to the right. Questions 3 and 4 require spatial reasoning and the right hemisphere, which should elicit more eye movement to the left.

   Try the same test on at least four other friends or family members. You will note two major points: (1) Cerebral lateralization is a matter of degree—not all or nothing, and (2) Individual differences do exist, especially among left-handers.

the brain is dominant for movement in left-handers, other types of skills are often localized in the same brain areas as for right-handers.

   Although left-handers have some difficulty living in a right-handed world, being left-handed might have some benefits. For example, history shows that a disproportionate number of lefties have achieved greatness in art, music, sports, and architecture, including Leonardo da Vinci, Michelangelo, Picasso, and M. C. Escher. Because the right hemisphere is superior at imagery and visualizing three-dimensional objects, it may help to use the left hand for drawing, painting, or drafting (Springer & Deutsch, 1998). Moreover, left-handers tend to recover better from strokes that damage the language areas in the brain, which may be because the nonspeech hemisphere in left-handers is better able to compensate (Geschwind, 1979).

The Myth of the "Neglected Right Brain"

Courses and books directed at "right-brain thinking" and "drawing on the right side of the brain" often promise to increase your intuition, creativity, and artistic abilities by waking up your neglected and underused right brain (e.g., Bragdon & Gamon, 1999; Edwards, 1999). The fact is that the two hemispheres work together in a coordinated, integrated way, with each making important contributions. If you are a married student with small children, you can easily understand this principle. Just as you and your partner often "specialize" in different jobs (one giving the kids their baths, the other washing the dinner dishes), the hemispheres also divide their workload. However, both parents and both hemispheres are generally aware of what the other "half" is doing.

   In our tour of the nervous system, the principles of *localization of function* and *specialization* are common—dendrites receive information, the occipital lobe specializes in vision, and so on. Keep in mind, however, that all parts of the brain and nervous system play *overlapping* and *synchronized* roles.

Application

CRITICAL THINKING

The Biology of Critical Thinking
(Contributed by Thomas Frangicetto)

Many students find this chapter difficult because of the large number of unfamiliar terms and concepts. This exercise will help you:

- Review key biological terms that may appear on exams.
- Apply these terms to critical thinking components.
- Check your answers in Appendix B.

Part I: Match each term from Chapter 2 with the correct abbreviated description.

1. ___Amygdala
2. ___Corpus Callosum
3. ___Dopamine
4. ___Frontal Lobes
5. ___Hypothalamus
6. ___Left Hemisphere
7. ___Cerebellum
8. ___Occipital Lobes
9. ___Parasympathetic Nervous System
10. ___Parietal Lobes
11. ___Right Hemisphere
12. ___Serotonin
13. ___Sympathetic Nervous System
14. ___Temporal Lobes

a. arousal
b. language/analytical
c. mood, impulsivity, depression
d. vision/visual perception
e. hearing/language
f. coordination
g. internal environment
h. calming
i. connects two hemispheres
j. bodily sensations
k. emotion
l. motor, speech, and higher functions
m. nonverbal abilities
n. movement, attention, schizophrenia

ACTIVE LEARNING

Part II: As mentioned earlier, your brain and nervous system control everything you do, feel, see, or think. They also control your critical thinking. For each of situations below, first identify which critical thinking component (CTC) from the Prologue (pp. xxx–xxxiv) is being described. And then decide which area of the brain or nervous system listed in Part I would most likely be involved in the application of this CTC. (Tip: If you need help, review the related text content for each term, not just the abbreviated description above.)

1. Tamara wrote several children's storybooks and attempted to do the illustrations herself. After many failed attempts, she accepted her limitations and hired a professional artist.

   CTC:_____ Biological Area (s):_____

2. Samantha was falling behind in her college courses primarily because she was not paying close attention during class lectures. She decided to carefully listen and to take detailed notes, and her grades dramatically improved.

   CTC:_____ Biological Area (s):_____

3. After two weeks on a new job, Alex was so stressed and overwhelmed he planned to quit, but his boss persuaded him to stay on. Once Alex accepted his boss's reassurance that uncertainty and mistakes are a normal part of getting adjusted to a new job, his symptoms of stress (shortness of breath and increased blood pressure) soon disappeared.

   CTC:_____ Biological Area (s):_____

Assessment

CHECK & REVIEW

The Cerebral Cortex and Two Brains in One?

The **cerebral cortex,** the thin surface layer on the cerebral hemispheres, regulates most complex behaviors and higher mental processes. The left and right cerebral hemispheres make up most of the weight of the brain, and each hemisphere is divided into four lobes. The two **frontal lobes** control movement, speech, and higher functions. The two **parietal lobes** are the receiving area for sensory information. The two **temporal lobes** are concerned with hearing, language, memory, and some emotional control. The two **occipital lobes** are dedicated to vision and visual information processing.

The two hemispheres are linked by the **corpus callosum,** through which they communicate and coordinate. **Split-brain** research shows that each hemisphere performs somewhat separate functions. In most people, the left hemisphere is dominant in verbal skills, such as speaking and writing, and analytical tasks. The right hemisphere appears to excel at nonverbal tasks, such as spatiomanipulative skills, art and music, and visual recognition.

Questions

1. The bumpy, convoluted area making up the outside surface of the brain is the_____.
2. You are giving a speech. Name the cortical lobes involved in the following behaviors:
   a. Seeing faces in the audience

www.wiley.com/college/huffman

b. Hearing questions from the audience
c. Remembering where your car is parked when you are ready to go home
d. Noticing that your new shoes are too tight and hurting your feet
3. The_____lobes regulate our personal-

ity and are largely responsible for much of what makes us uniquely human. (a) frontal; (b) temporal; (c) parietal; (d) occipital
4. Although the left and right hemispheres of the brain are specialized, they are normally in close communication because of the_____. (a) recipro-

cating circuits; (b) thalamus; (c) corpus callosum; (d) cerebellum

Check your answers in Appendix B.

CLICK & REVIEW
for additional assessment options:
www.wiley.com/college/huffman

OUR GENETIC INHERITANCE

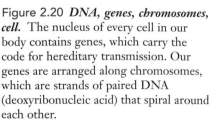

Achievement

How are heredity and evolution linked to human behavior?

Behavioral Genetics *Study of the relative effects of heredity and environment on behavior and mental processes*

Evolutionary Psychology *Branch of psychology that studies the ways in which natural selection and adaptation can explain behavior and mental processes*

Chromosome *Threadlike molecule of DNA (deoxyribonucleic acid) that carries genetic information*

Gene *A segment of DNA (deoxyribonucleic acid) that occupies a specific place on a particular chromosome and carries the code for hereditary transmission*

Some of what we are today results from evolutionary forces at play thousands of years before you or I were even on this planet. During that time, our ancestors foraged for food, fought for survival, and passed on traits that were selected and transmitted down through the generations. How do these transmitted traits affect us today? Are our modern-day violent crimes, murders, and international conflicts a result of aggressive genes inherited from these ancient ancestors? Or is this the result of our current environment? If you are sociable and outgoing like your mother or father, was this inherited or learned? To answer these questions, psychologists often turn to **behavioral genetics,** the study of the relative effects of heredity and environment on behavior and mental processes. Answers are also found in **evolutionary psychology,** which studies the ways in which natural selection and adaptation are connected to behavior and mental processes.

Behavioral Genetics: Is It Nature or Nurture?

With a good heredity, nature deals you a fine hand at cards; and with a good environment, you learn to play the hand well.

WALTER C. ALVAREZ

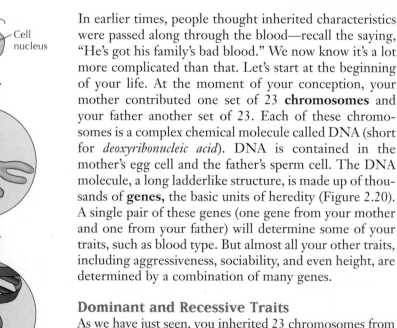

Figure 2.20 *DNA, genes, chromosomes, cell.* The nucleus of every cell in our body contains genes, which carry the code for hereditary transmission. Our genes are arranged along chromosomes, which are strands of paired DNA (deoxyribonucleic acid) that spiral around each other.

In earlier times, people thought inherited characteristics were passed along through the blood—recall the saying, "He's got his family's bad blood." We now know it's a lot more complicated than that. Let's start at the beginning of your life. At the moment of your conception, your mother contributed one set of 23 **chromosomes** and your father another set of 23. Each of these chromosomes is a complex chemical molecule called DNA (short for *deoxyribonucleic acid*). DNA is contained in the mother's egg cell and the father's sperm cell. The DNA molecule, a long ladderlike structure, is made up of thousands of **genes,** the basic units of heredity (Figure 2.20). A single pair of these genes (one gene from your mother and one from your father) will determine some of your traits, such as blood type. But almost all your other traits, including aggressiveness, sociability, and even height, are determined by a combination of many genes.

Dominant and Recessive Traits

As we have just seen, you inherited 23 chromosomes from each parent. And for many characteristics, you received a pair of genes for each of your traits. Whether or not specific genes from your mother or father express themselves in your own individual case depends on whether the gene is dominant or recessive. A *dominant* gene reveals its trait whenever the gene is present. In contrast, a *recessive* gene is expressed only if the other gene in the pair is also recessive.

It was once assumed that characteristics such as eye color, hair color, or height were the result of either one dominant gene or two paired recessive genes. But modern geneticists believe that each of these characteristics is *polygenic*, meaning they are controlled by multiple genes. Many polygenic traits like height or intelligence are also *multifactorial*. This means that in addition to being influenced by several genes, they are also affected by environmental and social factors. For example, children who are malnourished may not reach their full potential genetic height or maximum intelligence. As described in Figure 2.21, tongue curling is one of the few traits that depend on only one dominant gene.

Fortunately, most serious genetic disorders are not transmitted through a dominant gene. Can you understand why? From an evolutionary perspective, seriously diseased offspring would generally not survive long enough to transmit the disorder to their own children. However, certain recessive gene disorders, such as cystic fibrosis, Tay-Sachs disease, or sickle-cell anemia, can be passed on to children if they receive the same recessive gene from each biological parent. Prospective parents who fear they may be carriers of genetic disorders can obtain *genetic counseling*, which helps calculate the risk of their offspring inheriting a genetic disorder.

Methods for Studying Inheritance in Humans

Having reviewed some of the basic terminology and concepts behind behavioral genetics, let's talk about how scientists might research human inheritance. If you wanted to determine the relative influences of heredity or environment on complex traits like aggressiveness, intelligence, or sociability, how would you go about it? For very simple studies of inheritance in plants, you could simply breed one type of plant with another to see what your desired trait would be like in the next generation. But how would you conduct research on humans? Scientists cannot use selective breeding experiments—for obvious ethical reasons. Instead, they generally rely on four less direct methods:

1. *Twin studies.* Psychologists are especially interested in the study of twins because they have a uniquely high proportion of shared genes. Identical (*monozygotic*—one egg) twins share 100 percent of the same genes. Fraternal (*dizygotic*—two egg) twins share, on average, 50 percent. The difference between 50 and 100 percent is explained by the way the two kinds of twins are formed. As you can see in Figure 2.22, identical twins are created when a fertilized mother's egg divides into two separate (but identical) cells. These cells then go on to produce two complete individuals with identical (100 percent) genetic information. Fraternal twins, who share only 50 percent of the same genes, occur when different sperm from the father fertilize two separate

Can you curl your tongue lengthwise?

Tongue curling is one of the few traits that depends on only one dominant gene. If you can curl your tongue, at least one of your biological parents can also curl his or her tongue. However, if both of your parents are "noncurlers," they both must have recessive genes for curling.

Courtesy Karen Huffman

Figure 2.21 *A dominant gene in action.*

Figure 2.22 *Identical and fraternal twins.* Identical twins occur when a fertilized egg divides into two separate (but identical) cells that go on to produce two individuals with identical (100 percent) genetic material. Fraternal twins are created when two separate eggs are fertilized by different sperm and go on to develop into two separate individuals sharing on average 50 percent of the same genes.

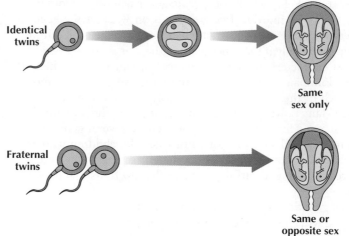

eggs from the mother. Although these twins experience approximately the same moment of fertilization, womb environment, and time of birth, they are genetically no more alike than brothers and sisters born at different times. Fraternal twins are simply nine-month "womb mates."

Identical and fraternal twins have differing percentages of shared genes. However, they still share the same biological parents and normally are reared in relatively the same environment. Can you see how twin studies provide a valuable type of "natural experiment?" Researchers collect data on both sets of twins. If they find significant differences in fraternal versus identical twins, the differences point directly to respective differences in their differing genetic inheritance. In other words, if a trait or behavior is influenced to some degree by heredity, identical twins should be more alike than fraternal twins.

Twin studies have provided a wealth of information on the relative effects of heredity on behavior. For example, studies of intelligence show that identical twins have almost identical IQ scores. In contrast, fraternal twins are only slightly more similar in their IQ scores than are siblings who are not twins (Bouchard, 2004; Plomin, 1999). The difference suggests a genetic influence on intelligence.

2. *Family studies.* Why would a psychologist interested in behavioral genetics study families? If a specific trait is inherited, there should be increased trait similarity among biological, blood relatives. And those relatives who share more genes, like siblings or twins, should exhibit more similarity than cousins. Using data from the genetic history of blood relatives (siblings, parents, aunts, uncles, cousins, etc.), family studies have shown that many traits and mental disorders, such as intelligence, sociability, and depression, do indeed run in families—as we will see in upcoming chapters.

3. *Adoption studies.* Another "natural experiment," adoption, also contributes significant information to our understanding of the relative effects of heredity or environment on behavior. Can you see why? If adopted children more closely resemble their biological parents (and biological siblings) in personality, mental disorders, or other traits, even though they were not raised in that family, then genetic factors probably had the greater influence. Conversely, if adopted children resemble their adopted family, even though they do not share similar genes, then environmental factors may predominate.

4. *Genetic abnormalities.* Research in behavioral genetics also explores disorders and diseases that result when genes malfunction. For example, an extra twenty-first chromosome fragment usually causes a condition called *Down syndrome.* People with Down syndrome often have distinctive round faces, with small folds of skin across the inner edge of the eyes. They also generally have impaired psychomotor and physical development, as well as mental retardation. Abnormalities in several genes or chromosomes are also suspected factors in *Alzheimer's disease,* which involves serious brain deterioration and memory loss, and *schizophrenia,* a severe mental disorder characterized by loss of contact with reality.

Heritability *A measure of the degree to which a characteristic is related to genetic, inherited factors*

Findings from these four methods have allowed behavioral geneticists to estimate the **heritability** of various traits. That is, to what degree are individual differences a result of genetic, inherited factors rather than differences in the environment? If genetics contributed *nothing* to the trait, it would have a heritability estimate of 0 percent. If a trait were *completely* due to genetics, we would say it had a heritability estimate of 100 percent.

pplication

APPLYING PSYCHOLOGY TO EVERYDAY LIFE

Overcoming Genetic Misconceptions

Behavioral genetics and heritability are hot topics in the general press—and in modern psychology. Each day we are bombarded with new discoveries regarding genes and the supposed heritability of intelligence, sexual orientation, and athletic abilities. But press reports are often misleading and invite misunderstanding. As you hear estimates of heritability, there are a few cautions to keep in mind:

1. *Genetic traits are not fixed or inflexible.* After listening to the latest research, some people become unreasonably discouraged. They fear they are destined for heart disease, breast cancer, depression, alcoholism, or other problems because of their particular biological inheritance. Keep in mind that genes may have a strong influence on diseases and behaviors. But these genetic studies do not reflect how an environmental intervention might change the outcome. If you inherited a possible genetic predisposition for some undesirable trait, you can significantly affect your odds by learning all you can about this trait. In addition, adopting lifestyle changes can sometimes prevent the development or minimize the effect of certain genetic problems. (Also, remember that nothing in life is 100 percent inherited—except sex. If your parents did not have it, it is 100 percent sure that you won't.)

2. *Heritability estimates do not apply to individuals.* When you hear media reports that intelligence or athletic talents are 30 to 50 percent inherited, do you assume this applies to you as an individual? Do you believe that if intelligence is 50 percent inherited, then 50 percent is due to your parents and 50 percent to your environment? This is a common misconception. Heritability statistics are mathematical computations of the proportion of total variance in a trait that is explained by genetic variation within a group—not *individuals*. Height, for example, has one of the highest heritability estimates—around 90 percent (Plomin, 1990). However, your own personal height may be very different from that of your parents or other blood relatives. We each inherit a unique combination of genes (unless we are identical twins). Therefore, it is impossible to predict your individual height from a heritability estimate. You can only estimate for the group as a whole.

3. *Genes and the environment are inseparable.* As first discussed in Chapter 1 (and throughout upcoming chapters), biological, psychological, and social forces all influence one another and are inseparable—the *biopsychosocial model*. Imagine your inherited genes as analogous to water, sugar, salt, flour, eggs, baking powder, and oil. When you mix these ingredients and pour them on a hot griddle (one environment), you get pancakes. Add more oil (a different combination of genes) and a waffle iron (a different environment), and you get waffles. With another set of ingredients and environments (different pans and an oven), you can have crepes, muffins, or cakes. How can you separate the effects of ingredients and cooking methods?

■ Evolutionary Psychology: Darwin Explains Behavior and Mental Processes

As we have seen, behavioral genetics studies help explain the role of heredity (nature) and the environment (nurture) in our individual behavior. To increase our understanding of genetic predispositions, we also need to look at universal behaviors transmitted from our evolutionary past.

FEEDING TIME AT THE NATURAL SELECTION ZOO

Non Sequitur by Wiley ©2000. Distributed by
Universal Press Syndicate. All Rights Reserved.

Natural Selection *The driving
mechanism behind evolution that allows
individuals with genetically influenced
traits that are adaptive in a particular
environment to stay alive and produce
offspring*

Evolutionary psychology suggests that many behavioral commonalities,
from eating to fighting with our enemies, emerged and remain in human
populations because they helped our ancestors (and ourselves) survive. This
perspective is based on the writings of Charles Darwin (1859), who suggested that natural forces select traits that are adaptive to the organism's
survival. This process of **natural selection** occurs when one particular
genetic trait gives a person a reproductive advantage over others. Some people mistakenly believe that natural selection means "survival of the fittest."
What really matters is *reproduction*—the survival of the genome. Because of
natural selection, the fastest or otherwise most fit organisms will be more
likely than the less fit to live long enough to mate, and thus pass on their
genes to the next generation.

Imagine that you are camping alone in a remote area and see a large
grizzly bear approaching. According to the principles of *natural selection*,
your chance for survival depends on how quickly and intelligently you
respond to the threat. What if you and your child, and a group of strangers
and their children, are also camping in the same spot? Whom do you
protect?

Most parents would "naturally" choose to help their own child. Why?
Why does this feel so "natural" and automatic? According to evolutionary
psychologists, natural selection favors animals whose concern for kin is proportional to their degree of biological relatedness. Thus, most people will devote
more resources, protection, love, and concern to close relatives. This helps ensure
their "genetic survival."

In addition to natural selection, *genetic mutations* also help explain behavior. Given
that each of us inherits literally thousands of genes, the probability is high that everyone carries at least one gene that has *mutated*, or changed from the original. The vast
majority of mutated genes have no effect on behavior whatsoever. But, on occasion, a
mutated gene will change an individual's behavior. It might cause someone to be more
social, more risk taking, or more careful. If the gene then gives the person reproductive advantage, he or she will be more likely to pass on the gene to future generations.
Note, however, that this mutation does not guarantee long-term survival. A genetic
mutation can sometimes produce a population perfectly adapted to a current environment, which later perishes when the environment changes.

Achievement
Gender & Cultural Diversity

The Evolution of Sex Differences

According to evolutionary theory, modern men and women have several sex differences that helped our ancestors adapt to their environment and hence to survive and
reproduce. As you can see in Figure 2.23, some research shows a difference in lateralization of function between men and women. Figure 2.24 also illustrates how men
tend to score higher on tests of mathe-
matical reasoning and spatial relationships. Women score higher on tests
involving mathematical calculation and
tasks requiring perceptual speed. Men
also tend to be more accurate in target-
directed motor skills. Women tend to
be more efficient in skills requiring fine
motor coordination. What accounts for
these differences?

Figure 2.23 *Sex differences in lateralization.* These are composite MRI scans
of the brains of men (left) and women
(right) during a verbal task involving
rhyming. Note how activation is largely
confined to only one hemisphere for men,
whereas it occurs in both hemispheres for
women.

B.A. Shaywitz et al., 1995 NMR/Yale Medical School

Figure 2.24 *Problem-solving tasks favoring women and men.*

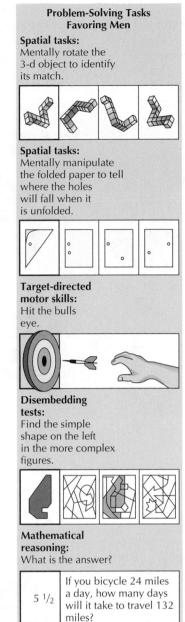

Problem-Solving Tasks Favoring Women

Perceptual speed:
As quickly as possible identify matching items.

Displaced objects:
After looking at the middle picture, tell which item is missing from the the picture on the right.

Verbal fluency:
List words that begin with the same letter. (Women also tend to perform better in ideational fluency tests, for example, listing objects that are the same color.)

B _ _ _   Bat, big, bike, bang, bark, bank, bring, brand, broom, bright, brook, bug, buddy, bunk

Precision manual tasks:
Place the pegs in the holes as quickly as possible.

Mathematical calculation:
Compute the answer.

72    $6(18+4)-78+\frac{36}{2}$

Problem-Solving Tasks Favoring Men

Spatial tasks:
Mentally rotate the 3-d object to identify its match.

Spatial tasks:
Mentally manipulate the folded paper to tell where the holes will fall when it is unfolded.

Target-directed motor skills:
Hit the bulls eye.

Disembedding tests:
Find the simple shape on the left in the more complex figures.

Mathematical reasoning:
What is the answer?

5 1/2   If you bicycle 24 miles a day, how many days will it take to travel 132 miles?

One possible answer from evolutionary psychologists is that ancient societies typically assigned men the task of "hunters" and women as "gatherers." The man's superiority on many spatial tasks and target-directed motor skills, for example, may have evolved from the adaptive demands of hunting. Similarly, activities such as gathering, child-rearing, and domestic tool construction and manipulation may have contributed to the woman's language superiority (Farber, 2000; Joseph, 2000; Silverman & Phillips, 1998). Some critics, however, suggest that evolution progresses much too slowly to account for this type of behavioral adaptation. furthermore, evolutionary explanations of sex differences are highly speculative and obviously difficult to test scientifically (Denmark, Rabinowitz, & Sechzer, 2005; Eagly & Wood, 1999).

Evolutionary psychology research emphasizes heredity and early biological processes in determining gender differences in cognitive behavior. Keep in mind, however, that almost all sex differences are *correlational*. The mechanisms involved in the actual *cause* of certain human behaviors have yet to be determined. Furthermore, it is important to remember that all known variations *between* the two sexes are much smaller than differences *within* each sex. Finally, to repeat a theme discussed throughout this text, it is extremely difficult to separate the effects of biological, psychological, and social forces—the biopsychosocial model.

Assessment

CHECK & REVIEW

Our Genetic Inheritance

Neuroscience studies how biological processes relate to behavioral and mental processes. **Genes** hold the code for certain traits that are passed on from parent to child, and they can be dominant or recessive. Genes are segments of the DNA molecules called **chromosomes,** which are present in every cell of our body. **Behavioral geneticists** use twin studies, family studies, adoption studies, and genetic abnormalities to explore genetic contributions to behavior and make estimates of **heritability**.

Evolutionary psychology is the branch of psychology that looks at evolutionary changes related to behavior. Several different processes, including **natural selection,** mutations, and social and cultural factors can affect evolution.

Questions

1. Threadlike strands of DNA that carry genetic information are known as_____. (a) stem cells; (b) genes; (c) neurons; (d) chromosomes
2. What are the four chief methods used to study behavioral genetics?
3. Evolutionary psychology is the branch of psychology that looks at_____. (a) how fossil discoveries affect behavior; (b) the relationship between genes and the environment; (c) the relationship between evolutionary changes and behavior; (d) the effect of culture change on behavior
4. According to evolutionary theorists, why are people more likely to help their family members than strangers?

Check your answers in Appendix B.

CLICK & REVIEW
for additional assessment options:
www.wiley.com/college/huffman

Application

RESEARCH HIGHLIGHT

Better Living Through Neuroscience

Imagine being completely paralyzed and unable to speak. Each year, thousands of people suffer serious brain and spinal cord injuries. Until recently, these injuries were considered permanent and beyond medical help. Scientists long believed that after the first two or three years of life, humans, and most nonhuman animals, lacked the capacity to repair or replace damaged neurons in the brain or spinal cord. Nerves in the peripheral nervous system sometimes repaired and regenerated themselves, but supposedly not in the central nervous system.

Thanks in part to recent research, we now know that the human brain is capable of lifelong neuroplasticity and neurogenesis. Let's begin with **neuroplasticity.** Rather than being a solid fixed organ, our brains are flexible and "plastic." Throughout our life, neurons in our brains reorganize and change their structure and function as a result of usage and experience (Abbott, 2004; Neumann et al., 2005). The basic brain organization (cerebellum, cortex, and so on) is irreversibly established well before birth. But details are subject to revision. As you are learning a new sport or a foreign language, your brain changes and "rewires" itself. New synapses form and others disappear. Some dendrites grow longer and sprout new branches. Others are "pruned" away. This is what makes our brains so wonderfully adaptive.

Courtesy Dr. Fred Gage, The Salk Institute

Can adult brains grow new neurons? *Neuroscientists once believed that each of us was born with all the brain cells we would ever have. But Fred Gage and others have shown that neurons are renewed throughout our life span.*

Neuroplasticity *The brain's lifelong ability to reorganize and change its structure and function*

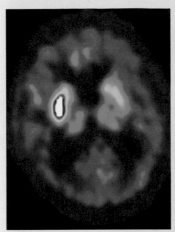 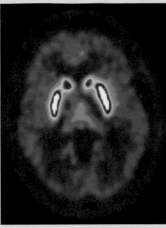

From P. Piccini et al., "Nautre Neuroscience 2," 1137 1999]

Stem cell research and Parkinson's disease. *A fetal graft implanted in the brain of a Parkinson's patient 10 years ago still produces significant levels of dopamine (the red and white area in the brain scan on the left). Note, however, that the activity of this area of the brain is still below that of the normal brain on the right.*

Remarkably, this rewiring has even helped the brain "remodel" itself following strokes. For example, psychologist Edward Taub and his colleagues (2002, 2004) have had success with constraint-induced (CI) movement therapy in stroke patients. Immobilizing the unaffected ("good") arm (or leg) of the patient has restored function in some patients as long as 21 years after their strokes. Rather than coddling the affected arm, Taub requires rigorous and repetitive exercise. He believes these repetitions cause intact parts of the brain to take over for the stroke-damaged areas. In effect, Taub "recruits" intact brain cells. This treatment would be analogous to an electrician's wiring a shunt around the damaged part of an electrical circuit.

Obviously, there are limits to neuroplasticity. Even with the best "rewiring," most of us will never become another Tiger Woods or Albert Einstein. However, the fact that our brains continually reorganize themselves throughout our lives has enormous implications.

Perhaps the most dazzling recent finding is **neurogenesis**—the production of nerve cells. Until very recently, it was believed that we were born with all the neurons we would ever have and that life was a slow process of dying neurons and increasing loss of brain tissue.

Today, however, we know that 80-year-olds have just as many neurons as 20-year-olds. We do lose hundreds of cells each day. But our brains replenish themselves with new cells that originate deep within the brain and migrate to become part of the brain's circuitry. The source of these newly created cells is neural **stem cells.** These rare, precursor ("immature") cells can grow and develop into any type of cell depending on the chemical signals they receive as they grow (Abbott, 2004; Kim, 2005).

To date, physicians have used stem cells for bone marrow transplants, and other clinical applications have already begun. For example, clinical trials using stem cells to repopulate or replace cells devastated by injury or disease have helped patients suffering from strokes, Alzheimer's, Parkinson's, epilepsy, stress, leukemia, and depression (Chang et al., 2005; Gruber et al., 2004; Kim et al., 2002; Wickelgren, 2002).

Does this mean that people paralyzed from spinal cord injuries might be able to walk again? At this point, neurogenesis in the brain and spinal cord is minimal. But one possible bridge might be to transplant embryonic stem cells in the damaged area of the spinal cord. In research with rats, researchers have transplanted mouse embryonic stem cells into a damaged rat spinal cord (Jones, Anderson, & Galvin, 2003; McDonald et al., 1999). When the damaged spinal cord was viewed several weeks later, the implanted cells had survived and spread throughout the injured spinal cord area. More important, the transplant rats also showed some movement in previously paralyzed parts of their bodies. Medical researchers have also begun human trials using nerve grafts to repair damaged spinal cords (Lopez, 2002; Saltus, 2000).

Although it is unwise to raise unrealistic hopes, we are making remarkable breakthroughs in neuroscience. The rewiring, repairing, and transplanting we have discussed in this section are just a small part of what has been discovered in the last 10 years. Can you imagine what the next step (or the next decade) might bring?

Mark Mainz/Getty Images

Oscar winning actress Halle Berry suffers from diabetes. *She actively campaigns for increased stem cell research because it offers promising leads toward a cure for diabetes.*

Neurogenesis [nue-roh-JEN-uh-sis] *The division and differentiation of nonneuronal cells to produce neurons*

Stem Cell *Precursor (immature) cells that give birth to new specialized cells; a stem cell holds all the information it needs to make bone, blood, brain—any part of a human body—and can also copy itself to maintain a stock of stem cells*

KEY TERMS

To assess your understanding of the **Key Terms** *in Chapter 2, write a definition for each (in your own words), and then compare your definitions with those in the text.*

neuroscience (p. 54)

Neural Bases of Behavior
action potential (p. 57)
axon (p. 55)
cell body (p. 55)
dendrites (p. 55)
endocrine [EN-doh-krin] system
    (p. 61)
endorphins [en-DOR-fins] (p. 58)
glial cells (p. 55)
hormones (p. 61)
myelin [MY-uh-lin] sheath (p. 56)
neuron (p. 62)
neurotransmitters (p. 57)
synapse [SIN-aps] (p. 57)

Nervous System Organization
autonomic nervous system (ANS)
    (p. 66)
central nervous system (CNS) (p. 63)
interneurons (p. 66)
motor neurons (p. 66)

parasympathetic nervous system (p. 66)
peripheral nervous system (PNS)
    (p. 63)
reflexes (p. 64)
sensory neurons (p. 66)
somatic nervous system (SNS) (p. 66)
sympathetic nervous system (p. 66)

A Tour Through the Brain
association areas (p. 78)
brainstem (p. 68)
cerebellum [sehr-uh-BELL-um] (p. 69)
cerebral cortex (p. 73)
corpus callosum [CORE-pus] [cah-
    LOH-suhm] (p. 79)
forebrain (p. 70)
frontal lobes (p. 74)
hindbrain (p. 68)
hypothalamus [hi-poh-THAL-uh-
    muss] (p. 71)
lateralization (p. 78)
limbic system (p. 71)
localization of function (p. 68)

medulla [muh-DUL-uh] (p. 68)
midbrain (p. 70)
occipital [ahk-SIP-ih-tal] lobes (p. 77)
parietal [puh-RYE-uh-tuhl] lobes
    (p. 76)
pons (p. 69)
reticular formation (RF) (p. 70)
split brain (p. 79)
temporal lobes (p. 77)
thalamus [THAL-uh-muss] (p. 71)

Our Genetic Inheritance
behavioral genetics (p. 84)
chromosomes (p. 84)
evolutionary psychology (p. 84)
genes (p. 84)
heritability (p. 86)
natural selection (p. 88)
neurogenesis [nue-roe-JEN-uh-sis]
    (p. 91)
neuroplasticity (p. 90)
stem cells (p. 91)

WEB RESOURCES

Huffman Book Companion Site

http://www.wiley.com/college/huffman

This site is loaded with free Interactive Self-Tests, Internet Exercises, Glossary and Flashcards for key terms, web links, Handbook for Non-Native Speakers, and other activities designed to improve your mastery of the material in this chapter.

Dissections of a real human brain and spinal cord

http://www.vh.org/Providers/Textbooks/BrainAnatomy/BrainAnatomy.html

Provides detailed photographs and drawings allowing an inside look at the internal structures, appearance, and organization of the brain and spinal cord.

Brain diseases

http://www.mic.ki.se/Diseases/c10.228.html

Contains a wealth of information related to brain diseases, including Alzheimer's, Parkinson's, stroke, and even migraine headaches.

Neuroscience for kids

http://faculty.washington.edu/chudler/neurok.html

A dynamic site designed for all ages to facilitate exploration of the human brain and nervous system.

Visual SUMMARY

□ Neural Bases of Behavior

What Is a Neuron?

Neurons: Individual nerve cells that transmit information throughout the body.
Glial cells: Provide structural, nutritional, and other support for neurons, as well as some information transfer.

Key features of a neuron
- **Dendrites**: Receive information and send impulses to cell body.
- **Cell body**: Integrates incoming information and nourishes neuron.
- **Axon**: Carries information from cell body to other neurons.

(**Myelin Sheath**: Fatty insulation around some axons that speeds up action potential.)

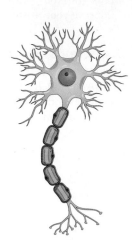

How Do Neurons Communicate?

- Communication *within the neuron* is through the **action potential**, a neural impulse that carries information along the axon.
- Communication *between neurons* occurs when an action potential reaches the axon terminal and stimulates the release of **neurotransmitters** into the **synapse.**

How Do Neurotransmitters and Hormones Affect Us?

Two key chemical messengers:
1) **Neurotransmitters**: Chemicals manufactured and released by neurons that alter activity in other neurons, which thereby affects behavior and mental processes.
2) **Hormones**: chemicals released from the endocrine system into the bloodstream, which affect the nervous system.

◇ Nervous System Organization

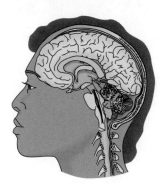

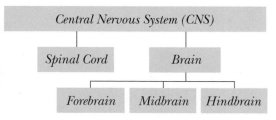

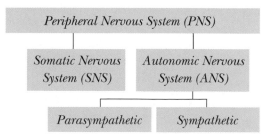

The Cerebral Cortex

The cerebral cortex is responsible for all higher mental processes and is divided into four sections

Frontal Lobes

Motor control, speech production, and higher functions (thinking, personality, emotion, and memory).

Parietal Lobes

Sensory processing (pressure, pain, touch, and temperature).

Temporal Lobes

Audition, language comprehension, memory, and some emotional control.

Occipital Lobes

Vision and visual perception.

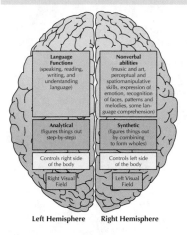

Language Functions (speaking, reading, writing, and understanding language)

Nonverbal abilities (music and art, perceptual and spatiomanipulative skills, expression of emotion, recognition of faces, patterns and melodies, some language comprehension)

Analytical (figures things out step-by-step)

Synthetic (figures things out by combining to form wholes)

Controls right side of the body

Controls left side of the body

Right Visual Field

Left Visual Field

Left Hemisphere   **Right Hemisphere**

Two Brains in One

Splitting the **corpus callosum**, which normally transfers neural impulses between the brain's left and right hemispheres, is a treatment for some forms of epilepsy. **Split-brain** research on these patients shows some specialization of functions in each hemisphere.

Behavioral Genetics

Each of the 46 human **chromosomes** is composed of DNA, which is made up of **genes**.

Genetics studies are done with twins, adopted children, families, and genetic abnormalities. Such studies allow estimates of **heritability**.

Evolutionary Psychology

Studies evolutionary principles, like **natural selection** and genetic mutations, which affect adaptation to the environment and help explain commonalities in behavior.

The brain can reorganize and change its structure and function throughout the lifespan (**neuroplasticity**), and create new nerve cells (**neurogenesis**) from **stem cells** (immature cells that produce specialized cells).

www.wiley.com/college/huffman

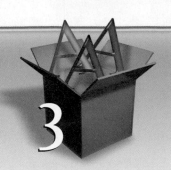

3

STRESS AND HEALTH PSYCHOLOGY

Achievement

Core Learning Outcomes

As you read Chapter 3, keep the following questions in mind and answer them in your own words:

▷ What is stress, and what are its major sources and effects?

▷ How is stress related to serious illness?

▷ How is health psychology involved with tobacco, alcohol, and chronic pain?

▷ What techniques and resources are available to help people stay healthy and cope with stress?

■ Achievement
■ Assessment
■ Application

WHY STUDY PSYCHOLOGY?

Jose Luis Pelaez/CorbisImages

Chapter 3 will explore interesting questions, such as Did you know...

▶ ...graduating from college and getting married are major sources of stress?

▶ ...procrastinating on homework can be harmful to your health as well as to your grades?

▶ ...friends are one of your best health resources?

▶ ...assembly-line jobs are a prime source of stress?

▶ ...small, everyday hassles can impair your immune system functioning?

▶ ...police officers, nurses, doctors, social workers, and teachers are particularly prone to "burnout"?

▶ ...having few choices or little control can be dangerous to your health?

▶ ...having a cynical, hostile Type A personality contributes to heart disease?

▶ ...prolonged stress can lead to death?

▶ ...hardy personality types may be more resistant to stress?

What do you remember about the terrorist attacks of September 11, 2001? What about the late summer of 2005 when Hurricane Katrina devastated a huge area of the southern United States? How did you feel? Have you been the victim of a robbery, rape, or wartime trauma? These are perhaps the most obvious events that come to mind when we think about being stressed. However, stress is all around us. It is an integral part of our physical and mental health. Throughout history, people have believed that emotions and thoughts affect physical health. However, in the late 1800s, the discovery of biological causes for infectious diseases, such as typhoid and syphilis, encouraged scientists to lessen their interest in psychological factors. Today, the major causes of death have shifted from contagious diseases (such as pneumonia, influenza, tuberculosis, and measles) to noncontagious diseases (such as cancer, cardiovascular disease, and chronic lung disease). And the focus has returned to psychological behaviors and lifestyles (National Center for Health Statistics, 2004).

In this chapter, we will explore how biological, psychological, and social factors (the *biopsychosocial model*) affect illness as well as health and well-being. We begin with "Understanding Stress," which examines the causes and effects of stress. The next section, "Stress and Illness," explores the role stress plays in serious illnesses, such as cancer and heart disease. "Health Psychology in Action" addresses how the field of health psychology can help with problems related to tobacco, alcohol, and chronic pain. And the chapter concludes with "Health and Stress Management," which presents suggestions for dealing with stress and having an overall healthier life.

UNDERSTANDING STRESS

Stress *Nonspecific response of the body to any demand made on it; the arousal, both physical and mental, to situations or events that we perceive as threatening or challenging*

Hans Selye (SELL-yay), a physiologist renowned for his research and writing in the area of stress since the 1930s, defines **stress** as the nonspecific response of the body to any demand made on it. The trigger that prompts the stressful reaction is called a *stressor.* When you play two nonstop tennis matches in the middle of a heat wave, your body responds with a fast heartbeat, rapid breathing, and an outpouring of perspiration. When you suddenly remember that the term paper you just started is due today rather than next Friday, your body has the same physiological stress response to a very different stressor. Stress reactions can occur to either internal, cognitive stimuli or external, environmental stimuli (Sanderson, 2004; Sarafino, 2005).

The body is nearly always in some state of stress, whether pleasant or unpleasant, mild or severe. *Anything* placing a demand on the body can cause stress. A total absence of stress would mean a total absence of stimulation, which would eventually lead to death. When stress is beneficial, such as moderate exercise, it is called **eustress**. When it is objectionable, as from chronic illness, it is called **distress** (Selye, 1974). Because health psychology has been chiefly concerned with the negative effects of stress, we will adhere to convention and use the word *stress* to refer primarily to harmful or unpleasant stress.

Eustress *Pleasant, desirable stress*

Distress *Unpleasant, objectionable stress*

■ Sources of Stress: Seven Major Stressors

Although stress is pervasive in our lives, some things cause more stress than others. The seven major sources of stress are cataclysmic events, chronic stressors, life changes, hassles, occupation burnout, frustration, and conflict (Figure 3.1).

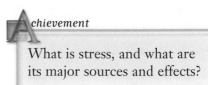

Achievement

What is stress, and what are its major sources and effects?

Cataclysmic Events

The terrorist attacks in America on September 11, 2001, the tsunami waves following the Indian Ocean earthquake on December 26, 2004, and Hurricane Katrina in August 2005 are what stress researchers call *cataclysmic events*. They occur suddenly and generally affect many people simultaneously. Politicians and the public often imagine that such catastrophes inevitably create huge numbers of seriously depressed and permanently scarred survivors. Relief agencies typically send large numbers of counselors to help with the psychological aftermath. Ironically, these events may not be as psychologically stressful as we think. Researchers have found that because the catastrophe is shared by so many others, there is a great deal of mutual social support from those with firsthand experience with the same disaster, which may help people cope (Collocan,

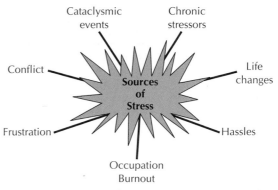

Figure 3.1 *Seven major sources of stress.*

Stress and cataclysmic events. Hurricane Katrina in 2005 and the Southeast Asia tsunami in 2004 provided recent examples of what most people would consider extremely stressful events. But it may not be as stressful as you imagine (see text for an explanation).

www.wiley.com/college/huffman

The stress of life changes.

Tuma, & Fleischman, 2004; Gorman, 2005). On the other hand, these cataclysmic events are clearly devastating to all parts of the victims' lives. And some survivors may develop a prolonged and severe stress reaction, known as *posttraumatic stress disorder (PTSD)*, which we will discuss later in this chapter.

Chronic Stressors

Not all stressful situations are single events such as a terrorist attack, a death, or a birth. A bad marriage, poor working conditions, or an intolerable political climate can be a *chronic stressor*. Even the stress of low-frequency noise is associated with measurable hormonal and cardiac changes (Waye et al., 2002). Our social lives can also be chronically stressful, because making and maintaining friendships involve considerable thought and energy (Sias et al., 2004).

Perhaps the largest source of chronic stress is work. People often experience stress associated with keeping or changing jobs or with job performance (Moore, Grunberg, & Greenberg, 2004). However, the most stressful jobs are those that make great demands on performance and concentration but allow little creativity or opportunity for advancement (Angenendt, 2003; Lewig & Dollard, 2003). Assembly-line work ranks very high in this category.

Researchers have documented that stress at work can also cause serious stress at home. And, of course, in our private lives, divorce, child and spouse abuse, alcoholism, and money problems can place severe stress on all members of a family (DiLauro, 2004; Luecken & Lemery, 2004).

Life Changes

Early stress researchers Thomas Holmes and Richard Rahe (1967) believed that change of any kind that required some adjustment in behavior or lifestyle could cause stress. Moreover, they believed that exposure to numerous stressful events within a short period could have a direct, detrimental effect on health.

To investigate the relationship between change and stress, Holmes and Rahe created a Social Readjustment Rating Scale (SRRS) that asked people to check off all the life events they had experienced in the last year (Table 3.1). Each event is assigned a numerical rating expressed in *life change units* (LCUs). To score yourself on this scale, add up the LCUs for all life events you have experienced during the last year. Now compare your total score with the following standards: 0–149 = No significant problems; 150–199 = Mild life crisis (33 percent chance of illness); 200–299 = Moderate life crisis (50 percent chance of illness); 300 and above = Major life crisis (80 percent chance of illness).

The SRRS scale is an easy and popular way to measure stress, and cross-cultural studies have shown that most people rank the magnitude of stressful events in similar

TABLE 3.1 MEASURING LIFE CHANGES

Social Readjustment Rating Scale			
Life Events	**Life Change Units**	**Life Events**	**Life Change Units**
Death of spouse	100	Son or daughter leaving home	29
Divorce	73	Trouble with in-laws	29
Marital separation	65	Outstanding personal achievement	28
Jail term	63	Spouse begins or stops work	26
Death of a close family member	63	Begin or end school	26
Personal injury or illness	53	Change in living conditions	25
Marriage	50	Revision of personal habits	24
Fired at work	47	Trouble with boss	23
Marital reconciliation	45	Change in work hours or conditions	20
Retirement	45	Change in residence	20
Change in health of family member	44	Change in schools	20
Pregnancy	40	Change in recreation	19
Sex difficulties	39	Change in church activities	19
Gain of a new family member	39	Change in social activities	18
Business readjustment	39	Mortgage or loan for lesser purchase (car, major appliance)	17
Change in financial state	38	Change in sleeping habits	16
Death of a close friend	37	Change in number of family get-togethers	15
Change to different line of work	36	Change in eating habits	15
Change in number of arguments with spouse	35	Vacation	13
Mortgage or loan for major purchase	31	Christmas	12
Foreclosure on mortgage or loan	30	Minor violations of the law	11
Change in responsibilities at work	29		

Source: Reprinted from Journal of Psychosomatic Research, Vol III; Holmes and Rahe: "The Social Readjustment Rating Scale," 213–218, 1967, with permission from Elsevier.

ways (De Coteau, Hope, & Anderson, 2003; Scully, Tosi, & Banning, 2000). However, the SRRS is not foolproof. First, it only shows a *correlation* between stress and illness. And as you recall from Chapter 1, *correlation does not prove causation*. Illnesses could be caused by stress, or they also could be caused by other (yet unknown) factors.

In addition, stress varies according to the individual. Any one event may be perceived as a stressful ordeal, a neutral occurrence, or even an exciting opportunity. It depends on your personal interpretation and appraisal (Holt & Dunn, 2004). You might find moving to another state a terrible sacrifice and a tremendous stressor. Your friend might see the same move as a wonderful opportunity and experience little or no stress. Some people have better coping skills, physical health, healthier lifestyles, or even better genetics that help them cope with change.

Hassles

We also experience a great deal of daily stress from **hassles**. These little problems of daily living are not significant in themselves, but they sometimes pile up to become a major source of stress. Some hassles tend to be shared by all: time pressures (getting to work or school on time, finding a parking place, fighting traffic jams), problems with family and coworkers (equitable sharing of work, scheduling conflicts, gossip), and financial concerns (competing demands for available funds, increasing prices). But our reactions to hassles may vary. For example, compared to women, men tend to have more impairment of their immune system and an increased heart rate in response to hassles (Delahanty et al., 2000).

Some authorities believe hassles can be more significant than major life events in creating stress (Kraaij, Arensman, & Spinhoven, 2002; Lazarus, 1999). For example, divorce is extremely stressful. For many families, the biggest stressors are the increased number of hassles—change in finances, child-care arrangements, longer working hours, and so on.

Occupation Burnout

Chronic exposure to high levels of stress and little personal control can lead to a state of psychosocial and physical exhaustion known as **burnout** (Sarafino, 2005). Although

Hassles *Small problems of daily living that accumulate and sometimes become a major source of stress*

Burnout *State of psychological and physical exhaustion resulting from chronic exposure to high levels of stress and little personal control*

TRY THIS

YOURSELF

Application

What Are Your Major Hassles?

Write down the top 10 hassles you most commonly experience. Then compare your answers to the following list:

The 10 Most Common Hassles for College Students

Corbis Images

	Percentage of Times Checked
1. Troubling thoughts about the future	76.6
2. Not getting enough sleep	72.5
3. Wasting time	71.1
4. Inconsiderate smokers	70.7
5. Physical appearance	69.9
6. Too many things to do	69.2
7. Misplacing or losing things	67.0
8. Not enough time to do the things you need to do	66.3
9. Concerns about meeting high standards	64.0
10. Being lonely	60.8

Source: Kanner, A. D., Coyne, J. C., Schaefer, C., & Lazarus, R. S. (1981). Comparison of two modes of stress measurement: Daily hassles and uplifts versus major life events. *Journal of Behavioral Medicine, 4,* 1–39.

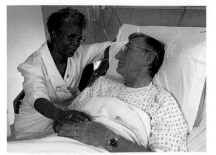

Will & Deni McIntyre/PhotoResearchers

Why is nursing a stressful career? *People who think of their profession as a calling may lose their idealism when faced with ongoing stresses and emotional turmoil. Over time, they may suffer a type of mental and physical exhaustion known as burnout.*

Frustration *Unpleasant tension, anxiety, and heightened sympathetic activity resulting from a blocked goal*

Conflict *Forced choice between two or more incompatible goals or impulses*

Approach–Approach Conflict *Forced choice between two or more desirable alternatives*

Avoidance–Avoidance Conflict *Forced choice between two or more undesirable alternatives*

Approach–Avoidance Conflict *Forced choice between two or more alternatives that have both desirable and undesirable results*

Lisa Peardon/Getty Images

Can you explain this man's approach–avoidance conflict?

the term has become an overused buzzword, health psychologists use it to describe a specific syndrome that develops most commonly in idealistic people who are involved in chronically stressful and emotionally draining professions (Hätinen et al., 2004; Linzer et al., 2002). People who think of their job as a "calling" enter their careers with a high sense of motivation and commitment. But over time, some become emotionally drained and disillusioned and feel a loss of personal accomplishment. They "burn out." The result may be increased absences from work, a sharp downturn in productivity, and an increased risk of physical problems.

Police officers, nurses, doctors, social workers, and teachers are particularly vulnerable to burnout. But who else experiences stress to the point of *burnout?* Type in the word "burnout" at amazon.com and over 500 book titles will be listed. Do a Google search and over 2 *million* links will appear! Clearly, burnout is no longer just a career "buzzword" (Skoglund, 2001).

Frustration

Frustration is a negative emotional state generally associated with a blocked goal, such as not being accepted for admission to your first-choice college. The more motivated we are, the more frustration we experience when our goals are blocked. After getting stuck in traffic and missing an important appointment, we may become very frustrated. On the other hand, if the same traffic jam causes us to be five minutes late to a painful medical appointment, we may experience little or no frustration.

Conflict

Another source of stress is conflict, which arises when one is forced to make a choice between at least two incompatible alternatives. The amount of stress produced by these forced choices depends on the complexity of the conflict itself and the difficulty involved in resolving it. There are three basic types of conflict: *approach–approach*, *avoidance–avoidance*, and *approach–avoidance*.

In an **approach–approach conflict**, a person must choose between two or more *favorable alternatives*. Thus, no matter what choice is made, the result will be desirable. At first, it might seem that this type of conflict should be stress free. But imagine having to choose between two great summer jobs. One job is at a resort where you will meet interesting people and have a good time. The other will provide you with valuable experience and look impressive on your résumé. No matter which job you choose, you will benefit in some way. In fact, you would like to take both jobs, but you cannot. Being forced to choose is the source of stress.

An **avoidance–avoidance conflict** involves a forced choice between two or more unpleasant alternatives both of which lead to negative results. In the book (and film) *Sophie's Choice*, Sophie and her two children are sent to a German concentration camp. A soldier demands that she give up (apparently to be killed) either her daughter or her son. If she doesn't choose, they both will be killed. Obviously, neither alternative is acceptable. Although this is an extreme example, avoidance–avoidance conflicts can lead to intense stress.

An **approach–avoidance conflict** occurs when a person must choose between alternatives that will have both desirable and undesirable results. During the evacuation before Hurricane Katrina made landfall in 2005, residents were told they could not take their pet animals with them to the shelters. For many people, this was an approach–avoidance conflict. They wanted to avoid the dangers of the hurricane, but they couldn't leave their beloved pets in harm's way. This conflict thus led to a great deal of ambivalence. In an approach–avoidance conflict, we experience both good and bad results from any alternative we choose.

Generally, the approach–approach conflict is the easiest to resolve and produces the least stress. The avoidance–avoidance conflict, on the other hand, is usually the most difficult because all choices lead to unpleasant results. Approach–avoidance conflicts are somewhat less stressful than avoidance–avoidance conflicts and are usually moderately difficult to resolve. Keep in mind that in addition to the stress of a forced choice, the longer any conflict exists, or the more important the decision, the more stress a person will experience.

Assessment

CHECK & REVIEW

Sources of Stress

Stress is the body's arousal, both physical and mental, to situations or events that we perceive as threatening or challenging. A situation or event, either pleasant or unpleasant, that triggers arousal and causes stress is known as a stressor.

The major sources of stress are cataclysmic events, chronic stressors, life changes, hassles, occupation burnout, frustration, and conflict. Cataclysmic events are stressors that occur suddenly and affect many people simultaneously. Chronic stressors are ongoing events such as poor working conditions. **Hassles** are little everyday life problems that pile up to cause major stress. Persistent hassles and a loss of initial idealism in your work situation can lead to a form of physical, mental,

and emotional exhaustion known as **burnout. Frustration** results from blocked goals. **Conflict** involves two or more competing goals. Conflicts can be classified as **approach–approach, avoidance–avoidance,** or **approach–avoidance.**

Questions

1. John was planning to ask Susan to marry him. When he saw Susan kissing another man at a party, he was quite upset. In this situation, John's seeing Susan kissing another man is _____, and it illustrates _____. (a) a stressor, distress; (b) eustress, a stressor; (c) distress, a stressor; (d) a stressor, eustress

2. The Social Readjustment Rating Scale constructed by Holmes and Rahe measures the stress situation in a person's life based on _____. (a) life changes; (b) stress tolerance; (c) daily hassles; (d) the balance between eustress and distress

3. Frustration is a negative emotional state that is generally associated with _____, whereas _____ is a negative emotional state caused by difficulty in choosing between two or more incompatible goals or impulses.

4. Give an example for each of the three types of conflict: approach–approach, approach–avoidance, and avoidance–avoidance.

Check your answers in Appendix B.

CLICK & REVIEW
for additional assessment options:
www.wiley.com/college/huffman

Effects of Stress: How the Body Responds

When stressed either mentally or physically, your body undergoes several major and minor physiological changes. The *sympathetic nervous system* and the *HPA axis* control most of these bodily changes (Figure 3.2).

Stress and the Sympathetic Nervous System

As you recall from Chapter 2, under low-stress conditions, the *parasympathetic* branch of the autonomic nervous system tends to reduce heart rate and blood pressure, while increasing muscle movement in the stomach and intestines. This allows the body to conserve energy, absorb nutrients, and maintain normal functioning. Under stressful conditions, however, the *sympathetic* part of the autonomic nervous system is dominant. It increases heart rate, blood pressure, respiration, and muscle tension; decreases the movement of stomach muscles; constricts blood vessels; and so on.

Stress also has an interesting domino effect. As one domino falls, it topples the next. As you can see on the left side of Figure 3.2, stress first activates the hypothalamus. The hypothalamus then signals the sympathetic nervous system, which then activates the central part of the adrenal glands (the adrenal medulla) to release large amounts of norepinephrine and epinephrine. The net result is increased energy to help us "fight or flee" from a threat.

Stress and the HPA Axis

The sympathetic nervous system obviously prepares us for immediate action. We see a shark and we quickly swim to shore. Once we're safe, our parasympathetic nervous

www.wiley.com/college/huffman

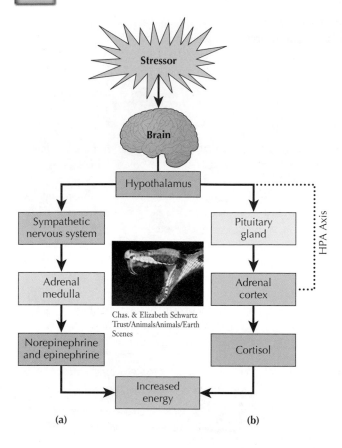

(a)   (b)

Chas. & Elizabeth Schwartz Trust/AnimalsAnimals/Earth Scenes

HPA Axis *The hypothalamus, pituitary gland, and adrenal cortex, which are activated by stress*

Psychoneuroimmunology [sye-koh-NEW-roh-IM-you-NOLL-oh-gee] *Interdisciplinary field that studies the effects of psychological factors on the immune system*

Damon Kiesow/GettyImages News and Sport Services

The visible effects of stress. *Would you like to be president of the United States? Note how the stress of this office has aged George W. Bush, as it has other presidents.*

Figure 3.2 *How our bodies respond to stress—an interrelated system.* (a) The sympathetic nervous system helps us respond immediately to stress (such as seeing a snake). (b) The pituitary allows us to maintain this vigilant response and deal with chronic stressors (like a bad job).

system calms us and restores normal functioning. But what happens to our bodies when we face chronic stressors, like bad jobs or bad marriages?

To deal with chronic stress, we have another stress response team that reacts a little more slowly and stays on the job. It is called the **HPA axis**—the *H*ypothalamus, *P*ituitary gland, and *A*drenal cortex system. Look again at Figure 3.2, but this time look at the right hand side. Note how stimulation of the hypothalamus activates the pituitary gland, which in turn activates the covering of the adrenal glands (the adrenal cortex). The adrenal glands then release the hormone known as *cortisol*. Once again, the net effect is increased energy.

It is important to understand the HPA axis because cortisol plays a critical role in the long-term effects of stress. Researchers call it a "stress hormone," and the level of circulating cortisol is the most commonly employed physiological measure of stress. During the initial crisis, cortisol increases blood sugar and metabolism, which helps us cope. However, with long-term stressors, the HPA axis remains in service and cortisol stays in the bloodstream. Prolonged elevation of cortisol has been linked to increased levels of depression, posttraumatic stress disorder (PTSD), memory problems, unemployment, drug and alcohol abuse, and even low birth weight for newborns (Bremner et al., 2004; Cowen, 2002; Sinha et al., 2003; Wüst et al., 2005). Perhaps most important, increased cortisol is directly related to impairment of immune system functioning.

Stress and the Immune System

The discovery of the relationship between stress and the immune system is very important. This system is our major defense against aging and many diseases, including bursitis, colitis, Alzheimer's disease, rheumatoid arthritis, periodontal disease, and even the common cold (Cohen et al., 2002; Hawkley & Cacioppo, 2004; Segerstrom & Miller, 2004; Theoharides & Cochrane, 2004).

The connection between stress and the immune system also has had a great impact on the field of psychology. Knowledge that psychological factors have considerable control over infectious diseases has upset long-held assumptions in biology and medicine that these diseases are "strictly physical." The clinical and theoretical implications are so important that a new field of biopsychology has emerged. That field is **psychoneuroimmunology**, and it studies the interactions of psychological factors ("psycho"), the nervous and endocrine systems ("neuro"), and the immune system ("immunology").

Selye's General Adaptation Syndrome (GAS)

Stress clearly causes physiological changes that can be detrimental to health. Hans Selye (1936), who was mentioned earlier in our def-

Alex Wong/Getty Images News and Sport Services

A. Operti/AmericanMuseum of Natural HistoryLibrary

Stress in ancient times. *As shown in these ancient cave drawings, the automatic "fight-or-flight" response was adaptive and necessary for early human survival. However, in modern society it occurs as a response to ongoing situations where we often cannot fight or flee. This repeated arousal could be detrimental to our health.*

General Adaptation Syndrome (GAS) *Selye's three-phase (alarm, resistance, and exhaustion) reaction to severe stress*

inition of *stress*, described a generalized physiological reaction to severe stressors that he called the **general adaptation syndrome (GAS)**. Figure 3.3 shows the three phases of this reaction. In the initial phase, called the *alarm reaction*, the body reacts to the stressor by activating the sympathetic nervous system (with increases in heart rate, blood pressure, secretion of hormones, and so on). The body has abundant energy and is alert and ready to deal with the stressor.

If the stressor remains, the body enters the *resistance phase*. Physiological arousal declines somewhat but remains higher than normal as the body tries to adapt to the stressor. According to Selye, one outcome of this stage is that some people develop what he called *diseases of adaptation*, including asthma, ulcers, and high blood pressure. This adaptation and resistance phase is very taxing, and long-term exposure to the stressor may eventually lead to the *exhaustion phase* if the resistance is not successful. During this final stage, all adaptation energy becomes depleted and our susceptibility to illness increases. In severe cases, long-term exposure to stressors can be life threatening because we become vulnerable to serious illnesses such as heart attack, stroke, and cancer.

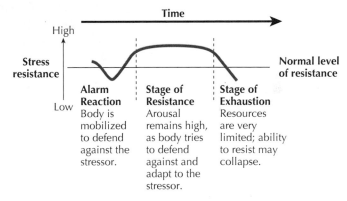

Figure 3.3 ***The general adaptation syndrome (GAS).*** According to Hans Selye, when the body is exposed to severe, prolonged stress, it goes from an initial alarm reaction to an increased level of resistance. If the stress is prolonged, as it is for workers in some high-risk occupations, it may lead to exhaustion and even death.

Application
APPLYING PSYCHOLOGY TO STUDENT LIFE

Why You Shouldn't Procrastinate

If your professor assigned a term paper for this class, have you already started working on it? Or are you putting it off until the last minute? Have you ever wondered if working continuously on a term paper from the first day of class until the paper is due might ultimately be more stressful than putting off the paper until the last minute?

To answer this question, Dianne Tice and Roy Baumeister (1997) at Case Western Reserve University assigned a term paper in their health psychology class at the beginning of the semester. Throughout the semester, they carefully monitored the stress, health, and procrastination levels of 44 student volunteers from the class. After the term papers were submitted at the end of the course, Tice and Baumeister found that procrastinators suffered significantly more stress and developed more health problems than nonprocrastinators. They were also more likely to turn in their papers late and earn lower grades on those papers.

In the "Tools for Student Success" section in Chapter 1, you learned that research shows that spacing out your studying rather than cramming the night before produces higher scores on exams. Now you have additional research showing that distributed work also produces better grades on term papers—as well as less stress. The bottom line is this: *Do not procrastinate.* It can be hazardous to your health as well as to your grades (Burka & Yuen, 2004).

A*ssessment*

CHECK & REVIEW

Effects of Stress

When stressed, the body undergoes physiological changes. The sympathetic branch of the autonomic nervous system is activated, increasing heart rate and blood pressure. Stressors also activate the **HPA axis** (hypothalamus, pituitary gland, and adrenal cortex), which increases the stress hormone cortisol. Increased cortisol decreases immune system functioning, which can render the body susceptible to a number of diseases.

Hans Selye described a generalized physiological reaction to severe stressors,

which he called the **general adaptation syndrome (GAS).** It has three phases: the alarm reaction, the resistance phase, and the exhaustion phase.

Questions

1. How do the sympathetic and parasympathetic nervous systems differ in their response to stress?
2. How does the HPA axis respond to stress?
3. The GAS consists of three phases: the _____ reaction, the _____ phase, and the _____ phase.
4. As Michael watches his instructor pass

out papers, he suddenly realizes this is the first major exam, and he is unprepared. Which phase of the GAS is he most likely experiencing? (a) resistance; (b) alarm; (c) exhaustion; (d) phase out.

Check your answers in Appendix B.

 CLICK & REVIEW
for additional assessment options:
www.wiley.com/college/huffman

A*chievement*

> How is stress related to serious illness?

STRESS AND ILLNESS

As we have just seen, stress has dramatic effects on our bodies. In this section, we will explore how stress is related to four serious illnesses—*cancer, coronary heart disease, post-traumatic stress disorder (PTSD),* and *gastric ulcers.*

▣ Cancer: A Variety of Causes—Even Stress

The word *cancer* is frightening to nearly everyone, and for good reason. Cancer is among the leading causes of death for adults in the United States. It occurs when a particular type of primitive body cell begins rapidly dividing and then forms a tumor that invades healthy tissue. Unless destroyed or removed, the tumor eventually damages organs and causes death. To date, over 100 types of cancer have been identified. They appear to be caused by an interaction between environmental factors and inherited predispositions.

To understand how the environment contributes to cancer, it helps to know what normally happens to cancerous cells. Whenever cancer cells start to multiply, the immune system checks the uncontrolled growth by attacking the abnormal cells (see the photo at the top of page 107). This goes on constantly, with abnormal cells arising and, in a healthy person, the immune system keeping cancer cells in check.

Something different happens when the body is stressed. As you read earlier, the stress response involves the release of adrenal hormones that suppress immune system functioning. The compromised immune system is less able to resist infection and cancer development. An experiment with nonhuman animals found that stress inhibited immune system defenses against cancer—thereby increasing tumor growth (Wu et al., 2000). Other research with humans suggests that stress can also suppress lymphocytes, the main immune system cells that control cancer (Goebel & Mills, 2000; Shi et al., 2003).

The good news is that we can substantially reduce our risk of cancer by making changes that reduce our stress level and enhance our immune system. For example, when researchers interrupted the sleep of 23 men and then measured their *natural killer cells* (a type of immune system cell), they found the number of killer cells was 28 percent below average (Irwin et al., 1994). Can you see how staying up late studying for an exam (or partying) can decrease the effectiveness of your immune system? Fortunately, these researchers also found that a normal night's sleep after the deprivation returned the killer cells to their normal levels.

◼ Cardiovascular Disorders: The Leading Cause of Death in the United States

Cardiovascular disorders cause over half of all deaths in the United States (American Heart Association, 2004). Understandably, health psychologists are concerned because stress is a major contributor to these deaths. *Heart disease* is a general term for all disorders that eventually affect the heart muscle and lead to heart failure. *Coronary heart disease* results from *arteriosclerosis*, a thickening of the walls of the coronary arteries that reduces or blocks the blood supply to the heart. Arteriosclerosis causes *angina* (chest pain due to insufficient blood supply to the heart) or *heart attack* (death of heart muscle tissue). Controllable factors that contribute to heart disease include stress, smoking, certain personality characteristics, obesity, a high-fat diet, and lack of exercise (Brummett et al., 2004; David et al., 2004; Hirao-Try, 2003).

How does stress contribute to heart disease? Recall that one of the major autonomic nervous system "fight-or-flight" reactions is the release of epinephrine and cortisol into the bloodstream. These hormones increase heart rate and release fat and glucose from the body's stores to give muscles a quickly available source of energy.

If no physical action is taken (as often happens in our modern lives), the fat released into the bloodstream is not burned as fuel and may become fatty deposits on the walls of blood vessels (Figure 3.4). These deposits are a major cause of blood supply blockage that causes heart attacks.

Personality Types
The effects of stress on heart disease may be amplified if an individual tends to be hard-driving, competitive, ambitious, impatient, and hostile. People with such **Type A personalities** are chronically on edge, feel intense time urgency, and are preoccupied with responsibilities. The antithesis of the Type A personality is the **Type B personality**, having a laid-back, calm, relaxed attitude toward life.

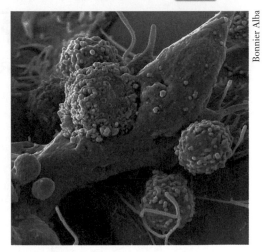

The immune system in action. The round structure near the left center of this photomicrograph is a T-lymphocyte, a type of white blood cell produced by the immune system. It has just killed a cancer cell, the sweet potato–shaped structure.

Type A Personality *Behavior characteristics including intense ambition, competition, exaggerated time urgency, and a cynical, hostile outlook*

Type B Personality *Behavior characteristics consistent with a calm, patient, relaxed attitude*

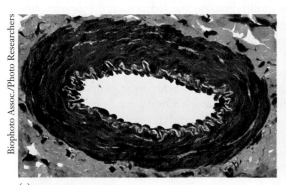
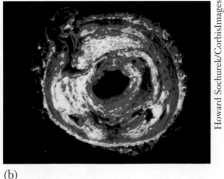

(a)

(b)

Figure 3.4 *Fatty deposits in arteries.* One major cause of heart disease is the blockage of arteries that supply blood to the heart. The artery at the left is normal; the one on the right is almost completely blocked. Reducing stress, exercising, and eating a low-fat diet can help prevent the buildup of fatty deposits in the arteries.

www.wiley.com/college/huffman

Two cardiologists, Meyer Friedman and Ray Rosenman (1959), were the first to identify and describe the Type A personality. The story goes that in the mid-1950s, an upholsterer who was recovering the waiting room chairs in Friedman's office noticed an odd wear pattern. He mentioned to Friedman that the chairs looked like new except for the front edges, which were badly worn, as if all the patients sat only on the edges of the chairs. Initially, this did not seem too important to Friedman. However, he later came to believe that this chronic sense of time urgency, being literally "on the edge of your seat," was a possible contributing factor to heart disease and the hallmark of the Type A personality.

Initial research into Type A behavior suggested that Friedman and Rosenman were right. But when later researchers examined the relationship between characteristics of the Type A behavior pattern and heart disease, they found that the critical component and *strongest* predictor of heart disease was *hostility*— not Type A personality (Krantz & McCeney, 2002; Mittag & Maurischat, 2004).

Actually, *cynical* hostility appears to be the most important factor in the Type A relationship to heart disease. Cynical people always expect problems and are constantly alert and "on watch," trying to foresee problems and possibly avert them. This attitude produces a nearly constant state of stress, which translates physiologically into higher blood pressure and heart rate, and production of stress-related hormones. Because of their hostile, suspicious, argumentative, and competitive style, these people also tend to have more frequent interpersonal conflicts. Such conflicts can lead to a loss of social support and heightened autonomic activation, which can then lead to increased risk of cardiovascular disease (Boyle et al., 1004; Bruck & Allen, 2003; Vanderwerker & Prigerson, 2004).

Can people with a Type A personality change their behavior? Health psychologists have developed two types of behavior modification to help people with Type A personality—the *shotgun approach* and the *target behavior approach*. The *shotgun approach* aims to change all the behaviors that relate to the Type A personality. Friedman and his colleagues (1986) use the shotgun approach in their Recurrent Coronary Prevention Program. The program provides individual counseling, dietary advice, exercise, drugs, and group therapy to eliminate or modify Type A behaviors. Type A's are specifically encouraged to slow down and perform tasks incompatible with their personalities. For example, they might try to listen to other people without interrupting or they could deliberately choose the longest supermarket line. The major criticism of the shotgun approach is that it may decrease *desirable* Type A traits, such as ambition, as well as *undesirable* traits, like cynicism and hostility.

The alternative therapy, the *target behavior approach*, focuses on only those Type A behaviors that are likely to cause heart disease—namely, cynical hostility. This approach is based on the belief that by modifying specific behaviors, the person will likely reduce his or her risk of heart disease.

Hardiness

In addition to Type A and Type B personalities, other personality patterns may affect the way we respond to stress? Have you ever wondered how some people survive in the face of great tragedy and stress? Suzanne Kobasa was among the first to study this question (Kobasa, 1979; Maddi, 2004; Turnipseed, 2003). Examining male executives with high levels of stress, she found that some people are more resistant to stress than others because of a personality factor called **hardiness**, a resilient type of optimism that comes from three distinctive attitudes:

Hardiness *Resilient personality that includes a strong commitment to personal goals, control over life, and viewing change as a challenge rather than a threat*

1. **Commitment.** Hardy people feel a strong sense of commitment to both their work and their personal life. They also make intentional commitments to purposeful activity and problem solving.

2. **Control.** Hardy people see themselves as being in control of their lives rather than as victims of their circumstances.

3. **Challenge.** Finally, hardy people look at change as an opportunity for growth and improvement—not as a threat. They welcome challenges.

The important lesson from this research is that hardiness is a *learned behavior*—not something based on luck or genetics. If you are not one of the *hardy* souls, you can develop the trait. The next time you face a bad stressor, such as four exams in one week, try using the 3 C's: "I am fully *committed* to my college education." "I can *control* the number of tests by taking one or two of them earlier than scheduled, or I can rearrange my work schedule." "I welcome this *challenge* as a final motivation to enroll in those reading improvement and college success courses I've always planned to take."

Before we go on, it is also important to note that Type A personality and lack of hardiness are not the only controllable risk factors associated with heart disease. Smoking, obesity, diet, and lack of exercise are very important factors. Smoking restricts blood circulation, and obesity stresses the heart by causing it to pump more blood to the excess body tissue. A high-fat diet, especially one high in cholesterol, contributes to the fatty deposits that clog blood vessels. Lack of exercise contributes to weight gain. It also prevents the body from obtaining important exercise benefits, including strengthened heart muscle, increased heart efficiency, and the release of neurotransmitters such as serotonin that alleviate stress and promote well-being.

Posttraumatic Stress Disorder (PTSD): A Disease of Modern Times?

Perhaps the most powerful example of the effects of severe stress is **posttraumatic stress disorder (PTSD)**. Children, as well as adults, can experience PTSD. Symptoms of PTSD include feelings of terror and helplessness during the trauma and recurrent flashbacks, nightmares, impaired concentration, and/or emotional numbing afterward. These symptoms may continue for months or years after the event itself. To reduce the stress, some victims of PTSD turn to alcohol and other drugs, which often compound the problem (Schnurr & Green, 2004).

We have an interesting history with the diagnosis of PTSD. During the Industrial Revolution, workers who survived horrific railroad accidents sometimes developed a condition very similar to PTSD. But they called it "railway spine" because they believed the problems resulted from a twisting or concussion of the spine. In later times, PTSD was primarily associated with military combat. Doctors called it "shell shock" because they believed it was a response to the physical concussion caused by exploding artillery. Today, we know that PTSD is caused by any exposure to extraordinary stress.

The essential feature of PTSD is *severe anxiety* (a state of constant or recurring alarm and fearfulness). The anxiety develops after experiencing a traumatic event (such as rape, natural disaster, or war), learning about a violent or unexpected death of a family member, or even being a witness or bystander to violence (American Psychiatric Association, 2002).

According to the Facts for Health website (http://www.factsforhealth.org), approximately 10 percent of Americans have had or will have PTSD at some point in their lives. The primary symptoms of PTSD are summarized in Table 3.2. The table also includes five important tips for coping with traumatic events.

Posttraumatic Stress Disorder (PTSD) *Anxiety disorder following exposure to a life-threatening or other extreme event that evoked great horror or helplessness; characterized by flashbacks, nightmares, and impaired functioning*

TABLE 3.2 IDENTIFYING PTSD AND COPING WITH CRISIS

Primary Symptoms of Posttraumatic Stress Disorder (PTSD)
- Re-experiencing the event through vivid memories or flashbacks
- Feeling "emotionally numb"
- Feeling overwhelmed by what would normally be considered everyday situations
- Diminished interest in performing normal tasks or pursuing usual interests
- Crying uncontrollably
- Isolating oneself from family and friends and avoiding social situations
- Relying increasingly on alcohol or drugs to get through the day
- Feeling extremely moody, irritable, angry, suspicious, or frightened
- Having difficulty falling or staying asleep, sleeping too much, and experiencing nightmares
- Feeling guilty about surviving the event or being unable to solve the problem, change the event, or prevent the disaster
- Feeling fear and sense of doom about the future

Five Important Tips for Coping with Crisis
1. Recognize your feelings about the situation and talk to others about your fears. Know that these feelings are a normal response to an abnormal situation.
2. Be willing to listen to family and friends who have been affected and encourage them to seek counseling if necessary.
3. Be patient with people. Tempers are short in times of crisis, and others may be feeling as much stress as you.
4. Recognize normal crisis reactions, such as sleep disturbances and nightmares, withdrawal, reverting to childhood behaviors, and trouble focusing on work or school.
5. Take time with your children, spouse, life partner, friends, and coworkers to do something you enjoy.

Source: American Counseling Association and adapted from Pomponio, 2001.

CASE STUDY / PERSONAL STORY

"Surviving" 9/11

On the morning of September 11, 2001, the woman in this photograph, Marcy Borders, was standing at a copying machine on the 81st floor of Tower One at the World Trade Center. She was busily daydreaming about her new job and thinking, "Here I am, in New York, doing something with my life." In the next moment, everything changed. The terrorists' plane hit and the building started "swaying like it was going to break off." Marcy frantically ran down the 81 flights of stairs and escaped to a world of panic and chaos.

Outside, rescue workers screamed to her, "Run! Don't look back! Run!" But Marcy couldn't move. She was paralyzed by the horror that surrounded her—huge walls of smoke barreling down the street, people hanging out of windows, and then jumping to their death. The smoke soon became so thick she could no longer see. Marcy stood alone in the dark screaming, "Help me, I don't want to die!"

Four months after the terrorist attack, Marcy was still having trouble adjusting. She was so depressed and terrified that she seldom left her apartment. Haunted by fears and memories of the attack, she could not work and lived "off Lipton's chicken noodle soup." Officials from the Red Cross and other organizations tried to help but found that she seemed reluctant to reach out. "I don't want to seem like I am taking away from the people who lost loved ones."

Alone at night, Marcy drank alcohol to try to fall asleep. Unfortunately, when she succeeded she had nightmares of missiles flying overhead or visions of her mother making her funeral arrangements. "Everything I've built up seems gone.... My mother is so disappointed in me. She thinks I should bounce back. But she wasn't there on the 81st floor."

ADAPTED FROM CANNON, 2002.

Application

RESEARCH HIGHLIGHT

Does Stress Cause Gastric Ulcers?

Do you have gastric ulcers or know someone who does? If so, you know that these lesions to the lining of the stomach (and duodenum—the upper section of the small intestine) can be quite painful. In extreme cases, they may even be life threatening. Have you been told ulcers are caused by bacteria and not by stress, as previously thought? Would you like to know what modern science believes?

Beginning in the 1950s, psychologists reported strong evidence that stress can lead to ulcers. Correlational studies have found that people who live in stressful situations develop a higher incidence of ulcers. And numerous experiments with laboratory animals have shown that stressors, such as shock or confinement to a very small space for a few hours, can produce ulcers in some laboratory animals (Andrade & Graeff, 2001; Bhattacharya & Muruganandam, 2003; Gabry et al., 2002; Landeira-Fernandez, 2004).

The relationship between stress and ulcers seemed well established until researchers reported a bacterium (Helicobacter pylori or H. pylori) that appears to be associated with ulcers. Because many people prefer medical explanations, like bacteria or viruses, to psychological ones, the idea of stress as a cause of ulcers has been largely abandoned by many people.

Is this warranted? Let's take a closer look at the research. First, most ulcer patients do have the H. pylori bacterium in their stomachs, and it clearly damages the stomach wall. In addition, antibiotic treatment does help many patients. However, approximately 75 percent of normal control subjects' stomachs also have the bacterium. This suggests that the bacterium may cause the ulcer, but only in people who are compromised by stress. Furthermore, behavior modification and other psychological treatments, used alongside antibiotics, can help ease ulcers. Finally, studies of the amygdala (a part of the brain involved in emotional response) show that it plays an important role in gastric ulcer formation (Henke, 1992; Tanaka, Yoshida, Yokoo, Tomita, & Tanaka, 1998).

Apparently, stressful situations and direct stimulation of the amygdala cause an increase in stress hormones and hydrochloric acid, as well as a decrease in blood flow in the stomach walls. This combination leaves the stomach more vulnerable to attack by the H. pylori bacteria.

In sum, it appears that H. pylori, increased hydrochloric acid, stress hormones, and decreased blood flow all lead to the formation of gastric ulcers. Once again, we see how biological, psychological, and social forces interact with one another (the biopsychosocial model). And, for now, the psychosomatic explanation for ulcers is back in business (Overmier & Murison, 2000).

Psychosomatic illness is not the same as an imagined, hypochondriacal, illness. Psychosomatic (psyche means "mind" and soma means "body") refers to symptoms or illnesses that are caused or aggravated by psychological factors, especially stress (Lipowski, 1986). Most researchers and health practitioners believe that almost all illnesses are partly psychosomatic in this sense.

Assessment

CHECK & REVIEW

Stress and Illness

Cancer appears to result from an interaction of heredity, environmental insults (such as smoking), and immune system deficiency. Stress may be an important cause of decreased immunity. During times of stress, the body may be less able to check cancer cell multiplication because the immune system is suppressed.

The leading cause of death in the United States is heart disease. Risk factors include smoking, stress, obesity, a high-fat diet, lack of exercise, and **Type A personality** (if it includes cynical hostility). The two main approaches to modifying Type A

behavior are the shotgun approach and the target behavior approach.

People with psychological **hardiness** are less vulnerable to stress because of three distinctive personality characteristics—commitment, control, and challenge.

Exposure to extraordinary stress (like war or rape) may lead to **posttraumatic stress disorder (PTSD)**. Current opinion suggests gastric ulcers are caused by the H. pylori bacterium. However, psychological research shows that stress also plays a contributing role.

Questions

1. Stress can contribute to heart disease by releasing the hormones _____ and _____, which increase the level of fat in the blood.
2. Which of the following is not among the characteristics associated with Type A personality? (a) time urgency; (b) patience; (c) competition; (d) hostility
3. Explain how the three characteristics of the hardy personality help reduce stress.
4. What is the essential feature of PTSD?

Check your answers in Appendix B.

CLICK & REVIEW
for additional assessment options:
www.wiley.com/college/huffman

HEALTH PSYCHOLOGY IN ACTION

Achievement

How is health psychology involved with tobacco, alcohol, and chronic pain?

Health psychology, the study of how biological, psychological, and social factors affect health and illness, is a growing field in psychology. In this section, we will consider the psychological components of two major health risks—*tobacco* and *alcohol*. We will also explore the psychological factors that increase and decrease *chronic pain*. But first, we must learn a little about the field of health psychology and what health psychologists have learned about promoting healthy behaviors.

Application

APPLYING PSYCHOLOGY TO WORK

Health Psychology *Studies how biological, psychological, and social factors affect health and illness*

Would You Like to Be a Health Psychologist?

Health psychologists study how people's lifestyles and activities, emotional reactions, ways of interpreting events, and personality characteristics influence their physical health and well-being. They work primarily in research or directly with physicians and other health professionals to implement research findings.

As researchers, health psychologists are particularly interested in the relationship between stress and the immune system. As we discovered earlier, a normally functioning immune system helps detect and defend against disease. And a suppressed immune system leaves the body susceptible to a number of diseases.

As practitioners, health psychologists can work as independent clinicians or as consultants alongside physicians, physical and occupational therapists, and other health care workers. Their goal is to reduce psychological distress or unhealthy behaviors. They also help patients and families make critical decisions and prepare psychologically for surgery or other treatment. Health psychologists have become so involved with health and illness that medical centers are one of their major employers (Careers in Health Psychology, 2004).

In addition to their work as researchers and practitioners, health psychologists also educate the public about health *maintenance*. They provide information about the effects of stress, smoking, alcohol, lack of exercise, and other health issues. In addition, health psychologists help people cope with chronic problems, such as pain, diabetes, and high blood pressure, as well as unhealthful behaviors, such as anger expression and lack of assertiveness. Due to space limitations, only a brief overview of the wide variety of work activities and interests of health psychologists can be provided here. If you are seriously interested in pursuing a career in this field, you may want to check with the counseling or career center on your campus. Also try exploring the career website included at the end of this chapter.

■ Tobacco: Hazardous to Your Health

> A custom loathsome to the eye, hateful to the nose, harmful to the brain, dangerous to the lungs, and in the black, stinking fume thereof, nearest resembling the horrible Stygian smoke of the pit that is bottomless.
>
> KING JAMES I (1604)

This is what King James I wrote about smoking in 1604, shortly after Sir Walter Raleigh introduced tobacco to England from the Americas. Today, more than 400 years later, many people would agree with the king's tirade against the practice. According to the latest U.S. Public Health Service report, tobacco is the single most preventable cause of death and disease in the United States and the second major cause of death in the world (World Health Organization, 2004). Smoking is a major risk factor for coronary heart disease and lung cancer. It also contributes to cancers of the mouth, larynx, throat, esophagus, bladder, and pancreas (Centers for Disease Control, 2003, 2004). In addition, smoking contributes to chronic bronchitis, emphysema, and ulcers. Moreover, smoking shortens life (Figure 3.5). This is true for both the smoker and those who breathe secondhand smoke.

What about all the new antismoking laws? Do they help? Ironically, the antismoking laws passed in the 1990s may have made quitting smoking even more difficult for some. Why? Smokers have to leave smoke-free environments and group together outdoors on the hottest summer days and the coldest winter days. This forced isolation creates a strong social bond. Cigarette companies knowingly play to this group loyalty (and the individual's "independence" and "perseverance") by showing smokers sitting high up on the ledges of office buildings and on the wings of airplanes in flight "going to any lengths" to have a cigarette. Also, when people cannot smoke in offices, on airplanes, in restaurants, or other public places, the interval between nicotine doses increases, which increases the severity of the withdrawal symptoms (Palfai, Monti, Ostafin, & Hutchinson, 2000).

Nick Baker/Cartoon Stock

"Must I really go outside to smoke?"

Smoking Prevention

The first puff on a cigarette is rarely pleasant. Most people also know that smoking is bad for their health and that the more they smoke, the more at risk they are. Why, then, do people ever start smoking? The answer is complex.

First, smoking usually starts when people are young. The *European School Survey Project on Alcohol and Other Drugs* (ESPAD) (2001) reported that tobacco smoking was well established by the mid-teens in most European countries. It also showed few signs of diminishing since the previous ESPAD survey in 1995. A similar survey of U.S. middle schools, grades 6 to 8, found that one in eight students were experimenting with some form of tobacco, such as cigarettes, cigars, and chewing tobacco (Kaufman, 2000). There are many reasons people begin to smoke at such a young age, but peer pressure and imitation of role models (such as celebrities) are particularly strong factors. Young smokers want to look mature and be accepted by their social peers.

Second, regardless of the age at which a person begins smoking, once he or she begins to smoke, there is a biological need to continue. Evidence suggests that nicotine addiction is very similar to heroin, cocaine, or alcohol addiction (Brody et al., 2004). When we inhale tobacco smoke, it takes only seconds for the nicotine to reach the brain. Once inside the brain, nicotine increases the release of the neurotransmitters acetylcholine and norepinephrine, which increase alertness, concentration, memory, and feelings of pleasure. Nicotine also stimulates the release of dopamine, the neurotransmitter most closely related to reward centers in the brain (Brody et al., 2004; Noble, 2000).

Finally, social pressures and physical addiction combine to create additional benefits (Brandon et al., 2004). Smoking is often paired with pleasant things, such as good food, friends, sex, and the nicotine high. In contrast, smokers who are deprived of cigarettes go through extremely unpleasant physical withdrawal. Unfortunately, when

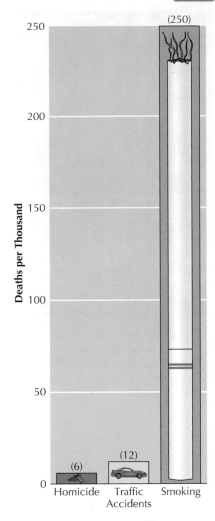

Figure 3.5 ***Smoking shortens your life.*** According to the World Health Organization, among 20-year-olds in the United States who smoke cigarettes regularly, the risk of dying before age 70 would be about 6 per 1000 from homicide, 12 per 1000 from traffic accidents, and 250 per 1000 from smoking. *Source:* World Health Organization, 2004. http://www.who.int/topics/smoking/en

Health psychology in action. *As part of California's antismoking campaign, this billboard may reduce the desire to start smoking. Source: California Department of Health Service.*

they get their next puff, the nicotine immediately relieves the symptoms. Smoking is rewarded and not smoking is punished. Can you see why many health psychologists and other scientists believe the best way to reduce the number of smokers may be to stop people from ever taking that first puff?

If most people begin smoking during adolescence, shouldn't prevention be aimed at this group? Prevention programs for teens face a tough uphill battle. For adolescents, the long-term health disadvantages of heart disease and cancer seem irrelevant. In contrast, smoking provides immediate short-term rewards from peers and the addictive, reinforcing properties of nicotine. Many smoking prevention programs therefore focus on immediate short-term problems with smoking, such as bad breath and interference with athletic performance.

Through films and discussion groups, teens also are educated about peer pressure and the media's influence on smoking. In addition, teens are given opportunities to role-play refusal skills, taught general social and personal skills needed in decision making, and given strategies for coping with the stresses of adolescence and daily life. Unfortunately, research shows that the effect of these psychosocial prevention programs is small (Tait & Hulse, 2003; Unger et al., 2004). To have even a modest effect, these programs must begin early and continue for many years.

To reduce the health risk and help fight peer pressure among college students, many universities now ban smoking in college buildings and provide more smoke-free dormitories. Another possible deterrent to college smoking may come from the increasing cost of cigarettes. Expensive legal battles and settlements by the tobacco industry create expenses that are passed on to consumers. This increase, added to state and local taxes, brings the cost to over $4 per pack in most states. For a student who smokes a pack of cigarettes a day, the annual cost is nearly $1500—more than twice the cost of textbooks for an entire academic year.

Stopping Smoking

To cease smoking is the easiest thing I ever did; I ought to know, for I have done it a thousand times.

MARK TWAIN

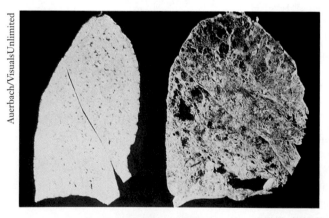

A hidden cost of smoking. *Would people continue to smoke if they could see what it does to their lungs? Compare the healthy tissue of the lung of a nonsmoker on the left to the blackened, unhealthy lung of the smoker on the right.*

Unfortunately, Mark Twain was never able to quit for very long, and many ex-smokers say that stopping smoking was the most difficult thing they ever did. Although some people find the easiest way for them to cope with the physical withdrawal from nicotine is to suddenly and completely stop, the success rate for this "cold turkey" approach is extremely low. Even with medical aids, such as patches, gum, or pills, it is still difficult to quit.

Any program designed to help smokers break their habit must combat the social rewards of smoking as well as the physical addiction to nicotine (Koop, Richmond, & Steinfeld, 2004). Sometimes the best approach is a combination of cognitive and behavioral techniques and nicotine replacement therapy.

Cognitively, smokers can learn to identify stimuli or situations that make them feel like smoking. They can then change or avoid them (Brandon, Collins, Juliano, & Lazev, 2000). They can also refocus their attention on something other than smoking or remind themselves of the benefits of not smoking (Taylor, Harris, Singleton, Moolchan, & Heishman, 2000). Behaviorally, they might cope with the urge to smoke by chewing gum, exercising, or chewing on a toothpick after a meal instead of lighting a cigarette. No program to quit smoking will work without strong personal motivation. However, the payoffs of a healthier and longer life are worth it.

■ Alcohol: Both a Personal and Social Health Problem

In the United States, considerable attention is given to the problem of illegal drugs such as marijuana and cocaine. But did you know that that the American Medical Association considers alcohol to be the most dangerous and physically damaging of all drugs (American Medical Association, 2003)? After tobacco, it is the leading cause of premature death in the United States and most European countries (Cohen et al., 2004; Grilly, 2006; Joh & Hanke, 2003).

In addition, alcohol may cause serious damage to your brain (Crews et al., 2004). The fact that alcohol seems to increase aggression also helps explain why it is a major factor in most murders, suicides, spousal assaults, child abuse, and accidental deaths (Pappas et al., 2004; Sebre et al., 2004; Sher, Grekin, & Williams, 2005).

Thanks to heavy advertising, most people are now aware of the major risks of alcohol and driving—heavy fines, loss of driver's license, serious injuries, possible jail time, and even death. But did you know that simply *drinking* alcohol itself can be fatal? Because alcohol depresses neural activity throughout the brain, if blood levels of alcohol rise to a certain point, the brain's respiratory center stops functioning and the person dies.

This is why binge drinking is so dangerous. **Binge drinking** is defined as having more than four (for women) or five (for men) drinks at a time on at least three occasions during a two-week period. Do you remember news reports of two freshmen at the Massachusetts Institute of Technology who died from alcohol poisoning after binge drinking at fraternity parties? One of the students had a blood alcohol level of .5888 percent. This is the equivalent of more than 20 beers in one hour. It is also over seven times the legal driving limit in most states. A national survey of college students found that between 1993 and 2001, approximately 44 percent of college students were binge drinkers (Wechsler et al., 2002). This survey also found that white students are more likely to drink heavily (50.2 percent) than are students of other ethnicities, such as Hispanic (34.4 percent), Native American Indian/Other (33.6 percent), Asian/Pacific Islander (26.2 percent), and black/African American (21.7 percent).

Alcohol is a serious health problem for all college-age students. For those who drink, research shows that because of alcohol use every year:

- 1400 college students die from alcohol-related causes.

- 500,000 students suffer nonfatal injuries.

- 1.2–1.5 percent of students attempt suicide because of alcohol or other drug use.

- 400,000 students have unprotected sex, and more than 100,000 are too intoxicated to know whether they consented to sexual intercourse (Task Force of the National Advisory, 2002).

Alcohol also has an effect on students who abstain or are only moderate drinkers. For example, for those who live on campus or in sorority or fraternity houses:

- 60 percent had their study or sleep interrupted by an alcohol user.

- 47.6 percent had to take care of a drunken student.

- 19.5 percent of female respondents experienced an unwanted sexual advance.

- 8.7 percent had been pushed, hit, or assaulted (Wechsler et al., 2002).

Unfortunately, many college students believe that heavy drinking is harmless fun and a natural part of "college life." College administrators, however, are increasingly aware of the problems of binge drinking and other types of alcohol abuse. They are developing and implementing policies and programs that go beyond traditional educational programs to include the physical, social, legal, and economic environment on college campuses and the surrounding communities (Kapner, 2004).

Binge Drinking *Occurs when a man consumes five or more drinks in a row, or a woman consumes four or more drinks at a time, on at least three occasions during a two-week period*

Binge drinking can be fatal. *On many college campuses, it is a tradition to "drink your age" on your 21st birthday. Following this tradition, Bradley McCue, a University of Michigan junior, drank 21 shots of alcohol plus three more to break his friend's record. He died on the morning of his 21st birthday from alcohol poisoning. For more information, contact www.Brad21.org.*

TRY THIS

YOURSELF

Application

College fun or a serious problem? Binge drinking among young adults is a growing problem, and many teenage and college women are drinking as much as men.

Do You Have an Alcohol Problem?

In our society, drinking alcoholic beverages is generally considered a normal and appropriate way to modify mood or behavior. Having a few beers after work or wine with dinner is commonplace. But as we have just seen, many people also abuse alcohol. If you would like a quick check of your own drinking behavior, place a mark next to each of the symptoms that describes your current drinking behavior. *(Note: Before you can improve your health, you must fully acknowledge and recognize your patterns of behavior. Be honest in your self-appraisal and responses.)*

Seven Signs of Alcohol Dependence Syndrome

___• Drinking increases, sometimes to the point of almost continuous daily consumption.

___• Drinking is given higher priority than other activities, in spite of its negative consequences.

___• More and more alcohol is required to produce behavioral, subjective, and metabolic changes; large amounts of alcohol can be tolerated.

___• Even short periods of abstinence bring on withdrawal symptoms, such as sweatiness, trembling, and nausea.

___• Withdrawal symptoms are relieved or avoided by further drinking, especially in the morning.

___• The individual is subjectively aware of a craving for alcohol and has little control over the quantity and frequency of intake.

___• If the person begins drinking again after a period of abstinence, he or she rapidly returns to the previous high level of consumption and other behavioral patterns.

Source: World Health Organization, 2004.

Achievement

Gender & Cultural Diversity

Binge Drinking Around the World

After reading the previous section on binge drinking, you may think it is a problem unique to college students in the United States. Unfortunately, binge drinking is a worldwide problem.

• The European School Survey Project (2001) found an overall increase in binge drinking since 1995, especially in Britain, Denmark, Ireland, and Poland. More than 30 percent of schoolchildren in those countries reported binge drinking three or more times in the last month.

• In Mexico, a study of drinking patterns at 16 religious fiestas and 13 nonreligious fiestas in the community of Santa María Atzompa found that nearly all the men qualified as binge drinkers at every fiesta. Furthermore, the binge drinking contributed to several outbreaks of violence at the fiestas (Perez, 2000).

• A study in Spain and South America found that young men who reported binge drinking were more likely than others to behave aggressively toward people outside their family (Orpinas, 1999).

• Scientists in Denmark compared the drinking patterns of 56,970 men and women with respect to their preferred drink, beer, wine, or spirits (Gronbaek, Tjonneland, Johansen, Stripp, & Overvad, 2000). Results showed that beer drinkers were the least likely of the different types of drinkers to binge, whereas wine drinkers were the most likely to binge.

- Research on alcohol consumption in Russia shows that 44 percent of men are binge drinkers (Bobak, McKee, Rose, & Marmot, 1999).

▪ Chronic Pain: An Ongoing Threat to Health

Imagine having all your pain receptors removed so that you could race cars, downhill ski, skateboard, and go to the dentist without ever worrying about pain. Does this sound too good to be true? Think again. Pain is essential to the survival and well-being of humans and all other animals. It alerts us to dangerous or harmful situations and forces us to rest and recover from injury (Watkins & Maier, 2000). In contrast, **chronic pain**, the type that comes with a chronic disease or continues long past the healing of a wound, does not serve a useful function.

Chronic Pain *Continuous or recurrent pain over a period of six months or longer*

To treat chronic pain, health psychologists often focus their efforts on psychologically oriented treatments, such as behavior modification, biofeedback, and relaxation. Although psychological factors may not be the source of the chronic pain, they frequently encourage and intensify it and increase the related anguish and disability (Currie & Wang, 2004; Eriksen et al., 2003; Keefe, Abernathy, & Campbell, 2005).

Behavior Modification

Chronic pain is a serious problem with no simple solution. For example, exercise is known to produce an increase in *endorphins*, naturally produced chemicals that attach themselves to nerve cells in the brain and block the perception of pain (Chapter 2). However, chronic pain patients tend to decrease their activity and exercise. In addition, well-meaning family members often ask chronic pain sufferers, "How are you feeling?" "Is the pain any better today?" Unfortunately, talking about pain focuses attention on it and increases its intensity (Sansone, Levengood, & Sellbom, 2004). Furthermore, as the pain increases, anxiety increases. The anxiety itself then increases the pain, which further increases the anxiety, which further increases the pain!

To counteract these hidden personal and family problems and negative cycles, health psychologists may begin a behavior modification program for both the patient with chronic pain and his or her family. The effectiveness of such programs for treating chronic pain was first shown in the late 1970s (Cairns & Pasino, 1977). Researchers established individualized pain management programs and monitored each patient's adherence to their pain treatment programs (daily exercise, use of relaxation techniques, and so on). Compared with a control group, patients who used these techniques experienced substantially reduced pain. Today, many pain control programs incorporate similar techniques for rewarding "well behaviors."

Biofeedback

In *biofeedback*, information about physiological functions, such as heart rate or blood pressure, is monitored, and the feedback helps the individual learn to control these functions. Such feedback helps reduce some types of chronic pain. Most biofeedback with chronic pain patients is done with the *electromyograph (EMG)*. This device measures muscle tension by recording electrical activity in the skin. The EMG is most helpful when the pain involves extreme muscle tension, such as tension headache and lower back pain. Electrodes are attached to the site of the pain, and the patient is instructed to relax. When sufficient relaxation is achieved, the machine signals with a tone or a light. The signal serves as feedback, enabling the patient to learn how to relax.

Pain control through biofeedback. Using an electromyograph (EMG), one can record muscular tension and the patient is taught specific relaxation techniques that reduce tension and help relieve chronic pain.

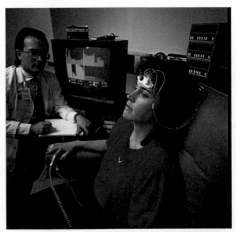

James Schnepf

Research shows that biofeedback is helpful and sometimes as effective as more expensive and lengthier forms of treatment (Engel, Jensen, & Schwartz, 2004; Hammond, 2005; Hawkins & Hart, 2003). Apparently, it is successful because it teaches patients to recognize patterns of emotional arousal and conflict that affect their physiological responses. This self-awareness, in turn, enables them to learn self-regulation skills that help control their pain.

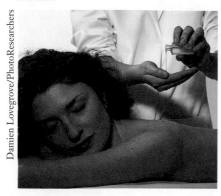

Relaxation techniques. Massage is a healthy way to reduce stress and tension-related pain.

Damien Lovegrove/PhotoResearchers

Relaxation Techniques

Because the pain always seems to be there, chronic pain sufferers tend to talk and think about their pain whenever they are not thoroughly engrossed in an activity. Watching TV shows or films, attending parties, or performing any activity that diverts attention from the pain seems to reduce discomfort. Attention might also be diverted with special *relaxation techniques* like those that are taught in some prepared childbirth classes. These techniques focus the birthing mother's attention on breathing and relaxing the muscles, which helps distract her attention from the fear and pain of the birthing process. Similar techniques also can be helpful to chronic pain sufferers (Astin, 2004). Remember, however, that these techniques do not eliminate the pain. They merely allow the person to ignore it for a time.

Application

APPLYING PSYCHOLOGY TO WORK

Is My Job Too Stressful?

Health psychologists (and industrial/organizational psychologists) have studied numerous factors in job-related stress. Their findings suggest that one way to prevent these stresses is to gather lots of information before making a career decision.

If you would like to apply this thinking to your own career plans, start by identifying what you like and do not like about your current (and past) jobs. With this information in hand, you will then be prepared to research jobs that will better suit your interests, needs, and abilities and avoid the stress caused by jobs failing to meet these criteria. To start your analysis, answer yes or no to these questions:

1. Is there a sufficient amount of laughter and sociability in my workplace?

2. Does my boss notice and appreciate my work?

3. Is my boss understanding and friendly?

4. Am I embarrassed by the physical conditions of my workplace?

5. Do I feel safe and comfortable in my place of work?

6. Do I like the location of my job?

7. If I won the lottery and were guaranteed a lifetime income, would I feel truly sad if I also had to quit my job?

8. Do I watch the clock, daydream, take long lunches, and leave work as soon as possible?

9. Do I frequently feel stressed and overwhelmed by the demands of my job?

10. Compared to others with my qualifications, am I being paid what I am worth?

11. Are promotions made in a fair and just manner where I work?

12. Given the demands of my job, am I fairly compensated for my work?

Now score your answers. Give yourself one point for each answer that matches the following: 1. No; 2. No; 3. No; 4. Yes; 5. No; 6. No; 7. No; 8. Yes; 9. Yes; 10. No; 11. No; 12. No.

The questions you just answered are based on four factors that research shows are conducive to increased job satisfaction and reduced stress: supportive colleagues, supportive working conditions, mentally challenging work, and equitable rewards (Robbins, 1996). Your total score reveals your overall level of dissatisfaction. A look at specific questions can help identify which of these four factors is most important to your job satisfaction—and most lacking in your current job.

Age Fotostock America, Inc.

Supportive colleagues (items 1, 2, 3): For most people, work fills important social needs. Therefore, having friendly and supportive colleagues and superiors leads to increased satisfaction.

Supportive working conditions (items 4, 5, 6): Not surprisingly, most employees prefer working in safe, clean, and relatively modern facilities. They also prefer jobs close to home.

Mentally challenging work (items 7, 8, 9): Jobs with too little challenge create boredom and apathy, whereas too much challenge creates frustration and feelings of failure.

Equitable rewards (items 10, 11, 12): Employees want pay and promotions based on job demands, individual skill levels, and community pay standards.

CHECK & REVIEW

Health Psychology in Action

Health psychology studies how biological, psychological, and social factors affect health and illness. Because smoking is the single most preventable cause of death and disease in the United States, prevention and cessation of smoking are of primary importance to all health practitioners.

Smoking prevention programs involve educating the public about short- and long-term consequences of smoking, trying to make smoking less socially acceptable, and helping nonsmokers resist social pressures to smoke. Most approaches to help people quit smoking include cognitive and behavioral techniques to aid smokers in their withdrawal from nicotine, along with nicotine replacement therapy (using patches, gum, and pills).

Alcohol is one of our most serious health problems. In addition to posing health risks to the individual, alcohol also plays a major role in social issues, such as murder, suicide, spousal abuse, and accidental death. **Binge drinking** also is a serious problem that occurs when a man has five or more drinks in a row or a woman has four or more drinks at one time, on at least three occasions during a two-week period.

Chronic pain is continuous or recurrent pain that persists over a period of six months or more. Although psychological factors rarely are the source of chronic pain, they can encourage and intensify it. Increased activity, exercise, and dietary changes help to reduce chronic pain. Health psychologists also use behavior modification, biofeedback, and relaxation techniques to treat chronic pain.

Questions

1. Knowing smoking is very dangerous, why is it so difficult for many people to stop?
2. If you are mounting a campaign to prevent young people from taking up smoking, you are likely to get the best results if you emphasize the_____. (a) serious, unhealthy, long-term effects of tobacco use; (b) number of adults who die from smoking; (c) value of having a relatively healthy retirement; (d) short-term detrimental effects of tobacco use
3. The American Medical Association considers _____ to be the most dangerous and physically damaging of all drugs.
4. An increase in activity and exercise levels benefits patients with pain because exercise increases the release of _____. (a) endorphins; (b) insulin; (c) acetylcholine; (d) norepinephrine

Check you answers in Appendix B.

 CLICK & REVIEW for additional assessment options: www.wiley.com/college/huffman

HEALTH AND STRESS MANAGEMENT

Everyone encounters pressure at work and school, long lines at the bank, and relationship problems. Because we cannot escape stress, we need to learn how to effectively cope with it. Lazarus and Folkman (1984) defined *coping* as "constantly changing cognitive and behavioral efforts to manage specific external and/or internal demands that are appraised as taxing or exceeding the resources of the person." In simpler terms, coping is an attempt to manage stress in some effective way. It is not one single act but a process that allows us to deal with various stressors. In this section, we

 Achievement
What techniques and resources are available to help people stay healthy and cope with stress?

 www.wiley.com/college/huffman

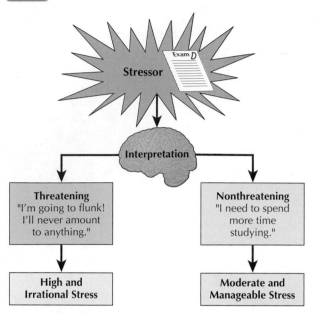

Figure 3.6 *Is stress in the eye of the beholder?* Lazarus (1999) suggests that our emotional reaction to stress is largely a result of how we interpret it. Therefore, we can learn to cope with stress by using cognitive, emotional, and behavioral strategies—instead of feeling threatened.

Emotion-Focused Forms of Coping *Coping strategies based on changing one's perceptions of stressful situations*

Defense Mechanisms *Unconscious strategies used to distort reality and relieve anxiety and guilt*

Problem-Focused Forms of Coping *Coping strategies that use problem-solving strategies to decrease or eliminate the source of stress*

will first discuss *emotion-focused* forms of coping that deal with our interpretation of problems. Then we will discuss *problem-focused* strategies that deal directly with our reactions. We close with a look at ways to determine whether your job is stressful and a review of helpful resources for stress management.

Emotion- and Problem-Focused Coping: Two Different Approaches

As you can see in Figure 3.6, our level of stress generally depends on both our interpretation of and reaction to the stressors (Gaab, Rohleder, Nater, & Ehlert, 2005; Lazarus, 1999). **Emotion-focused forms of coping** are emotional or cognitive strategies that change how we view a stressful situation. Suppose you are refused a highly desirable job or rejected by a desired lover. You might reappraise the situation and decide that the job or lover might not have been the right match for you. You could also decide that you were not really qualified or ready for that specific job or relationship.

In addition to these conscious forms of emotion-focused coping, we often resort to **defense mechanisms**. The use of unconscious defense mechanisms reduces anxiety and often helps us cope with unavoidable stress. For instance, *fantasizing* about what you will do once you graduate from college or during the summer break can relax you when you're feeling stressed over final exams. On the other hand, defense mechanisms can sometimes be destructive. You might decide you did not get the job or the lover because you did not have the right "connections" or "the perfect body." This is known as *rationalization*, fabricating excuses when frustrated in attaining particular goals. Not seeing the situation more clearly and realistically might prevent you from developing skills or qualities that could get you a desirable job or lover in the future.

Emotion-focused forms of coping that are accurate reappraisals of stressful situations, and do not distort reality, may alleviate stress in some situations (Giacobbi, Foore, & Weinberg, 2004; Patterson et al., 2004). Many times, however, it is necessary and more effective to use **problem-focused forms of coping**. This approach deals directly with the situation or the stressor to eventually decrease or eliminate it (Bond & Bunce, 2000). Problem-focused coping includes identifying the stressful problem, generating possible solutions, selecting the appropriate solution, and applying the solution to the problem—thus eliminating the stress.

To illustrate the difference between emotion- and problem-focused styles of coping, imagine you are flying to Denver to be in your best friend's wedding. You have an important exam that lets out at 10:00 and your plane leaves at noon. Although the wedding is at 4:00, you decide that you can make it. Unfortunately, on the way to the airport, the taxi has a flat tire. You can cognitively evaluate the situation and remind yourself that because this is your best friend, he'll understand that you did everything you could to be there. It wasn't your fault that the taxi had a flat (emotion-focused approach). Or you could ask the driver to immediately call for another taxi to come and take you to the airport (problem-focused approach).

Can people use both forms of coping strategies at once? Yes, most stressful situations are complex. People often combine problem-focused and emotion-focused coping strategies. Furthermore, as you know from your own life, stressful situations change. The type of strategy we use depends not only on the stressor but also on the changing nature of the stressor. In some situations, we may first need to use an emotion-focused strategy, which allows a step back from an especially overwhelming problem. Then, later on, when we have regained our emotional strength, we can reappraise the situation and use the problem-focused approach to look for solutions.

We also may use one coping strategy to prepare us to use the other. Imagine that you are anxiously awaiting your first exam in a difficult course. To calm yourself, start with an emotion-focused approach. Say to yourself, "Relax and take a deep breath. It can't be as bad as I'm imagining." With reduced anxiety, you can then use problem-focused coping techniques and fully concentrate on the test.

Resources for Healthy Living: From Good Health to Money

A person's ability to cope effectively depends on the stressor itself—its complexity, intensity, and duration—and on the type of coping strategy used (emotion- or problem-focused). It also depends on available resources. Researchers have identified seven important resources for healthy living and stress management.

1. ***Health and exercise.*** All stressors cause physiological changes. Therefore, an individual's health significantly affects his or her ability to cope. Look again at Figure 3.3 on the *general adaptation syndrome.* The resistance stage is the coping stage. The stronger and healthier you are, the better you can cope with stress. Also, if you exercise and keep yourself physically fit, you will experience less anxiety and depression. Interestingly, researchers have found that people engaging in *strenuous exercise* experience greater reductions in anxiety than do those in *moderate* programs (Broman-Fulks et al., 2004; Hong, 2000).

   Exercise reduces the negative effects of stress in several ways. First, it reduces the stress hormones secreted into the bloodstream, which helps speed up the immune system's return to normal functioning. Second, exercise can help reduce muscular tension. Third, exercise increases strength, flexibility, and stamina for encountering future stressors. Most important, it increases the efficiency of the cardiovascular system. The best exercise for all these purposes is aerobic exercise—brisk walking, jogging, bicycling, swimming, and dancing.

2. ***Positive beliefs.*** A positive self-image and a positive attitude are also significant coping resources. Research shows that even temporarily raising self-esteem reduces the amount of anxiety caused by stressful events (Greenberg et al., 1993). Also, hope can sustain a person in the face of severe odds. This is often documented in news reports of people who have triumphed over seemingly unbeatable circumstances. According to Lazarus and Folkman (1984), hope can come from a belief in oneself, which can enable us to devise our own coping strategies. It also comes from a belief in others, such as medical doctors whom we feel can effect positive outcomes, or a belief in a higher spiritual power.

3. ***Social skills.*** Social situations—meetings, discussion groups, dates, parties, and so on—are often a source of pleasure. But they can also be a source of stress. Merely meeting someone new and trying to find something to talk about can be very stressful for some people. Therefore, people who acquire social skills (know appropriate behaviors for certain situations, have conversation-starters "up their sleeves," and express themselves well) suffer less anxiety than people who do not. In fact, people lacking social skills are more at risk for developing illness (Cohen & Williamson, 1991).

   Social skills help us not only interact with others but also communicate our needs and desires. In addition, social skills help us enlist help when we need it, and decrease hostility in tense situations. If you have weak social skills, observe others and ask people with good social skills for advice. Then practice your new skills by role-playing before applying them in real life.

4. ***Social support.*** Having the support of others helps offset the stressful effects of divorce, loss of a loved one, chronic illness, pregnancy, physical abuse, job loss, and work overload (Greeff & Van Der Merwe, 2004; Shen, McCreary, & Myers, 2004; Southwick, Vythilingam, & Charney, 2005). When we are faced with stressful

People need people. *An important resource for coping with stress is social support from friends, families, and support groups.*

©AP/Wide World Photos

www.wiley.com/college/huffman

External Locus of Control *Believing that chance or outside forces beyond one's control determine one's fate*

Internal Locus of Control *Believing that one controls one's own fate*

Coping with stress. *Exercise and friends are important resources for effective stress reduction. As the song says, "I get by with a little help from my friends." John Lennon and Paul McCartney, Sgt. Pepper's Lonely Hearts Club Band, 1967.*

circumstances, our friends and family often help us take care of our health, listen and "hold our hand," make us feel important, and provide stability to offset the changes in our lives. Professional support groups, like those for alcoholics and families of alcoholics, help people cope not only because they provide other people to lean on but also because people can learn techniques for coping from others with similar problems (see Chapter 15).

5. **Material resources.** We have all heard the saying "Money isn't everything." But when it comes to coping with stress, money, and the things money can buy, can be very important resources. Money increases the number of options available to eliminate sources of stress or reduce the effects of stress. When faced with the minor hassles of everyday living, chronic stressors, or major catastrophes, people with money (and the skills to effectively use that money) generally fare better and experience less stress than people without money (Chi & Chou, 1999; Ennis, Hobfoll, & Schroeder, 2000).

6. **Control.** Do you believe that what happens to you is primarily the result of luck and chance or your own actions? People with an **external locus of control** are more likely to believe in bad luck or fate. They feel powerless to change their circumstances and are less likely to make healthy changes, follow treatment programs, or positively cope with a situation.

   Conversely, people with an **internal locus of control** believe they are in charge of their own destiny. And they tend to use positive coping strategies. For example, "internals" who believe their heart attacks happened because of their unhealthy choices, such as smoking or having a stressful job, are more likely to change their unhealthy behaviors and recover more quickly (Ewart & Fitzgerald, 1994). Studies in China, Taiwan, and the United Kingdom found that those who had a higher internal locus of control experienced less psychological stress than did those with a higher external locus of control (Hamid & Chan, 1998; Lu, Kao, Cooper, & Spector, 2000).

7. **Relaxation.** One of the most effective ways to reduce stress is to make a conscious decision to relax during the stressful situation. A variety of relaxation techniques is available. As we discovered in an earlier section, biofeedback is often used in the treatment of chronic pain. It also helps people relax and manage their stress (Ham-

TRY THIS

YOURSELF

Application

Progressive Relaxation

You can use progressive relaxation techniques anytime and anywhere you feel stressed, such as before or during an exam. Here's how:

1. Sit in a comfortable position, with your head supported.
2. Start breathing slowly and deeply.
3. Let your entire body relax. Release all tension. Try to visualize your body getting progressively more relaxed with each breath.
4. Systematically tense and release each part of your body. Beginning with your

toes, curl them tightly while counting to 10. Now, release them. Note the difference between the tense and relaxed state. Next, tense your feet to the count of 10. Then relax them and feel the difference. Continue upward with your calves, thighs, buttocks, abdomen, back muscles, shoulders, upper arms, forearms, hands and fingers, neck, jaw, facial muscles, and forehead.

Try practicing progressive relaxation twice a day for about 15 minutes. You will be surprised at how quickly you can learn to relax—even in the most stressful situations.

mond, 2005). In addition to biofeedback, progressive relaxation helps reduce or relieve the muscular tension commonly associated with stress (Khandai, 2004; Vocks et al., 2004). Using this technique, patients first tense and then relax specific muscles, such as in the neck, shoulders, and arms. Progressive relaxation helps people recognize the difference between tense and relaxed muscles.

 pplication

CRITICAL THINKING　　　　　ACTIVE LEARNING

Reducing Stress Through Critical Thinking
(Contributed by Thomas Frangicetto)

According to cognitive therapist Albert Ellis, "If people look at what they are telling themselves, look at their thinking, at their irrational beliefs and self-defeating attitudes . . . they can then experience *healthy* stressful reactions" (Palmer & Ellis, 1995). Of all the useful coping resources described in this chapter, examining our thinking (also known as *critical thinking*) is undoubtedly one of the most important. This exercise will help you:

- Understand the link between how we cognitively interpret a stressor and the the amount and type of stress we actually experience (Lazarus, 1999).
- Review important text content your professor may include on exams.
- Practice applying numerous critical thinking components.

Part I. Fill in the letter from the list of key terms and concepts that best applies to each of the 10 stressful situations. (Tip: *Italicized* words reflect verbatim content from Chapter 3.)

Text Key Terms and Concepts
a. Approach-Avoidance Conflict
b. Avoidance-Avoidance Conflict
c. Binge Drinking
d. Burnout
e. Defense Mechanisms
f. External Locus of Control
g. Frustration
h. Posttraumatic Stress Disorder
i. Procrastination
j. Type A Personality

Stressful Situation

___1. Wendy is *forced to choose* between the *undesirable alternative* of studying boring subjects AND the *undesirable alternative* of poor grades.

___2. John, *fabricates excuses* for his failures, which helps protect *his ego from the anxiety and guilt* that might result from taking personal responsibility.

___3. Marci was fortunate to escape the terrorist attack on September 11, 2001. But ever since that *life-threatening day,* her functioning has been impaired by *flashbacks, nightmares,* and an overwhelming sense of *anxiety, helplessness, and emotional numbing.*

___4. Jason is a college freshman who is pledging a fraternity. During the "hazing": "They made me do as many beers as I could until I threw up. They had buckets nearby ready for it. I did about *10 jello shots* in an hour or so. They said this was a *normal part of the Greek life.* I just wanted to fit in, that's all I ever wanted."

___5. Rodney is a high-powered executive whose *intense ambition and competitiveness* seem to have paid off. However, his wife complains about his *exaggerated sense of time urgency* and his *persistent cynicism* and *hostility.*

___6. Juanita is trapped in a traffic jam on her way to an important exam. She feels *tension and anxiety* building because she is being *blocked from achieving her goal.*

___7. Jennifer's job is *emotionally demanding* and she feels *physically, emotionally,* and *mentally exhausted.*

___8. Derek has been *putting off* working on a paper assigned three months ago. With one week to go, he is experiencing *tremendous stress and has developed a lingering cold.*

___9. Selena believes that all of the bad things that happen to her are the result of *bad luck or fate,* and she feels *powerless to change* her situation.

__10. James is a high achieving college student, but he recently met a wonderful person and his grades are falling. He feels *forced to choose* between dating and high grades.

Part II. On a separate sheet of paper, choose FIVE of the situations above, and then identify ONE critical thinking component (CTC) from the Prologue of this text (pp. xxx–xxxiv) and describe how it could be used to help each individual "cope more effectively." Try to use a different CTC for each situation.

CHECK & REVIEW

Health and Stress Management

The two major forms of coping with stress are *emotion-focused* and *problem-focused*. **Emotion-focused coping** strategies change how we view stressful situations, and one of the most common forms is the use of **defense mechanisms**. **Problem-focused coping** deals directly with the situation or the factor causing the stress to decrease or eliminate it. The ability to cope with a stressor also depends on the resources available to a person, including health and exercise, positive beliefs, social skills, social support, material resources, control, and relaxation.

Questions

1. Imagine that you forgot your best friend's birthday. Now, identify the form of coping you would be using in each of the following reactions. (a) "I can't be expected to remember everyone's birthday"; (b) "I'd better put Cindy's birthday on my calendar so this won't happen again."
2. What is the payoff of defense mechanisms, and why should people avoid overusing them?
3. People with a(n) _____ locus of control are better able to cope with stress.
4. What are the seven major resources for healthy living and stress management? Which resource is most helpful for you? Least helpful?

Check your answers in Appendix B.

CLICK & REVIEW
for additional assessment options:
www.wiley.com/college/huffman

KEY TERMS

*To assess your understanding of the **Key Terms** in Chapter 3, write a definition for each (in your own words), and then compare your definitions with those in the text.*

Understanding Stress

approach–approach conflict (p. 102)
approach–avoidance conflict (p. 102)
avoidance–avoidance conflict (p. 102)
burnout (p. 101)
conflict (p. 102)
distress (p. 99)
eustress (p. 99)
frustration (p. 102)
general adaptation syndrome (GAS)
  (p. 105)
hassles (p. 101)
HPA axis (p. 104)

psychoneuroimmunology (p. 104)
stress (p. 98)

Stress and Illness
hardiness (p. 111)
posttraumatic stress disorder (PTSD)
  (p. 111)
Type A personality (p. 107)
Type B personality (p. 107)

Health Psychology in Action
binge drinking (p. 115)
chronic pain (p. 117)

health psychology (p. 112)

Health and Stress Management
defense mechanisms (p. 120)
emotion-focused forms of coping
  (p. 120)
external locus of control (p. 122)
internal locus of control (p. 122)
problem-focused forms of coping
  (p. 120)

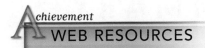

Achievement
WEB RESOURCES

Huffman Book Companion Site
http://www.wiley.com/college/huffman

This site is loaded with free Interactive Self-Tests, Internet Exercises, Glossary and Flashcards for key terms, web links, Handbook for Non-Native Speakers, and other activities designed to improve your mastery of the material in this chapter.

Stanford University health information library
http://healthlibrary.stanford.edu/

A general source of scientifically based medical information to help you make informed decisions about your health and health care.

Stress and its management
http://stress.about.com/?once=true&

An excellent site with useful information and tips for handling stress, such as time management, financial problems, and night eating.

Free health risk assessment
http://www.youfirst.com/

Contains a free personal health assessment useful for identifying your greatest risk factors and links to related information.

Focus on stress
http://helping.apa.org/work/index.html

Provides a series of interesting articles about stress.

Burnout test
http://www.prohealth.com/articles/burnout.htm

Offers a short self-test on job burnout.

Interested in a career in health psychology?
http://www.healthpsych.com/

This website was listed as an "APA Website of the Month" due to its practical and informative links and articles related specifically to a career in health psychology.

Visual Summary

◻ Understanding Stress

Sources of Stress

- *Life changes*: Holmes and Rahe Scale measures stress caused by important life events.
- *Chronic stressors*: Ongoing, long-term stress related to political world, family, work, etc.
- **Hassles**: Small, everyday problems that accumulate.
- **Occupation Burnout**: Exhaustion resulting from emotionally demanding situations.
- **Frustration**: Negative emotional state from blocked goals.
- **Conflict**: Negative emotional state from 2 or more incompatible goals.

There are 3 types of conflict

Approach-approach conflict:

Forced choice between two or more desirable alternatives

Avoidance-avoidance conflict:

Forced choice between two or more undesirable alternatives

Approach-avoidance conflict:

Forced choice between two or more alternatives with both desirable and undesirable outcomes

Effects of Stress

- *Sympathetic nervous system activation* increases heart rate, blood pressure, respiration, and muscle tension, and releases stress hormones.
- **HPA axis** increases the stress hormone cortisol, which decreases immune system functioning.
- *Suppressed immune system* leaves body vulnerable to disease.

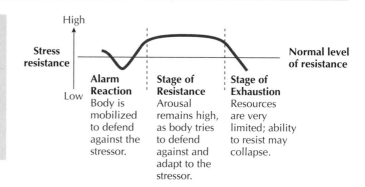

◇ Stress and Illness

Cancer

Caused by hereditary dispositions and environmental factors that lead to changes in body chemistry and the immune system.

Cardiovascular Disorders

Contributing factors:
- Behaviors such as smoking, obesity, lack of exercise
- Stress hormones
- **Type A personality**
- Lack of hardiness

Posttraumatic Stress Disorder (PTSD) and Gastric Ulcers

Exposure to extraordinary stress may lead to PTSD, and chronic stress may increase vulnerability to the *H. pylori* bacterium, which causes gastric ulcers.

Health Psychology in Action

Tobacco

- *Why do people smoke?* Peer pressure; imitation of role models; addiction (nicotine increases release of neurotransmitters that increase alertness, memory, and well-being, and decrease anxiety, tension, and pain); learned associations with positive results.
- *Prevention?* Educate about short- and long-term consequences, make smoking less socially acceptable, and help nonsmokers resist social pressures.
- *Stopping?* Use cognitive and behavioral techniques to deal with withdrawal; supplement with nicotine replacement therapy (patches, gum, and pills).

Alcohol

Alcohol is one of our most serious health problems.

Binge drinking: When a man consumes 5 or more drinks in a row, or a woman consumes 4 or more at least three times in a two-week period.

Chronic Pain

Chronic pain: Pain lasting over 6 months.

How to reduce?

- Increase activity and exercise.
- Use behavior modification strategies to reinforce changes.
- Employ *biofeedback* with *electromyograph (EMG)* to reduce muscle tension.
- Use relaxation techniques.

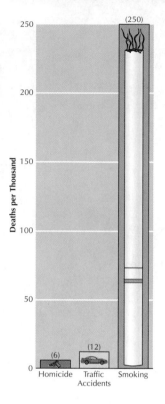

Health and Stress Management

Emotion-Focused Coping

Emotional and cognitive strategies that change how one appraises a stressful situation. **Defense mechanisms** are unconscious strategies that protect the ego and avoid anxiety by distorting reality.

Problem-Focused Coping

Strategies that deal directly with the stressful situation by applying problem-solving techniques to decrease or eliminate it.

Resources for Healthy Living

- Health and exercise
- Positive beliefs
- Social skills
- Social support
- Material resources
- Control (e.g., **internal locus of control**)
- Relaxation

4

SENSATION AND PERCEPTION

A*chievement*

Core Learning Outcomes

As you read Chapter 4, keep the following questions in mind and answer them in your own words:

▷ How do our sensory organs gather sensory information and convert it into signals our brain can understand?

▷ How do our eyes and ears enable us to see and hear?

▷ How do our other senses enable us to experience the world?

▷ How do we decide what to pay attention to in our environment?

▷ How do we organize stimuli to perceive form, constancy, depth, and color?

▷ What factors influence how we interpret sensations?

☐ *Achievement*
☐ *Assessment*
☐ *Application*

David Young-Wolff/Stone/Getty Images

Chapter 4 will explain how...

▷ People can experience excruciating pain in limbs that have been amputated.

▷ You can see a candle burning 30 miles away (on a clear, dark night), hear the tick of a watch at 20 feet (under quiet conditions), taste 1 teaspoon of sugar dissolved in 2 gallons of water, and smell one drop of perfume in a six-room apartment.

▷ You have a "blind spot" on the back of each eye that transmits no visual information to your brain.

▷ Loud music (or other loud noises) can lead to permanent hearing loss.

▷ Some people commonly experience *synesthesia,* which is a blending of sensory experiences. They "see" colors that feel warm or cold, "hear" sounds that are orange and purple, and "taste" foods that feel like different shapes.

Bettman/CORBIS

Through the sense of touch I know the faces of friends, the illimitable variety of straight and curved lines, all surfaces, the exuberance of the soil, the delicate shapes of flowers, the noble forms of trees, and the range of mighty winds. ... Footsteps, I discover, vary tactually according to the age, the sex, and the manners of the walker. ... I know by smell the kind of house we enter. I have recognized an old-fashioned country house because it has several layers of odors, left by a succession of families, of plants, perfumes, and draperies.

(KELLER, 1962, PP. 43–44, 46, 68–69)

Sensation *Process of receiving, converting, and transmitting raw sensory information from the external and internal environments to the brain*

Perception *Process of selecting, organizing, and interpreting sensory information*

Helen Keller, who wrote these words, was a renowned author and lecturer who lost both her vision and hearing at the age of 19 months. The story of Helen Keller is often used as an inspiring example of how people can overcome sensory deficiencies in one or two areas by fully developing their other senses. Her writing also provides a fascinating glimpse into an entirely different way of sensing and perceiving the world. Imagine being able to recognize your friends by a touch of their face or a house by the smell of its previous occupants. Most of us take sensation and perception for granted. But I think this chapter might help change that. For proof, stop and take time to savor the information in "Why Study Psychology?" Then try the activities in the "Try This Yourself" on the next page.

Now that I have you "hooked" on the potential interest of this chapter, let's get started with a few definitions and key concepts necessary for full appreciation of the material. This chapter focuses on two separate, but inseparable, topics—sensation and perception. Like chewing and swallowing food, these two processes are similar, yet somewhat different. Also like chewing and swallowing, the boundary between these two processes is not precise—there is considerable overlap.

Sensation is the process of receiving, converting, and transmitting raw sensory information from the external and internal environment to our brain. **Perception** refers to the selecting, organizing, and interpreting of this sensory information. As

Sensation or perception?

(a) When you stare at this drawing (known as the Necker cube), which area is the top, front, or back of the cube? (b) Now look at this drawing of a woman. Do you see a young woman looking back over her shoulder, or an older woman with her chin buried in the fur of her jacket?

In the process of *sensation*, your visual sensory system receives an assortment of light waves when looking at these two drawings. This sensory data is then converted and transmitted to your brain. In contrast, during *perception* your brain learns to *interpret* sensory information into lines and patterns that form a geometric shape called a cube. Interestingly, if you stare at either the cube or the woman long enough, your perception/interpretation will inevitably change. Although basic sensory input stays the same, your brain's attempt to interpret ambiguous stimuli creates a type of perceptual dance, shifting from one interpretation to another (Gaetz, Rzempoluck, & Jantzen, 1998).

(a)   (b)

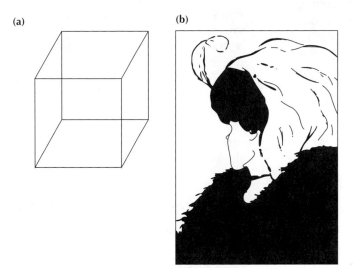

you can see in Figure 4.1, sensation occurs in your sense organs (eyes, ears, nose, skin, tongue), whereas perception takes place in your brain.

The first section, "Understanding Sensation, introduces the basic operations of sensation. "How We See and Hear" and "Our Other Senses" explore what are commonly known as the five basic senses—vision, hearing, taste, smell, and touch. These sections also examine other senses that provide the brain with data from inside the body: the *vestibular sense* (balance) and *kinesthesia* (bodily position and movement). "Understanding Perception" explores how we select, organize, and interpret the information from our senses. In that section, you will discover how we decide what to pay attention to, how we perceive distance, and how we see different colors. The chapter concludes with a "Research Highlight" that examines popular beliefs and scientific research on two controversial topics—subliminal perception and extrasensory perception (ESP).

Figure 4.1 *Sensation and perception.* Sensation involves the processing of raw data provided by our sensory receptors. But to make sense of these sensations, we also need perception.

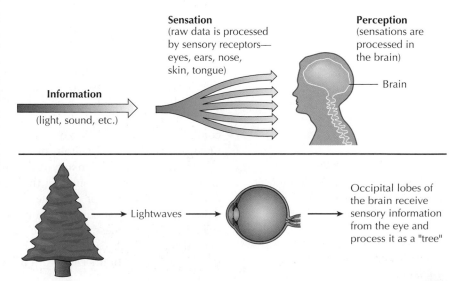

Sensation
(raw data is processed by sensory receptors—eyes, ears, nose, skin, tongue)

Perception
(sensations are processed in the brain)

Brain

Information
(light, sound, etc.)

Lightwaves

Occipital lobes of the brain receive sensory information from the eye and process it as a "tree"

www.wiley.com/college/huffman

UNDERSTANDING SENSATION

chievement

How do our sensory organs gather sensory information and convert it into signals the brain can understand?

When presented with a high-pitched tone, a famous musician reported, "It looks like fireworks tinged with a pink-red hue. The strip of color feels rough and unpleasant, and it has an ugly taste—rather like that of a briny pickle" (Luria, 1968). Do you understand what this person is saying? Probably not. This musician has a rare condition known as **synesthesia**, which literally means "mixing of the senses." People with synesthesia routinely blend their sensory experiences. They may "see" colors that feel warm or cold, "hear" sounds that are orange and purple, and "taste" foods that feel like different shapes.

To appreciate this musician's experience, we must first understand the basic processes of normal, *nonblended* sensations. For example, how do we turn light and sound waves from the environment into something our brain can comprehend? To do this, we first must have a way to receive the sensory signals from our external and internal environment. Then we need to convert the detected stimuli into a language the brain can understand. Let's take a closer look at how our sensory organs accomplish both tasks.

Synesthesia *A mixing of sensory experiences (e.g., "seeing" colors when a sound is heard)*

■ Processing: Getting the Outside Inside

Our eyes, ears, skin, and other sense organs all contain special cells called *receptors*, which receive and process sensory information from the environment. For each sense, these specialized cells respond to a distinct stimulus, such as light or sound waves or chemical molecules.

Through a process called **transduction**, the receptors convert the stimulus into neural impulses, which are then sent to the brain. In hearing, for example, tiny receptor cells in the inner ear convert mechanical vibrations (from sound waves) into electrochemical signals. These signals are then carried by neurons to specific areas of the brain for further processing. Interestingly, during the process of transduction we also have structures that purposefully reduce the amount of stimuli we receive.

Transduction *Converting a stimulus to a receptor into neural impulses*

Why would we want to reduce the sensory information? Can you imagine what would happen if you did not have some natural filtering of stimuli? You would constantly hear blood rushing through your veins and continually feel your clothes brushing against your skin. Some level of filtering is needed so that the brain is not overwhelmed with unnecessary information. It needs to be free to respond to those stimuli that have meaning for survival. Each of our senses is therefore custom designed to respond to only a select range of potential sensory information.

All species have evolved selective receptors that suppress or amplify information to allow survival. For example, hawks have an acute sense of vision but a poor sense of smell. Similarly, we humans cannot sense many stimuli, such as ultraviolet light, microwaves, the ultrasonic sound of a dog whistle, or infrared heat patterns from warm-blooded animals (which rattlesnakes can). However, we can see a candle burning 30 miles away on a dark, clear night; hear the tick of a watch at 20 feet under quiet conditions; smell one drop of perfume in a six-room apartment; and taste 1 teaspoon of sugar dissolved in 2 gallons of water.

Sensory Reduction *Filtering and analyzing incoming sensations before sending a neural message to the cortex.*

In the process of **sensory reduction**, we not only filter incoming sensations, we also analyze the sensations sent through before a neural impulse is finally sent to the cortex of the brain. For example, sudden loud noises will generally awaken sleeping animals (both human and nonhuman). This is because cells in the *reticular formation* (Chapter 2) send messages via the thalamus to alert the cortex. However, these reticular formation cells can learn to screen out certain messages, while allowing others to go on to higher brain centers. This explains why parents of a newborn can sleep through passing sirens and blaring stereos, yet still awaken to the slightest whimper of their baby.

How does the brain differentiate between sensations, such as sounds and smells? It depends on the number and type of sensory cells that are activated, on the precise nerve that is stimulated, and, ultimately, on the part of the brain that the nerve stimulates. Through a process known as **coding**, sounds and smells are interpreted as distinct sensations. This is not because of the environmental stimuli that activate them. It is because their respective neural impulses travel by different routes and arrive at different parts of the brain. Figure 4.2 illustrates the parts of the brain involved in sensory reception.

Figure 4.2 *Sensory areas of the brain.* Neural impulses travel from the sensory receptors to various parts of the brain.

Motor cortex
Movement of muscles
Sensory information from body
Plans for movement
Somatosensory cortex
Visual information
Auditory information
Temporal lobe pulled down to expose inner surface

Coding *Process that converts a particular sensory input into a specific sensation*

Thresholds: Testing Our Sensitivity

How do we know that humans can hear a watch ticking at 20 feet or smell one drop of perfume in a six-room apartment? The answer comes from **psychophysics**, an area of psychology that examines how physical stimuli (such as sound and smell) are related to an individual's psychological reactions to those stimuli. Using knowledge from both physics and psychology, psychophysicists study how the strength or intensity of a stimulus affects an observer.

Suppose you are the parent of a school-age daughter who has just suffered from a serious illness accompanied by high fever. During her period of recovery, you notice that she does not seem to hear as well as before her illness. You decide to take her to a hearing specialist.

During her test for hearing loss, the specialist uses a tone generator that produces sounds of differing pitches and intensities. Your daughter listens to the sounds over earphones and is asked to indicate the earliest point at which she can hear a tone. This is her **absolute threshold**, or the smallest amount of a stimulus (the tone) that she can detect (Table 4.1). To test your daughter's **difference threshold**, or *just noticeable difference* (JND), the examiner presents a small change in volume and asks her to respond when she notices a difference. By noting these absolute and difference thresholds and comparing them with thresholds of people with normal hearing, the specialist can determine whether your daughter has a hearing loss and, if so, the extent of the loss.

Psychophysics *Study of the relation between attributes of the physical world and our psychological experience of them*

Absolute Threshold *Smallest amount of a stimulus needed to detect that the stimulus is present*

Difference Threshold *Minimal difference needed to notice a stimulus change; also called the "just noticeable difference" (JND)*

TABLE 4.1 ABSOLUTE THRESHOLDS FOR VARIOUS SENSES

Sense	Stimulus	Absolute Threshold
Vision	Light energy	A candle flame seen from 30 miles away on a clear, dark night
Hearing	Sound waves	The tick of a watch at 20 feet
Taste	Chemical substances that contact the tongue	One teaspoon of sugar in two gallons of water
Smell	Chemical substances that enter the nose	One drop of perfume spread throughout a six-room apartment
Touch	Movement of, or pressure on, the skin	A bee's wing falling on your cheek from a height of about half an inch

ColorBlind Images/GettyImages

Controlling sensations *By adding a sleeping mask and special noise eliminating headphones, this traveler obtains welcome relief from unwanted sensations. The headphones work by creating opposing sound waves that cancel sounds from the environment.*

How does he do it? The fact that this man willingly endures such normally excruciating pain illustrates the complex mixture of psychological and biological factors in the experience of pain.

Sensory Adaptation *Repeated or constant stimulation decreases the number of sensory messages sent to the brain, which causes decreased sensation*

Gate-Control Theory of Pain *Theory that pain sensations are processed and altered by mechanisms within the spinal cord*

Sensory thresholds exist not only for hearing but also for vision, taste, smell, and the skin senses. Much of the research done in all areas of sensation originally began with the study of various thresholds.

Adaptation: Weakening Our Sensitivity

Your friends have invited you to come by to visit their wonderful new baby son. As they greet you at their front door, you are overwhelmed by the unpleasant odor of a nearby diaper pail. Even the baby smells bad! You wonder what's wrong. Why don't they do something about the smell? The answer is **sensory adaptation**. When a constant stimulus (like the smelly diapers or baby) is presented for a length of time, sensation often fades or disappears. Receptors higher up in the sensory system get "tired" and actually fire less frequently. (To test this for yourself, stop and place your pencil you're using for notetaking above your ear. Do you notice the change in the touch receptors on your skin? This increased sensitivity only lasts for a short while. Your receptors will soon "tire" of sending touch messages to your brain. They will only "notify" you when the pencil falls.)

Sensory adaptation makes sense from an evolutionary perspective. To survive, we can't afford to waste attention and time on unchanging, normally unimportant stimuli. "Turning down the volume" on repetitive information helps the brain cope with an overwhelming amount of sensory stimuli. Sensory adaptation also allows our brains time and space for paying attention to *change*. This decreased sensitivity helps your friends adapt to their smelly baby. And if you stay long enough, your senses also will adapt! Unfortunately, sensory adaptation can also be dangerous. People have died because they failed to respond to the faint smell of gas they first noticed when they walked into their house.

Some senses like smell and touch adapt quickly. Interestingly, we never completely adapt to visual stimuli because our eyes are constantly moving. They quiver just enough to guarantee a constantly changing sensory information. Otherwise, if we stared long enough at an object, it would vanish from sight! We also don't adapt to extremely intense stimuli, such as the heat of the desert sun or the pain of a cut hand. Again, from an evolutionary perspective, these limitations on sensory adaptation aid survival. They remind us to avoid intense heat and to do something about the damaged tissue on that cut hand.

If we don't adapt to pain, how do athletes keep playing despite painful injuries? In certain situations, the body releases natural painkillers called *endorphins* (see Chapter 2). Endorphins are neurotransmitters that act in the same way as morphine. They relieve pain by inhibiting pain perception. Pleasant stimuli, like the "runner's high," as well as unpleasant stimuli, such as injuries, can cause a release of endorphins. Pain relief through endorphins may also be the secret behind *acupuncture*, the ancient Chinese technique of gently twisting thin needles placed in the skin (Molsberger et al., 2002; Ternov et al., 2001).

In addition to endorphin release, one of the most accepted explanations of pain perception is the **gate-control theory**. First proposed by Ronald Melzack and Patrick Wall (1965), this theory suggests the experience of pain depends partly on whether the neural message gets past a "gatekeeper" in the spinal cord. This gatekeeper either blocks pain signals or allows them to pass on to the brain. Normally, the gate is kept shut by impulses coming down from the brain. It also can be kept closed by messages coming into the spinal cord from large-diameter fibers that conduct most sensory signals, such as touch and pressure. However, when body tissue is damaged, impulses from smaller pain fibers open the gate.

Have you noticed that rubbing your banged elbow helps relieve the pain? The gate-control theory helps explain why touch and pressure can reduce pain. The large fibers carry competing *pressure* messages that help block some of the pain. Messages from the brain itself can also control the pain gate. This explains how athletes and soldiers can carry on despite what should be excruciating pain. As mentioned in Chapter 3, we are capable of ignoring strong pain messages when we are distracted by competition or fear.

In contrast, when we get anxious or dwell on our pain by talking about it constantly, we can intensify it (Sansone, Levengood, & Sellbom, 2004; Sullivan, Tripp, & Santor, 1998). Ironically, well-meaning friends who ask chronic pain sufferers about their pain may unintentionally reinforce and increase it (Jolliffe & Nicholas, 2004).

Research also suggests that the pain gate may be chemically controlled. A neurotransmitter called *substance P* reportedly opens the pain gate and endorphins close it (Cesaro & Ollat, 1997; Liu, Mantyh, & Basbaum, 1997). Other research finds that the brain not only responds to incoming signals from sensory nerves but also is capable of *generating* pain (and other sensations) entirely on its own (Melzack, 1999; Vertosick, 2000). Have you heard of *tinnitus*, the ringing-in-the-ears sensation that sometimes accompanies hearing loss? In the absence of normal sensory input, nerve cells send conflicting messages ("static") to the brain, and in this case the brain interprets the static as "ringing." A similar process happens with the strange phenomenon of *phantom pain*, in which people continue to feel pain (and itching or tickling) long after a limb is amputated. The brain interprets the static as pain because it arises in the area of the spinal cord responsible for pain signaling. Interestingly, when amputees are fitted with prosthetic limbs and begin using them, phantom pain generally disappears (Gracely, Farrell, & Grant, 2002).

Each of the sensory principles we've discussed thus far—transduction, reduction, coding, thresholds, and adaptation—applies to all the senses. Yet the way in which each sense is processed is uniquely different, as we will see in the remainder of the chapter.

Assessment

CHECK & REVIEW

Understanding Sensation

Sensation refers to the process of receiving, converting, and transmitting information from the outside world. **Perception** is the process of selecting, organizing, and interpreting raw sensory data into useful mental representations of the world.

Sensory processing includes transduction, reduction, and coding. **Transduction** converts stimuli into neural impulses that are sent to the brain. We cope with the vast quantities of sensory stimuli through the process of **sensory reduction**. Each sensory system is also specialized to **code** its stimuli into unique sets of neural impulses that the brain interprets as light, sound, touch, and so on.

The **absolute threshold** is the smallest *magnitude* of a stimulus we can detect. The **difference threshold** is the smallest *change* in a stimulus that we can detect. The process of **sensory adaptation** decreases our sensitivity to constant, unchanging stimuli.

Questions

1. The key functions of sensation and perception are, respectively, _____. (a) stimulation and transduction; (b) transmission and coding; (c) reduction and transduction; (d) detection and interpretation; (e) interpretation and transmission

2. If a researcher were testing to determine the dimmest light a person could perceive, the researcher would be measuring the _____.

3. Why can't you smell your own perfume or aftershave after a few minutes?

4. The _____ theory of pain helps explain why it sometimes helps to rub or massage an injured thumb. (a) sensory adaptation; (b) gate-control; (c) just noticeable difference; (d) Lamaze

Check your answers in Appendix B.

CLICK & REVIEW
for additional assessment options:
www.wiley.com/college/huffman

HOW WE SEE AND HEAR

Achievement

How do our eyes and ears enable us to see and hear?

While on a long train trip, an aunt improvised a doll for 6-year-old Helen Keller out of a few towels. It had no nose, no mouth, no ears, and no eyes—nothing to indicate a face. Helen found this disturbing. Most disturbing to her, however, was the lack of eyes. It agitated her so much that she was not content until she found some beads and her aunt attached them for eyes. Uncomprehending as she was of the myriad sensations our eyes bring us, Helen still seemed to remember the importance of having eyes.

■ Vision: The Eyes Have It

Did you know major league batters can hit a 90-mile-per-hour fastball four-tenths of a second after it leaves the pitcher's hand? How can the human eye receive and process information that quickly? To fully appreciate the marvels of sight, we first need to examine the properties of light waves. We will then examine the structure and function of the eye and, finally, the way in which visual input is processed.

Waves of Light

Wavelength *Distance between the crests (or peaks) of light or sound waves; the shorter the wavelength, the higher the frequency*

Frequency *How often a light or sound wave cycles (i.e., the number of complete wavelengths that pass a point in a given time)*

Amplitude *Height of a light or sound wave—pertaining to light, it refers to brightness; for sound, it refers to loudness*

Vision (and also hearing) is based upon wave phenomena. To understand this, let's consider ocean waves. If you are standing on a pier, you see that waves have a certain distance between them (called the **wavelength**), and they pass by you at intervals. If you counted the number of passing waves in a set amount of time (e.g., 5 waves in 60 seconds), you could calculate what is called the **frequency**. In this case, it would be 5 waves divided by 60 seconds, or $\frac{1}{12}$ wave per second. Because waves near a pier typically move at about the same speed (not tsunami waves, which travel much faster), their frequency is inversely related to their wavelength. Larger wavelength means smaller frequency, and vice versa. Waves also have the characteristic of height (technically called **amplitude**) — some large (an exciting surf ride), and others small. Some waves have a very simple, uniform shape and would be considered good to ride with a surfboard. Others are made up of a combination of waves having different wavelengths and heights, and the result is a wave too irregular for surfing.

Vision is based on light waves, which have the same characteristics as ocean waves, although they are very much smaller and faster moving. Technically, light is waves of electromagnetic energy of a certain wavelength. As you can see in Figure 4.3, there are many different types of electromagnetic waves. Together they form what is known as the *electromagnetic spectrum*. Keep in mind that most wavelengths are invisible to the human eye. Only a small part of the spectrum, known as the *visible spectrum*, can be detected by our visual receptors.

Let's consider how the wave characteristics we discussed with regard to ocean waves apply to light waves and our seeing them. The *wavelength* determines the hue (color) we see. (We could also say the *frequency* determines the color, since they are inversely related. But by convention, we use wavelength when talking about light waves.) The *amplitude* (height) of the light waves determines the brightness of the light we see. And the complexity or mix of light waves determines whether we see a pure color or one which is a mix of different colors.

Eye Anatomy and Function

The eye is uniquely designed to capture light and focus it on receptors at the back of the eyeball. The receptors, in turn, convert light energy into neural signals to be interpreted by the brain. Several structures in the eye are involved in the process (Figure 4.4). Let's trace the path of light through these structures—the cornea, iris, pupil, lens, and retina.

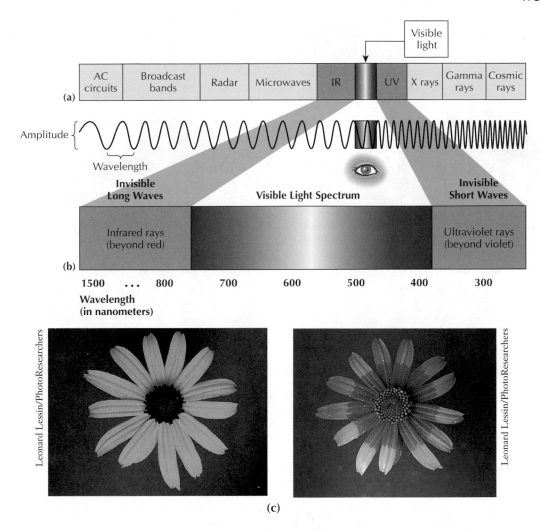

Figure 4.3 *The electromagnetic spectrum.* (a) The full spectrum of electromagnetic waves contains very long wavelength AC circuits and radio waves at one end, and relatively short cosmic ray waves at the other. (b) The visible light spectrum contains only the light waves we can see, in the middle of the electromagnetic spectrum. Note how the longest visible wavelengths are the light waves that we see as red, and the shortest are those we perceive as blue. In between are the rest of the colors. (c) The flower on the left looks normal to the human eye. The one on the right was photographed under ultraviolet light. Because insects like butterflies have ultraviolet receptors, this may be what it's like to see like a butterfly!

Cornea, Iris, Pupil, and Lens

Light first enters the eye through the *cornea*, a protective, transparent tissue that, because of its convex (outward) curvature, helps focus incoming light rays. Directly behind the cornea is the *iris*, which provides the color (usually brown or blue) of the eye. Muscles in the iris allow the *pupil* (or opening) to dilate or constrict in response to light intensity—or even to inner emotions. (Recall from Chapter 2 that our pupils dilate when we're in sympathetic arousal and constrict when we're in parasympathetic dominance.)

Behind the iris is the *lens*, which adds to the focusing begun by the cornea. Unlike the cornea, the lens is adjustable. Small muscles change its shape to allow us to focus on objects close to the eye or farther away. This focusing process is known

www.wiley.com/college/huffman

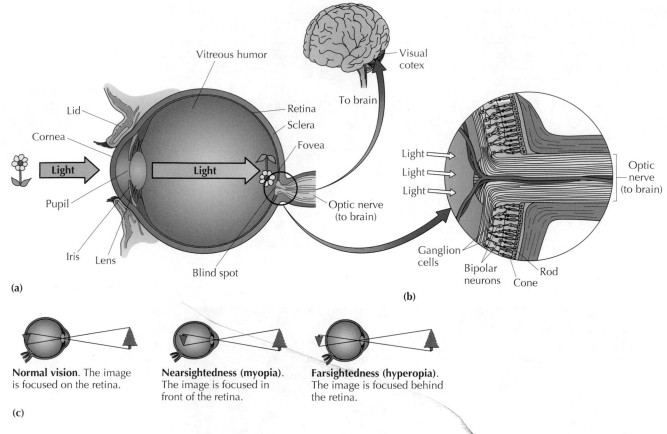

(a)

(b)

Normal vision. The image is focused on the retina.

Nearsightedness (myopia). The image is focused in front of the retina.

Farsightedness (hyperopia). The image is focused behind the retina.

(c)

Figure 4.4 *The path of light and anatomy of the eye.* (a) Note how light waves travel from the outside world, enter the eye at the cornea, and pass through the pupil and lens to the retina. In the retina, light waves are transduced (or changed) into neural impulses that move along the optic nerve to the brain. (b) The retina of the eye is a complicated structure with many different types of cells. The most important are the rods and cones, but light must first pass through the ganglion cells and bipolar neurons. (c) Note the slight changes in eyeball shape that help explain myopia and hyperopia.

Accommodation *Automatic adjustment of the eye, which occurs when muscles change the shape of the lens so that it focuses light on the retina from objects at different distances*

Nearsightedness (Myopia) *Visual acuity problem resulting from cornea and lens focusing an image in front of the retina*

Farsightedness (Hyperopia) *Visual acuity problem resulting from the cornea and lens focusing an image behind the retina.*

as **accommodation**. When you look at a faraway object, your lens accommodates by thinning and flattening to focus. When your glance shifts to a near object, such as this book you're reading, your lens accommodates by thickening and curving.

Small abnormalities in the eye sometimes interfere with accommodation, as you can see in Figure 4.4. If you have normal vision, your lens focuses the image of any object—near or far—on the retina at the back of your eye. If you are **nearsighted**, however, your eyeball is deeper than normal in relation to its lens or your cornea may be too sharply curved. The light rays are focused at a point in front of the retina and, at the retina, the image is blurred. The opposite occurs if you are **farsighted**. Your eyeball is shorter than normal and the light is focused on a point beyond the retina, leading to an inability to focus on objects at close range. Nearsightedness *(myopia)* and farsightedness *(hyperopia)* can occur at any age. However, at about age 40, most people find that they need reading glasses. This is because the lenses start to lose elasticity and the ability to accommodate for near vision *(presbyopia)*. Both nearsightedness and farsightedness are easily remedied with corrective lenses. Advances in laser surgery also make it possible to change the shape of the cornea to correct some visual acuity problems.

Retina

After light waves enter the eye through the cornea, they pass through the pupil and lens, and ultimately end up on the **retina**. This is an area at the back of the eye that contains blood vessels and a network of neurons that transmit neural information to the occipital lobes of the brain. The retina also contains special light-sensitive cells called **rods** and **cones**, so named for their distinctive shapes (see again Figure 4.4). There are about 6 million cones and 120 million rods tightly packed together at the back of the retina (Carlson, 2005).

The rods, besides being much more numerous, are also more sensitive to light than the cones. They enable us to see in dim light. This greater sensitivity, however, is achieved at the expense of fine detail and color vision, which are provided by the cones.

Cones function better in bright light and diminish in function as the light dims. They enable us not only to see things in fine detail but also to see in color. All cones are sensitive to many wavelengths. But each is maximally sensitive to one color—red, green, or blue. You may have noticed that it is impossible to see the color and fine detail of a flower in near-dark conditions, when only the rods are functioning.

Rods and cones also differ in their distribution in the eye. Cones are more numerous toward the center of the retina. In the center of the retina we have a **fovea**, a tiny pit filled with cones, responsible for our sharpest vision. Interestingly, near the fovea lies an area that has no visual receptors at all and absolutely no vision. This aptly named "blind spot" is where blood vessels and nerve pathways enter and exit the eyeball. Normally, we are unaware of our blind spot because our eyes are always moving. We fill in the information missing from the blind spot with information from adjacent areas on the retina or with images from the other eye.

When the brightness level suddenly changes, how do the rods "take over" from the cones, and vice versa? Think back to the last time you walked into a dark movie theater on a sunny afternoon and were momentarily blinded. This happens because in bright light the pigment inside the rods is bleached and they are temporarily nonfunctional. Going from a very light to a very dark setting requires a rapid shift from cones to rods. During the changeover, there is a second or two before the rods are functional enough for you to see. They continue to adjust for 20 to 30 minutes, until your maximum light sensitivity is reached. This process is known as *dark adaptation*. The visual adjustment that takes place when you leave the theater and go back into the sunlight—*light adaptation*—takes about 7 to 10 minutes and is the work of the cones. This adaptation process is particularly important to remember when driving your car from a brightly lit garage into a dark night. As we age, the adaptation takes longer.

Retina *Light-sensitive inner surface of the back of the eye, which contains the receptor cells for vision (rods and cones)*

Rods *Receptor cells in the retina that detect shades of gray and are responsible for peripheral vision and are most sensitive in dim light*

Cones *Receptor cells, concentrated near the center of the retina, responsible for color vision and fine detail; most sensitive in brightly lit conditions*

Fovea *A tiny pit in the center of the retina filled with cones and responsible for sharp vision*

TRY THIS YOURSELF

Application

Do you have a blind spot?

Everyone does. To find yours, hold this book about one foot in front of you, close your right eye, and stare at the X with your left eye. Very slowly, move the book closer to you. You should see the worm disappear and the apple become whole.

Hearing: A Sound Sensation

Helen Keller said she "found deafness to be a much greater handicap than blindness.... Blindness cuts people off from things. Deafness cuts people off from people." What is it about hearing that makes it so important? In discussing vision, we talked first about waves of light, then about the anatomy of the eye, and, finally, about problems with vision. We will follow the same pattern with **audition**, the sense of hearing.

Audition *Sense of hearing*

Cochlea[KOK-lee-uh] *Three-chambered, snail-shaped structure in the inner ear containing the receptors for hearing*

Waves of Sound

Have you heard the philosophical question, "If a tree falls in the forest, and there is no one to hear it, does it make a sound?" The answer depends on whether you define *sound* as a sensation (which requires a receptor such as a person's ear) or as a physical stimulus. As a physical phenomenon, sound is based upon pressure waves in air. These pressure variations can result from an impact, such as a tree hitting the ground, or from a vibrating object, like a guitar string. Sound waves (like light waves) have the characteristics of *wavelength* (or frequency), *amplitude* (height), and *complexity* (mix).

When talking about sound waves, we generally use the term frequency rather than wavelength. The *frequency* of the sound wave determines the *pitch* of the sound we hear. High frequency waves produce high notes, and low frequency waves produce the bass tones. The *amplitude* determines the *loudness* of the sound we hear. And the *complexity* determines what is called *timbre*. A sound could be a pure tone of a single frequency (we seldom hear pure tones, except during a hearing test). Sound can also be a complex mix of frequencies and amplitudes. In this latter case, the timbre is what allows us to distinguish whether a C note is played on a piano or on a trumpet. Timbre is also what allows us to distinguish all the many human voices we hear.

Ear Anatomy and Function

The ear has three major sections. The *outer ear* gathers and delivers sound waves to the *middle ear*, which amplifies and concentrates the sounds. The *inner ear* contains the receptor cells that ultimately transduce the mechanical energy created by sounds into neural impulses. As we trace the path of sound waves through the ear, it will help to refer to Figure 4.6.

Sound waves are gathered and funneled into the outer ear by the *pinna*, the external, visible part of the ear that we automatically envision when we think of an ear. The pinna channels the sound waves into the *auditory canal*, a tubelike structure that focuses the sound. At the end of the auditory canal is a thin, tautly stretched membrane known as the *eardrum*, or *tympanic membrane*. As sound waves hit the eardrum, it vibrates. The vibrating eardrum causes the three tiniest bones in the human body, the *malleus* (hammer), the *incus* (anvil), and the *stapes* (stirrup), to vibrate. (Together, these three bones are referred to as the *ossicles*.) The stapes bone presses on a membrane, the *oval window*, causing it to vibrate.

This vibration of the oval window then creates waves in the fluid that fills the **cochlea**. The cochlea is a snail-shaped

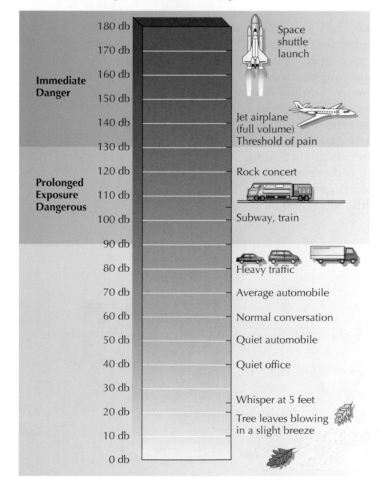

Figure 4.5 *Loudness.* The loudness of a sound is measured in decibels. One decibel is the faintest sound a normal person can hear. This figure lists some familiar sounds and their decibel levels. Normal conversation is about 60 decibels. Constant noise above about 90 decibels can cause permanent nerve damage to the ear.

Immediate Danger

180 db
170 db
160 db
150 db
140 db — Jet airplane (full volume)
130 db — Threshold of pain

Space shuttle launch

Prolonged Exposure Dangerous

120 db — Rock concert
110 db
100 db — Subway, train
90 db
80 db — Heavy traffic
70 db — Average automobile
60 db — Normal conversation
50 db — Quiet automobile
40 db — Quiet office
30 db
20 db — Whisper at 5 feet
10 db — Tree leaves blowing in a slight breeze
0 db

structure that contains the *basilar membrane* with receptors for hearing. The hearing receptors are known as *hair cells*, and they do, in fact, resemble hairs. As the waves travel through the cochlear fluid, the hair cells bend from side to side. It is at this point that the mechanical energy of the wave is transduced into electrochemical impulses that are carried by the *auditory nerve* to the brain.

We hear different *pitch* (low to high) and *loudness* (soft to loud) by a combination of mechanisms, depending on the frequency and intensity of the sound. According to **place theory**, we hear high-pitched sounds corresponding to the *place* along the *basilar membrane* that is most stimulated. When we hear a particular high-pitched sound, it causes the eardrum, the ossicles, and the oval window to vibrate. This vibration produces a "traveling wave" through the fluid in the cochlea. This wave causes some bending of hair cells all along the basilar membrane. But there is a single point where the hair cells are maximally bent for each distinct pitch.

How do we hear lower-pitched sounds? According to **frequency theory**, low-pitched sound causes hair cells along the basilar membrane to bend and fire neural messages (action potentials) at the same rate as the frequency of that sound. For example, a sound with a frequency of 90 hertz would produce 90 action potentials per second in the auditory nerve.

Why are some sounds louder than others? It depends on the *intensity* of the sound waves. Waves with high peaks and low valleys produce loud sounds. Those that are relatively small produce soft sounds.

Is it true that loud music can damage your hearing? Yes. There are basically two types of deafness. **Conduction deafness**, or middle-ear deafness, results from problems with the mechanical system that conducts sound waves to the inner ear. **Nerve deafness**, or inner-ear deafness, involves damage to the cochlea, hair cells, or auditory nerve. Disease and biological changes associated with aging can cause nerve deafness. But the most common (and preventable) cause of nerve deafness is continuous exposure to loud noise, which can damage hair cells and lead to permanent hearing loss. Even brief exposure to really loud sounds, like a stereo or headphones at full blast, a jackhammer, or a jet airplane engine, can cause nerve deafness.

Because damage to the nerve or receptor cells is almost always irreversible, the only current treatment for nerve deafness is a small electronic device called a *cochlear implant*. If the auditory nerve is intact, the implant bypasses hair cells and directly stimulates the nerve. At present, a cochlear implant produces only a crude approximation of hearing, but the technology is improving. The best bet is to protect your sense of hearing. That means avoiding exceptionally loud noises (rock concerts, jackhammers, stereo headphones at full blast), wearing earplugs when

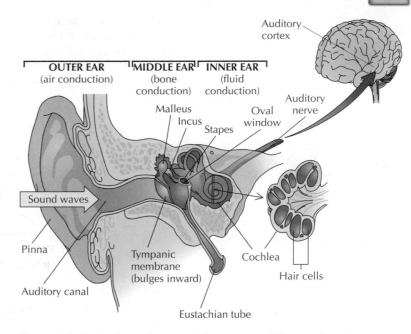

Figure 4.6 ***Path of sound waves and anatomy of the ear.*** Sound waves enter the outer ear, are amplified and concentrated in the middle ear, transduced in the inner ear, and then carried through the auditory nerve to the brain.

Place Theory *Explains how we hear higher-pitched sounds; different high-pitched sounds bend the basilar membrane hair cells at different locations in the cochlea*

Frequency Theory *Explains how we hear lower-pitched sounds; hair cells in the basilar membrane bend and fire neural messages (action potentials) at the same rate as the sound frequency*

Conduction Deafness *Middle-ear deafness resulting from problems with transferring sound waves to the inner ear.*

Nerve Deafness *Inner-ear deafness resulting from damage to the cochlea, hair cells, or auditory nerve*

©AP/Wide World Photos

Loud noise and nerve deafness. *Members of the music group Green Day (and their audience) are potential victims of noise-induced nerve deafness that is irreversible.*

www.wiley.com/college/huffman

such situations cannot be avoided, and paying attention to bodily warnings. These warnings include a change in your normal hearing threshold and *tinnitus*, a whistling or ringing sensation in your ears. These are often the first signs of hearing loss. Although normal hearing generally returns after exposure to a loud concert, keep in mind that permanent damage will accumulate with repeated exposure.

Assessment

CHECK & REVIEW

How We See and Hear

Light is a form of energy that is part of the electromagnetic spectrum. The **wavelength** of a light determines its hue, or color. The **amplitude,** or the height, of a light wave, determines its intensity or brightness. And the range of a light wave determines its complexity or saturation. The function of the eye is to capture light and focus it on visual receptors in the retina that convert light energy to neural impulses. Cells in the **retina** called **rods** are specialized for night vision, whereas **cones** are specialized for color and fine detail.

The sense of hearing is known as **audition.** We hear sound via sound waves, which result from rapid changes in air pressure caused by vibrating objects. The wavelength of these sound waves is sensed as the pitch of the sound. The amplitude of the waves is perceived as loudness. And the range of sound waves is sensed as timbre, the purity or complexity of the tone. The outer ear conducts sound waves to the middle ear, which in turn conducts vibrations to the inner ear. Hair cells in the inner ear are bent by a traveling wave in the fluid of the **cochlea** and transduced into neural impulses. The neural message is then carried along the auditory nerve to the brain.

Questions

1. Trace the path of light information as it enters the eye and leaves to go to the brain.
2. The lens of the eye focuses by _____ and _____. The focusing process is known as _____.
3. Trace the path of sound information as it enters the ear and leaves to go to the brain.
4. Explain how place theory differs from frequency theory.

Check your answers in Appendix B.

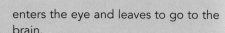

CLICK & REVIEW
for additional assessment options:
www.wiley.com/college/huffman

OUR OTHER SENSES

Vision and audition may be the most prominent of our senses, but taste, smell, and the body senses are also important for gathering information about our environment. The enjoyment of a summer's day comes not only from the visual and auditory beauty of the world but also from the taste of a fresh garden tomato, the smell of honeysuckle, and the feel of a warm gentle breeze.

Achievement

How do our other senses enable us to experience the world?

■ Smell and Taste: Sensing Chemicals

Smell and taste are sometimes referred to as the *chemical senses* because they involve *chemoreceptors*, which are sensitive to certain chemical molecules rather than to electromagnetic or mechanical vibrations. Have you noticed how food seems bland when your nose is blocked by a cold and you cannot smell your food? Smell and taste receptors are located near each other and often interact so closely that we have difficulty separating the sensations.

Olfaction

Our sense of smell, or **olfaction,** is remarkably useful and sensitive. We can detect over 10,000 distinct smells (floral, musky, rotten, and so on). And we can smell smoke

Olfaction *Sense of smell*

long before the most sensitive household detector is activated. Interestingly, those who are blind can learn to recognize others by their unique odors, and sighted people can do the same with extensive practice.

Our sense of smell results from stimulation of receptor cells in the nose (Figure 4.7). These receptors are embedded in a mucus-coated membrane called the *olfactory epithelium*. The olfactory receptors are actually modified neurons, with branched dendrites extending out into the epithelium. When chemical molecules in the air passing through the nose come in contact with the dendrites, they initiate a neural impulse. The impulse travels along the neuron's axon directly to the *olfactory bulb*, a brain structure just below the frontal lobes. Most olfactory information is processed in this area before being sent to other parts of the brain.

Figuring out how we distinguish different odors is complicated. Did you know we have over 1000 types of receptors that allow us to detect 10,000 distinct smells? According to the most popular current theory, each odorous chemical excites a specific portion of the olfactory bulb. Each odor is then coded and detected according to the stimulated area (Dalton, 2002).

Does smell affect sexual attraction? **Pheromones,** chemical, airborne odors, have been found in a number of nonhuman animal species. They are used to mark trails to food, define territory, and increase sexual arousal and mating behaviors. Although some research supports the idea that pheromones increase sexual behaviors in humans (Jacob, McClintock, Zelano, & Ober, 2002; Pierce, Cohen, & Ulrich, 2004; Thornhill et al., 2003), other findings question the results (Hays, 2003).

Gustation

In modern times, **gustation** (the sense of taste) may be the least critical of our senses. In the past, however, it played a vital role in our survival. The major function of taste is to provide information about substances that are entering our digestive tract so that we can screen out those that may be harmful. This function is aided by other senses, such as smell, temperature, and touch. Humans have five major taste sensations— sweet, sour, salty, bitter, and *umami*. You are undoubtedly familiar with the first four. But *umami* (which means "delicious" or "savory") has only recently been added to the list (Damak et al., 2003; Nelson et al., 2002). Umami is a separate taste and type of taste receptor that is sensitive to *glutamate* (the taste of protein). And glutamate is found in meats, meat broths, and monosodium glutamate (MSG). It is a major contributor to the taste of many natural foods, such as meats, fish, and cheese.

Like smell receptors, taste receptors respond differentially to the varying shapes of food and liquid molecules. The major taste receptors (or *taste buds*) are clustered on our tongues within little bumps called *papillae* (Figure 4.8). A small number of taste receptors are also found in the palate and the back of our mouths. Thus, even people without a tongue experience some taste sensations.

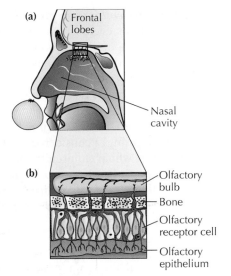
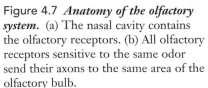

Figure 4.7 ***Anatomy of the olfactory system.*** (a) The nasal cavity contains the olfactory receptors. (b) All olfactory receptors sensitive to the same odor send their axons to the same area of the olfactory bulb.

Pheromones [FARE-oh-mones] *Airborne chemicals that affect behavior, including recognition of family members, aggression, territorial marking, and sexual mating*

Gustation *Sense of taste*

Surface of the tongue (magnified about 50 times)

Omikron/PhotoResearchers

Cross-section of a papilla

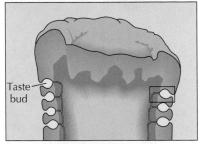

A taste bud

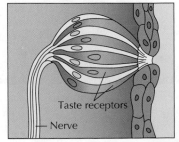

Figure 4.8 ***Taste sensation.*** When liquids enter the mouth or food is chewed and dissolved, the fluid runs over the papillae (the lavender circular areas) and into the pores to the taste buds, which contain the receptors for taste. (The cells shown in blue are support cells.)

Why are children so picky about food? In young people, taste buds die and are replaced about every seven days. As we age, however, the buds are replaced more slowly, so taste diminishes. Thus, children, who have abundant taste buds, often dislike foods with strong or unusual tastes (such as liver and spinach). But as they grow older and lose taste buds, they often come to like these foods.

Some pickiness is also related to learning. Many food and taste preferences result from childhood experiences and cultural influences. Many Japanese children eat raw fish and some Chinese children eat chicken feet as part of their normal diet. American children might consider these foods "yucky." However, most American children love cheese, which children in many other cultures find equally repulsive.

Pickiness also relates to the fact that the sense of taste normally enables human and nonhuman animals to discriminate between foods that are safe to eat and foods that are poisonous. Because many plants that taste bitter contain toxic chemicals, an animal is more likely to survive if it avoids bitter-tasting plants (Cooper et al., 2002; Guinard et al., 1996). On the other hand, human and nonhuman animals have a preference for sweet foods, which are generally nonpoisonous and good sources of energy. Unfortunately, this evolutionary preference for sweet foods now contributes to obesity problems in affluent countries where such high-calorie foods are easily available.

▨ The Body Senses: More Than Just Touch

Imagine for a moment that you are an Olympic downhill skier, anxiously awaiting the starting signal that will begin your once-in-a-lifetime race for the gold medal. What senses will you need to manage the subtle and ever-changing balance adjustments required for Olympic-level skiing? How will you make your skis carve the cleanest, shortest, fastest line from start to finish? What will enable your arms, legs, and trunk to work in perfect harmony so that you can record the shortest time and win the gold? The senses that will allow you to do all this, and much more, are the *body senses*. They tell the brain how the body is oriented, where and how the body is moving, the things it touches or is touched by, and so on. These senses include the *skin senses*, the *vestibular sense*, and *kinesthesia*.

The Skin Senses

The skin senses are vital. Skin not only protects the internal organs but also provides the brain with basic survival information. With nerve endings in the various layers of skin, our skin senses tell us when a pot is dangerously hot, when the weather is freezing cold, and when we have been hurt. Researchers have "mapped" the skin by applying probes to all areas of the body. Mapping shows there are three basic skin sensations: touch (or pressure), temperature, and pain. Receptors for these sensations occur in various concentrations and depths in the skin. For example, touch (pressure) receptors are maximally concentrated on the face and fingers and minimally in the back and legs. As your hands move over objects, pressure receptors register the indentations created in the skin, allowing perception of texture. For people who are blind, this is the principle underlying their ability to learn to read the raised dots that constitute Braille.

The relationship between the types of sensory receptors and the different sensations is not clear. It used to be thought that each receptor responded to only one type of stimulation. But we now know that some receptors respond to more than one. For example, because sound waves are a type of air pressure, our skin's pressure receptors also respond to certain sounds. And itching, tickling, and vibrating sensations seem to be produced by light stimulation of both pressure and pain receptors.

In conducting studies on temperature receptors, researchers have found that the average square centimeter of skin contains about six cold spots where only cold can be sensed, and one or two warm spots where only warmth can be felt. Interestingly, we don't seem to have separate "hot" receptors. Instead, our cold receptors detect not

Bob Krist/Corbis

The power of the skin senses. *Babies are highly responsive to touch, partly because of the density of their skin receptors.*

only coolness but also extreme temperatures—both hot and cold (Craig & Bushnell, 1994). See Figure 4.9.

The Vestibular Sense

The *vestibular sense* is the sense of body orientation and position with respect to gravity and three-dimensional space. In other words, it is the sense of balance. Even the most routine activities—riding a bike, walking, or even sitting up—would be impossible without this sense (Lackner & Di Zio, 2005). The vestibular apparatus is located in the inner ear and is composed of the vestibular sacs and the semicircular canals. The *semicircular canals* provide the brain with balance information, particularly information about rotation of the head. As the head moves, liquid in the canals moves and bends hair cell receptors. At the end of the semicircular canals are the *vestibular sacs*, which contain hair cells sensitive to the specific angle of the head—straight up and down or tilted. Information from the semicircular canals and the vestibular sacs is converted to neural impulses, which are then carried to the appropriate section of the brain.

What causes motion sickness? Information from the vestibular sense is used by the eye muscles to maintain visual fixation and, sometimes, by the body to change body orientation. If the vestibular sense gets overloaded or becomes confused by boat, airplane, or automobile motion, the result is often dizziness and nausea. Random versus expected movements also are more likely to produce motion sickness. Thus, automobile drivers are better prepared than passengers for upcoming movement and are less likely to feel sick (Rolnick & Lubow, 1991). Motion sickness also seems to vary with age. Infants are generally immune, children between ages 2 and 12 years have the highest susceptibility, and the incidence declines in adulthood.

Kinesthesia

Kinesthesia (from the Greek word for "motion") is the sense that provides the brain with information about bodily posture and orientation, as well as bodily movement. Unlike the receptors for sight, hearing, smell, taste, and balance, which are clumped together in one organ or area, kinesthetic receptors are found throughout the muscles, joints, and tendons of the body. As we sit, walk, bend, lift, turn, and so on, our kinesthetic receptors respond by sending messages to the brain. They tell which muscles are being contracted and which relaxed, how our body weight is distributed, and where our arms and legs are in relation to the rest of our body. Without these sensations, we would literally have to watch every step or movement we make.

We rely on kinesthesis constantly. But we seldom acknowledge it because this sense is rarely disturbed in our everyday lives. In one study, an experimenter intentionally disturbed participants' wrist tendon receptors by producing certain vibrations. Interestingly, participants reported sensations of having multiple forearms and impossible positions of their arms (Craske, 1977). However, we don't have to go through experimental procedures to appreciate our kinesthetic sense. All we have to do is observe children learning new skills or remember when we were first learning to ride a bike or catch a football. During the initial learning process, we appreciate our kinesthetic sense as we deliberately and consciously move

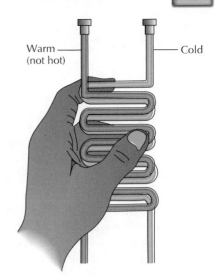

Warm (not hot) — Cold

Figure 4.9 ***How do we experience "hot"?*** Researchers use an instrument called a "heat grill"—two pipes twisted together, one containing warm water and the other cold. If you grasp both pipes, you experience intense heat because both warm and cold receptors are activated simultaneously. We do not have separate "hot" receptors.

Kinesthesia *Sensory system for body posture and orientation*

Bob Barbour/Stone/GettyImages

How does he do it? This surfer's finely tuned vestibular and kinesthetic senses allow him to ride his board in perfect balance, constantly compensating for the changing shape of the wave.

www.wiley.com/college/huffman

certain body parts and muscles. Once the skill is well learned, we are no longer conscious of these movements. Our kinesthetic sense is now on "automatic pilot."

CHECK & REVIEW

Our Other Senses

The sense of smell (**olfaction**) and the sense of taste (**gustation**) are called the chemical senses and are closely interrelated. The receptors for olfaction are at the top of the nasal cavity. The receptors for gustation are located primarily on the tongue and are sensitive to five basic tastes: salty, sweet, sour, bitter, and umami.

The body senses include the skin senses, the vestibular sense, and **kinesthesia.** The skin senses detect pressure, temperature, and pain. They protect the internal organs and provide basic survival information. The vestibular apparatus is located in the inner ear and provides balance information. The kinesthetic sense provides the brain with information about body posture and orientation, as well as body movement. The kinesthetic receptors are spread throughout the body in muscles, joints, and tendons.

Questions

1. Human and nonhuman animals may be affected by chemical scents found in natural body odors, which are called _____.

2. The weightlessness experienced by space travelers from zero gravity has its greatest effect on the _____

senses. (a) visceral; (b) reticular; (c) somasthetic; (d) vestibular

3. Receptors located in the muscles, joints, and tendons of the body provide _____ information to maintain bodily posture, orientation, and movement.

4. The skin senses include _____. (a) pressure; (b) pain; (c) warmth and cold; (d) all of these

Check your answers in Appendix B.

 CLICK & REVIEW
for additional assessment options:
www.wiley.com/college/huffman

UNDERSTANDING PERCEPTION

At this point, we are ready to move from sensation and the major senses to perception. Keep in mind, however, that the boundary between the two is ambiguous. Look, for example, at Figure 4.10a. What do you see? Most people see splotches of light and dark, but they perceive no real pattern. If you stare long enough, your brain will try to organize the picture into recognizable shapes or objects, as it does when you lie on your back outdoors and gaze at the clouds on a summer's day. Have you seen the image in the photo yet? If not, turn the page and look at Figure 4.10b. Before you *perceived* the cow, you *sensed* only light and dark splotches. Only when you could select relevant splotches and organize them into a meaningful pattern were you able to interpret them as the face of a cow.

Normally, our perceptions agree with our sensations, but there are times when they do not. This results in an **illusion**. Illusions are false or misleading perceptions that can be produced by actual physical distortions, as in desert mirages, or by errors in the perceptual process, as in the illusions shown in Fig-

Illusion *False or misleading perceptions*

 Study Tip

Be careful not to confuse illusion with hallucination or delusion [Chapters 5 and 14]. Hallucinations are imaginary sensory perceptions that occur without an external stimulus, such as hearing voices during a schizophrenic episode or seeing "pulsating flowers" after using LSD [lysergic acid diethylamide] and other hallucinogenic drugs. Delusions refer to false beliefs, often of persecution or grandeur, which also may accompany drug or psychotic experiences. (a)

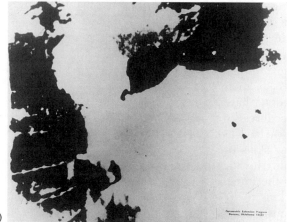

Courtesy Optometric Extension Program
Foundation, Santa Ana, CA

Figure 4.10a *What is it?*

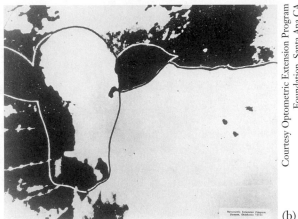

Courtesy Optometric Extension Program Foundation, Santa Ana, CA

(b)

Figure 4.10b *It's a cow!* Now go back to Figure 4.10a and you will easily perceive a cow.

ures 4.11 and 4.12. Besides being amusing, illusions provide psychologists with a tool for studying the normal process of perception (e.g., Nicholls, Searle, & Bradshaw, 2004; Vroomen & de Gelder, 2004).

Selection: Extracting Important Messages

The first step in perception is *selection*—choosing where to direct our attention. Three major factors are involved in the act of paying attention to some stimuli in our environment and not to others: *selective attention*, *feature detectors*, and *habituation*.

Selective Attention

In almost every situation, there is an excess of sensory information, but the brain manages to sort out the important messages and discard the rest (Folk & Remington, 1998; Kramer, Hahn, Irwin, & Theeuwes, 2000). As you sit reading this chapter, you may be ignoring sounds from another room or the discomfort of the chair you're sitting on. When you are in a group of people, surrounded by various conversations, you can still select and attend to the voices of people you find interesting. This process is known as **selective attention**.

Feature Detectors

The second major factor in selection is the presence of specialized neurons in the brain called **feature detectors** (or *feature analyzers*) that respond only to certain sensory information. In 1959, researchers discovered specialized neurons in the optic nerve of a frog. They called these receptors "bug detectors" because they respond only to moving bugs (Lettvin, Maturana, McCulloch, & Pitts, 1959). Later researchers found feature detectors in cats that respond to specific lines and angles (Hubel & Wiesel, 1965, 1979).

Similar studies with humans have found feature detectors in the temporal and occipital lobes that respond maximally to faces. Damage to these areas can produce a condition called *prosopagnosia* (*prospon* means "face" and *agnosia* means "failure to

Achievement

How do we decide what to pay attention to in our environment?

Selective Attention *Filtering out and attending only to important sensory messages*

Feature Detectors *Specialized neurons that respond only to certain sensory information*

Figure 4.11 *The horizontal-vertical illusion.* Which is longer, the horizontal (flat) or the vertical (standing) line? People living in areas where they regularly see long straight lines, such as roads and train tracks, perceive the horizontal line as shorter because of their environmental experiences.

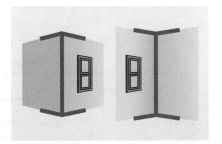

Figure 4.12 *The Müller–Lyer illusion.* Which vertical line is longer? Both are actually the same length, but people who live in urban environments normally see the vertical line on the right as longer than the line on the left. This is because they have learned to make size and distance judgments from perspective cues created by right angles and horizontal and vertical lines of buildings and streets. They perceive the right figure as a distant corner and thus compensate for its distance by judging it as longer.

know") (Barton, Press, Keenan, & O'Connor, 2002; Galaburda & Duchaine, 2003). Interestingly, people with prosopagnosia can recognize that they are looking at a face. But they cannot say whose face is reflected in a mirror, even if it is their own or that of a friend or relative.

Certain basic mechanisms for perceptual selection are thus built into the brain. However, a certain amount of interaction with the environment is apparently necessary for feature detector cells to develop normally (Crair, Gillespie, & Stryker, 1998). One well-known study demonstrated that kittens raised in a cylinder with only vertically or horizontally striped walls develop severe behavioral and neurological impairments (Blakemore & Cooper, 1970) (Figure 4.13). When "horizontal cats"—those raised with only horizontal lines in their environment—were removed from the cylinder and allowed to roam, they could easily jump onto horizontal surfaces. But they had great difficulty negotiating objects with vertical lines, such as chair legs. The reverse was true for the "vertical cats." They could easily avoid table and chair legs but never attempted to jump onto horizontal structures. Examination of the visual cortex of these cats showed they had failed to develop their potential feature detectors for either vertical or horizontal lines.

Habituation

Habituation *Tendency of the brain to ignore environmental factors that remain constant*

Another physiological factor important in selecting only certain sensory data is **habituation**. The brain seems "prewired" to pay more attention to changes in the environment than to stimuli that remain constant. We quickly *habituate* (or respond less) to predictable and unchanging stimuli. For example, when you buy a new CD, you initially listen carefully to all the songs. Over time, your attention declines and you can play the entire CD and not really notice it. This may not matter with CDs—we can always replace them when we become bored. But this same habituation phenomenon also applies to your friends and love life. And people aren't as easily replaced. Have you noticed how attention and compliments from a stranger are almost always more exciting and "valuable" than those from long-time friends and lovers? Unfortunately, some people misinterpret and overvalue this new attention. Some may even leave good relationships, not realizing that they will soon *habituate* to the new person. (Understanding the dangers of habituation is another payoff for studying psychology!)

VISUAL QUIZ

Courtesy Colin Blake more from Schmitt & Worden, "The Neurosciences Third Study Program," MIT Press

Figure 4.13 *Nature versus nurture.* Researchers found that kittens reared in a vertical world fail to develop their innate ability to detect horizontal lines or objects. On the other hand, kittens restricted to only horizontal lines cannot detect vertical lines. Can you explain why?

Answer: Without appropriate stimulation, brain cells sensitive to vertical or horizontal lines deteriorate during a critical (and irreversible) period in visual development.

How does habituation differ from sensory adaptation? Habituation is a perceptual process that occurs in the brain. Sensory adaptation occurs when sensory receptors (in the skin, eyes, ears, and so on) actually decrease the number of sensory messages they send to the brain. Sensory adaptation occurs when you first put on your shoes in the morning. Pressure/touch receptors in your feet initially send multiple messages to your brain. But with time they *adapt* and send fewer messages. You also habituate and your brain "chooses to ignore" the fact that you're wearing shoes. You only notice when something changes—when you break a buckle or shoelace, or get a blister from new shoes.

When given a wide variety of stimuli to choose from, we automatically select stimuli that are *intense, novel, moving, contrasting,* and *repetitious.* Parents and teachers often use these same attention-getting principles. But advertisers and politicians have spent millions of dollars developing them into a fine art. The next time you're watching TV, notice the commercial and political ads. Are they louder or brighter than the regular program (intensity)? Do they use talking cows to promote California cheese or computers (novelty)? Is the promoted product or candidate set in *favorable* contrast to the competition? No need to ask about repetition. This is the foundation of all commercial and political ads. Surprisingly, obnoxious advertising does not always deter people from buying the advertised product (or candidate). For sheer volume of sales, the question of whether you like the ad is irrelevant. If it gets your attention, that's all that matters.

ssessment

CHECK & REVIEW

Selection

The selection process allows us to choose which of the billions of separate sensory messages will eventually be processed. **Selective attention** allows us to direct our attention to the most important aspect of the environment at any one time. **Feature detectors** are specialized cells in the brain that distinguish between different sensory inputs. The selection process is very sensitive to changes in the environment. We **habituate** to unchanging stimuli and pay attention when stimuli change in intensity, novelty, location, and so on.

Questions

1. Explain how illusions differ from delusions and hallucinations.
2. Specialized cells in the brain called _____ respond only to certain types of sensory information.
3. Explain why "horizontal cats" can jump only onto horizontal surfaces.
4. You write a reminder of an appointment on a Post-it and stick it on the door, where you see it every day. A month later, you forget your appointment because of your brain's tendency to ignore constant stimuli. This is known as _____. (a) sensory adaptation; (b) selective perception; (c) habituation; (d) selective attention

Check your answers in Appendix B.

CLICK & REVIEW
for additional assessment options:
www.wiley.com/college/huffman

■ Organization: Form, Constancy, Depth, and Color

Having selected incoming information, we must organize it into patterns and principles that will help us understand the world. Raw sensory data are like the parts of a watch. They must be assembled in a meaningful way before they are useful. We organize sensory data in terms of *form*, *constancy*, *depth*, and *color*.

chievement

How do we organize stimuli in order to perceive form, constancy, depth, and color?

Form Perception

Look at the first drawing in Figure 4.14 (on page 156). What do you see? Can you draw a similar object on a piece of paper? This is known as an "impossible figure." The second part of the figure shows a painting by M. C. Escher, a Dutch painter who created striking examples of perceptual distortion. Although drawn to represent three-dimensional objects or situations, the parts don't assemble into logical wholes. Like the illusions studied earlier, impossible figures and distorted painting help us understand perceptual principles—in this case, the principle of *form organization*.

Gestalt psychologists were among the first to study how the brain organizes sensory impressions. The German word *gestalt* means "whole" or "pattern." Rather than perceiving its discrete parts as separate entities, the Gestaltists emphasized the importance of organization and patterning in enabling us to perceive the whole stimulus. The Gestaltists proposed laws of organization that specify how people perceive form. The most fundamental Gestalt principle, or law of organization, is the tendency to distinguish between *figure* and *ground*. For example, while you are reading this material, your eyes are receiving sensations of black lines and white paper. But your brain is organizing these sensations into letters and words that are perceived against a backdrop of white pages. The letters constitute the figure, and the pages constitute the ground. The discrepancy between figure and ground is sometimes so vague that we have difficulty perceiving which is which. This is known as a *reversible figure* (see Figure 4.15). Figure and ground and other basic Gestalt principles are summarized in Figure 4.16. Although these examples are all visual, each principle also applies to other modes of perception, such as audition.

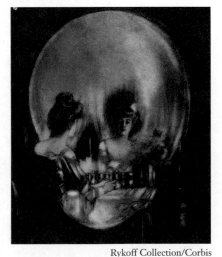

Figure 4.15 *Figure and ground.* This so-called reversible figure demonstrates alternating figure-ground relations. It can be seen as a woman looking in a mirror or as a skull depending on what you see as figure or ground.

Rykoff Collection/Corbis

www.wiley.com/college/huffman

Assessment

VISUAL QUIZ

(a)

Figure 4.14 *Can you explain these "impossible figures"?*

(b)

Concave and Convex by M.C. Escher/impossible figures Cordon Art b.v.

Answer: When you first glance at figure (a) and the famous painting by M. C. Escher in (b), you detect specific features of the stimuli and judge them as sensible figures. But as you try to sort and organize the different elements into a stable, well-organized whole, you realize they don't add up—they're illogical or "impossible." The point of the illustration is that there is no one-to-one correspondence between your actual sensory input and your final perception. The same stimuli looked at from another perspective can lead to very different perceptions.

Achievement
Gender & Cultural Diversity

Are the Gestalt Laws Universally True?

Gestalt psychologists conducted most of their work with formally educated people from urban European cultures. A.R. Luria (1976) was one of the first to question whether their laws held true for all participants, regardless of their education and cultural setting. Luria recruited a wide range of participants living in what was then the USSR. He included Ichkeri women from remote villages (with no formal education), collective farm activists (who were semiliterate), and female students in a teachers' school (with years of formal education).

Luria found that when presented with the stimuli shown in Figure 4.17, the formally trained female students were the only ones who identified the first three shapes by their categorical name of "circle." Whether circles were made of solid lines, incomplete lines, or solid colors, they called them all circles. However, participants with no formal education named the shapes according to the objects they resembled. They called a circle a watch, plate, or moon, and referred to the square as a mirror, house, or apricot-drying board. When asked if items 12 and 13 from Figure 4.17 were alike, one woman answered, "No, they're not alike. This one's not like a watch, but that one's a watch because there are dots" (p. 37).

Apparently, the Gestalt laws of perceptual organization are valid only for people who have been schooled in geometrical concepts. But an alternative explanation for Luria's findings has also been suggested. Luria's study, as well as most research on visual perception and optical illusions, relies on two-dimensional presentations—either on a piece of paper or projected on a screen. It may be that experience with pictures and photographs (not formal education in geometrical concepts) is necessary for learning to interpret two-dimensional figures as portraying three-dimensional forms. Westerners who have had years of practice learning to interpret two-dimensional drawings of three-dimensional objects may not remember how much practice it took to learn the cultural conventions about judging the size and shape of objects drawn on paper (Matsumoto & Juang, 2004; Price & Crapo, 2002).

Figure-Ground:
The ground is always seen as farther away than the figure.

Proximity:
Objects that are physically close together are grouped together. (In this figure, we see 3 groups of 6 hearts, not 18 separate hearts.)

Continuity:
Objects that continue a pattern are grouped together.

When we see this,

we normally see this

plus this.

Not this.

Closure:
The tendency to see a finished unit (triangle, square, or circle) from an incomplete stimulus.

Similarity:
Similar objects are grouped together (the green colored dots are grouped together and perceived as the number 5).

Summary Figure 4.16 *Basic Gestalt principles of organization.* Figure-ground, proximity, continuity, closure, and similarity are shown here. The Gestalt principle of contiguity cannot be shown because it involves nearness in time, not visual nearness.

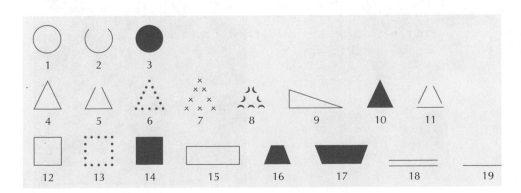

Figure 4.17 *Luria's stimuli.* When you see these shapes, you readily identify them as circles, triangles, and other geometric forms. According to cross-cultural research, this is due to your formal educational training. If you were from a culture without formal education, you might identify them instead as familiar objects in your environment —"the circle is like the moon."

www.wiley.com/college/huffman

Perceptual Constancy *Tendency for the environment to be perceived as remaining the same even with changes in sensory input*

Perceptual Constancies

Now that we have seen how form perception contributes to organization, we will examine **perceptual constancies**. As noted earlier with sensory adaptation and habituation, we are particularly alert to change. However, we also manage to perceive a great deal of consistency in the environment. Without perceptual constancy, our world would be totally chaotic. Things would seem to grow as we got closer to them, to change shape as our viewing angle changed, and to change color as light levels changed. The four best-known constancies are size, shape, color, and brightness (Figure 4.18).

1. *Size constancy.* Most perceptual constancies are based on prior experience and learning. For example, preschoolers express wonder at the fact that the car parked down the street is only "this high" (as they show about 2 inches between their fingers). Their size judgment is mistaken because they haven't yet had the experiences necessary for learning size constancy. According to this principle, the perceived size of an object remains the same even though the size of its retinal image changes (Figure 4.18a).

   Anthropologist Colin Turnbull (1961) provided a now-classic example of an adult who had never developed a sense of size constancy. While studying the Twa people living in the dense rain forest of the Congo River Valley in Africa, Turnbull took a native named Kenge for a Jeep ride to the African plains. Kenge had lived his entire life in an area so dense with foliage that he had never seen distances farther than about 100 yards. Now he was suddenly able to see for almost 70 miles.

   Lacking perceptual experience with such wide-open spaces, Kenge had great difficulty judging sizes. When he first saw a herd of water buffalo in the distance, he thought they were insects. When Turnbull insisted they were buffalo that were very far away, Kenge was insulted and asked, "Do you think that I am ignorant?" To Kenge's surprise, as they drove toward the "insects," the creatures seemed to grow into buffalo. He concluded that witchcraft was being used to fool him. After Turnbull showed him a lake so large that its opposite shore couldn't be seen, he asked to be taken back to his rain forest.

Figure 4.18 *Four types of perceptual constancies.* (a) Although the buffalo in the distance appears much smaller, we perceive it as similar in size to the buffalo in the foreground because of size constancy in relation to the tree. (b) As the coin is rotated it changes shape, but we perceive it as the same coin because of shape constancy. (c) Although this cat's fur appears different in the shade versus the sun, we know they are the same because of color and brightness constancy.

(a)

(b)

(c)

Jerry Shulman/Superstock

(a)   (b)

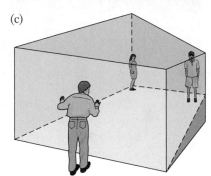

(c)

Figure 4.19 *The Ames room illusion.* (a, b) In the left photo, note how the woman on the right appears much taller than the boy on the left, but when they reverse positions (the right photo), the boy is taller. How do we explain this? (c) To the viewer peering through the peephole, the room appears perfectly normal. However, in this specially constructed room, the trapezoidal shape and sloping ceilings and floors provide misleading depth cues. Because the brain assumes the two people are the same distance away, it compensates for the differences in retinal size by making the person on the left appear much smaller.

2. *Shape constancy.* When you look at a chair directly from the front or the back, it has a rectangular shape. When you look at it directly from the side, it has an *h* shape. Yet you still perceive the chair as having a single shape. This is because your brain remembers past experiences with objects that only seemed to change shape as you moved but actually remained constant. This is known as *shape constancy* (Figure 4.18b).

An ophthalmologist named Adelbert Ames demonstrated the power of shape and size constancies by creating what is now known as the Ames room (see Figure 4.19). On examining Figure 4.19a, you might conclude that the person on the left is a midget and the person on the right is a giant. In actuality, both people are of normal size. This illusion is based on the unusual construction of the room. As can be seen in the diagram in Figure 4.19c, perspective tricks the observer into perceiving the room as square when it is actually shaped like a trapezoid. The illusion is so strong that when a person walks from the left corner to the right, the observer perceives the person to be "growing."

We know this is impossible, so why does this illusion still work? Our brain has had a lifetime of interaction with normally constructed rooms. And our desire to perceive the room according to our experience is so powerful that we overrule the truth. This is not a breakdown in perception. It results from trying to apply the standard perceptual processes of shape and size constancy to an unusual situation.

3. *Color constancy and* 4. *Brightness constancy.* Other forms of constancy that add stability to our world are *color constancy* and *brightness constancy* (See Figure 4.18c). These constancies enable us to perceive things as retaining the same color or brightness levels even though the amount of light may vary. For example, if you place a piece of gray paper in bright sunlight and a piece of white paper in shade, you will still perceive the white as lighter and the gray as darker. This is true regardless of the amount of reflected light actually coming from their surfaces. If you know an object from prior experience, you expect it will be the same color and the same

www.wiley.com/college/huffman

relative brightness in bright light as in low light. That is, you expect it to be its "right" color.

As is the case with shape and size constancy, color constancy and brightness constancy are learned from experience with familiar objects. If an object is unfamiliar, we determine its color and brightness by the actual wavelength of reflected light in combination with the color and brightness of the background.

Depth Perception *The ability to perceive three-dimensional space and to accurately judge distance*

BIZARRO By DAN PIRARO

Universal Press Syndicate

Depth Perception

The role of experience and learning in organizing perceptions is particularly clear in depth perception. **Depth perception** allows us to accurately estimate the distance of perceived objects and thereby perceive the world in three dimensions. It is possible to judge the distance of objects with nearly all senses. If a person enters a dark room and walks toward you, his or her voice and footsteps get louder, body smells grow stronger, and you may even be able to feel the slight movement of air from his or her approaching movement. In most cases, however, we rely most heavily on vision to perceive distance. When you add the ability to accurately perceive distance to the ability to judge the height and width of an object, you are able to perceive the world in three dimensions. But no matter which sense you use to perceive the three-dimensional world, perception of depth is primarily learned.

Take the classic example of a patient known as S.B. Blind since the age of 10 months, his sight was restored at age 52. Following the operation that removed cataracts from both eyes, S.B. had great difficulty learning to use his newly acquired vision for judging distance and depth. On one occasion, he even tried to crawl out of the window of his hospital room. He thought he would be able to lower himself by his hands to the ground below, even though the window was on the fourth floor.

Didn't S.B. have some inborn depth and distance perception? The answer is not clear. As you recall from Chapter 1, one of the most enduring debates in psychology (and other sciences) is the question of "nature versus nurture," inborn versus learned. In this case, naturists argue that depth perception is inborn. Nurturists insist it is learned. Today, most scientists think there is some truth in both viewpoints.

Evidence for the innate (inborn) position comes from a set of interesting experiments with an apparatus called the *visual cliff* (Figure 4.20). The apparatus consists of a tabletop with a slightly raised platform across the middle. On one side of the platform the tabletop is clear glass. Beneath the glass, a red-and-white-checked pattern runs down the side of the table and onto the floor several feet below the glass, simulating a steep cliff.

When an infant is placed on the platform and coaxed by his or her mother to crawl to the opposite side of the table, the infant will readily move to the "shallow" side but will hesitate or refuse to move to the clear glass "deep" side (Gibson & Walk, 1960). This reaction is given as evidence of innate depth perception—the infant's hesitation is attributed to fear of the apparent cliff.

Some researchers have argued that by the time infants are old enough to be tested, they have been crawling and may have *learned* to perceive depth. However, research with babies at 2 months of age has shown a change in their heart rate when they are placed on the deep side of the cliff but not when they are placed on the shallow side (Banks & Salapatek, 1983). Similar research with baby chickens, goats, and lambs (animals that walk almost immediately after birth) supports the hypothesis that some depth perception is inborn. These animals also hesitate to step onto the steep side. Once again, the *nature–nurture* debate continues.

We all recognize that in our three-dimensional world, the ability to perceive depth and distance is essential. But how do we perceive a three-dimensional world with a two-dimensional receptor system? One mechanism is the interaction of both eyes to produce **binocular cues**. The other mechanism involves **monocular cues**, which work with each eye separately. Keep in mind that having two eyes (binocular cues) does help with depth perception. However, we also get similar results with only one eye (monocular cues), as evidenced by the occasional major league football and baseball players who are blind in one eye.

1. Binocular cues. One of the most important cues for depth perception comes from **retinal disparity** (Figure 4.21). Because our eyes are about 2 ¹/₂ inches apart, each retina receives a slightly different view of the world. You can demonstrate this for yourself by pointing at some distant object across the room with your arm extended straight in front of you. Holding your pointing finger steady, close your left eye and then your right. You will notice that your finger seems to jump from one position to another as you change eyes. This "jumping" is the result of retinal disparity. The brain fuses the different images received by the two eyes into one overall visual image. Such *stereoscopic vision* provides important cues to depth.

As we move closer and closer to an object, a second binocular (and neuromuscular) cue, **convergence**, helps us judge depth. The closer the object, the more our eyes are turned inward toward our noses (Figure 4.22). Hold your index finger at arm's length in front of you and watch it as you bring it closer and closer until it is right in front of your nose. The amount of strain in your eye muscles created by the *convergence*, or turning inward of the eyes, is used as a cue by your brain to interpret distance.

Knowing how convergence operates might help you improve your performance in athletic endeavors. Allen Souchek (1986) found that depth perception is better when looking directly at an object, rather than out of the corner of your eye. Thus, if you turn your body or your head so that you look straight at your tennis

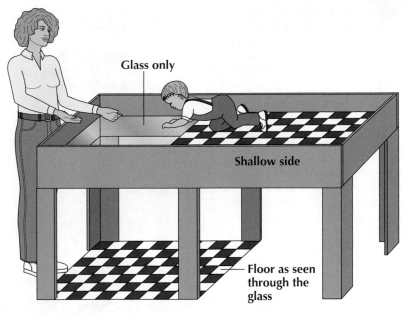

Figure 4.20 *The visual cliff.* Crawling infants generally refuse to move across this glass surface, designed to look like the edge of an elevated platform, even when their mothers stand on the opposite side and coax them. This suggests they are able to perceive depth.

Binocular Cues *Visual input from two eyes that allows perception of depth or distance*

Monocular Cues *Visual input from a single eye alone that contributes to perception of depth or distance*

Retinal Disparity *Binocular cue to distance where the separation of the eyes causes different images to fall on each retina*

Convergence *Binocular depth cue in which the closer the object, the more the eyes converge, or turn inward*

Figure 4.21 *Retinal disparity.* (a) Stare at your two index fingers a few inches in front of your eyes with their tips half an inch apart. Do you see the "floating finger"? Move it farther away and the "finger" will shrink. Move it closer and it will enlarge. (b) Because of retinal disparity, objects at different distances (such as the "floating finger") project their images on different parts of the retina. Far objects project on the retinal area near the nose, whereas near objects project farther out, closer to the ears. (c) "Magic Eye" images take advantage of retinal disparity. To see the three-dimensional image, stare at this drawing for several minutes, while focusing your eyes beyond it.

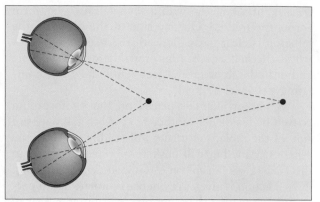

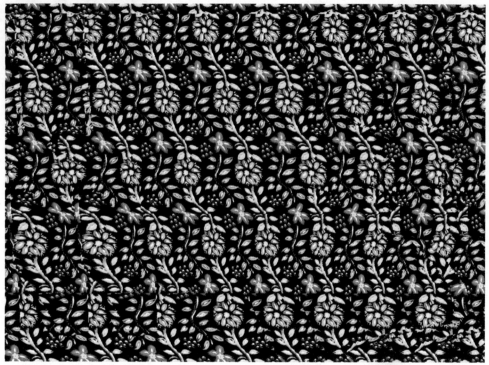

©2005 Magic Eye Inc. www.magiceye.com

opponent or the pitcher, you will more accurately judge the distance of the ball and thereby be more likely to swing at the right time.

2. Monocular cues. Retinal disparity and convergence are inadequate in judging distances longer than the length of a football field. According to R. L. Gregory (1969), "we are effectively one-eyed for distances greater than perhaps 100 meters." Luckily, we have several monocular cues available separately to each eye. Artists use these same monocular cues to create an illusion of depth on a flat canvas, a three-dimensional world on a two-dimensional surface. Figure 4.23 demonstrates six different monocular cues.

Two additional monocular cues—cues that cannot be used by artists—are *accommodation* of the lens of the eye and *motion parallax*. As you learned earlier in the chapter, *accommodation* refers to changes in the shape of the lens of the eye in response to the distance of the object on which you are focusing. For near objects, the lens bulges;

for far objects, it flattens. Neural impluses send information from the muscles that move the lens to the brain. The brain then interprets the signal and perceives the distance of the object.

Motion parallax (also known as *relative motion*) refers to the fact that when an observer is moving, objects at various distances move at different speeds across the retinal field. Close objects appear to whiz by, farther objects seem to move slowly, and very distant objects appear to remain stationary. This effect can easily be seen when traveling by car or train. Telephone poles and fences next to the road or track seem to move by very rapidly. Houses and trees in the midground seem to move by relatively slowly. And the mountains in the distance seem not to move at all.

Color Perception

We humans may be able to discriminate among seven million different hues. Is such color perception inborn and culturally universal? Research on many cultures with many different languages suggests that we all seem to see essentially the same colored world (Davies, 1998). Furthermore, studies of infants old enough to focus and move their eyes show that they are able to see color nearly as well as adults (Knoblauch, Vital-Durand, & Barbur, 2000; Werner & Wooten, 1979).

Although we know color is produced by different wavelengths of light, the actual way in which we

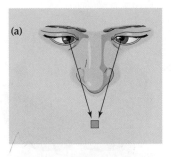
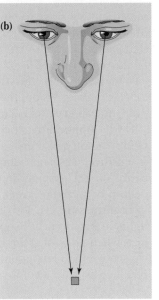

Figure 4.22 *Convergence.* (a) Your eyes turn in to view close objects and (b) turn out to view distant objects.

Hilarie Kavanagh/Stone/GettyImages

Figure 4.23 *Monocular depth cues.* Several monocular depth cues can be seen in this photo of the Taj Mahal in India. (a) Linear perspective results when parallel lines converge in the distance. Note how the lines of the sidewalk converge at the top of the photo. (b) Interposition occurs when a close object obscures part of a distant object. The tree in the left foreground is understood to be closer because it obscures the sidewalk and larger tree behind it. (c) Relative size is the result of close objects projecting a larger retinal image than distant objects. The red planters in the left foreground appear closer than the woman because of their relatively larger size. (d) Texture gradient results from the change in perceived texture as the background recedes into the distance. Notice how the breaks in the walkways next to the planters and the woman appear richer in texture than the walkways near the Taj Mahal. (e) Aerial perspective means that faraway objects look fuzzy and blurred compared with near objects because of intervening particles of dust or haze in the atmosphere. (f) Light and shadow depth cues occur when brighter objects are perceived as closer and darker objects are perceived as farther away.

www.wiley.com/college/huffman

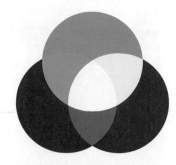

Figure 4.24 *Primary colors.*
Thomas Young showed that the three primary colors (red, green, and blue) can be combined to form all colors by varying their brightnesses. For example, a combination of green and red creates yellow.

Trichromatic Theory. *Young's theory that color perception results from mixing three distinct color systems—red, green, and blue*

Opponent-Process Theory *Hering's theory that color perception is based on three systems of color opposites— blue–yellow, red–green, and black–white*

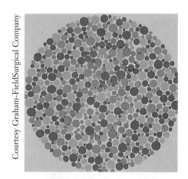

Figure 4.25 *Color-deficient vision.*
People who suffer red–green deficiency have trouble perceiving the number within the design.

Achievement

What factors influence how we interpret sensations?

perceive color is a matter of scientific debate. Traditionally, there have been two theories of color vision, the trichromatic (three-color) theory and the opponent-process theory. The **trichromatic theory** (from the Greek *tri* meaning "three," and *chroma* meaning "color") was first proposed by Thomas Young in the early nineteenth century. It was later refined by Hermann von Helmholtz and others. Apparently, we have three "color systems," as they called them—one system that is maximally sensitive to blue, another maximally sensitive to green, and another maximally sensitive to red (Young, 1802). The proponents of this theory demonstrated that mixing lights of these three colors could yield the full spectrum of colors we perceive (Figure 4.24).

Unfortunately, this theory has two major flaws. One is that it doesn't explain defects in color vision; the other is that it doesn't explain *color aftereffects*, a phenomenon you can experience in the "Try This Yourself" feature on the next page.

The **opponent-process theory**, proposed by Ewald Hering later in the nineteenth century, also proposed three color systems. But he suggested that each system is sensitive to two opposing colors—blue and yellow, red and green, black and white— in an "on–off" fashion. In other words, each color receptor responds either to blue or yellow, or to red or green, with the black-or-white system responding to differences in brightness levels. This theory makes a lot of sense because when different-colored lights are combined, people are unable to see reddish greens and bluish yellows. In fact, when red and green lights or blue and yellow lights are mixed in equal amounts, we see white. The opponent-process theory helps explain color vision defects. Most people who have a color weakness are unable to see either red and green or blue and yellow.

Are you color blind? Figure 4.25 provides a test for red–green color deficiency. Actually, most color vision defects are weaknesses—color *confusion* rather than color *blindness*. Many people who have some color blindness are not even aware of it.

Two Correct Theories

Judging from the discussion so far, it would seem the opponent-process theory is the correct one. Actually, however, both theories are correct. In 1964, George Wald demonstrated that there are indeed three different types of cones in the retina, each with its own type of photopigment. One type of pigment is sensitive to blue light, one is sensitive to green light, and the third is sensitive to red light.

At nearly the same time that Wald was doing his research on cones, R. L. DeValois (1965) was studying electrophysiological recording of cells in the optic nerve and optic pathways to the brain. DeValois discovered cells that respond to color in an opponent fashion in the thalamus. Thus, it appears that both theories have been correct all along. Color is processed in a trichromatic fashion at the level of the retina (in the cones) and in an opponent fashion at the level of the optic nerve and the thalamus (in the brain).

▮ Interpretation: Explaining Our Perceptions

After selectively sorting through incoming sensory information and organizing it into patterns, the brain uses this information to explain and make judgments about the external world. This final stage of perception—*interpretation*—is influenced by several factors, including perceptual adaptation, perceptual set, frame of reference, and bottom-up or top-down processing.

1. *Perceptual adaptation.* What would it be like if your visual field was inverted and reversed? You would certainly have trouble getting around. Things that you

Testing the Power of Color Aftereffects

Try staring at the dot in the middle of this color-distorted United States flag for 60 seconds. Then stare at a plain sheet of white paper. You should get interesting color aftereffects—red in place of green, blue in place of yellow, and white in place of black. You perceive a "genuine" red, white, and blue U.S. flag. (If you have trouble seeing it, blink, and try again.)

What happened? This is a good example of the *opponent-process* theory. As you stared at the figure, the green stripes stimulated only the green channel of the red–green opponent color cells. Several minutes of continuous stimulation fatigued the green channel. However, the nonstimulated red channel was not fatigued. When you looked at the blank piece of white paper, the white stimulated both the red and the green channels equally. Because the green channel was fatigued, the red channel fired at a higher rate and you saw a red color aftereffect. Without first staring at the white dot, the red and green receptors would have canceled each other out and you would have seen white when you looked at the white paper.

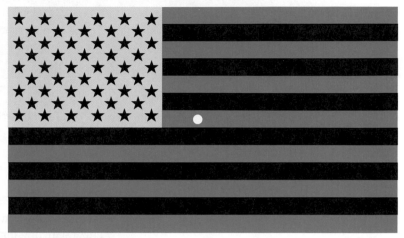

expected to be on your right would be on your left. Things you expected to be above your head would be below your head. Do you think you could ever *adapt* to this distorted world?

To answer such a question, psychologist George Stratton (1897) wore special lenses for eight days. For the first few days, Stratton had a great deal of difficulty navigating in this environment and coping with everyday tasks. But by the third day, his experience had begun to change and he noted:

> *Walking through the narrow spaces between pieces of furniture required much less care than hitherto. I could watch my hands as they wrote, without hesitating or becoming embarrassed thereby.*

By the fifth day, Stratton had almost completely adjusted to his strange perceptual environment. His expectations of how the world should be arranged had changed. As this experiment shows, we are able to adapt our perceptions by retraining our brains to create a newly coherent and familiar world.

2. *Perceptual set (or expectancies).* Our previous experiences, assumptions, and expectations also affect how we interpret and perceive the world. If a car backfires, runners at a track meet may jump the gun. People who believe that extraterrestrials occasionally visit the earth may interpret a weather balloon or an odd-shaped cloud as a spaceship. These mental predispositions, or **perceptual sets**, prepare us in a certain way and greatly influence our perception. In other words, we largely see what we expect to see.

For example, studies using the famous reversible figure of the young/old woman that you saw on page 131, found that when people are led to expect either a young woman or an old woman, they generally saw "what they expected to see" (Leeper, 1935). Another study recruited participants from a Jewish organization and briefly flashed pictures on a screen (Erdelyi & Applebaum, 1973). When the center symbol was a swastika, the Jewish participants were less likely to recognize and remember the symbols around the edges (Figure 4.26). Can you see how the

Perceptual Set *Readiness to perceive in a particular manner based on expectations*

Figure 4.26 *Perceptual set and life experiences.* Can you see why members of a Jewish organization would be less likely to pay attention to (and remember) the other stimuli in this photo when the center item is a swastika?

www.wiley.com/college/huffman

Perceptual Set

Do you notice anything unusual in this photo? What happens when you turn the book upside down? Despite the extreme distortion, most people see the first photo as normal. Can you explain why?

Answer: Because of perceptual set, we expect both photos to be the same.

Mitchell Gerber/Corbis

life experiences of the Jewish subjects led them to create a perceptual set for the swastika? Can you also see how expressions like "stingy jew," "lazy mexican," "crazy schizo," "dirty fag," or even "nerd" can lead to painful and dangerous forms of prejudice and discrimination (Chapters 12, 14, 16)?

3. *Frame of reference.* Our perceptions of people, objects, or situations are also affected by their frame of reference, or context. An elephant is perceived as much larger when it is next to a mouse than when it stands next to a giraffe.

4. *Bottom-up or top-down processing.* We began this chapter discussing how we receive sensory information and worked our way upward to the top levels of perceptual processing. Psychologists refer to this type of information processing as **bottom-up processing**, taking sensory data in through the sensory receptors, such as the eyes, ears, nose, and tongue, and sending it "upward" to the brain for analysis. In contrast, **top-down processing** begins with "higher," "top"-level, processing involving thoughts, previous experiences, expectations, language, and cultural background. It then works down to the sensory level. When first learning to read, we all used *bottom-up processing.* We initially learned that certain arrangements of lines and "squiggles" represented specific letters. Only later did we realize that these letters joined together to make up words. However, after years of experience and language training, we quickly perceive the words in this sentence *before* the individual letters—*top-down processing.* Although top-down processing is far superior for reading, both bottom-up and top-down processing are important to perception.

Bottom-Up Processing *Information processing that begins "at the bottom" with raw sensory data that feed "up" to the brain*

Top-Down Processing *Information processing that starts "at the top," with the observer's thoughts, expectations, and knowledge, and works down*

Why can't these two students shake hands with one another? *The student on the right is wearing inverting lenses that literally turn the world upside down—the sky is down, the ground is up. The one on the left is wearing displacement goggles that shift the apparent location of objects 40 degrees to the left. Interestingly, the human brain adapts to this type of distortion relatively quickly. Within a few days, the upside-down or displaced world would appear normal. While wearing these glasses, both students could easily shake hands, ride a bike, and even read this book!*

Courtesy Karen Huffman

A Final Note

We have seen that a number of internal and external factors can affect sensation as well as all three stages of perception—selection, organization, and interpretation. In upcoming chapters, we will continue our study of perception by examining how incoming sensory information is processed and retrieved in the different types of memory (Chapter 7), how perception develops in infants (Chapter 9), and how we perceive ourselves and others (Chapter 16).

Application
CASE STUDY / PERSONAL STORY

Helen Keller's Triumph and Advice

Helen Keller recognized how crucial sensation and perception are to our lives. She learned to "see" and "hear" with her sense of touch and often recognized visitors by their smell or by vibrations from their walk. Helen Keller wasn't born deaf and blind. When she was 19 months old, she suffered a fever that left her without sight or hearing and thus virtually isolated from the world. Keller's parents realized they had to find help for their daughter. After diligently searching, they found Anne Sullivan, a young teacher who was able to break through Keller's barrier of isolation by taking advantage of her sense of touch. One day, Sullivan took Keller to the pumphouse and, as Sullivan (1902) wrote:

Bettman/CORBIS

> I made Helen hold her mug under the spout while I pumped. As the cold water gushed forth, filling the mug, I spelled "w-a-t-e-r" in Helen's free hand. The word coming so close upon the sensation of cold water rushing over her hand seemed to startle her. She dropped the mug and stood as one transfixed. A new light came into her face. (p. 257)

That one moment, brought on by the sensation of cold water on her hand, was the impetus for a lifetime of learning about, understanding, and appreciating the world through her remaining senses. In 1904, Helen Keller graduated cum laude from Radcliffe College and went on to become a famous author and lecturer, inspiring physically limited people throughout the world.

Despite her incredible accomplishments, Keller often expressed a lifelong yearning to experience a normal sensory world. She offered important advice to all whose senses are "normal":

> I who am blind can give one hint to those who see: use your eyes as if tomorrow you would be stricken blind. And the same method can be applied to the other senses. Hear the music of voices, the song of a bird, the mighty strains of an orchestra as if you would be stricken deaf tomorrow. Touch each object as if tomorrow your tactile sense would fail. Smell the perfume of flowers, taste with relish each morsel as if tomorrow you could never smell and taste again. Make the most of every sense; glory in all the facets of pleasure and beauty that the world reveals to you through the several means of contact which nature provides. (Keller, 1962, p. 23)

Assessment
CHECK & REVIEW

Organization—Depth and Color— and Interpretation

Depth perception allows us to accurately estimate the distance of perceived objects and thereby perceive the world in three dimensions. But how do we perceive a three-dimensional world with two-dimensional receptors called eyes? There are two major types of cues: **binocular cues,** which require two eyes, and **monocular cues,** which require only one eye. Two binocular cues are **retinal disparity** and **convergence.** Monocular cues include *linear perspective, interposition, relative size, texture gradient, aerial perspective, light and shadow, accommodation,* and *motion parallax.*

Color perception is explained by a combination of two color theories. The **trichromatic theory** proposes three color systems maximally sensitive to blue, green, and red. The **opponent-process theory** also proposes three color systems but holds that each is sensitive to two opposing colors—blue and yellow, red and green, and black and white—and that

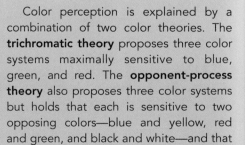

www.wiley.com/college/huffman

they operate in an on–off fashion. The trichromatic system operates at the level of the retina. The opponent-process system occurs in the brain.

Interpretation, the final stage of perception, can be influenced by perceptual adaptation, **perceptual set**, frame of reference, and **bottom-up** or **top-down processing**.

Questions

1. The visual cliff is an apparatus designed to study _____ in young children and animals. (a) color discrimination; (b) shape constancy; (c) depth perception; (d) monocular vision

2. Since Jolly Roger, the pirate, lost one eye in a fight, he can no longer use _____ as a cue for the perception of depth and distance. (a) accommodation; (b) retinal disparity; (c) motion parallax; (d) aerial perspective

3. After staring at a bright red rectangle for a period of time, a phenomenon known as _____ occurs, which means that if you look away and at a white background, you will see a _____.

4. Explain how the trichromatic theory of color perception differs from the opponent-process theory.

5. George Stratton's research is important because it demonstrated _____. (a) the role of learning in perception; (b) innate factors in human perception; (c) the difference between sensation and perception; (d) the ability of the retina to invert images

Check your answers in Appendix B.

CLICK & REVIEW
for additional assessment options:
www.wiley.com/college/huffman

Application

RESEARCH HIGHLIGHT

Is There Scientific Evidence for Subliminal Perception and ESP?

Years ago many people believed movie theaters were manipulating consumers by subliminally presenting messages like "Eat popcorn" and "Drink Coca-Cola." And record companies were supposedly embedding subliminal messages in rock music that encouraged violence and sex in listeners. The words on the movie screen and the messages in the music were allegedly presented so quickly that they were below the threshold for awareness. Most people were both fascinated and outraged. Politicians rushed to pass laws against the "invisible sell" and the "moral corruption" of our youth. Were they right to be concerned? Is there even such a thing as subliminal messages? What about extrasensory perception (ESP)? Do you believe it exists? Is there anything wrong with believing in ESP? These are the questions and answers we'll explore in this section.

Subliminal Perception

Two major questions surround *subliminal perception*. First, is it possible to perceive something without conscious awareness? The answer is clearly yes. Scientific research on **subliminal** (literally, "below the threshold") stimuli demonstrates that information processing does occur even when we are not aware of it (Luecken, Tartaro, & Appelhans, 2004; Nuñez & de Vicente, 2004; Todorov & Bargh, 2002).

Experimental studies commonly use an instrument called a *tachistoscope* to flash images too quickly for conscious recognition, but slowly enough to be registered. For example, in one study experimenters flashed one of two pictures subliminally (either a happy or an angry face) followed by a neutral face. They found this subliminal presentation evoked matching unconscious facial expressions in the participant's own facial muscles (Dimberg, Thunberg, & Elmehed, 2000). As you will discover in Chapter 12, the fact that participants were unaware of the subliminal stimuli, as well as their own matching facial response, also raises questions regarding our own emotional states. Do we unconsciously become a little happier when we're exposed to good-natured, pleasant peo-

Reprinted with special permission of King Features Syndicate

Subliminal *Pertaining to any stimulus presented below the threshold of conscious awareness*

ple? And upset when we are around those who are angry?

Although this research shows that subliminal perception does occur, the second—and perhaps more important—question is, "Does it lead to *subliminal persuasion?*" The answer to this question is less clear. Subliminal stimuli are basically *weak* stimuli. At most, they have a modest (if any) effect on consumer behavior. And, according to research, absolutely *no effect* on the minds of youth listening to rock music or citizens' voting behavior (Begg, Needham, & Bookbinder, 1993; Trappey, 1996). If you're wondering about buying subliminal tapes promising to help you lose weight or relieve stress, save your money. Blank "placebo" tapes appear to be just as "effective" as subliminal tapes.

In sum, evidence exists that subliminal perception occurs, but the effect on subliminal persuasion is uncertain. When it comes to commercials and self-help tapes, advertisers are better off using *above*-threshold messages—the loudest, clearest, and most attention-getting stimuli possible. And your money and time for weight loss are better spent on the old-fashioned methods of exercise and diet.

Extrasensory Perception

What about a so-called sixth sense beyond vision, hearing, touch, and so on? Do some people have the ability to perceive things that cannot be perceived with the usual sensory channels, by using **extrasensory perception (ESP)**? People who claim to have ESP profess to be able to read other people's minds (*telepathy*), perceive objects or events that are inaccessible to their normal senses (*clairvoyance*), predict the future (*precognition*), or move or affect objects without touching them (*psychokinesis*). Popular tabloids are filled with accounts of psychics claiming to be able to find lost children, talk to the

"What do you mean you didn't know that we were having a pop quiz today?"

dead, or even predict the stock market (Jaroff, 2001; McDonald, 2001).

Scientific investigations of ESP began in the early 1900s with Joseph B. Rhine. Many of these early experiments, as well as those done by subsequent ESP researchers, involved Zener cards. This deck of 25 cards included five different symbols—a plus sign, a square, a star, a circle, and wavy lines. When experimenters want to study telepathy, for instance, they ask a "sender" to concentrate on a card. Then they ask a "receiver" to try to "read the mind" of the sender. By chance alone, the receiver will guess the symbols on about 5 of the 25 cards correctly. A participant who consistently scores above "chance" is credited with having ESP.

Using Zener cards, Rhine apparently found a few people who scored somewhat better than chance. But his methodology has been severely criticized, particularly in the area of experimental control. In many early experiments, for example, the Zener cards were so cheaply printed that a faint outline of the symbol could be seen from the back. Also, because experimenters knew which cards were correct, they could

unknowingly give participants cues through subtle facial gestures.

The most important criticism of both experimental and casual claims of ESP is their lack of stability and replicability—a core requirement for scientific acceptance. Findings in ESP are notoriously "fragile" (Hyman, 1996). A meta-analysis of 30 studies using scientific controls, such as double-blind procedures and maximum security and accuracy in record keeping, reported absolutely no evidence of ESP (Milton & Wiseman, 1999, 2001). As one critic pointed out, positive ESP results usually mean "Error Some Place" (Marks, 1990).

If ESP is so unreliable, why do so many people believe in it? Our fast-paced technological world and rapid scientific progress lead many people to believe that virtually anything is possible. And *possible* is often translated as *probable*. Because ESP is by nature subjective and extraordinary, some people also tend to accept it as the best explanation for out-of-the-ordinary experiences. Moreover, as mentioned earlier in the chapter, our motivations and interests often influence our perceptions. Because research participants and researchers are strongly motivated to believe in ESP, they *selectively attend* to things they want to see or hear.

A large number of people want to believe in ESP, as evidenced by the popularity of *The Medium*, children's fairy tales, comic books, and popular movies. It seems that release from natural law is one of the most common and satisfying human fantasies. When it comes to ESP, people eagerly engage in a process known as "the willing suspension of disbelief." We seem to have a hard time accepting our finiteness, and a belief in psychic phenomena offers an increased feeling of infinite possibilities.

Extrasensory Perception (ESP) *Perceptual, or "psychic," abilities that supposedly go beyond the known senses (e.g., telepathy, clairvoyance, precognition, and psychokinesis)*

www.wiley.com/college/huffman

CRITICAL THINKING   ACTIVE LEARNING

Problems with Believing in Extrasensory Perception

The subject of extrasensory perception (ESP) often generates not only great interest but also strong emotional responses. And when individuals feel strongly about an issue, they sometimes fail to recognize the faulty reasoning underlying their beliefs. Belief in ESP is particularly associated with illogical, noncritical thinking. This exercise gives you a chance to practice your critical thinking skills as they apply to ESP. Begin by studying the following types of faulty reasoning:

1. **Fallacy of positive instances.** *Noting and remembering events that confirm personal expectations and beliefs (the "hits") and ignoring nonsupportive evidence (the "misses").* Remembering the time the palmist said you would receive a call in the middle of the night (a "hit") but ignoring that she also said that you had three children (a "miss").
2. **Innumeracy.** *Failing to recognize chance occurrences for what they are owing to a lack of training in statistics and probabilities.* Unusual events are misperceived as statistically impossible (such as predicting a president's illness). And extraordinary explanations, such as ESP, are seen as the logical alternative.

3. **Willingness to suspend disbelief.** *Refusing to engage one's normal critical thinking skills because of a personal need for power and control.* Although few people would attribute a foreign country's acquisition of top-secret information to ESP, some of these same individuals would willingly believe that a psychic could help them find their lost child.
4. **The "vividness" problem.** *Remembering and preferring vivid information.* Human information processing and memory storage and retrieval are often based on the initial "vividness" of the information. Sincere personal testimonials, theatrical demonstrations, and detailed anecdotes easily capture our attention and tend to be remembered better than rational, scientific descriptions of events. This is the heart of most stories about extraterrestrial visitations.

Using these four types of faulty reasoning, decide which one best describes each of the following. Although more than one type may be applicable, enter only one number beside each report. Comparing your answers with your classmates' and friends' answers will further sharpen your critical thinking skills.

_____ John hadn't thought of Paula, his old high school sweetheart, for years.

Yet one morning he woke up thinking about her. He was wondering what she looked like and whether she was married now, when suddenly the phone rang. For some strange reason, he felt sure the call was from Paula. He was right. John now cites this call as evidence for his personal experience with extrasensory perception.

_____ A psychic visits a class in introductory psychology. He predicts that out of this class of 23 students, two individuals will have birthdays on the same day. When a tally of birthdays is taken, his prediction is supported and many students leave class believing that the existence of ESP has been supported.

_____ A National League baseball player dreams of hitting a bases-loaded triple. Two months later, during the final game of the World Series, he gets this exact triple and wins the game. He informs the media of his earlier dream and the possibility that ESP exists.

_____ A mother sitting alone in her office at work suddenly sees a vivid image of her home on fire. She calls home and awakens the sitter. The sitter then notices smoke coming under the door and quickly extinguishes the fire. The media attribute the mother's visual images to ESP.

CHECK & REVIEW

Subliminal Perception and ESP

Subliminal (below the threshold) messages can be perceived without our knowing awareness. However, there is little or no evidence of subliminal persuasion. **Extrasensory perception (ESP)** is the supposed ability to perceive things that go beyond the normal senses. ESP research has produced "fragile" results, and critics condemn its lack of experimental control and replicability.

Questions

1. A subliminal stimulus refers to any stimulus that _____. (a) manipulates people without their knowing it; (b) is presented below the threshold of conscious awareness; (c) takes advantage of perceptual set and expectancies; (d) none of the above
2. Experiments on subliminal perception have _____. (a) supported the existence of the phenomenon, but it has little or no effect on persuasion; (b) shown that subliminal perception

occurs only among children and some adolescents; (c) shown that subliminal messages affect only people who are highly suggestible; (d) failed to support the existence of the phenomenon
3. The supposed ability to read other people's minds is called _____, perceiving objects or events that are inaccessible to the normal senses is known as _____, predicting the future is called _____, and moving or affecting objects without touching them is known as _____.

4. A major criticism of studies that indicate the existence of ESP is that they _____.

CLICK & REVIEW
for additional assessment options:
www.wiley.com/college/huffman

Check your answers in Appendix B.

ssessment
KEY TERMS

*To assess your understanding of the **Key Terms** in Chapter 4, write a definition for each (in your own words), and then compare your definitions with those in the text.*

perception (p. 130)
sensation (p. 130)

Understanding Sensation
absolute threshold (p. 133)
coding (p. 133)
difference threshold (p. 133)
gate-control theory of pain (p. 134)
psychophysics (p. 133)
sensory adaptation (p. 134)
sensory reduction (p. 131)
synesthesia (p. 131)
transduction (p. 131)

How We See and Hear
accommodation (p. 138)
amplitude (p. 136)
audition (p. 140)
cochlea (p. 140)

conduction deafness (p. 141)
cones (p. 139)
farsightedness (hyperopia) (p. 138)
fovea (p. 139)
frequency (p. 136)
frequency theory (p. 141)
nearsightedness (myopia) (p. 138)
nerve deafness (p. 141)
place theory (p. 141)
retina (p. 139)
rods (p. 139)
wavelength (p. 136)

Our Other Senses
gustation (p. 143)
kinesthesia (p. 145)
olfaction (p. 142)
pheromones [FARE-oh-mones] (p. 143)

Understanding Perception
binocular cues (p. 155)
bottom-up processing (p. 160)
convergence (p. 155)
depth perception (p. 154)
extrasensory perception (ESP) (p. 163)
feature detectors (p. 147)
habituation (p. 148)
illusion (p. 146)
monocular cues (p. 155)
opponent-process theory (p. 158)
perceptual constancy (p. 152)
perceptual set (p. 159)
retinal disparity (p. 155)
selective attention (p. 147)
subliminal (p. 162)
top-down processing (p. 160)
trichromatic theory (p. 158)

chievement
WEB RESOURCES

Huffman Book Companion Site
http://www.wiley.com/college/huffman
This site is loaded with free Interactive Self-Tests, Internet Exercises, Glossary and Flashcards for key terms, web links, Handbook for Non-Native Speakers, and other activities designed to improve your mastery of the material in this chapter.

Grand illusions
http://www.grand-illusions.com/
Offers an extensive and exciting gathering of optical illusions, scientific toys, visual effects, and even a little magic.

How we see
http://webvision.med.utah.edu/
Provides a wealth of information on the organization of the retina and visual system, color vision, and related topics.

Interactive tutorials
http://psych.hanover.edu/Krantz/tutor.html
Exceptional website offering numerous demonstrations and activities that are both fun and educational.

Visual Summary

Understanding Sensation

Processing

- **Receptors**: Body cells that detect and respond to stimulus energy.
- **Transduction**: A process of converting receptor energy into neural impulses the brain can understand.
- **Sensory reduction**: Filtering and analyzing of sensations before messages are sent to the brain.
- **Coding**: A three-part process that converts sensory input into specific sensations (sight, sound, touch, etc.).

Thresholds

Absolute threshold: Smallest *magnitude* of a stimulus we can detect.

Difference threshold: Smallest *change* in a stimulus we can detect.

Adaptation

Sensory adaptation: Decreased sensory response to continuous stimulation.

How We See and Hear

Vision

Light is a form of energy and part of the *electromagnetic spectrum*. Light waves vary in:
1) *Length* (the **wavelength** of a light determines **frequency**, which creates hue, or color).
2) *Height* (the **amplitude** determines intensity or brightness).
3) *Range* (the mixture of lengths and amplitudes determines complexity or saturation).

Eye anatomy and function

- *Cornea*: Clear bulge at front of eye, where light enters.
- *Pupil*: Hole through which light passes into eye.
- *Iris*: Colored muscles that surround pupil.
- *Lens*: Elastic structure that bulges and flattens to focus an image on retina (a process called **accommodation**).
- **Retina**: Contains visual receptor cells, called **rods** (for night vision) and **cones** (for color vision and fine detail).
- **Fovea**: Pit in the retina responsible for sharp vision.

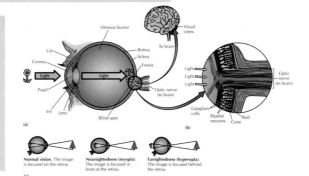

Normal vision. The image is focused on the retina.

Nearsightedness (myopia). The image is focused in front of the retina.

Farsightedness (hyperopia). The image is focused behind the retina.

Hearing

Audition (or hearing) occurs via *sound waves*, which result from rapid changes in air pressure caused by vibrating objects.

Sound waves vary in:
1) *Length* (the wavelength of a sound wave determines frequency, which corresponds to **pitch**).
2) *Height* (the amplitude of a sound wave determines **loudness**).
3) *Range* (the mixture of frequencies and amplitudes in sound waves determines timbre).

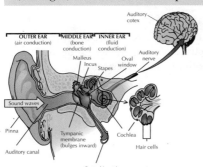

Ear Anatomy and Function

Outer ear conducts sound waves to *eardrum*, which vibrates tiny bones of middle ear that conduct sound vibrations to oval window. Movement of the oval window creates waves in fluid in the **cochlea**, which contains *hair cells* (receptors for hearing) that convert sound energy to neural impulses sent along to the brain.

Our Other Senses

Smell and Taste

Olfaction (sense of smell) Receptors located at the top of the nasal cavity.
Gustation (sense of taste) Five basic tastes: salty, sweet, sour, bitter, and umami.

The Body Senses

Skin senses detect touch (pressure), temperature, and pain. *Vestibular sense* (or sense of balance) results from receptors in inner ear.
Kinesthesia (body posture, orientation, and body movement) results from receptors in muscles, joints, and tendons.

Understanding Perception

Selection

Three major factors:
1) **Selective attention**: The brain sorts out and only attends to most important sensory messages.
2) **Feature detectors**: Specialized brain cells that only respond to specific sensory information.
3) **Habituation**: Tendency of brain to ignore environmental factors that remain constant.

Organization

Four general attributes:
1) **Form**: *Figure and ground, proximity, continuity, closure, contiguity,* and *similarity*.
2) **Constancy**: *Size constancy, shape constancy, color constancy,* and *brightness constancy*.
3) **Depth**: **Binocular** (2 eyes) **cues** involve **retinal disparity** and **convergence**. **Monocular** (one eye) **cues** include *linear perspective, interposition,* and so on.
4) **Color**: Color perception is explained by a combination of two theories: **trichromatic theory** and **opponent-process theory**.

Interpretation

Four major factors:
1) *Perceptual adaptation*: The brain adapts to changed environment.
2) **Perceptual set**: A readiness to perceive based on expectations.
3) *Frame of reference*: Based on context of situation.
4) **Bottom-up** and **top-down processing**: Information processing style that affects interpretation.

Subliminal Perception and ESP

Subliminal stimuli occur below the threshold of our conscious awareness.
Extrasensory perception (ESP) is the unproven ability to perceive things through unknown senses.

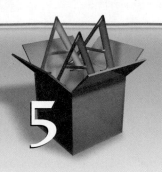

5

STATES OF CONSCIOUSNESS

A*chievement*

Core Learning Outcomes

As you read Chapter 5, keep the following questions in mind and answer them in your own words:

▷ How can we define and describe consciousness?

▷ What happens to consciousness while we sleep and dream?

▷ How do psychoactive drugs affect consciousness?

▷ How do alternate states of consciousness, like hypnosis and meditation, affect consciousness?

▪ Achievement
▪ Assessment
▪ Application

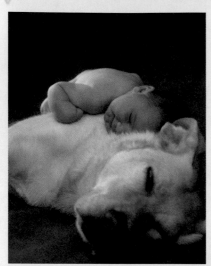

Chapter 5 contains interesting facts, such as . . .

▶ Virtually everyone dreams while they're sleeping.

▶ Approximately two-thirds of all American adults suffer from sleep problems.

▶ Sleep deprivation and shift work are key contributors to industrial and automobile accidents.

▶ People who suffer from narcolepsy may fall instantly asleep while walking, talking, or driving a car.

▶ People cannot be hypnotized against their will.

▶ The American Medical Association considers alcohol the most dangerous and physically damaging of all psychoactive drugs.

▶ Even small initial doses of cocaine can be fatal because they interfere with the electrical signals of the heart.

▶ An amount of LSD the size of an aspirin table is enough to produce psychoactive effects in over 3000 people.

▶ A survey of 488 societies around the world found that 90 percent engaged in institutionally recognized methods of changing consciousness.

Paul Kuroda/SUPERSTOCK

> Our normal waking consciousness is but one special type of consciousness, whilst all about it, parted from it by the filmiest of screens, there lie potential forms of consciousness entirely different.
>
> WILLIAM JAMES

As you may remember from Chapter 1, William James (1842–1910) was one of the most famous early psychologists. What did he mean by "normal waking consciousness" and "entirely different forms of consciousness"? You and I commonly use the term *consciousness*, but what exactly does it mean? Is it simple "awareness"? What would it be like to be "unaware"? How can we study the contents of our consciousness when the only tool of discovery is the object itself? How can the mind's awareness study itself? Consciousness is a fundamental concept in the field of psychology, yet it eludes simple definition (Damasio, 1999).

To answer these questions, our first section "Understanding Consciousness," begins with a general look at the definition and description of consciousness. "Sleep and Dreams" examines how consciousness changes as a result of circadian rhythms, sleep, and dreams. "Psychoactive Drugs" looks at psychoactive drugs and their effects on consciousness. And our final section, "Healthier Ways to Alter Consciousness," explores other routes to altered consciousness, such as meditation and hypnosis.

Consciousness *An organism's awareness of its own self and surroundings (Damaslo, 1999)*

UNDERSTANDING CONSCIOUSNESS

■ How Do We Define It? The Participant as the Inquirer

Our definition of **consciousness** is fairly simple and currently popular: *an organism's awareness of its own self and surroundings*. In the late nineteenth century, when psychology first became a scientific discipline separate from philosophy, it defined itself as "the study of human consciousness." But such a nebulous area of study eventually led to great dissatisfaction within the field. One group, the behaviorists, led by John Watson, believed that *behavior*, not consciousness, was the proper focus of the new science. in fact, Watson declared, "the time seems to have come when psychology must discard all references to consciousness; when it need no longer delude itself into thinking that it is making mental states the object of observation." (1913, p. 164).

In recent years, psychology has renewed its original interest in consciousness thanks to research in cognitive and cultural psychology. In addition, advances in scientific technology, such as the electroencephalogram (EEG), positron emission tomography (PET), and functional magnetic resonance imaging (fMRI), allow scientific study of brain activity during various **alternate states of consciousness (ASCs)**. ASCs include sleep and dreaming, chemically induced changes from psychoactive drugs, daydreaming, fantasies, hypnosis, fasting, meditation, and even the so-called runner's high. Many neuroscientists believe that normal everyday consciousness, as well as ASCs, will ultimately be linked to patterns of neural activity in the brain. The precise location or functioning of this "seat of consciousness" has not yet been discovered.

Alternate States of Consciousness (ASCs) *Mental states, other than ordinary waking consciousness, found during sleep, dreaming, psychoactive drug use, hypnosis, and so on*

How Do We Describe It? A Flowing Stream with Varying Depths

Consciousness may be easier to *describe* than to define. The first American psychologist, William James, likened consciousness to a stream that's constantly changing, yet always the same. It meanders and flows, sometimes where the person wills and sometimes not. However, through the process of *selective attention* (Chapter 4), we can control our consciousness by deliberate concentration and full attention. For example, at the present moment you are (I hope) fully awake and concentrating on the words on this page. At times, however, your control may weaken, and your stream of consciousness may drift to thoughts of a computer you want to buy, your job, or an attractive classmate.

In addition to meandering and flowing, your "stream of consciousness" also varies in depth. Consciousness is not an all-or-nothing phenomenon—conscious or unconscious. Instead, it exists along a continuum. As you can see in Table 5.1, this continuum from high awareness and sharp, focused alertness at one extreme, to middle levels of awareness such as daydreaming, to unconsciousness and coma at the other extreme.

Controlled Versus Automatic Processes

In addition to existing along a continuum, consciousness also involves both *controlled* and *automatic* processes. When you're working at a demanding task or learning something new, such as how to drive a car, consciousness is at the high end of the continuum. These **controlled processes** demand focused attention and generally interfere with other ongoing activities. Have you ever been so absorbed during an exam that you completely forgot your surroundings until the instructor announced, "Time is up," and asked for your paper? This type of focused attention is the hallmark of controlled processes.

In contrast, **automatic processes** require minimal attention and generally do not interfere with other ongoing activities. Think back to your childhood when you first marveled at your parents' ability to drive a car. Are you surprised that you can now listen to the radio, think about your classes, and talk to fellow passengers, all while driving? Learning a new task requires complete concentration and *controlled processing*. Once that task is well learned, you can relax and rely on your *automatic processes* (Geary, 2005).

Automatic processes are generally helpful. However, there are times when we are on "automatic pilot" and don't want to be. Consider the problems of novelist Colin Wilson (1967):

> When I learned to type, I had to do it painfully and with much nervous wear and tear. But at a certain stage a miracle occurred, and this complicated operation was

Controlled Processes *Mental activities requiring focused attention that generally interfere with other ongoing activities*

Automatic Processes *Mental activities requiring minimal attention and having little impact on other activities*

SUMMARY TABLE 5.1 LEVELS OF CONSCIOUSNESS

High Level of Awareness	*Controlled processes* (high level of awareness, focused attention required)	 Patrick Ramsey/ImageState
Middle Level of Awareness	*Automatic process* (awareness, but minimal attention required) *Daydreaming* (low level of awareness and conscious effort, somewhere between active consciousness and dreaming while asleep)	 Walter Hodges/Stone/GettyImages  Richard Hutchings/PhotoResearchers
Minimal or No Awareness	*Unconscious mind* (a Freudian concept discussed in Chapter 11 consisting of unacceptable thoughts, feelings, and memories too painful or anxiety provoking to be admitted to consciousness) *Unconscious* (biologically based lowest level of awareness due to head injuries, disease, anesthesia during surgery, or coma)	 Zigy Kaluzny/GettyImages  David Madison/DuomoPhotography, Inc.

"learned" by a useful robot that I conceal in my subconscious mind. Now I only have to think about what I want to say; my robot secretary does the typing. He is really very useful. He also drives the car for me, speaks French (not very well), and occasionally gives lectures at American universities. [My robot] is most annoying when I am tired, because then he tends to take over most of my functions without even asking me. I have even caught him making love to my wife. (p. 98)

Assessment

CHECK & REVIEW

Understanding Consciousness

Most of our lives are spent in normal, waking **consciousness,** an organism's awareness of its own self and surroundings.

However, we also spend considerable time in various **alternate states of consciousness (ASCs),** such as sleep and dreaming, daydreams, psychoactive drugs, hypnosis, and meditation.

Consciousness has always been difficult to study and define. William James described it as a "flowing stream." Modern researchers emphasize that consciousness exists along a continuum. **Controlled**

processes, which require focused attention, are at the highest level of this continuum. **Automatic processes,** which require minimal attention, are found in the middle. Unconsciousness and coma are at the lowest level.

Questions

1. _____ is (are) best defined as our awareness of our environments and

ourselves. (a) Alternate states of consciousness (ASCs); (b) Consciousness; (c) States of consciousness; (d) Selective attention

2. Why were early psychologists reluctant to study consciousness?

3. Controlled processes require _____ attention, whereas automatic processes need _____ attention.

4. As you read this text, you should

_____. (a) be in an alternate state of consciousness; (b) employ automatic processing; (c) let your stream of consciousness take charge; (d) employ controlled processing

Check your answers in Appendix B.

CLICK & REVIEW
for additional assessment options:
www.wiley.com/college/huffman

SLEEP AND DREAMS

Having explored the definition and description of everyday, waking consciousness, we now turn to two of our most common alternate states of consciousness (ASCs)—sleep and dreaming. These ASCs are fascinating to both scientists and the general public. Why are we born with a mechanism that forces us to sleep and dream for approximately a third of our lives? How can an ASC that requires reduced awareness and responsiveness to our environment be healthy? What are the functions and causes of sleep and dreams?

Achievement

What happens to consciousness while we sleep and dream?

TRY THIS

YOURSELF

Application

Common Myths About Sleep and Dreams

Before reading on, test your personal knowledge of sleep and dreaming by reviewing the common myths below.

- Myth: *Everyone needs 8 hours of sleep a night to maintain sound mental and physical health.* Although most of us average 7.6 hours of sleep a night, some people get by on an incredible 15 to 30 minutes. Others may need as much as 11 hours (Doghramji, 2000; Maas, 1999).

- Myth: *It is easy to learn complicated things, like a foreign language, while asleep.* Although some learning can occur during the lighter stages (1 and 2) of sleep, the processing and retention of this material is minimal (Aarons, 1976; Ogilvie, Wilkinson, & Allison, 1989). Wakeful learning is much more effective and efficient.

- Myth: *Some people never dream.* In rare cases, adults with certain brain injuries or disorders do not dream (Solms, 1997). But otherwise, virtually all adults regularly dream. Even people who firmly believe they never dream report dreams if they are repeatedly awakened during an

overnight study in a sleep laboratory. Children also dream regularly. For example, between ages 3 and 8, they dream during approximately 20 to 28 percent of their sleep time (Foulkes, 1982, 1993). Apparently, almost everyone dreams, but some people don't remember their dreams.

- Myth: *Dreams last only a few seconds.* Research shows that some dreams seem to occur in "real time." For example, a dream that seemed to last 20 minutes probably did last approximately 20 minutes (Dement & Wolpert, 1958).

- Myth: *When genital arousal occurs during sleep, it means the sleeper is having a sexual dream.* When sleepers are awakened during this time, they are no more likely to report sexual dreams than at other times.

- Myth: *Dreaming of dying can be fatal.* This is a good opportunity to exercise your critical thinking skills. Where did this myth come from? Has anyone ever personally experienced and recounted a fatal dream? How would we scientifically prove or disprove this belief?

Circadian [ser-KAY-dee-an]
Rhythms *Biological changes that occur
on a 24-hour cycle (circa = "about" and
dies = "day")*

The Power of Circadian Rhythms: Sleep and the 24-Hour Cycle

To understand sleep, you first need to understand that sleep is an integral part of several daily biological rhythms. Each day, our planet circles the sun, causing our environment to cycle from light to dark and back again. Most human and nonhuman animals have adapted to this change by developing a 24-hour cycle of activities, or circadian rhythms—in Latin, *circa* means "about" and *dies* means "day."

Have you noticed that your energy level, mood, and efficiency change throughout the day? Research shows that alertness, moods, learning efficiency, as well as blood pressure, cortisol levels, metabolism, and pulse rate all follow circadian rhythms (Ariznavarreta et al., 2002; Ice et al., 2004; Kunz & Hermann, 2000; Lauc et al., 2004). For most people, these activities reach their peak during the day and their low point at night. This corresponds to the fact that humans are awake during the light times of the circadian cycle and asleep during the dark periods.

What controls these circadian rhythms? Research shows that the "clock" that regulates these 24-hour rhythms is located in a part of the hypothalamus called the *suprachiasmatic nucleus* (the SCN). Damage to this area of the brain causes human and nonhuman animals to fall asleep or wake up at random times (Dawson, 2004; Ruby et al., 2002; Vitaterna, Takahashi, & Turek, 2001). Human circadian rhythms are also affected by the *pineal gland*, an endocrine gland in the middle of the brain. The pineal gland helps regulate sleep and arousal by secreting large quantities of the hormone *melatonin* during the night and little or none during the day.

Many people now take over-the-counter versions of melatonin as a "sleeping pill." And some research shows that it does improve sleep quality (e.g., Ivanenko et al., 2003; Smits et al., 2003). However, other studies have found little or no effect (Montes et al., 2003). Before taking it yourself consider that melatonin is a naturally occurring powerful hormone, and the synthetic versions available as dietary supplements have not been approved by the FDA. Furthermore, there is limited research on the long-term consequences of taking melatonin, how it interacts with other medications, or even its overall safety.

Disrupted Circadian Rhythms

Despite the warnings, a growing number of people use melatonin to treat "jet lag" and reset their sleep cycles after working late nights or being on rotating shifts. The desire to reset the biological clock is understandable. Studies clearly show that disruptions in circadian rhythms lead to increased fatigue, decreased concentration, sleep disorders, and other health problems (Bovbjerg, 2003; Garbarino et al., 2002; Valdez, Ramirez, & Garcia, 2003; Yesavage et al., 2004). As a student, you may be comforted to know how your late-night study sessions and full- or part-time night jobs help explain your fatigue and other complaints. Less comforting is the knowledge that 20 percent of employees in the United States (primarily in the fields of health care, data processing, and transportation) have rotating work schedules that create many of the same problems (Maas, 1999). Most physicians, nurses, police, and other workers manage to function well despite work schedules that change from day to day or week to week. However, studies do find that shift work and sleep deprivation lead to decreased concentration and productivity, as well as increased accidents (Connor et al., 2002; Dement & Vaughan, 1999; Garbarino et al., 2002).

For example, in a major review of Japanese near-collision train incidents, 82 percent took place between midnight and morning (Charland, 1992). Also, some of the worst recent disasters, including the Union Carbide chemical accident in Bhopal, India, the nuclear power plant disaster in Chernobyl, and the Alaskan oil spill from the *Exxon Valdez*, occurred during the night shift. And official investigations of airline crashes often cite pilot shift work and sleep deprivation as possible contributing factors.

Catastrophic accidents can also be traced to simple, but unusual, coincidences. However, we need to recognize that shift workers may be fighting a dangerous battle with their own circadian rhythms. What can be done to help? Some research shows that workers find it easier to adjust when their schedules are shifted from days to evenings to nights (8–4, 4–12, 12–8). This may be because it's easier to go to bed later than normal rather than earlier. Also, when shifts are rotated every three weeks, rather than every week, productivity increases and accidents decrease. Finally, some research suggests that brief naps for shift workers (or anyone) can help increase performance and learning potential (Purnell, Feyer, & Herbison, 2002; Tietzel & Lack, 2001).

Not only can rotating work schedules disrupt circadian cycles, but so can flying across several time zones. Have you ever taken a long airline flight and felt fatigued, sluggish, and irritable for the first few days after arriving? If so, you experienced symptoms of *jet lag*. Like rotating shift work, jet lag correlates with decreased alertness, decreased mental agility, exacerbation of psychiatric disorders, and overall reduced efficiency (Dawson, 2004; Iyer, 2001; Katz, Knobler, Laibel, Strauss, & Durst, 2002). Jet lag also tends to be worse when we fly eastward rather than westward. This is because our bodies adjust more readily to going to sleep later, rather than earlier.

Sleep Deprivation

Disruptions in circadian cycles due to shift work and jet lag can have serious effects. But what about long-term sleep deprivation? History tells us that during Roman times and in the Middle Ages, sleep deprivation was a form of torture. Today, the armed forces of the United States and other countries sometimes use loud, blaring music and noise to disrupt their enemy's sleep.

Scientifically exploring the effects of severe sleep loss is limited by obvious ethical concerns. Research is also hampered by practical considerations. For example, after about 72 hours without sleep, research participants unwillingly slip into brief, repeated periods of "microsleep" lasting a few seconds at a time. To complicate things further, sleep deprivation increases stress, making it difficult to separate the effects of sleep deprivation from those of stress.

Despite these problems, sleep researchers have documented several hazards related to sleep deprivation that coincide with the previously mentioned effects of disrupted circadian cycles. Sleep deprivation is correlated with significant mood alterations, decreased self-esteem, reduced concentration and motivation, increased irritability, lapses in attention, reduced motor skills, and increased cortisol levels (a sign of stress) (Bourgeois-Bougrine et al., 2003; Carskadon & Dement, 2002; Cho, 2001; Graw et al., 2004). Severe sleep deprivation in rats results in even more serious, and sometimes fatal, side effects (Rechtschaffen et al., 2002; Rechtschaffen & Bergmann, 1995). In addition, lapses in attention among sleep-deprived pilots, physicians, truck drivers, and other workers can also cause serious accidents and cost thousands of lives (McCartt, Rohrbaugh, Hammer, & Fuller, 2000; Oeztuerk, Tufan, & Gueler, 2002; Paice et al., 2002).

Interestingly, however, many physiological functions are not significantly disrupted by periods of sleep deprivation (Walsh & Lindblom, 1997). In fact, in 1965, a 17-year-old student named Randy Gardner, who wanted to earn a place in the *Guinness Book of World Records*, stayed awake for 264 consecutive hours. He did become irritable and had to remain active to stay awake. But he did not become incoherent or psychotic (Coren, 1996; Spinweber, 1993). After his marathon sleep deprivation, Randy slept a mere 14 hours and then returned to his usual 8-hour sleep cycle (Dement, 1992).

www.wiley.com/college/huffman

Sleep deprivation. *Insufficient sleep can seriously affect your college grades, as well as your physical health, motor skills, and overall mood.*

Are You Sleep Deprived?

Take the following two-part test and find out.

Part 1 A typical task used by sleep deprivation researchers is to ask people to trace a star using their nondominant hand while watching their hand in a mirror. Set up a small mirror next to the text and see if you can copy the star below. The task is difficult, and sleep-deprived people typically make many errors.

Part 2 Now give yourself one point each time you answer yes to the following questions:

Do you often fall asleep...

watching TV?

during boring meetings or lectures or in warm rooms?

after heavy meals or after a small amount of alcohol?

while relaxing after dinner?

within five minutes of getting into bed?

In the morning, do you generally...

need an alarm clock to wake up at the right time?

struggle to get out of bed?

hit the snooze bar several times to get more sleep?

During the day, do you...

feel tired, irritable, and stressed out?

have trouble concentrating and remembering?

feel slow when it comes to critical thinking, problem solving, and being creative?

feel drowsy while driving?

need a nap to get through the day?

have dark circles around your eyes?

According to Cornell University psychologist James Maas (1999), if you answered yes to three or more items, you are probably sleep deprived.

Source: Quiz adapted and reprinted from Maas, 1999, with permission.

▪ Stages of Sleep: How Scientists Study Sleep

Sleep is an important component of our circadian rhythms. Each night, we go through four to five cycles of distinct sleep stages. And each stage has its own rhythm and corresponding changes in brain activity and behavior. How do we know this? How can scientists study private mental events like sleep?

Surveys and interviews can provide some information about the nature of sleep. But perhaps the most important tool for sleep researchers is the *electroencephalograph* (EEG), an apparatus that detects and records brain waves. As we move from a waking state to deep sleep, our brains show complex and predictable changes in electrical activity. The EEG records these brain-wave changes by means of small disklike electrodes placed on the scalp. The electrodes pick up electrical changes in the nerve cells of the cerebral cortex. The changes are then amplified and recorded on a long roll of paper or a computer monitor. These recordings, or *electroencephalograms*, allow researchers to observe the brain's activity while its owner is asleep. Sleep researchers also use other recording devices, such as those seen in Figure 5.1.

Cycling Through the Stages of Sleep

Perhaps the best way to appreciate the methods and findings of sleep researchers is to pretend for a moment that you are a participant in a sleep experiment. When you arrive at the sleep lab, you are assigned one of several "bedrooms." The researcher hooks you up to various physiological recording devices. These devices include the *electroencephalograph* (EEG) to measure brain waves, the *electromyograph* (EMG) to measure muscular activity, and the *electrooculograph* (EOG) to measure eye movements. If you are like other participants, you will probably need a night or two to adapt to the equipment and return to a normal mode of sleeping.

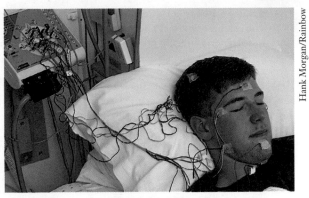

Hank Morgan/Rainbow

Early Stages of Sleep

Once adapted, you are ready for the researchers to monitor your typical night's sleep. As your eyes close and you begin to relax, the researcher in the next room notices that your EEG recordings have moved from the wave pattern associated with normal wakefulness, *beta waves*, to the slower *alpha waves*, which indicate drowsy relaxation (Figure 5.2). During this relaxed "presleep" period, you may experience a *hypnagogic state*. This state is characterized by feelings of floating, weightlessness, visual images (such as flashing lights or colors), or swift, jerky movements and a corresponding feeling of slipping or falling. Hypnagogic experiences are sometimes incorporated into fragmented dreams and remembered in the morning. They also may explain reported accounts of alien abduction. These alleged encounters typically occur while the victim is falling asleep, and many abductees report "strange flashes of light" and "floating off the bed."

As you continue relaxing, your brain's electrical activity slows even further. You are now in *Stage 1* sleep. During this stage, your breathing becomes more regular, your heart rate slows, and your blood pressure decreases. But you could still be readily awakened. No one wakens you, though, so you relax more deeply and slide gently into *Stage 2* sleep. This stage is noted on your electroencephalograph by occasional short bursts of rapid, high-amplitude brain waves known as *sleep spindles*. During Stage 2 sleep, you become progressively more relaxed and less responsive to the exter-

Figure 5.1 How sleep is studied. Researchers in a sleep laboratory use sophisticated equipment to record physiological changes during sleep. *Electroencephalograph* (EEG) electrodes are taped to the scalp to measure brain-wave activity. *Electromyograph* (EMG) electrodes are applied to the chin and jaw to measure muscular activity. *Electrooculograph* (EOG) electrodes are taped near the eyes to record eye movements. Other devices not shown in this photo record heart rate, respiration rate, and genital arousal.

Figure 5.2 Electroencephalograph patterns during sleep. Note as you move from being awake to deeply asleep how your brain waves decrease in frequency (cycles per second) and increase in amplitude (height). Also note how the REM (rapid-eye-movement) sleep waves most closely resemble the pattern in the alert (beta waves) state. The brain is more aroused during REM sleep than it is in the lightest level of NREM sleep, Stage 1.

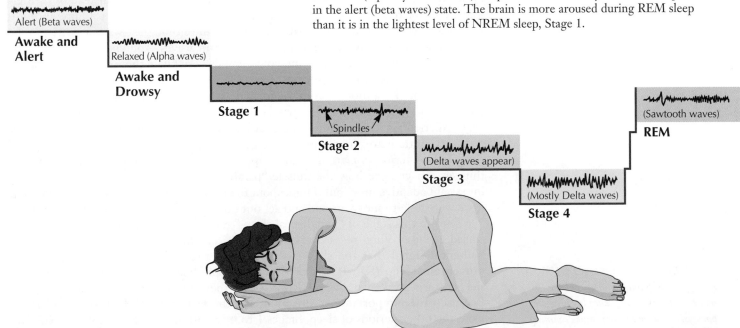

Alert (Beta waves)
Awake and Alert
Relaxed (Alpha waves)
Awake and Drowsy
Stage 1
Spindles
Stage 2
(Delta waves appear)
Stage 3
(Mostly Delta waves)
Stage 4
(Sawtooth waves)
REM

www.wiley.com/college/huffman

Figure 5.3 **Stages in a typical night's sleep.** During a normal night's sleep, the sleeper moves in and out of various stages of sleep. Starting off alert, the sleeper gradually shifts downward into NREM (non-rapid-eye-movement) Stage 1, then NREM Stages 2, 3, and 4. The sleep cycle then reverses. At the peak of the return trip, the sleeper spends some time in REM (rapid-eye-movement) sleep and then the cycle starts downward again. As the night continues, the sleeper repeats the general cycle four to five times. (The dotted lines indicate the boundaries of each cycle.) Note that the periods of Stage 4 and then Stage 3 sleep diminish during the night, whereas REM periods increase in duration. *Source:* Adapted from Julien, 2001, with permission.

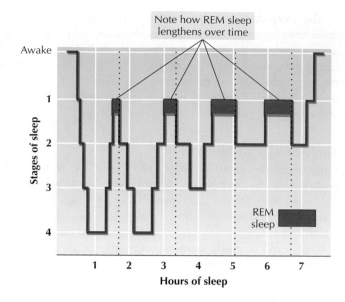

nal environment. Even deeper levels of sleep follow Stage 2—*Stages 3 and 4.* As shown in Figure 5.2, these stages are marked by the appearance of slow, high-amplitude *delta* waves. It is very hard to awaken you in stages 3 and 4, even by shouting and shaking. Stage 4 sleep also is the time when children are most likely to wet the bed and when sleepwalking occurs. (Can you see why it is difficult to learn foreign languages or other material from tapes while sound asleep [Wyatt & Bootzin, 1994]?)

In about an hour, you have progressed through all four stages of sleep. Then the sequence begins to reverse itself (see Figure 5.3). Keep in mind that we don't necessarily go through all four sleep stages in this exact sequence. However, during the course of a night, people usually complete four to five cycles of light to deep sleep and back. And each cycle lasts about 90 minutes.

REM Sleep

Figure 5.3 also shows an interesting phenomenon that occurs at the end of the first cycle. You reverse back through Stage 3, and then to Stage 2. But instead of reentering the calm, relaxed Stage 1, something totally different happens. Quite abruptly, your scalp recordings display a pattern of small-amplitude, fast-wave activity, similar in many ways to an awake, vigilant person's brain waves. Your breathing and pulse rates become fast and irregular. And your genitals very likely show signs of arousal (an erection or vaginal lubrication).

Interestingly, although your brain and body are giving many signs of active arousal, your musculature is deeply relaxed and unresponsive. The sleeper is in some ways experiencing the deepest stage of sleep. Yet, in other ways the lightest. Because of these contradictory qualities, this stage is sometimes referred to as "paradoxical sleep." The term *paradoxical* means "apparently self-contradictory." (As a critical thinker, can you see how the muscle "paralysis" of paradoxical sleep may serve an important adaptive function? Think about the problems and dangers that would ensue if we were able to move around and act out our dreams while we were sleeping.)

During this stage of "paradoxical sleep," rapid eye movements occur under your closed eyelids. When researchers discovered that these eye movements are a clear, biological signal that the sleeper is dreaming, they labeled this stage **rapid-eye-movement sleep (REM)**. Although some people believe they do not dream, when sleepers are awakened during REM sleep they almost always report dreaming. Because of the importance of dreaming and the fact that REM sleep is so different from the other periods of sleep, Stages 1 to 4 are often collectively called *NREM* (or

Rapid-Eye-Movement (REM) Sleep
A stage of sleep marked by rapid eye movements, high-frequency brain waves, paralysis of large muscles, and dreaming

The Sleep Cycle in Cats

During NREM (non-rapid-eye-movement) sleep, cats often sleep in an upright position. With the onset of REM sleep, the cat rolls over on its side. Can you explain why?

Answer: During REM sleep, large muscles are temporarily paralyzed, which causes the cat to lose motor control and lie down.

---

non-rapid-eye-movement) sleep. Dreaming sometimes occurs during NREM sleep, but less frequently. NREM dreams usually contain a simple experience, such as "I dreamed of a house" (Hobson, 2002; Squier & Domhoff, 1998).

What is the purpose of REM and NREM sleep? In addition to the need for dreaming, which will be discussed in the next section, scientists believe REM sleep may be important for complex brain functions, such as learning and consolidating new memories (Kavanau, 2000; Maquet et al., 2003; Squier & Domhoff, 1998). For example, the amount of REM sleep increases after periods of stress or intense learning. And fetuses, infants, and young children spend a large percentage of their sleep time in this stage (Figure 5.4). In addition, REM sleep occurs only in mammals of higher intelligence and is absent in nonmammals such as reptiles (Rechtschaffen & Siegel, 2000).

Non-Rapid-Eye-Movement (NREM) Sleep *Stages 1 to 4 of sleep with Stage 1 as the lightest level and Stage 4 as the deepest level*

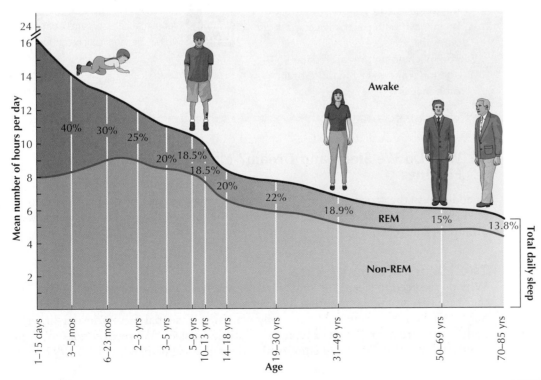

Figure 5.4 Sleep and dreaming over the life span. Notice that as you get older, the overall amount of sleep and the proportion of REM (rapid-eye-movement) sleep both decrease. The most dramatic changes occur during the first two to three years of life. As an infant, you spent almost eight hours a day in REM sleep. At age 70, you spend less than an hour.

www.wiley.com/college/huffman

There also is general agreement that REM serves an important biological need. When researchers selectively deprive sleepers of REM sleep (by waking them each time they enter the state), most people experience REM *rebound*. That is, they try to "catch up" on REM sleep on subsequent occasions by spending more time than usual in this state (Dement & Vaughan, 1999).

REM sleep is important to our biological functioning. However, the need for NREM sleep may be even greater. When people are deprived of *total* sleep, rather than just REM sleep, and then allowed full recovery sleep, their first uninterrupted night has a greater proportion of NREM sleep (Borbely, 1982). In addition, as you may remember from Figure 5.3, when you initially begin to sleep, you spend more time in Stage 1 sleep through Stage 4 sleep (NREM). After this need has been satisfied, the latter parts of the night are devoted to more REM sleep.

The idea that nature first satisfies its need for NREM sleep before going on to REM sleep is also supported by studies showing that adults who are "short sleepers" (five or fewer hours each night) spend less time in REM sleep than do "long sleepers" (nine or more hours each night). Similarly, infants get more sleep and have a higher percentage of REM sleep than do adults (see Figure 5.4). Apparently, the greater the total amount of sleep, the greater the percentage of REM sleep.

CHECK & REVIEW

Circadian Rhythms and Stages of Sleep

Circadian rhythms affect our sleep and waking cycle and disruptions due to shift work and jet lag can cause serious problems. A typical night's sleep consists of four to five 90-minute cycles. The cycle begins in Stage 1 and then moves through Stages 2, 3, and 4. After reaching the deepest level of sleep, the cycle reverses up to **REM (rapid-eye-movement) sleep,** in which the person often is dreaming.

Questions

1. Biological rhythms that occur on a daily basis are called _____ rhythms. (a) circuitous; (b) chronobiology; (c) calendrical; (d) circadian

2. Jet lag results from _____. (a) sleep deprivation; (b) disruption of the circadian rhythms; (c) the effect of light on the pineal gland; (d) disruption of brain-wave patterns that occur at high altitudes.

3. The machine that measures the voltage (or brain waves) that the brain produces is _____.

4. Just before sleep, brain waves move from _____ waves, indicating normal wakefulness, to _____ waves associated with drowsy relaxation. (a) beta, alpha; (b) theta, delta; (c) alpha, beta; (d) sigma, chi

Check your answers in Appendix B.

CLICK & REVIEW
for additional assessment options:
www.wiley.com/college/huffman

■ Why Do We Sleep and Dream? Major Theories and Recent Findings

In addition to the growing body of facts that we now know about sleep and dreaming, scientists also have developed several important, overarching theories, which we'll explore in this section.

Two Major Theories of Sleep

Why do we need to sleep? No one knows precisely all the functions sleep serves, but there are two prominent theories. The **repair/restoration theory** suggests that sleep helps us recuperate from depleting daily activities. Essential factors in our brain or body are apparently repaired or replenished while we sleep. We recover not only from physical fatigue but also from emotional and intellectual demands (Maas, 1999).

Repair/Restoration Theory *Sleep serves a recuperative function, allowing organisms to repair or replenish key factors*

In contrast, the **evolutionary/circadian theory** emphasizes the relationship of sleep to basic circadian rhythms. According to this view, sleep evolved so that human and nonhuman animals could conserve energy when they were not foraging for food or seeking mates. Sleep also serves to keep them still at times when predators are active (Hirshkowitz, Moore, & Minhoto, 1997). The evolutionary/circadian theory helps explain differences in sleep patterns across species (Figure 5.5). Opossums sleep many hours each day because they are relatively safe in their environment and are able to easily find food and shelter. In comparison, sheep and horses sleep very little because their diets require constant foraging for food. In addition, their only defense against predators is vigilance and running away.

Which theory is correct? Both theories have merit. Obviously, we need to repair and restore ourselves after a busy day. But bears don't hibernate all winter simply to recover from a busy summer. Like humans and other nonhuman animals, they also need to conserve energy when the environment is hostile. It may be that sleep initially served to conserve energy and keep us out of trouble. Over time it may have evolved to allow for repair and restoration.

Three Major Theories of Dreams

Is there special meaning and information in our dreams? Why do we have bad dreams? Why do we dream at all? These questions have long fascinated writers and poets, as well as psychologists.

The Psychoanalytic/Psychodynamic View   One of the oldest and most scientifically controversial explanations for why we dream is Freud's *psychoanalytic view*. In one of his first books, *The Interpretation of Dreams* (1900), Freud proposed that dreams are "the royal road to the unconscious." According to Freud, dreaming is a special state

Richard Cummins/Corbis

Dreams and butterflies. *Throughout the ages, humans have wondered about dreams. After dreaming he was a butterfly, Chuang Tzu, a Chinese Taoist (third century* B.C.*), spoke about the interplay of reality and dreams: "Suddenly I woke up and I was indeed Chuang Tzu. Did Chuang Tzu dream he was a butterfly? Or did the butterfly dream he was Chuang Tzu?"*

Evolutionary/Circadian Theory *As a part of circadian rhythms, sleep evolved to conserve energy and as protection from predators*

Figure 5.5 **Average daily hours of sleep for different mammals.** Why does an opossum spend almost 20 hours a day sleeping, yet a horse spends only 2 hours?

Answer: According to the evolutionary/circadian theory of sleep, animals that sleep the longest are least threatened by the environment and can easily find food and shelter. Note how the opossum and cat spend longer hours in sleep than the horse and sheep, presumably because of differences in diet and the number of predators.

www.wiley.com/college/huffman

Manifest Content *According to Freud, the surface content of a dream, which contains dream symbols that distort and disguise the dream's true meaning*

Latent Content *The true, unconscious meaning of a dream, according to Freudian dream theory*

Ric Frazier/Age FotostockAmerica, Inc.

Dream images. Have you ever had a dream like this? How would you interpret this dream according to the three theories discussed in the text?

Activation–Synthesis Hypothesis *Hobson's theory that dreams are by-products of random stimulation of brain cells; the brain attempts to combine (or synthesize) this spontaneous activity into coherent patterns, known as dreams*

in which normally repressed and personally unacceptable desires rise to the surface of consciousness. Supposedly, the main purpose of dreams is *wish fulfillment*. Therefore, listening to a patient's dreams reportedly offers direct insight into his or her unconscious. When a lonely person dreams of romance or an angry child dreams of getting even with the class bully, they may be expressing wish fulfillment.

More often, though, the dream content is so threatening and anxiety producing that it must be couched in symbols. A journey in a dream is supposedly a symbol for death. Horseback riding and dancing are considered symbols for sexual intercourse. And a gun might represent a penis. Freud referred to these symbols (the journey, horseback riding, or the gun) as the **manifest content** (or the story line) of the dream. The underlying, true meaning (death, sex, penis) is called the **latent content**. According to Freud, by disguising the forbidden unconscious needs as symbols, the dreamer avoids anxiety and remains asleep.

What is the scientific evidence for Freud's theory of dreams? Most modern research finds little or no scientific support for Freud's idea that dreams represent the fulfillment of repressed wishes or that the manifest content of dreams are disguised symbols of the dream's true meaning (Domhoff, 2003; Fisher & Greenberg, 1996). Critics also say that Freud's theory is highly subjective. The symbols can be interpreted according to the particular analyst's view or training. After being confronted about the symbolic nature of his beloved cigars, even Freud supposedly remarked, "Sometimes a cigar is just a cigar."

The Biological View In contrast to the Freudian perspective, the **activation–synthesis hypothesis** suggests dreams are a by-product of random stimulation of brain cells during REM sleep (Hobson, 1988, 2005). Based on research conducted on the brain activity of cats during REM sleep, Alan Hobson and Robert McCarley (1977) proposed that specific neurons in the brainstem fire spontaneously during REM sleep. The cortex then struggles to "synthesize" or make sense out of this random stimulation by manufacturing dreams.

Have you ever dreamed that you were trying to run away from a frightening situation but found that you could not move? The activation–synthesis hypothesis might explain this dream as random stimulation of the amygdala. As you recall from Chapter 2, the amygdala is a specific brain area linked to strong emotions, especially fear. If your amygdala is randomly stimulated and you feel afraid, you may try to run. But you can't move because your major muscles are temporarily paralyzed during REM sleep. To make sense of this conflict, you might create a dream about a fearful situation in which you were trapped in heavy sand or someone was holding on to your arms and legs.

This is *not* to say that Hobson believes dreams are totally meaningless. He suggests that even if dreams begin with more or less random activity in various brain areas, your interpretation of this activity is not random (1988, 2005). The dream that is constructed depends on your individual personality, motivations, memories, and life experiences.

The Cognitive View According to the cognitive view, dreams are an extension of everyday life—a form of thinking during sleep. Rather than being mysterious messages from the unconscious or the result of random brain stimulation, dreams are simply another type of *information processing*. They help us sift and sort our everyday experiences and thoughts. The brain periodically shuts out sensory input so that it can process, assimilate, and update information. The cognitive view sees dreams as a type of *mental housecleaning* similar to disk defragmentation on your computer.

The cognitive view of dreaming is supported by the fact that REM sleep increases following stress and intense learning periods. Furthermore, other research reports strong similarities between dream content and waking thoughts, fears, and concerns (Domhoff, 1999, 2005; Erlacher & Schredl, 2004). For example, college students often report "examination-anxiety" dreams. You can't find your classroom, you're running out of time, your pen or pencil won't work, or you've completely forgotten a scheduled exam and show up totally unprepared (Van de Castle, 1995). (Sound familiar?)

In Sum The psychoanalytic/psychodynamic, biological, and cognitive views of dreaming offer three widely divergent perspectives. And numerous questions remain. How would the psychoanalytic/psychodynamic theory explain why human fetuses show REM patterns? Is the fetus working out suppressed wishes and anxieties in the womb? On the other hand, how would the activation–synthesis hypothesis explain complicated, storylike dreams or recurrent dreams? What does a fetus have to dream about in response to random brain activity? Finally, according to the information-processing approach, how can a fetus sift and sort its "waking" experiences? And how is it that the same dream can often be explained by many theories?

Achievement
Gender & Cultural Diversity

Dream Variations and Similarities

Do men and women dream about different things? Are there differences between cultures in dream content? In reference to gender, research shows that men and women tend to share many common dream themes. But women are more likely to dream of children, family and familiar people, household objects, and indoor events. Men, on the other hand, more often dream about strangers, violence, weapons, sexual activity, achievement, and outdoor events (Domhoff, 2003; Murray, 1995; Schredl et al., 2004). Interestingly, recent evidence suggests that as gender differences and stereotypes lessen, segregation of dream content by gender becomes less distinct (Domhoff, Nishikawa, & Brubaker, 2004; Hobson, 2002).

Likewise, researchers have found both similarities and differences in dream content across cultures. Dreams involving basic human needs and fears (like sex, aggression, and death) seem to be found in all cultures. And children around the world often dream about large, threatening wild animals. People of all ages and cultures dream of falling, being chased, and being unable to do something they need to do. In addition, dreams around the world typically include more misfortune than good fortune, and the dreamer is more often the victim of aggression than the cause of it (Domhoff, 1996, 2003; Hall & Van de Castle, 1996).

Yet there are some cultural differences. The Yir Yoront, an Australian hunting-and-gathering group, generally prefer marriage between a man and his mother's brother's daughter (Schneider & Sharp, 1969). Therefore, it is not uncommon (or surprising) that young, single men in the group often report recurrent dreams of aggression from their mother's brother (their future father-in-law) (Price & Crapo, 2002). Similarly, Americans often report embarrassing dreams of being naked in public. Such dreams are rare in cultures where few clothes are worn.

How people interpret and value their dreams also varies across cultures (Matsumoto, 2000; Price & Crapo, 2002; Wax, 2004). The Iroquois of North America believe that one's spirit uses dreams to communicate unconscious wishes to the conscious mind (Wallace, 1958). They often share their dreams with religious leaders, who help them interpret and cope with their underlying psychic needs to prevent illness and even death. On the other hand, the Maya of Central America share their dreams and interpretations at communal gatherings as an important means of teaching cultural folk wisdom (Tedlock, 1992). (As a critical thinker, do you notice the close similarity between Freudian theory and the Iroquois concept of dreaming? Some historians believe that Freud borrowed many concepts from the Iroquois—without giving appropriate credit.)

Application

CRITICAL THINKING

Interpreting Your Dreams

Television, movies, and other popular media often portray dreams as highly significant and easily interpreted. However, scientists are deeply divided about the meaning of dreams and their relative importance. These differences in scientific opinion provide an excellent opportunity for you to practice the critical thinking skill of tolerance for ambiguity.

To improve your tolerance for ambiguity (and learn a little more about your own dreams), begin by briefly jotting down one of your most recent and vivid dreams. It should be at least three or four paragraphs in length. Now analyze your dream using the following perspectives:

1. According to the psychoanalytic/psychodynamic view, what might be the forbidden, unconscious fears, drives, or desires represented by your dream? Can you identify the manifest content versus the latent content?
2. How would the biological view, the activation–synthesis hypothesis, explain your dream? Can you identify a specific thought that might have been stimulated and then led to this particular dream?
3. Psychologists from the cognitive perspective believe dreams provide important information, help us make needed changes in our life, and even suggest solutions to real-life problems.

ACTIVE LEARNING

Do you agree or disagree? Does your dream provide an insight that increases your self-understanding?

Having analyzed your dream from each perspective, can you see how difficult it is to find the one right answer? Higher-level critical thinkers recognize that competing theories are akin to the story of the four blind men who are each exploring separate parts of an elephant. By listening to their description of the trunk, tail, leg, and so on, critical thinkers can synthesize the information and develop a greater understanding. But no one part—or single theory—reveals the whole picture.

Assessment

CHECK & REVIEW

Theories of Sleep and Dreams

The exact function of sleep is not known. But according to the **repair/restoration theory,** sleep is thought to be necessary for its restorative value, both physically and psychologically. According to **evolutionary/circadian theory,** it also has adaptive value.

Three major theories attempt to explain why we dream. According to the psychoanalytic/psychodynamic view, dreams are disguised symbols of repressed anxieties and desires. The biological perspective (**activation–synthesis hypothesis**) argues that dreams are simple

by-products of random stimulation of brain cells. The cognitive view suggests that dreams are an important part of information processing of everyday experiences.

Questions

1. How does the repair/restoration theory of sleep differ from the evolutionary/circadian theory?
2. Freud believed that dreams were the "royal road to the _____." (a) therapeutic alliance; (b) psyche; (c) latent content; (d) unconscious
3. _____ theory states that dreams are by-products of random stimulation of

brain cells. In contrast, the _____ view suggests dreams serve an information-processing function and help us sift and sort our everyday experiences and thoughts. (a) Biological, learning; (b) Cognitive, wish-fulfillment; (c) Activation–synthesis, cognitive; (d) Psychodynamic, infodynamic
4. After periods of stress and intense learning, _____ sleep increases.

Check your answers in Appendix B.

 CLICK & REVIEW
for additional assessment options:
www.wiley.com/college/huffman

▪ Sleep Disorders: When Sleep Becomes a Problem

Are you one of the lucky people who takes sleep for granted? If so, you may be surprised to discover the following facts (based on Dement & Vaughan, 1999; Doghramji, 2000; Hobson, 2005; National Sleep Foundation, 2004):

- An estimated two-thirds of American adults suffer from sleep problems, and about 25 percent of children under age 5 have a sleep disturbance.

- One in five adults is so sleepy during the day that sleepiness interferes with their daily activities. Each year Americans spend more than $98 million on over-the-counter sleep aids and another $50 million on caffeine tablets to keep them awake during the day.

- Twenty percent of all automobile drivers have fallen asleep for a few seconds (microsleep) at the wheel.

The costs of sleep disorders are enormous, not only for the individual but also for the public. Psychologists and other mental health professionals divide sleep disorders into two major diagnostic categories: (1) *dyssomnias*, which involve problems in the amount, timing, and quality of sleep, and (2) *parasomnias*, which include abnormal disturbances occurring during sleep.

Dyssomnias

There are at least three prominent examples of dyssomnias:

1. *Insomnia.* The term *insomnia* literally means "lack of sleep." People with **insomnia** have persistent difficulty falling asleep or staying asleep, or they wake up too early. Many people think they have insomnia if they cannot sleep before an exciting event, which is normal. They also wrongly assume that everyone must sleep eight hours a night. Sometimes, too, people think they are not sleeping when they really are.

    However, a significant percentage of the population (as much as 10 percent) genuinely suffers from insomnia, and nearly everyone occasionally experiences unwanted sleeplessness (Doghramji, 2000; Riemann & Volderholzer, 2003). A telltale complaint of insomnia is that the person feels poorly rested the next day. Most people with serious insomnia have other medical or psychological disorders as well, such as alcohol and other drug abuse, anxiety disorders, and depression (Reimann & Volderholzer, 2003; Taylor, Lichstein, & Durrence, 2003).

    Unfortunately, the most popular treatment for insomnia is drugs—either over-the-counter pills, such as Sominex, or prescription tranquilizers and barbiturates. The problem with nonprescription pills is that they generally don't work. Prescription pills, on the other hand, do help you sleep. But they decrease Stage 4 and REM sleep, thereby seriously affecting the quality of sleep. Frequently prescribed drugs like Ambien, Lunesta, Xanax, and Halcion may be helpful in treating sleeping problems related to anxiety and specific stressful situations, such as losing a loved one. However, chronic users run the risk of psychological and physical drug dependence (Leonard, 2003; McKim, 2002). In sum, sleeping pills may be useful for occasional, short-term (two to three nights) use, but they may create more problems than they solve.

2. *Sleep apnea.* A second major dyssomnia, closely related to insomnia, is sleep apnea. *Apnea* literally means "no breathing." Many people have either irregular breathing or occasional periods of 10 seconds or less without breathing during their sleep. People with sleep apnea, however, may fail to breathe for a minute or longer and then wake up gasping for breath. When they do breathe during their sleep, they often snore. Repeated awakenings result in insomnia and leave the person feeling

Insomnia *Persistent problems in falling asleep, staying asleep, or awakening too early*

Sleep Apnea *Repeated interruption of breathing during sleep because air passages to the lungs are physically blocked or the brain stops activating the diaphragm*

www.wiley.com/college/huffman

tired and sleepy during the day. Unfortunately, people are often unaware of these frequent awakenings and may fail to recognize the reason for their daytime fatigue.

Sleep apnea seems to result from blocked upper airway passages or from the brain ceasing to send signals to the diaphragm, thus causing breathing to stop. If you snore loudly or have repeated awakenings followed by gasps for breath, you may be suffering from sleep apnea and should seek medical attention. Recent research shows that sleep apnea may kill neurons in your brain that are critical for learning and memory. It also can lead to high blood pressure, stroke, and heart attack (Miller, 2004; National Sleep Foundation, 2004; Young, Skatrud, & Peppard, 2004).

Treatment for sleep apnea depends partly on its severity. If the problem occurs only when you're sleeping on your back, sewing tennis balls on the back of your pajama top may help remind you to sleep on your side. Obstruction of the breathing passages is also related to obesity and heavy alcohol use (Christensen, 2000), so dieting and alcohol restriction are often recommended. For others, surgery, dental appliances that reposition the tongue, or ventilating machines may be the answer.

For many years, researchers assumed that snoring (without the accompanying stoppages of breathing in sleep apnea) was a minor problem—except for bed partners. Recent findings, however, suggest that even this "simple snoring" can also lead to heart disease and possible death (Peppard, Young, Palta, & Skatrud, 2000). Although occasional mild snoring may be normal, chronic snoring is a possible "warning sign that should prompt people to seek help" (Christensen, 2000, p. 172).

Narcolepsy [NAR-co-lep-see]
Sudden and irresistible onsets of sleep during normal waking hours. (narco = "numbness" and lepsy = "seizure")

Louis Psihoyos

Louis Psihoyos

Narcolepsy. *William Dement and his colleagues at Stanford's Sleep Disorders Center have bred a colony of narcoleptic dogs. Note how the dog in the left photo lapses suddenly from alert wakefulness to deep sleep in the right photo.*

3. Narcolepsy. A serious sleep disorder that is somewhat the opposite of insomnia is narcolepsy—sudden and irresistible onsets of sleep during normal waking hours. Narcolepsy afflicts about one person in 2000 and generally runs in families (Kryger, Walld, & Manfreda, 2002; Siegel, 2000). During an attack, REM-like sleep suddenly intrudes into the waking state of consciousness. Victims may experience sudden attacks of muscle weakness or paralysis (known as *cataplexy*). Such people may fall asleep while walking, talking, or driving a car. These attacks are obviously dramatic and can be incapacitating. Can you imagine what it would be like to be driving along the highway or walking across campus and suddenly having a narcoleptic attack?

Long daily naps and stimulant or antidepressant drugs may help reduce the frequency of narcoleptic attacks. But the causes and cure of narcolepsy are still unknown. Stanford University's Sleep Disorders Center was among the first to selectively breed a group of narcoleptic dogs, which has increased our understanding of the genetics of this disorder. Research on these specially bred dogs has found degenerated neurons in certain areas of the brain (Siegel, 2000). Whether human narcolepsy results from similar degeneration is a question for future research.

Nightmares *Anxiety-arousing dreams generally occurring near the end of the sleep cycle, during REM sleep*

Night Terrors *Abrupt awakenings from NREM (non-rapid-eye-movement) sleep accompanied by intense physiological arousal and feelings of panic*

Parasomnias

The second category of sleep disorders, parasomnias, includes abnormal sleep disturbances such as nightmares and night terrors. **Nightmares**, or bad dreams, occur toward the end of the sleep cycle, during REM sleep. Less common, but more frightening, are **night terrors**. These parasomnias occur earlier in the cycle, during Stage 3 or Stage 4 of NREM sleep. The sleeper experiences panic, and may hallucinate, sit bolt upright, scream in terror, walk around, talk incoherently, and still be almost impossible to awaken.

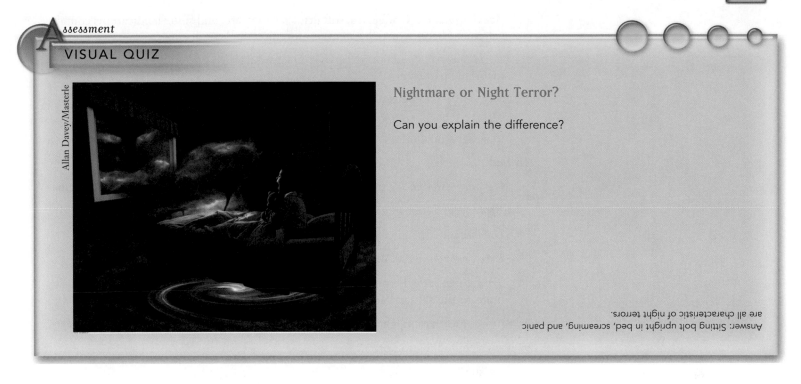

Allan Davey/Masterle

Nightmare or Night Terror?

Can you explain the difference?

Answer: Sitting bolt upright in bed, screaming, and panic are all characteristic of night terrors.

Sleepwalking, which tends to accompany night terrors, also occurs during NREM sleep (which explains why movement is possible). *Sleeptalking*, on the other hand, occurs with about equal probability in REM and NREM sleep. It can include single, indistinct words or long, articulate sentences. It is even possible to engage some sleeptalkers in a limited conversation.

Nightmares, night terrors, sleepwalking, and sleeptalking are all more common among young children. But they can also occur in adults, usually during times of stress or major life events (Hobson & Silvestri, 1999; Muris, Merckelbach, Gadet, & Moulaert, 2000). Patience and soothing reassurance at the time of the sleep disruption are usually the only treatment recommended for both children and adults.

Application
APPLYING PSYCHOLOGY TO EVERYDAY LIFE

Self-Help for Sleep Problems
Are you wondering what is recommended for sleep problems other than drugs? A recent large-scale study reported good success from behavior therapy (Smith et al., 2003). You can use these same techniques in your own life. For example, when you're having a hard time going to sleep, don't keep checking the clock and worrying about your loss of sleep. Instead, remove all TVs, stereos, and books, and limit the use of the bedroom to sleep (and sex). If you need additional help, try some of the relaxation techniques suggested by the *Better Sleep Council*, a nonprofit education organization in Burtonsville, Maryland.

During the day

> *Exercise.* Daily physical activity works away tension. But don't exercise vigorously late in the day, or you'll get fired up instead. Keep regular hours. An erratic schedule can disrupt biological rhythms. Get up at the same time each day.

www.wiley.com/college/huffman

Avoid stimulants. Coffee, tea, soft drinks, chocolate, and some medications contain caffeine. Nicotine may be an even more potent sleep disrupter.

Avoid late meals and heavy drinking. Overindulgence can interfere with your normal sleep pattern.

Stop worrying. Focus on your problems at a set time earlier in the day.

Use presleep rituals. Follow the same routine every evening: listen to music, write in a diary, meditate.

In bed

Use progressive muscle relaxation. Alternately tense and relax various muscle groups.

Apply yoga. These gentle exercises help you relax.

Use fantasies. Imagine yourself in a tranquil setting. Feel yourself relax.

Use deep breathing. Take deep breaths, telling yourself you're falling asleep.

Try a warm bath. This can induce drowsiness because it sends blood away from the brain to the skin surface.

For more information, check these websites:

- www.sleepfoundation.org
- www.stanford.edu/~dement

 Assessment

CHECK & REVIEW

Sleep Disorders

Sleep disorders fall into two major diagnostic categories—*dyssomnias* (including insomnia, sleep apnea, and narcolepsy) and *parasomnias* (such as nightmares and night terrors).

People who have repeated difficulty falling or staying asleep, or awakening too early, experience **insomnia.** A person with **sleep apnea** temporarily stops breathing during sleep, causing loud snoring or poor-quality sleep. **Narcolepsy** is excessive daytime sleepiness characterized by sudden sleep attacks. **Nightmares** are bad

dreams that occur during REM (rapid-eye-movement) sleep. **Night terrors** are abrupt awakenings with feelings of panic that occur during NREM sleep.

Questions

Following are four descriptions of people suffering from sleep disorders. Label each type.

1. George awakens many times each night and feels fatigued and poorly rested the next day.
2. While sleeping, Joan often snores loudly and frequently stops breathing temporarily.
3. Tyler is a young child who often wakes up terrified and cannot describe what has happened. These episodes occur primarily during NREM sleep.
4. Xavier complains to his physician about sudden and irresistible onsets of sleep during his normal work day.

Check your answers in Appendix B.

CLICK & REVIEW
for additional assessment options:
www.wiley.com/college/huffman

Psychoactive Drugs
Chemicals that change conscious awareness, mood, or perception

 Achievement

How do psychoactive drugs affect consciousness?

PSYCHOACTIVE DRUGS

Since the beginning of civilization, people of all cultures have used—and abused—psychoactive drugs (Grilly, 2006; Kuhn, Swartzwelder, & Wilson, 2003). **Psychoactive drugs** are generally defined as chemicals that change conscious awareness or perception. Do you (or does someone you know) use caffeine (in coffee, tea, chocolate, or cola) or nicotine (in cigarettes) as a pick-me-up? How about alcohol (in beer, wine, and cocktails) as a way to relax and lessen inhibitions? All three—caffeine, nico-

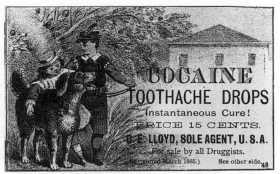

The New York Historical Society

The New York Historical Society

History of psychoactive drugs. Before the Food and Drug Administration (FDA) regulated the sale of such drugs as heroin, opium, and cocaine, they were commonly found in over-the-counter, non-prescription drugs.

tine, and alcohol—are psychoactive drugs. How use differs from abuse, and how chemical alterations in consciousness affect a person both psychologically and physically, are important topics in psychology. In this section, we begin by clarifying differences in terminology. We then go on to look at the four major categories of psychoactive drugs and "club drugs" like MDMA, or ecstasy.

◾ Understanding Psychoactive Drugs: Important Terminology

Have you noticed how difficult it is to have a logical, nonemotional discussion about drugs? In our society, where the most popular drugs are caffeine, tobacco, and ethyl alcohol, people often become defensive when these drugs are grouped with illicit drugs such as marijuana and cocaine. Similarly, users of marijuana are disturbed that their drug of choice is grouped with "hard" drugs like heroin. Most scientists believe there are good and bad uses of *all* drugs. To facilitate our discussion and understanding, we need to clarify several confusing terms and concepts.

Misconceptions and Confusing Terminology

Is drug abuse the same as drug addiction? The term **drug abuse** generally refers to drug taking that causes emotional or physical harm to the individual or others. The drug consumption is also typically compulsive, frequent, and intense. **Addiction** is a broad term referring to a condition in which a person feels compelled to use a specific drug. In recent times, the term *addiction* has been used to describe almost any type of compulsive activity (Coombs, 2004). People talk about being "addicted" to TV, work, physical exercise, and even the Internet.

Because of problems associated with the terms *addiction* and *drug abuse*, many drug researchers now use **psychological dependence** to refer to the mental desire or craving to achieve the effects produced by a drug. And they use the term **physical dependence** to refer to changes in bodily processes that make a drug necessary for minimum daily functioning. Physical dependence is shown most clearly when the drug is withheld, and the user undergoes painful **withdrawal** reactions, including physical pain and intense cravings.

After repeated use of a drug, many of the body's physiological processes adjust to higher and higher levels of the drug, producing a

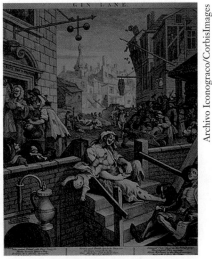

Archivo Iconografico/CorbisImages

Early abuse of drugs. William Hogarth's eighteenth-century engraving of the social chaos caused by the "gin epidemic." Infant mortality was so high that only one of four babies survived to the age of 5. In one section of London, one out of five houses was a gin shop (cited in Levinthal, 2002, p. 188).

Drug Abuse *Drug taking that causes emotional or physical harm to the drug user or others*

Addiction *Broad term describing a compulsion to use a specific drug or engage in a certain activity*

Psychological Dependence *Desire or craving to achieve the effects produced by a drug*

Physical Dependence *Bodily processes have been so modified by repeated use of a drug that continued use is required to prevent withdrawal symptoms*

Withdrawal *Discomfort and distress, including physical pain and intense cravings, experienced after stopping the use of addictive drugs*

Culture and marijuana. *These young Jamaican girls are members of the Rasta-farian Church, which considers marijuana a "wisdom weed." Can you see how culture also affects attitudes toward terms like drug abuse and addiction?*

Tolerance *Decreased sensitivity to a drug brought about by its continuous use*

©2002 Daniel Laine/MatrixInternational, Inc.

decreased sensitivity called **tolerance**. Tolerance leads many users to escalate their drug use and to experiment with other drugs in an attempt to re-create the original pleasurable altered state. In some cases, use of one drug increases tolerance for another. This is known as *cross-tolerance*. Despite the benign sound of the words *tolerance* and *cross-tolerance*, it's important to remember that the brain, heart, liver, and other body organs can be seriously damaged.

Although psychological dependence is sometimes considered less dangerous than physical dependence, the effects on the drug user's life can be even more damaging. The craving in psychological dependence can be so strong that the user ingests the drug regularly and maintains a constant drug-induced state. In addition, the psychological aspects of drug taking are often so powerful that an "addict" will return to a drug habit even after all signs of physical dependence are removed.

TRY THIS YOURSELF

Application

Are You Physically or Psychologically Dependent on Alcohol or Other Drugs?

Before we go on, you may want to take the following test.

1. Have you gotten into financial difficulties due to drinking or using other drugs?
2. Has drinking alcohol or using other drugs ever been behind your losing a job?
3. Has your efficiency or ambition decreased due to drinking and using other drugs?
4. Is your drinking and drug use jeopardizing your academic performance?
5. Does drinking or using other drugs cause you to have difficulty sleeping?
6. Have you ever felt remorse after drinking and using other drugs?
7. Do you crave a drink or other drug at a definite time daily, or do you want a drink or other drug the next morning?
8. Have you ever had a complete or partial loss of memory because of drinking or using other drugs?
9. Have you ever been to a hospital or institution because of drinking or other drug use?

If you answered yes to these questions, you are more likely to be a substance abuser than someone who answered no.

Source: Bennett et al., "Identifying Young Adult Substance Abusers: The Rutgers Collegiate Substance Abuse Screening Test." *Journal of Studies on Alcohol* 54: 522–527. Copyright 1993 Alcohol Research Documentation, Inc., Piscataway, NJ. Reprinted by permission. The RCSAST is to be used only as part of a complete assessment battery because more research needs to be done with this instrument.

Four Major Categories of Psychoactive Drugs: Depressants, Stimulants, Opiates, and Hallucinogens

For convenience, psychologists divide psychoactive drugs into four broad categories: depressants, stimulants, opiates, and hallucinogens (Table 5.2). In this section, we also explore a modern concern with "club drugs" like ecstasy.

SUMMARY TABLE 5.2 EFFECTS OF THE MAJOR PSYCHOACTIVE DRUGS

	Category	Desired Effects
 John E. Kelly/Stone/GettyImages	**Depressants (Sedatives)** Alcohol, barbiturates, antianxiety drugs (Valium), Rohypnol (roofies), Ketamine (special K), CoHB	Tension reduction, euphoria, disinhibition, drowsiness, muscle relaxation
 Joe Pellegrini/Foodpix/PictureArts Corp.	**Stimulants** Cocaine, amphetamine, methamphetamine (crystal meth), MDMA (Ecstacy)	Exhilaration, euphoria, high physical and mental energy, reduced appetite, perception of power, sociability
	Caffeine	Increased alertness
Adam Hart-Davis/PhotoResearchers	Nicotine	Relaxation, increased alertness, sociability
 Uwe Schmid/OKAPIA/PhotoResearchers	**Opiates (Narcotics)** Morphine, heroin, codeine	Euphoria, "rush" of pleasure, pain relief, prevention of withdrawal discomfort
 ©AP/Wide World Photos	**Hallucinogens (Psychedelics)** LSD (lysergic acid diethylamide)	Heightened aesthetic responses, euphoria, mild delusions, hallucinations, distorted perceptions and sensations
	Marijuana	Relaxation, mild euphoria, increased appetite

Depressants *Psychoactive drugs that act on the central nervous system to suppress or slow bodily processes and reduce overall responsiveness*

Drunk driving. *As in this fatal car accident in Austin, Texas, drunk drivers are responsible for almost half of all highway-related deaths in America.*

Stimulants *Drugs that act on the brain and nervous system to increase their overall activity and general responsiveness*

Depressants

Depressants (sometimes called *downers*) depress the central nervous system, causing relaxation, sedation, loss of consciousness, and even death. This category includes ethyl alcohol, barbiturates like Seconal, and antianxiety drugs like Valium. Because tolerance and dependence (both physical and psychological) are rapidly acquired with these drugs, there is strong potential for abuse.

One of the most widely used (and abused) depressant drugs around the world is alcohol. Why? It is primarily a depressant. However, at low doses it has stimulating effects, thus explaining its reputation as a "party drug." The first few drinks seem to relax the inhibitions and thus enliven a person at the same time. But as drinking increases, symptoms of drunkenness appear: Reactions slow, speech slurs, and skilled performance deteriorates (Table 5.3). At the highest doses, the depressant effects can leave the drinker "out of control" and incapable of voluntary action. If blood levels reach 0.5 percent, there is risk of coma and even death from respiratory depression (Kuhn, Swartzwelder, & Wilson, 2003). One college fraternity pledge, for example, died after a seven-hour drinking binge and approximately 24 drinks. His blood alcohol level was measured at 0.58, which was six to seven times the legally established limit for driving a car (Cohen, 1997).

Keep in mind that alcohol's effect is determined primarily by the amount that reaches the brain. Because the liver breaks down alcohol at the rate of about 1 ounce per hour, the number of drinks and the speed of consumption are both very important. Interestingly, men's bodies are more efficient at breaking down alcohol than women's. Even after accounting for differences in size and muscle-to-fat ratio, women have a higher blood alcohol level than do men following equal consumption.

Why is mixing alcohol and barbiturates so dangerous? Alcohol should not be combined with *any* other drug. But combining alcohol and barbiturates—both depressants—is particularly dangerous. Together, they can relax the diaphragm muscles to such a degree that the person literally suffocates. Actress Judy Garland is only one of many who have died from a barbiturate-and-alcohol mixture.

Stimulants

Whereas depressants are downers, **stimulants** are uppers. They act on the central nervous system to increase its overall activity and responsiveness. Stimulant drugs (such as caffeine, nicotine, amphetamines, and cocaine) produce alertness, excite-

TABLE 5.3 ALCOHOL'S EFFECT ON THE BODY AND BEHAVIOR

Number of drinks in two hours[a]	Blood Alcohol Content (%)[b]	Effect
(2)	0.05	Relaxed state; increased sociability
(3)	0.08	Everyday stress lessened
(4)	0.10	Movements and speech become clumsy
(7)	0.20	Very drunk; loud and difficult to understand; emotions unstable
(12)	0.40	Difficult to wake up; incapable of voluntary action
(15)	0.50	Coma and/or death

[a] A drink refers to one 12-ounce beer, a 4-ounce glass of wine, or a 1.25-ounce shot of hard liquor.

[b] In America, the legal blood alcohol level for "drunk driving" varies from 0.05 to 0.12.

ment, elevated mood, decreased fatigue, and sometimes increased motor activity. They also may lead to serious problems. Let's look more closely at nicotine and cocaine.

Nicotine Like caffeine, nicotine is a widely used legal stimulant. But unlike caffeine, it kills many of its users. A sad, ironic example of the dangers of nicotine addiction is Wayne McLaren, the rugged Marlboro Man in cigarette ads, who died of lung cancer at age 51. But McLaren was only one of 400,000 who die from smoking-related illnesses each year in the United States. Tobacco kills more than AIDS, legal drugs, illegal drugs, road accidents, murder, and suicide combined (CDC, 2004).

When smoking doesn't kill, it can result in chronic bronchitis, emphysema, and heart disease (CDC, 2004). Countless others are affected by secondhand smoke, by smoking-related fires, and by prenatal exposure to nicotine (Chapters 3 and 9). The U.S. Public Health Service considers cigarette smoking the single most preventable cause of death and disease in the United States (Baniff, 2004).

As scientific evidence of the dangers of smoking accumulates, and as social pressure from nonsmokers increases, many smokers are trying to kick the habit. Although some succeed, others find it extremely difficult to quit smoking. Researchers have found that nicotine activates the same brain areas (nucleus accumbens) as cocaine—a drug well known for its addictive potential (Grilly, 2006; Pich et al., 1997). The reported pleasures of smoking (relaxation, increased alertness, diminished pain and appetite) are so powerfully reinforcing that some smokers continue to smoke even after having a cancerous lung removed.

Cocaine Cocaine is a powerful central nervous system stimulant extracted from the leaves of the coca plant. It can be sniffed as a white powder, injected intravenously, or smoked in the form of crack. It produces feelings of alertness, euphoria, well-being, power, energy, and pleasure.

Although cocaine was once considered a relatively harmless "recreational drug," its potential for physical damage and severe psychological dependence is now recognized (Bonson et al., 2002; Franklin et al., 2002; Parrott et al., 2004). Sigmund Freud often is cited as a supporter of cocaine use. But few people know that in his later writings Freud called cocaine the "third scourge" of humanity, after alcohol and heroin. Even small initial doses can be fatal because cocaine interferes with the electrical system of the heart, causing irregular heartbeats and, in some cases, heart failure. It also can produce heart attacks and strokes by temporarily constricting blood vessels (Kuhn, Swartzwelder, & Wilson, 2003; Zagnoni & Albano, 2002). The most dangerous form of cocaine is the smokeable, concentrated version known as crack or rock. Its lower price makes it affordable and attractive to a large audience. But its greater potency also makes it more quickly addictive and dangerous.

Opiates

Opiates (or narcotics), which include morphine and heroin, numb the senses and thus are used medically to relieve pain (Kuhn, Swartzwelder, & Wilson, 2003). The classification term *opiates* is used because the drugs are derived from (or are similar to those derived from) the opium poppy. They are attractive to people seeking an alternate state of consciousness because they produce feelings of relaxation and euphoria. They produce their effect by mimicking the brain's own natural chemicals for pain control and mood elevation, called *endorphins*. (Recall from Chapter 2 that the word *endorphin* literally means "endogenous morphine.")

This mimicking of the body's natural endorphins creates a dangerous pathway to drug abuse. After repeated flooding with artificial opiates, the brain eventually reduces or stops the production of its own opiates. If the user later attempts to stop, the brain

"There's no shooting—we just make you keep smoking."

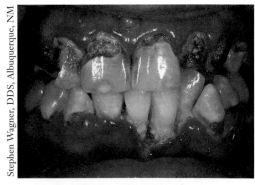

Stephen Wagner, DDS, Albuquerque, NM

Another problem with methamphetamine? *The key ingredients in methamphetamine burn and irritate the sensitive skin inside the mouth. The teeth of chronic meth users are often rotted to the gum line from the corrosive effect of the smoke's swirling vapors. Even snorting meth can lead to similar damage because the nasal passages drain into the back of the throat causing serious destruction to the teeth and gums.*

Opiates *Drugs derived from opium that function as an analgesic or pain reliever (The word opium comes from the Greek word meaning "juice.")*

©AP/Wide World Photos

Opium field. This farmer in Afghanistan is harvesting raw opium from a field of opium poppies. He starts by making shallow incisions into the seed capsules, allowing the fluid to ooze out. After exposure to air, the fluid oxidizes and hardens into the consistency of heavy syrup and is then collected plant by plant.

Hallucinogens [hal-LOO-sin-oh-jenz] *Drugs that produce sensory or perceptual distortions called hallucinations*

Tom & DeeAnn McCarthy/Corbis

Vision from an LSD trip?

lacks both the artificial and normal level of painkilling chemicals. And withdrawal becomes excruciatingly painful.

The euphoria, pain relief, and avoidance of withdrawal all contribute to make opiates, like heroin, extremely addictive. Interestingly, when opiates are used medically to relieve intense pain, they are very seldom habit-forming. However, when taken recreationally, they are strongly addictive (Coombs, 2004; Levinthal, 2006).

Hallucinogens

One of the most intriguing alterations of consciousness comes from **hallucinogens**. These drugs produce sensory or perceptual distortions, including visual, auditory, or kinesthetic hallucinations. According to some reports, colors are brighter and more luminous, patterns seem to pulsate and rotate, and senses may seem to fuse—that is, colors are "heard" or sounds "tasted."

Some cultures have used hallucinogens for religious purposes, as a way to experience "other realities" or to communicate with the supernatural. In Western societies, most people use hallucinogens for their reported "mind-expanding" potential. For example, hallucinogens are highly valued by some artists as a way of increasing creativity. But the experience is not always positive. Terror-filled "bad trips" can occur. Also, dangerous flashbacks may unpredictably recur long after the initial ingestion. The flashback experience may be brought on by stress, fatigue, marijuana use, illness, emerging from a dark room, and occasionally by the individual's intentional effort (Grilly, 2006).

Hallucinogens are also commonly referred to as *psychedelics* (from the Greek for "mind manifesting"). They include mescaline (derived from the peyote cactus), psilocybin (from mushrooms), phencyclidine (chemically derived), and LSD (lysergic acid diethylamide, derived from ergot, a rye mold). Marijuana (pot, grass, or hashish) is sometimes classified as a hallucinogen. In sufficient dosages, it can produce mental effects similar to the stronger hallucinogens. We will focus on LSD and marijuana in our discussion because they are the most widely used hallucinogens.

Lysergic acid diethylamide (LSD) LSD is a synthethic substance that produces dramatic alterations in sensation and perception. This odorless, tasteless, and colorless substance is also one of the most potent drugs known. As little as 10 micrograms of LSD can produce a measurable psychoactive effect in one individual. An amount the size of an aspirin is enough to produce effects in 3000 people. In 1943 Albert Hofman, the Swiss chemist who first synthesized LSD in a laboratory, accidentally licked some of the drug off his finger and later recorded this in his journal:

> Last Friday, April 16, 1943, I was forced to stop my work in the laboratory in the middle of the afternoon and to go home, as I was seized by a peculiar restlessness associated with a feeling of mild dizziness. Having reached home, I lay down and sank in a kind of drunkenness which was not unpleasant and which was characterized by extreme activity of imagination. As I lay in a dazed condition with my eyes closed (I experienced daylight as disagreeably bright) there surged upon me an uninterrupted stream of fantastic images of extraordinary plasticity and vividness and accompanied by an intense, kaleidoscope-like play of colors. This condition gradually passed after about two hours. (Hofman, 1968, pp. 184–185)

Perhaps because the LSD experience is so powerful, few people actually "drop acid" on a regular basis. This may account for its relatively low reported abuse rate. However, LSD use by high school and college students has been increasing (Connolly, 2000; Hedges & Burchfield, 2006; Yacoubian, Green, & Peters, 2003). LSD can be a dangerous drug. Bad LSD trips can be terrifying and may lead to accidents, death, or suicide.

Marijuana Although marijuana is generally classified as a hallucinogen, it has some of the properties of a depressant (including drowsiness and lethargy) and a narcotic (acting as a weak painkiller). In low doses, it also produces mild euphoria. Moderate doses lead to an intensification of sensory experiences and the illusion that time is passing very slowly. At the highest doses, marijuana may produce hallucinations, delusions, and distortions of body image (Hedges & Burchfield, 2006). Regardless of its classification, it is one of the most popular of all illegal consciousness-altering drugs in the Western world (Compton et al., 2004).

The active ingredient in marijuana (cannabis) is THC, or tetrahydracannabinol, which attaches to receptors that are abundant throughout the brain. The presence of these receptors implies that the brain produces some THC-like chemicals of its own. In fact, researchers have discovered a brain chemical (called anandamide) that binds to the same receptors that THC was previously found to use. In 1997, a second THC-like chemical (2-AG) was also discovered (Stella, Schweitzer, & Piomelli, 1997). At this point, no one knows the function of anandamide or 2-AG or why the brain has its own marijuana-like receptors.

With the exception of alcohol during the time of Prohibition, there has never been a drug more hotly debated than marijuana. On the positive side, some research has found marijuana therapeutic in the treatment of glaucoma (an eye disease), in alleviating the nausea and vomiting associated with chemotherapy, in increasing appetite, and in treating asthma, seizures, epilepsy, and anxiety (Darmani & Crim, 2005; Iversen, 2003; Zagnoni & Albano, 2002).

But some marijuana users also report impaired memory, attention, and learning—especially the first few times they use the drug. In addition, chronic marijuana use can lead to throat and respiratory disorders, impaired lung functioning, decreased immune response, declines in testosterone levels, reduced sperm count, and disruption of the menstrual cycle and ovulation (Hedges & Burchfield, 2006; Iversen, 2003; Nahas et al., 2002; Roth et al., 2004). Some research also suggests that marijuana's effects on the brain are disturbingly similar to those produced by drugs like heroin, cocaine, alcohol, and nicotine (Blum et al., 2000; Tanda & Goldberg, 2004). However, other studies have found little or no lasting negative health effects (e.g., Eisen et al., 2002).

Marijuana also can be habit-forming, but few users experience the intense cravings associated with cocaine or opiates. Withdrawal symptoms are mild because the drug dissolves in the body's fat and leaves the body very slowly, which explains why a marijuana user can test positive for days or weeks after the last use.

Politics and drug use. Protestors have long called for legalization of marijuana. Is this a good idea? Why or why not?

Application
APPLYING PSYCHOLOGY TO EVERYDAY LIFE

Club Drug Alert!

As you may know from television or newspapers, psychoactive drugs like Rohypnol (the date rape drug) and MDMA (ecstasy) are fast becoming some of our nation's most popular drugs of abuse—especially at "raves" and other all-night dance parties. Other "club drugs," like GHB (gamma-hydroxybutyrate), ketamine (Special K), methamphetamine (crystal meth), and LSD, also are gaining in popularity (Agar & Reisinger, 2004; Martins, Mazzotti, & Chilcoat, 2005; Yacoubian, Green, & Peters, 2003). Although these drugs can produce desirable effects (e.g., ecstasy's feeling of great empathy and connectedness with others), it's important to note that almost all psychoactive drugs may cause serious health problems. And, in some cases, even death (National Institute on Drug Abuse, 2005).

High doses of MDMA, for example, can cause dangerous increases in body temperature and blood pressure that may lead to seizures, heart attacks, and strokes

Club drugs developed for Generation X.

(Albadalejo et al., 2003; Landry, 2002). In addition, research shows that chronic use of MDMA may affect neurons that release the neurotransmitter serotonin (National Institute on Drug Abuse, 2005; Roiser et al., 2005). As you recall from Chapter 2, serotonin is critical to emotional regulation, learning, memory, and other cognitive functions.

Club drugs, like all illicit drugs, are particularly dangerous because there are no truth-in-packaging laws to protect buyers from unscrupulous practices. Sellers often substitute unknown cheaper, and possibly even more dangerous, substances for the ones they claim to be selling. Also, club drugs (like most psychoactive drugs) affect the motor coordination, perceptual skills, and reaction time necessary for safe driving.

Impaired decision making is a serious problem as well. Just as "drinking and driving don't mix," club drug use may lead to risky sexual behaviors and increased risk of AIDS (acquired immunodeficiency syndrome) and other sexually transmitted diseases. Add in the fact that some drugs, like Rohypnol, are odorless, colorless, tasteless, and can easily be added to beverages by individuals who want to intoxicate or sedate others, and you can see that the dangers of club drug use go far beyond the drug itself (Fernandez et al., 2005; National Institute on Drug Abuse, 2005). If you would like more information on the specific dangers and effects of these club drugs, check http://www.drugabuse.gov/clubalert/"clubdrugalert.html.

Explaining Drug Use: Psychoactive Drugs and ASCs

After an exploration of the four major categories of drugs and the problem with club drugs, a basic question remains: How do psychoactive drugs create alternate states of consciousness?

How Drugs Work

Psychoactive drugs influence the nervous system in a variety of ways. Alcohol, for example, has a diffuse effect on neural membranes throughout the entire nervous system. Most psychoactive drugs, however, act in a more specific manner, and most drug action occurs at one of four steps of neural transmission (Figure 5.6).

Step 1: *Production or synthesis.* Both psychoactive and therapeutic drugs often work by altering the production or synthesis of neurotransmitters. For example, patients with Parkinson's disease have decreased activity in cells that produce dopamine. Usually, the treatment is the drug L-dopa (levodopa) because it is converted in the brain to dopamine. Producing what the brain itself cannot, the drug sometimes relieves the tremors, rigidity, and difficulty in movement characteristic of patients with Parkinson's disease. L-dopa can provide added years of nearly normal life. But the disease is progressive and the benefits decrease over time. Finding the early onset of Parkinson-like symptoms in young people, like actor Michael J. Fox, offers important research clues to a major degenerative disease of our aging population. If people destined to develop Parkinson's disease in later life can be identified earlier, it may be possible to intervene with some treatment and prevent the disease from developing fully.

Step 2: *Storage and release.* Drugs also work by changing the amount of neurotransmitter stored or released by a neuron. As an example, venom from a black widow spider increases the release of the neurotransmitter acetylcholine. More acetylcholine available to the receiving neurons creates an exaggerated stimulant effect: extreme arousal, heightened anxiety, and dangerous increases in blood pressure and heart rate.

Step 3: *Reception.* Drugs also can alter the effect of neurotransmitters on the receiving site of the receptor neuron. As you recall from Chapter 2, some drugs, called receptor *agonists*, have a molecular structure very similar to that of the body's

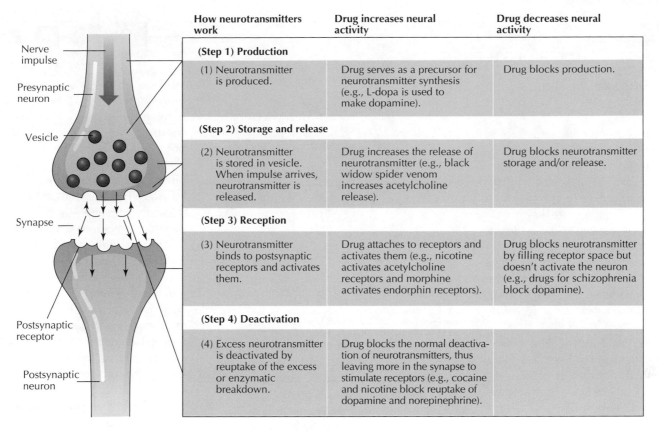

	How neurotransmitters work	Drug increases neural activity	Drug decreases neural activity
(Step 1) Production			
	(1) Neurotransmitter is produced.	Drug serves as a precursor for neurotransmitter synthesis (e.g., L-dopa is used to make dopamine).	Drug blocks production.
(Step 2) Storage and release			
	(2) Neurotransmitter is stored in vesicle. When impulse arrives, neurotransmitter is released.	Drug increases the release of neurotransmitter (e.g., black widow spider venom increases acetylcholine release).	Drug blocks neurotransmitter storage and/or release.
(Step 3) Reception			
	(3) Neurotransmitter binds to postsynaptic receptors and activates them.	Drug attaches to receptors and activates them (e.g., nicotine activates acetylcholine receptors and morphine activates endorphin receptors).	Drug blocks neurotransmitter by filling receptor space but doesn't activate the neuron (e.g., drugs for schizophrenia block dopamine).
(Step 4) Deactivation			
	(4) Excess neurotransmitter is deactivated by reuptake of the excess or enzymatic breakdown.	Drug blocks the normal deactivation of neurotransmitters, thus leaving more in the synapse to stimulate receptors (e.g., cocaine and nicotine block reuptake of dopamine and norepinephrine).	

Figure 5.6 **Psychoactive drugs and neurotransmitters.** Most psychoactive drugs produce their effects by changing the body's supply of neurotransmitters at one of four steps. They can alter production or synthesis (step 1), storage and release (step 2), reception by the next neuron (step 3), or the normal deactivation of excess neurotransmitters (step 4). Because the extra neurotransmitters remain in the synapse in step 4, the adjacent neurons continue to fire and the stimulation effects are increased.

own neurotransmitters. Nicotine is similar to the neurotransmitter acetylcholine, so when it fills the acetylcholine receptors, it produces similar effects (increased stimulation).

Other drugs are similar enough to occupy the same sites as the neurotransmitter but dissimilar enough that they do not cause a response in the receiving neuron. They are called receptor *antagonists.* The problem is that as long as they are attached to the receptors, they prevent the "real" neurotransmitter from getting its message through. As you will see in Chapter 14, many researchers believe an excess of dopamine is related to some forms of schizophrenia. Thus, it is often treated with antipsychotic drugs that act as receptor antagonists. These drugs fill the sites and block the action of the excess dopamine. For many patients, antipsychotic drugs help relieve the major symptoms of schizophrenia.

Step 4: *Deactivation.* After neurotransmitters carry their message across the synapse, the sending neuron normally deactivates the excess, or leftover, neurotransmitter in two ways: *reabsorption* (or *reuptake*) and *enzymatic breakdown.* If the excess is not removed or broken down, the receiving neurons continue to respond as if they were receiving fresh messages. Both nicotine and cocaine work by blocking the reuptake or enzymatic breakdown of dopamine and other neurotransmitters. The normal mood-enhancing effects of these neurotransmitters are thereby increased.

Application

RESEARCH HIGHLIGHT

Addictive Drugs as the Brain's "Evil Tutor"

Why do alcoholics and other addicts continue to take drugs that are clearly destroying their lives? One explanation may be that the brain "learns" to be addicted. Scientists have long known that various neurotransmitters are key to all forms of normal learning. Now evidence suggests that addictive drugs (acting on certain neurotransmitters) teach the brain to want more and more of the destructive substances—whatever the cost. Drugs become the brain's "evil tutor" (Wickelgren, 1998, p. 2045).

How does this happen? The neurotransmitter dopamine has been a primary focus of drug abuse research because of its well-known effect on a part of the brain's reward system known as the nucleus accumbens (Adinoff, 2005; Balfour, 2004). Nicotine and amphetamines, for example, stimulate the release of dopamine, and cocaine blocks its reuptake. Drugs that increase dopamine activity are most likely to result in physical dependence.

Recently, however, evidence points to the importance of another neurotransmitter, glutamate. Although surges in dopamine caused by drug use appear to activate the brain's reward system, glutamate may explain compulsive drug taking. Even after the initial effects of a drug

"That is not one of the seven habits of highly effective people."

©The New Yorker Collection 1998 Leo Cullum from cartoonbank.com. All Rights Reserved.

disappear, glutamate-induced learning encourages the addict to want more and more of the drug and directs the body to get it. Glutamate apparently creates lasting memories of drug use by changing the nature of "conversations" between neurons. Changes in neuronal connections result whenever we learn something and store it in memory. But in this case, glutamate "teaches" the brain to be addicted.

Glutamate's lesson is rarely forgotten. Even when users are highly motivated to end the vicious cycle of drug abuse, glutamate-related changes in the brain keep them "hooked." In addition to the well-known intense cravings and pain of withdrawal, the addicted brain also creates

cravings at the mere sight of drug-related items. When 13 cocaine addicts and 5 controls watched films of people using both neutral objects and drug-associated items (such as glass pipes and razor blades), the addicts reported significant cravings. During this same time, positron emission tomography (PET) scans of the addicts' brains showed significant neural activity in brain regions known to release glutamate (Grant et al., 1996). Apparently, activating the glutamate system—through drug use or some reminder of the drug—creates strong cravings, which helps explain the common problem of drug relapse.

As a critical thinker, are you wondering how this new research might help with drug abuse and relapse? Recalling earlier information about *agonists* and *antagonists,* what about developing and trying a glutamate antagonist? When shown drug-related objects, long-term drug addicts who received a glutamate antagonist reported a significant reduction in cravings and less drug-seeking behavior (Herman & O'Brien, 1997). Drugs that interfere with glutamate transmission are also being tested for the treatment of general drug abuse (Wickelgren, 1998).

Assessment

CHECK & REVIEW

Psychoactive Drugs

Psychoactive drugs change conscious awareness or perception. **Drug abuse** refers to drug taking that causes emotional or physical harm to the individual or others. **Addiction** is a broad term referring to

a person's feeling of compulsion to use a specific drug or to engage in certain activities.

Psychoactive drug use can lead to psychological dependence or physical dependence or both. **Psychological dependence** is a desire or craving to

achieve the effects produced by a drug. **Physical dependence** is a change in bodily processes due to continued drug use that results in **withdrawal** symptoms when the drug is withheld. **Tolerance** is a decreased sensitivity to a drug brought about by its continuous use.

The major categories of psychoactive drugs are **depressants, stimulants, opiates,** and **hallucinogens.** Depressant drugs slow the central nervous system, whereas stimulants activate it. Opiates numb the senses and relieve pain. And hallucinogens produce sensory or perceptual distortions.

Drugs act primarily by changing the effect of neurotransmitters in the brain. Drugs that act as *agonists* mimic neurotransmitters. *Antagonists* oppose or block normal neurotransmitter functioning.

Questions

1. Drugs that change conscious awareness or perception are called _____. (a) addictive; (b) hallucinogenic; (c) psychoactive; (d) mind altering
2. Drug taking that causes emotional or physical harm to the drug user or others is known as _____. (a) addiction; (b) physical dependence; (c) psychological dependence; (d) drug abuse
3. How does physical dependence differ from psychological dependence?

4. Describe four ways psychoactive drugs act on neurotransmitters.

Check your answers in Appendix B.

CLICK & REVIEW
for additional assessment options:
www.wiley.com/college/huffman

HEALTHIER WAYS TO ALTER CONSCIOUSNESS

As we have just seen, alternate states of consciousness (ASCs) may be reached through everyday activities such as sleep and dreaming or psychoactive drugs. But there are also less common, and perhaps healthier, routes to alternate states. In this section, we will explore the fascinating world of meditation and hypnosis.

Getting "High" on Meditation: A Positive Route to Altered Consciousness?

> Suddenly, with a roar like that of a waterfall, I felt a stream of liquid light entering my brain through the spinal cord. The illumination grew brighter and brighter, the roaring louder. I experienced a rocking sensation and then felt myself slipping out of my body, entirely enveloped in a halo of light. I felt the point of consciousness that was myself growing wider, surrounded by waves of light. (Khrishna, 1999, pp. 4–5)

This is how spiritual leader Gopi Khrishna describes his experience with meditation. Does it sound attractive? Most people in the beginning stages of meditation report a simpler, mellow type of relaxation, followed by a mild euphoria. With long practice some advanced meditators experience feelings of profound rapture and joy or strong hallucinations (Aftanas & Golosheikim, 2003; Castillo, 2003; Harrison, 2005).

What is **meditation**? The term is generally used to refer to a group of techniques designed to refocus attention, block out all distractions, and produce an alternate state of consciousness. Success in meditation requires controlling the mind's natural tendency to wander.

Some meditation techniques involve body movements and postures, as in the centuries-old Eastern practices of t'ai chi and hatha yoga. In other techniques, the meditator remains motionless, attending to a single focal point—gazing at a stimulus (such as a candle flame), observing the breath, or silently repeating a mantra. (A mantra is a special sound, word, or phrase used for mind concentration or spiritual worship.)

Meditation has been commonly practiced in some parts of the world for centuries. But it has only recently gained acceptance and popularity in the United States, primarily for its value in promoting relaxation and reducing anxiety. Some practitioners believe that meditation leads to a higher and more enlightened form of consciousness, superior to all other levels. They also believe that it allows them to have remarkable control over their bodily processes (Kim et al., 2005; Surawy, Roberts, & Silver, 2005). With sophisticated electronic equipment, researchers have verified that

Achievement

How do alternate states of consciousness, like hypnosis and meditation, affect consciousness?

Meditation *A group of techniques designed to refocus attention, block out all distractions, and produce an alternate state of consciousness*

Want the Benefits of Meditation?

Try this relaxation technique developed by Herbert Benson (1977):

1. Pick a focus word or short phrase that is calming and rooted in your personal value system (such as love, peace, one, shalom).
2. Sit quietly in a comfortable position, close your eyes, and relax your muscles.
3. Focusing on your breathing, breathe through your nose, and as you breathe out, say your focus word or phrase silently to yourself. Continue for 10 to 20 minutes. You may open your eyes to check the time, but do not use an alarm. When you have finished, sit quietly for several minutes, first with closed eyes and later with opened eyes.
4. Maintain a passive attitude throughout the exercise—permit relaxation to occur

Mischa Richter/TheCartoon Bank, Inc.

at its own pace. When distracting thoughts occur, ignore them and gently return to your repetition.
5. Practice the technique once or twice daily, but not within two hours after a meal—the digestive processes seem to interfere with a successful relaxation response.

meditation can produce dramatic changes in basic physiological processes such as brain waves, heart rate, oxygen consumption, and sweat gland activity. For the one in four Americans who suffers from high blood pressure, it may be useful to know that meditation also has been proven somewhat successful in reducing stress and lowering blood pressure (Kim et al., 2005; Harrison, 2005; Labiano & Brusasca, 2002).

Hypnosis *A trancelike state of heightened suggestibility, deep relaxation, and intense focus*

■ The Mystery of Hypnosis: Recreational and Therapeutic Uses

Relax … your body is so tired … your eyelids are so very heavy … your muscles are becoming more and more relaxed … your breathing is becoming deeper and deeper … relax … your eyes are closing and your whole body feels like lead … let go … relax.

These are the types of suggestions most hypnotists use to begin hypnosis. Once hypnotized, some people can be convinced they are standing at the edge of the ocean listening to the sound of waves and feeling the ocean mist on their faces. Invited to eat a delicious apple that is actually an onion, the hypnotized person may relish the flavor. Told they are watching a very funny or sad movie, they may begin to laugh or cry at their self-created visions.

Stage hypnosis. *Many people mistakenly believe that people can be hypnotized against their will. Stage hypnotists generally use eager volunteers who want to be hypnotized and willingly cooperate with their suggestions and directions.*

What is hypnosis? Scientific research has removed much of the mystery surrounding **hypnosis**. It is defined as a trancelike state of heightened suggestibility, deep relaxation, and intense focus. It is characterized by one or more of the following: (1) narrowed, highly focused attention (the participant is able to "tune out" competing sensory stimuli); (2) increased use of imagination and hallucinations (in the case of visual hallucinations, a person may see things that aren't there or not see things that are); (3) a passive and receptive attitude; (4) decreased responsiveness to

©AP/Wide World Photos

pain; and (5) heightened suggestibility (a willingness to respond to proposed changes in perception—"this onion is an apple") (Barber, 2000; David & Brown, 2002; Gay, Philoppot, & Luminet, 2002; Hilgard, 1986, 1992; Spiegel, 1999).

Therapeutic Uses

From the 1700s to modern times, hypnosis has been used (and abused) by entertainers and quacks. At the same time, it also has been employed as a respected clinical tool by physicians, dentists, and therapists. This curious dual existence began with Franz Anton Mesmer (1734–1815). Mesmer believed that all living bodies were filled with magnetic energy, and he claimed to use this "knowledge" to cure diseases. After lulling his patients into a deep state of relaxation and making them believe completely in his curative powers, Mesmer passed magnets over their bodies and told them their problems would go away. For some people, it worked—hence the term *mesmerized.*

Mesmer's theories were eventually discredited. But James Braid, a Scottish physician, later put people in this same trancelike state for surgery. Around the same time, however, powerful and reliable anesthetic drugs were discovered, and interest in Braid's technique dwindled. It was Braid who coined the term *hypnosis* in 1843, from the Greek word for "sleep."

Today, even with available anesthetics, hypnosis is occasionally used in surgery and for the treatment of chronic pain and severe burns (Harandi, Esfandani, & Shakibaei, 2004; Montgomery, Weltz, Seltz, & Bovbjerg, 2002). Hypnosis has found its best use, however, in medical areas in which patients have a high degree of anxiety, fear, and misinformation, such as dentistry and childbirth. Because pain is strongly affected by tension and anxiety, any technique that helps the patient relax is medically useful.

In psychotherapy, hypnosis can help patients relax, remember painful memories, and reduce anxiety. It has been used with modest success in the treatment of phobias and in efforts to lose weight, stop smoking, and improve study habits (Ahijevych, Yerardi, & Nedilsky, 2000; Dobbin et al., 2004; Gemignani et al., 2000).

Many athletes use self-hypnosis techniques (mental imagery and focused attention) to improve performance. Long-distance runner Steve Ortiz, for example, mentally relives all his best races before a big meet. He says that by the time the race actually begins, "I'm almost in a state of self-hypnosis. I'm just floating along" (cited in Kiester, 1984, p. 23).

Five Common Myths and Controversies

Although hypnotism has been well researched, several myths and controversies persist.

1. *Forced hypnosis.* One of the most common misconceptions is that people can be hypnotized against their will. Hypnosis requires a willing participant who makes a conscious choice to relinquish control of his or her consciousness to someone else. It is virtually impossible to hypnotize someone who is unwilling. As a matter of fact, about 8 to 9 percent of people cannot be hypnotized even when they are willing and trying very hard to cooperate. The notion that people can be hypnotically brainwashed and turned into mindless robots is false. The best potential subjects are those who are able to focus attention, are open to new experiences, and are capable of imaginative involvement or fantasy (Barber, 2000; Liggett, 2000).

2. *Unethical behavior.* A related myth is that hypnosis can make a person behave immorally or take dangerous risks against his or her will. Generally, people will not go against their strongest and most basic values while hypnotized. Participants retain the ability to control their behavior during hypnosis. They are aware of their surroundings and can refuse to comply with the hypnotist's suggestions (Kirsch & Braffman, 2001; Kirsch & Lynn, 1995).

Hypnosis or simple trick? You can re-create a favorite trick that stage hypnotists promote as evidence of superhuman strength under hypnosis. Simply arrange two chairs as shown in the picture. You will see that hypnosis is not necessary—all that is needed is a highly motivated volunteer willing to stiffen his or her body.

3. *Exceptional memory.* Another myth is that hypnotized people can recall things they otherwise could not. Some research has found that recall memory for some information is occasionally improved under hypnosis because the participant is able to relax and focus intently. However, the number of errors also increases! Furthermore, when pressed to re-create details, hypnotized participants have more difficulty separating fact from fantasy and are more willing to guess (Perry, Orne, London, & Orne, 1996; Stafford & Lynn, 2002). As you will see in Chapter 7, all memory recollection is ultimately a *reconstruction* rather than a *reproduction*. Therefore, because memory is normally filled with fabrication and distortion, hypnosis generally increases the potential for error. Consequently, a growing number of judges and state bar associations ban the use of hypnosis and the testimony of hypnotized individuals from the courtroom (Brown, Scheflin, & Hammond, 1997; McConkey, 1995).

4. *Superhuman strength.* It is also a misconception that, under hypnosis, people can perform acts of special, superhuman strength. When nonhypnotized people are simply asked to try their hardest on tests of physical strength, they generally can do anything that a hypnotized person can (Druckman & Bjork, 1994).

5. *Fakery.* Are hypnosis participants faking it and simply playing along with the hypnotist? Or are they actually in a special state of consciousness that changes normal awareness and perception? Although most participants are not consciously faking hypnosis, some researchers believe the effects result from a blend of conformity, relaxation, obedience, suggestion, and role-playing (Baker, 1996, 1998; Lynn, Vanderhoff, Shindler, & Stafford, 2002; Stafford & Lynn, 2002). According to this *relaxation/role-playing theory*, hypnosis is a normal mental state in which deeply relaxed, suggestible people allow the hypnotist to direct their fantasies and behavior.

In contrast, the *altered-state theorists* believe that hypnotic effects result from a special altered state of consciousness (Bowers & Woody, 1996; Hilgard, 1978, 1992). They doubt that relaxation, role-playing, and suggestion explain instances in which patients endure complex surgeries without drug-induced anesthesia. As in other controversial areas of psychology, there is a group of "unified" theorists here. These theorists suggest that hypnosis is a combination of both relaxation/role-playing and a unique alternate state of consciousness.

Assessment

CHECK & REVIEW

Healthier Ways to Alter Consciousness

Meditation is a group of techniques designed to focus attention, block out all distractions, and produce an alternate state of consciousness. Meditation can produce dramatic changes in physiological processes, including heart rate and respiration.

Hypnosis is an alternate state of heightened suggestibility characterized by relax- ation and intense focus. Hypnosis has been used to reduce pain, to increase concentration, and as an adjunct to psychotherapy.

Questions

1. _____ is a group of techniques designed to focus attention and produce an alternate state of consciousness. (a) Hypnosis; (b) Scientology; (c) Parapsychology; (d) Meditation
2. List the five major characteristics of hypnosis.

3. Why is it almost impossible to hypnotize an unwilling participant?
4. Compare and contrast relaxation/role-playing theory versus the altered-state theory of hypnosis.

Check your answers in Appendix B.

CLICK & REVIEW
for additional assessment options:
www.wiley.com/college/huffman

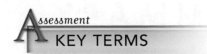

KEY TERMS

*To assess your understanding of the **Key Terms** in Chapter 5, write a definition for each (in your own words), and then compare your definitions with those in the text.*

Understanding Consciousness
alternate states of consciousness
    (ASCs) (p. 171)
automatic processes (p. 171)
consciousness (p. 170)
controlled processes (p. 171)

Sleep and Dreams
activation–synthesis hypothesis (p. 182)
circadian [ser-KAY dee-an] rhythms
    (p. 174)
evolutionary/circadian theory (p. 181)
insomnia (p. 185)
latent content (p. 182)
manifest content (p. 182)

narcolepsy [NAR co-lep-see] (p. 186)
night terrors (p. 186)
nightmares (p. 186)
non-rapid-eye-movement (NREM)
    sleep (p. 179)
rapid-eye-movement (REM) sleep
    (p. 178)
repair/restoration theory (p. 180)
sleep apnea (p. 185)

Psychoactive Drugs
addiction (p. 189)
depressants (p. 192)
drug abuse (p. 189)

hallucinogens [hal LOO-sin-o-jenz]
    (p. 194)
opiates (p. 193)
physical dependence (p. 189)
psychoactive drugs (p. 188)
psychological dependence (p. 189)
stimulants (p. 192)
tolerance (p. 190)
withdrawal (p. 189)

Healthier Ways to Alter Consciousness
hypnosis (p. 200)
meditation (p. 199)

WEB RESOURCES

Huffman Book Companion Site
http://www.wiley.com/college/huffman
    This site is loaded with free Interactive Self-Tests, Internet Exer-
    cises, Glossary and Flashcards for key terms, web links, Hand-
    book for Non-Native Speakers, and other activities designed to
    improve your mastery of the material in this chapter.

The Association for the Scientific Study of Consciousness
http://www.assc.caltech.edu/
    Includes transcripts of seminars on various topics in conscious-
    ness research, journal articles, bibliographies, and links that cover
    current and historical issues in consciousness.

Circadian rhythms
http://stanford.edu/~dement/circadian.html
    Offers a wealth of information about the biology of circadian
    rhythms.

Worried about your sleep?
http://www.sleepfoundation.org/
    Provides a self-test for sleep-related problems, links to finding
    sleep services in your community, recent updates in the field, and
    other vital information.

Everything you wanted to know about sleep but were too tired to ask!
http://www.sleepnet.com/
    An educational, noncommercial site developed to improve sleep
    health worldwide. It contains a sleep test, a forum on sleep issues,
    and many links to sleep lab sites and to sleep disorders.

Worried about your drug use?
http://www.ca.org/ http://www.alcoholics-anonymous.org/
    http://www.marijuana-anonymous.org/
    Offers basic information and advice on how to deal with problem
    drug abuse and use. If you want more information, try
    http://www.nida.nih.gov/ Sponsored by the National Institute on
    Drug Abuse, this website contains comprehensive, up-to-date
    information and national statistics on drug use and related links.

Want more information about MDMA or ecstasy?
http://www.dancesafe.org
    Promotes health and safety within the rave and nightclub com-
    munity. Click on the link "Your Brain on Ecstasy," and you will
    discover an incredible slide show detailing precisely how ecstasy
    creates its effects. Also try, http://faculty.washington.edu/
    chudler/mdma.html This website provides additional information
    on ecstasy, as well as GHB, Rohypnol, and other popular psy-
    choactive drugs.

Interested in hypnosis?
http://www.hypnosis.org
    Offers extensive information and services related to hypnosis,
    including free e-books and free articles.

American Society of Clinical Hypnosis (ASCH)
http//www.asch.net/
    A site provided by the largest U.S. organization for health and
    mental health care professionals using clinical hypnosis; presents
    information and links for the general public, as well as for mem-
    bers of the organization. A good first stop for researching possi-
    ble referral services.

Visual SUMMARY

◻ Understanding Consciousness

Consciousness: Awareness of self and surroundings.
Alternate states of consciousness: State other than ordinary waking consciousness.
Controlled processes: Require focused attention.
Automatic processes: Require minimal attention.

◇ Sleep and Dreams

- *Sleep as a Biological Rhythm*: 24-hour cycles (**circadian rhythms**) affect our sleep and waking cycle. Disruptions due to shift work, jet lag, and sleep deprivation can cause serious problems.
- *Stages of Sleep*: Typical night's sleep has four to five 90-minute cycles. NREM cycle begins in Stage 1 and then moves through Stages 2, 3, and 4. After reaching deepest level, cycle reverses up to REM state.

NREM Sleep (Stages 1-4)
Function: Required for basic biological functioning.

REM Sleep (paradoxical sleep)
Function: Important for memory, learning, and basic biological functioning. Rapid eye movement often signals dreaming.

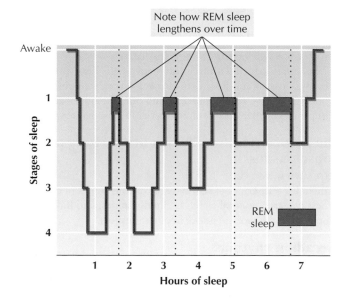

Theories of Sleep
1) **Repair/Restoration**: Allows recuperation from physical, emotional, and intellectual fatigue.
2) **Evolutionary/Circadian**: Sleep is part of circadian cycle, and evolved to conserve energy and protect from predators.

Theories of Dreaming
1) Psychoanalytic/psychodynamic view: Dreams are disguised symbols (**manifest** versus **latent content**) of repressed desires and anxieties.
2) Biological view: Random stimulation of brain cells (**activation-synthesis hypothesis**).
3) Cognitive view: Dreams help sift and sort everyday experiences (information processing theory).

Sleep and Dreams

Sleep Disorders

Insomnia
Repeated difficulty falling or staying asleep or awakening too early.

Sleep Apnea
Temporary stopping of breathing during sleep.

Narcolepsy
Sudden and irresistible onsets of sleep during waking hours.

Nightmares
Bad dreams generally occuring during REM sleep.

Night Terrors
Panic, hallucinations, and abrupt awakenings during NREM sleep.

Psychoactive Drugs

Important Terminology

Drug abuse: Drug taking that causes emotional or physical harm to the individual or others.
Addiction: Broad term referring to feelings of compulsion.
Psychological dependence: Desire or craving to achieve effects produced by a drug.
Physical dependence: Change in bodily processes due to continued drug use that results in withdrawal symptoms when the drug is withheld.
Tolerance: Decreased sensitivity to a drug due to its continuous use.
Withdrawal: Discomfort and distress after stopping addictive drugs.

Four Major Categories of Drugs

1) **Depressants** or "downers" (alcohol and barbiturates) slow down CNS.
2) **Stimulants** or "uppers" (caffeine, nicotine, and cocaine) activate CNS.
3) **Opiates** (heroin or morphine) numb senses and relieve pain.
4) **Hallucinogens** or psychedelics (LSD or marijuana) produce sensory or perceptual distortions.

Tom & DeeAnn McCarthy/Corbis

Healthier Ways to Alter Consciousness

Meditation:
Group of techniques designed to refocus attention, and block out all distractions.

Hypnosis:
Trancelike state of heightened suggestibility, deep relaxation, and intense focus.

www.wiley.com/college/huffman

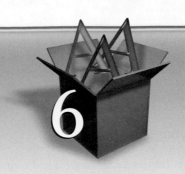

6

LEARNING

A*chievement*

Core Learning Outcomes

As you read Chapter 6, keep the following questions in mind and answer them in your own words:

▷ What is classical conditioning, and how can we apply it in everyday life?

▷ What is operant conditioning, and how can we apply it in everyday life?

▷ How do we learn according to cognitive-social theory, and how can we use it in everyday life?

▷ What neurological changes take place during and after learning? What are the evolutionary advantages of learning?

▷ What are the practical applications of conditioning principles?

■ *Achievement*
■ *Assessment*
■ *Application*

Andy Sacks/Stone/GettyImages

Studying Chapter 6 can:

▷ *Expand your understanding and control of behavior.* A core research finding from learning theory is that people (and nonhuman animals) *do not persist in behaviors that are not reinforced.* Using this information, we can remove reinforcers of destructive or undesirable behaviors and recognize that bad habits will continue until we change the reinforcers. Keep in mind that behavior is not random! There's a reason for everything we do.

▷ *Improve the predictability of your life.* Another key finding from research in learning is that the *best predictor of future behavior is past behavior.* People can (and do) change, and all learned behavior can be unlearned. However, the statistical odds are still high that old patterns of behavior will persist in the future. If you want to predict whether the person you're dating is good marriage material, look to his or her past.

▷ *Enhance your enjoyment of life.* Unfortunately, many people (who haven't taken introductory psychology) choose marital partners hoping to change or "rescue" them. Or they pursue jobs they hate because they want to "make a lot of money." If you carefully study and actively apply the information in this chapter, you can avoid these mistakes and thereby greatly enrich your life.

▷ *Help you change the world!* Reinforcement also motivates greedy business practices, unethical political and environmental decisions, prejudice, and war. Knowing this, if we all work together to remove the inappropriate reinforcers, we can truly change the world. Admittedly, this sounds grandiose and simplistic. But I sincerely believe in the power of education and the usefulness of the material in this chapter. Your life and the world around you can be significantly improved with a "simple" application of learning principles.

Learning *A relatively permanent change in behavior or mental processes resulting from practice or experience*

Greg Smith/Corbis

On Sunday morning, June 7, 1998, James Byrd, a disabled 49-year-old African American, was walking home along Martin Luther King Boulevard in Jasper, Texas. Three young white men pulled up and offered him a ride. But they had no intention of taking him home. Instead, they chained Mr. Byrd by his ankles to the back of their rusted 1982 pickup and dragged him along an old logging road outside of town until his head and right arm were ripped from his body.

What was the reason for this grisly murder? Byrd was a black man. His three murderers were "white supremacists" who want the United States to be a white-only society. Although white supremacists form only a tiny fraction of the American population, hate crimes are a serious and growing problem around the world. People are ridiculed, attacked, and even murdered simply because of their ethnicity, sexual orientation, gender, or religious preference. Why? Where does such hatred come from? Is prejudice learned?

In the everyday sense, *learning* usually refers to classroom activities, such as math and reading, or motor skills, like riding a bike or playing the piano. But to psychologists, **learning** is much broader. It is formally defined as a *relatively permanent change in behavior or mental processes resulting from practice or experience.* This *relative permanence* of learning applies to all learned behavior or mental processes, from using a spoon to writing great novels. Once you've learned how to use a spoon (or chopsticks) for eating, you will likely be able to use this skill for the rest of your life.

Most of psychology emphasizes learning. For example, developmental psychologists examine how children learn language and other cognitive and motor skills. Clinical and counseling psychologists explore how previous learning and experiences help explain present-day problems. And social psychologists study how attitudes, social behaviors, and prejudices, such as those evidenced by James Byrd's murderers, are learned through experience.

Tragedies like the murder of James Byrd show us the dark side of human learning. However, the very fact that racism and hatred are *learned* offers great hope. What is learned can be unlearned (or at least suppressed). In this chapter, we will discover how we learn hatred, racism, phobias, and superstitions, as well as love and generosity. Much of this chapter focuses on the most basic form of learning, called **conditioning**, which is the process of learning associations between environmental stimuli and behavioral responses. We begin with the two most common types of conditioning—classical and operant. Then we look at cognitive-social learning, followed by the biological factors in learning. The chapter concludes with how learning theories and concepts can be used to improve everyday life.

Conditioning *The process of learning associations between environmental stimuli and behavioral responses*

CLASSICAL CONDITIONING

Have you noticed that when you're hungry and see a large slice of chocolate cake or a juicy steak, your mouth starts to water? It seems natural that your mouth should water if you put food into it. But why do you salivate at just the sight of the food?

Achievement

What is classical conditioning, and how can we apply it in everyday life?

Pavlov and Watson's Contributions: The Beginnings of Classical Conditioning

The answer to this question was accidentally discovered in the Leningrad laboratory of Ivan Pavlov (1849–1936). Pavlov was a Russian physiologist who was awarded the Nobel Prize for his work on the role of saliva in digestion. One of Pavlov's experiments involved salivary responses in dogs. He attached a glass funnel to the experimental dogs' salivary glands to collect and measure the output (Figure 6.1). Pavlov wanted to know whether dry food required more saliva than moist food and whether nonfood objects required varying amounts of saliva, depending on how hard it was to spit them out.

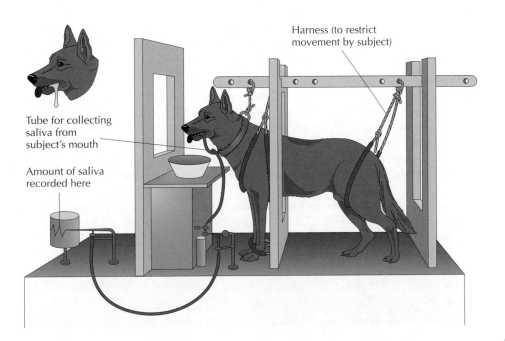

Harness (to restrict movement by subject)

Tube for collecting saliva from subject's mouth

Amount of saliva recorded here

Figure 6.1 *Pavlov's original classical conditioning apparatus.* During Pavlov's initial experiments, a tube was attached to the dog's salivary glands to collect and measure the saliva produced under different experimental conditions.

Pavlov's (Accidental) Discovery

In the course of Pavlov's research, one of his students noticed that many dogs began to salivate at the mere sight of the food or the food dish, the smell of the food, or even the sight of the person who delivered the food. This salivation occurred long *before* food was placed in their mouth! (This is the important *accidental* part of the discovery, which might have gone unnoticed if the collection tubes had not been in place.) Although this "unscheduled" salivation interfered with Pavlov's research design and irritated him, it also was intriguing. Salivation is a *reflex response*, a largely involuntary, automatic response to an external stimulus. Why were his dogs reflexively salivating *before* the food was even presented? Why did they salivate to extraneous stimuli other than food?

Pavlov's scientific training helped him appreciate the significance of what had at first seemed just annoying. A reflex (salivation) that occurred *before* the appropriate stimulus (food) was presented is clearly not inborn and biological. It had to have been acquired through experience—through *learning*. Excited by this accidental discovery, Pavlov and his students conducted several experiments. His most basic method involved sounding a tone on a tuning fork just before food was placed in the dog's mouth. After several pairings of tone and food, the dogs would salivate on hearing the tone alone. Using this same procedure, Pavlov and later experimenters went on to show that all sorts of things can be conditioned stimuli for salivation if they are paired with food—the ticking of a metronome, a bell, a buzzer, a light, and even the sight of a circle or triangle drawn on a card.

The type of learning that Pavlov discovered came to be known as **classical conditioning** (as in first [*classical*] learning [*conditioning*]). Classical conditioning is officially defined as *learning that occurs when a neutral stimulus (NS) becomes paired (associated) with an unconditioned stimulus (UCS) to elicit a conditioned response (CR)*.

To understand this definition, you need to learn five key terms describing each element of the classical conditioning process: *unconditioned stimulus* (UCS), *unconditioned response* (UCR), *neutral stimulus* (NS), *conditioned stimulus* (CS), and *conditioned response* (CR).

Before Pavlov's dogs *learned* to salivate at something extraneous like the sight of the experimenter, the original salivary reflex was inborn and biological. It consisted of an **unconditioned stimulus (UCS)**, food, and an **unconditioned response (UCR)**, salivation.

Pavlov's accidental discovery (and great contribution to psychology) was that learning can occur when a **neutral stimulus (NS)** (a stimulus that does not evoke or bring out a response) is regularly paired with an unconditioned stimulus (UCS). The neutral stimulus then becomes a **conditioned stimulus (CS)**, which elicits or produces a **conditioned response (CR)**. (*Study tip:* If you're finding this confusing, note that *conditioning* is just another word for *learning*. When you see words like *unconditioned stimulus* and *unconditioned response*, mentally rearrange and think "unlearned stimulus" and "unlearned response." Picture a newborn baby with little or no initial learning. Now imagine what stimuli would cause him or her to respond. With conditioning, these *unlearned stimuli* and *unlearned responses* could become *conditioned stimuli* and *conditioned responses*. For additional help, read through the diagram in Figure 6.2, which provides a visual organizer and detailed example from Pavlov's research.)

Does the neutral stimulus always come first? Researchers have investigated four different ways to pair stimuli (Table 6.1) and found that both the timing and the order in which the NS is presented are very important (Chang, Stout, & Miller, 2004; Delamater, LoLordo, & Sousa, 2003). For example, *delayed conditioning*, in which the NS is presented before the UCS and remains until the UCR begins, generally yields the fastest learning. On the other hand, *backward conditioning*, in which the UCS is presented before the NS, is the least effective.

Classical Conditioning *Learning that occurs when a neutral stimulus (NS) becomes paired (associated) with an unconditioned stimulus (UCS) to elicit a conditioned response (CR)*

Unconditioned Stimulus (UCS) *Stimulus that elicits an unconditioned response (UCR) without previous conditioning*

Unconditioned Response (UCR) *Unlearned reaction to an unconditioned stimulus (UCS) that occurs without previous conditioning*

Neutral Stimulus (NS) *A stimulus that, before conditioning, does not naturally bring about the response of interest*

Conditioned Stimulus (CS) *Previously neutral stimulus that, through repeated pairings with an unconditioned stimulus (UCS), now causes a conditioned response (CR)*

Conditioned Response (CR) *Learned reaction to a conditioned stimulus (CS) that occurs because of previous repeated pairings with an unconditioned stimulus (UCS)*

Drawing by John Chase

Before conditioning
The neutral stimulus produces no relevant response. The unconditioned stimulus elicits the unconditioned response.

Figure 6.2 *Pavlov's classical conditioning.* Before conditioning occurs, the neutral stimulus does not elicit a relevant or consistent response. During conditioning, the neutral stimulus is paired several times with an unconditioned stimulus. It now becomes a conditioned stimulus that elicits a conditioned response.

During conditioning
The neutral stimulus is repeatedly paired with the unconditioned stimulus, which produces the unconditioned response.

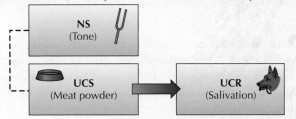

After conditioning
The neutral stimulus has become a conditioned stimulus (CS). This CS now produces a conditioned response (CR) that is usually similar to the unconditioned response (UCR).

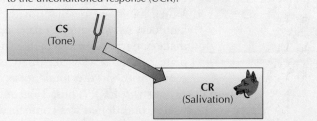

Summary
An originally neutral stimulus comes to elicit a response that it did not previously elicit.

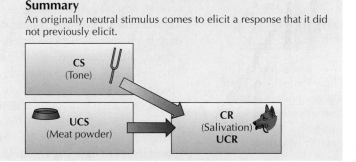

𝒮tudy𝒯ip 💡

Use this figure to help you visualize and organize the three major stages of classical conditioning and their associated key terms.

Watson's Contribution to Classical Conditioning

At this point, you may be wondering what a dog salivating to the sound of a tone has to do with your life—other than explaining why you salivate at the sight of delicious food. Classical conditioning has been shown to be the most basic and fundamental way that all animals, including humans, learn most new responses, emotions, and attitudes. Your love for your parents (or significant other), the hatred and racism that led to the murder of James Byrd, and your drooling at the sight of chocolate cake are largely the result of classical conditioning.

www.wiley.com/college/huffman

SUMMARY TABLE 6.1 CONDITIONING SEQUENCES

Delayed conditioning (most effective)	NS presented before UCS and remains until UCR begins	Tone presented before food
Simultaneous conditioning	NS presented at the same time as UCS	Tone and food presented simultaneously
Trace conditioning	NS presented and then taken away, or ends before UCS presented	Tone sounds, but food presented only once the sound stops
Backward conditioning (least effective)	UCS presented before NS	Food presented before the tone

NS = neutral stimulus; UCR = unconditioned response; UCS = unconditioned stimulus.

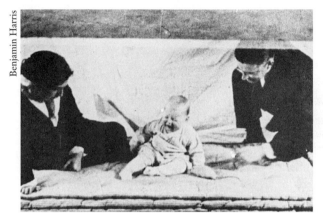

Benjamin Harris

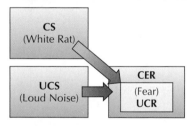

Figure 6.3 *Watson and Rayner.* This diagram shows how Little Albert's fear of rats was conditioned using a loud noise. In the photo, Watson and Rayner are shown with Little Albert, who's crying from the loud noise.

Conditioned Emotional Response (CER) *A classically conditioned emotional response to a previously neutral stimulus (NS)*

In one of the most famous (and controversial) psychological studies, John Watson and Rosalie Rayner (1920, 2000) experimentally demonstrated how the emotion of fear could be classically conditioned. Albert, a healthy 11-month-old normal child, was tested in Watson's lab at Johns Hopkins University (Figure 6.3). He was first allowed to play with a white laboratory rat to find out if he was afraid of rats. Like most infants, "Little Albert" was curious and reached for the rat, showing no fear. Using the fact that infants are naturally frightened (UCR) by loud noises (UCS), Watson stood behind Albert and again put the rat (NS) near him. When the infant reached for the rat, Watson banged a steel bar with a hammer. As you might imagine, the loud noise frightened Albert and made him cry. After several pairings of the white rat (NS) with the immediate loud noise (UCS), Albert began to cry when just the rat was presented without the loud noise. Albert's fear is called a **conditioned emotional response (CER)**. Thus, Watson and Rayner's original hypothesis that fears are classically conditioned was confirmed.

Watson and Rayner's experiment could not be performed today because it violates several ethical guidelines for scientific research (Chapter 1). Moreover, Watson and Rayner ended their experiment without *extinguishing* (removing) Albert's fear, although they knew that such a conditioned emotional response (CER) could endure for a long period. This disregard for Albert's well-being is a serious criticism of Watson and Rayner's study. Their research methodology also has been criticized. Rather than objectively measuring Albert's fear, Watson and Rayner only subjectively evaluated it, which raises doubt about the degree of fear conditioned (Paul & Blumenthal, 1989).

Despite such criticisms, John B. Watson made important and lasting contributions to psychology. At the time he was conducting research, psychology's early founders were defining the field as the *scientific study of the mind* (Chapter 1). Watson criticized this focus on internal mental activities, insisting that they were impossible to study objectively. Instead, he emphasized strictly *observable* behaviors. Watson is also credited with founding the new approach known as *behaviorism*, which explains behavior as a result of observable *stimuli* (in the environment) and observable *responses* (behavioral actions). In addition, Watson's study of Little Albert showed us that many of our likes, dislikes, prejudices, and fears are *conditioned emotional responses*. In Chapter 15, you will also see how Watson's research in *producing* Little Albert's fears later led to powerful clinical tools for *eliminating* extreme, irrational fears known as *phobias*.

Historical note: Shortly after the Little Albert experiment, Watson was fired from his academic position. And no other university would hire him, despite his international fame and scientific reputation. His firing resulted from his scandalous and highly publicized affair with his graduate student Rosalie Rayner and subsequent divorce. Watson later married Rayner and became an influential advertising executive. He is credited with many successful ad campaigns based on classical conditioning, including those for Johnson & Johnson baby powder, Maxwell House coffee, and Lucky Strike cigarettes (Goodwin, 2005; Hunt, 1993).

Assessment

CHECK & REVIEW

Pavlov and Watson's Contributions

In **classical conditioning,** the type of learning investigated by Pavlov and Watson, an originally **neutral stimulus (NS)** is paired with an **unconditioned stimulus (UCS)** that causes an **unconditioned response (UCR).** After several pairings, the neutral stimulus becomes a **conditioned stimulus (CS),** which alone will produce a **conditioned response (CR)** or **conditioned emotional response (CER)** similar to the original reflex response.

There are four conditioning sequences: *delayed conditioning, simultaneous conditioning, trace conditioning,* and *backward conditioning.* Delayed conditioning is the most effective, and backward conditioning is the least effective.

Pavlov's work laid a foundation for Watson's later insistence that psychology must be an objective science, studying only overt behavior without considering internal mental activity. Watson called this position *behaviorism.* His controversial "Little Albert" study demonstrated how emotional responses can be classically conditioned.

Questions

1. Eli's grandma gives him a Tootsie Roll every time she visits. When Eli sees his grandma arriving, his mouth begins to water. In this example the conditioned stimulus (CS) is _____. (a) hunger; (b) grandma; (c) the Tootsie Roll; (d) the watering mouth
2. After conditioning, the _____ elicits the _____.

3. In John Watson's demonstration of classical conditioning with Little Albert, the unconditioned stimulus was _____. (a) symptoms of fear; (b) a rat; (c) a bath towel; (d) a loud noise
4. An Iraqi War veteran experiences an intense emotional reaction to a clap of thunder. His emotional response is an example of a(n) _____. (a) CS; (b) UCS; (c) CER; (d) UCR

Check your answers in Appendix B.

CLICK & REVIEW
for additional assessment options:
www.wiley.com/college/huffman

■ Basic Principles: Fine-Tuning Classical Conditioning

Now that you understand the major key terms in classical conditioning and how they explain CERs, we can build on this foundation. In this section, we will discuss five important principles of classical conditioning: *stimulus generalization, stimulus discrimination, extinction, spontaneous recovery,* and *higher-order conditioning.*

Generalization and Discrimination

One of Pavlov's early experiments conditioned dogs to salivate at the sound of low-pitched tones. Pavlov and his students later demonstrated that the dogs would also salivate to higher-pitched tones. Although at first the conditioning was to one specific low- and one specific high-pitched tone, the dogs quickly showed conditioning to other high and low tones resembling the conditioned tones.

When an event similar to the originally conditioned stimulus triggers the same conditioned response (salivation), it is called **stimulus generalization**. The more the stimulus resembles the conditioned stimulus, the stronger the conditioned response (Hovland, 1937). Have you ever felt afraid when you were driving a car and noticed another car with a rack of lights on its roof following close behind? If so, your fear of police cars (which typically have lights on their roofs) has *generalized* to all cars with lights on their roofs. Stimulus generalization also occurred in Watson's experiment with Albert. After conditioning, Albert feared not only rats but also other objects that shared features with the white rat, including a rabbit, dog, and a Santa Claus mask.

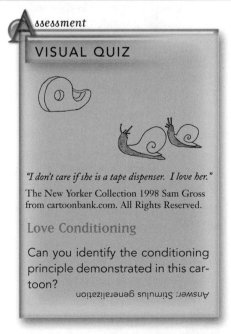

Assessment

VISUAL QUIZ

"I don't care if she is a tape dispenser. I love her."
The New Yorker Collection 1998 Sam Gross from cartoonbank.com. All Rights Reserved.

Love Conditioning

Can you identify the conditioning principle demonstrated in this cartoon?

Answer: Stimulus generalization

Stimulus Generalization *Learned response to stimuli that are like the original conditioned stimulus*

www.wiley.com/college/huffman

Would Little Albert still be afraid of a Santa Claus mask as he grew older? Probably not. As a child in the United States, he undoubtedly had numerous encounters with Santa Claus masks, and would have learned to recognize differences between rats and other stimuli. This process of learning responses to a specific stimulus, but not to other similar stimuli is called **stimulus discrimination**.

Although stimulus generalization seems to follow naturally from initial classical conditioning, organisms only learn to distinguish (or *discriminate*) between an original conditioned stimulus (CS) and similar stimuli if they have enough experience with both. Just as you learn to discriminate between the sound of your cellular phone and the ringing of others, when Pavlov repeatedly presented food following a high-pitched tone, but not with a low-pitched tone, the dogs gradually learned to distinguish between the two tones. Thus, both Little Albert and Pavlov's dogs produced conditioned responses only to specific stimuli—*stimulus discrimination*.

Extinction and Spontaneous Recovery

Classical conditioning, like all learning, is only *relatively* permanent. Most responses that are learned through classical conditioning can be weakened or suppressed through **extinction**. Extinction occurs when the unconditioned stimulus (UCS) is repeatedly withheld whenever the conditioned stimulus (CS) is presented, so that the previous association is weakened. For instance, when Pavlov sounded the tone again and again without presenting food, the dogs' salivation gradually declined. Similarly, if you have a classically conditioned fear of the sound of a dentist's drill and later start to work as a dental assistant, your fear will gradually diminish. Can you see the usefulness of this information if you're trying to get over a destructive love relationship? Rather than thinking, "I'll always be in love with this person," remind yourself that given time and repeated contact in a nonloving situation, your feelings will gradually lessen (Figure 6.4).

Does extinction cause us to "unlearn" a classical conditioned response? No, extinction is not *unlearning* (Bouton, 1994). A behavior becomes *extinct* when the response rate decreases and the person or animal no longer responds to the stimulus. It does not mean the person or animal has "erased" the previous learned connection between the stimulus and the response. In fact, if the stimulus is reintroduced, the conditioning is much faster the second time. Furthermore, Pavlov found that if he allowed several hours to pass after the extinction procedure and then presented the tone again, the salivation would spontaneously reappear. This reappearance of a conditioned response after extinction is called **spontaneous recovery**.

Knowing this term will help you understand why you suddenly feel excited at the sight of your old high school sweetheart even though years have passed (and extinction has occurred). Some people (who haven't read this book and studied this phenomenon) might mislabel this renewed excitement as "lasting love." You, on the other hand, would recognize it as simple *spontaneous recovery*. This phenomenon also explains why couples who've recently broken up sometimes misinterpret and overvalue a similar sudden flareup of feelings. They may even return to doomed relationships, despite knowing they were painful and destructive (Figure 6.5).

Higher-Order Conditioning

Children are not born salivating at the sign of McDonald's golden arches. So why do they want to stop and eat at one of the restaurants after simply seeing the golden arches on a passing billboard? It is because of **higher-order conditioning**. This type

Stimulus Discrimination *Learned response to a specific stimulus but not to other, similar stimuli*

Extinction *Gradual weakening or suppression of a previously conditioned response (CR)*

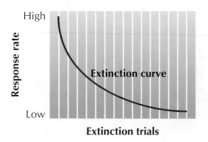

Figure 6.4 *The process of extinction.* This is a hypothetical graph from a typical extinction experiment. Note how the response rate decreases over time and with additional extinction trials.

Spontaneous Recovery *Reappearance of a previously extinguished conditioned response (CR)*

Figure 6.5 *Spontaneous recovery.* In this hypothetical graph from a standard extinction experiment, note how the extinguished response can "spontaneously reappear."

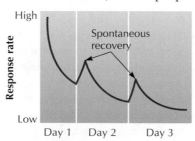

Higher-Order Conditioning *A neutral stimulus (NS) becomes a conditioned stimulus (CS) through repeated pairings with a previously conditioned stimulus (CS)*

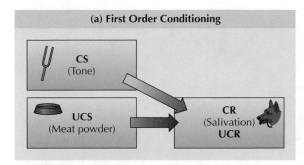

(a) First Order Conditioning

CS (Tone)

UCS (Meat powder)

CR (Salivation) UCR

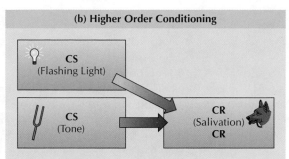

(b) Higher Order Conditioning

CS (Flashing Light)

CS (Tone)

CR (Salivation) CR

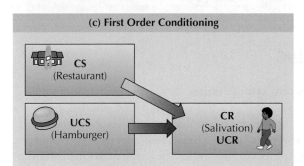

(c) First Order Conditioning

CS (Restaurant)

UCS (Hamburger)

CR (Salivation) UCR

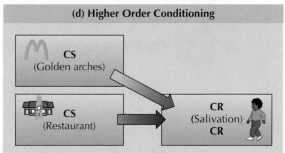

(d) Higher Order Conditioning

CS (Golden arches)

CS (Restaurant)

CR (Salivation) CR

Figure 6.6 *How children learn to salivate for McDonald's.* As you can see in the top two boxes (a and b), higher-order conditioning is a two-stage process. In the first stage, a neutral stimulus (such as a tone from a tuning fork) is paired with an unconditioned stimulus (such as meat powder). The NS then becomes a conditioned stimulus that elicits a conditioned response (salivation). During the second stage (higher-order conditioning), a different neutral stimulus (such as a flashing light) is paired with the tone until it also becomes a conditioned stimulus. Now examine the bottom two boxes (c and d). Can you see how the same two-stage type of higher-order conditioning helps explain why children become so excited (and salivate) when they see the golden arches?

of conditioning occurs when a neutral stimulus (NS) becomes a conditioned stimulus (CS) through repeated pairings with a previously conditioned stimulus (CS).

If you wanted to demonstrate higher-order conditioning in Pavlov's dogs, you would first condition the dogs to salivate to the sound of the tone. Then you would pair a flash of light to the ringing of the tone. Eventually, the dog would salivate to the flash of light alone (Figures 6.6a, and 6.6b). In a similar fashion, children first learn to pair McDonald's restaurant with food and later learn that two golden arches are a symbol for McDonald's (Figures 6.6c, and 6.6d). Their salivation and desire to eat at the restaurant are a classic case of higher-order conditioning (and successful advertising).

 Assessment

CHECK & REVIEW

Basic Principles of Classical Conditioning

In classical conditioning, **stimulus generalization** occurs when stimuli similar to the original conditioned stimulus (CS) elicit the conditioned response (CR). **Stimulus discrimination** takes place when only the CS elicits the CR. **Extinction** occurs when the unconditioned stimulus (UCS) is repeatedly withheld, and the association between the CS and the UCS is weakened. **Spontaneous recovery** occurs when a CR that had been extinguished suddenly reappears. In **higher-order conditioning,** the neutral stimulus (NS) is paired with a CS to which the participant has already been conditioned, rather than with a UCS.

Questions

1. Like most college students, your heart rate and blood pressure greatly increase when the fire alarm sounds. If the fire alarm system was malfunctioning and rang every half hour, by the end of the day, your heart rate and blood pressure would no longer

increase. Using classical conditioning terms, explain this change in your reponse.

2. A baby is bitten by a dog and then is afraid of all small animals. This is an example of _____. (a) stimulus discrimination; (b) extinction; (c) reinforcement; (d) stimulus generalization.

3. When a conditioned stimulus is used to reinforce the learning of a second conditioned stimulus, _____ has occurred.

4. If you wanted to use higher-order conditioning to get Little Albert to fear Barbie dolls, you would present a Barbie doll with _____. (a) the loud noise;

(b) the original unconditioned response; (c) the white rat; (d) the original conditioned response

Check your answers in Appendix B.

CLICK & REVIEW

for additional assessment options: www.wiley.com/college/huffman

OPERANT CONDITIONING

*A*chievement

What is operant conditioning, and how can we apply it in everyday life?

Operant Conditioning *Learning in which voluntary responses are controlled by their consequences (also known as instrumental or Skinnerian conditioning)*

Reinforcement *Strengthens a response and makes it more likely to recur*

Punishment *Weakens a response and makes it less likely to recur*

Law of Effect *Thorndike's rule that the probability of an action being repeated is strengthened when it is followed by a pleasant or satisfying consequence*

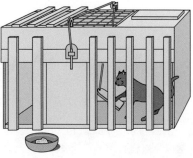

Figure 6.7 *Thorndike box.* Thorndike used a box like this in his trial-and-error experiments with cats. When a cat stepped on a pedal inside the box, the door latch was released and a weight attached to the door pulled it open so the cat could exit. (From Thorndike, 1898).

Consequences are the heart of **operant conditioning**. In classical conditioning, consequences are irrelevant—Pavlov's dog still got the meat powder whether or not it salivated. But in operant conditioning, the organism performs a behavior (an *operant*) that produces an effect on the environment. These effects, *reinforcement* or *punishment*, influence whether the response will occur again in the future. **Reinforcement** strengthens the response and makes it more likely to recur. **Punishment** weakens the response and makes it less likely to recur. If your friends smile and laugh when you tell a joke, your future joke telling is likely to increase. However, if they frown, groan, or ridicule you, your joke telling is likely to decrease.

In addition to differences in their emphasis on consequences, the two types of conditioning differ in another important way. In classical conditioning, the organism's response is *passive* and *involuntary*. It "happens to" the organism when a UCS follows a NS. In operant conditioning, however, the organism's response is *active* and *voluntary*. The learner "operates" on the environment and produces effects. These effects (or consequences) influence whether the behavior will be repeated.

It's important to note that these distinctions between classical and operant conditioning are *generally* true—but not *always* true. Technically speaking, classical conditioning does sometimes influence voluntary behavior, and operant conditioning can influence involuntary, reflexive behavior. Furthermore, both forms of conditioning often interact to produce and maintain behavior. But for most purposes, the distinction holds. In most cases, classical conditioning refers to involuntary responses and operant conditioning refers to voluntary responses.

In the sections that follow, we will examine the historical contributions of Thorndike and Skinner, and the general principles of operant conditioning. The chapter closes with interesting applications of operant conditioning to everyday life.

▪ Thorndike and Skinner's Contributions: The Beginnings of Operant Conditioning

Edward Thorndike (1874–1949), a pioneer of operant conditioning, was among the first to examine how voluntary behaviors are influenced by their consequences. In one of his famous experiments, he put a cat inside a specially built *puzzle box* (Figure 6.7). The only way the cat could get out was by pulling on a rope or stepping on a pedal. Through trial and error, the cat would eventually (and accidentally) pull on the rope or step on the pedal that opened the door. With each additional success, the cat's actions became more purposeful, and it soon learned to open the door immediately.

According to Thorndike's **law of effect**, the probability of an action being repeated is *strengthened* if it is followed by a pleasant or satisfying consequence. In short, rewarded behavior is more likely to reoccur (Thorndike, 1911). Thorndike's law of effect was a first step in understanding how active *voluntary* behaviors can be modified by their consequences.

B. F. Skinner (1904–1990) extended Thorndike's law of effect to more complex behaviors. As a strict behaviorist, however, Skinner avoided terms like *pleasant*, *desired*, and *voluntary* because they make unfounded assumptions about what an organism feels and wants. The terms also imply that behavior is due to conscious choice or intention. Skinner believed that to understand behavior, we should consider only observable, external, or environmental stimuli and responses. We must look outside the learner, not inside.

To scientifically test his theories, Skinner conducted systematic research. The typical Skinner experiment used an animal, usually a pigeon or a rat, and an apparatus that has come to be called a Skinner box (Figure 6.8). Skinner trained a rat or other animal to push a lever to receive a food pellet. The animal got a pellet each time it pushed the lever, and the number of responses made by the rat was recorded. Skinner used this basic experimental design to demonstrate a number of operant conditioning principles.

In keeping with his focus on external, observable behavior, Skinner emphasized that reinforcement (which increases the likelihood of a response) and punishment (which decreases it) are always defined *after the fact*. This emphasis on only reinforcing or punishing *after* the behavior is important. Suppose you ask to borrow the family car on Friday night, but your parents say you have to wash the car first. If they let you put off washing the car until the weekend, what is the likelihood that you will do it? From their own "trial-and-error" experiences, most parents have learned to make sure the payoff comes *after* the car washing is completed—not before!

In addition to warning that both reinforcement and punishment must come after the response, Skinner also cautions us to check the respondent's behavior to see if it increases or decreases. Sometimes we *think* we're reinforcing or punishing when we're doing the opposite. For example, a professor may think she is encouraging shy students to talk by repeatedly praising them each time they speak up in class. But what if shy students are embarrassed by this attention? If so, they may decrease the number of times they talk in class. Similarly, men may buy women candy and flowers after they accept first dates with them because they *know* all women like these things. However, some women hate candy (imagine that!) or may be allergic to flowers. In this case, the man's attempt at reinforcement becomes a punishment! Skinner suggests we should watch our target's *actual* responses—not what we *think* the other person *should* like or do.

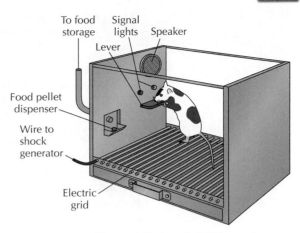

Figure 6.8 *A typical Skinner box.* Note how food pellets are delivered in the small receiving tray. The lights, speaker, and electric floor grid can all be used to adjust the learning environment.

🔲 Basic Principles: Understanding Operant Conditioning

If you want additional help using operant conditioning to improve your everyday life, you need to understand several important principles. Let's start with factors involved in *strengthening a response* (primary and secondary reinforcers, positive and negative reinforcement, schedules of reinforcement, and shaping). Then we'll explore ways to *weaken a response* (positive and negative punishment). We conclude with a look at the pros and cons of punishment and a review of terms that are shared between classical and operant conditioning.

Reinforcement—Strengthening a Response

Earlier, we said that Skinner was a strict behaviorist who insisted that scientific observation be limited to that which can be observed. Therefore, instead of using words like *rewards* (which focus on feelings), Skinner talked about reinforcers and reinforcement in terms of "strengthening the response." As you can see in Table 6.2, reinforcers can be grouped into two types, *primary* or *secondary*. These reinforcers also function as either *positive* or *negative* reinforcement.

SUMMARY TABLE 6.2 HOW REINFORCEMENT STRENGTHENS AND INCREASES BEHAVIORS

	Positive Reinforcement *Adds to (+) and* *strengthens behavior*	Negative Reinforcement *Takes away (–) and* *strengthens behavior*
Primary Reinforcers	You do a favor for a friend and she buys you lunch in return. You wash your friend's car and she hugs you.	You do the dishes and your roommate stops yelling. You take an aspirin for your headache, which takes away the pain.
Secondary Reinforcers	You increase profits and receive $200 as a bonus. You study hard and receive a good grade on your psychology exam.	After high sales, your boss says you won't have to work on weekends. Professor says you won't have to take the final exam because you did so well on your unit exam.

Primary Reinforcers *Stimuli that increase the probability of a response because they satisfy a biological need, such as food, water, and sex*

Secondary Reinforcers *Stimuli that increase the probability of a response because of their learned value, such as money and material possessions*

Positive Reinforcement *Adding (or presenting) a stimulus, which strengthens a response and makes it more likely to recur*

Negative Reinforcement *Taking away (or removing) a stimulus, which strengthens a response and makes it more likely to recur*

1. *Primary and secondary reinforcers.* One of the chief methods for strengthening a response is with primary and secondary reinforcers. Reinforcers such as food, water, and sex are called **primary reinforcers** because they normally satisfy an unlearned biological need. In contrast, reinforcers such as money, praise, attention, and material possessions that have no intrinsic value are called **secondary reinforcers**. Their only power to reinforce behavior results from learning. A baby, for example, would find milk much more reinforcing than a $100 bill. Needless to say, by the time this baby has grown to adolescence, he or she will have learned to prefer the money. Among Westerners, money may be the most widely used secondary reinforcer because of its learned association with desirable commodities.

2. *Positive and negative reinforcement.* Adding or taking away certain stimuli also strengthens behavior. Suppose you tickle your baby and he smiles at you. His smile increases (or strengthens) the likelihood that you will tickle him again in the future. The smile itself is a *positive reinforcer* for you. This is called **positive reinforcement**. On the other hand, suppose your baby is upset and crying, so you hug him and he stops crying. This time the removal of crying is a *negative reinforcer*. The *process* is called **negative reinforcement** because the "taking away" of the crying by the hugging increases (or strengthens) the likelihood that you will hug him again in the future when he cries. Both responses reinforce or strengthen your smiling and hugging behavior.

(As a critical thinker, you may be wondering what's happening for the baby in this example. As a parent, you were both *positively* and *negatively reinforced*. In the same two examples your baby was only *positively reinforced*. He learned that his smile caused you to tickle him more and that his crying caused you to hug him. If you're worried that reinforcing the crying with hugs will create bigger problems, you can relax. Your baby soon will learn to talk and develop "better" ways to communicate.)

Why Negative Reinforcement Is Not Punishment

Many people hear the term *negative reinforcement* and automatically think of punishment. But it's important to remember that these two terms are completely opposite procedures. Reinforcement (either positive or negative) *strengthens a behavior*. As we will see in the next section, punishment *weakens a behavior*.

My students find it easier if they think of positive and negative reinforcement in the *mathematical* sense (as shown in Table 6.2) rather than as personal values of posi-

Reinforcement in action. Is this father's attention a primary or secondary reinforcer?

Andy Sacks/Stone/GettyImages

tive as "good" or negative as "bad." Think of positive reinforcement as something being added (+) that increases the likelihood that the behavior will increase. Conversely, think of negative reinforcement as something being taken away (–) that also increases the likelihood that the behavior will continue. For example, if your boss compliments you on a job well done, the compliment is added (+) as a consequence of your behavior. And, therefore, your hard work is likely to increase (positive reinforcement). Similarly, if your boss tells you that you no longer have to do a boring part of your job because of your excellent work, the taking away (–) of the boring task is a negative reinforcement. And your hard work is also likely to increase.

When I make myself study before I let myself go to the movies, is this negative reinforcement? No, this is actually a form of *positive reinforcement*. Because you *add* "going to the movies" only *after* you study, this should increase (positively reinforce) your studying behaviors.

In this same example, you're also using the **Premack principle**. Psychologist David Premack believes any naturally occurring, high-frequency response can be used to reinforce and increase low-frequency responses. Recognizing that you love to go to movies, you intuitively tied your less desirable low-frequency activity (studying) to your high-frequency or highly desirable behavior (going to the movies). You also can use the Premack principle in other aspects of your college life, such as making yourself write 4 pages on your term paper or read 20 pages before you allow yourself to call a friend or have a snack.

Premack Principle *Using a naturally occurring high-frequency response to reinforce and increase low-frequency responses*

Should I use the Premack principle every time I want to go to the movies or just occasionally? The answer is complex and depends on your most desired outcome. To make this decision, you need to understand various *schedules* of *reinforcement*, rules that determine when a response will be rewarded and when it will not (Terry, 2003).

Schedules of Reinforcement

The term *schedule of reinforcement* refers to the rate or interval at which responses are reinforced. Although there are numerous schedules of reinforcement, the most important distinction is whether they are *continuous* or *partial*. When Skinner was training his animals, he found that learning was most rapid if the response was reinforced each time it occurred—a procedure called **continuous reinforcement**. However, real life seldom provides continuous reinforcement. You do not get an A each time you write a paper or a date each time you ask. But your behavior persists because your efforts are occasionally rewarded. Most everyday behavior is similarly rewarded on a **partial (or intermittent) schedule of reinforcement**, which involves reinforcing only some responses, not all of them (Sangha et al., 2002).

Continuous Reinforcement *Every correct response is reinforced*

Partial (Intermittent) Reinforcement *Some, but not all, correct responses are reinforced*

For effective use of these principles in your own life, remember that continuous reinforcement leads to faster learning than does partial reinforcement. For example, if children (or adults) are rewarded every time they blast an alien starship in a video game *(continuous reinforcement)*, they will learn how to play faster than if they are rewarded for every third or fourth hit *(partial reinforcement)*. On the other hand, imagine having to reward your children every morning for getting up, brushing their teeth, making their beds, dressing, and so on. You simply cannot reward someone constantly for every appropriate response. Although a continuous schedule of reinforcement leads to faster initial learning, it is *not* an efficient system for maintaining long-term behaviors.

It is therefore important to move to a partial schedule of reinforcement once a task is well learned. Why? Because under partial schedules, behavior is more resistant to extinction. Have you noticed that people spend long hours pushing buttons and pulling levers on slot machines in hopes of winning the jackpot? This high response rate and the compulsion to keep gambling in spite of significant losses are evidence of

Study Tip 💡

Remember that interval is time based, whereas ratio is response based.

Fixed Ratio (FR) Schedule
Reinforcement occurs after a predetermined set of responses; the ratio (number or amount) is fixed

Variable Ratio (VR) Schedule
Reinforcement occurs unpredictably; the ratio (number or amount) varies

Fixed Interval (FI) Schedule
Reinforcement occurs after a predetermined time has elapsed; the interval (time) is fixed

Variable Interval (VI) Schedule
Reinforcement occurs unpredictably; the interval (time) varies

Shaping *Reinforcement delivered for successive approximations of the desired response*

Positive Punishment *Adding (or presenting) a stimulus that weakens a response and makes it less likely to recur*

Negative Punishment *Taking away (or removing) a stimulus that weakens a response and makes it less likely to recur*

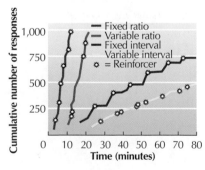

Figure 6.9 *Which schedule is best?*
Each of the different schedules produces its own unique pattern of response. The best schedule depends on the specific task—see Table 6.3. (The "stars" on the lines represent the delivery of a reinforcer.) (Adapted from Skinner, 1961.)

the strong resistance to extinction with partial schedules of reinforcement. This type of partial, intermittent reinforcement also helps parents maintain behaviors like tooth brushing and bed making. After the child has initially learned these behaviors with continuous reinforcement, you should move on to occasional, partial reinforcement.

Four Partial (Intermittent) Schedules of Reinforcement

There are four partial schedules of reinforcement: **fixed ratio (FR)**, **variable ratio (VR)**, **fixed interval (FI)**, and **variable interval (VI)**. Table 6.3 defines these terms and provides examples.

How do I know which schedule to choose? The type of partial schedule selected depends on the type of behavior being studied and on the speed of learning desired (Neuringer, Deiss, & Olson, 2000). For example, suppose you want to teach your dog to sit. Initially, you reinforce your dog with a cookie every time he sits (continuous reinforcement). To save on your cookie bill, and to make his training more resistant to extinction, you eventually switch to one of the partial reinforcement schedules. Using the *fixed ratio* schedule, you would give your dog a cookie after he sits a certain number of times. (The dog must make a fixed number of responses before he receives the reinforcement.) As you can see in Figure 6.9, a fixed ratio leads to the highest overall response rate. But each of the four types of partial schedules has different advantages and disadvantages (see Table 6.3).

Shaping

Each of the four schedules of partial reinforcement is important for maintaining behavior. But how do you teach new or complex behaviors like playing the piano or speaking a foreign language? **Shaping** teaches a desired response by reinforcing a series of successively improving steps leading to the final goal response. It is especially effective for teaching complex or novel behaviors that aren't likely to occur naturally. Skinner believed that shaping explains a wide variety of skills and abilities that each of us possesses, from eating with a fork, to playing a musical instrument, to driving a stick-shift car.

Parents, athletic coaches, teachers, and animal trainers all use shaping techniques. For example, if you want to shape a child to make his bed, you could begin by reinforcing when he first gets the sheets and pillows on the bed—even if it's sloppily done. Over time, you would stop reinforcing that level of behavior. You would only reinforce when he gets the bedspread on the bed and tucked over the pillows. Eventually you would stop reinforcing unless he gets the bedspread on, tucked over the pillows, and most of the wrinkles removed. Each step in shaping moves slightly beyond the previously learned behavior. This allows the person to link the new step to the behavior previously learned.

Punishment—Weakening a Response

Now that you understand how to *strengthen* a response, we will examine ways to *weaken* undesirable behaviors. Like reinforcement, punishment affects behavior. But it has the opposite effect. Punishment *decreases* the strength of the response—that is, the likelihood that a behavior will be repeated again is weakened. Just as with reinforcement, there are two kinds of punishment, *positive* and *negative* (Gordon, 1989; Skinner, 1953). Also, as with reinforcement, remember to think in mathematical terms of adding and taking away, rather than good and bad (Table 6.4).

Positive punishment is the addition (+) of a stimulus that decreases (or weakens) the likelihood of the response occurring again. If a parent adds new chores each time the child is late getting home, the parent is applying positive punishment. **Negative punishment** is the taking away (–) of a stimulus that decreases (or weakens) the

SUMMARY TABLE 6.3 FOUR SCHEDULES OF REINFORCEMENT

		Definitions	Response Rates	Examples
Ratio Schedules (response based)	**Fixed ratio (FR)**	Reinforcement occurs after a predetermined set of responses; the ratio (number or amount) is fixed	Produces a high rate of response, but a brief dropoff just after reinforcement	Car wash employee receives $10 for every 3 cars washed. In a laboratory, a rat receives a food pellet every time it presses the bar 7 times.
	Variable ratio (VR)	Reinforcement occurs unpredictably; the ratio (number or amount) varies	High response rates, no pause after reinforcement, and very resistant to extinction	Slot machines are designed to pay out after an average number of responses (maybe every 10 times), but any one machine may pay out on the first response, then seventh, then the twentieth.
Interval Schedules (time based)	**Fixed interval (FI)**	Reinforcement occurs after a predetermined time has elapsed; the interval (time) is fixed	Responses tend to increase as the time for the next reinforcer is near, but drop off after reinforcement and during interval	You get a monthly paycheck. Rat's behavior is reinforced with a food pellet when (or if) it presses a bar after 20 seconds have elapsed.
	Variable interval (VI)	Reinforcement occurs unpredictably; the interval (time) varies	Relatively low response rates, but they are steady because the nonhuman animal or person cannot predict when reward will come	Rat's behavior is reinforced with a food pellet after a response and a variable, unpredictable interval of time. In a class with pop quizzes, you study at a slow but steady rate because you can't anticipate the next quiz.

TABLE 6.4 HOW PUNISHMENT WEAKENS AND DECREASES BEHAVIORS

Positive Punishment *Adds stimulus (+) and weakens the behavior*	**Negative Punishment** *Takes stimulus away (–) and weakens the behavior*
You must run 4 extra laps in your gym class because you were late.	You're excluded from gym class because you were late.
A parent adds chores following a child's poor report card.	A parent takes away a teen's cell phone following a poor report card.
Your boss complains about your performance.	Your boss reduces your expense account after a poor performance.

www.wiley.com/college/huffman

VISUAL QUIZ

Kaku Kurita

Operant conditioning in action

Momoko, a five-year-old female monkey, is famous in Japan for her water-skiing, deep-sea diving, and other amazing abilities. Can you imagine how her trainers used shaping to teach this type of behavior?

Answer: The trainers would begin by reinforcing Momoko (with a small food treat) for standing or sitting on the water ski. Then they would reinforce her each time she put her hands on the pole. Next, they would slowly drag the water ski on dry land, and reinforce her for staying upright and holding the pole. Then they would take Momoko to a shallow and calm part of the ocean and reinforce her for staying upright and holding the pole as the ski moved in the water. Finally, they would take her into the deep part of the ocean, and reinforce her for holding on and successfully water-skiing.

likelihood of the response occurring again. Parents use negative punishment when they take the car keys away from a teen who doesn't come home on time. Notice that in *both* positive and negative punishment, the behavior has been punished and the behavioral tendencies have been weakened.

The Tricky Business of Punishment

When we hear the word *punishment*, most people think of disciplinary procedures used by parents, teachers, and other authority figures. But punishment is much more than parents giving a child a time-out for misbehaving or teachers giving demerits. Any process that adds or takes away something and causes the behavior to decrease is *punishment*. By this definition, if parents ignore all the A's on their child's report card and ask repeated questions about the B's and C's, they may unintentionally punish and weaken the likelihood of future A's. Dog owners who yell at or spank their dogs for finally coming to them after being called several times are actually punishing the desired behavior—coming when called. Similarly, college administrators who take away "leftover" money from a department's budget because it wasn't spent by the end of the year are punishing desired behavior—saving money. (Yes, I did add this last example as a subtle message to our college administrators!)

As you can see, punishment is a tricky business. But an advantage of studying psychology is that you now understand how positive and negative punishment (and positive and negative reinforcement) operate. You can use this knowledge to become a better parent, teacher, and authority figure, as well as a better friend and lover. To help you in these roles, consider the following general discussion and specific suggestions.

First, it's important to acknowledge that punishment plays a significant and unavoidable role in our social world. In his book *Walden Two* (1948), Skinner described a utopian (ideal) world where reinforcers almost completely replaced punishment. Unfortunately, in our real world, reinforcement is not enough. Dangerous criminals must be stopped and, possibly, removed from society. Parents must stop their children from running into the street and their teenagers from drinking and driving. Teachers must stop disruptive students in the classroom and bullies on the playground.

There is an obvious need for punishment. But it can be problematic (Javo et al., 2004; Reis et al., 2004; Saadeh, Rizzo, & Roberts, 2002). To be effective, punishment should be immediate and consistent. However, in the real world, this is extremely hard to do. Police officers cannot immediately stop every driver every time he or she speeds.

To make matters worse, when punishment is not immediate, during the delay the undesirable behavior is likely to be reinforced, which unintentionally places it on a *partial schedule of reinforcement*. Sadly, this makes the undesirable behavior even more resistant to extinction. Think about gambling. For almost everyone, it should be a *punishing* situation—on most occasions, you lose far more money than you win. However, the fact that you occasionally win keeps you "hanging in there."

Perhaps, most important, even if punishment immediately follows the misbehavior, the recipient may learn what *not* to do but not learn what he or she *should* do. Imagine trying to teach a child the word *dog* by only saying "No!" each time she said *dog* when it was inappropriate. The child (and you) would soon become very frustrated. It's much more efficient to teach someone by giving him or her clear examples of correct behavior, such as showing a child pictures of dogs and saying *dog* after each photo. Punishment has several other serious side effects, as Table 6.5 shows.

SUMMARY TABLE 6.5 SIDE EFFECTS OF PUNISHMENT

1. *Increased aggression.* Because punishment often produces a decrease in undesired behavior, at least for the moment, the punisher is in effect rewarded for applying punishment. Thus, a vicious circle may be established in which both the punisher and recipient are reinforced for inappropriate behavior—the punisher for punishing and the recipient for being fearful and submissive. This side effect partially explains the escalation of violence in family abuse and bullying (Javo et al., 2004; Larzelere & Johnson, 1999). In addition to fear and submissiveness, the recipient also might become depressed and/or respond with his or her own form of aggression.

2. *Passive aggressiveness.* For the recipient, punishment often leads to frustration, anger, and eventually aggression. But most of us have learned from experience that retaliatory aggression toward a punisher (especially one who is bigger and more powerful) is usually followed by more punishment. We therefore tend to control our impulse toward open aggression and instead resort to more subtle techniques, such as showing up late or forgetting to mail a letter for someone. This is known as *passive aggressiveness* (Gilbert, 2003; Stormshak, Bierman, McMahon, & Lengua, 2000).

Photo Researchers, Inc.

3. *Avoidance behavior.* No one likes to be punished, so we naturally try to avoid the punisher. If every time you come home a parent or spouse starts yelling at you, you will delay coming home or find another place to go.

4. *Modeling.* Have you ever seen a parent spank or hit a child for hitting another child? The punishing parent may unintentionally serve as a "model" for the same behavior he or she is attempting to stop.

5. *Temporary suppression.* Do you notice that car drivers quickly slow down when they see a police car but quickly resume their previous speed once the police officer is out of sight? Punishment generally suppresses the behavior only temporarily during the presence of the punishing person or circumstances.

6. *Learned helplessness.* Why do some people stay in abusive homes or marital situations? Research shows that if you repeatedly fail in your attempts to control your environment, you acquire a general sense of powerlessness or *learned helplessness* and you may make no further attempts to escape (Alloy & Clements, 1998; Seligman, 1975; Shors, 2004; Zhukov & Vinogradova, 2002).

Assessment

VISUAL QUIZ

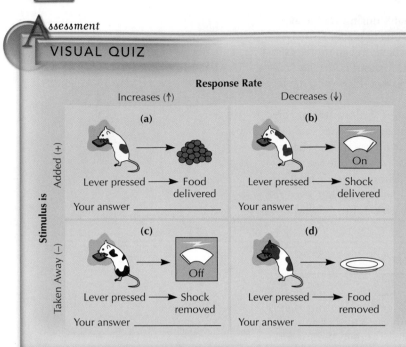

Response Rate

Increases (↑)   Decreases (↓)

Stimulus is

Added (+)

(a)
Lever pressed ⟶ Food delivered
Your answer _____

(b)
On
Lever pressed ⟶ Shock delivered
Your answer _____

Taken Away (−)

(c)
Off
Lever pressed ⟶ Shock removed
Your answer _____

(d)
Lever pressed ⟶ Food removed
Your answer _____

Test Yourself

Is this positive reinforcement, negative reinforcement, positive punishment, or negative punishment? Check your understanding by reviewing this figure and filling in your answer in the space provided in each box.

Answers: (a) positive reinforcement, (b) positive punishment, (c) negative reinforcement, (d) negative punishment.

TRY THIS YOURSELF

Application

Tips for Reinforcement and Punishment

After studying basic learning principles, can you effectively apply them in your own life? The best method seems to be a combination of the major principles: Reinforce appropriate behavior, extinguish inappropriate behavior, and save punishment for the most extreme cases (such as a 2-year-old running into the street). Here are additional tips:

1. *Feedback.* When using both reinforcement and punishment, be sure to provide immediate and clear feedback to the person or nonhuman animal whose behavior you wish to change. When using punishment, it is particularly important to make clear the desired response because punishment is merely an indication that the response is undesirable. In other words, give the participant an alternative response to the punished one.
2. *Timing.* Reinforcers and punishers should be presented as close in time to the response as possible. The old policy of "wait till your father gets home" is obviously inappropriate for many rea-

sons. In this case, it is because the delayed punishment is no longer associated with the inappropriate response. The same is true for reinforcement. If you're trying to lose weight, don't say you'll buy yourself a new wardrobe when you lose 30 pounds. Instead, reward yourself with a small treat (like a new blouse or shirt) after every few pounds.

3. *Consistency.* To be effective, both reinforcement and punishment must be consistent. Have you ever seen a child screaming for candy in a supermarket? Parents often begin by saying "no!" But when the child gets louder or throws a temper tantrum, the parents often give in and buy the candy. Although the parents are momentarily relieved (negatively reinforced) when the screaming stops, can you see how they're creating bigger and longer lasting problems?

First, the child is being positively reinforced for the screaming and temper tantrum, so this behavior will increase. To make matters worse, the parents' inconsistency (saying "no" and then occasionally giving in) places begging for candy on a partial schedule of reinforcement.

This makes temper tantrums highly resistant to extinction. Like a gambler who continues playing despite the odds, the child will continue the begging, screaming, and temper tantrums in hopes of the occasional payoff.

Because effective punishment requires constant surveillance and consistent responses, it's almost impossible to be a "good punisher." It's best (and easiest) to use consistent reinforcement for good behavior and extinction for bad behavior. Praise the child for happy and cooperative behavior in the supermarket. Extinguish the temper tantrum by consistently refusing the request and ignoring the tantrum.

4. *Order of presentation.* As a teenager, did you ever ask for an extra few dollars as an advance on your allowance? Did you later "forget" your promise to mow the grass on Saturday? As a parent, have you ever made your teen come home much earlier than their friends because you know that "all teenagers get into trouble after midnight"? Can you see why the reward of extra money must come after the lawn mowing and why punishment that comes before the behavior may create frustration and resentment? Both reinforcement and punishment should come after the behavior, never before.

Summarizing and Comparing Classical and Operant Conditioning

Are you feeling overwhelmed with all the important (and seemingly overlapping) terms and concepts for both classical and operant conditioning? This is a good time to stop and carefully review Table 6.6, which summarizes all the key terms and compares the two major types of conditioning.

SUMMARY TABLE 6.6 COMPARING CLASSICAL AND OPERANT CONDITIONING

	Classical Conditioning	**Operant Conditioning**
Pioneers	Ivan Pavlov John B. Watson	Edward Thorndike B. F. Skinner
Major Terms	Neutral stimulus (NS) Unconditioned stimulus (UCS) Conditioned stimulus (CS) Unconditioned response (UCR) Conditioned response (CR) Conditioned emotional response (CER)	Reinforcers (primary and secondary) Reinforcement (positive and negative) Punishment (positive and negative) Shaping Reinforcement schedules (continuous and partial)
Example	Cringing at the sound of a dentist's drill	A baby cries and you pick it up
Shared Terms	Generalization Discrimination Extinction Spontaneous recovery	Generalization Discrimination Extinction Spontaneous recovery
Major Differences	Learning based on paired associations Involuntary (subject is passive)	Learning based on consequences Voluntary (subject is active and "operates" on the environment)
Order of Effects	NS comes *before* the UCS	Reinforcement or punishment come *after* the behavior

Corbis Images

Discriminative stimuli in everyday life.

Discriminative Stimulus *A cue that signals when a specific response will lead to the expected reinforcement*

As you can see, there are several areas of similarity in classical and operant conditioning. For example, in our earlier discussion of the principles of classical conditioning, you learned about *stimulus generalization*, *stimulus discrimination*, *extinction*, and *spontaneous recovery*. These same terms also are used in operant conditioning. Just as 11-month-old Albert generalized his fear of rats to rabbits and Santa Claus masks, operantly conditioned responses also generalize. After learning the word for *Daddy* (through the operant conditioning procedure of *shaping*), children often use this same word for all adult men. This would be a form of *stimulus generalization* (and potential embarrassment to the parents). After parents explain the distinction, the child learns to differentiate (stimulus discrimination) and to call only one man Daddy.

In both classical and operant conditioning, *extinction* occurs when the original source of the learning is removed. In classical conditioning, the CR (Albert's fear of the rat) is extinguished if the CS (the rat) is repeatedly presented without the UCS (the loud noise). In operant conditioning, if the reinforcement (the rat's food) is removed, the response (bar pressing) will gradually decline. Following extinction in either classical or operant conditioning, you also sometimes have *spontaneous recovery*. Just as the classically conditioned fear of rats may spontaneously return, the operantly conditioned bar-pressing behaviors may recur.

One final comparison: In classical conditioning, we talked about *higher-order conditioning*. This occurs when a neutral stimulus (NS) is paired with a conditioned stimulus (CS), which is another stimulus that already produces a learned response. We said that if you wanted to demonstrate higher-order conditioning in Pavlov's dogs, you would first condition the dogs to salivate to the sound of the tone. Then you would pair the flash of light to the sound of the tone. Eventually, the dog would salivate only to the flash of light.

A similar process, with a different name, also occurs in operant conditioning. If a rat learns that bar pressing produces food *only* when a light is flashing, the rat will soon learn to respond only when the light is flashing. The light has become a **discriminative stimulus**, which signals whether or not a response will pay off. We depend on discriminative stimuli many times every day. We pick up the phone only when it rings. We look for the *Women* or *Men* signs on bathroom doors. And children quickly learn to ask grandparents for toys.

Assessment

VISUAL QUIZ

DENNIS THE MENACE

"I THINK MOM'S USING THE CAN OPENER."

DENNIS THE MENACE® used by permission of Hank Ketcham Enterprises, Inc. and © by North America Syndicate.

Conditioning in Action

Can you explain how this is both classical and operant conditioning?

Answer: In the beginning, the dog involuntarily paired up the sound of the can opener with food (classical conditioning). Later, the dog voluntarily ran toward the sound of the can opener and was positively reinforced with food (operant conditioning).

*A*pplication

CRITICAL THINKING   ACTIVE LEARNING

Using Learning Principles to Succeed in College

Psychological theory and research have taught us that an active approach to learning is rewarded by better grades. Active learning means using the SQ4R (Survey, Question, Read, Recite, Review, and wRite) study techniques discussed in the "Tools for Student Success" (pages 43–49). An active learner also rises above old, easy patterns of behavior and applies new knowledge to everyday situations. When you transfer ideas or concepts you learn from class to your personal life, your insight grows.

Now that you have studied the principles of learning, use the following activity to help you apply your new knowledge to achieve your education goals and have an enjoyable college experience:

1. List three ways you can positively reinforce yourself for studying, completing assignments, and attending class.
2. Discuss with friends how participating in club and campus activities can reinforce your commitment to education.

3. Examine the time and energy you spend studying for an exam in a course you like with your study effort in a course you don't like. How could you apply the Premack principle to your advantage in this situation?
4. When you take exams, are you anxious? How might this be a classically conditioned response? Describe how you could use the principle of extinction to weaken this response.

---

*A*ssessment

CHECK & REVIEW

Operant Conditioning

In **operant conditioning,** humans and nonhuman animals learn by the consequences of their responses. Whether behavior is reinforced or punished (consequences) influences whether the response will occur again. Thorndike and Skinner are the two major contributors to operant conditioning. Thorndike's **law of effect** states that rewarded behavior is more likely to recur. Skinner extended Thorndike's work to more complex behaviors but emphasized only external, observable behaviors.

Operant conditioning involves several important terms and principles. **Reinforcement** is any procedure that strengthens or increases a response. **Punishment** is any procedure that results in a weakening or decrease. To strengthen a response, we use **primary reinforcers.** These reinforcers satisfy an unlearned biological need (e.g., hunger, thirst). We also use **secondary reinforcers,** which

have learned value (e.g., money). **Positive reinforcement** (adding something) and **negative reinforcement** (taking something away) increase the likelihood the response will occur again. According to the **Premack principle,** activities or behaviors that are more common or probable in one's life will act as reinforcers for activities that are less probable. **Continuous reinforcement** rewards each correct response. A **partial (intermittent) schedule** reinforces for some, not all, designated responses. The four partial reinforcement schedules are **variable ratio (VR), variable interval (VI), fixed ratio (FR),** and **fixed interval (FI).** Complex behaviors can be trained through **shaping**—reinforcing successive approximations of the desired behavior.

Positive punishment (adding something) and **negative punishment** (taking something away) decrease the likelihood the response will occur again. Although some punishment is essential, it has serious side effects.

Questions

1. Define operant conditioning and explain how it differs from classical conditioning.
2. Negative punishment _____ and negative reinforcement _____ the likelihood the response will continue. (a) decreases, decreases; (b) increases, decreases; (c) decreases, increases; (d) increases, increases
3. Partial reinforcement schedules make responses more _____ to extinction.
4. Marshall is very disruptive in class and his teacher uses various forms of punishment hoping to decrease his misbehavior. List five potential problems with this approach.

Check your answers in Appendix B.

CLICK & REVIEW
for additional assessment options:
www.wiley.com/college/huffman

COGNITIVE-SOCIAL LEARNING

Achievement

How and when do we learn according to cognitive-social theory, and how can we use it in everyday life?

Cognitive-Social Theory *Emphasizes the roles of thinking and social learning in behavior*

Insight *Sudden understanding of a problem that implies the solution*

Is this insight? *Grande, one of Wolfgang Köhler's chimps, has just solved the problem of how to get the banana. Is this insight or trial and error? (Also, the chimp in the foreground is engaged in observational learning—our next topic.)*

American Philosophical Society

So far, we have examined learning processes that involve associations between a stimulus and an observable behavior. Some behaviorists believe that almost all learning can be explained in such stimulus–response terms. Other psychologists feel there is more to learning than can be explained solely by operant and classical conditioning. **Cognitive-social theory** (also called *cognitive-social learning* or *cognitive-behavioral theory*) incorporates the general concepts of conditioning. But rather than a simple S–R (stimulus and response), this theory emphasizes the interpretation or thinking that occurs within the organism—S–O–R (stimulus–organism–response). According to this view, people (as well as rats, pigeons, and other nonhuman animals) have attitudes, beliefs, expectations, motivations, and emotions that affect learning. Furthermore, both human and nonhuman animals are social creatures capable of learning new behaviors through observation and imitation of others. We begin with a look at the *cognitive* part of cognitive-social theory, followed by an examination of the *social* aspects of learning.

◼ Insight and Latent Learning: Where Are the Reinforcers?

As you'll discover throughout this text, cognitive factors play a large role in human behavior and mental processes. Given that these factors are covered in several other chapters (such as those on memory and thinking/language/intelligence), our discussion here is limited to the classic research of Wolfgang Köhler and Edward Tolman and their studies of *insight* and *latent learning*.

Köhler's Study of Insight

Early behaviorists likened the mind to a "black box," whose workings could not be observed directly. German psychologist Wolfgang Köhler wanted to look inside the box. He believed there was more to learning—especially learning to solve a complex problem—than responding to stimuli in a trial-and-error fashion. In several experiments conducted during World War I, Köhler posed different types of problems to chimpanzees and apes to see how they learned to solve them. In one experiment, he placed a banana just outside the reach of a caged chimpanzee. To reach the banana, the chimp would have to use a stick placed near the cage to extend its reach. The chimp did not solve this problem in the random trial-and-error fashion of Thorndike's cats or Skinner's rats and pigeons. Köhler noticed that he seemed to sit and think about the situation for a while. Then, in a flash of **insight** (a sudden understanding), the chimp picked up the stick and maneuvered the banana within its grasp (Köhler, 1925).

Another one of Köhler's chimps, an intelligent fellow named Sultan, was put in a similar situation. However, this time two sticks were made available to him and the banana was placed even farther away, too far to reach with a single stick. Sultan seemingly lost interest in the banana but continued to play with the sticks. When he later discovered that the two sticks could be interlocked, he instantly used the now-longer stick to pull the banana within reach. Köhler designated this type of learning *insight learning*. Some internal mental event that we can only describe as "insight" went on between the presentation of the banana and the use of the stick to retrieve it.

Tolman's Study of Latent Learning

Previous researchers suggested that rats learned mazes through trial-and-error and rewards. Edward C. Tolman (1898–1956) believed they underestimated the rat's cognitive processes and cognitive learning. He noted that rats placed in experimental mazes seemed to pause at certain intersections, almost as if they were *deciding* which route to take. When allowed to roam aimlessly in a maze with no food reward at the end, the rats also seemed to develop a **cognitive map**, or mental representation, of the maze.

To test the idea of cognitive learning, Tolman allowed one group of rats to explore a maze in an aimless fashion with no reinforcement. A second group was always reinforced with food whenever they reached the end of the maze. The third group was not rewarded initially (during the first 10 days of the trial). But starting on day 11 they found food at the end of the maze. As expected from simple operant conditioning, the first and third groups were slow to learn the maze. The second group, which had reinforcement, showed fast, steady improvement. However, when the third group started receiving reinforcement (on the 11th day), their learning of the maze quickly matched the performance of the group that had been reinforced every time (Tolman & Honzik, 1930). For Tolman, this was significant. It proved that the nonreinforced rats had been thinking and building cognitive maps of the area during their aimless wandering. Their hidden **latent learning** only showed up when there was a reason to display it (the food reward).

Cognitive learning is not limited to rats. If a new log is placed in its territory, a chipmunk will explore it for a time. But will soon move on if no food is found. When a predator comes into the same territory, however, the chipmunk heads directly for and hides beneath the log. Similarly, as a child you may have casually ridden a bike around your neighborhood with no particular reason or destination in mind. You only demonstrated your hidden knowledge of the area when your dad was later searching for the closest mailbox. The fact that Tolman's nonreinforced rats quickly caught up to the reinforced ones, that the chipmunk knew about the hiding place under the log, that you knew the location of the mailbox, and recent experimental evidence (Burgdorf, Knutson, & Panksepp, 2000) all provide clear evidence of latent learning and the existence of internal cognitive maps.

Cognitive Map *A mental image of a three-dimensional space that an organism has navigated*

Latent Learning *Hidden learning that exists without behavioral signs*

■ Observational Learning: What We See Is What We Do

After watching her first presidential debate, my friend's 5-year-old daughter asked, "Do we like him, Mommy?" What form of learning is this? In addition to classical and operant conditioning and cognitive processes (such as insight and latent learning), this child's question shows that we also learn many things through observation and imitation of others—thus the name **observational learning** (or *social learning* or *modeling*). From birth to death, observational learning is very important to our biological, psychological, and social survival (the *biopsychosocial* model). Watching others helps us avoid dangerous stimuli in our environment, teaches us how to think and feel, and shows us how to act and interact in social situations.

Some of the most compelling examples of observational learning come from the work of Albert Bandura and his colleagues (Bandura, 2003; Bandura, Ross, & Ross, 1961; Bandura & Walters, 1963). Wanting to know whether children learn to be aggressive by watching others be aggressive, Bandura and his colleagues set up several experiments. They allowed children to watch a live or televised adult model kick, punch, and shout at a large inflated Bobo doll. Later, the children were allowed to play in the same room with the same toys (see the photo on this page). As Bandura hypothesized, children who had seen the live or televised aggressive model were much more aggressive with the Bobo doll than children who had not seen the aggression. In other words, "Monkey see, monkey do."

We obviously don't copy or model everything we see, however. According to Bandura, learning by observation requires at least four separate processes:

1. *Attention.* Observational learning requires attention. This is why teachers insist on students watching their demonstrations.

Observational Learning *Learning new behavior or information by watching others (also known as social learning or modeling)*

Courtesy Albert Bandura

Bandura's classic Bobo doll study. *This child watched while an adult hit the Bobo doll and then imitated the behavior.*

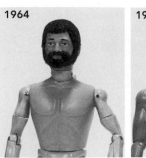
1964

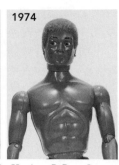
1974

1994

1998

©AP/Wide World Photos

All GI Joe images courtesy of Dr. Harrison G. Pope, Jr.

Observational learning and modeling. *Note how the bicep circumference of the G.I. Joe action figure has more than doubled since 1964. Can you see how this type of modeling might help explain why men today worry more about their chest and bicep size? Or why they sometimes use steroids to increase their muscle development? [Source: As G.I. Joe bulks up, concern for the 98-pound weakling (May 30, 1999, New York Times, p. D2)]*

2. *Retention.* To learn a complex new dance step, we need to carefully note and remember the instructor's directions and demonstrations.

3. *Motor reproduction.* Observational learning cannot occur if we lack the motor skills necessary to imitate the model. One of the worst arguments I've ever had with my husband was during his attempts to teach me to downhill ski. Although I paid close attention and remembered his instructions, I repeatedly failed at even the most basic skills—like standing up! Because he was an expert skier of many years, he had forgotten several important steps in the initial learning process. My beginner's motor skills were not up to the task of starting beyond the basics. Our argument was stopped (and our marriage saved) by the arrival of the *professional* ski instructor. (Did you note the way I emphasized "professional"?)

4. *Reinforcement.* We also decide whether we want to repeat the modeled behavior based on whether the model was reinforced. If we see a large number of people making lots of money in the stock market, we're likely to copy their behavior. We're less likely to do so when the market collapses.

Application

RESEARCH HIGHLIGHT

"The Theory Heard Round the World."
(Contributed by Thomas Frangicetto)

Bandura's "Bobo doll" study is considered a classic in social psychology. It proved that children will imitate models they observe on television. Why is this new or important? Parents, educators, and politicians have long complained about all the negative things children learn from television. But what about the positive effects? Around the world, billions of people spend a large portion of their lives watching television. Could these hours of observational learning be put to good use?

Yes! According to a recent article, researchers working with television producers have created long-running, entertaining, serial dramas that feature attractive characters who model positive behaviors and good outcomes (Putting the power of television to good use, 2005). Fortunately, these "soap operas" have had a dramatic effect on social problems like illiteracy, HIV, overpopulation, and gender discrimination. Consider the following:

• In 1975, Mexican television executive Miguel Sabido produced the soap opera *Ven Conmigo* ("Come with Me") to entertain and advocate for adult literacy.

The show was incredibly successful. The attendance in adult literacy classes was nine times higher than the year before.

• In the early 1990s, in the African country of Tanzania, life-threatening myths and misinformation were abundant. According to one report, Tanzanians believed that HIV "was transmitted through mosquitoes and having sex with a condom could cause the virus" (Smith, 2002). In 1993 an educational radio program aired in the Swahili language, *Twende na Wakati* ("Let's Go With the Time"), began broadcasting twice a week. Again, the results were spectacularly successful.

Interestingly, the social cognitive theory of Albert Bandura played a pivotal role—not just in Mexico and Tanzania, but also in China and areas in the Caribbean (Smith, 2002). According to Smith, Bandura's theory "is the foundation of television and radio shows that have changed the lives of millions." How do we know this?

"Sabido contacted Bandura," Smith writes, "explaining that he was using Bandura's work on modeling and social learning to produce *Ven Conmigo* and then showed him episodes of the drama." Bandura was duly impressed, "I thought this is a remarkably creative implementation of theory into practice," he told Smith. "I was amazed at the ingenuity." Sabido was not officially trained in psychology, but was able to "apply Bandura's theories to the real world" (Smith, 2002, p. 30).

But how can we be sure that the outcomes reported in Mexico and Tanzania were really the result of *cause and effect* and not *correlational*? How do we know, for example, that the changes in Tanzania—more Tanzanians knowing that unprotected sex could result in HIV infection, and decreasing their sexual partners while increasing condom use—were directly caused by observational learning and the radio soap opera *Twende nao Wakati*? Could other factors have been involved? Would the changes have occurred without the soap opera?

"The challenge," according to researcher Peter Vaughan (2004), "is to know how much of the change was caused by the program (cause and effect) and how much of the change was caused by other things that were going on in the country at the same time (correlation)." Vaughan, the director of *Population Communication International* (PCI), an agency that produces educational soap operas globally, admitted the difficulty of constructing a control group in these mass media studies. However, "in Tanzania we were actually able to do that." PCI divided a map of Tanzania into two areas. One group could hear the broadcasts of *Twende na Wakati* and the other could not. Increases in positive behavioral and attitudinal changes were *much* higher where *Twende* was aired. A full explanation of their findings can be found at PCI's website http://www.population.org/entsummit/transcript04_vaughan.shtm.

On this same website, PCI also explains that its "methodology" is based on "a theory of social learning developed by Professor Albert Bandura of Stanford University." In the spirit of Bandura's model, PCI trains their creative teams to "...include positive characters who are rewarded, negative characters who are punished, and transitional characters whose experiences embody the difficult choices we all face in life." And the crucial connection between "art and audience" that must take place if change is to occur does so here because "audience members tend to bond with the transitional characters who move to more positive behaviors, whether protecting themselves against HIV/AIDS, pursuing education, or keeping their children in school" (PCI, 2005). That is truly "psychology in action" and it is a legacy of which Albert Bandura can be justly proud.

Active Learning Questions

1. What role has observational learning played in your life? Can you think of specific examples of learning from the behavior of role models? Who were they and what qualities did they have that were worth emulating? Have you experienced *negative* role modeling? Does observational learning contradict good critical thinking? For example, does learning from observing the behaviors of others violate being an *independent thinker*?

2. Consider the PCI research described by Peter Vaughan. Identify the following terms in this study: hypothesis, experimental group, control group, independent variable, and dependent variable. Do you find PCIs conclusions convincing? Do you have any problem with PCI doing the research on the effectiveness of their own dramatic productions? Explain.

3. A recent American Psychological Association (APA) press release highlighted the prevalence of self-destructive behaviors such as "smoking, alcohol abuse, and a sedentary lifestyle" (Winerman, 2005) in the United States. One major problem, according to psychologist James Prochaska, is that "the American health-care system has yet to fully integrate behavior change into treatment." He encourages "psychologists to work to change that." Given what we know about the power of stories to engage the emotions of people (Giles, 2004), do you think that an American version of *Twende na Wakati* or *Ven Conmigo* would be effective? Explain.

*A*chievement
Gender & Cultural Diversity

Scaffolding as a Teaching Technique in Different Cultures

Learning in the real world is often a combination of classical conditioning, operant conditioning, and cognitive-social learning. This is especially evident in informal situations in which an individual acquires new skills under the supervision of a master teacher. The ideal process used by teachers in these situations is known as *scaffolding*

www.wiley.com/college/huffman

(Wood, Bruner, & Ross, 1976). Like the temporary platform on which construction workers stand, a cognitive *scaffold* provides temporary assistance while a learner acquires new skills. During this type of cognitive scaffolding, a more experienced person adjusts the amount of guidance to fit the student's current performance level. In most cases, scaffolding also combines *shaping* and *modeling*. The teacher selectively reinforces successes of the student and models more difficult parts of the task.

Patricia Marks Greenfield (1984, 2004) has described how scaffolding helps young girls learn to weave in Zinacantán, Mexico. Weaving is an important part of the culture of the Zinacantecos, who live in the highlands of southern Mexico. Greenfield videotaped 14 girls at different levels of learning to weave. Each girl was allowed to complete what she was able to do with ease. A more experienced weaver then created a scaffold by reinforcing correct weaving and modeling more difficult techniques. Interestingly, the teachers appear oblivious of their teaching methods or of the fact that they are teaching at all. Most of the Zinacanteco women believe that girls learn to weave by themselves. Similarly, in our Western culture, many believe that children learn to talk by themselves, ignoring how often children are reinforced (or scaffolded) by others.

CHECK & REVIEW

Cognitive-Social Learning

Cognitive-social theory incorporates concepts of conditioning but emphasizes thought processes, or cognitions, and social learning. According to this perspective, people learn through insight, latent learning, observation, and modeling.

Wolfgang Köhler, in working with chimpanzees, demonstrated that learning could occur with a sudden flash of **insight.** Tolman demonstrated that **latent learning** takes place in the absence of reward and remains hidden until some future time when it can be retrieved as needed. A **cognitive map** is a mental image of an area that a person or nonhuman animal has navigated.

According to Albert Bandura, **observa-** **tional learning** is the process of learning how to do something by watching others and performing the same behavior in the future. To imitate the behavior of others, we must pay attention, remember, be able to reproduce the behavior, and be motivated by some reinforcement.

Questions

1. _____ were influential in early studies of cognitive learning. (a) William James and Ivan Pavlov; (b) B. F. Skinner and Edward Thorndike; (c) Wolfgang Köhler and Edward Tolman; (d) Albert Bandura and R. H. Walters
2. Learning that occurs in the absence of a reward and remains hidden until some future time when it can be retrieved is called _____.
3. Mental images of an area that an organism has navigated are known as _____.
4. Bandura's observational learning studies focused on how _____. (a) rats learn cognitive maps through exploration; (b) children learn aggressive behaviors by observing aggressive models; (c) cats learn problem solving through trial and error; (d) chimpanzees learn problem solving through reasoning

Check your answers in Appendix B.

 CLICK & REVIEW for additional assessment options: www.wiley.com/college/huffman

THE BIOLOGY OF LEARNING

What neurological changes take place during and after learning? What are the evolutionary advantages to learning?

As you recall, learning is defined as a *relatively permanent change in behavior and mental processes resulting from practice or experience.* For this change in behavior to persist over time, lasting biological changes must occur within the organism. In this section, we will examine the neurological changes that occur during and after learning. We also will explore the evolutionary advantages of learning.

Neuroscience and Learning: The Adaptive Brain

Each time we learn something, either consciously or unconsciously, that experience changes our brains. We create new synaptic connections and alterations in a wide network of brain structures, including the cortex, cerebellum, hypothalamus, thalamus, and amygdala (Debaere et al., 2004; Fanselow & Poulos, 2005; Pelletier & Paré, 2004; Thompson, 2005).

Evidence that our brains change in structure because of experience first began to accumulate in the 1960s with studies of *enriched* and *deprived environments.* Research on this topic generally involves raising one group of rats in large cages with other rats and many objects to explore. This rat "Disneyland" is colorfully decorated, and each cage has ladders, platforms, and cubbyholes to investigate. In contrast, rats in the second group are raised in stimulus-poor, deprived environments. They live alone and have no objects to explore except food and water dispensers. After weeks in these environments, the brains of these two groups of rats are significantly different. The rats in the enriched environment typically develop a thicker cortex, increased nerve growth factor (NGF), more fully developed synapses, more dendritic branching, and improved performance on many tests of learning (Guilarte et al., 2003; Pham, Winblad, Granholm, & Mohammed, 2002; Rosenzweig & Bennett, 1996).

Admittedly, it is big leap from rats to humans. But research suggests that the human brain also responds to environmental conditions. For example, older adults exposed to stimulating environments generally perform better on intellectual and perceptual tasks than those who are in restricted environments (Schaie, 1994).

Evolution and Learning: Biological Preparedness and Instinctive Drift

So far, we have emphasized the learned aspects of behavior. But humans and other nonhuman animals are born with other innate, biological tendencies that help ensure their survival. When your fingers touch a hot object, you immediately pull your hand away. When a foreign object approaches your eye, you automatically blink. These simple *reflexes* involve making a specific automatic reaction to a particular stimulus. In addition to reflexes, many species also have a second set of adaptive responses called *instincts*, or species-specific behaviors. For example, the weaverbird is known to tie a particular grass knot to hold its nest together. Even when these birds are raised in total isolation for several generations, they will still tie the same knot.

Although these inborn, innate abilities are important to our evolutionary survival, they are inadequate for coping with a constantly changing environment. Reflexively withdrawing your fingers from a hot object is certainly to your advantage. But what if you saw a sign showing that the hot object was an unusual door handle that would allow you to escape a burning building? Numerous important stimuli in our environment require a flexible approach. Only through learning are we are able to react to spoken words, written symbols, and other important environmental stimuli. From an evolutionary perspective, *learning* is an adaptation that enables organisms to survive and prosper in a constantly changing world. In this section, we will explore how our biological heritage helps us learn some associations more easily than others (*biological preparedness*), while also restricting us from learning in other situations (*biological constraints*).

Classical Conditioning and Taste Aversions

Years ago, Rebecca (a student in my psychology class) was walking to class as she absentmindedly unwrapped a Butterfinger candy bar. Expecting the sweet chocolate taste and crunch of her favorite candy, she was momentarily confused by its unexpected bitter taste and wet, slimy texture. Her confusion was quickly replaced by horror—her candy bar was filled with small, wiggling maggots!

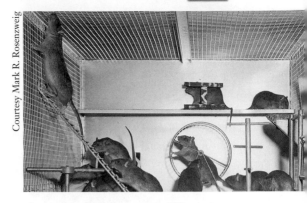

An enriched environment. When mice and rats live in cages with many objects to explore, their brains develop thicker cerebral cortexes and more efficient synapses.

Taste aversion. Coyotes find sheep an easy source of food. But if they are conditioned to develop a taste aversion to sheep, they will avoid them and seek other food.

www.wiley.com/college/huffman

Are you feeling slightly sick after reading this? Can you imagine how Rebecca felt? You're probably not surprised that many years later she still feels nauseated when she sees a Butterfinger candy bar. But can you explain why she doesn't feel similarly nauseated by the sight of her boyfriend, who bought her the candy?

I use Rebecca's graphic (and true!) story to illustrate an important evolutionary process. When a food or drink is associated with nausea or vomiting, that particular food or drink can become a conditioned stimulus (CS) that triggers a conditioned **taste aversion**. Like other classically conditioned responses, taste aversions develop involuntarily.

Can you see why this automatic response would be adaptive? If our cave-dwelling ancestors became ill after eating a new plant, it would increase their chances for survival if they immediately developed an aversion to that plant—but not to other family members who might have been present at the time. Similarly, people tend to develop phobias to snakes, darkness, spiders, and heights more easily than to guns, knives, and electric outlets. We apparently inherit a built-in (innate) readiness to form associations between certain stimuli and responses, known as **biological preparedness**.

Laboratory experiments have provided general support for both taste aversion and biological preparedness. For example, Garcia and his colleagues (1966) produced taste aversion in lab rats by pairing flavored water (NS) and a drug (UCS) that produced gastrointestinal distress (UCR). After being conditioned and recovering from the illness, the rats refused to drink the flavored water (CS) because of the conditioned taste aversion. Remarkably, however, Garcia discovered that only certain neutral stimuli could produce the nausea. Pairings of a noise (NS) or a shock (NS) with the nausea-producing drug (UCS) produced no taste aversion. Garcia suggested that when we are sick to our stomachs, we have a natural, evolutionary tendency to attribute it to food or drink. Being *biologically prepared* to quickly associate nausea with food or drink is adaptive. It helps us avoid that or similar food or drink in the future (Cooper et al., 2002; Domjan, 2005; Garcia, 2003).

This research calls into question early learning theorists who believed they could condition virtually any stimulus and any response—as long as the organism was physically capable of performing the behavior. In his research, however, Garcia found that taste–nausea associations were almost impossible to prevent. Other associations (noise–nausea and shock–nausea) were virtually impossible to produce!

Garcia's findings on taste aversion are important for at least two reasons. First, identifying exceptions to classical conditioning leads to a better understanding of biological preparedness. Second, he and his colleagues used their basic research to help solve an economic problem for western ranchers. Coyotes were killing sheep and the ranchers wanted to kill the coyotes. But this "solution" would have created a larger ecological problem because coyotes eat rabbits and small rodents.

In a form of applied research, Garcia and his colleagues used classical conditioning to teach the coyotes not to eat sheep (Gustavson & Garcia, 1974). The researchers began by lacing freshly killed sheep with a chemical that causes extreme nausea and vomiting in coyotes that eat the tainted meat. The conditioning worked so well that the coyotes would voluntarily run away from the mere sight and smell of sheep. Taste aversion research has since been widely tested and applied both in the wild and in the laboratory (Aubert & Dantzer, 2005; Cooper et al., 2002; Domjan, 2005; Nakajima & Masaki, 2004).

Operant Conditioning and Instinctive Drift

As we've just seen, behavior is influenced by an organism's evolutionary history. This history, in turn places limits, or *biological constraints*, on learning. Just as Garcia couldn't produce noise–nausea associations, other researchers have found that an animal's natural behavior pattern can interfere with operant conditioning. For example,

Taste Aversion *A classically conditioned negative reaction to a particular taste that has been associated with nausea or other illness*

Biological Preparedness *Built-in (innate) readiness to form associations between certain stimuli and responses*

$\mathscr{A}$ssessment

VISUAL QUIZ

Can you explain this?

Raccoons can easily learn to play basketball, but they have a very difficult time learning to add coins to a small piggy bank.

Marian Breland Bailey/Animal Behavior Enterprises

Answer: Because of instinctive drift, the raccoons rub the coins together in an instinctive food-washing response rather than placing them in the piggy bank.

the Brelands (1961) tried to teach a chicken to play baseball. Through shaping and reinforcement, the chicken first learned to pull a loop that activated a swinging bat. It later learned to actually hit the ball. But instead of running to first base, it would chase the ball as though it were food. Regardless of the lack of reinforcement for chasing the ball, the chicken's natural behavior took precedence. This biological constraint is known as **instinctive drift**, when an animal's conditioned responses tend to shift (or *drift*) toward innate response patterns.

Human and nonhuman animals can be operantly conditioned to perform a variety of novel behaviors (like jumping through hoops, turning in circles, and even water skiing). However, reinforcement alone does not determine behavior. There is a biological tendency to favor natural inborn actions. In addition, learning theorists initially believed that the fundamental laws of conditioning would apply to almost all species and all behaviors. However, later researchers have identified several constraints (such as biological preparedness and instinctive drift) that limit the generality of conditioning principles. As you discovered in Chapter 1, scientific inquiry is a constantly changing and evolving process.

Instinctive Drift *Conditioned responses shift (or drift) back toward innate response patterns*

USING CONDITIONING AND LEARNING PRINCIPLES

Do you remember what I "promised" in the "Why Study Psychology" box at the start of this chapter? I claimed that studying this chapter would *expand your understanding and control of behavior, improve the predictability of your life, enhance your enjoyment of life,* and even *help you change the world!* I sincerely believe each of these claims. Unfortunately, many introductory psychology students focus only on studying all the terms and concepts. They fail to see "the forest for the trees." I don't want this to happen to you. To help you understand and appreciate the profound (and practical) benefits of this material, let's examine several applications for classical conditioning, operant conditioning, and cognitive-social learning.

Achievement

What are the practical applications of conditioning principles?

Application

APPLYING PSYCHOLOGY TO EVERYDAY LIFE

Classical Conditioning—From Marketing to Medical Treatments

Do you know that advertisers, politicians, film producers, music artists, and others routinely and deliberately use classical conditioning to market their products and manipulate our purchases, votes, emotions, and motivation? Classical conditioning also helps explain how (and why) we learn to be prejudiced and experience problems with phobias and certain medical procedures.

Classical conditioning in action. Have you every wondered why politicians kiss babies? Or why beautiful women are so often used to promote products?

Marketing

Beginning with John B. Watson's academic firing and subsequent career in advertising in the 1920s, marketers have employed numerous classical conditioning principles

Bill Aaron/PhotoEdit

to promote their products. For example, TV commercials, magazine ads, and business promotions often pair their products or company logo (the neutral stimulus/NS) with pleasant images, such as attractive models and celebrities (the conditioned stimulus/CS). Through higher-order conditioning, these attractive models then trigger favorable responses (the conditioned response/CR). Advertisers know that after repeated viewings, the previously neutral stimulus (their products or logo) will become a conditioned stimulus that elicits favorable responses (CR)—purchasing their products. Psychologists caution that these ads also help produce visual stimuli that trigger conditioned responses such as urges to smoke, overeat, and drink alcohol (Dols, Willems, van den Hout, & Bittoun, 2000; Martin et al., 2002; Tirodkar & Jain, 2003; Wakfield et al., 2003).

Prejudice

Are children born with prejudice? Or are they the victims of classical conditioning? In a classic study in the 1930s, Kenneth Clark and Mamie P. Clark (1939) studied children's reactions to black dolls and to white dolls. They found that given a choice, both black and white children preferred the white dolls. When asked which doll was good and which was bad, both groups of children also responded that the white doll was good and nice. The black doll was seen as bad, dirty, and ugly. The Clarks reasoned that the children, as well as many others in the United States, had *learned* to associate inferior qualities with darker skin and positive qualities with light skin. The Clark study exemplifies the negative effects of classical conditioning. In addition, their findings played a pivotal role in the famous *Brown v. Board of Education of Topeka* decision in 1954, which ruled that segregation of public facilities was unconstitutional. (Interestingly, this was the first time social science research was formally cited in a U.S. Supreme Court case to support a legal argument.)

If you're thinking this 1930 study no longer applies, follow-up research in the late 1980s found that 65 percent of the African-American children and 74 percent of the white children still preferred the white doll (Powell-Hopson & Hopson, 1988).

The Clark study provided important insights into the negative effects of prejudice on the victims—African-American children. But what about the white children who also strongly preferred the white doll? Was their preference also due to classical conditioning? And did a similar type of classical conditioning contribute to the vicious murder of James Byrd? We can't be sure how the hatred and racism that took James

Byrd's life originally started. However, prejudice of many types (racism, ageism, sexism, homophobia, and religious intolerance) can be classically conditioned, as Figure 6.10 shows.

Medical Treatments

Examples of classical conditioning are also found in the medical field. For example, a program conducted by several hospitals in California gives an *emetic* (a nausea-producing drug) to their alcohol-addicted patients. But before the nausea begins, the patient gargles with his or her preferred alcoholic beverage to maximize the taste and odor cues paired with nausea. As a form of classical conditioning, the smell and taste of various alcoholic drinks (neutral stimulus/NS) are paired with the nausea-producing drug (the unconditioned stimulus/UCS). The drug then makes the patient vomit or feel sick (the unconditioned response/UCR). Afterward, just the smell or taste of alcohol (the conditioned stimulus/CS) makes the person sick (the conditioned response/CR). Some patients have found this treatment successful, but not all (Chapter 15).

Nausea is deliberately produced in this treatment for alcoholism. Unfortunately, it is an unintended side effect of many cancer treatments. The nausea and vomiting produced by chemotherapy increase the patient's discomfort and often generalize to other environmental cues, such as the hospital room color or odor (Stockhorst et al., 2000). Using their knowledge of classical conditioning to change associations, therapists can help cancer patients control their nausea and vomiting response.

Phobias

Do you know someone who "freaks out" at the sight of a cockroach? At some time during his or her lifetime, this person probably learned to associate the NS (cockroach) with a UCS (perhaps hearing a parent scream at the sight of a cockroach) until a CR (fear at the sight of a cockroach) was conditioned. Researchers have found that most everyday fears are classically conditioned emotional responses. As you'll see in Chapter 15, classical conditioning also produces most *phobias*, exaggerated and irrational fears of a specific object or situation (Rauhut, Thomas, & Ayres, 2001; Ressler & Davis, 2003). The good news is that extreme fear of cockroaches, hypodermic needles, spiders, closets, and even snakes can be effectively treated with *behavior modification* (Chapter 15).

Discovering Classical Conditioning in Your Own Life

To appreciate the influences of classical conditioning on your own life, try this:

1. Look through a popular magazine and examine several advertisements. What images are used as the unconditioned stimulus (UCS) or conditioned stimulus (CS)? Note how you react to these images.

2. While watching a movie or a favorite TV show, identify what sounds and images are serving as conditioned stimuli (CS). (Hint: Certain types of music are used to set the stage for happy stories, sad events, and fearful situations.) What are your conditioned emotional responses (CERs)?

3. Read the words below and pay attention to your emotional response. Your reactions—positive, negative, or neutral—are a result of your own personal classical conditioning history. Can you trace back to the UCS for each of these stimuli?

| father | final exams | spinach |
| Santa Claus | beer | mother |

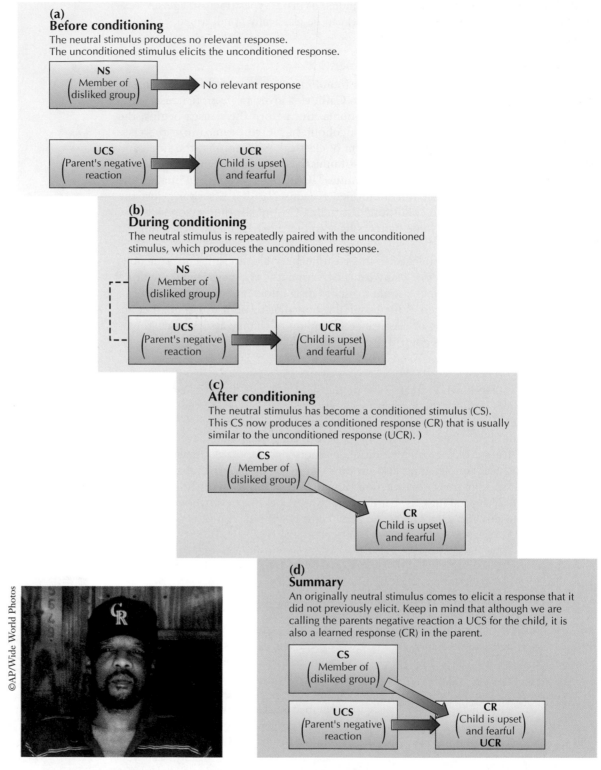

(a)
Before conditioning
The neutral stimulus produces no relevant response.
The unconditioned stimulus elicits the unconditioned response.

NS
(Member of disliked group) → No relevant response

UCS
(Parent's negative reaction) → UCR (Child is upset and fearful)

(b)
During conditioning
The neutral stimulus is repeatedly paired with the unconditioned stimulus, which produces the unconditioned response.

NS
(Member of disliked group)

UCS
(Parent's negative reaction) → UCR (Child is upset and fearful)

(c)
After conditioning
The neutral stimulus has become a conditioned stimulus (CS).
This CS now produces a conditioned response (CR) that is usually similar to the unconditioned response (UCR).)

CS
(Member of disliked group) → CR (Child is upset and fearful)

(d)
Summary
An originally neutral stimulus comes to elicit a response that it did not previously elicit. Keep in mind that although we are calling the parents negative reaction a UCS for the child, it is also a learned response (CR) in the parent.

CS
(Member of disliked group) → CR (Child is upset and fearful) UCR

UCS
(Parent's negative reaction)

©AP/Wide World Photos

Figure 6.10 *How prejudice may be acquired through classical conditioning.* As described in the chapter opener, James Byrd was viciously murdered because of his skin color. How did this prejudice develop? (a) Before children are conditioned to be prejudiced, they show no response to a member of a different group. (b) Given that children are naturally upset and fearful when they see their parents upset, they can learn to be upset and fearful (UCR) if they see their parents respond negatively (UCS) to a member of a disliked group (NS). (c) After several pairings of the person from this group with their parents' negative reactions, the sight of the other person becomes a conditioned stimulus (CS). Being upset and fearful becomes the conditioned response (CR). (d) A previously unbiased child has now learned to be prejudiced.

Application

APPLYING PSYCHOLOGY TO EVERYDAY LIFE

Operant Conditioning—Prejudice, Biofeedback, and Superstition

Operant conditioning has numerous and important applications in everyday life. Here we talk about *prejudice*, *biofeedback*, and *superstitious behavior*.

Prejudice

Consider again the murder of James Byrd. What might have reinforced such behavior? Could it have been attention, notoriety, or something else? As you discovered earlier, people can learn prejudice through classical conditioning. We also can learn prejudice through operant conditioning. Demeaning others gains attention and sometimes approval from others, as well as increasing one's self-esteem (at the victim's expense) (Fein & Spencer, 1997; Hayes et al., 2002). People also may have a single punishing experience with a specific member of a group. They then generalize and apply it to all members of the group (Vidmar, 1997). Can you see how this is another example of stimulus generalization?

But the men who killed James Byrd were sentenced to death or life imprisonment. Why would people do something that they know could bring the death penalty? Punishment does weaken and suppress behavior. But, as mentioned earlier, to be effective it must be consistent and immediate. Unfortunately, this seldom happens. Even worse, when punishment is inconsistent and the criminal gets away with one or more crimes, that criminal behavior is put on a *partial (intermittent) schedule of reinforcement*. Thus making it more likely to be repeated and to become more resistant to *extinction*.

Biofeedback

Sit quietly for a moment and try to determine your blood pressure. Is it high or low? Is it different from what it was a few minutes ago? You can't tell, can you? For most people, it is impossible to learn to control blood pressure consciously. But if you were hooked up to a monitor that recorded, amplified, and displayed this information to you by visual or auditory means, you could learn to control it (Figure 6.11). In this type of **biofeedback** (short for *biological feedback* and sometimes called *neurofeedback*), information about some biological function, such as heart rate, is conveyed to the individual through some type of signal.

Researchers have successfully used biofeedback to treat hypertension and anxiety by lowering blood pressure and muscle tension. It's also used to treat epilepsy by changing brain-wave patterns; urinary incontinence by gaining better pelvic muscle control; and cognitive functioning, chronic pain, and headache by redirecting blood flow (Hammond, 2005; Moss, 2004; Penzien, Rains, & Andrasik, 2002; Stetter & Kupper, 2002; Tatrow, Blanchard, & Silverman, 2003).

Biofeedback involves several operant conditioning principles. Something is added (feedback) that increases the likelihood that the behavior will be repeated—*positive reinforcement*. The biofeedback itself is a *secondary reinforcer*

Biofeedback *An involuntary bodily process (such as blood pressure or heart rate) is recorded, and the information is fed back to an organism to increase voluntary control over that bodily function*

Figure 6.11 *Biofeedback.* In biofeedback training, internal bodily processes (like blood pressure or muscle tension) are electrically recorded. The information is then amplified, and reported back to the patient through headphones, signal lights, and other means. This information helps the person learn to control bodily processes not normally under voluntary control.

www.wiley.com/college/huffman

because of the learned value of the relief from pain or other aversive stimuli *(primary reinforcer)*. Finally, biofeedback involves *shaping*. The person watches a monitor screen (or other instrument) that provides graphs or numbers indicating his or her blood pressure (or other bodily states). Like a mirror, the biofeedback reflects back the results of the various strategies the participant uses to gain control. Through trial and error, the participant gets progressively better at lowering heart rate (or making other desired changes). Biofeedback techniques are limited, however. They are most successful when used in conjunction with other techniques, such as behavior modification (Chapter 15).

Accidental Reinforcement and Superstitious Behavior
B. F. Skinner (1948, 1992) conducted a fascinating experiment to show how accidental reinforcement could lead to *superstitious behaviors*. He set the feeding mechanism in the cages of eight pigeons to release food once every 15 seconds. No matter what the birds did, they were reinforced at 15-second intervals. Interestingly, six of the pigeons acquired behaviors that they repeated over and over, even though the behaviors were not necessary to receive the food. For example, one pigeon kept turning in counterclockwise circles and another kept making jerking movements with its head.

Why did the pigeons engage in such repetitive and unnecessary behavior? Recall that a *reinforcer* increases the probability that a response just performed will be repeated. Skinner was not using the food to reinforce any particular behavior. However, the pigeons associated the food with whatever behavior they were engaged in when the food was randomly dropped into the cage. Thus, if the bird was circling counterclockwise when the food was presented, it would repeat that motion to receive more food.

Like Skinner's pigeons, we humans also believe in many superstitions that may have developed from accidental reinforcement. In addition to the superstitions shown in Table 6.7, professional and Olympic-level athletes sometimes carry lucky charms or

TABLE 6.7 COMMON WESTERN SUPERSTITIONS

Behavior		Superstition
	**Wedding plans:** *Why do brides wear something old and something borrowed?*	The something old is usually clothing that belongs to an older woman who is happily married. Thus, the bride will supposedly transfer that good fortune to herself. Something borrowed is often a relative's jewelry. This item should be golden, because gold represents the sun, which was once thought to be the source of life.
	**Spilling salt:** *Why do some people throw a pinch of salt over their left shoulder?*	Years ago, people believed good spirits lived on the right side of the body and bad spirits on the left. When a man spilled salt, he believed his guardian spirit had caused the accident to warn him of evil nearby. At the time, salt was scarce and precious. Therefore, to bribe the spirits who were planning to harm him, he would quickly throw a pinch of salt over his left shoulder.
	**Boasting, making a prediction, or speaking of good fortune:** *Why do some people knock on wood?*	Down through the ages, people have believed that trees were homes of gods, who were kind and generous if approached in the right way. A person who wanted to ask a favor of the tree god would touch the bark. After the favor was granted, the person would return to knock on the tree as a sign of thanks.

USING CONDITIONING AND LEARNING PRINCIPLES **241**

perform a particular ritual before every competition. Phil Esposito, a hockey player with the Boston Bruins and the New York Rangers for 18 years, always wore the same black turtleneck and drove through the same tollbooth on his way to a game. In the locker room, he put on all his clothes in the same order and laid out his equipment in exactly the same way he had for every other game. All this because once when he had behaved that way years before, he had been the team's high scorer. Alas, the power of accidental reinforcement.

Application
APPLYING PSYCHOLOGY TO EVERYDAY LIFE

Cognitive-Social Learning—We See, We Do?

We use cognitive-social learning in many ways in our everyday lives. Two of the most powerful examples are frequently overlooked—*prejudice* and *media influences*. As you can see in Figure 6.12, one of James Byrd's murderers, Bill King, had numerous tattoos on his body that proudly proclaimed his various prejudices. Did King and his two accomplices learn some of their hatred and prejudice through observation and modeling? King's family and friends insist that he was pleasant and quiet until he began serving an eight-year prison sentence for burglary (Galloway, 1999). What did he learn about prejudice during his prison sentence? Did he model his killing of Byrd after his uncle's well-known killing of a gay traveling salesman a number of years earlier? Or did he learn his prejudices during his numerous years of active membership with the KKK?

Some forms of prejudice are developed and maintained through the media. Experimental and correlational research clearly show that when we watch television, go to movies, and read books and magazines that portray minorities, women, and other groups in demeaning and stereotypical roles, we often learn to expect these behaviors and to accept them as "natural." Exposure of this kind initiates and reinforces the learning of prejudice (Blaine & McElroy, 2002; Neto & Furnham, 2005).

The media also can teach us what to eat, what toys to buy, what homes and clothes are most fashionable, and what constitutes "the good life." When a TV commercial shows children enjoying a particular cereal and beaming at their Mom in gratitude (and Mom is smiling back), both children and parents in the audience are participating in a form of observational learning. They learn that they, too, will be rewarded for buying the advertised brand (with happy children) or punished (with unhappy children who won't eat) for buying a competitor's product.

Unfortunately, observational learning also encourages destructive behaviors. Correlational evidence from more than 50 studies indicates that observing violent behavior is related to later desensitization and increased aggression (Anderson, 2004; Coyne, 2004; Kronenberger et al., 2005). As a critical thinker, you may be automatically noting that correlation is not causation. However, over 100 *experimental* studies have shown a causal link between observing violence and later performing it (Primavera & Herron, 1996).

What about video games? How do they affect behavior? Researchers are just beginning to study these questions. For example, studies have found that students who played more violent video games in junior high and high school engage in more aggressive behaviors (Anderson & Bushman, 2001; Bartholow & Anderson, 2002; Carnagey & Anderson, 2004). Craig Anderson and Karen Dill (2000) also experimentally assigned 210 students to first play either a violent or a nonviolent video game and later allowed them to punish their opponent with a loud sound blast. Those who played the violent game punished the opponent not only for a longer period of time but also with greater intensity. The researchers hypothesize that video games are more likely to model aggressive behavior because, unlike TV and other media, they

Figure 6.12 *John William "Bill" King.* King was sentenced to death for the murder of James Byrd. Note the tattoos on his arm. They include a Satanic image of the Virgin Mary holding a horned baby Jesus, Nazi and racist prison gang insignias, Ku Klux Klan symbols, and the figure of a lynched black man (Galloway, 1999).

Video games and aggression. *According to research, playing violent video games increases aggression. These young boys identify with the aggressor and may be more likely to imitate this behavior (Bartholow & Anderson, 2002). What do you think? Do video games affect your behavior or that of your friends?*

www.wiley.com/college/huffman

Those who won't forget. *Ross Byrd, left, and Renee Mullins, children of murder victim James Byrd, leaving the Jasper County Courthouse after John "Bill" King was convicted of capital murder.*

are interactive, engrossing, and require the player to identify with the aggressor. Virtual reality games are of particular concern (Unsworth & Ward, 2001).

A Final Note

I began this chapter with the story of James Byrd because prejudice is a worthy (but unusual) topic for a learning chapter. And his story deserved retelling. The death of James Byrd shocked many Americans into facing the terrible hatred and racism that still exist in our country. Sadly, his death (like others) is too quickly forgotten. The good news is that little (if anything) about prejudice is biologically driven. It is *learned*. Using the *biopsychosocial model*, you can see that the *psychological* component of prejudice (thoughts, values, and beliefs) and *sociocultural* forces (modeling, TV, and other media) are the result of experience and exposure (learning). Fortunately, *what we learn can be unlearned* through retraining, counseling, and self-reflection.

Assessment
CHECK & REVIEW

Using Conditioning and Learning Principles

Classical conditioning has many applications in everyday life. It explains how people market their products, how we sometimes learn negative attitudes toward groups of people (prejudice), and how we sometimes have problems with certain medical treatments and phobias.

Operant conditioning has similar applications. It helps explain how we learn prejudice through positive reinforcement and stimulus generalization. **Biofeedback,** another application, is the feeding back of biological information, such as heart rate or blood pressure, which a person uses to control normally automatic functions of the body. Operant conditioning also helps explain many superstitions, which involve accidentally reinforced behaviors that are continually repeated because they are believed to cause desired effects.

Cognitive-social theory helps to further explain prejudice and media influences. People often learn their prejudices by imitating what they've seen modeled by friends, family, and the media. The media affect our purchasing behaviors as well as our aggressive tendencies. Video games may have a particularly strong influence.

Questions

1. Politicians often depict their opponent as immoral and irresponsible because they know it helps create a ___ toward their rival. (a) classically conditioned phobia; (b) negative social-learning cue; (c) conditioned aversive response; (d) negative conditioned emotional response

2. Biofeedback reinforces desired physiological changes that have beneficial results. This makes it a(n) ___. (a) operant conditioner; (b) primary reinforcer; (c) secondary reinforcer; (d) biological marker

3. You insist on wearing a red sweater each time you take an exam because you believe it helps you get higher scores. This is an example of ___. (a) classical conditioning; (b) secondary reinforcement; (c) superstition; (d) redophilia reinforcement

4. Explain why video games may increase aggressive tendencies.

Check your answers in Appendix B.

 CLICK & REVIEW for additional assessment options: www.wiley.com/college/huffman

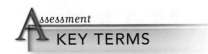

Assessment
KEY TERMS

*To assess your understanding of the **Key Terms** in Chapter 6, write a definition for each (in your own words), and then compare your definitions with those in the text.*

conditioning (p. 209)
learning (p. 208)

Classical Conditioning
classical conditioning (p. 210)
conditioned emotional response (CER)
 (p. 212)
conditioned response (CR) (p. 210)
conditioned stimulus (CS) (p. 210)
extinction (p. 214)
higher-order conditioning (p. 214)
neutral stimulus (NS) (p. 210)
spontaneous recovery (p. 214)
stimulus discrimination (p. 214)
stimulus generalization (p. 213)
unconditioned response (UCR)
 (p. 210)
unconditioned stimulus (UCS)
 (p. 210)

Operant Conditioning
continuous reinforcement (p. 219)
discriminative stimulus (p. 226)
fixed interval (FI) schedule (p. 220)
fixed ratio (FR) schedule (p. 220)
law of effect (p. 216)
negative punishment (p. 220)
negative reinforcement (p. 218)
operant conditioning (p. 216)
partial (intermittent) reinforcement
 (p. 219)
positive punishment (p. 220)
positive reinforcement (p. 218)
Premack principle (p. 219)
primary reinforcers (p. 218)
punishment (p. 216)
reinforcement (p. 216)
secondary reinforcers (p. 218)
shaping (p. 220)

variable interval (VI) schedule (p. 220)
variable ratio (VR) schedule (p. 220)

Cognitive-Social Learning
cognitive map (p. 229)
cognitive-social theory (p. 228)
insight (p. 228)
latent learning (p. 229)
observational learning (p. 229)

The Biology of Learning
biological preparedness (p. 234)
instinctive drift (p. 235)
taste aversion (p. 234)

**Using Conditioning and Learning
Principles**
biofeedback (p. 239)

Achievement
WEB RESOURCES

Huffman Book Companion Site
http://www.wiley.com/college/huffman
> This site is loaded with free Interactive Self-Tests, Internet Exercises, Glossary and Flashcards for key terms, web links, Handbook for Non-Native Speakers, and other activities designed to improve your mastery of the material in this chapter.

Want to learn more about classical conditioning?
http://www.brembs.net/classical/classical.html
> Introduces principles of classical conditioning and links to additional sites with important applications of learning techniques.

Interested in Ivan Pavlov?
http://www.almaz.com/nobel/medicine/1904a.html
> A Nobel Prize Internet Archive providing extensive links and background information on the life and accomplishments of Ivan Petrovich Pavlov.

Want more information about operant conditioning?
http://chiron.valdosta.edu/whuitt/col/behsys/_operant.html
> Provides an overview of operant conditioning, including a brief history, general principles, schedules of reinforcement, examples, and applications.

Interested in biofeedback?
http://www.questia.com/Index.jsp?CRID=behavior__modification&OFFID=se1
> In addition to background information and related links on the use of biofeedback, offers information and links to other complementary therapies.

Animal training at Sea World
http://www.seaworld.org/infobooks/training/home.html
> Gives a fascinating look at how operant conditioning, including positive reinforcers, and observational learning are used to train marine animals.

Want more information on cognitive-social learning or observational learning?
http://chiron.valdosta.edu/whuitt/col/soccog/soclrn.html
> Provides an overview of the field, including a brief summary of Bandura's work, research findings, and some general principles.

Interested in the use of taste aversion and wildlife management?
http://www.conditionedtasteaversion.net/
> Provides a wealth of fascinating information and links related to the use of conditioned taste aversion (CTA) in wildlife.

www.wiley.com/college/huffman

VisuaL Summary

Classical Conditioning

Pavlov and Watson's Contributions

Process: Involuntary

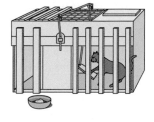

1) Before **conditioning**, originally **neutral stimulus (NS)** causes no relevant response, whereas **unconditioned stimulus (UCS)** causes **unconditioned response (UCR)**.
2) During conditioning, NS is paired with UCS that elicits the UCR.
3) After conditioning, previous NS becomes **conditioned stimulus (CS)**, which now causes a **conditioned response (CR)** or **conditioned emotional response (CER)**.

Principles of Classical Conditioning

- **Stimulus generalization**: Stimuli similar to original CS elicit CR.
- **Stimulus discrimination**: Only the CS elicits the CR.
- **Extinction**: Gradual suppression of a learned behavior by repeatedly presenting the CS without the UCS.
- **Spontaneous recovery**: Sudden reappearance of a previously extinguished CR.
- **Higher order conditioning**: The NS is paired with the CS to which the organism has already been conditioned.

Operant Conditioning

Thorndike and Skinner's Contributions

Process: Voluntary

Organisms learn through consequences of their behavior. When responses are reinforced, they are strengthened and likely to increase; when punished, they are weakened and likely to decrease.

Principles of Operant Conditioning

Strengthening a response occurs through:

1) Primary and secondary reinforcers: **Primary reinforcers**, like food, satisfy a biological need. The value of **secondary reinforcers**, such as money, is learned.
2) Positive and negative reinforcement: **Positive reinforcement** adds something that increases the likelihood of the response. **Negative reinforcement** takes away something that increases the likelihood of the response.

Additional concepts:

In a **continuous schedule of reinforcement**, every correct response is reinforced. In a **partial** (or **intermittent**) **schedule** only some responses are reinforced. Partial schedules include **fixed ratio (FR)**, **variable ratio (VR)**, **fixed interval (FI)**, and **variable interval (VI)**.

Shaping involves reinforcement for successive approximations of the desired response.

Weakening a response occurs through:

1) **Positive punishment** — adds something that decreases the likelihood of the response.
2) **Negative punishment** — takes away something that decreases the likelihood of the response.

Cognitive–Social Learning

Insight and Latent Learning

- *Köhler*: Learning can occur with a sudden flash of understanding (**insight**).
- *Tolman*: Learning can happen without reinforcement and remain hidden until needed (**latent learning**). After navigating their environments, people and nonhuman animals create **cognitive maps**.

Observational Learning

- *Bandura*: **Learning** occurs after watching and imitating others.

Courtesy Albert Bandura

The Biology of Learning

Learning and conditioning produce relatively permanent changes in neural connections and various parts of the brain. Evolutionary theorists believe some behavior is unlearned (e.g., reflexes or instincts), and that learning and conditioning are further adaptations that enable organisms to survive and prosper in a constantly changing world.

Using Conditioning Principles

Applying Classical Conditioning to Everyday Life

- *Marketing*: Products (NS) are repeatedly paired with pleasant images (UCS) until they become a (CS).
- *Prejudice*: Negative perceptions of others acquired through classical conditioning processes.
- *Medical treatments*: Using nausea producing drugs, alcoholics learn to pair alcohol (CS) with nausea (CR).
- *Phobias*: Irrational fears developed through association of a feared object with the UCS.

Applying Operant Conditioning to Everyday Life

- *Prejudice*: Negative perceptions of others acquired through operant conditioning.
- *Biofeedback*: "Feeding back" biological information (heart rate or blood pressure) for control of normally automatic body functions.
- *Superstitious behavior*: Develops from accidental rewarding of specific behaviors.

Applying Cognitive-Social Learning to Everyday Life

- *Prejudice*: Learned by imitating and modeling prejudiced behavior of others.
- *Media influences*: Consumerism, aggression, and other behaviors are partially learned from media models.

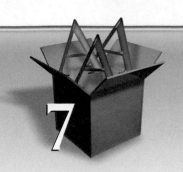

MEMORY

Achievement

Core Learning Outcomes

As you read Chapter 7, keep the following questions in mind and answer them in your own words:

▷ What are the four major memory models?

▷ Why do we forget, and how can we prevent forgetting?

▷ How do we form memories, and where do we store them?

▷ How is memory related to the legal system?

▷ How can we improve our memory?

▢ Achievement
▢ Assessment
▢ Application

WHY STUDY PSYCHOLOGY?

Chapter 7 explores interesting facts, such as . . .

▷ Eyewitness testimony is common in many legal cases, but research shows it to be highly unreliable.

▷ Without long-term memory, you would be unable to recognize new friends, doctors, movie stars, or politicians regardless of how many times you saw or talked talk with them.

▷ Long-lasting "flashbulb" memories for intense emotional events, like the 9/11 ter-

rorist attack on the United States, may be influenced by "fight-or-flight" hormones.

▷ People can be led to create false memories they later believe to be true.

▷ Long-term memory is like a magical credit card with unlimited cash and no known expiration date.

▷ Memory tricks and techniques (called *mnemonics*) can help improve your memory.

Digital Vision/AgeFotostock America, Inc.

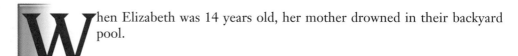

When Elizabeth was 14 years old, her mother drowned in their backyard pool.

In her diary Elizabeth wrote:

Today, July 10, 1959, was the most tragic day of my life. My dearly beloved mother, whom I had just gotten to be really close with, died. We woke up this morning and she was missing, and an hour later we found her in the swimming pool. Only God knows what happened. I know that life must go on and that we all must be brave.

(LOFTUS, 2002, P. 70)

As she grew older, the details surrounding her mother's death became increasingly vague for Elizabeth. At a family reunion some 30 years later, a relative told Elizabeth that she had been the one to find her mother's drowned body. Despite her initial shock and denial, over the next few days the memories slowly started coming back.

I could see myself, a thin, dark-haired girl, looking into the flickering blue-and-white pool. My mother, dressed in her nightgown, is floating face down. I start screaming. I remember the police cars, their lights flashing, and the stretcher with the clean, white blanket tucked in around the edges of the body. The memory had been there all along, but I just couldn't reach it.

(LOFTUS & KETCHAM, 1994, P. 45)

This is the true story of Elizabeth Loftus, who today is a well-known experimental psychologist specializing in the study of memory. Compare her life story with the memory problems of H.M.

When H.M. was 27 years old, portions of his temporal lobes and underlying parts of the limbic system were surgically removed to treat his severe epileptic seizures that could not be controlled even by high doses of anticonvulsant medication. The surgery successfully reduced the severity and number of seizures. But something was clearly wrong with his long-term memory. Two years after the surgery, he still believed he was 27. When his uncle died, he grieved in a normal way. But soon after, he began to ask why his uncle never visited him. H.M. had to be repeatedly reminded of his uncle's

Michelle Chang

death, and each reminder would begin a new mourning process. Today, over 50 years after the operation, H.M. cannot recognize the people who care for him daily, the scientists who have studied him for decades, or even the room where he lives. He spends his days in a perpetually unfamiliar nursing home. He often reads the same books and magazines over and over and laughs at the same jokes—each time as though it were the first. H.M. also thinks he is still 27 and no longer recognizes a photograph of his own face (Corkin, 2002).

Can you imagine what it would be like to be Elizabeth or H.M.? How could a child forget finding her mother's body? What would it be like to be H.M.—existing only in the present moment, unable to learn and form new memories? How can we remember our first phone number and our second-grade teacher's name, and then forget an important phone number and name of someone we met just five minutes ago?

In this chapter, you will discover answers to these and other fascinating questions about memory. We begin with a brief overview of the four most popular theories and models that help explain "What is memory?" We then examine several possible theories and answers to "Why (and how quickly) do we forget?" We also explore the biological bases of memory. Our "Research Highlight" looks at special issues associated with memory and the criminal justice system. The chapter concludes with helpful tips for memory improvement.

THE NATURE OF MEMORY

The charm, one might say the genius, of memory is that it is choosy, chancy, and temperamental.
ELIZABETH BOWEN (IRISH NOVELIST AND SHORT STORY AUTHOR, 1899–1973)

Among psychologists, **memory** is most often defined as "an internal record or representation of some prior event or experience" (Purdy, Markham, Schwartz, & Gordon, 2001, p. 9). Can you see how this internal record is critical to our psychological and physical survival? Without memory, we would have no past or future. We could not dress or feed ourselves, communicate, or even recognize ourselves in a mirror. Memory allows us to learn from our experiences and adapt to ever-changing environments.

However, as we've seen with the opening stories of Elizabeth Loftus and H.M., our memories are also highly fallible. Some people think of memory as a gigantic library or an automatic tape recorder. But our memories are *not* faithful storehouses or exact recordings of events. Instead, memory is a **constructive process**. We actively organize and shape information as it is processed, stored, and retrieved. As you might expect, this construction often leads to serious errors and biases discussed throughout this chapter.

Memory *An internal record or representation of some prior event or experience*

Constructive Process *Organizing and shaping of information during processing, storage, and retrieval of memories*

Four Models of Memory: A Brief Overview

To understand memory (and its constructive nature), you first need a model of how it operates. Over the years, psychologists have developed numerous models for memory. In this section, we begin with a brief overview of the four major approaches (Table 7.1) and then explore the most popular model in some depth.

Achievement

What are the four major memory models?

Information-Processing Approach
Memory is faulty and fragile. It's also highly functional and biologically well adapted for everyday life. Every moment of the day we filter and sort through a barrage of information, and then we store and retrieve information important to our survival. According to this *information-processing model*, information goes through three basic operations—*encoding*, *storage*, and *retrieval*. Each of these three processes represents a

SUMMARY TABLE 7.1 FOUR COMMON MEMORY MODELS

Information-Processing Approach 	Memory is *a process*, analogous to a computer, where information goes through three basic processes—*encoding, storage, and retrieval.*
Parallel Distributed Processing Model 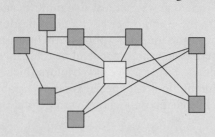	Memory is distributed across a wide network of interconnected neurons located throughout the brain. When activated, this network works simultaneously (in a *parallel* fashion) to process information.
Levels of Processing Approach 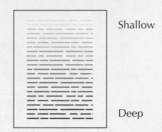 Shallow / Deep	Memory depends on the degree or depth of mental processing occurring when material is initially encountered. Shallow processing leads to little memory, whereas deeper processing adds meaning and greater memory.
Traditional Three-Stage Memory Model 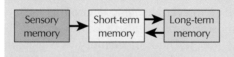	Memory requires three different storage boxes or stages to hold and process information for various lengths of time. *Sensory memory* holds information for exceedingly short intervals, *short-term memory* (STM) retains information for approximately 30 seconds or less (unless renewed), and *long-term memory* (LTM) provides relatively permanent storage.

Encoding *Translating information into neural codes (language)*

Storage *Retaining neurally coded information over time*

Retrieval *Recovering information from memory storage*

different function that is closely analogous to the parts and functions of a computer (Figure 7.1).

To input data into a computer, you begin by typing letters and numbers on the keyboard. The computer then translates these key strokes into its own electronic language. In a roughly similar fashion, your brain **encodes** sensory information (sound, visual image, and other senses) into a neural code (language) it can understand and use. Once computer or human information is encoded, it must be **stored.** Computer information is stored on a disk or hard drive. Human memories are stored in the brain. To **retrieve** information from either the computer or brain, you must search and locate the appropriate "files." Then you bring the information up on the computer monitor or to your short-term, working memory where it can be used.

This is not to say that psychologists believe computers and brains operate in exactly the same way. Like all analogies, this information-processing ("memory as a

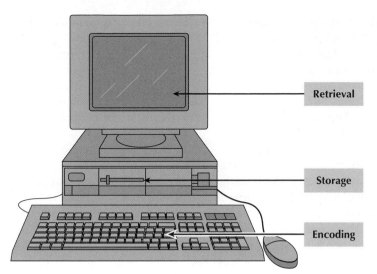

Figure 7.1 *Memory as a computer.* The encoding, storage, and retrieval model uses a computer metaphor to explain the three basic functions of our memory system. Similar to a computer, incoming information is first encoded (typed on a keyboard and translated into computer language). It is then stored on a disk or the hard drive, and later retrieved and brought to the computer screen to be used.

Retrieval

Storage

Encoding

computer") model has its limits. Human memories are often fuzzy and fragile compared to the literal, "hard" data stored on a computer disk or hard drive. Furthermore, computers process instructions and data *sequentially*. Units of computer information follow one after another in a logical, orderly fashion. Human memory, however, occurs *simultaneously*, through the action of multiple networks.

Parallel Distributed Processing Model

Noting these differences between computers and humans, some cognitive scientists prefer the **parallel distributed processing (PDP)**, or *connectionist*, model of memory (McClelland, 1995; Rogers et al., 2004). As the name implies, instead of recognizing patterns as a sequence of information bits (like a computer), our brain and memory processes perform multiple *parallel* operations all at one time. In addition, memory is spread out, or *distributed*, throughout an entire weblike network of processing units. If you're swimming in the ocean and see a large fin nearby, your brain does not conduct a complete search of all fish with fins before urging you to begin a rush to the beach. Instead, you conduct a mental *parallel* search. You note the color of the fish, the fin, and the potential danger all at the same time. Because the processes are parallel, you can quickly process the information—and possibly avoid being eaten by the shark!

The PDP model seems consistent with neurological information of brain activity (Chapter 2). It also has been useful in explaining perception (Chapter 4), language (Chapter 8), and decision making (Chapter 8). And it allows a faster response time. As we just noted, survival in our environment requires instantaneous information processing. However, the previous information processing model remains better at explaining the processing of new information and memory for single events.

Levels of Processing Model

Rather than focusing on computer analogies or on how information is processed, Fegus Craik and Robert Lockhart's (1972) **levels of processing** model suggests that memory relies on how *deeply* we process initial information. During shallow processing, we're only aware of basic incoming sensory information. Little or no memory is formed. However, when we do something more with the information, such as adding meaning, developing organizations and associations, or relating it to things we already know, the information is deeply processed and can be stored for a lifetime.

Imagine having to learn the names of all the students in your psychology class. If you obtained a copy of all the student names and simply repeated them, "James, Gloria, Enrique, Angelica...," you would be processing the information at a shallow,

Parallel Distributed Processing (PDP) *Memory results from weblike connections among interacting processing units operating simultaneously, rather than sequentially (also known as the connectionist model)*

Levels of Processing *The degree or depth of mental processing that occurs when material is initially encountered determines how well it's later remembered*

www.wiley.com/college/huffman

superficial level. And you would remember very few names. If you thought about each name and grouped all the names according to the first initial, you would be processing at a slightly deeper level and your memory would be somewhat better. Imagine the results if you stopped to think about each name both carefully and *deeply*, made associations with each person, and identified some distinguishing feature or personality trait for each student (e.g., "James is Jolly, Gloria has Glorious hair, Enrique is Energetic, and Angelica is Angelic"). Can you see how this approach would greatly improve your memory for names?

In addition, this levels of processing model has several practical applications for your college life. For example, if you're casually reading this text and are giving the words little thought (shallow processing), you will retain the information only for the briefest period of time. (And you'll remember little or nothing on exams or quizzes!) But if you stop and think deeply about the meaning of the words and relate them to your own experiences, you'll greatly increase your learning and memory for the material. Similarly, rote memorization of the chapter's key terms involves only a shallow level of processing. You need to deeply process each key term if you want to have long-term retention.

Traditional Three-Stage Memory Model

Since the late 1960s, one of the most widely used models in memory research has been the *traditional three-stage memory model* or the *three-box model* (Atkinson & Shiffrin, 1968; Healy & McNamara, 1996). According to this model, memory requires three different storage "boxes," or stages, to hold and process information for various lengths of time. The first stage holds information for exceedingly short intervals. The second stage retains information for approximately 30 seconds or less (unless renewed). And the third stage provides relatively permanent storage. Because information must pass through each of these stages to get to the next, they are often depicted as three boxes with directional arrows indicating the flow of information (Figure 7.2). Each of these three stages (*sensory*, *short-term*, and *long-term*) has a somewhat different purpose, duration, and capacity.

The traditional three-stage memory model remains the leading paradigm in memory research because it offers a convenient way to organize the major findings.

Figure 7.2 *Traditional three-stage memory model.* Each "box" represents a separate memory system that differs in purpose, duration, and capacity. When information is not transferred from sensory memory or short-term memory, it is assumed to be lost. Information stored in long-term memory can be retrieved and sent back to short-term memory for use.

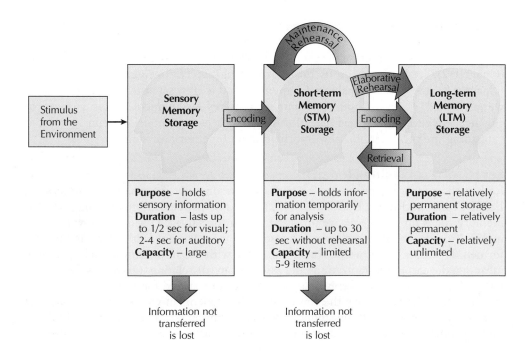

Now that we've briefly explored the four major models of memory, we can use this general information to explore in depth each of the stages of this traditional three-stage memory model—sensory, short-term, and long-term memory.

Sensory Memory: The Brief First Stage of Memory

Everything we see, hear, touch, taste, and smell first enters our **sensory memory**. The *purpose* of sensory memory is to retain a relatively exact image of each sensory experience just long enough to locate and focus on relevant bits of information and transfer them to the next stage of memory. The *duration* of sensory memory varies according to the specific sense. Researchers believe our sensory memory briefly stores information from each of our senses (vision, hearing, smell, taste, touch), but only vision and hearing have been extensively studied. For visual information, known as *iconic memory*, the visual icon (or image) lasts about one-half of a second. Auditory information (what we hear) is held in sensory memory about the same length of time as visual information, one-quarter to one-half of a second. However, a weaker "echo," or *echoic memory*, of this auditory information can last up to four seconds (Lu, Williamson, & Kaufman, 1992; Neisser, 1967).

How can such brief sensory messages be measured in a laboratory? One of the earliest researchers, George Sperling (1960), designed a clever experiment that briefly showed people visual arrays of 12 letters arranged in rows (Figure 7.3). Sperling rapidly flashed this three-letter by four-letter matrix on a screen. Immediately after the letters flashed off, he asked the participants to recall the letters. Participants generally recalled only four or five letters. But they also insisted they had seen more letters before the memory slipped away. To test this possibility, Sperling devised a "partial report" experiment. Rather than reporting everything from the display, he asked participants to report the first row of letters if they heard a high tone, the second row if they heard a medium tone, and the third row when they heard a low tone. Whatever row or column the participants were asked to recall, they were able to name the letters without any trouble, which indicates that they had memory access to all letters in the matrix for at least a few thousandths of a second. This suggests that all objects in the visual field are available in sensory memory if they can be attended to quickly.

From this and other studies, early researchers assumed that sensory memory had an unlimited capacity. However, later research suggests that sensory memory does have its limits. Furthermore, the stored images are fuzzier than was once thought (Best, 1999; Grondin, Ouellet, & Roussel, 2004).

Short-Term Memory (STM): Memory's Second Stage

Sensory memory maintains environmental stimuli only long enough for the brain to decide whether to send it on to the second stage. Similarly, this second stage, called **short-term memory (STM)** only temporarily stores and processes the sensory image until the brain decides whether or not to send it along to the third stage (long-term memory).

Sensory and short-term memory (STM) share a similar *purpose*. However, STM does not store exact *duplicates* of sensory information but rather a mixture of perceptual analyses. For example, when your sensory memory registers the sound of your professor's voice, it holds the actual auditory information for a few seconds. If the information requires further processing, it moves on to STM. While being transferred from sensory memory, the sound of your professor's words is converted into a larger, more inclusive type of message capable of being analyzed and interpreted

K	Z	R	A
Q	B	T	P
S	G	N	Y

Sensory Memory *First memory stage that holds sensory information; relatively large capacity, but duration is only a few seconds*

Figure 7.3 *Experiments with sensory memory.* When George Sperling flashed an arrangement of letters like these for 1/20 of a second, most people could only recall 4 or 5 (of 12). But when instructed to report the top, middle, or bottom row, depending on whether they heard a high, medium, or low tone, they reported almost all the letters correctly. Apparently, all 12 letters are held in sensory memory right after viewing them. But only those that are immediately attended to (with the tone) are noted and processed.

Short-Term Memory (STM) *Second memory stage that temporarily stores sensory information and decides whether to send it on to long-term memory (LTM); capacity is limited to five to nine items and duration is about 30 seconds*

Testing Iconic and Echoic Memory

If you'd like a simple demonstration of the duration of visual information, or *iconic memory*, swing a flashlight in a dark room. Because the image, or *icon*, lingers for a fraction of a second after the flashlight is moved, you see the light as a continuous stream rather than a succession of individual points. Would you like a similar test of auditory information, or echoic memory? Think back to times when someone interrupted you while you were deeply absorbed in a task. Did you ask "What?" and then immediately find you could answer the question without a repeat? Now you know why. If we divert our attention from the absorbing task quickly enough, we can "hear again" the echo of what was asked.

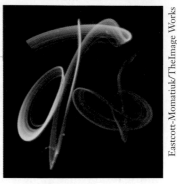

Eastcott-Momatiuk/TheImage Works

during short-term memory. If the information is important (or may be on a test), STM organizes and sends this information along to relatively permanent storage, called long-term memory (LTM).

Both the *duration* and *capacity* of STM are relatively limited. Although some researchers extend the time to a few minutes, most research shows that STM holds information for approximately 30 seconds. STM also holds a restricted *amount* of new information, five to nine items (Best, 1999; Kareev, 2000). As with sensory memory, information in STM either is transferred quickly into the next stage (LTM) or it decays and is lost.

Maintenance Rehearsal *Repeating information over and over to maintain it in short-term memory (STM)*

Chunking *Grouping separate pieces of information into a single unit (or chunk)*

©AP/Wide World Photos

How can I increase the duration and capacity of my STM? Look back to the memory model in Figure 7.2. Note the looping arrow at the top labeled "maintenance rehearsal." You can extend the *duration* of your STM almost indefinitely if you consciously and continuously repeat the information over and over again. This is called **maintenance rehearsal**. You are using maintenance rehearsal when you look up a phone number and repeat it over and over until you dial the number.

Unfortunately, this technique requires constant vigilance. If you stop repeating the phone number it's quickly lost. Like juggling a set of plates, the plates stay in perfect shape only as long as you keep juggling them. Once you stop, the plates fall and are destroyed. (In the case of memory, the memory is lost).

To extend the *capacity* of STM, you can use **chunking**—grouping separate pieces of information into a single unit (or *chunk*) (Boucher & Dienes, 2003; Miller, 1956). Have you noticed that numbers on credit cards, your Social Security identification, and telephone number are all grouped into three or four units separated by hyphens? This is because most people find it easier to remember numbers in chunks like *(760) 744–1129* rather than as a string of single digits. Similarly, in reading-improvement courses, students are taught to chunk groups of words into phrases. This allows fewer

Chunking and chess. Expert chess players like Garry Kasparov also use chunking to organize the information on a game board into meaningful patterns or units (Amidzic et al., 2001; Huffman, Matthews, & Gagne, 2001). Researchers have found that novice players who look at a standard chessboard with the pieces arranged in a typical play position can remember the positions of only a few pieces. Expert chess players generally remember all the positions. Just as you group the letters of this sentence into meaningful words and remember them long enough to understand the meaning, expert chess players group the chess pieces into patterns (or chunks) that can be easily recalled.

eye movements and the brain can process the phrases as units rather than as individual words.

If I have room for five to nine units or chunks, why doesn't chunking help me remember even three or four names during introductions? The limited capacity and brief duration of STM both work against you in this situation. Instead of concentrating on the name of someone you meet for the first time, you sometimes use all your short-term memory capacity wondering how you look and thinking about what to say. You might even fill STM space worrying about your memory!

People who are good at remembering names repeat the name of each person out loud or silently to keep it entered in STM (maintenance rehearsal). Keep in mind, however, that maintenance rehearsal saves the name only while you're actively rehearsing. If you want to really learn that name, you will need to transfer it into long-term memory.

Short-Term Memory as a "Working Memory"

Does it sound as if short-term memory (STM) is just a *passive*, temporary "holding area?" Most current researchers (Baddeley, 1992, 2000; Bleckley et al., 2003; DeStefano & LeFevre, 2004) emphasize that *active* processing of information also occurs in STM. Our short-term memory not only receives information from our sensory memory, it also sends and retrieves information from our long-term memory. In fact, all our conscious thought (reasoning, computing, perception) occurs in our STM. Therefore, today we think of STM as a three-part *working memory* (Figure 7.4):

1. *Visuospatial sketchpad.* The first component of working memory is the visual workplace. This so-called visuospatial sketchpad holds and manipulates visual images and spatial information (Best, 1999; Kemps et al., 2004). Imagine yourself as a food server who's taking multiple orders from three customers at a small table. Your mind's visuospatial "sketchpad" allows you to mentally visualize how to fit all the plates of food on their table.

2. *Phonological rehearsal loop.* The second component is responsible for holding and manipulating verbal information (Best, 1999; Jiang et al., 2000; Noël et al., 2001). Picture yourself again as the same food server. Your customers have given you the following orders: "I want the breakfast special with two scrambled eggs, orange juice, and coffee." "Give me the ham, very well done, with the stack of pancakes, and nothing to drink." "I'll have oatmeal without the raisins, dry toast, coffee, and grapefruit juice." Like the previously mentioned juggling example for *maintenance rehearsal*, you can mentally "juggle" the food orders by subvocally repeating them. This is why this component is called a phonological (auditory) *rehearsal loop*. You rehearse the order until you reach the kitchen and pass it along to the chef.

3. *Central executive.* This "executive" supervises and coordinates the other two components, along with material retrieved from long-term memory. When you mentally combine the verbal food orders (the phonological loop) and their spatial layout on the table (the visuospatial sketchpad), you are using your central executive.

Ken Fisher/Stone/GettyImages

Visuospatial sketchpad
(visual and spatial material)

Central executive
(coordinates material)

Phonological loop
(speech, words, numbers)

Figure 7.4 *Working memory as a central executive.* According to this model, working memory serves as a central executive that coordinates the visuospatial sketchpad and the phonological loop.

Problems with short-term memory?
When being introduced to several people at a party, you will be more apt to remember the person's name if you repeat it several times. It also helps to focus solely on the person rather than on other interfering factors.

www.wiley.com/college/huffman

Long-Term Memory (LTM): The Third Stage of Memory

Think back to the opening story of H.M. If you were to meet him, you might not recognize his problem. But if you walked away and then ran into one another again 10 minutes later, H.M. would not remember ever having met you. His surgery was successful in stopping the severe epileptic seizures. Unfortunately, it also apparently destroyed the mechanism that transfers information from short-term to long-term memory.

What would it be like to live eternally in just the present—without your long-term memory? The *purpose* of the third stage, **long-term memory (LTM)**, is to serve as a storehouse for information that must be kept for long periods of time. Once information is transferred from STM, it is organized and integrated with other information in LTM. It remains there until we need to retrieve it. Then it is sent back to STM for our use.

Compared to sensory memory and short-term memory, long-term memory has relatively unlimited *capacity* and *duration* (Klatzky, 1984). It's like a magical credit card that lets you spend an unlimited amount of money for an unlimited time. In fact, the more you learn, or the more money you spend, the better it is!

But why do I feel like the more I learn, the harder it is to find things? During the transfer of information from STM to LTM, incoming information is "tagged" or filed, hopefully in the appropriate place. If information is improperly stored, it creates major delays and problems during retrieval. The better we label and arrange things (whether it's our CD collection, bills, or memory), the more likely they'll be accurately stored and readily available for retrieval.

Types of Long-Term Memory

Given that LTM is believed to be generally unlimited in duration and capacity, we obviously collect a vast amount of information over a lifetime. How do we store it? As you can see in Figure 7.5, several types of LTM exist. At the top of the figure, you can see that LTM is divided into two major systems—*explicit (declarative) memory* and *implicit (nondeclarative) memory*.

1. ***Explicit (declarative) memory.*** *Explicit memory* refers to intentional learning or conscious knowledge. It is *memory with awareness*. If asked to remember your Social Security number, your first kiss, the name of your first-grade teacher, and the name of your current psychology professor, you can report the answers directly (explicitly). This type of memory is also known as *declarative memory* because, if asked, you can "declare" it (or state it in words). When people think of memory, they often are referring to this type of explicit (declarative) memory (Best, 1999; Hayne, Boniface, & Barr, 2000).

Explicit (declarative) memory is also further subdivided into two parts—*semantic memory* and *episodic memory*. **Semantic memory** is memory for facts and general knowledge (e.g., names of objects, days of the week). It is our internal mental dictionary or encyclopedia of stored knowledge. If you read and remember terms like *semantic, episodic, explicit (declarative)*, and *implicit (nondeclarative)*, it is because you have stored them in your semantic memory.

In contrast, **episodic memory** is the explicit memory of our own past experiences—our personal mental diary. It records the major events (or *episodes*) that happen to us or take place in our presence. Some of our episodic memories are short-lived (what you ate for breakfast today). Others can last a lifetime (your first romantic kiss, your high school graduation, the birth of your first child).

Have you ever wondered why toddlers are quite capable of remembering events they experienced in previous months, yet most of us as adults can recall almost nothing of those years before the age of 3? Why don't we remember our birth, our second

---

Long-Term Memory (LTM) *Third stage of memory that stores information for long periods of time; its capacity is virtually limitless, and its duration is relatively permanent*

Explicit (Declarative) Memory *Subsystem within long-term memory that consciously stores facts, information, and personal life experiences*

Semantic Memory *A part of explicit/declarative memory that stores general knowledge; a mental encyclopedia or dictionary*

Episodic Memory *A part of explicit/declarative memory that stores memories of personally experienced events; a mental diary of a person's life*

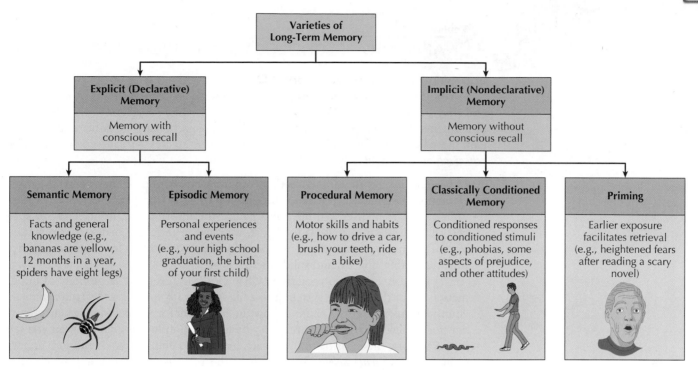

Figure 7.5 *Types of LTM.* Note how LTM is divided and subdivided into various types of memory. Taking time to study and visualize these separate systems and subsystems will improve your understanding and mastery of this material because it involves a deeper level of processing.

birthday, or our family's big move to a new city? These were major events at that point in our life. Research suggests that a concept of "self," sufficient language development, and growth of the frontal lobes of the cortex (along with other structures) may be necessary before these early events (or episodes) can be encoded and retrieved many years later (Simcock & Hayne, 2002; Sluzenski, Newcombe, & Offinger, 2004; Suzuki & Amaral, 2004; Uehara, 2000).

2. *Implicit (nondeclarative) memory.* Unlike explicit memory, *implicit memory* refers to unintentional learning or unconscious knowledge. It is memory *without awareness.* Can you describe how you tie your shoelaces without demonstrating the actual behavior? Because your memory of this skill is unconscious and hard to describe in words (to "declare"), implicit memory is also referred to as *nondeclarative.*

Implicit (nondeclarative) memory consists of *procedural* motor skills like tying your shoes, riding a bike, and brushing your teeth. It also includes simple, classically conditioned responses, such as fears or taste aversions. As you recall from Chapter 6, my student who ate the Butterfinger candy bar with the crawling maggots has a conditioned emotional response (or *implicit memory*). This memory makes her immediately and (unconsciously) nauseated whenever she sees or thinks about this particular candy.

In addition to procedural motor skills and classically conditioned responses, implicit memory also includes **priming**. This form of memory occurs when a prior exposure to a stimulus (or *prime*) facilitates or inhibits the processing of new information (Burton et al., 2004; McCarley et al., 2004; Tulving, 2000). Such priming effects may occur even when we do not consciously remember being exposed to the prime. Have you noticed how your fears are heightened after reading a Stephen King novel? Or that your romantic feelings increase after watching a romantic movie? This is because your previous experiences *prime* you to more easily notice and recall related instances. (It also suggests a practical way to improve your love life—go to romantic movies!)

Implicit (Nondeclarative) Memory
Subsystem within long-term memory that consists of unconscious procedural skills, simple classically conditioned responses, and priming

Priming *Prior exposure to a stimulus (or prime) facilitates or inhibits the processing of new information, even when one has no conscious memory of the initial learning and storage*

Application

APPLYING PSYCHOLOGY TO STUDENT LIFE

Improving Long-Term Memory (LTM)

After reading through all the terms and concepts associated with long-term memory, you may be wondering, "Why do I need to know this?" Understanding LTM has direct beneficial applications to your everyday life—particularly to college success. To gain these benefits, you need to focus on three key strategies—*organization*, *elaborative rehearsal*, and *retrieval cues*.

1. ***Organization.*** As mentioned earlier, organization is one of the most important elements in memory. To extend the capacity of short-term memory (five to nine units), we earlier discussed how to organize the information into *chunks*. To successfully encode information for LTM, we need to organize material into *hierarchies*. This involves arranging a number of related items into a few broad categories that are further divided and subdivided.

   For instance, do you recall how Chapter 2 organized the large body of information about the nervous system into a hierarchy with smaller and smaller units or chunks? Look at Figure 7.6. Note how the hierarchy for the nervous system is similar to our newly created hierarchy for the information in this chapter. Can you see how arranging the information into such hierarchies helps make them more understandable and *memorable?* This is one of the reasons I use so many hierarchies throughout this text (in the form of diagrams, tables, and end-of-chapter "Visual Summaries"). It also explains why chapters in almost all college textbooks are hierarchically arranged. Chapter outlines at the beginning of each chapter present small subsets of ideas grouped together as subheadings under a larger, main heading.

   If you want to improve your memory in this and other courses, study these hierarchies carefully. Better still, try making your own hierarchies when studying for exams. This may sound difficult, but keep in mind that you already possess all the basic skills. Think back to the first day you walked around your college campus. You probably felt overwhelmed by all the buildings, sidewalks, and parking lots. You needed a map just to find your classes. After being on campus for a while, however, you discarded the map because you "naturally" organized all the information into personally meaningful chunks (science building, library, cafeteria). These chunks were further organized into an overall personal hierarchy. Can you see how you could use these same skills to arrange the large assortment of facts and concepts required for a typical college exam?

Figure 7.6 *Hierarchies are a natural part of LTM.* Just as the diagram of the nervous system helped organize the material in Chapter 2, a similar diagram of the current information on memory helps you order and arrange the various terms. Encoding, storage, and retrieval in LTM are all improved through the use of hierarchies. This is why this text contains so many tables, figures, and end-of-chapter "Visual Summaries."

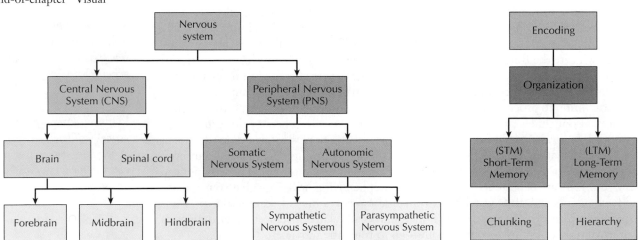

Admittedly, organization takes time and work. But you'll be happy to know that some memory organization and filing are done automatically while you sleep (Maquet et al., 2003; Smith & Smith, 2003; Wagner et al., 2003). Other research shows that sleep itself improves memory (Koulack, 1997; Wixted, 2004).

What about advertising that says you can use tape recordings to learn new skills like foreign languages during sleep? Do they work? In one early study, participants' brain waves were recorded while they listened to tapes as they slept. Afterward, they were asked questions about the information they heard. Participants who listened to the tapes while in a drowsy state could answer 50 percent of the questions. Listeners in a transition state between drowsiness and light sleep could answer only 5 percent of the questions. And listeners who were fully asleep did not remember any information at all (Simon & Emmons, 1956).

2. ***Elaborative Rehearsal.*** Like organization, rehearsal also improves encoding for both short-term memory (STM) and long-term memory (LTM). As we learned earlier, if you need to hold information in STM longer than 30 seconds, you can do a type of juggling act called *maintenance rehearsal.* You simply keep repeating the information over and over. This type of *shallow processing* works for information that you don't need in long-term memory.

Storage in LTM requires *deeper levels of processing*, called **elaborative rehearsal** (see Figure 7.2, page 252). When we *elaborate*, we expand. We think *deeply* about new information and tie it into previously stored memories. The previous com-

Elaborative Rehearsal *Linking new information to previously stored material (also known as deeper levels of processing)*

Improving Elaborative Rehearsal

As we discovered earlier, because LTM is relatively unlimited in capacity and duration, it's like a magical credit card with an unlimited amount of money and unlimited time. Using elaborative rehearsal, you can access even more of that unlimited bounty each time you go on a spending spree! How can this be true? Think about the students in your college classes. Have you noticed that older students often tend to get better grades? This is because they've lived longer and stored more information in their LTM. Older students can tag into a greater wealth of previously stored material. If you're a younger student (or an older student just returning to college), you can learn to process information at a deeper level and build your elaborative rehearsal skills by:

- *Expanding (or elaborating on) the information.* The more you elaborate or try to understand something, the more likely you are to remember it. To store the term "long-term memory," think about what it would be like if you only

had STM and could store information for only 30 seconds. Picture the life of H.M. (the man introduced at the beginning of the chapter).

If you can't easily tag information to what you already know, create a new link or "tag." For instance, to encode and store the term *echoic memory,* look for examples of this in other people or in yourself. Make a mental note when you find an example and store it with the term *echoic memory.*

- *Actively exploring and questioning new information.* Think about the term *iconic memory.* Ask yourself, "Why did they use this term?" Look up the term *icon* in the dictionary. You'll learn that it comes from the Greek word for "image" or "likeness."
- *Trying to find meaningfulness.* When you meet people at a party, don't just maintenance-rehearse their name. Ask about their favorite TV shows, their career plans, political beliefs, or anything else that requires deeper analysis. You'll be much more likely to remember their names.

Figure 7.7 *Recognition memory.* In this study of recognition memory, participants were asked to identify pictures of their high school classmates. As you can see, picture recognition is higher overall than name recognition. This is because name recognition requires greater recall.

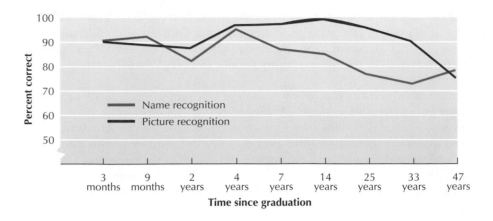

parison of the encoding, storage, and retrieval model to a computer is a good example of *elaborative rehearsal*. When you think deeply about this model and compare it to your previous knowledge of computers, it helps you learn and remember the new model. The immediate goal of elaborative rehearsal is to *understand*—not to memorize. Fortunately, this attempt to understand is one of the best ways to encode new information into long-term memory.

3. *Retrieval Cues.* A **retrieval cue** is any stimulus that can begin a retrieval process from LTM (Klatzky, 1984). There are basically two types of retrieval cues—*specific* and *general*. When you retrieve a memory using a specific cue, it is called **recognition.** You only have to identify (or "recognize") the correct response, as in a multiple-choice exam. When you use a general cue, it is called **recall.** You must retrieve (or recall) previously learned material, as in an essay exam.

A similar process occurs when you pick out a particular face you have previously seen from a police lineup. You use *recognition* to check the specific cue (the face) against your LTM contents to see if something matches (Figure 7.7). If, on the other hand, you remember someone's name from a description of that person (a general cue), you are using *recall*, which is a much more difficult task. During recall, you use a general cue to generate a list of materials associated with that cue. You then search through LTM to find something that matches the cue (Best, 1999). This general cue often isn't enough to locate a single piece of information because the list of possible matches is often quite large. Therefore, the more specific the cue, the more likely you are to retrieve the needed information from your memory.

Don't hesitate to ask questions of your professor during exams. Most professors allow questions, and their answers often provide valuable retrieval cues.

Retrieval Cue *A clue or prompt that helps stimulate recall or retrieval of a stored piece of information from long-term memory*

Recognition *Retrieving a memory using a specific cue*

Recall *Retrieving a memory using a general cue*

TRY THIS

YOURSELF

Application

A Test for Recall

Close your eyes and try to *recall* the names of Santa's nine reindeer. Most people can only recall four to five names. Now turn to page 261 for a *recognition* test on the same material.

Michel Tcherevkoff Ltd. /The Image Bank/GettyImages

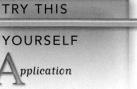

A Test for Recognition

Now that you've completed the recall test on page 260, see if you can recognize the correct names from the following list:

Rudolph, Dancer, Cupid, Lancer, Comet, Blitzen, Crasher, Donder, Prancer, Dasher, Vixen.

Although you may not need them, the answers are provided in Appendix B. Can you see why recognition tasks generally are much easier than recall?

Using Retrieval Strategies on Exams

As we've just seen, retrieval cues, both specific and general, are frequently used on exams. One lesser known strategy is to re-create the original learning conditions. The ease of retrieval depends on the match between the way information is encoded and the way it is later retrieved. This is known as the **encoding specificity principle** (Tulving & Thompson, 1973). Three important research findings related to this principle may help you improve your exam scores:

- *Context and retrieval.* Have you noticed that you do better on a test when you take it in the same seat and classroom where you originally studied the material? This happens because the location is a retrieval cue to the material you studied. Godden and Baddeley (1975) demonstrated how context affects learning and memory in a clever study some years ago. They had underwater divers learn a list of 40 words either on land or underwater. The divers had better recall for lists they had encoded underwater. But this happened only if they also were underwater at retrieval. Conversely, lists encoded above water were better recalled above water. This can be one reason you feel confident about material while studying at home. But you later may have trouble recalling it at school.

- *Mood congruence.* When you're sad or angry, do you tend to remember similar events and circumstances when you were sad or angry in the past? The idea that a given mood tends to evoke memories that are consistent with that mood is called *mood congruence.*

Research shows that people remember something better if their emotional moods are the same at the time when they learn something and during the time when they try to retrieve it (Kenealy, 1997). If you suffer from test anxiety, you might try re-creating the relaxed mood you had while studying. Take deep breaths and reassure yourself during exams. In addition, you might want to artificially increase your anxiety level while studying. Deliberately remind yourself of the importance of good grades or your long-range career plans. By lowering your test anxiety and upping your study anxiety, you create a better balance or match between your exam mood and your study mood. This should improve your retrieval.

- *State-dependent retrieval.* Research also has shown that if you learn something while under the influence of a drug, such as caffeine, you will remember it more easily when you take that drug again (Baddeley, 1998). Some students have found that drinking a cup of coffee while studying and before an exam does improve their performance.

Encoding Specificity Principle
Retrieval of information is improved when conditions of recovery are similar to the conditions when information was encoded

Callahan cartoon ©Callahan. Distributed by Levin Represents

"I wonder if you'd mind giving me directions. I've never been sober in this part of town before."

CHECK & REVIEW

The Nature of Memory

The information-processing model sees analogies between human memory and a computer. Like typing on a keyboard, **encoding** translates information into neural codes that match the brain's language. **Storage** retains neural coded information over time, like saving material on the computer's hard drive or a disk. **Retrieval** gets information out of LTM storage and sends it to STM to be used, whereas the computer retrieves information and displays it on the monitor.

According to the **parallel distributed processing (PDP)**, or connectionist, model, the contents of our memory exist as a vast number of interconnected units distributed throughout a huge network, all operating simultaneously in parallel. According to the **levels of processing** model, the degree or depth of mental processing that occurs when material is initially encountered determines how well it is later remembered.

The traditional three-stage memory model proposes that information must pass through each of three stages before being stored: sensory memory, short-term memory, and long-term memory. **Sensory memory** preserves a brief replica of sensory information. It has a large capacity, and information lasts from a fraction of a second to four seconds. Selected information is sent to short-term memory. **Short-term memory (STM)**, also called working memory, involves memory for current thoughts. Short-term memory can hold five to nine items for about 30 seconds before they are forgotten. Information can be stored longer than 30 seconds through **maintenance rehearsal**, and the capacity of STM can be increased with *chunking*. *Long-term memory (LTM)* is relatively permanent memory storage with an unlimited capacity.

Storage in LTM is divided into two major systems—**explicit (declarative)** and **implicit (nondeclarative) memory**. Explicit memory is further subdivided into two parts—**semantic** and **episodic memory**. Implicit memory is subdivided into procedural memory, classically conditioned memory, and **priming**. To improve LTM, we can use organization, **elaborative rehearsal,** and **retrieval cues** (**recognition** and **recall**).

Questions

1. During _____, your brain translates information into a neural language it can understand, and during _____ this neurally coded information is retained over time.
2. How do the PDP and levels of processing models explain memory?
3. According to the three-stage memory model, information must first enter _____, then transfer to _____ and then to _____ to be retained in our memory system.
4. What is the difference between semantic and episodic memory?
5. Multiple-choice questions require _____, whereas essay questions require _____.

Check your answers in Appendix B.

CLICK & REVIEW
for additional assessment options:
www.wiley.com/college/huffman

FORGETTING

Memory is what makes you wonder what you've forgotten.

ANONYMOUS

> Why do we forget, and how can we prevent forgetting?

Think about what your life would be like if you couldn't forget. Your LTM would be filled with meaningless data, such as what you ate for breakfast every morning of your life. Similarly, think of the incredible pain and sorrow you would continuously endure if you couldn't distance yourself from tragedy through forgetting. The ability to forget is essential to the proper functioning of memory. But what about those times when forgetting is an inconvenience or even dangerous?

■ How Quickly Do We Forget? Research Findings

Hermann Ebbinghaus, a pioneer memory researcher who often used himself as his only subject, first introduced the experimental study of learning and forgetting in 1885. To measure memory performance, he calculated how long it took him to learn a list of *nonsense syllables*. For his trials, Ebbinghaus chose three-letter nonsense syllables such as *SIB* and *RAL* because they were equally difficult to learn. Furthermore, nonsense syllables don't have the meanings and associations that words do, thus avoiding the complications of previous learning.

After Ebbinghaus memorized lists of nonsense syllables until he knew them perfectly, he retested his memory at regular intervals. He found that one hour after he knew a list perfectly, he remembered only 44 percent of the syllables. A day later, he recalled 35 percent. A week later only 21 percent. Figure 7.8 presents his famous (and somewhat depressing) "forgetting curve."

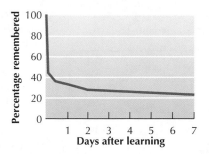

Figure 7.8 *Ebbinghaus's forgetting curve.* Note how rapidly nonsense syllables are forgotten, especially in the first few hours after learning.

Do we forget everything this fast? If you were to forget textbook materials and lecture notes this rapidly, you would be able to pass a test only if you took it immediately after studying the material. An hour later, you would fail the test because you would remember less than half of what you had studied. Keep in mind, however, that the forgetting curve in Figure 7.8 applies to meaningless nonsense syllables. Meaningful material is much less likely to be forgotten. The material you study for a test can be retained much longer if you make an effort to make it meaningful through elaborative rehearsal. But meaningful or not, you will still forget some of what you have studied.

On a more cheerful note, after some time passed and he had forgotten the list, Ebbinghaus also calculated the time it took to relearn the same list. He found that relearning a list took less time than the initial learning period. This is known as **relearning** (or the *savings method*). Ebbinghaus's research suggests that we often retain some memory for things we have learned, even when we seem to have forgotten them completely. This finding should be encouraging to you if you studied a foreign language years ago. You may be unable to fully recall or recognize the vocabulary at this time. But you can expect to relearn the material more rapidly the second time.

■ Why Do We Forget? Five Key Theories

Five major theories have been offered to explain why forgetting occurs: *decay, interference, motivated forgetting, encoding failure,* and *retrieval failure*. Each theory focuses on a different stage of the memory process or on a particular type of problem in processing information.

Decay Theory

Decay theory is based on the commonsense assumption that memory, like all biological processes, degrades with time. Because memory is processed and stored in a physical form—for example, in a network of neurons—the relevant connections between neurons could be expected to decrease over time. It is well documented that skills and memory are degraded if they are not used for a long period of time (Rosenzweig, Barnes, & McNaughton, 2002; Villarreal, Do, Haddad, & Derrick, 2002). In other words, "use it or lose it." But it also is important to point out that conclusive experimental support for decay theory is difficult to obtain. As we discovered in Chapter 4's discussion of extrasensory perception (ESP), it is impossible to *prove* ESP (or a previously stored memory) does *not* exist.

Interference Theory

Interference theory suggests that forgetting is caused by one memory competing with, or trying to replace, another memory (Anderson, Bjork, & Bjork, 1994; Conway & Pleydell-Pearce, 2000; Wixted, 2004). Interference is particularly strong among memories for similar events or with similar retrieval cues.

At least two types of interference exist: *retroactive* and *proactive* (Figure 7.9). When new information leads to forgetting old material, it is called **retroactive interference** (acting backward in time). Learning your new

Relearning *Learning material a second time, which usually takes less time than original learning (also called the savings method)*

Study**T**ip 🔆

If you want to remember the five theories, think of how forgetting involves memories that grow "dimmer." Note that the first letter of each theory has almost the same spelling—D-I-M-E-R.

Retroactive Interference *New information interferes with remembering old information; backward-acting interference*

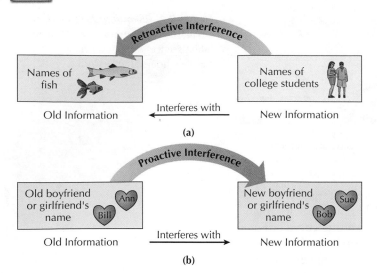

(a)

(b)

Figure 7.9 *Two types of interference.* (a) *Retroactive* (backward-acting) *interference* occurs when new information interferes with old information. This example comes from a story about an absent-minded icthyology professor (fish specialist) who refused to learn the name of his college students. Asked why, he said, "Every time I learn a student's name, I forget the name of a fish!" (b) *Proactive* (forward-acting) *interference* occurs when old information interferes with new information. Have you ever been in trouble because you used an old partner's name to refer to your new partner? You now have a guilt-free explanation—proactive interference.

phone number often causes forgetting of your old phone number (old, "retro" information is forgotten). Conversely, when old information leads to forgetting of new information, it is called **proactive interference** (acting forward in time). Old information (like the Spanish you learned in high school) may interfere with your ability to learn and remember your new college course in French.

In addition to retroactive and proactive interference, recent research suggests that a great deal of our everyday forgetting comes from simple everyday activities and a type of *consolidation failure* (Wixted, 2005). In Chapter 6, we learned that neurons and synapses in our brain change in response to new learning. We also know that it takes a certain amount of time for these neural changes to become fixed and stable in long-term memory, a process known as **consolidation.** Recently formed memories that have not yet "set up" and become permanently stored are vulnerable to a host of factors that may interfere and block consolidation. Consolidation is somewhat analogous to wet cement. If you place your hand print in wet cement, it takes time for it to set up and become permanent. While it is setting up, events can happen that erase your hand print.

Retroactive and proactive interference both involve interference from material that is similar to what was previously learned. In contrast, this alternative consolidation failure theory suggests that simply watching television or talking with friends after studying can interfere with the consolidation of the studied material. This also explains why going to sleep immediately after studying can help prevent forgetting!

Another way to remember the difference between retroactive and proactive interference is to emphasize where the interference is occurring. In retroactive interference, forgetting occurs with old ("retro") information. During proactive interference, forgetting occurs with new information.

Proactive Interference *Old information interferes with remembering new information; forward-acting interference*

Consolidation *Process by which neural changes associated with recent learning become durable and stable*

Motivated Forgetting Theory

A third theory of forgetting focuses on our sometimes unconscious wish to forget something unpleasant. According to the *motivated forgetting theory*, we forget for a reason. We inhibit the retrieval. Forgetting the name of an instructor who gave you a low grade, your dental appointment, or that embarrassing speech you made in eighth grade are all examples of motivated forgetting.

People obviously try to inhibit unpleasant or anxiety-producing thoughts or feelings. According to Freudian theory (Chapter 13), when they do this consciously, telling themselves not to worry about an upcoming final exam, it is called *suppression*. When they do it unconsciously, it is called *repression*. Sigmund Freud claimed that people repressed painful memories to avoid anxiety. If this is the case, appropriate therapy might overcome the repressive mechanisms and cause the repressed memory to be recovered. Memories of child abuse, sexual assault, war atrocities, and the death of loved ones may create such painful experiences that the individual is highly motivated to forget them. The controversy surrounding *repressed memories* is discussed later in this chapter.

Encoding Failure Theory

Whose head is on a U.S. penny? What is written at the top of a penny? Despite having seen a real penny thousands of times in our lives, most of us have difficulty rec-

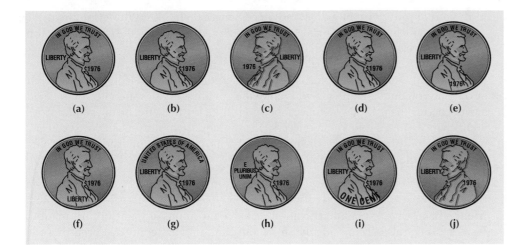

Figure 7.10 *Encoding failure.* Can you identify a drawing of a real penny among fakes?

ognizing the details (Figure 7.10). The U.S. penny has eight easily distinguishing characteristics (Lincoln's head, the date it was minted, which way Lincoln is facing, and so on). However, the average person can only remember three (Nickerson & Adams, 1979). This is a great example of *encoding failure*. Unless we are coin collectors, we have little motivation to properly encode the details of a penny. Our sensory memory certainly received the information and passed it along (encoded it) to STM. But during STM, we probably decided there was no need to remember the precise details of the penny. Because we can easily recognize pennies by their size and color, we don't encode the fine details and pass them on for storage in LTM.

Retrieval Failure Theory

If you've ever "blanked out" during an exam or a conversation and remembered the "forgotten" information later, you've had firsthand experience with the *retrieval failure* (or *cue-dependent*) *theory of forgetting*. According to this theory, memories stored in LTM aren't forgotten. They're just momentarily inaccessible as a result of such things as interference, faulty cues, or emotional states.

One of the most common experiences of *retrieval failure* is the **tip-of-the-tongue (TOT) phenomenon.** Have you ever felt that at any second, a word or event you are trying to remember will pop out from the "tip of your tongue" (Abrams, White, & Eitel, 2003; Brown & McNeill, 1966; Gollan & Acenas, 2004)? Even though you can't say the word, you can often tell how many syllables it has, the beginning and ending letters, or what it rhymes with.

As you might imagine, it is difficult to distinguish retrieval failure from encoding failure. In fact, most memory failures are probably due to poor encoding rather than to retrieval failure (Howe & O'Sullivan, 1997).

Tip-of-the-Tongue (TOT) Phenomenon *Feeling that specific information is stored in long-term memory but of being temporarily unable to retrieve it*

Application APPLYING PSYCHOLOGY TO STUDENT LIFE

Overcoming Problems with Forgetting

Following Ebbinghaus's original research, scientists have discovered numerous factors that contribute to forgetting. Four of the most important to your life as a student are the *serial position effect*, *source amnesia*, *sleeper effect*, and *spacing of practice*.

1. ***Serial position effect.*** When study participants are given lists of words to learn and are allowed to recall them in any order they choose, they remember the words at the beginning (*primacy effect*) and the end of the list (*recency effect*) better than those

Serial Position Effect *Information at the beginning and end of a list is remembered better than material in the middle.*

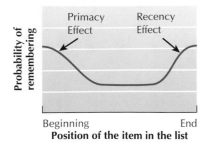

Figure 7.11 *The serial position effect.* If you try to recall a list of similar items, you'll tend to remember the first and last items best.

Source Amnesia *Forgetting the true source of a memory (also called source confusion or source misattribution)*

Sleeper Effect *Information from an unreliable source, which was initially discounted, later gains credibility because the source is forgotten*

Distributed Practice *Practice (or study) sessions are interspersed with rest periods*

Massed Practice *Time spent learning is grouped (or massed) into long, unbroken intervals (also known as cramming)*

in the middle (Burns et al., 2004; Golob & Starr, 2004; Suhr, 2002) (Figure 7.11). This effect, including both primacy and recency, is known as the **serial position effect.** The reasons for this effect are complex.

Can you see how the serial position effect helps explain why material at the beginning and end of a chapter is better remembered than that in the middle? It also helps you understand why you remember the first and last people you meet at a party better than those you meet inbetween. Finally, this effect can even improve your chances for employment success. If a potential employer calls to set up an interview, you can increase their memory of you (and your application) by asking to be either the first or last candidate.

2. **Source amnesia.** Have you ever chosen a wrong answer on a test because you thought you heard that "fact" from your professor—when it actually came from a friend? Each day we read, hear, and process an enormous amount of information. It's easy to confuse "who said what to whom" and in what context. Forgetting the true source of a memory is known as **source amnesia** (Drummey & Newcombe, 2002; Leichtman & Ceci, 1995; Oakes & Hyman, 2001). As a critical thinker, can you see why advertisers of shoddy services or products might benefit from "channel surfing"? If television viewers are skipping from news programs to cable talk shows to infomercials, they may give undue credit to the inferior services or products. Now that you're aware of source amnesia, can you use your new information to avoid some of the potential problems it creates?

3. **Sleeper effect.** In addition to source amnesia, with the passage of time we also tend to confuse reliable information with unreliable. Research on this aptly named **sleeper effect** finds that when we first hear something from an unreliable source, we tend to disregard that information in favor of a more reliable source. However, over time, the source of the information is forgotten (source amnesia). And the unreliable information is no longer discounted (the sleeper effect) (Kumkale & Albarracin, 2004; Underwood & Pezdek, 1998). This sleeper effect can be a significant problem when reliable and unreliable information are intermixed. Can you see how you might initially discount an opinion from a movie star about a weight-loss diet but later forget to discount this as an unreliable source?

4. **Spacing of practice.** Despite their best intentions, students often study in ways that encourage forgetting. Do you ever study in noisy places where your attention is easily diverted and interference is maximized? Do you attempt to memorize too much at one time by "cramming" the night before an exam? As the "Tools for Student Success" section in Chapter 1 emphasized, the single most important key to improving grades may be *distributed study*. **Distributed practice** refers to spacing your learning periods, with rest periods between sessions. Cramming is called **massed practice** because the time spent learning is *massed* into long, unbroken intervals. John Donovan and David Radosevich (1999) compared 63 separate studies and found that distributed practice produced superior memory and learning compared with massed practice. Unfortunately, research shows that most students (who haven't taken introductory psychology and studied this chapter) do most of their studying right before the test (Taraban, Maki, & Rynearson, 1999).

chievement

Gender & Cultural Diversity

Cultural Differences in Memory and Forgetting

How do you remember the dates for all your quizzes, exams, and assignments in college? What memory aids do you use if you need to buy 15 items at the supermarket? Most people from industrialized societies rely on written shopping lists, calendars, books, notepads, or computers to store information and prevent forgetting. Can you imagine living in a culture without these aids? What would it be like if you had to rely solely on your memory to store and retrieve all your learned information? Would you develop better memory skills if you couldn't write things down? Do people raised in preliterate societies with rich oral traditions develop better memory skills than do people raised in literate societies?

Ross and Millson (1970) designed a cross-cultural study to explore these questions. They compared American and Ghanaian college students' abilities to remember stories that were read aloud. Students listened to the stories without taking notes and without being told they would be tested. Two weeks later, all students were asked to write down as much as they could remember. As you might expect, the Ghanaian students had better recall than the Americans. Their superior performance was attributed to their culture's long oral tradition, which requires developing greater skill in encoding oral information (Matsumoto, 2000).

Does this mean that people from cultures with an oral tradition simply have better memories? Recall from Chapter 1 that a core requirement for scientific research is *replication* and the generation of related hypotheses and studies. In this case, when other researchers orally presented nonliterate African participants with lists of words instead of stories, they did *not* perform better (Cole, Gray, Glick, & Sharp, 1971). However, when both educated Africans and uneducated Africans were compared for memory of lists of words, the educated Africans performed very well (Scribner, 1979). This suggests that formal schooling helps develop memory strategies for things like lists of words. Preliterate participants may see such lists as unrelated and meaningless.

Wagner (1982) conducted a study with Moroccan and Mexican urban and rural children that helps explain the effect of formal schooling. Participants were presented with seven cards that were placed facedown in front of them, one at a time. They were then shown a card and asked to point out which of the seven cards was its duplicate. Everyone, regardless of culture or amount of schooling, was able to recall the latest cards presented (the *recency effect*). However, the amount of schooling significantly affected overall recall and the ability to recall the earliest cards presented (*primacy effect*).

Wagner suggests that the primacy effect depends on *rehearsal*—the silent repetition of things you're trying to remember—and that this strategy is strongly related to schooling. As a child in a typical classroom, you were expected to memorize letters, numbers, multiplication tables, and a host of other basic facts. This type of formal schooling provides years of practice in memorization and in applying these skills in test situations. According to Wagner, memory has a "hardware" section that does not change across culture. It also contains a "software" part that develops particular strategies for remembering, which are learned.

M. & E. Bernheim/Woodfin Camp & Associates

Culture and memory. *In many societies, tribal leaders pass down vital information through stories related orally. Because of this rich oral tradition, children living in these cultures have better memories for information related through stories than do other children.*

www.wiley.com/college/huffman

In summary, research indicates that the "software" (or programming) part of memory is affected by culture. In cultures in which communication relies on oral tradition, people develop good strategies for remembering orally presented stories. In cultures in which formal schooling is the rule, people learn memory strategies that help them remember lists of items. From these studies, we can conclude that, across cultures, people tend to remember information that matters to them. They develop memory skills to match the demands of their environment.

Assessment

CHECK & REVIEW

Forgetting

Hermann Ebbinghaus was one of the first researchers to study forgetting extensively. His famous "curve of forgetting" shows that it occurs most rapidly immediately after learning. However, Ebbinghaus also showed that **relearning** usually takes less time than original learning.

The *decay theory* of forgetting simply states that memory, like all biological processes, deteriorates as time passes. The *interference theory* of forgetting suggests that memories are forgotten because of either retroactive or proactive interference. **Retroactive interference** occurs when new information interferes with previously learned information. **Proactive interference** occurs when old information interferes with newly learned information. The *motivated forgetting theory* states that people forget things that are painful, threatening, or embarrassing. According to *encoding failure theory*, some material is forgotten because it was never encoded from short-term memory

to long-term memory (LTM). *Retrieval failure theory* suggests information stored in LTM is not forgotten but may at times be inaccessible.

To prevent problems with forgetting, you should be aware of four important factors: the **serial position effect** (remembering material at the beginning and end of the list better than material in the middle); **source amnesia** (forgetting the true source of a memory); the **sleeper effect** (initially discounting information from an unreliable source but later judging it as reliable because the source is forgotten); and spacing of practice (in which **distributed practice** is found to be superior to **massed practice**).

Questions

1. Which theory of forgetting is being described in each of the following examples?
   a. You are very nervous about having to introduce all the people at a party, and you forget a good friend's name.
   b. You meet a friend you haven't seen for 25 years and you cannot remember his name.
   c. .You were kidnapped as a child and have forgotten many events surrounding the kidnapping.
2. When taking an exam, students often do better with items taken from the first and last of the chapter covered by the exam. This demonstrates _____. (a) the superiority of distributed practice; (b) source amnesia; (c) the state-dependent effect; (d) the serial position effect.
3. How would you study for a test using distributed practice? Using massed practice?
4. Briefly describe a personal example of source amnesia and the sleeper effect from your own life.

Check your answers in Appendix B.

CLICK & REVIEW
for additional assessment options:
www.wiley.com/college/huffman

BIOLOGICAL BASES OF MEMORY

Achievement

> How do we form memories, and where do we store them?

The previous sections have emphasized the theories and models of memory and forgetting. Now we focus on the biological aspects of memory. We first explore how memories are formed and where they are located in the brain. Then we examine memory problems related to biological factors.

■ How Are Memories Formed? The Biological Perspective

It is obvious that something physical must happen in the brain and nervous system when we learn something new. (How else could we later recall and use this information?)

Neuronal and Synaptic Changes in Memory

As you will recall from Chapters 2 and 6, learning modifies the brain's neural networks. As a response is learned, specific neural pathways are established that become progressively more excitable and responsive. When learning to play tennis, the repeated practice builds neural "pathways" that make it easier and easier for you to get the ball over the net. This prolonged strengthening of neural firing, called **long-term potentiation (LTP)**, happens in at least two ways:

Long-Term Potentiation (LTP)
Long-lasting increase in neural excitability, which may be a biological mechanism for learning and memory

1. ***Repeated stimulation of a synapse can strengthen the synapse by causing the dendrites to grow more spines*** (Barinaga, 1999). Repeated stimulation results in more synapses, more receptor sites, and more sensitivity. As seen in Chapter 6, such structural changes were first demonstrated when rats placed in enriched environments grew more sprouts on their dendrites compared to those of rats raised in deprived environments (Rosenzweig, Benet, & Diamond, 1972).

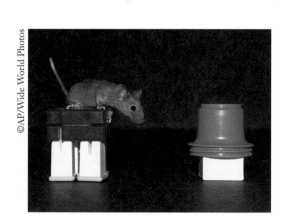

How does a sea slug learn and remember? The sea slug *Aplysia* can be classically conditioned to reflexively withdraw its gills when squirted with water. They learn to do this more quickly because they release more neurotransmitters at certain synapses. These neurotransmitters allow the circuit to communicate more efficiently. Similar structural changes in human synapses also occur after we learn and remember new information.

2. ***The ability of a particular neuron to release its neurotransmitters can be increased or decreased.*** This is shown from research with *Aplysia*. These sea slugs can be classically conditioned to reflexively withdraw their gills when squirted with water. After the conditioning occurs, the slugs release more neurotransmitters at certain synapses. And these synapses become more efficient at transmitting signals (see Chapter 6). Further evidence comes from researchers at Princeton University, who have created mice with an added gene that results in additional receptors for a neurotransmitter named NMDA (*N*-methyl-D-aspartate). These genetically mutated "smart mice" performed significantly better on memory tasks than did normal mice (Tang, Wang, Feng, Kyin, & Tsien, 2001; Tsien, 2000). Obviously, it is difficult to generalize from sea slugs and mice. However, research on long-term potentiation (LTP) in humans also has been widely supportive (Kikusui, Aoyagi, & Kaneko, 2000; Wixted, 2004).

Hormonal Changes and Memory

Hormones also have a significant effect on memory. When stressed or excited, we naturally produce "fight or flight" hormones that arouse the body, such as epinephrine and cortisol (see Chapter 3). These hormones in turn affect the amygdala (a subcortical limbic system structure involved in emotion). The amygdala then stimulates the hippocampus and cerebral cortex (other parts of the brain important for memory storage). Research on human and nonhuman laboratory animals has shown that direct injections of epinephrine or cortisol, or electrical stimulation of the amygdala, will increase the encoding and storage of new information (Akirav & Richter-Levin, 1999; Buchanan & Lovallo, 2001; McGaugh & Roozendaal, 2002). However, prolonged or extreme stress (and increased levels of cortisol) can interfere with memory (Al'absi, Hugdahl, & Lovallo, 2002; Heffelfinger & Newcomer, 2001; McAllister-Williams & Rugg, 2002).

Can you see why heightened (but not excessive) arousal might enhance memory? To survive, human or nonhuman animals must remember exactly how they got into a dangerous situation and how they got out of it. The naturally produced surge of hormones apparently alerts our brains to "pay attention and remember!"

Improving memory through genetic engineering. Scientists have created mice with an added gene that greatly improves their memory. These genetically altered mice were named "Doogie" after the boy genius on the television show Doogie Howser, M.D. This "Doogie" mouse stands on an object used in one of their standard learning and memory tests.

©AP/Wide World Photos

September 11, 2001. The terrorist attack on the World Trade Center is a flashbulb memory for most people in the United States.

The powerful effect of hormones on memory can be seen in what are known as *flashbulb memories*—vivid images of circumstances associated with surprising or strongly emotional events (Brown & Kulik, 1977; Edery-Halpern & Nachson, 2004). Do you remember the moment you learned about the September 11, 2001 terrorist attacks on the World Trade Center and the Pentagon? Is this memory so clear that it seems like a flashbulb went off, capturing every detail of the event in your memory? Assassinations (John Kennedy, Robert Kennedy, Martin Luther King Jr.), important personal events (graduation, illnesses, birth of a child), and, of course, horrific terrorist attacks have lasting effects on memory. We secrete fight-or-flight hormones when we initially hear of the event. We later replay these events in our minds again and again, which further strengthens our memories.

Despite their intensity, flashbulb memories are not as accurate as you might think (Squire, Schmolck, & Buffalo, 2001). For example, when asked how he heard the news of the September 11 attacks, George W. Bush, the president of the United States at the time, gave answers that contained numerous inconsistencies (Greenberg, 2004). Thus, not even flashbulb memories are immune to alteration. It also is important to note the problems with "hormonally induced memory." Have you ever become so anxious that you "blanked out" during an exam or while giving a speech? If so, you understand how extreme arousal and stress hormones can interfere with both the formation and retrieval of memories.

■ Where Are Memories Located? Tracking Down Memory Traces

So far, our discussion of the biological bases of memory has focused on the formation of memories as a result of neural changes or hormonal influences. But where is memory stored? What parts of the brain are involved?

One of the first scientists to explore these questions was Karl Lashley (1890–1958). Believing that memory was localized, or stored in a specific brain area, Lashley began with a standard learning maze experiment for rats. Once the maze was learned, he surgically removed tiny portions of the rats' brains. He then retested their memory of the maze. After three decades of frustrating research, Lashley found that rats were still able to run the maze regardless of the area of cortex he removed (Lashley, 1929, 1950). Lashley joked, "I sometimes feel in reviewing the evidence on localization of the memory trace, the necessary conclusion is that learning is not possible" (1950, p. 477).

Failing to locate a single brain site for memory, Lashley ultimately decided that memories were not localized. Instead, they were distributed throughout the cortex. Later research suggests that Lashley was both right and wrong. Memory tends to be localized not in a single area, but in many discrete locations throughout the brain—not just in the cortex.

Since Lashley's time, the brain structures involved in long-term memory (LTM) have been under investigation for many years. Today, research techniques are so advanced that we can experimentally induce and measure memory-related brain changes as they occur—on-the-spot reporting! For example, James Brewer and his colleagues (1998) used functional magnetic resonance imaging (fMRI) to locate areas of the brain responsible for encoding memories of pictures. They showed 96 pictures of indoor and outdoor scenes to participants while scanning their brains. And later tested them on their ability to recall those pictures. Brewer and his colleagues identified the right prefrontal cortex and the parahippocampal cortex as the most active regions of the brain during the encoding of the pictures. As you can see in Figure 7.12, these are only two of several brain regions involved in memory storage. These multiple storage areas may frustrate you as a student of psychology. However, keep in mind that this same complexity is what makes our human brains so wonderfully adaptive and responsive to our increasingly complex environment.

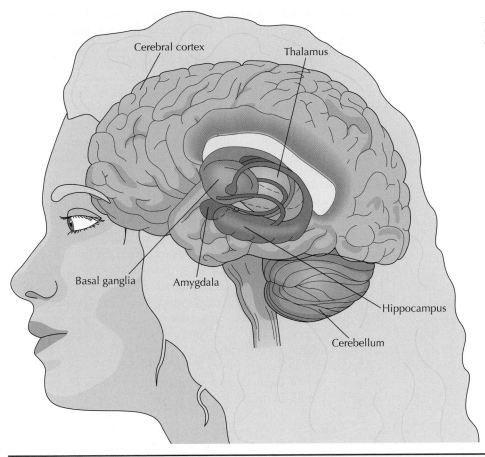

Figure 7.12 *Brain and memory formation.*
Damage to any one of these areas can affect
encoding, storage, and retrieval of memories.

Brain Area	Known or Suspected Relationship to Memory
Amygdala	Emotional memory (Blair et al., 2005; McGaugh & Roozendaal, 2002)
Basal Ganglia and Cerebellum	Creation and storage of the basic memory trace and implicit (nondeclarative) memories (such as skills, habits, and simple classical conditioned responses) (Christian & Thompson, 2005; Frank, 2005; Thompson, 2005)
Hippocampal Formation (Hippocampus and Surrounding Area)	Memory recognition; implicit, explicit, spatial, episodic memory; declarative long-term memory; sequences of events (Bachevalier & Varga-Khadem, 2005; Thompson, 2005)
Thalamus	Formation of new memories and spatial and working memory (Mendrek et al., 2005; Ridley et al., 2005; Sarnthein et al., 2005)
Cortex	Encoding of explicit (declarative) memories; storage of episodic and semantic memories; skill learning; priming; working memory (Pasternak & Greenlee, 2005; Reed et al., 2005; Thompson, 2005)

■ Biology and Memory Loss: Injury and Disease

What happens when people abruptly lose all memory of their past in cases of amnesia or slowly lose it with Alzheimer's? Imagine a total loss of memory. With no memories of the past and no way to make new memories, there would be no way to

www.wiley.com/college/huffman

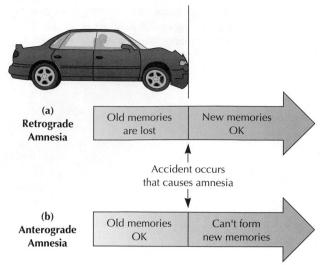

(a) Retrograde Amnesia

| Old memories are lost | New memories OK |

Accident occurs that causes amnesia

(b) Anterograde Amnesia

| Old memories OK | Can't form new memories |

Figure 7.13 *Two types of amnesia.* (a) In retrograde amnesia, the individual loses some or all of his or her memories before the brain injury. This type of amnesia is commonly portrayed in TV soap operas and movies, where the main characters lose almost all memory of their previous jobs, family members, and even their own name. (b) In anterograde amnesia, the individual cannot form new memories for events that occur after the brain injury.

Retrograde Amnesia *Loss of memory for events before a brain injury; backward-acting amnesia*

Anterograde Amnesia *Inability to form new memories after a brain injury; forward-acting amnesia*

use our previous skills or to learn new ones. We wouldn't know each other, nor would we know ourselves. In fact, our very survival would be in question.

Some memory problems are the result of injury and disease (organic pathology). When people are in serious accidents, suffer strokes, or encounter other events that cause trauma to the brain, memory loss or deterioration can occur. Disease also can alter the physiology of the brain and nervous system and thereby affect memory processes. This section focuses on two of the most common causes of biological memory failure: *brain injury* and *Alzheimer's disease.*

The Injured Brain

Have you ever wondered why parents and health professionals are so insistent about wearing helmets during most sports activities? *Traumatic brain injury* occurs when the skull has a sudden collision with another object. The compression, twisting, and distortion of the brain inside the skull all cause serious and sometimes permanent damage to the brain. The frontal and temporal lobes often take the heaviest hit because they directly impact against the bony ridges inside the skull. Traumatic brain injury is the leading cause of neurological disorders among Americans ages 15 to 25. These injuries most commonly result from car accidents, falls, blows, and gunshot wounds.

What happens to our memory when we have a serious head injury or trauma? Loss of memory as a result of brain injury or trauma is called *amnesia*, and there are two major types—*retrograde* and *anterograde* (Figure 7.13). In **retrograde amnesia** (acting backward in time), the person loses memory (is amnesic) for events that occurred *before* the brain injury. However, the same person has no trouble remembering things that happened after the injury. As the name implies, only the old, "retro" memories are lost.

What causes retrograde amnesia? In cases where the individual is only amnesic for the events right before the brain injury, the cause may be a failure of consolidation. We learned earlier that during long-term potentiation (LTP) our neurons change to accommodate new learning. We also learned that it takes a certain amount of time for these neural changes to become fixed and stable in long-term memory, a process known as *consolidation.* Returning to our earlier analogy of consolidation as being similar to wet cement, the brain injury "wipes away" unstable memories because the cement has not had time to harden (*retrograde amnesia*).

In addition to retrograde amnesia, some people lose memory for events that occur *after* a brain injury, which is called **anterograde amnesia** (acting forward in time). This type of amnesia generally results from a surgical injury or from diseases such as chronic alcoholism. Continuing our analogy with wet cement, anterograde amnesia would be like having permanently hardened cement. You can't lay down new long-term memories because the cement is hardened.

Are you confused about these two similar sounding forms of amnesia? Think back to the story of H.M. (the man introduced at the start of this chapter). H.M. suffers from both forms of amnesia. He has a mild memory loss for events in his life that happened the year or two *before* the operation (*retrograde amnesia*). Because his surgery destroyed the mechanism that transfers information from short-term memory to long-term memory, he also cannot form new lasting memories for events after the operation (*anterograde amnesia*) (Corkin, 2002). In most cases, retrograde amnesia is temporary and patients generally recover slowly over time. Unfortunately, anterograde amnesia is usually permanent. But patients also show surprising abilities to learn and remember implicit/nondeclarative tasks (such as procedural motor skills).

Alzheimer's Disease

Alzheimer's disease (AD) is a progressive mental deterioration that occurs most commonly in later life (Figure 7.14). The most noticeable early symptoms are disturbances in memory, beginning with typical incidents of forgetfulness that everyone experiences from time to time. With Alzheimer's, however, the forgetfulness progresses. In the final stages, the person fails to recognize loved ones, needs total nursing care, and ultimately dies.

Not all types of memory are affected equally. One of the major differences between normal memory loss and memory loss due to Alzheimer's is the extreme decrease in explicit declarative memory in Alzheimer's disease (Ballesteros & Manuel Reales, 2004; Mitchell et al., 2002). Alzheimer's patients fail to recall facts, information, and personal life experiences. However, they still retain some implicit/nondeclarative memories, such as simple classically conditioned responses and procedural tasks like tying their shoelaces.

What causes this disease? Autopsies of the brains of people with Alzheimer's disease (AD) show unusual *tangles* (structures formed from degenerating cell bodies) and *plaques* (structures formed from degenerating axons and dendrites). Hereditary Alzheimer's runs in families and generally strikes its victims between the ages of 45 and 55. Some experts believe the cause of Alzheimer's is primarily genetic. But others think genetic makeup may make some people more susceptible to environmental triggers (Bernhardt, Seidler, & Froelich, 2002; Khachaturian et al., 2004; Vickers et al., 2000).

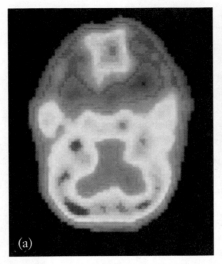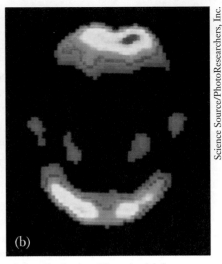

Figure 7.14 *The effect of Alzheimer's disease on the brain.* Note the high amount of red and yellow (signs of brain activity) in the positron emission tomography scans of the normal brain on the left. Compare this to the reduced activity in the brain of the Alzheimer's disease patient on the right. The loss is most significant in the temporal and parietal lobes. This is because these areas are particularly important for storing memories.

Alzheimer's [ALTS-high-merz] Disease *Progressive mental deterioration characterized by severe memory loss*

Science Source/PhotoResearchers, Inc.

Assessment

CHECK & REVIEW

Biological Bases of Memory

The biological perspective of memory focuses on changes in neurons (through **long-term potentiation**) and hormones, as well as on searching for the locations of memory in the brain. Memory tends to be localized and distributed throughout the brain—not just in the cortex.

Some memory problems are the result of injury and disease (organic pathology). Problems that result from serious brain injuries or trauma are called *amnesia*. In **retrograde amnesia**, memory for events that occurred before an accident is lost. In **anterograde amnesia**, memory for events that occur after an accident is lost. **Alzheimer's disease** is a progressive mental deterioration and severe memory loss occurring most commonly in later life.

Questions

1. Describe the two processes involved in LTP.
2. Your vivid memory of what you were doing when you learned about the attack on the World Trade Center is an example of _____. (a) the encoding specificity principle; (b) long-term potentiation; (c) latent learning; (d) a flashbulb memory
3. Forgetting that results from brain damage or trauma is called _____.
4. Ralph couldn't remember anything that happened to him before he fell through the floor of his tree house. His lack of memory for events before his fall is called _____ amnesia. (a) retroactive; (b) proactive; (c) anterograde; (d) retrograde

Check your answers in Appendix B.

 CLICK & REVIEW for additional assessment options: www.wiley.com/college/huffman

Memory and the Criminal Justice System

As you will discover throughout this text, our perception of the world is frequently biased and distorted. For example, we often "see what we want to see" (review *perceptual sets* in Chapter 4). We also keep on seeing what we want to see (known as *confirmation bias* and *functional fixedness* in Chapter 8, or *prejudice* in Chapter 16).

Our memories are subject to similar errors. When these errors involve the criminal justice system, they may lead to wrongful judgments of guilt or innocence and even life or death. Let's explore two of the most well-known problems—*eyewitness testimony* and *repressed memories*.

Eyewitness Testimony

Misremembering the name of your new friend or forgetting where you left your car keys may be relatively harmless memory problems. But what if police mistakenly arrest and convict an innocent man because of your erroneous eyewitness testimony (Figure 7.15)? You've heard that "seeing is believing." But can we really trust what we see—or *think we see*? In the past, one of the best forms of trial evidence a lawyer could have was an eyewitness. "I was there. I saw it with my own eyes." Unfortunately for lawyers, numerous research studies have identified several problems with eyewitness testimony (Lindsay et al., 2004; Loftus, 2000, 2001; Yarmey, 2004).

In one eyewitness study, participants were shown a film of a car driving through the countryside. Members of one group were asked to estimate how fast the car was going when it passed the barn. Participants in the other group, who saw the same film, were also asked to estimate the car's speed. But a barn was not mentioned! All participants were later asked if they saw a barn in the film. Six times as many in the group given the misinformation about the barn reported having seen

it, even though it never appeared in the film (Loftus, 1982).

It is impossible to determine how often eyewitnesses are mistaken in their recollections of events. However, experimental evidence indicates that the error rate might be disturbingly high. For example, in an experiment at the University of Nebraska, participants watched people committing a staged crime. About an hour later, they were asked to pick out suspects from mug shots and, a week later, from a lineup. None of the participants in the staged crime appeared in the mug shots or lineups. However, 20 percent of the eyewitnesses identified innocent people in the mug shots and 8 percent identified innocent people in the lineup (Brown, Deffenbacher, & Sturgill, 1977).

How could the research participants have been so mistaken? Several properties of memory could combine to create the type of mistaken identity that occurred at the lineup stage. First, we know that seeing a mug shot would lead to familiarity, which might lead to false recognition during the later lineup. Next, we know that memory is constructive. The participants might have constructed an inaccurate memory of the crime situation using memories instilled by the mug shots.

These problems are so well established and important that judges now allow expert testimony on the unreliability of eyewitness testimony. They also routinely instruct jurors on its limits (Durham & Dane, 1999; Ramirez, Zemba, & Geisel-

Corbis Images

Figure 7.15 *Dangers of eyewitness testimony.* Seven eyewitnesses identified the man in the far left photo (Father Pagano) as the "Gentleman Bandit" accused of several armed robberies. However, the man in the right photo (Robert Clouser) later confessed and was convicted of the crimes.

man, 1996). If you serve as a member of a jury or listen to accounts of crimes in the news, remind yourself of these problems. Also, keep in mind that research participants in eyewitness studies generally report their inaccurate memories with great self-assurance and strong conviction (Migueles & Garcia-Bajos, 1999). Eyewitnesses to actual crimes may similarly identify—with equally high confidence—an innocent person.

False Versus Repressed Memories

> Nothing fixes a thing so intensely in the memory as the wish to forget it.
>   MICHEL DE MONTAIGNE (1533–1592)

> Memory is the greatest of artists, and effaces from your mind what is unnecessary.
>   MAURICE BARING (1874–1945)

Which is true? Is it impossible to forget painful memories? Or can we erase what is unnecessary? The topic of false versus repressed memories is one of the hottest debates in memory research. Do you recall the opening story of Elizabeth, who sud-

Photo by Jean Greenwald. Courtesy Elizabeth Loftus

Elizabeth Loftus

denly remembered a childhood scene of finding her mother's drowned body? Elizabeth's recovery of these gruesome childhood memories, though painful, initially brought great relief. "I started putting everything into place. Maybe that's why I'm such a workaholic." It also seemed to explain why she had always been fascinated by the topic of memory and had spent so many years on its research.

After all this relief and resolution, however, her brother called to say there had been a mistake! The relative who told Elizabeth that she had been the one to discover her mother's body later remembered it had actually been Aunt Pearl, not Elizabeth Loftus. Other relatives also confirmed that it was Aunt Pearl. Like the eyewitnesses who erroneously recalled seeing a nonexistent barn, Loftus, an expert on memory distortions, had unknowingly created her own personal example of a *false memory*.

As we've seen throughout this chapter, our memories are frequently faulty, and researchers have demonstrated that it is relatively easy to create false memories (Dodd & MacLeod, 2004; Greenberg, 2004; Loftus, 1993, 1997, 2001).

So what about repressed memories? Can people recover true childhood memories? *Repression*, which was mentioned earlier as a part of motivated forgetting, is the supposed unconscious coping mechanism by which anxiety-provoking thoughts are prevented from reaching consciousness. Therefore, thoughts or memories that are extremely frightening to a person, such as memories of childhood sexual abuse, might be repressed. According to some research, these memories are *actively* and *consciously* "forgotten" in an effort to avoid the pain of their retrieval (Anderson et al., 2004). Others suggest that some memories are so painful they exist only in an *unconscious* corner of the brain, which reportedly makes them inaccessible to the individual (Bertram & Widener, 1999). In these cases, therapy would be necessary to unlock these hidden memories (Davies, 1996).

As you might imagine, this is a complex and controversial topic in psychology. No one doubts that some memories are forgotten and later recovered. When cued by a remark or experience, many people remember long-forgotten events—a childhood trip to Disneyland, the move from one house to another, or details surrounding a painful event. What is questioned is the concept of *repressed memories* of painful experiences (especially childhood sexual abuse) and their storage in the unconscious mind (Goodman et al., 2003; Kihlstrom, 2004; Loftus & Polage, 1999). Critics suggest that most people who have witnessed or experienced a violent crime, or are adult survivors of childhood sexual abuse, have intense, persistent memories. They have trouble *forgetting*, not remembering.

Some critics also wonder whether therapists retrieve actual memories or inadvertently create false memories for their clients during therapy. As you recall from Chapter 1, a scientist's *experimenter bias* may unintentionally influence participants' responses. Clinicians who sincerely believe a client might have been abused as a child may similarly unintentionally influence that client's recall of information. Furthermore, if the clinician mentions possible abuse, the client's own constructive processes may lead him or her to create a false memory.

Remember how Loftus used her relative's suggestion that she found her mother's body to create her own detailed false memory? As a critical thinker, can you see how clients might respond similarly to their therapist's suggestions? Even though the clinician only suggests the possibility of abuse, the client might think about movies and books portraying other people's experiences and then incorporate this information into his or her own memory. Unfortunately, they also tend to forget the original source *(source amnesia)*. Over time, the client might also forget these originally unreliable sources and see them as reliable (the *sleeper effect*).

Thus, the question "Are recovered memories true or false?" may be impossible to answer. As we've noted before, research clearly demonstrates that *all* memories are imperfectly *constructed* during encoding. They are also imperfectly *reconstructed* during retrieval. Attempting to label some memories as "true" and others as "false" may be misleading and oversimplifying.

The so-called repressed memory debate, however, has grown increasingly bitter. And research on both sides is hotly contested. This is not just an "academic debate." It has serious implications because civil lawsuits and criminal prosecutions are sometimes based on recovered memories of childhood sexual abuse. Families are also sometimes irreparably damaged by false accusations.

We will return to this hotly debated issue of repressed memories in Chapter 14. In the meantime, it is important to remember that child sexual abuse is a fact, not a disputed issue. We must be careful not to ridicule or condemn people who recover true memories of abuse. In the same spirit, we must protect the innocent from wrongful accusations that come from false memories. We look forward to a time when we can justly balance the interests of the victim with those of the accused.

(For more information about this continuing controversy, call or write the American Psychological Association in Washington, D.C. Ask for the pamphlet "Questions and Answers About Memories of Childhood Abuse." Also check the *Psychology in Action* website.)

Assessment

CHECK & REVIEW

Memory and the Criminal Justice System

Memories are not exact duplicates. We actively shape and *construct* information as it is encoded, stored, and retrieved. Two major memory problems have potentially serious effects on the legal system—eyewitness testimony and repressed memories. Eyewitness accounts are highly persuasive in the courtroom. But they're filled with potential errors. Psychologists continue to debate whether recovered memories are accurate recollections or

false memories. Concern about the reliability of eyewitness testimony and the possibility of false recovered memories has led many experts to encourage a cautious approach.

Questions

1. According to research, eyewitnesses generally report _____ confidence in the accuracy of their inaccurate memories. (a) very little; (b) little; (c) moderate; (d) high
2. _____ memories are related to anxiety-provoking thoughts or events that

are supposedly prevented from reaching consciousness. (a) Suppressed; (b) Flashback; (c) Motivated; (d) Repressed
3. Researchers have found that it is relatively _____ to create false memories.
4. Explain the difference between false memories and repressed memories.

Check your answers in Appendix B.

CLICK & REVIEW
for additional assessment options:
www.wiley.com/college/huffman

USING PSYCHOLOGY TO IMPROVE OUR MEMORY

Achievement

How can we improve our memory?

One of my first memories would date, if it were true, from my second year. I can still see, most clearly, the following scene, in which I believed until I was about fifteen. I was sitting in my pram, which my nurse was pushing in the Champs-Élysées, when a man tried to kidnap me. I was held in by the strap fastened round me while my nurse bravely tried to stand between the thief and me. She received various scratches, and I can still see vaguely those on her face. Then a crowd gathered, a policeman with a short cloak and a white baton came up, and the man took to his heels. I can still see the whole scene, and can even place it near the tube station. When I was about fifteen, my parents received a letter from my former nurse saying that she had been converted to the Salvation Army. She wanted to confess her past faults, and in particular to return the watch she had been given as a reward on this occasion. She had made up the whole story, faking the scratches. I, therefore, must have heard, as a child, the account of this story, which my parents believed, and projected it into the past in the form of a visual memory, which was a memory of a memory, but false. (Piaget, 1962, pp. 187–188)

This is the self-reported childhood memory of Jean Piaget, a brilliant and world-famous cognitive and developmental psychologist (Chapter 9). Why did Piaget create such a strange and elaborate memory for something that never happened?

Understanding Memory Distortions: The Need for Logic, Consistency, and Efficiency

Like Piaget, everyone tends to shape, rearrange, and distort their memories. One of the most common reasons is our need for logic and consistency. When we're initially forming new memories or sorting through old ones, we fill in missing pieces, make "corrections," and rearrange information to make it logical and consistent with our previous experiences.

In addition to our need for logic and consistency, we also shape and construct our memories because it is more efficient to do so. Think about a recent, important lec-

A Memory Test

Carefully read through all the words in the following list.

Bed	Awake	Tired	Dream	Wake	Snooze	Snore
Rest	Blanket	Doze	Slumber	Nap	Peace	Yawn
Drowsy	Nurse	Sick	Lawyer	Medicine	Health	Hospital
Dentist	Physician	Patient	Stethoscope	Curse	Clinic	Surgeon

Now cover the list and write down all the words you remember.

Number of correctly recalled words:
21 to 28 words = excellent memory
16 to 20 words = better than most
12 to 15 words = average
8 to 11 words = below average
7 or fewer = you might need a nap

How did you do? Do you have a good or excellent memory? Did you recall seeing the words *sleep* and *doctor*? Look back over the list. These words are not there. However, over 65 percent of students commonly report seeing these words. Can you explain why?

ture from your psychology instructor that you (hopefully) encoded for storage in LTM. You obviously did not record a word-for-word copy of the lecture. You summarized, augmented, and tied it in with related memories you have in LTM. Similarly, when you need to retrieve the stored lecture from your LTM, you recover only the general ideas or facts that were said.

After discussing all the problems and biases in our memories, it's important to emphasize that our memories are normally quite efficient and serve us well in most situations. Our memories have evolved to encode, store, and retrieve information vital to our survival. While working to secure our food and shelter, we constantly search and monitor our potentially dangerous environment. Even while sleeping, we process and store important memories. However, when faced with tasks like remembering precise details in a college text, the faces and names of potential clients, or where we left our house keys, our brains are simply not as well equipped.

Tips for Memory Improvement: Eight Surefire Ways to Improve Your Memory

The beauty of the human brain is that we can recognize the limits and problems of memory and then develop appropriate coping mechanisms. Our ancestors domesticated wild horses and cattle to overcome the physical limits of the human body. We can develop similar approaches to improve our memory for fine detail.

The field of psychology provides numerous helpful theories and concepts for improving memory. And everyone can improve his or her memory. The harder you work at it, the better your memory will become. In this section, I have summarized key points from the chapter that you can put into practice to improve your memory. (You might also recognize several points that were presented earlier in the "Tools for Student Success" in Chapter 1.)

www.wiley.com/college/huffman

- **Pay attention and reduce interference.** If you really want to remember something, you must pay attention to it. When you're in class, focus on the instructor and sit away from people who might distract you. When you study, choose a place with minimal interferences.

- **Use rehearsal techniques.** Remember that the duration of STM is about 30 seconds. To lengthen this time, use *maintenance rehearsal.* To effectively encode memory into LTM, use *elaborative* rehearsal, which involves thinking about the material and relating it to other information that has already been stored. Hopefully, you've noticed that I formally define each key term immediately in the text, in the margin, and in the glossary at the back of the book. I also give a brief explanation and one or two examples for each of these terms. While studying this text, use these tools to help your elaborative rehearsal. Also try making up your own examples. The more elaborate the encoding of information, the more memorable it will be.

- **Improve your organization.** This may be the most important key to a good memory. Although the capacity of STM is only around five to nine items, you can expand the capacity of STM by *chunking* (organizing) information into a few groups. To improve your LTM, create *hierarchies* that organize the material in meaningful patterns. The tables in this book and the "Visual Summaries" at the end of each chapter are examples of hierarchies that help you organize chapter material. Be sure to study them carefully—and make up your own whenever possible.

- **Counteract the serial position effect.** Because we tend to remember information that occurs at the beginning or end of a sequence, spend extra time with the information in the middle. When reading or reviewing the text, start at different places—sometimes at the second section, sometimes at the fourth.

- **Manage your time.** Study on a regular basis and avoid cramming. *Distributed* (spaced) learning sessions are more efficient than *massed* practice (cramming). In other words, five separate half-hour sessions tend to produce better encoding and storage than one session of 2½ hours. When you learn something new, take the time to associate it with what you already know. By doing this, you'll be organizing the new information so that you can easily retrieve it later on. Also, get plenty of sleep, for two reasons: (1) We don't remember information acquired when we're drowsy as well as that gained when we're alert, and (2) during REM sleep we process and store most of the new information we acquired when awake.

- **Use the encoding specificity principle.** When we form memories, we store them with links to the way we thought about them at the time. Therefore, the closer the retrieval cues are to the original encoding situation, the better the retrieval. Because you encode a lot of material during class time, avoid "early takes" or makeup exams, which are generally scheduled in other classrooms. The *context* will be different and your retrieval may suffer. Similarly, when you take a test, try to remain calm and reinstate the same psychological and physiological state that you were in when you originally learned the material. According to the *mood congruence* effect, you will recall more if the mood of your test taking matches the mood of the original learning. Also, according to the *state-dependent memory* research, if you normally drink a cup of coffee while studying, you might want to have a cup of coffee before your exam.

- **Employ self-monitoring and overlearning.** When studying a text, you should periodically stop and test your understanding of the material. This is why I included numerous "Check & Review" sections throughout each chapter. Stopping to read these reviews and completing the short quiz section will provide personal feedback on your mastery of the material. Even when you are studying a single sentence, you need to monitor your understanding. Poor readers tend to read at the same speed for both easy and difficult material. Good readers tend to recognize when they are having difficulty. They slow down or repeat difficult sentences.

When you finish reading a chapter, wait a few minutes and then do an additional monitoring of your understanding. If you evaluate your learning only while you're actively reading the material, you may overestimate your understanding (because the information is still in STM). However, if you delay making your judgment (for at least a few minutes), your evaluation will be more accurate (Weaver & Kelemen, 1997). The best way to ensure your full understanding of material (and success on an exam) is through *overlearning*—studying information even after you think you already know it. Don't just study until you *think* you know it. Work hard until you *know* you know it!

- *Use mnemonics.* **Mnemonic devices** (derived from the Greek word for "memory") are memory aids (or tricks) based on encoding items in a special way. Some memory experts use mnemonics to perform amazing feats of recall. And simple mnemonics can be helpful with shopping lists and some academic tasks. However, for many people spending too much time on mnemonics may be more trouble than it's worth. My students do better with the well-researched principles discussed in the chapter and reviewed above.

  Here are four of the most popular mnemonic techniques:

Mnemonic [nih-MON-ik] Device
Memory-improvement technique based on encoding items in a special way

1. The *method of loci* was developed by early Greek and Roman orators to keep track of the many parts of their long speeches. *Loci* is the Latin word for "physical places." Orators would imagine the parts of their speeches attached to places inside a building or, if they were outside, in a courtyard. For example, if an opening point in a speech was the concept of *justice*, they might visualize a courtroom placed in the first corner of their garden to remind them of this point. As they mentally walked around their garden during their speech, they would encounter each of the points to be made in their appropriate order.

2. To use the *peg-word* mnemonic, you first need to memorize a set of 10 visual images that you can use as pegs (or markers) on which to hang ideas. The easiest system of peg-words is to learn 10 items that rhyme with the numbers they stand for (e.g., *one in a bun, two in a shoe, three in a tree*, and so on). When you can mentally produce the peg-word image for each number, you are ready to use the images as pegs to hold the items of any list. Try it with items you might want to buy on your next trip to the grocery store: milk, eggs, bread, and razor blades. Visualize the first item (milk) with a bun, the second (eggs) with a shoe, and so on. Imagine a soggy bun in a bowl of milk. Imagine a giant shoe stepping on a carton of eggs, slices of bread hanging on a tree, and a giant razor blade as a door, complete with doorknob.

"YOU SIMPLY ASSOCIATE EACH NUMBER WITH A WORD, SUCH AS 'TABLE' AND 3,467,009."

Sidney Harris

3. The *substitute word* method is useful for when you are learning many new and complicated terms. To remember some of the terms associated with the brain, break the word to be remembered into parts or use words that sound similar that can be visualized. The word *occipital* can be converted into *ox, sip it, tall*. Then create a vivid image. (You might visualize an ox on stilts sipping something through a straw.) Try a similar strategy with *parietal* (*pear, eye, it all*).

4. The *method of word associations* is a mnemonic device that creates verbal associations for items to be learned. If you're taking a physics course and need to learn the colors of the spectrum, think of a man's name: *Roy G. Biv* (*R*ed, *O*range, *Y*ellow, *G*reen, *B*lue, *I*ndigo, *V*iolet). Or, to recall the names of the Great Lakes for a geography course, think of *HOMES on a great lake* (*H*uron, *O*ntario, *M*ichigan, *E*rie, *S*uperior).

A Final Note

As we have seen throughout this chapter, our memories are remarkable—yet highly fickle. Recognizing these limits will make us better jurors in the courtroom. It will also

PhotoEdit

Memory problems. Unfortunately, some memories persevere even when they cause tremendous pain and suffering.

make us better consumers of daily news reports when we assess accounts of "eyewitness testimony" and "repressed memories." Knowing the frailties of memory might similarly improve our skills as students, teachers, and friends.

Unfortunately, sometimes our memories are better than we would like. Traumatic and extremely emotional memories can persist even when we would very much like to forget. Though painful, these memories can sometimes provide important insights. As Elizabeth Loftus suggests in a recent letter to her deceased mother:

I thought then [as a 14-year-old] that eventually I would get over your death. I know today that I won't. But I've decided to accept that truth. What does it matter if I don't get over you? Who says I have to? David and Robert still tease me: "Don't say the M word or Beth will cry." So what if the word *mother* affects me this way? Who says I have to fix this? Besides, I'm too busy (Loftus, 2002, p. 70).

Application

CRITICAL THINKING

Memory and Metacognition

Metacognition is the ability to review and analyze your own mental processes—to "think about your thinking." It is also a vital part of critical thinking because it helps you objectively examine your thoughts and cognitive strategies and then to evaluate their appropriateness and accuracy. In the context of this chapter, you can use metacognition to examine and successfully employ the memory improvement tips we have just discussed.

Start by placing a "+" mark by those skills and strategies that you are currently using and a "–" by those that you avoid or that cause you problems. Now carefully review those items you've identified with a "–" mark. Why are you avoiding or not employing these particular skills? Are your reasons rational? Can you think of areas of your life where these skills might be useful? If so, go back and place a mark by those items you want to develop. Use these checkmarks as the starting point for your personal memory improvement plan.

ACTIVE LEARNING

_____ Pay attention and reduce interference.

_____ Use rehearsal techniques.

_____ Improve your organization.

_____ Counteract the serial position effect.

_____ Manage your time.

_____ Use the encoding specificity principle.

_____ Employ self-monitoring and overlearning.

_____ Use mnemonic devices.

Assessment

CHECK & REVIEW

Using Psychology to Improve Our Memory

This section offers eight concrete strategies for improving memory. These strategies include paying attention and reducing interference, using rehearsal techniques (both maintenance and elaborative rehearsal), improving your organization (by chunking and creating hierarchies), counteracting the serial position effect, managing your time, using the encoding specificity principle,

employing self-monitoring and overlearning, and **mnemonic devices.**

Questions

1. How can maintenance rehearsal and elaborative rehearsal improve your memory?
2. Explain how you can overcome the serial position effect while studying.
3. The best way to ensure your full understanding of material (and success on an exam) is through_____.

4. Which mnemonic device is being described in each of the following situations?
   a. You remember items to bring to a meeting by visualizing them in association with a previously learned sequence.
   b. You remember a speech for your communications class by forming visual images of the parts of your speech and associating them with areas in the classroom.

c. You remember errands you need to run by making up the rhyme "First go to the store, then get books galore. Get my ring and then some gas, and the cleaners at the last."

d. You remember a new acquaintance's name, Paul Barrington, by linking it to words that can be visualized: *pall-bearing town*.

Check your answers in Appendix B.

CLICK & REVIEW
for additional assessment options:
www.wiley.com/college/huffman

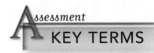

Assessment
KEY TERMS

*To assess your understanding of the **Key Terms** in Chapter 7, write a definition for each (in your own words), and then compare your definitions with those in the text.*

The Nature of Memory
chunking (p. 254)
constructive process (p. 249)
elaborative rehearsal (p. 259)
encoding (p. 249)
encoding specificity principle (p. 261)
episodic memory (p. 256)
explicit (declarative) memory (p. 256)
implicit (nondeclarative) memory (p. 257)
levels of processing (p. 251)
long-term memory (LTM) (p. 256)
maintenance rehearsal (p. 254)
memory (p. 249)
parallel distributed processing (251)
priming (p. 257)
recall (p. 260)

recognition (p. 260)
retrieval (p. 249)
retrieval cue (p. 260)
semantic memory (p. 256)
sensory memory (p. 253)
short-term memory (STM) (p. 253)
storage (p. 249)

Forgetting
consolidation (p. 264)
distributed practice (p. 266)
massed practice (p. 266)
proactive interference (p. 264)
relearning (p. 263)
retroactive interference (p. 263)
serial position effect (p. 266)
sleeper effect (p. 266)

source amnesia (p. 266)
tip-of-the-tongue (TOT) phenomenon (p. 265)

Biological Bases of Memory
Alzheimer's [ALTS-high-merz] disease (AD) (p. 273)
anterograde amnesia (p. 272)
long-term potentiation (LTP) (p. 269)
retrograde amnesia (p. 272)

Using Psychology to Improve Our Memory
mnemonic [nih-MON-ik] device (p. 279)

Achievement
WEB RESOURCES

Huffman Book Companion Site
http://www.wiley.com/college/huffman
This site is loaded with free Interactive Self-Tests, Internet Exercises, Glossary and Flashcards for key terms, web links, Handbook for Non-Native Speakers, and other activities designed to improve your mastery of the material in this chapter.

Would you like to test your memory?
http://www.exploratorium.edu/memory/index.html
Contains numerous articles, lectures, self-tests, online exhibits, and even a sheep brain dissection that help you explore and understand memory processes. The Exploratory Memory Exhibit is from the Exploratorium Science Museum in San Francisco, California.

Want to improve your memory?
http://www.mindtools.com/memory.html
A website created to enhance memory processes through knowledge and skills related to learning, memory, and processing.

Need further help with your memory?
http://www.premiumhealth.com/memory/
Provides a wealth of tutorials, activities, tips, and tricks to improve your overall memory skills.

Need help with your study habits?
http://www.mtsu.edu/~studskl/mem.html
Provides a list of memory and learning principles directly related to study skills; also offers explanations of what brain research has discovered about each of these principles. Be sure to check out the links to "organization" and "distributed practice."

Visual Summary

The Nature of Memory

Four Memory Models

- **Information Processing:** Memory is a *process* (**encoding**, **storage**, and **retrieval**) analogous to a computer.
- **Parallel Distributed Processing:** Memory is distributed across a network of neurons working simultaneously (in a *parallel* fashion).
- **Levels of Processing:** Memory depends on the depth of processing when material is initially encountered.
- **Traditional Three-Stage Memory:** Memory requires three different storage boxes or stages to hold and process information. **Sensory memory** holds information for exceedingly short intervals, **short-term memory** (**STM**) retains information for approximately 30 seconds or less (unless renewed), and **long-term memory** (**LTM**) provides relatively permanent storage.

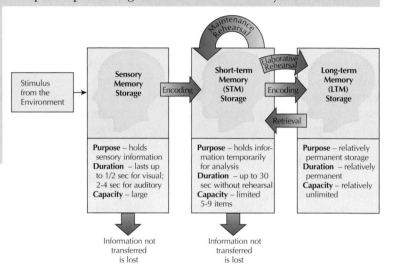

Forgetting

Why Do We Forget?

- *Decay*   Memory deteriorates over time.
- *Interference*   Memories forgotten due to **proactive interference** (old information interferes with new) or **retroactive interference** (new information interferes with old).
- *Motivated Forgetting*   Painful, threatening, or embarassing memories are forgotten.
- *Encoding Failure*   Material from STM to LTM was never successfully encoded.
- *Retrieval Failure* Information is not forgotten, just temporarily inaccessible.

Problems with Forgetting

- **Serial position effect:** Remembering material at the beginning and end of a list better than material in the middle.
- **Source amnesia:** Forgetting the true source of a memory.
- **Sleeper effect:** Delayed effectiveness of a message from an unreliable source.
- **Spacing of practice: Distributed practice** is better than **massed practice**.

Biological Bases of Memory

Formation and Location of Memory

The biological perspective of memory focuses on changes in neurons (through **long-term potentiation**) and hormones, as well as on searching for the location of memory in the brain. Memory tends to be localized and distributed throughout the brain—not just in the cortex.

Biology and Memory Loss

- *Brain injuries or trauma*: **Retrograde amnesia**, memory is lost for events that occured before the accident. **Anterograde amnesia** memory is lost for events that occur after an accident.
- *Disease*: **Alzheimer's disease** is a progressive mental deterioration and severe memory loss occurring most commonly in old age.

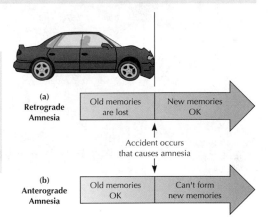

(a) Retrograde Amnesia | Old memories are lost | New memories OK

Accident occurs that causes amnesia

(b) Anterograde Amnesia | Old memories OK | Can't form new memories

Using Psychology to Improve Our Memory

Specific Tips and Mnemonics

- Pay attention and reduce interference.
- Use rehearsal techniques (maintenance for STM and elaborative for LTM).
- Improve organization (chunking for STM and hierarchies for LTM).
- Counteract the serial position effect.
- Use time management (distributed versus massed practice).
- Use the encoding specificity principle (including context, mood congruence, and state-dependent retrieval).
- Employ self-monitoring and overlearning.
- Use **mnemonic devices** (method of loci, peg-word, substitute word, and method of word associations).

8

THINKING, LANGUAGE, AND INTELLIGENCE

Achievement

Core Learning Outcomes

As you read Chapter 8, keep the following questions in mind and answer them in your own words:

▷ How do we think, solve problems, and be creative?

▷ What is language? How is language related to thinking? Do nonhuman animals use language?

▷ What is intelligence, and how do we measure it?

▷ Why is intelligence testing so controversial?

Achievement
Assessment
Application

Application

WHY STUDY PSYCHOLOGY?

National Archives/Taxi/GettyImages

Chapter 8 will explore interesting facts, such as . . .

▷ Thomas Edison patented over 1000 inventions, yet some believe he added little to scientific knowledge.

▷ Shortly after the 9/11 terrorist attack on the World Trade Center, surveys found most Americans believed they had a 20.5 percent chance of being hurt in a terrorist attack within the next year.

▷ Children all over the world go through similar stages in language development at about the same age, and their babbling is the same in all languages.

▷ Chimps and dolphins can use nonvocal language to make simple sentences and communicate with human trainers.

▷ Many cultures have no language equivalent for our notion of intelligence.

▷ Overall IQ scores have increased in the last 20 years in over 20 countries.

Martin Harvey/CorbisImages

Have you heard about Koko, the gorilla who reportedly speaks more than 1000 words in American Sign Language (ASL)? According to her teacher, Penny Patterson, Koko has used ASL to converse with others, talk to herself, rhyme, joke, and even lie (Linden, 1993; Patterson, 2002). Koko also uses signs to communicate her personal preferences, including a strong attraction to cats. Do you think Koko is using true language? Do you consider Koko intelligent?

What about the famous case of the "wild child" Genie? From the age of 20 months until authorities rescued her at the age of 13, Genie lived in a tiny, windowless room in solitary confinement. By day, she sat naked and tied to a chair with nothing to do and no one to talk to. At night, she was put in a kind of straitjacket and caged in a covered crib. Genie's abusive father forbade anyone to speak to her for the entire 13 years and refused to have a radio or TV in the home. If Genie made any noise, her father would beat her, while he barked and growled like a dog. After she was discovered at age 13, linguists and psychologists worked with her intensively for many years. Sadly, Genie never progressed much beyond sentences like "Genie go" (Curtiss, 1977; La Pointe, 2005; Rymer, 1993). With her limited language skills, would you say Genie is intelligent?

What about Thomas Edison, the famous inventor of the light bulb? Despite having attended school for only three months and suffering progressive deafness throughout his life, Edison patented over 1000 inventions—more than any other single individual in history. He has been called the "greatest inventor in American history" (Israel, 1998). Yet others have labeled him a "technologist rather than a scientist, adding little to original scientific knowledge" (Baldwin, 2001). Would you consider Thomas Edison intelligent?

Being the "greatest inventor in American history" obviously requires a large repertoire of thinking processes and intellectual agility. But Genie's survival and Koko's use of sign language also require some form of intelligence. To be intelligent, you must be able to think and to learn. To express this thinking and intelligence, you need language. The three topics of this chapter—"Thinking", "Language", and

"Intelligence"—are often studied together under the larger umbrella of **cognition**, *the mental activities of acquiring, storing, retrieving, and using knowledge.* In a real sense, we discuss cognition throughout the text (e.g., chapters on sensation and perception, consciousness, learning, and memory). Psychology is "the scientific study of behavior and *mental processes.*"

Cognition *Mental activities involved in acquiring, storing, retrieving, and using knowledge*

THINKING

What is *thinking*? Every time you use information and mentally act on it by forming ideas, reasoning, solving problems, drawing conclusions, expressing thoughts, or comprehending the thoughts of others, you are thinking. We begin this section by exploring how our brains perform this basic (but seemingly magical) act. Next, we examine the building blocks of thoughts—*images* and *concepts*. Then, we discuss the mental processes involved in *problem solving* and *creativity.*

Achievement

What is thinking, and what are its building blocks? How do we solve problems, and what is creativity?

■ Cognitive Building Blocks: The Foundation of Thought

Do you remember the story of Phineas Gage from Chapter 2? He was the railroad supervisor who had difficulty controlling his thoughts and emotions after his frontal lobes were accidentally pierced by an iron rod. Thought processes are distributed throughout the brain in networks of neurons. However, as Gage's case shows, the frontal lobes are primarily responsible for higher functions like the ability to plan ahead or to synthesize and evaluate information.

The frontal lobes also link to other important areas of the brain, such as the limbic system (Heyder, Suchan, & Daum, 2004; Saab & Willis, 2003). Because the limbic system is largely responsible for generating emotions, Gage and people with comparable injuries have difficulty controlling their emotions and making connections between their feelings and thoughts (Damasio, 1999). Similar problems occur with heavy drinking. Have you wondered why drinkers are more apt to get into fights or to drink and drive despite repeated warning and serious dangers? Alcohol disrupts communication between the thinking and decision making capability of the frontal lobes and the primitive emotions of the limbic system.

Now that we know the definition and general location of thinking, we need to study its three basic components—*mental images, concepts,* and *language.* When you're thinking about your sweetheart, you have a mental *image* of him or her in your mind. You think of him or her in terms of *concepts* or categories, such as woman, man, strong, happy. And you may have in mind *linguistic* statements such as "I wish I could be with him or her right now instead of reading this text."

In this section, we will consider the role of images and concepts in thinking. Language is discussed later in the chapter.

Study Tip

Are your studies disrupted by images, thoughts, or linguistic statements related to your dating partner, feelings of hunger, or other distractions? Remember the Premack principle from Chapter 6—using any naturally occurring, high-frequency response to reinforce low-frequency response. In this case, don't call your sweetheart or get a snack until you've finished studying a preassigned section of your text.

Mental Images

Imagine yourself on a warm, sandy ocean beach. Do you see tall palms swaying in the wind? Can you smell the salty ocean water and hear the laughter of the children playing in the surf? What you've just created in your mind's eye is a **mental image**, a mental representation of a previously stored sensory experience, that may include visual, auditory, olfactory, tactile, motor, and gustatory imagery (McKellar, 1972).

Where are mental images located in the brain? According to research, we all have a mental space, similar to the screen of a computer monitor, where we mentally visualize and manipulate our sensory images (Brewer & Pani, 1996; Hamm, Johnson, & Corballis, 2004). Some of our most creative moments come when we are forming mental images and manipulating them. Albert Einstein said that his first insight into relativity theory occurred when he pictured a beam of light and imagined himself chasing after it at its own speed.

Mental Image *Mental representation of a previously stored sensory experience, including visual, auditory, olfactory, tactile, motor, or gustatory imagery (e.g., visualizing a train and hearing its horn)*

www.wiley.com/college/huffman

Mental imagery. *Can you imagine what this runner is visualizing in her "mind's eye"? Constant use of mental imagery is critical to her success.*

Alan Thornton/Stone/GettyImages

Concepts

Concept *Mental representation of a group or category that shares similar characteristics (e.g., the concept of a river groups together the Nile, the Amazon, and the Mississippi because they share the common characteristic of being a large stream of water that empties into an ocean or lake)*

In addition to mental images, our thinking involves **concepts**—mental representations of a group or category. We form concepts by grouping together objects, events, activities, or ideas that share similar characteristics (Smith, 1995). Our mental concept of *car* represents a large group of objects that share similar characteristics (vehicles with four wheels, seating space for at least one person, and a generally predictable shape). We also form concepts for abstract ideas, such as *honesty, intelligence,* or *pornography.* These abstract ideas, however, are often our own individual constructions. They may or may not be shared by others. Therefore, it is generally harder to communicate about honesty than about a car.

Concepts are an essential part of thinking and communication because they simplify and organize information. Imagine being Genie, the "wild child" described at the beginning of the chapter. If you had been confined to a small, windowless room your entire life, how would you process the world around you without the use of concepts? Normally, when you see a new object or encounter a new situation, you relate it to your existing conceptual structure and categorize it according to where it fits. If you see a rectangular box with moving pictures and sound, and people are staring at it, you safely assume it is a TV set. Although you have never encountered this specific brand before, you understand the concept of a *TV set.* But if you were

---

TRY THIS YOURSELF

Application

Manipulating Mental Images

Look at the four geometrical patterns to the right. Can you see why the two forms in (a) are the same but the two forms in (b) are different? Solving this problem requires mental manipulation of the patterns. (Those of you who are familiar with the computer game Tetris might find this puzzle rather simple. Others might want to turn to Appendix B for an explanation of the answer.)

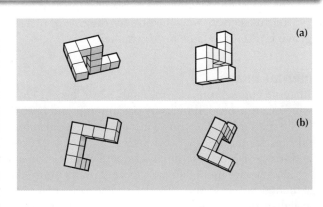

Genie, how would you identify a TV set, a telephone, or even a bathroom, having never seen them and compared them to other TVs, telephones, and rooms?

How do we learn concepts? They develop through the creation and use of three major strategies: *artificial concepts, natural concepts/prototypes,* and *hierarchies:*

1. *Artificial concepts.* We create some of our concepts from logical rules or definitions. Consider the definition of *triangle:* "a geometric figure with three sides and three angles." Using this definition, we group together and classify all three-sided geometric forms as triangles. If any of the defining features were missing, we would not include the object in the *concept* of triangle. Concepts like *triangle* are called *artificial* (or *formal*) because the rules for inclusion are sharply defined. As you have seen in this and other college texts, artificial concepts are often a core part of the sciences and other academic disciplines.

2. *Natural concepts/prototypes.* In everyday life, we seldom use precise, artificial definitions. When we see birds in the sky, we do not think "warm-blooded animals that fly, have wings, and lay eggs"—an *artificial concept.* Instead, we use *natural concepts,* called **prototypes.** Prototypes are based on a personal "best example" or a typical representative of that concept (Rosch, 1973). When we see flying animals, we can quickly identify them as birds by using our previous prototype or natural concept for a bird. Most of us have a model bird, or prototype—such as a robin or a sparrow—that captures for us the essence of "birdness."

Is this your prototype for a sport? *Most Americans readily recognize baseball as a prototype for sports. However, if you were from Bermuda, where most people watch or play cricket, you would have a different sports prototype.*

Prototypes provide an efficient mental shortcut. But what happens when we encounter a new item, like *penguin,* where we cannot use our prototype robin? In this case, we tend to use our more time consuming artificial concept (the definition of *bird*). Because the penguin does not fly (although it does lay eggs and is warm-blooded), it takes longer to classify. It is easier to classify a robin because our prototype robin is a "birdier bird" than a penguin.

3. *Hierarchies.* Some of our concepts also develop when we create *hierarchies,* in which specific concepts are grouped as subcategories within broader concepts. Note in the hierarchy depicted in Figure 8.1a how the top (superordinate) category of *animals* is very broad and includes lots of members. The midlevel categories of *bird* and *dog* are more specific but still rather general. And the lowest (subordinate) categories of *parakeet* and *poodle* are the most specific.

Interestingly, research shows that when we first learn something, we use the middle categories, which are called *basic-level* concepts (Rosch, 1978). For example, children tend to learn *bird* or *dog* before they learn higher, superordinate concepts like *animals* or lower, subordinate concepts like *parakeet* and *poodle.* Even as adults, when shown a picture of a parakeet, we first classify it as a bird before thinking of the higher concept of *animal* or the lower concept of *parakeet.*

Prototype *A representation of the "best" or most typical example of a category (e.g., baseball is a prototype of the concept of sports)*

 Study Tip

Recall from Chapter 7 that organization and hierarchies are essential to efficient encoding and storage in long-term memory (LTM). Imagine not having a mental hierarchy for animal, bird, and parakeet. How would you describe their respective similarities and differences? You experience the same problem when you try to memorize all the key terms in this book in preparation for exams. It is much easier to learn and remember a large number of items when they are organized into a hierarchy. This is why I have included so many tables and figures throughout this text and created "Visual Summaries" at the end of each chapter. Built-in hierarchies like these will help you master the material. However, it is even better if you develop your own.

www.wiley.com/college/huffman

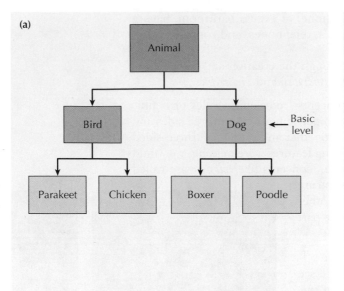

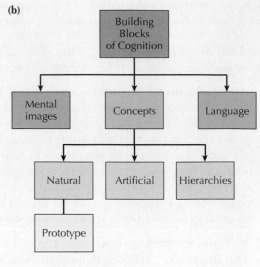

Figure 8.1 *Can hierarchies improve both thinking and exam scores?* (a) When we think, we naturally organize concepts according to superordinate and subordinate classes. We organize concepts, like *animals* or *birds*, with the most general concept at the top and the most specific at the bottom. Research also shows that we use the middle, basic level when we are initially categorizing objects, later adding the upper and lower levels. Although they may look complicated, hierarchies significantly reduce the time and effort necessary for learning. For example, when you learn that all animals have mitochondria in their cells, you don't have to relearn that fact each time you learn a new animal species. (b) Hierarchies can be generated from almost any set of interrelated facts and can be used to provide a similar savings in time and effort. For example, instead of focusing on and attempting to memorize the key terms *concept*, *mental image*, and *prototype*, you should begin by making a hierarchy of how these terms are interrelated. Once you have this "big picture," it speeds up your mastery of the material, which translates into better exam scores.

Assessment

CHECK & REVIEW

Cognitive Building Blocks

Cognition, or thinking, is defined as mental activities involved in acquiring, storing, retrieving, and using knowledge. Thought processes are distributed throughout the brain in neural networks. However, during problem solving and decision making, our thoughts are localized within the frontal lobes.

The frontal lobes link to other areas of the brain. One of their most important connections is with the emotional centers of the limbic system. Without connecting thoughts to feelings, solving problems and making decisions would be difficult.

The three basic building blocks of cognition are mental images, concepts, and language. **Mental images** are mental representations of a sensory experience, including visual, auditory, olfactory, tactile, motor, and gustatory imagery. **Concepts** are mental categories that group objects, events, activities, or ideas that share similar characteristics. (Language is discussed in a later section.)

We learn concepts in three ways: (1) Artificial concepts are formed by logical, specific rules or characteristics. (2) Natural concepts are formed by experience in everyday life. When we are confronted with a new item, we compare it with a **prototype** (most typical example) of a concept. (3) Concepts are generally organized into hierarchies. We most frequently use the middle, basic-level concepts when first learning material.

Questions

1. All of the following are examples of concepts except _____. (a) trees; (b) tools; (c) blue; (d) umbrellas
2. How do we learn concepts?
3. When asked to describe the shape and color of an apple, you probably rely on a _____.
4. For most psychologists, consciousness is a(n) _____ concept, whereas for the layman it is a(n) _____ concept. (a) automatic, health; (b) artificial, natural; (c) mental image, natural; (d) superordinate, basic-level

Check your answers in Appendix B.

CLICK & REVIEW
for additional assessment options:
www.wiley.com/college/huffman

Problem Solving: Three Steps to the Goal

Several years ago in Los Angeles, a 12-foot-high tractor-trailer rig tried to pass under a bridge 11 feet 6 inches high. As you might expect, the truck got stuck, unable to move forward or back, thus causing a huge traffic jam. After hours of towing, tugging, and pushing, the police and transportation workers were stumped. About this time, a young boy happened upon the scene and asked, "Why don't you let some air out of the tires?" It was a simple, creative suggestion—and it worked.

Our everyday lives are filled with problems, some easier to solve than others. For example, figuring out a way to make coffee without a filter is much easier than rescuing 118 Russian Navy seamen trapped inside a submarine at the bottom of the Barents Sea. In all cases, however, problem solving requires moving from a *given state* (the problem) to a *goal state* (the solution), a process that usually involves three steps (Bourne, Dominowski, & Loftus, 1979).

Step 1: Preparation

To help you appreciate the three steps for problem solving, let's look at a common problem. Are you, or is someone you know, looking for a long-term love relationship? There are at least three separate components to successful preparation:

- ***Identifying given facts.*** To find lasting love, it is important to identify your most basic, *nonnegotiable* limits and desires. For example, do you want children? Are you willing to move to another city to find love or to be with someone you love? Does your partner have to share your religion?

- ***Separating relevant from irrelevant facts.*** What are your *negotiable* items? What do you consider irrelevant and easily compromised? Would you consider a relationship with someone who is 10 years older than you? What about 10 years younger? Do you want someone who is college educated, or is that negotiable?

- ***Defining the ultimate goal.*** This part of the preparation stage may seem easy, but think again. Are you interested in a long-term relationship with the ultimate goal of marriage and children? If so, dating someone who wants to travel his or her entire life and never have children is probably not a safe bet. Similarly, if your major enjoyments are camping and outdoor sports, you may not want to date a big-city museum lover.

Step 2: Production

During the *production step*, the problem solver produces possible solutions, called *hypotheses*. Two major approaches to generating hypotheses are *algorithms* and *heuristics*:

- An **algorithm** is a step-by-step procedure that, if followed correctly, will always produce the solution. Math problems are ideal for demonstrating algorithms. An algorithm for solving the problem 10×2 is $2 + 2 + 2 + 2 + 2 + 2 + 2 + 2 + 2 + 2$. Algorithms will eventually lead to the correct answer. But they may take a long time—especially for complex problems.

  Few people really enjoy the stresses and uncertainty of years of dating. Therefore, you are unlikely to use algorithms in your search for lasting love. But they are very useful if you want to balance your checkbook or compute your grade point average. Computers are especially well suited for algorithms because they can quickly perform millions of calculations and logical operations in a systematic search for a solution to a problem.

- A **heuristic** is a simple rule or strategy for problem solving that provides shortcuts but does not guarantee a solution. It works most of the time, but not always. If you consult friends or family members regarding your dating problems, they may offer

Successful problem solving? *Why hasn't this motorized scooter become a popular way to travel?*

Looking for love in all the wrong places. *Are singles' bars a good place to find lasting love? Why or why not?*

Algorithm *A set of steps that, if followed correctly, will eventually solve the problem*

Heuristics *Strategies, or simple rules, used in problem solving and decision making that do not guarantee a solution but offer a likely shortcut to it*

SUMMARY TABLE 8.1 PROBLEM-SOLVING HEURISTICS

Problem-solving Heuristics	Description	Example
Working backward	An approach that starts with the solution, a known condition, and works backward through the problem. Once the search has revealed the steps to be taken, the problem is solved.	Deciding you want to be an experimental psychologist, you ask your psychology professor and career counselor to recommend courses, graduate and undergraduate colleges and universities, areas to emphasize, and so on. Then you write to the recommended colleges or universities requesting information on their admission policies and standards. You then plan your current college courses accordingly and work hard to meet (or exceed) the admission standards.
Means–end analysis	The problem solver determines what measure would reduce the difference between the given state and the goal. Once the means to reach the goal are determined, the problem is solved.	Knowing that you need good grades to get into a good graduate school for experimental psychology, you want an A in your psychology course. You ask your professor for suggestions, interview several A students to compare and contrast their study habits, assess your own study habits, and then determine the specific means (the number of hours and which study techniques) required to meet your end goal of an A.
Creating subgoals	Large, complex problems are broken down into a series of small subgoals. These subgoals then serve as a series of stepping-stones that can be taken one at a time to reach the original large goal.	Getting a good grade or even passing many college courses requires writing a successful term paper. To do this, you choose a topic, go to the library and Internet to locate information related to the topic, organize the information, write an outline, write the paper, review the paper, rewrite, rewrite again, and submit the final paper on or before the due date.

advice (or *heuristics*) such as, "Do what you naturally love to do [dancing, skiing, movies], and you'll find someone with similar interests." In addition to this possible "dating heuristic," Table 8.1 demonstrates how heuristics can be usefully applied to college courses and career plans.

TRY THIS YOURSELF

Application

Are you a good problem solver?

If you want a more hands-on experience with problem solving, try this classic thinking problem (Bartlett, 1958). Your task is to determine the numerals 0 through 9 that are represented by letters, with each letter representing a separate, distinct number. You get one hint before you start: *D* = 5.

```
   D O N A L D
 + G E R A L D
 ─────────────
   R O B E R T
```

Given there are 362,880 possible combinations of letters and numbers, algorithms obviously won't work. At the rate of 1 combination per minute, 8 hours per day, 5 days a week, 52 weeks a year, it would take nearly 3 years to try all the possible combinations.

If you successfully solved the problem, you probably used the "creating subgoals" heuristic in Table 8.1. You employed previous knowledge of arithmetic to set subgoals, such as determining what number *T* represents (if *D* = 5, then *D* + *D* = 10, so *T* = 0, with a carryover of 1 into the tens column). The complete answer is at the end of the next "Check & Review."

Several heuristics can be particularly helpful in college, including (1) working backward, (2) means–end analysis, and (3) creating subgoals (see Table 8.1). Successful college students seem to be particularly good at breaking down a solution into subgoals. When you are faced with a heavy schedule of exams and term papers, try creating subgoals to make the immediate problems more manageable and increase the likelihood of reaching your final goal—a college degree.

Step 3: Evaluation

Once the hypotheses (possible solutions) are generated, they must be evaluated to see if they meet the criteria defined in step 1. If one or more of the hypotheses meet the criteria, the problem is solved—you know what you want in a partner and the best place to find him or her. If not, then you must return to the production stage and produce alternate solutions. Keep in mind, however, that "action must follow solution." Once the little boy solved the "stuck-truck" problem, someone had to follow through and actually let some air out of the tires. Similarly, once you identify your path to the goal, you must follow through and implement the necessary solution.

Application
APPLYING PSYCHOLOGY TO EVERYDAY LIFE

Recognizing Barriers to Problem Solving

Do you find that you can solve some problems easily but seem to have a mental block when it comes to others? You are not alone. Everyone frequently encounters barriers that prevent effective problem solving. The most common barriers are: *mental sets, functional fixedness, confirmation bias, the availability heuristic,* and the *representativeness heuristic:*

1. ***Mental sets.*** Like the police and transportation workers who were trying to pull or shove the truck that was stuck under the bridge, have you ever persisted in attacking problems using solutions the same as, or similar to, ones that have worked in the past? This is known as a **mental set.** Although pulling or shoving may occasionally work, in this instance the old solution created a mental barrier to new, and possibly more effective, solutions (such as deflating the tires). The habit (or *mental set*) of working arithmetic problems from the right (ones) column to the left also explains why most people fail to see the solution to the DONALD + GERALD problem. In the same way, looking for love only by going to singles' bars can be a barrier to good dating. To practice overcoming mental sets, try the nine-dot problem in Figure 8.2 and check your answer with the solution shown in Figure 8.3.

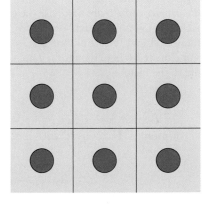

2. ***Functional fixedness.*** The tendency to view objects as functioning only in the usual or customary way is known as **functional fixedness.** Suppose you wanted to make coffee in your automatic coffeemaker but were out of filters. Would you dig through the trash looking for an old, dirty filter without thinking of using a paper towel? What if you were given the objects shown in Figure 8.4 and asked to mount the candle on the wall so that it could be easily lit in the normal fashion, with no

Problem solving in action. *Graduating from college requires many skills, including the successful use of several problem solving heuristics.*

Mental sets also block some college students from using the SQ4R (Survey, Question, Read, Recite, Review, and wRite) method or other study techniques described in the "Tools for Student Success" at the end of Chapter 1. Their reliance on past study habits blocks them from considering newer and more efficient strategies. If we try to be flexible in our thinking, we can offset the natural tendency toward mental sets.

Figure 8.2 ***The nine-dot problem.*** Draw no more than four lines that run through all nine dots on this page without lifting your pencil from the paper. (See Figure 8.3, page 294, for the solution.)

Mental Set *Persisting in using problem-solving strategies that have worked in the past rather than trying new ones*

Functional Fixedness *Tendency to think of an object functioning only in its usual or customary way*

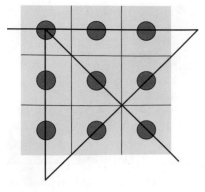

Figure 8.3 *Solution to the nine-dot problem.* People find this puzzle difficult because they see the arrangement of dots as a square. This mental set limits possible solutions because they "naturally" assume they can't go out of the boundaries of the square.

Figure 8.4 *Overcoming functional fixedness.* Can you use these supplies to mount the candle on a wall so that it can be lit in a normal way—without toppling over?

Confirmation Bias *Preferring information that confirms preexisting positions or beliefs, while ignoring or discounting contradictory evidence*

Figure 8.5 *One solution to the candle problem in Figure 8.4.* Use the tacks to mount the matchbox tray to the wall. Light the candle and use some melted wax to mount the candle to the matchbox.

danger of toppling (Duncker, 1945)? How would you do this? Think about it before you read on.

The solution is to empty the box, use the tacks to attach it to the wall, light the candle, drop some melted wax on the box, and then set the candle in the dripped wax (Figure 8.5). In the research test of this problem, participants had a much more difficult time solving the problem when the box was filled with matches than when it was presented with the matches separate. In the former situation, the participants saw the box only as a container for matches and overlooked it as a useful item in itself. When a child uses sofa cushions to build a fort, or you use a table knife instead of a screwdriver to tighten a screw, you both have successfully avoided functional fixedness. Similarly, the individual who discovered a way to retrofit diesel engines to allow them to use discarded restaurant oil as fuel has overcome functional fixedness—and may become a very rich man! (Unfortunately, I cannot find an example of functional fixedness and love relationships. If you have a suggestion, please e-mail me <khuffman@palomar.edu>.)

3. ***Confirmation bias.*** We frequently complain about politicians who readily accept opinion polls that support their political views—and ignore those that conflict. But have you recognized the same bias in your own thinking? Do you pay greater attention to common sayings that support your personal biases (e.g., "opposites attract") and overlook contradictory findings (e.g., "similarity is the best predictor of long-term relationships")? This preference for information that confirms our preexisting positions or beliefs, while ignoring or discounting contradictory evidence, is known as the **confirmation bias** (Nickerson, 1998; Reich, 2004).

British researcher Peter Wason (1968) was the first to demonstrate this phenomenon. He started with a question, like this:

Can you guess the rule?	2	4	6

In addition to finding a rule for this set of three numbers, Wason's participants were also asked to generate additional sets of numbers that conformed to their hypothesized rule. Respondents offered sets such as 4, 6, 8, or 1, 3, 5. These sets reflected their commonly shared (but unspoken) guess that the rule was "numbers increasing by 2." (Is this the same rule you generated?)

Each time the participants presented their list of numbers, Wason assured them their set of numbers conformed to the rule. However, when Wason later informed them that the rule "numbers increasing by 2" was incorrect, they were very frustrated. The actual rule was "numbers in increasing order of magnitude."

(Did you guess the correct rule?) The barrier to solving this problem was that participants searched only for confirming information and failed to look for evidence that would disprove their hypothesis. If they had proposed a series such as 1, 3, 4 instead, they would have discovered that their initial hypothesis was incorrect and they could have easily discovered the correct rule.

4. **Availability heuristic.** Earlier in the chapter we talked about heuristics as simple rules used in problem solving and decision making that do not guarantee a solution but offer a likely shortcut to it. Cognitive psychologists Amos Tversky and Daniel Kahneman have found that these heuristics often provide handy mental shortcuts to problem solving. But they also may lead us to ignore other relevant information (Kahneman, 2003; Tversky & Kahneman, 1974, 1993).

The **availability heuristic** helps explain why even the smartest people often make foolish decisions. They judge the likelihood or probability of an event based on how easily recalled, or readily *available*, other instances of the event are in their memories. If previous instances are easily recalled, we assume they are common and typical, and therefore more likely to occur again in the future (McKelvie & Drumheller, 2001; Oppenheimer, 2004).

Ease of recall often *is* correlated with actual data—but not always. For example, a national study conducted shortly after the horrific attacks on the World Trade Center on 9/11 found that average Americans believed they had a 20.5 percent chance of being hurt in a terrorist attack within the next year (Lerner, Gonzalez, Small, & Fischoff, 2003). Can you see how the vivid media coverage of the attacks created this—thankfully—erroneous availability heuristic and unreasonably high perception of risk? Similarly, casinos use loud bells and bright flashing lights to attract attention when someone wins a slot machine jackpot. Although casino owners may not be familiar with Tversky and Kahneman's research on the availability heuristic, their business experience has taught them that calling attention to winners creates a vivid impression. This, in turn, causes nearby gamblers to overestimate the likelihood of winning (and to increase their own gambling).

5. **Representativeness heuristic.** Tversky and Kahneman identified a second type of heuristic that sometimes leads to erroneous decisions and ineffective problem solving. When using the **representativeness heuristic**, we estimate the probability of something based on how well the event, person, or object matches (or *represents*) our previous prototype. (*Remember:* A prototype is your most common or representative example.) For instance, if you were looking through questionnaires and noted that John is 6 feet 5 inches tall with very sloppy handwriting, would you guess that he's a bank president or an NBA basketball player? Because this description matches (or represents) most people's prototype of a basketball player (Beyth-Marom, Shlomith, Gombo, & Shaked, 1985), you might overestimate the probability that this is, in fact, John's occupation. Statistically, this is not a wise guess. Although the representative heuristic is often adaptive and beneficial, in this case it ignores *base-rate information*—the probability of a characteristic occurring in the general population. In the United States, bank presidents outnumber NBA players by about 50 to 1. Therefore, it is much more likely that John is a bank president.

Availability Heuristic *Judging the likelihood or probability of an event based on how readily available other instances of the event are in memory*

Fast food and representative heuristics. *McDonald's, Dunkin' Donuts, and other fast-food franchise restaurants have found that using the same ingredients and methods at every location helps increase their sales. But do they know why? It's primarily because this repetition creates a representative heuristic for their specific restaurant. For example, after a few experiences with different McDonald's in various locations, you create a prototype that guides your expectations about how long it will take to get your food and what it will taste like. When traveling and looking for a quick "bite to eat," your "McDonald's representative heuristic" makes it easier for you to choose their restaurant over the competition.*

Representativeness Heuristic *Estimating the probability of something based on how well the circumstances match (or represent) our previous prototype*

Application

Solving Problems in College Life

Critical thinking requires adaptive, flexible approaches to thinking and problem solving. The following exercise offers practice in critical thinking, new insights into common college-related problems, and a quick review of terms and concepts discussed in this section.

Be sure to use the major problem-solving approaches we have discussed—algorithms (step-by-step procedures that guarantee solutions) and heuristics (shortcuts to possible solutions based on previous knowledge and experience). See

Table 8.1 for three specific heuristics: working backward, means–end analysis, and creating subgoals.

Problem 1 It is the end of the semester and you have a term paper due Friday. Thursday night you try to print your previously prepared paper, and you can't find the file on your computer.

Problem 2 The financial aid office has denied your student loan until you verify your income and expenses from last year. You need to find all your pay stubs and receipts.

For each problem, answer the following:

1. What was your first step in approaching the problem?
2. Which problem-solving approach did you select and why?
3. Did you experience mental sets, functional fixedness, confirmation bias, the availability heuristic, and the representativeness heuristic during the problem-solving process?

Assessment

CHECK & REVIEW

Problem Solving

Problem solving entails three stages: preparation, production, and evaluation. During the preparation stage, we identify given facts, separate relevant from irrelevant facts, and define the ultimate goal.

During the production stage, we generate possible solutions, called hypotheses. We typically generate hypotheses by using **algorithms** and **heuristics**. Algorithms, as problem-solving strategies, are guaranteed to lead to an eventual solution. But they are not practical in many situations. Heuristics, or simplified rules based on experience, are much faster but do not guarantee a solution. Three common heuristics are working backward, means–end analysis, and creating subgoals. The evaluation stage in problem solving involves judging the hypotheses

generated during the production stage against the criteria established in the preparation stage.

Five major barriers to successful problem solving are **mental sets, functional fixedness, confirmation bias, the availability heuristic,** and the **representativeness heuristic.**

Questions

1. List and describe the three stages of problem solving.
2. Rosa is shopping in a new supermarket and wants to find a specific type of mustard. Which problem-solving strategy would be most efficient? (a) algorithm; (b) heuristic; (c) instinct; (d) mental set
3. Before a new product arrives in the store, a manufacturer goes through several stages, including designing,

building, testing a prototype, and setting up a production line. This approach is called _____. (a) working backward; (b) means–end analysis; (c) divergent thinking; (d) creating subgoals
4. List the five major barriers to problem solving.

Check your answers in Appendix B.

CLICK & REVIEW
for additional assessment options:
www.wiley.com/college/huffman

Solution to the DONALD + GERALD = ROBERT problem:

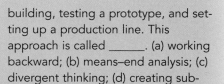

```
    5  2  6  4  8  5
 +  1  9  7  4  8  5
 ─────────────────────
    7  2  3  9  7  0
```

■ Creativity: Finding Unique Solutions

Are you a creative person? Like many students, you may think of only painters, dancers, and composers as creative and may fail to recognize examples of your own creativity. Even when doing ordinary tasks, such as taking notes in class, you are being somewhat creative—unless you're copying the lecture verbatim. Similarly, if you've ever tightened a screw with a penny or used a magazine to splint a broken arm, you've found creative solutions to problems. All of us, to a greater or lesser degree, exhibit a certain amount of creativity in some aspects of life. Whether a solution or performance is considered creative often depends on its need and usefulness at the time. Definitions of *creativity* vary among psychologists and among cultures. But it is generally agreed that **creativity** is the *ability to produce valued outcomes in a novel way* (Bink & Marsh, 2000; Boden, 2000).

Creativity *The ability to produce valued outcomes in a novel way*

Measuring Creativity

Creative thought is associated with three special characteristics: *originality*, *fluency*, and *flexibility*. As you can see in Table 8.2, Thomas Edison's invention of the light bulb offers a prime example of each of these characteristics. Creativity also involves **divergent thinking**, whereby many alternatives are developed from a single starting point (Baer, 1994). The opposite of divergent thinking is **convergent thinking**, or *conventional thinking*. In this case, lines of thinking *converge* (come together) on one correct answer. You used convergence in the DONALD + GERALD problem to find the one correct number represented by each letter.

Divergent Thinking *Thinking that produces many alternatives or ideas; a major element of creativity (e.g., finding as many uses as possible for a paper clip)*

Divergent thinking is the focus of most tests of creativity. In the *Unusual Uses Test*, you would be asked to think of as many uses as possible for an object (such as "How many ways can you use a brick?"). In the *Anagrams Test*, you would need to reorder the letters in a word to make as many new words as possible. Try rearranging the letters in these words to make new words. Then decide what they share in common. (Answers appear in the "Check & Review" on page 299.)

Convergent Thinking *Narrowing down a list of alternatives to converge on a single correct answer (e.g., standard academic tests generally require convergent thinking)*

1. grevenidt_____
2. neleecitlgni_____
3. ytliibxilef_____

4. ptoyroper_____
5. yvitcearti_____

National Archives/Taxi/Getty Images

Creativity in action. *Thomas Edison with his most famous invention—the light bulb.*

TABLE 8.2 THREE ELEMENTS OF CREATIVE THINKING

	Explanations	Thomas Edison Examples
Originality	Seeing unique or different solutions to a problem	After noting that electricity passing through a conductor produces a glowing red or white heat, Edison imagined using this light for practical uses.
Fluency	Generating a large number of possible solutions	Edison tried literally hundreds of different materials to find one that would heat to the point of glowing white heat without burning up.
Flexibility	Shifting with ease from one type of problem-solving strategy to another	When he couldn't find a long-lasting material, Edison tried heating it in a vacuum—thereby creating the first light bulb.

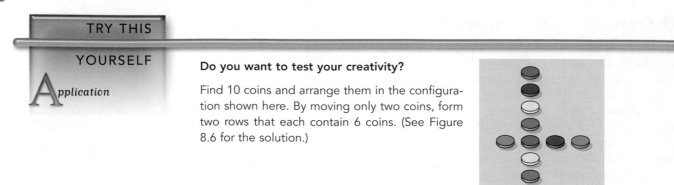

TRY THIS

YOURSELF

*A*pplication

Do you want to test your creativity?

Find 10 coins and arrange them in the configuration shown here. By moving only two coins, form two rows that each contain 6 coins. (See Figure 8.6 for the solution.)

Researching Creativity

Some researchers view creativity as a special talent or ability. Therefore, they look for common personality traits among people they define as creative (Guilford, 1967; Jausovec & Jausovec, 2000). Other researchers explain the distinction between creative and noncreative people in terms of cognitive processes. That is, creative and noncreative people differ in how they encode information, in how they store it, and in what information they generate to solve problems (Bink & Marsh, 2000; Cooper, 2000; Jacoby, Levy, & Steinbach, 1992).

According to Sternberg and Lubart's *investment theory* (1992, 1996), creative people are also willing to "buy low and sell high" in the realm of ideas. They buy low by championing ideas that they feel have potential but that most people think are worthless or worth very little. Once their creative ideas are supported and highly valued, they "sell high" and move on to another unpopular but promising idea.

Investment theory also suggests that creativity requires the coming together of six different but interrelated resources: intellectual ability, knowledge, thinking style, personality, motivation, and environment (Kaufman, 2002; Sternberg & Lubart, 1996). These resources are summarized in Table 8.3. One way to improve your personal creativity is to study this list and then strengthen yourself in those areas that you think need improvement.

TABLE 8.3 RESOURCES OF CREATIVE PEOPLE

Intellectual Ability	Knowledge	Thinking Style	Personality	Motivation	Environment
Enough intelligence to see problems in a new light	Sufficient basic knowledge of the problem to effectively evaluate possible solutions	Novel ideas and ability to distinguish between the worthy and worthless	Willingness to grow and change, take risks, and work to overcome obstacles	Sufficient motivation to accomplish the task and more internal than external motivation	An environment that supports creativity

*A*ssessment

CHECK & REVIEW

Creativity

Creativity is the ability to produce valued outcomes in a novel way. Creative thinking involves originality, fluency, and flexibility. **Divergent thinking**—generating as many solutions as possible—is a special type of thinking involved in creativity. In contrast, **convergent thinking**—or conventional thinking—works toward a single correct answer.

Creative people may have a special talent or differing cognitive processes. The investment theory of creativity proposes that creative people "buy low" by pursuing promising but unpopular ideas. They then "sell high" when these ideas are widely accepted. It also proposes that creativity depends on six specific resources: intellectual ability, knowledge, thinking style, personality, motivation, and environment.

Questions

1. Which of the following items would most likely appear on a test measuring creativity? (a) How long is the Ohio River? (b) What are the primary colors? (c) List all the uses of a pot. (d) Who was the first governor of New York?
2. Identify the type of thinking for each of these examples.
   a. You create numerous excuses ("reasons") for not studying.
   b. On a test, you must select one correct answer for each question.
   c. You make a list of ways to save money.
3. According to investment theory, what are the six resources necessary for creativity?

Check your answers in Appendix B.

CLICK & REVIEW
for additional assessment options:
www.wiley.com/college/huffman

Solutions to the Anagrams Test

1. divergent
2. intelligence
3. flexibility
4. prototype
5 creativity

Note that the answers are also key terms found in this chapter.

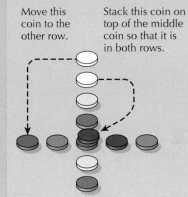

Move this coin to the other row.   Stack this coin on top of the middle coin so that it is in both rows.

Figure 8.6 *Coin problem solution.*

LANGUAGE

Any discussion of human thought processes must include a discussion of language. As mentioned earlier, language (along with mental images and concepts) is one of the three building blocks of thinking. Language enables us to mentally manipulate symbols, thereby expanding our thinking. Most importantly, whether it's spoken, written, or signed, language allows us to communicate our thoughts, ideas, and feelings.

■ Characteristics of Language: Structure and Production

What is language? Do beavers slapping their tails, birds singing their songs, and ants laying their trails use language? Not according to a strict scientific definition. As we discussed earlier, scientists develop precise definitions and restrictions for certain *artificial concepts*. Psychologists, linguists, and other scientists define **language** as a form of communication using sounds and symbols combined according to specified rules.

Building Blocks of Language
To produce language, we first build words using *phonemes* and *morphemes*. Then we string words into sentences using rules of *grammar* (*syntax* and *semantics*) (Table 8.4):

*A*chievement

What is language, and how is it related to thinking?

Language *Form of communication using sounds and symbols combined according to specified rules*

SUMMARY TABLE 8.4 BUILDING BLOCKS OF LANGUAGE

Blocks	Description	Example
Phonemes	The smallest units of sound that make up every language.	*p* in *pansy; ng* in *sting*
Morphemes	The smallest units that carry meaning; they are created by combining phonemes. (*Function morphemes* are prefixes and suffixes. *Content morphemes* are root words.)	*unthinkable = un • think • able* (prefix = *un*, root word = *think*, suffix = *able*)
Grammar	A system of rules (syntax and semantics) used to generate acceptable language that enables us to communicate with and understand others.	*They were in my psychology class.* versus *They was in my psychology class.*
Syntax	A system of rules for putting words in order.	*I am happy.* versus *Happy I am.*
Semantics	A system of using words to create meaning.	*I went out on a limb for you.* versus *Humans have several limbs.*

Phoneme [FOE-neem] *Smallest basic unit of speech or sound*

Morpheme [MOR-feem] *Smallest meaningful unit of language, formed from a combination of phonemes*

Grammar *Rules that specify how phonemes, morphemes, words, and phrases should be combined to express thoughts*

Syntax *Grammatical rules that specify how words and phrases should be arranged in a sentence to convey meaning*

"GOT IDEA. TALK BETTER. COMBINE WORDS. MAKE SENTENCES."

Sidney Harris.

1. *Phonemes.* The smallest basic units of speech or sound are called **phonemes**. These basic speech sounds make up every language. The English language has about 40 phonemes. Each one has distinctive features. Examples include variations in sound (like the letter *a* in *am* and *ape*) or unvoiced versus voiced components (when we say *s*, we simply hiss; when we say *z*, we do the same but add the voice).

2. *Morphemes.* Phonemes are combined to form the second building block of language, morphemes. **Morphemes** are the smallest *meaningful* units of language. Morphemes are divided into two types: (a) *content morphemes*, which hold the basic meaning of a word, such as *cat*, and (b) *function morphemes*, which are prefixes and suffixes, such as *un-, dis-, -able*, and *-ing*. Function morphemes add additional meaning to the word.

3. *Grammar.* Phonemes, morphemes, words, and phrases are joined together by the third building block of language, the rules of **grammar**. Grammatical rules govern how we combine phonemes into morphemes and words. They also control how we use various classes of words (nouns, verbs, etc.) and their inflections (plurals, verb tenses, etc.), and how we choose and order words to form meaningful sentences. Grammar is made up of two components, syntax and semantics.

   • Syntax. The grammatical rules for ordering words in sentences are known as rules of **syntax**. By the time we are able to read, our syntactical sense is so highly developed that even a sentence composed of nonsense words sounds as if it makes sense, as long as it follows proper syntax. Consider Lewis Carroll's poem "Jabberwocky":

   'Twas brillig, and the slithy toves

   Did gyre and gimble in the wabe…

   Can you see how the word arrangement follows the rules of English syntax so well that we feel we know what Carroll is talking about?

Syntax varies from language to language. In English, for example, the verb is usually the second element in a sentence ("He *has driven* to New York"). But in German, the main verb often comes at the very end of a sentence (German word order would be "He *has* to New York *driven*"). English speakers always put the adjective before the noun (my *precious* love), but Italian speakers sometimes place the adjective before, and sometimes after, depending on the intended meaning: *Una carrisima amore* means "a very dear, precious love." *Un' amore carrisima* means "a very expensive love," one that costs a lot to keep kindled!

- Semantics. The choosing of words according to the meaning we want to convey is known as **semantics**. When we add *-ed* to the word *walk*, it refers to walking in the past. If we want to refer to a baby sheep, we use the word *lamb*, not the word *limb*, which means something entirely different. Actually, *limb* has several meanings, so we must depend on context to know whether the speaker is referring to an arm, leg, or one of the larger branches of a tree. Then there is the expression "to go out on a limb," which means not that someone literally climbs a tree but rather that someone takes a risk. Meaning depends on many factors—including word choice, context, and whether the intent is literal or figurative, to name just a few.

Semantics *Meaning, or the study of meaning, derived from words and word combinations*

Language and Thought: A Complex Interaction

Our cognitive processes and language are intricately related. Does the fact that you speak English versus Spanish—or Chinese versus Swahili—mean that you reason, think, and perceive the world differently? According to linguist Benjamin Whorf (1956), the language a person speaks largely determines that person's thoughts. As proof of this *linguistic relativity* hypothesis, Whorf offered a now-classic example: Eskimos [Inuits] have many words to describe different kinds of snow (*apikak* for "first snow falling," *pukak* for "snow for drinking water," etc. Therefore, their richer vocabulary supposedly enables them to perceive and think about snow differently from English speakers, who have only one word—*snow*. People who speak different languages reportedly have different conceptions of the world around them.

Whorf's hypothesis is certainly intriguing. But most research does not support it. For one thing, he apparently exaggerated the number of Inuit words for snow (Pullum, 1991). He also ignored the fact that English speakers have a number of terms for snow like *slush, sleet, hard pack, powder,* and so on. More importantly, Eleanor Rosch (1973) found counterevidence for Whorf's hypothesis when she experimentally tested his ideas with the Dani tribe in New Guinea. The Dani language has only two color names—one indicating cool, dark colors and the other warm, bright colors. In contrast to Whorf's hypothesis, Rosch found that the Dani could discriminate among color hues just as well as people speaking languages with multiple names for colors. In other words, although it may be easier to express a particular idea in one language than in another, language does not necessarily determine how or what we think.

Whorf apparently went too far with his theory that language *determines* thought. But there is no doubt that language *influences* thought (Lillard, 1998). For example, what happens when people speak two or more languages? Studies have found that people who are bilingual report feeling a different sense of self, depending on the language they are using (Matsumoto, 2000). When using Chinese, they found they tended to behave in ways appropriate to Chinese cultural norms. When speaking English, they tended to adopt Western norms.

The influence of language on thought is readily apparent in our choice of words. When companies want to alter workers' perceptions, they don't *fire* employees. Instead, they are *outplaced, dehired,* or *nonrenewed.* Similarly, the military uses terms like *preemptive strike* to cover the fact that they attacked first and *tactical redeployment* to refer to a retreat of their troops.

Our choice of words also has had some embarrassing and financial consequences for North American businesses. When Pepsi-Cola used its "Come alive with Pepsi" slogan

Nature or nurture? *Children learn to communicate in the first few months of life. What does this say about the biological basis for language acquisition?*

Figure 8.7 ***Can you identify this emotion?*** Infants as young as 2.5 months can nonverbally express emotions, such as joy, surprise, or anger.

Cooing *Vowel-like sounds infants produce beginning around 2 to 3 months of age*

Babbling *Vowel/consonant combinations that infants begin to produce at about 4 to 6 months of age*

Overextension *Overly broad use of a word to include objects that do not fit the word's meaning (e.g., calling all men "Daddy")*

Telegraphic Speech *Two- or three-word sentences of young children that contain only the most necessary words*

in Japan, they later learned that it translated as "Pepsi brings your dead ancestors back from the grave." Similarly, Chevrolet Motor Company had great difficulty marketing its small Nova car in Mexico because they didn't understand that *No va* means "doesn't go" in Spanish. Words evoke different images and value judgments. Our words, therefore, *influence* not only our thinking but also the thinking of those who hear them.

Language Development: From Crying to Talking

From birth, a child has a multitude of ways to communicate. Through such nonverbal means as facial expressions, eye contact, and body gestures, babies only hours old begin to "teach" their parents and caregivers when and how they want to be held, fed, and played with. As early as the late 1800s, Charles Darwin proposed that most emotional expressions, such as smiles, frowns, and looks of disgust, are universal and innate (Figure 8.7). Darwin's contention is supported by the fact that children who are born blind and deaf exhibit the same facial expressions for emotions as sighted and hearing children.

Stages of Language Development

In addition to nonverbal communication, children also communicate verbally. The *prelinguistic stage* begins with the newborn baby's reflexive cry. Within a short time, crying becomes more purposeful. At least three distinct patterns of crying have been identified: hunger, anger, and pain (Wolff, 1969). Some parents and child-care texts suggest that each of these cries can be easily identified and responded to by the primary caregivers. However, most parents find that they must learn, through a process of trial and error, what each cry means and what actions will satisfy their child.

At about 2 to 3 months, babies begin **cooing**, producing vowel-like sounds ("ooooh" and "aaaah"). Then around 4 to 6 months, they start **babbling**, adding consonants to their vowels ("bahbahbah" and "dahdahdah"). Some parents mark babbling as the beginning of language and consider their child's vocalizations as "words." They do this despite the fact that the child typically does not associate a "word" with a specific object or person, and all children babble in the same fashion.

The true *linguistic stage* begins toward the end of the first year of life. The babbling begins to sound more like the language of the child's home and the child seems to understand that sound is related to meaning. At the beginning of the linguistic stage, the child is generally limited to a single-utterance vocabulary such as "mama," "go," "juice," or "up." Children manage to get a lot of mileage out of these singular utterances. "Mama" can be used to mean, "I want you to come get me," "I'm hurt," and "I don't like this stranger." However, their expressive ability more than doubles once they begin to join words into short phrases such as "Go bye-bye," "Daddy, milk," and "No night-night!"

At this age, children occasionally overextend the words they use. **Overextension** is using words to include objects that do not fit the word's meaning. For example, having learned the word *doggie*, a child often overextends the word to include all small, furry animals (e.g., kittens, bunnies).

Around age 2, most children are creating short but intelligible sentences by linking several words. However, they leave out nonessential connecting words: "Me want cookie;" "Grandma go bye-bye?" This pattern is called **telegraphic speech**. Like telegrams of days gone by, a two-year-old's speech includes only words directly relevant to meaning, and nothing more.

Children increase their vocabulary at a phenomenal rate during these early years. They also acquire a wide variety of rules for grammar, such as adding *-ed* to indicate

Are you having difficulty differentiating between overextension and overgeneralization? Remember the g in overgeneralize as a cue that this term applies to problems with grammar.

the past tense and *-s* to form plurals. They occasionally make mistakes, however, because they **overgeneralize**, or *overuse* the basic rules of grammar. This results in novel constructions like "I goed to the zoo" and "Two mans."

By age 5, most children have mastered the basic rules of grammar and typically use about 2000 words. (Many foreign-language instructors consider this level of mastery adequate for getting by in any given culture.) Past this point, our vocabulary and grammar acquisition continue to improve throughout our entire life span.

Theories of Language Development

What motivates children to develop language? Some theorists believe language capability is innate. Others claim it is learned through imitation and reinforcement (the nature–nurture controversy again). Although both sides have staunch supporters, most psychologists find neither of these extreme positions satisfactory. Most believe that language acquisition is a combination of both nature and nurture—the interactionist position (Casti, 2000; Van Hulle, Goldsmith, & Lemery, 2004).

According to the nature position, language acquisition is primarily a matter of growth and development. The most famous advocate of this viewpoint, Noam Chomsky (1968, 1980), suggests that children are born "prewired" to learn language. They possess neurological ability, known as a **language acquisition device (LAD)**, that needs only minimal exposure to adult speech to unlock its potential. The LAD enables the child to analyze language and extract the basic rules of grammar.

To support his viewpoint, Chomsky points out that children all over the world go through similar stages in language development at about the same age. And they do this in a pattern that parallels motor development. He also cites the fact that babbling is the same in all languages and that deaf babies babble just like hearing babies.

Although the nativist position enjoys considerable support, it fails to adequately explain individual differences. Why does one child learn rules for English, for example, whereas another learns rules for Spanish? The "nurturists" can explain individual differences and distinct languages. From their perspective, children learn language through a complex system of rewards, punishments, and imitation. Any vocalization attempt ("mah" or "dah") from an English speaking infant is quickly rewarded with smiles and other forms of encouragement. When the infant later babbles "mama" or "dada," proud parents respond even more enthusiastically. (As a critical thinker, can you see how these parents are unknowingly using a type of *shaping*—a concept we discussed in Chapter 6?)

▣ Animals and Language: Can the Human Animal Talk to Nonhuman Animals?

In addition to the nature–nurture debate on human language development, controversy also exists over whether nonhuman animals use language or can be taught to use language. Without question, nonhuman animals communicate. Most species send warnings, signal sexual interest, share the location of food sources, and so on. But are nonhuman animals capable of mastering the rich complexity of human language?

One of the earliest attempts to answer this question came from psychologists Winthrop and Luella Kellogg (1933). They raised a baby chimpanzee for several years alongside their son of about the same age. Although the chimp learned a few rudimentary communicative gestures, she never uttered sounds that resembled language. Early animal language researchers concluded that the Kelloggs probably failed because apes do not have the necessary anatomical structure to vocalize the way humans do. Therefore, subsequent studies focused on teaching apes nonvocal languages.

Beatrice and Allen Gardner (1969) conducted one of the most successful nonvocal language studies. Recognizing the manual dexterity of chimpanzees and their ability to imitate gestures, the Gardners used American Sign Language (ASL) with a chimp named Washoe. Their success story speaks for itself. By the time Washoe was

Overgeneralize *Applying the basic rules of grammar even to cases that are exceptions to the rule (e.g., saying "mans" instead of "men")*

Language Acquisition Device (LAD) *According to Chomsky, an innate mechanism that enables a child to analyze language and extract the basic rules of grammar*

Georgia State University Language Research Center

Computer-aided communication.
Using symbols on a computer, chimps have learned to press specific buttons to get food, drink, or a tickle from the trainers. Does this qualify as true language? Why or why not?

4 years old, she had learned 132 signs. And she was able to combine them into simple sentences such as: "Hurry, give me toothbrush" and "Please tickle more."

Following the Gardners' success with Washoe, several other language projects have been conducted with apes (Itakura, 1992; Savage-Rumbaugh, 1990). David Premack (1976) taught a chimp named Sarah to "read" and "write" by arranging plastic symbols on a magnetic board. Sarah learned not only to use the plastic symbols but also to follow certain grammatical rules in communicating with her trainers.

Another well-known study was conducted with a chimp named Lana. She learned to push symbols on a computer to get things she wanted. Examples included food, a drink, a tickle from her trainers, or having her curtains opened (Rumbaugh et al., 1974). And, of course, there is the famous gorilla Koko discussed at the beginning of the chapter. Penny Patterson (2002) reportedly taught Koko over 1000 signs in ASL.

A number of language studies also have been done with dolphins using hand signals or audible commands. The commands may be spoken by trainers or generated by computer and transmitted through an underwater speaker system. In one typical study, dolphins were given commands made up of two- to five-word sentences, such as "Big ball—square—return." This set of signals told the dolphins they should go get the big ball, put it in the floating square, and return to the trainer (Herman, Richards, & Woltz, 1984).

The interesting part of this experiment was that the commands varied in syntax and content, both of which altered meaning. For example, the next command might be "Square—big ball—return." This new set of signals meant the dolphin should go to the square first, then get the big ball, then return to the trainer with the ball. Or the command might refer to one of the other objects floating in the pool. "Triangle—little ball—square" required the dolphin to discriminate among various shapes and various sizes of balls to carry out the command. The study demonstrated that dolphins could carry out a great variety of commands that differed in both content and syntax.

Communicating through art? *Dolphins have learned to respond to complicated hand signals and vocal commands from their trainers. They've even learned to "express themselves" through art. But is this simple communication, operant conditioning, or true language?*

Evaluating Animal Language Studies

These ape and dolphin language studies are impressive. Most scientists agree that nonhuman animals *communicate*, but they question whether this qualifies as true *language*. Compared with humans, nonhuman animals express a limited repertoire of ideas. In addition, the average length of sentences produced and understood by humans is significantly greater than the two- to five-word sentences used by other animals. Moreover, critics claim that apes and dolphins are unable to learn the rules of grammar and syntax that humans use to convey subtle differences in meaning. They question whether nonhuman animals can use language in ways that are considered creative or unique. And they point out that these animals do not express the concept of time (*tomorrow, last week*), request information (*How do birds fly*)?, comment on the feelings of others (*Penny is sad*), express similarities (*That cloud looks like a tree*), or propose possibilities (*The cat might sit on my lap*) (Jackendoff, 2003).

Other critics raise the issue of operant conditioning (Chapter 6). They claim that nonhuman animals do not have a conceptual understanding of the complex signs and symbols of language. Animals that do engage in simple human language are merely imitating symbols to receive rewards. In short, nonhuman animals are not really trying to communicate with humans. They're simply performing operantly conditioned responses (Savage-Rumbaugh, 1990; Terrace, 1979). Finally, other critics suggest that much of the data regarding animal language has been anecdotal—and not always well documented. For example, the most spectacular claims of Koko's abilities have yet to be published in scientific journals (Lieberman, 1998; Willingham, 2001).

Proponents of animal language are quick to point out that chimpanzees and gorillas can use language creatively and have

"ALTHOUGH HUMANS MAKE SOUNDS WITH THEIR MOUTHS AND OCCASIONALLY LOOK AT EACH OTHER, THERE IS NO SOLID EVIDENCE THAT THEY ACTUALLY COMMUNICATE WITH EACH OTHER."

even coined some words of their own. For example, Washoe called a refrigerator "open eat drink" and a swan a "water bird" (Gardner & Gardner, 1971). Koko reportedly signed "finger bracelet" to describe a ring and "eye hat" to describe a mask (Patterson & Linden, 1981). Proponents also argue that, as demonstrated by the dolphin studies, nonhuman animals can be taught to understand basic rules of sentence structure.

Still, the fact remains that the gap between language as spoken and understood by humans and that generated and understood by other animals is considerable. Current evidence suggests that nonhuman animals can learn and use many basic forms of language. But their language is less complex, creative, and rule-laden than language used by humans. (As a critical thinker, have you ever thought about an opposite approach to this type of language research? Why don't humans learn nonhuman animal language? Could humans be taught to comprehend and use chimpanzee, whale, or elephant communication systems, for example?)

Assessment
CHECK & REVIEW

Language

Human language is a form of communication using sounds and symbols combined according to a set of specified rules. **Phonemes** are the basic speech sounds. They are combined to form **morphemes,** the smallest meaningful units of language. Phonemes, morphemes, words, and phrases are put together by rules of **grammar** (syntax and semantics). **Syntax** refers to the grammatical rules for ordering words in sentences. **Semantics** refers to meaning in language.

According to Benjamin Whorf's linguistic relativity hypothesis, language shapes thought. Generally, Whorf's hypothesis is not supported. However, our choice of vocabulary can influence our mental imagery and social perceptions.

Children go through two stages in their acquisition of language: prelinguistic (crying, **cooing, babbling**) and linguistic (single utterances, **telegraphic speech**, and the acquisition of rules of grammar).

Nativists believe that language is an inborn capacity and develops primarily by maturation. Chomsky suggests that human brains possess a **language acquisition device (LAD)** that needs only minimal environmental input. Nurturists emphasize the role of the environment and suggest that language development results from rewards, punishments, and imitation of models.

The most successful nonhuman animal language studies have been done with apes using American Sign Language and written symbols. Dolphins also have been taught to comprehend sentences that vary in syntax and meaning. Some psychologists believe that nonhuman animals can truly learn human language. Others suggest the nonhuman animals are merely responding to rewards.

Questions

1. The basic speech sounds /ch/ and /v/ are known as _____. The smallest meaningful units of language, such as *book*, *pre-*, and *-ing*, are known as _____.

2. A child says "I hurt my foots." This is an example of _____.

3. Chomsky believes we possess an inborn ability to learn language known as a _____. (a) telegraphic understanding device (TUD); (b) language acquisition device (LAD); (c) language and grammar translator (LGT); (d) over-generalized neural net (ONN)

4. Human language differs from the communication of nonhuman animals in that it is _____. (a) used more creatively to express thoughts and ideas; (b) the expression of an innate capability; (c) essential for thought; (d) composed of sounds

Check your answers in Appendix B.

CLICK & REVIEW
for additional assessment options:
www.wiley.com/college/huffman

INTELLIGENCE

Achievement
What is intelligence, and how is it measured?

Are Koko, Genie, and Thomas Edison intelligent? What exactly is intelligence? Many people equate intelligence with "book smarts," which conflicts with the common jokes and stereotypes about "absentminded professors" and geniuses with no common or practical sense. For others, what is judged as intelligent depends on the characteristics and skills valued in a particular social group or culture (Sternberg, 2005; Sternberg &

www.wiley.com/college/huffman

Hedlund, 2002; Suzuki & Aronson, 2005). For example, did you know that many languages have no word that corresponds to our Western notion of intelligence? The closest Mandarin word is a Chinese character meaning "good brain and talented" (Matsumoto, 2000). Interestingly, this Chinese word is commonly associated with traits like imitation, effort, and social responsibility (Keats, 1982).

Even among Western psychologists, considerable debate exists over the definition of *intelligence*. In this discussion, I will rely on a formal definition developed by psychologist David Wechsler (WEX-ler) (1944, 1977). Wechsler defined **intelligence** as *the global capacity to think rationally, act purposefully, and deal effectively with the environment*. In other words, intelligence is your ability to effectively use your thinking processes to cope with the world. An advantage of this definition is that it incorporates most modern viewpoints as well as most cultural and social influences.

Before going on, I want to emphasize that intelligence is not a *thing*. It has no mass. It occupies no space. There are no specific sites within the brain where intelligence resides. When people talk about intelligence as though it were a concrete, tangible object, they commit an error in reasoning, known as *reification*. Like the concepts of consciousness, learning, memory, and personality, intelligence is a *hypothetical, abstract construct*.

Intelligence *Global capacity to think rationally, act purposefully, and deal effectively with the environment*

■ What Is Intelligence? Do We Have One or Many Intelligences?

Because of the difficulty in identifying and defining intelligence, it remains a complex and controversial topic. For many Western psychologists, one of the prime areas of debate is: What are the properties of intelligence? Is it a single general ability or several distinct kinds of mental abilities (intelligences)? In this section, we will discuss several theories that attempt to answer these questions, beginning with Charles Spearman's early theory of *general intelligence (g)*.

Intelligence as a Single Ability
In the early years of intelligence testing, psychologists viewed intelligence as innate. And as a broad mental ability that included all the cognitive functions. However, Charles Spearman (1923) proposed that intelligence is a single factor, which he termed *general intelligence (g)*. He based his theory on his observation that high scores on separate tests of mental abilities, such as spatial and reasoning abilities, tend to correlate with each other. Thus, Spearman believed general intelligence (g) underlies all intellectual behavior, including reasoning, solving problems, and performing well in all areas of cognition. Based on Spearman's work, standardized tests have been widely used in the military, schools, and business to measure this general intelligence (Deary et al., 2004; Johnson et al., 2004; Lubinski & Dawis, 1992).

Intelligence as Multiple Abilities
About a decade later, L. L. Thurstone (1938) proposed seven primary mental abilities: verbal comprehension, word fluency, numerical fluency, spatial visualization, associative memory, perceptual speed, and reasoning. He felt that Spearman's concept of general intelligence (g) had little, if any, value. Naturally, at the time, Thurstone's view was rather radical. Many years later, J. P. Guilford (1967) expanded on this number and proposed that as many as 120 factors were involved in the structure of intelligence.

Intelligence Again as a Single Ability
About the same time that Guilford was working, Raymond Cattell (1963, 1971) reanalyzed Thurstone's data and argued against the idea of multiple intelligences. He agreed with Spearman that an overall general intelligence (g) does exist. But Cattell suggested there are two subtypes:

Fluid Intelligence *Aspects of innate intelligence, including reasoning abilities, memory, and speed of information processing, that are relatively independent of education and tend to decline as people age*

1. **Fluid intelligence** *(gf)* refers to reasoning abilities, memory, and speed of information processing. If you were asked to solve analogies or remember a long set of

numbers, you would be relying on your fluid intelligence. Being relatively independent of education and experience, it reflects an inherited predisposition. And, like other biological capacities, fluid intelligence declines with advancing age (Burns, Nettelbeck, & Cooper, 2000; Li et al., 2004; Rozencwajg et al., 2005).

2. **Crystallized intelligence** (*gc*) refers to knowledge and skills gained through experience and education (Facon & Facon-Bollengier, 1999). You would rely on your crystallized intelligence if you were asked to explain the rules of baseball or the difference between a "bear" and "bull" stock market. Crystallized intelligence tends to increase over the life span. This explains why physicians, teachers, musicians, politicians, and people in many other occupations often become more successful with age and can continue working well into old age.

Recent findings show increased frontal lobe activity during very complex tasks, which helps support the idea of *g* (Duncan, 2005). Recall from Chapter 1, however, that correlation does not necessarily imply causation. Moreover, other studies find that more intelligent people are likely to show less, not more, frontal lobe activation. This may be because tasks are not as challenging to them as to those who are less intelligent (Haier et al., 1995; Sternberg, 1999, 2005).

A Return to Multiple Intelligences

Today there is considerable support for the concept of general intelligence (*g*) as a measure of academic smarts. But we all know people who are wizards at math or science yet poor in verbal abilities. Many contemporary cognitive theorists believe that intelligence is not a single general factor but a collection of many separate specific abilities.

Gardner's Theory of Multiple Intelligences   One of these theorists, Howard Gardner, believes that people have many kinds of intelligences. The fact that brain-damaged patients often lose some kinds of intellectual abilities, while retaining others, suggests to Gardner that different intelligences are located in discrete areas throughout the brain. Gardner (1983, 1998, 1999) developed a *theory of multiple intelligences* (Figure 8.8) identifying eight (or possibly nine) distinct intelligences, shown in Table 8.5. According to Gardner, people have different *profiles of intelligence* because

Crystallized Intelligence *Knowledge and skills gained through experience and education that tend to increase over the life span*

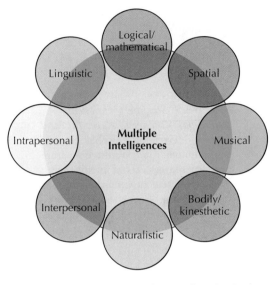

Figure 8.8 *Gardner's theory of multiple intelligences.* Howard Gardner believes that there are numerous forms of intelligence and that the value of these intelligences may change according to culture. Gardner also proposed a possible ninth intelligence, spiritual/existential, shown in Table 8.5.

TABLE 8.5 GARDNER'S MULTIPLE INTELLIGENCES AND POSSIBLE CAREERS

Linguistic: language, such as speaking, reading a book, writing a story	Spatial: mental maps, such as figuring out how to pack multiple presents in a box or how to draw a floor plan	Bodily/ kinesthetic: body movement, such as dancing, gymnastics, or figure skating	Intra-personal: understanding oneself, such as setting achievable goals or recognizing self-defeating emotions	Logical/ mathematical: problem solving or scientific analysis, such as following a logical proof or solving a mathematical problem	Musical: musical skills, such as singing or playing a musical instrument	Inter-personal: social skills, such as managing diverse groups of people	Naturalistic: being attuned to nature, such as noticing seasonal patterns or using environmentally safe products	(Possible) Spiritual/ existential: attunement to meaning of life and death and other conditions of life
Careers: novelist, journalist, teacher	Careers: engineer, architect, pilot	Careers: athlete, dancer, ski instructor	Careers: increased success in almost all careers	Careers: mathematician, scientist, engineer	Careers: singer, musician, composer	Careers: salesperson, manager, therapist, teacher	Careers: biologist, naturalist	Careers: philosopher, theologian

Source: Adapted from Gardner, 1983, 1999.

www.wiley.com/college/huffman

they are stronger in some areas than others. They also use their intelligences differently to learn new material, perform tasks, and solve problems. For example, talk show host Oprah Winfrey would undoubtedly score high on both *intrapersonal* and *interpersonal intelligences*. Einstein would have scored at the top in *logical/mathematical* intelligence.

Gardner's theory has wide-reaching implications for intelligence testing and for education. He believes intelligence testing should consist of assessing a person's strengths rather than coming up with a single "IQ score." He challenges our education system to present material in a variety of learning modes rather than only the traditional linguistic and logical/mathematical. He also suggests we should develop multiple means of assessment rather than the traditional paper-and-pencil tests.

Sternberg's Triarchic (Three-Part) Theory of Successful Intelligence Research with brain-damaged patients led Howard Gardner to his theory of multiple intelligences. Research on information processing similarly prompted Robert Sternberg to propose his *triarchic theory of successful intelligence* (Figure 8.9). Sternberg (1985, 1999) believes that even more important than the outward products of intelligence, such as correct answers on an intelligence test, are the thinking processes we use to arrive at the answers. He proposed three aspects of intelligence—*analytical*, *creative*, and *practical* (Grigorenko, Jarvin, & Sternberg, 2002; Sternberg, 1999). Table 8.6 briefly describes each aspect.

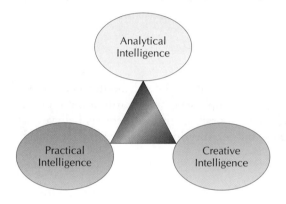

Figure 8.9 *Sternberg's triarchic (three-part) theory of successful intelligence.* According to Robert Sternberg's model, there are three separate and different aspects of intelligence. Each of these components is learned, not the result of genetics. Therefore, each can be strengthened or improved.

The value of Sternberg's theory of intelligence is that he emphasizes the process underlying thinking rather than just the end product. He also stresses the importance of applying mental abilities to real-world situations rather than testing mental abilities in isolation (e.g., Sternberg 2005; Sternberg & Hedlund, 2002). Sternberg (1998) introduced the term *successful intelligence* to describe the ability to adapt to, shape, and select environments in order to accomplish personal and societal goals. Gardner and Sternberg differ on a number of points in their theories. But they agree that intelligence involves multiple abilities.

TABLE 8.6 STERNBERG'S TRIARCHIC THEORY OF SUCCESSFUL INTELLIGENCE

	Analytical Intelligence	**Creative Intelligence**	**Practical Intelligence**
Sample Skills	Good at analysis, evaluation, judgment, and comparison skills	Good at invention, coping with novelty, and imagination skills	Good at application, implementation, execution, and utilization skills
Methods of Assessment	These skills are assessed by intelligence or scholastic aptitude tests. Questions ask about meanings of words based on context and how to solve number-series problems.	These skills are assessed in many ways, including open-ended tasks, writing a short story, drawing a piece of art, or solving a scientific problem requiring insight.	Although these skills are more difficult to assess, they can be measured by asking for solutions to practical and personal problems.

CHECK & REVIEW

What Is Intelligence?

Today, **intelligence** is commonly defined as the global capacity to think rationally, act purposefully, and deal effectively with the environment. Several theorists have debated whether intelligence is one or many abilities. Spearman viewed intelligence as one factor, called *g*, for general intelligence. Thurstone saw it as seven distinct mental abilities. Guilford believed it was composed of 120 or more separate abilities. And Cattell viewed it as two types of general intelligence (*g*), which he called **fluid intelligence** and **crystallized intelligence.**

In addition to these early theorists, Gardner's theory of multiple intelligences identifies eight (and possibly nine) types of intelligence. He believes that both teaching and assessing should take into account people's learning styles and cognitive strengths. Sternberg's triarchic theory of successful intelligence (*analytical, creative,* and *practical*) emphasizes the thinking process rather than the end product (the answer).

Questions

1. The *g* factor, originally proposed by Spearman, is best defined as _____. (a) skill in the use of language as a tool for thought; (b) general intelligence; (c) the ability to adapt to the environment; (d) the type of intelligence we call common sense

2. What is the difference between fluid and crystallized intelligences?

3. _____ suggested that people differ in their "profiles of intelligence" and that each person shows a unique pattern of strengths and weaknesses. (a) Spearman; (b) Binet; (c) Wechsler; (d) Gardner

4. Explain Sternberg's triarchic theory of successful intelligence.

Check your answers in Appendix B.

CLICK & REVIEW
for additional assessment options:
www.wiley.com/college/huffman

■ How Do We Measure Intelligence? IQ Tests and Scientific Standards

As you've just seen, intelligence is difficult to define. And the scientific community remains divided over whether it is one or multiple abilities. Despite this uncertainty, most college admissions officers and scholarship committees, as well as many employers, commonly use scores from intelligence tests as a significant part of their selection criteria. How good are these tests? Are they good predictors of student and employee success?

Many different kinds of intelligence (IQ) tests exist, and each approaches the measurement of intelligence from a slightly different perspective. Most, however, attempt to measure abilities that allow the test to be a good predictor of academic performance. In other words, most IQ tests are designed to predict grades in school. To see how that's done, let's examine the most commonly used IQ tests.

Individual IQ Tests

Alfred Binet [bih-NAY] created the first widely used IQ test in France around the turn of the last century. In the United States, Lewis Terman (1916) developed the Stanford–Binet (at Stanford University), which added items and revised Binet's scoring procedure. This test is revised periodically—the latest (fifth) edition consists of 10 subtests. The test items are administered individually (one test-giver and one test-taker). And they involve such tasks as copying geometric designs, identifying similarities, and repeating a sequence of numbers.

In the original version of the Stanford–Binet, results were expressed in terms of a mental age. For example, if a 7-year-old's score equaled that of an average 8-year-old, the child was considered to have a mental age of 8, as measured by the test. To determine the child's *intelligence quotient (IQ)*, mental age was divided by the child's chronological age (actual age in years) and multiplied by 100, as follows:

$$IQ = \frac{MA}{CA} \times 100 = \frac{8}{7} \times 100 = 1.14 \times 100 = 114$$

Thus, a 7-year-old with a mental age of 8 would have an IQ of 114. A "normal" child should have a mental age equal to his or her chronological age. (*Normal* in this case refers to the norms or statistics used to standardize the test.)

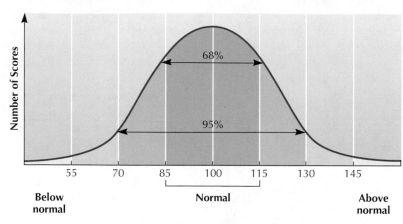

Figure 8.10 *The normal distribution of IQ scores.* Notice that over two-thirds of the people taking the test, 68 percent have an IQ within the normal range.

Today, most intelligence tests, including the Stanford–Binet, no longer compute an IQ. Instead, the test scores are expressed as a comparison of a single person's score to a national sample of similar-aged people. These deviation IQs are based on how far the person's score on the test deviates from the national average. As you can see in Figure 8.10, on a standardized IQ test, the majority of people score within 1 standard deviation (15 points) above, or 1 standard deviation (15 points) below, the national average of 100 points.

Figure 8.10 also shows how the distribution of IQ scores follows a bell-shaped curve. The majority of individuals (68 percent) who take the test score within the normal range—85 to 115. Even though the actual IQ is no longer calculated, the term *IQ* remains as a shorthand expression for intelligence test scores.

The Wechsler Tests

David Wechsler developed the most widely used intelligence test, the *Wechsler Adult Intelligence Scale* (WAIS), now in a third edition (WAIS III). He also created a similar test for school-age children, the *Wechsler Intelligence Scale for Children* (WISC-III; Table 8.7), and one for preschool children, the *Wechsler Preschool and Primary Scale of Intelligence* (WPPSI), now revised as WPPSI-R.

Like the Stanford–Binet, the Wechsler tests yield a final intelligence score. But they have separate *verbal* (vocabulary, comprehension, knowledge of general information) and *performance* scores (arranging pictures to tell a story, arranging blocks to match a given pattern). Wechsler's approach has three advantages: (1) The WAIS, WISC, and WPPSI were specifically designed for different age groups. (2) Different abilities can be evaluated either separately or together. (3) People who are unable to speak or understand English can still be tested. The verbal portion of the test doesn't have to be administered because each subtest yields its own score.

Scientific Standards for Psychological Tests

What makes a good test? How are the tests developed by Binet and Wechsler any better than those created by popular magazines and television programs? To be scientifically acceptable, all psychological tests must fulfill three basic requirements: *standardization*, *reliability*, and *validity*.

Standardization *Establishment of the norms and uniform procedures for giving and scoring a test*

1. **Standardization.** To be useful, intelligence tests (as well as personality, aptitude, and most other tests) must be *standardized*. The term **standardization** has two meanings as it applies to testing (Hogan, 2003). First, every test must have *norms*, or average scores. To develop norms, the test is given to a *representative sample*—a large sample of diverse people who resemble those for whom the test was intended. Norms determine whether an individual's particular score is considered high, low, or average in comparison to the representative sample. Second, *testing procedures* must be standardized. Uniform conditions are strictly followed for all aspects of

TABLE 8.7 SUBTESTS OF THE WISC-III

<table>
<tr><td colspan="2" align="center">Example*</td></tr>
<tr><td colspan="2">Verbal Subtests</td></tr>
<tr><td>Information</td><td>How many senators are elected from each state?</td></tr>
<tr><td>Similarities</td><td>How are computers and books alike?</td></tr>
<tr><td>Arithmetic</td><td>If one baseball card costs three cents, how much will five baseball cards cost?</td></tr>
<tr><td>Vocabulary</td><td>Define lamp.</td></tr>
<tr><td>Comprehension</td><td>What should you do if you accidentally break a friend's toy?</td></tr>
</table>

Performance Subtests Example below:

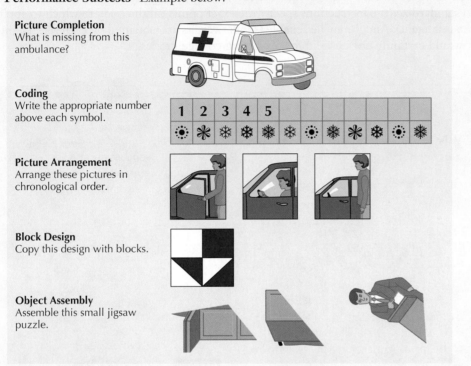

Picture Completion
What is missing from this ambulance?

Coding
Write the appropriate number above each symbol.

Picture Arrangement
Arrange these pictures in chronological order.

Block Design
Copy this design with blocks.

Object Assembly
Assemble this small jigsaw puzzle.

* These examples are similar to those used on the actual test.

taking, giving, and scoring the test. For example, all test-takers are given the same instructions, questions, and time limits. In addition, all test administrators follow the same objective standards in their scoring.

2. **Reliability.** Imagine having a stopwatch or oven thermometer that gave different readings each time you measured. Obviously, every measuring device (including tests) must be consistent. That is, repeated measurements should produce reasonably similar findings. This stability, or **reliability,** of a test is usually determined by retesting to determine whether test scores have changed significantly (Hogan, 2003). Retesting can be by the *test–retest method*, comparing participants' scores on two separate administrations of a test. Researchers can also use the *split-half method*, splitting a test into two equivalent parts and comparing the degree of similarity between the two halves (e.g., whether scores from odd- and even-numbered questions agree).

3. **Validity.** The third important principle of test construction is **validity,** the ability of a test to measure what it is designed to measure. There are several types of

Reliability *A measure of the consistency and stability of test scores when the test is readministered*

Validity *Ability of a test to measure what it was designed to measure*

validity. The most important is *criterion-related validity*, or the accuracy with which test scores can be used to predict another variable of interest (known as the *criterion*). Criterion-related validity is expressed as the *correlation* between the test score and the criterion (or standard). (Recall from Chapter 1 that a correlation is a standard measure of how two variables are related.) A high correlation indicates the two variables are closely related. A low or zero correlation indicates there is little or no relationship between them. If two variables are highly correlated, then one variable can be used to predict the other. Thus, if a test is valid, its scores will be useful in predicting people's behavior in some other specified situation, such as using intelligence test scores to predict grades in college.

Can you see why a test that is standardized and reliable, but *not* valid, is worthless? Suppose you are giving someone a test for skin sensitivity. Such a test may be easy to standardize (the instructions specify the exact points on the body to which to apply the test agent). And it may be reliable (similar results are obtained on each retest). But it would certainly not be valid for predicting college grades.

 ssessment

CHECK & REVIEW

How Do We Measure Intelligence?

Although there are many tests for intelligence, the Stanford-Binet and Wechsler are the most widely used. Both tests compute an *intelligence quotient (IQ)* by comparing the deviation of a person's test score to the norms for that person's age group.

For any test to be useful, it must be standardized, reliable, and valid. **Standardization** refers to (a) giving a test to a large number of people in order to determine norms and (b) using identical procedures in administering a test so that everyone takes the test under exactly the same testing conditions. **Reliability** refers to the stability of test scores over time.

Validity refers to how well the test measures what it is intended to measure.

Questions

1. What is the major difference between the Stanford–Binet and the Wechsler Intelligence Scales?
2. If a 10-year-old's score on an original version of the Stanford-Binet test was the same as an average 9-year-old, the child would have an IQ of _____.
3. Identify which testing principle—standardization, reliability, or validity—is being described in each of the following statements:
   a. _____ ensures that if a person takes the same test two weeks after taking it the first time, his or her

score will not significantly change.
   b. _____ ensures that a test or other measurement instrument actually measures what it purports to measure.
   c. _____ ensures that the test has been given to large numbers of people to determine which scores are average, above average, and below average—in short, which scores are representative of the general population.

Check your answers in Appendix B.

 CLICK & REVIEW
for additional assessment options:
www.wiley.com/college/huffman

 chievement

How do we measure extremes in intelligence? What roles do biology, genetics, the environment, and ethnicity play in intelligence?

THE INTELLIGENCE CONTROVERSY

As noted earlier, intelligence is extremely difficult to define. Psychologists also differ on whether it is composed of a single factor (*g*) or multiple abilities. Therefore, how valid is it to develop tests that measure intelligence? Furthermore, is intelligence inherited, or is it a result of environment? Are IQ tests culturally biased against certain ethnic groups? Intelligence testing has long been the subject of intense interest and great debate. In this section, we explore the use of intelligence tests for measuring extremes in intelligence (mental retardation and giftedness). Then we examine three possible explanations for overall differences in intelligence (the brain, genetics, and the environment). We close with a look at proposed ethnic differences in intelligence.

Extremes in Intelligence: Mental Retardation and Giftedness

If you want to judge the validity of any test (academic, intelligence, personality, etc.), one of the best methods is to compare people who score at the extremes. Students who get an A on a major exam should clearly know more than those who fail. As you will see, the validity of IQ tests is somewhat supported by the fact that individuals who score at the lowest level on standard IQ tests *do* have clear differences in intellectual abilities compared to those who score at the top. Intelligence tests provide one of the major criteria for diagnosing *mental retardation* and *giftedness*.

Mental Retardation

According to clinical standards, the label *mentally retarded* is applied when someone is significantly below average in general intellectual functioning (IQ less than 70) and has significant deficits in adaptive functioning (such as communicating with others, living independently, social or occupational functioning, and maintaining safety and health) (American Psychiatric Association, 2000). Mental retardation (like most aspects of human behavior) is on a continuum that ranges from mildly to severely retarded. As you can see in Table 8.8, less than 1 to 3 percent of the general population would be classified as mentally retarded. And of this group, 85 percent are only *mildly* retarded.

What causes mental retardation? Some forms of retardation stem from genetic causes. Examples include *Down syndrome*, which results from an extra chromosome in the body's cells; *fragile-X syndrome*, an abnormality of the X chromosome caused by a defective gene; and *phenylketonuria (PKU)*, a metabolic disorder resulting from an inherited enzyme deficiency. Newborn babies in the United States are routinely tested for the presence of PKU. If detected early, it is treatable by minimizing phenylalanine in the child's diet.

Other causes of retardation are environmental, including alcohol and other drug abuse during pregnancy, extreme deprivation or neglect in early life, and postnatal

SUMMARY TABLE 8.8 DEGREES OF MENTAL RETARDATION

Level of Retardation	IQ Scores	Percent of Mentally Retarded Population	Characteristics
Mild	50–70	85	Usually able to become self-sufficient: may marry, have families, and secure full-time jobs in unskilled occupations
Moderate	35–49	10	Able to perform simple unskilled tasks; may contribute to a certain extent to their livelihood
Severe	20–34	3–4	Able to follow daily routines, but with continual supervision; with training, may learn basic communication skills
Profound	below 20	1–2	Able to perform only the most rudimentary behaviors, such as walking, feeding themselves, and saying a few phrases

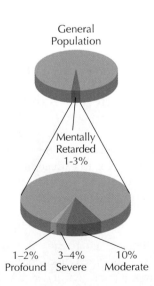

General Population

Mentally Retarded 1-3%

1–2% Profound 3–4% Severe 10% Moderate

An unusual form of intelligence. In the movie *Rain Man,* Dustin Hoffman portrayed a savant with exceptional mathematical ability.

Savant Syndrome *A condition in which a person with mental retardation exhibits exceptional skill or brilliance in some limited field*

accidents that damage parts of the brain. However, in many cases, there is no known cause.

It's important to keep in mind that children classified as mildly retarded are not easily distinguished from their classmates until they've been in school for several years. Moreover, once they leave academic settings, their mental limits are less noticeable. Many become self-supporting, integrated members of the community. Even those who are part of the moderately retarded group can learn vocational skills that allow them to live in supervised group homes. Furthermore, people can score low on some measures of intelligence and still be average or even gifted in others. The most dramatic examples are people with **savant syndrome**. Although these individuals score very low on IQ tests (usually between 40 and 70), they also demonstrate exceptional skills or brilliance in specific areas, such as rapid calculation, art, memory, or musical ability (Bonnel et al., 2003; McMahon, 2002; Pring & Hermelin, 2002). In the movie *Rain Man,* Dustin Hoffman portrayed a *savant* with exceptional mathematical ability.

Mental Giftedness

At the other end of the intelligence spectrum, we have people with especially high IQs (typically defined as being in the top 1 or 2 percent). Have you ever wondered what happens to people with such superior intellectual abilities?

In 1921, Lewis Terman used teacher recommendations and IQ tests to identify 1500 gifted children with IQs of 140 or higher. He then tracked their progress through adulthood. His study of these gifted children—affectionately nicknamed the "Termites"—destroyed many myths and stereotypes about gifted people. As children, these Termites not only received excellent grades but were also found to be socially well adjusted. In addition, they were taller and stronger than their peers of average IQ. By the age of 40, the number of individuals who became research scientists, engineers, physicians, lawyers, or college teachers, or who were highly successful in business and other fields, was many times the number a random group would have provided (Leslie, 2000; Terman, 1954).

On the other hand, not every Termite was successful. There were some notable failures. The members who were the most successful tended to have extraordinary motivation and someone at home or school who was especially encouraging (Goleman, 1980). However, many in this gifted group were like others their age of average intelligence. They became alcoholics, got divorced, and committed suicide at close to the national rate (Leslie, 2000). A high IQ is therefore no guarantee for success in every endeavor. It only offers more intellectual opportunities.

Application

RESEARCH HIGHLIGHT

Explaining Differences in IQ

Some people are mentally gifted, some are mentally retarded, and most are somewhere in between. To explain these differences, we need to look at the brain, genetics, and the environment.

The Brain's Influence on Intelligence

A basic tenet of neuroscience is that all mental activity (including intelligence) results from neural activity in the brain.

Three major questions have guided neuroscience research on intelligence:

1. Does a bigger brain mean greater intelligence? It makes logical sense. After all, humans have relatively large brains. And, as a species, we are more intelligent than dogs, which have smaller brains. Some nonhuman animals, such as whales and dolphins, do have larger brains than humans. But the brains of humans are larger in relation to the size

of our bodies. Since the early 1800s, researchers have asked whether "bigger is better," and modern studies using magnetic resonance imaging (MRI) have found a significant correlation between brain size (adjusted for body size) and intelligence (Ivanovic et al., 2004; Posthuma et al., 2002; Stelmack, Knott, & Beauchamp, 2003).

On the other hand, anatomical studies of Einstein's brain found that it was not heavier or larger than normal

(Witelson, Kigar, & Harvey, 1999). Some areas were, in fact, smaller than average. However, the area of the brain responsible for processing mathematical and spatial information (the lower region of the parietal lobe) was 15 percent larger. Also, we cannot know if Einstein was born with this difference, or if his brain changed due to his scientific pursuits. Rather than focusing on brain size, therefore, most of the recent research on the biology of intelligence has focused on brain functioning.

2. Is a faster brain more intelligent? The public seems to think so, and neuroscientists have found that a faster response time is indeed related to higher intelligence (Bowling & Mackenzie, 1996; Deary & Stough, 1996, 1997; Posthuma, deGeus, & Boomsma, 2001). A standard experiment flashes simple images like the one in Figure 8.11, and participants must inspect them quickly and make an accurate decision. As simple as it may seem, those participants who respond most quickly also tend to score highest on intelligence tests.

3. Does a smart brain work harder? As you read in Chapter 1, PET scans measure brain activity by recording the amount of radioactive glucose used in different parts of the brain. (A more active area of the brain uses more glucose than a less active area). Surprisingly, as can be seen in Figure 8.12, researchers have found that areas of the brain involved in problem solving show *less* activity in people of high intelligence than in people of lower intelligence when they are given the same problem-solving tasks (Haier et al., 1995; Neubauer et al., 2004; Posthuma, Neale, Boomsma, & de Geus, 2001). Apparently, intelligent brains work smarter, or more efficiently, than less intelligent brains.

Genetic and Environmental Influences on Intelligence

The central tenet of neuroscience is that all mental activity is linked to the brain and

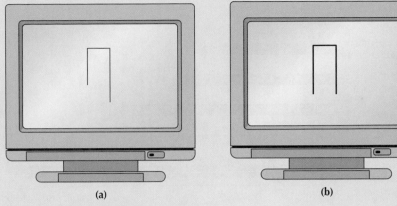

(a)   (b)

Figure 8.11 *A test for intelligence?* Which "leg" of the drawing in (a) is longer, the right or the left? Although the answer seems simple, researchers have found that when images like these are flashed for a few milliseconds on a computer screen, the amount of time people need to make correct judgments may reveal something about their intelligence. The second figure (b) appears immediately after figure (a) to block, or "mask," the lingering afterimage.

other parts of the nervous system. A similar, repeated theme of this text (and most areas of psychology) is that nature and nurture play interacting, *inseparable* roles. In the case of intelligence, any similarities between family members are due to *heredity* (family members share similar genetic material) combined with *environmental* factors (family members share similar living arrangements).

Researchers interested in the role of heredity in intelligence often focus on *twin studies.* Recall from Chapter 2 that one of the most popular ways to study the relative effects of genetics versus the environment is to use monozygotic (identical, one-egg) twins. Such studies have found significant hereditary influences for intelligence (Figure 8.13), personality, and psychopathology (Bouchard et al., 1998; Davalos et al., 2004; Kaye et al., 2004; Jensen, Nyborg, & Nyborg, 2003; Lynn, 2002; Rushton, 2001).

Perhaps the most important and most extensive of all twin studies is the Min-

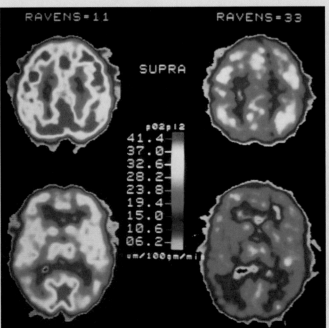

Courtesy Richard J. Haier, University of California-Irvine

Figure 8.12 *Do intelligent brains work harder?* The PET scans in the left column are from a person with a tested low IQ. The scans on the right are from someone with a high IQ. Note that when solving problems, the brain on the left is more active. (Red and yellow indicate more brain activity.) Contrary to popular opinion, this research suggests that lower-IQ brains actually work harder, but less efficiently, than higher IQ brains.

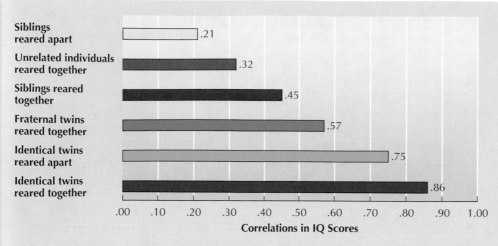

Figure 8.13 *Genetic and environmental influences.* Note the higher correlations between identical twins' IQ test scores compared to correlations between all other pairs. This suggests that genes play a significant role in intelligence. (Based on Bouchard & McGue, 1981; Bouchard et al., 1998; McGue et al., 1993.)

nesota Study of Twins. Beginning in 1979 and continuing for more than two decades, researchers from the University of Minnesota have been studying identical twins who grew up in different homes (Bouchard, 1994, 1999; Bouchard, McGue, Hur, & Horn, 1998; Markon et al., 2002). Each of these "reared-apart" twins was separated from his or her sibling and adopted by a different family early in life. They were reunited only as adults. Because each twin has identical genetic material but was raised in a different family, researchers have a unique natural experiment that can be used to distinguish the effects of genetics from the effects of the environment. When the IQ data were collected and the statistics computed, researchers found that genetic factors appear to play a surprisingly large role in the IQ score of monozygotic (identical) twins reared apart.

How would you critique these findings? First, adoption agencies tend to look for similar criteria in their choice of adoptive parents. Therefore, the homes of these reared-apart twins could have been quite similar. In addition, these twins also shared the same nine-month prenatal environment, which might have influenced their brain development and intelligence (White, Andreasen, & Nopoulos, 2002).

What about the famous reunited "Jim twins" who had the same name and almost the same personality? This is one of the most widely publicized cases of the entire Minnesota study. These two children were separated 37 days after their birth and reared with no contact until 38 years later. Despite this lifelong separation, James Lewis and James Springer both had divorced and remarried women named Betty, had undergone police training, loved carpentry, vacationed at the same beach each summer, and had named their firstborn sons James Allan and James Alan (Holden, 1980).

This is only a short list of their incredible similarities.

Heredity undoubtedly plays an important role, but can you think of other explanations? One study of *unrelated* pairs of students of the same age and gender also found a striking number of similarities (Wright et al., 1984). People of the same age apparently share a common historical time that influences large aspects of their personality. In addition, do you recall our earlier discussion of the *confirmation bias* (the tendency to seek out and pay attention to information that confirms our existing positions or beliefs, while ignoring contradictory data)? Imagine suddenly finding your long-lost identical twin. Wouldn't you be highly excited and thrilled with all your similarities and disinclined to note the differences?

As you can see, the research is inconclusive. Although heredity equips each of us with innate intellectual capacities, the environment significantly influences whether a person will reach his or her full intellectual potential (Dickens & Flynn, 2001; Sangwan, 2001). For example, early malnutrition can cause retarded brain development, which in turn affects the child's curiosity, responsiveness to the environment, and motivation for learning—all of which can lower the child's IQ. We are reminded once again that nature and nurture are inseparable.

Identical twins reared apart. Jerry Levy and Mark Newman, twins separated at birth, first met each other as adults at a firefighters' annual convention.

Gender & Cultural Diversity

Are IQ Tests Culturally Biased?
How would you answer the following questions?

1. A symphony is to a composer as a book is to a(n) _____. (a) musician; (b) editor; (c) novel; (d) author

2. If you throw dice and they land with a 7 on top, what is on the bottom? (a) snake eyes; (b) box cars; (c) little Joes; (d) eleven

Can you see how the content and answers to these questions might reflect *cultural bias*? People from some backgrounds will find the first question easier. Other groups will more easily answer the second. Which of these two questions do you think is most likely to appear on standard IQ tests?

One of the most hotly debated and controversial issues in psychology has to do with the accuracy of intelligence tests and what group differences in test scores really mean. In 1969, Arthur Jensen began a heated debate when he argued that intelligence is largely genetic in origin. Therefore, genetic factors are "strongly implicated" as the cause of ethnic differences in intelligence. A book by Richard J. Herrnstein and Charles Murray titled *The Bell Curve: Intelligence and Class Structure in American Life* reignited this debate in 1994 when the authors claimed that African Americans score below average in IQ because of their "genetic heritage."

Psychologists have responded to these claims with several points:

- *Some ethnic groups do score differently on IQ tests* (Blanton, 2000; Herrnstein & Murray, 1994; Jensen, Nyborg, & Nyborg, 2003; Rushton & Jensen, 2005; Templer et al., 2003). In the United States, Asian-American children score slightly higher on standardized IQ tests than European-American children, who in turn score higher than African-American, Latino, or Native American children (Brody, 1992; Lynn, 1995; Williams & Ceci, 1997).

- *Lack of cultural exposure to the concepts required on IQ tests can result in lowered IQ scores.* Therefore, the tests may not be an accurate measure of true capability—they may be culturally biased (Ginsberg, 2003; Manly et al., 2004; Naglieri & Ronning, 2000).

- *Group differences in IQ may have more to do with socioeconomic differences than ethnicity* (McLoyd, 1998; Reifman, 2000). African Americans, and most other minorities, are far more likely than whites to live in poverty. The environmental effects of poverty, such as poor prenatal care, poorly funded schools, and lack of textbooks and other resources, clearly influence intellectual development (Solan & Mozlin, 2001).

- *IQ does have a substantial genetic component.* Racial and ethnic differences may reflect underlying hereditary differences (Jensen, Nyborg, & Nyborg, 2003; Plomin, 1999; Plomin & DeFries, 1998; Rushton & Jensen, 2005). Note, however, that race and ethnicity, like intelligence itself, are almost impossible to define. For example, depending on the definition that you use, there are between 3 and 300 races, and no race is pure in a biological sense (Beutler et al., 1996; Yee, Fairchild, Weizmann, & Wyatt, 1993).

- *Intelligence is not a fixed characteristic.* A comparison of intelligence scores over recent years indicates that IQ scores have increased from one generation to the next. Furthermore, this increase is found in over 20 different countries (Flynn, 1987, 2000, 2003; Neisser, 1998; Resing & Nijland, 2002). *Fluid intelligence* scores, typically measured with problem-solving tasks, have increased about 15 points per

"YOU CAN'T BUILD A HUT, YOU DON'T KNOW HOW TO FIND EDIBLE ROOTS AND YOU KNOW NOTHING ABOUT PREDICTING THE WEATHER. IN OTHER WORDS, YOU DO TERRIBLY ON OUR I.Q. TEST."

www.wiley.com/college/huffman

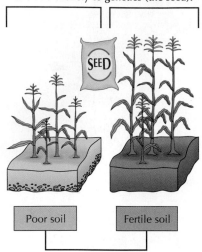

Differences <u>within</u> groups are due entirely to genetics (the seed).

Poor soil | Fertile soil

Differences <u>between</u> groups are due <u>entirely</u> to environment (the soil).

Figure 8.14 *If plants could talk!* Note that even when you begin with the exact same package of seeds (genetic inheritance), the average height of corn plants in the fertile soil will be greater than those in the poor soil (environmental influences). The same is true for intelligence. Therefore, no conclusions can be drawn about possible genetic contributions to the differences between groups.

Stereotype Threat *Negative stereotypes about minority groups cause some members to doubt their abilities*

generation. *Crystallized intelligence* scores, generally assessed by vocabulary and math skills, have increased about 9 points per generation. Interestingly, there also has been a steady increase in the verbal ability scores of African Americans over time and a slight decline for white Americans (Huang & Hauser, 1998).

James Flynn (2000, 2003) believes such increases may reflect the fact that intelligence tests aren't actually measuring intelligence but rather some weak link to intelligence. The explanation is unclear. But there are at least three possible contributors to this so-called *Flynn effect:* (1) The level of public education has increased, (2) people have become more proficient test-takers, and (3) intelligence increases with better nutrition.

Looking beyond what possibly caused these increases, the simple fact that overall IQ scores have increased in recent years suggests the *environment* is a significant contributor to ethnic and other differences in intelligence. As a critical thinker, can you think of other possible explanations for the so-called *Flynn effect?*

- *Differences in IQ scores reflect motivational and language factors.* In some ethnic groups, a child who excels in school is ridiculed for trying to be different from his or her classmates. Moreover, children grow up speaking the language of their culture and the dialect of their neighborhood. If this language or dialect does not match the educational system of which they are a part or the IQ test they take, they are obviously disadvantaged (Tanner-Halverson, Burden, & Sabers, 1993).

- *Members of every ethnic group can be found to have scores at all levels of the IQ scale.* The bell curves of all groups show considerable overlap, and IQ scores and intelligence have their greatest relevance in terms of individuals, not groups (Garcia & Stafford, 2000; Myerson, Rank, Raines, & Schnitzler, 1998; Reifman, 2000). For example, many individual African Americans receive higher IQ scores than many individual white Americans. Most important, even if a trait is primarily genetic (which does not appear to be the case with intelligence), group differences can still be wholly due to the environment (Figure 8.14).

- *As we've seen earlier, there are multiple intelligences, and traditional IQ tests do not measure many of them* (Gardner, 1999; Sternberg & Hedlund, 2002).

- *Finally, stereotype threats can significantly reduce the test scores of people in stereotyped groups* (Gonzales, Blanton, & Williams, 2002; Josephs, Newman, Brown, & Beer, 2003; Steele, 2003). The central thesis of **stereotype threat** is that an individual's performance on an IQ test depends in part on the individual's expectations about how he or she will do. These expectations are often shaped by cultural stereotypes about the abilities of an individual's particular age, ethnicity, gender, or socioeconomic class. If the dominant cultural stereotype says, "You can't teach old dogs new tricks" or "Women aren't good at math," you can imagine how this might affect many older individuals and women when they take an IQ test.

Claude Steele and Joshua Aronson (1995) first revealed stereotype threat in an experiment at Stanford University. They recruited African American and white students to take a *performance exam* and informed them that their individual intellectual abilities would be examined. Participants were matched on ability levels prior to the exam, and the exam was composed of questions similar to the Graduate Records Exam (GRE). The results revealed that the African-American students performed well below the white students. The researchers later repeated the same procedure and told students it was a *laboratory task* instead of a performance exam. This time there was no difference between African American scores and white scores.

What explains the difference in results? Subsequent work by Steele and others shows that stereotype threat occurs because members of the stereotyped groups doubt their own abilities. Simply being aware that you are not expected to do well lowers your score—you unintentionally fulfill the negative "self-fulfilling prophecy." Members fear that they will be evaluated in terms of the stereotype. This worry then translates into anxiety, which in turn lowers both the speed and accuracy of their responses to test questions. On the other hand, some individuals cope by "disidentifying." They say to themselves, "The test scores have no influence on how I feel about myself!" (Major, Spencer, Schmader, Wolfe, & Crocker, 1998). Unfortunately, this attitude also decreases performance because of the lessened motivation.

Studies show that stereotype threat affects the test performance of many groups, including African Americans, women, Native Americans, Latinos, low-income people, elderly people, and white male athletes (e.g., Ford et al., 2004; Gonzales, Blanton, & Williams, 2002; Major & O'Brien, 2005; Steele, 2003; Steele, James, & Barnett, 2002). This research helps explain some group differences in intelligence and achievement tests. Unfortunately, employers, educators, and clinicians routinely use such tests for many purposes. Yet there is more to intelligence (and achievement) than what is measured by an exam. Relying solely on these tests to make critical decisions affecting individual lives is not warranted and possibly is even unethical.

A Final Note

Think back to the questions we asked at the very beginning of our discussion of intelligence: Are Koko, Genie, and Thomas Edison intelligent? How would you answer these questions now? Hopefully, you now understand that all three cognitive processes discussed in this chapter (thinking, language, and intelligence) are complex phenomena, which are greatly affected by numerous interacting factors. As evidence, let's update our story of Genie. Her life, as you might have guessed, does not have a happy Hollywood ending. Genie's tale is a heartbreaking account of the lasting scars from a disastrous childhood. At the time of her rescue, at age 13, Genie's intellectual performance was at the level of a normal 1-year-old. Over the years, she was given thousands of hours of special training and rehabilitation, so that by the age of 19 she could use public transportation and was adapting well to her foster home and special classes at school (Rymer, 1993).

Genie was far from normal, however. Her intelligence scores were still close to the cutoff for mental retardation. And, as noted earlier, her language skills were similar to those of a 2- or 3-year-old. To make matters worse, she was also subjected to a series of foster home placements—one of which was abusive. At last report, Genie was living in a home for mentally retarded adults (Rymer, 1993).

CHECK & REVIEW

The Intelligence Controversy

Intelligence testing has long been the subject of great debate. To determine whether these tests are valid, you can examine people who fall at the extremes of intelligence. People with IQs of 70 and below (identified as mentally retarded) and those with IQs of 135 and above (identified as gifted) do differ in their respective intellectual abilities.

Research on the brain's role in intelligence has focused on three major questions: (1) Does a bigger brain mean greater intelligence? (Answer: "Not necessarily.") (2) Is a faster brain more intelligent? (Answer: "A qualified yes." And (3) Does a smart brain work harder? (Answer: "No, the smarter brain is more efficient.")

Another topic of debate is whether intelligence is inherited or due to the environment. According to the Minnesota

Study of Twins Reared Apart (1979 to present), heredity and environment are important, inseparable factors in intellectual development. Heredity equips each of us with innate capacities. The environment significantly influences whether an individual will reach full potential.

Perhaps the most hotly debated topic is whether ethnic differences on IQ tests are primarily "genetic in origin." Although some ethnic groups do score differently

 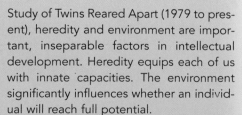

on IQ tests, cultural exposure, socioeconomic differences, motivation, language, and **stereotype threats** have been found to be contributing factors in score differences.

Questions

1. People with _____ are often categorized as mentally retarded, but they also possess incredible abilities in specific areas, such as musical memory or math calculations. (a) IQ scores below 70; (b) phenylketonuria (PKU); (c) fragile-X syndrome; (d) savant syndrome

2. A longitudinal study of the "Termites" found that high intelligence is correlated with _____. (a) higher academic success; (b) better athletic ability; (c) higher occupational achievement; (d) all of the above

3. The more efficient brain uses fewer _____ to solve problems than a less efficient brain. (a) parts of the brain; (b) neurotransmitters; (c) synapses, (d) energy resources

4. Which is more important in determining intelligence—heredity or environment?

Check your answers in Appendix B.

CLICK & REVIEW
for additional assessment options:
www.wiley.com/college/huffman

Assessment

KEY TERMS

*To assess your understanding of the **Key Terms** in Chapter 8, write a definition for each (in your own words), and then compare your definitions with those in the text.*

cognition (p. 287)

Thinking
algorithm (p. 291)
availability heuristic (p. 295)
concept (p. 288)
confirmation bias (p. 294)
convergent thinking (p. 297)
creativity (p. 297)
divergent thinking (p. 297)
functional fixedness (p. 293)
heuristics (p. 291)
mental image (p. 287)
mental set (p. 293)
prototype (p. 289)
representativeness heuristic (p. 295)

Language
babbling (p. 302)
cooing (p. 302)
grammar (p. 300)
language (p. 299)
language acquisition device (LAD) (p. 303)
morpheme [MOR-feem] (p. 300)
overextension (p. 302)
overgeneralize (p. 303)
phoneme [FOE-neem] (p. 300)
semantics (p. 301)
syntax (p. 300)
telegraphic speech (p. 302)

Intelligence
crystallized intelligence (p. 307)
fluid intelligence (p. 306)
intelligence (p. 306)
reliability (p. 311)
standardization (p. 310)
validity (p. 311)

The Intelligence Controversy
savant syndrome (p. 314)
stereotype threat (p. 318)

Achievement WEB RESOURCES

Huffman Book Companion Site
http://www.wiley.com/college/huffman
>This site is loaded with free Interactive Self-Tests, Internet Exercises, Glossary and Flashcards for key terms, web links, Handbook for Non-Native Speakers, and other activities designed to improve your mastery of the material in this chapter.

Interested in more information on problem solving?
http://www.big6.com/showarticle.php?id=415
>This is the home page for the Big6 information literacy model, which was developed by Mike Eisenberg and Bob Berkowitz. Thousands of K-12 schools, colleges, universities, and corporate and adult training programs have successfully applied this model to their personal, social, and global problems.

Want to compete in an Internet Problem Solving Contest (IPSC)?
http://ipsc.ksp.sk/
>This site offers an annual online contest for teams consisting of up to three people who all have computers with access to the Internet. Registration forms, guidelines, technical information, and practice sessions are all provided and clearly explained.

Want to increase your creativity at work?
http://ilearn.senecac.on.ca/careers/goals/creativity.html
>Provides numerous resources for developing personal creativity and organizational innovation in the workplace.

Chimp talk debate
http://www.santafe.edu/~johnson/articles.chimp.html
>A fascinating and detailed paper exploring the pros and cons of animal language.

Need more information about language?
http://www-csli.stanford.edu/
>The home page for the Center for the Study of Language and Information, an independent research center founded by researchers from Stanford University, provides information concerning current and past research and publications.

Want to learn more about the development of IQ tests?
http://www.indiana.edu/~intell/map.html
>This site for intelligence theory and testing presents an interactive map detailing the history of influences on the development of intelligence testing and theory.

Want to test your IQ?
http://www.brain.com/
>Offers a wide range of timed tests of intelligence, mental performance, memory, emotional states, and more.

☐ Thinking

Cognitive Building Blocks

1) **Mental image**: Mind's representation of a sensory experience.
2) **Concepts**: Mental categories that group according to similar characteristics. Concepts arise out of logical rules and definitions (artificial concepts). We also create natural categories or concepts (**prototypes**) and then organize them into successive ranks (hierarchies).

Animal → Bird, Dog ← Basic level

Bird → Parakeet, Chicken

Dog → Boxer, Poodle

Problem Solving

Step 1: Preparation
- Identify given facts.
- Separate relevant facts.
- Define ultimate goal.

→

Step 2: Production
Create hypotheses using **algorithms** and **heuristics**.

→

Step 3: Evaluation
Judge the hypotheses from Step 2 against criteria from Step 1.

Barriers to problem solving: **Mental sets**, **functional fixedness**, **confirmation bias**, **availability heuristic**, and **representativeness heuristic**.

Creativity

- *Elements of creativity*: Originality, fluency, and flexibility.
- *Measuring creativity*: **Divergent thinking** versus **convergent thinking**.
- *Researching creativity*: Investment theory says creativity is a combination of intellectual ability, knowledge, thinking style, personality, motivation, and environment.

◇ Language

Characteristics of Language

Language is produced from words using **phonemes** (basic speech sounds) and **morphemes** (the smallest meaningful units of language). The words are strung together into sentences using rules of **grammar**, which include **syntax** (the grammatical rules for ordering words) and **semantics** (meaning in language).

Language Development

Stages
- *Prelinguistics*: Crying → **cooing** (vowel sounds) → **babbling** (vowel/consonant combinations).
- *Linguistic*: One-word utterances → **telegraphic speech** (omits unnecessary, connecting words) → grammatical speech.
- *Problems*: **Overextension**(e.g., "bunnies" called "dogs") and **overgeneralization** (e.g., "foots," "goed").

Theories
- *Nature*: Language results from maturation. Chomsky's innate **language acquisition device** (LAD).
- *Nurture*: Environment and rewards or punishments explain language.

Intelligence

What Is Intelligence?

Competing theories and definitions:

- Spearman→Intelligence is "g," a general intelligence.
- Thurstone→Intelligence is seven distinct mental abilities.
- Guilford→Intelligence is composed of 120 or more separate abilities.
- Cattell→Intelligence is two types of "g" (**fluid intelligence** and **crystallized intelligence**).
- Gardner→Eight or possibly nine types of intelligence.
- Sternberg→Triarchic theory of intelligence (analytical, creative, and practical).

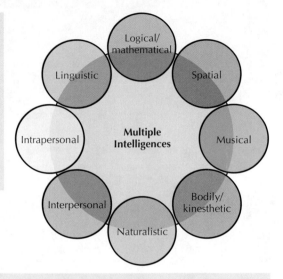

How Do We Measure Intelligence?

Intelligence quotient (IQ) tests are widely used in our culture.

- *Stanford-Binet* measures cognitive abilities of children ages 3 to 16.
- *Wechsler* measures cognitive and nonverbal abilities of three distinct age levels.

Elements of a useful test:

1) **Standardization**: Test is given to a representative sample to establish norms, and uniform administration procedures are used.
2) **Reliability**: The scores are stable over time.
3) **Validity**: The test measures what it is designed to measure.

The Intelligence Controversy

Extremes and Differences in Intelligence

- Individuals with IQs of 70 and below are identified as mentally retarded. Individuals with IQs of 135 and above are identified as gifted.
- Neuroscientists ask: 1) Does a bigger brain mean greater intelligence? Not necessarily. 2) Is a faster brain more intelligent? A qualified yes. 3) Does a smart brain work harder? No, the smarter brain is more efficient.
- The Minnesota Study of Twins Reared Apart found heredity and environment are important, inseparable factors in intellectual development.

www.wiley.com/college/huffman

9

LIFE SPAN DEVELOPMENT I

Achievement

Core Learning Outcomes

As you read Chapter 9, keep the following questions in mind and answer them in your own words:

▷ How is research in developmental psychology different from research in other areas of psychology?

▷ What are the major physical changes that occur throughout our life span?

▷ How does cognition, or the way we think about the world, change during our life cycle?

▷ How do attachment and parenting styles affect development?

▢ Achievement
▢ Assessment
▢ Application

325

WHY STUDY PSYCHOLOGY?

Davis Barber/Photoedit

Chapter 9 will explore questions, such as "Did you know that..."

▶ At the moment of conception, you were smaller than the period at the end of a sentence?

▶ During the last few months of pregnancy, you (as a fetus) could hear sounds outside your mother's womb?

▶ At birth, your head was approximately one-fourth of your total body size, but as an adult it's only one-eighth?

▶ Within the first few days of life, breast-fed newborns can recognize and show prefer-

ence for the odor and taste of their mother's milk over another mother's?

▶ Children in many cultures sleep alongside their parents for several years—not in a separate bed or room?

▶ According to Piaget, teenagers tend to believe they are alone and unique in their thoughts and feelings—"no one has ever felt like this before"?

Developmental Psychology *Study of age-related changes in behavior and mental processes from conception to death*

I magine for a moment that you are on a magical carpet ride and can go back to the moment right before your conception—when your father's sperm met your mother's egg—and can change who will be either your father or your mother. Would you? Would you still be "you" if you had a different father or mother? What if you could skip ahead to your childhood and change your hometown, change your school, or add or subtract siblings? What would you change? How might such changes affect who you are today?

As you can see from this brief fantasy, "you" are truly a product of your past—and future! What you are now is a reflection of thousands of contributors from the past, and what you will be tomorrow is still unwritten. Life doesn't stand still. You are in a state of constant change and development throughout your entire life. You and I (and every other human on this planet) will be many people in our lifetime—infant, child, teenager, adult, and senior citizen.

Would you like to know more about yourself at each of these ages? There is an entire field of knowledge, called **developmental psychology**, which *studies age-related changes in behavior and mental processes from conception to death* (Table 9.1). In this chapter, we will study how developmental psychologists conduct their research

THE FOUR AGES OF MAN

INFANCY   CHILDHOOD   YOUTH   MATURITY

©The New Yorker Collection 1991Michael Crawford from cartoonbank.com. All Rights Reserved.

TABLE 9.1 LIFE SPAN DEVELOPMENT

Stage	Approximate Age
Prenatal	Conception to birth
Infancy	Birth to 18 months
Early childhood	18 months to 6 years
Middle childhood	6–12 years
Adolescence	12–20 years
Young adulthood	20–45 years
Middle adulthood	45–60 years
Later adulthood	60 years to death

and how our physical bodies change over the life span. Then we will explore life span changes in our cognitive (or thought) processes and our social-emotional development.

To emphasize that development is an ongoing, lifelong *process*, throughout this chapter we also will take a topical approach (as opposed to a chronological approach, which arbitrarily divides the field into two periods—childhood–adolescence and adulthood). Thus, in this chapter, we will trace physical, cognitive, and social-emotional development—one at a time—from conception to death.

Then, in the next chapter, we will explore moral development, personality development, and special issues related to grief and death—again, one topic at a time. The topical approach allows us to see how any one aspect of development affects an individual over the entire life span.

STUDYING DEVELOPMENT

In all fields of psychology, certain theoretical issues guide the basic direction of research. First, we look at what those issues are in human development, and then we examine how developmental psychologists conduct their research.

Theoretical Issues: Ongoing Debates

The three most important debates or questions in human development are about *nature versus nurture*, *continuity versus stages*, and *stability versus change*.

1. *Nature versus nurture.* The issue of *nature versus nurture* has been with us since the beginning of psychology. Even the ancient Greeks had the same debate—Plato arguing for innate knowledge and abilities, and Aristotle, for learning through the five senses.

   According to the nature position, human behavior and development are governed by automatic, genetically predetermined signals in a process known as **maturation**. Just as a flower unfolds in accord with its genetic blueprint, we humans crawl before we walk and walk before we run. Furthermore, there is an optimal period shortly after birth, one of several **critical periods** during our lifetime, when an organism is especially sensitive to certain experiences that shape the capacity for future development.

   Nurturists make up the other side of the debate. Early philosophers proposed that at birth our minds are a *tabula rasa* (or blank slate) and that the environment determines what messages are written on the slate. Those who hold an extreme nurturist position would argue that development occurs by learning through personal experience and observation of others.

2. *Continuity versus stages.* Continuity proponents maintain that development is continuous, with new abilities, skills, and knowledge gradually added at a relatively uniform pace. The continuity model, then, suggests that adult thinking and intelligence differ quantitatively from a child's. We simply have more math or verbal skills than children. Stage theorists, on the other hand, believe development occurs at different rates, alternating between periods of little change and periods of abrupt, rapid change. In this chapter and the next, we discuss several stage theories: Piaget's theory of cognitive development, Erikson's psychosocial theory of personality development, and Kohlberg's theory of moral development.

3. *Stability versus change.* Have you generally maintained your personal characteristics as you matured from infant to adult (stability)? Or does your current personality bear little resemblance to the personality you displayed during infancy (change)? Psychologists who emphasize stability in development hold

Achievement

How is research in developmental psychology different from research in other areas of psychology?

Maturation *Development governed by automatic, genetically predetermined signals*

Critical Period *A period of special sensitivity to specific types of learning that shapes the capacity for future development*

that measurements of personality taken during childhood are important predictors of adult personality. Of course, psychologists who emphasize change disagree.

Which of these positions is more correct? Most psychologists do not take a hard line either way. Rather, they prefer an *interactionist perspective*. In the age-old *nature-versus-nurture* debate, for example, psychologists generally believe that development emerges from each individual's unique genetic predisposition *and* from individual experiences in the environment (Gottesman & Hanson, 2005; McCrae, 2004; Olson, 2004; Sullivan, Kendler, & Neale, 2003). More recently, the interactionist position has evolved into the *biopsychosocial model* mentioned throughout this text. In this model, biological factors (genetics, brain functions, biochemistry, and evolution), psychological influences (learning, thinking, emotion, personality, and motivation), and social forces (family, school, culture, ethnicity, social class, and politics) all affect and are affected by one another.

As with the nature-versus-nurture debate, so with the issues of continuity versus stages and stability versus change. Perspectives are not a matter of either/or. Physical development and motor skills, for example, are believed to be primarily continuous in nature. In contrast, cognitive skills usually develop in discrete stages. Similarly, some traits are stable, whereas others vary greatly across the life span.

We will return to these three questions several times in this chapter. Now we turn our attention to another aspect of studying development—how developmental psychologists collect their information.

■ Research Methods: Two Basic Approaches

To study development, psychologists use either a *cross-sectional* or *longitudinal* method. The **cross-sectional method** examines individuals of various ages (e.g., 20, 40, 60, and 80 years) at one point in time—and gives information about age differences. The **longitudinal method** follows a single individual or group of individuals (e.g., only 20-year-olds at the beginning of the study) over an extended period and gives information about age changes (Figure 9.1).

Cross-Sectional Method *Measures individuals of various ages at one point in time and gives information about age differences*

Longitudinal Method *Measures a single individual or group of individuals over an extended period and gives information about age changes*

Figure 9.1 *Cross-sectional versus longitudinal research.* Note that cross-sectional research uses different participants and is interested in age-related differences, whereas longitudinal research studies the same participants over time to find age-related changes.

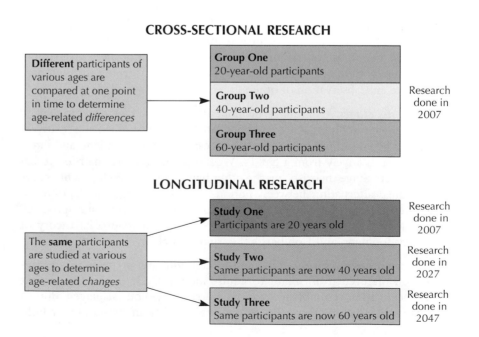

CROSS-SECTIONAL RESEARCH

Different participants of various ages are compared at one point in time to determine age-related *differences*

Group One 20-year-old participants
Group Two 40-year-old participants
Group Three 60-year-old participants

Research done in 2007

LONGITUDINAL RESEARCH

The **same** participants are studied at various ages to determine age-related *changes*

Study One Participants are 20 years old — Research done in 2007
Study Two Same participants are now 40 years old — Research done in 2027
Study Three Same participants are now 60 years old — Research done in 2047

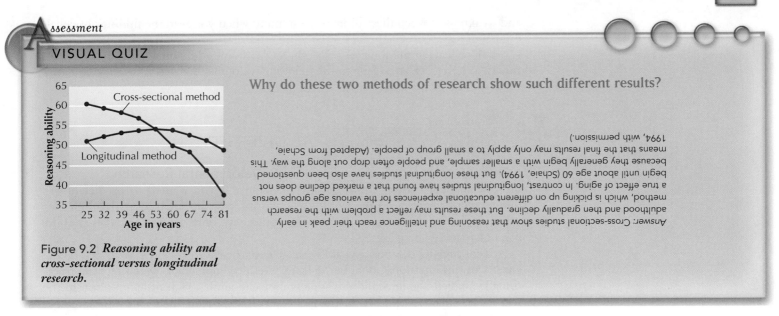

Why do these two methods of research show such different results?

Answer: Cross-sectional studies show that reasoning and intelligence reach their peak in early adulthood and then gradually decline. But these results may reflect a problem with the research method, which is picking up on different educational experiences for the various age groups versus a true effect of aging. In contrast, longitudinal studies have also been questioned begin until about age 60 (Schaie, 1994). But these longitudinal studies have also been questioned because they generally begin with a smaller sample, and people often drop out along the way. This means that the final results may only apply to a small group of people. (Adapted from Schaie, 1994, with permission.)

Figure 9.2 *Reasoning ability and cross-sectional versus longitudinal research.*

Imagine you are a developmental psychologist interested in studying intelligence in adults. Which method would you choose—cross-sectional or longitudinal? Before you decide, note the different research results shown in Figure 9.2.

Researchers suggest that the different results may reflect a central problem with cross-sectional studies. They often confuse genuine age differences with *cohort effects*—differences that result from specific histories of the age group studied (Elder, 1998). As you can see in Figure 9.2, the 81-year-olds measured by the cross-sectional method have dramatically lower scores than the 25-year-olds. But is this due to aging or possibly to broad environmental differences, such as less formal education or poorer nutrition? Because the different age groups, called *cohorts*, grew up in different historical periods, the results may not apply to people growing up at other times. With the cross-sectional method, age effects and cohort effects are hopelessly tangled.

Longitudinal studies also have their limits. They are expensive in terms of time and money, and their results are restricted in *generalizability*. Because participants often drop out or move away during the extended test period, the experimenter may end up with a self-selected sample that differs from the general population in important ways. As you can see in Table 9.2, each method of research has its own strengths

TABLE 9.2 ADVANTAGES AND DISADVANTAGES OF CROSS-SECTIONAL AND LONGITUDINAL RESEARCH DESIGNS

	Cross-Sectional	**Longitudinal**
Advantages	Gives information about age differences Quick Less expensive Typically larger sample	Gives information about age changes Increased reliability More in-depth information per participant
Disadvantages	Cohort effects are difficult to separate Restricted generalizability (measures behaviors at only one point in time)	More expensive Time consuming Restricted generalizability (typically smaller sample and dropouts over time)

and weaknesses. Keep these differences in mind when you read the findings of developmental research.

Before leaving the topic of research, let's examine the unique contributions cultural psychologists have made to the field of developmental psychology.

chievement
GENDER & CULTURAL DIVERSITY

Cultural Psychology's Guidelines for Developmental Research

How would you answer the following question: "If you wanted to predict how a human child anywhere in the world was going to grow up, what his or her behavior was going to be like as an adult, and you could have only one fact about that child, what fact would you choose to have?"

According to cultural psychologists like Patricia Greenfield (1994, 2004), the answer to this question should be "culture." Yet developmental psychology has traditionally studied people (children, adolescents, and adults) with little attention to the sociocultural context. In recent times, however, psychologists are paying increasing attention to the following points:

1. ***Culture may be the most important determinant of development.*** If a child grows up in an individualistic/independent culture (such as North America or most of Western Europe), we can predict that this child will probably be competitive and question authority as an adult. Were this same child reared in a collectivist/interdependent culture (common in Africa, Asia, and Latin America), she or he would most likely grow up to be cooperative and respectful of elders (Delgado-Gaitan, 1994; Berry et al., 2002).

2. ***Human development, like most areas of psychology, cannot be studied outside its sociocultural context.*** In parts of Korea, most teenagers see a strict, authoritarian style of parenting as a sign of love and concern (Kim & Choi, 1995). Korean-American and Korean-Canadian teenagers, however, see the same behavior as a sign of rejection. Thus, rather than studying specific behaviors, such as "authoritarian parenting styles," discussed later in this chapter, researchers in child development suggest that children should be studied only within their *developmental niche*. A developmental niche has three components: the physical and social contexts in which the child lives, the culturally determined rearing and educational practices, and the psychological characteristics of the parents (Bugental & Johnston, 2000).

3. ***Each culture's ethnotheories are important determinants of behavior.*** Within every culture, people have a prevailing set of ideas and beliefs that attempt to explain the world around them (an *ethnotheory*) (Amorim & Rossetti-Ferreira, 2004; Keller, Yovsi, & Voelker, 2002). In the area of child development, for example, cultures have specific ethnotheories about how children should be trained. As a critical thinker, you can anticipate that differing ethnotheories can lead to problems between cultures. Even the very idea of "critical thinking" is part of our North American ethnotheory regarding education. And it, too, can produce culture clashes.

Concha Delgado-Gaitan (1994) found that Mexican immigrants from a rural background have a difficult time adjusting to North American schools, which teach children to question authority and think for themselves. In their culture of origin, these children are trained to respect their elders, be good listeners, and participate in conversation only when their opinion is solicited. Children who argue with adults are reminded not to be *malcriados* (naughty or disrespectful).

Cultural influences on development. How might these two groups differ in their physical, social-emotional, cognitive, and personality development?

Wojnarowicz/The Image Works

Hugh Sitton/Stone/Getty Images

4. ***Culture is largely invisible to its participants.*** Culture consists of ideals, values, and assumptions that are widely shared among a given group and that guide specific behaviors (Brislin, 2000). Precisely because these ideals and values are widely shared, they are seldom discussed or directly examined. Just as a "fish doesn't know it's in water," we take our culture for granted, operating within it, although being almost unaware of it.

TRY THIS YOURSEL*F* *Application*

Culture Invisibility

If you would like a personal demonstration of the invisibility of culture, try this simple experiment: The next time you walk into an elevator, don't turn around. Remain facing the rear wall. Watch how others respond when you don't turn around or stand right next to them rather than going to the other side of the elevator. Our North American culture has rules that prescribe the "proper" way to ride in an elevator, and people become very uncomfortable when these rules are violated.

*A*ssessment
CHECK & REVIEW

Studying Development

Developmental psychology is concerned with describing, explaining, predicting, and sometimes modifying age-related behaviors across the entire life span. Three important research issues are nature versus nurture, continuity versus stages, and stability versus change.

Researchers in developmental psychology generally use **cross-sectional** (different participants of various ages at one point in time) or **longitudinal** (same participants over an extended period) **methods.** Each has advantages and disadvantages.

Cultural psychologists suggest that developmental researchers keep the following points in mind:

- Culture is the most important determinant of development.
- Human development cannot be studied outside its sociocultural context.
- Each culture's ethnotheories are important determinants of behavior.
- Culture is largely invisible to its participants.

Questions

1. Briefly define developmental psychology.
2. What three major questions are studied in developmental psychology?
3. Differences in age groups that reflect factors unique to a specific age group are called _____ effects. (a) generational; (b) social-environmental; (c) operational; (d) cohort
4. _____ studies are the most time-efficient method, whereas _____ studies provide the most in-depth information per participant. (a) Correlational, experimental; (b) Fast-track, follow-up; (c) Cross-sectional, longitudinal; (d) Cohort-sequential, cohort-intensive

Check your answers in Appendix B.

CLICK & REVIEW
for additional assessment options:
www.wiley.com/college/huffman

PHYSICAL DEVELOPMENT

After studying my photos in Figure 9.3, or looking at your own child and adult photos, you may be amused and surprised by the dramatic changes in physical appearance. But have you stopped to appreciate the incredible underlying process that transformed all of us from birth to our current adult bodies? In this section, we will explore the fascinating world of physical development. We begin with the prenatal period and early childhood, followed by adolescence and adulthood.

*A*chievement

What are the major physical changes that occur throughout our life span?

www.wiley.com/college/huffman

Images courtesy of Karen Huffman

Figure 9.3 *Changes in physical development.* These are photos of this text's author at ages 1, 4, 10, 30, and 55. Although physical changes are the most obvious signs of aging and development, our cognitive, social, moral, and personality processes and traits also change across the life span.

Prenatal Period and Early Childhood: A Time of Rapid Change

Do you remember being a young child and feeling like it would "take forever to grow up"? Contrary to a child's sense of interminable, unchanging time, the early years of development are characterized by rapid and unparalleled change. In fact, if you continued to develop at the same rapid rate that marked your first two years of life, you would weigh several tons and be over 12 feet tall as an adult! Thankfully, physical development slows, yet it is important to note that change continues until the very moment of death. Let's look at some of the major physical changes occurring throughout the life span.

Prenatal Physical Development

Your prenatal development began at *conception,* when your mother's egg, or *ovum,* united with your father's *sperm* cell (Figure 9.4). At that time, you were a single cell barely $1/175$ of an inch in diameter—smaller than the period at the end of this sentence. This new cell, called a *zygote,* then began a process of rapid cell division that resulted in a multimillion-celled infant (you) some nine months later.

Figure 9.4 *The moment of conception.* (a) Note the large number of sperm surrounding the ovum. (b) Although a "joint effort" is required to break through the outer coating, only one sperm will actually fertilize the egg.

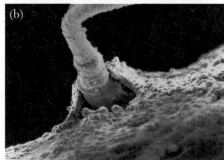

Francis Leroy, Biocosmos/PhotoResearchers, Inc.

Bonnier Alba

The vast changes that occur during the nine months of a full-term pregnancy are usually divided into three stages (Figure 9.5). The **germinal period** begins with fertilization and ends with implantation of the rapidly dividing mass of cells (the zygote) in the wall of the uterus. The outer portion of the zygote forms part of the placenta and umbilical cord, whereas the inner portion becomes the *embryo.* The **embryonic period**, the second stage, begins after implantation and lasts through the eighth week. During this time, the embryo's major organ systems begin to develop. The final stage is the **fetal period**, from the end of the second month until birth. During this period, the *fetus* continues to grow and the organs begin to function. Prenatal growth, as well as growth during the first few years after birth, is *proximodistal* (near to far), with the innermost parts of the body developing before the outermost parts. Thus, a fetus's arms develop before its hands and fingers. Development

Germinal Period *First stage of prenatal development, which begins with conception and ends with implantation in the uterus (the first two weeks)*

Embryonic Period *Second stage of prenatal development, which begins after uterine implantation and lasts through the eighth week*

Fetal Period *The third, and final, stage of prenatal development (eight weeks to birth), characterized by rapid weight gain in the fetus and the fine detailing of body organs and systems*

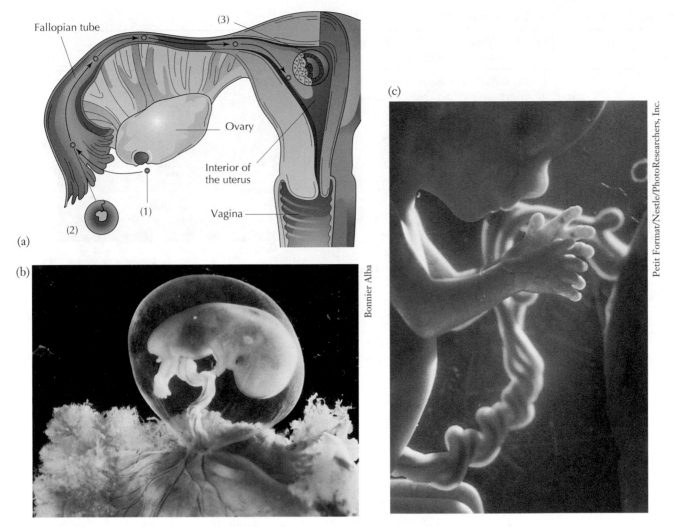

Figure 9.5 *Prenatal development.* (a) *From ovulation to implantation.* After discharge from either the left or right ovary (number 1 on the diagram), the ovum travels to the opening of the fallopian tube. If fertilization occurs (2), it normally takes place in the first third of the fallopian tube. The fertilized ovum is referred to as a zygote. When the zygote reaches the uterus, it implants itself in the wall of the uterus (3) and begins to grow tendril-like structures that intertwine with the rich supply of blood vessels located there. After implantation, the organism is known as an embryo. (b) *Embryonic period.* This stage occurs from implantation to 8 weeks. At 8 weeks, the major organ systems have become well differentiated. Note that at this stage, the head grows at a faster rate than other parts of the body. (c) *Fetal stage.* This is the period from the end of the second month to birth. At four months, all the actual body parts and organs are established. The fetal stage is primarily a time for increased growth and "fine detailing."

also proceeds *cephalocaudally* (head to tail). Thus, a fetus's head is disproportionately large compared to the lower part of its body.

Hazards to Prenatal Development

During pregnancy, the *placenta* (the vascular organ that unites the fetus to the mother's uterus) serves as the link for food and excretion of wastes. It also screens out some, but not all, harmful substances. Environmental hazards such as X-rays or toxic waste, drugs, and diseases such as rubella (German measles) can cross the *placental barrier* (Table 9.3). These influences generally have their most devastating effect during the first three months of pregnancy—making this a *critical period* in development.

The pregnant mother obviously plays a primary role in prenatal development because her nutrition and health directly influence the child she is carrying. Further-

GASP   www.gasp.org.uk

SUMMARY TABLE 9.3 THREATS TO PRENATAL DEVELOPMENT

Maternal Factors	Possible Effects on Embryo, Fetus, Newborn, or Young Child	
Malnutrition	Low birth weight, malformations, less developed brain, greater vulnerability to disease	 Streissguth, A.P., & Little, R.E. (1994). "Unit 5:Alcohol, Pregnancy, and the Fetal Alcohol Syndrome: SecondEdition" of the Project)
Stress exposure	Low birth weight, hyperactivity, irritability, feeding difficulties	
Exposure to X-rays	Malformations, cancer	
Legal and illegal drugs	Inhibition of bone growth, hearing loss, low birth weight, fetal alcohol syndrome, mental retardation, attention deficits in childhood, and death.	 ***Fetal alcohol syndrome.** In addition to facial abnormalities and stunted growth, children suffering from fetal alcohol syndrome (FAS) also have brains that are smaller and underdeveloped compared to those of normal children.*
Diseases German measles (rubella), herpes, AIDS, and toxoplasmosis	Blindness, deafness, mental retardation, heart and other malformations, brain infection, spontaneous abortion, premature birth, low birth weight, and death	

Sources: Abadinsky, 2004; Hyde & DeLamater, 2006; Lee, Mattson, & Riley, 2004; Rybacki & Long, 1999; Watson, Mednick, Huttunen, & Wang, 1999.

Teratogen [Tuh-RAT-uh-jen]
Environmental agent that causes damage during prenatal development; the term comes from the Greek word teras, meaning "malformation"

Fetal Alcohol Syndrome (FAS) *A combination of birth defects, including organ deformities and mental, motor, and/or growth retardation, that results from maternal alcohol abuse*

more, almost everything she ingests can cross the placental barrier (a better term might be *placental sieve*). However, the father also plays a role—other than just fertilization. Environmentally, the father's smoking may pollute the air the mother breathes, and genetically, he may transmit heritable diseases. In addition, research suggests that alcohol, opiates, cocaine, various gases, lead, pesticides, and industrial chemicals all can damage the father's sperm (Bandstra et al., 2002; Grilly, 2006; Richardson et al., 2002).

Perhaps the most important, and generally avoidable, danger to the developing fetus comes from drugs—both legal and illegal. Nicotine and alcohol are two of the most important **teratogens**, environmental agents that cause damage during prenatal development. Mothers who smoke tobacco have significantly higher rates of spontaneous abortions, premature births, low-birth-weight infants, and fetal deaths (American Cancer Society, 2004; Bull, 2003; Oliver 2002). Children of women who smoke during pregnancy also show increased behavioral abnormalities and cognitive problems (Roy, Seidler, & Slotkin, 2002; Thapar et al., 2003).

Alcohol also readily crosses the placenta, affects fetal development, and can result in a neurotoxic syndrome called **fetal alcohol syndrome (FAS)**. Prenatal exposure to alcohol can cause facial abnormalities and stunted growth. But the most disabling features of FAS are neurobehavioral problems, ranging from hyperactivity and learning disabilities to mental retardation, depression, and psychoses (Korkman, Kettunen, & Autti-Ramo, 2003; Lee, Mattson, & Riley, 2004; Sokol, Delaney-Black, & Nordstrom, 2003).

Early Childhood Physical Development
Although Shakespeare described newborns as capable of only "mewling and puking in the nurse's arms," they are actually capable of much more. Let's explore three key areas of change in early childhood: *brain, motor,* and *sensory/perceptual development.*

1. *Brain development.* As you recall from Chapter 2, the human brain is divided into three major sections—the *hindbrain*, *midbrain*, and *forebrain*. Note in Figure 9.6 how the prenatal brain begins as a fluid-filled neural tube and then rapidly progresses. The brain and other parts of the nervous system grow faster than any other part of the body during both prenatal development and the first two years of life. At birth, a healthy newborn's brain is one-fourth its full adult size and will grow to about 75 percent of its adult weight and size by the age of 2. At age 5, the child's brain is nine-tenths its full adult weight (Figure 9.7).

Rapid brain growth during infancy and early childhood slows down in later childhood. Further brain development and learning occur primarily because neurons grow in size and because the number of axons and dendrites, as well as the extent of their connections, increases (DiPietro, 2000). As children learn and develop, synaptic connections between active neurons strengthen, and dendritic connections become more elaborate (Figure 9.8). *Synaptic pruning* (reduction of unused synapses) helps support this process. *Myelination*, the accumulation of fatty tissue coating the axons of nerve cells, continues until early adulthood. Myelin increases the speed of neural impulses, and the speed of information processing shows a corresponding increase (Chapter 2). In addition, synaptic connections in the frontal lobes and other parts of the brain continue growing and changing throughout the entire life span (Chapter 2 and 6).

2. *Motor development.* Compared to the hidden, internal changes in brain development, the orderly emergence of active movement skills, known as *motor development*, is easily observed and measured. The newborn's first motor abilities are limited to *reflexes*—involuntary responses to stimulation. For example, the rooting reflex occurs when something touches a baby's cheek: The infant will automatically turn its head, open its mouth, and root for a nipple.

In addition to simple reflexes, the infant soon begins to show voluntary control over movements of

The effects of maturation on motor development. Some Hopi Indian infants spend a great portion of their first year of life being carried in a cradleboard, rather than crawling and walking freely on the ground. Yet by age 1, their motor skills are very similar to those of infants who have not been restrained in this fashion (Dennis & Dennis, 1940).

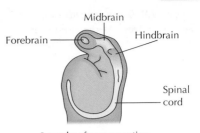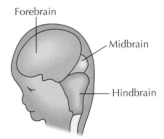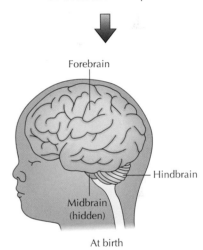
Figure 9.6 *Prenatal brain development.*

Wind River Victor Englebert/PhotoResearchers

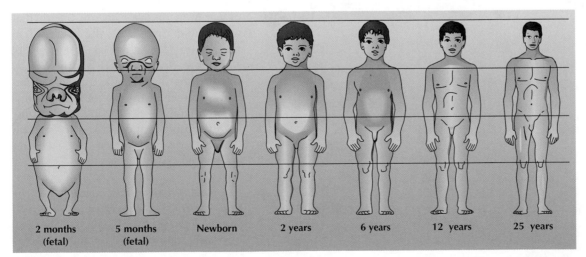
2 months (fetal) 5 months (fetal) Newborn 2 years 6 years 12 years 25 years

Figure 9.7 *Changes in body proportions.* Notice how body proportions change as we grow older. At birth, an infant's head is one-fourth its total body's size. In adulthood, the head is one-eighth the body size.

 www.wiley.com/college/huffman

Figure 9.8 *Brain growth in the first two years.* As the child learns and acquires new abilities, his or her brain develops increased connections between neurons.

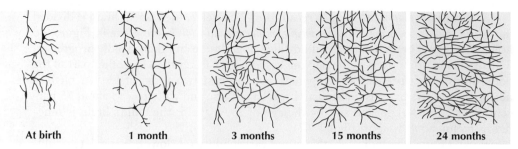

At birth   1 month   3 months   15 months   24 months

Figure 9.9 *Milestones in motor development.* In the typical progression of motor abilities, "chin up" occurs at approximately age 2.2 months. However, no two children are exactly alike; all follow their own individual timetable for physical development. (Adapted from Frankenburg et al., 1992, with permission.)

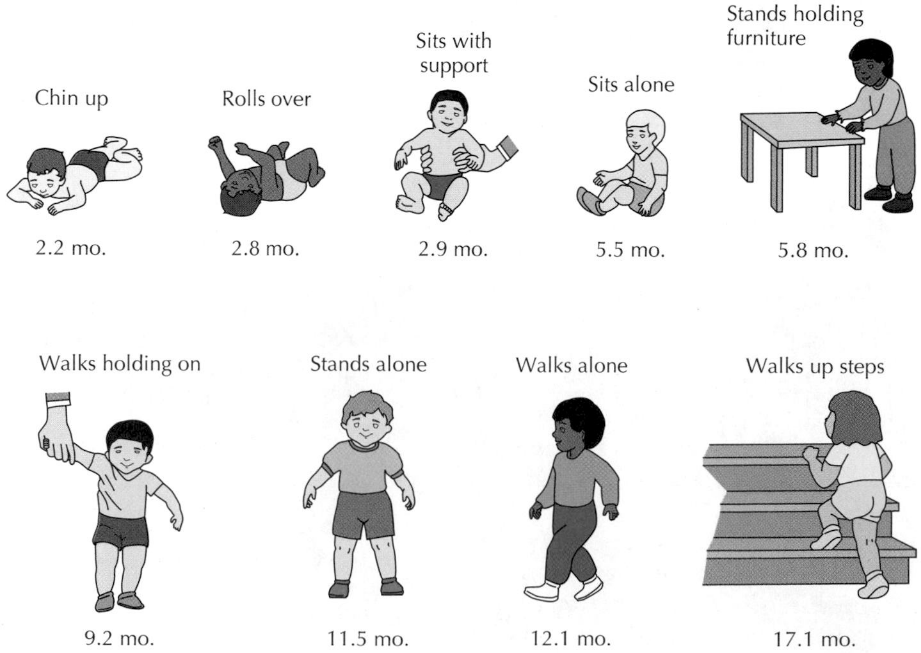

various body parts. As you can see in Figure 9.9, a helpless newborn who cannot even lift her head is soon transformed into an active toddler capable of crawling, walking, and climbing. Keep in mind that motor development is largely due to natural maturation, but it can also be affected by environmental influences like disease and neglect.

3. *Sensory and perceptual development.* At birth, a newborn can smell most odors and distinguish between sweet, salty, and bitter tastes. Breast-fed newborns also recognize and show preference for the odor and taste of their mother's milk over another mother's (DiPietro, 2000). In addition, the newborn's sense of touch and pain is highly developed, as evidenced by reactions to circumcision and heel pricks for blood testing (Williamson, 1997).

The sense of vision, however, is poorly developed. At birth, a newborn is estimated to have vision between 20/200 and 20/600 (Haith & Benson, 1998). If you have normal 20/20 vision, you can imagine what the infant's visual life is like. An infant sees at 20 feet the level of detail you see at 200 or 600 feet. Within the first few months, vision quickly improves, and by 6 months, it is 20/100 or better. At 2 years, visual acuity reaches a near-adult level of 20/20 (Courage & Adams, 1990).

One of the most interesting findings in infant sensory and perceptual research concerns hearing. Not only can the newborn hear quite well at birth (Matlin & Foley, 1997) but also, during the last few months in the womb, the fetus can apparently hear sounds outside the mother's body (Vaughan, 1996). This raises the interesting possibility of fetal learning, and some have advocated special stimulation for the fetus as a way of increasing intelligence, creativity, and general alertness (e.g., Van de Carr & Lehrer, 1997).

Studies on possible fetal learning have found that newborn infants easily recognize their own mother's voice over that of a stranger (Kisilevsky et al., 2003). They also show preferences for children's stories (such as *The Cat in the Hat* or *The King, the Mice, and the Cheese*) that were read to them while they were still in the womb (DeCasper & Fifer, 1980; Karmiloff & Karmiloff-Smith, 2002). On the other hand, some experts caution that too much or the wrong kind of stimulation before birth can be stressful for both the mother and fetus. They suggest that the fetus gets what it needs without any special stimulation.

How can scientists measure perceptual abilities and preferences in such young babies? Newborns and infants obviously cannot talk or follow direc-

Chin up   Rolls over   Sits with support   Sits alone   Stands holding furniture

2.2 mo.   2.8 mo.   2.9 mo.   5.5 mo.   5.8 mo.

Walks holding on   Stands alone   Walks alone   Walks up steps

9.2 mo.   11.5 mo.   12.1 mo.   17.1 mo.

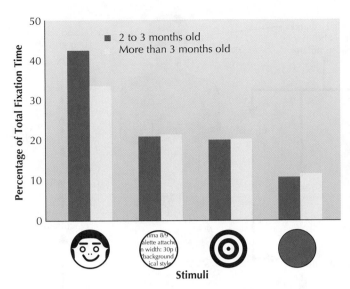

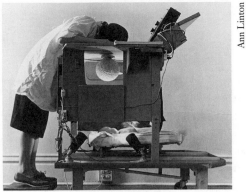

Figure 9.10 *Fantz's "looking chamber."* Using this specially designed testing apparatus, Fantz and his colleagues measured the length of time infants stared at various stimuli. They found that infants preferred complex rather than simple patterns and pictures of faces rather than nonfaces.

tions, so researchers have had to create ingenious experiments to evaluate their perceptual skills. One of the earliest experimenters, Robert Fantz (1956, 1963), designed a "looking chamber" in which infants lie on their backs and look at visual stimuli (Figure 9.10).

Researchers also use newborns' heart rate and innate abilities, such as the sucking reflex, to study how they learn and how their perceptual abilities develop. To study the sense of smell, researchers measure changes in the newborns' heart rates when different odors are presented. Presumably, if they can smell one odor but not the other, their heart rate will change in the presence of the first but not the second. From research such as this, we now know that the senses develop very early in life.

▣ Adolescence and Adulthood: A Time of Both Dramatic and Gradual Change

Whereas the adolescent years are marked by dramatic changes in appearance and physical capacity, middle age and later adulthood are times of gradual physical changes. We begin with a look at adolescence.

Adolescence

Think back for a moment to your teen years. Were you concerned about the physical changes you were going through? Did you worry about how you differed from your classmates? Changes in height and weight, breast development and menstruation for girls, and a deepening voice and beard growth for boys are important milestones for adolescents. **Puberty**, the period of adolescence when a person becomes capable of reproduction, is a major physical milestone for everyone. It is a clear biological signal of the end of childhood.

Although commonly associated with puberty, *adolescence* is the loosely defined psychological period of development between childhood and adulthood. In the United States, it roughly corresponds to the teenage years. It is important to recognize that adolescence is not a universal concept. Some nonindustrialized countries have no need for such a slow transition, and children simply assume adult responsibilities as soon as possible.

The clearest and most dramatic physical sign of puberty is the *growth spurt*, characterized by rapid increases in height, weight, and skeletal growth (Figure 9.11) as well as significant changes in reproductive structures and sexual characteristics. Maturation and hormone secretion cause rapid development of the ovaries, uterus, and

Puberty *Biological changes during adolescence that lead to an adult-sized body and sexual maturity*

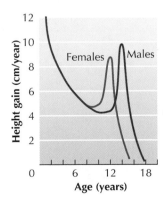

Figure 9.11 *Adolescent growth spurt.* Note the gender differences in height gain during puberty. Most girls are about two years ahead of boys in their growth spurt and therefore are taller than most boys between the ages of 10 and 14.

www.wiley.com/college/huffman

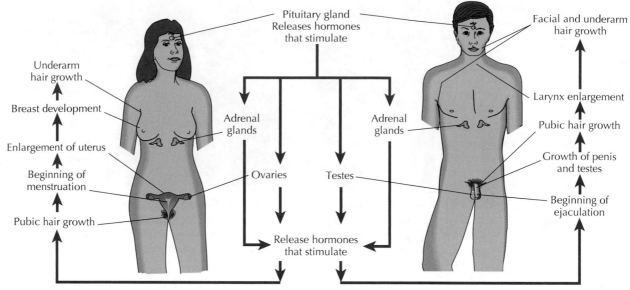

Figure 9.12 *Secondary sex characteristics.* Complex physical changes in puberty primarily result from hormones secreted from the ovaries and testes, the pituitary gland in the brain, and adrenal glands near the kidneys.

vagina and the onset of menstruation *(menarche)* in the adolescent female. In the adolescent male, the testes, scrotum, and penis develop, and he undergoes *spermarche* (the first ejaculation). The ovaries and testes in turn produce hormones that lead to the development of *secondary sex characteristics,* such as the growth of pubic hair, deepening of the voice, growth of facial hair, growth of breasts, and so on (Figure 9.12).

Once the large and obvious pubertal changes have occurred, further age-related physical changes are less dramatic. Other than some modest increase in height and muscular development during the late teens and early twenties, most individuals experience only minor physical changes until middle age.

Middle Age

For women, *menopause,* the cessation of the menstrual cycle, which occurs somewhere between ages 45 and 55, is the second most important life milestone in physical development. The decreased production of estrogen (the dominant female hormone) produces certain physical changes. However, the popular belief that menopause (or "the change of life") causes serious psychological mood swings, loss of sexual interest, and depression is *not* supported by current research (Hvas, 2001; Matlin, 2003; Morrison & Tweedy, 2000). One large-scale study of postmenopausal American women found that almost two-thirds felt relief that their menstrual periods had stopped, and over 50 percent did not experience hot flashes (Brim, 1999). When psychological problems exist, they may reflect the social devaluation of aging women, not the physiological process of menopause itself. Given our Western society in which women are highly valued for their youth and beauty, can you understand why such a biological landmark of aging may be difficult for some women? Or why women in cultures that derogate aging tend to experience more anxiety and depression during menopause (Mingo, Herman, & Jasperse, 2000; Sampselle, Harris, Harlow, & Sowers, 2002; Winterich, 2003)?

For men, youthfulness is less important, and the physical changes of middle age are less obvious. Beginning in middle adulthood, men experience a gradual decline in the production of sperm and testosterone (the dominant male hormone), although they may remain capable of reproduction into their eighties or nineties. Physical changes such as unexpected weight gain, decline in sexual responsiveness, loss of muscle strength, and graying or loss of hair may lead some men (and women as well) to feel depressed and to question their life progress. They often see these alterations as a biological signal of aging and mortality. Such physical and psychological changes in men are known as the *male climacteric*.

Late Adulthood

After middle age, most physical changes in development are gradual and occur in the heart and arteries and sensory receptors. For example, cardiac output (the volume of blood pumped by the heart each minute) decreases, whereas blood pressure increases due to the thickening and stiffening of arterial walls. Visual acuity and depth perception decline, hearing acuity lessens, especially for high-frequency sounds, and smell and taste sensitivity decreases (Atchley & Kramer, 2000; Kiessling et al., 2003; Wahl et al, 2004).

This all sounds depressing. Can anything be done about it? Television, magazines, movies, and advertisements generally have portrayed aging as a time of balding and graying hair, sagging parts, poor vision, hearing loss, and, of course, no sex life. Such negative portrayals contribute to our society's widespread **ageism**, prejudice or discrimination based on physical age. However, as advertising companies pursue the revenue of the huge aging baby-boomer population, there has been a recent shift toward a more accurate portrayal of aging also as a time of vigor, interest, and productivity (Figure 9.13). Recent research also shows that cognitive functioning in older adults can be greatly enhanced with simple aerobic training (Benloucif et al., 2004; Lytle et al., 2004).

What about memory problems and inherited genetic tendencies toward Alzheimer's disease and other serious diseases of old age? There's good news on this front, too. The public and most researchers have long thought aging is accompanied by widespread death of neurons in the brain. Although this decline does happen with degenerative disorders like Alzheimer's disease, it is no longer believed to be a part of normal aging (Chapter 2). It is also important to remember that age-related memory problems are not on a continuum with Alzheimer's disease (Wilson et al., 2000). That is, normal forgetfulness "does not reflect a predisposition" for serious dementia.

Use it or lose it? *Research shows exercise may be the most important factor in maintaining mental and physical abilities throughout the life span.*

Ageism *Prejudice or discrimination based on physical age*

Figure 9.13 *Achievement in later years.* Note the high level of productivity among some of the world's most famous figures. When Georgia O'Keeffe, the famous American painter, began to lose her eyesight, she turned to ceramics, shaping beautifully rounded forms and pottery (Leveton, 2002).

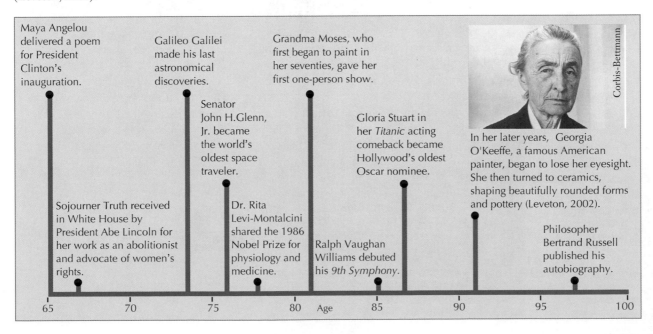

Maya Angelou delivered a poem for President Clinton's inauguration.

Galileo Galilei made his last astronomical discoveries.

Grandma Moses, who first began to paint in her seventies, gave her first one-person show.

Senator John H. Glenn, Jr. became the world's oldest space traveler.

Gloria Stuart in her *Titanic* acting comeback became Hollywood's oldest Oscar nominee.

In her later years, Georgia O'Keeffe, a famous American painter, began to lose her eyesight. She then turned to ceramics, shaping beautifully rounded forms and pottery (Leveton, 2002).

Sojourner Truth received in White House by President Abe Lincoln for her work as an abolitionist and advocate of women's rights.

Dr. Rita Levi-Montalcini shared the 1986 Nobel Prize for physiology and medicine.

Ralph Vaughan Williams debuted his *9th Symphony*.

Philosopher Bertrand Russell published his autobiography.

65   70   75   80   Age   85   90   95   100

*"As I get older, I find I rely more and more
on these sticky notes to remind me."*

Arnie Levin ©The New Yorker Collection/
The Cartoon Bank, Inc.

Aging does seem to take its toll on the *speed* of information processing, however. Recall from Chapter 7 that decreased speed of processing may reflect problems with *encoding* (putting information into long-term storage) and *retrieval* (getting information out of storage). If memory is like a filing system, older people may have more filing cabinets, and it may take them longer to initially file and later retrieve information. Although mental speed declines with age, general information processing and much of memory ability are largely unaffected by the aging process (Lachman, 2004; Whitbourne, 2005).

What causes us to age and die? If we set aside aging and deaths resulting from disease, abuse, or neglect, we are left to consider *primary aging* (gradual, inevitable age-related changes in physical and mental processes). There are two main theories explaining primary aging and death—programmed theory and damage theory (Cristofalo, 1996; Medina, 1996; Wallace, 1997).

According to *programmed theory*, aging is genetically controlled. Once the ovum is fertilized, the program for aging and death is set and begins to run. Researcher Leonard Hayflick (1977, 1996) found that human cells seem to have a built-in life span. After about 50 doublings of laboratory-cultured cells, they cease to divide—they have reached the *Hayflick limit*. The other explanation of primary aging is *damage theory*, which proposes that an accumulation of damage to cells and organs over the years ultimately causes death.

Whether aging is genetically controlled or caused by accumulated damage over the years, scientists generally agree that humans appear to have a maximum life span of about 110 to 120 years. Although we can try to control secondary aging in an attempt to reach that maximum, so far we have no means to postpone primary aging.

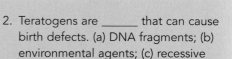

Assessment

CHECK & REVIEW

Physical Development

The prenatal period of development consists of three major stages: the **germinal, embryonic,** and **fetal periods.** Development can be affected by environmental influences at any of these stages. Both legal and illegal drugs are potentially **teratogenic** (capable of producing birth defects). Doctors advise pregnant women to avoid all unnecessary drugs, especially nicotine and alcohol.

During the prenatal period and the first two years of life, the brain and nervous system grow faster than any other part of the body. Early motor development (crawling, standing, and walking) is largely the result of maturation, not experience. Except for vision, the sensory and perceptual abilities of newborns are relatively well developed.

At **puberty,** the individual becomes capable of reproduction and experiences a sharp increase in height, weight, and skeletal growth, called the *pubertal growth spurt.* Both men and women experience bodily changes in middle age.

Although many of the changes associated with physical aging (such as decreases in cardiac output and visual acuity) are the result of primary aging, others are the result of disease, abuse, or neglect. Physical aging may be genetically built in from the moment of conception (programmed theory), or it may result from the body's inability to repair damage (damage theory).

Questions

1. What are the three stages of prenatal development?

2. Teratogens are _____ that can cause birth defects. (a) DNA fragments; (b) environmental agents; (c) recessive genes; (d) dominant genes

3. The period of life when an individual first becomes capable of reproduction is known as _____. (a) the age of fertility; (b) adolescence; (c) puberty; (d) the adolescent climacteric

4. Gradual, inevitable age-related changes in physical and mental processes are called _____.

Check your answers in Appendix B.

CLICK & REVIEW

for additional assessment options:
www.wiley.com/college/huffman

COGNITIVE DEVELOPMENT

The following fan letter was written to Shari Lewis (1963), a children's television performer, about her puppet Lamb Chop:

Dear Shari:

All my friends say Lamb Chop isn't really a little girl that talks. She is just a puppet you made out of a sock. I don't care even if it's true. I like the way Lamb Chop talks. If I send you one of my socks will you teach it how to talk and send it back?

RANDI

Randi's understanding of fantasy and reality is certainly different from an adult's. Just as a child's body and physical abilities change, his or her way of knowing and perceiving the world also grows and changes. This seems intuitively obvious. But early psychologists—with one exception—focused on physical, emotional, language, and personality development. The one major exception was Jean Piaget (Zhan Pee-ah-ZHAY).

Piaget demonstrated that a child's intellect is fundamentally different from an adult's. He showed that an infant begins at a cognitively "primitive" level and that intellectual growth progresses in distinct stages, motivated by an innate need to know. Piaget's theory, developed in the 1920s and 1930s, has proven so comprehensive and insightful that it remains the major force in the cognitive area of developmental psychology today.

To appreciate Piaget's contributions, we need to consider three major concepts: schemas, assimilation, and accommodation. **Schemas** are the most basic units of intellect. They act as patterns that organize our interactions with the environment, like architect's drawings or builder's blueprints.

In the first few weeks of life, for example, the infant apparently has several schemas based on the innate reflexes of sucking, grasping, and so on. These schemas are primarily motor skills and may be little more than stimulus-and-response mechanisms—the nipple is presented and the baby sucks. Soon, however, other schemas emerge. The infant develops a more detailed schema for eating solid food, a different schema for the concepts of *mother* and *father*, and so on. It is important to recognize that schemas, our tools for learning about the world, are enlarged and changed throughout our lives. For example, music lovers previously accustomed to LP records have had to develop different schemas for playing tapes, CDs, and MP3s.

Assimilation and accommodation are the two major processes by which schemas grow and change over time. **Assimilation** is the process of absorbing new information into existing schemas. For instance, infants use their sucking schema not only in sucking nipples but also in sucking blankets or fingers. Similarly, if you go out on a blind date and are pleasantly surprised at the attractiveness of your date, it is because you easily assimilated the appearance of your new date into your preexisting schema for attractiveness.

Accommodation occurs when new information or stimuli cannot be assimilated. New schemas must be developed, or old schemas must be changed to better fit with the new information. An infant's first attempt to eat solid food with a spoon is a good example of accommodation. When the spoon first enters her mouth, the child attempts to assimilate it by using the previously successful sucking schema—shaping lips and tongue around the spoon as around a nipple. After repeated trials, she accommodates by adjusting her lips and tongue in a way that moves the food off the spoon and into her mouth. Similarly, if you meet someone through an online chat room and later feel shocked when you talk face to face, it is because of the unexamined schemas you constructed. The awkwardness and discomfort you now feel is due, in part, to the work involved in accommodating your earlier schemas to match the new reality.

Achievement

How does cognition, or the way we think about the world, change during our life cycle?

Erik Soh/Asia Images/Getty Images, Inc.

Early experimentation. *Piaget believed children are natural experimenters biologically driven to explore their environment.*

Schema *Cognitive structures or patterns consisting of a number of organized ideas that grow and differentiate with experience*

Assimilation *In Piaget's theory, absorbing new information into existing schemas*

Accommodation *In Piaget's theory, adjusting old schemas or developing new ones to better fit with new information*

Study the "impossible figure" to the right.

Using a clean sheet of paper, try to draw this same figure without tracing it. Students with artistic training generally find it relatively easy to reproduce, whereas the rest of us find it "impossible." This is because we lack the necessary artistic schema and cannot assimilate what we see. With practice and training, we could accommodate the new information and easily draw the figure.

■ Stages of Cognitive Development: Birth to Adolescence

According to Piaget, all children go through approximately the same four stages of cognitive development, regardless of the culture in which they live (Table 9.4). And no stage can be skipped because skills acquired at earlier stages are essential to mastery at later stages. Let's take a closer look at these four stages: sensorimotor, preoperational, concrete operational, and formal operational.

Sensorimotor Stage *Piaget's first stage (birth to approximately age 2 years), in which schemas are developed through sensory and motor activities*

Object Permanence *Piagetian term for an infant's understanding that objects (or people) continue to exist even when they cannot be seen, heard, or touched directly*

Michael Ventura/Image State

Can you see why this stage is called "sensorimotor"?

The Sensorimotor Stage

During the **sensorimotor stage**, lasting from birth until "significant" language acquisition (about age 2), children explore the world and develop their schemas primarily through their senses and motor activities—hence the term *sensorimotor*.

One important concept acquired during this stage is **object permanence**. At birth and for the next three or four months, children lack object permanence. They seem to have no schemas for objects they cannot see, hear, or touch—out of sight is truly out of mind (Figure 9.14).

VISUAL QUIZ

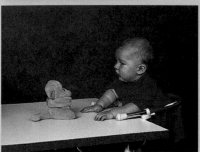

Doug Goodman/PhotoResearchers, Inc.

Figure 9.14 *Sensorimotor stage of development.* The child in these two photos seems to believe the toy no longer exists once it is blocked from sight. Can you explain why?

Answer: According to Piaget, young infants lack object permanence—an understanding that objects continue to exist even when they cannot be seen, heard, or touched.

SUMMARY TABLE 9.4 PIAGET'S FOUR STAGES OF COGNITIVE DEVELOPMENT

Birth to 2	***Sensorimotor*** Abilities: Uses senses and motor skills to explore and develop cognitively. Limits: Beginning of stage lacks *object permanence* (understanding things continue to exist even when not seen, heard, or felt).	
Age 2–7	***Preoperational*** Abilities: Has significant language and thinks symbolically. Limits: • Cannot perform "operations." • *Egocentric* thinking (inability to consider another's point of view). • *Animistic* thinking (believing all things are living).	
Age 7–11 	***Concrete Operational*** Abilities: • Can perform "operations" on concrete objects. • Understands *conservation* (realizing changes in shape or appearance can be reversed). Limits: Cannot think abstractly and hypothetically.	
Age 11 and up	***Formal Operational*** Abilities: Can think abstractly and hypothetically. Limits: *Adolescent egocentrism* at the beginning of this stage, with related problems of the *personal fable* and *imaginary audience*.	

Preoperational Stage

During the **preoperational stage** (roughly age 2 to 7), language advances significantly, and the child begins to think *symbolically*—using symbols, such as words, to represent concepts. Three other qualities characterize this stage:

1. ***Concepts are not yet operational.*** Piaget labeled this period "preoperational" because the child lacks *operations*, reversible mental processes. For instance, if a preoperational boy who has a brother is asked, "Do you have a brother?" he will easily respond, "Yes." However, when asked, "Does your brother have a brother?" he will answer, "No!" To understand that his brother has a brother, he must be able to *reverse* the concept of "having a brother."

2. ***Thinking is egocentric.*** Children at this stage have difficulty understanding that there are points of view other than their own. **Egocentrism** refers to the preoperational child's limited ability to distinguish between his or her own perspective and someone else's. Egocentrism is not the same as "selfishness." Preschoolers who move in front of you to get a better view of the TV or repeatedly ask questions while you are talking on the telephone are not being selfish. They are demonstrating egocentric thought processes. They naively assume that others see, hear, feel, and think exactly as they do. Consider the following telephone conversation between a 3-year-old, who is at home, and her mother, who is at work:

Preoperational Stage *Piaget's second stage (roughly age 2 to 7), characterized by the ability to employ significant language and to think symbolically, but the child lacks operations (reversible mental processes), and thinking is egocentric and animistic*

Egocentrism *The inability to consider another's point of view, which Piaget considered a hallmark of the preoperational stage*

Concrete Operational Stage
Piaget's third stage (roughly age 7 to 11); the child can perform mental operations on concrete objects and understand reversibility and conservation, but abstract thinking is not yet present

Conservation *Understanding that certain physical characteristics (such as volume) remain unchanged, even when their outward appearance changes*

MOTHER: Emma is that you?

EMMA: (Nods silently.)

MOTHER: Emma, is Daddy there? May I speak to him?

EMMA: (Twice nods silently.)

Egocentric preoperational children fail to understand that the phone caller cannot see their nodding head. Charming as this is, preoperational children's egocentrism also sometimes leads them to believe their "bad thoughts" caused their sibling or parent to get sick or that their misbehavior caused their parents' marital problems. Because they think the world centers on them, they often cannot separate reality from what goes on inside their own head.

3. ***Thinking is animistic.*** Children in the preoperational stage believe that objects such as the sun, trees, clouds, and bars of soap have motives, feelings, and intentions (for example, "dark clouds are angry" and "soap sinks to the bottom of the bathtub because it is tired"). *Animism* refers to the belief that all things are living (or animated). Our earlier example of Randi's letter asking puppeteer Shari Lewis to teach her sock to talk like Lamb Chop is also an example of animistic thinking.

Can preoperational children be taught how to use operations and to avoid egocentric and animistic thinking? Although some researchers have reported success in accelerating the preoperational stage, Piaget did not believe in pushing children ahead of their own developmental schedule. He believed children should be allowed to grow at their own pace, with minimal adult interference (Elkind, 1981, 2000). Piaget thought Americans were particularly guilty of pushing children, calling American childhood the "Great American Kid Race."

Concrete Operational Stage

Between the approximate ages of 7 and 11, children are in the **concrete operational stage**. During this stage many important thinking skills emerge. Unlike the preoperational stage, concrete operational children are able to perform operations on *concrete* objects. Because they understand the concept of *reversibility*, they recognize that certain physical attributes (such as volume) remain unchanged, although the outward appearance is altered, a process known as **conservation** (Figure 9.15).

Figure 9.15 ***Test for conservation.*** (a) In the classic conservation-of-liquids test, the child is first shown two identical glasses with liquid at the same level. (b) The liquid is poured from one of the short, wide glasses into the tall, thin one. (c) When asked whether the two glasses have the same amount, or if one has more, the preoperational child replies that the tall, thin glass has more. In contrast, a concrete operational child will recognize they still contain the same amount.

MR 'Ellen B. Senisi/TheImage Works

TABLE 9.5 SAMPLE PIAGETIAN TASKS

Type of Conservation Task (Average age at which concept is grasped)	Your task as experimenter...	Child is asked...
Length (ages 6-7)	**Step 1** Center two sticks of equal length. Child agrees that they are of equal length. **Step 2** Move one stick.	**Step 3** *"Are these two sticks the same length?"* Preoperational child will say that one of the sticks is longer. Child in concrete stage will say that they are both the same length.
Substance amount (ages 6-7)	**Step 1** Center two identical clay balls. Child acknowledges that the two have equal amounts of clay. **Step 2** Flatten one of the balls.	**Step 3** *"Do the two pieces have the same amount of clay?"* Preoperational child will say that the flat piece has more clay. Child in concrete stage will say that the two pieces have the same amount of clay.
Area (ages 8-10)	**Step 1** Center two identical sheets of cardboard with wooden blocks placed on them in identical positions. Child acknowledges that the same amount of space is left open on each piece of cardboard. **Step 2** Scatter the blocks on one piece of the cardboard.	**Step 3** *"Do the two pieces of cardboard have the same amount of open space?"* Preoperational child will say that the cardboard with scattered blocks has less open space. Child in concrete stage will say that both pieces have the same amount of open space.

If you know children in the preoperational or concrete operational stages, you may enjoy testing their grasp of conservation by trying some of the experiments shown in Table 9.5. The equipment is easily obtained, and you will find their responses fascinating. Keep in mind that this should be done as a game. Do not allow the child to feel that he or she is failing a test or making a mistake.

Formal Operational Stage
The final period in Piaget's theory is the **formal operational stage**, which typically begins around age 11. In this stage, children begin to apply their operations to abstract

Formal Operational Stage *Piaget's fourth stage (around age 11 and beyond), characterized by abstract and hypothetical thinking*

concepts in addition to concrete objects. In this stage, children find it much easier to master the abstract thinking required for geometry and algebra. For example, $(a + b)^2 = a^2 + 2ab + b^2$. They also become capable of hypothetical thinking ("What if?"), which allows systematic formulation and testing of concepts.

Adolescents considering part-time jobs, for example, may think about possible conflicts with school and friends, the number of hours they want to work, and the kind of work for which they are qualified before they start filling out applications. Formal operational thinking also allows the adolescent to construct a well-reasoned argument based on hypothetical concepts and logical processes. Consider the following argument:

1. If you hit a glass with a feather, the glass will break.

2. You hit the glass with a feather.

What is the logical conclusion? The correct answer, "The glass will break," is contrary to fact and direct experience. Therefore, the child in the concrete operational stage would have difficulty with this task, whereas the formal operational thinker understands that this problem is about abstractions that need not correspond to the real world.

Problems with Early Formal Operational Thinking

Along with the benefits of this cognitive style come several problems. Adolescents in the early stages of the formal operational period demonstrate a type of *egocentrism* different from that of the preoperational child. Although adolescents do recognize that others have unique thoughts and perspectives, they often fail to differentiate between what others are thinking and their own thoughts. This *adolescent egocentrism* has two characteristics that may affect social interactions as well as problem solving:

1. *Personal fable.* Given their unique form of egocentrism, adolescents may conclude that they alone are having certain insights or difficulties and that no one else could understand or sympathize. David Elkind (1967, 2000, 2001) described this as the formation of a *personal fable*, an intense investment in their own thoughts and feelings, and a belief that these thoughts are unique. One student in my class remembered being very upset in junior high when her mother tried to comfort her over the loss of an important relationship. "I felt like she couldn't possibly know how it felt—no one could. I couldn't believe that anyone had ever suffered like this or that things would ever get better."

    Several forms of risk taking, such as engaging in sexual intercourse without contraception, driving dangerously, and experimenting with drugs, also seem to arise from the personal fable (Coley & Chase-Lansdale, 1998; Flavell, Miller, & Miller, 2002; Greene et al., 2000). Although adolescents will acknowledge the risks of these activities, they don't feel personally endangered because they feel uniquely invulnerable and immortal.

2. *Imaginary audience.* In early adolescence, people tend to believe they are the center of others' thoughts and attentions, instead of considering that everyone is equally wrapped up in his or her own concerns and plans. In other words, adolescents picture all eyes focused on their behaviors. Elkind referred to this as the *imaginary audience.* This egocentrism may explain what seems like extreme forms of self-consciousness and concern for physical appearance ("Everyone knows I don't know the answer"; or "They're noticing how fat I am and this awful haircut").

    If the imaginary audience results from an inability to differentiate the self from others, the personal fable is a product of differentiating too much. Thankfully, these two forms of adolescent egocentrism tend to decrease during later stages of the formal operational period.

Dennis Novak/Photographer's Choice/Getty Images

Personal fable in action? *Can you see how this type of risk-taking behavior may reflect the personal fable—adolescents' tendency to believe they are unique and special and that dangers don't apply to them?*

■ Assessing Piaget's Theory: Criticisms and Contributions

As influential as Piaget's account of cognitive development has been, it has received significant criticisms. Let's look briefly at two major areas of concern: underestimated abilities and underestimated genetic and cultural influences.

Underestimated Abilities

Research shows that Piaget may have underestimated young children's cognitive development. For example, researchers report that very young infants have a basic concept of how objects move, are aware that objects continue to exist even when screened from view, and can recognize speech sounds (Baillargeon, 2000; Streri et al., 2004).

Research on infant imitation of facial expression also raises questions about Piaget's estimates of early infant abilities. In a series of well-known studies, Meltzoff and Moore (1977, 1985, 1994) found that newborns could imitate such facial movements as tongue protrusion, mouth opening, and lip pursing (Figure 9.16). At age 9 months, infants will imitate facial actions a full day after seeing them (Heimann & Meltzoff, 1996).

Nonegocentric responses also appear in the earliest days of life. For example, newborn babies tend to cry in response to the cry of another baby (Dondi, Simion, & Caltran, 1999). And preschoolers will adapt their speech by using shorter, simpler expressions when talking to 2-year-olds rather than to adults.

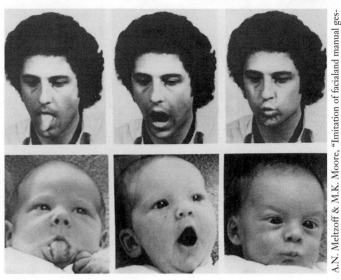

Figure 9.16 *Infant imitation?* When an adult models a facial expression, even very young infants will respond with a similar expression. Is this true imitation or a simple stimulus–response reflex?

A.N. Meltzoff & M.K. Moore, "Imitation of facial and manual gestures by human neonates." Science, 1977, 198, 75–78

Underestimated Genetic and Cultural Influences

Piaget's model, like other stage theories, has also been criticized for not sufficiently taking into account genetic and cultural differences (Flavell, Miller, & Miller, 2002; Matusov & Hayes, 2000; Maynard & Greenfield, 2003). During Piaget's time, the genetic influences on cognitive abilities were poorly understood, but as you know from earlier chapters and discussions in this text, there has been a rapid explosion of information in this field in the last few years. In addition, formal education and specific cultural experiences can significantly affect cognitive development. Consider the following example from a researcher attempting to test the formal operational skills of a farmer in Liberia (Scribner, 1977):

> RESEARCHER: All Kpelle men are rice farmers. Mr. Smith is not a rice farmer. Is he a Kpelle man?
>
> KPELLE FARMER: I don't know the man. I have not laid eyes on the man myself.

Instead of reasoning in the "logical" way of Piaget's formal operational stage, the Kpelle farmer reasoned according to his specific cultural and educational training, which apparently emphasized personal knowledge. Not knowing Mr. Smith, the Kpelle farmer did not feel qualified to comment on him. Thus, Piaget's theory may have underestimated the effect of culture on a person's cognitive functioning.

Despite criticisms, Piaget's contributions to psychology are enormous. As one scholar put it, "assessing the impact of Piaget on developmental psychology is like assessing the impact of Shakespeare on English literature or Aristotle on philosophy—impossible" (cited in Beilin, 1992, p. 191).

Ellen Senisi/The Image Works

Are preoperational children always egocentric? Contrary to Piaget's beliefs, children at this age often do take the perspective of another.

■ Information Processing: A Computer Model of Cognition

An alternative to Piaget's theory of cognitive development is the *information-processing model*, which compares the workings of the mind to a computer and studies how information is received, encoded, stored, organized, retrieved, and used by people of different ages. This model offers important insights into two major areas of cognition: attention and memory.

Attention

Attention refers to focusing awareness on a narrowed range of stimuli. Infants pay attention to their environment for only short periods of time. Even toddlers, who can pay attention for longer periods, are easily distracted. When watching television, for example, 2-year-olds talk more to other people, play more with toys, and look around the room more than 4-year-olds. As they get older, children's attention spans improve and they learn to discriminate between what is and what is not important to concentrate on at any given time (Bjorklund, 1995).

Memory

After children attend to information and take it into their information-processing system, they must remember it. Attention determines what information enters the "computer," whereas memory determines what information is saved.

Like attention, memory skills also improve gradually throughout childhood and adolescence (Hayne, Boniface, & Barr, 2000; Richards, 1997). Two-year-olds can repeat back about two digits immediately after hearing them, but 10-year-olds can repeat about six. Improvement comes as children acquire strategies during the school years for storing and retrieving information. For example, they learn to rehearse or repeat information over and over, to use mnemonics (like "*i* before *e* except after *c*"), and to organize their information in ways that facilitate retrieval (Chapter 7).

As people grow older, their use of information-processing strategies and overall memory continues to change. Recall from Chapter 8 that *fluid intelligence* (requiring speed or rapid learning) tends to decrease with age, whereas *crystallized intelligence* (knowledge and information gained over the life span) continues to increase until advanced old age.

Despite concerns about "keeping up with 18-year-olds," older returning students often do as well or better than their younger counterparts in college classes. This superior performance by older adult students is due in part to their generally greater academic motivation, but it also reflects the importance of prior knowledge. Cognitive psychologists have demonstrated that the more people know, the easier it is for them to lay down new memories (Leahy & Harris, 1997; Matlin, 2005). Older students, for instance, generally find this chapter on development easier to master than younger students. Their interactions with children and greater knowledge about life changes create a framework on which to hang new information.

In summary, the more you know, the more you learn. Thus, having a college degree and stimulating occupation may help you stay mentally sharp in your later years (Mayr & Kliegl, 2000; Whitbourne, 2005).

Haven't studies also shown decreases in older adults' memory capabilities? As mentioned at the beginning of the chapter, this may reflect problems with cross-sectional versus longitudinal research. In addition, earlier studies often asked participants to memorize simple lists of words or perform paired association tasks, which older people often find meaningless and uninteresting. When the information is meaningful, an older person's rich web of existing knowledge helps them remember it (Graf, 1990).

Contrary to popular stereotypes of the frail and forgetful elderly, growing old, for most of us, will probably be better than expected—and, of course, far better than the alternative!

Assessment

CHECK & REVIEW

Cognitive Development

According to Piaget, cognitive development occurs in an invariant sequence of four stages: **sensorimotor** (birth to age 2), **preoperational** (between 2 and 7), **concrete operational** (between 7 and 11), and **formal operational** (age 11 and up).

In the sensorimotor stage, children acquire **object permanence.** During the preoperational stage, children are better equipped to use symbols. But their language and thinking is limited by their lack of operations, **egocentrism,** and animism.

In the concrete operational stage, children learn to perform operations (to think about concrete things while not actually doing them). They understand the principles of **conservation** and reversibility. During the formal operational stage, the adolescent is able to think abstractly and

deal with hypothetical situations but again is prone to a type of adolescent egocentrism.

Although Piaget has been criticized for underestimating abilities and genetic and cultural influences, he remains one of the most respected psychologists in modern times.

Psychologists who explain cognitive development in terms of the information-processing model have found this model especially useful in explaining attention and memory changes across the life span. In contrast to pessimistic early studies, recent research is much more encouraging about age-related changes in information processing.

Questions

1. _____ was one of the first scientists to prove that a child's cognitive processes are fundamentally different

from an adult's. (a) Baumrind; (b) Beck; (c) Piaget; (d) Elkind
2. Match the following list of key terms with the correct Piagetian stage:
 ___1. Egocentrism, animism
 ___2. Object permanence
 ___3. Abstract and hypothetical thinking
 ___4. Conservation, reversibility
 ___5. Personal fable, imaginary audience
 a. Sensorimotor
 b. Preoperational
 c. Concrete operational
 d. Formal operational
3. Briefly summarize the major contributions and criticisms of Jean Piaget.

Check your answers in Appendix B.

 CLICK & REVIEW
for additional assessment options:
www.wiley.com/college/huffman

SOCIAL-EMOTIONAL DEVELOPMENT

The poet John Donne wrote, "No man is an island, entire of itself." In addition to physical and cognitive development, developmental psychologists are very interested in social-emotional development. That is, they study how our social relations and emotions grow and change over the life span. Two of the most important topics in social-emotional development are those of *attachment* and *parenting styles.*

■ Attachment: The Importance of Bonding

An infant arrives in the world with a multitude of behaviors that encourage a strong bond of attachment with primary caregivers. **Attachment** can be defined as a strong affectional bond with special others that endures over time. Most research has focused on the attachment between mother and child. However, infants also form attachment bonds with fathers, grandparents, and other caregivers.

In studying attachment behavior, researchers are often divided along the lines of the now-familiar nature-versus-nurture debate. Those who advocate the innate or biological position cite John Bowlby's work (1969, 1989, 2000). He proposed that newborn infants are biologically equipped with verbal and nonverbal behaviors (such as crying, clinging, smiling) and with "following" behaviors (such as crawling and walking after the caregiver) that serve to elicit certain instinctive nurturing responses from the caregiver. The biological argument for attachment is also supported by Konrad Lorenz's (1937) early studies of **imprinting**. Lorenz's studies demonstrated

Achievement

What are some of the key themes and theories in social, moral, and personality development?

Attachment *A strong affectional bond with special others that endures over time*

Imprinting *An innate form of learning within a critical period that involves attachment to the first large moving object seen*

www.wiley.com/college/huffman

VISUAL QUIZ

Nina Leen/GettyImages/
Time Life Pictures

Why are these geese following so closely behind scientist Konrad Lorenz?

Answer: Because they instinctively form a strong attachment and imprint on the first large moving object they see. Usually it is the mother goose, but in this case it was Lorenz.

how baby geese attach to, and then follow, the first large moving object they see during a certain critical period in their development.

Feeding or Contact Comfort?

According to Freud, infants become attached to the caregiver who provides oral pleasure (Chapter 13). But is there scientific evidence to support Freud's claim? In what is now a classic experiment, Harry Harlow and Robert Zimmerman (1959) set out to experimentally investigate the variables that might affect attachment. They started by

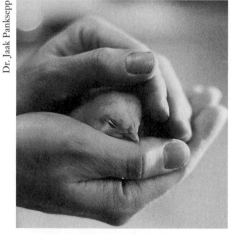

Dr. Jaak Panksepp

Is contact comfort biological? When nestled next to a hen, or held in a person's cupped hands, chicks will almost immediately "relax" and close their eyes.

creating two types of wire-framed *surrogate* (substitute) "mother" monkeys: one covered by soft terry cloth and one left uncovered. The infant monkeys were fed by either the cloth or the wire mother and had access to both mothers (Figure 9.17).

Harlow and Zimmerman found those monkeys who were "reared" by a cloth mother spent significant amounts of time clinging to the soft material of their surrogate mother. They also developed greater emotional security and curiosity than did monkeys assigned to the wire mother. Monkeys who were given free choice of both mothers also showed strong attachment behaviors toward the cloth mother—even when the wire-framed mother provided all food!

Further evidence of the importance of contact comfort came from later research by Harlow and Harlow (1966), in which monkey babies were exposed to various forms of rejection. Some of the "mothers" contained metal spikes that would suddenly protrude from the cloth covering and push the babies away; others had air jets that would sometimes blow the babies away. Nevertheless, the infant monkeys waited until the rejection was over and then clung to the cloth mother as tightly as before.

Based on these and related findings, Harlow concluded that what he called *contact comfort*, the pleasurable tactile sensations provided by a soft and cuddly "parent," is a powerful contributor to attachment. The satisfaction of other physical needs, such as food, is not enough.

Davis Barber/Photoedit

Contact comfort. Both parent and child benefit from cuddling.

Is contact comfort similarly important between human mothers and infants? Several studies suggest that it may be. Touching and massaging premature infants, for example, produce significant physical and emotional benefits (Dieter et al., 2003; Field & Hernandez-Reif, 2001; Gitau et al., 2002). Touch elicits positive emotions and attention from almost all babies. Mothers around the world tend to kiss, nuzzle, nurse, comfort, clean, and respond to their children with lots of physical contact.

For example, Japanese mothers and their children are rarely separated during the first months of life. The mothers touch their infants to communicate with them, breast-feed, carry them around on their backs, and take baths with them. Japanese infants do not sleep in separate beds (Matsumoto, 2000). In many cultures, children sleep alongside their mothers for several years. If a new baby comes along, the older child moves to a bed in the same room or shares a bed with another family member (Javo, Ronning, & Heyerdahl, 2004; Morelli, Oppenheim, Rogoff, & Goldsmith, 1992; Rothrauff, Middlemiss, & Jacobsen, 2004).

As you can see, attachment seems to depend, at least in part, on the hugging, cuddling, and caresses babies naturally receive from their mothers. I use the word *mother* because almost all research in this area has focused on mothers and their infants. However, research also shows that the same results apply to fathers and other caregivers (Dietner et al., 2002; Grossmann et al., 2002; van Ijzendoorn & De Wolff, 1997).

What happens if a child does not form an attachment? Researchers have investigated this question in two ways: They have looked at children and adults who spent their early years in institutions without the stimulation and love of a regular caregiver or who lived at home but were physically isolated under abusive conditions.

Infants raised in impersonal or abusive surroundings suffer from a number of problems. They seldom cry, coo, or babble; they become rigid when picked up; and they have few language skills. As for their social-emotional development, they tend to form shallow or anxious relationships. Some appear forlorn, withdrawn, and uninterested in their caretakers, whereas others seem insatiable in their need for affection (Zeanah, 2000). They also tend to show intellectual, physical, and perceptual retardation; increased susceptibility to infection; and neurotic "rocking" and isolation behaviors: in some cases, they die from lack of attachment (Belsky & Cassidy, 1994; Bowlby, 1973, 1982, 2000; Spitz & Wolf, 1946).

Levels of Attachment

Although most children are never exposed to such extreme institutional conditions, developmental psychologist Mary Ainsworth and her colleagues (1967, 1978) have found significant differences in the typical level of attachment between infants and their mothers. Moreover, *level of attachment* affects long-term behaviors. Using a method called the *strange situation procedure,* in which a researcher observes infants in the presence or absence of their mother and a stranger, Ainsworth found that children could be divided into three groups: *securely attached, avoidant,* and *anxious/ambivalent.*

1. **Securely attached** (65 percent). When exposed to the stranger, the infant seeks closeness and contact with the mother, uses the mother as a safe base from which to explore, shows moderate distress on separation, and is happy when the mother returns.

2. **Avoidant** (25 percent). The infant does not seek closeness or contact with the mother, treats the mother much like a stranger, and rarely cries when the mother leaves the room.

3. **Anxious/ambivalent** (10 percent). The infant becomes very upset when the mother leaves the room. When she returns, the infant seeks close contact, and then squirms angrily to get away.

VISUAL QUIZ

Figure 9.17 *Attachment.* Why is this monkey clinging to the cloth figure on the left rather than to the one on the right that provides milk?

Answer: Harlow and Zimmerman found that infant monkeys spent more time on the terry-cloth-covered "mother," even when it was the wire "mother" that provided food. They concluded that contact comfort, rather than feeding, was the most important determinant of a monkey's attachment to its caregiver.

Nina Leen/Time Life Pictures/Getty Images

Ainsworth found that infants with a secure attachment style have caregivers who are sensitive and responsive to their signals of distress, happiness, and fatigue (Ainsworth et al., 1967, 1978; van Ijzendoorn & DeWolff, 1997). On the other hand, avoidant infants have caregivers who are aloof and distant, and anxious/ambivalent infants have inconsistent caregivers who alternate between strong affection and indifference.

Can you see why infants who are securely attached generally develop feelings of emotional security and trust in others? Or why avoidant infants learn to avoid others and suppress their attachment needs? Or why anxious/ambivalent infants tend to be temperamental and anxious that others will not return their affection? It is not surprising that follow-up studies found securely attached children were the most sociable, emotionally aware, enthusiastic, cooperative, persistent, curious, and competent (DeRosnay & Harris, 2002; Goldberg, 2000; Jacobsen & Hofmann, 1997).

Application

RESEARCH HIGHLIGHT

Romantic Love and Attachment

If you've been around young children, you've probably noticed how often they share toys and discoveries with a parent and seem much happier when a parent is near. You've probably also thought how cute and sweet it is when infants and parents coo and share baby talk with each other. But have you noticed that these very same behaviors often occur between you and your adult romantic partner?

Intrigued by these parallels, several researchers have studied the relationship between an infant's attachment to a parent figure and an adult's love for a romantic partner (Bachman & Zakahi, 2000; Diamond, 2004; Myers & Vetere, 2002). In one study, Cindy Hazan and Phillip Shaver (1987, 1994) discovered that adults who had an avoidant pattern in infancy are uncomfortable with intimacy as adults. They find it hard to trust others, difficult to self-disclose, and rarely report finding "true love" (Cooper, Shaver, & Collins, 1998; Fraley & Shaver, 1997). Anxious/ambivalent infants as adults also have difficulty with intimate relationships, but unlike avoidants, they tend to be obsessed with their romantic partners, fearing their intense love will not be reciprocated. Individuals who are securely attached as infants easily become close to others, expect intimate relationships to endure, and perceive others as generally trustworthy.

Why do avoidant and anxious/ambivalent infants have trouble with their later romantic relationships? According to research, the avoidant lover may block intimacy by being emotionally aloof and distant, whereas the anxious/ambivalent lover may smother intimacy by being possessive and emotionally demanding. As you may expect, the securely attached lover has intimacy patterns that foster long-term relationships and is the most desired partner by the majority of adults, regardless of their own attachment styles (Klohnen & Bera, 1998; Pietromonaco & Carnelley, 1994). Studies of adult attachment are significant because they suggest that our earliest bonding experiences may have lasting effects. Bowlby (1979) believed that attachment behaviors "characterize human beings from the cradle to the grave" (p. 129).

Evaluating Attachment Theories

Although Hazan and Shaver's research and similar studies are consistent with infant attachment theory, the results are correlational rather than experimental. As you know from Chapter 1, it is always risky to infer causation from correlation. Accord-

Karen Huffman

Bill Bachmann/IndexStock

The importance of attachment. *Researchers have found that the degree and quality of attachments you formed as an infant are correlated with your adult romantic relationships.*

ingly, the relationship between romantic love style and early infant attachment is subject to several alternative causal explanations. Further research is necessary before we fully understand the link between infant attachment and adult intimate relationships.

Be aware that early attachment experiences may predict the future but do not determine it. Despite the significance of the initial infant–parent attachment bond, we are capable of learning new social skills and different attitudes toward relationships in our later interactions with peers, close friends, lovers, and spouses. Unlike diamonds, attachment styles are not necessarily forever.

What's Your Romantic Attachment Style?

Thinking of your current and past romantic relationships, place a check next to those statements that best describe your feelings.

1. I find it relatively easy to get close to others and am comfortable depending on them and having them depend on me. I don't often worry about being abandoned or about someone getting too close.

2. I am somewhat uncomfortable being close. I find it difficult to trust partners completely or to allow myself to depend on them. I am nervous when anyone gets close and love partners often want me to be more intimate than is comfortable for me.

3. I find that others are reluctant to get as close as I would like. I often worry that my partner doesn't really love me or won't stay with me. I want to merge completely with another person, and this desire sometimes scares people away.

According to research, 55 percent of adults agree with item 1 (secure attachment), 25 percent choose number 2 (avoidant attachment), and 20 percent choose item 3 (anxious/ambivalent attachment) (adapted from Fraley & Shaver, 1997; Hazan & Shaver, 1987). Note that the percentages for these adult attachment styles are roughly equivalent to the percentages for infant–parent attachment.

Karen Huffman

Friendship and attachment. *These 50-year-old women have remained close friends since kindergarten. Despite heavy schedules, they get together at least once a year for a "friendship reunion."*

■ Parenting Styles: Their Effect on Development

How much of our personality comes from the way our parents treat us as we're growing up? Researchers since the 1920s have studied the effects of different methods of child-rearing on children's behavior, development, and mental health. Studies done by Diana Baumrind (1980, 1995) found that parenting styles could be reliably divided into three broad patterns: *permissive, authoritarian,* and *authoritative.*

1. ***Permissive.*** Permissive parents come in two styles: (a) *permissive-indifferent,* the parent who sets few limits and provides little in the way of attention, interest, or emotional support, and (b) *permissive-indulgent,* the parent who is highly involved but places few demands or controls on the child. Children of permissive-indifferent parents have poor self-control (becoming demanding and disobedient) and poor social skills. Children of permissive-indulgent parents often fail to learn respect for others and tend to be impulsive, immature, and out of control.

2. ***Authoritarian.*** These parents are rigid and punitive. They value unquestioning obedience and mature responsibility from their children, while remaining aloof and detached. An authoritarian parent might say, "Don't ask questions. Just do it my way or else." Children of authoritarian parents are easily upset, moody, aggressive, and generally have poor communication skills.

3. ***Authoritative.*** These parents are tender, caring, and sensitive toward their children. But they also set firm limits and enforce them, while encouraging increasing responsibility. As you might expect, children do best with authoritative parents. They become self-reliant, self-controlled, and high achieving. They also seem more content, goal oriented, friendly, and socially competent in their dealings with others (Baumrind, 1995; Gonzalez, Holbein, & Quilter, 2002; Parke & Buriel, 1998).

Study **T**ip

These last two terms are very similar. An easy way to remember is to notice the R in Authorita-R-ian, and imagine a rigid ruler. Then note the T in Authorita-T-ive, and picture a tender teacher.

www.wiley.com/college/huffman

Evaluating Baumrind's Research

Before you conclude that the authoritative pattern is the only way to raise successful children, you should know that many children raised in the other styles also become caring, cooperative adults. Criticism of Baumrind's findings generally falls into three areas: *child temperament, child expectations,* and *parental warmth:*

1. ***Child temperament.*** Results may reflect the child's unique temperament and reactions to parental efforts rather than the parenting style per se (Clarke-Stewart, Fitzpatrick, Allhusen, & Goldberg, 2000; McCrae et al., 2000). That is, the parents of mature and competent children may have developed the authoritative style because of the child's behavior rather than vice versa.

2. ***Child expectations.*** Cultural research suggests that a child's expectations of how parents should behave also play an important role in parenting styles (Brislin, 2000; Valsiner, 2000). As we discovered at the beginning of this chapter, adolescents in Korea expect strong parental control and interpret it as a sign of love and deep concern. Adolescents in North America, however, would interpret the same behavior as a sign of parental hostility and rejection.

3. ***Parental warmth.*** Cross-cultural studies suggest that the most important variable in parenting styles and child development might be the degree of warmth versus rejection parents feel toward their children. Analyses of over 100 societies have shown that parental rejection adversely affects children of all cultures (Rohner, 1986; Rohner & Britner, 2002). The neglect and indifference shown by rejecting parents tend to be correlated with hostile, aggressive children who have a difficult time establishing and maintaining close relationships. These children also are more likely to develop psychological problems that require professional intervention.

Do fathers differ from mothers in their parenting style? Until recently, the father's role in discipline and child care was largely ignored. But as more fathers have begun to take an active role in child-rearing, there has been a corresponding increase in research. From these studies, we now know that fathers are absorbed with, excited about, and responsive to their newborns and that there are few differences in the way children form attachments to either parent (Diener, Mengelsdorf, McHale, & Frosch, 2002; Lopez & Hsu, 2002; Rohner & Veneziano, 2001). After infancy, the father becomes increasingly involved with his children, yet he still spends less overall time in direct child care than the mother does (Demo, 1992; Hewlett, 1992). But fathers are just as responsive, nurturing, and competent as mothers when they do assume child-care responsibilities.

Kaz Mori/Photographers Choice/Getty Images

Are fathers important? *Although over-looked in the past, the father's role in a child's development is now a topic of active research.*

Application

CRITICAL THINKING

The Development of "Suicide Bombers"
(Contributed by Thomas Frangicetto)

The war in Iraq. Suicide Bombers. The 9/11 World Trade Center terrorist attack. In varying degrees all of these horrific events are the result of culture clashes, misunderstandings, mistrust, and mistaken beliefs. They also reflect lethal hatred. A

recent *60 Minutes* broadcast, "The Mind of a Suicide Bomber," examined the psychology of two "failed" suicide bombers who were captured and interviewed by Dr. Eyad Sarraj, a Palestinian psychiatrist. These individuals are obviously violent killers, right? "No, on the contrary," says Sarraj. "They usually were very timid people, introverts, the problem for them was always ... communicating their feelings, so

ACTIVE LEARNING

they were not violent at all." But, as so many Americans tend to believe, are these people psychotic, or out of touch with reality? According to Dr. Ariel Merari, "I don't know of a single case of one of them who was really psychotic. And still, there is this absolute absence of fear..."

According to Sarraj and Merari, the decision to become a suicide bomber is positively reinforced by many sociocultural consequences that strengthen the appeal within the population. What are these sociocultural reinforcers for suicide bombers?

- They achieve the highest rank in their religion—martyrdom.
- Their families not only are rewarded monetarily, they also attain an exalted status within their culture.
- They are revered as heroes and serve as idols worthy of emulation.
- They are promised an automatic "ticket to Paradise" where they will be immediately married to 72 beautiful virgins.

Critical Thinking Application

Using the cultural psychology guidelines for developmental research (pp. 330 to 331) and other information found throughout Chapter 9, answer the following:

1. Would suicide bombing be more likely in an individualist or collectivist culture? Why?
2. Given that culture is largely invisible to its participants, what are the seldom discussed ideals and values in American culture that encourage young men and women to voluntarily sign up to go to war, but not to become suicide bombers?
3. Which of Piaget's four stages of cognitive development best describes the cognitive processes of suicide bombers? Why?
4. Do you think attachment theory could help explain suicide bombers? Explain why or why not.
5. Which of Baumrind's three parenting styles would be most and least likely to produce a suicide bomber?

CHECK & REVIEW

Social-Emotional Development

Nativists believe **attachment** is innate. Nurturists believe it is learned. The Harlow and Zimmerman experiments with monkeys raised by cloth or wire surrogate mothers found that contact comfort might be the most important factor in attachment.

Infants who fail to form attachments may suffer serious effects. When attachments are formed, they may differ in level or degree. Research that identified securely attached, avoidant, and anxious/ambivalent infants found that their early behavioral differences may persist into romantic relationships in adulthood.

Parenting styles fall into three major categories: permissive, authoritarian, and authoritative. Critics suggest that a child's unique temperament, expectations of parents, and the degree of warmth versus rejection from parents may be the three most important variables in parenting styles.

Questions

1. According to Harlow and Zimmerman's research with cloth and wire surrogate mothers, _____ is the most important variable for attachment. (a) availability of food; (b) contact comfort; (c) caregiver and infant bonding; (d) imprinting
2. List the three types of attachment reported by Ainsworth.
3. Using Hazan and Shaver's research on adult attachment styles, match the following adults with their probable type of infant attachment:
   ___ Mary is nervous around attractive partners and complains that lovers often want her to be more intimate than she finds comfortable.
   ___ Bob complains that lovers are often reluctant to get as close as he would like.
   ___ Rashelle finds it relatively easy to get close to others and seldom worries about being abandoned.
   (a) avoidant; (b) secure; (c) anxious/ambivalent
4. Briefly explain Baumrind's three parenting styles.

Check your answers in Appendix B.

CLICK & REVIEW
for additional assessment options:
www.wiley.com/college/huffman

KEY TERMS

*To assess your understanding of the **Key Terms** in Chapter 9, write a definition for each (in your own words), and then compare your definitions with those in the text.*

developmental psychology (p. 326)

Studying Development
critical period (p. 327)
cross-sectional method (p. 328)
longitudinal method (p. 328)
maturation (p. 327)

Physical Development
ageism (p. 339)
embryonic period (p. 332)

fetal alcohol syndrome (FAS) (p. 334)
fetal period (p. 332)
germinal period (p. 332)
puberty (p. 337)
teratogen [Tuh-RAT-uh-jen] (p. 334)

Cognitive Development
accommodation (p. 341)
assimilation (p. 341)
concrete operational stage (p. 344)
conservation (p. 344)

egocentrism (p. 343)
formal operational stage (p. 345)
object permanence (p. 342)
preoperational stage (p. 343)
schema (p. 341)
sensorimotor stage (p. 342)

Social-Emotional Development
attachment (p. 349)
imprinting (p. 349)

Achievement
WEB RESOURCES

Huffman Book Companion Site

http://www.wiley.com/college/huffman

This site is loaded with free Interactive Self-Tests, Internet Exercises, Glossary and Flashcards for key terms, web links, Handbook for Non-Native Speakers, and other activities designed to improve your mastery of the material in this chapter.

Want to know more about genetics?

http://www.exploratorium.edu/genepool/genepool_home.html

A site developed from the Exploratorium Science Museum in San Francisco, California, containing a wealth of information, including "DNA: Your Genetic Blueprint," "Learning from Our Relatives," and "Tools for Decoding DNA."

Would you like an inside view of prenatal development?

http://www.parentsplace.com/first9months/main.html

Contains an extremely detailed, interactive visual of the incredible journey through the first nine months of a baby's development—from conception to birth.

Interested in more information on Piaget and his stages of cognitive development?

http://chiron.valdosta.edu/whuitt/col/cogsys/piaget.html

This site offers detailed biographical information on Piaget and a wide assortment of informative links to other prominent figures in cognitive development, such as Vygotsky, Erikson, and Bruner. The site also provides a brief overview of Piaget's four stages of cognitive development with a link to specific examples of how to use Piagetian theory in teaching and learning.

Need tips or information on child development and parenting skills?

http://www.childdevelopmentinfo.com/index.htm

Recommended by the American Psychological Association (APA), this site offers a wealth of information on child development, parenting, learning, health and safety, as well as practical suggestions for parents covering toddlers to teens. It also provides information on childhood disorders such as attention deficit disorder, dyslexia, and autism.

Want more information on adult attachment theory?

http://www.psych.uiuc.edu/~rcfraley/attachment.htm

Created by R. Chris Fraley at the University of Illinois, this site offers a concise summary of the voluminous research on adult attachment. Beginning with Bowlby's original theory of attachment, Fraley then explains individual differences in infant attachment, and concludes with adult romantic relationships.

Visual Summary

Studying Development

Developmental Psychology
Studies age-related changes in behavior and mental processes from conception to death.

Theoretical Issues
Key Issues:
- Nature vs. Nurture
- Continuity vs. Stages
- Stability vs. Change

Research Methods
Cross–sectional: Different participants, various ages, one point in time. Major problem: Cohort effects (a given generation may be affected by specific cultural and historical events).

Longitudinal: Same participants, extended time period. Major problem: Expensive, time consuming.

Physical Development

Prenatal and Early Childhood
- Three prenatal stages: **germinal**, **embryonic**, and **fetal**.
- **Teratogens:** Environmental agents capable of producing birth defects.
- Sensory and perceptual abilities are relatively well developed in newborns.
- Motor development primarily results from **maturation**.

Adolescence and Adulthood
- Adolescence: Psychological period between childhood and adulthood.
- **Puberty:** When sex organs become capable of reproduction.
- Menopause: Cessation of menstruation.
- Male climacteric: Physical and psychological changes in midlife.
- Primary aging: Inevitable, biological changes with age.
- Explanations of primary aging: *Programmed theory* (genetically built-in) and *damage theory* (body's inability to repair damage).

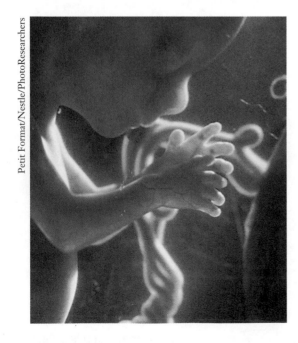

Petit Format/Nestle/PhotoResearchers

Cognitive Development

Paiget's Major Concepts:

- **Schema:** Cognitive structure for organizing ideas.
- **Assimilation:** Adding new information to an existing schema.
- **Accommodation:** Revising or developing new schemas to fit with new information.

Four Stages	Abilities	Limits
Sensorimotor (Birth to 2 years)	→ Uses senses and motor skills to explore and develop cognitively.	→ At beginning of stage, infant lacks **object permanence** (understanding things continue to exist even when not seen, heard, or felt).
Preoperational (Age 2 to 7)	→ Has significant language and thinks symbolically.	→ ■ Cannot perform "operations." ■ **Egocentric** thinking (inability to consider another's point of view). ■ Animistic thinking (believing all things are living).
Concrete Operational (Age 7 to 11)	→ ■ Can perform "operations" on concrete objects. ■ Understands **conservation** (realizes changes in shape or appearance can be reversed).	→ Cannot think abstractly and hypothetically.
Formal Operational (11 and up)	→ Can think abstractly and hypothetically.	→ Adolescent egocentrism at the beginning of this stage, with related problems of the *personal fable* and *imaginary audience*.

Social-Emotional Development

Attachment

- Infant attachment: **Imprinting:** Attaching to first moving object. Harlow's experiments found "contact comfort" very important to **attachment**. Infants who do not attach may suffer serious, lasting effects.
- Adult attachment: Patterns of infant attachment (secure, avoidant, and anxious/ambivalent) may carry over into adult romantic attachments.

Parenting Styles

There are three major categories (permissive, authoritarian, and authoritative), but critics suggest that a child's unique temperament, expectations of parents, and degree of warmth versus rejection from parents may be the most important determinants of parenting styles.

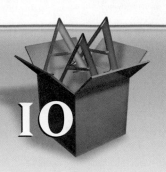

10

LIFE SPAN DEVELOPMENT II

Achievement

Core Learning Outcomes

As you read Chapter 10, keep the following questions in mind and answer them in your own words:

▷ How does morality change over the life span?

▷ How does personality change from infancy to old age?

▷ How can we have a successful adult life?

▷ Are there predictable stages of grief and death?

■ Achievement
■ Assessment
■ Application

Application

WHY STUDY PSYCHOLOGY?

Left Lane Productions/CorbisImages

Chapter 10 will explore fascinating facts, such as...

▶ A 5-year-old typically believes that *accidentally* breaking 15 cups is "badder" and more deserving of punishment than *intentionally* breaking 1 cup.

▶ Juvenile chimpanzees will soothe a frightened or injured peer. And adult female chimps will "adopt" a motherless baby.

▶ One of the most influential factors in early personality development is goodness of fit between a child's nature and the social and environmental setting.

▶ Erikson believed that adolescents who fail to resolve their "identity crises" may later have difficulty in maintaining close personal relationships and be more prone to delinquency.

▶ Parents typically experience their highest levels of marital satisfaction before children are born and after they leave home.

▶ Kübler-Ross believed that most people go through five predictable psychological stages when facing death.

Rubberball/SUPERSTOCK

In Europe, a woman was near death from a special kind of cancer. There was one drug that doctors thought might save her. It was a form of radium that a druggist in the same town had recently discovered. The drug was expensive to make. But the druggist was charging 10 times what the drug cost him to make. He paid $200 for the radium and charged $2,000 for a small dose of the drug.

The sick woman's husband, Heinz, went to everyone he knew to borrow the money. However, he could get together only about $1,000, which is half of what it cost. He told the druggist that his wife was dying and asked him to sell it cheaper or let him pay later. But the druggist said, "No, I discovered the drug, and I'm going to make money from it." So Heinz got desperate and broke into the man's store to steal the drug for his wife.

(KOHLBERG, *1964, PP. 18–19*)

Was Heinz right to steal the drug? What would you have done in this situation? Is morality "in the eye of the beholder," with everyone simply arguing for his or her own self-interest? Or are there universal truths and principles? Whatever your answer, your ability to think, reason, and respond to Heinz's dilemma demonstrates another type of development that is very important to psychology—moral development.

As we discussed in Chapter 9, developmental psychology is devoted to the study of age-related changes in behavior and mental processes from conception to death. Chapter 9 explored life span changes in physical development, cognitive development, and social-emotional development. In this chapter, we continue our study with moral development, personality development, special challenges of adulthood, and grief and death.

Achievement

How does morality change over life span?

MORAL DEVELOPMENT

In Chapter 9, we noted that newborns cry when they hear another baby cry. But did you know that by age 2, most children use words like *good* or *bad* to evaluate actions that are aggressive or that might endanger their own or another's welfare (Kochanska, Casey, & Fukumoto, 1995)? Or that juvenile chimpanzees will soothe a frightened or injured peer, and adult female chimps will "adopt" a motherless baby (Goodall, 1990). How can we explain such early emergence and cross-species evidence of *morality*—the ability to take the perspective of, or empathize with, others and distinguish between right and wrong?

From a biological perspective, some researchers suggest that morality may be prewired and evolutionarily based (e.g., Green et al., 2001; Haidt, 2001; Rossano, 2003). Behaviors like infant empathic crying and adoption of motherless chimp babies help the species survive. Therefore, evolution may have provided us with biologically based provisions for moral acts. But as with most human behaviors, biology is only one part of the *biopsychosocial model*. In this section, we will focus our attention on the psychological and social factors that explain how moral thoughts, feelings, and actions change over the life span.

Kohlberg's Research: What Is Right?

One of the most influential researchers in moral development was Lawrence Kohlberg (1927–1987). He presented what he called "moral stories" like the Heinz dilemma to people of all ages. On the basis of his findings, he developed a highly influential model of moral development (1964, 1984).

What is the right answer to Heinz's dilemma? Kohlberg was not interested in whether participants judged Heinz right or wrong. He only studied the reasons they gave for their decision. On the basis of participants' responses, Kohlberg proposed three broad levels in the evolution of moral reasoning, each composed of two distinct stages (Table 10.1). Individuals at each stage and level may or may not support Heinz's stealing of the drug, but for different reasons.

Like Piaget's stages of cognitive development, Kohlberg believed his stages of moral development were *universal* and *invariant*. That is, they supposedly exist in all cultures, and everyone goes through each of the stages in a predictable fashion. The age trends that are noticed tend to be rather broad.

1. ***Preconventional level*** (Stages 1 and 2—birth to adolescence). At this level, moral judgment is *self-centered*. What is right is what one can get away with or what is personally satisfying. Moral understanding is based on rewards, punishments, and exchange of favors. This level is called **preconventional** because children have not yet accepted society's *(conventional)* rule-making processes.

   - ***Stage 1 (punishment and obedience orientation).*** Children at this stage focus on self-interest—obedience to authority and avoidance of punishment. They also have difficulty considering another's point of view. Thus, they generally ignore people's intentions in their moral judgments. A 5-year-old will often say that *accidentally* breaking 15 cups is "badder" and should receive more punishment than *intentionally* breaking 1 cup.

   - ***Stage 2 (instrumental-exchange orientation).*** During this stage, children become aware of another's perspective. But their morality is based on reciprocity—an equal exchange of favors. "I'll share my lunch with you because if I ever forget mine you'll share yours with me." "You scratch my back and I'll scratch yours" is the guiding philosophy.

2. ***Conventional level*** (Stages 3 and 4—adolescence and young adulthood). During this time, moral reasoning advances from being self-centered to *other-centered*. The individual personally accepts **conventional** societal rules because they help ensure social order and he judges morality in terms of compliance with these rules and values.

Preconventional Level *Kohlberg's first level of moral development, in which morality is based on rewards, punishment, and exchange of favors*

Conventional Level *Kohlberg's second level of moral development, where moral judgments are based on compliance with the rules and values of society*

www.wiley.com/college/huffman

SUMMARY TABLE 10.1 KOHLBERG'S THEORY OF MORAL DEVELOPMENT

Name of Stage	Moral Reasoning	Heinz's Dilemma Responses	
		Pro	**Con**
Preconventional level			
Stage 1: punish-ment–obedience orientation	Morality is what you can get away with	"If you let your wife die, you will get in trouble. You'll be blamed for not spending the money to save her and there'll be an investigation of you and the druggist for your wife's death."	"You shouldn't steal the drug, because you'll be caught and sent to jail. If you do get away, your conscience would bother you thinking how the police will catch up with you at any minute."
Stage 2: instrumen-tal-exchange orienta-tion	Obey rules to obtain rewards or favors	"If you do happen to get caught, you could give the drug back and you wouldn't get much of a sentence. It wouldn't bother you much to serve a little jail term if you had your wife when you got out."	"You may not get much of a jail term if you steal the drug, but your wife will probably die before you get out, so it won't do you much good. If your wife dies, you should-n't blame yourself; it isn't your fault she has cancer."
Conventional level			
Stage 3: good-child orientation	Obey rules to get approval	"No one will think you're bad if you steal the drug, but your family will think you're an inhuman husband if you don't. If you let your wife die, you'll never be able to look anybody in the face again."	"It isn't just the druggist who will think you're a criminal; everyone else will, too. After you steal it, you'll feel bad thinking how you've brought dishonor on your family and yourself, and you won't be able to face anyone again."
Stage 4: law-and-order orientation	Obey laws because they maintain the social order	"If you have any sense of honor, you won't let your wife die just because you're afraid to do the only thing that will save her. You'll always feel guilty that you caused her death if you don't do your duty to her."	"You're desperate and you may not know you're doing wrong when you steal the drug. But you'll know you did wrong after you're sent to jail. You'll always feel guilty for breaking the law."
Postconventional level			
Stage 5: social-con-tract orientation	Moral reasoning reflects belief in democratically accepted laws	"You'll lose other people's respect, not gain it, if you don't steal. If you let your wife die, it would be out of fear, not out of reasoning it out. So you'd lose self-respect and proba-bly the respect of others, too."	"You would lose your standing and respect in the community and vio-late the law. You'd lose respect for yourself if you're carried away by emotion and forget the long-range point of view."
Stage 6: universal-ethics orientation	Moral reasoning reflects individ-ual conscience	"If you don't steal the drug and let your wife die, you'll always con-demn yourself for it afterward. You wouldn't be blamed and you would have lived up to the outside rule of the law, but you wouldn't have lived up to your own standards of conscience."	"If you stole the drug, you wouldn't be blamed by other people, but you'd condemn yourself because you wouldn't have lived up to your own conscience and standards of honesty."

Sources: Adapted from Kohlberg, L. "Stage and Sequence: The Cognitive Developmental Approach to Socialization." in D. A. Aoslin, *The Handbook of Social-ization Theory and Research.* Chicago: Rand McNally, 1969. p. 376 (Table 6.2).

- *Stage 3 (good-child orientation).* At Stage 3, the primary moral concern is with being nice and gaining approval. People are also judged by their intentions and motives—"His heart was in the right place."

- *Stage 4 (law-and-order orientation).* During this stage, the individual takes into account a larger perspective—societal laws. Stage 4 individuals understand that if everyone violated laws, even with good intentions, there would be chaos. Thus, doing one's duty and respecting law and order are highly valued. According to Kohlberg, Stage 4 is the highest level attained by most adolescents and adults.

3. *Postconventional level* (Stages 5 and 6—adulthood). At this level, individuals develop personal standards for right and wrong. They also define morality in terms of abstract principles and values that apply to all situations and societies. A 20-year-old who judges the "discovery" and settlement of North America by Europeans as immoral because it involved the theft of land from native peoples is thinking in **postconventional** terms.

- *Stage 5 (social-contract orientation).* Individuals at Stage 5 appreciate the underlying purposes served by laws. When laws are consistent with the interests of the majority, they are obeyed because of the "social contract." However, laws can be morally disobeyed if they fail to express the will of the majority or maximize social welfare. For example, if someone said Heinz should steal the drug because his wife's right to life was more important than the druggist's property rights, this would be a Stage 5 type of moral reasoning.

- *Stage 6 (universal-ethics orientation).* At this stage, "right" is determined by universal ethical principles that *all* religions or moral authorities might view as compelling or fair. Examples of these universal principles might include nonviolence, human dignity, freedom, and equality. According to Stage 6 moral reasoning, these principles apply whether or not they conform to existing laws. Thus, Mohandas Gandhi, Martin Luther King, and Nelson Mandela intentionally broke laws that violated universal principles, such as human dignity.

  Few individuals actually achieve Stage 6 (about 1 or 2 percent of those tested worldwide). And Kohlberg found it difficult to separate Stages 5 and 6. Thus, in time, he combined the stages (Kohlberg, 1981).

Postconventional Level *Kohlberg's highest level of moral development, in which individuals develop personal standards for right and wrong, and define morality in terms of abstract principles and values that apply to all situations and societies*

Study Tip

This is a good point to stop and review your understanding of Kohlberg's theory by carefully studying Summary Table 10.1.

Assessing Kohlberg's Theory: Three Major Criticisms

Kohlberg has been credited with enormous insights and contributions. But his theories have also been the focus of three major areas of criticism.

1. *Moral reasoning versus behavior.* Are the people who achieve higher stages on Kohlberg's scale really more moral than others? Or do they just "talk a good game"? Some studies show a positive correlation between higher stages of reasoning and higher levels of moral behavior (Borba, 2001; Rest, Narvaez, Bebeau, & Thoma, 1999). But others have found that situational factors are better predictors of moral behavior (Bandura, 1986, 1991; Bruggeman & Hart, 1996; Nayda, 2002). For example, research participants are more likely to steal when they are told the money comes from a large company rather than from individuals (Greenberg, 2002). And both men and women will tell more sexual lies during casual relationships than during close relationships (Williams, 2001).

2. *Cultural differences.* Recall from Chapter 9 two of the basic questions that guide developmental researchers: "nature or nurture?" and "continuity or stages?" Cross-cultural research on morality confirms that children in different cultures generally do conform to Kohlberg's model. And they progress sequentially from his first level, the preconventional, to his second, the conventional (Rest, Narvaez, Bebeau, &

Jonathan Nourok/Stone/Getty Images

Gilligan Versus Kohlberg. *According to Carol Gilligan, women score "lower" on Lawrence Kohlberg's stages of moral development because they are socialized to assume more responsibility for the care of others.*

Thoma, 1999; Snarey, 1985, 1995). Thus, the nature and stage aspects of these two basic questions seem to be supported by cross-cultural studies.

At the same time, cultural *differences* suggest that nurture, or culture, also influence morality. For example, cross-cultural comparisons of responses to Heinz's moral dilemma show that Europeans and Americans tend to consider whether they like or identify with the victim in questions of morality. In contrast, Hindu Indians consider social responsibility and personal concerns two separate issues (Miller & Bersoff, 1998). Researchers suggest that the difference reflects the Indians' broader sense of social responsibility.

In India, Papua New Guinea, and China, as well as in Israeli kibbutzim, people don't choose between the rights of the individual and the rights of society (as the top levels of Kohlberg's model require). Instead, most people seek a compromise solution that accommodates both interests (Killen & Hart, 1999; Miller & Bersoff, 1998). Thus, Kohlberg's standard for judging the highest level of morality (the postconventional) may be more applicable to cultures that value individualism over community and interpersonal relationships.

3. ***Possible gender bias.*** Researcher Carol Gilligan has also criticized Kohlberg's model because on his scale women often tend to be classified at a lower level of moral reasoning than men. Gilligan suggested that this difference occurred because Kohlberg's theory emphasizes values more often held by men, such as rationality and independence. Kohlberg also supposedly ignores common female values, such as concern for others and belonging (Gilligan, 1977, 1990, 1993; Hoffman, 2000). Most follow-up studies of Gilligan's theory, however, have found few, if any, gender differences in level or type of moral reasoning (Hoffman, 2000; Jaffee & Hyde, 2000; Pratt, Skoe, & Arnold, 2004).

Application

CRITICAL THINKING

Morality and Academic Cheating
(Contributed by Thomas Frangicetto)

Recent research from *The Center for Academic Integrity* on cheating among American high school students found that: (1) cheating is widespread, (2) students have little difficulty rationalizing cheating, (3) the Internet is causing new concerns, and (4) students cheat for a variety of reasons. Do you think academic cheating is a moral issue? Consider the following moral dilemma:

It is close to final exam time in your psychology course, and you are on the border between a C or B grade. You go to your professor's office to see what you can do to make sure you get the B grade. But there's a note on the open door, "I'll be right back. Please wait." You notice the stack of exams for your upcoming final, and you could easily take one and leave without being seen.

Describe what you would do in this situation, and briefly explain your reasons.

_____
_____
_____
_____

After reviewing Kohlberg's six stages of moral development (Summary Table 10.1), can you label your stage of moral development on this moral dilemma? Stage # _____.

To further develop your critical thinking (and help prepare you for exams on this material), read and label the following responses to the same situation.

Student A: "I wouldn't take the exam because it would be wrong. What if *everybody* cheated every chance they got? What kind of credibility would grades have? It would cheapen the value of education and the whole system would be worthless." Stage # _____.

ACTIVE LEARNING

Student B: "I would take the exam because I really need the B in this course. Psychology is not my major, and I have to keep my scholarship. Otherwise, I will not be able to stay in school and my children will suffer." Stage # _____.

Student C: "I wouldn't take it because I would be too afraid of getting caught. With my luck, the teacher would return early and catch me in the act." Stage # _____.

Student D: "I wouldn't take the exam because I wouldn't be able to live with myself. I believe that cheating is the same as stealing and is therefore a crime. My own opinion of myself as an honest person of high integrity would be permanently damaged." Stage # _____.

Student E: "I wouldn't take it because if I got caught and my parents found out they would be devastated. I care too much about what they think of me to risk that. Stage # _____.

Student F: "I wouldn't do it because it wouldn't be fair to other students who have to take the exam without any advantages. The system is designed to work fairly for everyone and cheating definitely violates that ideal." Stage # _____.

Critical Thinking Application

Review the 21 critical thinking components (CTCs) from the Prologue (pp. xxx–xxxiv). Below are a few student com-

ments quoted in the report of The Center for Academic Integrity. Apply at least one CTC to each.

"I think that cheating has become so common that it's starting to become 'normal' in some cases." CTC: _____

"There is no way of stopping it. Only the students themselves have the power to do so. Restrictions aren't the problem, but the morals of students sure are." CTC: _____

"Cheating will always exist as long as parents place the emphasis on grades rather than learning. The parent–student relation adds greatly to the dumbing down of America." CTC: _____

"Unless someone makes teachers care about cheating, it won't be stopped. It is unfair that teachers don't take it seriously because then the honest students get the bad end of the deal." CTC: _____

Assessment

CHECK & REVIEW

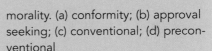

Moral Development

According to Kohlberg, morality progresses through three levels. Each level consists of two stages. At the **preconventional level,** morality is self-centered. What is right is what one can get away with (Stage 1). Or what is personally satisfying (Stage 2). **Conventional level** morality is based on a need for approval (Stage 3) and obedience to laws because they maintain the social order (Stage 4). **Postconventional level** morality comes from adhering to the social contract (Stage 5) and the individual's own principles and universal values (Stage 6). Kohlberg's the-

ory has been criticized for being politically, culturally, and gender biased.

Questions

1. According to Kohlberg's theory of morality, self-interest and avoiding punishment are characteristic of the _____ level, personal standards or universal principles characterize the _____ level, and gaining approval or following the rules describes the _____ level.

2. Calvin would like to wear baggy, torn jeans and a nose ring, but he is concerned that others will disapprove. Calvin is at Kohlberg's _____ level of

morality. (a) conformity; (b) approval seeking; (c) conventional; (d) preconventional

3. Five-year-old Tyler believes "bad things are what you get punished for." Tyler is at Kohlberg's _____ level of morality. (a) concrete; (b) preconventional; (c) postconventional; (d) punishment-oriented

4. Explain the possible cultural and gender bias in Kohlberg's theory.

Check your answers in Appendix B.

CLICK & REVIEW
for additional assessment options:
www.wiley.com/college/huffman

PERSONALITY DEVELOPMENT

■ Thomas and Chess's Temperament Theory: Biology and Personality Development

As an infant, did you lie quietly and seem oblivious to loud noises? Or did you tend to kick and scream and respond immediately to every sound? Did you respond warmly to people, or did you fuss, fret, and withdraw? Your answers to these questions help determine what developmental psychologists call your **temperament**, an individual's innate, biological behavioral style and characteristic emotional response.

One of the earliest and most influential theories regarding temperament came from the work of psychiatrists Alexander Thomas and Stella Chess (Thomas & Chess,

Achievement

How does personality change from infancy to old age?

Temperament *An individual's innate behavioral style and characteristic emotional response*

www.wiley.com/college/huffman

1977, 1987, 1991). Thomas and Chess found that approximately 65 percent of the babies they observed could be reliably separated into three categories:

1. *Easy children.* These infants were happy most of the time, relaxed and agreeable, and adjusted easily to new situations (approximately 40 percent).

2. *Difficult children.* Infants in this group were moody, easily frustrated, tense, and overreactive to most situations (approximately 10 percent).

3. *Slow-to-warm-up children.* These infants showed mild responses, were somewhat shy and withdrawn, and needed time to adjust to new experiences or people (approximately 15 percent).

Follow-up studies have found that certain aspects of these temperamental styles tend to be consistent and enduring throughout childhood and even adulthood (Caspi, 2000; Kagan, 1998; McCrae, 2004; Stams, Juffer, & van Ijzendoorn, 2002). That is not to say every shy, cautious infant ends up a shy adult. Many events take place between infancy and adulthood that shape an individual's development.

One of the most influential factors in early personality development is *goodness of fit* between a child's nature, parental behaviors, and the social and environmental setting (Eccles et al., 1999; Lindahl & Obstbaum, 2004; Realmuto, August, & Egan, 2004). For example, a slow-to-warm-up child does best if allowed time to adjust to new situations. Similarly, a difficult child thrives in a structured, understanding environment but not in an inconsistent, intolerant home. Alexander Thomas, the pioneer of temperament research, thinks parents should work with their child's temperament rather than trying to change it. Can you see how this idea of goodness of fit is yet another example of how nature and nurture interact?

■ Erikson's Psychosocial Theory: The Eight Stages of Life

Psychosocial Stages *Erikson's theory that individuals pass through eight developmental stages, each involving a crisis that must be successfully resolved*

Like Kohlberg, Erik Erikson (1902–1994) also developed a stage theory of development. Kohlberg described three levels of moral development and Erikson identified eight **psychosocial stages** of social development. Each Eriksonian stage is marked by a "psychosocial" crisis or conflict related to a specific developmental task.

The name for each psychosocial stage reflects the specific crisis encountered at that stage and two possible outcomes.. For example, the crisis or task of most young adults is *intimacy versus isolation* (Table 10.2). This means that this age group's developmental task is developing deep, intimate relations with others. Those who don't meet this developmental challenge risk social isolation. Erikson believed that the more successfully we overcome each psychosocial crisis, the better chance we have to develop in a healthy manner (Erikson, 1950).

Stage 1

In Erikson's first stage (birth to approximately 12 months), the major crisis is *trust versus mistrust*. When and how the infant's needs are met determines whether the infant decides the world is a good and satisfying place to live or a source of pain, frustration, and uncertainty.

Stages 2 to 4

According to Erikson, the second stage, *autonomy versus shame and doubt* (ages 1 to 3), is a time for developing self-awareness and independence. During the "terrible twos," toddlers continually assert their wills—"no, no" and "me, me." Parents who handle these beginning attempts at independence with patience and good-humored encouragement help their toddlers develop a sense of autonomy. Conversely, if parents are ridiculing, impatient, or controlling, the child develops feelings of shame and doubt.

SUMMARY TABLE 10.2 ERIKSON'S EIGHT STAGES

	Psychosocial Crisis (approximate age)	Description
Erikson's first stage	Trust versus mistrust (0–1)	Infants learn to trust that their needs will be met by the world, especially by the mother; if not, mistrust develops.
	Autonomy versus shame and doubt (1–3)	Toddlers learn to exercise will, to make choices, to control themselves; if not, they become uncertain and doubt they can do things by themselves.
Erikson's second stage	Initiative versus guilt (3–6)	Preschool children learn to initiate activities and enjoy their accomplishments; if not, they feel guilty for their attempts at independence.
	Industry versus inferiority (6–12)	Elementary school age children develop a sense of industry or competence and learn productive skills their culture requires; if not, they feel inferior.
Erikson's sixth stage	Identity versus role confusion (12–20)	Adolescents develop a coherent sense of self and their role in society or they face identity and role confusion.
	Intimacy versus isolation (20–30)	Young adults form intimate connections with others; if not, they may experience feelings of isolation.
Erikson's eighth stage	Generativity versus stagnation (30–65)	Middle-aged adults develop concern for establishing, guiding, and influencing the next generation; if not, they experience stagnation (a sense of life-lessness).
	Ego integrity versus despair (65+)	Older people enter a period of reflection and life review. They either achieve a sense of integrity for the lives they've lived and accept death, or yield to despair that their lives cannot be relived.

Photo credits (left margin): Dann Coffey/The ImageBank/Getty Images; Prof. Karen Huffman; Jeff Greenberg/PhotoResearchers; Jocelyn Boutin/IndexStock

Source: Adapted from Papalia, Olds, & Feldman (2001). *Human Development* (8 ed.). New York: McGraw-Hill.

During the third stage, *initiative versus guilt* (ages 3 to 6), the main issue is the child's desire to initiate activities and the guilt that comes from unwanted or unexpected consequences. When my son was 5 years old, he decided to make himself a grilled cheese sandwich in the toaster! Like all parents, I make mistakes with my children. But in this case I realized that he was "taking initiative" and avoided criticizing him—despite a considerable mess all over the entire kitchen and living room. According to Erikson, if caregivers' responses to self-initiated activities are supportive and encouraging (at least most of the time), the child will develop feelings of power and self-confidence instead of guilt and doubt.

During Erikson's fourth stage, *industry versus inferiority* (age 6 through 12), children develop a sense of industry, or competency, as they begin to practice skills they will use for a lifetime of productive work. Most children in industrialized countries learn to read, write, and count during this stage. How the external world responds to a child's successes and failures determines whether she or he develops feelings of competency and industriousness or feelings of insecurity and inferiority.

Stages 5 and 6

Erikson's fifth stage is the period of *identity versus role confusion* (ages 12 to 20). Erikson believed that each individual's personal identity develops from a period of serious questioning and intense soul searching. During this **identity crisis**, adolescents attempt to discover who they are, what their skills are, and what kinds of roles they are best suited to play for the rest of their lives. Failure to resolve the identity crisis may be related to a lack of stable identity, delinquency, or difficulty in maintaining close personal relationships in later life.

Once a firm sense of identity is established, Erikson believed the individual (now in young adulthood—ages 20 to 30) is ready to meet the challenges of *intimacy versus isolation*, Stage 6 of development. If close bonds are formed, a basic feeling of intimacy with others will result. If not, the individual may avoid interpersonal commitments and experience feelings of isolation. Erikson's model for Stages 5 and 6 suggests that if we are to have close, loving relationships with others, we must first learn who we are and how to be independent.

Stages 7 and 8

In the seventh stage, *generativity versus stagnation* (middle age—ages 30 to 65), the individual expands feelings of love and concern beyond the immediate family group to include all of society. One major drive for this age group is the assistance and guidance of younger generations. If this expansion and effort do not occur, an individual stagnates, becoming concerned solely with material possessions and personal well-being.

In the final years of life, adults enter the period of *ego integrity versus despair*, Stage 8. Those who have been successful in resolving their earlier psychosocial crises will tend to look back on their lives with feelings of accomplishment and satisfaction. Those who resolved their earlier crises in a negative way or who lived fruitless, self-centered lives may deeply regret lost opportunities or become despondent because they realize it is too late to start over. As the Danish philosopher Søren Kierkegaard said, "Life is lived forward, but understood backward."

Evaluating Erikson's Theory

Many psychologists agree with Erikson's general idea that psychosocial crises, which are based on interpersonal and environmental interactions, do contribute to personality development (Brendgen, Vitaro, & Bukowski, 2000; Bugental & Goodnow, 1998; Marcia, 2002). However, Erikson also has his critics. First, Erikson's psychosocial stages, like Freud's theories, are difficult to test scientifically. Second, the labels Erikson used to describe the eight stages may not be entirely appropriate cross-culturally. For example, in individualistic cultures, *autonomy* is highly preferable to *shame and doubt*. But in collectivist cultures, the preferred resolution might be *dependence* or *merging relations* (Matsumoto, 2000). In addition, it is difficult to squeeze an entire lifetime of development into one comprehensive theory.

Identity Crisis *Erikson's term for an adolescent's search for self, which requires intense self-reflection and questioning*

Despite their limits, Erikson's stages have greatly contributed to the study of North American and European psychosocial development. Moreover, Erikson was among the first theorists to suggest that development continues past adolescence. And his theory encouraged further research.

Myths of Development: Correcting Popular Misconceptions

Having completed our brief overview of two major theories of life span personality development, we need to clarify a few lingering misconceptions before going on. For example, until recently, most psychologists characterized adolescence as a time of *storm and stress*—great emotional turbulence and psychological strain. Research within the last 20 years, however, has found that storm and stress is largely a myth. Adolescence is no stormier than any other life transition—an observation supported by research in 186 societies (Schlegel & Barry, 1991). And, contrary to Erikson's predicted need for psychological separation from parents in order to establish identity, most teenagers of both sexes remain close to their parents and admire them (Diener & Diener, 1996; Lerner & Galambos, 1998; Van Wel, Linssen, & Abma, 2000).

Other popular beliefs about age-related crises are also not supported by research. The popular idea of a *midlife crisis* began largely as the result of Gail Sheehy's national best-seller *Passages* (1976). Sheehy drew on the theories of Daniel Levinson (1977, 1996) and psychiatrist Roger Gould (1975), as well as her own interviews. Sheehy popularized the idea that almost everyone experiences a "predictable crisis" at about age 35 for women and 40 for men. Middle age often *is* a time of reexamining one's values and lifetime goals. However, Sheehy's book led many people to automatically expect a midlife crisis with drastic changes in personality and behavior. Research suggests that a severe reaction or crisis may actually be quite rare and not typical of what most people experience during middle age (Horton, 2002; Lachman, 2004).

Many people also believe that when the last child leaves home, most parents experience an *empty nest syndrome*—a painful separation and time of depression for the mother, the father, or both parents. Again, research suggests that the empty nest syndrome may be an exaggeration of the pain experienced by a few individuals and an effort to downplay positive reactions (White & Rogers, 1997; Whyte, 1992). For example, one major benefit of the empty nest is an increase in marital satisfaction (Figure 10.1). Furthermore, parent–child relationships do continue once the child leaves home. As one mother said, "The empty nest is surrounded by telephone wires" (Troll, Miller, & Atchley, 1979).

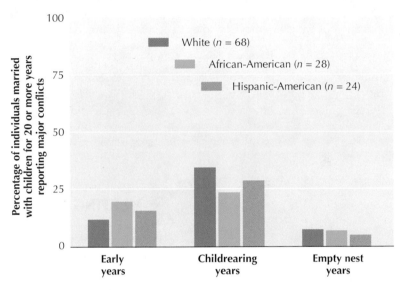

Figure 10.1 *Life span marital satisfaction.* Do you believe children make a marriage stronger? Do you think most parents experience a depressing empty nest syndrome when children grow up and leave home? If so, you'll be surprised to know that the highest levels of marital satisfaction and lowest levels of marital conflict occur *before* children are born and *after* they leave home (Mackey & O'Brien, 1998, p. 132).

CHECK & REVIEW

Personality Development

Thomas and Chess emphasized the genetic component of certain traits (such as sociability) and the fact that babies often exhibit differences in **temperament** shortly after birth.

Erikson proposed a theory of eight **psychosocial stages** of development covering the entire life span. The four stages that occur during childhood are trust versus mistrust, autonomy versus shame and doubt, initiative versus guilt, and industry versus inferiority. The major psychosocial **identity crisis** of adolescence is the search for identity versus role confusion. During young adulthood, the individual's task is to establish intimacy over isolation. During middle adulthood, the person must deal with generativity versus stagnation. At the end of life, the older adult must establish ego integrity or face overwhelming despair at the realization of lost opportunities.

Research shows that adolescent storm and stress, the midlife crisis, and the empty nest syndrome may be exaggerated accounts of a few individual's experiences and not typical of most people.

Questions

1. An infant's inborn disposition is known as _____. (a) personality; (b) reflexes; (c) temperament; (d) traits

2. Briefly describe Thomas and Chess's temperament theory.

3. Erikson suggested that problems in adulthood are sometimes related to unsuccessful resolution of one of his eight stages. For each of the following individuals, identify the most likely "problem" stage:
   a. Marcos has trouble keeping friends and jobs because he continually asks for guarantees and reassurance of his worth.
   b. Ann has attended several colleges without picking a major, has taken several vocational training programs, and has had numerous jobs over the last 10 years.
   c. Teresa is reluctant to apply for a promotion even though her coworkers have encouraged her to do so. She worries that she will be taking jobs from others and questions her worth.
   d. George continually obsesses over the value of his life. He regrets that he left his wife and children for a job in another country and failed to maintain contact.

4. Discuss the text's three common myths of development.

Check your answers in Appendix B.

CLICK & REVIEW
for additional assessment options:
www.wiley.com/college/huffman

MEETING THE CHALLENGES OF ADULTHOOD

Achievement

How can we have a successful adult life?

Having completed our whirlwind trip through the major theories and concepts explaining moral and personality development across the life span, you may be wondering how this information can be helpful in your current adult life. In this section, we will explore three of the most important developmental tasks we all face as adults: developing good marital relationships, coping with the challenges of family life, and finding rewarding work and retirement.

Marriage: Overcoming Unrealistic Expectations

> After years of advising other people on their personal problems, I was stunned by my own divorce. I only wish I had someone to write to for advice.
>
> ANN LANDERS

Although there has been a modest decline in the divorce rate since the 1970s, nearly one-half of marriages still end in divorce in the United States. As expected, these breakups have serious implications for both adult and child development (Abbey & Dallos, 2004; Lengua, Wolchik, Sandler, & West, 2000; Riggio, 2004). For the adults, both spouses generally experience emotional as well as practical difficulties. They are also at high risk for depression and physical health problems. However, many problems assumed to be due to divorce are actually present before marital disruption. In fact, for some, divorce can be life enhancing. In a "healthy" divorce, ex-spouses must accomplish three tasks: *let go, develop new social ties*, and, when children are involved, *redefine parental roles* (Everett & Everett, 1994).

In addition to stresses on the divorcing couple, some research shows that children also suffer both short-term and long-lasting effects. Compared with children in continuously intact two-parent families, children of divorce generally exhibit more behavioral problems, poorer self-concepts, more psychological problems, lower academic achievement, and more relationship and social difficulties (Ham, 2004; Hetherington & Stanley-Hagan, 2002; Pedro-Carroll, 2005; van Schaick & Stolberg, 2001). On the other hand, other research finds that children's psychological development is not affected by parental separation per se. Instead, it is related to issues such as level of attachment and the child's unique personality. It is also affected by the mother's income, education, ethnicity, child-rearing beliefs, depressive symptoms, and behavior (Clarke-Stewart et al., 2000; Ruschena et al., 2005; Torrance, 2004). Other researchers have suggested that children may also do better without the constant tension and fighting of an intact, but unhappy, home (Emery, 1999).

Whether children become "winners" or "losers" in a divorce depends on the (1) individual attributes of the child, (2) qualities of the custodial family, (3) continued involvement with noncustodial parents, and (4) resources and support systems available to the child and parents (Brauer et al., 2005; Carbone, 2000; Gottman, 1998; Grych, 2005; Torrance, 2004). If you or your parents are currently considering or going through divorce, you might want to keep these four factors in mind when making legal and other decisions about children.

Two different kinds of families. The *Cosby Show* and *The Sopranos.*

pplication

APPLYING PSYCHOLOGY TO EVERYDAY LIFE

Are Your Marital Expectations Unrealistic?

How can I have a good marriage and avoid divorce? One of the first steps is to examine your personal dreams and expectations for marriage. Where did they come from? Are they realistic? When you think about marriage and the roles of husband and wife, what do you imagine? Do you re-create images of television families like those on *The Cosby Show, Everybody Loves Raymond,* or even *The Sopranos*? Research shows that women are more likely than men to report trying to model their family life after what they have seen on TV situational comedies. They also tend to expect their significant other to act like the men they have seen on TV (Morrison & Westman, 2001).

When we look at men's expectations, research finds they are more likely to believe certain myths about marriage, such as "men are from Mars and women are from Venus" or "affairs are the main cause of divorce." Can you see how these expectations and myths could lead to marital problems? For both women and men, marriage therapists and researchers consistently find that realistic expectations are a key ingredient in successful marriages (Gottman & Levenson, 2002; Waller & McLanahan, 2005).

Are your expectations realistic? Two important components of realistic expectations are *recognizing personal biases* and *valuing truth above self-interest.* Try to use these two critical thinking skills as you compare your personal marital expectations with the following list of traits and factors based on long-term happy marriages (Gottman & Levenson, 2002; Gottman & Notarius, 2000; Greeff & Malherbe, 2001; Harker & Keltner, 2001; Heaton, 2002; Rosen-Grandon, Myers, & Hattie, 2004).

1. ***Established "love maps."*** In a happy marriage, both partners are willing to share their personal feelings and life goals. This sharing leads to detailed "love maps" of each other's inner emotional life and the creation of shared meaning in the relationship. Is this true for you? Or do you have the unrealistic expectation that this type of closeness "naturally" develops or that the "right partner" will automatically know your innermost thoughts and feelings?

2. ***Shared power and mutual support.*** Are you willing to fully share power and respect your partner's point of view, even if you disagree? Or have you unconsciously accepted the imbalance of power portrayed by TV sitcoms? Note how the

husbands on *The Cosby Show*, *Everybody Loves Raymond*, and *The Sopranos* are generally portrayed as the "head of the house." But the real power is secretly held by the "little woman." Can you see how this common portrayal might create unrealistic expectations for women and avoidance of marriage for men?

3. *Conflict management.* Successful couples work hard to solve their solvable conflicts, accept their unsolvable ones, and know the difference. Do you expect your partner to automatically change when you have conflict? Conflict resolution is not about making others change. It involves negotiation and accommodation. Do you idealistically expect to resolve most or all of your problems? Marriage counselors find that most marital conflicts are perpetual—they don't go away. Happy couples recognize these areas and avoid marital "gridlock" with dialogue, patience, and acceptance.

4. *Similarity.* Do you believe "opposites attract"? We all know couples who are very different and still happy. However, research finds that similarity (in values, beliefs, religion, and so on) is one of the best predictors of long-lasting relationships (Chapter 16).

5. *Supportive social environment.* Do you expect that "love conquers all"? Unfortunately, research finds several environmental factors that can overpower or slowly erode even the strongest love. These factors include age (younger couples have higher divorce rates), money and employment (divorce is higher among the poor and unemployed), parents' marriages (divorce is higher for children of divorced parents), length of courtship (longer is better), and premarital pregnancy (no pregnancy is better and waiting a while after marriage is better still).

6. *Positive emphasis.* Do you believe marriage is a place where you can indulge your bad moods and openly criticize one another? Think again. Positive interpretations (how you view your partner's actions), positive affect (cheery emotions, good moods), positive expressions, positive interactions, and a positive rebound to marital conflict are vitally important to lasting, happy marriages.

TRY THIS YOURSELF

Application

Would you like a simple test of the importance of a positive emphasis on all relationships?

Pick two or three of your most "troublesome" friends, family members, or coworkers, and try giving them four positive comments before allowing yourself to say anything even remotely negative. Note how their attitudes and behaviors quickly change. More important, pay attention to the corresponding change in your own feelings and responses toward this troublesome person when you apply this positive emphasis. Can you see how this type of positivism can dramatically improve marital satisfaction?

Families and personality. Does this remind you of your own family? How did your father, mother, and siblings affect your own personality development?

Mugshots/Corbis StockMarket

Families: Their Effect on Development

As we saw in the discussions of attachment and parenting styles in the last chapter, our families exert an enormous influence on our development. But it is not always for the best. Family violence as well as teen pregnancy and teen parenthood can have significant effects on development.

Family Violence

Families can be warm and loving. They also can be cruel and abusive. Maltreatment and abuse are more widely recognized than in the past. However, it is difficult to measure family violence because it usually occurs in private and victims are reluctant to report it out of shame, powerlessness, or fear of reprisal. Nevertheless, every year millions of cases of domestic violence, child abuse, and elderly abuse are reported to police and social service agencies (Cicchetti & Toth, 2005; Levinthal, 2006; Safarik, Jarvis, & Nussbaum, 2002).

What causes family violence? Violence occurs more often in families experiencing marital conflict, substance abuse, mental disorders, and economic stress (Field, Caetano, & Nelson, 2004; Holtzworth-Munroe et al., 2003; Levinthal, 2006). It is important to remember that abuse and violence occur at all socioeconomic levels. However, abuse and violence do occur more frequently in families disrupted by unemployment or other financial distress.

In addition to having financial problems, many abusive parents are also socially isolated and lack good communication and parenting skills. Their anxiety and frustration may explode into spouse, child, and elderly abuse. In fact, one of the clearest identifiers of abuse potential is *impulsivity*. People who abuse their children, their spouses, or their elderly parents seem to lack impulse control, especially when stressed. They also respond to stress with more intense emotions and greater arousal (Begic & Jokic-Begic, 2002; Cicchetti & Toth, 2005; Cohen et al., 2003). This impulsivity is related not only to psychosocial factors like economic stress and social isolation (with no one to turn to for help or feedback) but also to possible biological influences.

Biologically, three regions of the brain are closely related to the expression and control of aggression: the amygdala, the prefrontal cortex, and the hypothalamus (see Chapter 2 to review these regions). Interestingly, head injuries, strokes, dementia, schizophrenia, alcoholism, and abuse of stimulant drugs have all been linked to these three areas and to aggressive outbursts. Research also suggests that low levels of the neurotransmitters serotonin and GABA (gamma-aminobutyric acid) are associated with irritability, hypersensitivity to provocation, and impulsive rage (Goveas, Csernansky, & Coccaro, 2004; Halperin et al., 2003; Levinthal, 2006).

Is there anything that can be done to reduce this type of aggression? Treatment with antianxiety and serotonin-enhancing drugs like fluoxetine (Prozac) may lower the risk of some forms of impulsive violence. However, given the correlation between spousal, child, sibling, and elder abuse, and because violence affects other family members who are not victims or perpetrators, treatment generally includes the entire family (Becvar & Becvar, 2006; Emery & Laumann-Billings, 1998).

Most professionals advocate two general approaches in dealing with family violence. *Primary programs* attempt to identify "vulnerable" families and prevent abuse by teaching parenting and marital skills, stress management, and impulse control. These programs also publicize the signs of abuse and encourage people to report suspected cases. *Secondary programs* attempt to rehabilitate families after abuse has occurred. They work to improve social services, establish self-help groups such as Parents Anonymous and AMAC (Adults Molested as Children), and provide individual and group psychotherapy for both victims and abusers.

Teen Pregnancy and Parenthood

Another factor that may affect development is becoming a parent and starting a family at too early an age. Have you heard that the United States has one of the highest rates of teen pregnancy among major industrialized nations (Alan Guttmacher Institute, 2004; Boonstra, 2002)? Regrettably, this is a sad fact. But, ironically, today's rate is actually much lower than it has been throughout much of the twentieth century.

With this decline, why is everyone so worried about teen pregnancies? Although the total rate has declined substantially, the percentage of *unwed teen births* has increased (Boonstra, 2002; Hyde & DeLamater, 2006). The higher nonmarital rate is important because single-parent families headed by women are at great risk of

www.wiley.com/college/huffman

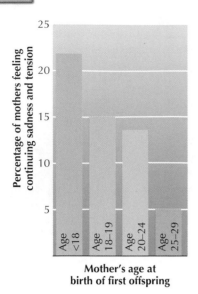

Figure 10.2 *Maternal age and satisfaction.* Note that the age of the mother directly relates to the percentage of reported feelings of sadness and tension.

Resiliency *The ability to adapt effectively in the face of threats*

poverty. In addition, pregnancy during adolescence also carries with it considerable health risk for both the mother and child (Chapter 9), decreased chances of marital success, and lower educational achievement (Barnet, Duggan, & Devoe, 2003; Endersbe, 2000; Philliber et al., 2003). Pregnancy, in fact, is the most common reason for dropping out of high school. In view of these facts, is it any wonder that teen mothers also report one of the highest levels of depression (Figure 10.2)?

What can be done to reduce the number of teen pregnancies? *Comprehensive education and health-oriented services* seem to be the most promising avenue for decreasing the rate of pregnancy among high-risk teenagers (Coley & Chase-Lansdale, 1998; Hyde & DeLamater, 2006). The Johns Hopkins Pregnancy Prevention Program, for example, provides complete medical care, contraceptive services, social services (such as counseling), and parenting education. This approach postponed the age of onset of sexual activity, increased contraception use, reduced the frequency of sex, and decreased the actual pregnancy rate in the experimental group by 30 percent. During the same period, pregnancy rates in a comparison school rose by 58 percent (Hardy & Zabin, 1991).

A number of other outreach programs are also working to enhance social development among adolescents through structured volunteer community service and classroom discussions of life choices, careers, and relationships. Research shows that many teen pregnancies are due to poverty and the resulting perception that life options and choices are limited (Stewart, 2003; Young et al., 2004).

Most research and social programs (like the two described here) focus on economics: how money (or the lack of it) affects teen pregnancies. But researchers Rebekah Coley and Lindsay Chase-Lansdale (1998) suggest we also should be exploring the *psychological* consequences of early parenting. If adolescence is a time for solidifying identity and developing autonomy from parents, what happens with teen parents? What are the effects on a teen mother if she lives with her mother? What happens to the life span development of the "early" grandparents? What about the teen father? How does early fatherhood affect his course of development? And what about the child who is being raised by a teen mother or teen father or grandparent? How does this affect his or her development? Answers to these questions rest with the next generation of researchers (perhaps some of you who are reading this text).

Application

RESEARCH HIGHLIGHT

Children Who Survive Despite the Odds

Children fortunate enough to grow up with days filled with play and discovery, nights that provide rest and security, and dedicated, loving parents usually turn out fine. But what about those who are raised in violent, impoverished, or neglectful situations? As we saw in the previous discussions of family violence, teen pregnancy and parenting, and divorce, a troubled childhood creates significantly higher risk of serious physical, emotional, and behavioral problems. There are exceptions to this rule. Some offspring of wonderful, lov-

ing parents have serious problems. And some children growing up amid major stressors are remarkably well adjusted.

What is it about children living in harsh circumstances that helps them survive and prosper—despite the odds? The answer holds great interest for both parents and society. Such resilient children can teach us better ways to reduce risk, promote competence, and shift the course of development in more positive directions (Masten, 2001). **Resiliency** refers to the ability to adapt effectively in the face of threats.

Resilience has been studied throughout the world in a variety of situations, including poverty, natural disasters, war, and

family violence (e.g., Cole & Brown, 2002; Horning & Rouse, 2002; Martindale & Palmes, 2005). Two researchers—Ann Masten at the University of Minnesota and Douglas Coatsworth at the University of Miami (1998)—identified several traits of the resilient child and the environmental circumstances that might account for the resilient child's success.

Most children who do well have (1) good intellectual functioning; (2) relationships with caring adults; and, as they grow older, (3) the ability to regulate their attention, emotions, and behavior. These traits obviously overlap. Good intellectual functioning, for example, may help resilient children solve problems or protect themselves from adverse conditions. Their intelligence may also attract the interest of teachers who serve as nurturing adults. These greater intellectual skills may also help resilient children learn from their experiences and from the caring adults, so in later life they have better self-regulation skills.

In times of growing concern about homelessness, poverty, abuse, teen pregnancy, violence, and divorce, studies of successful children can be very important. On the other hand, there is no such thing as an invulnerable child. Masten and Coatsworth (1998) remind us that "if we

Resiliency and 9/11. Following the terrorist attack on September 11, 2001, many children and teenagers in New York created moving drawings and letters to express their feelings. Note the red heart in the upper corner of this drawing. It was done by Angelina, a Queens high school student. Is this the sign of a resilient person?

Angelina Gallesi, Newcomers High School, September, 2001.

allow the prevalence of known risk factors for development to rise while resources for children fall, we can expect the competence of individual children and the human capital of the nation to suffer" (p. 216).

Are You Resilient?

Did you grow up in a "high-risk" environment? Are you a resilient child? A 30-year longitudinal study of resilience (Werner, 1993, 1999) identified several environmental factors of high-risk children. Place a check mark by each risk factor that applies to your childhood:

___ Born into chronic poverty
___ Stressful fetal or birth conditions (e.g., prenatal hazards, low birth weight)

___ Chronic discord in the family environment
___ Parents divorced
___ Mental illness in one or both parents

Two-thirds of the high-risk children who had experienced four or more of these factors by age 2 developed serious adjustment problems in later years. But one-third of the children who also experienced four or more such risk factors were resilient. They developed into competent, confident, and caring adults.

■ Work and Retirement: How They Affect Us

Throughout most of our adult lives, work defines us in fundamental ways. It affects our health, our friendships, where we live, and even our leisure activities. Too often, however, career choices are made from dreams of high income. Nearly 74 percent of college freshmen surveyed by the Higher Education Research Institute said that being "very well off financially" was "very important" or "essential." Seventy-one percent felt the same way about raising a family ("This Year's Freshmen," 1995). These young people understandably hope to combine both family and work roles and "live the good life." But many will find themselves in miserable, unsatisfying, "dead-end" jobs having to work long hours just to keep up with the rate of inflation.

How can I find a rewarding career that suits my personality and interests? Choosing an occupation is one of the most important decisions in our lives. Unfortunately, the task is becoming ever more difficult and complex as career options rapidly change due to increasing specialization and job fluctuations. The *Dictionary of Occupational Titles*, a government publication, currently lists more than 200,000 job categories. One way to learn more about these job categories and potential careers is to visit your college career center. These centers typically offer an abundance of books and pamphlets as well as interesting and helpful vocational interest tests. (You also can try the online version of several vocational interest inventories— http://www.keirsey.com/cgi-bin/newkts.cgi.)

In addition to visiting career counselors and taking vocational interest tests, you may want to consider what psychologist John Holland has to say. According to his *personality–job fit theory*, a match (or "good fit") between our individual personality and our career choice is a major factor in determining job satisfaction (Holland, 1985, 1994). Holland developed a *Self-Directed Search* questionnaire that scores each person on six personality types and then matches their individual interests and abilities to the job demands of various occupations. Research shows that a "good fit" between personality and occupation helps ensure job success and job satisfaction— people tend to like what they are good at (Brkich, Jeffs, & Carless, 2002; Kieffer, Schinka, & Curtiss, 2004; Spokane, Meir, & Catalano, 2000: Tett & Murphy, 2002).

Enjoying Retirement

Work and careers are a big part of adult lives and self-identity. But the large majority of men and women in the United States choose to retire sometime in their sixties. Like the midlife crisis and empty nest syndrome, the loss of self-esteem and depression that are commonly assumed to accompany retirement may be largely a myth. Life satisfaction after retirement appears to be most strongly related to good health, con-

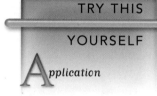

TRY THIS

YOURSELF

Application

Are You in the Right Job?

Choose the personality description in the left-hand column of Table 10.3 that most closely describes you. In the center and right-hand columns locate your "Holland Personality Type" and your suggested "Matching/Congruent Occupation."

TABLE 10.3 ARE YOU IN THE RIGHT JOB?

Personality Characteristics	Holland Personality Type	Matching/Congruent Occupation
Shy, genuine, persistent, stable, conforming, practical	1. Realistic: Prefers physical activities that require skill, strength, and coordination	Mechanic, drill press operator, assembly-line worker, farmer
Analytical, original, curious, independent	2. Investigative: Prefers activities that involve thinking, organizing, and understanding	Biologist, economist, mathematician, news reporter
Sociable, friendly, cooperative, understanding	3. Social: Prefers activities that involve helping and developing others	Social worker, counselor, teacher, clinical psychologist
Conforming, efficient, practical, unimaginative, inflexible	4. Conventional: Prefers rule-regulated, orderly, and unambiguous activities	Accountant, bank teller, file clerk, corporate manager
Imaginative, disorderly, idealistic, emotional, impractical	5. Artistic: Prefers ambiguous and unsystematic activities that allow creative expression	Painter, musician, writer, interior decorator
Self-confident, ambitious, energetic, domineering	6. Enterprising: Prefers verbal activities where there are opportunities to influence others and attain power	Lawyer, real estate agent, public relations specialist, small business manager

trol over one's life, social support, and participation in community services and social activities (Warr, Butcher, & Robertson, 2004; Yeh & Lo, 2004). This type of active involvement is the key ingredient to a fulfilling old age, according to the **activity theory** of aging. In contrast, other theorists believe that successful aging is a natural and graceful withdrawal from life, the **disengagement theory** (Achenbaum & Bengtson, 1994; Cummings & Henry, 1961; McKee & Barber, 2001; Neugarten, Havighurst, & Tobin, 1968; Rook, 2000).

For obvious reasons, the disengagement theory has been seriously questioned and largely abandoned. Successful aging does *not* require withdrawal from society. I mention this theory because of its historical relevance, and also because of its connection to an influential modern perspective, **socioemotional selectivity theory**. This latest model helps explain the predictable decline in social contact that almost everyone experiences as they move into their older years (Carstensen, Fung, & Charles, 2003; Lang & Carstensen, 2002). According to socioemotional selectivity theory, we don't naturally withdraw from society in our later years—we just become more *selective* with our time. We deliberately choose to decrease our total number of social contacts in favor of familiar people who provide emotionally meaningful interactions.

As you can see in Figure 10.3, when we begin life, our need for emotional connection is paramount. During childhood, adolescence, and early adulthood, this need declines, but it rises again during late adulthood. The reverse is true of our need for information and knowledge. Can you appreciate the intuitive appeal of this theory? Emotional support is essential to infant survival, information gathering is critical during childhood and early adulthood, and emotional satisfaction is more important in old age—we tend to invest time in those who can be counted on in time of need.

Walter Hodges/Stone/GettyImages

Disengagement versus activity. *The disengagement theory of aging suggests that older people naturally disengage and withdraw from life. However, judging by the people in this photo, activity theory may be a better theory of aging because it suggests that everyone should remain active and involved throughout the entire life span.*

Activity Theory *Successful aging is fostered by a full and active commitment to life*

Disengagement Theory *Successful aging is characterized by mutual withdrawal between the elderly and society*

Socioemotional Selectivity Theory *A natural decline in social contact occurs as older adults become more selective with their time*

Achievement
GENDER & CULTURAL DIVERSITY

Cultural Differences in Ageism

As we've seen in this and the previous chapter, there are losses and stress associated with the aging process—although much less than most people think. Perhaps the greatest challenge for the elderly, at least in the United States, is the *ageism* they

Assessment

VISUAL QUIZ

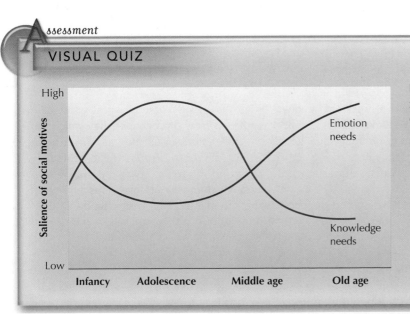

Figure 10.3 ***Socioemotional selectivity.*** Note how emotional needs are highest during infancy and late adulthood. Can you explain why?

Answer: An infant's survival depends on close attachment to its caregivers. Older adults recognize their time is limited and more highly value close relationships than the things they pursued in their middle years.

encounter. In societies that value older people as wise elders or keepers of valued traditions, the stress of aging is much less than in societies that view them as mentally slow and socially useless. In cultures like that in the United States in which youth, speed, and progress are strongly emphasized, a loss or decline in any of these qualities is deeply feared and denied (Powell, 1998).

Elder respect. *Native Americans generally revere and respect the elder members of their tribe. How would aging be different if being old was an honor and blessing versus a dreaded curse?*

Aren't there also cultures that honor their elderly? Yes. In Japan, China, and the United States among African Americans and most tribes of Native Americans, the elderly are more revered. Aging parents are generally respected for their wisdom and experience. They also are deferred to in family matters, and often are expected to live with their children until they die (Gattuso & Shadbolt, 2002; Klass, 2000; Miller et al., 2006). However, as these cultures become more urbanized and Westernized, there is often a corresponding decline in respect for the elderly. In Japan, for example, over 80 percent of the elderly lived with their adult children in 1957. This percentage declined to only 55 percent in 1994. Japan has recently made it a legal obligation to care for elderly relatives (Hashizume, 2000; Oshima et al., 1996).

Ageism, Gender, and Ethnicity in the United States

There also is considerable difference in the status and treatment of different subgroups of the elderly. In the United States, for example, studies show that older men have more social status, income, and sexual partners than do older women. Elderly women, on the other hand, have more friends and are more involved in family relationships. But they have lower status and income. Contrary to the popular stereotype of the "rich old woman," elderly females represent one of the lowest income levels in North America (Chrisler, 2003; U.S. Bureau of the Census, 2001).

Ethnicity also plays a role in aging in the United States. Ethnic minority elderly, especially African Americans and Latinos, face problems related to both ageism and racism. They are more likely to become ill but less likely to receive treatment. And they are overrepresented among the elderly poor living below the poverty line (Contrada et al., 2000; Miller et al., 2006).

Other research, however, reports that African Americans are more likely than Anglo Americans to regard elderly persons with respect (Mui, 1992). Also, compared with whites, other ethnic groups often have a greater sense of community and may have stronger bonds of attachment, owing to their shared traits and experiences with prejudice. Ethnicity itself may therefore provide some benefits. "In addition to shielding them from majority attitudes, ethnicity provides the ethnic elderly with a source of esteem" (Fry, 1985, p. 233).

Assessment

CHECK & REVIEW

Meeting the Challenges of Adulthood

A good marriage is one of the most important and difficult tasks of adulthood. Researchers have found six major traits and factors in happy marriages: established "love maps," shared power and mutual support, conflict management, similarity, a supportive social environment, and a positive emphasis.

Family violence, teenage pregnancy, and divorce have significant effects on development. However, **resilient** children who survive abusive and stress-filled childhoods usually have good intellectual functioning, a relationship with a caring adult, and the ability to regulate their attention, emotions, and behavior.

The kind of work we do and the occupational choices we make can play a critical role in our lives. One theory of successful aging, **activity theory,** says people should remain active and involved throughout the entire life span. The other major theory, **disengagement theory,** says the elderly naturally and gracefully withdraw from life because they welcome the relief from roles they can no longer fulfill. Although the disengagement theory is no longer in favor, the **socioemotional selectivity theory** does find that the elderly tend to decrease their total number of social contacts as they become more selective with their time.

Questions

1. Efforts to identify and prevent family violence are called _____ programs.

(a) directive; (b) redirective; (c) primary; (d) secondary

2. The _____ theory of aging suggests that you should remain active and involved until death, whereas the _____ theory suggests that you should naturally and gracefully withdraw from life.

3. _____ is prejudice against people based on their age. (a) Ethnocentrism; (b) Elder abuse; (c) Ageism; (d) Disengagement

4. Explain how ethnicity may help the elderly overcome some problems of aging.

Check your answers in Appendix B.

CLICK & REVIEW
for additional assessment options:
www.wiley.com/college/huffman

GRIEF AND DEATH

One unavoidable part of life is its end. How can we understand and prepare ourselves for the loss of our own life and those of loved others? In this section, we look at the four stages of grief. We then study cultural and age-related differences in attitudes toward death. We conclude with death itself as a final developmental crisis.

Achievement
Are there predictable stages of grief and death?

Grief: Lessons in Survival

What do I do now that you're gone? Well, when there's nothing else going on, which is quite often, I sit in a corner and I cry until I am too numbed to feel. Paralyzed motionless for a while, nothing moving inside or out. Then I think how much I miss you. Then I feel fear, pain, loneliness, desolation. Then I cry until I am too numbed to feel. Interesting pastime.

PETER McWILLIAMS, *HOW TO SURVIVE THE LOSS OF A LOVE*, P. 18

Have you ever felt like this? If so, you are not alone. Loss and grief are an inevitable part of all our lives. Feelings of desolation, loneliness, and heartache, accompanied by painful memories, are common reactions to loss, disaster, or misfortune. Ironically, such painful emotions may serve a useful function. Evolutionary psychologists suggest that bereavement and grief may be adaptive mechanisms for both human and nonhuman animals. The pain may motivate parents and children or mates to search for one another. Obvious signs of distress also may be adaptive because they bring the group to the aid of the bereaved individual.

What does it mean if someone seems emotionless after an important loss? Grieving is a complicated and personal process. Just as there is no right way to die, there is no right way to grieve. People who restrain their grief may be following the rules for emotional display that prevail in their cultural group. Moreover, outward signs of strong emotion may be the most obvious expression of grief. But this is only one of four stages in the "normal" grieving process (Koppel, 2000; Parkes, 1972, 1991).

In the initial phase of grief, *numbness*, bereaved individuals often seem dazed and may feel little emotion other than numbness or emptiness. They also may deny the death, insisting that a mistake has been made.

In the second stage of grief, individuals enter a stage of *yearning*, intense longing for the loved one, and pangs of guilt, anger, and resentment. The bereaved may also experience illusions. They "see" the deceased person in his or her favorite chair or in the face of a stranger, they have vivid dreams in which the deceased is still alive, or they feel the "presence" of the dead person. They also experience strong guilt feelings ("If only I had gotten her to a doctor sooner" "I should have been more loving") and anger or resentment ("Why wasn't he more careful?" "It isn't fair that I'm the one left behind").

Once the powerful feelings of yearning subside, the individual enters the third *disorganization/despair* phase. Life seems to lose its meaning. The mourner feels listless,

Grieving. *Individuals vary in their emotional reactions to loss. There is no right or wrong way to grieve.*

apathetic, and submissive. As time goes by, however, the survivor gradually begins to accept the loss both intellectually (the loss makes sense) and emotionally (memories are pleasurable as well as painful). This acceptance, combined with building a new self-identity ("I am a single mother" "We are no longer a couple"), characterizes the fourth and final stage of grief—the *resolution or reorganization* stage.

Grief is obviously not the same for everyone. People vary in they way they grieve, the stages of grief that they experience, and the length of time needed for "recovery" (Bonanno et al., 2005; Satterfield, Folkman, & Acree, 2002; Stroebe, Schut, & Stroebe, 2005). You can help people who are grieving by accepting these individual differences and recognizing that there is no perfect response. Simply say, "I'm sorry." And then let the person talk if he or she wishes. Your quiet presence and caring are generally the best type of support.

When it comes to dealing with your own losses and grief, psychologists offer several techniques that you may find helpful (Ingram, Jones, & Smith, 2001; Kranz & Daniluk, 2002; Napolitane, 1997; Wartik, 1996):

1. *Recognize the loss and allow yourself to grieve.* Despite feelings of acute loneliness, remember that loss is a part of everyone's life and accept comfort from others. Take care of yourself by avoiding unnecessary stress, getting plenty of rest, and giving yourself permission to enjoy life whenever possible.

2. *Set up a daily activity schedule.* One of the best ways to offset the lethargy and depression of grief is to force yourself to fill your time with useful activities (studying, washing your car, doing the laundry, and so on).

3. *Seek help.* Having the support of loving friends and family helps offset the loneliness and stress of grief. Recognize, however, that professional counseling may be necessary in cases of extreme or prolonged numbness, anger, guilt, or depression. (You will learn more about depression and its treatment in Chapters 14 and 15.)

Attitudes Toward Death and Dying: Cultural and Age Variations

Cultures around the world interpret and respond to death in widely different ways: "Funerals are the occasion for avoiding people or holding parties, for fighting or having sexual orgies, for weeping or laughing, in a thousand combinations" (Metcalf & Huntington, 1991, p. 62).

Similarly, subcultures within the United States also have different responses to death. Irish Americans are likely to believe the dead deserve a good send-off—a wake with food, drink, and jokes. On the other hand, African Americans traditionally regard funerals as a time for serious grief, demonstrated in some congregations by wailing and singing spirituals (Barley, 1997; Wartik, 1996). In contrast, most Japanese Americans try to restrain their grief and smile so as not to burden others with their pain. They also want to avoid the shame associated with losing emotional control (Cook & Dworkin, 1992).

In addition, attitudes toward death and dying vary with age. As adults, we understand death in terms of three basic concepts: (1) *permanence*—once a living thing dies, it cannot be brought back to life; (2) *universality*—all living things eventually die; and (3) *nonfunctionality*—all living functions, including thought, movement, and vital signs, end at death.

Research shows that permanence, the notion that death cannot be reversed, is the first and most easily understood concept. Preschoolers seem to accept the fact that the dead person cannot get up again, perhaps because of their experiences with dead butterflies and beetles found while playing outside (Furman, 1990).

Understanding of universality comes slightly later. By about the age of 7, most children have mastered nonfunctionality and have an adultlike understanding of death. Adults may fear that discussing death with children and adolescents will make them unduly anxious. But those who are offered open, honest discussions of death have an easier time accepting it (Christ, Siegel, & Christ, 2002; Kastenbaum, 1999; Pfeffer et al., 2002).

■ The Death Experience: Our Final Developmental Task

Have you thought about your own death? Would you like to die suddenly and alone? Or would you prefer to know ahead of time so you could plan your funeral and spend time saying good-bye to your family and friends? If you find thinking about these questions uncomfortable, it may be because most people in Western societies deny death. Unfortunately, avoiding thoughts and discussion of death and associating aging with death contribute to *ageism* (Atchley, 1997). Moreover, the better we understand death, and the more wisely we approach it, the more fully we can live until it comes.

During the Middle Ages (from about the fifth until the sixteenth century), people were expected to recognize when death was approaching so they could say their farewells and die with dignity, surrounded by loved ones (Aries, 1981). In recent times, Western societies have moved death out of the home and put it into the hospital and funeral parlor. Rather than personally caring for our dying family and friends, we have shifted responsibility to "experts"—physicians and morticians. We have made death a medical failure rather than a natural part of the life cycle.

This avoidance of death and dying may be changing, however. Since the late 1990s, right-to-die and death-with-dignity advocates have been working to bring death out in the open. And mental health professionals have suggested that understanding the psychological processes of death and dying may play a significant role in good adjustment.

Confronting our own death is the last major crisis we face in life. What is it like? Is there a "best" way to prepare to die? Is there such a thing as a "good death"? After spending hundreds of hours at the bedsides of the terminally ill, Elisabeth Kübler-Ross developed her stage theory of the psychological processes surrounding death (1983, 1997, 1999).

Based on extensive interviews with patients, Kübler-Ross proposed that most people go through five sequential stages when facing death: *denial* of the terminal condition ("This can't be true; it's a mistake!"), *anger* ("Why me? It isn't fair!"), *bargaining* ("God, if you let me live, I'll dedicate my life to you!"), *depression* ("I'm losing everyone and everything I hold dear"), and finally *acceptance* ("I know that death is inevitable and my time is near").

Evaluating Kübler-Ross's Theory

Critics of the stage theory of dying stress that each person's death is a unique experience. Furthermore, emotions and reactions depend on the individual's personality, life situation, age, and so on (Dunn, 2000; Wright, 2003). Others worry that popularizing such a stage theory will cause further avoidance and stereotyping of the dying ("He's just in the anger stage right now"). In response, Kübler-Ross (1983, 1997, 1999) agreed that not all people go through the same stages in the same way and regretted that anyone would use her theory as a model for a "good death." Dying, like living, is a unique, individual experience.

In spite of the potential abuses, Kübler-Ross's theory has provided valuable insights and spurred research into a long-neglected topic. **Thanatology**, the study of

Thanatology [than-uh-TALL-uh-gee] *The study of death and dying; the term comes from thanatos, the Greek name for a mythical personification of death, and was borrowed by Freud to represent the death instinct*

www.wiley.com/college/huffman

death and dying, has become a major topic in human development. Thanks in part to thanatology research, the dying are being helped to die with dignity by the *hospice* movement. This organization has trained staff and volunteers to provide loving support for the terminally ill and their families in special facilities, hospitals, or the patient's own home (McGrath, 2002; Parker-Oliver, 2002).

One of the most important contributions by Kübler-Ross (1975) may have been her suggestion that:

> It is the denial of death that is partially responsible for [people] living empty, purposeless lives; for when you live as if you'll live forever, it becomes too easy to postpone the things you know you must do. In contrast, when you fully understand that each day you awaken could be the last you have, you take the time that day to grow, to become more of whom you really are, to reach out to other human beings. (p. 164).

Application
APPLYING PSYCHOLOGY TO EVERYDAY LIFE

Dealing with Your Own Death Anxiety

Woody Allen once said, "It's not that I'm afraid to die. I just don't want to be there when it happens." Although some people who are very old and in poor health may welcome death, most of us have difficulty facing it. One of the most important elements of critical thinking is *self-knowledge*, which includes the ability to critically evaluate our deepest and most private fears.

Death Anxiety Questionnaire
To test your own level of death anxiety, indicate your response according to the following scale:

0	1	2
not at all	somewhat	very much

___1. Do you worry about dying?

___2. Does it bother you that you may die before you have done everything you wanted to do?

___3. Do you worry that you may be very ill for a long time before you die?

___4. Does it upset you to think that others may see you suffering before you die?

___5. Do you worry that dying may be very painful?

___6. Do you worry that the persons closest to you won't be with you when you are dying?

___7. Do you worry that you may be alone when you are dying?

___8. Does the thought bother you that you might lose control of your mind before death?

___9. Do you worry that expenses connected with your death will be a burden to other people?

___10. Does it worry you that your will or instructions about your belongings may not be carried out after you die?

___11. Are you afraid that you may be buried before you are really dead?

___12. Does the thought of leaving loved ones behind when you die disturb you?

___13. Do you worry that those you care about may not remember you after your death?

___14. Does the thought worry you that with death you may be gone forever?

___15. Are you worried about not knowing what to expect after death?

Source: H. R. Conte, M. B. Weiner, & R. Plutchik (1982). Measuring death anxiety: Conceptual, psychometric, and factor-analytic aspects. *Journal of Personality and Social Psychology*, 43, 775–785. Reprinted with permission.

How does your total score compare to the national average of 8.5? When this same test was given to nursing-home residents, senior citizens, and college students, researchers found no significant differences, despite the fact that those tested ranged in age from 30 to 80.

Assessment
CHECK & REVIEW

Grief and Death

Attitudes toward death and dying vary greatly across cultures and among age groups. Although adults understand the permanence, universality, and nonfunctionality of death, children often don't master these concepts until around age 7.

Grief is a natural and painful reaction to a loss. For most people, grief consists of four major stages—numbness, yearning, disorganization/despair, and resolution.

Kübler-Ross's theory of the five-stage psychological process when facing death (denial, anger, bargaining, depression, and acceptance) offers important insights into the last major crisis we face in life. The study of death and dying, **thanatology,**

has become an important topic in human development.

Questions

1. Explain how an adult's understanding of death differs from a preschool child's.
2. Grieving people generally begin with the _____ stage and end with the _____ stage. (a) numbness, bargaining; (b) grief, anger; (c) yearning, acceptance; (d) numbness, resolution
3. Match the following statements with Elisabeth Kübler-Ross's five-stage theory of death and dying:
   ___a. "I understand that I'm dying, but if I could just have a little more time…"
   ___b. "I refuse to believe the doctors. I want a fourth opinion."
   ___c. "I know my time is near. I'd better make plans for my spouse and children."
   ___d. "Why me? I've been a good person. I don't deserve this."
   ___e. "I'm losing everything. I'll never see my children again. Life is so hard."
4. The study of death and dying is known as _____. (a) gerontology; (b) ageism; (c) mortality; (d) thanatology

Check your answers in Appendix B.

CLICK & REVIEW
for additional assessment options:
www.wiley.com/college/huffman

Assessment
KEY TERMS

*To assess your understanding of the **Key Terms** in Chapter 10, write a definition for each (in your own words), and then compare your definitions with those in the text.*

Moral Development
conventional level (p. 363)
postconventional level (p. 365)
preconventional level (p. 363)

Personality Development
identity crisis (p. 370)

psychosocial stages (p. 368)
temperament (p. 367)

Meeting the Challenges of Adulthood
activity theory (p. 379)
disengagement theory (p. 379)
resiliency (p. 376)

socioemotional selectivity theory (p. 379)

Grief and Death
thanatology [than-uh-TALL-uh-gee] (p. 383)

Achievement
WEB RESOURCES

Huffman Book Companion Site
http://www.wiley.com/college/huffman
   This site is loaded with free Interactive Self-Tests, Internet Exercises, Glossary and Flashcards for key terms, web links, Handbook for Non-Native Speakers, and other activities designed to improve your mastery of the material in this chapter.

Want more information about moral development and moral education?
http://tigger.uic.edu/~lnucci/MoralEd
   The College of Education at the University of Illinois at Chicago developed this comprehensive website. Its stated mission is to serve "as a link for educators, scholars, and citizens interested in sharing their work and learning about research, practices, and activities in the area of moral development and education."

www.wiley.com/college/huffman

Visual SUMMARY

Moral Development

Kohlberg's Three Levels and Six Stages

Stage 1:
Punishment-obedience orientation.
Morality is what you can get away with.

Stage 2:
Instrumental-exchange orientation. Obeys
rules to obtain rewards or favors.

Stage 3:
Good-child orientation. Obeys rules to get approval.

Stage 4:
Law-and-order orientation. Obeys laws
because they maintain the social order.

Stage 5:
Social-contract orientation. Moral reasoning reflects
belief in democratically established laws.

Stage 6:
Universal ethics orientation. Moral
reasoning reflects individual conscience.

Preconventional Morality

Conventional Morality

Postconventional Morality

Personality Development

Thomas & Chess's Temperament Theory

Temperament: Basic, inborn disposition.
Three temperament styles: easy, difficult, and slow-to-warm-up. Styles seem consistent and enduring.

Erikson's Eight Psychosocial Stages

- Childhood: Trust vs. mistrust, autonomy vs. shame and doubt, initiative vs. guilt, industry vs. inferiority.
- Adolescence: Identity vs. role confusion.
- Young Adulthood: Intimacy vs. isolation.
- Middle Adulthood: Generativity vs. stagnation.
- Older Adult: Ego integrity vs. despair.

Dann Coffey/The
ImageBank/Getty Images

Families
- Family violence, teenage pregnancies, and divorce can damage personality development.
- **Resilience** helps some children survive an abusive or stress-filled childhood.

Mugshots/Corbis StockMarket

Occupational Choices
Occupational choice is critically important because most people channel their accomplishment needs into their work.

Aging
Three major theories of aging.

Active Theory (should remain active)

Disengagement Theory (should gracefully withdraw)

Socioemotional Selectivity: (elderly reduce social contacts because they're more selective)

Grief and Death

Grief
Grief: A natural and painful reaction to a loss, consists of four major stages:

1) numbness → 2) yearning → 3) disorganization and despair → 4) resolution

Attitudes
Attitudes toward death and dying vary greatly across cultures and among age groups. Children generally don't fully understand the *permanence*, *universality*, and *nonfunctionality* of death until around the age seven.

Thomas Ives/Corbis StockMarket

Death Experience
- Kübler-Ross proposes a five-stage psychological process when facing death (denial, anger, bargaining, depression, and acceptance).
- **Thanatology**: Study of death and dying.

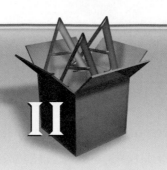

GENDER AND HUMAN SEXUALITY

Achievement

Core Learning Outcomes

As you read Chapter 11, keep the following questions in mind and answer them in your own words:

▷ How are sex and gender defined, and how do we develop our gender roles? What are the major sex and gender differences between men and women?

▷ How do scientists study a sensitive topic like sex?

▷ How are men and women alike and different in sexual arousal and response?

▷ What is the latest research on sexual orientation?

▷ What factors contribute to sexual dysfunction and sexually transmitted infections?

■ Achievement
■ Assessment
■ Application

Application

WHY STUDY PSYCHOLOGY?

PhotoDisc, Inc./GettyImages

Chapter 11 will explore numerous fascinating facts and widespread myths.

Before we begin, test yourself by answering true or false to the following statements. (Answers are at the bottom and expanded explanations are found throughout this chapter.)

1. The breakfast cereal Kellogg's Corn Flakes was originally developed to discourage masturbation.

2. Nocturnal emissions and masturbation are signs of abnormal sexual adjustment.

3. The American Academy of Pediatrics (AAP) no longer recommends routine circumcision for male babies.

4. The American Psychiatric Association and the American Psychological Association (APA) consider homosexuality a type of mental illness.

5. Men and women are more alike than different in their sexual responses.

6. Sexual skill and satisfaction are learned behaviors that can be increased through education and training.

7. If you're HIV-positive (have the human immunodeficiency virus), you cannot infect someone else. You must have AIDS (acquired immunodeficiency syndrome) to spread the disease.

8. Women cannot be raped against their will.

Answers: 1.T 2.F 3.T 4.F 5.T 6.T 7.F 8.F

"As Nature Made Him: The Boy Who Was Raised As A Girl", by John Colapinto. Courtesy of Harper-Collins Publishers

It was an unusual circumcision. The identical twin boys, Bruce and Brian, were already 8 months old when their parents took them to the doctor to be circumcised. For many years in the United States, most male babies have had the foreskin of their penis removed during their first week of life. This is done for religious and presumed hygienic reasons. It is also assumed that newborns will experience less pain. The most common procedure is cutting or pinching off the foreskin tissue. In this case, however, the doctor used an electrocautery device, which is typically used to burn off moles or small skin growths. The electrical current used for the first twin was too high, and the entire penis was accidentally removed. (The parents canceled the circumcision of the other twin.)

In anguish over the tragic accident, the parents sought advice from medical experts. Following discussions with John Money and other specialists at John Hopkins University, the parents and doctors made an unusual decision—they would turn the infant with the destroyed penis into a girl. (Reconstructive surgery was too primitive at the time to restore the child's penis.)

The first step in the reassignment process occurred at age 17 months, when the child's name was changed—Bruce became "Brenda" (Colapinto, 2000). Brenda was dressed in pink pants and frilly blouses, and "her" hair was allowed to grow long. At 22 months, surgery was performed. The child's testes were removed, and external female genitals and an internal, "preliminary" vagina were created. Further surgery to complete the vagina was planned for the beginning of adolescence, when the child's physical growth would be nearly complete. At this time she would also begin to take female hormones to complete the boy-to-girl transformation.

Corbis Images

What do you think about the parents' and experts' solution to this terrible accident? Is it possible that our sense of ourselves as men or women develops primarily from how our parents or others treat us? Or is biology the best predictor? You will learn more about "Brenda" and your own gender development and sexuality in the first section of this chapter. Then we will discuss four pioneers in sex research and cultural differences in sexual practices and attitudes. The third section describes sexual arousal, response, and orientation. Finally, the chapter covers sexual dysfunction and sexually transmitted infections, including AIDS (acquired immunodeficiency syndrome).

SEX AND GENDER

Why is it that the first question most people ask after a baby is born is "Is it a girl or a boy?" What would life be like if there were no divisions according to maleness or femaleness? Would your career plans or friendship patterns change? These questions reflect the importance of *sex* and *gender* in our lives. This section begins with a look at the various ways sex and gender can be defined, followed by a discussion of gender role development and sex and gender differences.

■ What Is "Maleness" and "Femaleness"? Defining Sex and Gender

When people ask if a newborn is a girl or boy, they're typically thinking of standard biological differences as seen in Figure 11.1. But when they buy gifts for children, they frequently demonstrate their expectations of *femininity* ("She'll like this pretty doll") versus *masculinity* ("This fire truck is perfect for him"). In the case of the male twin who was reassigned as a girl, do you still think of "her" as basically male? Is a man who cross-dresses a woman? The question of what is "male" and "female" can be confusing.

Achievement

How are sex and gender defined, and how do we develop our gender roles? What are the major sex and gender differences between men and women?

Figure 11.1 *Male and female internal and external sex organs.*

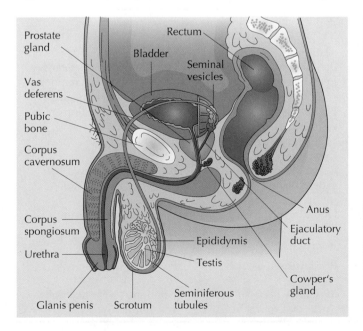
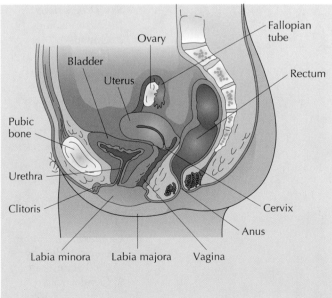

Sex *Biological maleness and femaleness, including chromosomal sex; also, activities related to sexual behaviors, such as masturbation and intercourse*

Gender *Psychological and sociocultural meanings added to biological maleness or femaleness*

Gender Identity *Self-identification as either a man or a woman*

Assessment

VISUAL QUIZ

This type of "dressing up" is a good example of which dimension of gender?

Answer: Gender role

In recent years, researchers have come to use the term **sex** to refer to biological elements (such as having a penis or vagina) or physical activities (such as masturbation and intercourse). **Gender**, on the other hand, encompasses the psychological and sociocultural meanings added to biology (such as "Men should be aggressive" and "Women should be nurturing"). There are at least seven dimensions or elements of *sex* and two of *gender* (Table 11.1).

If you apply the dimensions of sex and gender that are presented in Table 11.1 to the case of the reassigned twin, you can see why it is a classic in the field of human sexuality. Although born a chromosomal male, the child's genital sex was first altered by the doctor who accidentally removed the penis and later by surgeons who removed his testes and created a "preliminary" vagina. The question was whether surgery, along with female hormones and "appropriate" gender role expectations of the parents, would be enough to create a stable female **gender identity**. Would the child accept the sex reassignment and identify herself as a girl?

As you will discover in the upcoming case study, David ultimately rejected his assigned female gender despite strong pressure from his family and doctors. This indicates that the most important factor in gender identity may be biological. A recent longitudinal study offers additional evidence of a biological link. Researchers at Johns Hopkins Hospital tracked the development of 16 otherwise normal boys who had been born without a penis, a rare defect known as *cloacal exstrophy*. Fourteen of these boys had their testes removed and were raised as girls. Despite this radical treatment, researchers observed many signs of masculine behavior, including lots of "typical" male "rough-and-tumble" play. Eight of the 14 children, ranging in age from 5 to 16, later rejected their female reassignment and declared themselves to be boys (Reiner & Gearhart, 2004).

In addition to the gender difficulties involved in David's case and the cases of the boys born without a penis, other gender identity problems may develop when a person feels he or she is trapped in a body of the wrong sex. This is known as *transsexualism* (having a gender identity opposite to biological sex). Although some may see the case of Brenda/Bruce/David as a form of transsexualism, "true" transsexuals are born chromosomally and anatomically one sex. But they have a deep and lasting discomfort

TABLE 11.1 DIMENSIONS OF SEX AND GENDER

	Male	Female
Sex Dimensions		
1. Chromosomes	XY	XX
2. Gonads	Testes	Ovaries
3. Hormones	Predominantly androgens	Predominantly estrogens
4. External genitals	Penis, scrotum	Labia majora, labia minora, clitoris, vaginal opening
5. Internal accessory organs	Prostate gland, seminal vesicles, vas deferens, ejaculatory duct, Cowper's gland	Vagina, uterus, fallopian tubes, cervix
6. Secondary sex characteristics	Beard, lower voice, wider shoulders, sperm emission	Breasts, wider hips, menstruation
7. Sexual orientation	Heterosexual, gay, bisexual	Heterosexual, lesbian, bisexual
Gender Dimensions		
8. Gender identity (self-definition)	Perceives self as male	Perceives self as female
9. Gender role (societal expectations)	Masculine ("Boys like trucks and sports")	Feminine ("Girls like dolls and clothes")

with their sexual anatomy. They report feeling as if they are victims of a "birth defect," and they often seek corrective reassignment surgery (Bower, 2001). At one time, the number of men seeking reassignment was much higher than the number of women who wished to be men. But the ratio has narrowed considerably in recent years (Landen, Walinder, & Lundstrom, 1998).

Is a transsexual the same as a transvestite? No, *transvestism* involves individuals (almost exclusively men) who adopt the dress (cross-dressing), and often the behavior, typical of the opposite sex. Some homosexual men and women dress up as the other sex, and some entertainers cross-dress as part of their job. But for true transvestites, the cross-dressing is primarily for emotional and sexual gratification (Miracle, Miracle, & Baumeister, 2006). In contrast, transsexuals feel that they are really members of the opposite sex imprisoned in the wrong body. Their gender identity does not match their gonads, genitals, or internal accessory organs. Transsexuals may also cross-dress. But their motivation is to look like the "right" sex rather than to obtain sexual arousal. Transvestites should also be distinguished from female impersonators (who cross-dress to entertain) and from gay men who occasionally "go in drag" (cross-dress).

Are transvestites and transsexuals also homosexual? When a person is described as *homosexual*, it is because of a **sexual orientation** toward the same sex. (The preferred terms today are *gay* and *lesbian* rather than *homosexual*.) Transvestites are usually heterosexual (Bullough & Bullough, 1997). Transsexuality, on the other hand, has nothing to do with sexual orientation, only with gender identity. In fact, a transsexual can be heterosexual, gay, lesbian, or *bisexual* (being sexually attracted to both males and females).

◼ Gender Role Development: Two Major Theories

Sexual orientation and gender identity also should not be confused with **gender roles**—societal expectations for normal and appropriate female and male behavior. Gender roles influence our lives from the moment of birth (when we are wrapped in either a pink or blue blanket) until the moment of death (when we are buried in either a dress or a dark suit). By age 2, children are well aware of gender roles. They recognize that boys should be strong, independent, aggressive, dominant, and achieving. Conversely, girls should be soft, dependent, passive, emotional, and "naturally" interested in children (Kimmel, 2000; Renzetti et al., 2006). The gender role expectations learned in childhood apparently influence us throughout our life.

How do we develop our gender roles? The existence of similar gender roles in many cultures suggests that evolution and biology may play a role. However, most research emphasizes two major theories of gender role development: *social learning* and *cognitive developmental*.

Social Learning Theory

Social learning theorists emphasize the power of the immediate situation and observable behaviors on gender role development. They suggest that girls learn how to be "feminine" and boys learn how to be "masculine" in two major ways: (1) They receive rewards or punishments for specific gender role behaviors, and (2) they watch and imitate the behavior and attitudes of others—particularly the same-sex parent (Bandura, 1989, 2000; Fredrick & Eccles, 2005; Kulik, 2005). A boy who puts on his father's tie or baseball cap wins big, indulgent smiles from his parents. But can you imagine what would happen if he put on his mother's nightgown or lipstick? Parents, teachers, and friends generally reward or punish behaviors according to traditional boy/girl gender role expectations. Thus, a child "socially learns" what it means to be male or female.

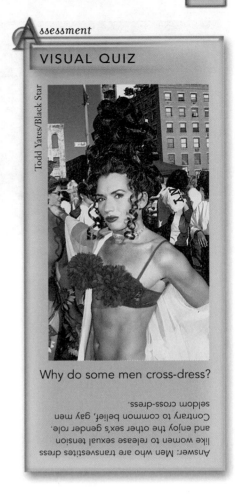

VISUAL QUIZ

Todd Yates/Black Star

Why do some men cross-dress?

Answer: Men who are transvestites dress like women to release sexual tension and enjoy the other sex's gender role. Contrary to common belief, gay men seldom cross-dress.

Sexual Orientation *Primary erotic attraction toward members of the same sex (homosexual, gay or lesbian), both sexes (bisexual), or other sex (heterosexual)*

Gender Role *Societal expectations for normal and appropriate male and female behavior*

Early gender role conditioning. Can you predict the long-term effects of this type of gender role training on young boys and girls? Are these effects primarily good or bad?

Cognitive Developmental Theory

Cognitive developmental theory acknowledges that social learning is part of gender development. But the social learning model sees gender development as a passive process. Cognitive developmentalists point out that children actively observe, interpret, and judge the world around them (Bem, 1981, 1993; Cherney, 2005; Giles & Heyman, 2005). As children process this information, they create internal rules governing correct behaviors for boys versus girls. Using these rules, they form *gender schemas* (mental images) of how they should act. (Recall from the discussion of Piaget in Chapter 9 that a *schema* is a cognitive structure, a network of associations, which guides perception.)

Thus, a little boy plays with fire trucks and building blocks because his parents smiled approvingly in the past. It is also because he has seen more boys than girls playing with these toys *(social learning theory)*. But his internal thought processes *(cognitive developmental theory)* also contribute to his choice of "masculine" toys. The child realizes he is a boy, and he has learned that boys "should" prefer fire trucks to dishes and dolls.

Application
CASE STUDY / PERSONAL STORY

The Tragic Tale of "John/Joan"

Corbis Images

What do you think happened to the baby boy who suffered the botched circumcision and was "reassigned" to be raised as a girl? According to John Money (Money & Ehrhardt, 1972), Bruce/Brenda moved easily into her new identity. By age three, Brenda wore nightgowns and dresses almost exclusively and liked bracelets and hair ribbons. She also reportedly preferred playing with "girl-type" toys and asked for a doll and carriage for Christmas. But her brother, Brian, asked for a garage with cars, gas pumps, and tools. By age 6, Brian was accustomed to defending his sister if he thought someone was threatening her. The daughter copied the mother in tidying and cleaning up the kitchen, whereas the boy did not. The mother agreed that she encouraged her daughter when she helped with the housework and expected the boy to be uninterested.

During their childhood, both Brenda/Bruce and her brother Brian were brought to Johns Hopkins each year for physical and psychological evaluation. The case was heralded as a complete success. It also became the model for treating infants born with ambiguous genitalia. The story of "John/Joan," (the name used by John Hopkins) was heralded as proof that gender is made—not born.

What first looked like a success was, in fact, a dismal failure. Follow-up studies report that Brenda never really adjusted to her assigned gender (Colapinto, 2004).

Despite being raised from infancy as a girl, she did not feel like a girl and avoided most female activities and interests. As she entered adolescence, her appearance and masculine way of walking led classmates to tease her and call her "cave woman." At this age, she also expressed thoughts of becoming a mechanic, and her fantasies reflected discomfort with her female role. She even tried urinating in a standing position and insisted she wanted to live as a boy (Diamond & Sigmundson, 1997).

By age 14, she was so unhappy that she contemplated suicide. The father tearfully explained what had happened earlier, and for Brenda, "All of a sudden everything clicked. For the first time things made sense, and I understood who and what I was" (Thompson, 1997, p. 83).

After the truth came out, "Brenda" reclaimed his male gender identity and renamed himself David. Following a double mastectomy (removal of both breasts) and construction of an artificial penis, he married a woman and adopted her children. David, his parents, and twin brother, Brian, all suffered enormously from the tragic accident and the no less tragic solution. He said, "I don't blame my parents." But they still felt extremely guilty about their participation in the reassignment. The family members later reconciled. But David remained angry with the doctors who "interfered with nature" and ruined his childhood.

Sadly, there's even more tragedy to tell. On May 4, 2004, thirty-eight-year old David committed suicide. Why? No one knows what went through his mind when he decided to end his life. But he had just lost his job, a big investment had failed, he was separated from his wife, and his twin brother had committed suicide shortly before (Walker, 2004). "Most suicides, experts say, have multiple motives, which come together in a perfect storm of misery" (Colapinto, 2004).

Sex and Gender Differences: Nature Versus Nurture

Now that we have looked at the different dimensions of sex and gender and examined gender role development, let's turn our attention to sex and gender differences between males and females.

Sex Differences

Physical anatomy is the most obvious biological difference between men and women (Figure 11.2). The average man is taller, heavier, and stronger than the average woman. He is also more likely to be bald and color-blind. In addition, men and women differ in their *secondary sex characteristics* (facial hair, breasts, and so on), their signs of reproductive capability (the menarche for girls and the ejaculation of sperm for boys), and their physical reactions to middle age or the end of reproduction (the female menopause and male climacteric).

There also are several functional and structural differences in the brains of men

Figure 11.2 *Major physical differences between the sexes.* Source: Miracle, Tina S., Miracle, Andrew, W., and Baumeister, R. F., Study Guide: Human sexuality: Meeting your basic needs, 2nd edition. ©2006. Reprinted by permission of Pearson Education, Inc., Upper Saddle River, NJ.

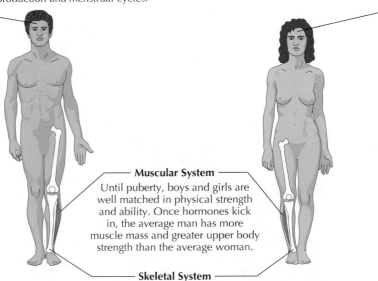

Body Size and Shape
The average man is 35 pounds heavier, has less body fat and is 5 inches taller than the average woman. Men tend to have broader shoulders, slimmer hips and slightly longer legs in proportion to their height.

Brain
The corpus callosum, the bridge joining the two halves of the brain, is larger in women; therefore they can integrate information from the two halves of the brain and more easily perform more than one task simultaneously.

An area of the hypothalamus causes men to have a relatively constant level of sex hormones; whereas, women have cyclic sex hormone production and menstrual cycles.

Differences in the cerebral hemispheres may help explain reported sex differences in verbal and spatial skills.

Muscular System
Until puberty, boys and girls are well matched in physical strength and ability. Once hormones kick in, the average man has more muscle mass and greater upper body strength than the average woman.

Skeletal System
Men produce testosterone throughout their life span, whereas estrogen production virtually stops when a women goes through menopause. Because estrogen helps rejuvenate bones, women are more likely to have brittle bones. Women also are more prone to knee damage because a woman's wider hips may place a greater strain on the ligaments joining the thigh to the knee.

and women. These differences result, at least in part, from the influence of prenatal sex hormones on the developing fetal brain. And the differences are most apparent in the *hypothalamus, corpus callosum,* and *cerebral hemispheres* (Chipman, Hampson, & Kimura, 2002; Lewald, 2004; McCarthy, Auger, & Perrot-Sinal, 2002; Swaab et al., 2003). For example, during puberty, the female's hypothalamus directs her pituitary gland to release hormones in a cyclic fashion (the menstrual cycle). In contrast, the male's hypothalamus directs a relatively steady production of sex hormones. The corpus callosum, the web of nerve fibers connecting the cerebral hemispheres, is larger in adult women and shaped differently in women than in men. Research suggests this difference may explain why men tend to rely on one hemisphere or the other in performing tasks, while women generally use both hemispheres at once. Researchers also have documented differences in the cerebral hemispheres of men and women that may account for reported differences in verbal and spatial skills, which are discussed in the next section (Lewald, 2004; Phillips et al., 2001; Skrandies, Reik, & Kunzie, 1999).

Gender Differences

Do you think there are inborn psychological differences between women and men? Do you believe that women are more emotional and more concerned with aesthetics? Or that men are naturally more aggressive and competitive? Scientists have identified several gender differences, which are summarized in Table 11.2. In this section, we will focus on two of their most researched differences—cognitive abilities and aggression.

TABLE 11.2 RESEARCH-SUPPORTED SEX AND GENDER DIFFERENCES

Type of Behavior	More Often Shown by Men	More Often Shown by Women
Sexual	• Begin masturbating sooner in life cycle and have higher overall occurrence rates. • Start sexual life earlier and have first orgasm through masturbation. • Are more likely to recognize their own sexual arousal. • Experience more orgasm consistency in their sexual relations.	• Begin masturbating later in life cycle and have lower overall occurrence rates. • Start sexual life later and have first orgasm from partner stimulation. • Are less likely to recognize their own sexual arousal. • Experience less orgasm consistency in their sexual relations.
Touching	• Are touched, kissed, and cuddled less by parents. • Exchange less physical contact with other men and respond more negatively to being touched. • Are more likely to initiate both casual and intimate touch with sexual partner.	• Are touched, kissed, and cuddled more by parents. • Exchange more physical contact with other women and respond more positively to being touched. • Are less likely to initiate either casual or intimate touch with sexual partner.
Friendship	• Have larger number of friends and express friendship by shared activities.	• Have smaller number of friends and express friendship by shared communication about self.
Personality	• Are more aggressive from a very early age. • Are more self-confident of future success. • Attribute success to internal factors and failures to external factors. • Achievement is task oriented; motives are mastery and competition. • Are more self-validating. • Have higher self-esteem.	• Are less aggressive from a very early age. • Are less self-confident of future success. • Attribute success to external factors and failures to internal factors. • Achievement is socially directed with emphasis on self-improvement; have higher work motives. • Are more dependent on others for validation. • Have lower self-esteem.
Cognitive Abilities	• Are slightly superior in mathematics and visuospatial skills.	• Are slightly superior in grammar, spelling, and related verbal skills.

Sources: Crooks & Baur, 2005; Masters & Johnson, 1961, 1966, 1970; Miracle, Miracle, & Baumeister, 2006.

1. *Cognitive abilities.* For many years, researchers have noted that females tend to score higher on tests of verbal skills. Conversely, males score higher on math and visuospatial tests (Gallagher et al., 2000; Quaiser-Pohl & Lehmann, 2002). As mentioned earlier, some researchers suggest that these differences may reflect biology—that is, structural differences in the cerebral hemispheres, hormones, or the degree of hemispheric specialization.

   One argument against such a biological model, however, is that male–female differences in verbal ability and math scores have declined in recent years (Brown & Josephs, 1999; Halpern, 1997, 2000; Lizarraga & Ganuza, 2003). The gap has not been narrowed, however, with men in the very highest IQ range. Men in this group still score higher than women on SAT math scores.

2. *Aggression.* One of the clearest and most consistent findings in gender studies is greater physical aggressiveness in males. From an early age, boys are more likely to engage in mock fighting and rough-and-tumble play. As adolescents and adults, men are more likely to commit aggressive crimes (Camodeca et al., 2002; Henning & Feder, 2004; Moffitt, Caspi, Harrington, & Milne, 2002; Ostrov & Keating, 2004). But gender differences are clearer for physical aggression (like hitting) than for other forms of aggression. Early research also suggested that females were more likely to engage in more indirect and relational forms of aggression, such as spreading rumors and ignoring or excluding someone (Bjorkqvist, 1994; Ostrov & Keating, 2004). But other studies have not found such clear differences (Cillessen & Mayeux, 2004; Feiring et al., 2002; Salmivalli & Kaukiainen, 2004).

What causes these gender differences in aggression? Those who take a nature perspective generally cite biological factors. For example, several studies have linked the male gonadal hormone testosterone to aggressive behavior (Book, Starzyk, & Qunisey, 2002; Ramirez, 2003; Trainor, Bird, & Marler, 2004). Other studies have found that aggressive men have disturbances in their levels of serotonin, a neurotransmitter inversely related to aggression (Berman, Tracy, & Coccaro, 1997; Holtzworth-Munroe, 2000; Nelson & Chiavegatto, 2001). In addition, studies on identical twins find that genetic factors account for about 50 percent of aggressive behavior (Cadoret, Leve, & Devor, 1997; Segal & Bouchard, 2000).

Nurturists suggest these gender differences result from environmental experiences with social dominance and pressures that encourage "sex-appropriate" behaviors and skills (Rowe et al., 2004). For example, children's picture books, video games, and TV programs and commercials frequently present women and men in stereotypical gender roles—men as pilots and doctors, women as flight attendants and nurses.

Androgyny

What if we don't like the negative parts of gender roles? What can we do? One way to overcome rigid or destructive gender role stereotypes is to encourage **androgyny**, expressing both the "masculine" and "feminine" traits found in each individual. Rather than limiting themselves to rigid gender-appropriate behaviors, androgynous men and women can be assertive and aggressive when necessary, but also gentle and nurturing.

Some people think *androgyny* is a new term for asexuality or transsexualism. However, the idea of androgyny has a long history referring to positive combinations of gender roles, like the *yin* and *yang* of traditional Chinese religions. Carl Jung (1946, 1959), an early psychoanalyst, described a woman's natural masculine traits and impulses as her "animus" and feminine traits and impulses in a man as his "anima." Jung believed we must draw on both our masculine and feminine natures to become fully functioning adults.

Using personality tests and other similar measures, modern researchers have found that *masculine* and *androgynous* individuals generally have higher self-esteem,

Androgyny [an-DRAW-juh-nee]
Combining characteristics considered typically male (assertive, athletic) with characteristics considered typically female (yielding, nurturant); from the Greek andro, meaning "male," and gyn, meaning "female"

academic scores, and creativity. They are also more socially competent and motivated to achieve, and exhibit better overall mental health (Choi, 2004; Hittner & Daniels, 2002; Venkatesh et al., 2004). It seems that androgyny and masculinity, but *not* femininity, are adaptive for both sexes.

How can you explain this? It seems that traditional masculine characteristics (analytical, independent) are more highly valued than traditional feminine traits (affectionate, cheerful). For example, in business a good manager is still perceived as having predominantly masculine traits (Powell, Butterfield, & Parent, 2002). Also, when college students in 14 different countries were asked to describe their "current self" and their "ideal self," the ideal self-descriptions for both men and women contained more masculine than feminine qualities (Williams & Best, 1990).

This shared preference for male traits helps explain why extensive observations of children on school playgrounds have found that boys who engage in feminine activities (like skipping rope or playing jacks) lose status. The reverse of this is not true for girls (Leaper, 2000). Even as adults, it is more difficult for males to express so-called female traits like nurturance and sensitivity than for women to adopt traditionally male traits of assertiveness and independence. In short, most societies prefer "tomboys" to "sissies."

Recent studies show that gender roles in our society are becoming less rigidly defined (Kimmel, 2000; Loo & Thorpe, 1998). Asian-American and Mexican-American groups show some of the largest changes toward androgyny. And African Americans remain among the most androgynous of all ethnic groups (Denmark & Rabinowitz, 2005; Harris, 1996; Huang & Ying, 1989; Renzetti et al., 2006).

TRY THIS YOURSELF

Application

Are You Androgynous?

Social psychologist Sandra Bem (1974, 1993) developed a personality measure that has been widely used in research. You can take this version of Bem's test by rating yourself on the following items. Give yourself a number between 1 (never or almost never true) and 7 (always or almost always true):

1. _____ Analytical
2. _____ Affectionate
3. _____ Competitive
4. _____ Compassionate
5. _____ Aggressive
6. _____ Cheerful
7. _____ Independent
8. _____ Gentle
9. _____ Athletic
10. _____ Sensitive

Now add up your points for all the odd-numbered items; then add up your points for the even-numbered items. If you have a higher total on the odd-numbered items, you are "masculine." If you scored higher on the even-numbered items, you are "feminine." If your score is fairly even, you may be androgynous.

Androgyny in action. *Combining the traits of both genders helps many couples meet the demands of modern life.*

Ranald Mackechnie/Stone/GettyImages

CRITICAL THINKING   ACTIVE LEARNING

Gender Differences and Critical Thinking
(Contributed by Thomas Frangicetto)

For each of the following:
- Fill in the blanks with terms and concepts from this chapter, including Table 11.2. This will help you review important text content that may appear on exams.
- Answer the associated critical thinking questions. They will improve your relationship skills and understanding of important gender and sexuality issues.

1. According to research, "one way to overcome rigid or destructive _____ is to encourage *androgyny*, expressing both the "masculine" and "feminine" traits found in each individual." Do you agree? Do you believe that children should be raised to be androgynous? Which of the 21 critical thinking components (CTCs) found in the Prologue (pp. xxx–xxxiv) do you think are essential in becoming an androgynous person? Are there any CTCs that women display more than men, or vice versa?

2. "Men are encouraged to bring a certain level of sexual knowledge into the relationship. In contrast, women are expected to stop male advances and refrain from sexual activity until marriage." This _____ still exists in modern Western societies. How does this common belief affect your personal relationships or sexual behaviors? Can you identify at least two CTCs that could be useful in overcoming possible problems or negative effects associated with this belief?

3. According to research cited in Table 11.2, men have a _____ number of friends and express their friendship by _____. Women have _____ friends and express their friendship by _____. Do you agree? Does this research help you understand differences between men and women? How might this difference create problems for married couples with few outside friendships?

4. Research cited in Table 11.2 also finds that men "have _____ self-esteem" and women "have _____ self-esteem." Can you identify additional content from that table that might help explain this difference? For example, what role does "self-validation" play in the formation of self-esteem? What about differences in their attributions for success or failure? Choose one to three CTCs that you think could help equalize these gender differences in self-esteem.

CHECK & REVIEW

Sex and Gender

The term **sex** is differentiated along seven dimensions: chromosomal sex, gonadal sex, hormonal sex, external genitals, internal accessory organs, secondary sex characteristics, and sexual orientation. **Gender,** on the other hand, is differentiated according to **gender identity** and **gender role.** Transsexualism is a problem with gender identity. Transvestism is cross-dressing for emotional and sexual gratification. **Sexual orientation** (gay, lesbian, bisexual, or heterosexual) is unrelated to either transsexualism or transvestism.

There are two main theories of gender role development. *Social learning theorists* focus on rewards, punishments, and imitation. *Cognitive developmental theorists* emphasize the active thinking processes of the individual.

Studies of male and female sex differences find several obvious physical differences, such as height, body build, and reproductive organs. There are also important functional and structural sex differences in the brains of human females and males. Studies find some gender differences (such as in aggression and verbal skills). But the cause of these differences (either nature or nurture) is still being debated.

Questions

1. Match the following dimensions of gender with their appropriate meaning:

___ Chromosomal sex
___ Gender identity
___ Gonadal sex
___ Gender role

a. Ovaries and testes
b. XX and XY
c. Estrogens and androgens
d. One's perception of oneself as male or female

___ Hormonal sex
___ Secondary sex characteristics
___ External genitals
___ Sexual orientation
___ Internal accessory organs

e. Breasts, beards, menstruation
f. Uterus, vagina, prostate gland, vas deferens
g. Labia majora, clitoris, penis, scrotum
h. Homosexual, bisexual, heterosexual
i. Differing societal expectations for appropriate male and female behavior

2. Individuals who have the genitals and secondary sex characteristics of one sex but feel as if they belong to the other sex are known as _____. (a) transvestites; (b) heterosexuals; (c) gays or lesbians; (d) transsexuals
3. Briefly summarize the two major theories of gender role development.
4. A combination of both male and female personality traits is called _____. (a) heterosexuality; (b) homosexuality; (c) transsexualism; (d) androgyny

Check your answers in Appendix B.

CLICK & REVIEW
for additional assessment options:
www.wiley.com/college/huffman

THE STUDY OF HUMAN SEXUALITY

chievement

How do scientists study a sensitive topic like sex?

Sex is used and abused in many ways. It is a major theme in literature, movies, and music, as well as a way to satisfy sexual desires. We also use and abuse sex to gain love and acceptance from partners and peer groups, to express love or commitment in a relationship, to end relationships through affairs with others, to dominate or hurt others, and, perhaps most conspicuously, to sell products.

People have probably always been interested in understanding their sexuality. But cultural forces have often suppressed and controlled this interest. During the nineteenth century, for example, polite society avoided mention of all parts of the body covered by clothing. The breast of chickens became known as "white meat," male doctors examined female patients in totally dark rooms, and some people even covered piano legs for the sake of propriety (Allen, 2000; Gay, 1983; Money, 1985a).

During this same Victorian period, medical experts warned that masturbation led to blindness, impotence, acne, and insanity (Allen, 2000; Michael, Gagnon, Laumann, & Kolata, 1994). Believing a bland diet helped suppress sexual desire, Dr. John Harvey Kellogg and Sylvester Graham developed the original Kellogg's Corn Flakes and Graham crackers and marketed them as foods that would discourage masturbation (Money, Prakasam, & Joshi, 1991). One of the most serious concerns of many doctors was nocturnal emissions (wet dreams), which were believed to cause brain damage and death. Special devices were even marketed for men to wear at night to prevent sexual arousal (Figure 11.3).

In light of modern knowledge, it seems hard to understand these strange Victorian practices and outrageous myths about masturbation and nocturnal emissions. One of the first physicians to explore and question these beliefs was Havelock Ellis (1858–1939). When he first heard of the dangers of nocturnal emissions, Ellis was frightened—he had had personal experience with the problem. His fear led him to frantically search the medical literature. But instead of a cure, he found predictions of gruesome illness and eventual death. He was so upset he contemplated suicide.

Granger Collection

One of the earliest sex scientists.
Havelock Ellis was one of the first sex researchers to celebrate eroticism and fully acknowledge female sexuality.

Ellis eventually decided he could give meaning to his life by keeping a detailed diary of his deterioration. He planned to dedicate the book to science when he died. However, after several months of careful observation, he realized the books were wrong. He wasn't dying. He wasn't even sick. Angry that he had been so misinformed by the "experts," he spent the rest of his life developing reliable and accurate sex information. Today, Havelock Ellis is acknowledged as one of the most important early pioneers in the field of sex research.

Another major contribution to sex research came from Alfred Kinsey and his colleagues (1948, 1953). Kinsey and his coworkers personally interviewed over 18,000 participants, asking detailed questions about their sexual activities and preferences. Their results shocked the nation. For example, they reported that 37 percent of men and 13 percent of women had engaged in adult same-sex behavior to the point of orgasm. However, Kinsey's data were criticized because most research participants were young, single, urban, white, and middle class. Despite the criticism, Kinsey's work is still widely respected, and his data are frequently used as a *baseline* for modern research. In recent years, hundreds of similar sex surveys and interviews have been conducted on such topics as contraception, abortion, premarital sex, and rape (Dodge et al., 2005; Laumann, Gagnon, Michael, & Michaels, 1994; Leskin & Sheikh, 2002). By comparing Kinsey's data to the responses found in later surveys, we can see how sexual practices have changed over the years.

In addition to surveys, interviews, and case studies, some researchers have employed direct laboratory experimentation and observational methods. To experimentally document the physiological changes involved in sexual arousal and response, William Masters and Virginia Johnson (1961, 1966, 1970) and their research colleagues enlisted several hundred male and female volunteers. Using intricate physiological measuring devices, the researchers carefully monitored participants' bodily responses as they masturbated or engaged in sexual intercourse. Masters and Johnson's research findings have been hailed as a major contribution to our knowledge of sexual physiology. Some of their results are discussed in later sections.

chievement
Gender & Cultural Diversity

A Cross-Cultural Look at Sexual Behaviors

Sex researchers interested in both universalities and variations in human sexual behavior conduct cross-cultural studies of sexual practices, techniques, and attitudes (Beach, 1977; Bhugra, 2000; Brislin, 1993, 2000; Ho & Tsang, 2002; Mackay, 2001). Their studies of different societies put sex in a broader perspective.

Cross-cultural studies of sex also help counteract *ethnocentrism*, the tendency we have to judge our own cultural practices as "normal" and preferable to those of other groups. For example, do you know that kissing is unpopular in Japan and unknown among some cultures in Africa and South America? Do you find it strange that Apinaye women in Brazil often bite off pieces of their mate's eyebrows as a natural part of sexual foreplay? Does it surprise you that members of Tiwi society, off the northern coast of Australia, believe that young girls will not develop breasts or menstruate unless they first experience intercourse? Do you know that the men and women of the Amazonian Yanomamo routinely wear nothing but a thin cord around their waists? Interestingly, if you were to ask a Yanomamo woman to remove the cord, she would respond in much the same way an American woman would if you asked her to remove her blouse (Hyde & DeLamater, 2006; Frayser, 1985; Gregerson, 1996; Goldstein, 1976; Miracle, Miracle, & Baumeister, 2006). In addition, the Sambia of New Guinea believe that young boys must swallow semen to achieve manhood (Herdt, 1981). Adolescent boys in Mangaia, a small island in the South Pacific, routinely undergo superincision, a painful initiation rite in which the foreskin of the penis is slit and folded back (Marshall, 1971). Figure 11.4 gives other examples of surprising cultural variation in sexuality.

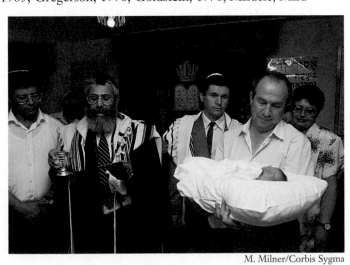

M. Milner/Corbis Sygma

Figure 11.3 *Victorian sexual practice.* During the nineteenth century, men were encouraged to wear spiked rings around their penises at night. Can you explain why?

Answer: The Victorians believed nighttime erections and emissions ("wet dreams") were dangerous. If the man had an erection, the spikes would cause pain and awaken him.

Circumcision and religion.
Although circumcision is an important part of some religions, it is relatively rare in most parts of the world.

Figure 11.4 *Cross-cultural differences in sexual behavior.* Note: "Inis Beag" is a pseudonym used to protect the privacy of residents of this Irish island. *Sources:* Crooks & Baur, 2005; Ford & Beach, 1951; Hyde & DeLamater, 2006; Marshall, 1971; Messenger, 1971; Miracle, Miracle, & Baumeister, 2006; Money et al., 1991.

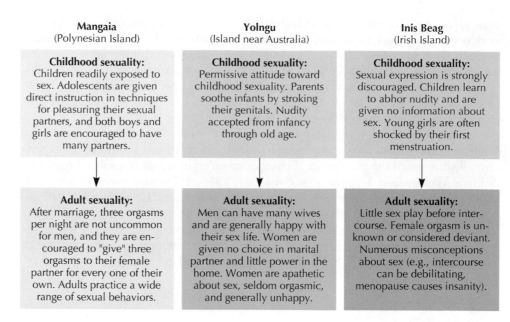

Mangaia
(Polynesian Island)

Childhood sexuality:
Children readily exposed to sex. Adolescents are given direct instruction in techniques for pleasuring their sexual partners, and both boys and girls are encouraged to have many partners.

Adult sexuality:
After marriage, three orgasms per night are not uncommon for men, and they are encouraged to "give" three orgasms to their female partner for every one of their own. Adults practice a wide range of sexual behaviors.

Yolngu
(Island near Australia)

Childhood sexuality:
Permissive attitude toward childhood sexuality. Parents soothe infants by stroking their genitals. Nudity accepted from infancy through old age.

Adult sexuality:
Men can have many wives and are generally happy with their sex life. Women are given no choice in marital partner and little power in the home. Women are apathetic about sex, seldom orgasmic, and generally unhappy.

Inis Beag
(Irish Island)

Childhood sexuality:
Sexual expression is strongly discouraged. Children learn to abhor nudity and are given no information about sex. Young girls are often shocked by their first menstruation.

Adult sexuality:
Little sex play before intercourse. Female orgasm is unknown or considered deviant. Numerous misconceptions about sex (e.g., intercourse can be debilitating, menopause causes insanity).

Although other cultures' practices may seem unnatural and strange to us, we forget that our own sexual rituals may appear equally curious to others. If the description of the Mangaian practice of superincision bothered you, how do you feel about our own culture's routine circumcision of infant boys? Before you object that infant circumcision in the United States is "entirely different" and "medically safe and necessary," you might want to consider the position now taken by the American Academy of Pediatrics (AAP). In 1999, they decided the previously reported medical benefits of circumcision were so statistically small that the procedure should *not* be routinely performed. However, the AAP does consider it legitimate for parents to take into account cultural, religious, and ethnic traditions in deciding whether to circumcise their sons.

If the controversy over infant male circumcision surprises you, so, too, may information about female genital mutilation. Throughout history and even today—in parts of Africa, the Middle East, Indonesia, and Malaysia—young girls undergo several types of *female genital mutilation* (FGM). FGM includes circumcision (removal of the clitoral hood), *clitoridectomy* (removal of the clitoris), and *genital infibulation* (removal of the clitoris and labia and stitching together of the remaining tissue to allow only a small opening for urine and menstrual flow) (Dandash, Refaat, & Eyada, 2001; El-Gibaly et al., 2002; Whitehorn, Ayonrinde, & Maingay, 2002). In most countries, the surgeries are performed on girls between ages 4 and 10 and often without anesthesia or antiseptic conditions (Abusharaf, 1998; McCormack, 2001). The young girls suffer numerous health problems because of these practices—the most serious from genital infibulation. Risks include severe pain, bleeding, chronic infection, and menstrual difficulties. As adults, these women frequently experience serious sexual problems, as well as dangerous childbirth complications or infertility.

What is the purpose of these procedures? The main objective is to ensure virginity before marriage (Oruboloye, Caldwell, & Caldwell, 1997). Without these procedures, young girls are considered unmarriageable and without status. As you might imagine, these practices create serious culture clashes. For example, physicians in Western societies are currently being asked by immigrant parents to perform these operations on their daughters. What should the doctor do? Should this practice be forbidden? Or would this be another example of ethnocentrism?

As you can see, it is a complex issue. Canada was the first nation to recognize female genital mutilation as a basis for granting refugee status (Crooks & Baur, 2005). And the United Nations has suspended its regular policy of nonintervention in the cultural practices of nations. The World Health Organization (WHO) and the United Nations International Children's Emergency Fund (UNICEF) have both issued statements opposing female genital mutilation. They also have developed programs to combat this and other harmful practices affecting the health and well-being of women and children.

ssessment

CHECK & REVIEW

The Study of Human Sexuality

Although sex has always been an important part of human interest, motivation, and behavior, it received little scientific attention before the twentieth century. Havelock Ellis was among the first to study human sexuality despite the repression and secrecy of nineteenth-century Victorian times.

Alfred Kinsey and his colleagues were the first to conduct large-scale, systematic surveys and interviews of the sexual practices and preferences of Americans during the 1940s and 1950s. The research team of William Masters and Virginia Johnson pioneered the use of actual laboratory measurement and observation of human physiological response during sexual activity. Cultural studies are important sources of scientific information on human sexuality.

Questions

1. During earlier times, it was believed that _____ led to blindness, impotence, acne, and insanity, whereas _____ caused brain damage and death. (a) female orgasms, male orgasms; (b) masturbation, nocturnal emissions; (c) menstruation, menopause; (d) oral sex, sodomy

2. Fill in the researchers name that matches their contributions to the study of human sexuality:
   a. _____ based his/their groundbreaking research into human sexuality on personal diaries
   b. _____ popularized the use of the survey method in studying human sexuality
   c. _____ pioneered the use of direct observation and physiological measurement of bodily responses during sexual activities

3. What are the advantages of cultural studies in sex research?

4. Viewing one's own ethnic group (or culture) as central and "correct" and then judging the rest of the world according to this standard is known as _____. (a) standardization; (b) stereotyping; (c) discrimination; (d) ethnocentrism

Check your answers in Appendix B.

CLICK & REVIEW
for additional assessment options:
www.wiley.com/college/huffman

SEXUAL BEHAVIOR

Are women and men fundamentally alike in their sexual responses? Or are they unalterably different? What causes a gay or lesbian sexual orientation? What is sexual prejudice? These are some of the questions we will explore in this section.

Sexual Arousal and Response: Gender Differences and Similarities

Males and females have obvious differences and similarities in their sexual arousal and response. But how would researchers scientifically test what happens to the human body when an individual or couple engage in sexual activities? As you can imagine, this is a highly controversial topic for research. William Masters and Virginia Johnson (1966) were the first to conduct actual laboratory studies. With the help of 694 female and male volunteers, they attached recording devices to the volunteers' bodies and monitored or filmed their physical responses as they moved from nonarousal to orgasm and back to nonarousal. They labeled the bodily changes during this series of events a **sexual response cycle** that included four stages: *excitement,*

chievement

How are men and women alike and different in sexual arousal and response? What is the latest research on sexual orientation?

Sexual Response Cycle *Masters and Johnson's description of the four-stage bodily response to sexual arousal, which consists of excitement, plateau, orgasm, and resolution*

www.wiley.com/college/huffman

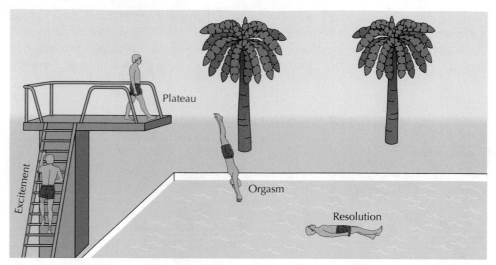

Figure 11.5 *Masters and Johnson's sexual response cycle.* One way to visualize (and remember) the four stages of the *sexual response cycle* is to compare it to diving off a high diving board. During the *excitement phase* (climbing up the ladder), both men and women become progressively more aroused and excited, resulting in penile and clitoral erection, and vaginal lubrication in women. In the *plateau phase* (walking across the diving board), sexual and physiological arousal continue at a heightened state. The *orgasm phase* (jumping off the diving board) involves rhythmic muscle contractions in both men and women and ejaculation of sperm by men. During the final *resolution phase* (resting and swimming back to the edge), physiological responses return to normal. Note, however, that this is a simplified description that does not account for individual variation. It should not be used to judge what's "normal."

Excitement Phase *First stage of the sexual response cycle, characterized by increasing levels of arousal and increased engorgement of the genitals*

Plateau Phase *Second stage of the sexual response cycle, characterized by a leveling off in a state of high arousal*

Orgasm Phase *Third stage of the sexual response cycle, when pleasurable sensations peak and orgasm occurs*

Resolution Phase *Final stage of the sexual response cycle, when the body returns to its unaroused state*

Refractory Period *Phase following orgasm, during which further orgasm is considered physiologically impossible for men*

plateau, orgasm, and *resolution* (Figure 11.5). Let's take a closer look at each of these stages.

Stage 1: In the **excitement phase**, which can last from a few minutes to several hours, arousal is initiated through physical factors, such as touching or being touched, or through psychological factors, such as fantasy or erotic stimuli. During this stage, heart rate, respiration, and vaginal lubrication increase. Blood flow to the pelvic region also increases, causing engorgement of the penis and clitoris. Both men and women may have nipples becoming erect, and both may experience a *sex flush*, or reddening of the upper torso and face.

Stage 2: If stimulation continues, the **plateau phase** begins and heartbeat, respiration rate, and blood pressure continue at a high level. In the man, the penis becomes more engorged and erect while the testes swell and pull up closer to the body. In the woman, the clitoris pulls up under the clitoral hood and the entrance to the vagina contracts while the uterus rises slightly. This movement of the uterus causes the upper two-thirds of the vagina to balloon, or expand. As arousal reaches its peak, both sexes may experience a feeling that orgasm is imminent and inevitable.

Stage 3: During the **orgasm phase**, the individual experiences a highly intense and pleasurable release of tension. In the woman, muscles around the vagina squeeze the vaginal walls in and out and the uterus pulsates. Muscles at the base of the penis contract in the man, causing *ejaculation*, the discharge of semen or seminal fluid.

Stage 4: Both male and female bodies gradually return to their preexcitement state during the **resolution phase**. After one orgasm, most men enter a **refractory period**, during which further excitement to orgasm is considered impossible. Many women (and some men), however, are capable of multiple orgasms in fairly rapid succession.

Achievement
Gender & Cultural Diversity

Are There Evolutionary Advantages to Female Nonmonogamy?

In many ways, women and men are similar in their general sexual responses. But it is our differences that attract the most attention. For example, have you heard that men have more sexual drive, interest, and activity than women do? How do scientists investigate such a common belief? There are two major perspectives—evolutionary and social role.

The *evolutionary perspective*, emphasizing the adaptive value of behaviors, suggests that sexual differences (such as men having more sexual partners) evolved from ancient mating patterns that helped the species survive (Buss, 1989, 2003, 2005; Chuang, 2002; Mathes, King, Miller, & Reed, 2002; Rossano, 2003). According to this *sexual strategies theory* (SST), men have a greater interest in sex and multiple partners. Men are also more sexually jealous and controlling because these behaviors maximize their chances for reproduction. Women, on the other hand, seek a good protector and provider to increase their chances for survival, as well as that of their offspring. These male and female sexual strategies reportedly serve to pass along their respective genes and ensure the survival of the species.

Can you see how this particular interpretation of the evolutionary perspective suggests that only men have a biological advantage in having multiple sex partners? Keep in mind, however, that in at least 18 societies around the world it is *female nonmonogamy* (women having multiple sex partners) that offers survival value to women and children (Beckerman et al., 1999). People in these cultures believe in *partible paternity* (one child having more than one biological father). And pregnant women openly acknowledge their extramarital lovers as "secondary fathers."

This belief that multiple men contribute to the initial impregnation and later "building of the child" seems to benefit both the pregnant woman and her children. Among the Bari of Venezuela and Colombia, Beckerman and his colleagues found that pregnant women with lovers were less likely to miscarry, possibly because of courtship gifts that boosted their nutrition. In addition, 80 percent of children with "extra" fathers lived to age 15, in contrast to 64 percent of children with lone dads.

The *social role approach* offers an important alternative to the evolutionary perspective and its biological emphasis. This perspective suggests that gender differences in sexual behavior result from the roles that men and women internalize from their society (Eagly, 1997; Megarry, 2001). For instance, in traditional cultural divisions of labor, women are childbearers and homemakers. Men are providers and protectors. But as women gain more reproductive freedom and educational opportunities, they also acquire more personal resources and status through means other than mates.

This hypothesis is directly supported by a reanalysis of Buss's original data collected from 37 cultures (Buss et al., 1990). Kasser and Sharma (1999) found that women did indeed prefer resource-rich men. But this only occurred when the women lived in cultures with little reproductive freedom and educational equality. Therefore, say Kasser and Sharma, the conflict between the evolutionary and social role perspectives may be resolved by examining patriarchal cultural systems that limit women's choices.

If strong patriarchies existed during the Pleistocene epoch, enough time may have passed for psychological mechanisms to evolve in reaction to such environments. If, however, patriarchy emerged only in the past 10,000 years, with the advent of agriculture (Miller & Fishkin, 1997), the time span is too short for evolutionary changes, and the social role approach may be the best explanation.

Sexual Orientation: Contrasting Theories and Myths

What causes homosexuality? What causes heterosexuality? Many have asked the first question, but few have asked the second. As a result, the roots of sexual orientation are poorly understood. However, research has identified several widespread myths and misconceptions about homosexuality (Drescher, 2003; Fone, 2000; Lamberg, 1998; LeVay, 2003; Mitchell, 2002). Keep in mind that each of the following popular "theories" is *false*!

- *Seduction theory.* Gays and lesbians were seduced as children by adults of their own sex.

- *"By default" myth.* Gays and lesbians were unable to attract partners of the other sex or have experienced unhappy heterosexual experiences.

- *Poor parenting theory.* Sons become gay because of domineering mothers and weak fathers. Daughters become lesbians because of weak or absent mothers and having only fathers as their primary role model.

- *Modeling theory.* Children raised by gay and lesbian parents usually end up adopting their parents' sexual orientation.

The precise cause or causes of sexual orientation are still unknown. However, most scientists believe genetics and biology play the dominant role (Bailey, Dunne, & Martin, 2000; Cantor, Blanchard, Paterson, & Bogaert, 2002; Hamer & Copeland, 1999; Rahman & Wilson, 2003). For example, a genetic predisposition toward homosexuality is supported by studies on identical male and female twins, fraternal twins, and adopted siblings (Kirk, Bailey, Dunne, & Martin, 2000; Lynch, 2003). These studies found that if one identical twin was gay, about 48 to 65 percent of the time so was the second twin. (Note that if the cause were totally genetic, the percentage would be 100.) The rate for fraternal twins was 26 to 30 percent and 6 to 11 percent for adopted brothers or sisters. Estimates of homosexuality in the general population run between 2 and 10 percent.

Some researchers have also hypothesized that prenatal hormone levels affect fetal brain development and sexual orientation. Animal experiments have found that administering male hormones prenatally can cause female offspring of sheep and rats to engage in the mounting behavior associated with male sheep and rats (Bagermihl, 1999). It is obviously unethical to experiment with human fetuses. Therefore, we cannot come to any meaningful conclusions about the effect of hormones on fetal development. Furthermore, no well-controlled study has ever found a difference in adult hormone levels between heterosexuals and gays and lesbians (Banks & Gartrell, 1995; LeVay, 2003).

The origin of sexual orientation remains a mystery. However, we do know that gays and lesbians are often victimized by society's prejudice against them. Research shows that many suffer verbal and physical attacks; disrupted family and peer relationships; and high rates of anxiety, depression, and suicide (Jellison, McConnell, & Gabriel, 2004; Meyer, 2003; Mills et al., 2004; Rosenberg, 2003).

Some of this prejudice supposedly stems from an irrational fear of homosexuality in oneself or others, which Martin Weinberg labeled *homophobia* in the late 1960s. Today, some researchers believe this term is too limited and scientifically unacceptable. It implies that antigay attitudes are limited to individual irrationality and pathology. Therefore, psychologist Gregory Herek (2000) prefers the term **sexual prejudice**, which emphasizes multiple causes and allows scientists to draw on the rich scientific research on prejudice.

In 1973 both the American Psychiatric Association and the American Psychological Association officially acknowledged that homosexuality is not a mental illness. However, it continues to be a divisive societal issue in the United States. Seeing *sexual prejudice* as a socially reinforced phenomenon rather than an individual pathology, coupled with political action by gays and lesbians, may help fight discrimination and hate crimes.

Evan Agostini/Liaison Agency, Inc./Getty Images

Sexual prejudice and hate crimes. *The vicious beating and murder of Matthew Shepard in 1998 is a tragic reminder of the costs of sexual prejudice.*

Sexual Prejudice *Negative attitudes toward an individual because of her or his sexual orientation*

Alison Wright/PhotoResearchers

Fighting back against sexual prejudice. *These protesters are working to increase public awareness and acceptance of different sexual orientations.*

Assessment

CHECK & REVIEW

Sexual Behavior

William Masters and Virginia Johnson identified a four-stage **sexual response cycle** during sexual activity—the **excitement, plateau, orgasm,** and **resolution phases.** There are numerous similarities and differences between the sexes, but differences are the focus of most research. According to the evolutionary perspective, men engage in more sexual behaviors with more sexual partners because it helps the species survive. The social role approach suggests this difference results from traditional cultural divisions of labor.

Although researchers have identified several myths concerning the causes of homosexuality, the origins remain a puzzle. In recent studies, the genetic and biological explanation has gained the strongest support. Despite increased understanding, sexual orientation remains a divisive issue in the United States.

Questions

1. Briefly describe Masters and Johnson's sexual response cycle.
2. How do the evolutionary and social role perspectives explain male and female differences in sexual behavior?
3. The genetic influence on sexual orientation has been supported by research reporting that _____. (a) between identical twins, if one brother is gay, the other brother has a 52 percent chance of also being gay; (b) gay men have fewer chromosomal pairs than straight men, whereas lesbians have larger areas of the hypothalamus than straight women; (c) between adoptive pairs of brothers, if one brother is gay, the other brother has an increased chance of also being gay; (d) parenting style influences adult sexual orientation for men but not for women
4. A homosexual orientation appears to be the result of _____. (a) seduction during childhood or adolescence by an older homosexual; (b) a family background that includes a dominant mother and a passive, detached; father; (c) a hormonal imbalance; (d) unknown factors

Check your answers in Appendix B.

 CLICK & REVIEW
for additional assessment options:
www.wiley.com/college/huffman

SEXUAL PROBLEMS

When we are functioning well sexually, we tend to take this part of our lives for granted. But what happens when things don't go smoothly? Why does normal sexual functioning stop for some people and never begin for others? What are the major diseases that can be spread through sexual behavior? We will explore these questions in the following section.

Sexual Dysfunction: The Biopsychosocial Model

There are many forms of **sexual dysfunction**, or difficulty in sexual functioning. And their causes are complex (Figure 11.6). In this section, we will discuss how biology, psychology, and social forces (the *biopsychosocial model*) all contribute to sexual difficulties.

Biological Factors

Although many people may consider it unromantic, a large part of sexual arousal and behavior is clearly the result of biological processes (Coolen et al., 2004; Hiller, 2004; Hyde & DeLamater, 2006). *Erectile dysfunction* (the inability to get or maintain an erection firm enough for intercourse) and *orgasmic dysfunction* (the inability to respond to sexual stimulation to the point of orgasm) often reflect lifestyle factors like cigarette smoking. They also involve medical conditions such as diabetes, alcoholism, hormonal deficiencies, circulatory problems, and reactions to certain prescription and nonprescription drugs. In addition, hormones (especially testosterone) have a clear effect on sexual desire in both men and women. But otherwise, the precise role of hormones in human sexual behavior is not well understood.

In addition to problems resulting from medical conditions and hormones, sexual responsiveness is also affected by the spinal cord and sympathetic nervous system

Achievement

What factors contribute to sexual dysfunction and sexually transmitted infections?

Sexual Dysfunction *Impairment of the normal physiological processes of arousal and orgasm*

Male ♂		Female ♀		Both Male ♂ and Female ♀	
Disorder	**Causes**	**Disorder**	**Causes**	**Disorder**	**Causes**
Erectile dysfunction (impotence) Inability to have (or maintain) an erection firm enough for intercourse *Primary erectile dysfunction* Lifetime erectile problems *Secondary erectile dysfunction* Erection problems occurring in at least 25 percent of sexual encounters	**Physical** — diabetes, circulatory conditions, heart disease, drugs, extreme fatigue, alcohol consumption, hormone deficiencies **Psychological** — performance anxiety, guilt, difficulty in expressing desires to partner, severe antisexual upbringing	**Orgasmic dysfunction** (anorgasmia, frigidity) Inability or difficulty in reaching orgasm *Primary orgasmic dysfunction* Lifetime history of no orgasm *Secondary orgasmic dysfunction* Regularly orgasmic, but no longer is *Situational orgasmic dysfunction* Orgasms occur only under certain circumstances	**Physical** — chronic illness, diabetes, extreme fatigue, drugs, alcohol consumption, hormone deficiencies, pelvic disorders, lack of appropriate or adequate stimulation **Psychological** — fear of evaluation, poor body image, relationship problems, guilt, anxiety, severe antisexual upbringing, difficulty in expressing desires to partner, prior sexual trauma, childhood sexual abuse	**Dyspareunia** Painful intercourse	**Primarily physical** — irritations, infections, or disorders of the internal or external genitals
				Inhibited sexual desire (sexual apathy) Avoids sexual relations due to disinterest	**Physical** — hormone deficiencies, alcoholism, drug use, chronic illness **Psychological** — depression, prior sexual trauma, relationship problems, anxiety
Premature ejaculation Rapid ejaculation beyond the man's control; partner is non-orgasmic in at least 50 percent of their intercourse episodes	**Almost always psychological** — because of guilt, fear of discovery while masturbating, and hurried experiences in cars or motels, man learns to ejaculate as quickly as possible	**Vaginismus** Involuntary spasms of the vagina and penile insertion is impossible or difficult and painful	**Primarily psychological** — learned association of pain or fear with intercourse, due to prior sexual trauma, severe antisexual upbringing, guilt, or lack of lubrication	**Sexual aversion** Avoids sex due to overwhelming fear or anxiety	**Psychological** — severe parental sex attitudes, prior sex trauma, partner pressure, gender identity confusion

Figure 11.6 *Major male and female sexual dysfunctions.* Although sex therapists typically divide sexual dysfunctions into "male," "female," or "both," problems should never be considered "his" or "hers." Couples are almost always encouraged to work together to find solutions. For more information, check www.goaskalice.columbia.edu/Cat6.html. *Sources:* Adapted from Crooks & Baur, 2005; Masters et al., 1995; Miracle, Miracle, & Baumeister, 2006.

(Coolen et al., 2004). The human brain is certainly involved in all parts of the sexual response cycle. However, certain key sexual behaviors do not require an intact cerebral cortex to operate. In fact, some patients in comas still experience orgasms (Halaris, 2003).

How is this possible? Recall from Chapter 2 that some aspects of human behavior are reflexive. They are unlearned, automatic, and occur without conscious effort or motivation. Sexual arousal for both men and women is partially reflexive and somewhat analogous to simple reflexes like the eye-blink response to a puff of air. For example, a puff of air produces an automatic closing of the eye. Similarly, certain stimuli, such as stroking of the genitals, can lead to automatic arousal in both men and women. In both situations, nerve impulses from the receptor site travel to the spinal cord. The spinal cord then responds by sending messages to target organs or glands. Normally the blood flow into organs and tissues through the arteries is balanced by an equal outflow through the veins. During sexual arousal, however, the arteries dilate beyond the capacity of the veins to carry the blood away. This results in erection of the penis in men and an engorged clitoris and surrounding tissue in women.

If this is so automatic, why do some people have difficulty getting aroused? Unlike simple reflexes such as the eye blink, negative thoughts or high emotional states may block sexual arousal. Recall from Chapter 2 that the autonomic nervous system (ANS) is intricately involved in emotional (and sexual) responses. The ANS is composed of two subsystems: the sympathetic, which prepares the body for "fight or flight," and the parasympathetic, which maintains bodily processes at a steady, even balance. The sympathetic branch is dominant during initial sexual excitement. However, sustained arousal (the plateau phase) requires parasympathetic dominance. The sympathetic branch dominates during ejaculation and orgasm.

Can you see why the parasympathetic branch *must* be in control during arousal? The body needs to be relaxed enough to allow blood to flow to the genital area. This helps explain why young women in our culture often have difficulty with sexual arousal and orgasm. The secretive and forbidden conditions of many early sexual experiences create strong anxieties and fear of discovery, fear of loss of respect, and fear of unwanted pregnancy. Many women later discover that they need locked doors, committed relationships, and reliable birth control to enjoy sexual relations.

What about men? Most men also prefer privacy, commitment, and freedom from pregnancy concerns. But as you can see in Table 11.3, relationship status has less of an effect on male orgasms than it does on female orgasms. Apparently, women relax more under these conditions, which allows them to stay in arousal and parasympathetic dominance long enough for orgasm to occur.

Most couples also recognize that both sexes have difficulty with arousal if they drink too much alcohol or when they are stressed, ill, or fatigued. But one of the least recognized blocks of sexual arousal is **performance anxiety**, the fear of being judged in connection with sexual activity. Men commonly experience problems with erections (especially after drinking alcohol) and wonder if their "performance" will satisfy their partner. At the same time, women frequently worry about their attractiveness and orgasms. Can you see how these performance fears can lead to sexual problems? Once again, increased anxiety causes the sympathetic nervous system to dominate, which blocks blood flow to the genitals.

TABLE 11.3 SEX AND RELATIONSHIPS

Men ♂	Women ♀	Always or Usually Have an Orgasm with Partner
94%	62%	Dating
95%	68%	Living together
95%	75%	Married

Source: Laumann, Gagnon, Michael, & Michaels, 1994.

Performance Anxiety *Fear of being judged in connection with sexual activity*

Double Standard *Beliefs, values, and norms that subtly encourage male sexuality and discourage female sexuality*

Psychological and Social Influences

Our bodies may be biologically prepared to become aroused and respond to erotic stimulation. But psychological and social forces also play a role (Mah & Binik, 2005). As we have just seen, fear of evaluation, or of the consequences of sexual activity, are learned, psychological factors that contribute to both male and female sexual dysfunction. *Gender role training*, the *double standard*, and *sexual scripts* are also important social influences.

Gender role training begins at birth and continually impacts all aspects of our life, as the story of "Brenda/David" from the beginning of this chapter shows. Can you imagine how traditional male gender roles—being dominant, aggressive, independent—could lead to different kinds of sexual thoughts and behaviors than traditional female gender roles—being submissive, passive, and dependent? Can you also imagine how this type of gender role training may lead to a **double standard**? Men are encouraged to explore their sexuality and bring a certain level of sexual knowledge into the relationship. Conversely, women are expected to stop male advances and refrain from sexual activity until marriage.

Although overt examples of this *double standard* are less evident in modern times, covert or hidden traces of this belief still exist. Look again at the gender differences in Figure 11.7. Can you see how items like men wanting women to "initiate sex more often" or women wanting men "to talk more lovingly" might be remnants of the double standard?

"Now, that's product placement!"

Dating Couples

Men Wish Their Partners Would:	Women Wish Their Partners Would:
Be more experimental	Talk more lovingly
Initiate sex more often	Be more seductive
Try more oral-genital sex	Be warmer and more involved
Give more instructions	Give more instructions
Be warmer and more involved	Be more complimentary

Married Couples

Men Wish Their Partners Would:	Women Wish Their Partners Would:
Be more seductive	Talk more lovingly
Initiate sex more often	Be more seductive
Be more experimental	Be more complimentary
Be wilder and sexier	Give more instructions
Give more instructions	Be warmer and more involved

Figure 11.7 *What do men and women want?* When asked what they wish they had more of in their sexual relationships, men tended to emphasize activities, whereas women focused more on emotions and the relationship. *Source:* Based on Hatfield & Rapson, 1996, p. 142.

Sexual Scripts *Socially dictated descriptions of "appropriate" behaviors for sexual interactions*

In addition to gender role training and the related double standard, we also learn explicit **sexual scripts** that teach us "what to do, when, where, how, and with whom" (Gagnon, 1990). During the 1950s, societal messages said the "best" sex was at night, in a darkened room, with a man on top and a woman on the bottom. Today, the messages are more bold and varied, partly because of media portrayals. Compare, for example, the sexual scripts portrayed in Figure 11.8.

Figure 11.8 *Changing sexual scripts.* (a) Television and movies in the 1950s and 1960s allowed only married couples to be shown in a bedroom setting (and only in long pajamas and separate twin-size beds). (b) Contrast this with modern times, where very young, unmarried couples are commonly portrayed in one bed, seemingly nude, and engaging in various stages of intercourse. (c, d) Also, note the change in body postures and clothing in these beach scenes from the 1960s and today.

Rob McEwan/EverettCollection, Inc.

Sexual scripts, gender roles, and the double standard may all be less rigid today, but a major difficulty remains. Many people and sexual behaviors do not fit society's scripts and expectations. Furthermore, we often "unconsciously" internalize societal messages. But we seldom realize how they affect our values and behaviors. For example, modern men and women generally say they want equality. Yet both sexes may feel more comfortable if the woman is a virgin and the man has had many partners. Sex therapy encourages partners to examine and sometimes modify inappropriate sexual scripts, gender roles, and beliefs in the double standard.

How do therapists work with sex problems? Clinicians usually begin with interviews and examinations to determine whether the problem is organic, psychological, or, more likely, a combination of both (Black, 2005; McCarthy, 2002). Organic causes of sexual dysfunction include medical conditions (such as diabetes mellitus and heart disease), medications (such as antidepressants), and drugs (such as alcohol and tobacco—see Table 11.4). Erectile disorders are the problems most likely to have an organic component. In 1998, a medical treatment for erectile problems, *Viagra*, quickly became the fastest-selling prescription drug in U.S. history. Other medications for both men and women are currently being tested—but they are not the answer to all sexual problems.

Years ago, the major psychological treatment for sexual dysfunction was long-term psychoanalysis. This treatment was based on the assumption that sexual problems resulted from *deep-seated conflicts* that originated in childhood. During the 1950s and 1960s, behavior therapy was introduced. It was based on the idea that sexual dysfunction was *learned*. (See Chapter 14 for a more complete description of both psychoanalysis and behavior therapy.) It wasn't until the early 1970s and the publication of Masters and Johnson's *Human Sexual Inadequacy* that sex therapy gained national recognition. Because the model that Masters and Johnson developed is still popular and used by many sex therapists, we will use it as our example of how sex therapy is conducted.

Masters and Johnson's Sex Therapy Program

Masters and Johnson's approach is founded on four major principles:

1. ***A relationship focus.*** Unlike forms of therapy that focus on the individual, Masters and Johnson's sex therapy focuses on the relationship between two people. To counteract any blaming tendencies, each partner is considered fully involved and affected by sexual problems. Both partners are taught positive communication and conflict resolution skills.

2. ***An integration of physiological and psychosocial factors.*** Medication and many physical disorders can cause or aggravate sexual dysfunctions. Therefore, Masters

Ira Wyman/Corbis Sygma

Experiments in sex? *William Masters and Virginia Johnson were the first researchers to use direct laboratory experimentation and observation to study human sexuality.*

TABLE 11.4 SEXUAL EFFECTS OF LEGAL AND ILLEGAL DRUGS

Drugs	Effects
Alcohol	Moderate to high doses inhibit arousal. Chronic abuse causes damage to testes, ovaries, and the circulatory and nervous systems.
Tobacco	It decreases blood flow to the genitals, thereby reducing the frequency and duration of erections and vaginal lubrication.
Cocaine and amphetamines	Moderate to high doses and chronic use result in inhibition of orgasm and decrease in erection and lubrication.
Barbiturates	They cause decreased desire, erectile disorders, and delayed orgasm.

Source: Grilly, 2006; Miracle, Miracle, & Baumeister, 2006; Tengs & Osgood, 2001.

If you would like to improve your own, or your children's current or future sexual functioning, sex therapists would recommend:

- *Beginning sex education as early as possible.* Children should be given positive feelings about their bodies and an opportunity to discuss sexuality in an open, honest fashion.
- *Avoiding goal- or performance-oriented approaches.* Therapists often remind clients that there really is no "right" way to have sex. When couples or individuals attempt to judge or evaluate their sexual

lives or to live up to others' expectations, they risk making sex a job rather than pleasure.

- *Communicating openly with your partner.* Mind reading belongs onstage, not in the bedroom. Partners need to tell each other what feels good and what doesn't. Sexual problems should be openly discussed without blame, anger, or defensiveness. If the problem does not improve within a reasonable time, consider professional help.

and Johnson emphasize the importance of medical histories and exams. They also explore psychosocial factors, such as how the couple first learned about sex and their current attitudes, gender role training, and sexual scripts.

3. ***An emphasis on cognitive factors.*** Recognizing that many problems result from fears of performance and *spectatoring* (mentally watching and evaluating responses during sexual activities), couples are discouraged from setting goals and judging sex in terms of success or failure.

4. ***An emphasis on specific behavioral techniques.*** Couples are seen in an intensive two-week counseling program. They explore their sexual values and misconceptions and practice specific behavioral exercises. "Homework assignments" usually begin with a *sensate focus* exercise in which each partner takes turns gently caressing the other and communicating what is pleasurable. There are no goals or performance demands. Later exercises and assignments are tailored to the couple's particular sex problem.

Application

RESEARCH HIGHLIGHT

Is Cybersex Harmful?

Lisa, a 42-year-old student, says:

We bought my son a new, powerful computer, and he showed me how to go online to get into chat rooms. I started to log on just to visit and chat. But I soon found my way to chat rooms, where the primary purpose was to discuss sexual fantasies. It was quite a turn-on. I was getting into these intimate discussions with

all kinds of men. We talked about our sex lives and what we liked to do in bed. Then it got personal—what we'd like to do to each other. I never wanted to meet these guys face-to-face, but I started to feel like I was still having sex with them.

It all came to a head when my husband saw one of the Internet bills and freaked—it was over $500 for the month. I had to explain the whole thing to him. He felt like I had cheated on him and considered sep-

aration. It took several weeks to restore his trust and convince him I still loved him. I have moved the computer into my son's room, and we've started seeing a family therapist. (Personal communication cited in Blonna & Levitan, 2000, p. 584).

The Internet is a great technological innovation. At school, work, and home, our computers help us work or study online, gather valuable information, or even recreationally "surf the Net." But, for some, the Internet can also be harmful (Bowker & Gray, 2004; McGrath & Casey, 2002; Roller, 2004). A survey among 18- to 64-year-old self-identified cybersex participants found several problems associated with their online sexual activities (Schneider, 2000). For example, two women with no prior history of interest in sado-masochistic sex discovered this type of behavior online and came to prefer it. Others in the survey reported increased problems with depression, social isolation, career loss or decreased job performance, financial consequences, and, in some cases, legal difficulties.

Like Lisa, some Internet users also use cyberspace chat rooms and e-mail as a way to secretly communicate with an intimate other or as outlets for sexual desires they're unwilling to expose or discuss with their partners. Although these secret liaisons may be exciting, sex therapists are finding that this behavior often leads to a worsening of the participants' relationships with spouses or partners and serious harm to their marriages or primary relationships. "Cybercheating," like

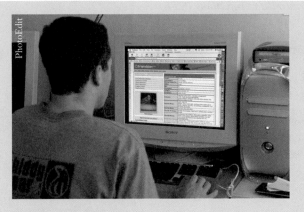

traditional infidelity or adultery, erodes trust and connection with the spouse or partner. The ongoing secrecy, lying, and fantasies also increase attraction to the "virtual" relationship.

What do you think? Does sex require physical contact to count as an "affair"? If you only exchange sexual fantasies with someone on the Internet, are you unfaithful? Is visiting sex sites harmful? When I ask this question in my college classes, some students consider it very harmful and eagerly talk about resulting relationship problems. In contrast, others think of

it as nothing more than an X-rated movie. They appear surprised that anyone would call it "cheating." I encourage them (and you) to openly discuss with their partners what each considers unacceptable in their relationships—both online and in everyday interactions.

Before going on, I also want to mention that many people have developed healthy, lasting relationships through the Internet. They report that these relationships are just as intimate (or even more so) than face-to-face ones. Others suggest that cyberconnecting can be a good rehearsal for the "real" thing. Even some sex therapists see a positive use for the Internet. They find its anonymity allows open, frank, and explicit discussions about sex, which are vital components to successful therapy. As you will see in Chapter 15, online sex therapy is part of the growing field of mental health therapy, called telehealth.

Sexually Transmitted Infections: The Special Problem of AIDS

Early sex education and open communication between partners are vitally important for full sexual functioning. They are also key to avoiding and controlling sexually transmitted infections (STIs), formerly called sexually transmitted diseases (STDs), venereal disease (VD), or social diseases. *STI* is the term used to describe the disorders caused by more than 25 infectious organisms transmitted through sexual activity.

Each year, of the millions of North Americans who contract one or more STIs, a substantial majority are under age 35 (Hopkins, Tanner & Raymond, 2004; Ross, 2002; Weinstock et al., 2004). Also, as Figure 11.9 shows, women are at much

Figure 11.9 *Male–female differences in susceptibility to sexually transmitted infections (STIs).* These percentages represent the chances of infection for men and women after a single act of intercourse with an infected partner. Note that women are at much greater risk than men for four of these six STIs. This is partly because female genitals are more internal.

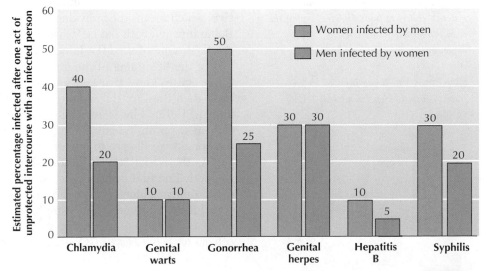

www.wiley.com/college/huffman

Figure 11.10 *Common sexually transmitted infections (STIs).* Note that you may have an STI without any of the danger signs but still acquire the complications. Seek medical attention if you suspect that you have come in contact with any of the infections! Follow all medical recommendations. This may include returning for a checkup to make sure that you are no longer infected. Take only medications prescribed by your doctor, and take all of them as directed. Don't share them. If you would like more information, check www.niaid.nih.gov/factsheets/stdinfo.htm. For information on protection from STIs, try www.safesex.org. *Sources:* Adapted from Crooks & Baur, 2005; Miracle, Miracle, & Baumeister, 2006.

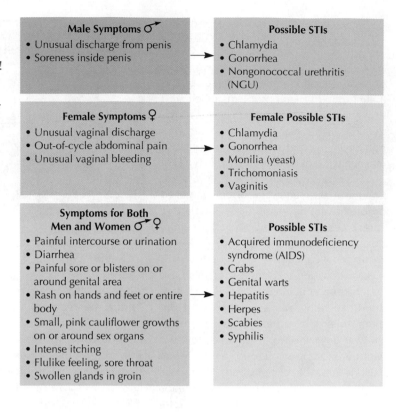

Male Symptoms ♂
- Unusual discharge from penis
- Soreness inside penis

Possible STIs
- Chlamydia
- Gonorrhea
- Nongonococcal urethritis (NGU)

Female Symptoms ♀
- Unusual vaginal discharge
- Out-of-cycle abdominal pain
- Unusual vaginal bleeding

Female Possible STIs
- Chlamydia
- Gonorrhea
- Monilia (yeast)
- Trichomoniasis
- Vaginitis

Symptoms for Both Men and Women ♂ ♀
- Painful intercourse or urination
- Diarrhea
- Painful sore or blisters on or around genital area
- Rash on hands and feet or entire body
- Small, pink cauliflower growths on or around sex organs
- Intense itching
- Flulike feeling, sore throat
- Swollen glands in groin

Possible STIs
- Acquired immunodeficiency syndrome (AIDS)
- Crabs
- Genital warts
- Hepatitis
- Herpes
- Scabies
- Syphilis

greater risk than men of contracting major STIs. It is extremely important for sexually active people to get medical diagnosis and treatment for any suspicious symptoms and to inform their partners. If left untreated, many STIs can cause severe problems, including infertility, ectopic pregnancy, cancer, and even death.

The good news is that most STIs are readily cured in their early stages. See Figure 11.10 for an overview of the signs and symptoms of the most common STIs. As you read through this table, remember that many infected people are *asymptomatic*, meaning lacking obvious symptoms. You can have one or more of the diseases without knowing it. And it is often impossible to tell if a sexual partner is infectious.

STIs such as genital warts and chlamydial infections have reached epidemic proportions. Yet, **AIDS (acquired immunodeficiency syndrome)** has received the largest share of public attention. AIDS results from infection with the *human immunodeficiency virus (HIV)*. A standard blood test can determine if someone is **HIV-positive**, which means the individual has been infected by one or more of the HIV viruses. Being infected with the HIV virus, however, is not the same as having AIDS. AIDS is the final stage of the HIV infection process.

In the beginning of the infection process, the HIV virus multiplies rapidly. It is important to know that newly infected individuals are 100 to 1000 times more infectious than they are throughout the remainder of the disease (Royce, Sena, Cates, & Cohen, 1997). This is especially troubling because most infected people are likely to remain symptom free for months or even years. Unfortunately, during this time, they can spread the disease to others—primarily through sexual contact.

As the initial HIV infection advances to AIDS, the virus progressively destroys the body's natural defenses against disease and infection. The victim's body becomes increasingly vulnerable to opportunistic infections and cancers that would not be a threat if the immune system were functioning normally. The virus may also attack the brain and spinal cord, creating severe neurological and cognitive deterioration. The official term *full-blown AIDS* includes anyone infected with HIV who also has a CD4

AIDS (Acquired Immunodeficiency Syndrome) *Human immunodeficiency viruses (HIVs) destroy the immune system's ability to fight disease, leaving the body vulnerable to a variety of opportunistic infections and cancers*

HIV Positive *Being infected by the human immunodeficiency virus (HIV)*

count of 200 cells per cubic millimeter of blood or less. (The HIV virus destroys CD4 lymphocytes, also called T-cells, which coordinate the immune system's response to disease.)

AIDS is considered one of the most catastrophic diseases of our time. An estimated 34 million people worldwide are infected with HIV (CDC, 2005). Recent advances in the treatment of AIDS have increased the survival time of victims. But for almost everyone, AIDS remains an ultimately fatal disorder, and some researchers doubt that a 100 percent effective vaccine will ever be developed. Despite the severity of this disease, there are signs of public complacency due to the false notion that drugs can now cure AIDS and to a reduced emphasis on prevention and education.

Reflecting cutbacks in sex education, AIDS myths are widespread. For instance, many people still believe AIDS can be transmitted through casual contact, such as sneezing, shaking hands, sharing drinking glasses or towels, social kissing, sweat, or tears. Some also think it is dangerous to donate blood. Sadly, others are paranoid about gays, because male homosexuals were the first highly visible victims. All of these are false beliefs.

Infection by HIV spreads only by direct contact with bodily fluids—primarily blood, semen, and vaginal secretions. Blood *donors* are at *no* risk whatsoever. Furthermore, AIDS is not limited to the homosexual community. In fact, the AIDS epidemic is now spreading most quickly among heterosexuals, women, African Americans, Hispanics, and children (CDC, 2005).

Application

APPLYING PSYCHOLOGY TO RELATIONSHIPS

Protecting Yourself and Others Against STIs

The best hope for curtailing the HIV/AIDS epidemic is through education and behavioral change. The following "safer sex" suggestions are not intended to be moralistic—but only to help reduce your chances of contracting both HIV/AIDS and other STIs.

1. *Remain abstinent or have sex with one mutually faithful, uninfected partner.* Be selective about sexual partners and postpone physical intimacy until laboratory tests verify that you are both free of STIs.

2. *Do not use intravenous illicit drugs or have sex with someone who does.* If you use intravenous drugs, do not share needles or syringes. If you must share, use bleach to clean and sterilize your needles and syringes.

3. *Avoid contact with blood, vaginal secretions, or semen.* Using latex condoms is the best way to avoid contact. (Until recently, scientists believed condoms and spermicides with nonoxynol-9 would help prevent spread of STIs. Unfortunately, recent research shows nonoxynol-9 may increase the risk, and the World Health Organization no longer recommends its use [WHO, 2002].)

4. *Avoid anal intercourse, with or without a condom.* This is the riskiest of all sexual behaviors.

5. *Do not have sex if you or your partner are impaired by alcohol or other drugs.* The same is true for your friends. "Friends don't let friends drive (or have sex) drunk."

Application

CRITICAL THINKING   ACTIVE LEARNING

Rape Myths and Rape Prevention

Sexuality can be a source of vitality and tender bonding. But it can also be traumatizing if it becomes a forcible act against the wishes of the other. Rape can be defined as oral, anal, or vaginal penetration forced on an unwilling, underage, or unconscious victim. As clear-cut as this definition seems, many people misunderstand what constitutes rape. To test your own knowledge, answer true or false to the following:

1. Women cannot be raped against their will.
2. A man cannot be raped by a woman.
3. If you are going to be raped, you might as well relax and enjoy it.
4. All women secretly want to be raped.
5. Male sexuality is biologically overpowering and beyond a man's control.

As you might have expected, all of these statements are false. Tragically, however, rape myths are believed by a large number of men and women (Carr & Van Deusen, 2004; Finch & Munro, 2005; Lee et al., 2005; Peterson & Muehlenhard, 2004). Using your critical thinking skills, can you explain how each of the following factors might contribute to rape myths?

- Gender role conditioning
- The double standard
- Media portrayals
- Lack of information

If you would like to compare your answers to ours or would like specific information regarding rape prevention, see Appendix B.

Assessment

CHECK & REVIEW

Sexual Problems

Many people experience **sexual dysfunction.** They often fail to recognize the role of biology in both sexual arousal and response. Ejaculation and orgasm are partially reflexive. The parasympathetic nervous system must be dominant for sexual arousal. The sympathetic nervous system must dominate for orgasm to occur. Several aspects of sexual arousal and response are also learned. Early gender role training, the **double standard,** and **sexual scripts** teach us what to consider the "best" sex.

Many sexual problems can be helped with sex therapy. William Masters and Virginia Johnson emphasize the couple's relationship, combined physiological and psychosocial factors, cognitions, and spe-cific behavioral techniques. Professional sex therapists offer important guidelines for everyone: Sex education should be early and positive, a goal or performance orientation should be avoided, and communication should be kept open.

The most publicized sexually transmitted infection (STI) is **AIDS (acquired immunodeficiency syndrome).** Although AIDS is transmitted only through sexual contact or exposure to infected bodily fluids, many people have irrational fears of contagion. At the same time, an increasing number of North Americans are **HIV-positive** and therefore carriers.

Questions

1. Briefly explain the roles of the sympathetic and parasympathetic nervous systems in sexual response.

2. Sexual learning that includes "what to do, when, where, how, and with whom" is known as _____. (a) appropriate sexual behavior; (b) sexual norms; (c) sexual scripts; (d) sexual gender roles
3. What are the four principles of Masters and Johnson's sex therapy program?
4. What are five "safer sex" ways to reduce the chances of AIDS and other STIs?

Check your answers in Appendix B.

 CLICK & REVIEW
for additional assessment options:
www.wiley.com/college/huffman

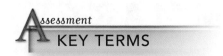

Assessment
KEY TERMS

*To assess your understanding of the **Key Terms** in Chapter 11, write a definition for each (in your own words), and then compare your definitions with those in the text.*

Sex and Gender
androgyny [an-DRAW-jah-nee]
  (p. 397)
gender (p. 392)
gender identity (p. 392)
gender role (p. 393)
sex (p. 392)
sexual orientation (p. 393)

Sexual Behavior
excitement phase (p. 404)
orgasm phase (p. 404)
plateau phase (p. 404)
refractory period (p. 404)
resolution phase (p. 404)
sexual prejudice (p. 406)
sexual response cycle (p. 403)

Sexual Problems
AIDS (acquired immunodeficiency
  syndrome) (p. 414)
double standard (p. 409)
HIV-positive (p. 414)
performance anxiety (p. 409)
sexual dysfunction (p. 407)
sexual scripts (p. 410)

Achievement
WEB RESOURCES

Huffman Book Companion Site
http://www.wiley.com/college/huffman
  This site is loaded with free Interactive Self-Tests, Internet Exercises, Glossary and Flashcards for key terms, web links, Handbook for Non-Native Speakers, and other activities designed to improve your mastery of the material in this chapter.

Want more general information about the field of human sexuality?
http://www.sexscience.org/
  The Society for the Scientific Study of Sexuality is an international organization dedicated to the advancement of knowledge about sexuality.
  In addition, http://www.indiana.edu/%7Ekinsey/, the Kinsey Institute for research in sex, gender, and reproduction, is designed to promote interdisciplinary research and assistance with an array of topics related to gender and sexuality. Another excellent website, http://www.siecus.org/, is maintained by the Sexuality Information and Education Council of the U.S. (SIECUS), a national, nonprofit organization that develops, collects, and disseminates information; promotes comprehensive education about sexuality; and advocates the right of individuals to make responsible sexual choices.

Do you have specific sex questions not answered in this chapter?
http://www.goaskalice.columbia.edu/
  Go Ask Alice! is the health question-and-answer Internet service produced by Columbia University Health Service. "Alice"

answers questions about relationships, sexuality, sexual health, nutrition, alcohol, and general health. The stated mission of this site is to increase access to "health information by providing factual, in-depth, straightforward, and nonjudgmental information to assist readers' decision-making about their physical, sexual, emotional, and spiritual health."

Need specific information about STIs?
http://www.cdc.gov/std
  This site offers frank, accurate details and practical information to prevent and treat STIs.

Would you like more information on gender roles and androgyny?
http://www.utdallas.edu/~waligore/digital/garvey.html
  Loosely based on the Bem Sex Role Inventory discussed in this chapter, this site features a humorous web project, entitled "Genderbender," which offers a self-administered questionnaire with scales to measure masculinity and femininity.

Visual Summary

Sex and Gender

Definitions

Sex: Biological dimensions of maleness or femaleness, and physical activities (such as intercourse).
Gender: Psychological and sociocultural meanings of maleness and femaleness.

Gender Role Development

Gender role: Social expectations for appropriate male and female behavior.
Two major theories:

Social learning (reward, punishment, and imitation).

Cognitive Developmental (active thinking processes).

Sex and Gender Differences

Sex differences: Physical differences (like height) and brain differences (function and structure).
Gender differences: Females tend to score somewhat higher in verbal skills. Males score somewhat higher in math and are more physically aggressive.
Androgyny: Combination of masculine and feminine personality traits.

Bill Gallery/Stock, Boston

Bob Daemmrich/The Image Works

Study of Human Sexuality

Havelock Ellis

Based his research on personal diaries.

Kinsey & Colleagues

Popularized the use of surveys and interviews.

Masters & Johnson

Used direct observation and measurement of human sexual response.

Cultural Studies

Provide insight into universalities and variations in sexual behavior across cultures.

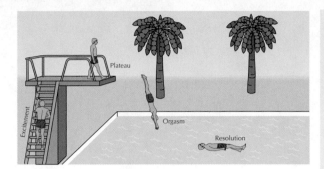

Sexual Arousal and Response

Masters and Johnson's **sexual response cycle: excitement, plateau, orgasm,** and **resolution**. There are numerous similarities of the sexes in this cycle, but differences are the focus of most research. According to the *evolutionary perspective*, males engage in more sexual behaviors with more sexual partneers because it helps the species survive, The *social role approach* suggests this difference results from traditional cultural divisions of labor.

Sexual Orientation

Two major theories

False theories: Seduction, "by default," poor parenting, and modeling.

Supported theories: Genetic/ biological contributors (genetic predisposition, prenatal biasing of the brain, and hormonal differences).

Sexual Problems

Sexual Dysfunctions

Possible causes:

Biological: Anxiety blocks arousal. Parasympathetic nervous system must dominate for sexual arousal to occur, whereas sympathetic nervous system must dominate for orgasm to happen.

Treatment: Masters and Johnson emphasize couple's relationship, combined physiological and psychosocial factors, cognitions, and specific behavioral techniques.

Psychological:

- Negative gender role training
- Unrealistic **sexual scripts**
- **Double standard** encourages male sexuality but discourages female's
- **Performance anxiety** created from fear of not meeting partner's sex expectations

Sexually Transmitted Infections (STIs)

Most publicized STI is **AIDS**. AIDS is transmitted only through sexual contact or exposure to infected bodily fluids, but irrational fears of contagion persist. An estimated one million in the U.S. are HIV positive and therefore are carriers.

12

MOTIVATION AND EMOTION

Achievement

Core Learning Outcomes

As you read Chapter 12, keep the following questions in mind and answer them in your own words:

▷ What major concepts and theories do I need to know to understand motivation?

▷ What causes hunger and drives us to achieve?

▷ What major theories and concepts do I need to know to understand emotion?

▷ How can I apply critical thinking to motivation and emotion?

▢ Achievement
▢ Assessment
▢ Application

WHY STUDY PSYCHOLOGY?

Alan Schein Photography/CorbisImages

Chapter 12 will explain why or how...

▷ Being too excited or too relaxed can interfere with test performance.

▷ Getting paid for your hobbies may reduce your overall creativity and enjoyment.

▷ Obesity in America has reached epidemic proportions.

▷ Smiling can make you feel happy and frowning can create negative feelings.

▷ Lie detector tests may be fooled by biting your tongue.

▷ People with high emotional intelligence (EI) are often more successful than people with a high intelligence quotient (IQ).

Motivation *Set of factors that activate, direct, and maintain behavior, usually toward a goal*

Emotion *A subjective feeling that includes arousal (heart pounding), cognitions (thoughts, values, and expectations), and expressions (frowns, smiles, and running)*

Why are you in college? What are your goals? How hard will you work to achieve your lifetime dreams? When you receive a grade on an exam, do you feel happy, sad, mad, frustrated? Why? Research in *motivation* and *emotion* attempts to answer such "what" and "why" questions and to explain emotional states such as happiness and sadness. **Motivation** refers to the set of factors that activate, direct, and maintain behavior, usually toward some goal. **Emotion**, on the other hand, refers to a subjective feeling that includes arousal (heart pounding), cognitions (thoughts, values, and expectations), and expressive behaviors (smiles, frowns, and running). In other words, motivation energizes and directs behavior. Emotion is the "feeling" response. (Both *motivation* and *emotion* come from the Latin *movere*, meaning "to move.")

Why do I cover both topics in one chapter? Motivation and emotion are inseparable. If you saw your loved one in the arms of another, you might experience a wide variety of emotions (jealousy, fear, sadness, anger). And your various motives would determine how you would respond in the situation. Your desire for revenge might lead you to search for another partner. Or your need for love and belonging might motivate you to look for ways to explain the behavior and protect your relationship.

Our first section, "Theories and Concepts of Motivation," discusses the major theories and concepts of motivation. "Motivation and Behavior" explores how research on motivation helps explain behaviors like hunger and eating, achievement, and sexuality. "Theories and Concepts of Emotion" identifies the basic theories and concepts related to emotion. The last section, "Critical Thinking About Motivation and Emotion," explores intrinsic versus extrinsic motivation, the polygraph as a lie detector, and emotional intelligence (EI).

THEORIES AND CONCEPTS OF MOTIVATION

What major concepts and theories do I need to know to understand motivation?

There are six major theories of motivation that fall into three general categories—biological, psychosocial, and biopsychosocial (Table 12.1). As we discuss each theory, see if you can identify the one that best explains your reasons for going to college.

TABLE 12.1 SIX MAJOR THEORIES OF MOTIVATION

Theory	View
Biological Theories	
1. Instinct	Motivation results from behaviors that are unlearned, uniform in expression, and universal in a species.
2. Drive-Reduction	Motivation begins with a physiological need (a lack or deficiency) that elicits a drive toward behavior that will satisfy the original need.
3. Arousal	Organisms are motivated to achieve and maintain an optimal level of arousal.
Psychosocial Theories	
4. Incentive	Motivation results from environmental stimuli that "pull" the organism in certain directions.
5. Cognitive	Motivation is affected by attributions, or how we interpret or think about our own or others' actions.
Biopsychosoical Theory	
6. Maslow's Hierarchy of Needs	Lower motives (such as physiological and safety needs) must be satisfied before advancing to higher needs (such as belonging and self-esteem).

Reuters/Corbis Images

What motivates this behavior? *Using the six theories summarized in Table 12.1, choose the one that best explains Lance Armstrong's incredible persistence and commitment to athletic excellence.*

■ Biological Theories: Looking for Internal "Whys" of Behavior

Many theories of motivation are biologically based. They focus on inborn, genetically determined processes that control and direct behavior. Among these biologically oriented theories are *instinct*, *drive-reduction*, and *arousal* theories.

Instinct Theories

In the earliest days of psychology, researchers like William McDougall (1908) proposed that humans had numerous "instincts," such as repulsion, curiosity, and self-assertiveness. Other researchers later added their favorite "instincts." By the 1920s, the list of recognized instincts had become so long it was virtually meaningless. One early researcher found listings for over 10,000 human instincts (Bernard, 1924).

In recent years, a branch of biology called *sociobiology* has revived the case for **instincts** when defined as fixed response patterns that are unlearned and found in almost all members of a species. Instinctual behaviors are obvious in many nonhuman animals: Birds build nests and salmon swim upstream to spawn. But sociobiologists such as Edward O. Wilson (1975, 1978) believe humans also have instincts, like competition or aggression. And that these instincts are genetically transmitted from one generation to another.

Martin Harvey/Peter Arnold, Inc.

Instinct theory in action? *Nurturing of the young is an instinctual behavior for many species.*

Instincts *Fixed response patterns that are unlearned and found in almost all members of a species*

Drive-Reduction Theory *Motivation begins with a physiological need (a lack or deficiency) that elicits a drive toward behavior that will satisfy the original need; once the need is met, a state of balance (homeostasis) is restored and motivation decreases*

Drive-Reduction Theory

In the 1930s, the concepts of drive and drive reduction began to replace the theory of instincts. According to **drive-reduction theory** (Hull, 1952), all living organisms have certain biological *needs* (such as food, water, and oxygen) that must be met if they are to survive. When these needs are unmet, a state of tension (known as a *drive*) is

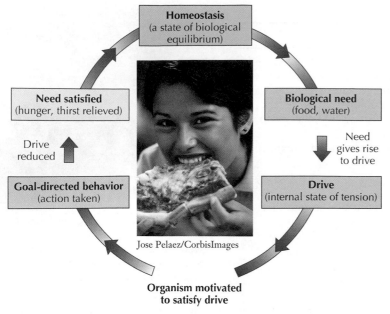

Jose Pelaez/CorbisImages

Figure 12.1 *Drive-reduction theory.* Homeostasis, the body's natural tendency to maintain a state of internal balance, is the foundation of drive-reduction theory. When you are hungry or thirsty, the imbalance creates a drive that motivates you to search for food or water. When the balance is restored, your motivation (to seek food or water) is also decreased.

Homeostasis *A body's tendency to maintain a relatively stable state, such as a constant internal temperature*

Arousal Theory *Organisms are motivated to achieve and maintain an optimal level of arousal*

created, and the organism is motivated to reduce it. When we are deprived of food, our biological need (the hunger *drive*) creates a state of tension, which motivates our search for food.

Drive-reduction theory is based largely on the biological concept of **homeostasis**—a state of balance or stability in the body's internal environment. (*Homeostasis* literally means "standing still.") Body temperature, blood sugar and oxygen level, and water balance are all normally maintained in a state of equilibrium (Chapter 2). When this balance is disrupted, a need arises (a drive is created), and we are motivated to restore homeostasis. Drive-reduction theory and homeostasis are summarized in Figure 12.1.

Arousal Theory—The Need for Stimulation

In addition to our obvious biological need for food and water, humans and other animals are innately curious and require a certain amount of novelty and complexity from the environment. This need for arousal and sensory stimulation begins shortly after birth and continues throughout the life span. Infants show a marked preference for complex versus simple visual stimuli, and adults pay more attention to complex and changing stimuli. Similarly, monkeys will perform various tasks for the simple "reward" of a brief look around an experimental laboratory. They also work hard opening latches for the sheer pleasure of satisfying their curiosity (Figure 12.2) (Butler, 1954; Harlow, Harlow, & Meyer, 1950).

Is there a limit to this need for arousal? What about overstimulation? According to **arousal theory**, organisms are motivated to achieve and maintain an optimal level of arousal that maximizes their performance. Take a close look at the inverted U-shaped curve in Figure 12.3, so named because the graph looks like an upside-down letter *U*. Note how performance is diminished when arousal is either too high or too low. Also note that we do our best when arousal is at its midrange, "optimal" level.

Figure 12.2 *Arousal-seeking behavior.* (a) Monkeys will work very hard at tasks like opening latches simply for the pleasure of satisfying their curiosity. (b) The arousal motive is also apparent in the innate curiosity and exploration of the human animal.

Harlow Primate Laboratory, University of Wisconsin

Robert E. Daemmrich/Stone/GettyImages

Have you noticed this optimal level of arousal effect while taking exams? When underaroused, your mind wanders. You may make careless errors like filling in the space for option A on a multiple-choice exam when you meant to fill in B. In contrast, when overaroused, you may become so anxious that you "freeze-up" and can't remember what you studied. This kind of forgetting results in part from anxiety and overarousal, which interfere with retrieving information from long-term memory (see Chapter 7).

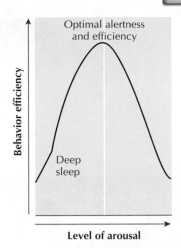

Application
APPLYING PSYCHOLOGY TO STUDENT LIFE

Overcoming Test Anxiety
If you do become overly aroused on exam day, you may want to take a class in study skills or test anxiety. You can also try these basic study tips:

Step 1: *Prepare in advance.* The single most important cure for test anxiety is advance preparation and *hard work*. If you are well prepared, you will feel calmer and more in control.

- Read your textbook using the SQ4R (Survey, Question, Read, Recite, Review, and wRite) method.

- Practice good time management and distribute your study time; don't cram the night before.

- Actively listen during lectures and take detailed, summarizing notes.

- Follow the general strategies for test taking in the "Tools for Student Success" (Chapter 1) and the tips for memory improvement (Chapter 7).

Step 2: *Learn to cope with the anxiety.* Performance is best at a moderate level of arousal, so a few butterflies before and during exams are okay and to be expected. However, too much anxiety can interfere with concentration and cripple your performance. To achieve the right amount of arousal:

- Replace anxiety with relaxed feelings. Practice deep breathing (which activates the parasympathetic nervous system) and the relaxation response described in Chapter 3, on page 118.

- Desensitize yourself to the test situation. See Chapter 15, page 551.

- Exercise regularly. This is a great stress reliever, while also promoting deeper and more restful sleep.

Figure 12.3 *Optimal level of arousal.* Our need for stimulation (the *arousal motive*) suggests that behavior efficiency increases as we move from deep sleep to increased alertness. However, once we pass the maximum level of arousal, our performance declines.

Psychosocial Theories: Incentives and Cognitions

Instinct and drive-reduction theories explain some motivations but not all. Why, for example, do we continue to eat after our biological need is completely satisfied? Why does someone work overtime when his or her salary is sufficient to meet all basic biological needs? These questions are better answered by psychosocial theories that emphasize incentives and cognition.

Incentive Theory—Environmental "Pulls"
Drive-reduction theory states that internal factors *push* people in certain directions. In contrast, **incentive theory** maintains that external stimuli *pull* people toward desirable goals or away from undesirable ones. People begin eating because their hunger "pushes" them (drive-reduction theory). But the sight of apple pie or ice cream "pulls" them toward continued eating (incentive theory).

Incentive Theory *Motivation results from external stimuli that "pull" the organism in certain directions*

www.wiley.com/college/huffman

Self-Test for Sensation Seeking

Everyone needs an optimal level of arousal, but how do we explain people who seem to have an extreme need for stimulation? What motivates people who hang-glide over deep canyons or go whitewater rafting down dangerous rivers? According to research, these "high sensation seekers" may be biologically "prewired" to need a higher level of stimulation (Zuckerman, 1979, 1994, 2004).

Are you a high, average, or low sensation seeker? To find out, in each of the following, circle the choice (**A** or **B**) that BEST describes you:

1. **A** I would like a job that requires a lot of traveling.
   B I would prefer a job in one location.
2. **A** I am invigorated by a brisk, cold day.
   B I can't wait to get indoors on a cold day.
3. **A** I get bored seeing the same old faces.
   B I like the comfortable familiarity of everyday friends.
4. **A** I would prefer living in an ideal society where everyone is safe, secure, and happy.
   B I would have preferred living in the unsettled days of our history.
5. **A** I sometimes like to do things that are a little frightening.
   B A sensible person avoids activities that are dangerous.
6. **A** I would not like to be hypnotized.
   B I would like to have the experience of being hypnotized.
7. **A** The most important goal of life is to live it to the fullest and experience as much as possible.
   B The most important goal of life is to find peace and happiness.
8. **A** I would like to try parachute jumping.
   B I would never want to try jumping out of a plane, with or without a parachute.
9. **A** I enter cold water gradually, giving myself time to get used to it.
   B I like to dive or jump right into the ocean or a cold pool.
10. **A** When I go on a vacation, I prefer the comfort of a good room and bed.
    B When I go on a vacation, I prefer the change of camping out.
11. **A** I prefer people who are emotionally expressive even if they are a bit unstable.
    B I prefer people who are calm and even-tempered.
12. **A** A good painting should shock or jolt the senses.
    B A good painting should convey a feeling of peace and security.
13. **A** People who ride motorcycles must have some kind of unconscious need to hurt themselves.
    B I would like to drive or ride on a motorcycle.

Scoring

Give yourself 1 point for each of the following items that you have circled: 1**A**, 2**A**, 3**A**, 4**B**, 5**A**, 6**B**, 7**A**, 8**A**, 9**B**, 10**B**, 11**A**, 12**A**, 13**B**. Add up your total and compare it with the following norms: 0–3 = very low need for sensation seeking; 4–5 = low; 6–9 = average; 10–11 = high; 12–13 = very high.

Source: Zuckerman, M. (1978, February). The search for high sensation, *Psychology Today*, pp. 38–46. Copyright © 1978 by the American Psychological Association. Reprinted by permission.

Research based on longer versions of this scale suggest four distinct factors that characterize sensation seeking (Diehm & Armatas, 2004; Johnson & Cropsey, 2000; Zuckerman, 2004): (1) thrill and adventure seeking (skydiving, driving fast, or trying to beat a train), (2) openness to experience (travel, unusual friends, drug experimentation), (3) disinhibition ("letting loose"), and (4) susceptibility to boredom (lower tolerance for repetition and sameness).

According to Zuckerman, if you scored very high or very low on this test, you may have difficulties with individuals who score toward the other extreme. This is true not just between partners or spouses but also between parent and child, therapist and patient, and employer and employee. For example, high sensation seekers may be underaroused in a routine clerical or assembly-line job. Low sensation seekers are likely to be overaroused and anxious in a highly challenging and variable occupation.

High sensation seeking? Would you enjoy sky diving? If not, you may be a low or average sensation seeker on Zuckerman's scale.

Joe McBride/Stone/GettyImages

Cognitive Theories—Explaining Things to Ourselves

If you receive a high grade in your psychology course, you can interpret that grade in several ways. You earned it because you really studied. You "lucked out." Or the textbook was exceptionally interesting and helpful (my preferred interpretation!). According to cognitive theories, motivation is directly affected by *attributions*, or how we interpret or think about our own and others' actions. Researchers have found that people who attribute their successes to personal ability and effort tend to work harder toward their goals than people who attribute their successes to luck (Cheung & Rudowicz, 2003; Meltzer, 2004; Weiner, 1972, 1982).

Expectancies are also important to motivation (Haugen, Ommundsen, & Lund, 2004; Sirin & Rogers-Sirin, 2004). Your anticipated grade on a test affects your willingness to study—"If I can get an A in the course, then I will study very hard." Similarly, your expectancies regarding future salary increases or promotions at work affect your willingness to work overtime for no pay.

Hierarchy of Needs *Maslow's theory that some motives (such as physiological and safety needs) must be met before going on to higher needs (such as belonging and self-actualization)*

▣ Biopsychosocial Theory: Interactionism Once Again

As we've seen throughout this text, research in psychology generally emphasizes either biological or psychosocial factors (nature or nurture). However, *biopsychosocial factors* (or *interactionism*) almost always provide the best explanation for behavior. Theories of motivation are no exception. One researcher who recognized this interactionism and developed a theory that accounts for biological, psychological, and social needs in motivation was Abraham Maslow (1954, 1970, 1999). Maslow believed that we all have numerous needs that compete for fulfillment. But some needs are more important than others. For example, your need for a good grade in psychology may compete with demands from other classes. In addition, your need for food and shelter is generally more important than college grades.

As Figure 12.4 shows, Maslow's **hierarchy of needs** *prioritizes* needs. He places survival needs at the bottom and self-actualization needs at the top. Maslow's theory is usually depicted as a pyramid to emphasize that human motivation rests on a foundation of basic biological needs that must be satisfied for survival before higher-level

Figure 12.4 *Maslow's hierarchy of needs.* According to Maslow, basic physical necessities must be satisfied before higher-growth needs can be addressed.

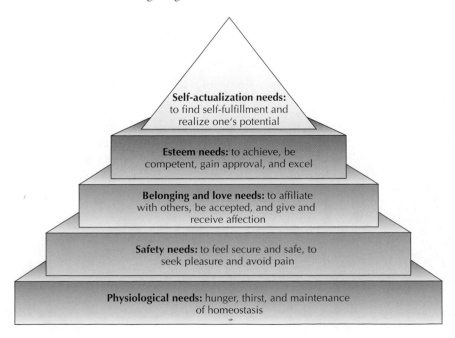

Self-actualization needs: to find self-fulfillment and realize one's potential

Esteem needs: to achieve, be competent, gain approval, and excel

Belonging and love needs: to affiliate with others, be accepted, and give and receive affection

Safety needs: to feel secure and safe, to seek pleasure and avoid pain

Physiological needs: hunger, thirst, and maintenance of homeostasis

Hierarchy of needs. How would Maslow label the needs of these people?

www.wiley.com/college/huffman

needs can be addressed. As a humanistic psychologist, Maslow also believed that we all have a compelling need to "move up"—to grow, improve ourselves, and ultimately become "self-actualized." (We'll revisit Maslow and other humanistic perspectives in Chapter 13.)

Maslow's hierarchy of needs seems intuitively correct. A starving person would first look for food, then seek love and friendship, then self-esteem, and finally self-actualization. This prioritizing and the concept of *self-actualization* are important contributions to the study of motivation (Frick, 2000; Harper, Harper, & Stills, 2003).

On the other hand, critics argue that parts of Maslow's theory are poorly researched and biased toward Western individualism. Furthermore, people also sometimes seek to satisfy higher-level needs even when lower-level needs have not been met (Cullen & Gotell, 2002; Hanley & Abell, 2002; Neher, 1991). In some nonindustrialized societies, people may be living in a war zone, subsisting on very little food, and suffering from injury and disease. Although they have not fulfilled Maslow's two lowest and most basic needs, they still seek the higher needs of strong social ties and self-esteem. In addition, during the famine and war in Somalia, many parents sacrificed their own lives to carry starving children hundreds of miles to food distribution centers. And parents at the centers often banded together to share the limited supplies. Because Maslow argued that each individual's own lower needs must be at least partially met before higher needs can influence behavior, these examples "stand Maslow's need hierarchy on its head" (Neher, 1991, p. 97). In sum, we're normally motivated to fulfill basic needs first. However, in certain circumstances we can bypass these lower stages and pursue higher-level needs.

A*ssessment*

CHECK & REVIEW

Theories and Concepts of Motivation

Motivations are the "whys" of behavior. **Emotions** are the feelings. Because motivated behaviors are often closely related to emotions, these two topics are frequently studied together. There are three general categories for motivation theories: *biological, psychosocial, and biopsychosocial.*

Among the biological approaches, **instinct** theories emphasize inborn, genetic components in motivation. **Drive-reduction theory** suggests that internal tensions (produced by the body's demand for **homeostasis**) "push" the organism toward satisfying basic needs. And **arousal theory** suggests organisms seek an optimal level of arousal that maximizes their performance.

Within the psychosocial approaches to motivation, **incentive theory** emphasizes the "pull" of external environmental stim-

uli. Cognitive theory focuses on the importance of attributions and expectations.

One example of the biopsychosocial approach is Maslow's **hierarchy of needs** (or motives). This theory suggests that basic survival needs must be satisfied before a person can attempt to satisfy higher needs and to become self-actualized.

Questions

1. Define instinct and homeostasis.
2. Match the following examples with their appropriate theory of motivation: (a) instinct; (b) drive-reduction; (c) arousal; (d) incentive; (e) cognitive; (f) Maslow's hierarchy of needs
   ____i. Joining a club because you want to be accepted by others
   ____ii. Two animals fighting because of their inherited, evolutionary desire for survival
   ____iii. Eating to reduce hunger
   ____iv. Studying hard for an exam because you expect that

studying will result in a good grade
   ____v. Skydiving because you love the excitement
3. _____ theory suggests we need a certain amount of novelty and complexity from our environment. (a) Sensory; (b) Social; (c) Drive-reduction; (d) Arousal
4. _____ theories emphasize the importance of attributions and expectancies in motivating behaviors. (a) Attribution; (b) Motivational; (c) Achievement; (d) Cognitive
5. According to _____ theory, basic survival and security needs must be satisfied before one can move on to such higher needs as self-actualization. (a) evolutionary; (b) instinct; (c) Maslow's (d) Weiner's

Check your answers in Appendix B.

CLICK & REVIEW
for additional assessment options:
www.wiley.com/college/huffman

MOTIVATION AND BEHAVIOR

Why do you spend hours playing a new computer game instead of studying for a major exam? Why do salmon swim upstream to spawn? Behavior results from many motives studied by psychologists. For example, the sleep motive was covered in Chapter 5, the sex drive was explored in Chapter 11, and aggression, altruism, and interpersonal attraction will be discussed in Chapter 16. Here, we will focus on the motives behind hunger and eating and achievement.

Achievement

What causes hunger and drives us to achieve?

Hunger and Eating: Multiple Biopsychosocial Factors

What motivates hunger? Is it your growling stomach? Or is it the sight of a juicy hamburger or the smell of a freshly baked cinnamon roll? Hunger is one of our strongest motivational drives. Numerous biological factors (stomach, biochemistry, the brain) and many psychosocial forces (visual cues and cultural conditioning) affect our eating behaviors.

The Stomach

Walter B. Cannon and A. L. Washburn (1912) conducted one of the earliest experiments exploring the internal factors in hunger. In this study, Washburn swallowed a balloon and then inflated it in his stomach. His stomach contractions and subjective reports of hunger feelings were then simultaneously recorded. Because each time Washburn reported having stomach pangs (or "growling") the balloon also contracted, the researchers concluded that stomach movement *caused* the sensation of hunger.

Can you identify what's wrong with this study? As you learned in Chapter 1, correlation does not mean causation. Furthermore, researchers must always control for the possibility of *extraneous variables*, factors that contribute irrelevant data and confuse the results. In this case, it was later found that an empty stomach is relatively inactive. The stomach contractions experienced by Washburn were an experimental artifact—something resulting from the presence of the balloon. Washburn's stomach had been tricked into thinking it was full and was responding by trying to digest the balloon!

In sum, sensory input from the stomach is not essential for feeling hungry. Dieters learn this the hard way when they try to "trick" their stomachs into feeling full by eating large quantities of carrots and celery and drinking lots of water. Also, humans and nonhuman animals without stomachs continue to experience hunger.

Does this mean there is no connection between the stomach and feeling hungry? Not necessarily. Receptors in the stomach and intestines detect levels of nutrients. And specialized pressure receptors in the stomach walls signal fullness or a feeling of emptiness. Furthermore, research has shown that the stomach and other parts of the gastrointestinal tract release chemicals that play a role in hunger (Donini, Savina, & Cannella, 2003; Woods, Schwartz, Baskin, & Seeley, 2000). These (and other) chemical signals are the topic of our next section.

Biochemistry

As we discovered in Chapter 2, the brain and other parts of the body (including the stomach and other parts of the gastrointestinal tract) produce numerous neurotransmitters, hormones, enzymes, and other chemicals that affect behavior. Research in this area is complex because of the large number of known (and unknown) bodily chemicals and the interactions between them. Hunger and eating are no exception.

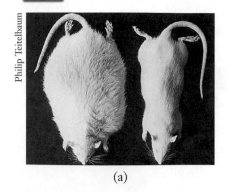

(a)

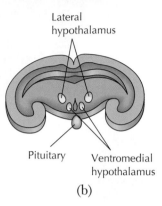

Lateral
hypothalamus

Pituitary   Ventromedial
              hypothalamus

(b)

Figure 12.5 *How does the brain affect eating?* (a) Note the size difference in these two rats. The one on the right is of normal size and weight. (b) Now, study this diagram, which shows a section of a rat's brain viewed from the front with the front half cut away. Note the positions of the ventromedial hypothalamus (VMH) and the lateral hypothalamus (LH). The ventromedial area of the hypothalamus of the rat on the left was destroyed, which led to a tripling of body weight.

For example, researchers have shown that glucose, insulin, cholecystokinin (CCK), adiponectin, glucagon, somatostatin, galanin, neuropeptide Y, leptin, serotonin, PPY3–36, and other bodily chemicals have an effect on hunger and *satiety* (a feeling of fullness, or satiation) (e.g., Chapelot et al., 2004; Hirosumi et al., 2002; Monteleone et al., 2003; Sawaya et al., 2001; Schwartz & Morton, 2002; Shimizu-Albergine, Ippolito, & Beavo, 2001).

It's unlikely that any one chemical controls our hunger and eating. Other internal factors, such as *thermogenesis* (the heat generated in response to food ingestion), also play a role (Subramanian & Vollmer, 2002). In addition, structures in our brains also influence hunger and eating.

The Brain

Recall from Chapter 2 that a part of the brain known as the *hypothalamus* helps regulate eating, drinking, and body temperature. Early research suggested that one area of the hypothalamus, the *lateral hypothalamus* (LH), stimulated eating. In contrast, the *ventromedial hypothalamus* (VMH), created feelings of satiation and signaled the animal to stop eating. When the LH area was destroyed in rats, early researchers found the animals starved to death if they were not force-fed. When the VMH area was destroyed, they overate to the point of extreme obesity (Figure 12.5).

Later research, however, showed that the LH and VMH areas are not simple on–off switches for eating. For example, lesions to the VMH make animals picky eaters—they reject food that doesn't taste good. Lesions also increase the secretion of insulin, which may, in turn, cause overeating (Challem, Berkson, Smith, & Berkson, 2000). Today, researchers know that although the hypothalamus plays an important role in hunger and eating, it is not the brain's "eating center." In fact, hunger and eating, like virtually all behavior, are influenced by numerous neural circuits that run throughout the brain (Berthoud, 2002).

In sum, several internal factors, including structures in the brain, numerous chemicals, and messages from the stomach and intestines, all seem to play important roles in hunger and eating. But even all these internal factors cannot completely explain what motivates us to reach for that chocolate milkshake.

Psychosocial Factors

As you (and I) know, we often eat for many reasons that are unrelated to internal needs. For example, have you ever ordered dessert after a heavy meal just because you saw a delectable treat on a nearby table? The sight of food and other stimulus cues (such as time of day and food advertisements) act as external triggers to hunger and eating.

In addition to these cues, one of the most important social influences on when, what, where, and why we eat is cultural conditioning. North Americans, for example, tend to eat their evening meal around 6:00 P.M.. People in Spain and South America tend to eat around 10:00 P.M. When it comes to *what* we eat, have you ever eaten rat, dog, or horse meat? If you are a typical North American, this might sound repulsive to you. Did you know most Hindus would feel a similar revulsion at the thought of eating meat from cows?

As you can see, hunger and eating are complex phenomena controlled by numerous biological, psychological, and social factors. These same biopsychosocial forces also play a role in three of our most serious eating disorders—obesity, anorexia nervosa, and bulimia nervosa.

Obesity

As you're well aware, Western cultures have a strong preference for thinness and an overt prejudice against being fat. However, obesity has reached epidemic proportions in the United States and many other developed nations. Well over half of all adults in the United States meet the current criterion for clinical *obesity* (e.g., having a body weight 15 percent or more above the ideal for one's height and age). Obesity is a serious and growing problem (no pun intended). It places us at increased risk for a number of medical problems, including heart disease, cancer, arthritis, diabetes, high blood pressure, strokes, and death (American Heart Association, 2003; Friedman, 2002; Kuritzky & Weaver, 2003; Mokdad et al., 2004). Each year, billions of dollars are spent treating these health-related problems. And consumers spend billions more on largely ineffective weight-loss products and services.

Felicia Martinez/Photoedit

Portion control? Can you see why it's difficult to lose pounds or maintain a healthy weight when "I just had a muffin for breakfast" means the one on the right?

Why are so many people overweight? The simple answer is overeating and not enough exercise. But obesity is much more than just an imbalance between caloric intake and energy expenditure. We all know some people who can eat anything they want and still not add pounds. As we've seen earlier, this may be a result of their ability to burn calories more effectively (thermogenesis), a higher metabolic rate, or other factors. Adoption and twin studies also suggest that genes may be the culprit. Adopted children of all weights (ranging from very thin to very obese) tend to resemble their biological parents more than their adoptive parents in body weight. Heritability for obesity is estimated to range between 30 and 70 percent (Hewitt, 1977; Schmidt, 2004). Unfortunately, identifying the genes for obesity is difficult. Researchers have isolated over 2000 genes that contribute to normal and abnormal weight (Camarena et al. 2004; Costa, Brennen, & Hochgeschwender, 2002; Devlin et al., 2000).

©AP/Wide World Photos

Is there anything that can be done to successfully lose weight? The search for a biological answer to obesity (in the form of drugs or even gene manipulation) is a multimillion-dollar industry. At the current time, however, diet and exercise remain the safest route. For Americans, this is a particularly difficult task. We are among the most sedentary peoples of all nations. We've also indulged ourselves with double (or triple) cheeseburgers, "Big Gulp" drinks, and huge servings of dessert (Lawrence, 2002; Smith, Orleans, & Jenkins, 2004). Europeans are often shocked by the size of food portions in America. In addition, we've learned that we should have meals at least three times a day (whether we are hungry or not); that "tasty" food means adding lots of salt, sugar, and fat; and that food is an essential part of almost all social gatherings and celebrations. To successfully lose weight (and maintain that loss), we must make permanent lifestyle changes regarding the amount and types of foods we eat and when we eat them.

Can the environment affect body weight? *Obesity is relatively common among modern Pima Indians living in the United States. However, their close relatives living nearby in Mexico who eat traditional foods are generally slim.*

Application

RESEARCH HIGHLIGHT

Obesity—Weighing the Evidence
(Contributed by Thomas Frangicetto)

"We can't afford to be complacent about this epidemic of obesity and certainly not based on findings from an analysis that is flawed." Dr. JoAnn Manson, Brigham & Women's Hospital in Boston (USATODAY, 2005).

"There are people who have made up their minds that obesity (and being) overweight are the biggest public health problem that we have to face. These numbers show that maybe it's not that big." Dr. Steven Blair, president, Cooper Institute (NYT, 2005).

The source of the disagreement between these two highly respected experts was a controversial study published in 2005 in the *Journal of the American Medical Association* (JAMA).

www.wiley.com/college/huffman

Researchers at the Centers for Disease Control and Prevention (CDC) and the National Cancer Institute combined their efforts to look at the effects of obesity. Surprisingly, their study found that people tend to live longer if they are slightly overweight (Flegal et al., 2005). Clearly contradicting numerous previous reports, this study caused an uproar in the medical community—and mass confusion in the public.

A month after its publication, critics from the Harvard School of Public Health and the American Cancer Society, reported that other studies, their own included, found that the likelihood of death from extra weight increased steadily from normal weight to being overweight to obesity. Calling the Flegal study "deeply flawed," they cited their own *Nurses' Health Study*, which followed over 120,000 women and found that as "body mass index increases, the death rate increases dramatically" (Kolata, 2005).

Dr. Katherine Flegal, the lead author of the controversial study, countered that she and her colleagues had carefully analyzed and reanalyzed the data and the results were always the same: "There was no mortality risk from being overweight and little from being obese, except for the extremely obese" (Flegal, 2005, p. 21).

The Flegal study authors also pointed to the Harvard group's study being exclusively with nurses. In contrast, the Flegal group used volunteers, which they suggest provide data more representative of the United States population.

More confusing still, the second half of the Flegal research team, the Centers for Disease Control and Prevention (CDC), then issued a press release generally retracting their original support. They stated, "Obesity remains an important cause of death in the United States, with 75% of excess deaths from obesity occurring in people younger than 70 years." Furthermore, CDC director Dr. Julie Gerberding proposed that, "It is not OK to be overweight. People need to be fit, they need to have a healthy diet, they need to exercise. I'm very sorry for the confusion that these scientific discussions have had…It is not healthy to be overweight" (Gerberding, 2005). Many scientists, including the CDC's former critics, expressed relief that the CDC was returning to the collective wisdom that obesity is a serious and growing health problem.

Critical Thinking/Active Learning Applications

1. What do you think of this controversy? For more information on the health risks associated with obesity, visit the CDC website at http://www.cdc.gov/ and type "body mass index" in the CDC search box. At this site, you'll find a chart like the one below. To calculate your own BMI (Body Mass Index), just click on the link provided or go to http://www.cdc.gov/nccdphp/dnpa/bmi/index.htm.
2. Based on the limited information provided here, do you think the Flegal group with its volunteers or the Har-

Weight Range	BMI	Considered
124 lbs or less	Below 18.5	Underweight
125 lbs to 168 lbs	18.5 to 24.9	Healthy weight
169 lbs to 202 lbs	25.0 to 29.9	Overweight
203 lbs or more	30 or higher	Obese

vard study of nurses made the better case? Who and what should we believe? To help you deal with the confusion, you can employ several critical thinking components such as *tolerating ambiguity*, *gathering data*, and *delaying judgment until adequate data is available* (see the *Prologue*, pp. xxx–xxxiv).

You can also consider the *weight of the evidence*. Before jumping to follow the latest hot new research topic, ask yourself, "Which opposing side has the greater number of studies and a longer history of support?" As you have learned from the studies cited in this chapter, cumulative, long-term research shows that obesity is a serious health problem. To deal with the contradictory findings from the Flegal study, most scientists would advocate an open mind and a "wait and see" attitude.

Anorexia Nervosa *Severe loss of weight resulting from self-imposed starvation and an obsessive fear of obesity*

Bulimia Nervosa *Consuming large quantities of food (bingeing), followed by vomiting, extreme exercise, and/or laxative use (purging)*

Anorexia Nervosa and Bulimia Nervosa

Interestingly, as obesity has reached epidemic proportions, we've seen a similar rise in two other eating disorders—**anorexia nervosa** (self-starvation and extreme weight loss) and **bulimia nervosa** (intense, recurring episodes of binge eating followed by purging through vomiting or taking laxatives). Contrary to myth, these eating disorders are not restricted to females from upper-middle-class backgrounds. Research shows that more than 50 percent of women in Western industrialized countries show some signs of an eating disorder and approximately 2 percent meet the official criteria for anorexia nervosa or bulimia nervosa (Porzelius et al., 2001). These disorders also are found in all socioeconomic levels. A few men occasionally develop eating disorders, but the incidence among them is rare compared with that among women (Barry, Grilo, & Masheb, 2002; Coombs, 2004; Jacobi et al., 2004).

Anorexia nervosa is characterized by an overwhelming fear of becoming obese, a disturbed body image, the need for control, and the use of dangerous measures to lose weight. The fear of fatness does not diminish even with radical and obvious weight loss. And the body image is so distorted that even a skeletal, emaciated body is perceived as fat. Many people with anorexia nervosa not only refuse to eat but also take up extreme exercise regimens—hours of cycling, running, or constant walking. The extreme malnutrition often leads to osteoporosis and bone fractures. Menstruation in women frequently stops, and computed tomography (CT) scans of the brain show enlarged ventricles (cavities) and widened grooves. Such signs generally indicate loss of brain tissue. A significant percentage of individuals with anorexia nervosa ultimately die of the disorder (Gordon, 2000; Werth et al., 2003). As you can see, this is a serious and chronic condition that needs immediate and ongoing treatment.

Occasionally, the person suffering from anorexia nervosa succumbs to the desire to eat and gorges on food, then vomits or takes laxatives. However, this type of bingeing and purging is more characteristic of bulimia nervosa. This disorder involves recurrent episodes of out-of-control eating followed by drastic measures (such as vomiting, taking laxatives, or exercising excessively) to purge the body of the unwanted calories. Individuals suffering from this disorder are not just impulsive eaters. They also show impulsivity in other areas, sometimes by excessive shopping, alcohol abuse, or petty shoplifting (Bulik, Sullivan, & Kendler, 2002; Kane et al., 2004; Steiger et al., 2003). The vomiting associated with both anorexia nervosa and bulimia nervosa causes eroded tooth enamel and tooth loss, severe damage to the throat and stomach, cardiac arrhythmias, metabolic deficiencies, and serious digestive disorders.

What causes anorexia nervosa and bulimia nervosa? There are almost as many suspected causes as there are victims. Some theories focus on physical causes such as hypothalamic disorders, low levels of various neurotransmitters, and genetic or hormonal disorders. Other theories emphasize psychological or social factors. These factors include a need for perfection, a perceived loss of control, destructive thought patterns, depression, dysfunctional families, distorted body image, and sexual abuse (e.g., Coombs, 2004; Jacobi et al., 2004; McCabe & Ricciardelli, 2003; Neumark-Sztainer, Wall, Story, & Perry, 2003).

Culture and Eating Disorders

Cultural factors also play important roles in eating disorders (Davis, Dionne, & Shuster, 2001; Dorian & Garfinkel, 2002). A number of cross-cultural studies have found important differences in perceptions and stereotypes about eating, thinness, and obesity. For instance, Asian and African Americans report fewer eating and dieting disorders and greater body satisfaction than do European Americans (Akan & Grilo, 1995). And Mexican students report less concern about their own weight and more acceptance of obese people than do Caucasian students (Crandall & Martinez, 1996).

Although social pressures for thinness certainly contribute to the development of eating disorders, it is interesting to note that anorexia nervosa also has been found in nonindustrialized areas like the Caribbean island of Curaçao (Hoek et al., 2005). On that island, being overweight is socially acceptable, and anorexia nervosa among the majority black population is virtually nonexistent. However, some minority mixed and caucasian women do suffer from anorexia nervosa. This research suggests that both culture and biology help explain eating disorders. Regardless of the causes, it is important to recognize the symptoms of anorexia and bulimia (Table 12.2) and seek therapy if the symptoms apply to you. Both disorders are unquestionably serious and require treatment.

"Gee, I had no idea you were married to a supermodel."

Ashley Gilbertson/Aurora& Quanta Productions

The media's role in eating disorders. *Can you see why the extreme thinness of high-fashion models and popular television stars may unintentionally contribute to anorexia and bulimia?*

TABLE 12.2 DSM-IV-TRᵃ SYMPTOMS OF ANOREXIA NERVOSA AND BULIMIA NERVOSA

Symptoms of Anorexia Nervosa	*Symptoms of Bulimia Nervosa*
• Body weight below 85% of normal for one's height and age • Intense fear of becoming fat or gaining weight, even though underweight • Disturbance in one's body image or perceived weight • Self-evaluation unduly influenced by body weight • Denial of seriousness of abnormally low body weight • Absence of menstrual periods • Purging behavior (vomiting or misuse of laxatives or diuretics)	• Normal or above-normal weight • Recurring binge eating • Eating an amount of food that is much larger than most people would consume • Feeling a lack of control over eating • Purging behavior (vomiting or misuse of laxatives or diuretics) • Excessive exercise to prevent weight gain • Fasting to prevent weight gain • Self-evaluation unduly influenced by body weight

ᵃ DSM-IV-TR = *Diagnostic and Statistical Manual of Mental Disorders*, fourth edition, revised

Achievement: The Need for Success

Do you wonder what motivates Olympic athletes to work so hard for so many years for the remote possibility of a gold medal? Or what about someone like Thomas Edison? Inventing the light bulb would seem to have been achievement enough for any person. But Edison also received patents for the microphone, the phonograph, and over 1,000 other inventions. Even as a child, he spent hours doing experiments and figuring out how things work. What drove Edison?

The key to understanding what motivates high-achieving individuals lies in what psychologist Henry Murray (1938) identified as a *high need for achievement* (nAch). **Achievement motivation** can be broadly defined as the desire to excel, especially in competition with others. One of the earliest tests for achievement motivation was devised by Christiana Morgan and Henry Murray (1935). Using a series of ambiguous pictures called the *Thematic Apperception Test* (TAT) (Figure 12.6), these researchers asked participants to make up a story about each picture. Their responses are scored for different motivational themes, including achievement. Since that time, other researchers have developed several questionnaire measures of achievement.

Before you read on, complete the following "Try This Yourself!" and "Critical Thinking/Active Learning" activities. They provide multiple tests of your own need for achievement.

Achievement Motivation *Desire to excel, especially in competition with others*

TRY THIS YOURSELF

Application

Using the TAT to Test nAch

The Thematic Apperception Test (TAT) measures achievement motivation by presenting a series of ambiguous pictures like the one shown in Figure 12.6. Look closely at the two women in the photo, and then write a short story answering the following questions:

1. What is happening in this picture, and what led up to it?
2. Who are the people in this picture, and how do they feel?
3. What is going to happen in the next few moments, and in a few weeks?

Figure 12.6 *Measuring achievement.* This card is a sample from the *Thematic Apperception Test* (TAT). The strength of an individual's need for achievement is reportedly measured by stories he or she tells about the TAT drawings.

Harvard University Press

Scoring

Give yourself 1 point each time any of the following is mentioned: (1) defining a problem, (2) solving a problem, (3) obstructions to solving a problem, (4) techniques that can help overcome the problem, (5) anticipation of success or resolution of the problem. The higher your score on this test, the higher your overall need for achievement.

Characteristics of High Achievers
(Contributed by Thomas Frangicetto)

Do you have a high need for achievement (nAch)? People with a high achievement orientation generally have more success in life and report more satisfaction with what they've accomplished in their lives. Here is a chance for you to:

- Review the six characteristics of high achievers.
- Rate yourself on those characteristics.
- Apply critical thinking components to improve your achievement motivation scores.

Part I: Researchers have identified several personality traits that distinguish people with a high nAch from those with a low nAch (McClelland, 1958, 1987, 1993; Mueller & Dweck, 1998; Wigfield & Eccles, 2000). To determine your own personal need for achievement, read the six characteristics below and rate yourself according to how accurately each one describes you.

RATING:
(Not like me at all)   0 1 2 3 4 5 6 7 8 9 10   (Describes me accurately)

1. *Preference for moderately difficult tasks.* I tend to avoid tasks that are too easy because they offer little challenge and avoid extremely difficult tasks because the chance of success is too low.
2. *Preference for clear goals with competent feedback.* I prefer tasks with a clear outcome and situations in which you can receive performance feedback. I also prefer criticism from a harsh but competent evaluator to one who is friendlier but less competent.
3. *Competitive.* I am more attracted to careers and tasks that involve competition and an opportunity to excel. I enjoy the challenge of having to prove myself.
4. *Responsible.* I prefer being personally responsible for a project, and when I am directly responsible I feel more satisfaction when the task is well done.
5. *Persistent.* I am highly likely to persist at a task even when it becomes difficult, and I gain satisfaction in seeing a task through to completion.
6. *More accomplished.* In comparison to others, I generally achieve more (e.g., I typically do better on exams and earn higher grades and/or receive top honors in sports, clubs, and other activities).

Add up your total need for achievement (nAch) points. 55–60 = Very high; 49–54 = High; 43–48 = Moderately high; 37–42 = Average; 31–36 = Below average; below 30 = Low.

Part II: Review your ratings and identify one critical thinking component (CTC) (Prologue, pp. xxx–xxxiv) that you believe could help increase your score on each trait. This is an important exercise. The closer your need for achievement reflects the characteristics of high achievers, the more likely you are to accomplish your goals. Here is an example for item #1:

Preference for moderately difficult tasks. High achievers know that succeeding at an easy task results in low satisfaction. On the other hand, overly difficult tasks lead to unnecessary frustration. Therefore, the CTC "Recognizing Personal Biases" is very important. Honestly facing the facts about our knowledge and abilities helps us recognize our limitations. It can also help prevent wasteful rationalizing and blaming others for our failures. Being realistic about our abilities without being overly self-critical achieves a healthy balance.

What causes some people to be more achievement oriented than others? Achievement orientation appears to be largely learned in early childhood, primarily through interactions with parents. Highly motivated children tend to have parents who encourage independence and frequently reward success (Maehr & Urdan, 2000). The culture that we are born and raised in also affects achievement needs (Lubinski & Benbow, 2000). Events and themes in children's literature, for example, often contain subtle messages about what the culture values. In North American and Western European cultures, many children's stories are about persistence and the value of hard work. In fact, a study by Richard de Charms and Gerald Moeller (1962) found a significant correlation between the achievement themes in children's literature and the actual industrial accomplishments of various countries.

www.wiley.com/college/huffman

CHECK & REVIEW

Motivation and Behavior

Hunger is one of the strongest motivational drives. Both biological factors (stomach, biochemistry, the brain) and psychosocial forces (stimulus cues and cultural conditioning) affect our eating behaviors. A large number of people have eating disorders. Obesity seems to result from biological factors, such as the individual's genetic inheritance, lifestyle factors, and numerous psychological factors.

Anorexia nervosa (extreme weight loss due to self-imposed starvation) and **bulimia nervosa** (excessive consumption of food followed by purging) are both related to an intense fear of obesity.

Achievement motivation refers to the desire to excel, especially in competition with others. People with high achievement needs prefer moderately difficult tasks and clear goals with competent feedback. They also tend to be more competitive, responsible, persistent, and accomplished.

Questions

1. Motivation for eating is found _____. (a) in the stomach; (b) in the ventromedial section of the hypothalamus; (c) throughout the brain; (d) throughout the body
2. Severe weight loss resulting from self-imposed starvation and an obsessive fear of obesity is called _____.
3. Juan has a need for success and prefers moderately difficult tasks, especially in competition with others. Juan probably has a high _____. (a) need for approval; (b) testographic personality; (c) power drive; (d) need for achievement.
4. What are the chief identifying characteristics of high achievers?

Check your answers in Appendix B.

CLICK & REVIEW
for additional assessment options:
www.wiley.com/college/huffman

THEORIES AND CONCEPTS OF EMOTION

What major theories and concepts do I need to know to understand emotion?

We have reviewed the major theoretical explanations for motivation and specific motives such as hunger and achievement. But as we mentioned at the beginning of this chapter, motivation is inextricably linked to emotion. In this section, we begin with an exploration of the three basic components of emotion (*physiological, cognitive,* and *behavioral*). Then we examine the four major theories that help us understand emotion (*James–Lange, Cannon–Bard, facial-feedback,* and *Schachter's two-factor*).

■ Three Components of Emotion: Physiological, Cognitive, and Behavioral

Emotions play an important role in our lives. They color our dreams, memories, and perceptions. When they are disordered they contribute significantly to psychological problems. But what do we mean by the term *emotion*? In everyday usage, we describe emotions in terms of feeling states—we feel "thrilled" when our political candidate wins an election, "defeated" when our candidate loses, and "miserable" when our loved ones reject us. Obviously, what you and I mean by these terms, or what we individually experience with various emotions, can vary greatly among individuals. In an attempt to make the study of emotions more reliable and scientific, psychologists define and study emotions according to their three basic components (*physiological, cognitive,* and *behavioral*).

The Physiological (Arousal) Component

Internal physical changes occur in our bodies whenever we experience an emotion. Imagine walking alone on a dark street in a dangerous part of town. You suddenly see someone jump from behind a stack of boxes and start running toward you. How do you respond? Like most of us, you would undoubtedly interpret the situation as threatening and would prepare to defend yourself or run. Your predominant emotion, fear, would involve several physiological reactions, including increased heart rate and blood pressure, dilated pupils, perspiration, dry mouth, rapid or irregular breathing, increased blood sugar, trembling, decreased gastrointestinal motility, and piloerection (goose bumps). These physiological reactions are controlled by many parts of your body. But certain brain regions and the autonomic nervous system (ANS) play especially significant roles.

The Brain   Our emotional experiences appear to result from important interactions among several areas of our brain, most particularly the cerebral cortex and limbic system (Langenecker et al., 2005; LeDoux, 2002; Panksepp, 2005). The cerebral cortex, the outermost layer of the brain, serves as our body's ultimate control and information-processing center, including our ability to recognize and regulate our emotions. Recall from Chapter 1 that when a 13-pound tamping iron accidentally slammed through Phineas Gage's cortex, he could no longer monitor or control his emotions.

In addition to the cortex, the limbic system is also essential to our emotions (Figure 12.7). Electrical stimulation of specific parts of the limbic system can produce an automatic "sham rage" that turns a docile cat into a hissing, slashing animal (Morris et al., 1996). Stimulating adjacent areas can cause the same animal to purr and lick your fingers. (The rage is called "sham" because it occurs in the absence of provocation and disappears immediately when the stimulus is removed.) Several studies have also shown that one area of the limbic system, the **amygdala**, plays a key role in emotion—especially the emotional response of fear. It sends signals to other areas of the brain, causing our hearts to speed up and all the other physiological reactions related to fear.

Interestingly, some forms of emotional arousal can occur without conscious awareness. Have you ever been hiking and suddenly jumped back because you thought you saw a snake on the trail, only to realize a moment later that it was just a stick? How does this happen? According to psychologist Joseph LeDoux (1996, 2002), when sensory inputs capable of eliciting emotions (the sight of the stick) arrive in the thalamus (our brain's sensory switchboard), it sends messages along two independent pathways—one going up to the cortex and the other going directly to the nearby amygdala. If the amygdala senses a threat, it immediately activates the body's alarm system, long before the cortex has had a chance to really "think" about the stimulus.

Although this dual pathway occasionally leads to "false alarms," such as mistaking a stick for a snake, LeDoux believes it is a highly adaptive warning system essential to our survival. He states that "the time saved by the amygdala in acting on the thalamic interpretation, rather than waiting for the cortical input, may be the difference between life and death."

The Autonomic Nervous System (ANS)   As you can see, the brain plays a vital role in emotion. However, it is the autonomic nervous system (ANS) that produces the obvious signs of emotional arousal (increased heart rate, fast and shallow breathing, trembling, and so on). These largely automatic responses result from interconnections between the ANS and various glands and muscles (Figure 12.8).

Recall from Chapter 2 that the ANS has two major subdivisions: the *sympathetic nervous system* and the *parasympathetic nervous system*. When you are emotionally aroused, the sympathetic branch increases heart rate, respiration, and so on (the fight-or-flight response). When you are relaxed and resting, the parasympathetic branch works to calm the body and maintain *homeostasis*. The combined action of both the sympathetic and parasympathetic systems allows you to respond to emotional arousal and then return to a more relaxed state.

Where does adrenaline fit into this picture? Adrenaline, or, more properly, *epinephrine*, is a hormone secreted from the adrenal glands at the direction of the hypo-

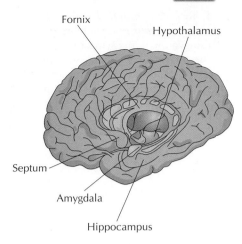

Figure 12.7 ***The limbic system and emotion.*** In addition to drive regulation, memory, and other functions, the limbic system is very important to emotions. It consists of several subcortical structures that form a border (or limbus) around the brainstem. (The red structure in the center is the thalamus.)

Amygdala *Area of the brain's limbic system involved in emotional responses*

Figure 12.8 *Emotion and the autonomic nervous system.* During emotional arousal, the sympathetic branch of the autonomic nervous system (in connection with the brain) prepares the body for fight or flight. The parasympathetic system is responsible for returning the body to its prearoused state.

Sympathetic		Parasympathetic
Pupils dilated	**Eyes**	Pupils constricted
Dry	**Mouth**	Salivating
Goose bumps, perspiration	**Skin**	No goose bumps
Respiration increased	**Lungs**	Respiration normal
Increased rate	**Heart**	Decreased rate
Increased epinephrine and norepinephrine	**Adrenal glands**	Decreased epinephrine and norepinephrine
Decreased motility	**Digestion**	Increased motility

thalamus. The sympathetic nervous system is almost instantaneously "turned on," along with the limbic system and frontal lobes. However, epinephrine and norepinephrine keep the system under sympathetic control until the emergency is over. The damaging effects of prolonged and excessive sympathetic arousal due to stress are discussed in Chapter 3.

The Cognitive (Thinking) Component

> There is nothing either good or bad, but thinking makes it so.
>
> SHAKESPEARE, *HAMLET*

Our thoughts, values, and expectations also help determine the type and intensity of our emotional responses. Consequently, emotional reactions are very individual. What you experience as intensely pleasurable may be boring or aversive for another.

To study the cognitive component of emotions, psychologists typically use self-report techniques such as paper-and-pencil tests, surveys, and interviews. But our cognitions (or thoughts) about our own and others' emotions are typically difficult to describe and measure scientifically. Individuals differ in their ability to monitor and report on their emotional states. In addition, some people may lie or hide their feelings because of social expectations or as an attempt to please the experimenter.

Furthermore, it is often impractical or unethical to artificially create emotions in a laboratory. How can we ethically create strong emotions like anger in a research participant just to study his or her emotional reactions? Finally, memories of emotions are not foolproof. You may remember that trip to Yellowstone as the "happiest camping trip ever." Your brother or sister may remember the same trip as the "worst." Our individual needs, experiences, and personal interpretations all affect the accuracy of our memories (Chapter 7).

The Behavioral (Expressive) Component

Having examined the cognitive and physiological components of emotions, we now turn our attention to how emotions are expressed—the *behavioral component.* Emotional expression is a powerful form of communication. An infant's smile can create instant bonding, a cry of "fire" can cause crowds to panic, and a sobbing friend can elicit heartbreaking empathy. Though we can talk about our emotions, we more often express them nonverbally through facial expressions; gestures; body position; and the use of touch, eye gaze, and tone of voice.

Facial expressions may be our most important form of emotional communication. And researchers have developed very sensitive measurement techniques allowing

(a)   (b)

Figure 12.9 *Duchenne smile.* To most people, the smile on the left looks more sincere than the one on the right? Do you know why?

Answer: (a) A smile of real joy is referred to as a Duchenne smile. Note how the muscles around the eyes also contract.(b) In a social smile, however, only the muscles around the mouth contract.

them to detect subtleties of feeling and differentiate honest expressions from fake ones. Perhaps most interesting is the difference between the "social smile" and the "Duchenne smile." The latter is named after French anatomist Duchenne de Boulogne, who first described it in 1862.

Look closely at the two photos in Figure 12.9. Which smile do you think is most natural and sincere? In a false, social smile, our voluntary cheek muscles are pulled back, but our eyes are unsmiling. Smiles of real pleasure, on the other hand, use the muscles not only around the cheeks but also around the eyes. According to Duchenne de Boulogne, the eye muscle "does not obey the will" and "is put in play only by the sweet emotions of the soul" (cited in Goode, Schrof, & Burke, 1991, p. 56). Studies find that people who show a Duchenne, or real, smile and laughter elicit more positive responses from strangers and enjoy better interpersonal relationships and personal adjustment (Keltner, Kring, & Bonanno, 1999; Prkachin & Silverman, 2002).

Four Major Theories of Emotion: James—Lange, Cannon—Bard, Facial-Feedback, and Schachter's Two-Factor

Researchers generally agree on the three components of emotion (physiological, cognitive, and behavioral). There is less agreement on *how* we become emotional. The four major theories are the James—Lange, Cannon—Bard, facial-feedback, and Schachter's two-factor. Each of these theories emphasizes different sequences or aspects of the three elements (cognitions, arousal, and expression). As you read about the different theories, you will find it helpful to refer to Figure 12.10.

James—Lange Theory

According to ideas originated by psychologist William James and later expanded by physiologist Carl Lange, emotions depend on feedback from our physiological arousal and behavioral expression. Contrary to popular opinion, which says we cry because we're sad, James wrote: "We feel sorry because we cry, angry because we strike, afraid because we tremble" (James, 1890).

Why would I tremble unless I first felt afraid? According to the **James—Lange theory**, your bodily response of trembling is a reaction to a specific stimulus such as seeing a large snake in the wilderness. In other words, you perceive an event, your body reacts, and then you interpret the bodily changes as a specific emotion (see Figure 12.10a). It is your perception of autonomic arousal (palpitating heart, sinking stomach, flushed cheeks), your actions (running, yelling), and changes in your facial

James—Lange Theory *Emotions result from physiological arousal and behavioral expression ("I feel sad because I'm crying"); in this view, each emotion is physiologically distinct*

Figure 12.10 *Four major theories of emotion.* (a) In the James–Lange theory, emotion occurs after the body is aroused. (b) In the Cannon–Bard theory, arousal and emotion occur simultaneously. (c) The facial-feedback hypothesis proposes that changes in facial expression produce arousal and emotions. (d) In Schachter's two-factor theory, arousal causes us to search for a reason for the arousal. Once the arousal is labeled, emotion occurs.

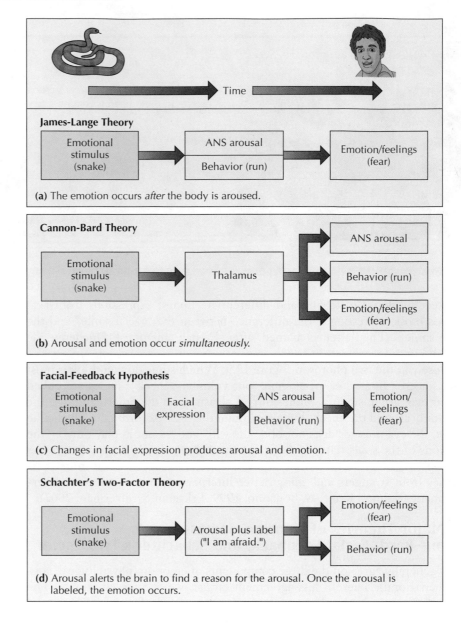

James-Lange Theory

Emotional stimulus (snake) → ANS arousal / Behavior (run) → Emotion/feelings (fear)

(a) The emotion occurs *after* the body is aroused.

Cannon-Bard Theory

Emotional stimulus (snake) → Thalamus → ANS arousal / Behavior (run) / Emotion/feelings (fear)

(b) Arousal and emotion occur *simultaneously.*

Facial-Feedback Hypothesis

Emotional stimulus (snake) → Facial expression → ANS arousal / Behavior (run) → Emotion/feelings (fear)

(c) Changes in facial expression produces arousal and emotion.

Schachter's Two-Factor Theory

Emotional stimulus (snake) → Arousal plus label ("I am afraid.") → Emotion/feelings (fear) / Behavior (run)

(d) Arousal alerts the brain to find a reason for the arousal. Once the arousal is labeled, the emotion occurs.

expression (crying, smiling, frowning) that produce what we refer to as emotions. In short, arousal and expression cause emotion. According to James-Lange theory, if there is no arousal or expression, there is no emotion.

Cannon—Bard Theory

The James–Lange theory argues that arousal and expression produce emotion and each emotion has its own distinct physiological reaction. In contrast, the **Cannon–Bard theory** holds that all emotions are physiologically similar and that arousal, behavior, and emotion occur simultaneously. Walter Cannon (1927) and Philip Bard (1934) proposed that after perception of the emotion-provoking stimulus (seeing a snake), a small part of the brain, called the thalamus, sends *simultaneous* messages to the brain and body. These simultaneous messages then lead to ANS arousal, behavioral reactions, and emotions (Figure 12.10b).

The major point of the Cannon–Bard theory is that all emotions are physiologically similar. In fact, arousal is not a necessary or even a major factor in emotion. Cannon supported his position with several experiments in which nonhuman animals were

Cannon—Bard Theory *Arousal, behavior, and emotions occur simultaneously; in this view, all emotions are physiologically similar*

surgically prevented from experiencing physiological arousal. Yet these surgically altered animals still showed observable behaviors (like growling and defensive postures) that might be labeled emotional reactions (Cannon, Lewis, & Britton, 1927).

Facial-Feedback Hypothesis

The third major explanation of emotion—the facial-feedback hypothesis—focuses on the *expressive* component of emotions. According to the **facial-feedback hypothesis**, facial changes correlate with and intensify emotions. They also *cause* or initiate the emotion itself (Ceschi & Scherer, 2001; Keillor et al., 2002; Soussignan, 2002). Contractions of the various facial muscles send specific messages to the brain, which help us identify each basic emotion. Like James, these researchers suggest that we don't smile because we are happy. We feel happy because we smile (see Figure 12.10c).

The facial-feedback hypothesis also supports Darwin's (1872) evolutionary theory that freely expressing an emotion intensifies it, whereas suppressing outward expression diminishes it. Interestingly, research suggests that even watching another's facial expressions causes an automatic, *reciprocal* change in our own facial muscles (Dimberg & Thunberg, 1998). When people are exposed to pictures of angry faces, for example, the eyebrow muscles involved in frowning are activated. In contrast, the smile muscles show a significant increase in activity when participants are shown photos of a happy face. In follow-up research using the *subliminal perception* techniques discussed in Chapter 4, scientists have shown that this automatic, matching response occurs even *without* the participant's attention or conscious awareness (Dimberg, Thunberg, & Elmehed, 2000).

This automatic, innate, and generally unconscious imitation of others' facial expressions has several important applications. Have you ever felt depressed after listening to a friend's problems? Your unconscious facial mimicry of the person's sad expression may have led to similar physiological reactions and similar feelings of sadness. This theory may also provide personal insights for therapists who constantly work with depressed clients and for actors who simulate emotions for their livelihood. In addition, studies show that "happy workers are generally more productive than unhappy workers" (Wright et al., 2002). Does this mean that unhappy coworkers or a constantly angry boss might affect the happiness (and productivity) of the general workforce? If Darwin was right that expressing an emotion intensifies it, and if watching others' emotions produces a matching response, should we reconsider traditional advice encouraging us to "express our anger"?

Facial-Feedback Hypothesis
Movements of the facial muscles produce or intensify emotional reactions

*A*ssessment

VISUAL QUIZ

David Young-Wolff/Photoedit

Testing the Facial-Feedback Hypothesis

Hold a pen or pencil between your teeth with your mouth closed, as shown in the left photo. Spend about 15 to 30 seconds in this position. How do you feel? Now hold the pencil between your teeth with your mouth open and your teeth showing, as in the right photo. During the next 15 to 30 seconds, pay attention to your feelings. According to research, pleasant feelings are more likely when teeth are showing. Can you explain why?

Source: Adapted from Strack, Martin, & Stepper, 1988.

www.wiley.com/college/huffman

Schachter's Two-Factor Theory

Schachter's Two-Factor Theory
Emotions result from physical arousal and cognitive labeling (or interpretation) of that arousal based on external cues

Psychologist Stanley Schachter agrees with James–Lange that our experience of an emotion comes from a cognitive awareness of our bodily arousal. But he also agrees with Cannon–Bard that emotions are physiologically similar. He reconciles the two theories by proposing that we look to *external* rather than *internal* cues to differentiate and label our emotions. According to **Schachter's two-factor theory**, emotions depend on two factors: (1) physical arousal and (2) cognitive labeling of that arousal. If we cry at a wedding, for example, we interpret our emotion as joy or happiness. If we cry at a funeral, we label our emotion as sadness.

In Schachter and Singer's classic study (1962), participants were given shots of epinephrine and told it was a type of vitamin. Their subsequent arousal and labeling were then investigated (Figure 12.11). One group of participants was *correctly* informed about the expected effects (hand tremors, excitement, and heart palpitations), and a second group was *misinformed* and told to expect itching, numbness, and headache. A third, *uninformed*, group was told nothing about the possible effects.

Following the injection, each participant was placed in a room with a *confederate* (a "stooge" who was part of the experiment but pretended to be a fellow volunteer). In one condition, the confederate was told to act happy and cheerful (throwing paper airplanes around the room and shooting wads of paper into the wastebasket). In the other condition, the confederate was told to act unhappy and angry (complaining and expressing general dissatisfaction with the entire experiment).

The results of the study confirmed the experimental hypothesis. Participants who did not have an appropriate cognitive label for their emotional arousal (the misinformed group and the uninformed group) tended to look to the situation for an explanation. Thus, those placed with a happy confederate became happy. Those placed with an unhappy confederate became unhappy. Participants who knew their physiological arousal was the result of the shot (the correctly informed group) were generally unaffected by the confederate.

Figure 12.11 *Schachter's two-factor theory.* A comparison of informed, misinformed, and uninformed participants in Schachter and Singer's classic experiment demonstrates the importance of cognitive labels in emotions.

Which theory is correct? As you may imagine, each theory has its limits. For example, the James–Lange theory fails to acknowledge that physical arousal can occur without emotional experience (e.g., when we exercise). This theory also requires a distinctly different pattern of arousal for each emotion. Otherwise, how do we know whether we are sad, happy, or mad? However, positron emission tomography (PET) scan studies of the brain do show subtle differences and general physical arousal with basic emotions, such as happiness, fear, and anger (Lane, Reiman, Ahern, & Schwartz, 1997; Levenson, 1992). But most people are not aware of these slight variations. Thus, there must be other explanations for why we experience emotion.

The Cannon–Bard theory (that the cortex and autonomic nervous system receive simultaneous messages from the thalamus) has received some experimental support. For instance, victims of spinal cord damage still experience emotions—often more intensely than before their injuries (Bermond, Fasotti, Nieuwenhuyse, & Schuerman, 1991). Instead of the thalamus, however, other research shows that it is the limbic system, hypothalamus, and prefrontal cortex that are most important in emotional experience (Langenecker et al., 2005; Panksepp, 2005).

Research on the facial-feedback hypothesis has found a distinctive physiological response for basic emotions such as fear, sadness, and anger—thus partially confirming James–Lange's initial position (Dimberg, Thunberg, & Elmehed, 2000; Wehrle, Kaiser, Schmidt, & Scherer, 2000). Facial feedback does seem to contribute to the intensity of our subjective emotional experience and our overall moods. Thus, if you want to change a bad mood or intensify a particularly good emotion, adopt the appropriate facial expression. Try smiling when you're sad and expanding your smiles when you're happy.

Finally, Schachter's two-factor theory correctly emphasizes the importance of cognitive processes in emotions. But his findings have been criticized. For example, research shows that some neural pathways involved in emotion bypass the cortex and go directly to the limbic system. Recall our earlier example of jumping at a strange sound in the dark and then a second later using the cortex to interpret what it was. This and other evidence suggest that emotions can take place without conscious cognitive processes. Thus, emotion is not simply the labeling of arousal (Dimberg, Thunberg, & Elmehed, 2000; LeDoux, 1996, 2002; Mineka & Oehman, 2002).

In sum, certain basic emotions are associated with subtle differences in arousal. These differences can be produced by changes in facial expressions or by organs controlling the autonomic nervous system. In addition, "simple" emotions (likes, dislikes, fears, and anger) do not initially require conscious cognitive processes. This allows a quick, automatic emotional response that can later be modified by cortical processes. On the other hand, "complex" emotions (jealousy, grief, depression, embarrassment, love) seem to require cognitive elements.

Assessment

CHECK & REVIEW

Theories and Concepts of Emotion

All emotions have three basic components: physiological arousal (e.g., heart pounding), cognitive (thoughts, values, and expectations), and behavioral expressions (e.g., smiles, frowns, running). Studies of the physiological component of emotion find that most emotions involve a general, nonspecific arousal of the nervous system. Self-report techniques, such as paper-and-pencil tests, surveys, and interviews, are used to study the cognitive component of emotions. The behavioral component of emotions refers to how we express our emotions, including facial expressions.

Four major theories explain what causes emotion. According to the **James–Lange theory,** we interpret the way we feel based on physiological arousal and behavioral expression, such as smiles, increased heart rate, and trembling. The **Cannon–Bard theory** suggests that arousal, cognitions, and behavioral expression of emotions occur simultaneously. According to the **facial-feedback hypothesis,** facial movements elicit specific emotions. **Schachter's two-factor theory** suggests that emotions depend on two factors—physical arousal and a cognitive labeling of the arousal. In other words, people notice what is going on around them, as well as their own bodily responses, and then label the emotion accordingly.

Questions

1. Identify the following examples with the appropriate emotional component: (a) cognitive; (b) physiological; (c) behavioral
   ___i. Increased heart rate
   ___ii. Crying during a sad movie
   ___iii. Believing crying is inappropriate for men
   ___iv. Shouting during a soccer match

2. When people are emotionally aroused, the _____ branch of the _____ nervous system works to increase heart rate and blood pressure and to activate other crisis responses.

3. We see a bear in the woods, our hearts race as we begin to run, and then we experience fear. This is best explained by _____. (a) the James–Lange theory; (b) the Cannon–Bard theory; (c) the facial-feedback hypothesis; (d) Schacter's two-factor theory

4. According to _____, physiological arousal must be labeled or interpreted for an emotional experience to occur.

(a) the Cannon–Bard theory; (b) the James–Lange theory; (c) the facial-feedback hypothesis; (d) Schacter's two-factor theory

5. The Cannon–Bard theory of emotion suggests that arousal, cognitions, and expression of emotions occur _____.

Check your answers in Appendix B.

CLICK & REVIEW
for additional assessment options:
www.wiley.com/college/huffman

Achievement

How can I apply critical thinking to motivation and emotion?

CRITICAL THINKING ABOUT MOTIVATION AND EMOTION

As you will recall from Chapter 1, critical thinking is a core part of psychological science and a major goal of this text. In this section, we will use our critical thinking skills as we explore four special (and sometimes controversial) topics in motivation and emotion—*intrinsic versus extrinsic motivation, the polygraph as a lie detector, emotional intelligence,* and *culture, evolution, and emotion.*

Intrinsic Versus Extrinsic Motivation: What's Best?

Intrinsic Motivation *Motivation resulting from personal enjoyment of a task or activity*

Extrinsic Motivation *Motivation based on obvious external rewards or threats of punishment*

When you were a child, did your parents reward you with money or prizes for your school grades? If so, was this a good idea? What about giving students rewards for good attendance? Many psychologists are concerned about the widespread practice of giving external, *extrinsic* rewards to motivate behavior (e.g., Deci et al., 1999; Henderlong & Lepper, 2002; Reeve, 2005). They're worried that it will seriously affect the individual's personal, *intrinsic* motivation. **Intrinsic motivation** comes from within the individual. The person engages in an activity for its own sake or for internal satisfaction, with no ulterior purpose or need for an external reward. In contrast, **extrinsic motivation** stems from external rewards or avoidance of punishment and is learned through interaction with the environment. Participation in sports and hobbies, like swimming or playing a guitar, is usually intrinsically motivated. Going to work is primarily extrinsically motivated.

As a critical thinker, can you see why using extrinsic rewards may create problems? What would happen if you were suddenly given money, praise, or other incentives for your intrinsically satisfying "play" activities like watching TV, playing cards, or even sex? You may be surprised to find that people in this situation often lose a lot of their enjoyment and interest. They may even decrease the time spent on the activity (Hennessey & Amabile, 1998; Kohn, 2000; Moneta & Siu, 2002).

One of the earliest experiments to demonstrate this effect involved preschool children who liked to draw (Lepper, Greene, & Nisbett, 1973). The children were all given artist's paper and felt-tipped pens. One group was promised a "Good Player" certificate with a gold seal and ribbon for their drawings. The second

Percentage of free time spent drawing

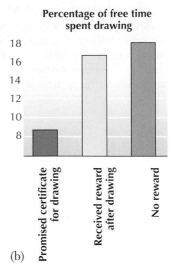

Promised certificate for drawing | Received reward after drawing | No reward

(a)

(b)

Figure 12.12 *Intrinsic versus extrinsic motivation.* (a) These children are obviously having fun finger painting. Why do we stop finger painting as adults? Is it because we're too busy now? Or is it because we were given grades, praise, or other extrinsic rewards that reduced our original intrinsic motivation? (b) As shown in this graph, children who were given no reward spent more free time drawing. *Source:* Lepper, Greene, & Nisbett, Understanding Children's Intrinsic Interest in Extrinsic Rewards, *Journal of Personality and Social Psychology, 28,* pp. 129–137.

group was asked to draw and then received an unexpected reward when they were done. A third group received no promise of a certificate, and no reward was given. A few weeks later, these same children were placed in a situation in which they could draw if they freely chose to do so. The amount of time they spent drawing was recorded.

What do you think happened? As Figure 12.12 shows, offers of a "Good Player" certificate greatly undermined the children's subsequent interest in drawing. How can we explain the results of these studies? Apparently, the critical factor in enjoyment of a task is how we interpret our motivation to ourselves. When we perform a task for no apparent reason, we use internal, personal reasons ("I like it"; "It's fun"). But when extrinsic rewards are added, the explanation shifts to external, impersonal reasons ("I did it for the money"; "I did it to please the boss"). This shift generally decreases enjoyment and negatively affects performance.

But doesn't getting a raise or receiving a gold medal increase enjoyment and productivity? Not all extrinsic motivation is bad (Covington & Mueller, 2001; Moneta & Siu, 2002). The problem seems to be in how extrinsic rewards are used. They are motivating if they are used to inform a person of superior performance or as a special treat. As you can see in Figure 12.13, extrinsic rewards do not work as motivators if the person experiences them as pressure or a form of control. In addition, research finds extrinsic rewards do not reduce intrinsic interest if they are based on competency (Deci, 1995). In fact, they may intensify the desire to do well again. Thus, getting a raise or gold medal can inform us and provide valuable feedback about our performance, which may increase enjoyment. On the other hand, if rewards are used to control, like giving children money or privileges for good grades, intrinsic motivation declines (Eisenberger & Armeli, 1997; Eisenberger & Rhoades, 2002).

Figure 12.13 *Motivation is in the eye of the beholder.* Do rewards increase motivation, or are they seen as coercion or bribery? It depends. Note how a controlling reward and external pressure both lead to extrinsic motivation, whereas an informing reward and "no strings" treat produce intrinsic motivation.

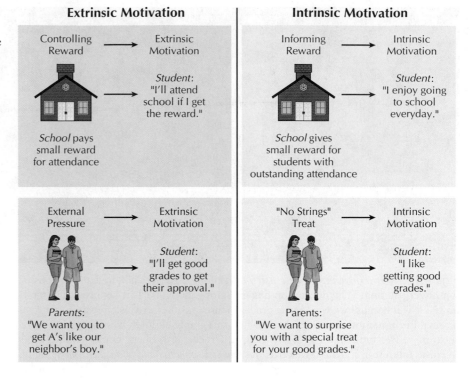

TRY THIS

YOURSELF

Application

Improving Motivation

Intrinsic–extrinsic motivation has important implications for raising children, running a business, or even studying this text. Consider the following guidelines:

1. *Limit concrete extrinsic rewards.* In general, it is almost always better to use the least possible extrinsic reward and for the shortest possible time period. When children are first learning to play a musical instrument, it may help to provide small rewards until they gain a certain level of mastery. But once a child is working happily or practicing for the sheer joy of it, it is best to leave him or her alone. Similarly, if you're trying to increase your study time, begin by rewarding yourself for every significant improvement. But don't reward yourself when you're handling a difficult assignment easily. Save rewards for when you need them. Keep in mind, that we're speaking primarily of concrete extrinsic rewards. Praise and positive feedback are generally safe to use and often increase intrinsic motivation (Carton, 1996; Henderlong & Lepper, 2002).

2. *Reward competency.* Use extrinsic rewards to provide feedback for competency or outstanding performance—not for simply engaging in the behavior. Schools can enhance intrinsic motivation by giving medals or privileges to students with no absences, rather than giving money for simple attendance. Similarly, you should reward yourself with a movie or a call to a friend after you've studied hard for your scheduled time period or done particularly well on an exam. Don't reward yourself for half-hearted attempts.

3. *Emphasize intrinsic reasons for behaviors.* Rather than thinking about all the people you'll impress with good grades or all the great jobs you'll get when you finish college, focus instead on personally satisfying, intrinsic reasons. Think about how exciting it is to learn new things or the value of becoming an educated person and a critical thinker.

Obviously, not all college classes or all aspects of our lives can be intrinsically interesting. Nor should they be. We all have to do many worthwhile things that are obviously extrinsically motivated—going to the dentist, cleaning the house, and studying for exams. It's a good idea, therefore, to save your external reinforcers for the times you're having trouble motivating yourself to do an undesirable task, and avoid "wasting" rewards on well-established intrinsic activities.

Reprinted with permission of King Features Syndicate.

The Polygraph as a Lie Detector: Does It Work?

If you suspected your friend of lying or your significant other of having an affair, would it help convince you if they took a polygraph test? Many people believe the **polygraph** can accurately detect when someone is lying. But can it? The polygraph is based on the theory that when people lie, they feel guilty and anxious. These feelings are then supposedly detected by the polygraph machine.

The polygraph does monitor the activity of the sympathetic and parasympathetic nervous systems—in particular, heart rate, breathing, and changes in skin conductance (Figure 12.14). But these machines don't necessarily detect lies. Research shows that lying is only loosely related to anxiety and guilt. Some people become nervous when telling the truth. Others remain perfectly calm when deliberately lying. In addition, a polygraph cannot tell *which* emotion is being felt (nervousness, excitement, sexual arousal, etc.). It also cannot identify whether a response is due to emotional arousal or something else, such as physical exercise, drugs, tense muscles, or even previous experience with polygraph tests. In fact, one study found that people can affect the outcome by about 50 percent by simply pressing their toes against the floor or biting their tongue (Honts & Kircher, 1994).

For all these reasons, most judges, psychologists, and other scientists have serious reservations about using polygraphs as lie detectors (DeClue, 2003). Although proponents contend that polygraph tests are 90 percent or more accurate, actual tests show error rates ranging between 25 and 75 percent. Thus, although people say the innocent have nothing to fear from a polygraph test, the research suggests otherwise (DeClue, 2003; Faigman, Kaye, Saks, & Sanders, 1997; Iacono & Lykken, 1997).

Is there any way to make the polygraph more reliable? One suggestion is to use "guilty knowledge" questions. These questions are based on specific information that only a guilty person would know (such as the time a robbery was committed). The idea is that a guilty person would recognize these specific cues and respond in a different way than an innocent person (Lykken, 1984, 1998; MacLaren, 2001; Verschuere et al., 2004). Expanding on this idea, psychologists have suggested using computers and statistical analyses to improve polygraph reliability and validity (Saxe & Ben-Shakhar, 1999; Spence, 2003).

Even with improvements, however, many psychologists and others still strongly object to using polygraphs to establish guilt or innocence. In fact, the National Research Council recently concluded that the polygraph lacks evidence to support its use in detecting deception and called for new methods to be developed (National Research Council, 2002). This continuing scientific controversy and public concern

Polygraph *Instrument that measures heart rate, respiration rate, blood pressure, and skin conductivity to detect emotional arousal, which in turn supposedly reflects lying versus truthfulness*

(a)

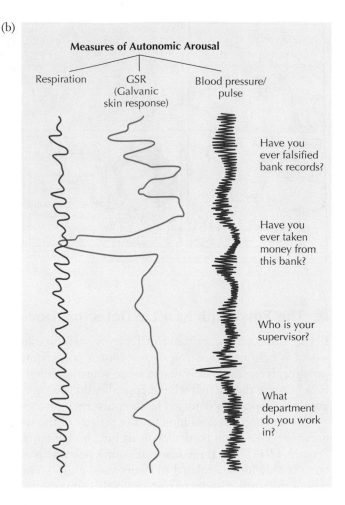

(b)

Figure 12.14 *Polygraph tests.* (a) During the administration of a polygraph—or lie detector—test, a band around the individual's chest measures breathing rate; a cuff monitors blood pressure; and finger electrodes measure sweating, or galvanic skin response (GSR). (b) Polygraph tests are sometimes used to detect lying or dishonesty in employees or suspected criminals. Note in this sample printout how the GSR rises sharply in response to the question, "Have you ever taken money from this bank?" Before you decide that this response proves the individual is lying, remember that research has found error rates ranging between 25 and 75 percent on the polygraph!

prompted the U.S. Congress to pass a bill that severely restricts the use of polygraphs in the courts, in government, and in private industry.

But what about alternative methods for lie detection? Why is lie detection focused only on the sympathetic and parasympathetic nervous systems? Why not study the source of all mental activity—the brain itself? Asking these same questions, scientists recently used functional magnetic resonance imaging (fMRI) to successfully identify five brain regions that are activated during lying compared to truth telling (Kozel, Padgett, & George, 2004). However, the researchers were careful to point out that their study was *not* designed to formally test the fMRI as a means of lie detection. This is a classic example of *basic* versus *applied* research. Once we understand the underlying brain processes involved in deception (basic research), then we may be able to develop a better method for lie detection in the future (applied research).

Emotional Intelligence (EI): Are You "Emotionally Smart"?

You've heard of IQ, the intelligence quotient, but what do you know about EI—emotional intelligence? According to Daniel Goleman (1995, 2000), **emotional intelligence** (EI) involves knowing and managing one's emotions, empathizing with others, and maintaining satisfying relationships. In other words, an emotionally intelligent person successfully combines the three components of emotions (cognitive, physiological, and behavioral).

Goleman suggests that having a high EI explains why people of modest IQ are often more successful than people with much higher IQ scores. He believes that traditional measures of human intelligence ignore a crucial range of abilities that char-

Emotional Intelligence *Goleman's term for the ability to know and manage one's emotions, empathize with others, and maintain satisfying relationships*

acterize people who excel in real life: self-awareness, impulse control, persistence, zeal and self-motivation, empathy, and social deftness.

Goleman also proposes that many societal problems, such as domestic abuse and youth violence, can be attributed to a low EI. Therefore, EI should be fostered in everyone. Proponents have suggested that law schools and other professional training programs should make EI training a curriculum staple. In addition, advocates suggest parents and educators can help children develop EI by encouraging them to identify their emotions and understand how these feelings can be changed and how they are connected to their actions (Reilly, 2005; Shriver & Weissberg, 2005). Schools that have instituted Goleman's ideas say students show not just "more positive attitudes about ways to get along with people. They also show improvements in critical thinking skills" (Mitchell, Sachs, & Tu, 1997, p. 62).

Critics argue that the components of EI are difficult to identify and measure (Gannon & Ranzijn, 2005; Springer, 2005). Others fear that a handy term like EI invites misuse. Paul McHugh, director of psychiatry at Johns Hopkins University, suggests that Goleman is "presuming that someone has the key to the right emotions to be taught to children. We don't even know the right emotions to be taught to adults" (cited in Gibbs, 1995, p. 68).

EI is a controversial concept, but most researchers are pleased that the subject of emotion is being taken seriously. Further research will increase our understanding of emotion and perhaps even reveal the ultimate value of Goleman's theory.

Digital Vision/GettyImages

Developing emotional intelligence.
Adults can help children identify and understand their own emotions as well as how to change them.

Application
CASE STUDY/PERSONAL STORY

The Emotional Intelligence of Abraham Lincoln
(Adapted from Goodwin, 2005)

How does a self-taught farm boy of humble origins grow up to become President of the United States? General William T. Sherman provided one answer: "Of all the men I ever met, he seemed to possess more of the elements of greatness, combined with goodness, than any other" ("Life behind the legend," 2005, p. 44).

Modern psychologists might call these same elements of greatness and goodness high emotional intelligence. Consider the following:

Alan Schein Photography/CorbisImages

Empathy Known for his great ability to empathize and put himself in the place of others, Lincoln refused to criticize and castigate the Southern slave owners like other antislavery orators. Instead, he argued: "They are just what we would be in their situation. If slavery did not now exist amongst them, they would not introduce it. If it did now exist amongst us, we should not instantly give it up" (Goodwin, 2005, p. 49).

Magnanimity Possessing a high-minded, generous spirit, Lincoln refused to bear grudges. Opponent Edwin Stanton called him a "long-armed ape" and deliberately shunned and humiliated him. However, when Lincoln needed a new War Secretary, he noble-mindedly appointed Stanton because he was the best man for this very important position.

Generosity of Spirit Lincoln often took the blame for others, shared credit for successes, and quickly conceded his errors. After General Grant's great battle at Vicksburg, Lincoln wrote, "I now wish to make the personal acknowledgment that you were right, and I was wrong" (Goodwin, 2005, p. 53).

Self-Control Rather than lashing out at others during moments of anger, Lincoln waited until his emotions settled down. He would often write hot letters to others, but would put them aside and seldom send them.

Humor Noted for his dark, depressive moods, Lincoln also possessed a wonderful self-effacing, sense of humor and a gift for storytelling. His jokes and stories not only entertained, but they also contained invaluable insights and wisdom. At the end of the Civil War, many debated the fate of the Southern Rebel leaders. Lincoln wished they could "escape the country," but could not say this publicly. Instead, he told General Sherman a story: "A man once had taken the total abstinence pledge. When visiting a friend, he was invited to take a drink, but declined, on the score of his pledge ... His friend suggested lemonade ... and said the lemonade would be more palatable if he were to pour in a little brandy ... [The] guest said, if he could do so 'unbeknown' to him, he would not object." Sherman immediately grasped the point. "Mr. Lincoln wanted [Jefferson] Davis to escape, 'unbeknown' to him" (Goodwin, 2005, p. 50).

Achievement Gender & Cultural Diversity

Culture, Evolution, and Emotion

Where do our emotions come from? Are they a product of our evolutionary past? Do they differ from one culture to the next, or are they the same? As you might suspect, researchers have found several answers.

Cultural Similarities

All people of all cultures have feelings and emotions, and all must learn to deal with them (Markus & Kitayama, 2003; Matsumoto, 2000). But are these emotions the same across all cultures? Given the seemingly vast array of emotions within our own culture, it may surprise you to learn that some researchers believe all our feelings can be condensed into 7 to 10 *culturally universal* emotions. Note the strong similarities among the four lists in Table 12.3.

Cultural differences in emotional expression. *Some Middle Eastern men commonly greet one another with a kiss. Can you imagine this same behavior among men in North America, who generally shake hands or pat one another's shoulders?*

How do we explain emotions not on the list, such as love? Love, like many other emotions, is believed to be a combination of primary emotions with variation in intensity. Robert Plutchik (1984, 1994, 2000) suggested that primary emotions, such as fear, acceptance, and joy, are like colors on a color wheel that combine to form secondary emotions, such as love, submission, awe, and optimism (Figure 12.15).

In addition to all cultures sharing the same basic emotions, some researchers believe that each of these emotions is expressed and recognized in essentially the same way in all cultures. They point to research that finds people from very different cultures displaying remarkably similar facial expressions when experiencing particular

TABLE 12.3 THE BASIC HUMAN EMOTIONS

Carroll Izard	Paul Ekman and Wallace Friesen	Robert Plutchik	Silvan Tomkins
Fear	Fear	Fear	Fear
Anger	Anger	Anger	Anger
Disgust	Disgust	Disgust	Disgust
Surprise	Surprise	Surprise	Surprise
Joy	Happiness	Joy	Enjoyment
Shame	—	—	Shame
Contempt	Contempt	—	Contempt
Sadness	Sadness	Sadness	—
Interest	—	Anticipation	Interest
Guilt	—	—	—
—	—	Acceptance	—
—	—	—	Distress

Figure 12.15 *Plutchik's wheel of emotions.* The inner circle represents the eight primary emotions that seem to exist in all cultures. Emotions in the inner circle combine to form secondary emotions located outside the circle. For example, joy and acceptance combine to form love. Robert Plutchik also found that emotions that lie next to each other are more alike than those located farther apart.

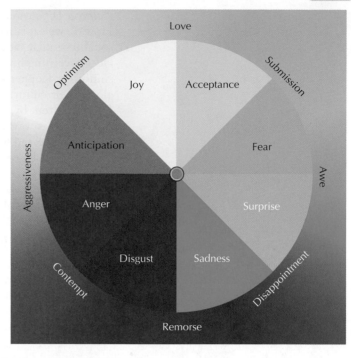

emotions (Biehl et al., 1997; Ekman, 1993, 2004; Matsumoto & Kupperbusch, 2001). Moreover, whether respondents are from Western or non-Western societies, they can reliably identify at least six basic emotions: happiness, surprise, anger, sadness, fear, and disgust (Buck, 1984; Matsumoto, 1992, 2000). In other words, across cultures, a frown is recognized as a sign of displeasure and a smile as a sign of pleasure (Figure 12.16).

The Role of Evolution
Charles Darwin first advanced the evolutionary theory of emotion in 1872. In his classic book *The Expression of the Emotions in Man and Animals*, Darwin proposed that expression of emotions evolved in different species as a part of survival and natural selection. For example, fear helps human and nonhuman animals avoid danger, and expressions of anger and aggression are useful when fighting for mates and necessary resources. Modern evolutionary theory further suggests that basic emotions (such as fear and anger) originate in the limbic system. Given that higher brain areas (the cortex) developed later than the subcortical limbic system, evolutionary theory proposes that basic emotions evolved before thought.

Cross-cultural studies of emotional expression tend to support the innate, evolutionary perspective. The idea of universal facial expressions makes adaptive sense because they signal others about our current emotional state (Ekman & Keltner, 1997). Studies with infants also point to an evolutionary basis for emotions. For example, did you know that infants only a few hours old show distinct expressions of emotions that closely match adult facial expressions (Field, Woodson, Greenberg, & Cohen, 1982)? Or that all infants, even those born deaf and blind, show similar facial expressions in similar situations (Eibl-Eibesfeldt, 1980b; Feldman, 1982)? This collective evidence points to a strong biological, evolutionary basis for emotional expression and decoding.

Figure 12.16 *Can you identify these emotions?* Most people can reliably identify at least six basic emotions—happiness, surprise, anger, sadness, fear, and disgust. On occasion, our facial expressions don't seem to match our presumed emotions, as is the case in the last photo. This woman has just won an important award, yet she looks sad rather than happy.

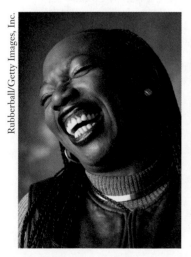

Cultural Differences

How do we explain cultural *differences* in emotions? Although we all seem to share reasonably similar facial expressions for some emotions, each culture has its own *display rules* governing how, when, and where to express emotions (Ekman, 1993, 2004; Matsumoto & Kupperbusch, 2001; Scherer & Wallbott, 1994). For instance, parents pass along their culture's specific display rules by responding angrily to some emotions in their children, by being sympathetic to others, and, on occasion, by simply ignoring them. In this way, children learn which emotions they may freely express and those they are expected to control. In Japanese culture, for instance, children learn to conceal negative emotions with a stoic expression or polite smile (Dresser, 1996). Young males in the Masai culture are similarly expected to conceal their emotions in public, but by appearing stern and stony-faced (Keating, 1994).

Public physical contact is also governed by display rules. North Americans and Asians are generally not touch-oriented. And only the closest family and friends might hug in greeting or farewell. In contrast, Latin Americans and Middle Easterners often embrace and hold hands as a sign of casual friendship (Axtell, 1998).

Assessment

CHECK & REVIEW

Critical Thinking About Motivation and Emotion

Intrinsic motivation comes from within the individual. **Extrinsic motivation** stems from external rewards or avoidance of punishment. Research shows that extrinsic rewards can lower interest and motivation if they are not based on competency.

A **polygraph** measures changes in emotional arousal (increased heart rate, blood pressure, and so on). But research shows it is a poor "lie detector." Emotional intelligence (EI) involves managing one's emotions, empathizing with others, and maintaining satisfying relationships.

Studies have identified 7 to 10 basic emotions that may be universal—experienced and expressed in similar ways across almost all cultures. Display rules for emotional expression differ across cultures. Most psychologists believe that emotions result from a complex interplay between evolution and culture.

Questions

1. Which of the following would be an example of extrinsic motivation? (a) money; (b) praise; (c) threats of being fired; (d) all of these options

2. An elementary school began paying students $5 for each day they attend school. Overall rates of attendance increased in the first few weeks and then fell below the original starting point. This is because _____. (a) the students felt going to school wasn't worth $5; (b) money is a secondary versus a primary reinforcer; (c) extrinsic rewards decreased the intrinsic value of attending school; (d) the student expectancies changed to fit the situation

3. The polygraph, or lie detector, measures primarily the _____ component of emotions. (a) physiological; (b) articulatory; (c) cognitive; (d) subjective

4. Knowing and managing one's emotions, empathizing with others, and maintaining satisfying relationships are the key factors in _____. (a) self-actualization; (b) emotional intelligence; (c) emotional metacognition; (d) empathic IQ

Check your answers in Appendix B.

CLICK & REVIEW
for additional assessment options:
www.wiley.com/college/huffman

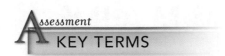

KEY TERMS

*To assess your understanding of the **Key Terms** in Chapter 12, write a definition for each (in your own words), and then compare your definitions with those in the text.*

emotion (p. 422)
motivation (p. 422)

Theories and Concepts of Motivation
arousal theory (p. 424)
drive-reduction theory (p. 424)
hierarchy of needs (p. 427)
homeostasis (p. 424)
incentive theory (p. 425)
instincts (p. 423)

Motivation and Behavior
achievement motivation (p. 434)
anorexia nervosa (p. 432)
bulimia nervosa (p. 432)

Theories and Concepts of Emotion
amygdala (p. 437)
Cannon–Bard theory (p. 440)
facial-feedback hypothesis (p. 441)
James–Lange theory (p. 439)
Schachter's two-factor theory (p. 442)

Critical Thinking About Motivation and Emotion
emotional intelligence (EI) (p. 448)
extrinsic motivation (p. 444)
intrinsic motivation (p. 444)
polygraph (p. 447)

WEB RESOURCES

Huffman Book Companion Site
http://www.wiley.com/college/huffman
This site is loaded with free Interactive Self-Tests, Internet Exercises, Glossary and Flashcards for key terms, web links, Handbook for Non-Native Speakers, and other activities designed to improve your mastery of the material in this chapter.

Want more information on eating disorders?
http://www.mentalhealth.com/p20-grp.html
The Internet Mental Health Eating Disorders site provides important information, diagnosis criteria, and treatment for eating disorders.

Explaining differences in either a high or low need for achievement.
http://mentalhelp.net/psyhelp/chap4/chap4j.htm
This site provides an excellent overview of past and current theories regarding the need for achievement beginning with the research of McClelland and Atkinson. It also explains how we learn our individual need for achievement and the family background of high achievers.

Want to learn more about the controversy surrounding the polygraph test?
http://antipolygraph.org/
This is the home page of the non-profit, AntiPolygraph.org. On their "What We Want" link they clearly state that their organization is dedicated to "the complete abolishment of polygraph 'testing' from the American workplace." It provides interesting reading about the controversy surrounding polygraph testing.

Need more information on how the polygraph works?
http://science.howstuffworks.com/question123.htm
Interesting Web site that provides background information about "How Lie Detectors Work," "Rules and Regulations for Polygraph Examiners," and "How to Sting the Polygraph."

Interested in more information on emotional intelligence (EI)?
http://www.eiconsortium.org/
This is the home site of the Consortium for Research on Emotional Intelligence in Organizations. It offers a host of research articles and full-text reports on topics such as, "EI: What is it and Why it Matters," "Economic Value of EI Programs," and "Do EI Programs Work?"

www.wiley.com/college/huffman

Visual SUMMARY

Theories and Concepts of Motivation

Biological Theories

- **Instinct**: Emphasizes inborn, genetic component in motivation.

- **Arousal**: Organisms seek *optimal level* of *arousal* that maximizes their performance.

- **Drive-reduction**: Internal tensions (produced by body's demand for **homeostasis**) "push" organism to satisfy basic needs.

Psychosocial Theories

- **Incentive**: Emphasizes the "pull" of environmental stimuli.

- *Cognitive*: Emphasizes attributions and expectations.

Biopsychosocial Theory

- Maslow's **hierarchy of needs**: Basic physiological and survival needs must be met before higher needs, such as love and self-actualization.

Motivation and Behavior

Hunger and Eating
- Both *biological* factors (stomach, biochemistry, brain) and *psychosocial* forces (stimulus cues and cultural conditioning) contribute to hunger and eating.
- Obesity, **anorexia nervosa**, and **bulimia nervosa** result from a combination of biological and psychosocial factors.

1) Obesity: Being significantly above the recommended weight level.

2) **Anorexia nervosa**: Extreme weight loss due to self-imposed starvation.

3) **Bulimia nervosa**: Excessive consumption of food followed by purging.

Achievement
- **Achievement motivation:** Need for success, doing better than others, and mastering challenging tasks.

Three Basic Components of Emotion

- Physiological (arousal): increased heart rate, respiration
- Cognitive (thinking): thoughts, values, expectations
- Behavioral (expressions): smiles, frowns, running

Four Major Theories of Emotion

James–Lange

Feelings are interpreted from physiological arousal and behavioral expressions (smile, racing heart).

Cannon–Bard

Arousal, cognitions, and behavioral expression of emotions occur simultaneously.

Facial–Feedback

Movement of facial muscles elicits specific emotions.

Schachter's Two–Factor

Emotions depend on two factors—physical arousal and cognitive labeling of the arousal.

Critical Thinking About Motivation and Emotion

- **Intrinsic** vs. **extrinsic motivation**: Research shows extrinsic rewards can lower interest and achievement motivation.

- **Polygraph**: Measures changes in emotional arousal but is not valid for measuring guilt or innocence.
- **Emotional intelligence (EI)**: Knowing and managing emotions, empathizing, and maintaining satisfying relationships.

- **Culture, Evolution, and Emotion**: Seven to ten basic, *universal* emotions suggest emotions that may be innate; however, display rules differ across cultures.

www.wiley.com/college/huffman

Photodisc Green/GettyImages, Inc.

PERSONALITY

A chievement

Core Learning Outcomes

As you read Chapter 13, keep the following questions in mind and answer them in your own words:

▷ What are the trait theories of personality?

▷ What is Freud's psychoanalytic theory, and how did his followers build on his theory?

▷ What do humanistic theorists believe about personality?

▷ What is the social-cognitive perspective on personality?

▷ How does biology contribute to personality?

▷ How do psychologists measure personality?

▷ How do sex, gender, and culture influence personality?

■ Achievement
■ Assessment
■ Application

Chapter 13 will help explain why or how...

Cameron/Corbis Images

▷ Sigmund Freud believed that between the ages of 3 and 6, little boys develop a sexual longing for their mother and jealousy and hatred for their father.

▷ Carl Rogers believed that children raised with conditional positive regard might later have poorer mental health as adults.

▷ In the 1800s phrenologists believed personality could be measured by reading the bumps on your skull.

▷ Some measures of personality require respondents to interpret inkblots.

▷ We tend to notice and remember events that confirm our expectations and ignore those that are nonconforming.

▷ Europeans and Americans have measurable personality differences from people in Asian and African cultures.

Consider the following personality description. How well does it describe you?

> *You have a strong need for other people to like and admire you. You have a tendency to be critical of yourself. You have a great deal of unused capacity that you have not turned to your advantage. Although you have some personality weaknesses, you are generally able to compensate for them. You pride yourself on being an independent thinker and do not accept other opinions without satisfactory proof. Disciplined and self-controlled outside, you tend to be worried and insecure inside. At times, you have serious doubts whether you have made the right decision or done the right thing.*
>
> (ADAPTED FROM ULRICH, STACHNIK, & STAINTON, 1963)

What do you think? Does this sound like you? This same personality description was given to a variety of research participants, and they were told that it was written specifically for them based on previous psychological tests. Although all participants were given identical personality descriptions, a high percentage reported that the description was "very accurate." Surprisingly, even when participants were informed that this was a made-up assessment based on generalized information, most still believed the description fit them better than a bona fide personality profile developed from scientifically designed tests (Hyman, 1981).

What about common newspaper horoscopes? Research shows that about 78 percent of women and 70 percent of men read their personal horoscopes, and many believe they are so correct that they were written especially for them (Halpern, 1998). Perhaps most surprising, in a study of nonpsychology and psychology majors and mental health professionals, researchers found widespread acceptance of vague and universal statements as valid descriptors of their individual personalities (Pulido & Marco, 2000).

Why are these pseudo personality assessments so popular? It could be that we think they somehow tap into our unique selves. Actually, however, the traits they supposedly reveal are generalizations shared by almost everyone. Furthermore, the traits are generally positive and flattering—or at least neutral. (Would we believe or accept assessments that characterize us as "irritable, selfish, and emotionally unstable"?) In this chapter, rather than using these nonscientific methods, we will focus on scientifically-based methods used by psychologists to assess personality.

Before we begin, we need to define *personality*. For most people, "personality" is a relatively simple, everyday concept, as in "He's got a great (or lousy) personality." But for psychologists, personality is an inherently complicated concept, with numerous definitions. One of the most widely accepted definitions is that **personality** is an individual's unique and relatively stable pattern of thoughts, feelings, and actions. Personality describes you as a *person*: how you are different from other people and what patterns of behavior are typical of you. You might qualify as an "extrovert," for example, if you are talkative and outgoing most of the time. Or you may be described as "conscientious" if you are responsible and self-disciplined most of the time. (Keep in mind that personality is not the same as *character*, which refers to your ethics, morals, values, and integrity.)

Personality *Unique and relatively stable pattern of thoughts, feelings, and actions*

Unlike the pseudopsychologies in supermarket tabloids and newspaper horoscopes, the descriptions presented by personality researchers are based on empirical studies—the *science* of personality. In line with the basic goals of psychology presented in Chapter 1, personality researchers seek to (1) *describe* individual differences in personality, (2) *explain* how those differences come about, and (3) *predict* individual behavior based on personality findings. The bulk of this chapter is dedicated to the five most prominent theories and findings in personality research: *trait, psychoanalytic/psychodynamic, humanistic, social-cognitive,* and *biological*. The chapter ends with "Personality Assessment," which discusses the tests and measurement techniques used by psychologists to measure personality.

TRAIT THEORIES

How would you describe your two or three best friends? Would you say they are funny, loyal, and good-natured? The terms you use to describe other people (and yourself) are called **traits**, relatively stable personal characteristics. Trait theorists are

Trait *Relatively stable personal characteristic that can be used to describe someone*

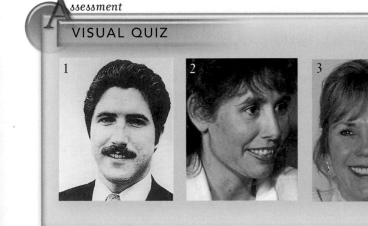
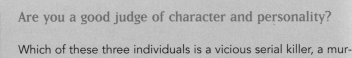

What are the trait theories of personality?

interested in first discovering how people differ (which key traits best describe them). They then want to measure how people differ (the degree of variation in traits within the individual and among individuals).

■ Early Trait Theorists: Allport, Cattell, and Eysenck

> Much of our lives is spent in trying to understand others and in wishing others understood us better than they do.
>
> GORDON ALLPORT

Identifying and measuring the essential traits that distinguish individual personalities sounds much easier than it actually is. Every individual differs from others in a great number of ways. An early study of dictionary terms found almost 18,000 words that could be used to describe personality. Of these, about 4500 were considered to fit the researchers' definition of personality *traits* (Allport & Odbert, 1936).

Faced with this enormous list of potential traits, Gordon Allport (1937) believed the best way to understand personality was to study an individual and then arrange his or her unique personality traits into a hierarchy. The most important and pervasive traits were listed at the top and the least important at the bottom.

Factor Analysis *Statistical procedure for determining the most basic units or factors in a large array of data*

Later psychologists reduced the wide array of possible personality traits with a statistical technique called **factor analysis**. Raymond Cattell (1950, 1965, 1990) condensed the list of traits to 30 to 35 basic characteristics. Hans Eysenck (1967, 1982, 1990) reduced the list even further. He described personality as a relationship among three basic types of traits—*extroversion–introversion*, *neuroticism*, (tendency toward insecurity, anxiety, guilt, and moodiness), and *psychoticism* (exhibiting some qualities commonly found among psychotics). These dimensions are assessed with the *Eysenck Personality Questionnaire*.

■ The Five-Factor Model: Five Basic Personality Traits

Factor analysis was also used to develop the most talked about (and most promising) modern trait theory—the **five-factor model (FFM)** (McCrae & Costa, 1990, 1999; McCrae et al., 2004). Combining all the previous research findings and the long list of possible personality traits, researchers discovered that several traits came up repeatedly, even when different tests were used. These five major dimensions of personality, often dubbed the "Big Five," are as follows.

Five-Factor Model (FFM) *Trait theory of personality that includes openness, conscientiousness, extroversion, agreeableness, and neuroticism*

1. *(O) Openness.* People who rate high in this factor are original, imaginative, curious, open to new ideas, artistic, and interested in cultural pursuits. Low scorers tend to be conventional, down to earth, narrower in their interests, and not artistic. [Interestingly, critical thinkers tend to score higher than others on this factor (Clifford, Boufal, & Kurtz, 2004).]

2. *(C) Conscientiousness.* This factor ranges from responsible, self-disciplined, organized, and achieving at the high end to irresponsible, careless, impulsive, lazy, and undependable at the other.

3. *(E) Extroversion.* This factor contrasts people who are sociable, outgoing, talkative, fun loving, and affectionate at the high end with introverted individuals who tend to be withdrawn, quiet, passive, and reserved.

4. *(A) Agreeableness.* Individuals who score high on this factor are good-natured, warm, gentle, cooperative, trusting, and helpful. Low scorers are irritable, argumentative, ruthless, suspicious, uncooperative, and vindictive.

Study **T**ip

You can easily remember the five factors by noting that the first letters of each of the five-factor dimensions spell the word "ocean."

5. *(N) Neuroticism (or emotional stability).* People high on neuroticism are emotionally unstable and prone to insecurity, anxiety, guilt, worry, and moodiness. People at the other end are emotionally stable, calm, even-tempered, easygoing, and relaxed.

Constructing Your Own Personality Profile

Study Figure 13.1, which is based on Raymond Cattell's factor analysis findings. Note how Cattell's 16 source traits exist on a continuum. There are extremes at either end, such as reserved and less intelligent at the far left and outgoing and more intelligent at the far right. Average falls somewhere in the middle.

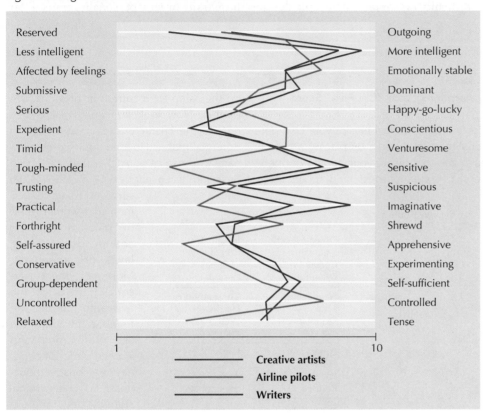

Figure 13.1 *Cattell's continuum of 16 source traits.*

Take a pen and make a dot on the line (from 1 to 10) that represents your own degree of reservation versus outgoingness. Then make a dot for yourself on the other 15 traits. Now connect the dots. How does your personality profile compare with the profiles of creative artists, airline pilots, and writers?

▪ Evaluating Trait Theories: The Pros and Cons

As you will see in the "Try This Yourself" exercise on the next page, David Buss and his colleagues (1990, 1999, 2003) found a strong correlation between their survey findings and the five-factor model (FFM). This may reflect an evolutionary advantage to people who are more open, conscientious, extroverted, and agreeable—and less neurotic. The evolutionary perspective also is confirmed by cross-cultural studies (Chuang, 2002; McCrae et al., 2004) and comparative studies with dogs, chimpanzees, and other species (Fouts, 2000; Gosling & John, 1999; Wahlgren & Lester, 2003).

www.wiley.com/college/huffman

Taken together, these studies suggest that the five-factor model may be a biologically based human universal. This model is the first to achieve the major goal of trait theory—to describe and organize personality characteristics using the fewest number of traits. Critics argue, however, that the great variation seen in personalities cannot be accounted for by only five traits. Furthermore, the Big Five model fails to offer *causal* explanations for these traits (Friedman & Schustack, 2006; Funder, 2000; Monte & Sollod, 2003). Trait theories, in general, are subject to three major criticisms:

1. ***Lack of explanation.*** Trait theories are good at *describing* personality. But they have difficulty *explaining* why people develop these traits or why personality traits differ

---

TRY THIS YOURSELF

Application

Determining Your "Big Five" Score

Use the figure below to plot your own personality profile. Begin by placing a dot on each line to indicate your degree of openness, conscientiousness, and so on. Then do the same for a current or previous love partner. Now look at Figure 13.2, which reports the characteristics most valued in potential mates. How do your scores compare to those of your love partner? David Buss and his colleagues (1989, 1999, 2003) surveyed over 10,000 men and women from 37 different countries and found a surprising level of agreement. Moreover, most personality traits of the five-factor model are found at the top of the list. Both men and women prefer *dependability* (conscientiousness), *emotional stability* (low neuroticism), *pleasing disposition* (agreeableness), and *sociability* (extroversion) to the alternatives.

Personality and marital stability. *According to long-term studies of personality, most changes in personality occur during childhood, adolescence, and young adulthood (McCrae et al., 2000). After age 30, most traits are relatively fixed, and changes after that point are few and small. Thus, people who marry after age 30 may have a more successful marriage because their personalities are more stable.*

Big Five Traits	Low Scorers	High Scorers
1 **O**penness	Down-to-earth / Uncreative / Conventional / Uncurious	Imaginative / Creative / Original / Curious
2 **C**onscientiousness	Negligent / Lazy / Disorganized / Late	Conscientious / Hard-working / Well-organized / Punctual
3 **E**xtroversion	Loner / Quiet / Passive / Reserved	Joiner / Talkative / Active / Affectionate
4 **A**greeableness	Suspicious / Critical / Ruthless / Irritable	Trusting / Lenient / Soft-hearted / Good-natured
5 **N**euroticism	Calm / Even-tempered / Comfortable / Unemotional	Worried / Temperamental / Self-conscious / Emotional

♂ What Men Want in a Mate
1. Mutual attraction — love
2. Dependable character
3. Emotional stability and maturity
4. Pleasing disposition
5. Good health
6. Education and intelligence
7. Sociability
8. Desire for home and children
9. Refinement, neatness
10. Good looks

♀ What Women Want in a Mate
1. Mutual attraction — love
2. Dependable character
3. Emotional stability and maturity
4. Pleasing disposition
5. Education and intelligence
6. Sociability
7. Good health
8. Desire for home and children
9. Ambition and industriousness
10. Refinement, neatness

Figure 13.2 ***The importance of various traits in mate selection around the world.*** Source: Buss et al., "International Preferences in Selecting Mates." *Journal of Cross-Cultural Psychology*, 21, pp. 5–47, 1990. Sage Publications, Inc.

across cultures. For example, cross-cultural research has found that people of almost all cultures can be reliably grouped into the FFM. However, trait theories fail to *explain* why people in cultures that are geographically close tend to have similar personalities or why Europeans and Americans tend to be higher in extroversion and openness to experience and lower in agreeableness than people in Asian and African cultures (Allik & McCrae, 2004).

2. ***Lack of specificity.*** Trait theorists have documented a high level of personality stability after age 30. But they haven't identified which characteristics last a lifetime and which are most likely to change. One cross-cultural study of the FFM did find that neuroticism, extroversion, and openness to experience tend to decline from adolescence to adulthood. Conversely, agreeableness and conscientiousness tend to increase (McCrae et al., 2004). (As a critical thinker, how would you explain these changes? Do you think they're good or bad?)

3. ***Ignoring situational effects.*** Trait theorists have been criticized for ignoring the importance of situational and environmental effects. One sad example of how the environment influences personality comes from a longitudinal study of the FFM with a group of young children. Psychologists Fred Rogosch and Dante Cicchetti (2004) found that 6-year-old children who were victims of abuse and neglect scored significantly lower on the traits of openness to experience, conscientiousness, and agreeableness and higher on the trait of neuroticism than did children who were not maltreated. The children were then reassessed at ages 7, 8, and 9. Unfortunately, the traits persisted. And these maladaptive personality traits create significant liabilities that may trouble these children throughout their lifetime. More research is obviously needed to identify ways to help maltreated children—and prevent the abuse itself.

As these examples show, the situation or environment can sometimes have a powerful effect on personality. For years, a heated debate—known as "trait versus situationism" or the "person–situation controversy"—existed in psychology. After two decades of continuing debate and research, both sides seem to have won. Just as nature and nurture are inseparable and interacting forces (see Chapter 9), the situation or environment also interacts with our relatively stable personality traits (Caspi, Roberts, & Shiner, 2005; Cervone, 2005; Segerstrom, 2003). We will return to this *interactionist* position later in this and other chapters.

*A*pplication

RESEARCH HIGHLIGHT

Do Nonhuman Animals Have Personality?

"It was exactly 33 years ago that I first met one of my oldest and dearest friends. To this day, the most outstanding aspect of her personality remains a quality I noticed the very first time I laid eyes on her: She is one of the most caring and compassionate people I know. She's also a chimpanzee" (Fouts, 2000, p. 68).

These are the words of a famous and highly respected comparative psychologist, Dr. Roger Fouts. What do you think? Do nonhuman animals have personality? Roger Fouts proposes that "like us, chimps are highly intelligent, cooperative and sometimes violent primates who nurture family bonds, adopt orphans, mourn the death of mothers, practice self-medication, struggle for power and wage war. And that only makes sense, because the chimp brain and the human brain both evolved from the same brain—that of our common ape ancestor" (Fouts, 2000, p. 68). Other scientists, however, are generally reluctant to ascribe personality traits, emotions, and cognitions to nonhuman animals, despite the often-cited statistic that humans have 98.4 percent of the same DNA as chimps.

Noting that previous studies on animal personality were scattered across multiple disciplines and various journals, researchers Samuel Gosling and Oliver John attempted to integrate and summarize this fragmented literature. They carefully reviewed 19 factor analytic personality studies of 12 different species:

Do nonhuman animals have personality? *Pet owners have long believed that their dogs and cats have unique personality traits, and recent research tends to agree with them (Fouts, 2000; Gosling et al., 2004; Gosling & John, 1999). For example, when 78 dogs of all shapes and sizes were rated by both owners and strangers, a strong correlation was found on traits such as affection vs. aggression, anxiety vs. calmness, and intelligence vs. stupidity. They also found that personalities vary widely within a breed, which means that not all pit bulls are aggressive and not all labradors are affectionate (Gosling et al., 2004).*

guppies, octopi, rats, dogs, cats, pigs, donkeys, hyenas, vervet monkeys, rhesus monkeys, gorillas, and chimpanzees. To integrate the diverse, multispecies information, Gosling and John used the human five-factor model discussed earlier. Interestingly, three human FFM dimensions—extroversion, neuroticism, and agreeableness—showed the strongest cross-species generality. How these personality traits are manifested, however, depends on the species. A human who scores low on extroversion "stays at home on Saturday night, or tries to blend into a corner at a large party. The [similarly low-scoring] octopus stays in its protective den during feedings and attempts to hide itself by changing color

or releasing ink into the water" (Gosling & John, 1999, p. 70).

One nonhuman dimension was also found to be important for describing animal personality—dominance. In adult humans, dominance is part of the extroversion dimension. But dominance has a wider range of personality implications in nonhuman animals. Gosling and John explain that unlike most species, humans have multiple dominance hierarchies. The class bully may dominate on the schoolyard, the academically gifted may dominate in the classroom, and the artist may win prizes for his or her creations.

Sex differences are another area where cross-species studies provide important information. For example, research on the human FFM consistently shows that women score higher on neuroticism than men (i.e., being more emotional and prone to worry) (Hrebickva, Cermak, & Osecka, 2000; McCrae et al., 1999). However, Gosling and John found a reversal of gender differences among hyenas. It was the males that were most neurotic—being more high-strung, fearful, and nervous (Figure 13.3). They explain that, among

hyenas, the female is larger and more dominant than the male. Furthermore, the hyena clan is matrilineal, with the mother recognized as the head of the family. Thus, it may be that sex differences in personality are related to the ecological niches (the place or function within the ecosystem) occupied by the two sexes in a species.

According to Gosling and John, comparative studies provide insight into the existence of nonhuman animal personality. They also offer a fresh perspective on the interplay between social and biological forces in human personality. As Roger Fouts suggested, "In the past few decades, scientific evidence on chimps and other nonhuman primates has poured in to support one basic fact: We have much more in common with apes than most people care to believe" (Fouts, 2000, p. 68).

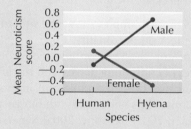

Figure 13.3 *Sex differences in standard (z) scores for neuroticism among humans and hyenas.* The ratings for hyenas are from Gosling (1998). The humans were described by peers on the same rating scales used for hyenas.

CHECK & REVIEW

Trait Theories

Trait theorists believe **personality** consists of relatively stable and consistent characteristics. Gordon Allport described individuals by their trait hierarchy. Raymond

Cattell and Hans Eysenck used **factor analysis** to identify the smallest possible number of traits. More recently, researchers identified a **five-factor model (FFM)** that can be used to describe most individuals. The five traits are openness,

conscientiousness, extroversion, agreeableness, and neuroticism.

General trait theories are subject to three major criticisms: *lack of explanation* (no explanation for why people develop certain traits and why traits sometimes change), *lack of specificity* (no specifics provided about which early characteristics endure and which are transient), and *ignoring situational effects*.

Questions

1. A relatively stable and consistent characteristic that can be used to describe someone is known as a _____. (a) character; (b) trait; (c) temperament; (d) personality

2. Match the following personality descriptions with their corresponding factor from the five-factor model (FFM): (a) openness; (b) conscientiousness; (c) introversion; (d) agreeableness; (e) neuroticism

___i. Tending toward insecurity, anxiety, guilt, worry, and moodiness

___ii. Being imaginative, curious, open to new ideas, and interested in cultural pursuits

___iii. Being responsible, self-disciplined, organized, and high achieving

___iv. Tending to be withdrawn, quiet, passive, and reserved

___v. Being good-natured, warm, gentle, cooperative, trusting, and helpful

3. Trait theories of personality have been criticized for _____. (a) failing to explain why people develop their traits; (b) not including a large number of central traits; (c) failing to identify which traits last and which are transient; (d) not considering situational determinants of personality; (e) all but one of these options.

Check your answers in Appendix B.

 CLICK & REVIEW
for additional assessment options:
www.wiley.com/college/huffman

PSYCHOANALYTIC/PSYCHODYNAMIC THEORIES

In contrast to trait theories that *describe* personality as it exists, *psychoanalytic* (or *psychodynamic*) theories of personality attempt to *explain* individual differences by examining how *unconscious* mental forces interplay with thoughts, feelings, and actions. The founding father of psychoanalytic theory is Sigmund Freud. We will examine Freud's theories in some detail and then briefly discuss three of his most influential followers—Alfred Adler, Carl Jung, and Karen Horney.

Achievement

What is Freud's psychoanalytic theory, and how did his followers build on his theory?

Freud's Psychoanalytic Theory: Four Key Concepts

Who is the best-known figure in all of psychology? Most people immediately name Sigmund Freud. Even before you studied psychology, you probably came across his name in other courses. Freud's theories have been applied in the fields of anthropology, sociology, religion, medicine, art, and literature. Working from about 1890 until he died in 1939, Freud developed a theory of personality that has been one of the most influential—and, at the same time, most controversial—in all of science (Allen, 2006; Domhoff, 2004; Gay, 1999).

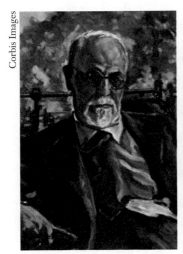

AP/Wide World

Freud and his famous couch. Sigmund Freud (1856–1939) was one of the most influential personality theorists. He also developed a major form of therapy (known as psychoanalysis) and treated many patients in the office pictured here.

In discussing Freud's theory, we will focus on four of his key concepts: *levels of consciousness, personality structure, defense mechanisms, and psychosexual stages of development.*

Levels of Consciousness

Freud called the mind the *psyche* [sie-KEY] and believed that it functioned on three levels of awareness or consciousness (Figure 13.4). Using the analogy of an iceberg, the first level of awareness, the **conscious**, can be compared to the part of the iceberg above water. This part of the mind consists of all thoughts or motives that we are currently aware of or are remembering.

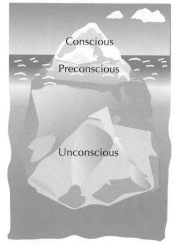

Figure 13.4 *Freud's three levels of consciousness.* The tip of the iceberg is often compared to the *conscious* mind, which is above the water and open to easy inspection. The preconscious (the area only shallowly submerged) contains information that can be viewed with a little extra effort. The large base of the iceberg is comparable to the *unconscious* mind, completely hidden from personal inspection. According to Freud, at this moment your conscious mind may be focusing on this text. But your preconscious may include feelings of hunger and thoughts of where you might go for lunch. Any repressed sexual desires, aggressive impulses, or irrational thoughts and feelings are reportedly stored in your unconscious.

Immediately below the conscious realm, and the water's surface, is the somewhat larger **preconscious**. The preconscious includes thoughts or motives that are not part of our current thoughts but are able to be readily brought to mind. For example, the smell of fried chicken at lunch may make you feel inexplicably happy. You are conscious of being happy. But without close examination you may not realize that the smell reminds you, preconsciously, of your grandmother, whom you adore.

The third level, the **unconscious**, lies below the preconscious and forms the bulk of the psyche. According to Freud, the unconscious stores our primitive, instinctual motives, plus anxiety-laden thoughts and memories blocked from normal awareness.

What would you think if you heard a flight attendant say, "It's been a real job serving you … I mean joy!"? From a Freudian perspective, this little slip of the tongue (known as a *Freudian slip*) supposedly reflects the flight attendant's true, unconscious feelings. Freud believed the unconscious is hidden from our personal awareness. But it still has an enormous impact on our behavior—and reveals itself despite our intentions. Just as the enormous mass of iceberg below the surface destroyed the ocean liner *Titanic*, the unconscious may similarly damage our psychological lives. Freud believed that most psychological disorders originate from repressed (hidden) memories and instincts (sexual and aggressive) stored in the unconscious.

Conscious *In Freudian terms, thoughts or motives that a person is currently aware of or is remembering*

Preconscious *Freud's term for thoughts, motives, or memories that can voluntarily be brought to mind*

Unconscious *Freud's term for thoughts, motives, and memories blocked from normal awareness*

"Good morning, beheaded—uh, I mean beloved."

To treat these disorders, Freud developed *psychoanalysis*—a type of therapy designed for identifying and resolving problems stored in the unconscious (See Chapter 15). As you can imagine, Freud's concepts of the conscious, preconscious, and unconscious mind, as well as his techniques for uncovering hidden, unconscious thoughts, motives, and memories are difficult to study scientifically. They have, therefore, been the subjects of great debate in psychology.

Personality Structure

In addition to proposing that the mind functions at three levels of awareness, Freud believed personality was composed of three interacting mental structures: *id*, *ego*, and *superego*. Each of these structures resides, fully or partially, in the unconscious mind (Figure 13.5). (Keep in mind that the id, ego, and superego are mental concepts—or hypothetical constructs. They are not physical structures you could see if you dissected a human brain.)

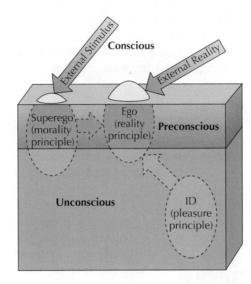

The Id According to Freud, the **id** is made up of innate, biological instincts and urges. It is immature, impulsive, irrational, and totally unconscious. When its primitive drives build up, the id seeks immediate gratification to relieve the tension. Thus, the id operates on the **pleasure principle**, the immediate and uninhibited seeking of pleasure and the avoidance of discomfort. In other words, the ID is like a newborn baby. It wants what it wants when it wants it!

If the id was not constrained by reality, we might seek pleasure (cheat on our spouses) and avoid pain (lie about our behavior) because this is what the id often urges us to do. However, Freud believed the other two parts of the psyche—the *ego* and the *superego*—develop to control and channel the id's potentially destructive energy.

The Ego As the infant grows older, the second part of the psyche, the **ego**, develops. The ego is responsible for planning, problem solving, reasoning, and controlling the id. Unlike the id, which lies entirely in the unconscious, the ego resides primarily in the conscious and preconscious. In Freud's system, the ego corresponds to the self—our conscious identity of ourselves as persons.

One of the ego's tasks is to channel and release the id's energy in ways that are compatible with the external environment. Contrary to the id's *pleasure principle*, the ego operates on the **reality principle**. This means the ego is responsible for delaying gratification until it is practical or appropriate.

Freud used the example of a rider and his horse to illustrate the relationship of the ego and id:

> In its relation to the id [the ego] is like a man on horseback, who has to hold in check the superior strength of the horse.... Often a rider, if he is not to be parted from his horse, is obliged to guide it where it wants to go; so in the same way the ego is in the habit of transforming the id's will into action as if it were its own.
>
> (FREUD, 1923/1961, P. 25)

The Superego The final part of the psyche to develop is the **superego**. This voice of conscience is made up of a set of ethical standards or rules for behavior that resides primarily in the preconscious and unconscious. The superego develops from internalized parental and societal standards. Some Freudian followers have suggested that it operates

Figure 13.5 *Freud's personality structure.* According to Freud, personality is composed of three structures—the *id*, *ego*, and *superego*. The id operates on the *pleasure principle*, the ego operates on the *reality principle*, and the superego is guided by the *morality principle*. Note how the ego is primarily conscious and preconscious, whereas the id is entirely unconscious.

Id *According to Freud, the source of instinctual energy, which works on the pleasure principle and is concerned with immediate gratification*

Pleasure Principle *In Freud's theory, the principle on which the id operates—seeking immediate pleasure*

Ego *In Freud's theory, the rational part of the psyche that deals with reality by controlling the id, while also satisfying the superego; from the Latin term ego, meaning "I"*

Reality Principle *According to Freud, the principle on which the conscious ego operates as it tries to meet the demands of the id and superego and the realities of the environment*

Superego *In Freud's theory, the part of the personality that incorporates parental and societal standards for morality*

Freudian theory in action? What might the id, ego, and superego be saying during this flirtation?

Morality Principle *The principle on which the superego may operate, which results in feelings of guilt if its rules are violated*

Defense Mechanisms *In Freudian theory, the ego's protective method of reducing anxiety by distorting reality*

Repression *Freud's first and most basic defense mechanism, which blocks unacceptable impulses from coming into awareness*

on the **morality principle** because violating its rules results in feelings of guilt. Have you ever felt the urge to copy someone else's paper during an exam? According to Freud, the desire to cheat and hopefully get a better grade comes from your id. The guilt and conscience that stops you from cheating comes from your superego.

The superego constantly strives for perfection. It is, therefore, as unrealistic as the id. Not only must the ego find objects and events that satisfy the id, but these same objects and events also must not violate the standards of the superego. For this reason, the ego is often referred to as the "harried executive" of the personality—managing, organizing, and directing behavior.

Defense Mechanisms

What happens when the ego fails to satisfy both the id and the superego? Anxiety slips into conscious awareness. Because anxiety is uncomfortable, people avoid it through **defense mechanisms**, which satisfy the id and superego by distorting reality. An alcoholic who uses his paycheck to buy drinks (a message from the id) may feel very guilty (a response from the superego). He may reduce this conflict by telling himself that he deserves a drink for working so hard. This is an example of the defense mechanism of *rationalization*.

Although Freud described many kinds of defense mechanisms, he believed repression was the most important. **Repression** is the mechanism by which the ego prevents the most anxiety-provoking or unacceptable thoughts and feelings from entering consciousness. It is the first and most basic form of anxiety reduction.

In recent years, repression has become a popular—and controversial—topic because of the number of lawsuits brought by adults who claim *repressed memories* of childhood sexual abuse. As we discussed in Chapter 7, however, it is difficult to determine the authenticity of such memories. Table 13.1 presents repression and several other Freudian defense mechanisms—all of which are reportedly unconscious.

"I'm sorry, I'm not speaking to anyone tonight. My defense mechanisms seem to be out of order."

©The New Yorker Collection 1985 Joseph Mirachi from cartoonbank. com. All rights reserved.

SUMMARY TABLE 13.1 SAMPLE PSYCHOLOGICAL DEFENSE MECHANISMS

Defense Mechanism	Description	Example
Repression	Preventing painful or unacceptable thoughts from entering consciousness	Forgetting the details of your parent's painful death
Sublimation	Redirecting unmet desires or unacceptable impulses into acceptable activities	Rechanneling sexual desires into school, work, art, sports, hobbies that are constructive
Denial	Protecting oneself from an unpleasant reality by refusing to perceive it	Alcoholics refusing to admit their addiction
Rationalization	Substituting socially acceptable reasons for unacceptable ones	Justifying cheating on an exam by saying "everyone else does it"
Intellectualization	Ignoring the emotional aspects of a painful experience by focusing on abstract thoughts, words, or ideas	Emotionless discussion of your divorce while ignoring underlying pain
Projection	Transferring unacceptable thoughts, motives, or impulses to others	Becoming unreasonably jealous of your mate while denying your own attraction to others
Reaction formation	Refusing to acknowledge unacceptable urges, thoughts, or feelings by exaggerating the opposite state	Promoting a petition against adult bookstores even though you are secretly fascinated by pornography
Regression	Responding to a threatening situation in a way appropriate to an earlier age or level of development	Throwing a temper tantrum when a friend doesn't want to do what you'd like
Displacement	Redirecting impulses toward a less threatening person or object	Yelling at a coworker after being criticized by your boss

I see people using defense mechanisms all the time. Is this bad? Defense mechanisms do twist the truth and distort reality. On the other hand, research supports Freud's belief that some misrepresentation seems to be necessary for our psychological well-being (Newman, Duff, & Baumeister, 1997; Taylor & Armor, 1996). During a gruesome surgery, for example, physicians and nurses may *intellectualize* the procedure as an unconscious way of dealing with their personal anxieties. By focusing on highly objective technical aspects of the situation, they do not become emotionally overwhelmed by the potentially tragic situations they often encounter. Occasional use of defense mechanisms can be healthy as long as it does not become extreme.

Sublimation in action?

Psychosexual Stages of Development

The concept of defense mechanisms has generally withstood the test of time. And they are an accepted part of modern psychology (e.g., Chapter 3). This is not the case for Freud's theory of psychosexual stages of development.

According to Freud, strong biological urges residing within the id supposedly push all children through five universal **psychosexual stages** during the first 12 or so years of life—oral, anal, phallic, latency, and genital (Figure 13.6). The term *psychosexual*

Psychosexual Stages *In Freudian theory, five developmental periods (oral, anal, phallic, latency, and genital) during which particular kinds of pleasures must be gratified if personality development is to proceed normally*

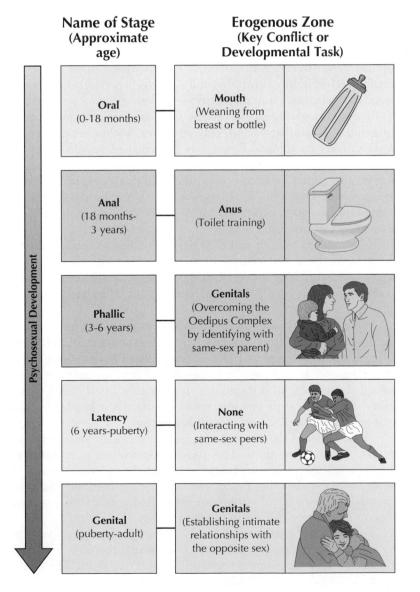

Name of Stage (Approximate age)	Erogenous Zone (Key Conflict or Developmental Task)	
Oral (0-18 months)	**Mouth** (Weaning from breast or bottle)	
Anal (18 months-3 years)	**Anus** (Toilet training)	
Phallic (3-6 years)	**Genitals** (Overcoming the Oedipus Complex by identifying with same-sex parent)	
Latency (6 years-puberty)	**None** (Interacting with same-sex peers)	
Genital (puberty-adult)	**Genitals** (Establishing intimate relationships with the opposite sex)	

Psychosexual Development

Figure 13.6 *Freud's five psychosexual stages of development.*

Photodisc Green/GettyImages

www.wiley.com/college/huffman

Michael Newman/PhotoEdit

The oral stage? *Is this an example of Freud's earliest stage of psychosexual development, or just a part of all infants' normal sucking behaviors?*

Oedipus [ED-uh-puss] Complex
Period of conflict during the phallic stage when children are supposedly attracted to the opposite-sex parent and hostile toward the same-sex parent

reflects Freud's emphasis on *infantile sexuality*—his belief that children experience sexual feelings from birth (although in different forms from those of adolescents or adults).

At each psychosexual stage, the id's impulses and social demands come into conflict. Therefore, if a child's needs are not met, or are overindulged, at one particular stage, the child may *fixate* and a part of the personality will remain stuck at that stage. Most individuals successfully pass through one or more of the five stages. But during stressful times, they may return (or *regress*) to an earlier stage in which earlier needs were badly frustrated or overgratified.

During the *oral stage* (birth to 12 to 18 months), the erogenous (or sexually arousing) zone is the mouth. The infant receives satisfaction through sucking, eating, biting, and so on. Because the infant is highly dependent on parents and other caregivers to provide opportunities for oral gratification, fixation at this stage can easily occur. If the mother overindulges her infant's oral needs, the child may fixate and as an adult become gullible ("swallowing" anything), dependent, and passive. The underindulged child, however, will develop into an aggressive, sadistic person who exploits others. According to Freud, orally fixated adults may also orient their life around their mouth—overeating, becoming an alcoholic, smoking, talking a great deal, and so on.

During the *anal stage* (between 12 to 18 months and 3 years), the erogenous zone shifts to the anus. The child receives satisfaction by having and retaining bowel movements. Because this is also the time when most parents begin toilet training, the child's desire to control his or her own bowel movements often leads to strong conflict. Adults who are fixated at this stage, in Freud's view, may display an *anal-retentive* personality and be highly controlled and compulsively neat. Or they may be very messy, disorderly, rebellious, and destructive—the *anal-expulsive* personality.

During the *phallic stage* (between 3 and 6 years), the major center of pleasure is the genitals. Masturbation and "playing doctor" with other children are common during this time. According to Freud, a 3- to 6-year-old boy also develops an unconscious sexual longing for his mother and jealousy and hatred for the rival father. This attraction creates a conflict Freud called the **Oedipus complex**, after Oedipus, the legendary Greek king who unwittingly killed his father and married his mother. The young boy eventually experiences guilt and fear of punishment from the rival father, perhaps by castration.

This *castration anxiety* and the Oedipus conflict are reportedly resolved when the boy represses his sexual feelings for his mother, gives up his rivalry with his father, and begins to *identify* with him instead. If this stage is not resolved completely or positively, the boy supposedly grows up resenting his father and generalizes this feeling to all authority figures.

What about the psychosexual development of young girls? Freud admitted being unsure, but he did believe girls develop a special attachment to their father. Unlike the young boy who develops castration anxiety, however, the young girl discovers that she lacks a penis. This supposedly causes her to develop *penis envy* and hostile feelings toward the mother, who she blames for the anatomical "deficiency." The conflict is resolved when the little girl suppresses her desire for her father, gives up her rivalry with her mother, and identifies with her instead.

Freud believed that most young girls never really overcome penis envy or fully identify with their mothers. This causes most women to reportedly develop a lower level of morality than men. (You are undoubtedly surprised or outraged by this statement, but remember that Freud was a product of his times. Sexism was common at this point in history. And most modern psychodynamic theorists reject Freud's notion of penis envy, as we will see in the next section.)

Following the phallic stage is the *latency stage* (from age 6 years to puberty). During this stage, children supposedly repress sexual thoughts and engage in nonsexual activities, such as developing social and intellectual skills. The task of this stage is to

Does art imitate life? Or does art imitate Freud? *According to Freudian interpretation, Shakespeare's* Hamlet *(upper left) portrayed unconscious Oedipal feelings—a young boy's wish to kill his father and marry his mother. The psychiatrist in the movie* Psycho *(top middle) also explained that "Oedipal problems" led to the bloody stabbing and murder scene in the shower. Similarly,* The Little Mermaid *(bottom left) might tap into the young girl's desire for her father and rivalry with her mother. In this and other Disney films, the mother is almost always either dead or absent, and the young girl has her father all to herself.*

develop successful interactions with same-sex peers and refinement of appropriate gender roles.

With the beginning of adolescence comes the *genital stage.* The genitals are again erogenous zones. Adolescents seek to fulfill their sexual desires through emotional attachment to members of the opposite sex. Unsuccessful outcomes at this stage lead to participation in sexual relationships based only on lustful desires, not on respect and commitment.

■ Neo-Freudian/Psychodynamic Theories: Revising Freud's Ideas

Some initial followers of Freud later rebelled and proposed theories of their own. Three of the most influential of these *neo-Freudians* were Alfred Adler, Carl Jung, and Karen Horney.

Adler's Individual Psychology

Alfred Adler (1870–1937) was the first to leave Freud's inner circle. Instead of seeing behavior as motivated by unconscious forces, he believed it is purposeful and goal-directed. He believed that each of us has the capacity to choose and to create. According to Adler's theory of *individual psychology,* our goals in life provide the source of our motivation—especially those goals that aim to obtain security and overcome feelings of inferiority. Adler believed that almost everyone suffers from an **inferiority complex**, deep feelings of inadequacy that arise from childhood.

Why are inferiority feelings so common? In Adler's view, we have inferiority feelings because we begin life as completely helpless infants. Every young child feels small, incompetent, and helpless when dealing with skilled adults. These early feelings of inadequacy supposedly result in a *will-to-power* that causes children to strive to

Inferiority Complex *Adler's idea that feelings of inferiority develop from early childhood experiences of helplessness and incompetence*

www.wiley.com/college/huffman

develop superiority over others or, more positively, to develop their full potential and gain mastery and control in their lives. Thus, the childhood inferiority complex can lead to negative adult traits of dominance, aggression, and envy. Or it can lead to positive traits such as self-mastery and creativity (Adler, 1964, 1998).

Adler also suggested that the will-to-power could be positively expressed through *social interest*—identifying with others and cooperating with them for the social good. In stressing social interest and the positive outcomes of inferiority feelings, Adlerian theory is more optimistic than Freudian theory.

Jung's Analytical Psychology

Another early follower turned dissenter, Carl Jung (yoong), developed *analytical psychology*. Like Freud, Jung (1875–1961) emphasized unconscious processes. But he believed the unconscious contains positive and spiritual motives as well as sexual and aggressive forces.

Collective Unconscious *Jung's concept of a reservoir of inherited, universal experiences that all humans share*

Archetypes [AR-KEH-types] *According to Jung, the images and patterns of thoughts, feelings, and behavior that reside in the collective unconscious*

Jung also thought we have two forms of unconscious mind, the *personal unconscious* and the *collective unconscious*. The personal unconscious is created from our individual experiences. Conversely, the **collective unconscious** is a reservoir of inherited, universal experiences that all humans share (Jung, 1936/1969). The collective unconscious consists of primitive images and patterns of thought, feeling, and behavior that Jung called **archetypes**. In other words, the collective unconscious is the ancestral memory of the human race, which explains the similarities in religion, art, symbolism, and dream imagery across cultures (Figure 13.7).

Because of archetypal patterns in the collective unconscious, we perceive and react in certain predictable ways. One set of archetypes refers to *gender roles* (Chapter 11). Jung claimed that both males and females have patterns for feminine aspects of personality *(anima)* and masculine aspects *(animus)*. The anima and animus within allow each of us to express both masculine and feminine personality traits and to understand and relate to the other sex.

Horney, Freud, and Penis Envy

Karen Horney (HORN-eye) accepted much of the Freudian theory, but she also added concepts of her own. For example, she strongly disagreed with Freud that differences in men and women were biologically based. Instead of "biology is destiny," Horney contended that male–female differences were largely the result of social and

Figure 13.7 *A collective unconscious?* According to Jung, humans around the world, and throughout history, tend to share basic images that are stored in the collective unconscious. Note the repeated symbol of the snake in the early Australian aboriginal bark painting and the ancient Egyptian tomb painting.

Charles & Josette Lenars/Corbis Images

Roger Wood/Corbis Images

cultural factors. Freud's concept of penis envy, for example, reflected women's feelings of cultural inferiority, not biological inferiority. According to Horney, the appropriate term should be *power envy*.

> The wish to be a man . . . may be the expression of a wish for all those qualities or privileges that in our culture are regarded as masculine, such as strength, courage, independence, success, sexual freedom, and the right to choose a partner.
> (HORNEY, 1926/1967, P. 108)

Corbis Images

Karen Horney (1885–1952). One of the few women who were trained by Freud, Horney disagreed with his emphasis on biological determinants of personality. She believed penis envy should be called power envy because it resulted from women's lower social status. Horney is also remembered for the concept of basic anxiety.

Horney is also known for her theories of personality development. If, as a child, you felt alone and isolated in a hostile environment and your needs were not met by nurturing parents, Horney believed you would experience extreme feelings of helplessness and insecurity. How people respond to this **basic anxiety**—a major concept in Horney's theory—greatly determines emotional health.

According to Horney, we all search for security in one of three basic and distinct ways. We can move toward people (by seeking affection and acceptance from others). We can move away from people (by striving for independence, privacy, and self-reliance). Or we can move against people (by trying to gain control and power over others). Emotional health requires a balance among these three styles. Exaggerating or overusing one constitutes a neurotic, or emotionally unhealthy, response.

Basic Anxiety *According to Horney, the feelings of helplessness and insecurity that adults experience because as children they felt alone and isolated in a hostile environment*

▇ Evaluating Psychoanalytic Theories: Criticisms and Enduring Influence

Freud and his psychoanalytic theories have been enormously influential. But as we said at the onset, his theories have also been the subject of great debate. Five major criticisms are presented here:

1. *Difficult to test.* From a scientific point of view, a major problem with psychoanalytic theory is that most of its concepts cannot be empirically tested (Domhoff, 2004; Esterson, 2002; Friedman & Schustack, 2006). How do you conduct an experiment on the id or unconscious conflicts? Scientific standards require testable hypotheses and operational definitions.

2. *Overemphasis on biology and unconscious forces.* Like many of the neo-Freudians, modern psychologists believe that Freud overemphasized biological determinants and did not give sufficient attention to learning and culture in shaping behavior.

3. *Inadequate empirical support.* Freud based his theories almost exclusively on the case histories of his adult patients. His data, therefore, were all subjective, leading critics today to wonder whether Freud saw what he expected to see and ignored the rest. Moreover, Freud's patients were almost exclusively upper-class Viennese women who sought his help because they had serious adjustment problems. Such a small and selective sample may mean that his theory describes only disturbed personality development in upper-class Viennese women in the late 1800s.

4. *Sexism.* Many psychologists reject Freud's theories as misogynistic, or derogatory toward women. For example, there is Freud's theory of *penis envy*, which, as you read earlier, Karen Horney, and others since, have rejected.

5. *Lack of cross-cultural support.* The Freudian concepts that ought to be most easily supported empirically—the biological determinants of personality—are generally not borne out by cross-cultural studies (Crews, 1997).

Granger Collection

Freud and his daughter. Despite criticisms of sexism, psychoanalysis was one of the few areas where women gained prominent positions in the early twentieth century. Here Freud is walking with his daughter Anna Freud (1895–1982), who also became an influential psychoanalyst.

www.wiley.com/college/huffman

PEANUTS reprinted by permission of United Features Syndicate, Inc.

Today there are few Freudian purists left. Modern psychodynamic theorists and psychoanalysts employ only some of his theories and techniques. Instead, they use empirical methods and research findings to reformulate and refine traditional Freudian theories and methods of assessment (Shaver & Mikulincer, 2005; Westen, 1998).

Many criticisms of Freud are quite legitimate. Nonetheless, many psychologists argue that, wrong as he was on many counts, Freud still ranks as one of the giants of psychology (Allen, 2006; Monte & Sollod, 2003; Weinberger & Westen, 2001). He should be credited and remembered for at least five reasons: (1) the emphasis on the unconscious and its influence on behavior; (2) the conflict among the id, ego, and superego and the resulting defense mechanisms; (3) open talk about sex in Victorian times; (4) the development of an influential form of therapy, *psychoanalysis;* and (5) the sheer magnitude of his theory.

In reference to this last point, Freud's impact on Western intellectual history cannot be overstated. He attempted to explain dreams, religion, social groupings, family dynamics, neurosis, psychosis, humor, the arts, and literature. It's easy to criticize Freud if you don't remember that he began his work at the start of the twentieth century and lacked the benefit of modern research findings and technology. To criticize his theory without historical perspective is like criticizing the Wright brothers for their crude airplane design. We can only imagine how our current theories will look 100 years from now.

Today, Freud's legacy lives on in our thinking and artistic imagination. Often without realizing the source, we talk about unconscious motives, oral fixations, and repression. We accuse people of being anal or egomaniacs. Right or wrong, Freud has a lasting place among the pioneers in psychology.

Assessment

CHECK & REVIEW

Psychoanalytic/Psychodynamic Theories

Sigmund Freud founded the psychoanalytic approach to personality, which emphasizes the power of the unconscious. The mind (or psyche) reportedly functions on three levels of awareness (**conscious, preconscious,** and **unconscious**). Similarly, the personality has three distinct structures (**id, ego,** and **superego**). The ego struggles to meet the demands of both the id and superego. When these demands conflict, the ego may resort to **defense mechanisms** to relieve anxiety. According to Freud, all human beings pass through five **psychosexual stages:** oral, anal, phallic, latency, and genital. How specific conflicts at each of these stages are resolved is important to personality development.

Three influential followers of Freud who later broke with him were Alfred Adler, Carl Jung, and Karen Horney. Known as neo-Freudians, they emphasized different issues. Adler emphasized the **inferiority complex** and the compensating will-to-power. Jung introduced the **collective unconscious** and **archetypes.** Horney stressed the importance of **basic anxiety** and refuted Freud's idea of penis envy, replacing it with power envy.

Critics of the psychoanalytic approach, especially Freud's theories, argue that the approach is difficult to test, overemphasizes biology and unconscious forces, has inadequate empirical support, is sexist, and lacks cross-cultural support. Despite these criticisms, Freud remains a notable pioneer in psychology.

HUMANISTIC THEORIES

Humanistic theories of personality emphasize internal experiences—feelings and thoughts—and the individual's own feelings of basic worth. In contrast to Freud's generally negative view of human nature, humanists believe people are naturally good (or, at worst, neutral). And that they possess a positive drive toward self-fulfillment.

According to this view, each individual's personality is created out of his or her unique way of perceiving and interpreting the world. Behavior is controlled by the individual's perception of reality, not by traits, unconscious impulses, or rewards and punishments. To fully understand another human being, you must know how he or she perceives the world. Humanistic psychology was developed largely from the writings of Carl Rogers and Abraham Maslow.

Achievement

What do humanistic theorists believe about personality?

Rogers's Theory: The Importance of the Self

To humanistic psychologist Carl Rogers (1902–1987), the most important component of personality is the *self*. This is the part of experience that a person comes to identify early in life as "I" or "me." Today, Rogerians (followers of Rogers) use the term **self-concept** to refer to all the information and beliefs you have as an individual regarding your own nature, unique qualities, and typical behaviors. Rogers was very concerned with the match between a person's self-concept and his or her actual experiences with life. He believed poor mental health and maladjustment developed from an incongruence or disparity between the self-concept and actual life experiences (Figure 13.8).

Self-Concept *Rogers's term for all the information and beliefs individuals have about their own nature, qualities, and behavior*

Mental Health, Congruence, and Self-Esteem

According to Rogers, there is an intimate connection among mental health, congruence, and *self-esteem—*

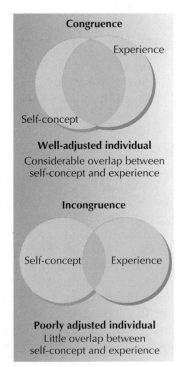

Congruence

Experience

Self-concept

Well-adjusted individual
Considerable overlap between self-concept and experience

Incongruence

Self-concept   Experience

Poorly adjusted individual
Little overlap between self-concept and experience

Figure 13.8 *Self-concept and adjustment.* According to Carl Rogers, mental health is related to the degree of congruence (or match) between our self-concept and life experiences. If our self-concept is reasonably consistent with our actual life experiences, our "self" is said to be congruent and we are well adjusted. The reverse is true when there is incongruity and little overlap.

Corbis Images

Carl Rogers (1902–1987). *As a founder of humanistic psychology, Rogers emphasized the importance of the self-concept. He believed our personality and individual self-esteem are heavily influenced by early childhood experiences, such as whether we received unconditional positive regard from our adult caregivers.*

www.wiley.com/college/huffman

Dear diary,
Sorry to
bother you again.

LOW SELF-ESTEEM

© The New Yorker Collection 1996 Mike Twohy
from cartoonbank.com. All Rights Reserved.

how we feel about ourselves. If our self-concept is congruent with (or matches) our life experiences, we generally have high self-esteem and better mental health. For example, an athletic child living in a family in which athletics are highly valued would have a better chance at higher self-esteem and better mental health than an artistic child in a family in which the arts aren't valued.

Mental health, congruence, and self-esteem are believed to be part of our innate biological capacities. All of us are born into the world with an innate need to survive, grow, and enhance ourselves. We naturally approach and value people and experiences that enhance our growth and fulfillment and avoid those that do not. Therefore, Rogers believed we can—and should—trust our own internal feelings to guide us toward mental health and happiness.

If everyone has an inborn, positive drive toward self-fulfillment, why do some people have low self-esteem and poor mental health? Rogers believed these outcomes generally result from early childhood experiences with parents and other adults who make their love *conditional.* That is, children learn that their acceptance is contingent on behaving in certain ways and expressing only certain feelings. When affection and love seem conditional, children block out the existence of negative impulses and feelings (which others label as "bad"). And their self-concepts and self-esteem become distorted. If a child is angry and hits his younger brother, for example, some parents might punish the child or deny his anger. They might say, "Nice children don't hit their brothers. They love them!" To gain parental approval, the child has to deny his true feelings of anger. But inside he secretly suspects he is not a "nice boy" because he *did* hit his brother and did not love him (at least at that moment).

Can you see how repeated incidents of this type might have a lasting effect on someone's self-esteem? If the child learns that his negative feelings and behaviors (which we all have) are totally unacceptable and unlovable, he may always doubt the love and approval of others because they don't know "the real person hiding inside."

Unconditional Positive Regard

Unconditional Positive Regard
Rogers's term for love and acceptance with no contingencies attached

PhotoDisc Green/GettyImages

To help a child develop to fullest potential, adults need to create an atmosphere of **unconditional positive regard**. That is, a setting in which children realize that they are loved and accepted with no conditions or strings attached. According to child expert Thomas Gordon:

> Acceptance is like the fertile soil that permits a tiny seed to develop into the lovely flower it is capable of becoming. The soil only enables the seed to become the flower. It releases the capacity of the seed to grow, but the capacity is entirely within the seed. As with the seed, a child contains entirely within the organism the capacity to develop. Acceptance is like the soil—it merely enables the child to actualize his potential.
>
> (GORDON, 1975, P. 31)

To some, unconditional positive regard and acceptance means we should allow people to do whatever they please. This is a common misinterpretation. Humanists separate the value of the person from his or her behaviors. They accept the person's positive nature and basic worth, while discouraging destructive or hostile behaviors. Hitting a playmate or yelling at a sales clerk is contrary to the child's or adult's positive nature as well as offensive to others.

Humanistic psychologists encourage children and adults to control their behavior so that they can develop a healthy self-concept and healthy relationships with others. In the previous example, they would encourage the parent to say, "I know you're angry with your brother, but we don't hit. You won't be allowed to play with him for a while if you can't control your anger."

◼ Maslow's Theory: The Search for Self-Actualization

Like Rogers, Abraham Maslow believed there is a basic goodness to human nature and a natural tendency toward self-actualization. He saw personality as the quest to fulfill basic physiological needs and then move upward toward the highest level of self-actualization (Figure 13.9).

What exactly is self-actualization? According to Maslow, **self-actualization** is the inborn drive to develop all one's talents and capacities. It involves understanding one's own potential, accepting oneself and others as unique individuals, and taking a problem-centered approach to life situations (Maslow, 1970). Self-actualization is an ongoing *process* of growth rather than an end *product* or accomplishment—more a road to travel than a final destination.

Maslow believed that only a few, rare individuals, such as Albert Einstein, Mohandas Gandhi, and Eleanor Roosevelt, become fully self-actualized. However, he saw self-actualization as part of every person's basic hierarchy of needs. (See Chapter 12 for more information on Maslow's theory.)

◼ Evaluating Humanistic Theories: Three Major Criticisms

Humanistic psychology was extremely popular during the 1960s and 1970s. It was a refreshing new perspective on personality after the negative determinism of the psychoanalytic approach and the mechanical nature of learning theories. Although this early popularity has declined, many humanistic ideas have been incorporated into approaches for counseling and psychotherapy (Kirschenbaum & Jourdan, 2005).

Ironically, the strength of the humanists, their focus on positivism and the subjective self experiences, is also why humanistic theories have been sharply criticized (e.g., Funder, 2000). Three of the most important criticisms are:

1. ***Naive assumptions.*** Critics suggest that the humanists are unrealistic, romantic, and even naive about human nature. Are all people as inherently good as they say? Our continuing history of murders, warfare, and other acts of aggression suggests otherwise.

Self-Actualization *Maslow's term for the inborn drive to develop all one's talents and capabilities*

"We do pretty well when you stop to think that people are basically good."

Dana Fradon/The CartoonBank, Inc.

Figure 13.9 *Maslow's hierarchy of needs.* According to Maslow, basic physical necessities must be satisfied before higher-growth needs can be addressed.

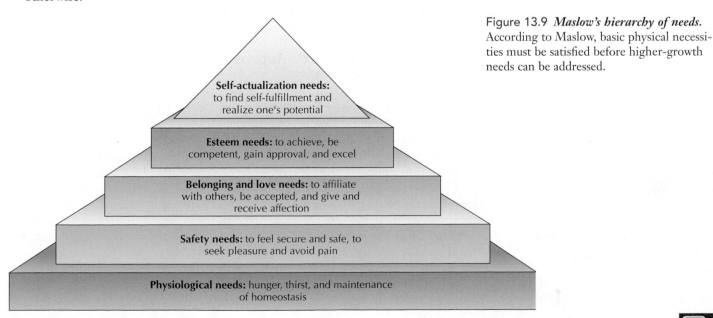

Self-actualization needs: to find self-fulfillment and realize one's potential

Esteem needs: to achieve, be competent, gain approval, and excel

Belonging and love needs: to affiliate with others, be accepted, and give and receive affection

Safety needs: to feel secure and safe, to seek pleasure and avoid pain

Physiological needs: hunger, thirst, and maintenance of homeostasis

www.wiley.com/college/huffman

2. ***Poor testability and inadequate evidence.*** Like many psychoanalytic terms and concepts, humanistic concepts (such as unconditional positive regard and self-actualization) are difficult to define operationally and test scientifically.

3. ***Narrowness.*** Like trait theories, humanistic theories have been criticized for merely *describing* personality, rather than *explaining* it. For example, where does the motivation for self-actualization come from? To say that it is an "inborn drive" doesn't satisfy those who favor experimental research and hard data as the way to learn about personality.

Assessment

CHECK & REVIEW

Humanistic Theories

Humanistic theories focus on internal experiences (thoughts and feelings) and the individual's **self-concept.** Carl Rogers emphasized mental health, congruence, self-esteem, and **unconditional positive regard.** Abraham Maslow emphasized the potential for **self-actualization.** Critics of the humanistic approach argue that these theories are based on naive assumptions and are not scientifically testable or well supported by empirical evidence. In addi-

tion, their focus on description, rather than explanation, makes them narrow.

Questions

1. If you took the _____ approach to personality, you would emphasize internal experiences, like feelings and thoughts, and the basic worth of the individual. (a) humanistic; (b) psychodynamic; (c) personalistic; (d) motivational

2. Rogers thought that _____ is necessary for a child's uniqueness and positive self-concept to unfold naturally. (a) per-

missive parenting; (b) a challenging environment; (c) unconditional positive regard; (d) a friendly neighborhood

3. Abraham Maslow's belief that all people are motivated toward personal growth and development is known as _____.

4. What are three major criticisms of humanistic theories?

Check your answers in Appendix B.

CLICK & REVIEW
for additional assessment options:
www.wiley.com/college/huffman

SOCIAL-COGNITIVE THEORIES

According to the social-cognitive perspective, each of us has a unique personality because of our individual history of interactions with the environment and because we *think* about the world and interpret what happens to us (Cervone & Shoda, 1999). Two of the most influential social-cognitive theorists are Albert Bandura and Julian Rotter.

Achievement

> What is the social-cognitive perspective on personality?

■ Bandura's and Rotter's Approaches: Social Learning Plus Cognitive Processes

Bandura's Self-Efficacy and Reciprocal Determinism

Although Albert Bandura is perhaps best known for his work on observational learning or social learning (Chapter 6), he has also played a major role in reintroducing thought processes into personality theory. Cognition is central to his concept of **self-efficacy**, which refers to a person's learned expectation of success (Bandura, 1997, 2000, 2003).

How do you generally perceive your ability to select, influence, and control the circumstances of your life? According to Bandura, if you have a strong sense of self-efficacy, you believe you can generally succeed, regardless of past failures and current obstacles. Most importantly, your self-efficacy will in turn affect the challenges you accept and the effort you expend in reaching goals.

Self-Efficacy *Bandura's term for a person's learned expectation of success*

Reciprocal Determinism *Bandura's belief that cognitions, behaviors, and the environment interact to produce personality*

Doesn't such a belief also affect how others respond to you and thereby affect your chances for success? Precisely! This type of mutual interaction and influence is a core part of another major concept of Bandura's—**reciprocal determinism**. According to Bandura, our cognitions (or thoughts), behaviors, and the environment are interdependent and interactive (Figure 13.10). Thus, a cognition ("I can succeed") will affect behaviors ("I will work hard and ask for a promotion"), which in turn will affect the environment ("My employer recognized my efforts and promoted me.").

Rotter's Locus of Control

Julian Rotter's theory is similar to Bandura's. He believes that prior learning experiences create *cognitive expectancies* that guide behavior and influence the environment (Rotter, 1954, 1990). According to Rotter, your behavior or personality is determined by (1) what you *expect* to happen following a specific action and (2) the *reinforcement value* attached to specific outcomes—that is, the degree to which you prefer one reinforcer to another.

To understand your personality and behavior, for instance, Rotter would want to know your expectancies and what you see as the source of life's rewards and punishments. To secure this information, Rotter might use personality tests that measure your internal versus external *locus of control* (Chapter 3). These tests ask people to respond "true" or "false" to a series of statements, such as "People get ahead in this world primarily by luck and connections rather than by hard work and perseverance" or "When someone doesn't like you, there is little you can do about it."

As you may suspect, people with an *external locus of control* think environment and external forces have primary control over their lives. Conversely, *internals* think they can control events in their lives through their own efforts. Numerous studies have found that having this type of an internal locus of control is positively associated with higher achievement and better mental health (Cheung & Rudowicz, 2003; Silvester et al., 2002; Sirin & Rogers-Sirin, 2004).

■ Evaluating Social-Cognitive Theory: The Pluses and Minuses

The social-cognitive perspective holds several attractions. First, it emphasizes how the environment affects, and is affected by, individuals. Second, it meets most standards for scientific research. It offers testable, objective hypotheses and operationally defined terms and relies on empirical data for its basic principles. Critics, however, believe social-cognitive theory is too narrow. It also has been criticized for ignoring unconscious and emotional aspects of personality (Carducci, 1998; Westen, 1998). For example, certain early experiences might have prompted a person to develop an external locus of control.

Both Bandura's and Rotter's theories emphasize cognition and social learning, but they are a long way from a strict behaviorist theory, which suggests that only environmental forces control behavior. They are also a long way from the biological theories that say inborn, innate qualities determine behavior and personality. Biological theories are the topic of our next section.

Self-efficacy in action. Research shows that self-defense training has significant effects on improving women's belief that they could escape from or disable a potential assailant or rapist (Weitlauf et al., 2001). But Bandura stresses that self-efficacy is always specific to the situation. For example, women who took this course reported greater self-defense efficacy, but this increased efficacy did not transfer over to other areas of their lives.

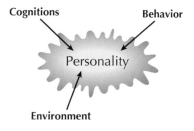

Figure 13.10 *Albert Bandura's theory of reciprocal determinism.* According to Bandura, thoughts (or cognitions), behavior, and the environment all interact to produce personality.

CHECK & REVIEW

Social-Cognitive Theories

Social-cognitive theorists emphasize the importance of our interactions with the environment and how we interpret and respond to these external events. Albert Bandura's social-cognitive approach focuses on **self-efficacy** and **reciprocal determinism.** Julian Rotter emphasizes cognitive expectancies and an internal or external locus of control.

Social-cognitive theory is credited for its attention to environmental influences and its scientific standards. However, it has been criticized for its narrow focus and lack of attention to the unconscious and emotional components of personality.

Questions

1. The social-cognitive approach to personality is most likely to analyze _____.

2. According to _____, thoughts (or cognitions), behavior, and the environment all interact to produce personality. (a) reciprocal determinism; (b) interactionism; (c) confluence theory; (d) reverberating circuits theory

3. According to Bandura, _____ involves a person's belief about whether he or she can successfully engage in behaviors related to personal goals. (a) self-actualization; (b) self-esteem; (c) self-efficacy; (d) self-congruence

4. People with an _____ expect the environment and external forces to control events, whereas those with an _____ believe in personal control.

Check your answers in Appendix B.

CLICK & REVIEW
for additional assessment options:
www.wiley.com/college/huffman

BIOLOGICAL THEORIES

Achievement

How does biology contribute to personality?

As you were growing up, you probably heard comments such as "You're just like your father" or "You're so much like your mother." Does this mean that biological factors you inherited from your parents were the major contributors to your personality? This is the question we first explore in this section. We conclude with a discussion of how all theories of personality ultimately interact within the biopsychosocial model.

■ Three Major Contributors: The Brain, Neurochemistry, and Genetics

Biological theories of personality focus on the brain, neurochemistry, and genetics. We begin our study with the brain.

The Brain

Do you remember the case study of Phineas Gage from Chapter 2? He was the railroad supervisor who survived a horrific mining accident that sent a 13-pound metal rod through his frontal lobe. As shown by Gage's case, brain damage can dramatically affect personality (Fukutake et al., 2002; Moretti et al., 2001). Modern biological research also suggests that activity in certain brain areas may contribute to some personality traits. Tellegen (1985), for example, proposes that extroversion and introversion are associated with particular areas of the brain, and research seems to support him. For instance, sociability (or extroversion) is associated with increased electroencephalographic (EEG) activity in the left frontal lobes of the brain. On the other hand, shyness (introversion) shows greater EEG activity in the right frontal lobes (Schmidt, 1999).

A major limitation to research on brain structures and personality is the difficulty of identifying which structures are uniquely connected with particular personality traits. Damage to one structure tends to have wide-ranging effects. Neurochemistry seems to offer more precise data on biological bases of personality. Jerome Kagan (1998), a major personality researcher, believes that most biologically based personality differences rest "on differences in neurochemistry rather than anatomy" (p. 59).

Neurochemistry

Do you enjoy skydiving and taking risks in general? Neurochemistry may explain why. Research has found a consistent relationship between sensation seeking and monoamine oxidase (MAO), an enzyme that regulates levels of neurotransmitters such as dopamine (Ibanez, Blanco, & Saiz-Ruiz, 2002; Zuckerman, 1994, 2004). Dopamine also seems to be correlated with novelty seeking and extroversion (Depue & Collins, 1999; Laine et al., 2001).

How can traits like sensation seeking, novelty seeking, and extroversion be related to neurochemistry? Studies suggest that high sensation seekers and extroverts tend to have lower levels of physiological arousal than introverts (Lissek & Powers, 2003). Their lower arousal apparently motivates them to seek out situations that will elevate their arousal. Moreover, it is believed that a lower threshold is inherited. In other words, personality traits like sensation seeking and extroversion may be inherited. (Also see Chapter 12 on arousal and sensation seeking.)

Genetics

Heredity is what sets the parents of a teenager wondering about each other.

LAURENCE J. PETER

Psychologists have only recently recognized the importance and influence of genetic factors in personality (Johnson et al., 2004; Murakami & Hayashi, 2002; Plomin & Crabbe, 2000; Sequeira et al., 2004). This relatively new area, called *behavioral genetics*, attempts to determine the extent to which behavioral differences among people are due to genetics as opposed to environment (Chapter 2).

To measure genetic influence, researchers rely mostly on two kinds of data. First, they compare similarities between identical twins and fraternal twins. Twin studies of the heritability of the five-factor model (FFM) personality traits range from 0.35 to about 0.70 (Bouchard, 1997; Eysenck, 1967, 1991; Lensvelt-Mulders & Hettema, 2001). These correlations suggest that genetic factors contribute about 40 to 50 percent of personality.

Second, researchers compare the personalities of parents, their biological children, and their adopted children. Research on the FFM traits of extroversion and neuroticism show that parents' traits correlate moderately with those of their biological children and very little with those of their adopted children (Bouchard, 1997; McCrae et al., 2004).

Overall, studies show a strong influence of hereditary factors on personality. At the same time, researchers are careful not to overemphasize the genetic basis (Deckers, 2005; Funder, 2001; Maccoby, 2000). Some believe the importance of the unshared environment (aspects of the environment that differ from one individual to another, even within a family) has been overlooked (Saudino, 1997). Others fear that research on "genetic determinism" could be misused to "prove" that an ethnic or racial group is inferior, that male dominance is natural, or that social progress is impossible. There is no doubt that genetics studies have produced exciting and controversial results. However, it is also clear that more research is necessary before we have a cohesive biological theory of personality.

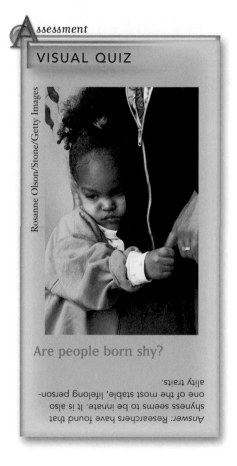

Assessment

VISUAL QUIZ

Rosanne Olson/Stone/Getty Images

Are people born shy?

Answer: Researchers have found that shyness seems to be innate. It is also one of the most stable, lifelong personality traits.

■ The Biopsychosocial Model: Integrating the Perspectives

With regard to personality, no one theory is more correct than another. Each provides a different perspective. And each offers different insights into how a person develops the distinctive set of characteristics we call "personality." As you can see in Figure 13.11, instead of adhering to any one theory, many psychologists believe in the *biopsychosocial* approach—the idea that several factors overlap in their contributions to personality (Higgins, 2004; McCrae, 2004). Hans Eysenck (1990), a leading personality theorist, believes that cer-

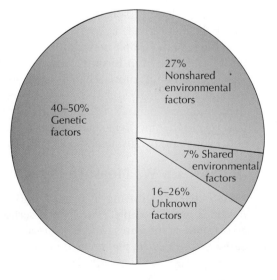

27% Nonshared environmental factors

40–50% Genetic factors

7% Shared environmental factors

16–26% Unknown factors

Figure 13.11 *Multiple influences on personality.* Researchers have concluded that personality can be broken down into four major factors: (1) genetics, inherited traits (40–50 percent); (2) nonshared environmental factors, or how each individual's genetic factors react and adjust to his or her particular environment (27 percent); (3) shared environmental factors, involving parental patterns and shared family experiences (7 percent); and (4) error, unidentified factors or problems with testing (16–26 percent). *Source:* Bouchard, 1997; Plomin, 1997; Talbot, Duberstein, King, Cox, & Giles, 2000; Wright, 1998.

www.wiley.com/college/huffman

tain traits (like introversion and extroversion) may reflect inherited patterns of cortical arousal, as well as social learning, cognitive processes, and the environment. Can you see how someone with an introverted personality, and therefore a higher level of cortical arousal, might try to avoid excessive stimulation by seeking friends and jobs with low stimulation levels?

Eysenck's work exemplifies how trait, biological, and social-cognitive theories can be combined to provide better insight into personality. This trend toward integration and the *biopsychosocial model* is reflected in a growing number of books and articles.

CHECK & REVIEW

Biological Theories

Biological theories emphasize brain structures, neurochemistry, and inherited genetic components of personality. Research on specific traits, such as extroversion and sensation seeking, support the biological approach. The biopsychosocial approach suggests that the major theories overlap and that each contributes to our understanding of personality.

Questions

1. _____ theories emphasize the importance of genetics in the development of personality. (a) Evolutionary; (b) Phenomenological; (c) Genological; (d) Biological

2. What concerns people about genetic explanations for personality?

3. What factor appears to have the greatest influence (40 to 50 percent) on personality? (a) the environment; (b) genetics; (c) learning; (d) unknown factors

4. The _____ approach represents a blending of several theories of personality. (a) unification; (b) association; (c) biopsychosocial; (d) phenomenological

Check your answers in Appendix B.

CLICK & REVIEW
for additional assessment options:
www.wiley.com/college/huffman

PERSONALITY ASSESSMENT

Achievement

How do psychologists measure personality?

Throughout history, people have sought information about their personality and that of others. Back in the 1800s, if you wanted to have your personality assessed, you would go to a *phrenologist*. This highly respected person would carefully measure your skull, examine the bumps on your head, and then give you a psychological profile of your unique qualities and characteristics. Phrenologists used a phrenology chart to determine which personality traits were associated with bumps on different areas of the skull (Figure 13.12).

Today, some people consult fortune-tellers, horoscope columns in the newspaper, tarot cards, and even fortune cookies in Chinese restaurants. But scientific research has provided much more reliable and valid methods for measuring personality. Clinical and counseling psychologists, psychiatrists, and other helping professionals use these modern methods to help with the diagnosis of patients and to assess their progress in therapy. Personality assessment is also used for educational and vocational counseling and by businesses to aid in hiring decisions.

How Do We Measure Personality: Do You See What I See?

Like a detective solving a mystery, modern psychologists typically use numerous methods and a complete *battery* (or series) of tests to fully *assess* personality. This assortment of measures can be grouped into a few broad categories: *interviews, observations, objective tests,* and *projective tests*.

Interviews

We all use informal "interviews" to get to know other people. When first meeting someone, we ask about their job, college major, family, and hobbies or interests. Psychologists use a more formal type of interview—both *structured* and *unstructured*. Unstructured interviews are often used for job and college selection and for diagnosing psychological problems. In an unstructured format, interviewers get impressions and pursue hunches. They also let the interviewee expand on information that promises to disclose unique personality characteristics. In structured interviews, the interviewer asks specific questions and follows a set of preestablished procedures so that the interviewee can be evaluated more objectively. The results of a structured interview are often charted on a rating scale that makes comparisons with others easier.

Observations

In addition to structured and unstructured interviews, psychologists also use direct behavioral observation to assess personality. Most of us enjoy casual "people watching." But, as you recall from Chapter 1, scientific observation is a much more controlled and methodical process. The psychologist looks for examples of specific behaviors and follows a careful set of evaluation guidelines. For instance, a psychologist might arrange to observe a troubled client's interactions with his or her family. Does the client become agitated by the presence of certain family members and not others? Does he or she become passive and withdrawn when asked a direct question? Through careful observation, the psychologist gains valuable insights into the client's personality, as well as family dynamics.

Objective Tests

Objective self-report personality tests, or *inventories*, are standardized questionnaires that require written responses. Answers to the typically multiple-choice or true–false questions help people to describe themselves—to "self-report." The tests are considered "objective" because they have a limited number of possible responses to items. They also have empirical standards for constructing test items and scoring. Another important advantage is that objective tests can be administered to a large number of people in a relatively short period of time and evaluated in a standardized fashion. These advantages help explain why objective tests are by far the most widely used method for assessing personality.

You have been introduced to several objective self-report personality tests in this textbook. We describe the sensation-seeking scale in Chapter 12, and earlier in this chapter we discussed Rotter's locus-of-control scale. The complete versions of these tests measure one specific personality trait and are used primarily in research. Often, however, psychologists in clinical, counseling, and industrial settings are interested in assessing a range of personality traits all at once. To do this, they generally use *multitrait* (or *multiphasic*) inventories.

The most widely studied and clinically used objective, multitrait test is the **Minnesota Multiphasic Personality Inventory (MMPI)**—or its revision, the MMPI-2 (Butcher, 2000; Butcher & Rouse, 1996). The test consists of over 500 statements that participants respond to with *True, False,* or *Cannot say.* The following are examples of the kinds of statements found on the MMPI:

My stomach frequently bothers me.

I have enemies who really wish to harm me.

I sometimes hear things that other people can't hear.

I would like to be a mechanic.

I have never indulged in any unusual sex practices.

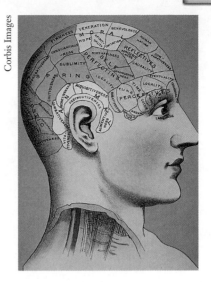

Corbis Images

Figure 13.12 *Is personality reflected in our skulls?* Yes, at least according Franz Gall, the founder of phrenology, which believed the skull takes its shape from the brain. Therefore, by examining the shape and unevenness of a head or skull, "scientists" could discover the underlying parts of the brain responsible for different psychological traits. For example, a large bump in the area above the right ear at the position attributed to *sublimity* would indicate that the individual had a "well-developed" organ in the brain responsible for squelching natural impulses, especially sexual ones. Can you imagine what traits might be measured if we still believed in phrenology? Would we find bumps and create terms like *technicity* (ability to adapt to rapidly changing technology) and *Scorcesity* (enjoyment of violent and terrifying movies)?

Minnesota Multiphasic Personality Inventory (MMPI) *The most widely researched and clinically used self-report personality test (MMPI-2 is the revised version)*

TABLE 13.2 SUBSCALES OF THE MMPI-2

Name of Subscale	Typical Interpretations of High Scores
Clinical Scales	
1. Hypochondriasis	Numerous physical complaints
2. Depression	Seriously depressed and pessimistic
3. Hysteria	Suggestible, immature, self-centered, demanding
4. Psychopathic deviate	Rebellious, nonconformist
5. Masculinity–femininity	Interests like those of other sex
6. Paranoia	Suspicious and resentful of others
7. Psychasthenia	Fearful, agitated, brooding
8. Schizophrenia	Withdrawn, reclusive, bizarre thinking
9. Hypomania	Distractible, impulsive, dramatic
10. Social introversion	Shy, introverted, self-effacing
Validity Scales	
1. L (lie)	Denies common problems, projects a "saintly" or false picture
2. F (confusion)	Answers are contradictory
3. K (defensiveness)	Minimizes social and emotional complaints
4. ? (cannot say)	Many items left unanswered

Why are some of these questions about really unusual, abnormal behavior? Although there are many "normal" questions on the full MMPI, the test is designed primarily for clinical and counseling psychologists to diagnose psychological disorders. Table 13.2 shows how MMPI test items are grouped into 10 *clinical scales*, each measuring a different disorder. Depressed people, for example, tend to score higher on one group of questions. People with schizophrenia score higher on a different group. Each group of items is called a *scale*. There are also four *validity scales* designed to reflect the extent to which respondents distort their answers, do not understand the items, or are being uncooperative. Research has found that the validity scales effectively detect those who may be faking psychological disturbances or trying to appear more psychologically healthy (Bagby, Rogers, & Buis, 1994).

Are these tests the same as career inventories? Personality tests like the MMPI are often confused with other objective self-report tests called *career inventories* or *vocational interest tests*. For example, the *Strong Vocational Interest Inventory* asks whether you would rather write, illustrate, print, or sell a book or whether you'd prefer the work of a salesperson or teacher. Your answers to these types of questions help identify occupations that match your unique traits, values, and interests.

Given your vocational interest test profile, along with your scores on *aptitude tests* (which measure potential abilities) and *achievement tests* (which measure what you have already learned), a counselor can help you identify the types of jobs that best suit you. Most colleges have career counseling centers where you can take vocational interest tests to guide you in your career decisions.

Projective Techniques

Unlike objective tests, **projective tests** use ambiguous, unstructured stimuli, such as inkblots, which can be perceived in many ways. As the name implies, *projective* tests supposedly allow each person to *project* his or her own unconscious conflicts, psychological defenses, motives, and personality traits onto the test materials. Troubled respondents are believed to be unable (or unwilling) to express their true feelings if asked directly. Therefore, the ambiguous stimuli reportedly provide an indirect, "psychological X-ray" of their hidden, unconscious processes (Hogan, 2003). Two of the

Projective Tests *Psychological tests using ambiguous stimuli, such as inkblots or drawings, which allow the test taker to project his or her unconscious onto the test material*

Index Stock

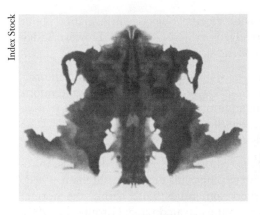

Harvard University Press

Figure 13.13 *What do you see?* If you were given a Rorschach test, you would be shown 10 inkblots like this one and asked to report what figures or objects you see. This is called a *projective* test because psychoanalysts believe that people will *project* the hidden, unconscious parts of their personality onto the ambiguous stimuli. (Reproduced with permission from APA.)

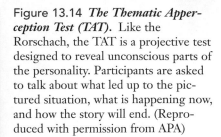

Figure 13.14 *The Thematic Apperception Test (TAT).* Like the Rorschach, the TAT is a projective test designed to reveal unconscious parts of the personality. Participants are asked to talk about what led up to the pictured situation, what is happening now, and how the story will end. (Reproduced with permission from APA)

most widely used projective tests are the *Rorschach Inkblot Test* and the *Thematic Apperception Test (TAT)*.

The Rorschach Inkblot Test, introduced in 1921 by Swiss psychiatrist Hermann Rorschach, consists of 10 inkblots. This test was originally developed by spilling ink on paper and folding the paper in half (Figure 13.13). You are asked to report what you see in each card. And the clinician records your responses verbatim while also observing your gestures and reactions. The clinician later interprets your answers as indications of your unconscious feelings and conflicts.

Created by personality researcher Henry Murray in 1938, the **Thematic Apperception Test (TAT)** is another of the most frequently used projective tests. It consists of a series of black-and-white ambiguous pictures, such as Figure 13.14. As mentioned in Chapter 12, the TAT is frequently used to measure achievement motivation. It also is used for personality assessment. If you were taking this test, you would be asked to create a story about the picture, including what the characters are feeling and how the story turns out. As with the Rorschach, your responses reportedly reflect your unconscious needs and conflicts. A person who sees a picture of a young girl looking at mannequins in a store window might create a story with angry references to the parents of the girl in the picture. Hearing this, the clinician might infer that the test-taker has hidden resentments toward his or her own parents (Davison, Neale, & Kring, 2004).

"RORSCHACH! WHAT'S TO BECOME OF YOU?"

Sidney Harris

◼ Are Personality Measurements Accurate? Evaluating the Methods

What do you think of these widely differing methods of personality assessment? Do they accurately measure true personality? Let's evaluate each of the four major methods: *interviews*, *observation*, *objective tests*, and *projective tests*.

- *Interviews and observations.* Both interviews and observations can provide valuable insights into personality. But they are time-consuming and therefore expensive. Furthermore, just as football fans can disagree over the relative merits of the same quarterback, raters of personality tests frequently disagree in their evaluations of the same individual. Interviews and observations also involve unnatural settings. And, as we saw in Chapter 1, the very presence of an observer can alter the behavior that is being studied.

Rorschach [ROAR-shock] Inkblot Test *A projective test that presents a set of 10 cards with symmetrical abstract patterns, known as inkblots, and asks respondents to describe what they "see" in the image; their response is thought to be a projection of unconscious processes*

Thematic Apperception Test (TAT) *A projective test that shows a series of ambiguous black-and-white pictures and asks the test-taker to create a story related to each; the responses presumably reflect a projection of unconscious processes*

www.wiley.com/college/huffman

- *Objective tests.* Tests like the MMPI-2 provide specific, objective information about a broad range personality traits in a relatively short period of time. However, they are also the subject of at least three major criticisms:

  1. *Deliberate deception and social desirability bias.* Some items on self-report inventories are easy to "see through." Thus, respondents may intentionally, or unintentionally, fake particular personality traits. In addition, some respondents want to look good and will answer questions in ways that they perceive as *socially desirable.* (The validity scales of the MMPI-2 are designed to help prevent these problems.)

  2. *Diagnostic difficulties.* When self-report inventories are used for diagnosis, overlapping items sometimes make it difficult to pinpoint a diagnosis (Graham, 1991). In addition, clients with severe disorders sometimes score within the normal range, and normal clients may score within the elevated range (Cronbach, 1990).

  3. *Possible cultural bias and inappropriate use.* Some critics think that the standards for "normalcy" on objective self-report tests fail to recognize the impact of culture. For example, Latinos—such as Mexicans, Puerto Ricans, and Argentineans—generally score higher than respondents from North American and Western European cultures on the masculinity–femininity scale of the MMPI-2 (Lucio-Gomez, Ampudia-Rueda, Duran-Patino, Gallegos-Mejia, & Leon-Guzman, 1999). The fact that these groups score higher may reflect their greater adherence to traditional gender roles and cultural training more than any individual personality traits.

- *Projective tests.* Projective tests are extremely time-consuming to administer and interpret. However, their proponents suggest that because they have no right or wrong answers, respondents are less able to deliberately fake their responses. In addition, because these tests are unstructured, respondents may be more willing to talk about sensitive, anxiety-laden topics.

  On the other hand, critics point out that the reliability and validity of projective tests are among the lowest of all tests of personality (Grove et al., 2002; Wood, Lilienfeld, Nezworski, & Garb, 2001). As you recall from Chapter 8's discussion of intelligence tests, the two most important measures of a good test are *reliability* (Are the results consistent?) and *validity* (Does the test measure what it's designed to measure?). One problem with the Rorschach, in particular, is that interpreting clients' responses depends in large part on the subjective judgment of the examiner. And some examiners are simply more experienced or skilled than others. Also, there are problems with *interrater reliability:* Two examiners may interpret the same response in very different ways.

In sum, each of these four methods has its limits. However, psychologists typically combine results from various methods to create a more complete understanding of an individual personality.

---

 pplication

CRITICAL THINKING

Why Are Pseudo Personality Tests So Popular?

Throughout this text, we have emphasized the value of critical thinking. By carefully evaluating the evidence and credibility of the source, critical thinkers recognize faulty logic and appeals to emotion. Applying these standards to the pseudo personality evaluations like the one in our introductory incident, we can identify at least three important logical fallacies: the *Barnum effect*, the *fallacy of positive instances*, and the *self-serving bias.*

ACTIVE LEARNING

The Barnum Effect

Pseudo personality descriptions and horoscope predictions are often accepted because we think they are accurate. We tend to believe these tests have somehow tapped into our unique selves. In fact they are ambiguous, broad statements that fit just about anyone. Being so readily disposed to accept such generalizations is known as the *Barnum effect*. This name is based on P.T. Barnum, the legendary circus promoter who said, "Always have a little something for everyone."

Reread the bogus personality profile in the chapter opening (p. 464). Can you see how the description, "You have a strong need for other people to like and admire you," fits almost everyone? Or do you know anyone who doesn't "at times have serious doubts whether [they've] made the right decision or done the right thing"? P.T. Barnum also said, "There's a sucker born every minute."

The Fallacy of Positive Instances

Look again at the introductory personality profile and count the number of times both sides of a personality trait are given.

("You have a strong need for other people to like you" and "You pride yourself on being an independent thinker.") According to the *fallacy of positive instances,* we tend to notice and remember events that confirm our expectations and ignore those that are nonconfirming. If we see ourselves as independent thinkers, for example, we ignore the "needing to be liked by others" part. Similarly, horoscope readers easily find "Sagittarius characteristics" in a Sagittarius horoscope. However, these same readers generally overlook Sagittarius predictions that miss or when the same traits appear for Scorpios or Leos.

The Self-Serving Bias

Now check the overall tone of the personality description. Can you see how the traits are generally positive and flattering—or at least neutral? According to the

self-serving bias, we tend to prefer information that maintains our positive self-image (Brown & Rogers, 1991; Gifford & Hine, 1997). In fact, research shows that the more favorable a personality description is, the more people believe it and the more likely they are to believe it is unique to themselves (Guastello, Guastello, & Craft, 1989). (The self-serving bias might also explain why people prefer pseudo personality tests to bona fide tests—they're generally more flattering!)

Taken together, these three logical fallacies help explain the belief in "pop psych" personality tests and newspaper horoscopes. They offer "something for everyone" (the *Barnum effect*). We pay attention only to what confirms our expectations (the *fallacy of positive instances*). And we like flattering descriptions (the *self-serving bias*).

VISUAL QUIZ

Can you identify the two fallacies in this cartoon?

Non Sequitur by Wiley ©1993 Washington PostWriter's Group, Distributed by Universal Press Syndicate. All Rights Reserved.

Answer: The self-serving bias and the Barnum effect.

Gender & Cultural Diversity

How Individualist and Collectivist Cultures Affect Personality

Up to this point, we have examined only Western theories of personality. In Western cultures, personality is seen as a composition of individual parts (traits and motives) and the self as a bounded individual—separate and autonomous from others (Markus & Kitayama, 2003; Matsumoto, 2000). Concepts like the *conscious, preconscious, unconscious, id, ego, superego, inferiority complex, basic anxiety, self-concept, self-esteem,* and *self-actualization* all assume a unique *self* composed of discrete traits, motives, and abilities.

www.wiley.com/college/huffman

Individualistic Cultures *The needs and goals of the individual are emphasized over the needs and goals of the group*

Collectivistic Cultures *The needs and goals of the group are emphasized over the needs and goals of the individual*

The self versus others. When engaged in exercise or recreation, people in collectivist cultures are more likely to emphasize group symmetry and connectedness. People in individualist cultures focus on independent movement and freedom to "do your own thing."

Joe Carini/The ImageWorks

AP/Wide World

This focus on the *self* also reflects an **individualistic culture**, where the needs and goals of the individual are emphasized over the needs and goals of the group. If asked "Who am I?" and to complete the statement, "I am…," people from individualistic cultures tend to respond with personality traits—"I am shy," "I am outgoing"—or their occupation—"I am a teacher," "I am a student."

In **collectivistic cultures**, however, the opposite is true. The person is defined and understood primarily by looking at his or her place in the social unit (McCrae, 2004; Montuori & Fahim, 2004; Tseng, 2004). Relatedness, connectedness, and interdependence are valued, as opposed to separateness, independence, and individualism. When asked to complete the statement, "I am…," people from collectivistic cultures tend to mention their families or nationality—"I am a daughter," "I am Chinese."

Are you part of an individualistic or collectivistic culture? As you can see in Table 13.3, if you are North American or Western European, you are more likely to be individualistic. And you may find the concept of a self, defined in terms of others, almost contradictory. A core selfhood seems intuitively obvious to you. Recognizing that over 70 percent of the world's population lives in collectivistic cultures, however, may improve your cultural sensitivity and prevent misunderstandings (Singelis et al., 1995). For example, North Americans generally define *sincerity* as behaving in accordance with one's inner feelings. Japanese, however, tend to see it as behavior that conforms to a person's role expectations (carrying out one's duties) (Yamada, 1997). Can you see how Japanese behavior might appear insincere to a North American and vice versa? Understanding how the individualistic perspective differs from that in collectivist cultures may improve our understanding of the cultural effects on personality. It also points out limits and biases in our current Western personality theories and the need for continued cross-cultural research.

TABLE 13.3 A WORLDWIDE RANKING OF CULTURES

Individualistic Cultures	Intermediate Cultures	Collectivistic Cultures
United States	Israel	Hong Kong
Australia	Spain	Chile
Great Britain	India	Singapore
Canada	Argentina	Thailand
Netherlands	Japan	West Africa region
New Zealand	Iran	El Salvador
Italy	Jamaica	Taiwan
Belgium	Arab region	South Korea
Denmark	Brazil	Peru
France	Turkey	Costa Rica
Sweden	Uruguay	Indonesia
Ireland	Greece	Pakistan
Norway	Phillipines	Colombia
Switzerland	Mexico	Venezuela

Cultural Effects on Personality

If asked to draw a circle with yourself in the center, and the people in your life as separate circles surrounding you, which of the two diagrams in Figure 13.15 comes closest to your personal view?

If you chose (a), you probably have an *individualistic* orientation, seeing yourself as an independent, separate self. However, if you chose (b), you're more closely aligned with a *collectivist* culture, seeing yourself as interdependent and interconnected with others (Markus & Kitayama, 2003).

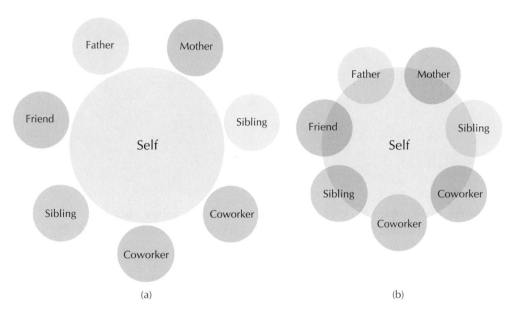

(a)   (b)

Figure 13.15 *The "self" in individualistic versus collectivistic cultures.*

ssessment

CHECK & REVIEW

Personality Assessment

Psychologists use four basic methods to measure or assess personality: interviews, observations, objective tests, and projective techniques. Interviews and observations can provide insights into personality. But they are time consuming and therefore expensive.

Objective tests, such as the **Minnesota Multiphasic Personality Inventory (MMPI-2),** use self-report questionnaires or inventories. These tests provide objec-

tive standardized information about a large number of personality traits. However, they are limited by respondents' deliberate deception and social desirability bias, diagnostic difficulties, and possible cultural bias and inappropriate use.

Projective tests, such as the **Rorschach Inkblot Test** and the **Thematic Apperception Test (TAT),** ask test-takers to respond to ambiguous stimuli. Although these tests reportedly provide insight into unconscious elements of personality, they have low reliability and validity.

Most Western theories of personality emphasize the concept of a self, which aligns with the **individualistic culture's** emphasis on personal needs and goals over those of the group. In **collectivistic cultures,** however, the opposite is true. The person is defined and understood primarily by looking at his or her place in the social unit. Relatedness, connectedness, and interdependence are valued, as opposed to separateness, independence, and individualism.

Questions

1. Match each personality test with its description:
   a. a projective test using inkblots
   b. an objective, self-report personality test
   c. a projective test using ambiguous drawings of ambiguous human situations
   ___i. MMPI-2
   ___ii. Rorschach
   ___iii. TAT

2. Two important criteria for evaluating the usefulness of tests used to assess personality are _____. (a) concurrence and prediction; (b) reliability and validity; (c) consistency and correlation; (d) diagnosis and prognosis

3. Describe the three logical fallacies that encourage acceptance of pseudo personality tests and horoscopes.

4. Explain how the Western concept of the self reflects an individualistic culture versus a collectivistic one.

Check your answers in Appendix B.

CLICK & REVIEW
for additional assessment options:
www.wiley.com/college/huffman

Assessment
KEY TERMS

*To assess your understanding of the **Key Terms** in Chapter 13, write a definition for each (in your own words), and then compare your definitions with those in the text.*

personality (p. 459)

Trait Theories
factor analysis (p. 460)
five-factor model (FFM) (p. 460)
trait (p. 459)

Psychoanalytic/Psychodynamic Theories
archetypes [AR-KEH-types] (p. 472)
basic anxiety (p. 474)
collective unconscious (p. 472)
conscious (p. 466)
defense mechanisms (p. 468)
ego (p. 467)
id (p. 467)

inferiority complex (p. 471)
morality principle (p. 468)
Oedipus [ED-uh-puss] complex (p. 470)
pleasure principle (p. 467)
preconscious (p. 466)
psychosexual stages (p. 469)
reality principle (p. 467)
repression (p. 468)
superego (p. 467)
unconscious (p. 466)

Humanistic Theories
self-actualization (p. 477)
self-concept (p. 475)
unconditional positive regard (p. 476)

Social-Cognitive Theories
reciprocal determinism (p. 478)
self-efficacy (p. 478)

Personality Assessment
collectivistic cultures (p. 488)
individualistic cultures (p. 488)
Minnesota Multiphasic Personality Inventory (MMPI-2) (p. 483)
projective tests (p. 484)
Rorschach [ROAR-shock] Inkblot Test (p. 485)
Thematic Apperception Test (TAT) (p. 485)

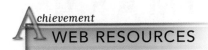

WEB RESOURCES

Huffman Book Companion Site

http://www.wiley.com/college/huffman

This site is loaded with free Interactive Self-Tests, Internet Exercises, Glossary and Flashcards for key terms, web links, Handbook for Non-Native Speakers, and other activities designed to improve your mastery of the material in this chapter.

Want more information about major personality theorists?

http://www.wynja.com/personality/theorists.html

This site offers detailed background material on most of the theories and theorists discussed in this chapter, including Freud, Maslow, and Rogers. It also provides information on lesser known theorists, such as Kelley, Lewin, and Tart. For even more information about Freudian theory, try http://psychoanalysis.org. This website, sponsored by the New York Psychoanalytic Institute and Society, contains a vast array of resources related to psychoanalytic theory and its application. If you want details about Maslow, try http://web.utk.edu/%7Egwynne/maslow.html. This website offers detailed information about Maslow's hierarchy of needs and its effect on motivation and personality development.

Are you painfully shy?

http://www.shyness.com/encyclopedia.html

Sponsored by the Palo Alto Shyness Clinic in Portola Valley, California, this website features a lengthy article written by Lynne Henderson and Philip Zimbardo—two renowned experts in the field. The article details the prevalence and diagnosis of shyness, a research summary, the genetic and environmental influences, as well as suggestions for treatment.

Would you like to take several tests?

http://www.2h.com/personality-tests.html

This commercial site offers a variety of tests, including the Keirsey Temperament Sorter, a Career Values Inventory, and VALS, a measure of your values, attitudes, and lifestyle. As noted in their stated mission, the sponsors of this site "do not give psychological advice and are not trained in that profession. Tests are only for your entertainment."

Interested in taking a free "Big Five" personality test?

http://www.outofservice.com/bigfive/

As noted in this chapter, the five-factor model is currently the most widely respected and well researched theory of personality. This site provides a free test of your own personality using this "Big Five" model, and you are encouraged to also submit responses for someone you know well, such as a close friend, coworker, spouse, or other family member.

Want to explore the great ideas in personality?

http://www.personalityresearch.org/

This site offers an excellent overview of past and current theories in personality, such as behaviorism, the five-factor model, cognitive social theories, and psychoanalysis. It also provides links to less well-known theories, including interpersonal theory and the PEN model.

Would you like to download a free electronic textbook on personality?

http://www.ship.edu/~cgboeree/perscontents.html

Dr. C. George Boeree at Shippensburg University has created a text that is copyrighted, but you may download or print it without permission as long as the material is used for your personal or educational purposes.

Interested in a career as a personality researcher?

http://www.rap.ucr.edu/overview.htm

This is the home page overview of a lab project currently being conducted by well respected personality researchers, including David Funder and Lawrence Wright. It will give you an idea of the type of research performed by personality researchers.

VISUAL SUMMARY

Major Personality Theories and Assessment Techniques

Theorists and Key Concepts

Five-Factor Model (FFM)

1. **O**penness
2. **C**onscientiousness
3. **E**xtroversion
4. **A**greeableness
5. **N**euroticism

Trait

Early theorists
- Allport: Arranged **traits** in hierarchy.
- Cattell (16PF) and Eysenck (Personality Questionnaire): Used **factor analysis** to reduce number of traits.

Modern theory
- **Five-factor model (FFM):** Openness, conscientiousness, extroversion, agreeableness, and neuroticism.

Determinants of Personality
Heredity and environment combine to create personality traits.

Methods of Assessment
Objective (self-report) inventories (e.g., MMPI), observation.

Psychoanalytic/Psychodynamic

Freud
- Levels of Consciousness—**conscious**, **preconscious**, and **unconscious**.
- Personality structure—**id (pleasure principle)**, **ego (reality principle)**, **superego (morality principle)**.
- Defense Mechanisms—**repression** and others.
- **Psychosexual Stages**—oral, anal, phallic, latency, and genital.

NeoFreudians
- Adler—individual psychology, **inferiority complex**, and will-to-power.
- Jung—analytical psychology, **collective unconscious**, and **archetypes**.
- Horney—power envy vs. penis envy and **basic anxiety**.

Determinants of Personality
Unconscious conflicts between id, ego, and superego lead to defense mechanisms.

Methods of Assessment
Interviews and **projective tests: Rorschach inkblot test, Thematic Apperception Test (TAT).**

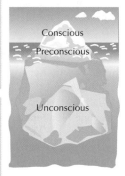

Conscious
Preconscious

Unconscious

Humanistic
- Rogers—**self-concept**, self-esteem, and **unconditional positive regard.**
- Maslow—**self-actualization.**

Determinants of Personality
Individual's subjective experience of reality.

Methods of Assessment
Interviews, objective (self-report) inventories.

Social/Cognitive
- Bandura—**self-efficacy** and **reciprocal determinism.**
- Rotter—cognitive expectancies and locus of control.

Determinants of Personality
Interaction between cognition and environment.

Methods of Assessment
Observation, objective (self-report) inventories.

Biological
- Brain structures like the frontal lobes may play a role.
- Neurochemistry (dopamine, MAO, and others) may play a role.
- Genetic factors also contribute to personality.

Determinants of Personality
Brain, neurochemistry, genetics.

Methods of Assessment
Animal studies and biological techniques.

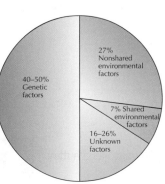

27% Nonshared environmental factors

40–50% Genetic factors

7% Shared environmental factors

16–26% Unknown factors

Personality Assessment

Psychologists use four methods to measure personality:

Interviews:
Can be either structured or unstructured.

Observations:
Psychologist uses direct behavioral observation with set of evaluation guidelines.

Objective Tests
(such as the **MMPI-2**) ask test-takers to self-report on paper-and-pencil questionnaires or inventories. These tests provide objective standardized information about a large number of personality traits, but they have their limits, including deliberate deception, social desirability bias, diagnostic difficulties and inappropriate use.

Projective Tests [such as the **Rorschach "inkblot"** or **Thematic Apperception Test (TAT)**] ask test-takers to respond to ambiguous stimuli. Though these tests are said to provide insight into unconscious elements of the personality, they are not very reliable or valid.

Reliability and **validity** are the major criteria for evaluating the accuracy of personality tests.

Cultural Contributions to Personality

Most theories of personality emphasize the concept of a self, and the Western, **individualistic culture's** emphasis on personal needs and goals over those of the group. In **collectivistic cultures**, the person is defined by his or her place in the social unit.

Roger Bamber/Alamy Images

14

PSYCHOLOGICAL DISORDERS

Achievement

Core Learning Outcomes

As you read Chapter 14, keep the following questions in mind and answer them in your own words:

▷ How do psychologists identify, explain, and classify abnormal behavior?

▷ What are anxiety disorders, and how do we explain them?

▷ When do disturbances in mood become abnormal?

▷ What are the symptoms and explanations for schizophrenia?

▷ How are substance-related, dissociative, and personality disorders identified?

▢ Achievement
▢ Assessment
▢ Application

Application

WHY STUDY PSYCHOLOGY?

Peterson Family/ZUMA/CorbisImages

Is Scott Peterson mentally ill? *This photo of the smiling parents-to-be was taken only a few days before Scott Peterson brutally killed his wife and unborn son.*

Chapter 14 will help clarify the following myths...

▶ *Myth #1: People with psychological disorders act in bizarre ways and are very different from normal people.*

Fact: This is true for only a small minority of individuals and during a relatively small portion of their lives. In fact, sometimes even mental health professionals find it difficult to distinguish normal from abnormal individuals without formal screening.

▶ *Myth #2: Mental disorders are a sign of personal weakness.*

Fact: Psychological disorders are a function of many factors, such as exposure to stress, genetic disposition, family background, and so on. Mentally disturbed individuals can't be blamed for their illness any more than we blame people who develop Alzheimer's or other physical illnesses.

▶ *Myth #3: Mentally ill people are often dangerous and unpredictable.*

Fact: Only a few disorders, such as some psychotic and antisocial personalities, are associated with violence. The stereotype that connects mental illness and violence persists because of prejudice and selective media attention.

▶ *Myth #4: A person who has been mentally ill never fully recovers.*

Fact: With therapy, the vast majority of people who are diagnosed as mentally ill eventually improve and lead normal pro-ductive lives. Moreover, mental disorders are generally only temporary. A person may have an episode that lasts for days, weeks, or months. Afterwards, they may go for years—even a lifetime—without further difficulty.

▶ *Myth #5: Most mentally ill individuals can work at only low-level jobs.*

Fact: Mentally disturbed people are individuals. As such, their career potentials depend on their particular talents, abilities, experience, and motivation, as well as their current state of physical and mental health. Many creative and successful people have suffered serious mental disorders. John Forbes Nash Jr., a recent Nobel Prize winner, has a lifetime history of schizophrenia. But he is now doing very well, as has been documented in the book and film *A Beautiful Mind (Famous People and Schizophrenia,* 2004). British Prime Minister Winston Churchill, Scottish soccer player Andy Goram, writer and poet Edgar Allan Poe, Pink Floyd band member Syd Barrett, Green Bay Packers sports star Lionel Aldridge, actress Patty Duke, painter Vincent Van Gogh, and billionaire Howard Hughes are all believed to have suffered from a serious mental disorder.

(*Sources:* Brown & Bradley, 2002; *Famous People and Schizophrenia,* 2004; *Famous People with Mental Illness,* 2004; Hansell & Damour, 2005; O'Flynn, 2001; Volavka, 2002.)

Mary's troubles first began in adolescence. She began to miss curfew, was frequently truant, and her grades declined sharply. During family counseling sessions, it was discovered that Mary also had been promiscuous and had prostituted herself several times to get drug money. She revealed a history of drug abuse, including "everything I can get my hands on." Mary also had ongoing problems with her peers. She quickly fell in love and overly idealized new friends. But when they quickly (and inevitably) disappointed her, she would angrily cast them aside. This pattern of poor grades, cutting classes, and unstable relationships continued throughout high school, two years of college, and a series of clerical jobs. Mary's problems, coupled with a preoccupation with inflicting pain on herself (by cutting and burning) and persistent thoughts of suicide, eventually led to her admittance to a psychiatric hospital at age 26.

(DAVISON, NEALE, & KRING, 2004, PP. 408–409)

Jim is a third-year medical student. Over the last few weeks, he has been noticing that older men appear to be frightened of him when he passes them on the street. Recently, he has become convinced that he is actually the director of the Central Intelligence Agency and that these men are secret agents of a hostile nation. Jim has found confirmatory evidence for his idea in the fact that a helicopter flies over his house every day at 8:00 A.M. and at 4:30 P.M. Surely, this surveillance is part of the plot to assassinate him.

(BERNHEIM & LEWINE, 1979, P. 4)

Ken Bianchi, the "Hillside Strangler," terrorized the Los Angeles area for more than a year. Working with his cousin, Bianchi used phony police badges to lure victims into his car or home, where they were later raped, systematically tortured, and then murdered. Bianchi and his cousin killed 10 women aged 12 to 28. Bianchi killed two more after moving to Washington State.

Scott Peterson smiled confidently before the jury's verdict was announced on November 12, 2004. After hearing that he was found guilty of killing his pregnant wife and their unborn son, he showed no apparent emotion. Four months later, Scott Peterson smiled once again as he entered the courtroom. His smile faded slightly when the judge upheld an earlier decision that he should die by lethal injection. But he remained motionless and emotion free as he listened to lengthy and heart wrenching victim impact statements.

(DORNIN, 2004, ON-LINE; MONTALDO, 2005, ON-LINE)

Each of these individuals has a severe psychological problem, and each case raises interesting questions. What caused Mary's unstable relationships and suicidal thoughts, Jim's paranoia, and Ken's and Scott's cold-blooded murders? Was there something in their early backgrounds to explain their later behaviors? Is there something medically wrong with them? What about less severe forms of abnormal behavior? Is a person who dreams of airplane crashes and refuses to fly mentally ill? What about a compulsively neat student who types all his lecture notes and refuses to write in any textbook? What is the difference between being eccentric and disordered? These are a few of the many topics we'll explore in this chapter.

The chapter begins with a discussion of the ways psychological disorders are identified, explained, and classified. The heart of the chapter explores six major categories of psychological disorders (anxiety disorders, mood disorders, schizophrenia, substance-related disorders, dissociative disorders, and personality disorders). Treatment for psychological disorders will be fully discussed in Chapter 15.

Achievement

How do psychologists identify, explain, and classify abnormal behavior?

STUDYING PSYCHOLOGICAL DISORDERS

As the introductory cases show, mental disorders vary in type and severity from person to person. Like personality, consciousness, and intelligence, *abnormal behavior* is difficult to define. In this section, we will explore how psychologists attempt to identify, explain, and classify abnormal behavior.

▪ Identifying Abnormal Behavior: Four Basic Standards

The behaviors of Mary, Jim, Ken, and Scott are clearly abnormal. However, most cases of abnormal behavior are not so clear-cut. Most people

"In the mental health profession, we try to avoid negative labels, like 'a hundred and fifty bucks an hour—that's <u>crazy!</u>' or 'three fifty-minute sessions a week—that's <u>insane!</u>'"

www.wiley.com/college/huffman

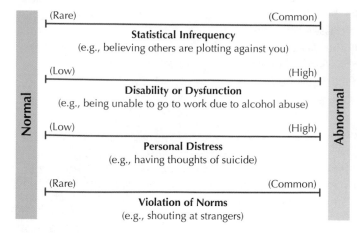

Figure 14.1 *The four criteria and a continuum of abnormal behavior.* There are at least four major criteria for judging abnormal behavior—statistical infrequency, disability or dysfunction, personal distress, and violation of norms. Rather than fixed categories, both "abnormal" and "normal" behaviors exist along a continuum from low to high and rare to common.

Abnormal Behavior *Patterns of emotion, thought, and action considered pathological (diseased or disordered) for one or more of these reasons: statistical infrequency, disability or dysfunction, personal distress, or violation of norms*

𝒜ssessment

VISUAL QUIZ

Would this behavior be considered abnormal?

Answer: This woman's extreme piercing do meet standards 1 and 4, but the term *abnormal behavior* is generally restricted to behavior that is considered pathological (diseased or disordered).

don't fall into one of two extreme categories—"crazy" versus "normal." As we've seen in previous chapters, traits like intelligence or creativity, and now abnormal behaviors, lie along a continuum. Most of the population falls somewhere between the two extreme end points.

Recognizing this continuum, how do we decide when behavior becomes abnormal? Let's begin with one of the most widely accepted definitions of **abnormal behavior**—patterns of emotion, thought, and action considered pathological (diseased or disordered) for one or more of the following reasons: statistical infrequency, disability or dysfunction, personal distress, or violation of norms (Davison, Neale, & Kring, 2004

As you can see in Figure 14.1, for each of these four criteria abnormal behavior falls along a continuum (Hansell & Damour, 2005). Keep in mind that each criterion has its merit and limits and that no single criterion is adequate for identifying all forms of abnormal behavior. Psychologists and other mental health professionals recognize this. They seldom label behavior as abnormal unless it meets several of these standards.

1. *Statistical infrequency.* (*How rare is the behavior?*) A behavior may be judged abnormal if it occurs infrequently in a given population. For example, believing that others are plotting against you is statistically abnormal. And it might be a sign of a serious problem called *delusions of persecution*. However, having great intelligence (Albert Einstein), exceptional athletic ability (Lance Armstrong), or an unusual artistic skill (Frida Kahlo) is *not* classified as abnormal by the public (or by psychologists). Therefore, we cannot use statistical infrequency as the sole criterion for determining what is normal versus abnormal.

2. *Disability or dysfunction.* (*Is there a loss of normal functioning?*) People who suffer from psychological disorders may be unable to get along with others, hold a job, eat properly, or clean themselves. Their ability to think clearly and make rational decisions also may be impaired. Therefore, when people's use of alcohol (or other drugs) is so extreme that it interferes with their normal social or occupational functioning, they may be diagnosed as having a *substance-related disorder*.

3. *Personal distress.* (*Is the person unhappy?*) The personal distress criterion focuses on the individual's own judgment of his or her level of functioning. For example, someone who drinks heavily every day may realize it is unhealthy and wish to stop. Unfortunately, many people with true *alcohol-dependence disorders* deny they have a problem. Also, some serious psychological disorders cause little or no emotional discomfort. A serial killer, for instance, can torture someone without feeling remorse or guilt. The personal distress criterion by itself, then, is not sufficient for identifying all forms of abnormal behavior.

4. *Violation of norms.* (*Is the behavior culturally abnormal?*) The fourth approach to identifying abnormal behavior is violation of, or nonconformance to, *social norms*, which are cultural rules that guide behavior in particular situations. Being in such a highly excited state that you forget to pay the rent but pass out $20 bills to strangers is a violation of norms. This type of behavior is common among individuals who are diagnosed with *bipolar disorder*.

A major problem with this criterion, however, is that cultural diversity can affect what people consider a *violation* of norms (Lopez & Guarnaccia, 2000). Abnormal behavior is often *culturally relative*—understandable only in terms of the culture in which it occurs. For example, believing in possession by spirits is common in some cultures. And it should probably not be taken as a sign that the believer in those cultures is mentally ill. In addition, there are also *culture-bound* disorders that are unique and found only in particular cultures, as well as *culture-*

general symptoms that are found in all cultures (Flaskerud, 2000; Green, 1999; Lopez & Guarnaccia, 2000). These terms are fully discussed later in this section.

What about the term insanity? Where does it fit in? **Insanity** is a legal term indicating that a person cannot be held responsible for his or her actions, or is judged incompetent to manage his or her own affairs, because of mental illness. In the law, the definition of mental illness rests primarily on a person's inability to tell right from wrong. Some critics have argued that insanity is misused as a type of "get out of jail free" card. However, the insanity plea is used in less than 1 percent of all cases that reach trial. Furthermore, when used, it is rarely successful (Kirschner, Litwack, & Galperin, 2004; Steadman, 1993).

For our purposes, it's important to keep in mind that insanity is a legal term. It is not the same as abnormal behavior. Consider the case of Andrea Yates, the mother who killed her five small children. Both the defense and prosecution agreed that Yates was mentally ill at the time of the murder, yet the jury still found her guilty and sentenced her to life in prison. How could the jury not find her insane? Her behavior was statistically infrequent, she was clearly dysfunctional and personally distressed (diagnosed by her doctor as suffering from psychotic postpartum depression), and her behavior was considered abnormal by almost everyone in our culture. Due to a legal technicality, Andrea Yates' conviction was later overturned, but she remains in prison under medical supervision.

AP/Wide World

Insanity *Legal term applied when people cannot be held responsible for their actions, or are judged incompetent to manage their own affairs, because of mental illness.*

The insanity plea. *Andrea Yates admitted drowning her five children and was sentenced to life imprisonment despite a vigorous defense and a plea of insanity. An appellate court overturned her conviction in 2005, primarily because of a mistake by the prosecution's star witness. He insisted Yates was copying a Law and Order episode from television, in which the woman was acquitted on an insanity plea. The problem? There was no such episode! (Note: Keep in mind that an insanity verdict normally results in the defendant being committed to a mental institution indefinitely—sometimes longer than a prison term for a similar crime.)*

chievement

Gender & Cultural Diversity

Avoiding Ethnocentrism

You will discover throughout this chapter that even strongly biological mental disorders, like schizophrenia, can differ greatly between cultures. Unfortunately, most research originates and is conducted primarily in Western cultures. Using your critical thinking skills, can you see how such a restricted sampling can limit our understanding of disorders in general? Or how it might lead to an ethnocentric view of mental disorders? How can you avoid this? You obviously can't randomly assign mentally ill people to different cultures and then watch how their disorders change and develop.

Fortunately, cross-cultural researchers have devised ways to overcome these difficulties, and there is a growing wealth of information (Draguns & Tanaka-Matsumi, 2003). For example, Robert Nishimoto (1988) has found several *culture-general* symptoms that are useful in identifying disorders across cultures. Using the Langer (1962) index of psychiatric symptoms, Nishimoto gathered data from three diverse groups, Anglo Americans in Nebraska, Vietnamese Chinese in Hong Kong, and Mexicans living in Texas and Mexico. (The Langer index is a screening instrument widely used to identify psychological disorders that disrupt everyday functioning but do not require institutionalization.) When asked to think about their lives, respondents who needed professional help all named one or more of the same 12 symptoms (Table 14.1).

In addition to the culture-general symptoms (such as "nervousness" or "trouble sleeping"), Nishimoto also found several *culture-bound* symptoms. For example, the Vietnamese Chinese reported "fullness in head," the Mexican respondents had "problems with my memory," and the Anglo Americans reported "shortness of breath" and "headaches." Apparently people *learn* to express their problems in ways acceptable to

TABLE 14.1 TWELVE CULTURE-GENERAL SYMPTOMS OF MENTAL HEALTH DIFFICULTIES

Nervous	Trouble sleeping	Low spirits
Weak all over	Personal worries	Restless
Feel apart, alone	Can't get along	Hot all over
Worry all the time	Can't do anything worthwhile	Nothing turns out right

Source: From *Understanding Culture's Influence on Behavior*, 2nd edition by BRISLIN. ©2000. Reprinted with permission of Wadsworth, a division of Thompson Learning. www.thompsonrights.com. Fax 800-730-2215.

others in the same culture (Brislin, 1997, 2000; Widiger & Sankis, 2000). In other words, most Americans learn that headaches are a common response to stress. Conversely, many Mexicans learn that others will understand their complaints about memory.

This division between culture-general and culture-bound symptoms also helps us understand depression. Research shows that certain symptoms of depression seem to exist across all cultures: (1) frequent and intense sad affect (emotion), (2) decreased enjoyment, (3) anxiety, (4) difficulty in concentrating, (5) lack of energy (Green, 1999; World Health Organization, 2000). On the other hand, there is evidence of some culture-bound symptoms. For example, feelings of guilt are found more often in North America and Europe. In China, *somatization* (converting depression into bodily complaints) is more frequent than in other parts of the world (Helms & Cook, 1999).

Just as there are culture-bound and culture-general *symptoms*, researchers have found that mental disorders are themselves sometimes culturally bound and sometimes culturally general. For example, schizophrenia is widely believed to be a culturally general disorder. However, *windigo psychosis*, in which victims believe they are possessed by the spirit of a *windigo* that causes delusions and cannibalistic impulses, is an example of a culture-bound disorder. It only shows up in a small group of Canadian Indians.

Why do cultures develop such unique, culture-bound disorders? In the case of *windigo psychosis*, one explanation is that the disorder developed after fur trade competition depleted game that the Canadian tribes used for food, leading to widespread famine (Bishop, 1974). Facing starvation could have led to cannibalism and the subsequent need to create a *windigo* spirit. Belief in spirit possession is a common feature of many cultures. In this case, people may have used it to explain a socially and psychologically abhorrent behavior, cannibalism (Faddiman, 1997).

Some researchers question the famine explanation for *windigo psychosis* and even the idea of culture-bound disorders (Dana, 1998; Hoek, Van Harten, Van Hoeken, & Susser, 1998). However, there is little doubt that some mental disorders are at least somewhat *culture-bound* (Guarnaccia & Rogler, 1999; Helms & Cook, 1999; Lopez & Guarnaccia, 2000). (See Figure 14.2.)

As you can see, culture has a strong effect on mental disorders. Studying the similarities and differences across cultures can lead to better diagnosis and understanding. It also helps mental health professionals who work with culturally diverse populations understand that culturally general and culturally bound symptoms exist, and what these are for any population.

■ Explaining Abnormality: From Superstition to Science

Having explored the criteria for defining abnormal behavior, the next logical question is, "How do we explain it?" Historically, evil spirits and witchcraft have been the primary suspects (Millon, 2005). During the Stone Age, for example, people believed that abnormal behavior resulted from demonic possession. The recommended "therapy" was to bore a hole in the skull to relieve pressure or release evil spirits—a process known as *trephining*.

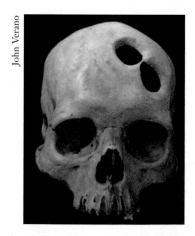

John Verano

An early "treatment" for abnormal behavior? *During the Stone Age, many believed that demonic possession was a primary cause of mental disorders, and one treatment was to bore holes in the skull to allow evil spirits to escape.*

Puerto Rican and other Latin cultures	Southeast Asian, Malaysian, Indonesian, Thai	West African	Ethiopia	South Chinese and Vietnamese	Western Nations
Ataque de nervios ("attack of nerves")	Running amok	Brain fog	Possession by the "Zar"	*Koro*	*Anorexia nervosa* (as other countries become Westernized they're showing some cases of anorexia)
Symptoms: Trembling, heart palpitations, and seizurelike episodes often associated with the death of a loved one, accidents, or family conflict	**Symptoms:** Wild, out-of-control, aggressive behaviors and attempts to injure or kill others	**Symptoms:** "Brain tiredness," a mental and physical response to the challenges of schooling	**Symptoms:** Involuntary movements, mutism, and incomprehensible language	**Symptoms:** Belief that the penis is retracting into the abdomen and that when it is fully retracted, death will result; attempts to prevent the supposed retraction may lead to severe physical damage	**Symptoms:** Occurs primarily among young women; preoccupied with thinness, they exercise excessively and refuse to eat; death can result

Figure 14.2 *Culture-bound disorders.* Keep in mind that some disorders are fading as remote areas become more Westernized, whereas other disorders (such as anorexia nervosa) are spreading as other countries adopt Western values. *Source:* Carmaciu, Anderson, & Markar, 2001; Davison, Neale, & Kring, 2004; Durand & Barlow, 2006; Guarnaccia & Rogler, 1999; Matsumoto, 2000.

During the European Middle Ages (from about the fifth to the fifteenth century A.D.), the troubled person was sometimes treated with a religious practice known as *exorcism.* Prayer, fasting, noise-making, beating, and drinking terrible-tasting brews were all used to make the body so uncomfortable it would be uninhabitable for the Devil.

This *demonological model* continued into the fifteenth century. Many people believed abnormal behavior resulted from inhabitation (or possession) by supernatural forces. They also believed some people could willingly *choose* to consort with the Devil. These "willing people" (usually women who somehow offended the social rules for feminine behavior) were often called witches. And many were tortured, imprisoned for life, or executed. How did they test for possession? One of the most "creative" methods was dunking, or the water-float test. It was known that during smelting impurities rise to the surface and pure metals sink to the bottom. Therefore, suspected witches could be tested by tying them up and dunking them in deep water. If the alleged witch sank and drowned, she was declared innocent. However, if she somehow managed to float to the top, she was obviously "impure" and would be handed over to the law for execution. This was the ultimate catch-22, or no-win situation.

Corbis Images

Witchcraft or mental illness? *During the fifteenth century, some people who may have been suffering from mental disorders were accused of witchcraft and tortured or hung.*

An early catch-22. *In the Middle Ages, "dunking tests" were used to determine whether people who behaved abnormally were possessed by demons. Individuals who did not drown while being dunked were believed to be guilty of possession and then punished (usually by hanging). Those who did drown were judged to be innocent.*

Asylums

As the Middle Ages ended, advances were made in the treatment of mental disorders. By the fifteenth and sixteenth centuries, special mental hospitals, called *asylums*, began to appear in Europe. Initially designed to provide patients quiet retreats from the world and to "protect" society from their abnormal behavior (Millon, 2005), the asylums later became overcrowded, inhumane prisons.

Improvement came in 1792 when Philippe Pinel, a French physician, was put in charge of a Parisian asylum. Inmates in these asylums were shackled to the walls of unlighted and unheated cells. But Pinel removed them from these dungeons and insisted they be treated humanely. Many inmates improved so dramatically they could be released. Pinel's belief that abnormal behavior was caused by "mental illness" and "sick" minds soon became the accepted way of viewing people who had previously been feared and punished for their abnormality.

Modern Times

Pinel's idea that disturbed individuals had an underlying *physical illness* predated our modern **medical model**, which views mental illness as having biological causes like other diseases. In turn, this medical model eventually gave rise to more scientific treatment and the modern specialty of **psychiatry**. Unfortunately, when we assume that a mental "disease" exists and label people "mentally ill," we may create new problems. One of the most outspoken critics of the medical model is psychiatrist Thomas Szasz (1960, 2000, 2004). Szasz believes the medical model encourages people to believe they have no responsibility for their actions and that they can find solutions in drugs, hospitalization, or surgery. He contends that mental illness is a "myth" used to label individuals who are peculiar or offensive to others (Wyatt, 2004). Furthermore, labels can become self-perpetuating. That is, the person begins behaving according to the diagnosed disorder.

A famous study done by David Rosenhan of Stanford University illustrates problems with diagnostic labels (Rosenhan, 1973). Rosenhan and several colleagues presented themselves to local mental hospitals complaining of hearing voices (a classic symptom of schizophrenia). Although they had no other complaints, they were admitted to the hospital with a diagnosis of schizophrenia. After admission, they stopped their claims of hearing voices and behaved in their normal fashion. The purpose?

Rosenhan wanted to see how long it would take the doctors and hospital staff to recognize they were not mentally ill. Surprisingly, none of the pseudopatients were ever recognized as phony. Once they were inside a mental ward with a label of "schizophrenia," staff members saw only what they expected to see. Interestingly, real patients were not so easily fooled. They were the first to realize that the pretend patients were not really mentally ill.

Rosenhan's study offers important insights into problems with labeling mental illness (Hock, 2001). But as you remember from Chapter 1, the scientific method requires operational definitions, control groups, single- and double-blind procedures, and replication. Unfortunately, none of these standards were met in the Rosenhan study. Despite its limits, though, the study does increase our awareness of the dangers of diagnostic labels in mental illness.

Today, the medical model remains a founding principle of *psychiatry*. And diagnosis and treatment of mental disorders continue to be based on the concept of mental *illness*. In contrast, *psychology* offers a multifaceted approach to explaining abnormal behavior. Each of the seven major perspectives in psychology—psychoanalytic, behavioral, humanistic, cognitive, biological, evolutionary, and sociocultural—offers alternative explanations. Figure 14.3 summarizes these perspectives.

Medical Model *Perspective that assumes diseases (including mental illness) have physical causes that can be diagnosed, treated, and possibly cured*

Psychiatry *Branch of medicine dealing with the diagnosis, treatment, and prevention of mental disorders*

Figure 14.3 *Seven major perspectives on abnormal behavior.* Each of the approaches emphasizes different factors believed to contribute to abnormal behavior, but they do overlap in varying degrees in actual practice.

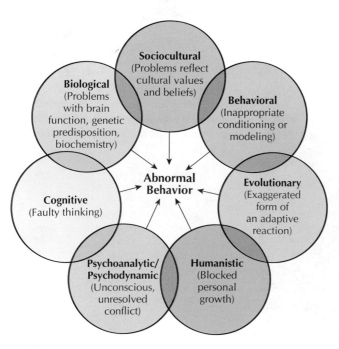

Classifying Abnormal Behavior: The Diagnostic and Statistical Manual IV-TR

Now that we have *identified* and *explained* abnormal behavior, we also need a clear and reliable system for *classifying* the wide range of disorders. Physicians obviously need specific terms for classifying one set of signs and symptoms as cancer and another as heart disease. Psychologists and psychiatrists also need specific terms to identify and differentiate abnormal behavior. Mary's disruptive behavior and broken relationships, as described in the opening vignette, are very different from Jim's paranoia. Without a uniform system for classifying and clearly describing psychological disorders, scientific research on them would be almost impossible. And communication among mental health professionals would be seriously impaired.

Fortunately, mental health specialists do share a uniform classification system. It is the ***Diagnostic and Statistical Manual of Mental Disorders***, fourth edition, text revision ***(DSM-IV-TR)*** (American Psychiatric Association, 2000). The "IV" simply designates that this is the fourth revision and the "TR" signals that this is the text revision of the fourth edition.

Why are there so many revisions of the DSM*?* Each revision has expanded the list of disorders and changed the descriptions and categories to reflect the latest advances in scientific research. Revisions also reflect changes in the way abnormal behaviors are viewed within our social context (First & Tasman, 2004; Smart & Smart, 1997). For example, the terms **neurosis** and **psychosis** as categories of disorders were significantly revised in *DSM-IV.* In previous editions, *neurosis* reflected Freud's theories about anxiety disorders. He believed that anxiety could be experienced directly (through phobias, obsessions, and compulsions) or that the unconscious could convert it into bodily complaints (somatoform disorders).

Over the years, mental health professionals decided Freud's emphasis on unconscious processes was too limiting and the category of neuroses was too large to be maximally useful. In the *DSM-IV,* conditions previously grouped together as neuroses were redistributed as anxiety disorders, somatoform disorders, and dissociative disorders. Despite these changes, the term *neurosis* continues as a part of our everyday language. And clinicians may occasionally use neurosis to describe disordered behavior presumed to be due to underlying anxiety.

Unlike neurosis, the term *psychosis* is still listed in the *DSM-IV-TR* because it helps distinguish the most severe mental disorders. Individuals with a psychosis suffer extreme mental disruption and loss of contact with reality. They often have trouble meeting the ordinary demands of life, making hospitalization necessary. Schizophrenia, some mood disorders, and some disorders due to medical conditions are described as psychoses.

Understanding the *DSM*

DSM-IV-TR is organized according to five major dimensions, called *axes*, which serve as guidelines for making decisions about symptoms (Figure 14.4). Axis I describes *state disorders* that reflect the patient's current condition, or "state." Depression and anxiety disorders are examples of Axis I disorders. Axis II describes *trait disorders*, which are long-running personality disturbances (like antisocial personality disorder) and mental retardation.

As you can see, mental disorders are *diagnosed* along Axis I and Axis II. The other three axes are used to record important supplemental information. Axis Ill lists medical conditions that may be important to the person's psychopathology (such as diabetes or hypothyroidism, which can affect mood). Axis IV is reserved for psychosocial and environmental stressors that could be contributing to emotional problems (such as job or housing troubles or the death of a family member). Axis V evaluates a person's overall level of functioning, on a scale from 1 (serious attempt

Diagnostic and Statistical Manual of Mental Disorders (DSM-IV-TR) *Classification system developed by the American Psychiatric Association used to describe abnormal behaviors; the "IV-TR" indicates it is the text revision (TR) of the fourth major revision (IV)*

Neurosis *Outmoded term for disorders characterized by unrealistic anxiety and other associated problems*

Psychosis *Serious mental disorders characterized by extreme mental disruption and loss of contact with reality*

Figure 14.4 *Five axes of DSM-IV-TR.* Each of these five axes serves as a broad category that helps organize the wide variety of mental disorders and acts as a guideline for making decisions. Reprinted with permission from the *Diagnostic and Statistical Manual of Mental Disorders*, copyright 2000, American Psychiatric Association.

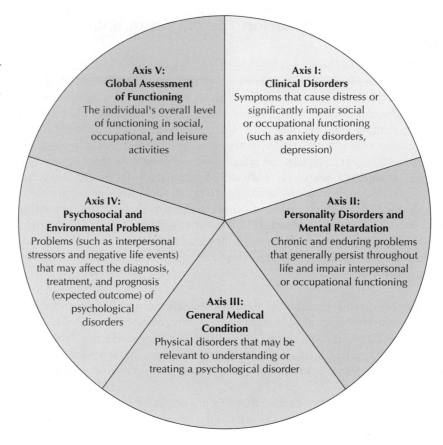

Axis V:
Global Assessment of Functioning
The individual's overall level of functioning in social, occupational, and leisure activities

Axis I:
Clinical Disorders
Symptoms that cause distress or significantly impair social or occupational functioning (such as anxiety disorders, depression)

Axis IV:
Psychosocial and Environmental Problems
Problems (such as interpersonal stressors and negative life events) that may affect the diagnosis, treatment, and prognosis (expected outcome) of psychological disorders

Axis II:
Personality Disorders and Mental Retardation
Chronic and enduring problems that generally persist throughout life and impair interpersonal or occupational functioning

Axis III:
General Medical Condition
Physical disorders that may be relevant to understanding or treating a psychological disorder

at suicide or complete inability to take care of oneself) to 100 (happy, productive, with many interests).

In sum, the *DSM* offers a comprehensive, well-defined system intended for the diagnosis and classification of psychological disorders. It does *not* suggest therapies or treatment. The current *DSM-IV-TR* contains over 200 diagnostic categories grouped into 17 major categories (Table 14.2). Due to space limitations, we will discuss only 6 of the 17 categories. We begin with three of the most common categories—*anxiety disorders*, *mood disorders*, and *schizophrenia*. We then explore substance-related, *dissociative*, and *personality disorders*.

Before going on, it is important to note that the *DSM-IV-TR* classifies disorders that people have, *not the people themselves*. To reflect this important distinction, this text (like the *DSM-IV-TR*) avoids the use of terms such as *schizophrenic*. Instead, we use the term *a person with schizophrenia*.

Evaluating the *DSM-IV-TR*

The *DSM-IV* has been praised for carefully and completely describing symptoms, standardizing diagnosis and treatment, and facilitating communication among professionals and between professionals and patients. It also is praised as a valuable educational tool. Critics, on the other hand, suggest it relies too heavily on the medical model and unfairly labels people (Cooper, 2004; Mitchell, 2003; Roelcke, 1997). The *DSM-IV* has also been criticized for its possible cultural bias. It does provide a culture-specific section and a glossary of culture-bound syndromes. But the classification of most disorders still reflects a Western European and American perspective (Dana, 1998; Matsumoto, 2000; Smart & Smart, 1997). In addition, some would

TABLE 14.2 SUMMARY OF MAIN CATEGORIES OF MENTAL DISORDERS AND THEIR DESCRIPTIONS IN DSM-IV-TR* (THE FIRST SIX DISORDERS ARE DISCUSSED IN THIS CHAPTER)

1. **Anxiety Disorders:** Problems associated with severe anxiety, such as *phobias, obsessive-compulsive disorder,* and *posttraumatic stress disorder.*

2. **Mood Disorders:** Problems associated with severe disturbances of mood, such as *depression, mania,* or alternating episodes of the two *(bipolar disorder).*

3. **Schizophrenia and other Psychotic Disorders:** A group of disorders characterized by major disturbances in perception, language and thought, emotion, and behavior.

4. **Dissociative Disorders:** Disorders in which the normal integration of consciousness, memory, or identity is suddenly and temporarily altered, such as *amnesia* and *dissociative identity disorder.*

5. **Personality Disorders:** Problems related to lifelong maladaptive personality traits, including *antisocial personality disorders.* (violation of others' rights with no sense of guilt) or *borderline personality disorders* (impulsivity and instability in mood and relationships).

6. **Substance-related Disorders:** Problems caused by alcohol, cocaine, tobacco, and other drugs.

7. **Somatoform Disorders:** Problems related to unusual preoccupation with physical health or physical symptoms with no physical cause.

8. **Factitious Disorders:** Disorders that the individual adopts to satisfy some economic or psychological need.

9. **Sexual and Gender Identity Disorders:** Problems related to unsatisfactory sexual activity, finding unusual objects or situations arousing, gender identity problems

10. **Eating Disorders:** Problems related to food, such as *anorexia nervosa* and *bulimia.*

11. **Sleep Disorders:** Serious disturbances of sleep, such as *insomnia* (too little sleep), *sleep terrors,* or *hypersomnia* (too much sleep).

12. **Impulse Control Disorders (not elsewhere classified):** Problems related to *kleptomania* (impulsive stealing), *pyromania* (setting of fires), and *pathological gambling.*

13. **Adjustment Disorders:** Problems involving excessive emotional reaction to specific stressors such as divorce, family discord, or economic concerns.

14. **Disorders usually first diagnosed in infancy, childhood, or early adolescence:** Problems that appear before adulthood, including mental retardation and language development disorders.

15. **Delirium, Dementia, Amnestic, and Other Cognitive Disorders:** Problems caused by known damage to the brain, including Alzheimer's disease, strokes, and physical trauma to the brain.

16. **Mental Disorders due to a general medical condition (not elsewhere classified):** Problems caused by physical deterioration of the brain due to disease, drugs, and so on.

17. **Other conditions that may be a focus of clinical attention:** Problems related to physical or sexual abuse, relational problems, occupational problems, and so forth.

* *Diagnostic Manual of Mental Disorders (DSM-IV-TR).*

Reprinted with permission from the *Diagnostic and Statistical Manual of Mental Disorders,* copyright 2000, American Psychiatric Association.

Anxiety disorders

Mood disorders

Substance-related disorders

prefer that disorders be described not just in terms of *categories* (e.g., anxiety disorders) but also in terms of *dimensions,* or degrees, of traits or behaviors.

Despite its faults, many consider this fourth revision of the *DSM* the most advanced scientifically based classification system yet (Durand & Barlow, 2006; First & Tasman, 2004). Like Winston Churchill's description of democracy: "It is the worst system devised by the wit of man, except for all the others."

Assessment

CHECK & REVIEW

Studying Psychological Disorders

Abnormal behavior refers to patterns of emotion, thought, and action considered pathological for one or more of these reasons: statistical infrequency, disability or dysfunction, personal distress, or violation of norms. **Insanity** is a legal term.

In ancient times, people commonly believed that demons were the cause of abnormal behavior. The **medical model,** which emphasizes disease, later replaced this demonological model. The *Diagnostic and Statistical Manual of Mental Disorders (DSM-IV-TR)* classification system provides detailed descriptions of symp-

toms. It also allows standardized diagnosis and improved communication among professionals and between professionals and patients.

The *DSM* has been criticized for relying too heavily on the medical model, for unfairly labeling people, and for not paying sufficient attention to cultural factors.

Questions

1. What are the four major standards for identifying abnormal behavior?
2. In early treatment of abnormal behavior, _____ was used to allow evil spirits to escape, whereas _____ was designed to make the body so uncom-

fortable it would be uninhabitable for the devil. (a) purging, fasting; (b) trephining, exorcism; (c) demonology, hydrotherapy; (d) the medical model, the dunking test
3. Briefly define neurosis, psychosis, and insanity.
4. What are the chief advantages and disadvantages of the DSM system of classifying mental disorders?

Check your answers in Appendix B.

 CLICK & REVIEW
for additional assessment options:
www.wiley.com/college/huffman

ANXIETY DISORDERS

Achievement

What are anxiety disorders, and how do we explain them?

Anxiety Disorder *Type of abnormal behavior characterized by unrealistic, irrational fear*

Bettman/Corbis

A scene from The Miracle Worker. As a young girl, Patty Duke won an Academy Award for her role as Helen Keller. But even at this early age the young actress suffered from a serious anxiety disorder.

I was 9 years old and sitting alone in the back of a cab as it rumbled over New York City's 59th Street bridge. I noticed the driver was watching me curiously. My feet began tapping and then shaking, and slowly my chest grew tight and I couldn't get enough air in my lungs. I tried to disguise the little screams I made as throat clearings, but the noises began to rattle the driver. I knew a panic attack was coming on, but I had to hold on, get to the studio, and get through the audition. Still, if I kept riding in that car I was certain I was going to die. The black water was just a few hundred feet below. "Stop!" I screamed at the driver. "Stop right here, please! I have to get out." "Young miss, I can't stop here." "Stop!" I must have looked like I meant it, because we squealed to a halt in the middle of traffic. I got out and began to run. I ran the entire length of the bridge and kept going. Death would never catch me as long as my small legs kept propelling me forward.

(ADAPTED FROM PEARCE & SCANLON, 2002, P. 69)

These are the words of actress Patty Duke describing an episode around the time she was starring as Helen Keller, the deaf and blind child in *The Miracle Worker*. Patty Duke's flight from the cab and other cases of **anxiety disorder** share one central defining characteristic—unreasonable, often paralyzing, anxiety or fear. The person feels threatened, unable to cope, unhappy, and insecure in a world that seems dangerous and hostile. Anxiety disorders are the most frequently occurring category of mental disorders in the general population. And they are diagnosed about twice as often in women as in men (National Institute of Mental Health, 1999; Swartz & Margolis, 2004). Fortunately, they also are among the easiest disorders to treat and have one of the best chances for recovery (see Chapter 15).

Four Major Anxiety Disorders: The Problem of Fear

Symptoms of anxiety, such as rapid breathing and increased heart rate, plague most of us during final exams and important job interviews. But some people experience unreasonable anxiety that is so intense and chronic it seriously disrupts their lives. We will consider four major types of these anxiety disorders: *generalized anxiety disorder, panic disorder, phobia,* and *obsessive-compulsive disorder.* (Posttraumatic stress disorder, another major anxiety disorder, was discussed in Chapter 3.) Although we discuss these disorders separately, it is important to remember that people with one anxiety disorder often have others (Barlow, Esler, & Vitali, 1998).

Generalized Anxiety Disorder

Generalized anxiety disorder is characterized by chronic, uncontrollable, and excessive fear and worry that last at least six months and that are not focused on any particular object or situation. It also is a common chronic problem that affects twice as many women as men and leads to considerable impairment (Brawman-Mintzer & Lydiard, 1996, 1997). As the name implies, the anxiety is *unspecific* or *free-floating.* People with this disorder feel afraid of *something* but are unable to articulate the specific fear. They fret constantly and have a hard time controlling their worries. Because of persistent muscle tension and autonomic fear reactions, they may develop headaches, heart palpitations, dizziness, and insomnia. These physical complaints, combined with the intense, long-term anxiety, make it difficult to cope with normal daily activities.

Panic Disorder

Generalized anxiety disorder involves chronic, free-floating worry. In contrast, **panic disorder** is marked by sudden and inexplicable *attacks* of intense apprehension that cause trembling and shaking, dizziness, and difficulty breathing. Patty Duke's feeling of suffocation and certainty that she would die if she didn't immediately get out of the cab are characteristic of panic attacks. The American Psychiatric Association (2000) defines a *panic attack* as fear or discomfort that arises abruptly and peaks in 10 minutes or less. Panic attacks may appear to come out of nowhere. But they generally happen after frightening experiences, prolonged stress, or even exercise.

Many people who have occasional panic attacks interpret them correctly—as resulting from a passing crisis or stress. Unfortunately, others begin to worry excessively, and some may even quit jobs or refuse to leave home to avoid future attacks. It is labeled *panic disorder* when several apparently spontaneous panic attacks lead to a persistent concern about future attacks. A common complication of panic disorder is the subsequent development of *agoraphobia*—anxiety about becoming trapped or helpless in a place or situation where escape is difficult or embarrassing (Craske, 2000; Gorman, 2000). Agoraphobia is one of the phobias discussed in the next section.

Phobias

Phobias involve a strong, irrational fear and avoidance of specific objects or situations. Phobic disorders differ from generalized anxiety disorders and panic disorder because a specific stimulus or situation elicits the strong fear response. The objective danger is often small or nonexistent and the person recognizes the fear as irrational. However, the experience is still one of overwhelming anxiety, and a full-blown panic attack may follow. Imagine how it would feel to be so frightened by a spider that you would try to jump out of a speeding car to get away from it. This is how a person suffering from phobia might feel.

Agoraphobia As discussed earlier, *agoraphobia* often develops following a panic attack. The term *agoraphobia* comes from the Greek words meaning "fear of the marketplace." People with agoraphobia restrict their normal activities because they fear being in busy, crowded places, in enclosed places like a bus or elevator, or alone in wide-open places like a deserted beach. Can you see what is common to all these places? The people fear being trapped somewhere from which they cannot easily

Generalized Anxiety Disorder *Persistent, uncontrollable, and free-floating anxiety*

Panic Disorder *Sudden and inexplicable panic attacks; symptoms include difficulty breathing, heart palpitations, dizziness, trembling, terror, and feelings of impending doom*

Phobia *Intense, irrational fear and avoidance of a specific object or situation*

Corbis Images

Do you have a snake phobia? *If so, you're probably not reading this caption because you've shut your eyes or turned the page. Phobias are intense, irrational fears.*

escape or where they would be unable to receive help in an emergency. The emergency they fear most is having another panic attack. In severe cases, people with agoraphobia become so frightened that they refuse to leave their home because this is the only place they feel really safe.

Simple phobias   A *simple phobia* is a fear of a specific object or situation, such as needles, heights, rats, or spiders. *Claustrophobia* (fear of closed spaces) and *acrophobia* (fear of heights) are the simple phobias most often treated by therapists. People with simple phobias have especially powerful imaginations. They vividly anticipate terrifying consequences from encountering the feared object or situation.

As with all phobias, people with simple phobias generally recognize that their fears are excessive and unreasonable. But they are unable to control their anxiety and will go to great lengths to avoid the feared stimulus. Years ago, a student who had taken my child psychology class wanted to take my general psychology class. However, her anxiety over the *possibility* that our text or the videos might have *pictures* of rats kept her from enrolling. Eventually, she did seek therapy and successfully completed the course.

Social phobias   Individuals with *social phobias* feel extremely insecure in social situations and have an irrational fear of embarrassing themselves. Fear of public speaking or of eating in public are the most common social phobias. Almost everyone experiences "stage fright" when speaking or performing in front of a group. But people with social phobias become so extremely anxious that performance may be out of the question. In fact, their fear of public scrutiny and potential humiliation may become so pervasive that normal life is impossible (den Boer, 2000; Swartz & Margolis, 2004).

Obsessive-Compulsive Disorder (OCD) *Intrusive, repetitive fearful thoughts (obsessions), urges to perform repetitive, ritualistic behaviors (compulsions), or both*

Obsessive-Compulsive Disorder

Do you remember the movie *The Aviator*? The main character, Howard Hughes, was endlessly counting, checking, and repeatedly washing his hands in a seemingly senseless, ritualistic pattern. What drives this behavior? The answer is **obsessive-compulsive disorder (OCD)**. This disorder involves persistent, unwanted fearful thoughts *(obsessions)* and/or irresistible urges to perform an act or repeat a ritual *(compulsions)*. The compulsions help relieve the anxiety created by the obsession. In adults, this disorder is equally common in men and women. However, it is more prevalent among boys when the onset is in childhood (American Psychiatric Association, 2000).

Consider the case of billionaire Howard Hughes:

> Due to his unreasonable fear of germs, he made people who worked with him wear white gloves, sometimes several pairs, when handling documents he would later touch. When newspapers were brought to him, they had to be in stacks of three so he could slide the middle one out by grasping it with a tissue. To escape contamination by dust, he ordered that masking tape be put around the doors and windows of his cars and houses.
>
> FOWLER (1986)

The Aviator. In this film, Leonardo DiCaprio portrays the obsessive-compulsive behaviors of famous billionaire Howard Hughes.

© Andrew Cooper/Miramax Films/ Bureau L.A. Collections/Corbis

I sometimes worry about germs and what others might have touched. Would this be an obsessive-compulsive disorder? Many people have obsessive thoughts or find they occasionally check stove burners, count steps, or clean their homes and offices past the point of normal standards. People even casually refer to this as "being OC" or "anal." There is a significant difference between an OCD and milder forms of obsession and compulsion. With OCD the repetitive thoughts and ritualistic actions become *uncontrollable* and seriously interfere with the person's life.

A woman with OCD who worries obsessively about germs, for example, might compulsively wash her hands hundreds of times a day until they are raw and bleeding. A man might check the lights, locks, oven, and furnace 10 times each night in a ritualistic pattern before he can go to sleep. Most sufferers of OCD do not enjoy these rituals and realize that their actions are senseless. But when they try to stop the behavior, they experience mounting anxiety that is relieved only by giving in to the urges. They simply cannot stop themselves.

Concerned family and friends generally understand that the person cannot stop the obsessive-compulsive behaviors. But they also may feel irritated, confused, and resentful. As with other psychological disorders, therapists may recommend family counseling as well as individual therapies (Chapter 15).

Explaining Anxiety Disorders: Multiple Roots

Why people develop anxiety disorders is a matter of considerable debate. Research has focused primarily on the roles of *psychological, biological,* and *sociocultural* processes (the *biopsychosocial model*).

Psychological

Two of the primary psychological contributions to anxiety disorders are faulty cognitions and maladaptive learning.

Faulty cognitions People with anxiety disorders have certain thinking, or cognitive, habits that make them vulnerable or prone to fear. They tend to be *hypervigilant*. They constantly scan their environment for signs of danger and seem to ignore signs of safety. They also tend to magnify ordinary threats and failures. For example, most people are anxious in a public speaking situation. But those who suffer from a social phobia are excessively concerned about others' evaluation, hypersensitive to any criticism, and obsessively worried about potential mistakes. This intense self-preoccupation intensifies the social anxiety. It also leads these people to think they have failed—even when they have been successful. As you will see in Chapter 15, changing the thinking patterns of anxious people can greatly lessen their fears (Alden, Mellings, & Laposa, 2004; Craske & Waters, 2005; Swartz & Margolis, 2004).

Jennifer Berman

Courtesy Susan Mineka, Northwestern University

Vicarious phobias. *Monkeys who watch artificially created videotapes of other monkeys being afraid of either a toy snake, toy rabbit, toy crocodile, or flowers will develop their own set of phobias. The fact that the viewing monkeys only develop fears of snakes and crocodiles, but not of flowers or toy rabbits, demonstrates that phobias are both learned and biological.*

Maladaptive learning According to learning theorists, phobias and other anxiety disorders generally result from *conditioning* (both classical and operant conditioning) and *social learning* (both modeling and imitation) (Bouton, Mineka, & Barlow, 2001; King, Clowes-Hollins, & Ollendick, 1997; Thomas & Ayres, 2004). (See Chapter 6 for a review of these terms.)

During classical conditioning, for example, a stimulus that is originally neutral, like a harmless spider, becomes paired with a frightening event (e.g., the sudden panic attack). The spider then becomes a conditioned stimulus that elicits anxiety. After this kind of classical conditioning, the spider phobia is typically maintained through operant conditioning. The person begins to avoid the anxiety-producing stimulus (in this case, spiders) because avoiding the stimulus reduces the unpleasant feelings of anxiety (a process known as negative reinforcement).

However, most people with phobias have no memory of specific instances that led to their fear. Furthermore, in the face of similar experiences some people develop phobias whereas others do not (Craske, 1999). This suggests that conditioning may not be the only (or best) explanation.

Social learning theorists believe some phobias result from modeling and imitation. Can you imagine how overprotective, fearful parents may make their children more prone to developing phobias and other anxiety disorders? Howard Hughes's mother, for instance, was extremely protective and worried constantly about his physical health.

Phobias may also be learned vicariously (in an indirect, secondhand way). One research team showed specially constructed videotapes to four groups of rhesus monkeys. The tapes were spliced together in a special way to show another monkey apparently experiencing extreme fear of a toy snake, a toy rabbit, a toy crocodile, and flowers (Cook & Mineka, 1989). The "viewing" monkeys were later afraid of the toy snake and crocodile. Interestingly, they were *not* afraid of the toy rabbit or flowers, which suggests that phobias have both a learned and biological component.

Biological

The fact that the rhesus monkeys selectively learned phobias for only the toy snake and toy crocodile may mean that we have an evolutionary predisposition to fear what was dangerous to our ancestors (Mineka & Oehman, 2002; Rossano, 2003). Studies show that anxiety disorders also may be due to a genetic predisposition, disrupted biochemistry, or unusual brain activity (Albert, Maina, Ravizza, & Bogetto, 2002; Camarena et al., 2004; Craske & Waters, 2005). For example, twin and family studies show that some individuals with panic disorder seem to be genetically predisposed toward an overreaction of the autonomic nervous system. These people apparently respond more quickly and intensely to stressful stimuli than others. Stress and arousal also seem to play a role in panic attacks. Drugs such as caffeine or nicotine or even hyperventilation (breathing deeper and faster than normal) can trigger an attack, which also suggests a biochemical disturbance.

Sociocultural

Have you heard that we are living in the "age of anxiety"? There has been a sharp rise in anxiety disorders in the past 50 years, particularly in Western industrialized countries. Sociocultural influences on anxiety may include our fast-paced life with decreased job security, increased mobility, and lack of stable family support. As we discovered in Chapter 3, our evolutionary ancestors were prewired to respond automatically to threatening stimuli. However, today our threats are less identifiable and immediate—but always with us. This may lead some of us to become hypervigilant and predisposed to anxiety disorders.

Further support for sociocultural influences on anxiety disorders is that anxiety disorders can take dramatically different forms in other cultures. For example, the

Japanese have a type of social phobia, called *taijin kyofusho* (TKS). Loosely translated this means "fear of people." But it is not a fear that people will criticize you, as in the Western version of social phobia. The Japanese disorder is a morbid dread that you will do something to embarrass others. TKS is extremely rare in Western cultures (Dinnel, Kleinknecht, & Tanaka-Matsumi, 2002). In the United States, "we don't think of the fear of embarrassing other people as a psychological syndrome" (cited in Goleman, 1995, p. C-3). But it is so common in Japan that TKS treatment centers, like weight clinics in the United States, are on almost every corner. Can you see how these differences between Western social phobias and TKS provide an example of how individualistic cultures (like ours) emphasize the individual, whereas collectivist cultures (like Japan) focus on others?

*A*ssessment

CHECK & REVIEW

Anxiety Disorders

People with **anxiety disorders** experience unreasonable, often paralyzing, anxiety or fear. In **generalized anxiety disorder,** there is a persistent, uncontrollable, and free-floating anxiety. In **panic disorder,** anxiety is concentrated into sudden and inexplicable panic attacks. **Phobias** are intense, irrational fears and avoidance of specific objects or situations. **Obsessive-compulsive disorder** involves persistent anxiety-arousing thoughts (obsessions) and/or ritualistic actions (compulsions).

Anxiety disorders are influenced by psychological, biological, and sociocultural factors (the biopsychosocial model). Psychological theories focus on faulty thinking (hypervigilance) and maladaptive learning from conditioning and social learning. Biological approaches emphasize genetic predisposition, brain differences, and biochemistry. The sociocultural perspective focuses on environmental stressors that increase anxiety and cultural socialization that produces distinct culture-bound disorders like *taijin kyofusho* (TKS).

Questions

1. Match the descriptions below with the following specific forms of anxiety disorder: (a) generalized anxiety disorder; (b) panic disorder; (c) phobia; (d) obsessive-compulsive disorder (OCD):

___i. Severe attacks of extreme anxiety

___ii. Long-term anxiety that is not focused on any particular object or situation

___iii. Irrational fear of an object or situation

___iv. Intrusive thoughts and urges to perform repetitive, ritualistic behaviors

2. Researchers believe that anxiety disorders are probably due to some combination of _____.

3. How do learning theorists and social learning theorists explain anxiety disorders?

Check your answers in Appendix B.

 CLICK & REVIEW
for additional assessment options:
www.wiley.com/college/huffman

MOOD DISORDERS

Ann had been divorced for eight months when she called a psychologist for an emergency appointment. Although her husband had verbally and physically abused her for years, she had had mixed feelings about staying in the marriage. She had anticipated feeling good after the divorce, but she became increasingly depressed. She had trouble sleeping, had little appetite, felt very fatigued, and showed no interest in her usual activities. She stayed home from work for two days because she "just didn't feel like going in." Late one afternoon, she went straight to bed, leaving her two small children to fend for themselves. Then, the night before calling for an emergency therapy appointment, she took five sleeping tablets and a couple of stiff drinks. As she said, "I don't think I wanted to kill myself; I just wanted to forget everything for awhile."

(MEYER & SALMON, 1988; P. 312)

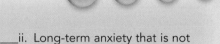

*A*chievement

When do disturbances in mood become abnormal?

www.wiley.com/college/huffman

Major Depressive Disorder *Long-lasting depressed mood that interferes with the ability to function, feel pleasure, or maintain interest in life*

Bipolar Disorder *Repeated episodes of mania (unreasonable elation and hyperactivity) and depression*

Ann's case is a good example of a *mood disorder* (also known as an *affective disorder*). This category encompasses not only excessive sadness, like Ann's, but also unreasonable elation and hyperactivity.

Understanding Mood Disorders: Major Depressive Disorder and Bipolar Disorder

As the name implies, mood disorders are characterized by extreme disturbances in emotional states. There are two main types of mood disorders—*major depressive disorder* and *bipolar disorder.*

Major Depressive Disorder

Depression has been recorded as far back as ancient Egypt, when the condition was called melancholia and was treated by priests. We all feel "blue" sometimes, especially following the loss of a job, end of a relationship, or death of a loved one. People suffering from **major depressive disorder**, however, may experience a lasting and continuously depressed mood without a clear trigger or precipitating event. In addition, their sadness is far more intense, interfering with their basic ability to function, feel pleasure, or maintain interest in life (Swartz & Margolis, 2004).

Clinically depressed people are so deeply sad and discouraged that they often have trouble sleeping, are likely to lose (or gain) weight, and may feel so fatigued that they cannot go to work or school or even comb their hair and brush their teeth. They may sleep both day and night, have problems concentrating, and feel so profoundly sad and guilty that they consider suicide. These feelings have no apparent cause and may be so severe that the individual loses contact with reality. As in the case of Ann, depressed individuals have a hard time thinking clearly or recognizing their own problems. Family or friends are often the ones who recognize the symptoms and encourage them to seek professional help.

Figure 14.5 *Mood disorders.* If major depressive disorders and bipolar disorders were depicted on a graph, they might look something like this.

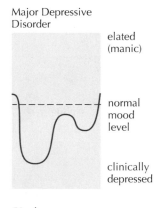

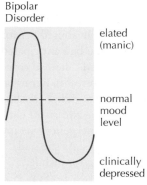

Bipolar Disorder

When depression is *unipolar*, the depressive episode eventually ends and people return to a "normal" emotional level. Some people, however, rebound to the opposite state, known as *mania*. In this type of **bipolar disorder**, the person experiences periods of depression as well as *mania* (an excessive and unreasonable state of overexcitement and impulsive behavior) (Figure 14.5).

During a manic episode, the person is overly excited, extremely active, and easily distracted. The person exhibits unrealistically high self-esteem and an inflated sense of importance or even delusions of grandeur. He or she often makes elaborate plans for becoming rich and famous. The individual is hyperactive and may not sleep for days at a time yet does not become fatigued. Thinking is speeded up and can change abruptly to new topics, showing "rapid flight of ideas." Speech is also rapid ("pressured speech"), and it is difficult for others to get a word in edgewise. Poor judgment is also common: A person may give away valuable possessions or go on wild spending sprees.

Manic episodes may last a few days to a few months and generally end abruptly. The person's previous manic mood, rapid thinking and speaking style, and hyperactivity are reversed. The following depressive episode generally lasts three times as long as the manic episode. The lifetime risk for developing bipolar disorder is low—somewhere between 0.5 and 1.6 percent. Unfortunately, it can be one of the most debilitating and lethal disorders, with a suicide rate between 10 and 20 percent (Goodwin et al., 2004; MacKinnon, Jamison, & DePaulo, 1997).

Achievement
Gender & Cultural Diversity

How Gender and Culture Affect Depression

Research shows that certain symptoms of depression seem to exist across cultures: (1) frequent and intense sad affect, (2) decreased enjoyment, (3) anxiety, (4) difficulty in concentrating, and (5) lack of energy (Green, 1999; World Health Organization, 2000). On the other hand, there is evidence of some culture-specific symptoms. For example, feelings of guilt are found more often in North America and Europe. In China, *somatization* (converting depression into bodily complaints) is more frequent than in other parts of the world (Helms & Cook, 1999).

Not only does culture have an impact on depression but so does gender. It is widely known that women are more likely than men to suffer depressive symptoms. In North America, the rate of clinical (or severe) depression for women is two to three times the rate for men. And this gender difference holds true in several other countries as well (Angst et al., 2002; Nolen-Hoeksema, Larson, & Grayson, 2000; Ohayon & Schatzberg, 2002; Parker & Brotchie, 2004).

Why are women more depressed? Research explanations can be grouped under *biological* influences (hormones, biochemistry, and genetic predisposition), *psychological* processes (ruminative thought processes), and *social* factors (greater poverty, work–life conflicts, unhappy marriages, and sexual or physical abuse) (Cheung, Gilbert, & Irons, 2004; Garnefski et al., 2004; Kornstein, 2002; Parker & Brotchie, 2004).

Perhaps the best answer is the *biopsychosocial model*, which combines the biological, psychological, and social factors. According to this model, some women may inherit a genetic or hormonal predisposition toward depression. This biological predisposition then combines with our society's socialization processes to help reinforce certain behaviors that increase the chances for depression (Alloy et al., 1999; Nolen-Hoeksema, Larson, & Grayson, 2000). For example, gender roles for women in our culture encourage greater emotional expression, passivity, and dependence. In contrast, men are socialized toward emotional suppression, activity, and independence.

Can you see how this explanation also suggests that we may underestimate male depression? If we socialize men to suppress their emotions and be the "stronger sex," they may be overlooking and underreporting their feelings of sadness and hopelessness. They also may be more reluctant to admit their depressive feelings. Furthermore, the traditionally identified symptoms of depression (sadness, low energy, feelings of helplessness) may cause us to overlook large numbers of depressed men. Interestingly, in Western society the expression of anger is the one emotion that is more acceptable in men than in women. So, how do men handle their depression? Often by acting out (aggression), impulsivity (reckless driving and petty crimes), and substance abuse. It may be that a great number of men are depressed and we just haven't recognized it. In recent years, a separate Gotland Male Depression Scale has been developed to help identify this type of *male depressive syndrome* (Walinder & Rutz, 2002).

Explaining Mood Disorders: Biological Versus Psychosocial Factors

Mood disorders differ in their *severity* (how often they occur and how much they disrupt normal functioning). They also differ in their *duration* (how long they last). In this section, we will examine the latest thinking on biological and psychosocial factors that attempts to explain mood disorders.

Biological Factors

Biological factors play a significant role in both major depression and bipolar disorder. Recent research shows that some patients with bipolar and depressive disorders show decreased gray matter and decreased overall functioning in the frontal lobes. This suggests that structural brain changes may contribute to (or cause) these mood disorders (Almeida et al., 2003; Lyoo et al., 2004; Steffens et al., 2003). Other research, however, points to imbalances of several neurotransmitters, including serotonin, norepinephrine, and dopamine (Delgado, 2004; Owens, 2004; Southwick, Vythilingam, & Charney, 2005).

This makes sense because these same neurotransmitters are involved in the capacity to be aroused or energized and in the control of other functions affected by depression such as sleep cycles and hunger. Moreover, drugs that alter the activity of these neurotransmitters also decrease the symptoms of depression (and hence are called *antidepressants*). Similarly, the drug *lithium* reduces or prevents manic episodes by preventing norepinephrine- and serotonin-sensitive neurons from being overstimulated (Chuang, 1998).

Evidence also suggests that major depressive disorders, as well as bipolar disorders, may be inherited (Baldessarini & Hennen, 2004; Horiuchi et al., 2004; Sequeira et al., 2004). For example, when one identical twin has a mood disorder, there is about a 50 percent chance that the other twin will also develop the illness (Swartz & Margolis, 2004). It is important to remember, however, that relatives generally have similar environments as well as similar genes.

Finally, the evolutionary perspective suggests that moderate depression may be an adaptive response to a loss that helps us step back and reassess our goals (Neese, 2000). Consistent with this theory is the observation that primates also show signs of depression when they suffer a significant loss (Suomi, 1991). Clinical, severe depression may just be an extreme version of this generally adaptive response.

Psychosocial Theories

Psychosocial theories of depression focus on environmental stressors and disturbances in the person's interpersonal relationships, thought processes, self-concept, and learning history (Cheung, Gilbert, & Irons, 2004; Hammen, 2005; Matthews & Macleod, 2005). The psychoanalytic explanation sees depression as anger turned inward against oneself when an important relationship or attachment is lost. Anger is assumed to come from feelings of rejection or withdrawal of affection, especially when a loved one dies. The humanistic school says depression results when a person's self-concept is overly demanding or when positive growth is blocked.

Another important contributor may be the **learned helplessness** theory of depression, developed by Martin Seligman (1975, 1994). Seligman has demonstrated that when human or nonhuman animals are repeatedly subjected to pain that they cannot escape, they develop such a strong sense of helplessness or resignation that they do not attempt to escape future painful experiences. In other words, when people (or nonhuman animals) learn they are unable to change things for the better, they're more likely to give up. Can you see how this might help explain citizens who accept brutally repressive governments, or people who stay in abusive relationships? Seligman also suggests that our general societal emphasis on individualism and less involvement with others make us particularly vulnerable to depression.

The learned helplessness theory may also involve a cognitive element, known as *attribution*, or the explanations people assign to their own and others' behavior. Once someone perceives that his or her behaviors are unrelated to outcomes (learned helplessness), depression is likely to occur. This is particularly true if the person attributes failure to causes that are *internal* ("my own weakness"), *stable* ("this weakness is long-standing and unchanging"), and *global* ("this weakness is a problem in lots of settings") (Chaney et al., 2004; Gotlieb & Abramson, 1999; Peterson & Vaidya, 2001).

Learned Helplessness *Seligman's term for a state of helplessness or resignation in which human or nonhuman animals learn that escape from something painful is impossible and depression results*

Suicide and Its Prevention

Suicide is a serious danger associated with severe depression. Because of the shame and secrecy surrounding the suicidal person, there are many misconceptions and stereotypes. Can you correctly identify which of the following is true or false?

1. People who talk about suicide are not likely to commit suicide.
2. Suicide usually takes place with little or no warning.
3. Suicidal people are fully intent on dying.
4. Children of parents who attempt suicide are at greater risk of committing suicide.
5. Suicidal people remain so forever.
6. Men are more likely than women to actually kill themselves by suicide.
7. When a suicidal person has been severely depressed and seems to be "snapping out of it," the danger of suicide decreases substantially.
8. Only depressed people commit suicide.
9. Thinking about suicide is rare.
10. Asking a depressed person about suicide will push him or her over the edge and cause a suicidal act that would not otherwise have occurred.

Compare your responses to the experts' answers and explanations (Baldessarini & Hennen, 2004; Besançon, 2004; Hansell & Damour, 2005; Joiner, Brown, & Wingate, 2005; Sequeira et al., 2004):

1. and 2. **False.** About 90 percent of people who are suicidal talk about their intentions. They may say, "If something happens to me, I want you to…" or "Life just isn't worth living." They also provide behavioral clues, such as giving away valued possessions, withdrawing from family and friends, and losing interest in favorite activities.
3. **False.** Only about 3 to 5 percent of suicidal people truly intend to die.

Brent C. Peterson/Corbis

Most are just unsure about how to go on living. They cannot see their problems objectively enough to realize that they have alternative courses of action. They often gamble with death, arranging it so that fate or others will save them. Moreover, once the suicidal crisis passes, they are generally grateful to be alive.

4. **True.** Children of parents who attempt or commit suicide are at much greater risk of following in their footsteps. As Schneidman (1969) puts it, "The person who commits suicide puts his psychological skeleton in the survivor's emotional closet" (p. 22).
5. **False.** People who want to kill themselves are usually suicidal only for a limited period.
6. **True.** Although women are much more likely to attempt suicide, men are more likely to actually commit suicide. Men are also more likely to use stronger methods, such as guns versus pills.
7. **False.** When people are first coming out of a depression, they are actually at greater risk! This is because they now have the energy to actually commit suicide.
8. **False.** Suicide rates are highest for people with major depressive disorders. However, suicide is also the leading cause of premature death in people who suffer from schizophrenia. In addition, suicide is a major cause of death in people with anxiety disorders and alcohol and other substance-related disorders. Furthermore, suicide is not limited to people with depression. Poor physical health, serious illness, substance abuse (particularly alcohol), loneliness, unemployment, and even natural disasters may push many over the edge.
9. **False.** Estimates from various studies are that 40 to 80 percent of the general public have thought about committing suicide at least once in their lives.
10. **False.** Because society often considers suicide a terrible, shameful act, asking directly about it can give the person permission to talk. In fact, *not asking* might lead to further isolation and depression.

How can you tell if someone is suicidal? If you believe someone is contemplating suicide, act on your beliefs. Stay with the person if there is any immediate danger. Encourage him or her to talk to you rather than withdraw. Show the person that you care, but do not give false reassurances that "everything will be okay." This type of response makes the suicidal person feel *more* alienated. Instead, openly ask if the person is feeling hopeless and suicidal. Do not be afraid to discuss suicide with people who feel depressed or hopeless, fearing that you will just put ideas into their heads. The reality is that people who are left alone or who are told they can't be serious about suicide often attempt it.

If you suspect someone is suicidal, it is vitally important that you help the person obtain counseling. Most cities have suicide prevention centers with 24-hour hotlines or walk-in centers that provide emergency counseling. Also, share your suspicions with parents, friends, or others who can help in a suicidal crisis. To save a life, you may have to betray a secret when someone confides in you.

www.wiley.com/college/huffman

Application

CRITICAL THINKING

How Your Thoughts Can Make You Depressed

Imagine that the following situations really happened to you. In each case, what do you think would be the most likely cause? Will the cause change in the future? Is the cause unique? Respond to each question by circling the number that most closely describes how you would feel in this same situation. Answering carefully and truthfully will improve your metacognitive critical thinking skills. It will also provide helpful insight into how your thoughts may cause your own mild to serious depression.

Situation 1

You are introduced to a new person at a party and are left alone to talk. After a few minutes, the person appears bored.

1. Is this outcome caused by you? Or is it something about the other person or the circumstances?

    1   2   3   4   5   6   7

    Other person or   Me
    circumstances

2. Will the cause of this outcome also be present in the future?

    1   2   3   4   5   6   7

    No   Yes

3. Is the cause of this outcome unique to this situation, or does it also affect other areas of your life?

    1   2   3   4   5   6   7

    Affects just   Affects all
    this situation   situations
                                      in my life

Situation 2

You receive an award for a project that is highly praised.

4. Is this outcome caused by you or something about the circumstances?

    1   2   3   4   5   6   7

    Circumstances   Me

5. Will the cause of this outcome also be present in the future?

    1   2   3   4   5   6   7

    No   Yes

6. Is the cause of this outcome unique to this situation, or does it also affect other areas of your life?

    1   2   3   4   5   6   7

    Affects just   Affects all
    this situation   situations
                                      in my life

You have just completed a modified version of the *Attributional Style Questionnaire*. This test measures people's explanations

ACTIVE LEARNING

for the causes of good and bad events. If you have a *depressive explanatory style*, you tend to explain *bad* events in terms of *internal* factors ("It's my fault"), a *stable* cause ("It will always be this way"), and a *global* cause ("It's this way in many situations"). In contrast, if you have an *optimistic explanatory style*, you tend to make *external* ("It's someone else's fault"), *unstable* ("It won't happen again"), and *specific* ("It's just in this one area") explanations.

When *good* things happen, however, the opposite occurs. People with a depressive explanatory style tend to make *external, unstable, specific* explanations. Those with an optimistic style tend to make *internal, stable, global* explanations.

	Depressive Explanatory Style	Optimistic Explanatory Style
Bad events	Internal, stable, global	External, unstable, specific
Good events	External, unstable, specific	Internal, stable, global

If you had mostly high scores (5–7) on questions 1, 2, and 3 and low scores (1–3) on questions 4, 5, and 6, you probably have a *depressive explanatory style*. If the reverse is true (low scores on the first three questions and high scores on the last three), you tend to have an *optimistic explanatory style*. Can you see how you can use this personal information to lift or avoid depressive feelings? When bad things happen, remind yourself of all the external factors that could explain the event. Research shows that people who attribute bad outcomes to themselves and good outcomes to external factors are more prone to depression than people who do the opposite (Abramson, Seligman, & Teasdale, 1978; Seligman, 1991, 1994). If you have a bad experience and then blame it on your personal (internal) inadequacies, interpret it as unchangeable (stable), and draw far-reaching (global) conclusions, you are obviously more likely to feel depressed. This self-blaming, pessimistic, and overgeneralizing explanatory style results in a sense of hopelessness (Abramson, Metalsky, & Alloy, 1989; Metalsky et al., 1993).

As expected, the idea that depression can be caused by attributional style has its critics. The problem lies in separating cause from effect. Does a depressive explanatory style cause depression? Or does depression cause a depressive explanatory style? Could another variable, such as neurotransmitters or other biological factors, cause both? Evidence suggests that both thought patterns and biology interact and influence depression. Biological explanations undoubtedly play an important role in major depressive disorders and professional help is needed. However, simply changing your explanatory style may help dispel mild or moderate depression.

Assessment

CHECK & REVIEW

Mood Disorders

Mood disorders are disturbances of affect (emotion). In **major depressive disorder,** individuals experience a long-lasting depressed mood that interferes with their ability to function, feel pleasure or maintain interest in life. The feelings have no apparent cause, and the individual may lose contact with reality (psychosis). In **bipolar disorder,** episodes of mania and depression alternate with normal periods. During the manic episode, the person is overly excited, his or her speech and thinking are rapid, and poor judgment is common. The person also may experience delusions of grandeur and act impulsively.

Biological theories of mood disorders emphasize brain function abnormalities and disruptions in neurotransmitters (especially serotonin, norepinephrine, and dopamine). Genetic predisposition also plays a role in both major depression and bipolar disorder.

Psychosocial theories of mood disorders emphasize disturbed interpersonal relationships, faulty thinking, poor self-concept, and maladaptive learning. According to **learned helplessness** theory, depression results from repeatedly failing to escape from a punishing situation. Suicide is a serious problem associated with depression. You can help others who may be contemplating suicide by becoming involved and showing concern.

Questions

1. The two main types of mood disorders are _____. (a) major depression, bipolar disorder; (b) mania, depression; (c) SAD, MAD; (d) learned helplessness, suicide

2. A major difference between major depressive disorder and bipolar disorder is that only in bipolar disorders do people have _____. (a) hallucinations or delusions; (b) depression; (c) manic episodes; (d) a biochemical imbalance

3. What is Martin Seligman's learned helplessness theory of depression?

4. According to attributional theories, depression is more likely to occur when someone attributes his or her failure to an _____ cause. (a) external, unstable, and specific; (b) internal, stable, and global; (c) internal, unstable, and global; (d) external, stable, and global

Check your answers in Appendix B.

CLICK & REVIEW
for additional assessment options:
www.wiley.com/college/huffman

SCHIZOPHRENIA

Imagine for the moment that your daughter has just left for college and you hear voices inside your head shouting, "You'll never see her again! You have been a bad mother! She'll die." Or what if you saw dinosaurs on the street and live animals in your refrigerator? These are actual experiences that have plagued Mrs. T for almost three decades (Gershon & Rieder, 1993).

Mrs. T suffers from **schizophrenia**, a disorder characterized by major disturbances in perception, language, thought, emotion, and behavior. All the disorders we have considered so far cause considerable distress. But most sufferers can still function in daily life. Schizophrenia, however, is often so severe that it is considered a *psychosis*, meaning that the person is out of touch with reality. People with schizophrenia often have serious problems caring for themselves, relating to others, and holding a job. In extreme cases, the individual may withdraw from others and from reality, often into a fantasy life of delusions and hallucinations. At this point, they may require institutional or custodial care. As we will see later in this chapter, the problems are worsened by the fact that many people with schizophrenia also engage in significant substance abuse, perhaps reflecting an attempt to self-medicate (Bates & Rutherford, 2003; Green et al., 2004; Teesson, Hodder, & Buhrich, 2004).

Researchers are divided on whether schizophrenia is a distinct disorder itself or a combination of disorders (schizophrenias). However, there is general agreement that it is one of the most widespread and devastating of all mental disorders. Approximately 1 of every 100 persons will develop schizophrenia in his or her lifetime. And approximately half of all people admitted to mental hospitals are diagnosed with this disorder (Getting the facts, 2004; Gottesman, 1991; Kendler, Gallagher, Abelson, & Kessler,

Achievement

What are the symptoms and explanations for schizophrenia?

Schizophrenia [skit-so-FREE-nee-uh] *Group of psychotic disorders involving major disturbances in perception, language, thought, emotion, and behavior; the individual withdraws from people and reality, often into a fantasy life of delusions and hallucinations*

"Jazz Band" by W. Wells, UNC-CH Schizophrenia Treatment & Evaluation Programs (STEP) Artist.

Symptoms of schizophrenia? *Disorganized thoughts, emotions, and perceptions are sometimes reflected in the artwork of people suffering from schizophrenia.*

1996; Kessler et al., 1994; Regier et al., 1993). Schizophrenia usually emerges between the late teens and the mid-thirties and only rarely prior to adolescence or after age 45. It also seems to be equally prevalent in men and women. For unknown reasons it is generally more severe and strikes earlier in men than in women (Salyers & Mueser, 2001).

Is schizophrenia the same as "split or multiple personality"? No. Schizophrenia means "split mind." When Eugen Bleuler coined the term in 1911, he was referring to the fragmenting of thought processes and emotions found in schizophrenic disorders (Neale, Oltmanns, & Winters, 1983). Unfortunately, the public often confuses "split mind" with "split personality." One study of college freshmen found that 64 percent thought having multiple personalities was a common symptom of schizophrenia (Torrey, 1998). But as you will read later, *multiple personality disorder* (now known as *dissociative identity disorder*) is the rare condition of having more than one distinct personality. Schizophrenia is a much more common—and altogether different—type of psychological disorder. What are the symptoms of schizophrenia? What are its causes? And how does it differ cross-culturally?

■ Symptoms of Schizophrenia: Five Areas of Disturbance

The two categories just discussed each have hallmark features. All people with anxiety disorders have anxiety. All people with mood disorders have depression and/or mania. People who suffer from schizophrenia are different. They can have significantly different symptoms yet all are given the same general label. This is because schizophrenia is a group or class of disorders. Each case is identified according to some kind of basic disturbance in one or more of the following areas: *perception, language, thought, emotions* (affect), and *behavior.*

Perception

The senses of people with schizophrenia may be either enhanced (as in the case of Mrs. T) or blunted. The filtering and selection processes that allow most people to concentrate on whatever they choose are impaired. Thus, sensory stimulation is jumbled and distorted. One patient reported:

> When people are talking, I just get scraps of it. If it is just one person who is speaking, that's not so bad, but if others join in then I can't pick it up at all. I just can't get in tune with the conversation. It makes me feel all open—as if things are closing in on me and I have lost control.

(MCGHIE & CHAPMAN, 1961, P. 106)

Hallucinations *Imaginary sensory perceptions that occur without external stimuli*

Because of these disruptions in sensation, people with schizophrenia may also experience **hallucinations**—imaginary sensory perceptions that occur without external stimuli. Hallucinations can occur in any of the senses (visual, tactile, olfactory). But auditory hallucinations (hearing voices and sounds) are most common in schizophrenia. As with Mrs. T, people with schizophrenia often hear voices speaking their thoughts aloud, commenting on their behavior, or telling them what to do. The voices seem to come from inside their own heads or from an external source such as an animal, telephone wires, or a TV set.

On rare occasions, people with schizophrenia will hurt others in response to their distorted internal experiences or the voices they hear. Unfortunately, these cases receive undue media attention and create exaggerated fears of "mental patients." In reality, a person with schizophernia is more likely to be self-destructive and suicidal than violent toward others.

Language and Thought

Have you heard the proverb "People who live in glass houses shouldn't throw stones?" When asked to explain the meaning of this proverb, a patient with schizophrenia said,

"People who live in glass houses shouldn't forget people who live in stone houses and shouldn't throw glass."

From this brief example, can you see how for people with schizophrenia their logic is sometimes impaired and their thoughts disorganized and bizarre? When language and thought disturbances are mild, an individual with schizophrenia jumps from topic to topic. In more severe disturbances, phrases and words are jumbled together (referred to as *word salad*). Or the person creates artificial words *(neologisms)*. The person might say "splisters" for *splinters* and *blisters* or "smever" for *smart* and *clever*.

The most common thought disturbance experienced by people with schizophrenia is the lack of contact with reality *(psychosis)*. Remember Jim, the med student in the chapter opener who believed people were plotting to assassinate him? Can you imagine how frightening it would be if you lost contact with reality and could no longer separate hallucinations and delusions from reality?

In addition to this general lack of contact with reality, another common thought disturbance of schizophrenia is that of **delusions**, mistaken beliefs based on misrepresentations of reality. We all experience exaggerated thoughts from time to time, such as thinking a friend is trying to avoid us or that our parents' divorce was our fault. But the delusions of schizophrenia are much more extreme. For example, Jim was completely convinced that others were trying to assassinate him (a *delusion of persecution*). And no one was able to reassure him or convince him otherwise. In *delusions of grandeur*, people believe they are someone very important, perhaps Jesus Christ or the queen of England. In *delusions of reference*, unrelated events are given special significance, as when a person believes a radio program or newspaper article is giving him or her a special message.

Delusions *Mistaken beliefs based on a misrepresentations of reality*

Emotion

It must look queer to people when I laugh about something that has got nothing to do with what I am talking about, but they don't know what's going on inside and how much of it is running around in my head. You see, I might be talking about something quite serious to you and other things come into my head at the same time that are funny and this makes me laugh. If I could only concentrate on one thing at the same time, I wouldn't look half so silly.

(MCGHIE & CHAPMAN, 1961, P. 104)

As you can see from this quote, the emotions of people suffering from schizophrenia are sometimes exaggerated and fluctuate rapidly in inappropriate ways. In other cases, emotions may become blunted or decreased in intensity. Some people with schizophrenia have *flattened affect*—meaning almost no emotional response of any kind.

Behavior

Disturbances in behavior may take the form of unusual actions that have special meaning. One patient shook his head rhythmically from side to side to try to shake the excess thoughts out of his mind. Another massaged his head repeatedly "to help clear it" of unwanted thoughts. In other cases, the affected person may grimace and display unusual mannerisms. These movements, however, may also be side effects of the medication used to treat the disorder (Chapter 15).

People with schizophrenia also may become *cataleptic* and assume an uncomfortable, nearly immobile stance for an extended period. A few people with schizophrenia have a symptom called *waxy flexibility*, a tendency to maintain whatever posture is imposed on them.

These abnormal behaviors are often related to disturbances in perceptions, thoughts, and feelings. For example, experiencing a flood of sensory stimuli or overwhelming confusion, a person with schizophrenia may hallucinate, experience delusions, and/or withdraw from social contacts and refuse to communicate.

Types of Schizophrenia: Recent Methods of Classification

For many years, researchers divided schizophrenia into *paranoid*, *catatonic*, *disorganized*, *undifferentiated*, and *residual* subtypes (Table 14.3). These terms are still included in the *DSM-IV-TR* and are sometimes used by the public. But critics suggest that they have little value in clinical practice and research. They contend that this classification by subtype does not differentiate in terms of prognosis (prediction for recovery), etiology (cause), or response to treatment. Furthermore, the undifferentiated type may be a catchall for cases that are difficult to diagnose (American Psychiatric Association, 2000).

For all these reasons, researchers have proposed an alternative classification system of two groups of symptoms instead of four:

1. *Positive symptoms* involve *additions* to or exaggerations of normal thought processes and behaviors, such as delusions and hallucinations. Positive symptoms are more common when schizophrenia develops rapidly (called *acute*, or *reactive*, schizophrenia), and positive symptoms are associated with better adjustment before the onset and a better prognosis for recovery.

2. *Negative symptoms* involve the *loss* or absence of normal thought processes and behaviors. Examples include impaired attention, limited or toneless speech, flattened affect (or emotions), and social withdrawal. Negative symptoms are more often found in slow-developing schizophrenia (*chronic*, or *process*, schizophrenia).

In addition to these two groups of positive or negative symptoms, the latest *DSM-IV-TR* suggests adding another dimension to reflect *disorganization of behavior*. Symptoms in this group would include rambling speech, erratic behavior, and inappropriate affect (or feelings). One advantage of either a two- or three-dimension model is the acknowledgement that schizophrenia is more than one disorder and that it has multiple causes.

Explaining Schizophrenia: Nature and Nurture Theories

Why do some people develop schizophrenia? Because the disorder comes in so many different forms, most researchers believe it results from multiple biological and psychosocial factors—the *biopsychosocial model*. (Walker et al., 2004).

"That's the doctor who is treating me for paranoia. I don't trust him."

If you're having difficulty understanding the distinction between positive and negative symptoms of schizophrenia, think back to what you learned in Chapter 6 regarding positive and negative reinforcement and punishment. Positive can be seen as "the addition of," whereas negative refers to the "removal or loss of."

TABLE 14.3 SUBTYPES OF SCHIZOPHRENIA

Paranoid	Dominated by delusions (persecution and grandeur) and hallucinations (hearing voices)
Catatonic	Marked by motor disturbances (immobility or wild activity) and echo speech (repeating the speech of others)
Disorganized	Characterized by incoherent speech, flat or exaggerated emotions, and social withdrawal
Undifferentiated	Meets the criteria for schizophrenia but is not any of the above subtypes
Residual	No longer meets the full criteria for schizophrenia but still shows some symptoms

Biological Theories

An enormous amount of scientific research exists concerning possible biological factors in schizophrenia. Some research suggests that prenatal viral infections, birth complications, immune responses, maternal malnutrition, and advanced paternal age all contribute to the development of schizophrenia (Beraki et al., 2005; Cannon et al., 2002; Dalman & Allebeck, 2002; Sawa & Kamiya, 2003; Zuckerman & Weiner, 2005). However, most biological theories of schizophrenia focus on three main factors: *genetics, neurotransmitters,* and *brain abnormalities.*

1. *Genetics.* Genes undoubtedly play a primary role in the development of schizophrenia. Although researchers are beginning to identify specific genes related to schizophrenia and have even identified the chromosomal locations of some of them, most genetic studies have focused on twins and adoptions (Crow, 2004; Davalos et al., 2004; Elkin, Kalidindi, & McGuffin, 2004; Hulshoff Pol et al., 2004; Lindholm et al., 2004; Petronis, 2000).

By most estimates, heritability for schizophrenia is around 48 percent for identical twins. Figure 14.6 shows the risk of developing schizophrenia in people with differing degrees of relatedness to a person with schizophrenia. As expected, the risk increases with genetic similarity. In other words, people who share more genes are more likely to develop the disorder. For example, if one identical twin develops schizophrenia, the other twin has a 48 to 83 percent chance of also developing schizophrenia (Berrettini, 2000; Cannon, Kaprio, Lonnqvist, Huttunen, & Koskenvuo, 1998). But if one sibling develops schizophrenia, the chances of the other sibling developing it are only 9 percent. If you compare these percentages with the risk for the general population (which is around 1 percent), you can appreciate the role of genetics in schizophrenia.

2. *Neurotransmitters.* Precisely how neurotransmitters contribute to schizophrenia is unclear. The most widely held view implicates a predisposition toward a dopamine imbalance (Ikemoto, 2004; Paquet et al., 2004). According to the **dopamine hypothesis**, overactivity of certain dopamine neurons in the brain may contribute to some forms of schizophrenia. This hypothesis is based on two important observations:

- Large doses of amphetamines increase the amount of dopamine in the brain (see Chapter 5). This oversupply of dopamine can then produce the positive symptoms of schizophrenia (such as delusions of persecution). Importantly, these amphetamine induced symptoms occur in people with no prior history of psychological disorders. In addition, low doses of amphetamines worsen symptoms in people who already have schizophrenia. Moreover, an amphetamine-induced psychosis is more likely to occur in individuals who have a genetic predisposition to but no signs of active schizophrenia.

- Drugs effective in treating schizophrenia, such as Haldol or Thorazine, block or reduce dopamine activity in the brain. As predicted by the dopamine hypothesis, this blockage or reduction then leads to a reduction or elimination of the positive symptoms of schizophrenia, such as hallucinations and delusions.

3. *Brain abnormalities.* The third major biological theory for schizophrenia involves abnormalities in brain function and structure. Researchers have found larger cerebral ventricles (the normal, fluid-filled spaces in the brain) in some people with schizophrenia (Delisi et al., 2004; Gaser et al., 2004). You can see this effect in the two

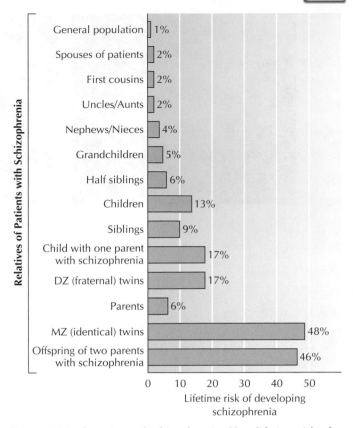

Figure 14.6 *Genetics and schizophrenia.* Your lifetime risk of developing schizophrenia depends, in part, on how closely you are genetically related to someone with schizophrenia. As you evaluate the statistics, bear in mind that the risk in the general population is a little less than 1 percent (the top line on the graph). Risk increases with the degree of genetic relatedness. *Source:* Gottesman, "Schizophrenia Genesis," 1991, W. H. Freeman and Company/Worth Publishers.

Dopamine Hypothesis *Theory that overactivity of dopamine neurons may contribute to some forms of schizophrenia*

www.wiley.com/college/huffman

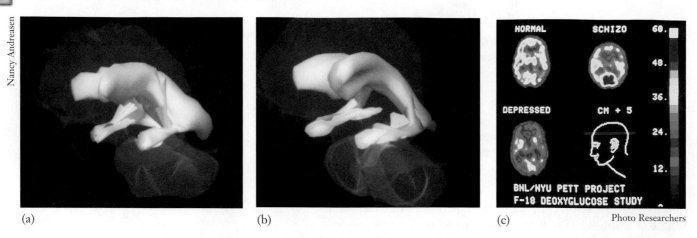

(a)   (b)   (c)

Nancy Andreasen

Photo Researchers

Figure 14.7 *Brain-scan views of schizophrenia.* (a) A three-dimensional magnetic resonance image (MRI) shows structural changes in the shrunken hippocampus (yellow) and enlarged ventricles (gray) of the brain of a patient with schizophrenia. (b) Compare the same regions (the yellow and gray areas) of this person without schizophrenia. (c) These positron emission tomography (PET) scans show variations in the brain activity of normal individuals, people with major depressive disorder, and individuals with schizophrenia. Levels of brain activity correspond to the colors and numbers at the far right of the photo. Higher numbers and warmer colors indicate increased activity.

magnetic resonance imaging (MRI) scans in Figure 14.7a and b. Enlarged cerebral ventricles were also found in the brain of John Hinckley Jr. This was the man who attempted to assassinate President Ronald Reagan, and remains in prison under treatment for schizophrenia.

Another type of brain abnormality associated with schizophrenia is revealed by positron emission tomography (PET) brain scans (Figure 14.7c). These scans show that some people with chronic schizophrenia tend to have a lower level of activity in the frontal and temporal lobes. Because the frontal and temporal lobes are involved in language, attention, and memory, damage and lower activity in these areas may explain the thought and language disturbances that characterize schizophrenia.

This lower level of brain activity, and schizophrenia itself, may also result from an overall loss of gray matter in the brain (Gogtay et al., 2004; Hulshoff Pol et al., 2004). (Recall from Chapter 2 that *gray matter* refers to the grayish-colored neurons of the cerebral cortex and spinal cord.)

In each of these cases of brain abnormalities, keep in mind that correlation does not mean causation. Abnormalities in the brain may indeed cause or worsen schizophrenia. But the disease itself could also cause the abnormalities. Furthermore, some people with schizophrenia do not show brain abnormalities, and these same abnormalities are often found in other psychological disorders.

Psychosocial Theories

We can understand the degree to which psychosocial factors contribute to the development of schizophrenia by looking at genetic statistics for *identical twins*. Remember that identical twins share *identical genes*. Therefore, if schizophrenia were completely inherited, and if one identical twin developed the disorder, what would be the percentage chance that the other twin would also develop schizophrenia? If you say 100 percent, you're right. Because the actual rate is only 48 percent, nongenetic factors must contribute the remaining percentage. Other biological factors (such as neurotransmitters and brain abnormalities) may take up part of the "leftover" percentage. But most psychologists believe there are at least two possible nonbiological contributors: *stress* and *family communication*.

1. **Stress.** In most theories of schizophrenia, stress plays an essential role in triggering schizophrenic episodes (Corcoran et al., 2003; Schwartz & Smith, 2004; Walker et al., 2004). According to the *diathesis-stress* model of schizophrenia, people inherit a predisposition (or *diathesis*) toward schizophrenia. If they then experience more stress than they can handle, a schizophrenic episode may be triggered.

2. **Family communication.** Some investigators suggest that communication disorders in parents and family members may be a predisposing factor for schizophrenia. Such disorders include unintelligible speech, fragmented communication, and contradictory messages sent by parents to their children. Given this environment, the child might withdraw into a private world and thereby set the stage for later schizophrenia.

Family communication patterns also can negatively affect the recovery of patients with schizophrenia. In several studies, researchers measured the degree of criticism and hostility the family directed at the family member with schizophrenia and their level of emotional overinvolvement in his or her life. Based on these measures of *expressed emotion* (EE), it was found that hospitalized patients who went home to high EE families experienced significantly greater relapse and worsening of symptoms (Hooley & Hiller, 2001; Lefley, 2000).

Evaluating the Theories

Critics of the dopamine hypothesis and the brain-abnormalities theory argue that they fit only some cases of schizophrenia. Moreover, with both theories, it is difficult to determine cause and effect. That is, does overactivity in dopamine neurons cause schizophrenia, or does schizophrenia cause overactivity in dopamine neurons? Similarly, does brain damage cause schizophrenia, or does schizophrenia cause brain damage? Or is there a third, as yet unknown, factor? Some researchers believe that genetic predisposition may be the strongest contributing factor in schizophrenia. But, as mentioned earlier, the highest correlation, found in identical twins, is only about 50 percent.

The psychosocial theories for schizophrenia are subject to the same criticisms as the biological theories. And the research is equally inconclusive. This uncertainty points to the fact that schizophrenia is probably the result of a combination of known and unknown interacting factors (Beck & Rector, 2005; Gottesman & Hanson, 2005) (Figure 14.8).

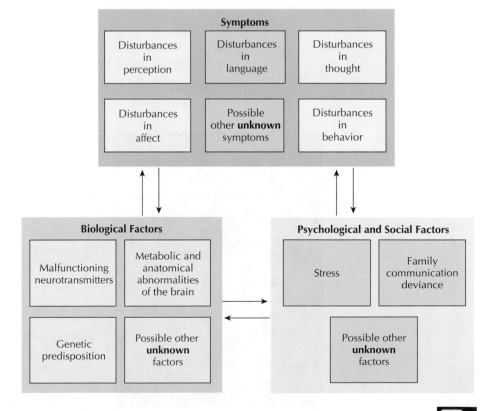

Figure 14.8 *The biopsychosocial model and schizophrenia.* Research shows that biological factors interact with psychological and social factors to produce schizophrenia. *Source:* Reprinted from *Biological Psychiatry,* Meltzer, G. "Genetics and Etiology of Schizophrenia and Bipolar Disorder," 2000, pp. 171–178, with permission from Society of Biological Psychiatry.

www.wiley.com/college/huffman

chievement

Gender & Cultural Diversity

Schizophrenia Around the World

It is difficult to directly compare mental disorders across cultures because people tend to experience mental disorders in a wide variety of ways. However, schizophrenia seems to have a large biological component. Therefore, it may provide the best opportunity for understanding the impact of culture on abnormal behavior.

1. ***Prevalence.*** Schizophrenia has been found to occur in all countries and cultural groups studied so far. But there are also some interesting differences within these cultures. In Norway, men tend to develop the disease three to four years earlier than women. They also have more and longer hospitalizations and have poorer social functioning (Raesaenen, Pakaslahti, Syvaelahti, Jones, & Isohanni, 2000). It is unclear whether these differences result from an actual difference in prevalence of the disorder or from differences in definition, diagnosis, or reporting (Kleinman & Cohen, 1997; Lefley, 2000).

2. ***Form.*** The form and symptoms of expression of schizophrenia also vary across cultures (Stompe et al., 2003). In Nigeria, for example, the major symptom of schizophrenia is intense suspicion of others, accompanied by bizarre thoughts of personal danger (Katz et al., 1988). In Western nations, the major symptom is auditory hallucinations. Interestingly, the "sources" of these auditory hallucinations have changed with technological advances. In the 1920s, the voices that people heard came from the radio. During the 1950s, these voices came from television. In the 1960s, patients reported voices from satellites in outer space. And in the 1970s and 1980s, the voices often came from microwave ovens (Brislin, 2000).

3. ***Onset.*** As we discussed earlier, some theories suggest that stress may trigger the onset of schizophrenia. Cross-cultural research in sites such as Algeria, Asia, Europe, South America, and the United States supports the relationship between stress and schizophrenia (Al-Issa, 2000; Browne, 2001; Neria et al., 2002; Torrey & Yolken, 1998). Some stressors were shared by many cultures, such as the unexpected death of a spouse or loss of a job. But others were culturally specific, such as feeling possessed by evil forces or being the victim of witchcraft.

4. ***Prognosis.*** The *prognosis* (or prediction) for recovery from, schizophrenia also varies among cultures. Given the advanced treatment facilities and wider availability of trained professionals and drugs in industrialized nations, are you surprised that the prognosis for people with schizophrenia is better in nonindustrialized societies? This may be because the core symptoms of schizophrenia (poor rapport with others, incoherent speech, etc.) make it more difficult to function in highly industrialized countries. In addition, individualism is highly encouraged in most industrialized nations. Therefore, families and other support groups are less likely to feel responsible for relatives and friends with schizophrenia (Brislin, 2000; Lefley, 2000).

Cultural effects on schizophrenia. The prevalence, form, onset, and prognosis for schizophrenia differ across cultures. Surprisingly, the prognosis, or prediction for recovery, is better for people suffering from schizophrenia in nonindustrialized countries than for those in industrialized countries. Can you explain why?

Peter Johnson/Corbis

Can you see how these four *culturally specific* factors (prevalence, form, onset, and prognosis) support a sociocultural or psychological explanation of schizophrenia? On the other hand, the large number of *culturally general* symptoms and the fact that schizophrenia is found in almost every society also support biological explanations. Once again, we have an example of the interacting factors in the *biopsychosocial model.*

Schizophrenia

Schizophrenia is a serious psychotic mental disorder that afflicts approximately 1 of every 100 people. The five major symptoms are disturbances in perception (**hallucinations**), language (word salad and neologisms), thought (impaired logic and **delusions**), emotion (exaggerated, changeable, or blunted), and behavior (social withdrawal, bizarre mannerisms, catalepsy, waxy flexibility).

Symptoms of schizophrenia can be divided into a positive and negative symptom classification system. *Positive* symptoms involve addition to or exaggeration of normal thought processes and behaviors (e.g., delusions and hallucinations). *Negative* symptoms involve loss or absence of normal thought processes and

behaviors (e.g., toneless voice and flat emotions).

Biological theories of schizophrenia emphasize the role of genetics (people inherit a predisposition), disruptions in neurotransmitters (the **dopamine hypothesis**), and abnormal brain structure and function (such as enlarged ventricles and lower levels of activity in the frontal and temporal lobes). Psychosocial theories of schizophrenia focus on the roles of stress and disturbed communication.

Questions

1. _____ refers to "split mind," whereas _____ refers to "split personality." (a) Psychosis, neurosis; (b) Insanity, multiple personalities; (c) Schizophrenia, dissociative identity disorder; (d) Paranoia, borderline

2. Schizophrenia is also a form of _____, a term describing general lack of contact with reality.

3. Perceptions for which there are no appropriate external stimuli are called _____, and the most common type among people suffering from schizophrenia is _____. (a) hallucinations, auditory; (b) hallucinations, visual; (c) delusions, auditory; (d) delusions, visual

4. List three biological and two psychosocial factors that may contribute to schizophrenia.

Check your answers in Appendix B.

 CLICK & REVIEW
for additional assessment options:
www.wiley.com/college/huffman

OTHER DISORDERS

We have now discussed anxiety disorders, mood disorders, and schizophrenia. In this section, we will briefly describe three additional disorders—*substance-related, dissociative,* and *personality disorders.*

Achievement

How are substance-related, dissociative, and personality disorders identified?

■ Substance-Related Disorders: When Drug Use Becomes Abnormal

Do you consider having wine with dinner or a few beers at a party to be an acceptable way to alter mood and behavior? In the *DSM-IV-TR,* drug use becomes a disorder when the person becomes physically or psychologically dependent. As you can see in Table 14.4, **substance-related disorders** are subdivided into two general groups—*substance abuse* and *substance dependence*—each with specific symptoms. When drug use interferes with a person's social or occupational functioning, it is called *substance abuse.* Drug use becomes *substance dependence* when it also causes physical reactions, including *tolerance* (requiring more of the drug to get the desired effect) and *withdrawal* (negative physical effects when the drug is removed).

Can people use drugs and not develop a substance-related disorder? Of course. Most people drink alcohol without creating problems in their social relationships or occupations. Unfortunately, researchers have not been able to identify ahead of time those who can safely use drugs versus those who might become abusers. Substance-related disorders also commonly coexist with other mental disorders, including anxiety disorders, mood disorders, schizophrenia, and personality disorders (Goodwin, Fergusson, & Horwood, 2004; Green et al., 2004; Grilly, 2006). This type of co-occurrence of disorders is known as **comorbidity**, and it creates serious problems.

Substance-Related Disorders *Abuse of, or dependence on, a mood- or behavior-altering drug*

Comorbidity *Co-occurrence of two or more disorders in the same person at the same time, as when a person suffers from both depression and alcoholism*

www.wiley.com/college/huffman

TABLE 14.4 *DSM-IV-TR* SUBSTANCE ABUSE AND SUBSTANCE DEPENDENCE

Criteria for Substance Abuse (alcohol and other drugs)	Criteria for Substance Dependence (alcohol and other drugs)
Maladaptive use of a substance shown by one of the following: • Failure to meet obligations • Repeated use in situations where it is physically dangerous • Continued use despite problems caused by the substance • Repeated substance-related legal problems	*Three or more of the following:* • Tolerance • Withdrawal • Substance taken for a longer time or greater amount than intended • Lack of desire or efforts to reduce or control use • Social, recreational, or occupational activities given up or reduced • Much time spent in activities to obtain the substance • Use continued despite knowing that psychological or physical problems are worsened by it

How can we identify the appropriate cause or treatment for someone if we're dealing with a combination of disorders? And what causes this type of multiple disorder? Perhaps the most influential hypothesis is that of self-medication—individuals use drugs to reduce their symptoms (Batel, 2000; Goswami et al., 2004; Green, 2000). One of the most common comorbid disorders is alcohol use disorder (AUD). Research shows a high genetic correlation between alcohol use disorders and other conditions, such as depression and personality disorders (Heath et al., 2003). On the other hand, several environmental variables also predict substance abuse disorders and comorbid conditions in adolescence. These variables include reduced parental monitoring, distance from teachers, selective socialization with deviant peers, and disaffiliation with peers (Fisher & Harrison, 2005; Sher, Grekin, & Williams, 2005).

Although it may seem contradictory to have both genetic and environmental explanations, we see once again that nature and nurture interact. Researchers suggest that the interaction might result from the fact that an alcohol-abusing youth might tend to seek out deviant peers. In addition, the same genes that contribute to a parent's lax monitoring might also contribute to his or her child's early experimentation with alcohol (Sher, 2000).

Regardless of the causes or correlates of alcohol abuse disorders and comorbid conditions, it is critical that patients, family members, and clinicians recognize and deal with comorbidity if treatment is to be effective. Alcohol abuse disorders often accompany serious depression, and simply stopping drinking is not a total solution (though certainly an important first step). Similarly, people suffering from schizophrenia are far more likely to relapse into psychosis, require hospitalization, neglect their medications, commit acts of violence, or kill themselves when they also suffer from AUDs (Batel, 2000; Besançon, 2004; Goswami et al., 2004). Recognizing this pattern and potential danger, many individual and group programs that treat schizophrenia now also include methods used in drug abuse treatment.

Dennis MacDonald/PhotoEdit

The high cost of alcohol abuse. *Children of alcoholic parents are at much greater risk of also abusing alcohol and developing related disorders. Is this because of a genetic predisposition, modeling by the parents, or the emotional devastation of growing up with an alcoholic parent?*

▉ Dissociative Disorders: When the Personality Splits Apart

Have you seen the movie *The Three Faces of Eve* or the movie *Sybil?* Both films dramatized and popularized cases of **dissociative disorders**. There are several types of dissociative disorders. But all involve a splitting apart (a *dis*-association) of significant aspects of experience from memory or consciousness. Individuals dissociate from the core of their personality by failing to recall or identify past experience (*dissociative amnesia*), by leaving home and wandering off (*dissociative fugue*), by losing the sense of

Dissociative Disorder *Amnesia, fugue, or multiple personalities resulting from a splitting apart of experience from memory or consciousness*

reality and feeling estranged from the self *(depersonalization disorder)*, or by developing completely separate personalities *(dissociative identity disorder;* previously known as *multiple personality disorder).*

Why would someone react this way? We've all had the experience of traveling somewhere, arriving at our destination, and then realizing we don't remember a single detail of the trip. This is a very mild form of dissociation. To understand what a dissociative *disorder* might be like, imagine witnessing a loved one's death in a horrible car accident. Can you see how your mind might cope with the severe emotional pain by blocking out all memory of the event? Putnam (1992) described a heart-wrenching example of a dissociative disorder in a young girl who saw both her parents blown to bits in a minefield. And how she tried to carefully piece their bodies back together, bit by bit.

The major problem underlying all dissociative disorders is the need to escape from anxiety. By developing amnesia, running away, or creating separate personalities, the individual avoids the anxiety and stress that threaten to overwhelm him or her. Unlike most psychological disorders, environmental variables are reported to be the primary cause, with little or no genetic influence (Waller & Ross, 1997).

Dissociative Identity Disorder

The most severe dissociative disorder is **dissociative identity disorder (DID)**, previously known as *multiple personality disorder* (MPD). In this disorder, two or more distinct personalities exist within the same person at different times. Each personality has unique memories, behaviors, and social relationships. Transition from one personality to another occurs suddenly and is often triggered by psychological stress. Usually, the original personality has no knowledge or awareness of the existence of the alternate subpersonalities. But all of the different personalities may be aware of lost periods of time. Often, the alternate personalities are very different from the original personality. They may be of the other sex, a different race, another age, or even another species (such as a dog or lion). The disorder is diagnosed more among women than among men. Women also tend to have more identities, averaging 15 or more, compared with men, who average 8 (American Psychiatric Association, 2000).

The book and movie *Sybil* portrayed one of the best known cases of DID. Sybil Dorsett was a midwestern schoolteacher with 16 personalities that took turns controlling her body. Instead of thinking of herself as one person who behaved differently at times, Sybil had lapses of memory when she became "another person." When she was "Peggy Lou," she was aggressive and capable of anger. As "Vickie," she was a confident and sophisticated woman who knew of the other personalities.

DID is a controversial diagnosis. Some researchers and mental health professionals suggest that many cases are faked or result from false memories and an unconscious need to please the therapist (Kihlstrom, 2005; Loftus, 1997; McNally, 2004; Stafford & Lynn, 2002). These skeptics also believe that therapists may be unintentionally encouraging, and thereby overreporting, the incidence of DID.

Even the authenticity of "Sybil" is now being questioned (Miller & Kantrowitz, 1999). The real-life patient, Shirley Ardell Mason, died in 1998, and some experts are now disputing the original diagnosis of her condition. They suggest that Shirley was highly hypnotizable and suggestible and that her therapist, Cornelia Wilbur, unintentionally "suggested" the existence of multiple personalities.

On the other side of the debate are psychologists who accept the validity of DID and believe the condition is underdiagnosed (Brown, 2001; Lipsanen et al., 2004; Spiegel & Maldonado, 1999). Consistent with this view, DID cases have been documented in many cultures around the world. And there has been a rise in the number of reported cases (American Psychiatric Association, 2000). (Critics suggest this also may reflect a growing public awareness of the disorder.)

Dissociative Identity Disorder (DID) *Presence of two or more distinct personality systems in the same individual at different times; previously known as multiple personality disorder*

Photofest

Dissociative identity disorder (DID). *Actress Sally Field won an Emmy for her sensitive portrayal of a woman suffering from dissociative identity disorder (DID) in the TV drama Sybil. Joanne Woodward portrayed the psychiatrist who guided her back to mental health. Although this drama was based on a real-life patient, experts have recently questioned the validity of the case and the diagnosis of DID. Source: Miller & Kantrowitz, 1999.*

www.wiley.com/college/huffman

■ Personality Disorders: Antisocial and Borderline

In Chapter 13, *personality* was defined as a unique and relatively stable pattern of thoughts, feelings, and actions. What would happen if these stable patterns, called personality, were so inflexible and maladaptive that they created significant impairment of someone's ability to function socially and occupationally? This is what happens with **personality disorders**. Unlike anxiety or mood disorders, which also involve maladaptive functioning, people with personality disorders generally do not feel upset or anxious about their behavior and may not be motivated to change. Several types of personality disorders are included in this category in *DSM-IV-TR*. In this section we will focus on the best-known type, *antisocial personality disorder*, and one of the most common, *borderline personality disorder*.

Antisocial Personality Disorder

The term **antisocial personality** describes behavior so far outside the usual ethical and legal standards of society that many consider it the most serious of all mental disorders. Unlike the previous disorders, people with this diagnosis focus solely on their own interests, while totally disregarding the rights of others. They also experience little or no remorse. Unfortunately, their maladaptive personality traits generally bring considerable harm and suffering to others (Hervé et al., 2004; Kirkman, 2002; Nathan et al., 2003). It might seem that such people would inevitably end up in jail. However, many people with this disorder avoid problems with the law and harm people in less dramatic ways as con artists, ruthless businesspeople, and "crooked" politicians and CEOs.

Symptoms Scott Peterson, the murderer described in the opening pages of this chapter, demonstrated four of the key traits of an antisocial personality disorder: *egocentrism*, *lack of conscience*, *impulsive behavior*, and *superficial charm*. Egocentrism refers to a preoccupation with one's own concerns and insensitivity to the needs of others. Dr. Robert Hare described individuals with an antisocial personality disorder as "social predators who charm, manipulate, and ruthlessly plow their way through life, leaving a broad trail of broken hearts, shattered expectations, and empty wallets. Completely lacking in conscience and empathy, they selfishly take what they want and do as they please, violating social norms and expectations without the slightest sense of guilt or regret" (Hare, 1993, p. xi).

Unlike most adults, who have learned to sacrifice immediate gratification for the sake of long-range goals, these individuals act on their impulses, without giving thought to the consequences. They are usually serene and poised when confronted with their destructive behavior and feel contempt for anyone they are able to manipulate. They change jobs and relationships suddenly and often have a history of truancy from school and of being expelled for destructive behavior. Even after repeated punishment, they seem to lack insight into the connection between their behavior and its consequences.

Interestingly, people with antisocial personalities can be quite charming and persuasive. They also have remarkably good insight into the needs and weaknesses of other people. Even while exploiting someone, they generally inspire feelings of trust. Mass murderer Ken Bianchi was so good at charming others that he convinced a woman he knew only casually to give him an alibi for some of the killings. Bianchi had been charged with several murders and was behind bars when he persuaded her to help him (Magid & McKelvey, 1987).

Why some individuals develop antisocial personality disorder is not completely understood (Lynam & Gudonis, 2005). Evidence for biological factors comes from twin and adoption studies that suggest a possible genetic predisposition (Bock & Goode, 1996; Jang et al., 2003). Other studies have found abnormally low autonomic activity during stress, right-hemisphere abnormalities, and reduced gray matter in the frontal lobes (Kiehl et al., 2004; Raine, Lencz, Bihrle, LaCasse, & Colletti, 2000).

Evidence also exists for environmental or psychological contributors. Studies have found a high correlation between antisocial personalities and both abusive par-

Personality Disorders *Inflexible, maladaptive personality traits that cause significant impairment of social and occupational functioning*

Antisocial Personality Disorder *Profound disregard for, and violation of, the rights of others*

©AP/Wide World Photos

A recent example of an antisocial personality disorder. Do you remember listening to audiotapes of Scott Peterson flirting and lying to his girlfriend while others frantically searched for his "missing" wife? This is a good example of the traits and behaviors of an antisocial personality disorder.

enting styles and inappropriate modeling. (Farrington, 2000; Pickering, Farmer, & McGuffin, 2004). People with antisocial personality disorder often come from homes characterized by emotional deprivation, harsh and inconsistent disciplinary practices, and antisocial behaviors on the part of parents. Still other studies show a strong interaction between both heredity and environment (Paris, 2000; Rutler, 1997).

Borderline Personality Disorder

Borderline personality disorder (BPD) is among the most commonly diagnosed personality disorders (Markovitz, 2004). The core features of this disorder are impulsivity and instability in mood, relationships, and self-image. Although "borderline" sounds like it might be a relatively minor disorder, it's not. Originally, the term implied that the person was on the *borderline* between neurosis and schizophrenia (Davison, Neale, & Kring, 2004). The modern conceptualization no longer has this connotation. But the disorder remains one of the most complex and debilitating of all the personality disorders.

Mary's story of chronic, lifelong dysfunction, described in the chapter opener, illustrates the serious problems associated with this disorder. People with borderline personality disorder experience extreme difficulties in relationships and engage in destructive, impulsive behaviors, like Mary's sexual promiscuity and self-mutilation. Others have problems with drinking, gambling, and eating sprees, which also are self-damaging and potentially lethal (Chabrol et al., 2004; Trull, Sher, Minks-Brown, Durbin, & Burr, 2000). Subject to chronic feelings of depression, emptiness, and intense fear of abandonment, BPD sufferers may attempt suicide and sometimes engage in self-mutilating behavior, such as slicing into their forearms or legs with a razor blade (Bohus et al., 2004; McKay, Gavigan, & Kulchycky, 2004; Paris, 2004).

Have you known someone who fits Mary's description? If so, you know that being a friend, lover, or parent to someone like Mary can be extremely difficult. They can be exciting, friendly, and totally charming one moment, and angry, argumentative, irritable, and sarcastic the next. They also tend to see themselves and everyone else in *absolutes*—perfect or worthless (Mason & Kreger, 1998). Partly because of their fragile identity, they constantly seek reassurance from others and may quickly erupt in anger at the slightest sign of disapproval or rejection. A simple gesture, missed appointment, or wrong turn of phrase can trigger an angry outburst, even in public situations, that would embarrass most people. People with BPD typically have a long history of broken friendships, divorces, and lost jobs.

Explanations   Research finds that borderline personality disorder is commonly associated with a childhood history of neglect, emotional deprivation, and physical, sexual, or emotional abuse (Goodman & Yehuda, 2002; Helgeland & Torgersen, 2004; Schmahl et al., 2004). This disorder also tends to run in families. In addition, some researchers have found a relationship with impaired functioning of the brain's frontal lobes and limbic system, areas that control impulsive behaviors (Schmahl et al., 2004; Tebartz et al., 2003).

What can be done to help these people? Some therapists have had success with drug therapy and behavior therapy (Bohus et al., Markovitz, 2004). Sadly, in most cases, the prognosis is not favorable. In one study, seven years after treatment, about 50 percent of the original group still had the disorder (Links, Heslegrave, & Van Reekum, 1998). People with BPD appear to have a deep well of intense loneliness and a chronic fear of abandonment. They go from friend to friend, lover to lover, and therapist to therapist, looking for someone to "complete" them. Unfortunately, given their troublesome personality traits, friends, lovers, and therapists often do "abandon" them—thus creating a tragic self-fulfilling prophecy and life long entrapment in BPD.

Borderline Personality Disorder (BPD) *Impulsivity and instability in mood, relationships, and self-image*

pplication

APPLYING PSYCHOLOGY TO STUDENT LIFE

Testing Your Knowledge of Abnormal Behavior

Applying abstract terminology is an important component of critical thinking. Test your understanding of the six major diagnostic categories of psychological disorders by matching the disorders with the possible diagnosis. Check your answers in Appendix B.

Description of Disorder

1. Julie mistakenly believes she has lots of money and is making plans to take all her friends on a trip around the world. She has not slept for days. Last month, she could not get out of bed and talked of suicide.

2. Steve is exceptionally charming and impulsive and apparently feels no remorse or guilt when he causes great harm to others.

3. Chris believes he is president of the United States and hears voices saying the world is ending.

4. Each day, Kelly repeatedly checks and rechecks all stove burners and locks throughout her house and washes her hands hundreds of times.

5. Lee has repeated bouts of uncontrollable drinking, frequently misses his Monday morning college classes, and was recently fired for drinking on the job.

6. Susan wandered off and was later found living under a new name, with no memory of her previous life.

Possible Diagnosis

a. Anxiety disorder

b. Schizophrenia

c. Mood disorder

d. Dissociative disorder

e. Personality disorder

f. Substance-related disorder

ssessment

CHECK & REVIEW

Other Disorders

Substance-related disorders involve abuse of, or dependence on, a mood- or behavior-altering drug. People with substance-related disorders also commonly suffer from other psychological disorders, a condition known as **comorbidity.**

In **dissociative disorders,** critical elements of personality split apart. This split is manifested in a dis-association of significant aspects of experience from memory or consciousness. Developing completely separate personalities [**dissociative identity disorder (DID)**] is the most severe dissociative disorder.

Personality disorders involve inflexi-

ble, maladaptive personality traits. The best-known type is the **antisocial personality,** characterized by a profound disregard for, and violation of, the rights of others. Research suggests this disorder may be related to genetic inheritance, defects in brain activity, or disturbed family relationships. **Borderline personality disorder (BPD)** is the most commonly diagnosed personality disorder. It is characterized by impulsivity and instability in mood, relationships, and self-image.

Questions

1. The major underlying problem for all dissociative disorders is the psychological need to escape from _____.

2. What is DID?

3. A serial killer would likely be diagnosed as a(n) _____ personality in the Diagnostic and Statistical Manual of Mental Disorders, fourth edition, text revision.

4. One possible biological contributor to BPD is _____. (a) childhood history of neglect; (b) emotional deprivation; (c) impaired functioning of the frontal lobes; (d) all these options.

Check your answers in Appendix B.

CLICK & REVIEW
for additional assessment options:
www.wiley.com/college/huffman

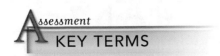

Assessment
KEY TERMS

*To assess your understanding of the **Key Terms** in Chapter 14, write a definition for each (in your own words), and then compare your definitions with those in the text.*

Studying Psychological Disorders
abnormal behavior (p. 498)
Diagnostic and Statistical Manual of Mental Disorders (DSM-IV-TR) (p. 503)
insanity (p. 499)
medical model (p. 502)
neurosis (p. 503)
psychiatry (p. 502)
psychosis (p. 503)

Anxiety Disorders
anxiety disorder (p. 506)
generalized anxiety disorder (p. 507)

obsessive-compulsive disorder (OCD) (p. 508)
panic disorder (p. 507)
phobia (p. 507)

Mood Disorders
bipolar disorder (p. 512)
learned helplessness (p. 514)
major depressive disorder (p. 512)

Schizophrenia
delusions (p. 519)
dopamine hypothesis (p. 521)
hallucinations (p. 518)

schizophrenia [skit-so-FREE-nee-uh], (p. 517)

Other Disorders
antisocial personality disorder (p. 528)
borderline personality disorder (BPD) (p. 529)
comorbidity (p. 526)
dissociative disorder (p. 526)
dissociative identity disorder (DID) (p. 527)
personality disorders (p. 528)
substance-related disorders (p. 525)

Achievement
WEB RESOURCES

Huffman Book Companion Site
http://www.wiley.com/college/huffman
This site is loaded with free Interactive Self-Tests, Internet Exercises, Glossary and Flashcards for key terms, web links, Handbook for Non-Native Speakers, and other activities designed to improve your mastery of the material in this chapter.

Want more detailed information about all the disorders discussed in this chapter, plus others?
http://www.apa.org/science/lib.html
Created by the American Psychological Association (APA), this website offers articles, books, library searches, and links for all the disorders listed in the *DSM-IV-TR*. If you'd like additional information, try http://www.mentalhealth.com/p20-grp.html. Sponsored by the Internet Mental Health Group, this site provides a wealth of resources and information about all the major disorders, including description, diagnosis, treatment, research, and recommended booklets. Also try http://www.mhsource.com/. Designed primarily for mental health professionals, this website offers valuable resources and links to information on specific disorders, their cause, diagnosis, and treatment.

Would you like to see a complete listing of DSM-IV mental disorders?
http://www.behavenet.com/capsules/disorders/dsm4classification.htm
Although the listing is somewhat obsolete because it is based on the *DSM-IV*, not the newer *DSM-IV-TR*, this website does provide a sample of the exhaustive list of mental disorders and their classification.

Are you depressed?
http://www.medicinenet.com/Depression/article.htm
Sponsored by MedicineNet.com, this website offers over 80 articles related to depression. Written by medical authors and editors, these articles discuss the diagnosis, causes, self-help, and professional therapy for depression. If you would like more information, try http://www.blarg.net/_~charlatn/Depression.html. This website offers numerous resources related to depression and its treatment.

Are you, or is someone you know, feeling suicidal?
http://www.spanusa.org/
Sponsored by the Suicide Prevention Action Network (SPANUSA), this website is "dedicated to the creation and implementation of effective National Suicide Prevention Strategies." It offers information and tools for suicide prevention. But, as stated on the opening page, "This site is not intended as a crisis line or hotline. Local crisis hotline numbers can be found in the front of your local phone book, or call 911."

Need additional information about schizophrenia?
http://www.mhsource.com/schizophrenia/index.html
The home page for the *Psychiatric Times*, the number-one psychiatric publication. Although targeted at mental health professionals, this website offers valuable general information and resources for the diagnosis and treatment of schizophrenia.

Visual Summary

Studying Psychological Disorders

Identifying Abnormal Behavior

Abnormal behavior: Pattern of emotion, thought, and action considered pathological for one or more of four reasons (statistical infrequency, disability or dysfunction, personal distress, or violation of norms).

©AP/Wide World Photos

Explaining Abnormality

Stone Age—demonology model; treated with *trephining*.	Middle Ages—demonology model; treated with exorcism, torture, imprisonment, death.	18th century—Pinel reforms inhumane asylums to treat the mentally ill.	Modern times—**medical model** dominates (e.g., **psychiatry**).

Classifying Abnormal Behavior

The **Diagnostic and Statistical Manual of Mental Disorders (DSM–IV–TR)** categorizes disorders according to major similarities and differences and provides detailed descriptions of symptoms.

- *Benefits*: Standardized diagnosis, improved communication among professionals and between professionals and patients.
- *Problems*: Insufficient attention to cultural factors, overreliance on medical model, and labels may become self-perpetuating.

Anxiety Disorders

Persistent feelings of threat in facing everyday problems

Generalized Anxiety Disorder	**Panic Disorder**	**Phobias**	**Obsessive-Compulsive Disorder**
Persistent free-floating or nonspecific anxiety	Anxiety concentrated into brief or lengthy episodes of panic attacks	Exaggerated fears of specific objects or situations	Persistent anxiety-arousing thoughts (obsessions) relieved by ritualistic actions (compulsions) such as hand washing

Mood Disorders

Mood disorders are disturbances of affect (emotion) that may include psychotic distortions of reality. Two types:

- **Major depressive disorder**: Long-lasting depressed mood, feelings of worthlessness, and loss of interest in most activities. Feelings are without apparent cause and person may lose contact with reality.
- **Bipolar disorder**: Episodes of mania and depression alternate with normal periods. During manic episode, speech and thinking are rapid, and the person may experience delusions of grandeur and act impulsively.

Schizophrenia

Schizophrenia: Serious psychotic mental disorder afflicting approximately one out of every 100 people.

Five major symptoms: Disturbances in

1) Perception (impaired filtering and selection, **hallucinations**).
2) Language (word salad, neologisms).
3) Thought (impaired logic, **delusions**).
4) Emotion (either exaggerated or blunted emotions).
5) Behavior (social withdrawal, bizarre mannerisms, catalepsy, waxy flexibility).

Two-type Classification System:

Positive symptoms—distorted or excessive mental activity (e.g., delusions and hallucinations).

Negative symptoms—behavioral deficits (e.g., toneless voice, flattened emotions).

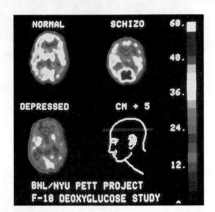

Other Disorders

Substance-Related Disorders	Dissociative Disorders	Personality Disorders	
	Dissociative Identity Disorder	Antisocial Personality	Borderline Personality Disorder (BPD)

Photofest

THERAPY

Achievement

Core Learning Outcomes

As you read Chapter 15, keep the following questions in mind and answer them in your own words:

▷ What are the core treatment techniques in insight therapy?

▷ How are learning principles used in behavior therapy?

▷ What are the major biomedical therapies?

▷ How can I use critical thinking to improve my understanding of therapy?

☐ *Achievement*
☐ *Assessment*
☐ *Application*

Application

WHY STUDY PSYCHOLOGY?

Michael Goldman/Masterfile

Chapter 15 will help you overcome myths such as...

▶ Myth: *There is one best therapy.*

Fact: Many problems can be treated equally well with many different forms of therapy.

▶ Myth: *Therapists can read minds.*

Fact: Good therapists often seem to have an uncanny ability to understand how their clients are feeling and to know when someone is trying to avoid certain topics. This is not due to any special mind-reading ability. It reflects their specialized training and daily experience working with troubled people.

▶ Myth: *People who go to therapists are crazy or just weak.*

Fact: Most people seek counseling because of stress in their lives or because they realize that therapy can improve their level of functioning. It is difficult to be objective about our own problems. Seeking therapy is a sign not only of wisdom but also of personal strength.

▶ Myth: *Only the rich can afford therapy.*

Fact: Therapy can be expensive. But many clinics and therapists charge on a sliding scale based on the client's income. Some insurance plans also cover psychological services.

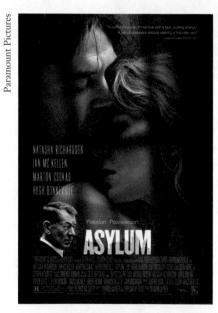

Paramount Pictures

Hollywood's take on psychotherapy.

Did you see the latest version of the movie The House on Haunted Hill? "A sanitarium of horrors, overseen by a surgeon gone mad" *is how the fake newsreel coverage of the events describes the scene. Compare this dimly lit, overcrowded insane asylum with the painfully bright, clinical-looking mental facility in* One Flew over the Cuckoo's Nest *or* Terminator 2: Judgment Day.

Consider, too, how mentally ill people themselves are generally portrayed. They are either cruel, sociopathic criminals (Hannibal Lecter, played by Anthony Hopkins, in Silence of the Lambs) *or helpless victims who will never be believed again after being labeled insane (Sarah Connor in* Terminator 2, *Jack Nicholson in* One Flew over the Cuckoo's Nest, *and Winona Ryder in* Girl Interrupted).

Since the beginning of the movie age, from The Cabinet of Dr. Caligari *to* Terminator 2, *from* Silence of the Lambs *to* A Beautiful Mind, *mentally ill people and their treatment have been the subject of some of Hollywood's most popular and influential films. The mad or heartless doctors and nurses, the "crazy" or bizarre patients, and the brutal treatment of mentally ill patients perfectly suit the needs of Hollywood directors hoping to boost ticket sales (adapted from Koenig, 2000).*

What's wrong with these films? Are they only "harmless entertainment," or do they perpetuate harmful stereotypes? According to the Surgeon General's *Report on Mental Health*, the shame and embarrassment caused by the stigma that surrounds a diagnosis of mental illness is the "most formidable obstacle to future progress in the arena of mental illness and health." Remarking on the film industry's distorted and largely negative portrayal of mental illness and its treatment, the Surgeon General also stated: "We want to help overcome the stereotypes, and help people realize that, just as things go wrong with the heart, the liver and the kidney, things can go wrong with the brain, and there should be no shame in that" (Adams, 2000).

The Surgeon General's Report also found that nearly two-thirds of all people who have mental disorders avoid seeking treatment because of financial problems, limited access, lack of awareness, or other reasons. At least a part of their resistance to therapy may be due to Hollywood's negative one-sided portrayals. This is unfortunate. As you will see in this chapter, modern therapy can be very effective and prevent much needless suffering (Blanco et al., 2003; Ellis, 2004; Nordhus & Pallesen, 2003; Shadish & Baldwin, 2003; Swanson, Swartz, & Elbogen, 2004).

In our coverage of modern forms of therapy, I hope to offset what you might have "learned" from Hollywood films with a balanced, factual presentation of the latest research. It's important to emphasize that not everyone who seeks professional help is suffering from mental illness. Psychological disorders are much more prevalent than most people realize (Chapter 14). But for a large number of people the major goal of therapy is to help with everyday problems in living, such as parent–child conflicts, unhappy marriages, the death of a loved one, or adjustment to retirement. In addition, some people enjoy therapy for their gains in self-knowledge and personal fulfillment.

People often talk about going to their family and friends (or even their barber or hair stylist) for "therapy." In the strictest sense, **psychotherapy** refers only to techniques used by professionals (e.g., psychoanalysis, behavior modification, client-centered therapy). Psychologists involved in psychotherapy include clinical and counseling therapists. Outside psychology, psychiatrists, psychiatric nurses, social workers, counselors, and members of the clergy with special training in pastoral counseling also provide professional therapy.

This chapter focuses on the therapies used primarily by psychologists. The one exception is our discussion of *biomedical therapies* [drug treatments, electroconvulsive therapy (ECT), and psychosurgery]. Although psychiatrists and other medical professionals are generally the ones who practice biomedical techniques, they often work with psychologists to design the best treatment for clients. It is also becoming clear that the effects of psychotherapy and biomedical therapy overlap. For example, clients often need drugs to calm their anxieties or relieve their depression. But they also need psychotherapy to change their dysfunctional thoughts and behaviors. Interestingly, successful biomedical therapy and psychotherapy both tend to alter brain functions.

As you'll discover throughout this chapter, there are numerous forms of psychotherapy. According to one expert (Kazdin, 1994), there may be over 400 approaches to treatment. Figure 15.1 organizes the most representative and widely used treatments into three like-minded groups. This chapter begins with "Insight Therapies," which

Psychotherapy *Techniques employed to improve psychological functioning and promote adjustment to life*

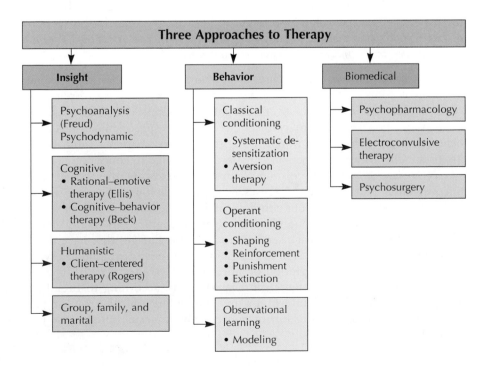

Figure 15.1 *An overview of the three major approaches to therapy.*

emphasize personal understanding and self-knowledge. Our second group, the "Behavior Therapies," focuses on changing maladaptive behaviors. Our third topic, "Biomedical Therapy," explores abnormal behavior as a mental illness and therefore emphasizes medical treatments, such as drugs. The chapter concludes with several issues related to therapy, including effectiveness and how to find a good therapist.

INSIGHT THERAPIES

Achievement

What are the core treatment techniques in insight therapy?

What do you think of when you hear the word *therapy*? When I ask my students this question, they usually describe a small, cluttered office with a sofa where patients recline and tell their secrets to a male therapist with a beard. Does this description match the one in your own mind? If so, it's probably due once again to Hollywood films. In most films, "therapy" is either biomedical (drugs, electroconvulsive therapy and psychosurgery) or "talk therapy" with a bearded therapist listening to a patient reclining on a couch. This stereotype has little to do with the realities of modern therapy.

We begin our discussion of insight therapy with traditional psychoanalysis (which often *does* use a couch) and its modern counterpart, psychodynamic therapy. Then we explore cognitive, humanistic, group, and family therapies. Each of these therapies is significantly different from the others. But they're often grouped together under the title "insight therapies" because they generally seek to increase self-knowledge and understanding (insight) into the client's difficulties. The belief is that once people understand what motivates them, they can gain greater control over and improvement in their thoughts, feelings, and behaviors.

Modern therapy in action.

Psychoanalysis/Psychodynamic Therapies: Unlocking the Secrets of the Unconscious

Psychoanalysis means just what the name implies. A person's *psyche* (or mind) is *analyzed*. During psychoanalysis, the therapist (or psychoanalyst) works to bring unconscious conflicts, which are believed to date back to early childhood experiences, into consciousness. The patient comes to understand the reasons for his or her behavior and realizes that the childhood conditions under which the conflicts developed no longer exist. Once this realization (or *insight*) occurs, the conflicts can be resolved and the patient is free to develop more adaptive behavior patterns. In this section we will discuss Freud's five major methods of psychoanalysis: *free association, dream analysis, analyzing resistance, analyzing transference,* and *interpretation.*

1. *Free association.* Have you ever let your mind wander without attempting to monitor or control the direction of your thinking? According to Freud, when you remove conscious censorship over thoughts—a process called **free association**—interesting and even bizarre connections seem to spring into awareness. Freud believed that the first (uncensored) thing to come to a patient's mind was often an important clue to what the person's unconscious wanted to conceal.

2. *Dream analysis.* According to Freud, dreams are the "royal road to the unconscious." This is because defenses are supposedly lowered during sleep and forbidden desires and unconscious conflicts can be freely expressed. Even while dreaming, however, these feelings and conflicts are recognized as being unacceptable. Therefore, they must be disguised as *dream symbols* (images that have deeper symbolic meaning). Freud suggested the therapist must move beyond these symbols and the superficial, surface description of a dream (the *manifest content*) to uncover the true, underlying meaning (the *latent content*). Thus, according to Freudian **dream analysis**, a therapist might interpret a dream of riding a horse or driving a car (the manifest content) as a desire for, or concern about, sexual intercourse (the latent content).

Psychoanalysis *Freudian therapy designed to bring unconscious conflicts, which usually date back to early childhood experiences, into consciousness; also Freud's theoretical school of thought emphasizing unconscious processes*

Free Association *In psychoanalysis, reporting whatever comes to mind without monitoring its contents*

Dream Analysis *In psychoanalysis, interpreting the underlying true meaning of dreams to reveal unconscious processes*

3. *Analyzing resistance.* During free association or dream analysis, Freud found that patients often show **resistance**—an inability or unwillingness to discuss or reveal certain memories, thoughts, motives, or experiences. While talking about a painful childhood memory, the individual might suddenly "forget" what he or she was saying, or competely change the subject. It is the therapist's job to identify these cases of resistance, help patients face their problems, and learn to deal with them in a realistic manner.

Why would someone pay money to a therapist and then be resistant to talk? People generally enter therapy to gain personal insight into their problems. But they also resist exposing their most painful or embarrassing feelings. The closer the patient and analyst come to the source of the anxiety, the more the patient is motivated to run from it. A classic joke about psychoanalysis may help you understand (and remember) the concept of resistance: "If patients arrive on time for their appointment, they're compulsive; if they're early, they're dependent; and if late, they're resistant."

4. *Analyzing transference.* During psychoanalysis, patients disclose intimate feelings and memories that they've probably never shared with anyone else. As a result, the relationship between the therapist and patient may become complex and emotionally charged. Patients often come to see the analyst as a symbol for other significant figures from the past, perhaps a parent or lover. They then apply (or *transfer*) some of their unresolved emotions and attitudes onto the therapist. This process of **transference** is considered a valuable part of psychoanalysis. The therapist uses it to help the patient "relive" painful past relationships in a safe, therapeutic setting. Once the patient "works through" his or her previously repressed feelings and unconscious conflicts, he or she can move on to healthier relationships.

5. *Interpretation.* The core of all psychoanalytic therapy is **interpretation**. During free association, dream analysis, resistance, and transference, the analyst listens closely and observes patterns and hidden conflicts. At the right time, the therapist explains (or *interprets*) the true, underlying meanings to the client. For instance, during therapy a man who has trouble with intimacy might look out the window and change the subject whenever anything touches on closeness or feelings. The analyst will attempt to interpret these defensive behaviors and help the patient recognize how he avoids the topic (Davison, Neale, & Kring, 2004). The goal is to provide *insight*. This helps the patient uncover and resolve previously repressed memories, thoughts, and unconscious conflicts.

Evaluation

As you can see, most of psychoanalysis rests on the assumption that repressed memories and unconscious conflicts actually exist. But as you may remember from Chapters 7 and 13, this assumption is questioned by modern scientists and has become the subject of a heated, ongoing debate. In addition to this questionable assumption, critics also point to two other problems:

1. *Limited applicability.* Freud's methods were developed in the early 1900s for a particular clientele—upper-class Viennese people (primarily women). Although psychoanalysis has been refined over the years, critics say it still seems to suit only a select group of individuals. Success appears to be best with less severe disorders, such as anxiety disorders, and with highly motivated, articulate patients. Critics jokingly proposed the acronym *YAVIS* to describe the perfect psychoanalysis patient: young, attractive, verbal, intelligent, and successful (Schofield, 1964).

In addition, psychoanalysis is time consuming (often lasting several years with four to five sessions a week) and expensive. And it seldom works well with severe mental disorders, such as schizophrenia. This is logical because psychoanalysis is based on verbalization and rationality—the very abilities most significantly disrupted by serious disorders. Critics suggest that spending years on a couch chasing unconscious

Resistance *In psychoanalysis, the person's inability or unwillingness to discuss or reveal certain memories, thoughts, motives, or experiences*

"I dreamt I had a Harem, but they all wanted to talk about the relationship."

Transference *In psychoanalysis, the patient may displace (or transfer) unconscious feelings about a significant person in his or her life onto the therapist*

Interpretation *A psychoanalyst's explanation of a patient's free associations, dreams, resistance, and transference; more generally, any statement by a therapist that presents a patient's problem in a new way*

conflicts from the past allows patients to escape from the responsibilities and problems of adult life—in effect, the patient becomes "couchridden."

2. ***Lack of scientific credibility.*** The goals of psychoanalysis are explicitly stated—to bring unconscious conflicts to conscious awareness. But how do you know when this goal has been achieved? If patients accept the analyst's interpretations of their conflicts, their "insights" may be nothing more than cooperation with the therapist's belief system.

On the other hand, if patients refuse to accept the analyst's interpretations, the analyst may say they're exhibiting resistance. Moreover, the therapist can always explain away a failure. If patients get better, it's because of their insights. If they don't, then the insight was not real—it was only intellectually accepted. Such reasoning does not meet scientific standards. The ability to prove or disprove a theory is the foundation of the scientific approach.

Psychoanalysts acknowledge that it is impossible to scientifically document certain aspects of their therapy. However, they insist that most patients benefit (Gabbard, Gunderson, & Fonagy, 2002; Ward, 2000). Many analysands (patients) agree.

Modern Psychodynamic Therapy

Partly in response to criticisms of traditional psychoanalysis, more streamlined forms of psychoanalysis have been developed. In modern psychoanalytic therapy (known as **psychodynamic therapy**), treatment is briefer. Therapists and patients usually meet only one to two times a week, rather than several times a week, and for only a few weeks or months versus several years. The patient is also seen face to face (rather than reclining on a couch). In addition, the therapist takes a more directive approach (rather than waiting for a gradual unveiling of the unconscious).

Psychodynamic Therapy *A briefer, more directive, and more modern form of psychoanalysis that focuses on conscious processes and current problems*

*A*ssessment

VISUAL QUIZ

PT: Sometimes it doesn t seem worth the effort to continue.

TH: Have you had any thoughts of wanting to kill yourself?

PT: No, not really.

TH: What have you thought of doing?

PT: Nothing that s worth mentioning.

TH: Have you ever thought of taking an overdose of pills?

PT: No, I haven t.

TH: What about cutting yourself or jumping off a bridge?

PT: No, those options aren t very good. You might not die.

TH: Have you thought of a way you think might be more certain, perhaps like using a gun?

PT: (long pause) I have thought of shooting myself.

No small segment of therapy can truly convey an actual full-length therapy session. However, this brief excerpt of an exchange between a patient (PT) and therapist (TH) using a psychodynamic approach does demonstrate several psychoanalytic/psychodynamic techniques. See if you find examples of free association, dream analysis, resistance, or transference in this discussion.

Answer: The clearest example is resistance. When the therapist asks her about thoughts of suicide, she initially resists and then admits she has thought of shooting herself. Keep in mind that all therapists in this situation would probe beyond this point to follow up on the patient's suicide risk.

Also, although contemporary psychodynamic therapists try to help clients gain insight into their early childhood experiences and unconscious roots of problems, they focus more attention on conscious processes and current problems. Such refinements have helped make psychoanalysis shorter, more available, and more effective for an increasing number of people (Guthrie et al., 2004; Hilsenroth et al., 2003; Siqueland et al., 2002).

Interpersonal therapy (IPT) is a psychodynamically based, and particularly influential, brief form of therapy. As the name implies, *interpersonal* therapy focuses almost exclusively on the client's current relationships and issues that arise from those relationships. The goal of IPT is to relieve immediate symptoms and help the client learn better ways to solve future interpersonal problems. The assumption is that emotional problems and psychiatric disorders are inextricably linked with relationship problems. Once clients identify and improve their social skills, their psychological problems will also improve. IPT was originally designed for acute depression. But it is similarly effective for a variety of disorders, including marital conflict, eating disorders, parenting problems, and drug addiction (Guthrie et al., 2004; Markowitz, 2003; Weissman, Markowitz, & Klerman, 2003; Wilfley et al., 2002).

Assessment

CHECK & REVIEW

Psychoanalysis/Psychodynamic Therapies

Sigmund Freud developed the psychoanalytic method of therapy to uncover unconscious conflicts and bring them into conscious awareness. The five major techniques of **psychoanalysis** are **free association, dream analysis,** analyzing **resistance,** analyzing **transference,** and **interpretation.** Like psychoanalytic theories of personality, psychoanalysis is the subject of great debate. It is criticized primarily for its limited availability (it is time-consuming, expensive, and suits only a small group of people) and its lack of sci-

entific credibility. Modern **psychodynamic therapies** overcome some of these limitations.

Questions

1. The system of psychotherapy developed by Freud that seeks to bring unconscious conflicts into conscious awareness is known as _____. (a) transference; (b) cognitive restructuring; (c) psychoanalysis; (d) the "hot seat" technique
2. Which psychoanalytic concept best explains the following situations?
   a. Mary is extremely angry with her therapist, who seems unresponsive and uncaring about her personal needs.
   b. Although John is normally very punctual in his daily activities, he is frequently late for his therapy session.
3. What are the two major criticisms of psychoanalysis?
4. How does modern psychodynamic therapy differ from psychoanalysis?

Check your answers in Appendix B.

 CLICK & REVIEW
for additional assessment options:
www.wiley.com/college/huffman

Cognitive Therapies: A Focus on Faulty Thoughts and Beliefs

The mind is its own place, and in itself can make a Heavn' of Hell, a Hell of Heav'n
JOHN MILTON, *PARADISE LOST,* LINE 247

Cognitive therapy assumes that faulty thought processes and beliefs create problem behaviors and emotions. For example, a cognitive therapist would say that feelings of depression are created by such beliefs as "If I don't do everything perfectly, I am worthless" or "I'm helpless to change my life, so I'll never be happy." When people hold beliefs that are irrational, that are overly demanding, or that fail to match reality, their emotions and behaviors may become disturbed (Dowd, 2004; Ellis, 1996, 2003, 2004; Luecken et al., 2004).

Cognitive therapists, like psychoanalysts, analyze a person's thought processes, believing that altering destructive thoughts will enable the person to live more

Cognitive Therapy *Therapy that focuses on faulty thought processes and beliefs to treat problem behaviors*

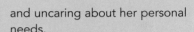 www.wiley.com/college/huffman

effectively. Like psychoanalysts, cognitive therapists assume that many of the beliefs that create problem behaviors operate at an unexamined (but not necessarily "unconscious") level.

Cognitive therapists also agree with psychoanalysts that exploring an unexamined belief system can produce insight into the reasons for disturbed behaviors. However, instead of believing that a change in behavior occurs because of the insight itself, cognitive therapists believe that insight into negative **self-talk**, the unrealistic things a person has been telling himself or herself, is most important.

This insight allows the individual to challenge his or her thoughts, to directly change how he or she interprets events, and, ultimately, to change maladaptive behaviors. For example, the irrational statement "If I don't do everything perfectly, I am worthless" can be changed to more adaptive thoughts like "I can accept my limits" or "I can make constructive changes in my behavior." **Cognitive restructuring** is the name for this process of changing destructive thoughts or inappropriate interpretations.

Albert Ellis and Rational-Emotive Therapy

One of the best-known cognitive therapists is Albert Ellis, a former psychoanalytic therapist who developed his own approach, known as **rational-emotive behavior therapy (REBT)** (1961, 2003, 2004). Ellis calls REBT an A–B–C–D approach, referring to the four steps involved in creating and dealing with maladaptive thinking: (A) an *activating event*, which is some type of stimulus, such as criticism from a boss or a failing grade; (B) the *belief system*, which is the person's interpretation of the activating experience; (C) the emotional and behavioral *consequences* that the person experiences; and (D) the *disputing*, or challenging, of the erroneous belief (Figure 15.2).

Ellis claims that unless we stop to think about our interpretation of events, we will automatically go from A (the activating event) to C (the emotional and behavioral consequences). We fail to see that step B (the belief system) actually creates the subsequent emotion and behavior. Receiving a failing grade on an exam, for example, does not *cause* the emotion of depression. It is step B (the belief that "I'll never get through college") that is the culprit.

Self-Talk *Internal dialogue; the things people say to themselves when they interpret events*

Cognitive Restructuring *Process in cognitive therapy to change destructive thoughts or inappropriate interpretations*

Rational-Emotive Behavior Therapy (REBT) *Ellis's cognitive therapy to eliminate self-defeating beliefs through rational examination*

Figure 15.2 *The development and treatment of irrational misconceptions.* How do our thoughts and beliefs make us unhappy? According to Albert Ellis, our emotional reactions are produced by our interpretation of an event, not by the event itself. For example, if you receive a low exam score, you might explain to yourself and others that your bad mood was a direct result of the low grade. Ellis would argue that the self-talk ("I'll never get through college") that occurs between the event and the feeling is what upset you. Furthermore, the bad mood causes you to ruminate on all the other bad things in your life, which maintains your negative emotional state. Ellis's therapy emphasizes disputing, or challenging, these irrational beliefs, which, in turn, causes changes in maladaptive emotions—it breaks the vicious cycle.

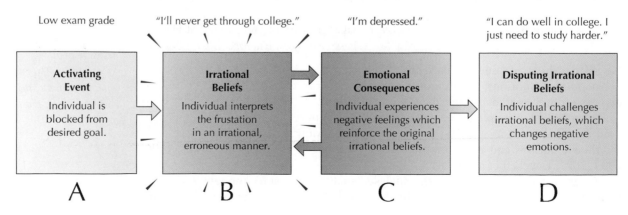

When he originally formulated his theory, Ellis emphasized a number of specific irrational beliefs resulting from his A–B–C–D model, such as "I must have love from everyone" and "I must be thoroughly competent." In recent years, however, he has shifted to a general concept of "demandingness" (David, Schnur, & Belloiu, 2002; Ellis, 1997, 2003, 2004). When people *demand* certain "musts" and "shoulds" from themselves and others, they create emotional distress and behavioral dysfunction that often require therapeutic intervention. For example, a divorced man whose wife left him for another man might engage in this self-talk: "I *must* be loved by everyone. She *should* not and *must* not reject me. I *demand* that she come back to me, or I'll get even."

Ellis believes that such unrealistic, unproductive self-talk, "demandingness," and "musturbation" ("He *must* love me" "I *must* get into graduate school") generally go unexamined unless the client is confronted directly. In therapy, Ellis often argues with clients, cajoling and teasing them, sometimes in very blunt language. Many clients are shocked by his bluntness—and by their own irrational beliefs.

Once clients recognize their self-defeating thoughts, Ellis begins working with them on how to *behave* differently—to test out new beliefs and to learn better coping skills. Reflecting this increased attention to behavioral change, he renamed his original rational-emotive therapy (RET) *rational-emotive behavior therapy* (REBT) (Crosby, 2003). According to Ellis (2003), we hold ourselves prisoner to the past. This is because we are still propagandizing ourselves with irrational nonsense. By controlling how we think in the present, we can liberate ourselves from the "scars" of the past.

Aaron Beck and Cognitive-Behavior Therapy

Another well-known cognitive therapist is Aaron Beck (1976, 2000). Like Ellis, Beck believes that psychological problems result from illogical thinking and from destructive self-talk. Ellis and psychoanalysts encourage the client to express thoughts and

---

TRY THIS YOURSELF

Application

Overcoming Irrational Misconceptions

Albert Ellis believes that most people require the help of a therapist to allow them to see through their defenses and force them to challenge their self-defeating thoughts. However, you may be able to improve some of your own irrational beliefs and responses with the following suggestions:

1. *Identify your belief system.* Identify your irrational beliefs by asking yourself why you feel the particular emotions you do. Ellis believes that by confronting your beliefs, you can discover the irrational assumptions that are creating the problem consequences.

2. *Evaluate the consequences.* Emotions such as anger, anxiety, and depression often seem "natural." But they don't have to happen. Rather than perpetuating negative emotions by assuming they must be experienced, focus on whether your reactions make you more effective and enable you to solve your problems.

3. *Dispute the self-defeating beliefs.* Once you have identified an overly demanding or irrational belief, argue against it. For example, it is gratifying when people you cherish love you in return, but if they do not, continuing to pursue them or insisting that they must love you will only be self-defeating.

4. *Practice effective ways of thinking.* Continue to examine your emotional reactions to events and situations to create opportunities to dispute irrational beliefs and substitute realistic perceptions. Practice behaviors that are more effective by rehearsing them at home and imagining outcomes that are more successful.

Cognitive-Behavior Therapy *Beck's system for confronting and changing behaviors associated with destructive cognitions*

feelings to gain insight into the origins of maladaptive behaviors. In contrast, Beck takes a much more active approach. He seeks to provide clients with experiences, both inside and outside the therapy session, that will alter their negative talk in a favorable way. The overall goal is to directly confront and change the behaviors associated with destructive cognitions—hence the term **cognitive-behavior therapy**. (The upcoming section in this chapter offers a full discussion of behavior therapy.)

One of the most successful applications of Beck's theory has been in the treatment of depression. Beck has identified several thinking patterns that he believes are associated with depression. These are among the most important:

1. *Selective perception.* Depression-prone people tend to focus selectively on negative events while ignoring positive events.

2. *Overgeneralization.* Based on limited information, depressed people often overgeneralize and draw negative conclusions about their self-worth. Believing you are worthless because you lost a promotion or failed an exam is a good example of overgeneralization.

3. *Magnification.* Depressed people tend to exaggerate the importance of undesirable events or personal shortcomings. They also see them as catastrophic and unchangeable.

4. *All-or-nothing thinking.* Depressed people tend to see things in black-or-white categories. Everything is either totally good or bad, right or wrong, a success or a failure.

Beck's cognitive-behavior therapy works like this: To begin, clients are taught to recognize and keep track of their thoughts. Examples might be: "How come I'm the only one alone at this party" (selective perception) and "If I don't get straight A's, I'll never get a good job" (all-or-nothing thinking). Next, the therapist trains the client to develop ways to test these automatic thoughts against reality. If the client believes that straight A's are necessary for a certain job, the therapist needs to find only one instance of this not being the case to refute the belief. Obviously, the therapist chooses the tests carefully so that they do not confirm the client's negative beliefs but lead instead to positive outcomes.

This approach—identifying dysfunctional thoughts followed by active testing—helps depressed people discover that negative attitudes are largely a product of unrealistic or faulty thought processes. At this point, Beck introduces the second phase of therapy, persuading the client to actively pursue pleasurable activities. Depressed individuals often lose motivation, even for experiences they used to find enjoyable. Simultaneously taking an active rather than a passive role and reconnecting with enjoyable experiences help in recovering from depression.

" I wish you'd stop being so negative."

Cartoon Stock

Evaluating Cognitive Therapies

Considerable evidence suggests that cognitive therapies are highly effective with depression, anxiety disorders, bulimia nervosa, anger management, addiction, and even some symptoms of schizophrenia and insomnia (Beck & Rector, 2005; Ellis, 2003, 2004; Reeder et al., 2004; Secker et al., 2004; Turkington et al., 2004).

Both Beck and Ellis are criticized, however, for ignoring or denying the client's unconscious dynamics, overemphasizing rationality, and minimizing the importance of the client's past (Butler, 2000; Hammack, 2003). In addition, Ellis is criticized for "preaching an ethical system" (Davison, Neale, & Kring, 2004, p. 579). By labeling his patients' beliefs "irrational" and insisting that they be replaced with "rational" thoughts, Ellis is imposing his own set of standards. Other critics suggest cognitive therapies are successful because they employ behavior techniques. It is not because they change the underlying cognitive structure (Bandura, 1969, 1997; Wright & Beck, 1999).

◼ Humanistic Therapies: Blocked Personal Growth

When you first started reading this chapter, you might have imagined that psychotherapy is reserved for only the most serious psychological problems. But humanistic approaches, like almost all other forms of therapy, are also very helpful for people with "simple" relationship or self-image problems. Humanists believe human potential includes the freedom to become what one wants to be as well as the responsibility to make choices.

Humanistic therapy, therefore, assumes that people with problems are suffering from a blockage or disruption of their normal growth potential. This blockage creates a defective self-concept. Remove these blocks and the individual is free to become the self-accepting, genuine person everyone is capable of being. Imagine for a minute how you feel when you are with someone who believes you are a good person with unlimited potential, a person whose "real self" is unique and valuable. These are the feelings that are nurtured in humanistic therapy.

Carl Rogers and Client-Centered Therapy

One of the best-known humanistic therapists, Carl Rogers (1961, 1980), developed an approach that encourages people to actualize their potential and relate to others in genuine ways. His approach is referred to as **client-centered therapy**. Using the term *client* instead of *patient* was very significant to Rogers. He believed the label "patient" implied being sick or mentally ill rather than responsible and competent. Treating people as clients demonstrates *they* are the ones in charge of the therapy. It also emphasizes the equality of the therapist–client relationship.

Client-centered therapy, like psychoanalysis and cognitive therapies, explores thoughts and feelings to obtain insight into the causes for behaviors. But clients are responsible for discovering their own maladaptive patterns. The job of the therapist is to provide an accepting atmosphere in which the client can freely explore important thoughts and feelings.

How does the therapist create such an atmosphere? Rogerian therapists create a therapeutic relationship by focusing on four important qualities of communication: *empathy, unconditional positive regard, genuineness,* and *active listening.*

1. **Empathy** is a sensitive understanding and sharing of another person's inner experience. When we put ourselves in other people's shoes, we enter their inner world. Therapists watch body language and listen for subtle cues to help them understand the emotional experiences of clients. When clients express feelings verbally, they are encouraged to explore them further. The therapist uses open-ended statements such as "You found that upsetting" or "You haven't been able to decide what to do about this" rather than asking questions or offering explanations.

2. **Unconditional positive regard** is genuine caring for people based on their innate value as individuals. Because humanists believe human nature is positive and each person is unique, clients can be respected and cherished without their having to prove themselves worthy of the therapist's esteem. Unconditional positive regard allows the therapist to trust that clients have the best answers for their own lives.

   To maintain a climate of unconditional positive regard, the therapist avoids making evaluative statements such as "That's good" and "You did the right thing." Such comments give the idea that the therapist is judging them and that clients need to receive approval. Humanists believe that when people receive unconditional caring from others, they become better able to value themselves in a similar way.

3. **Genuineness**, or *authenticity*, is being aware of one's true inner thoughts and feelings and being able to share them honestly with others. When people are genuine,

Humanistic Therapy *Therapy to maximize personal growth through affective restructuring (emotional readjustment)*

Client-Centered Therapy *Rogers's therapy emphasizing the client's natural tendency to become healthy and productive; techniques include empathy, unconditional positive regard, genuineness, and active listening*

Empathy *In Rogerian terms, an insightful awareness and ability to share another's inner experience*

Unconditional Positive Regard *Rogers's term for love and acceptance with no contingencies attached*

Genuineness *In Rogerian terms, authenticity or congruence; the awareness of one's true inner thoughts and feelings and being able to share them honestly with others*

"Just remember, son, it doesn't matter whether you win or lose—unless you want Daddy's love."

Pat Byrnes/The CartoonBank, Inc.

www.wiley.com/college/huffman

they are not artificial, defensive, or playing a role. If a Rogerian therapist were pleased or displeased with a client's progress, he or she would feel free to share those feelings. When therapists are genuine with their clients, they believe their clients will in turn develop self-trust and honest self-expression.

Active Listening *Listening with total attention to what another is saying; involves reflecting, paraphrasing, and clarifying what the person says and means*

4. **Active listening** involves reflecting, paraphrasing, and clarifying what the client says and means. To *reflect* is to hold a mirror in front of the person, enabling that person to see him- or herself. To *paraphrase* is to summarize in different words what the client is saying. To *clarify* is to check that both the speaker and listener are on the same wavelength.

Noticing the client's furrowed brow and clenched hands while the client is discussing his marital problems, the clinician might respond, "Sounds like you're angry with your wife and feeling pretty miserable right now." With this one statement, the clinician reflects the client's anger, paraphrases his complaint, and gives feedback to clarify the communication. By being an *active listener*, the clinician communicates that he or she is genuinely interested in what the client is saying.

Evaluating Humanistic Therapies

Supporters say there is empirical evidence for the efficacy of client-centered therapy (e.g., Kirschenbaum & Jourdan, 2005; Teusch et al., 2001). But critics argue that the basic tenets of humanistic therapy, such as self-actualization and self-awareness, are difficult to test scientifically. Most of the research on the outcomes of humanistic therapy relies on client self-reports. However, people undergoing any type of therapy are motivated to justify their time and expense. In addition, research on specific therapeutic techniques, such as Rogerian "empathy" and "active listening," has had mixed results (Gottman, Coan, Carrere, & Swanson, 1998).

TRY THIS YOURSELF — Application

Client-Centered Therapy in Action

Would you like to check your understanding of empathy, unconditional positive regard, genuineness, and active listening? Identify the techniques being used in the following excerpt (Shea, 1988, pp. 32–33). Check your responses with those in Appendix B.

THERAPIST (TH): What has it been like coming down to the emergency room today?

CLIENT (CL): Unsettling, to say the least. I feel very awkward here, sort of like I'm vulnerable. To be honest, I've had some horrible experiences with doctors. I don't like them.

TH: I see. Well, they scare the hell out of me, too (smiles, indicating the humor in his comment).

CL: (Chuckles) I thought you were a doctor.

TH: I am (pauses, smiles)—that's what's so scary.

CL: (Smiles and laughs)

TH: Tell me a little more about some of your unpleasant experiences with doctors, because I want to make sure I'm not doing anything that is upsetting to you. I don't want that to happen.

CL: Well, that's very nice to hear. My last doctor didn't give a hoot about what I said, and he only spoke in huge words.

In case you're wondering, this is an excerpt from an actual session—humor and informality can be an important part of the therapeutic process.

CHECK & REVIEW

Cognitive and Humanistic Therapies

Cognitive therapy emphasizes the importance of faulty thought processes, beliefs, and negative **self-talk** in the creation of problem behaviors. Albert Ellis's rational-emotive behavior therapy (REBT) aims to replace a client's irrational beliefs with rational beliefs and accurate perceptions of the world. Aaron Beck's **cognitive-behavior therapy** takes a more active approach with clients by emphasizing changes in both thought processes and behavior.

Evaluations of cognitive therapies find Beck's procedures particularly effective for relieving depression. And Ellis has had success with a variety of disorders. Both Beck and Ellis, however, are criticized for ignoring the importance of unconscious processes and the client's history. Some critics also attribute any success with cognitive therapies to the use of behavioral techniques.

Humanistic therapies are based on the premise that problems result when an individual's normal growth potential is blocked. In Carl Rogers's **client-centered therapy,** the therapist offers **empathy, unconditional positive regard, genuineness,** and **active listening** as means of facilitating personal growth. Humanistic therapies are difficult to evaluate scientifically, and research on specific therapeutic techniques has had mixed results.

Questions

1. Cognitive therapists assume that problem behaviors and emotions are caused by _____. (a) faulty thought processes and beliefs; (b) a negative self-image; (c) incongruent belief systems; (d) lack of self-discipline
2. What are the four steps (the A–B–C–D) of Ellis's REBT?
3. Beck identified four destructive thought patterns associated with depression (selective perception, overgeneralization, magnification, and all-or-nothing thinking). Using these terms, label the following thoughts:
   _____ a. Mary left me, and I'll never fall in love again. I'll always be alone.
   _____ b. My ex-spouse is an evil monster, and our entire marriage was a sham.
4. Label each of the following Rogerian therapy techniques:
   _____ a. A sensitive understanding and sharing of another's inner experience
   _____ b. The honest sharing of inner thoughts and feelings
   _____ c. A nonjudgmental and caring attitude toward another that does not have to be earned

Check your answers in Appendix B.

CLICK & REVIEW
for additional assessment options:
www.wiley.com/college/huffman

Group, Family, and Marital Therapies: Healing Interpersonal Relationships

The therapies described thus far all consider the individual as the unit of analysis and treatment. In contrast, group, family, and marital therapies treat multiple individuals simultaneously.

Group Therapy

Group therapy began as a response to the need for more therapists than were available and for a more economical form of therapy. What began as a practical and economic necessity, however, has become a preferred approach in its own right. In **group therapy**, multiple people meet together to work toward therapeutic goals. Typically, 8 to 10 people meet with a therapist on a regular basis, usually once a week for two hours. The therapist can work from any of the psychotherapeutic orientations discussed in this chapter. And, like individual therapy, members of the group talk about problems in their own lives.

A variation on group therapy is the **self-help group**. Unlike other group therapy approaches, a professional does not guide these groups. They are simply groups of people who share a common problem and meet to give and receive support. For example, people who are learning to deal with painful life crises find support in organizations like AMAC (Adults Molested as Children), Formerly Employed, and Parents of Murdered Children. Individuals who need help with destructive lifestyles can find it

Group Therapy *A number of people meet together to work toward therapeutic goals*

Self-Help Group *Leaderless or nonprofessionally guided groups in which members assist each other with a specific problem, as in Alcoholics Anonymous*

in Alcoholics Anonymous, Debtors Anonymous, and Gamblers Anonymous. Some support groups also use their shared pain for public service, like MADD (Mothers Against Drunk Driving). There are even groups for people in happy situations (New Parents, Parents of Twins) where the help may be more instructional than emotional.

Although group members don't get the same level of individual attention found in one-on-one therapies, group and self-help therapies provide their own unique advantages (Davison, Neale, & Kring, 2004; Porter, Spates, & Smitham, 2004; White & Freeman, 2000):

1. *Less expense.* In a typical group of eight or more, the cost of traditional one-on-one therapy can be divided among all members of the group. Self-help groups, which typically operate without a professional therapist, are even more cost-saving.

2. *Group support.* During times of stress and emotional trouble, it is easy to imagine we are alone and that our problems are unique. Knowing that others have similar problems can be very reassuring. In addition, seeing others improve can be a source of hope and motivation.

3. *Insight and information.* Because group members typically have comparable problems, they can learn from each other's mistakes and share insights. Furthermore, when a group member receives similar comments about his or her behavior from several members of the group, the message may be more convincing than if it comes from a single therapist.

4. *Behavior rehearsal.* Group members can role-play one another's employer, spouse, parents, children, or prospective dates. By role-playing and observing different roles in relationships, people gain practice with new social skills. They also gain valuable feedback and insight into their problem behaviors.

Therapists often refer their patients to group therapy and self-help groups to supplement individual therapy. Someone who has a problem with alcohol, for example, can find comfort and help with others who have "been there." They exchange useful information, share their coping strategies, and gain hope by seeing others overcome or successfully manage their shared problems. Research on self-help groups for alcoholism, obesity, and other disorders suggests they can be very effective—either alone or in addition to individual psychotherapy (Bailer et al., 2004; Davidson et al., 2001; Magura et al., 2003).

Family Therapy *Treatment to change maladaptive interaction patterns within a family*

Tony Freeman/Photoedit

What happens in family and marital therapy? *Rather than one-on-one counseling, family therapists generally work with the entire family to improve communication and resolve conflicts.*

Family and Marital Therapies

> Mental health problems do not affect three or four out of five persons but one out of one.
>
> DR. WILLIAM MENNINGER

Therapists have long known that dealing with an individual's problem may not be enough. Because a family or marriage is a system of interdependent parts, the problem of any one individual unavoidably affects all the others. Family and marital therapy can help everyone involved (Becvar & Becvar, 2006; Cavacuiti, 2004; Shadish & Baldwin, 2003). A teen's delinquency or a spouse's drug problem affects both members of the couple and each individual within the family.

Sometimes the problems parents have with a child arise from conflicts in the marriage. Other times a child's behavior creates distress in an otherwise well-functioning couple. The line between *marital* (or *couples*) therapy and *family therapy* is often blurred. Given that most married couples have children, our discussion will focus on **family therapy**, in which the primary aim is to change maladaptive family interaction patterns. All members of the family attend therapy sessions. At times the therapist may also see family members individually or in twos or threes. (The therapist, incidentally, may take any orientation—behavioral, cognitive, etc.)

Many families initially come into therapy believing that one member is *the* cause of all their problems ("Johnny's delinquency" or "Mom's drinking"). However, family therapists generally find that this "identified patient" is the scapegoat (a person blamed for someone else's problems) for deeper disturbances. For example, instead of confronting their own problems with intimacy, the parents may focus all their attention and frustration on the delinquent child (Hanna & Brown, 1999). It is usually necessary to change ways of interacting within the family system to promote the health of individual family members and the family as a whole.

Family therapy is also useful in treating a number of disorders and clinical problems. As we discussed in Chapter 14, patients with schizophrenia are more likely to relapse if their family members express emotions, attitudes, and behaviors that involve criticism, hostility, or emotional overinvolvement (Hooley & Hiller, 2001; Lefley, 2000; Quinn et al., 2003). Family therapy can help family members modify their behavior toward the patient. It also seems to be the most favorable setting for the treatment of adolescent drug abuse (Kumfer, Alvarado, & Whiteside, 2003; Stanton, 2004).

Application

CRITICAL THINKING

ACTIVE LEARNING

Hunting for Good Therapy Films
(Contributed by Thomas Frangicetto)

This chapter opened with Hollywood's generally negative and unrealistic portrayals of therapy. There are notable exceptions, like *Good Will Hunting*. But even this film has a few overly dramatic and unprofessional scenes. For example, during the first therapy session between Will Hunting (played by Matt Damon) and his therapist Sean (played by Robin Williams), Sean grabs Will by the throat and threatens him for insulting his deceased wife.

Despite its limits, *Good Will Hunting* provides a reasonably accurate portrayal of several therapy techniques. It also provides an opportunity to review important terms related to insight therapy and improve your critical thinking skills. If you haven't seen the film, here's a brief summary:

Will Hunting, a janitor at MIT, is an intellectual genius. But he is low in emotional intelligence (EI) (Chapter 12). Will's need for revenge gets him into a fight, and he is court-ordered to go into therapy. A number of therapists attempt to work with Will and fail. Sean proves to be up to the task because he "speaks his language"—the language of the streets.

Key Term Review

Read the following descriptions and identify which insight therapy term is being illustrated.

1. From the moment Will first walks into Sean's office, he engages in a highly creative and relentless avoidance of the therapist's attempts to get him to talk about himself. This is an example of _____.

2. Despite Will's insults and verbal attacks, Sean continues working with him while expressing a nonjudgmental attitude and genuine caring for Will. Sean is displaying _____.

3. During the therapy sessions, Sean often shares his true inner thoughts and feelings with Will. This type of honest communication is called _____.

4. Will believes he is unlovable and blames himself for the abuse he received as a child. Will's low emotional intelligence and antisocial behavior are the effect of those causes. How would Ellis's rational-emotive-behavior therapy explain this in terms of the A–B–C–D approach? The *activating event* (A) is _____. The *irrational belief* (B) is _____. And the

emotional consequence (C) is _____. Can you think of a *disputing irrational beliefs* (D) statement that Will could use to challenge this irrational belief?

5. Sean listens to Will focusing on the negative aspects of his life and ignoring anything positive that happens to him. Sean says, "All you see is every negative thing 10 miles down the road." With this statement, Sean wants Will to recognize that he is using _____, one of Beck's thinking patterns associated with depression.

Critical Thinking Application

Sean is a therapist in need of therapy himself—he is still grieving the death of his wife. A competent therapist would never behave the way Sean does in certain scenes. However, he does effectively portray several characteristics of good professional therapy. In addition, he displays many of the critical thinking components (CTCs) found in the Prologue (pp. xxx–xxxiv). *Empathy* and *active listening* are two of the most obvious components that Sean—and all therapists—employ. Can you identify other CTCs that you think a good therapist might use?

www.wiley.com/college/huffman

Assessment

CHECK & REVIEW

Group, Family, and Marital Therapies

In **group therapy,** a number of people (usually 8 to 10) come together to work toward therapeutic goals. A variation on group therapy is the **self-help group** (like Alcoholics Anonymous), which is not guided by a professional. Although group members do not get the same level of attention as in individual therapy, group therapy has other advantages. First, it is less expensive. It also provides group support, insight and information, and opportunities for behavior rehearsal.

The primary aim of marital and **family therapy** is to change maladaptive family interaction patterns. Because a family is a system of interdependent parts, the problem of any one member unavoidably affects all the others.

Questions

1. In _____, multiple people meet together to work toward therapeutic goals. (a) encounter groups; (b) behavior therapy; (c) group therapy; (d) conjoint therapy
2. What are the four major advantages of group therapy?
3. Why do individual therapists often refer their patients to self-help groups?
4. _____ treats the family as a unit, and members work together to solve problems. (a) Aversion therapy; (b) An encounter group; (c) A self-help group; (d) Family therapy

Check your answers in Appendix B.

CLICK & REVIEW
for additional assessment options:
www.wiley.com/college/huffman

BEHAVIOR THERAPIES

Achievement

How are learning principles used in behavior therapy?

Behavior Therapy *Group of techniques based on learning principles used to change maladaptive behaviors*

Have you ever understood why you were doing something that you would rather not do, but continued to do it anyway? Sometimes having insight into a problem does not automatically solve it. Take the example of Mrs. D, an agoraphobic woman who had not left her house for 3½ years except with her husband. She had undergone 1½ years of insight-based therapy and had become very aware of the causes of her problem, but she did not change her behavior. She finally sought the help of a different type of therapist. Rather than working on her understanding of her problems or attempting to restructure her feelings, Mrs. D's behavior therapist systematically trained her to *behave* differently. After less than two months, Mrs. D was able to leave her house and travel alone to appointments (Lazarus, 1971).

Behavior therapy uses learning principles to change behaviors. Behavior therapists do not believe it is necessary to obtain insight or restructure feelings before changes in behavior can occur. Their focus is on the problem behavior itself, rather than on any underlying causes. That is not to say that the person's feelings and interpretations are disregarded; they are just not emphasized.

In behavior therapy, the therapist diagnoses the problem by listing the maladaptive behaviors that occur and the adaptive behaviors that are absent. The therapist then attempts to decrease the frequency of maladaptive behaviors and increase the frequency of adaptive ones.

To accomplish this type of change, a behavior therapist draws on principles of classical conditioning, operant conditioning, and observational learning.

Classical Conditioning Techniques: The Power of Association

Behavior therapists use the principles of classical conditioning. These principles are derived from Pavlov's model for associating two stimulus events. They work to decrease maladaptive behavior by creating

Sidney Harris

new stimulus associations and behavioral responses to replace faulty ones. Two techniques based on these principles are *systematic desensitization* and *aversion therapy*.

1. *Systematic desensitization*. Mrs. D's behavior therapist used *systematic desensitization*, a procedure developed by Joseph Wolpe (Wolpe & Plaud, 1997), to extinguish her agoraphobia. **Systematic desensitization** begins with relaxation training, followed by imagining or directly experiencing various versions of a feared object or situation while remaining deeply relaxed.

The goal is to replace an anxiety response with a relaxation response when confronting the feared stimulus (Heriot & Pritchard, 2004). Recall from Chapter 2 that the parasympathetic nerves control autonomic functions when we are relaxed. Because the opposing sympathetic nerves are dominant when we are anxious, it is physiologically impossible to be both relaxed and anxious at the same time.

Desensitization is a three-step process. First, a client is taught how to maintain a state of deep relaxation that is physiologically incompatible with an anxiety response. Next, the therapist and client construct a *hierarchy*, or ranked listing of 10 or so anxiety-arousing images (Figure 15.3). In the final step, the relaxed client mentally visualizes or physically experiences items at the bottom of the hierarchy. The client then works his or

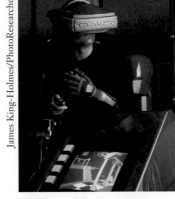

James King-Holmes/PhotoResearchers

Systematic Desensitization *A gradual process of extinguishing a learned fear (or phobia) by working through a hierarchy of fear-evoking stimuli while staying deeply relaxed*

Virtual reality therapy. *Rather than mental imaging or actual physical experiences of a fearful situation, modern therapy can use the latest in computer technology—virtual reality headsets and data gloves. A client with a fear of heights, for example, can have experiences ranging from climbing a stepladder all the way to standing on the edge of a tall building, while never leaving the therapist's office.*

Figure 15.3 *Systematic desensitization for a driving phobia.* During systematic desensitization, the client begins by constructing a hierarchy, or ranked listing, of anxiety-arousing images or situations starting with one that produces very little anxiety and escalating to those that arouse extreme anxiety. To extinguish a driving phobia, the patient begins with images of actually sitting behind the wheel of a nonmoving car and ends with driving on a busy expressway.

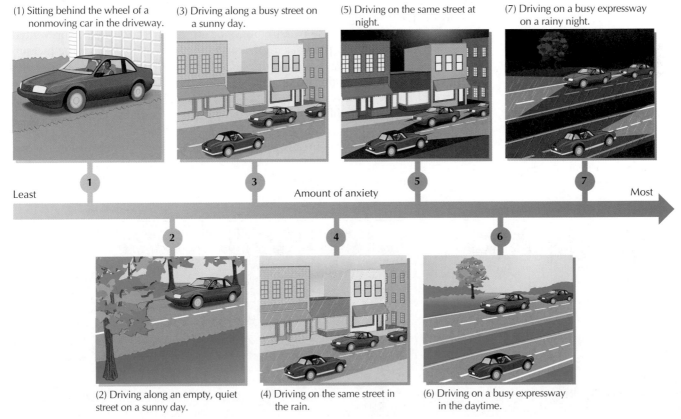

(1) Sitting behind the wheel of a nonmoving car in the driveway.

(3) Driving along a busy street on a sunny day.

(5) Driving on the same street at night.

(7) Driving on a busy expressway on a rainy night.

Least   Amount of anxiety   Most

(2) Driving along an empty, quiet street on a sunny day.

(4) Driving on the same street in the rain.

(6) Driving on a busy expressway in the daytime.

Do You Have Test Anxiety?

Nearly everyone is somewhat anxious before an important exam. If you find this anxiety helpful and invigorating, skip ahead to the next section. However, if the days and evenings before a major exam are ruined by your anxiety and you sometimes "freeze up" while taking the test, you can benefit from an informal type of systematic desensitization.

Step 1: Review and practice the relaxation technique taught in Chapter 3.

Step 2: Create a 10-step "test-taking" hierarchy—starting with the least anxiety-arousing image (perhaps the day your instructor first mentions an upcoming exam) and ending with actually taking the exam.

Step 3: Beginning with the least arousing image—hearing about the exam—picture yourself at each stage. While maintaining a calm, relaxed state, work your way through all 10 steps. If you become anxious at any stage, stay there, repeating your relaxation technique until the anxiety diminishes.

Step 4: If you start to feel anxious the night before the exam, or even during the exam itself, remind yourself to relax. Take a few moments to shut your eyes and review how you worked through your hierarchy.

Aversion Therapy *Pairing an aversive (unpleasant) stimulus with a maladaptive behavior*

her way upward to the most anxiety-producing images at the top of the hierarchy. If at any time an image or situation begins to create anxiety, the client stops momentarily and returns to a state of complete relaxation. Eventually, the fear response is extinguished.

2. Aversion therapy. In sharp contrast to systematic desensitization, **aversion therapy** uses principles of classical conditioning to create anxiety rather than extinguish it. People who engage in excessive drinking, for example, build up a number of pleasurable associations. These pleasurable associations cannot always be prevented. However, aversion therapy provides *negative associations* to compete with the pleasurable ones. Someone who wants to stop drinking, for example, could take a drug called Antabuse that causes vomiting whenever alcohol enters the system. When the new connection between alcohol and nausea has been classically conditioned, engaging in the once desirable habit will cause an immediate negative response (Figure 15.4).

Aversion therapy has had some limited success. But it has always been controversial. Is it ethical to hurt someone (even when the person has given permission)? It also

Figure 15.4 *Aversion therapy for alcoholism.* Using the principles of classical conditioning, a nausea-producing drug (Antabuse) is paired with alcohol to create an aversion to drinking.

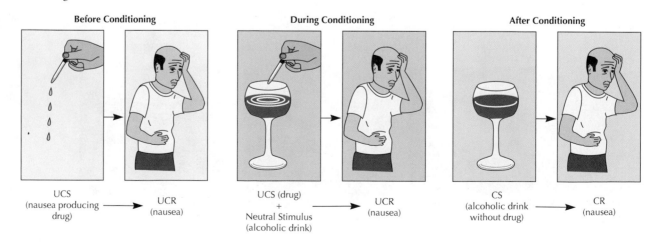

has been criticized because it does not provide lasting relief (Seligman, 1994). Do you recall the taste aversion studies in Chapter 6? It was discovered that when sheep meat was tainted with a nausea-producing drug, coyotes quickly learned to avoid sheep. Why doesn't it work with people? Interestingly, humans understand that the nausea is produced by the Antabuse and do not generalize their learning to the alcohol itself. Once they leave treatment, most alcoholics go back to drinking (and do not continue taking the Antabuse).

Operant Conditioning Techniques: Increasing the "Good" and Decreasing the "Bad"

Operant conditioning techniques use shaping and reinforcement to increase adaptive behaviors, and punishment and extinction to decrease maladaptive behaviors. Like the techniques used in the popular TV program *The Nanny*, behavior therapists may train parents to reward children for appropriate behavior. They also train parents to withdraw attention (extinction) or to use *time-out* procedures (punishment) to weaken or eliminate inappropriate behavior.

In behavior therapy, a behavior to be acquired is called the *target behavior*. *Shaping*—being rewarded for successive approximations of the target behavior—is one operant technique for eventually performing the target behavior. One of the most successful applications of shaping and reinforcement has been with autistic children. Children with *autism* do not communicate or interact normally with other people. Shaping has been used to develop their language skills. The child is first rewarded for any sounds but later only for words and sentences.

Shaping is also used to help people acquire social skills. If you are painfully shy, for example, a behavior therapist might first ask you to role-play simply saying hello to someone you find attractive. Then, you might practice behaviors that gradually lead you to suggest a get-together or date. During such *role-playing*, or *behavior rehearsal*, the clinician would give you feedback and reinforcement.

Behavior rehearsal is also the technique behind *assertiveness training*, which teaches people to stand up for themselves. Clients begin with simple situations and progress to practicing effective verbal responses and adaptive behaviors. In treating Mrs. D's agoraphobia, for example, her therapist used role-playing to shape assertive behaviors such as standing up to her domineering father.

Overcoming agoraphobia. Behavior therapists would use shaping and reinforcement to treat this woman's agoraphobia.

Adaptive behaviors can also be taught or increased with techniques that provide immediate reinforcement in the form of tokens (Sarafino, 2000). *Tokens* are secondary (conditioned) reinforcers, such as poker chips, "credit" cards, or other tangible objects that can be exchanged for primary rewards such as food, treats, watching TV, a private room, or outings. In an inpatient treatment facility, patients are sometimes rewarded with tokens as they are gradually shaped toward desirable activities such as taking medication, attending group therapy sessions, or taking part in recreational programs. Patients can also be "fined" for inappropriate behaviors by having tokens taken away.

Doesn't this approach depend too much on the tokens to have any lasting effect? Advocates point out that tokens help people acquire beneficial behaviors that become rewarding in themselves. A full-fledged behavior management program has a series of levels, each requiring increasingly complex behavior. For example, patients might at first be given tokens for merely attending group therapy sessions. Once this behavior is established, they will be rewarded only for actually participating in the sessions. Eventually, the tokens can be discontinued when the patient receives the reinforcement of being helped by participation in the therapy sessions. Tokens have been successfully used in a wide variety of settings, including hospitals, programs for delinquents, classrooms, and individual homes (Field et al., 2004; Filcheck et al., 2004).

Modeling Therapy *Watching and imitating models that demonstrate desirable behaviors*

Observational Learning Techniques: The Power of Modeling

In addition to using classical and operant conditioning techniques, behavioral therapists also use techniques from observational learning. Recall from Chapter 6 that we all learn many things through observing others. We can directly watch what they do, read about them, or view them on television or in movies. Therapists use this type of observation in **modeling therapy**, which asks clients to observe and imitate appropriate *models* as they perform desired behaviors.

This type of modeling can be very effective. For example, Bandura and his colleagues (1969) asked clients with snake phobias to watch other (nonphobic) people handle snakes. After only two hours of exposure, over 92 percent of the phobic observers allowed a snake to crawl over their hands, arms, and neck. When the client combines live modeling with direct and gradual practice, it is called *participant modeling*.

Modeling is also part of social skills training and assertiveness training. Clients learn how to interview for a job by first watching the therapist role-play the part of the interviewee. The therapist models the appropriate language (assertively asking for a job), body posture, and so forth. The client then imitates the therapist's behavior and plays the same role. Over the course of several sessions, the client becomes gradually desensitized to the anxiety of interviews and learns valuable interview skills.

Evaluating Behavior Therapies: How Well Do They Work?

Research suggests that behavior therapy based on classical and operant conditioning and observational learning has been effective with various problems, including phobias, obsessive-compulsive disorder, eating disorders, autism, mental retardation, and delinquency (Heriot & Pritchard, 2004; Herrera, Johnston, & Steele, 2004; Sarafino, 2000; Wilson, 2005). Some patients have even returned to their homes and communities after years of institutionalization.

Critics of behavior therapy raise important questions that fall into two major categories:

1. *Generalizability.* What happens after the treatment stops? Can the results be generalized? Critics argue that because patients are not consistently reinforced in the "real world," their newly acquired behaviors may disappear. To deal with this possibility, behavior therapists work to gradually shape clients toward rewards that are typical of life outside the clinical setting.

2. *Ethics.* Is it ethical for one person to control another's behavior? Are there some situations in which behavior therapy should not be used? In the classic movie *A Clockwork Orange*, dangerously powerful people used behavior modification principles to control the general population. Behaviorists reply that rewards and punishments already control our behaviors. Behavior therapy only increases a person's freedom by making these controls *overt*. Furthermore, they believe behavior therapy increases self-control by teaching people how to change their own behavior and how to maintain those changes when they leave the clinical setting.

Assessment

CHECK & REVIEW

Behavior Therapies

Behavior therapies use learning principles to change maladaptive behaviors. Classical conditioning principles are used to change faulty associations. In **system-** atic **desensitization,** the client replaces anxiety with relaxation, and in **aversion therapy,** an aversive stimulus is paired with a maladaptive behavior. Shaping and reinforcement are behavior therapy techniques based on operant conditioning principles. **Modeling therapy** is based on acquisition of skills or behaviors through observation.

Behavior therapies have been successful with a number of psychological disorders. But they are also criticized for lack of generalizability and the questionable ethics of controlling behavior.

Questions

1. A group of techniques based on learning principles that are used to change maladaptive behaviors is known as _____.

2. In behavior therapy, _____ techniques use shaping and reinforcement to increase adaptive behaviors. (a) classical conditioning; (b) modeling; (c) operant conditioning; (d) social learning

3. Describe how shaping can be used to develop desired behaviors.

4. What are the two criticisms of behavior therapy?

Check you answers in Appendix B.

 CLICK & REVIEW
for additional assessment options:
www.wiley.com/college/huffman

BIOMEDICAL THERAPIES

Biomedical therapies are based on the premise that mental health problems are caused, at least in part, by chemical imbalances or disturbed nervous system functioning. In most cases, a psychiatrist, rather than a psychologist, must prescribe biomedical therapies. But psychologists commonly work with patients receiving biomedical therapies. They also conduct research programs to evaluate therapy's effectiveness.

Despite Hollywood's persistent linking of mental illness with asylums and hospitals, today only people with the most severe and intractable disturbances are institutionalized. And abuses like those portrayed in most films are virtually nonexistent. Most people with psychological disorders can be helped with drugs, psychotherapy, or a combination of the two. In this section, we will discuss three forms of biomedical therapies: *psychopharmacology, electroconvulsive therapy (ECT)*, and *psychosurgery*.

Psychopharmacology: Treating Psychological Disorders with Drugs

Since the 1950s, drug companies have developed an amazing variety of chemicals to treat abnormal behaviors. In some cases discoveries from **psychopharmacology** (the study of drug effects on mind and behavior) have helped correct a chemical imbalance. In these instances, using a drug is similar to administering insulin to people with diabetes, whose own bodies fail to manufacture enough. In other cases, drugs are used to relieve or suppress the symptoms of psychological disturbances even when underlying cause is not known to be biological. Psychiatric drugs are classified into four major categories: antianxiety, antipsychotic, mood stabilizer, and antidepressant. Table 15.1 summarizes some of the most common medications prescribed in each category.

Antianxiety Drugs
Antianxiety drugs (also known as minor tranquilizers) produce relaxation or reduce anxiety in addition to relieving muscle tension. They also are among the most used and abused drugs. As discussed in Chapter 14, anxiety is one of the most common psychological disorders. Antianxiety drugs, such as Valium and Xanax, lower the sympathetic activity of the brain—the crisis mode of operation—and anxiety responses are diminished or prevented (Blanco et al., 2003; Swartz & Margolis, 2004). These drugs work by increasing the effectiveness of the neurotransmitter *gamma-aminobutyric acid* (GABA), which has an inhibitory (or calming) effect on neurons.

Antipsychotic Drugs
The medications used to treat schizophrenia and other acute psychotic states are called **antipsychotic drugs**, or *neuroleptics*. They are often referred to as major

Achievement

What are the major biomedical therapies?

Biomedical Therapy *Using physiological interventions (drugs, electroconvulsive therapy, and psychosurgery) to reduce or alleviate symptoms of psychological disorders*

Psychopharmacology *The study of drug effects on mind and behavior*

Antianxiety Drugs *Medications used to treat anxiety disorders*

Antipsychotic Drugs *Medications used to diminish or eliminate hallucinations, delusions, withdrawal, and other symptoms of psychosis; also known as neuroleptics or major tranquilizers*

TABLE 15.1 DRUG TREATMENTS FOR PSYCHOLOGICAL DISORDERS

Type of Drug	Psycological Disorder	Chemical Group	Generic Name	Brand Name
Antianxiety drugs	Anxiety disorders	Benzodiazepines	Alprazolam	Xanax
			Diazepam	Valium
		Glycerol derivatives	Meprobamate	Miltown
				Equanil
Antipsychotic drugs	Schizophrenia	Phenothiazines	Chlorpromazine	Thorazine
			Fluphenazine	Prolixin
			Thioridazine	Mellaril
		Butyrophenones	Haloperidol	Haldol
		Dibenzodiazepine	Clozapine	Clozaril
		Atypical antipsychotics	Résperidone	Risperdal
Mood stabilizer drugs	Bipolar disorder	Antimanic	Lithium carbonate	Lithonate
				Lithane
			Carbamazepine	Tegretol
Antidepressant drugs	Depressive disorders	Tricyclic antidepressants	Imipramine	Tofranil
			Amitriptyline	Elavil
		Monoamine oxidase inhibitors (MAOIs)	Phenelzine	Nardil
		Selective serotonin reuptake inhibitors (SSRIs)	Paroxetine	Paxil
			Fluoxetine	Prozac
		Atypical antidepressants	Buspirone	Buspar
			Venlafaxine	Effexor

tranquilizers, creating the mistaken impression that they invariably have a strong calming or sedating effect. Some antipsychotic drugs, such as Haldol, do reduce hallucinations and delusions. However, other antipsychotic drugs, such as Clozaril, energize and animate patients. The main intended effect of antipsychotic drugs is to diminish or eliminate psychotic symptoms, including hallucinations, delusions, withdrawal, and apathy. They are not designed to sedate the patient. Unfortunately, they do not "cure" schizophrenia or ensure that there will be no further psychotic episodes. However, a large majority of patients show marked improvement when treated with antipsychotic drugs.

How do these drugs work? Traditional antipsychotics reduce certain symptoms of schizophrenia (such as hallucinations) by decreasing activity at the dopamine synapses, which further supports the theory that excessive dopamine contributes to schizophrenia (Chapter 14). Given the multiple types of dopamine receptors in different parts of the brain, newer drugs like Clozaril may be more effective because they target specific dopamine receptors (as well as serotonin receptors) and avoid interfering with others (Kapur, Sridhar, & Remington, 2004).

Mood Stabilizer and Antidepressant Drugs

For people suffering from bipolar disorders, *mood stabilizer* drugs such as lithium can help manic episodes and depression. Because lithium acts relatively slowly, however, it can be three or four weeks before it takes effect. Its primary use is in preventing *future* episodes and helping to break the manic-depressive cycle.

People with depression are usually treated with one of four types of **antidepressant drugs** (e.g., Gomez-Gil et al., 2004; Harmer et al., 2004; Wada et al., 2004):

1. *Tricyclics* (named for their chemical structure, which contains three rings), such as Tofranil, act on multiple neurochemical pathways in the brain, increasing levels of serotonin and catecholamines.

Antidepressant Drugs *Medications used to treat depression, some anxiety disorders, and certain eating disorders (such as bulimia)*

"Before Prozac, she loathed company."

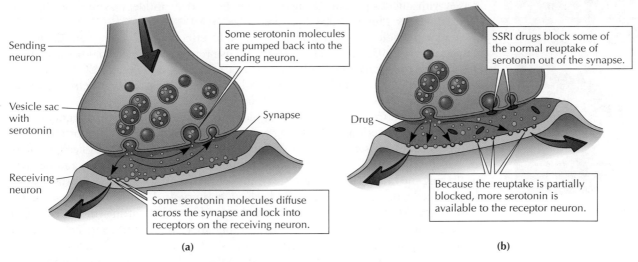

(a) **(b)**

Figure 15.5 *How Prozac and other SSRI antidepressants work.* (a) Under normal conditions, a nerve impulse (or action potential) travels down the axon to the terminal buttons of a sending neuron. If the vesicle sac of this particular neuron contains the neurotransmitter serotonin, the action potential will trigger its release. Some of the serotonin will travel across the synapse and lock into the receptors on the receiving neuron. Excess serotonin within the synapse will be pumped back up into the sending neuron for storage (the "serotonin reuptake"). (b) When selective serotonin reuptake inhibitors (SSRIs), like Prozac, are taken to treat depression and other disorders, they block the normal reuptake of excess serontonin that lingers in the synaptic gap after being released from the sending neuron. This leaves more serotonin molecules free to stimulate receptors on the receiving neuron, which enhances its mood lifting effects.

2. *Monoamine oxidase inhibitors* (MAOIs), such as Nardil, block the enzyme *monoamine oxidase*. Because this enzyme inactivates serotonin and catecholamines, blocking it increases the availability of these helpful neurochemicals.

3. *Selective serotonin reuptake inhibitors* (SSRIs), such as Prozac, work like the tricyclics, but they selectively affect only serotonin (Figure 15.5). They are by far the most commonly prescribed antidepressants.

4. *Atypical antidepressants*, such as Buspar or Effexor, are a miscellaneous group of drugs used for patients who fail to respond to the other drugs or for people who experience certain side effects (like decreased sexual function) that are common to other antidepressants.

Electroconvulsive Therapy and Psychosurgery: Promising or Perilous?

In **electroconvulsive therapy (ECT)**, also known as *electroshock therapy* (EST), a current of moderate intensity is passed through the brain between two electrodes placed on the outside of the head (Figure 15.6). The electrical current is applied for less than a second. But it triggers widespread firing of neurons, also known as convulsions. The convulsions produce many changes in the central and peripheral nervous systems, including activation of the autonomic nervous system, increased secretion of various hormones and neurotransmitters, and changes in the blood–brain barrier.

During the early years of ECT, some patients received hundreds of treatments (Fink, 1999). Today most receive 12 or fewer treatments. Sometimes the electrical current is applied only to the right hemisphere, which causes less interference with verbal memories and left-hemisphere functioning. Modern ECT is used primarily in cases of severe depression that do not respond to antidepressant drugs or psychotherapy. It also

Electroconvulsive Therapy (ECT)
Biomedical therapy based on passing electrical current through the brain; used almost exclusively to treat serious depression when drug therapy does not work

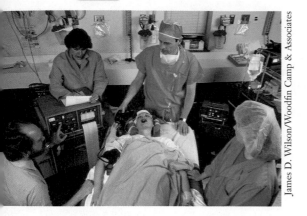

James D. Wilson/Woodfin Camp & Associates

Figure 15.6 *Electroconvulsive therapy (ECT).* During ECT, electrodes on the forehead apply electric current to the brain, creating a brief cortical seizure. Although ECT is controversial and may seem barbaric to you, for some severely depressed people it is the only hope, and it can be effective in lifting depression.

Psychosurgery *Operative procedures on the brain designed to relieve severe mental symptoms that have not responded to other forms of treatment*

Lobotomy *Outmoded medical procedure for mental disorders, which involved cutting nerve pathways between the frontal lobes and the thalamus and hypothalamus*

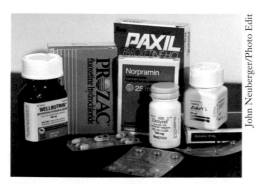

John Neuberger/Photo Edit

The pros and cons of drug therapy. Psychotherapeutic drugs like Prozac often help relieve suffering and symptoms associated with psychological disorders. However, they also have major and minor side effects. Physicians and patients must carefully weigh both the costs and the benefits.

is used with suicidal patients because it works faster than antidepressant drugs (Birken-häger, Renes, & Pluijms, 2004; Sylvester et al., 2000).

Clinical studies of ECT conclude that it is effective for very severe depression (Carney et al., 2003; Prudic et al., 2004). Its use remains controversial because it creates massive functional (and perhaps structural) changes in the brain. ECT is also controversial because we simply don't know why it works. Most likely it helps reestablish levels of neurotransmitters that control moods.

The most extreme, and least used, biomedical therapy is **psychosurgery**—brain surgery to reduce serious, debilitating psychological problems. (It is important to note that psychosurgery is *not* the same as brain surgery used to remove physical problems, such as a tumor or blood clot.) Attempts to change disturbed thinking and behavior by altering the brain have a long history. In Roman times, for example, it was believed that a sword wound to the head could relieve insanity. In 1936, a Portuguese neurologist, Egaz Moniz, treated uncontrollable psychoses by cutting the nerve fibers between the frontal lobes (where association areas for monitoring and planning behavior are found) and lower brain centers (Pressman, 1998; Valenstein, 1998). Thousands of patients underwent this procedure, called a **lobotomy**, before it was eliminated because of serious complications. Today lobotomies are almost never used. Psychiatric drugs offer a less risky and more effective treatment.

▪ Evaluating Biomedical Therapies: Are They Effective?

Like all forms of therapy, the biomedical therapies have both proponents and critics. We will summarize the research in this area.

1. *Psychopharmacology.* Several potential problems are associated with drug therapy. First, although drugs may provide relief of symptoms, they seldom provide "cures" or long-term solutions. Researchers also are still learning about the long-term effects and potential interactions. Furthermore, not all patients are helped by these drugs, and some show only modest improvement. Some patients also develop tolerance to the drugs and become physically dependent. Withdrawal symptoms (such as convulsions and hallucinations) can occur if they suddenly stop taking the drugs. Overdosing with psychotherapeutic drugs intentionally (to get a stronger effect) or unintentionally (by combining them with other drugs, such as alcohol) can be fatal.

Controlling negative side effects is another important issue with drug therapy. For example, reactions to antipsychotic drugs range from reduced alertness and drowsiness to symptoms similar to Parkinson's disease, including muscle rigidity, tremors, and an unusual shuffling way of walking (Parrott, Morinan, Moss, & Scholey, 2004; Tarsy, Baldessarini, & Tarazi, 2002).

One of the most serious side effects of antipsychotic drugs is a movement disorder called *tardive dyskinesia*, which develops in 15 to 20 percent of the patients. The symptoms generally appear after the drugs have been taken for long periods of time (hence the term *tardive*, from the Latin root for "slow"). They include involuntary movements of the tongue, face, and sometimes other muscles (*dyskinesia*, meaning "disorder of movement") that can be severely disabling. When my students see films about schizophrenia, they often confuse the patient's sucking and smacking of the lips or lateral jaw movements as signs of the disorder rather than signs of the motor disturbances of tardive dyskinesia.

Like antipsychotic medications, antidepressant drugs and mood stabilizers also have major and minor side effects. Antidepressants may cause dry mouth, fatigue, sexual dysfunction, weight gain, and memory difficulties; mood stabilizer drugs, such as lithium, can impair memory and cause weight gain. In excessive dosages, lithium can be fatal. Thus, as with other drug therapies, it is important to carefully monitor dosage level and patient reactions (Breggin, 2004).

Despite the problems associated with psychotherapeutic drugs, they have led to revolutionary changes in mental health. Before the use of drugs, some patients were destined for a lifetime in psychiatric institutions. Today, most improve enough to return to their homes and live successful lives if they continue to take their medication to prevent relapse.

2. *ECT and psychosurgery.* After nearly half a century of use of ECT, we do not fully understand why an ECT-induced convulsion alleviates depression. Partly because we cannot explain *why* it works, but also because it seems barbaric, ECT is a controversial treatment (Baldwin & Oxlad, 2000; Cloud, 2001; Pearlman, 2002). Unlike ECT portrayals in movies like *One Flew over the Cuckoo's Nest* and *The Snake Pit*, patients show few, if any, visible reactions to modern ECT. This is because modern muscle-relaxant drugs dramatically reduce muscle contractions during the seizure. Most ECT patients are also given an anesthetic, such as sodium pentothal, to block their memory of the treatment. However, some patients still find the treatment extremely uncomfortable (Johnstone, 1999). But many others find it life-saving.

Problems with ECT may become obsolete thanks to *repetitive transcranial magnetic stimulation* (rTMS), which delivers a brief (but powerful) electric current through a coil of wire placed on the head. Unlike ECT, which passes a strong electric current directly through the brain, the rTMS coil creates a strong magnetic field that is applied to certain areas in the brain. When used to treat depression, the coil is usually placed over the left prefrontal cortex, a region linked to deeper parts of the brain that regulate mood. Some studies have found that rTMS has a significant positive effect on major depression. It also has fewer side effects than ECT, such as memory loss (Fitzgerald et al., 2003; Jorge et al., 2004; Kauffmann, Cheema, & Miller, 2004). However, other studies have reported no significant benefits (Aarre et al., 2003; Martin et al., 2003).

Because all forms of psychosurgery have potentially serious or fatal side effects and complications, some critics suggest it should be banned altogether. Furthermore, the consequences are irreversible. For these reasons, psychosurgery is considered experimental and remains a highly controversial treatment.

The Kobal Collection

One Flew over the Cuckoo's Nest. *In this film, the lead character, McMurphy (played by Jack Nicholson), is a persistent problem for the hospital staff. To punish and control him, the staff first used drug therapy, then ECT, and finally psychosurgery—a prefrontal lobotomy. Although this was a popular movie, it also deepened public fear and misconceptions about biomedical therapy.*

Assessment

CHECK & REVIEW

Biomedical Therapies

Biomedical therapies use biological techniques to relieve psychological disorders. Treatment with drugs is the most common form by far. **Antianxiety drugs** (Valium, Xanax) are used to treat anxiety disorders, **antipsychotic drugs** (Haldol, Navane) treat the symptoms of schizophrenia, **antidepressant drugs** (Prozac, Effexor) treat depression, and mood stabilizers (lithium) can help patients with bipolar disorders. Drug therapy has been responsible for major improvements in many disorders. However, there are also problems with dosage levels, side effects, and patient cooperation.

Electroconvulsive therapy (ECT) is used primarily to relieve serious depression when medication has not worked. But it is risky and considered a treatment of last resort. **Psychosurgeries,** such as a **lobotomy,** have been used in the past but are rarely used today.

Questions

1. The dramatic reduction in numbers of hospitalized patients today compared to past decades is primarily attributable to _____. (a) biomedical therapy; (b) psychoanalysis; (c) psychosurgery; (d) drug therapy.

2. What are the four major categories of psychiatric drugs?

3. The effectiveness of antipsychotic drugs is thought to result primarily from blockage of _____ receptors. (a) serotonin; (b) dopamine; (c) acetylcholine; (d) epinephrine

4. ECT is used primarily to treat _____. (a) phobias; (b) conduct disorders; (c) depression; (d) schizophrenia

Check your answers in Appendix B.

CLICK & REVIEW
for additional assessment options:
www.wiley.com/college/huffman

THERAPY AND CRITICAL THINKING

As you discovered in the Prologue to this text and throughout the individual chapters, critical thinking is one of the most important skills you'll develop while studying psychology. Nowhere is this more important than in this chapter. For example, we mentioned at the start of this chapter that there are over 400 forms of therapy. How are you going to choose one of these for yourself or someone you know?

In the first part of this section, we discuss the five goals that are common to all psychotherapies. Then we explore the key cultural similarities and differences in therapies around the world. We conclude with specific tips for finding a therapist. Can you see how these discussions help you see the overall "big picture"? Noncritical thinkers often fail to *synthesize* large bodies of information. When it comes to therapy, they may get lost "in the trees" and give up their search for therapists because they can't step outside and see "the forest."

Achievement

How can I use critical thinking to improve my understanding of therapy?

▪ Therapy Essentials: Five Common Goals

All major forms of therapy are designed to help the client in five specific areas (Figure 15.7). Depending on the individual therapist's training and the client's needs, one or more of these five areas may be emphasized more than the others.

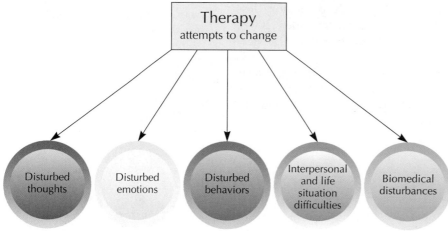

1. ***Disturbed thoughts.*** Troubled individuals typically suffer some degree of confusion, destructive thought patterns, or blocked understanding of their problems. Therapists work to change these thoughts, provide new ideas or information, and guide individuals toward finding solutions to problems.

2. ***Disturbed emotions.*** People who seek therapy generally suffer from extreme emotional discomfort. Therapists help clients understand and control their emotions and relieve the discomfort.

3. ***Disturbed behaviors.*** Therapists help clients eliminate troublesome behaviors and guide them toward more effective lives.

4. ***Interpersonal and life situation difficulties.*** Therapists help clients improve their relationships with family, friends, and coworkers. They also help them avoid or minimize sources of stress in their lives, such as job demands or family conflicts.

5. ***Biomedical disturbances.*** Troubled individuals sometimes suffer biological disruptions that directly cause or contribute to psychological difficulties (e.g., chemical imbalances that lead to depression). Therapists help relieve these problems, primarily with drugs.

Figure 15.7 *The five most common goals of therapy.* Most therapies focus on one or more of these five goals. After having read about each therapy, can you identify which goal(s) would be of most interest to a psychoanalyst, a cognitive therapist, a behaviorist, and a psychiatrist? Doing so will help you differentiate between the various approaches to therapy—and it might even help you in an exam on this chapter.

Although most therapists work with clients in several of these areas, the emphasis varies according to the therapist's training. As you learned earlier in this chapter, psychoanalysts and psychodynamic therapists generally emphasize unconscious thoughts and emotions. Cognitive therapists focus on their client's faulty thinking and belief patterns. And humanistic therapists attempt to alter the client's negative emotional responses. Behavior therapists, as the name implies, focus on changing maladaptive behaviors, and therapists who use biomedical techniques attempt to change biological disorders.

Keep in mind that the terms *psychoanalyst* and *cognitive therapist* simply refer to the theoretical background and framework that guide a clinician's thinking. Just as

Democrats and Republicans approach political matters in different ways, behavior and cognitive therapists approach therapy differently. And just as Democrats and Republicans borrow ideas from one another, clinicians from different perspectives also share ideas and techniques. Clinicians who regularly borrow freely from various theories are said to take an **eclectic approach**.

Eclectic Approach *Combining techniques from various theories to find the most appropriate treatment*

Application
APPLYING PSYCHOLOGY TO WORK

Careers in Mental Health

Do you enjoy helping people and think you would like a career as a therapist? Have you wondered how long you will have to go to college or the type of training that is required to be a therapist? Most colleges have counseling or career centers with numerous resources and trained staff who can help you answer these (and other) questions. To get you started, I have included a brief summary in Table 15.2 of the major types of mental health professionals, their degrees, years of required education beyond the bachelor's degree, and type of training.

TABLE 15.2 MAJOR TYPES OF MENTAL HEALTH PROFESSIONALS

Occupational Title	Degree	Years of Graduate Education Required and Nature of Training
Clinical Psychologist	Ph.D. (Doctor of Philosophy), Psy.D. (Doctor of Psychology)	(5–7 years) Most often have a doctoral degree with training in research and clinical practice, and a supervised one-year internship in a psychiatric hospital or mental health facility. As clinicians, they work with patients suffering from mental disorders, but many also work in colleges and universities as teachers and researchers in addition to having their own private practice.
Counseling Psychologist	M.A. (Master of Arts), Ph.D. (Doctor of Philosophy), Psy.D. (Doctor of Psychology), Ed.D. (Doctor of Education)	(3–7 years) Similar training to clinical psychologists, but counseling psychologists usually have a master's degree with more emphasis on patient care and less on research. They generally work in schools or other institutions and focus on problems of living rather than mental disorders.
Psychiatrist	M.D. (Doctor of Medicine)	(7–10 years) After four years of medical school, an internship and residency in psychiatry are required, which involves supervised practice in psychotherapy techniques and biomedical therapies. M.D.s are the only mental health specialists who can regularly prescribe drugs.
Psychiatric Social Worker	M.S.W. (Master in Social Work), D.S.W. (Doctorate in Social Work), Ph.D. (Doctor of Philosophy)	(2–5 years) Usually have a master's degree in social work, followed by advanced training and experience in hospitals or outpatient settings working with people who have psychological problems.
Psychiatric Nurse	R.N. (Registered Nurse), M.A. (Master of Arts), Ph.D. (Doctor of Philosophy)	(0–5 years) Usually have a bachelor's or master's degree in nursing, followed by advanced training in the care of mental patients in hospital settings and mental health facilities.
School Psychologist	M.A. (Master of Arts), Ph.D. (Doctor of Philosophy), Psy.D. (Doctor of Psychology), Ed.D. (Doctor of Education)	(3–7 years) Usually begin with a bachelor's degree in psychology, followed by graduate training in psychological assessment and counseling involving school-related issues and problems.

Application

RESEARCH HIGHLIGHT

Therapy in the Electronic Age

I never think of the future. It comes soon enough.

ALBERT EINSTEIN

Would you like to talk to a therapist over the phone or only on the Internet? Or is this too impersonal and high-tech for you? Like it or not, the electronic age of therapy has arrived.

Today millions of people seek advice and "therapy" from radio call-in programs, telephone services with 900 numbers, and websites for online therapy. The newest mental health therapy, called tele-health, has approximately 200 websites and between 350 and 1000 online counselors offering counseling, group support chats, e-mail correspondence, private instant messages, and videoconferencing therapy (Davison, Pennebaker, & Dickerson, 2000; Kicklighter, 2000; Newman, 2001). These online counselors are psychologists, psychiatrists, social workers, licensed counselors, nonlicensed "helpers," and outright quacks. Together, they treat an estimated 10,000 clients each week (Kicklighter, 2000).

As you might expect, many qualified therapists and academic institutions are concerned about this new form of therapy. They fear, among other things, that without a governing body to regulate this type of therapy, there are no checks and bal-

ances to protect the client from unethical and unsavory practices. Many of these concerns were recently addressed by the formulation of 10 Interdisciplinary Principles for Professional Practice in Tele-Health. According to these principles, psychologists would be required to follow the basic ethical policies of confidentiality, informed consent, and integrity as prescribed by the APA (American Psychological Association) Ethics Code (Newman, 2001). However, questions remain regarding interstate and international licensing conflicts for psychologists and the lack of consumer protection against those practicing without any license at all.

Why would anyone want to use an online counselor? The Internet and other electronic forms of therapy may sometimes be more effective than traditional therapy. For example, Enid M. Hunkeler and her colleagues (2000) found that depressed patients who received standard care as well as weekly phone calls from health professionals were significantly more likely to show improvement in their depressive symptoms than were patients who did not receive such calls. In another study, Andrew Winzelberg and his colleagues (2000) evaluated an Internet-based program designed for college students with eating disorders and found a significant improvement in body image and a decrease in drive for thinness.

Studies have long shown that success rates for both physical and mental health are improved with increased contact between patients and their health care providers. Electronic forms of therapy may be the easiest and most cost-effective way of increasing this contact (Schopp, Johnstone, & Merrell, 2000). Online clients appreciate having increased access to their therapist, especially during times of crisis. Clients also tend to feel safer discussing sensitive topics in the privacy of their own homes.

On the other hand, critics claim that online therapy is a contradiction in terms—an oxymoron. They say that psychotherapy is based on both verbal and nonverbal communication. They suggest it may be impossible for online therapists to give appropriate therapeutic advice to clients without face-to-face contact. Others are concerned about sending private and confidential thoughts into unsecured cyberspace to a person who may not be a qualified therapist (e.g., Bloom, 1998). David Nickelson, director of technology policy and projects for the APA, advises people to first seek face-to-face therapy. "We still need research," Nickelson says, and we "may find that there are just some things therapists and their patients can't do over the Internet" (http://www.apa.org/practice/pf/aug97/tele-heal.html).

Achievement
Gender & Cultural Diversity

Similarities and Differences

All the therapies we have described in this chapter are based on Western European and North American culture. But what about other, less traditional, therapies? Do our psychotherapists do some of the same things that, say, a native healer or shaman does? Or are there fundamental cultural differences between therapies? What about women? Do they have different issues in therapy? As mentioned earlier, looking at each of these questions requires critical thinking. Let's carefully consider these issues one at a time.

Cultural Similarities

When we look at therapies in all cultures, we find that they have certain key features in common (Corey, 2001b; Jennings & Skovholt, 1999; Lee, 2002; Matsumoto, 2000). Richard Brislin (1993) has summarized some of these features:

1. **Naming the problem.** One important step toward improving psychological functioning is labeling the problem. People often feel better just by knowing that others experience the same problem and that the therapist has had experience with this particular problem.

2. **Qualities of the therapist.** Clients must feel the therapist is caring, competent, approachable, and concerned with finding solutions to their problem.

3. **Establishing credibility.** Word-of-mouth testimonials and status symbols (such as diplomas on the wall) establish the therapist's credibility. Among native healers, in lieu of diplomas, credibility may be established by having served as an apprentice to a revered healer.

4. **Placing the problem in a familiar framework.** If the client believes evil spirits cause psychological disorders, the therapist will direct treatment toward these spirits. Similarly, if the client believes in the importance of early childhood experiences and the unconscious mind, psychoanalysis will be the likely treatment of choice.

5. **Applying techniques to bring relief.** In all cultures, therapy involves action. Either the client or the therapist must do something. Moreover, what they do must fit the client's expectations. For example, people who believe evil spirits possess them expect the shaman to perform a ceremony to expel the demons. In the Western European and American model, clients expect to reveal their thoughts and feelings and provide background information. This "talk therapy" may also have biological or behavioral components. But those who seek therapy generally expect to talk about their problem.

6. **A special time and place.** The fact that therapy occurs outside the client's everyday experiences seems to be an important feature of all therapies. People apparently need to set aside a special time and go to a special place to concentrate on their problems.

Cultural Differences

There are clear similarities in therapies across cultures, but there are also important differences. In the traditional Western European and American model, clients are encouraged toward self-awareness, self-fulfillment, self-actualization, and modifying self-behavior. The emphasis is on the "self" and on independence and control over one's life—qualities that are highly valued in individualistic cultures. When we look at therapies in collectivist cultures, however, the focus is on interdependence and accepting the realities of one's life (Sue & Sue, 2002).

Japanese *Naikan* therapy is a good example of a collectivist culture's approach to psychological disorders. In *Naikan* therapy, the patient sits quietly from 5:30 A.M. to 9 P.M. for seven days and is visited by an interviewer every 90 minutes. During this time, the patient is instructed to look at his or her relationships with others from three perspectives: *care received* (recollect and reexamine the care and kindness you have received from others), *repayment* (recall what you have done to repay the care and kindness of others), and *troubles caused* (think about the troubles and worries you have caused others) (Berry, Poortinga, Segall, & Dasen, 1992; Ryback, Ikemi, & Miki, 2001).

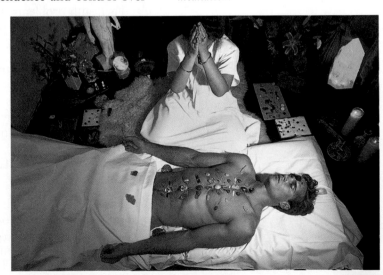

Alternative therapies. In all cultures, therapy involves specific actions or treatments. In this photo, the therapist is using crystal healing, laying on of stones, and meditation.

Alan Levenson/Stone/GettyImages

The goals of *Naikan* therapy are to discover personal guilt for having been ungrateful and troublesome to others. And to develop gratitude toward those who have been helpful. When these goals are attained, the person will have a better self-image and interpersonal attitude.

As you can see, there are pronounced differences between *Naikan* therapy goals and the methods and therapies we have described in this chapter. Culture affects the types of therapy that are developed. It also influences the perceptions of the therapist. For this reason, recognizing cultural differences is very important for building trust between therapists and clients and for effecting behavioral change. Clinicians who work with clients from different cultural backgrounds should learn about their clients' cultures. They also should be aware of cultural disparities in access to care and of their own cultural and ethnic-based values and beliefs (Snowden & Yamada, 2005; Tseng, 2004).

Women and Therapy

In addition to sensitivity to their clients' cultural backgrounds, therapists must also be responsive to gender differences. Within individualistic Western culture, men and women present different needs and problems to therapists. For example, compared with men, women are more comfortable and familiar with their emotions, have fewer negative attitudes toward therapy, and are more likely to seek psychological help (Komiya, Good, & Sherrod, 2000). However, research has identified five unique concerns related to women and psychotherapy (Chaikin & Prout, 2004; Holtzworth-Munroe, 2000; Whitney, Kusznir, & Dixie, 2002).

1. ***Rates of diagnosis and treatment of mental disorders.*** Research has found that women are diagnosed and treated for mental illness at a much higher rate than men. Is this because women are "sicker" than men as a group? Or are they just more willing to admit their problems? Perhaps the categories for illness may be biased against women. More research is needed to answer this question.

2. ***Stresses of poverty.*** Poverty is an important contributor to many psychological disorders. Therefore, women bring special challenges to the therapy situation because of their overrepresentation in the lowest economic groups.

3. ***Stresses of multiple roles.*** Women today are mothers, wives, homemakers, wage earners, students, and so on. The conflicting demands of their multiple roles often create special stresses.

4. ***Stresses of aging.*** Aging brings special concerns for women. They live longer than men do. Women also tend to be poorer, to be less educated, and to have more serious health problems. Elderly women, primarily those with age-related dementia, account for over 70 percent of the chronically mentally ill who live in nursing homes in the United States.

5. ***Violence against women.*** Rape, violent assault, incest, and sexual harassment all take a harsh toll on women's mental health. With the exception of violent assault, these forms of violence are much more likely to happen to women than to men. These violent acts may lead to depression, insomnia, posttraumatic stress disorder, eating disorders, and other problems.

Institutionalization: Treating Chronic and Serious Mental Disorders

We all believe in the right to freedom. Should people be involuntarily committed to protect them from their own mental disorders? What about people who threaten suicide or are potentially violent? Despite Hollywood film portrayals, forced institutionalization of the mentally ill poses serious ethical problems. It is generally reserved for only the most serious and life-threatening situations.

Involuntary Commitment

The legal grounds for involuntary commitment vary from state to state. But, generally, people can be sent to psychiatric hospitals if:

- They are believed to be dangerous to themselves (usually suicidal) or dangerous to others (potentially violent).

- They are believed to be in serious need of treatment (indicated by bizarre behavior and loss of contact with reality).

- There is no reasonable, less restrictive alternative.

In emergencies, psychologists and other professionals can authorize temporary commitment for 24 to 72 hours. During this observation period, laboratory tests can be performed to rule out medical illnesses that could be causing the symptoms. The patient can also receive psychological testing, medication, and short-term therapy.

Deinstitutionalization

Although the courts have established stringent requirements for involuntary commitment, abuses do occur. There are also problems with long-term chronic institutionalization. And properly housing and caring for the mentally ill is very expensive. In response to these problems, many states have a policy of *deinstitutionalization*, discharging patients from mental hospitals as soon as possible and discouraging admissions.

Deinstitutionalization has been a humane and positive step for many (Lariviere et al., 2002; Priebe et al., 2002). But some patients are discharged without continuing provision for their protection. Many of these people end up living in rundown hotels or understaffed nursing homes, in jails, or on the street with no shelter or means of support. [It is important to note that a sizable percentage of homeless people do have mental disorders. The rise in homelessness is also due to such economic factors as increased unemployment, underemployment, and a shortage of low-income housing (Becker & Kunstmann, 2001; Seager, 1998; Torrey, 1998).]

What else can be done? Rather than returning patients to state hospitals, most clinicians suggest expanding and improving community care (Duckworth & Borus, 1999; Lamb, 2000). They recommend that general hospitals be equipped with special psychiatric units where acutely ill patients receive inpatient care. For less disturbed individuals and chronically ill patients, they recommend walk-in clinics, crisis intervention services, improved residential treatment facilities, and psychosocial and vocational rehabilitation. State hospitals can then be reserved for the most unmanageable patients.

Deinstitutionalization. *Keeping people locked in large mental institutions creates problems. But deinstitutionalization also creates problems because it forces many former patients onto the streets with no home or medical care.*

Peter Turnley/Corbis

Gavin Hellier/Stone/GettyImages

www.wiley.com/college/huffman

Community Mental Health (CMH) Centers

These organizations are a prime example of an alternative to institutionalization. CMH centers provide outpatient services such as individual and group therapy and prevention programs. They also coordinate short-term inpatient care and programs for discharged mental patients, such as halfway houses and aftercare services. Psychiatrists, social workers, nurses, and volunteers who live in the neighborhood generally staff CMH centers.

As you can imagine, CMH centers and their support programs are also expensive. Investing in primary prevention programs could substantially reduce these costs. Instead of waiting until someone loses his or her job, home, and family, we could develop more intervention programs for high-risk individuals and offer short-term immediate services during crises.

■ Evaluating and Finding Therapy: Does It Work? How to Choose?

Have you ever thought about going to a therapist? If you've gone, was it helpful? In this section, we will discuss questions about the effectiveness of therapy and how to find a therapist.

Judging Effectiveness

Scientifically evaluating the effectiveness of therapy can be tricky. How can you trust the perception and self-report of clients or clinicians? Both have biases and a need to justify the time, effort, and expense of therapy.

To avoid these problems, psychologists use controlled research studies. Clients are randomly assigned to different forms of therapy or to control groups who receive no treatment. After therapy, clients are independently evaluated, and reports from friends and family members are collected. Until recently, these studies were simply compared. But with a new statistical technique called *meta-analysis*, which combines and analyzes data from many studies, years of such studies and similar research can be brought together to produce a comprehensive report.

The good news, for both consumers and therapists, is that after years of controlled research and meta-analysis we have fairly clear evidence that therapy does work! Forty to 80 percent of people who receive treatment are better off than people who do not. Furthermore, short-term treatments can be as effective as long-term treatments (Blanco et al., 2003; Ellis, 2004; Nordhus & Pallesen, 2003; Shadish & Baldwin, 2003; Storosum et al., 2004; Swanson, Swartz, & Elbogen, 2004). In addition, some therapies are more effective than others for specific problems. For example, phobias seem to respond best to systematic desensitization, and obsessive-compulsive disorders can be significantly relieved with cognitive-behavior therapy accompanied by medication.

Finding a Therapist

How do we find a good therapist for our specific needs? If you have the time (and the money) to explore options, take the time to "shop around" for a therapist best suited to your specific goals. Consulting your psychology instructor or college counseling system for referrals can be an important first step. However, if you are in a crisis—you have suicidal thoughts, you have failing grades, or you are the victim of abuse—get help fast (Besançon, 2004; Beutler, Shurkin, Bongar, & Gray, 2000; First, Pincus, & Frances, 1999). Most communities have telephone hotlines that provide counseling on a 24-hour basis. And most colleges and universities have counseling centers that provide immediate, short-term therapy to students free of charge.

If you are encouraging someone else to get therapy, you might offer to help locate a therapist and go with them for their first visit. If he or she refuses help and the problem affects you, it is often a good idea to seek therapy yourself. You will gain insights and skills that will help you deal with the situation more effectively.

Application
APPLYING PSYCHOLOGY TO EVERYDAY LIFE

The Kobal Collection

What's Wrong with Movie Portrayals of Therapy

In the film *The Prince of Tides*, Barbra Streisand portrays a psychiatrist who falls in love and has sex with her client, Nick Nolte. What's wrong with this picture? Can you use your critical thinking skills to briefly describe how this portrayal of sex between a therapist and client might create serious and lasting problems for the therapist, client, and the viewing public?

Therapist: _____

Client: _____

Viewing Public: _____

Now, compare your responses to the discussion below.

As we discussed in the chapter opener, movie portrayals of harmful therapy and unethical therapists create dangerous stereotypes and lasting misconceptions. In this case, the movie treats the sexual relationships between therapist and client as just another romantic encounter. It fails to acknowledge that the therapist is in serious violation of professional ethics, which may lead to a loss of license and possible criminal charges. Romance may enliven a movie. But in real life, therapists must uphold the highest standards of ethical behavior. Sex between patient and therapist is not only unethical in several states it's also a criminal offense (Dalenberg, 2000; Sloan, Edmond, Rubin, & Doughty, 1998).

In addition to ignoring the professional problems for the therapist, movie portrayals of sexual trysts during therapy ignore the fact that the client is seeking help and occupies a less powerful position, which unfairly increases his or her vulnerability. Intimacy also destroys the professional relationship required to help the client. Perhaps the most overlooked danger in these portrayals is the damage to the viewing public. Because these movies trivialize (and romanticize) a serious breach of professional ethics, they may create a false (and possibly lasting) bad impression that may discourage troubled people from seeking valuable therapy.

What's wrong with this picture?
Romantic, sexual relationships between therapists and their clients are a common theme in Hollywood films, as was the case in this film, Prince of Tides, with Barbra Streisand (therapist) and Nick Nolte (client).

Assessment

CHECK & REVIEW

Therapy and Critical Thinking

There are numerous forms of therapy. But they all focus treatment on five basic areas of disturbance—thoughts, emotions, behaviors, interpersonal and life situations, and biomedical problems. Many therapists take an **eclectic approach** and combine techniques from various theories.

Therapies in all cultures share six culturally universal features: naming a problem, qualities of the therapist, establishing credibility, placing the problems in a familiar framework, applying techniques to bring relief, and a special time and place. Impor-tant cultural differences in therapies also exist. For example, therapies in individualistic cultures emphasize the self and control over one's life, whereas therapies in collectivist cultures emphasize interdependence. Japan's *Naikan* therapy is a good example of a collectivist culture's therapy.

Therapists must take five considerations into account when treating women clients: higher rate of diagnosis and treatment of mental disorders, stresses of poverty, stresses of multiple roles, stresses of aging, and violence against women.

People believed to be mentally ill and dangerous to themselves or others can be involuntarily committed to mental hospitals for diagnosis and treatment. Abuses of involuntary commitments and other problems associated with state mental hospitals have led many states to practice *deinstitutionalization*—discharging as many patients as possible and discouraging admissions. Community services such as community mental health (CMH) centers try to cope with the problems of deinstitutionalization. Research on the effectiveness of psychotherapy has found that 40 to 80 percent of those who receive treatment are better off than those who do not receive treatment.

Questions

1. Match the following therapists with their primary emphasis:
   ___ psychoanalysts
   ___ humanistic therapists
   ___ biomedical therapists
   ___ cognitive therapists
   ___ behaviorist therapists

   (a) faulty thinking and belief patterns
   (b) unconscious thoughts
   (c) biological disorders
   (d) negative emotions
   (e) maladaptive behaviors

2. Name the six features of therapy that are culturally universal.
3. A Japanese therapy designed to help clients discover personal guilt for having been ungrateful and troublesome to others and to develop gratitude toward those who have helped them is known as _____. (a) Kyoto therapy; (b) Okado therapy; (c) Naikan therapy; (d) Nissan therapy
4. What are the five major concerns about women in therapy?
5. The policy of discharging as many people as possible from state hospitals and discouraging admissions is called _____. (a) disengagement; (b) reinstitutionalization; (c) maladaptive restructuring; (d) deinstitutionalization

Check your answers in Appendix B.

CLICK & REVIEW
for additional assessment options:
www.wiley.com/college/huffman

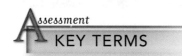

ssessment

KEY TERMS

*To assess your understanding of the **Key Terms** in Chapter 15, write a definition for each (in your own words), and then compare your definitions with those in the text.*

psychotherapy (p. 537)

Insight Therapies
active listening (p. 546)
client-centered therapy (p. 545)
cognitive-behavior therapy (p. 544)
cognitive restructuring (p. 542)
cognitive therapy (p. 541)
dream analysis (p. 538)
empathy (p. 546)
family therapy (p. 548)
free association (p. 538)
genuineness (p. 545)
group therapy (p. 547)
humanistic therapy (p. 545)
interpretation (p. 539)

psychoanalysis (p. 538)
psychodynamic therapy (p. 540)
rational-emotive behavior therapy (REBT) (p. 542)
resistance (p. 539)
self-help group (p. 547)
self-talk (p. 542)
transference (p. 539)
unconditional positive regard (p. 545)

Behavior Therapies
aversion therapy (p. 552)
behavior therapy (p. 550)
modeling therapy (p. 554)
systematic desensitization (p. 551)

Biomedical Therapies
antianxiety drugs (p. 555)
antidepressant drugs (p. 556)
antipsychotic drugs (p. 555)
biomedical therapy (p. 555)
electroconvulsive therapy (ECT) (p. 557)
lobotomy (p. 558)
psychopharmacology (p. 555)
psychosurgery (p. 558)

Therapy and Critical Thinking
eclectic approach (p. 561)

WEB RESOURCES

Huffman Book Companion Site

http://www.wiley.com/college/huffman

This site is loaded with free Interactive Self-Tests, Internet Exercises, Glossary and Flashcards for key terms, web links, Handbook for Non-Native Speakers, and other activities designed to improve your mastery of the material in this chapter.

Interested in more information on types of therapy?

http://www.grohol.com/therapy.htm

A website that offers a brief overview of four major therapies: psychodynamic/psychoanalytic, cognitive-behavioral/behavioral, humanistic/existential, and eclectic.

Want help finding a therapist?

http://www.helping.apa.org/brochure/index.html

Sponsored by the American Psychological Association (APA), this website provides general information on psychotherapy as well as advice on how to choose a psychotherapist. If you want more information, try www.psychologytoday.com. The homepage of *Psychology Today* magazine, this website features the most commonly asked questions in selecting a therapist, help in locating a therapist, and individual consultations with an expert online.

Want more detailed information about a specific problem and its treatment?

http://www.apa.org/science/lib.html

Created by the American Psychological Association (APA), this website offers articles, books, library searches, and links for all the disorders listed in the *DSM-IV-TR*. If you'd like additional information, try http://www.mentalhealth.com/p20-grp.html. Sponsored by the Internet Mental Health group, this site provides a wealth of resources and information about all the major disorders, including description, diagnosis, treatment, research, and recommended booklets. Also try http://www.mhsource.com/. Designed primarily for mental health professionals, this website offers valuable resources and links to specific disorders and their causes, diagnosis, and treatment.

Want help with a substance abuse disorder?

http://www.health.org/

The National Clearinghouse for Alcohol and Drug Information sponsors this site, which provides numerous links to the prevention and treatment of substance abuse. For even more information, try http://www.drugnet.net/metaview.htm. This website offers a wealth of information and links to resources around the globe.

Visual SUMMARY

Insight Therapies

Description/Major Goals

- **Psychoanalysis/psychodynamic therapies**: Bring unconscious conflicts into conscious awareness.

- **Cognitive therapies**: Analyze faulty thought processes, beliefs, and negative **self-talk**, and change these destructive thoughts with **cognitive restructuring**.

- **Humanistic therapies**: Work to facilitate personal growth.

- **Group, family, and marital therapies**: Several clients meet with one or more therapists to resolve personal problems.

Techniques/Methods

Five major techniques:
- **Free association**
- **Dream analysis**
- **Resistance**
- **Transference**
- **Interpretation**

Ellis's **rational-emotive behavior therapy (REBT)** replaces irrational beliefs with rational beliefs and accurate perceptions of the world.

Beck's **cognitive-behavior therapy** emphasizes change in both thought processes and behavior.

Roger's **client-centered therapy** offers **empathy**, **unconditional positive regard**, **genuineness**, and **active listening** to facilitate personal growth.

Provide group support, feedback, information, and opportunities for behavior-rehearsal.
- **Self-help groups** (like Alcoholics Anonymous) are sometimes considered group therapy, but professional therapists do not conduct them.
- **Family therapies**: Work to change maladaptive family interaction patterns.

Behavior Therapies

Description/Major Goals

- **Behavior therapies**: Use learning principles to eliminate mal-adaptive behaviors and substitute healthy ones.

Techniques/Methods

- Classical conditioning techniques, including **systematic de-sensitization** (client replaces anxiety with relaxation) and **aversion therapy** (an aversive stimulus is paired with a maladaptive behavior).
- Operant conditioning techniques, including shaping and reinforcement.
- Observational learning techniques, including **modeling therapy** (clients watch and imitate positive role models).

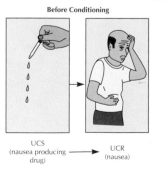
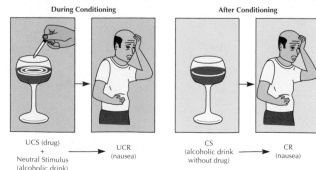

Before Conditioning

UCS
(nausea producing drug) → UCR
(nausea)

During Conditioning

UCS (drug)
+
Neutral Stimulus
(alcoholic drink) → UCR
(nausea)

After Conditioning

CS
(alcoholic drink without drug) → CR
(nausea)

Biomedical Therapies

Description/Major Goals

- **Biomedical therapies**: Use biological techniques to relieve psychological disorders. →

Techniques/Methods

Drug therapy is the most common biomedical treatment.
- **Antianxiety drugs** used to treat anxiety disorders.
- **Antipsychotic drugs** relieve symptoms of psychosis.
- **Mood stabilizers** help stabilize bipolar disorders.
- **Antidepressants** used to treat depression.

Electroconvulsive therapy (ECT) used primarily to relieve serious depression, when medication fails.

Psychosurgeries, such as a **lobotomy**, are seldom used today.

Therapy and Critical Thinking

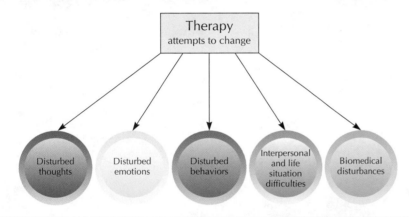

Therapy attempts to change

- Disturbed thoughts
- Disturbed emotions
- Disturbed behaviors
- Interpersonal and life situation difficulties
- Biomedical disturbances

Women in Therapy

Higher rate of diagnosis and treatment of mental disorders due to stresses of poverty, multiple roles, aging, and violence against women.

Cultural Issues

- *Common features of therapy in all cultures:* Naming a problem, qualities of the therapist, establishing credibility, placing the problem in a familiar framework, applying techniques to bring relief, and a special time and place.
- *Differences in therapy between cultures:* Individualistic cultures emphasize the "self" and control over one's life. However, therapies in collectivist cultures, like Japan's Naikan therapy, emphasize interdependence.

Institutionalization

- People believed to be mentally ill and dangerous to themselves or others can be involuntarily committed to mental hospitals for diagnosis and treatment.
- Abuses of involuntary commitment and other problems led to *deinstitutionalization*—discharging as many patients as possible and discouraging admissions.
- Community services such as Community Mental Health (CMH) centers offset some problems of deinstitutionalization.

Seeking Therapy

- Forty to 80 percent of those who receive treatment are better off than those who do not.
- Take time to "shop around," but a crisis requires immediate help.
- If others' problems affect you, get help yourself.

www.wiley.com/college/huffman

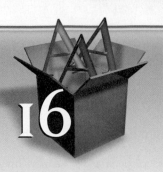

16

SOCIAL PSYCHOLOGY

Achievement

Core Learning Outcomes

As you read Chapter 16, keep the following questions in mind and answer them in your own words:

▷ How do our thoughts affect how we explain and judge others?

▷ What feelings are most important in our social interactions?

▷ How do our actions toward others affect their lives and our own?

▷ How can we use social psychology to help resolve social problems?

■ Achievement
■ Assessment
■ Application

Application

WHY STUDY PSYCHOLOGY?

Chris Fortuna/GettyImages, Inc.

Chapter 16 will explain why or how...

▶ Groups generally make more risky decisions than a single individual does.

▶ Most people judge others more harshly than they judge themselves.

▶ Looks are the primary factor in our initial feelings of attraction, liking, and romantic love.

▶ Opposites don't really attract.

▶ Romantic love rarely lasts longer than one or two years.

▶ Inducing cognitive dissonance is a great way to change attitudes.

▶ There are positive as well as negative forms of prejudice.

▶ Watching a violent sports match or punching a pillow is a not a good way to let off steam and reduce aggression.

▶ When people are alone, they are more likely to help another individual than when they are in a group.

Photo courtesy of Washington Post/GettyImages

Social psychology in action? *Was the torture of prisoners in the Abu Ghraib prison the result of a few "rogue U.S. soldiers"? Or was it predictable (and preventable)?*

Social Psychology *The study of how others influence our thoughts, feelings, and actions*

o you remember the prisoner abuse scandal at the Iraqi Abu Ghraib prison in 2004? People around the world were shocked and outraged by the degrading photos of the smiling U.S. military guards as they posed next to naked prisoners whom they had forced to form a human pryamid with their bodies. Politicians and military officials claimed the crimes were the "vile acts of a few bad soldiers" and a "gross aberration for U.S. soldiers" (Ripley, 2004; Warner, 2004). Social psychologists believed otherwise. As you'll discover later in this chapter, researchers have discovered that ordinary people, under the right circumstances, will do horrible, unimaginable things, including mistreating prisoners and obeying orders that seem to cause serious injury to others—and even the loss of their own lives. Social psychologists also study other, more positive elements of human social behaviors, such as interpersonal attraction and helping behaviors.

A combination of confusion and fascination over social behaviors is what draws many students and researchers to the field of **social psychology**—the study of how other people influence an individual's thoughts, feelings, and actions. But, unlike other fields of psychology that focus on internal personality dynamics or individual pathology, social psychologists emphasize external social forces and the environment. They work to understand how groups, attitudes, social roles, and norms encourage us to behave cruelly or aggressively as well as lovingly and altruistically. Using the tools of science (experiments, surveys, case studies, self-reports, and so on), social psychologists seek scientific answers to *social* questions—hence the term *social psychology*.

Almost everything we do is social. Thus, the subject matter of social psychology is enormous and varied. We will therefore organize our study by looking at each individual component of the definition (thoughts, feelings, and actions). The chapter begins with topics related to "Our Thoughts About Others" (attribution and attitudes). Then we examine "Our Feelings About Others" by looking at prejudice, discrimination, and interpersonal attraction. (Prejudice and discrimination could also be discussed under thoughts or actions. But here they are included under feelings toward others because negative emotions are the central defining characteristic of prejudice.)

The next section explores "Our Actions Toward Others" (social influence, group processes, aggression, and altruism). And the chapter concludes with a discussion of how social psychology can help reduce prejudice, discrimination, and destructive forms of obedience.

OUR THOUGHTS ABOUT OTHERS

How could a mother brutalize and torture her child? Why would someone run into a burning building to rescue a stranger? Why do we fall in love with some people and not others? Trying to understand the social world often means trying to understand other people's behavior. We look for reasons and explanations for others' behavior (the process of attribution). We also develop thoughts and beliefs (attitudes) about others.

Achievement

How do our thoughts affect how we explain and judge others?

Attribution: Explaining Others' Behavior

When we observe the world around us, we need to understand and explain why people think, feel, or act as they do and why events occur as they do. We start by asking questions: "Why did the American soldiers abuse the prisoners in Abu Ghraib?" "Why did my friend not invite me to the party?" "Why did my college tuition increase so much last year?" Then we answer our questions by *attributing* the behaviors or events to various causes: "The soldiers were just weak or sadistic." "My friend is mad at me." "Tuitions are rising because tax revenues are decreasing."

Attribution *An explanation for the cause of behaviors or events*

Why are we so interested in making attributions? Fritz Heider (1958) spent many years studying this question. He concluded that people need to see the world as coherent and controllable. When we develop "logical" explanations for why things happen, we feel safer and more in control. Heider also noted a pattern in the way people make their attributions. Most people begin with a basic question: Does the behavior stem mainly from the person's internal *disposition* or from the external *situation*? If you concluded that the military guards at Abu Ghraib prison acted because of their own personal characteristics, motives, and intentions, you would be making a *dispositional attribution*. On the other hand, if you decided they responded to situational demands and environmental pressures, you would be making a *situational attribution*.

Attribution. *How would you explain why these people are so willing to crowd around this one television set?*

Mistaken Attributions

The choice between disposition and situation is central to accurate judgments of why people do what they do. Unfortunately, our attributions are frequently marred by two major errors: the *fundamental attribution error* and the *self-serving bias*.

1. ***The fundamental attribution error—judging the behavior of others.*** When we recognize and take into account environmental influences on behavior, we generally make accurate attributions. However, given that people have enduring personality traits (Chapter 13) and a tendency to take cognitive shortcuts (Chapter 8), we more often choose dispositional attributions. In short, we blame the person. This bias toward personal, dispositional factors rather than environmental factors is so common in individualistic cultures that it is called the **fundamental attribution error (FAE)** (Fernández-Dols, Carrera, & Russell, 2002; Gawronski, 2003; O'Sullivan, 2003).

For example, noting that your instructor seems relaxed and talkative in front of the class, you might decide that he or she is an extroverted and outgoing person—a

Fundamental Attribution Error (FAE) *Misjudging the causes of others' behavior as due to internal (dispositional) causes rather than external (situational) ones*

www.wiley.com/college/huffman

dispositional attribution. However, outside of class you may be surprised to find him or her shy and awkward in a one-on-one situation. Similarly, many Americans thought the abusing soldiers in the Abu Ghraib prison scandal were "sadistic," "perverted," or "weak-willed" individuals just following the orders of the commanding officers. They blamed the person (dispositional attribution). They overlooked and underestimated the power of the environment (situational attribution).

Saliency Bias *Focusing on the most noticeable (salient) factors when explaining the causes of behavior*

Why do we tend to jump to internal, personal explanations? There are several possible explanations. The most important may be that human personalities and behaviors are more *salient* (or noticeable) than situational factors. This **saliency bias** helps explain why we focus on the soldiers in the Abu Ghraib prisoner abuse versus the larger, more ambiguous situational factors. It also helps explain why some people blame women for being raped or homeless people for being homeless. It's easier (and more salient) to "blame the victim."

Self-Serving Bias *Taking credit for our successes and externalizing our failures*

2. ***The self-serving bias—judging our own behavior.*** When we judge others' behavior, we tend to emphasize internal personality factors over external situational causes. But when we explain our own behavior, we favor internal personal attributions for our *successes* and external environmental attributions for our *failures*. This **self-serving bias** is motivated by a desire to maintain our self-esteem as well as a desire to look good to others (Goerke et al., 2004; Higgins & Bhatt, 2001; Ross et al., 2004).

Students who do well on an exam often take personal credit ("I really studied hard," or "I'm smart!"). If they fail the test, however, they tend to blame the instructor, the textbook, or the "tricky" questions. Similarly, studies find young children blame their siblings for conflicts. Both partners in divorced couples are also more likely to see themselves as the victim, as less responsible for the breakup, and as being more willing to reconcile (Gray & Silver, 1990; Wilson et al., 2004).

Assessment

VISUAL QUIZ

PEANUTS; drawings by Charles Schulz; 1989 United Features Syndicate, Inc. Reprinted by permission of UFS, Inc.

Can you use terms from this chapter to explain this cartoon?

Answer: Lucy's criticism of Linus may be the result of the fundamental attribution error. Her overlooking of her own faults may be the self-serving bias.

Culture and Attributional Biases

Both the fundamental attribution error and the self-serving bias may depend in part on cultural factors (Kudo & Numazaki, 2003; Matsumoto, 2000). As we discussed in earlier chapters, some cultures tend to be *individualistic*, whereas others are more *collectivistic*. In highly individualistic cultures, like the United States, people are defined and understood as individual selves—largely responsible for their successes and failures. But in highly collectivistic cultures, like China, people are defined and understood as members of their social network. They are largely responsible for doing what is expected of them by others. Using your critical thinking skills, can you predict how people from these two cultures might differ in their attributional styles?

As you may have guessed, many studies have found that the fundamental attribution error is far less common in collectivistic cultures than in those that are individualistic (Gilovich, Griffin, & Kahneman, 2002; Norenzayan & Nisbett, 2000; Triandis, 2001). Why are collectivists less susceptible to this attribution error? Compared to Westerners, who tend to believe individuals are responsible for their own actions, people in many Eastern countries are more group oriented and tend to be more aware of situational constraints on behavior. If you were watching a baseball game in China and the umpire made a bad call, as a Westerner you would probably make a personality attribution ("He's a lousy umpire"). In contrast, a Chinese spectator would tend to make a situational attribution ("He's under pressure").

Like the fundamental attribution error, the self-serving bias is also much less common in Eastern nations. In Japan, for instance, the ideal person is someone who is aware of his or her shortcomings and continually works to overcome them. It is not someone who thinks highly of himself or herself (Heine & Renshaw, 2002). In the East, where people do not define themselves as much in terms of their individual accomplishments, self-esteem is not related to doing better than others. Rather, fitting in and not standing out from the group is stressed. As the Japanese proverb says, "The nail that sticks up gets pounded down."

This emphasis on group relations in Asian cultures is also true of many Native Americans. For example, when the Wintun Native Americans originally described being with a close relation or intimate friend, they would not say, for example, "Linda and I," but rather, "Linda we" (Lee, 1950). This attachment to community relations instead of individual *selfhood* often seems strange to people in contemporary Western, individualist societies. But it remains common in collectivist cultures (Markus & Kitayama, 2003).

■ Attitudes: Our Learned Predispositions Toward Others

An **attitude** is a learned predisposition to respond cognitively, affectively, and behaviorally to a particular object in a particular way. The object can be anything from pizza to people, from diseases to drugs, from abortion to psychology.

Attitude *Learned predisposition to respond cognitively, affectively, and behaviorally to a particular object*

Components of Attitudes

Social psychologists generally agree that most attitudes have three components (Figure 16.1): cognitive, affective, and behavioral. The *cognitive component* consists of thoughts and beliefs, such as "Marijuana is a relatively safe drug" or "The dangers of marijuana are greatly underestimated." The *affective*, or *emotional*, *component* involves feelings, such as frustration that our legal system has not legalized marijuana or, conversely, that some people want it legalized. The *behavioral component* consists of a *predisposition* to act in certain ways toward an attitude object. Someone who held a positive attitude toward marijuana might write to textbook authors and publishers complaining that we are too critical in our discussion of drugs in Chapter 5. Someone with a negative attitude, on the other hand, might write to complain that even the use of marijuana as an example could encourage its use.

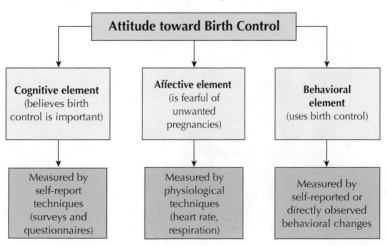

Figure 16.1 *Three components of all attitudes.* When social psychologists study attitudes, they measure each of the three components—cognitive, affective, and behavioral.

VISUAL QUIZ

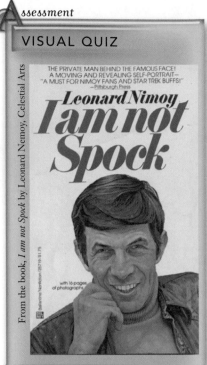

From the book, *I am not Spock* by Leonard Nimoy, Celestial Arts

THE PRIVATE MAN BEHIND THE FAMOUS FACE!
A MOVING AND REVEALING SELF-PORTRAIT—
"A MUST FOR NIMOY FANS AND STAR TREK BUFFS!"
—Pittsburgh Press

Leonard Nimoy
I am not Spock

with 16 pages of photographs

Mistaking Nimoy for Spock. Leonard Nimoy has complained that people continue to think of him as the character he portrayed on Star Trek—a long-running popular television series. He even called his autobiography, *I Am Not Spock*. Mistaking Nimoy for Spock is a good example of what component of all attitudes?

Answer: The cognitive component.

Cognitive Dissonance *A feeling of discomfort caused by a discrepancy between an attitude and a behavior or between two competing attitudes*

Spencer Grant/PhotoEdit

Cognitive dissonance in action. Using information from this section, can you imagine how this doctor explains her smoking behavior?

Cognitive Dissonance Theory

| People are motivated to maintain consistency in their thoughts, feelings, and actions. | When inconsistencies or conflicts exist between thoughts, feelings, and/or actions it can... | lead to | Strong tension and discomfort (cognitive dissonance) | To reduce this tension or dissonance, we change our original attitude or behavior |

Figure 16.2 *Cognitive dissonance theory.* When differences exist between our strongly held attitudes, or when there are large inconsistencies between our attitudes and behavior, we experience discomfort (dissonance) and a need to change either the attitude or the behavior.

Attitude Change Through Cognitive Dissonance

We are not born with our attitudes—they are learned. From earliest childhood, we form them through direct experience (we eat pizza and like the taste), and through indirect learning or observation (we listen to testimonials or watch others happily eating pizza). Although attitudes begin in early childhood, they are not permanent. Advertisers and politicians spend millions of dollars on campaigns because they know attitudes can be shaped and changed throughout the entire life span.

Attitude change often results from persuasive appeals (such as TV ads like "Friends Don't Let Friends Drive Drunk"). An even more efficient method is by creating **cognitive dissonance**, a feeling of discomfort caused by a discrepancy between an attitude and a behavior or between two competing attitudes (Prinstein & Aikins, 2004; Thorgersen, 2004; Van Overwalle & Jordens, 2002). *Dissonance* comes from disagreement or conflict. According to Leon Festinger (1957), when we notice a conflict between our attitudes and behaviors, or between two conflicting attitudes, the contradiction makes us uncomfortable. This discomfort (cognitive dissonance) makes us want to change our attitude to agree with our behaviors or to match our other attitudes (Figure 16.2).

Cigarette smokers undoubtedly know tobacco is related to heart disease, lung cancer, and other serious diseases. Their behavior and attitude are inconsistent. How do they deal with the resulting cognitive dissonance? They could quit smoking (change their behavior). But that is very difficult to do. Like most people, they probably choose the easier route—they change their attitudes. They convince themselves that smoking isn't that dangerous. They reassure themselves with personal examples like their Uncle Charlie and Grandma Betsy who lived to be a hundred. Or they simply ignore or discount all the contradictory information. Obviously, this is maladaptive, irrational thinking and a threat to health and life. But it does reduce the pain and discomfort of cognitive dissonance.

The theory of cognitive dissonance has been widely tested in a large number of experiments. One of the best-known studies was conducted by Leon Festinger and J. Merrill Carlsmith (1959). Students selected as participants were given excruciatingly boring tasks for an hour. After finishing the task, participants were approached by the experimenter and asked for a favor. The experimenter asked if they would serve as research assistants and tell the next "participant" (who was really a confederate of the experimenter) that the task was "very enjoyable" and "fun." In one experimental condition, the person was offered $1 for helping. In the second condition, the person was offered $20. If the person lied to the incoming participant and was paid, he or she was then led to another room and asked about his or her true feelings toward the experimental tasks.

The participants were obviously coaxed into doing something (lying) that was inconsistent with their actual experiences and attitudes. What do you think happened? Most people expect that those who were paid $20 for lying would feel more positive toward the task than would those paid $1. Ironically, the reverse occurred.

Can you explain this? Cognitive dissonance theory is essentially a *drive-reduction theory* (Chapter 12). Just as the discomfort of being hungry motivates us to search for food, the discomfort or tension of cognitive dissonance motivates us to search for ways to eliminate the discrepancy between our behavior and attitudes and the resulting tension. People strive for consistency in their cognitions and behaviors. In the boring task experiment, participants faced a mismatch between their attitude toward the experiment ("That was boring!") and their behavior ("I told another participant it was interesting!"). To relieve the resulting tension, all participants changed their original attitude from boredom to "I enjoyed the task."

Interestingly, participants who were paid $20 changed their attitudes less than those paid $1 because they could readily explain their behavior in terms of the larger payment. ($20 was a considerable amount in the late 1950s.) Being paid well for their actions helped relieve the logical inconsistency (the cognitive dissonance) between what they truly believed about the boring task and what they told others. In contrast, the participants who received $1 had *insufficient justification* for lying to another participant. Thus, they had more cognitive dissonance and stronger motivation to change their attitudes.

Culture and Dissonance

The experience of cognitive dissonance may not be the same in other cultures. It may presume a particular way of thinking about and evaluating the self that is distinctively

Assessment

VISUAL QUIZ

Cognitive Dissonance and Home Buying

This family has just purchased this new home. Using cognitive dissonance theory, can you predict whether they will like this house more or less after they move in?

Tom & Dee Ann McCarthy/Corbis Images

Answer: Moving to a new home involves a great deal of effort and money. Therefore, the family will need to justify their decision. By focusing only on the positives, they will reduce any cognitive dissonance (and increase their liking of their new home).

www.wiley.com/college/huffman

Can you imagine how cognitive dissonance might affect these two teams from differing cultures?

©AP/Wide World Photos

Western. As noted in earlier chapters, North Americans are highly individualistic and independent. For them, making a bad choice or decision has strong, negative effects on self-esteem and results in a greater motivation for attitude change because we believe this bad choice reflects somehow on our worth as an individual.

Asians, on the other hand, tend to be much more collectivist and interdependent. Consequently, they feel more tension over a potential loss of connection with others than with a threat to their individual self-esteem. Research comparing Japanese and other Asian participants with Canadian and U.S. participants supports this position (Choi & Nisbett, 2000; Markus & Kitayama, 1998, 2003).

Assessment

CHECK & REVIEW

Our Thoughts About Others

We explain people's behavior (make **attributions**) by determining whether their actions resulted from internal, dispositional factors (their own traits and motives) or external, situational factors (other people or the environment). Attribution is subject to several forms of error and bias. The **fundamental attribution error** is the tendency to overestimate internal personality influences when judging the behavior of others. When we explain our own behavior, however, we tend to attribute positive outcomes to internal factors and negative outcomes to external causes (the **self-serving bias**).

Attitudes are learned predispositions toward a particular object. Three components of all attitudes are the cognitive responses (thoughts and beliefs), affective responses (feelings), and behavioral tendencies (predispositions to actions). We sometimes change our attitudes because of **cognitive dissonance,** a feeling of discomfort caused by a discrepancy between an attitude and a behavior or between two competing attitudes. This mismatch and resulting tension motivate us to change our attitude or behavior to restore balance.

Questions

1. The principles people follow in making judgments about the causes of events, others' behavior, and their own behavior are known as ___. (a) impression management; (b) stereotaxic determination; (c) attributions; (d) person perception

2. What is the fundamental attribution error?

3. After hearing about the shocking behavior of the soldiers at Abu Ghraib prison, most people strongly believe they would have acted differently. They also easily remember instances in which they have refused to obey others. This may be an example of _____. (a) cognitive illusions; (b) groupthink; (c) the illusion of invulnerability; (d) the self-serving bias

4. According to _____ theory, people are motivated to change their attitudes because of tension created by a mismatch between two or more competing attitudes or between their attitudes and behavior.

Check your answers in Appendix B.

CLICK & REVIEW
for additional assessment options:
www.wiley.com/college/huffman

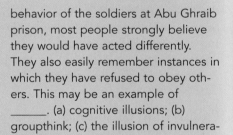

OUR FEELINGS ABOUT OTHERS

Having explored our thoughts about others (attribution and attitudes), we now turn our attention to our feelings about others. We begin by examining the negative feelings (and thoughts and actions) associated with *prejudice* and *discrimination*. We will then explore the generally positive feelings of *interpersonal attraction*.

■ Prejudice and Discrimination: It's the Feeling That Counts

Prejudice, which literally means "prejudgment," is a learned, generally *negative* attitude directed toward specific people solely because of their membership in an identified group. Prejudice is not innate. It is learned. It also creates enormous problems for its victims and limits the perpetrator's ability to accurately judge others and process information.

Positive forms of prejudice do exist, such as "all women love babies" or "African Americans are natural athletes." However, most research and definitions of prejudice focus on the negative forms. (It is also interesting to note that even positive forms of prejudice can be harmful. For example, women might think there must be something wrong with them if they don't like being around babies. Similarly, African Americans might see athletics or entertainment as their only routes to success.)

Like all attitudes, prejudice is composed of three elements: (1) a *cognitive component* or **stereotype**, thoughts and beliefs held about people strictly because of their membership in a group; (2) an *affective component*, consisting of feelings and emotions associated with objects of prejudice; and (3) a *behavioral component*, consisting of predispositions to act in certain ways toward members of the group (**discrimination**).

Although the terms *prejudice* and *discrimination* are often used interchangeably, there is an important difference between them. *Prejudice* refers to an *attitude*. **Discrimination** refers to *action* (Fiske, 1998). Discrimination often results from prejudice, but not always (Figure 16.3). People don't always act on their prejudices.

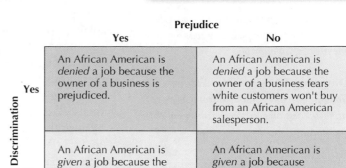
Achievement

What feelings are most important in our social interactions?

	Prejudice	
	Yes	**No**
Discrimination **Yes**	An African American is *denied* a job because the owner of a business is prejudiced.	An African American is *denied* a job because the owner of a business fears white customers won't buy from an African American salesperson.
No	An African American is *given* a job because the owner of a business hopes to attract African-American customers.	An African American is *given* a job because he or she is the best suited for it.

Figure 16.3 *Prejudice and discrimination.* Note how prejudice can exist without discrimination and vice versa. The only condition in this example without prejudice or discrimination is when someone is given a job simply because he or she is the best candidate.

Major Sources of Prejudice and Discrimination

How do prejudice and discrimination originate? Why do they persist? As we explore these questions, you may find your values and beliefs challenged. Use this opportunity to apply your highest critical thinking skills to evaluate your attitudes. We will look at the four most commonly cited sources of prejudice: *learning, mental shortcuts, economic and political competition,* and *displaced aggression.*

1. ***Prejudice as a learned response.*** People learn prejudice in the same way they learn attitudes toward abortion, divorce, or pizza—through classical and operant conditioning and social learning (Chapter 6). Children often watch TV and movies and read books and magazines that portray minorities and women in demeaning and stereotypical roles. Through these stereotypical portrayals they learn that such images must be acceptable. Similarly, when children hear their parents, friends, and teachers expressing prejudice, they imitate them. Exposure of this kind initiates and reinforces the learning of prejudice (Anderson & Hamilton, 2005; Bennett et al., 2004; Blaine & McElroy, 2002; Neto & Furnham, 2005).

People also learn their prejudices through direct experience. They derogate

Prejudice *A learned, generally negative, attitude toward members of a group; it includes thoughts (stereotypes), feelings, and behavioral tendencies (possible discrimination)*

Stereotype *A set of beliefs about the characteristics of people in a group that is generalized to all group members; also, the cognitive component of prejudice*

Discrimination *Negative behaviors directed at members of a group*

THE FAMILY CIRCUS   By Bil Keane

12-15
©1998 Bil Keane, Inc.
Dist. by Cowles Synd., Inc.

BIL KEANE

"That's the DOLL aisle, Daddy. Somebody might see us!"

©Bill Keane, Inc. Reprinted with special permission of King Features Syndicate.

others and experience a rise in their own self-esteem (Fein & Spencer, 1997; Plummer, 2001). In addition, they receive attention, and sometimes approval, for expressing racist or sexist remarks. Finally, people may have a single negative experience with a specific member of a group that they then generalize and apply to all members of the group (Vidmar, 1997).

2. *Prejudice as a mental shortcut.* According to some researchers, prejudice develops from stereotyping, normal thought processes, and everyday attempts to explain a complex social world (Kulik, 2005; Philipsen, 2003). Stereotypes (the cognitive component of prejudice) are a by-product of how we cognitively simplify the world through categorization. Stereotyping allows us to make quick judgments about others, thus freeing our mental resources for other activities.

Biologists classify all living things into categories, and mental health professionals classify mental disorders in the *DSM-IV-TR* (see Chapter 14). In a similar way, people use stereotypes to classify others by membership in a specific group ("jocks," "Mexicans," "chicks," and so on). Because people generally classify themselves as part of the preferred group, they also create ingroups and outgroups. An *ingroup* is any category that people see themselves belonging to. An *outgroup* consists of all others. People tend to see ingroup members as being more attractive, having better personalities, and engaging in more socially accepted forms of behavior than outgroup members. In other words, they practice **ingroup favoritism** (Aboud, 2003; Bennett et al., 2004). In addition to ingroup favoritism, people tend to see more diversity among members of their own ingroup and less among the outgroup (Carpenter & Radhakrisknan, 2002; Guinote & Fiske, 2003). This "they all look alike to me" tendency is termed the **outgroup homogeneity effect.**

Outgroup homogeneity bias can be particularly dangerous. When members of minority groups are not perceived as varied and complex individuals who have the same needs and feelings as the dominant group, it is easier to perceive them as faceless objects and treat them in discriminatory ways. During the Vietnam War, for example, Asians were labeled "gooks" for whom "life is cheap." Facelessness made it easier to kill large numbers of Vietnamese civilians (Johnson, 1999).

3. *Prejudice as the result of economic and political competition*. Other theorists think prejudice develops out of competition for limited resources. And it is maintained because it offers significant economic and political advantages to the dominant group (Esses et al., 2001; Pettigrew, 1998). The competition for resources idea is supported by findings that lower-class whites in the United States have more racist attitudes than higher-class whites. It may be that the upper class can afford to be less prejudiced because minorities represent less threat to their employment, status, and income. In addition, prejudice is maintained because it serves a function—protecting the interests of the dominant class. The stereotype that blacks are inferior to whites, for example, helps justify a social order in the United States where whites hold disproportionate power (Conyers, 2002).

4. *Prejudice as a form of displaced aggression.* Have you ever wondered why lower-class groups tend to blame each other rather than the upper class or the socioeconomic class system itself? As you will see in the section on aggression, frustration often leads people to attack the source of frustration. But when the source is bigger and capable of retaliating, or when the cause of the frustration is ambiguous, people often displace their aggression on an alternative, nonthreatening target. The innocent victim of displaced aggression is known as a *scapegoat* (Dervin, 2002; Poppe, 2001). There is strong historical evidence for the power of scapegoating. During the Great Depression of the 1930s, Hitler used Jews as scapegoats that Germans could blame for their economic troubles. If it is true that a picture is worth a thousand words, then the

Ingroup Favoritism *Viewing members of the ingroup more positively than members of an outgroup*

Outgroup Homogeneity Effect *Judging members of an outgroup as more alike and less diverse than members of the ingroup*

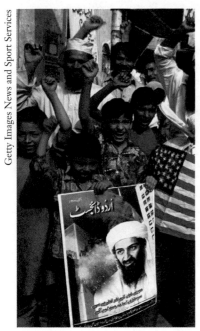

Getty Images News and Sport Services

Prejudice and war. *This group is supporting Osama Bin Laden and demonstrating against the United States. How would you explain their loyalty to Bin Laden and prejudice against Americans?*

(a)

©AP/Wide World Photos

(b)

Granger Collection

(c)

Anthony Njuguna/Reuters/Corbis

Figure 16.4 *The price of prejudice.* Here are several examples of atrocities associated with prejudice: (a) the Holocaust, when millions of Jews, and other minorities, were exterminated by the Nazis, (b) slavery in the United States, where Africans were bought and sold as slaves, and (c) recent acts of genocide in Sudan, where thousands have been slaughtered.

photos in Figure 16.4 speak volumes about the atrocities resulting from displaced aggression, prejudice, and discrimination.

Understanding the causes of prejudice is only the first step in overcoming it. At the close of the chapter, we will consider several interesting and effective ways psychologists have developed to reduce prejudice, a learned attitude that is so harmful to the human race.

Interpersonal Attraction: Why We Like and Love Others

Stop for a moment and think about someone you like very much. Now picture someone you really dislike. Can you explain your feelings? Social psychologists use the term **interpersonal attraction** to refer to the degree of positive feelings toward another. Attraction accounts for a variety of social experiences—admiration, liking, friendship, intimacy, lust, and love. In this section, we will discuss several factors that explain interpersonal attraction.

Interpersonal Attraction *Positive feelings toward another*

Three Key Factors in Attraction—Physical Attractiveness, Proximity, and Similarity

Social psychologists have identified three compelling factors in interpersonal attraction—*physical attractiveness*, *proximity*, and *similarity*. Physical attractiveness and proximity are most influential in the beginning stages of relationships. However, similarity is more important in maintaining long-term relationships.

Physical Attractiveness   Can you remember what first attracted you to your best friend or romantic partner? Was it his or her warm personality, sharp intelligence, or great sense of humor? Or was it looks? Research consistently shows that *physical attractiveness* (size, shape, facial characteristics, and manner of dress) is one of the most important factors in our initial liking or loving of others (Buss, 2003, 2005; Buunk et al., 2002; Li et al., 2002; Sprecher & Regan, 2002; Waynforth, 2001).

Like it or not, attractive individuals are seen by both men and women as more poised, interesting, cooperative, achieving, sociable, independent, intelligent, healthy, and sexually warm (Fink & Penton-Voak, 2002; Langlois et al., 2000; Watkins & Johnston, 2000; Zebrowitz et al., 2002). Perhaps even more distressing, premature infants who are rated as physically more attractive by nurses caring for them thrive

www.wiley.com/college/huffman

better during their hospital stay. They gain more weight and are released earlier than infants perceived as less attractive, presumably because they receive more nurturing (Badr & Abdallah, 2001). In another study comparing actual court cases, researchers found that judges gave longer prison sentences to unattractive than to attractive defendants—even when they were convicted of comparable crimes (Stewart, 1985).

Gender & Cultural Diversity

Is Beauty in the Eye of the Beholder?

If you found the previous list of advantages of physical attractiveness unnerving, you'll be even more surprised to know that some research also shows that judgments of attractiveness appear consistent across cultures. For example, in 37 cultures around the world, women are judged more beautiful if they are youthful in appearance (Buss, 1989, 1999, 2003, 2005; Cunningham, Roberts, Barbee, Druen, & Wu, 1995; Langlois et al., 2000; Rossano, 2003). In these same studies, male attractiveness is judged more on maturity and financial resources.

Culture and attraction. *Which of these women do you find most attractive? Can you see how your cultural background might train you to prefer one look to the others?*

How can this be so universally true? Evolutionary psychologists would suggest that both men and women prefer attractive people because good looks generally indicate good health, sound genes, and high fertility. For example, facial and body symmetry appear to be key elements in attractiveness (Fink et al., 2004; Gangestad & Thornhill, 2003), and symmetry seems to be correlated with genetic health. The fact that across cultures men prefer youthful appearing women is reportedly because this is a sign of their future fertility. Similarly, women prefer men with maturity and financial resources because the responsibility of rearing and nurturing children more often falls on women's shoulders. Therefore, they prefer mature men "who will stick around" and men with greater resources to invest in children.

In contrast to this seeming universal agreement on standards of attractiveness, evidence also exists that beauty is in "the eye of the beholder." What we judge as beautiful varies somewhat from era to era and culture to culture. For example, the Chinese once practiced foot binding because small feet were considered beautiful in women. All the toes except the big one were bent under a young girl's foot and into the sole. The physical distortion made it almost impossible for her to walk. And she suffered excruciating pain, chronic bleeding, and frequent infections throughout her life (Dworkin, 1974). Even in modern times, cultural demands for attractiveness encourage an increasing number of women (and men) to undergo expensive and often painful surgery to *increase* the size of their eyes, breasts, lips, chest, and penis. They also undergo surgery to *decrease* the size of their nose, ears, chin, stomach, hips, and thighs (Atkins, 2000; Etcoff, 1999).

Given that only a small percentage of people are as attractive as Cameron Diaz or Denzel Washington or have the money (or inclination) for extensive cosmetic surgery, how do the rest of us ever find mates? The good news is that perceived attractiveness for *known* people, in contrast to *unknown* people, is strongly influenced by nonphysical traits (Kniffin & Wilson, 2004). This means that traits like respect and familiarity increase our judgments of beauty in friends and family. Also, what people judge as "ideally attractive" may be quite different from what they eventually choose for a mate. According to the *matching hypothesis*, men and women of approximately equal physical attractiveness tend to select each other as partners (Reagan, 1998; Sprecher & Regan, 2002). Further good news, as you will see in the following application section, is that *flirting* offers a "simple" way to increase attractiveness.

Application
APPLYING PSYCHOLOGY TO RELATIONSHIPS

The Art and Science of Flirting

Picture yourself watching a man (Tom) and woman (Kaleesha) at a singles' bar.

> As Tom approaches the table, Kaleesha sits up straighter, smiles, and touches her hair. Tom asks her to dance. Kaleesha quickly nods and stands up while smoothing her skirt. During the dance, she smiles and sometimes glances at him from under her lashes. When the dance finishes, Kaleesha waits for Tom to escort her back to her chair. She motions him to sit in the adjacent chair, and they engage in a lively conversation. Kaleesha allows her leg to briefly graze his. When Tom reaches for popcorn from the basket in front of Kaleesha, she playfully pulls it away. This surprises Tom, and he frowns at Kaleesha. She quickly turns away and starts talking to her friends. Despite his repeated attempts to talk to her, Kaleesha ignores him.

What happened? Did you recognize Kaleesha's sexual signals? Did you understand why she turned away at the end? If so, you are skilled in the art and science of flirting. If not, you may be very interested in the work of Monica Moore at the University of Missouri (1998). Moore is a scientist interested in describing and understanding flirting and the role it plays in human courtship. She has observed and recorded many scenes—in singles' bars and shopping malls—like the one with Tom and Kaleesha. Although she prefers the term *nonverbal courtship signaling*, what Moore and her colleagues have spent thousands of hours secretly observing is *flirting*.

Charles Gupton/Stock, Boston

From these naturalistic observations, we know a great deal more about what works, and doesn't work, in courtship. First of all, both men and women flirt. But women generally initiate a courtship. The woman signals her interest with glances that may be brief and darting, or direct and sustained. Interested women often smile at the same time they gesture with their hands—often with an open or extended palm. Primping (adjusting clothing or patting hair) is also common. A flirting woman will also make herself more noticeable by sitting straighter, with stomach pulled in and breasts pushed out.

Once contact is made and the couple is dancing or sitting at a table, Moore noticed the woman increases the level of flirting. She orients her body toward his, whispers in his ear, and frequently nods and smiles in response to his conversation. Most significant, she touches the man or allows the man to touch her. Like Kaleesha with Tom, allowing her leg to graze his is a powerful indication of her interest.

Women also use play behaviors to flirt. They tease, mock-hit, and tell jokes. They do this to inject humor, while also testing the man's receptivity to humor. As in the case of Tom's reaction to the popcorn tease, when a man doesn't appreciate the playfulness, a woman often uses rejection signals to cool or end the relationship. Other studies confirm Moore's description of women's nonverbal sexual signaling (Lott, 2000).

Now that you know what to look for, watch for flirting behavior in others—or perhaps in your own life. According to Moore and other researchers, flirting may be the single most important thing a woman can do to increase her attractiveness. Because the burden of making the first approach is usually the man's, men are understandably cautious and uncomfortable. They generally welcome a woman clearly signaling her interest.

Two cautions are in order. First, signaling interest does not mean that the woman is ready to have sex with the man. She flirts because she wants to get to know the man better. She'll later decide whether she wants to develop a relationship (Allgeier & Allgeier, 2000). Second, Moore reminds women to "use their enhanced flirting skills only when genuinely interested" (1997, p. 69). Flirting should be reserved for times when you genuinely want to attract and keep the attention of a particular partner.

Proximity   Attraction also depends on people being in the same place at the same time. Thus, **proximity**, or geographic nearness, is another major factor in attraction. A study of friendship in college dormitories found that the person next door was more often liked than the person two doors away, the person two doors away was liked more than someone three doors away, and so on (Priest & Sawyer, 1967).

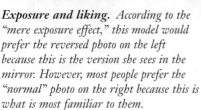

Proximity *Attraction based on geographic closeness*

Why is proximity so important? It's largely because of *mere exposure*. Just as familiar people become more physically attractive over time, repeated exposure also increases overall liking (Monin, 2003; Rhodes, Halberstadt, & Brajkovich, 2001; Rossanom, 2003). This makes sense from an evolutionary point of view. Things we have seen before are less likely to pose a threat than novel stimuli. It also explains why modern advertisers tend to run highly redundant ad campaigns with familiar faces and jingles (Zajonc, 1968, 1998). Repeated exposure increases our liking—and purchases.

We even like *ourselves* better when we see ourselves in a familiar way. When researchers showed college students pictures of themselves or reversed photos (the mirror image), students strongly preferred the reversed photos. They liked the image they were used to seeing in the mirror! Close friends of the same students preferred the regular photos of their friend. They were used to seeing this image (Mita, Dermer, & Knight, 1977). (This also explains why people often complain that photos of themselves "never really look like them!")

Bernhard Kuhmsted/Retna

Exposure and liking. *According to the "mere exposure effect," this model would prefer the reversed photo on the left because this is the version she sees in the mirror. However, most people prefer the "normal" photo on the right because this is what is most familiar to them.*

One caution: Repeated exposure to a *negative* stimulus can *decrease* attraction, as evidenced by the high number of negative political ads. Politicians have learned that repeatedly running an attack ad associating an opposing candidate with negative cues (like increased taxes) decreases the viewers' liking of the opponent. On the other hand, running ads showing themselves in a positive light (kissing babies, helping flood victims) helps build positive associations and increased liking.

Similarity   Once we've had repeated opportunity to get to know someone through simple physical proximity, and assuming we find him or her attractive, we then need something to hold the relationship together over time. The major cementing factor for long-term relationships, whether liking or loving, is *similarity*. We tend to prefer, and stay with, people (and organizations) who are most like us, those who share our ethnic background, social class, interests, and attitudes (Chen & Kenrick, 2002; Peretti & Abplanalp, 2004; Wakimoto & Fujihara, 2004). In other words, "Birds of a feather flock together."

What about the old saying "opposites attract"? It does seem that this bit of common folklore is contradictory. But the term *opposites* here probably refers to personality traits rather than to social background or values. An attraction to a seemingly opposite person is more often based on the recognition that in one or two important areas that person offers something we lack (Dryer & Horowitz, 1997). If you are a talkative and outgoing person, for example, your friendship with a quiet and reserved individual may endure because each of you provides important resources for the other. Psychologists refer to this as **need complementarity**, as compared with the **need**

Need Complementarity *Attraction toward those with qualities we admire but personally lack*

Reprinted with special permission of King Features Syndicate.

Based on your reading of this section, can you explain what is wrong with Kvack's love for the wooden dummy?

Answer: Research shows that similarity is the best predictor of long-term relationships. As shown here, however, many people ignore dissimilarities and hope that their chosen partner will change over time.

compatibility represented by similarity. In sum, lovers can enjoy some differences, but the more alike people are, the more their liking endures (Byrne, 1971).

Need Compatibility *Attraction based on sharing similar needs*

Loving Others

To complete our discussion of interpersonal attraction, we will explore three perspectives on the mystery of love: liking versus loving, romantic love, and companionate love.

Liking Versus Loving   Because love relationships often develop from friendships and initial feelings of liking for one another, Zick Rubin (1970, 1992) developed two paper-and-pencil tests to explore the relationship between liking and loving (Table 16.1).

In spite of the apparent simplicity of Rubin's scales, they have proven to be useful indicators of both liking and loving. For example, Rubin hypothesized that "strong love" couples would spend more time gazing into one another's eyes than "weak love" couples. To test his hypothesis, while the couples were waiting for the experiment to begin, Rubin and his assistants secretly recorded the actual amount of eye contact between all couples. As predicted, couples who scored highest on the love scale also spent more time looking into one another's eyes. In addition, Rubin found that both partners tended to match each other on their love scores. But women liked their dating partners significantly more than they were liked in return.

TABLE 16.1 SAMPLE ITEMS FROM RUBIN'S LIKING AND LOVING TEST

Love Scale
1. I feel that I can confide in _____ about virtually everything.
2. I would do almost anything for _____.
3. If I could never be with _____, I would feel miserable.

Liking Scale
1. I think that _____ is unusually well adjusted.
2. I would highly recommend _____ for a responsible job.
3. In my opinion, _____ is an exceptionally mature person.

Source: Rubin, Z. (1970). "Measurement of romantic love," *Journal of Personality and Social Psychology, 16,* 265–273. Copyright © 1970 by the American Psychological Association. Reprinted by permission of the author.

www.wiley.com/college/huffman

How does love differ from liking on Rubin's scales? Rubin found that liking involves a favorable evaluation of another, as reflected in greater feelings of admiration and respect. He found that love is more intense than liking. And that love is composed of three basic elements:

- *Caring*, the desire to help the other person, particularly when help is needed

- *Attachment*, the need to be with the other person

- *Intimacy*, a sense of empathy and trust that comes from close communication and self-disclosure to and from another

Romantic Love   When you think of romantic love, do you think of falling in love, a magical experience that puts you on cloud nine? **Romantic love**, also called *passionate love* or *limerence*, has been defined as "any intense attraction that involves the idealization of the other, within an erotic context, with the expectation of enduring for some time in the future" (Jankowiak, 1997, p. 8).

Romantic love has intrigued people throughout history. Its intense joys and sorrows have also inspired countless poems, novels, movies, and songs around the world. A cross-cultural study by anthropologists William Jankowiak and Edward Fischer found romantic love in 147 of the 166 societies they studied. The researchers concluded that "romantic love constitutes a human universal or, at the least, a near universal" (1992, p. 154).

Problems with Romantic Love   Romantic love may be almost universal, but it's not problem free. First, romantic love is typically short lived. Even in the most devoted couples, the intense attraction and excitement generally begin to fade after 6 to 30 months (Hatfield & Rapson, 1996; Livingston, 1999). Although this research finding may disappoint you, as a critical thinker do you really think any emotion of this intensity could last forever? What would happen if other intense emotions, such as anger or joy, were eternal? Moreover, given the time-consuming nature of romantic love, what would happen to other parts of our lives, such as school, career, and family?

Another major problem with romantic love is that it is largely based on mystery and fantasy. People fall in love with others not necessarily as they are but as they want them to be (Fletcher & Simpson, 2000; Levine, 2001). What happens to these illusions when we are faced with everyday interactions and long-term exposure? Our "beautiful princess" isn't supposed to snore. And our "knight in shining armor" doesn't look very knightly flossing his teeth. And, of course, no princess or knight would ever notice our shortcomings, let alone comment on them.

Is there any way to keep love alive? If you mean romantic love, one of the best ways to fan the flames is through some form of frustration that keeps you from fulfilling your desire for the presence of your love. Researchers have found that this type of interference (for example, the parents in Shakespeare's *Romeo and Juliet*) often increases the feelings of love (Driscoll, Davis, & Lipetz, 1972).

Because romantic love depends on uncertainty and fantasy, it can also be kept alive by situations in which we never really get to know the other person. This may explain why computer chat room romances or old high school sweethearts have such a tug on our emotions. Because we never really get to test these relationships, we can always fantasize about what might have been.

One of the most constructive ways of keeping romantic love alive is to recognize its fragile nature and nurture it with carefully planned surprises, flirting, flattery, and special dinners and celebrations. In the long run, however, romantic love's most important function might be to keep us attached long enough to move on to companionate love.

Romantic Love *Intense feeling of attraction to another within an erotic context and with future expectations*

Symbols of romantic love? *Do you consider this a romantic gesture? How might other cultures signal their attraction and love for one another?*

Companionate Love **Companionate love** is based on admiration and respect, combined with deep feelings of caring for the person and commitment to the relationship. Studies of close friendships show that satisfaction grows with time as we come to recognize the value of companionship and of having an intimate confidante (Kim & Hatfield, 2004). Unlike romantic love, which is very short lived, companionate love seems to grow stronger with time and often lasts a lifetime (Figure 16.5).

Companionate love is what we feel for our best friends. It also is the best bet for a strong and lasting marriage. But finding and keeping a long-term companionate love is no easy task. Many of our expectations for love are based on romantic fantasies and unconscious programming from fairy tales and TV shows in which everyone lives happily ever after. Therefore, we are often ill equipped to deal with the hassles and boredom that come with any long-term relationship.

One tip for maintaining companionate love is to *overlook each other's faults.* Studies of both dating and married couples find that people report greater satisfaction with—and stay longer in—relationships where they have a somewhat idealized or unrealistically positive perception of their partner (Campbell et al., 2001; Fletcher & Simpson, 2000). This makes sense in light of research on cognitive dissonance (discussed earlier). Idealizing our mates allows us to believe we have a good deal—and hence avoids the cognitive dissonance that might naturally arise every time we saw an attractive alternative. As Benjamin Franklin wisely put it, "Keep your eyes wide open before marriage, half shut afterwards."

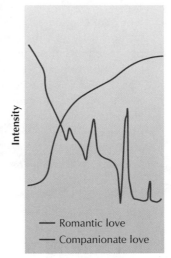

Companionate Love *Strong and lasting attraction characterized by trust, caring, tolerance, and friendship*

Intensity

—— Romantic love
—— Companionate love

Years of relationship

Figure 16.5 *Love over the life span.* Romantic love is high in the beginning of a relationship but tends to diminish over time, with periodic resurgences or "spikes." Companionate love usually increases over time.

Karen Huffman

The benefits of companionate love. *This couple just celebrated their 60th wedding anniversary. Unlike romantic love, which rarely lasts longer than 6 to 30 months, companionate love can last a lifetime.*

Assessment

CHECK & REVIEW

Our Feelings About Others

Prejudice is a generally negative attitude directed toward specific people because of their membership in an identified group. It contains all three components of attitudes—cognitive, affective, and behavioral. (The cognitive component is also known as **stereotypes.**)

Discrimination is not the same as prejudice. It refers to actual negative behaviors directed at members of a group. People do not always act on their prejudices.

The four major sources of prejudice are learning (classical and operant conditioning and social learning), mental shortcuts

(categorization), economic and political competition, and displaced aggression (scapegoating). When using mental shortcuts, people view members of their ingroup more positively than members of the outgroup (**ingroup favoritism**) and see less diversity in the outgroup (**outgroup homogeneity effect**).

Physical attractiveness is very important to **interpersonal attraction.** Physically attractive people are often perceived as more intelligent, sociable, and interesting than less attractive people. Physical **proximity** also increases one's attractiveness. If you live near someone or work alongside someone, you are more likely to like that person. Although people commonly

believe that "opposites attract" (**need complementarity**), research shows that similarity (**need compatibility**) is a much more important factor in maintaining long-term relationships.

Love can be defined in terms of caring, attachment, and intimacy. **Romantic love** is highly valued in our society. However, because it is based on mystery and fantasy, it is hard to sustain. **Companionate love** relies on mutual trust, respect, and friendship and seems to grow stronger with time.

Questions

1. Explain how prejudice differs from discrimination.

2. Saying that members of another ethnic group "all look alike to me" may be an example of _____. (a) ingroup favoritism; (b) the outgroup homogeneity effect; (c) outgroup negativism; (d) ingroup bias

3. Cross-cultural research on physical attractiveness has found all but one of the following. (a) The Chinese once practiced foot binding because small feet were considered attractive in women. (b) Across most cultures, men prefer youthful appearing women. (c) In most Eastern cultures, men prefer women with power and financial status over beauty. (d) For men, maturity and financial resources are more important than appearance in their ability to attract a mate.

4. Compare the dangers associated with romantic love with the benefits of companionate love.

Check your answers in Appendix B.

CLICK & REVIEW
for additional assessment options:
www.wiley.com/college/huffman

OUR ACTIONS TOWARD OTHERS

Achievement

How do our actions toward others affect their lives and our own?

Having just completed our whirlwind examination of how our thoughts and emotions influence others—and vice versa—we turn to topics associated with actions toward others. We begin with a look at social influence (conformity and obedience) and then continue with group processes (membership and decision making). We conclude by exploring two opposite kinds of behavior—aggression and altruism.

Social Influence: Conformity and Obedience

The society and culture into which we are born influence us from the moment of birth until the moment of death. Our culture teaches us to believe certain things, feel certain ways, and act in accordance with these beliefs and feelings. These influences are so strong and so much a part of who we are that we rarely recognize them. Just as a fish doesn't know it's in water, we are largely unaware of the strong impact cultural and social factors have on all our behaviors. In this section, we will discuss two kinds of *social influence:* conformity and obedience.

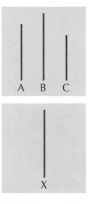

Figure 16.6 *Solomon Asch's study of conformity.* Participants were shown four lines such as these and then asked which line (A, B, or C) was most similar to the one on the bottom (X).

Conformity—Going Along with Others

Imagine for a moment that you have volunteered for a psychology experiment on perception. You find yourself seated around a table with six other students. You are all shown a card with three lines labeled A, B, and C, as in Figure 16.6. You are then asked to select the line that is closest in length to a fourth line, X. Each of you is asked to state your choice out loud, in order, around the table. At first, everyone agrees on the correct line, and the experiment seems pretty boring. On the third trial, however, the first participant gives what is obviously a wrong answer. You know that line B is correct, but he says line A. When the second, third, fourth, and fifth participants also say line A, you really start to wonder: "What's going on here? Are they blind? Or am I?"

What do you think you would do at this point in the experiment? Would you stick with your convictions and say line B, regardless of what the others have answered? Or would you go along with the group? In the original version of this experiment, conducted by Solomon Asch (1951), six participants were actually confederates of the experimenter. And seating was arranged so that the one participant who was the real subject was always in the next-to-last position. The six confederates were instructed ahead of time to respond incorrectly on the third trial and selected later trials. This setup was designed to test the participant's degree of **conformity**, or changing one's behavior because of real or imagined group pressure.

Conformity *Changing behavior because of real or imagined group pressure*

How did Asch's participants respond? More than one-third conformed and agreed with the group's obviously incorrect choice. This level of conformity is particularly intriguing when it is compared with responses in the control group. Partici-

Conformity in action? What's "in" during the latest fashion trends changes dramatically over the years. But note how both groups from different eras generally conform to their group's overall "dress code."

pants in this group experienced no group pressure and made the correct choice virtually 100 percent of the time. Asch's study has been conducted dozens of times, in at least 17 countries, and always with similar results (Bond & Smith, 1996).

Why would so many people conform? To the onlooker, conformity is often difficult to understand. And even the conformer sometimes has a hard time explaining his or her behavior. We can better understand Asch's participants and our own forms of conformity if we look at three factors: (1) *normative social influence*, (2) *informational social influence*, and (3) the role of *reference groups*.

Normative Social Influence The first factor, **normative social influence**, refers to conformity to group pressure out of a need for approval and acceptance by the group. A **norm** is a cultural rule for behavior prescribing what is acceptable in a given situation. Norms are society's definition of how we "should" behave. They are sometimes explicit. But most often norms are quite subtle and implicit. Have you ever asked what others are wearing to the party or watched your neighbor's table manners to be sure you pick up the right fork? Such behavior reflects your desire to conform and the power of normative social influence.

An important norm that we conform to in every culture is *personal space* (Axtell, 1998; Hall, 1966, 1983; Sommer, 1969). If someone invades the invisible "personal bubble" that we like to maintain around our bodies, we generally feel very uncomfortable. Imagine yourself as the typical American traveling in several Middle Eastern countries. How would you respond when a local citizen answers your question while standing close enough that you can feel his or her breath? Most Americans, Canadians, and Northern Europeans feel very uncomfortable at this distance (unless talking with a lover). But most Middle Easterners like to be close enough to "read" one another's eyes. If you "naturally" back away during the conversation, the Middle Easterner might think you are cold and standoffish. Sadly, at the same time you might consider him or her rude and intrusive.

Why do some people like to stand closer than others do? There are a number of possible explanations. First, culture and socialization have a lot to do with personal space. For example, people from Mediterranean, Muslim, and Latin American countries tend to maintain smaller interpersonal distances than do North Americans and Northern Europeans (Axtell, 1998; Steinhart, 1986). Children also tend to stand very close to others until they are socialized to recognize and maintain a greater personal distance. In addition, certain relationships, situations, and personalities affect inter-

Normative Social Influence *Conforming to group pressure out of a need for approval and acceptance*

Norm *Cultural rule of behavior prescribing what is acceptable in a given situation*

Testing Personal Space

If you want to personally experience the power of social norms, approach a fellow student on campus and ask for directions to the bookstore, library, or some other landmark. As you are talking, move toward the person until you invade his or her personal space. You should be close enough to almost touch toes. How does the person respond? How do you feel? Now repeat the process with another student. This time try standing 5 to 6 feet away while asking directions. Which procedure was most difficult for you? Most people think this will be a fun assignment. However, they often find it extremely difficult to willingly break our culture's unwritten norms for personal space.

personal distances. Friends stand closer than strangers, women tend to stand closer than men, and violent prisoners prefer approximately three times the personal space of nonviolent prisoners (Axtell, 1998; Gilmour & Walkey, 1981; Roques, Lambin, Jeunier, & Strayer, 1997).

Informational Social Influence Have you ever bought a specific brand of ski equipment or automobile simply because of a friend's recommendation? You may have conformed because you hoped to gain the friend's approval (*normative social influence*). But in this particular case, you probably conformed because you assumed your friend had more information than you did. Given that participants in Asch's experiment observed all the other participants give unanimous decisions on the length of the lines, they also may have conformed because they believed the others had more information. Conforming out of a need for information or direction is known as **informational social influence.**

Reference Groups Have you wondered why movie or sports stars are paid millions of dollars to endorse their products? Advertisers know that consumers are more likely to buy these endorsed products because we tend to conform more to our **reference groups**—people we like, admire, or want to resemble. Lots of people want to be as admired as Lance Armstrong, as cool as Wesley Snipes, or as beautiful as Jennifer Lopez. But we also have other important reference groups, including family, friends, parents, spouses, teachers, religious leaders, and so on.

Informational Social Influence
Conforming because of a need for information and direction

Reference Groups *People we conform to, or go along with, because we like and admire them and want to be like them*

Obedience *Following direct commands, usually from an authority figure*

Obedience—Going Along with a Command

A second form of social influence, **obedience**, involves going along with a direct command, usually from someone in a position of authority. Under orders from an experimenter, would you shock a man with a known heart condition who is screaming and asking to be released? As you'll see shortly, most people assume that few people would do so. But research shows otherwise.

Stop for a moment and imagine you are one of several people responding to an ad in the local newspaper calling for volunteers for a study on memory. As you arrive at the Yale University laboratory, you are introduced to the experimenter and another participant in the study. The experimenter explains he is studying the effects of punishment on learning and memory. One of you will play the role of the learner and the other will be the teacher. You draw lots. On your paper is written "teacher." The experimenter leads you into a room where he straps the other participant—the "learner"—into an "electric chair" apparatus that looks escape-proof. The experimenter then applies electrode paste to the learner's wrist "to avoid blisters and burns" and attaches an electrode that is connected to a shock generator.

You, the "teacher," are shown into an adjacent room and asked to sit in front of this same shock generator, which is wired through the wall to the chair of the learner. As you can see in Figure 16.7, the shock machine consists of 30 switches. Each switch represents successively higher levels of shock in 15-volt increments. Written labels appear below each group of levers, ranging from Slight Shock to Danger: Severe Shock, all the way to XXX. The experimenter explains it is your job to teach the learner a list of word pairs. And you must punish any errors by administering a shock. With each wrong answer, you are to give a shock one level higher on the shock generator. For example, at the first wrong response, you give a shock of 15 volts; at the second wrong response, 30 volts; and so on.

As the study begins, the learner seems to be having problems with the task. The responses are often wrong. Before long, you are inflicting shocks that must be extremely painful. Indeed, after you administer 150 volts, the learner begins to protest and demands, "Get me out of here. ... I refuse to go on."

You hesitate and wonder what to do. The experimenter asks you to continue. He insists that even if the learner refuses, you must keep increasing the shock levels. But the other person is obviously in pain. What should you do?

Actual participants in this series of studies suffered real conflict and distress when confronted with this problem. The following dialogue took place between the experimenter and one of the "teachers":

TEACHER: I can't stand it. I'm not going to kill that man in there. You hear him hollering?

EXPERIMENTER: As I told you before, the shocks may be painful. But there is no permanent tissue damage.

© 1965 by Stanley Milgram. From the film Obedience, distributed by the New York University Film Library.

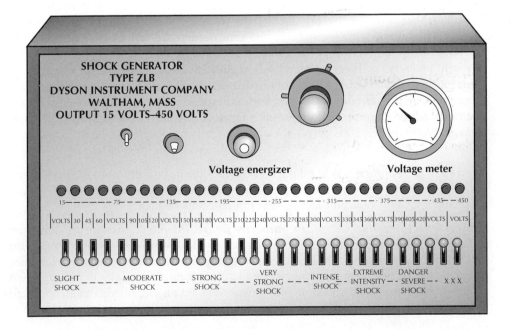

Figure 16.7 *Milgram's shock generator.* Research participants were told to give increasing levels of shocks to someone they had watched being strapped down and connected to this machine. Note how the shock levels are clearly labeled, starting with Slight Shock, moving to Very Strong Shock, Danger: Severe Shock, and ultimately XXX. How would you respond? Would you refuse from the beginning, or would you stop after a few shocks and complaints from the recipient? Would you go all the way to 450 volts?

LEARNER (screaming): Let me out of here, you have no right to keep me here. Let me out of here, let me out, my heart's starting to bother me, let me out! (Teacher shakes head, pats the table nervously.)

TEACHER: You see, he's hollering. Hear that? Gee, I don't know.

EXPERIMENTER: The experiment requires…

TEACHER (interrupting): I know it does, sir, but I mean—huh! He don't know what he's getting in for. He's up to 195 volts!

(Following this exchange, the teacher continues through 210 volts, 225 volts, 240 volts, 255 volts, and 270 volts. At this point the teacher, with evident relief, runs out of word-pair questions.)

EXPERIMENTER: You'll have to go back to the beginning of that page and go through them again until he's learned them all correctly.

TEACHER: Aw, no, I'm not going to kill that man. You mean I've got to keep going up with the scale? No, sir. He's hollering in there. I'm not going to give him 450 volts.

(MILGRAM, 1974, pp. 73–74)

What do you think happened? Did the man continue? This particular "teacher" continued giving shocks—despite the learner's strong protests. He even continued after the learner refused to give any more answers.

As you might have guessed, this research was not about punishment and learning. The psychologist who designed the study, Stanley Milgram, was actually investigating *obedience to authority*. Would participants see the experimenter as an authority figure and obey his prompts and commands to shock another human being? In Milgram's public survey, fewer than 25 percent thought they would go beyond 150 volts. And no respondents predicted they would go past the 300-volt level. Surprisingly, a full *65 percent* of the teacher-participants in this series of studies obeyed completely—going all the way to the end of the scale.

Even Milgram was surprised by his results. When he polled a group of psychiatrists before the study began, they predicted that most people would refuse to go beyond 150 volts. They also predicted that less than 1 percent of those tested would "go all the way." Only someone who was "disturbed and sadistic" would obey to the fullest extent. But as Milgram discovered, most of his participants, both men and women, of all ages and from all walks of life, administered the highest voltage.

Like the stories of the prisoner abuse scandal in Abu Ghraib, many people thought Milgram's findings were just a one-time occurrence with a few "sadistic" individuals. Unfortunately, as we've learned from both Abu Ghraib and Milgram's study, this is not the case. Milgram's study was replicated many times and in many other countries with similarly high levels of obedience. Milgram also replicated his original experiment with a series of follow-up studies designed to identify the specific conditions that either increase or decrease obedience (Blass, 1991, 2000; Meeus & Raaijmakers, 1989; Snyder, 2003).

Factors in Obedience What did Milgram discover in his follow-up studies? Using basically the same setup as the original study, he manipulated several variables and found at least four important factors that influence obedience:

1. *Legitimacy and closeness of the authority figure.* People in positions of authority have an extraordinary, and often underestimated, power to elicit obedience. But this authority figure must be perceived as legitimate and be nearby. As Figure 16.8b shows, when an ordinary person (a "confederate") gave the orders or when the experimenter left the room and gave orders by phone, obedience dropped to about 20 percent.

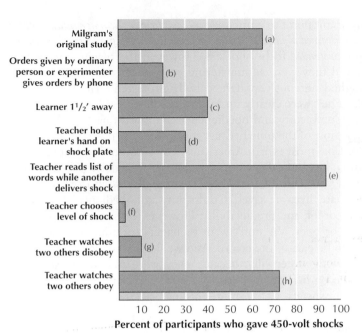

Milgram's original study (a)
Orders given by ordinary person or experimenter gives orders by phone (b)
Learner 1½′ away (c)
Teacher holds learner's hand on shock plate (d)
Teacher reads list of words while another delivers shock (e)
Teacher chooses level of shock (f)
Teacher watches two others disobey (g)
Teacher watches two others obey (h)

10 20 30 40 50 60 70 80 90 100

Percent of participants who gave 450-volt shocks

Figure 16.8 *Participants' response to Milgram's different research conditions.* Milgram conducted a series of studies to discover the specific conditions that either increased or decreased obedience to authority. As you can see in the first bar on the graph (a), 65 percent of the participants in Milgram's original study gave the learner the full 450-volt level of shocks. In the second bar (b), note that when orders came from an ordinary person, and when the experimenter left the room and gave orders by phone, the participants' obedience dropped to 20 percent. Now look at the third and fourth bars (c and d), and note that the remoteness of the victim had an important impact. When the "learner" was only 1½ feet away from the teacher, obedience dropped to 40 percent. And when the teacher had to actually hold the learner's hand on the shock plate, obedience was only 30 percent. Looking at bars (e) and (f), note the dramatic importance of the teacher's level of responsibility. The levels of obedience dropped from 90 percent to 3 percent! Finally, looking at bars (g) and (h), recognize the incredible power of modeling and imitation. When the teachers watched two others disobey, obedience was only 10 percent, but when they watched others follow orders, their own obedience jumped to over 70 percent (Milgram, 1963, 1974).

2. *Remoteness of the victim.* Look again at Figure 16.8(c), (d). Note that when the learner was only 1½ feet from the participant, only 40 percent obeyed fully. And when the teacher-participant was required to force the learner's hand down on a simulated "shock plate," only 30 percent followed orders. Can you see how these results relate to some aspects of modern warfare? Think how much harder it might be to obey a military command to directly stab and kill one person, compared to the "ease" of dropping a bomb from a high-flying airplane that might kill thousands. Or think how many more prisoners in Abu Ghraib might have been abused if the abuser only had to push a button rather than engage in direct physical contact.

3. *Assignment of responsibility.* Research has also found that when participants are reminded that they will be held responsible for any harm to the victim, obedience is sharply reduced (Hamilton, 1978). Note the level of obedience in Figure 16.8(e), (f) when participants were asked to just read the list of words while another teacher delivered the shock. Now compare this to the much lower second condition, when the participant was responsible for choosing the level of shock.

4. *Modeling/imitation.* Watching others either cooperate or rebel also can have a tremendous impact on participant obedience. Look again at Figure 16.8(g), (h). When two confederates (who were acting like teachers) were instructed to either openly rebel and refuse to continue or to fully obey, actual participants copied either the obedient or the disobedient model.

Important Reminders Like students in my on-campus class, you're probably surprised by these findings and, perhaps, upset by the treatment of research participants. Please keep in mind that deception is a necessary part of some research projects. However, the degree of deception and discomfort of the study's participants in Milgram's research is viewed as highly unethical by today's scientific standards. His study would never be undertaken today. On the other hand, Milgram carefully debriefed everyone after the study and followed up with the participants for several months. Most participants reported the experience as being personally informative and valuable.

Chuck Savage/Corbis

The advantages of conformity and obedience. These people willingly stand in long lines knowing that their needs will be met in an orderly and fair manner. Can you imagine what would happen to our everyday social functioning if most people did not go along with the crowd and generally obey orders?

There's another important point to emphasize. *No participant-learner in any part of Milgram's experiments ever received an actual shock.* The learner was an accomplice of the experimenter and simply *pretended* to be shocked. However, the teachers were true participants. They believed they were administering real shocks, and they sweated, trembled, stuttered, laughed nervously, and repeatedly protested that they did not want to hurt the learner. They were clearly upset. *But still they obeyed.*

One final reminder: Conformity and obedience aren't always bad. In fact, most people conform and obey most of the time because it is in their own best interest (and everyone else's) to do so. Like most North Americans, you stand in line at the movie theater instead of pushing ahead of others. And this allows an orderly purchasing of tickets. Similarly, you and your officemates obey the firefighters who order you to evacuate a building. And many lives are saved. Conformity and obedience allow social life to proceed with safety, order, and predictability. However, on some occasions it is important *not* to conform or obey. We don't want teenagers (or adults) engaging in risky sex or drug use just to be part of the crowd. And we don't want soldiers (or anyone else) mindlessly following orders just because they were told to do so by an authority figure. Because recognizing and resisting destructive forms of obedience are particularly important to our society, we'll explore this material in greater depth at the end of this chapter.

Foot-in-the-Door Technique *A first, small request is used as a setup for later, larger requests*

Application

CRITICAL THINKING

When Should We Obey?

One common intellectual illusion that hinders critical thinking about obedience is the belief that only evil people do evil things or that evil announces itself. For example, the experimenter in Stanley Milgram's study looked and acted like a reasonable person who was simply carrying out a research project. Because he was not seen as personally corrupt and evil, the participants' normal moral guard was down and obedience was maximized.

This relaxed moral guard also might explain obedience to a highly respected military officer or the leader of a religious cult. One of the most infamous cult leaders, Jim Jones, was well known and highly revered for his kindness and "good works"—at least in the beginning. Perhaps because of their relaxed moral guard (combined with the four factors discussed earlier), in 1978 over 900 members of the People's Temple in Guyana committed mass suicide on Jones's order. People who resisted were murdered. But the vast majority took their lives willingly by drinking cyanide-laced Kool-Aid.

In addition to a relaxed moral guard, the gradual nature of many obedience situations may explain why so many people were willing to give the maximum shocks in Milgram's study. The initial mild level of shocks may have worked as a **foot-in-the-door technique,** in which a first, small request is used as a setup for later, larger requests. Once Milgram's participants complied with the initial request, they might have felt obligated to continue (Chartrand, Pinckert, & Burger, 1999; Sabini & Silver, 1993).

Take this opportunity to think critically about extreme forms of destructive obedience in your own life. Then compare them to everyday examples like the following. Rank each situation by placing a 1 next to the one you believe is the most ethical act of obedience and a 3 next to the least ethical.

____ Jane is 19 and wants to become a commercial artist. She is offered a scholarship to a good art school, but her parents strongly object to her career choice. After considerable pressure, she gives in and enrolls at

ACTIVE LEARNING

the same engineering school her father attended.

____ Tom is 45 and having serious doubts about his employer's shady business practices, such as double-billing the clients. He believes his boss is dishonest and unethical. But he stays silent and cooperates because he really needs the job.

____ Mary is 20 and a senior in college. She desperately wants to get into a graduate program at a very prestigious school but is failing an important class. The instructor has suggested she could get an A in his course if she would sexually "cooperate." She agrees.

There are no right or wrong answers to your ranking. However, exploring your thinking about others' responses may help you use what you have learned in this chapter about conformity and obedience to clarify situations in your past where you were unethically persuaded—and perhaps prevent future problems.

Assessment

CHECK & REVIEW

Social Influence

The process of social influence teaches important cultural values and behaviors that are essential to successful social living. Two of the most important forms of social influence are conformity and obedience.

Conformity refers to changes in behavior in response to real or imagined pressure from others. People conform for approval and acceptance **(normative social influence)**, out of a need for more information **(informational social influence)**, and to match the behavior of those they admire and feel similar to (their **reference group**). **Obedience** involves giving

in to a command from others. Milgram's study showed that a surprisingly large number of people would obey orders even when another human being is physically threatened.

Conformity and obedience can be maladaptive and destructive. But people also go along with the crowd or obey orders because it is often adaptive to do so.

Questions

1. Explain how conformity differs from obedience.
2. The classic study showing the power of authority on people's behavior was conducted by _____. (a) Zimbardo; (b) Bandura; (c) Asch; (d) Milgram

3. Milgram's participants thought they were participating in an experiment designed to study the effect of _____. (a) obedience to authority; (b) arousal on memory; (c) punishment on learning; (d) electric shock on brain-wave activity
4. What percentage of people in Milgram's study were willing to give the highest level of shock (450 volts)? (a) 45 percent; (b) 90 percent; (c) 65 percent; (d) 10 percent

Check your answers in Appendix B.

CLICK & REVIEW
for additional assessment options:
www.wiley.com/college/huffman

Group Processes: Membership and Decision Making

Have you noticed that you talk and behave differently with your friends than with your parents, your employer, or your roommates? Or have you ever been with friends and done something like a Halloween prank that you would not have done alone? In each situation, your behavior is largely the result of group processes. We seldom recognize the power of group membership, but social psychologists have identified several important ways that groups affect us.

Group Membership

In simple groups, such as couples or families, as well as complex groups, like classes or sports teams, each person generally plays one or more *roles*. These *roles* (or sets of behavioral patterns connected with particular social positions) are specifically spelled out and regulated in some groups (e.g., the different roles of teachers and students). Other roles, like being a parent, are assumed through informal learning and inference.

Roles   How do these roles affect behavior? To explore this question, social psychologist Philip Zimbardo carefully screened 20 well-adjusted young college men from Stanford University. Each student was paid $15 a day for participating in a simulation of prison life (Haney, Banks, & Zimbardo, 1978; Zimbardo, 1993).

To appreciate Zimbardo's prison study, pretend you are one of the 20 college students who volunteered to be a participant. During initial evaluations, you are randomly assigned to play the role of "prisoner." Later, you're watching TV at home when you unexpectedly hear a loud knock. When you open the door, several uniformed police officers take you outside, spread-eagle you against the police car, frisk you, and inform you that you are being arrested. At the police station, you are photographed, fingerprinted, and booked. You are then blindfolded and driven to your final destination—the "Stanford Prison." Here you are given an ID number (in place of your name) and deloused! You are then issued a shapeless gown to wear and a tight nylon cap to conceal your hair—but no underwear. All prisoners are in similar

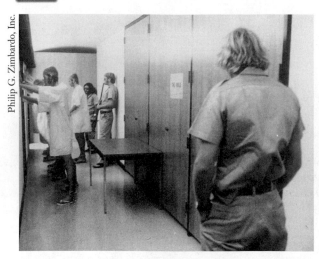

Philip G. Zimbardo, Inc.

Power corrupts. *Zimbardo's prison study showed how the demands of roles and situations could produce dramatic changes in behavior. Can you see the similarities between Zimbardo's study and what happened at the Abu Ghraib prison in Iraq in 2004?*

Deindividuation *Reduced self-consciousness, inhibition, and personal responsibility that sometimes occurs in a group, particularly when the members feel anonymous*

Deindividuation. *In the classic movie To Kill a Mockingbird, a young girl (named Scout) asked one of the angry lynch mob members about his son. Her simple question destroyed the mob's feeling of anonymity and deindividuation. Once this happened, their anger subsided and they slowly (and harmlessly) dispersed.*

The Kobal Collection

prisoner clothes. In contrast, students chosen to be "guards" are provided official-looking guard uniforms, billy clubs, and whistles. You and the other prisoners are then locked in your cells. The guards are given complete control over you and your fellow prisoners. What do you think happened next?

Not even Zimbardo foresaw what actually happened. Some guards turned out to be "good guys" who did little favors for the prisoners and others were "tough but fair." But all guards engaged in some abuse of power. They insisted that prisoners quickly obey all prison rules and willingly accept the guards' arbitrary punishments. The slightest disobedience was followed by degrading tasks (such as cleaning the toilet with bare hands) or the loss of "privileges" (such as eating, sleeping, and washing).

Most prisoners initially responded to the bossing and punishment with good-humored acceptance. But as demands increased and abuses began, they became passive and depressed. Only one prisoner fought back with a hunger strike. His lone act of disobedience ended with his forced feeding by the guards. The stresses were so severe that four prisoners had to be released within the first four days due to their uncontrollable sobbing, fits of rage, severe depression, and, in one case, a psychosomatic rash over the prisoner's entire body.

The original study was planned to last two weeks. But it was stopped after only six days due to alarming psychological changes in *all* participants. The guards were seriously abusing their power, and the traumatized prisoners were becoming progressively more depressed and dehumanized.

Note that this was not a true experiment. It lacked control groups and a clear measure of the dependent variable. However, this simulated prison does offer insights into the potential power of roles on individual behavior. According to interviews conducted after the study, the students apparently became so absorbed in their roles that they forgot they were *volunteers* in a university study (Zimbardo, Ebbeson, & Maslach, 1977). For them the *simulated* roles of prisoner or guard became real—too real.

Although many have criticized the ethics of Zimbardo's study, it alerts us to potentially serious dangers inherent in roles and group membership. Consider the following: If this type of personality disintegration and abuse of power could be generated in a mere six days in a mock prison with fully informed *volunteers*, what happens during life imprisonment, six-year sentences, or even overnight jail stays? Similarly, what might happen when military personnel, who are under tremendous pressure, are put in charge of guarding deadly enemies?

Deindividuation Zimbardo's prison study shows that the roles we play as members of a group can have a powerful effect on behavior. His study also demonstrates an interesting phenomenon called **deindividuation**. To be deindividuated means that you feel less self-conscious, less inhibited, and less personally responsible as a member of a group than when you're alone. This is particularly likely under conditions of anonymity. To increase allegiance and conformity, groups sometimes actively encourage deindividuation, such as by requiring uniforms or masks. Unfortunately, deindividuation sometimes leads to abuses of power, angry mobs, rioters, and tragic consequences like gang rapes, lynchings, and hate crimes (Silke, 2003).

There are also positive forms of deindividuation. We all enjoy being swept along with a crowd's joyous celebration on New Year's Eve and the raucous cheering and shouting during an exciting sports competition. Deindividuation also encourages increased helping behaviors and even heroism, as we will see later in this chapter.

What causes deindividuation? There are several possible explanations. But one of the most compelling is the fact that the simple presence of others tends to increase arousal and generally diminishes our sense of responsibility. Deindividuation is even more extreme and common when group members feel anonymous. For example, in one experiment, women who wore KKK-like disguises that completely covered their faces and bodies delivered twice as much electric shock to a victim than did women who were not disguised and wore large nametags (Zimbardo, 1970). It seems that *anonymity* is a powerful disinhibitor, which also helps explain why Halloween masks seem to increase vandalism and why most crimes and riots occur at night—under the cover of darkness. It is important to emphasize, however, that not everyone in a crowd becomes deindividuated. Some people do resist and do maintain their personal values and beliefs. (Also keep in mind, as in all such experiments, the "victim" was a confederate who did *not* receive actual shocks.)

Group Decision Making

Are two heads truly better than one? Does the presence of others improve decision making? Do juries make better decisions than a judge? There are no simple answers to these questions. To formulate some response, we need to consider how group discussions affect individual opinions (group polarization). We also need to study how group membership affects access to accurate information (groupthink).

Group Polarization Most people assume that group decisions are more conservative, cautious, and "middle of the road" than individual decisions. But is this true? Initial investigations indicated that after discussing an issue, groups actually supported *riskier* decisions than decisions they made as individuals before the discussion (Stoner, 1961).

Partly because it contradicted the common belief about group caution and moderation, this *risky-shift* concept sparked a great deal of research. Subsequent research shows that the risky-shift phenomenon is only part of the picture in group decision making. Some groups do, in fact, make riskier decisions. But others become extremely conservative (Liu & Latané, 1998). Whether the final decision is risky or conservative depends primarily on the dominant preexisting tendencies of the group. That is, as individuals interact and discuss their opinions, their initial positions become more exaggerated. This movement toward one polar extreme or the other is known as **group polarization**.

Why does this happen? The tendency toward group polarization generally results from increased exposure to *persuasive arguments* (Liu & Latané, 1998). People who hear arguments from others are exposed to new information. Because most informal, political, or business groups consist of likeminded individuals, the "new" information generally only reinforces the group's original opinion. Thus, the group's preexisting tendencies are strengthened by the group discussion.

Groupthink Group decision making is often affected by group polarization. But another related and equally dangerous tendency is that of **groupthink**. Irving Janis (1972, 1989) defines *groupthink* as "a mode of thinking that people engage in when they are deeply involved in a cohesive in-group, and when the members' strivings for unanimity override their motivation to realistically appraise alternative courses of action" (p. 9). That is, when groups are strongly cohesive (a family, a panel of military advisers, an athletic team), they generally share a strong desire for agreement (to see themselves as one). This desire may lead them to ignore important information or

John Neubauer/Photoedit

Juries and group polarization. Is group polarization a desirable part of jury deliberation? Yes and no. In an ideal world, attorneys from both sides present the facts of the case. Then, after careful deliberation, the jury moves from its initially neutral position toward the defendant to a more extreme position— either conviction or acquittal. In a not-so-ideal world, the quality of legal arguments from opposing sides may not be equal, the individual members of the jury may not be neutral at the start, and some jurors may unduly influence other jurors.

Group Polarization *Group's movement toward either riskier or more conservative behavior, depending on the members' initial dominant tendency*

Groupthink *Faulty decision making that occurs when a highly cohesive group strives for agreement and avoids inconsistent information*

© Sidney Harris

points of view held by outsiders or critics (Hergovich & Olbrich, 2003; Vaughn, 1996).

As outlined in Figure 16.9, the process of groupthink begins with group members feeling a strong sense of cohesiveness and relative isolation from the judgments of qualified outsiders. Add a directive leader and little chance for debate, and you have the recipe for a potentially dangerous decision. During the actual discussion process, the members also come to believe they are invulnerable, tend to develop common rationalizations and stereotypes of the outgroup, and exert considerable pressure on anyone who dares to offer a dissenting opinion. Some members actually start to play the role of group "mindguards." These mindguards operate like bodyguards to isolate and protect the group from all differences in opinion. The tendency toward groupthink is strongest when members feel threatened and begin to defend their view rather than searching for the best solution.

ESBIN-Anderson/The Image Works

Figure 16.9 *An example of groupthink?* Few people realize that the decision to marry can be a form of groupthink. (Remember that a "group" can have as few as two members.) While dating, the couple may show several of the antecedent conditions (top box). This includes a strong need for cohesiveness ("We agree on almost everything"), insulation from outside influences ("We do almost everything as a couple"), and failure to carefully consider the pros and cons of alternative actions. When planning for marriage, they also sometimes show symptoms of groupthink (middle box). These symptoms include an illusion of invulnerability ("We're different—we won't ever get divorced"), collective rationalizations ("Two can live more cheaply than one"), shared stereotypes of the outgroup ("Couples with problems just don't know how to communicate"), and pressure on dissenters ("If you don't support our decision to marry, we don't want you at the wedding!")

Antecedent Conditions

1 A highly cohesive group of decision makers
2 Insulation of the group from outside influences
3 A directive leader
4 Lack of procedures to ensure careful consideration of the pros and cons of alternative actions
5 High stress from external threats with little hope of finding a better solution than that favored by the leader

Strong desire for group consensus—The groupthink tendency

Symptoms of Groupthink

1 Illusion of invulnerability
2 Belief in the morality of the group
3 Collective rationalizations
4 Stereotypes of outgroups
5 Self-censorship of doubts and dissenting opinions
6 Illusion of unanimity
7 Direct pressure on dissenters

Symptoms of Poor Decision Making

1 An incomplete survey of alternative courses of action
2 An incomplete survey of group objectives
3 Failure to examine risks of the preferred choice
4 Failure to reappraise rejected alternatives
5 Poor search for relevant information
6 Selective bias in processing information
7 Failure to develop contingency plans

Low probability of successful outcome

Presidential errors, such as Franklin Roosevelt's failure to anticipate the attack on Pearl Harbor, John F. Kennedy's disastrous backing of the Bay of Pigs invasion of Cuba, Lyndon Johnson's escalation of the Vietnam War, Richard Nixon's cooperation with the Watergate coverup, and Ronald Reagan's Iran–Contra scandal, have all been blamed on groupthink. It also may have contributed to the 1986 explosion of the space shuttle *Challenger*, the loss in 2003 of *Columbia*, the terrorist attack of 9/11,

©AP/Wide World Photos

Another possible example of group-think? *Two days before the Columbia broke apart in 2003, a NASA engineer warned his supervisors of possible catastrophes on reentry. His message was not forwarded up the chain of command, and all seven astronauts died in the disaster (Schwartz & Broder, 2003).*

and the war in Iraq (Ehrenreich, 2004; Janis, 1972, 1989; Landay & Kuhnehenn, 2004; Schwartz & Broder, 2003). Before the September 11, 2001 attacks on the World Trade Center and the Pentagon, most Americans and many of our leaders believed we were somehow immune from terrorist attacks (illusion of invulnerability). As a critical thinker, can you identify other symptoms of groupthink that might help explain why we were so surprised by the 9/11 attack?

Assessment

CHECK & REVIEW

Group Processes

Group membership affects us through the roles we play. The importance of roles in determining and controlling behavior was dramatically demonstrated in Zimbardo's Stanford Prison Study.

Group membership can also lead to **deindividuation,** a reduced self-consciousness, inhibition, and personal responsibility. **Group polarization** research shows that if most group members initially tend toward an extreme idea, the entire group will polarize in that direction. This is because the like-minded members reinforce the preexisting tendencies. **Groupthink** is a faulty type of thinking that occurs when a highly cohesive group strives for agreement and avoids inconsistent information.

Questions

1. Zimbardo stopped his prison study before the end of the scheduled two weeks because _____.
2. The critical factor in deindividuation is _____. (a) loss of self-esteem; (b) anonymity; (c) identity diffusion; (d) group cohesiveness
3. What are the major symptoms of groupthink?
4. In a groupthink situation, the person who takes responsibility for seeing that dissenting opinions are not expressed is called the _____. (a) censor; (b) mindguard; (c) monitor; (d) whip

Check your answers in Appendix B.

 CLICK & REVIEW
for additional assessment options:
www.wiley.com/college/huffman

Aggression: Explaining and Controlling It

Aggression is any form of behavior intended to harm or injure another living being. Why do people act aggressively? We will explore a number of possible explanations for aggression—both *biological* and *psychosocial*. Then we will look at how aggression can be controlled or reduced.

Aggression *Any behavior intended to harm someone*

Biological Factors in Aggression

1. *Instincts.* Because aggression has such a long history and is found among all cultures, many theorists believe humans are instinctively aggressive. After personally witnessing the massive death and destruction that occurred during World War I, Sigmund Freud stated that aggressive impulses are inborn. He argued that the drive for violence arises from a basic instinct and that, therefore, human aggression cannot be eliminated (Gay, 1999, 2000; Goodwin, 2005).

Najlah Feanny-Hicks/Corbis

Nature or nurture? *From a very early age, Andrew Golden was taught to fire hunting rifles. At the age of 11, he and his friend Mitchell Johnson killed four classmates and a teacher at an elementary school in Jonesboro, Arkansas. Was this tragedy the result of nature or nurture?*

Evolutionary psychologists and *ethologists* (scientists who study animal behavior) propose another instinct theory. They believe that aggression evolved because it contributes to Darwin's survival of the fittest. Freud saw aggression as destructive and disruptive. But ethologists believe aggression prevents overcrowding and allows the strongest animals to win mates and reproduce the species (Dabbs & Dabbs, 2000; Lorenz, 1981; Rossano, 2003). Most social psychologists tend to reject both Freud's and the evolutionary ethological view of instinct as the major source of aggression.

2. *Genes.* Twin studies suggest that some individuals are genetically predisposed to have hostile, irritable temperaments and to engage in aggressive acts (Miles & Carey, 1997; Segal & Bouchard, 2000; Wasserman & Wachbroit, 2000). Remember from Chapter 1, however, that this does not mean that these people are doomed to behave aggressively. Aggression develops from a complex interaction of biology, social forces, and psychological factors within each individual.

3. *The brain and nervous system.* Electrical stimulation or severing specific parts of an animal's brain has a direct effect on aggression (Delgado, 1960; Delville, Mansour, & Ferris, 1996; Roberts & Nagel, 1996). Research with brain injuries and organic disorders has also identified possible aggression circuits in the brain—in particular, the hypothalamus, amygdala, and other parts of the brain (Davidson, Putnam, & Larson, 2000; Raine et al., 1998).

4. *Substance abuse and other mental disorders.* Substance abuse (particularly alcohol) among the general public is a major factor in most forms of aggression—child abuse, spousal assault, robberies, murders, and so on (Badawy, 2003; Gerra et al., 2004; Levinthal, 2006). Homicide rates are also somewhat higher among men with schizophrenia and antisocial disorders, particularly if they also abuse alcohol (Raesaenen et al., 1998; Tiihonen, Isohanni, Rasanen, Koiranen, & Moring, 1997).

5. *Hormones and neurotransmitters.* Several studies have linked the male gonadal hormone testosterone to aggressive behavior (Mong & Pfaff, 2003; O'Connor, Archer, Hair, & Wu, 2002; Trainer, Bird & Marler, 2004). However, the relationship between human aggression and testosterone is complex. Testosterone seems to increase aggression and dominance. But dominance itself increases testosterone (Mazur & Booth, 1998). Violent behavior has also been linked with low levels of the neurotransmitters serotonin and GABA (gamma-aminobutyric acid) (Goveas, Csernansky, & Coccaro, 2004; Halperin et al., 2003).

Psychosocial Factors in Aggression

1. *Aversive stimuli.* Research shows that aversive stimuli such as noise, heat, pain, insults, and foul odors can increase aggression (Anderson, 2001; Anderson, Anderson, Dorr, DeNeve, & Flanagan, 2000; Twenge et al., 2001). Traffic congestion (road rage), cramped airliners (airplane rage), and excessive demands at work (office rage) all reflect another aversive stimulus—*frustration*. Being blocked from achieving a goal increases aggressive tendencies.

John Dollard and his colleagues (1939) noted this relationship between frustration and aggression more than half a century ago. According to the **frustration–aggression hypothesis**, frustration creates anger, which for some may lead to aggression. This does not mean that if you get mad at your boss, you will punch him or her in the nose. You may displace your aggression and take out your anger on your family or friends. Or you may turn your aggression toward yourself, becoming self-destructive or withdrawing, giving up, and becoming depressed.

2. *Culture and learning.* As discussed in Chapter 6, observational or social learning theory suggests that we learn by watching others. Thus, people raised in a culture with aggressive models will learn more aggressive responses (Matsumoto, 2000) and the opposite is also true. In Japan, for example, children are taught very early to value social harmony, and Japan has one of the lowest rates of violence in all industrialized nations (Nisbett, Peng, Choi, & Norenzayan, 2000; Zahn-Waxler, Friedman, Cole, Mizuta, &

Frustration–Aggression Hypothesis *Blocking of a desired goal (frustration) creates anger that may lead to aggression*

Himura, 1996). In contrast, the United States is one of the most violent nations, and our children grow up with numerous models for aggression, which they tend to imitate.

3. *Violent media and video games.* Many believe that violence in movies, TV, and video games is only harmless entertainment. However, considerable evidence exists that media portrayals of violence directly contribute to aggression in both children and adults (Anderson, 2004; Bartholow & Anderson, 2002; Kronenberger et al., 2005; Uhlmann & Swanson, 2004). For example, video games such as *Grand Theft Auto*, *Mortal Kombat*, and *Half-Life* all feature realistic sound effects and gory depictions of "lifelike" violence. Research shows these games may teach children that violence is exciting and acceptable. Obviously, most children who play violent video games and watch violent movies and TV shows do not go on to become dangerous killers. However, children do imitate what they see on TV (and, presumably, video games) and seem to internalize as a value that violence is acceptable behavior.

Culture and learning. *People vary in their practice and acceptance of aggression. Acts of aggression are extremely rare among the Efe, shown here.*

Could it be that aggressive children just tend to prefer violent television and video games? Research suggests it is a two-way street. Laboratory studies, correlational research, and cross-cultural studies among children in five different countries (Australia, Finland, Israel, Poland, and the United States) have all found that exposure to TV violence did increase aggressiveness and that aggressive children tend to seek out violent programs (Aluja-Fabregat & Torrubia-Beltri, 1998; Singer, Slovak, Frierson, & York, 1998).

Controlling or Eliminating Aggression

Some therapists advise people to release aggressive impulses by engaging in harmless forms of aggression, such as exercising vigorously, punching a pillow, or watching competitive sports. But studies suggest that this type of *catharsis,* or "draining the aggression reservoir," doesn't really help (Bushman, 2002; Bushman, Baumeister, & Stack, 1999). In fact, as we pointed out in Chapter 12, expressing an emotion, anger or otherwise, tends to intensify the feeling rather than reduce it.

A second approach, which does seem to effectively reduce or control aggression, is to introduce *incompatible responses.* Certain emotional responses, such as empathy and humor, are incompatible with aggression. Thus, purposely making a joke or showing some sympathy for the other person's point of view can signifantly reduce anger and frustration (Harvey & Miceli, 1999; Kaukiainen et al., 1999; Oshima, 2000).

A third approach to controlling aggression is to improve social and communication skills. Studies show that people with the most deficient communication skills account for a disproportionate share of the violence in society (Trump, 2000; Vance, Fernandez, & Biber, 1998). Unfortunately, little effort is made in our schools or families to teach basic communication skills or techniques for conflict resolution.

"It's a guy thing."

Application

RESEARCH HIGHLIGHT

America's "Anger/Rudeness Epidemic"

Two supermarket shoppers get in a fistfight over who should be first in a newly opened checkout lane.

A Continental Airlines flight returns to the Anchorage airport after a passenger allegedly throws a can of beer at a flight attendant and bites a pilot.

A father beats another father to death in an argument over rough play at their sons' hockey practice.

A subway rider loudly complains about a fellow rider's loud cell phone conversation.

What do you think of these media reports? Americans experienced a brief time of closeness and increased civility following the horrific terrorist attacks on September 11, 2001. But today experts believe the nation has returned to our previous "anger and rudeness epidemic," ranging from tantrums in supermarkets and on airplanes to deadly fights over a children's hockey practice (Carson, 2002; Gilligan, 2000; Peterson, 2000).

Perhaps most disturbing is the increase in teen violence (Zanigel & Ressner, 2001). One of the most dramatic examples of teen violence occurred on April 20, 1999, in Littelton, Colorado. On that infamous day, Eric Harris and Dylan Klebold shot and killed 12 fellow Columbine High School students and 1 teacher, and wounded many others. They then turned the guns on themselves and committed suicide. Armed with a semiautomatic rifle, two sawed-off shotguns, a semiautomatic handgun, and dozens of homemade bombs, these two young men joined a growing list of recent school shootings in the United States.

Juvenile massacres are still an aberration. But the slaughter at Columbine High "opened a sad national conversation about what turns two boys' souls into poison" (Gibbs, 1999, p. 25). What causes kids to gun down other kids? Can we identify high-risk children at early ages? Is aggressiveness a personality trait that is malleable or is it highly resistant to change?

These are the kinds of questions addressed by researchers Rolf Loeber and Magda Stouthamer-Loeber (1998) of the University of Pittsburgh. The numbers of juvenile perpetrators and victims have gradually increased over the past decades. And these researchers also found research showing highly aggressive children are at risk for adult crime, alcoholism, drug abuse, unemployment, divorce, and mental illness.

Research on juvenile antisocial behavior is voluminous. Loeber and Stouthamer-Loeber identified five major misconceptions and controversies that block our understanding of the problem and future research.

Misconception #1: *Stability of childhood aggression.* Correlation studies give the impression that aggression is highly stable from childhood to adulthood (a review of the literature shows coefficients range from .63 to .92—very high). In other words, individuals who are aggressive as children are likely to be aggressive as adults. However, Loeber and Stouthamer-Loeber think we are stopping short of the real challenge. We should be researching why some children don't go on to become aggressive adults. They cite studies showing that preschool boys commonly show aggressive behaviors and that aggression decreases from preschool to elementary school and from adolescence to adulthood. Knowing why some individuals outgrow aggression could greatly help mental health professionals intervene in high-risk cases.

Misconception #2: *Beginnings of aggression.* All serious aggression begins in early childhood. Loeber and Stouthamer-Loeber suggest we need additional research into violent individuals without a history of early aggression. They go on to suggest three developmental types of aggressive individuals: (a) a life-course type (characterized by aggression in childhood that persists and worsens into adulthood), (b) a limited-duration type (individuals who outgrow aggression), and (c) a late-onset type (individuals without a history of aggression). This three-type classification could be more helpful to clinicians, probation officers, and others working with children.

Misconception #3: *Controversy over single or multiple pathways.* Loeber and Stouthamer-Loeber suggest researchers should spend less time debating whether one *single* pathway leads to antisocial behavior and violence. (By "pathway,"

they mean causes such as genes, culture, learning, or any of the other possible causes discussed at the beginning of this section). Instead, we should research multiple pathways because "casting a wide net" is more likely to produce results than looking at each possibility one at a time.

Misconception #4: *Simple versus complex causes of aggression.* Loeber and Stouthamer-Loeber looked at three possible causes of aggression in children—family factors, physiology, and genetics. They report that a more complex relationship exists than was previously thought.

Studies of family factors, for example, show a relationship exists between children who live with aggressive parents in a conflict filled home and children who commit personal or violent crimes, but not children who commit property crimes. Similarly, physiological studies link certain hormones (such as testosterone) and neurotransmitters (such as serotonin) to juvenile aggression. But not to property crimes. Genetic studies have produced conflicting results.

Misconception #5: *Gender differences in aggression.* Loeber and Stouthamer-Loeber say the assumption that violence develops in much the same way in women and men is erroneous. Few gender differences have been recorded in toddlerhood. But beginning in preschool and throughout adulthood boys show more personal and physical aggression. For these reasons, Loeber and Stouthamer-Loeber believe major gender differences exist in aggression. At the same time, they stress that these variations are pieces of the bigger puzzle that must be addressed by future research.

◼ Altruism: Why We Help (and Don't Help) Others

After reading about prejudice, discrimination, and aggression, you will no doubt be relieved to discover that human beings also behave in positive ways. People help and support one another by donating blood, giving time and money to charities, helping stranded motorists, and so on. There are also times when people do not help. Consider the following:

In 1964, a woman named Kitty Genovese was raped and stabbed repeatedly by a knife-wielding assailant as she returned from work to her apartment in Queens, New York. It was about 3:00 A.M., but 38 of her neighbors watched as she struggled to fight off her attacker and heard her screams and pleas for help: "Oh my God, he stabbed me! Please help me! Please help me!" The attack lasted for over half an hour; yet no one came to help her. By the time one neighbor finally called the police, it was too late. Kitty Genovese had died.

How could such a thing have happened? Why didn't her neighbors help? More generally, under what conditions do people sometimes help and sometimes ignore others' pleas for help?

Why Do We Help?

Altruism (or prosocial behavior) refers to actions designed to help others with no obvious benefit to the helper. Evolutionary theory suggests that altruism is an instinctual behavior that has evolved because it favors survival of one's genes (Bower, 2000; Ozinga, 2000; 2002; Rossano, 2003). As evidence, these theorists cite altruistic acts among lower species (e.g., worker bees cooperatively working and living only for their mother, the queen). They also point out that altruism in humans is strongest toward one's own children and other relatives. Altruism protects not the individual but the individual's genes. By helping, or even dying for, your child or sibling, you increase the odds that the genes you share will be passed on to future generations.

Other research suggests that helping may actually be a form of egoism or disguised self-interest. According to this **egoistic model**, helping is always motivated by some degree of anticipated gain. We help others because we hope for later reciprocation, because it makes us feel good about ourselves, or because it helps us avoid feelings of distress and guilt that loom if we don't help (Cialdini, 2001; Williams, Haber, Weaver, & Freeman, 1998).

Opposing the egoistic model is the **empathy–altruism hypothesis** proposed by C. D. Batson and his colleagues (Batson, 1991, 1998; Batson & Ahmad, 2001). As Figure 16.10 shows, Batson thinks some altruism is motivated by simple, selfish concerns (the top part of the diagram). In other situations, however, helping is truly selfless and motivated by concern for others (the bottom part of the diagram).

According to the empathy–altruism hypothesis, simply seeing another person's suffering or hearing of his or her need can create *empathy*, a subjective grasp of that person's feelings or experiences. When we feel empathic toward another, we focus on

Altruism *Actions designed to help others with no obvious benefit to the helper*

Egoistic Model *Helping that's motivated by anticipated gain—later reciprocation, increased self-esteem, or avoidance of distress and guilt*

Empathy—Altruism Hypothesis *Helping because of empathy for someone in need*

Figure 16.10 *Two major explanations for helping.* Do you think the egoistic or the empathy–altruism model is best shown in this photo? Would the young child be motivated to help his pet? Why? According to C. D. Batson and his colleagues, both models motivate helping. Can you explain?

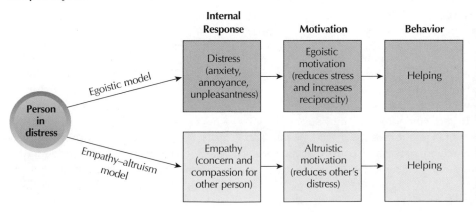

that person's distress, not our own. We're also more likely to help the person for his or her own sake. The ability to empathize may even be innate. Research with infants in the first few hours of life shows that they become distressed and cry at the sound of another infant's cries (Hay, 1994; Hoffman, 1993).

Why Don't We Help?

Many theories have been proposed to explain why people help, but few explain why we do not. How do we explain why Kitty Genovese's neighbors did not help her? One of the most comprehensive explanations for helping or not helping comes from the research of Bibb Latané and John Darley (1970). They found that whether or not someone helps depends on a series of interconnected events and decisions. The potential helper must first *notice* what is happening, must clarify and *interpret* the event as an emergency, must accept *personal responsibility* for helping, and then must *decide how to help* and actually initiate the helping behavior.

Where did the sequence break down for Kitty Genovese? Kitty's neighbors obviously noticed what was happening and interpreted it as an emergency. The breakdown came at the third stage—*taking personal responsibility for helping.* Newspaper interviews with each of the neighbors described a great deal of anguish. Each individual failed to intervene because they were certain that someone must already have called the police. Latané and Darley called this the **diffusion of responsibility** phenomenon—the dilution (or diffusion) of personal responsibility for acting by spreading it among all other group members. If you see someone drowning at the beach and you are the only person around, then responsibility falls squarely on you. But if others are present, there may be a diffusion of responsibility. It is ironic that if only one neighbor had seen the brutal attack, and thought that there were no other witnesses, Kitty might still be alive today.

Diffusion of Responsibility *The dilution (or diffusion) of personal responsibility for acting by spreading it among all other group members*

How Can We Promote Helping?

The most obvious way to increase altruistic behavior is to clarify when help is needed and then assign responsibility. For example, if you notice a situation in which it seems unclear whether someone needs help, simply ask. On the other hand, if you are the one in need of help, look directly at anyone who may be watching and give specific directions, such as "Call the police. I am being attacked!"

Helping behaviors could also be encouraged through societal rewards. Some researchers suggest that states need to enact more laws that protect the helper from potential suits. Certain existing police programs, such as Crime Stoppers, actively recruit public compliance in reporting crime, give monetary rewards, and ensure anonymity. Such programs have apparently been highly effective in reducing crime.

Assessment

CHECK & REVIEW

Aggression and Altruism

Aggression is any behavior intended to harm someone. Some researchers believe it is caused by biological factors, such as instincts, genes, the brain and nervous system, substance abuse and other mental disorders, and hormones and neurotransmitters. Other researchers emphasize psy-

chosocial factors, such as aversive stimuli, culture and learning, and violent media and video games. Releasing aggressive feelings through violent acts or watching violence (catharsis) is not an effective way to reduce aggression. Introducing incompatible responses (such as humor) and teaching social and communication skills are more efficient.

Altruism refers to actions designed to help others with no obvious benefit to oneself. Evolutionary theorists believe altruism is innate and has survival value. Psychological explanations for altruism emphasize the **egoistic model,** which suggests that helping is motivated by anticipated gain. In contrast, the **empathy–altruism hypothesis** proposes that helping increases when the helper feels empathy for the victim.

Whether or not someone helps depends on a series of interconnected events, starting with noticing the problem and ending with a decision to help. Some people don't help because of the ambiguity of many emergencies or because of **diffusion of responsibility** (assuming someone else will respond). To increase the chances of altruism, we should reduce ambiguity, increase the rewards for helping, and decrease the costs.

Questions

1. What are the five major biological and three chief psychosocial factors that contribute to aggression?
2. According to research, what are the best ways to reduce aggression?
3. How do evolutionary theorists, the egoistic model, and the empathy–altruism hypothesis explain altruism?
4. Kitty Genovese's neighbors failed to respond to her cries for help because

of the _____ phenomenon. (a) empathy–altruism; (b) egoistic model; (c) inhumanity of large cities; (d) diffusion of responsibility

Check your answers in Appendix B.

CLICK & REVIEW
for additional assessment options:
www.wiley.com/college/huffman

APPLYING SOCIAL PSYCHOLOGY TO SOCIAL PROBLEMS

Each and every day of your life you're confronted with social problems. Driving or riding to work, you note how the freeways get busier each year. Camping in the wilderness, you find your favorite remote site occupied by other campers and cluttered with trash. Watching television, you check to see if the terror level is elevated and wonder if and when terrorists will attack. Reading the newspaper, you ask yourself what makes someone a suicide bomber.

Unfortunately, social psychology has been more successful in describing, explaining, and predicting social problems than in solving them. However, researchers have found several helpful techniques. In this section, we'll first explore what scientists have discovered about reducing prejudice. We'll then discuss effective ways to cope with destructive forms of obedience.

A*chievement*

How can we use social psychology to help resolve social problems?

▪ Reducing Prejudice and Discrimination

> Let's go hand in hand, not one before another.
>
> WILLIAM SHAKESPEARE

What can be done to combat prejudice? Five major approaches can be used: *cooperation, superordinate goals, increased contact, cognitive retraining,* and *cognitive dissonance.*

1, 2. *Cooperation and superordinate goals.* Research shows that one of the best ways to combat prejudice is to encourage *cooperation* rather than *competition* (Brewer, 1996; Walker & Crogan, 1998). Muzafer Sherif and his colleagues (1966, 1998) conducted an ingenious study to show the role of competition in promoting prejudice. The researchers artificially created strong feelings of ingroup and outgroup identification in a group of 11- and 12-year-old boys at a summer camp. They did this by physically separating the boys in different cabins and assigning different projects to each group, such as building a diving board or cooking out in the woods.

Once each group developed strong feelings of group identity and allegiance, the researchers set up a series of competitive games, including tug-of-war and touch football. They awarded desirable prizes to the winning teams. Because of this treatment, the groups began to pick fights, call each other names, and raid each other's camps. Researchers pointed to these behaviors as evidence of the experimentally-produced prejudice.

"I WISH WE COULD HAVE MET
UNDER DIFFERENT CIRCUMSTANCES . . ."

Universal Press Syndicate

 www.wiley.com/college/huffman

After using competition to create prejudice between the two groups, the researchers demonstrated how cooperation could be successfully used to eliminate it. They created "minicrises" and tasks that required expertise, labor, and cooperation from both groups. And once again prizes were awarded to all. The hostilities and prejudice between the groups slowly began to dissipate. At the end of the camp experience, the boys voted to return home in the same bus. And the self-chosen seating did not reflect the earlier camp divisions. Sherif's study demonstrated the importance of cooperation as opposed to competition. They also showed how *superordinate goals* (resolving the minicrises) can help reduce prejudice (Der-Karabetian, Stephenson, & Poggi, 1996).

3. **Increased contact.** A third approach to reducing prejudice is increasing contact between groups (Brown et al., 2003; London et al., 2002; Philipsen, 2003). But as you just discovered with Sherif's study of the boys at the summer camp, contact can sometimes increase prejudice. Increasing contact only works under certain conditions: (1) *close interaction* (if minority students are "tracked" into vocational education courses and white students are primarily in college prep courses, they seldom interact and prejudice is increased), (2) *interdependence* (both groups must be involved in superordinate goals that require cooperation), and (3) *equal status* (everyone must be at the same level). Once people have positive experiences with a group, they tend to generalize to other groups (Pettigrew, 1998).

Only equals can be friends.

ETHIOPIAN PROVERB.

4. **Cognitive retraining.** One of the most recent strategies in prejudice reduction requires taking another's perspective or undoing associations of negative stereotypical traits (Galinsky & Ku, 2004; Galinsky & Moskowitz, 2000; Phillipsen, 2003). For example, in a computer training session, North American participants were asked to *try not* to think of cultural associations when they saw a photograph of an elderly person. They were also asked to press a *no* button when they saw a photograph of an elderly person with a trait stereotypically associated with elderly people (e.g., slow, weak). Conversely, they were instructed to press a *yes* button when they saw a photograph of an elderly person with a trait not normally associated with the elderly. After a number of trials, their response times became faster and faster, indicating they were undoing negative associations and learning positive ones. Following the training, participants were less likely to activate any negative stereotype of elderly people in another activity than were others who did not participate in the training exercise (Kawakami et al., 2000).

People can also learn to be nonprejudiced if they are taught to selectively pay attention to *similarities* rather than *differences* (Phillips & Ziller, 1997). When we focus on how "black voters feel about affirmative action" or how Jewish people feel about "a Jewish candidate for vice president of the United States," we are indirectly encouraging stereotypes and ingroups versus outgroups. Can you see how this might also apply to gender? By emphasizing gender differences (*Men Are from Mars, Women Are from Venus*), we may be perpetuating gender stereotypes (Powlishta, 1999).

You cannot judge another person until you have walked a mile in his moccasins.

AMERICAN INDIAN PROVERB

5. **Cognitive dissonance.** As mentioned earlier, prejudice is a type of attitude that has three basic components—affective (feelings), behavioral tendencies, and cognitive (thoughts). And one of the most efficient methods to change an attitude uses the principle of *cognitive dissonance*, a perceived discrepancy between an attitude and a behavior or between an attitude and a new piece of information (Cook, 2000; D'Alessio & Allen, 2002). Each time we meet someone who does not conform to our prejudiced views, we experience dissonance—"I thought all gay men were effeminate. This guy is a deep-voiced professional athlete. I'm confused." To resolve the dissonance, we can maintain our stereotypes by saying, "This gay man is an exception to the rule." However, if we continue our contact with a large variety of gay men, this "exception to the rule" defense eventually breaks down and attitude change occurs.

©AP/Wide World Photos

(a)

Chris Graythen/AFP/Getty Images

(b)

The media's role in prejudice. *After Hurricane Katrina ripped through New Orleans in 2005, newspapers featured numerous photos of people taking food and supplies from local grocery stores. Criticism arose because the caption under one photo of a black person (a) mentioned he was "looting." In contrast, the caption for the photo of a white couple (b) said they were "finding" bread and soda. If this was an example of media biases and the reporters' covert prejudice, how would you use information in this section to help reduce prejudice in the media and prevent possible carryover to the viewing public?*

As a critical thinker, can you see how social changes, such as school busing, integrated housing, and increased civil rights legislation, might initially create cognitive dissonance that would lead to an eventual reduction in prejudice? Moreover, do you recognize how the five methods of reducing prejudice we just described also involve cognitive dissonance? Cooperation, superordinate goals, increased contact, and cognitive retraining all create cognitive dissonance for the prejudiced person. And this uncomfortable dissonance motivates the individual to eventually change his or her attitudes, thereby reducing their prejudice.

Cognitive dissonance? *Does this photo of an active, healthy senior citizen conflict with your stereotypes of frail, ill elderly people? Can you explain how this conflict, or cognitive dissonance, might lead to prejudice reduction?*

■ Overcoming Destructive Obedience: When Is It Okay to Say No?

Obedience to authority is an important part of our lives. If people routinely refused to obey police officers, firefighters, and other official personnel, our individual safety and social order would collapse. However, there are also many times when obedience may be unnecessary and destructive—and should be reduced.

For example, do you remember the story of Jim Jones? In 1978, over 900 members of the People's Temple in Guyana committed mass suicide because he ordered them to do so. People who resisted were murdered. But the vast majority took their lives willingly by drinking cyanide-laced Kool-Aid. A less depressing example of mass obedience occurred in 1983 when 2075 identically dressed couples were married by the Reverend Sun Myung Moon in Madison Square Garden. Although most partners were complete strangers to one another, they married because the Reverend Moon ordered them to do so.

How do we explain (and hopefully reduce) destructive obedience? In addition to all the factors associated with Milgram's study discussed earlier, social psychologists have developed other helpful theories and concepts on the general topic of obedience.

- ***Socialization.*** As mentioned before, our society and culture have a tremendous influence on all our thoughts, feelings, and actions. Obedience is no exception. From very early childhood, we're taught to respect and obey our parents, teachers, and other authority figures. Without this obedience we would have social chaos. Unfortunately, this early (and lifelong) socialization often becomes so deeply ingrained that we no longer consciously recognize it. This helps explain many instances of mindless obedience to immoral requests from people in positions of authority. For example, participants in Milgram's study came into the research lab with a lifetime of socialization toward the value of scientific research and respect for the experimenter's authority. They couldn't suddenly step outside themselves and question the morality of this particular experimenter and his orders. American soldiers accused of atrocities in Iraq or in the Abu Ghraib prison shared this general socialization toward respect for authority combined with military training requiring immediate, unquestioning obedience. Unfortunately, history is replete with instances of atrocities committed because people were "just following orders."

Overcoming destructive obedience. *New military recruits understand that effective military action requires quick and immediate obedience. However, social psychological principles, such as socialization, the power of the situation, and groupthink also encourage these individuals to willingly do push-ups in response to their officer's orders. Can you explain why?*

- ***Power of the situation.*** Situational influences also have a strong impact on obedience. For example, the roles of police officer or public citizen, teacher or student, and parent or child all have built-in guidelines for appropriate behavior. One person is ultimately "in charge." The other person is supposed to follow along. Because these roles are so well socialized, we mindlessly play them and find it difficult to recognize the point where they become maladaptive. As we discovered earlier with the Zimbardo prison study, well-adjusted and well-screened college students became so absorbed in their roles of prisoners and guards that their behaviors clearly passed the point of moral behaviors. The "simple" role of being a research participant in Milgram's study—or a soldier in Vietnam, Iraq, or Afghanistan—helps explain many instances of destructive obedience.

- ***Groupthink.*** When discussing Milgram's study and other instances of destructive obedience, most people believe that they and their friends would never do such a

www.wiley.com/college/huffman

Lawrence Migdale/Photo Researchers

Foot-in-the-door technique. *If this homeowner allows the salesperson to give him a small gift (a "foot-in-the-door" technique), he's more likely to agree to buy something. Can you explain why?*

thing. Can you see how this might be a form of *groupthink*, a type of faulty thinking that occurs when group members strive for agreement and avoid inconsistent information? When we smugly proclaim that Americans would never follow orders like some German people did during World War II, we're demonstrating several symptoms of groupthink—stereotypes of the outgroup, the illusion of unanimity, belief in the morality of the group, and so on.

- **Foot-in-the-door.** The gradual nature of many obedience situations may also help explain why so many people were willing to give the maximum shocks in Milgram's study. The initial mild level of shocks may have worked as a *foot-in-the-door technique*, in which a first, small request is used as a setup for later, larger requests. Once Milgram's participants complied with the initial request, they might have felt obligated to continue (Chartrand, Pinckert, & Burger, 1999; Sabini & Silver, 1993).

- **Relaxed moral guard.** One common intellectual illusion that hinders critical thinking about obedience is the belief that only evil people do evil things or that evil announces itself. For example, the experimenter in Milgram's study looked and acted like a reasonable person who was simply carrying out a research project. Because he was not seen as personally corrupt and evil, the participants' normal moral guard was down and obedience was maximized. This relaxed moral guard might similarly explain why so many people followed Hitler's commands to torture and kill millions of Jews during World War II. Although most believe only "monsters" would obey such an order, Milgram's research suggests otherwise. He revealed the conditions that breed obedience as well as the extent to which ordinary, everyday people will mindlessly obey an authority. As philosopher Hannah Arendt has suggested, the horrifying thing about the Nazis was not that they were so deviant but that they were so "terrifyingly normal."

Final Note

In addition to recognizing and understanding the power of these forces, it's equally important to remember that each of us must be personally alert to immoral forms of obedience. On occasion, we also need the courage to stand up and say "No!" One of the most beautiful and historically important examples of just this type of bravery occurred in Alabama in 1955. Rosa Parks boarded a bus and, as expected in those times, she obediently sat in the back section marked "Negroes." When the bus became crowded, the driver told her to give up her seat to a white man. Surprisingly for those days, Parks refused and was eventually forced off the bus by police and arrested. This single act of disobedience was an important catalyst for the small, but growing, civil rights movement and the later repeal of Jim Crow laws in the South. Her courageous stand also inspires the rest of us to think about when it is good to obey authorities and when to disobey unethical demands from authorities.

William Philpott/Reuters/Corbis Images

The power of one! *In late October 2005, Americans mourned the passing of Rosa Parks—the "mother of the civil rights movement." History books typically emphasize her 1955 arrest and jailing for refusing to give up her bus seat to a white man. They fail to mention that this "simple" refusal threatened her job and possibly her life. (Both her mother and husband warned her that she might be lynched for her actions.) They also overlook that long before this one defiant bus ride, Parks fought hard and courageously against segregated seating on buses and for voting rights for blacks.*

Assessment

CHECK & REVIEW

Applying Psychology to Social Problems

Research in social psychology can help reduce or eliminate social problems. Cooperation, superordinate goals, increased contact, cognitive retraining, and cognitive dissonance reduction are five methods for reducing prejudice and discrimination.

To understand how to reduce dangerous forms of destructive obedience, we need to examine socialization, the power of the situation, groupthink, the foot-in-the-door technique, and a relaxed moral guard.

Questions

1. If your college and hometown were suddenly threatened by a raging wildfire, prejudice might decrease because groups would come together to fight the fire and help rebuild the community. This is an example of how _____ is (are) important in reducing prejudice. (a) outgroup homogeneity; (b) scapegoating; (c) displaced competition; (d) superordinate goals

2. Cooperation, superordinate goals, increased contact, and cognitive retraining all create _____ for a prejudiced person.

3. A social influence technique in which a first, small request is used as a setup for later requests is known as _____. (a) the lowball technique; (b) the foot-in-the-door technique; (c) the infiltration technique; (d) ingratiation

4. Explain why Rosa Parks is a good example of the power of disobedient models in reducing obedience.

Check your answers in Appendix B.

CLICK & REVIEW
for additional assessment options:
www.wiley.com/college/huffman

Assessment
KEY TERMS

*To assess your understanding of the **Key Terms** in Chapter 16, write a definition for each (in your own words), and then compare your definitions with those in the text.*

social psychology (p. 574)

Our Thoughts About Others
attitude (p. 577)
attribution (p. 575)
cognitive dissonance (p. 578)
fundamental attribution error (FAE) (p. 575)
saliency bias (p. 576)
self-serving bias (p. 576)

Our Feelings About Others
companionate love (p. 589)
discrimination (p. 581)

ingroup favoritism (p. 582)
interpersonal attraction (p. 583)
need compatibility (p. 587)
need complementarity (p. 586)
outgroup homogeneity effect (p. 582)
prejudice (p. 581)
proximity (p. 586)
romantic love (p. 588)
stereotype (p. 581)

Our Actions Toward Others
aggression (p. 601)
altruism (p. 605)
conformity (p. 590)

deindividuation (p. 598)
diffusion of responsibility (p. 606)
egoistic model (p. 605)
empathy–altruism hypothesis (p. 605)
foot-in-the-door technique (p. 596)
frustration–aggression hypothesis (p. 602)
group polarization (p. 599)
groupthink (p. 599)
informational social influence (p. 592)
norm (p. 591)
normative social influence (p. 591)
obedience (p. 592)
reference groups (p. 592)

Achievement
WEB RESOURCES

Huffman Book Companion Site
http://www.wiley.com/college/huffman
This site is loaded with free Interactive Self-Tests, Internet Exercises, Glossary and Flashcards for key terms, web links, Handbook for Non-Native Speakers, and other activities designed to improve your mastery of the material in this chapter.

Want more general information about social psychology?
http://www.socialpsychology.org/
Sponsored by the Social Psychology Network, this website is the best starting place for information about the field. As stated on the opening page, this is "the largest social psychology database on the Internet. In these pages, you'll find more than 5,000 links related to psychology."

Interested in love and attraction?
http://www.socialpsychology.org/social.htm
As part of the Social Psychology Network, this link offers tips on online romance, shyness, top 10 rejection lines by women and men, and other interesting topics.

Want to learn more about prejudice and its reduction?
http://www.tolerance.org/
This website offers self-tests for hidden bias, 101 tools for tolerance, 10 ways to fight hate, and a host of other important topics.

Interested in social influence and persuasion techniques?
http://www.influenceatwork.com/
This is a commercial website for the Influence at Work consulting services group. Robert Cialdini, a renowned expert on influence, is the president of this organization. You'll find interesting links describing its training and services.

Need information about cults and psychological manipulation?
http://www.csj.org/
An interdisciplinary network that studies psychological manipulation, cult groups, sects, and new religious movements. Through its publications, workshops, programs, and services, it offers practical educational services for families, former group members, professionals, and educators.

www.wiley.com/college/huffman

Our Thoughts About Others

Attribution

Attribution: Explaining others' behavior by deciding that their actions resulted from internal (dispositional) factors (their own traits and motives) or external (situational) factors. Problems: **fundamental attribution error** and **self-serving bias**.

Attitudes

Attitudes: Learned pre-dispositions toward a particular object. Three components of all attitudes: cognitive, affective, and be-havioral tendencies.

Cognitive Dissonance Theory

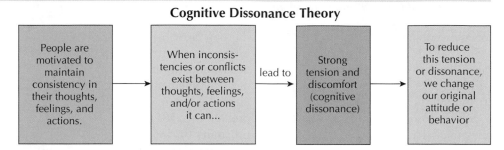

People are motivated to maintain consistency in their thoughts, feelings, and actions. → When inconsis-tencies or conflicts exist between thoughts, feelings, and/or actions it can... → lead to → Strong tension and discomfort (cognitive dissonance) → To reduce this tension or dissonance, we change our original attitude or behavior

Our Feelings About Others

Prejudice and Discrimination

Prejudice: Generally negative attitude directed toward people solely because of their membership in a specific group. Contains all three components of attitudes—cognitive (**stereotype**), affective, and behavioral (**discrimination**).

Discrimination: Refers to the actual negative behavior directed at members of a group. People do not always act on their prejudices. Four major sources of prejudice:

Learning: Classical and operant conditioning and social learning

Cognitive processes: **Ingroup favoritism, outgroup homogeneity effect**

Economic and political competition

Displaced aggression: Scapegoating

Interpersonal attraction

Three key factors:

Physical **proximity** increases attraction largely due to the *mere exposure effect.*

Physical attractiveness is im-portant to initial attraction and more important to men than women.

Although many believe "opposites attract" (**need complementarity**), re-search shows **similarity (need compatibility)** is more important.

Karen Huffman

- *Love*: Rubin defines it in terms of caring, attachment, and intimacy.
- **Romantic love** highly valued in our society, but it's based on mystery and fantasy; thus, hard to sustain.
- **Companionate love** relies on mutual trust, respect, and friendship and grows stronger with time.

Our Actions Toward Others

Social Influence

Conformity: Changes in behavior in response to real or imagined pressure from others.

Four reasons we conform:

For approval and acceptance (**normative social influence**).	Need for more information (**informational social influence**).
To match behavior of those we admire and feel similar to (**reference group**).	We also conform because it is often adaptive to do so.

Obedience: Going along with a direct command. Milgram's study showed a high degree of obedience. Why?

Power of authority	Distance between teacher and learner	Assignment of respon-sibility	Modeling/ imitation

Aggression

Aggression: Deliberate attempt to harm another living being who is motivated to avoid such treatment.
- *Biological causes*: Instincts, genes, the brain and nervous system, substance abuse, and other mental disorders, hormones, and neurotransmitters.
- *Psychosocial causes*: Aversive stimuli, learning, violent media, and videogames.
- *Treatment*: Incompatible responses (like humor), social skills, and improved communication help reduce aggression, but expressing it doesn't.

Group Processes

- *Group membership* affects us through the roles we play or through **deindividuation**
- *Group decision making* is affected by two key factors:

Group polarization: When most group members initially tend toward an extreme idea, the entire group will move toward that extreme.	**Groupthink**: Dangerous type of decision making where group's desire for agreement overrules critical evaluation.

Altruism

Altruism: Actions designed to help others with no obvious benefit to oneself.

Why do we help?
- Evolutionary theorists believe altruism is innate and has survival value.
- Psychological explanations suggest helping is motivated by anticipated gain (**egoistic model**) or when helper feels empathy for the victim (**empathy-altruism hypothesis**).

Why don't we help?
- It depends on a series of interconnected events, starting with noticing the problem and ending with a decision to help.
- Many emergency situations are ambiguous.
- We assume others will respond (**diffusion of responsibility**).

How do we increase altruism?
- Reduce ambiguity by giving clear directions to observers.
- Increase rewards, while decreasing costs.

Applying Social Psychology to Social Problems

Social psychological research applied to social problems:
- Cooperation, superordinate goals, increased contact, cognitive retraining, and cognitive dissonance reduction may help reduce prejudice and discrimination.
- Understanding socialization, the power of the situation, groupthink, the foot-in-the-door, and a relaxed moral guard may help reduce destructive obedience.

www.wiley.com/college/huffman

APPENDIX A
Statistics and Psychology

We are constantly bombarded by numbers: "On sale for 30 percent off," "70 percent chance of rain," "9 out of 10 doctors recommend…" The president uses numbers to try to convince us that the economy is healthy. Advertisers use numbers to convince us of the effectiveness of their products. Psychologists use statistics to support or refute psychological theories and demonstrate that certain behaviors are indeed results of specific causal factors.

When people use numbers in these ways, they are using statistics. **Statistics** is a branch of applied mathematics that uses numbers to describe and analyze information on a subject.

Statistics make it possible for psychologists to quantify the information they obtain in their studies. They can then critically analyze and evaluate this information. Statistical analysis is imperative for researchers to describe, predict, or explain behavior. For instance, Albert Bandura (1973) proposed that watching violence on television causes aggressive behavior in children. In carefully controlled experiments, he gathered numerical information and analyzed it according to specific statistical methods. The statistical analysis helped him substantiate that the aggression of his subjects and the aggressive acts they had seen on television were related, and that the relationship was not mere coincidence.

Although statistics is a branch of applied mathematics, you don't have to be a math whiz to use statistics. Simple arithmetic is all you need to do most of the calculations. For more complex statistics involving more complicated mathematics, computer programs are available for virtually every type of computer. What is more important than learning the mathematical computations, however, is developing an understanding of when and why each type of statistic is used. The purpose of this appendix is to help you understand the significance of the statistics most commonly used.

THE STAT FAMILY

Drawing by M. Stevens; © 1989 the New Yorker Magazine, Inc.

GATHERING AND ORGANIZING DATA

Psychologists design their studies to facilitate gathering information about the factors they want to study. The information they obtain is known as **data (data** is plural; its singular is **datum).** When the data are gathered, they are generally in the form of numbers; if they aren't, they are converted to numbers. After they are gathered, the data must be organized in such a way that statistical analysis is possible. In the following section, we will examine the methods used to gather and organize information.

Variables

When studying a behavior, psychologists normally focus on one particular factor to determine whether it has an effect on the behavior. This factor is known as a **variable,** which is in effect anything that can assume more than one value (see Chapter 1). Height, weight, sex, eye color, and scores on an IQ test or a video game are all factors that can assume more than one value and are therefore variables. Some will vary between people, such as sex (you are either male *or* female but not both at the same time). Some may even vary within one person, such as scores on a video game (the same person might get 10,000 points on one try and only 800 on another). Opposed to a variable, anything that remains the same and does not vary is called a **constant.** If researchers use only females in their research, then sex is a constant, not a variable.

In nonexperimental studies, variables can be factors that are merely observed through naturalistic observation or case studies, or they can be factors about which people are questioned in a test or survey. In experimental studies, the two major types of variables are independent and dependent variables.

Independent variables are those that are manipulated by the experimenter. For example, suppose we were to conduct a study to determine whether the sex of the debater influences the outcome of a debate. In this study, one group of subjects watches a videotape of a debate between a male arguing the "pro" side and a female arguing the "con"; another group watches the same debate, but with the pro and con roles reversed. In such a study, the form of the presentation viewed by each group (whether "pro" is argued by a male or a female) is the independent variable because the experimenter manipulates the form of presentation seen by each group. Another example might be a study to determine whether a particular drug has any effect on a manual dexterity task. To study this question, we would administer the drug to one group and no drug to another. The independent variable would be the amount of drug given (some or none). The independent variable is particularly important when using **inferential statistics,** which we will discuss later.

The **dependent variable** is a factor that results from, or depends on, the independent variable. It is a measure of some

A1

TABLE A.1 STATISTICS APTITUDE TEST SCORES FOR 50 COLLEGE STUDENTS

73	57	63	59	50
72	66	50	67	51
63	59	65	62	65
62	72	64	73	66
61	68	62	68	63
59	61	72	63	52
59	58	57	68	57
64	56	65	59	60
50	62	68	54	63
52	62	70	60	68

outcome or, most commonly, a measure of the subjects' behavior. In the debate example, each subject's choice of the winner of the debate would be the dependent variable. In the drug experiment, the dependent variable would be each subject's score on the manual dexterity task.

Frequency Distributions

After conducting a study and obtaining measures of the variable(s) being studied, psychologists need to organize the data in a meaningful way. Table A.1 presents test scores from a statistics aptitude test collected from 50 college students. This information

TABLE A.2 FREQUENCY DISTRIBUTION OF 50 STUDENTS ON STATISTICS APTITUDE TEST

Score	Frequency
73	2
72	3
71	0
70	1
69	0
68	5
67	1
66	2
65	3
64	2
63	5
62	5
61	2
60	2
59	5
58	1
57	3
56	1
55	0
54	1
53	0
52	2
51	1
50	3
Total	50

is called **raw data** because there is no order to the numbers. They are presented as they were collected and are therefore "raw."

The lack of order in raw data makes them difficult to study. Thus, the first step in understanding the results of an experiment is to impose some order on the raw data. There are several ways to do this. One of the simplest is to create a **frequency distribution,** which shows the number of times a score or event occurs. Although frequency distributions are helpful in several ways, the major advantages are that they allow us to see the data in an organized manner and they make it easier to represent the data on a graph.

The simplest way to make a frequency distribution is to list all the possible test scores, then tally the number of people (N) who received those scores. Table A.2 presents a frequency distribution using the raw data from Table A.1. As you can see, the data are now easier to read. From looking at the frequency distribution, you can see that most of the test scores lie in the middle with only a few at the very high or very low end. This was not at all evident from looking at the raw data.

This type of frequency distribution is practical when the number of possible scores is 20 or fewer. However, when there are more than 20 possible scores it can be even harder to make sense out of the frequency distribution than the raw data. This can be seen in Table A.3, which presents the Scholastic Aptitude Test scores for 50 students. Even though there are only 50 actual scores in this table, the number of possible scores ranges from a high of 1390 to a low of 400. If we included zero frequencies there would be 100 entries in a frequency distribution of this data, making the frequency distribution much more difficult to understand than the raw data. If there are more than 20 possible scores, therefore, a **group** frequency distribution is normally used.

In a **group frequency distribution,** individual scores are represented as members of a group of scores or as a range of scores (see Table A.4). These groups are called **class intervals.** Grouping these scores makes it much easier to make sense out of the distribution, as you can see from the relative ease in understanding Table A.4 as compared to Table A.3. Group frequency distributions are easier to represent on a graph.

When graphing data from frequency distributions, the class intervals are represented along the **abscissa** (the horizontal or x axis). The frequency is represented along the **ordinate** (the vertical or y axis). Information can be graphed in the form of a bar graph, called a **histogram,** or in the form of a point or line graph, called a **polygon.** Figure A.1 shows a histogram presenting the data from Table A.4. Note that the class intervals are represented along the bottom line of the graph (the x axis) and the

TABLE A.3 SCHOLASTIC APTITUDE TEST SCORES FOR 50 COLLEGE STUDENTS

1350	750	530	540	750
1120	410	780	1020	430
720	1080	1110	770	610
1130	620	510	1160	630
640	1220	920	650	870
930	660	480	940	670
1070	950	680	450	990
690	1010	800	660	500
860	520	540	880	1090
580	730	570	560	740

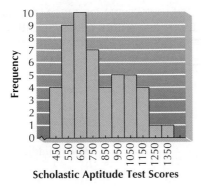

Figure A.1 A histogram illustrating the information found in Table A.4.

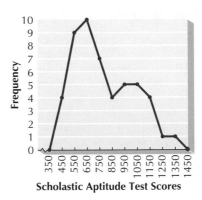

Figure A.2 A polygon illustrating the information found in Table A.4.

height of the bars indicates the frequency in each class interval. Now look at Figure A.2. The information presented here is exactly the same as that in Figure A.1 but is represented in the form of a polygon rather than a histogram. Can you see how both graphs illustrate the same information? Even though reading information from a graph is simple, we have found that many students have never learned to read graphs. In the next section we will explain how to read a graph.

How to Read a Graph

Every graph has several major parts. The most important are the labels, the axes (the vertical and horizontal lines), and the points, lines, or bars. Find these parts in Figure A.1.

The first thing you should notice when reading a graph are the labels because they tell what data are portrayed. Usually the data consist of the descriptive statistics, or the numbers used to measure the dependent variables. For example, in Figure A.1 the horizontal axis is labeled "Scholastic Aptitude Test Scores," which is the dependent variable measure; the vertical axis is labeled "Frequency," which means the number of occurrences. If a graph is not labeled, as we sometimes see in TV commercials or magazine ads, it is useless and should be ignored. Even when a graph

TABLE A.4 GROUP FREQUENCY DISTRIBUTION OF SCHOLASTIC APTITUDE TEST SCORES FOR 50 COLLEGE STUDENTS

Class Interval	Frequency
1300–1390	1
1200–1290	1
1100–1190	4
1000–1090	5
900–990	5
800–890	4
700–790	7
600–690	10
500–590	9
400–490	4
Total	50

is labeled, the labels can be misleading. For example, if graph designers want to distort the information, they can elongate one of the axes. Thus, it is important to pay careful attention to the numbers as well as the words in graph labels.

Next, you should focus your attention on the bars, points, or lines on the graph. In the case of histograms like the one in Figure A.1, each bar represents the class interval. The width of the bar stands for the width of the class interval, whereas the height of the bar stands for the frequency in that interval. Look at the third bar from the left in Figure A.1. This bar represents the interval "600 to 690 SAT Scores," which has a frequency of 10. You can see that this directly corresponds to the same class interval in Table A.4, since graphs and tables are both merely alternate ways of illustrating information.

Reading point or line graphs is the same as reading a histogram. In a point graph, each point represents two numbers, one found along the horizontal axis and the other found along the vertical axis. A polygon is identical to a point graph except that it has lines connecting the points. Figure A.2 is an example of a polygon, where each point represents a class interval and is placed at the center of the interval and at the height corresponding to the frequency of that interval. To make the graph easier to read, the points are connected by straight lines.

Displaying the data in a frequency distribution or in a graph is much more useful than merely presenting raw data and can be especially helpful when researchers are trying to find relations between certain factors. However, as we explained earlier, if psychologists want to make predictions or explanations about behavior, they need to perform mathematical computations on the data.

USES OF THE VARIOUS STATISTICS

The statistics psychologists use in a study depend on whether they are trying to describe and predict behavior or explain it. When they use statistics to describe behavior, as in reporting the average score on the Scholastic Aptitude Test, they are using **descriptive statistics.** When they use them to explain behavior, as Bandura did in his study of children modeling aggressive behavior seen on TV, they are using **inferential statistics.**

■ Descriptive Statistics

Descriptive statistics are the numbers used to describe the dependent variable. They can be used to describe characteristics of a **population** (an entire group, such as all people living in the United States) or a **sample** (a part of a group, such as a randomly selected group of 25 students from Cornell University). The major descriptive statistics include measures of central tendency (mean, median, and mode), measures of variation (variance and standard deviation), and correlation.

Measures of Central Tendency

Statistics indicating the center of the distribution are called **measures of central tendency** and include the mean, median, and mode. They are all scores that are typical of the center of the distribution. The **mean** is what most of us think of when we hear the word "average." The **median** is the middle score. The **mode** is the score that occurs most often.

Mean   What is your average golf score? What is the average yearly rainfall in your part of the country? What is the average reading test score in your city? When these questions ask for the average, they are really asking for the "mean." The arithmetic **mean** is the weighted average of all the raw scores, which is computed by totaling all the raw scores and then dividing that total by the number of scores added together. In statistical computation, the mean is represented by an "X" with a bar above it ($\bar{X}$, pronounced "X bar"), each individual raw score by an "X," and the total number of scores by an "N." For example, if we wanted to compute the $\bar{X}$ of the raw statistics test scores in Table A.1, we would sum all the X's ($?X$, with ? meaning sum) and divide by N (number of scores). In Table A.1, the sum of all the scores is equal to 3,100 and there are 50 scores. Therefore, the mean of these scores is

$$\bar{X} = \frac{3,100}{50} = 62$$

Table A.5 illustrates how to calculate the mean for 10 IQ scores.

TABLE A.5 COMPUTATION OF THE MEAN FOR 10 IQ SCORES

IQ Scores X
143
127
116
98
85
107
106
98
104
116
ΣX = 1,100

$$\text{Mean} = \bar{X} = \frac{\Sigma X}{N} = \frac{1,100}{10} = 110$$

TABLE A.6 COMPUTATION OF MEDIAN FOR ODD AND EVEN NUMBERS OF IQ SCORES

IQ	IQ
139	137
130	135
121	121
116	116
107	108 ← middle score
101	106 ← middle score
98	105
96 ← middle score	101
84	98
83	97
82	N = 10
75	N is even
75	
68	$\text{Median} = \dfrac{106 + 108}{2} = 107$
65	

N = 15
N is odd

Median   The **median** is the middle score in the distribution once all the scores have been arranged in rank order. If N (the number of scores) is odd, then there actually is a middle score and that middle score is the median. When N is even, there are two middle scores and the median is the mean of those two scores. Table A.6 shows the computation of the median for two different sets of scores, one set with 15 scores and one with 10.

Mode   Of all the measures of central tendency, the easiest to compute is the **mode,** which is merely the most frequent score. It is computed by finding the score that occurs most often. Whereas there is always only one mean and only one median for each distribution, there can be more than one mode. Table A.7 shows how to find the mode in a distribution with one mode (unimodal) and in a distribution with two modes (bimodal).

TABLE A.7 FINDING THE MODE FOR TWO DIFFERENT DISTRIBUTIONS

IQ	IQ
139	139
138	138
125	125
116 ←	116 ←
116 ←	116 ←
116 ←	116 ←
107	107
100	98 ←
98	98 ←
98	98 ←
Mode = most frequent score	Mode = 116 and 98
Mode = 116	

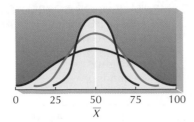

Figure A.3 Three distributions having the same mean but a different variability.

There are several advantages to each of these measures of central tendency, but in psychological research the mean is used most often. A book solely covering psychological statistics will provide a more thorough discussion of the relative values of these measures.

Measures of Variation

When describing a distribution, it is not sufficient merely to give the central tendency; it is also necessary to give a **measure of variation**, which is a measure of the spread of the scores. By examining the spread, we can determine whether the scores are bunched around the middle or tend to extend away from the middle. Figure A.3 shows three different distributions, all with the same mean but with different spreads of scores. You can see from this figure that, in order to describe these different distributions accurately, there must be some measures of the variation in their spread. The most widely used measure of variation is the standard deviation, which is represented by a lowercase s. The standard deviation is a standard measurement of how much the scores in a distribution deviate from the mean. The formula for the standard deviation is

$$s = \sqrt{\frac{\Sigma(X-\bar{X})^2}{N}}$$

Table A.8 illustrates how to compute the standard deviation.

Most distributions of psychological data are bell-shaped. That is, most of the scores are grouped around the mean, and the farther the scores are from the mean in either direction, the fewer the scores. Notice the bell shape of the distribution in Figure A.4. Distributions such as this are called **normal** distributions. In normal distributions, as shown in Figure A.4, approximately two-thirds of the scores fall within a range that is one standard deviation below the mean to one standard deviation above the mean. For example, the Wechsler IQ tests (see Chapter 7) have a mean of 100 and a standard deviation of 15. This means that approximately two-thirds of the people taking these tests will have scores between 85 and 115.

Correlation

Suppose for a moment that you are sitting in the student union with a friend. To pass the time, you and your friend decide to play a game in which you try to guess the height of the next male who enters the union. The winner, the one whose guess is closest to the person's actual height, gets a piece of pie paid for by the loser. When it is your turn, what do you guess? If you are like most peo-

TABLE A.8 COMPUTATION OF THE STANDARD DEVIATION FOR 10 IQ SCORES

IQ Scores X	$X - \bar{X}$	$(X - \bar{X})^2$
143	33	1089
127	17	289
116	6	36
98	–12	144
85	–25	625
107	–3	9
106	–4	16
98	–12	144
104	–6	36
116	6	36
$\Sigma X = 1100$		$\Sigma(X - \bar{X})^2 = 2424$

Standard Deviation = s

$$= \sqrt{\frac{\Sigma(X-\bar{X})^2}{N}} = \sqrt{\frac{2424}{10}}$$

$$= \sqrt{242.4} = 15.569$$

ple, you will probably try to estimate the mean of all the males in the union and use that as your guess. The mean is always your best guess if you have no other information.

Now let's change the game a little and add a friend who stands outside the union and weighs the next male to enter the union. Before the male enters the union, your friend says "125 pounds." Given this new information, will you still guess the mean height? Probably not — you will probably predict *below* the mean. Why? Because you intuitively understand that there is a **correlation**, a relationship, between height and weight, with tall people usually weighing more than short people. Given that 125 pounds is less than the average weight for males, you will probably guess a less-than-average height. The statistic used to measure this type of relationship between two variables is called a correlation coefficient.

Correlation Coefficient

A **correlation coefficient** measures the relationship between two variables, such as height and weight or IQ and SAT scores. Given any two variables, there are three

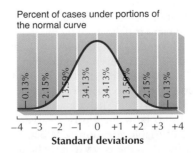

Figure A.4 The normal distribution forms a bell-shaped curve. In a normal distribution, two-thirds of the scores lie between one standard deviation above and one standard deviation below the mean.

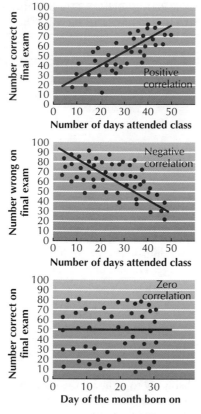

Figure A.5 Three types of correlation. Positive correlation (top): As the number of days of class attendance increases, so does the number of correct exam items. Negative correlation (middle): As the number of days of class attendance increases, the number of incorrect exam items decreases. Zero correlation (bottom): The day of the month on which one is born has no relationship to the number of exam items correct.

TABLE A.9 COMPUTATION OF CORRELATION COEFFICIENT BETWEEN HEIGHT AND WEIGHT FOR 10 MALES

Height (inches) X	X^2	Weight (pounds) Y	Y^2	XY
73	5,329	210	44,100	15,330
64	4,096	133	17,689	8,512
65	4,225	128	16,384	8,320
70	4,900	156	24,336	10,920
74	5,476	189	35,721	13,986
68	4,624	145	21,025	9,860
67	4,489	145	21,025	9,715
72	5,184	166	27,556	11,952
76	5,776	199	37,601	15,124
71	5,041	159	25,281	11,289
700	49,140	1,630	272,718	115,008

$$r = \frac{N \cdot \Sigma XY - \Sigma X \cdot \Sigma Y}{\sqrt{[N \cdot \Sigma X^2 - (\Sigma X)^2]} \sqrt{[N \cdot \Sigma Y^2 - (\Sigma Y)^2]}}$$

$$r = \frac{10 \cdot 115,008 - 700 \cdot 1,630}{\sqrt{[10 \cdot 49,140 - 700^2]} \sqrt{[10 \cdot 272,718 - 1,630^2]}}$$

$$r = 0.92$$

possible relationships between them: **positive, negative,** and **zero** (no relationship). A positive relationship exists when the two variables vary in the same direction (e.g., as height increases, weight normally also increases). A negative relationship occurs when the two variables vary in opposite directions (e.g., as temperatures go up, hot chocolate sales go down). There is no relationship when the two variables vary totally independently of one another (e.g., there is no relationship between peoples' height and the color of their toothbrushes). Figure A.5 illustrates these three types of correlations.

The computation and the formula for a correlation coefficient (correlation coefficient is delineated by the letter "r") are shown in Table A.9. The correlation coefficient (r) always has a value between +1 and −1 (it is never greater than +1 and it is never smaller than −1). When r is close to +1, it signifies a high positive relationship between the two variables (as one variable goes up, the other variable also goes up). When r is close to −1, it signifies a high negative relationship between the two variables (as one variable goes up, the other variable goes down). When r is 0, there is no linear relationship between the two variables being measured.

Correlation coefficients can be quite helpful in making predictions. Bear in mind, however, that predictions are just that: *predictions*. They will have some error as long as the correlation coefficients on which they are based are not perfect (+1 or −1). Also, correlations cannot reveal any information regarding causation. Merely because two factors are correlated, it does not mean that one factor causes the other. Consider, for example, ice cream consumption and swimming pool use. These two variables are positively correlated with one another, in that as ice cream consumption increases, so does swimming pool use. But nobody would suggest that eating ice cream *causes* swimming, or vice versa. Similarly, just because Michael Jordan eats Wheaties and can do a slam dunk it does not mean that you will be able to do one if you eat the same breakfast. The only way to determine the cause of behavior is to conduct an experiment and analyze the results by using inferential statistics.

Inferential Statistics

Knowing the descriptive statistics associated with different distributions, such as the mean and standard deviation, can enable us to make comparisons between various distributions. By making these comparisons, we may be able to observe whether one variable is related to another or whether one variable has a causal effect on another. When we design an experiment specifically to measure causal effects between two or more variables, we use **inferential** statistics to analyze the data collected. Although there are many inferential statistics, the one we will discuss is the t-test, since it is the simplest.

t-Test Suppose we believe that drinking alcohol causes a person's reaction time to slow down. To test this hypothesis, we recruit 20 participants and separate them into two groups. We

TABLE A.10 REACTION TIMES IN MILLISECONDS (MSEC) FOR SUBJECTS IN ALCOHOL AND NO ALCOHOL CONDITIONS AND COMPUTATION OF t

RT (msec) Alcohol X_1	RT (msec) No Alcohol X_2
200	143
210	137
140	179
160	184
180	156
187	132
196	176
198	148
140	125
159	120
$SX_1 = 1{,}770$	$SX_2 = 1{,}500$
$N_1 = 10$	$N_2 = 10$
$\bar{X}_1 = 177$	$\bar{X}_2 = 150$
$s_1 = 24.25$	$s_2 = 21.86$

$$\Sigma_{\bar{X}_1} = \frac{s}{\sqrt{N_1 - 1}} = 8.08 \qquad \Sigma_{\bar{X}_2} = \frac{s}{\sqrt{N_2 - 1}} = 7.29$$

$$S_{\bar{X}_1 - \bar{X}_2} = \sqrt{S_{\bar{X}_1}^2 + S_{\bar{X}_2}^2} = \sqrt{8.08^2 + 7.29^2} = 10.88$$

$$t = \frac{\bar{X}_1 - \bar{X}_2}{S_{\bar{X}_1 - \bar{X}_2}} = \frac{177 - 150}{10.88} = 2.48$$

$$t = 2.48, \, p < .05$$

ask the participants in one group to drink a large glass of orange juice with one ounce of alcohol for every 100 pounds of body weight (e.g., a person weighing 150 pounds would get 1.5 ounces of alcohol). We ask the control group to drink an equivalent amount of orange juice with no alcohol added. Fifteen minutes after the drinks, we have each participant perform a reaction time test that consists of pushing a button as soon as a light is flashed. (The reaction time is the time between the onset of the light and the pressing of the button.) Table A.10 shows the data from this hypothetical experiment. It is clear from the data that there is definitely a difference in the reaction times of the two groups: There is an obvious difference between the means. However, it is possible that this difference is due merely to chance. To determine whether the difference is real or due to chance, we can conduct a *t*-test. We have run a sample *t*-test in Table A.10.

The logic behind a *t*-test is relatively simple. In our experiment we have two samples. If each of these samples is from the *same* population (e.g., the population of all people, whether drunk or sober), then any difference between the samples will be due to chance. On the other hand, if the two samples are from *different* populations (e.g., the population of drunk people *and* the population of sober people), then the difference is a significant difference and not due to chance.

If there is a significant difference between the two samples, then the independent variable must have caused that difference. In our example, there is a significant difference between the alcohol and the no alcohol groups. We can tell this because *p* (the probability that this *t* value will occur by chance) is less than .05. To obtain the *p*, we need only look up the *t* value in a statistical table, which is found in any statistics book. In our example, because there is a significant difference between the groups, we can reasonably conclude that the alcohol did cause a slower reaction time.

APPENDIX B
Answers to Review Questions and
Try This Yourself Activities

Chapter 1 *Introducing Psychology Page 9* 1. scientific; behavior; mental processes. 2. The process of objectively evaluating, comparing, analyzing, and synthesizing information. 3. (a). *Description* tells "what" occurred. (b). An *explanation* tells "why" a behavior occurred. (c). *Prediction* specifies the conditions under which a behavior or event is likely to occur. (d). *Change* means applying psychological knowledge to prevent unwanted outcomes or bring about desired goals 4. (a) biopsychology or neuroscience, (b) developmental psychology, (c) cognitive psychology, (d) clinical and/or counseling psychology, (e) industrial/organizational psychology. *Origins of Psychology Page 17* 1. structuralist. 2. Functionalists. 3. Freud's theories are controversial because of his nonscientific approach, emphasis on sexual and aggressive impulses, and possible sexist bias in his writings and theories. 4. a. *The Science of Psychology Pages 23–24* 1. c. 2. a. 3. d. 4. c. 5. Obtaining informed consent from research participants and debriefing them after the research is conducted helps ensure the well-being of the participant and helps maintain high ethical standards. Deception is sometimes necessary in psychological research because if participants know the true purpose of the study, their response will be unnatural. *Experimental Research Page 31* 1. In an experiment, the experimenter manipulates and controls the variables, which allows them to isolate a single factor and examine the effect of that factor alone on a particular behavior. 2. d. 3. c. 4. The two primary problems for researchers are experimenter bias and ethnocentrism. The two problems for participants are sample bias and participant bias. To guard against **experimenter bias,** researchers employ blind observers, single-blind and **double-blind studies,** and **placebos.** To control for **ethnocentrism,** they use cross-cultural sampling. To offset participant problems with **sample bias,** researchers use random/representative sampling and **random assignment.** To control for participant bias, they rely on many of the same controls in place to prevent experimenter bias, such as double-blind studies. They also attempt to assure anonymity, confidentiality, and sometimes use deception. *Descriptive, Correlational, and Biological Research Page 40* 1. c. 2. d. 3. c. 4. CT, PET, MRI, fMRI.

Chapter 2 *Neural Bases of Behavior Pages 62–63* 1. Check your diagram with Figure 2.1. 2. c. 3. b. 4. Neurotransmitters are manufactured and released at the synapse, where the messages are picked up and relayed by neighboring neurons. Hormones are released from glands in the endocrine system directly into the bloodstream. *Nervous System Organization Pages 67–68* 1. central; peripheral. 2. d. 3. d. 4. The sympathetic nervous system arouses the body and mobilizes energy stores to deal with emergencies. The parasympathetic nervous system calms the body and conserves the energy stores. *Lower-Level Brain Structures Page 72* 1. medulla, pons, and cerebellum. 2. cerebellum. 3. b. 4. The amygdale is important because of its role in the production and regulation of emotions, particularly aggression and fear. *The Cerebral Cortex and Two Brains in One? Pages 83–84* 1. cerebral cortex. 2. occipital; temporal; frontal; parietal. 3. a. 4. c. *Our Genetic Inheritance Page 90* 1. d. 2. Behavioral geneticists use twin studies, adoption studies, family studies, and genetic abnormalities. 3. c. 4. Because natural selection favors animals whose concern for kin is proportional to their degree of biological relatedness, most people will devote more resources, protection, love, and concern to close relatives, which helps ensure their genetic survival.

Chapter 3 *Sources of Stress Page 103* 1. a. 2. a. 3. a blocked goal; conflict. 4. A forced choice between apple or pumpkin pie is an example of an approach-approach conflict. Having to choose between attending a desirable college versus not going to that college because you know your ex is also going there is an example of an approach-avoidance conflict. Taking an exam when you're underprepared or not taking the exam and receiving an automatic "F" is an example of an avoidance-avoidance conflict. *Effects of Stress Page 106* 1. Under stress, the sympathetic branch of the autonomic nervous system is activated, thereby increasing heart rate, blood pressure, etc. In contrast, the parasympathetic branch of the autonomic nervous system is activated under relaxed conditions and it lowers heart rate and blood pressure, while increasing activity in the stomach and intestines. 2. The HPA axis increases the level of cortisol, which decreases the resistance of the immune system. 3. alarm; resistance; exhaustion. 4. b. *Stress and Illness Page 111* 1. epinephrine; cortisol. 2. b. 3. A hardy personality is based on three qualities: a commitment to personal goals, control over life, and viewing change as a challenge rather than a threat. People with these qualities are more successful at dealing with stress because they take a more active, positive approach and assume responsibility for their stress. 4. Severe anxiety. *Health Psychology in Action Page 119* 1. In addition to social pressures that encourage smoking, nicotine is a powerfully addictive drug and smokers learn to associate positive things with smoking. 2. d. 3. alcohol. 4. a. *Health and Stress Management Page 124* 1. a. emotion-focused; b. problem-focused. 2. Defense mechanisms alleviate anxiety and help us cope with stress, but we should avoid overusing them because they distort reality. 3. internal. 4. The seven resources are health and exercise, positive beliefs, social skills, social support, material resources, control, and relaxation. Individual responses will vary depending on personality and individual life style.

Chapter 4 *Understanding Sensation Page 135* 1. d. 2. absolute threshold. 3. Your sensory receptors for smell adapt and send fewer messages to your brain. 4. b. *How We See and Hear Page 142* 1. Compare your diagram to Figure 4.4. 2. thinning and flattening; accommodation. 3. Compare your diagram to Figure 4.6. 4. Place theory explains higher-pitched sounds by where along the basilar membrane the hairs are bent. Frequency theory says low-pitched sounds are due to the hair cells firing action potentials at the same rate as the sound frequency. *Our Other Senses Page 146* 1. pheromones. 2. d. 3. kinesthetic. 4. d. *Selection Page 149* 1. Illusions are false or misleading perceptions of the physical world produced by actual physical distortions. Hallucinations are imaginary sensory perceptions that occur without an external stimulus. Delusions are false beliefs. 2. feature detectors. 3. "Horizontal cats" reared in a horizontal world fail to develop potential feature detectors for vertical lines or objects. 4. c. *Organization — Form and Constancies Page 154* 1. proximity, similarity, closure. 2. size constancy. 3. brightness constancy. 4. c. *Organization — Depth and Color—and Interpretation Page 161* 1. c. 2. b. 3. color aftereffects, green rectangle. 4. The trichromatic system operates at the level of the retina. The opponent-process system occurs at the level of the brain. 5. a. *Subliminal Perception and ESP Pages 164–165* 1. b. 2. a. 3. telepathy, clairvoyance, precognition, psychokinesis. 4. usually cannot be replicated.

Chapter 5 *Understanding Consciousness Pages 172–173* 1. b. 2. They considered it too unscientific and not the proper focus of psychology. 3.

focused, minimal. 4. d. *Circadian Rhythms and Stages of Sleep Page 180* 1. d. 2. b. 3. an electroencephalograph (EEG). 4. a. *Theories of Sleep and Dreams Page 184* 1. Repair/restoration theory suggests we sleep to physically restore our mind and body. Evolutionary/circadian theory says that sleep evolved because it helped conserve energy and provided protection from predators. 2. d. 3. c. 4. REM. *Sleep Disorders Page 188* 1. insomnia. 2. sleep apnea. 3. night terrors. 4. narcolepsy. *Psychoactive Drugs Pages 198–199* 1. c. 2. d. 3. Physical dependence refers to changes in the bodily processes that require continued use of the drug to prevent withdrawal symptoms. Psychological dependence refers to the mental desire or craving to achieve the effects produced by the drug. 4. Psychoactive drugs can alter the production or synthesis, affect storage or release, alter the reception, and block the deactivation of neurotransmitters. *Healthier Ways to Alter Consciousness Page 202* 1. d. 2. narrowed, highly focused attention; increased use of imagination and hallucinations; a passive and receptive attitude; decreased responsiveness to pain; and heightened suggestibility. 3. Hypnosis requires the subject to make a conscious decision to relinquish some personal control of his or her consciousness. 4. According to the *relaxation/role-playing theory*, hypnosis is a normal mental state in which deeply relaxed, suggestible people allow the hypnotist to direct their fantasies and behavior. In contrast, the *altered-state theory* suggests that hypnotic effects result from a special altered state of consciousness.

Chapter 6 *Pavlov and Watson's Contributions Page 213* 1. b. 2. conditioned stimulus, conditioned response. 3. d. 4. c. *Basic Principles of Classical Conditioning Pages 215–216* 1. You no longer respond to the sound of the fire alarm because your response has been extinguished, which occurs when the UCS is repeatedly withheld, and the association between the CS and the UCS is broken. 2. d. 3. higher-order conditioning. 4. c. *Operant Conditioning Page 227* 1. Operant conditioning occurs when organisms learn by the consequences of their responses, whereas in classical conditioning organisms learn by pairing up associations. Operant conditioning is voluntary, whereas classical conditioning is involuntary. 2. c. 3. resistant. 4. Answers may include punishment is often not immediate or consistent, the recipient of the punishment only learns what *not* to do, increased aggression, passive aggressiveness, avoidance behavior, modeling, temporary suppression, and learned helplessness. *Cognitive-Social Learning Page 232* 1. c. 2. latent learning. 3. cognitive maps. 4. b. *The Biology of Learning Page 235* 1. evolutionary. 2. Garcia and his colleagues laced freshly killed sheep with a chemical that caused nausea and vomiting in coyotes. After the coyotes ate the tainted meat and became ill, they avoided all sheep. 3. Biological preparedness refers to the fact that organisms are innately predisposed to form associations between certain stimuli and responses. 4. Instinctive drift. *Using Conditioning and Learning Principles Page 242* 1. d. 2. c. 3. c. 4. Video games may increase aggressive tendencies because they are interactive, engrossing, and require the player to identify with the aggressor.

Chapter 7 *Try This Yourself Page 261* Rudolph, Dancer, Cupid, Comet, Blitzen, Donner, Dasher, Prancer, Vixen. *The Nature of Memory Page 262* 1. encoding; storage. 2. According to the parallel distributed processing (PDP), or *connectionist*, model, memory resembles a vast number of interconnected units and modules distributed throughout a huge network, all operating in parallel — simultaneously. The levels of processing model suggests memory depends on the degree or depth of mental processing occurring when material is initially encountered. 3. sensory memory, short-term memory, long-term memory. 4. Semantic memory stores general knowledge, whereas episodic memory stores memories of events. 5. recognition, recall. *Forgetting Page 268* 1. Retrieval failure theory; decay theory; motivated forgetting theory. 2. d.

3. Using distributed practice, you would space your study time into many learning periods with rest periods in between; using massed practice, you would "cram" all your learning into long, unbroken periods. 4. Answers will vary. *Biological Bases of Memory Page 273* 1. Repeated stimulation of a synapse can strengthen the synapse by stimulating the dendrites to grow more spines, and the ability of a particular neuron to release its neurotransmitters can be increased or decreased. 2. d. 3. amnesia. 4. d. *Research Highlight—Memory and the Criminal Justice System Page 276* 1. d. 2. d. 3. easy. 4. False memories are imagined events constructed in the mind, whereas repressed memories are painful memories that are supposedly "forgotten" in an effort to avoid the pain of their retrieval. *Using Psychology to Improve Our Memory Pages 280–281* 1. Given that the duration of short-term memory is about 30 seconds, to lengthen this time use *maintenance rehearsal*, which involves continuously repeating the material. To effectively encode memory into long-term memory, use *elaborative rehearsal*, which involves thinking about the material and relating it to other information that has already been stored. 2. Because we tend to remember information that falls at the beginning or end of a sequence, we should spend extra time studying information in the middle of the chapter. 3. organization. 4. Peg-word system, method of loci, method of word associations, substitute word system.

Chapter 8 *Try This Yourself Page 288* The figures in b are not the same. To solve this problem, mentally rotate one of the objects and then compare the rotated image with the other object to see whether they matched or not. The figures in b were more difficult to solve because they required a greater degree of mental rotation. This is also true of real objects in physical space. It takes more time and energy to turn a cup 20 degrees to the right, than to turn it 150 degrees. *Cognitive Building Blocks Page 290* 1. c. 2. There are at least three methods — artificial concepts, natural concepts, and hierarchies. 3. prototype. 4. b. *Problem Solving Page 296* 1. *Preparation*, in which we identify the facts, determine which ones are relevant, and define the goal; *production*, in which we propose possible solutions, or hypotheses; and *evaluation*, in which we determine whether the solutions meet the goal. 2. b. 3. d. 4. mental sets, functional fixedness, confirmation bias, availability heuristic, and representativeness heuristic. *Creativity Page 299* 1. c. 2. divergent, convergent, divergent. 3. intellectual ability, knowledge, thinking style, personality, motivation, and environment. *Language Page 305* 1. phonemes, morphemes. 2. overgeneralization. 3. b. 4. a. *What Is Intelligence? Page 309* 1. b. 2. Fluid intelligence refers to reasoning abilities, memory, and speed of information processing. Crystallized intelligence refers to knowledge and skills gained through experience and education. 3. d. 4. Sternberg proposed that intelligence is composed of three aspects — analytic, creative, and practical. *How Do We Measure Intelligence Page 312* 1. The Stanford–Binet is a single test consisting of several sets of various age-level items. The Wechsler consists of three separate tests. 2. 90. 3. reliability, validity, standardization. *The Intelligence Controversy Pages 319–320* 1. d. 2. d. 3. d. 4. Heredity and environment are both important, interacting influences.

Chapter 9 *Studying Development Page 331* 1. Developmental psychology studies age-related changes in behavior and mental processes from conception to death. 2. nature or nurture, continuity or stages, stability or change. 3. d. 4. c. *Physical Development Page 340* 1. The three major stages are the germinal period, the embryonic period, and the fetal period. 2. b. 3. c. 4. primary aging. *Cognitive development Page 349* 1. c. 2. 1b, 2a, 3d, 4c, 5d. 3. Piaget has been criticized for underestimating abilities, genetic, and cultural influences, but his contributions to the understanding of a child's cognitive development offset these criticisms. *Social-Emotional Development Page 355* 1. b. 2. Securely attached, avoidant, and anxious-ambivalent; 3. 1a, 2c, 3. Mary shows an avoidant style. Bob demonstrates an anxious/ambivalent style. Rashelle shows a secure attachment style. 4. Permissive parents either set few limits and provide little attention (the permissive-indifferent), or they're highly involved but place few demands (the permissive-indulgent). Authoritarian parents value unquestioning obedience and mature responsibility from their children. Authoritative parents are caring and sensitive, but also set firm limits and enforce them.

Chapter 10 *Moral Development Page 367* 1. Preconventional, postconventional, conventional. 2. c. 3. b. 4. Kohlberg's theory may be culturally biased toward individualism versus community and interpersonal relationships. His theory may be gender biased because it supposedly favors the male perspective. *Personality Development Pages 371–372* 1. c. 2. Thomas and Chess describe three categories of temperament — easy, difficult, and slow-to-warm-up — that seem to correlate with stable personality differences. 3. a) trust versus mistrust, b) identity versus role confusion, c) initiative versus guilt, d) ego integrity versus despair. 4. Research shows that beliefs about adolescent storm and stress, the midlife crisis, and the empty nest syndrome may be exaggerated accounts of a few people's experiences and not those of most people. *Meeting the Challenges of Adulthood Pages 380–381* 1. c. 2. activity; disengagement. 3. c. 4. The social support may help reduce the losses that accompany aging. *Grief and Death Page 385* 1. Preschool children only understand the permanence of death, they do not yet comprehend the nonfunctionality or universality of death. 2. d. 3. a) bargaining, b) denial, c) acceptance, d) anger, e) depression. 4. d.

Chapter 11 *Sex and Gender Pages 399–400* 1. b) Chromosomal sex, d) gender identity a) gonadal sex, i) gender role c) hormonal sex e) secondary sex characteristics g) external genitals, h) sexual orientation, f) internal accessory organs. 2. d. 3. Social learning theory emphasizes learning through rewards, punishments, and imitation. Cognitive-developmental theory focuses on the active, thinking processes of the individual. 4. d. *The Study of Human Sexuality Page 403* 1. b. 2. Ellis based his research on personal diaries. Masters and Johnson pioneered the use of direct observation and measurement of bodily responses during sexual activities. Kinsey popularized the use of the survey method. 3. Cultural comparisons put sex in a broader perspective and help counteract ethnocentrism. 4. d. *Sexual Behavior Page 407* 1. Masters and Johnson identified a four-stage sexual response cycle (excitement, plateau, orgasm, and resolution) that acknowledged both similarities and differences between the sexes. However differences are the focus of most research. 2. According to the evolutionary perspective, males engage in more sexual behaviors with more sexual partners because it helps the species survive. The social role perspective suggests this difference reflects a double standard, which subtly encourages male sexuality while discouraging female sexuality. 3. c. 4. d. *Active Learning Exercise Page 416* Gender role conditioning — A main part of traditional gender conditioning is the belief that women should be the "gatekeepers" for sexuality and men should be the "pursuers." This belief contributes to the myth that male sexuality is overpowering and women are responsible for controlling the situation. Double standard — Female gender role also encourages passivity, and women are not taught how to aggressively defend themselves. People who believe the myth that women cannot be raped against their will generally overlook the fact that the female gender role encourages passivity and women are not taught how to aggressively defend themselves. Media portrayals — Novels and films typically portray a woman resisting her attacker and then melting into passionate responsiveness. This helps perpetuate the myth that women secretly want to be raped and the myth that she might as well "relax and enjoy it." Lack of information — The myth that women cannot be raped against their will overlooks the fact that most men are much stronger and much faster than most women, and a

woman's clothing and shoes further hinder her ability to escape. The myth that women cannot rape men ignores the fact that men can have erections despite negative emotions while being raped. Furthermore, an erection is unnecessary, since many rapists (either male or female) often use foreign objects to rape their victims. The myth that all women secretly want to be raped overlooks the fact that if a woman fantasizes about being raped she remains in complete control, whereas in an actual rape she is completely powerless. Also, fantasies contain no threat of physical harm, while rape does.

Tips for Rape Prevention Sex educators and researchers suggest the following techniques for reducing stranger rape (the rape of a person by an unknown assailant) and acquaintance (or date) rape (committed by someone who is known to the victim) (Allgeier & Allgeier, 2005; Crooks & Baur, 2005). To avoid stranger rape: 1. Follow commonsense advice for avoiding all forms of crime: lock your car, park in lighted areas, install dead-bolt locks on your doors, don't open your door to strangers, don't hitchhike, etc. 2. Make yourself as strong as possible. Take a self-defense course, carry a loud whistle with you, and demonstrate self-confidence with your body language. Research shows that rapists tend to select women who appear passive and weak (Richards et al., 1991). 3. During an attack, run away if you can, talk to the rapist as a way to stall, and/or attempt to alert others by screaming ("Help, rape, call the police") (Shotland & Stebbins, 1980). When all else fails, women should actively resist an attack, according to current research (Fischhoff, 1992; Furby & Fischhoff, 1992). Loud shouting, fighting back, and causing a scene may deter an attack. To prevent acquaintance rape: 1. Be careful on first dates — date in groups and in public places; avoid alcohol and other drugs (Gross & Billingham, 1998). 2. Be assertive and clear in your communication — say what you want and what you don't want. Accept a partner's refusal. If sexual coercion escalates, match the assailant's behavior with your own form of escalation — begin with firm refusals, get louder, threaten to call the police, begin shouting and use strong physical resistance. Don't be afraid to make a scene! *Sexual Problems Page 416* 1. The parasympathetic branch of the autonomic nervous system dominates during sexual arousal, whereas the sympathetic branch dominates during ejaculation and orgasm. 2. c. 3. Relationship focus, integration of physiological and psychosocial factors, emphasis on cognitive factors, emphasis on specific behavioral techniques. 4. Remain abstinent or have sex with one mutually faithful, uninfected partner. Do not use IV drugs or have sex with someone who does. If you do use IV drugs, sterilize or don't share equipment. Avoid contact with blood, vaginal secretions, and semen. Avoid anal intercourse. Don't have sex if either you or your partner is impaired by drugs.

Chapter 12 *Theories and Concepts of Motivation Page 428* 1. An instinct is an unlearned, behavioral pattern that is uniform in expression and universal in a species. Homeostasis is the state of balance or stability in the body's internal environment. 2. (a)ii, (b)iii, (c)v, (d)iv, (e)i. 3. d. 4. d. 5. c. *Motivation and Behavior Page 436* 1. d. 2. anorexia nervosa. 3. d. 4. preference for moderately difficult tasks, competitiveness, preference for clear goals with competent feedback, responsibility, persistence, more accomplishments. *Theories and Concepts of Emotion Pages 443–444* 1. (a)iii, (b)i, (c)ii and iv. 2. sympathetic, autonomic. 3. a. 4. d. 5. simultaneously. *Critical Thinking About Motivation and Behavior Page 452* 1. d. 2. c. 3. a. 4. b.

Chapter 13 *Trait Theories Pages 464–465* 1. b. 2. (a)ii, (b)iii, (c)iv, (d)v, (e)vi. 3. e. *Psychoanalytic/Psychodynamic Theories Pages 474–475* 1. The *conscious* is the tip of the iceberg and the highest level of awareness; the *preconscious* is just below the surface but can readily be brought to awareness; the *unconscious* is the large base of the iceberg and operates below the level of awareness. 2. b. 3. Freud believed an individual's adult personality reflected his or her resolution of the specific crisis presented in each psychosexual stage (oral, anal, phallic, latency, and genital). 4. (a) Adler, (b) Horney, (c) Jung, (d) Horney. *Humanistic Theories Page 478* 1. a. 2. c. 3. self-actualization. 4. Humanistic theories are criticized for their naive assumptions, poor testability and inadequate evidence, and narrowness in merely describing, not explaining, behavior. *Social-Cognitive Theories Pages 479–480* 1. how each individual thinks about the world and interprets experiences. 2. a. 3. c. 4. external locus of control, internal locus of control. *Biological Theories Page 482* 1. d. 2. Some researchers emphasize the importance of the unshared environment, while others fear that genetic determinism could be misused to "prove" certain ethnic groups are inferior, male dominance is natural, or that social progress is impossible. 3. b. 4. c. *Personality Assessment Pages 489–490* 1. (a)ii, (b)i, (c)iii. 2. b. 3. People accept pseudo personality tests because they offer generalized statements that apply to almost everyone (Barnum effect), they notice and remember events that confirm predictions and ignore the misses (fallacy of positive instances), and they prefer information that maintains a positive self-image (self-serving bias). 4. Western, individualistic countries emphasize the "self" as separate and autonomous from others, whereas collectivist cultures see the "self" as inherently linked to others.

Chapter 14 *Studying Psychological Disorders Page 506* 1. Statistical infrequency, disability or dysfunction, personal distress, and violation of norms. 2. b. 3. Early versions of the DSM used *neurosis* to refer to mental disorders related to anxiety. In contrast, *psychosis* is currently used to describe disorders characterized by loss of contact with reality and extreme mental disruption. *Insanity* is a legal term for people with a mental disorder that implies a lack of responsibility for behavior and an inability to manage their own affairs. 4. The chief advantages of the DSM is that it provides detailed descriptions of symptoms, which in turn allows standardized diagnosis and improved communication among professionals and between professionals and patients. The major disadvantage is that the label "mental illness" can lead to social and economic discrimination. *Anxiety Disorders Page 511* 1. (a)ii, (b)i, (c)iii, (d)iv. 2. psychological, biological, and sociocultural factors. 3. Learning theorists most often believe anxiety disorders result from classical and operant conditioning. Social learning theorists argue that imitation and modeling are the cause. *Mood Disorders Page 517* 1. a. 2. c. 3. Seligman believes the individual becomes resigned to pain and sadness and feels unable to change, which leads to depression. 4. b. *Schizophrenia Page 525* 1. c. 2. psychosis. 3. a. 4. Three biological causes include malfunctioning neurotransmitters, brain abnormalities, and genetic predisposition. Two possible psychosocial causes of schizophrenia may be stress and family communication problems. *Applying Psychology to Student Life Exercise Page 530* 1. c. 2. e. 3. b. 4. a. 5. f. 6. d. *Other Disorders Page 530* 1. anxiety. 2. Dissociative identity disorder (DID) refers to a dissociative disorder characterized by the presence of two or more distinct personality systems within the same individual. 3. Antisocial personality. 4. d.

Chapter 15 *Psychoanalysis/Psychodynamic Therapies Page 541* 1. c. 2. Mary is exhibiting transference, reacting to her therapist as she apparently did to someone earlier in her life. John is exhibiting resistance, arriving late because he fears what his unconscious might reveal. 3. Limited applicability, lack of scientific credibility. 4. Modern psychodynamic therapy is briefer, face-to-face, more directive, and emphasizes current problems and conscious processes. *Try This Yourself Page 546* All four techniques are shown in this example: empathy ("they scare the hell out

of me too"), unconditional positive regard (therapist's acceptance and nonjudgmental attitude and caring about not wanting to do "anything that is upsetting" to the client), genuineness (the therapist's ability to laugh and make a joke at his or her own expense); and active listening (therapist demonstrated genuine interest in what the client was saying). *Cognitive and Humanistic Therapies Page 547* 1. a. 2. The activating event, the belief system, the emotional consequence, and disputing irrational thoughts. 3. a) magnification, b) all-or-nothing thinking. 4. a) empathy, b) genuineness, c) unconditional positive regard. *Group, Family, and Marital Therapies Page 550* 1. c. 2. Less expense, group support, insight and information, behavior rehearsal. 3. Self-help groups are recommended as a supplement to individual therapy. 4. d. *Behavior Therapies Pages 554–555* 1. behavior therapy. 2. c. 3. By rewarding successive approximations of a target behavior, the patient is "shaped" toward more adaptive behaviors. 4. Behavior therapy is criticized for lack of generalizability and questionable ethics. *Biomedical Therapies Page 559* 1. d. 2. antianxiety, antipsychotic, antidepressant, and mood stabilizer. 3. a. 4. c. *Therapy and Critical Thinking Pages 567–568* 1. (a) cognitive therapists, (b) psychoanalysts, (c) biomedical therapists, (d) humanistic therapists, (e) behaviorists. 2. Naming the problem, qualities of the therapist, establishment of credibility, placing the problem in a familiar framework, applying techniques to bring relief, a special time and place. 3. c. 4. Rates of diagnosis and treatment of mental disorders, stresses of poverty, stresses of multiple roles, stresses of aging, violence against women. 5. d.

Chapter 16 *Our Thoughts about Others Page 580* 1. c. 2. When judging the causes of others' behaviors, we tend to overestimate internal personality factors and underestimate external situational factors. 3. d. 4. cognitive dissonance. *Our Feelings about Others Pages 589–590* 1. Prejudice is an attitude with behavioral tendencies that may or may not be activated. Discrimination is actual negative behavior directed at members of an outgroup. 2. b. 3. c. 4. Romantic love is short lived (6 to 30 months) and largely based on mystery and fantasy, which leads to inevitable disappointment. Companionate love is long lasting and grows stronger with time. *Social Influence Page 597* 1. Conformity involves changing behavior in response to real or imagined pressure from others. Obedience involves giving in to a command from others. 2. d. 3. c. 4. c. *Group Processes Page 601* 1. Guards were abusing their power and prisoners were becoming dehumanized and depressed. 2. b. 3. illusion of invulnerability, belief in the morality of the group, collective rationalizations, stereotypes of the outgroup, self-censorship of doubts and dissenting opinions, illusion of unanimity, and direct pressure on dissenters. 4. b. *Aggression and Altruism Pages 606–607* 1. The five major biological factors are instincts, genes, brain and nervous system, substance use and other mental disorders, hormones and neurotransmitters. The three key psychosocial factors are aversive stimuli, culture and learning, and violent media and video games. 2. Introduce incompatible responses and improve social and communication skills. 3. According to evolutionary theorists, altruism evolved because it favored overall genetic survival. The egoistic model says helping is motivated by anticipated gain for the helper. The empathy–altruism hypothesis suggests helping is activated when the helper feels empathy for the victim. 4. d. *Applying Social Psychology to Social Problems Pages 610–611* 1. d. 2. cognitive dissonance. 3. b. 4. Rosa Parks' act of disobedience was an important catalyst for the small but growing civil rights movement and the later repeal of Jim Crow laws in the South.

GLOSSARY

Abnormal Behavior Patterns of emotion, thought, and action considered pathological (diseased or disordered) for one or more of these reasons: statistical infrequency, disability or dysfunction, personal distress, or violation of norms *Page 498*

Absolute Threshold Smallest amount of a stimulus needed to detect that the stimulus is present *Page 133*

Accommodation Automatic adjustment of the eye, which occurs when muscles change the shape of the lens so that it focuses light on the retina from objects at different distances *Page 341*

Accommodation In Piaget's theory, adjusting old schemas or developing new ones to better fit with new information *Page 138*

Achievement Motivation Desire to excel, especially in competition with others *Page 434*

Action Potential Neural impulse that carries information along the axon of a neuron. The action potential is generated when positively charged ions move in and out through channels in the axon's membrane *Page 57*

Activation–Synthesis Hypothesis Hobson's theory that dreams are by-products of random stimulation of brain cells; the brain attempts to combine (or synthesize) this spontaneous activity into coherent patterns, known as dreams *Page 182*

Active Listening Listening with total attention to what another is saying; involves reflecting, paraphrasing, and clarifying what the person says and means *Page 546*

Activity Theory Successful aging is fostered by a full and active commitment to life *Page 379*

Addiction Broad term describing a compulsion to use a specific drug or engage in a certain activity *Page 189*

Ageism Prejudice or discrimination based on physical age *Page 339*

Aggression Any behavior intended to harm someone *Page 601*

AIDS (Acquired Immunodeficiency Syndrome) Human immunodeficiency viruses (HIVs) destroy the immune system's ability to fight disease, leaving the body vulnerable to a variety of opportunistic infections and cancers *Page 414*

Algorithm A set of steps that, if followed correctly, will eventually solve the problem *Page 291*

Alternate States of Consciousness (ASCs) Mental states other than ordinary waking consciousness, found during sleep, dreaming, psychoactive drug use, hypnosis, and so on *Page 171*

Altruism Actions designed to help others with no obvious benefit to the helper *Page 605*

Alzheimer's [ALTS-high-merz] Disease Progressive mental deterioration characterized by severe memory loss *Page 273*

Amplitude Height of a light or sound wave—pertaining to light, it refers to brightness; for sound, it refers to loudness *Page 136*

Amygdala Area of the brain's limbic system involved in emotional responses *Page 437*

Androgyny [an-DRAW-juh-nee] Combining characteristics considered typically male (assertive, athletic) with characteristics considered typically female (yielding, nurturant); from the Greek *andro*, meaning "male," and *gyn*, meaning "female" *Page 397*

Anorexia Nervosa Severe loss of weight resulting from self-imposed starvation and an obsessive fear of obesity *Page 432*

Anterograde Amnesia Inability to form new memories after a brain injury; forward-acting amnesia *Page 272*

Antianxiety Drugs Medications used to treat anxiety disorders *Page 555*

Antidepressant Drugs Medications used to treat depression, some anxiety disorders, and certain eating disorders (such as bulimia) *Page 556*

Antipsychotic Drugs Medications used to diminish or eliminate hallucinations, delusions, withdrawal, and other symptoms of psychosis; also known as neuroleptics or major tranquilizers *Page 555*

Antisocial Personality Disorder Profound disregard for, and violation of, the rights of others *Page 528*

Anxiety Disorder Type of abnormal behavior characterized by unrealistic, irrational fear *Page 506*

Applied Research Research designed to solve practical problems *Page 17*

Approach–Approach Conflict Having to choose between two or more desirable alternatives *Page 102*

Approach–Avoidance Conflict Forced choice between two or more alternatives that have both desirable and undesirable results *Page 102*

Archetypes [AR-KEH-types] According to Jung, the images and patterns of thoughts, feelings, and behavior that reside in the collective unconscious *Page 472*

Arousal Theory Organisms are motivated to achieve and maintain an optimal level of arousal *Page 424*

Assimilation In Piaget's theory, absorbing new information into existing schemas *Page 341*

Association Areas So-called quiet areas in the cerebral cortex involved in interpreting, integrating, and acting on information processed by other parts of the brain *Page 78*

Attachment A strong affectional bond with special others that endures over time *Page 349*

Attitude Learned predisposition to respond cognitively, affectively, and behaviorally to a particular object *Page 574*

Attribution An explanation for the cause of behaviors or events *Page 575*

Audition Sense of hearing *Page 140*

Automatic Processes Mental activities requiring minimal attention and having little impact on other activities *Page 171*

Autonomic Nervous System (ANS) Subdivision of the peripheral nervous system (PNS) that controls involuntary functions, such as heart rate and digestion. It is further subdivided into the sympathetic nervous system, which arouses, and the parasympathetic nervous system, which calms *Page 66*

Availability Heuristic Judging the likelihood or probability of an event based on how readily available other instances of the event are in memory *Page 295*

Aversion Therapy Pairing an aversive (unpleasant) stimulus with a maladaptive behavior *Page 552*

Avoidance–Avoidance Conflict Forced choice between two or more undesirable alternatives *Page 102*

Axon A long, tubelike structure that conveys impulses away from the neuron's cell body toward other neurons or to muscles or glands *Page 55*

Babbling Vowel/consonant combinations that infants begin to produce at about 4 to 6 months of age *Page 302*

Basic Anxiety According to Horney, the feelings of helplessness and insecurity that adults experience because as children they felt alone and isolated in a hostile environment *Page 473*

Basic Research Research conducted to advance scientific knowledge *Page 17*

Behavior Perspective Emphasizes objective, observable environmental influences on overt behavior *Page 12*

Behavior Therapy Group of techniques based on learning principles used to change maladaptive behaviors *Page 550*

Behavioral Genetics Study of the relative effects of heredity and environment on behavior and mental processes *Page 84*

Binge Drinking Occurs when a man consumes five or more drinks in a row, or a woman consumes four or more drinks at a time, on at least three occasions during a two-week period *Page 115*

Binocular Cues Visual input from two eyes that allows perception of depth or distance *Page 155*

Biofeedback An involuntary bodily process (such as blood pressure or heart rate) is recorded, and the information is fed back to an organism to increase voluntary control over that bodily function *Page 239*

Biological Preparedness Built-in (innate) readiness to form associations between certain stimuli and responses *Page 234*

Biological Research Scientific studies of the brain and other parts of the nervous system *Page 36*

Biomedical Therapy Using physiological interventions (drugs, electroconvulsive therapy, and psychosurgery) to reduce or alleviate symptoms of psychological disorders *Page 555*

Biopsychosocial Model Unifying theme of modern psychology that considers biological, psychological, and social processes *Page 16*

Bipolar Disorder Repeated episodes of mania (unreasonable elation and hyperactivity) and depression *Page 531*

Borderline Personality Disorder (BPD) Impulsivity and instability in mood, relationships, and self-image *Page 529*

Bottom-Up Processing Information processing that begins "at the bottom" with raw sensory data that feed "up" to the brain *Page 160*

Brainstem Area of the brain that houses parts of the hindbrain, midbrain, and forebrain, and helps regulate reflex activities critical for survival (such as heartbeat and respiration) *Page 68*

Bulimia Nervosa Consuming large quantities of food (bingeing), followed by vomiting, extreme exercise, and/or laxative use (purging) *Page 432*

Burnout State of psychological and physical exhaustion resulting from chronic expo-

sure to high levels of stress and little personal control *Page 101*

Cannon–Bard Theory Arousal, behavior, and emotions occur simultaneously; in this view, all emotions are physiologically similar *Page 440*

Case Study In-depth study of a single research participant *Page 33*

Cell Body The part of the neuron that contains the cell nucleus, as well as other structures that help the neuron carry out its functions; also known as the soma *Page 55*

Central Nervous System (CNS) The brain and spinal cord *Page 63*

Cerebellum [sehr-uh-BELL-um] Hindbrain structure responsible for coordinating fine muscle movement, balance, and some perception and cognition *Page 69*

Cerebral Cortex Thin surface layer on the cerebral hemispheres that regulates most complex behavior, including sensations, motor control, and higher mental processes *Page 73*

Chromosome Threadlike molecule of DNA (deoxyribonucleic acid) that carries genetic information *Page 84*

Chronic Pain Continuous or recurrent pain over a period of six months or longer *Page 117*

Chunking Grouping separate pieces of information into a single unit (or chunk) *Page 254*

Circadian [ser-KAY-dee-an] Rhythms Biological changes that occur on a 24-hour cycle (*circa* = "about" and *dies* = "day") *Page 174*

Classical Conditioning Learning that occurs when a neutral stimulus (NS) becomes paired (associated) with an unconditioned stimulus (UCS) to elicit a conditioned response (CR) *Page 210*

Client-Centered Therapy Rogers's therapy emphasizing the client's natural tendency to become healthy and productive; techniques include empathy, unconditional positive regard, genuineness, and active listening *Page 545*

Cochlea[KOK-lee-uh] Three-chambered, snail-shaped structure in the inner ear containing the receptors for hearing *Page 140*

Coding Process that converts a particular sensory input into a specific sensation *Page 133*

Cognition Mental activities involved in acquiring, storing, retrieving, and using knowledge *Page 287*

Cognitive-Behavior Therapy Beck's system for confronting and changing behaviors associated with destructive cognitions *Page 544*

Cognitive Dissonance A feeling of discomfort caused by a discrepancy between an

attitude and a behavior or between two competing attitudes *Page 578*

Cognitive Map A mental image of a three-dimensional space that an organism has navigated *Page 229*

Cognitive Perspective Focuses on thought, perception, and information processing *Page 13*

Cognitive Restructuring Process in cognitive therapy to change destructive thoughts or inappropriate interpretations *Page 542*

Cognitive-Social Theory Emphasizes the roles of thinking and social learning in behavior *Page 228*

Cognitive Therapy Therapy that focuses on faulty thought processes and beliefs to treat problem behaviors *Page 541*

Collective Unconscious Jung's concept of a reservoir of inherited, universal experiences that all humans share *Page 472*

Collectivistic Cultures The needs and goals of the group are emphasized over the needs and goals of the individual *Page 488*

Comorbidity Co-occurrence of two or more disorders in the same person at the same time, as when a person suffers from both depression and alcoholism *Page 526*

Companionate Love Strong and lasting attraction characterized by trust, caring, tolerance, and friendship *Page 589*

Concept Mental representation of a group or category that shares similar characteristics (e.g., the concept of a river groups together the Nile, the Amazon, and the Mississippi because they share the common characteristic of being a large stream of water that empties into an ocean or lake) *Page 288*

Concrete Operational Stage Piaget's third stage (roughly age 7 to 11); the child can perform mental operations on concrete objects and understand reversibility and conservation, but abstract thinking is not yet present *Page 344*

Conditioned Emotional Response (CER) A classically conditioned emotional response to a previously neutral stimulus (NS) *Page 212*

Conditioned Response (CR) Learned reaction to a conditioned stimulus (CS) that occurs because of previous repeated pairings with an unconditioned stimulus (UCS) *Page 210*

Conditioned Stimulus (CS) Previously neutral stimulus that, through repeated pairings with an unconditioned stimulus (UCS), now causes a conditioned response (CR) *Page 210*

Conditioning The process of learning associations between environmental stimuli and behavioral responses *Page 209*

Conduction Deafness Middle-ear deafness resulting from problems with transferring sound waves to the inner ear. *Page 141*

Cones Receptor cells, concentrated near the center of the retina, responsible for color vision and fine detail; most sensitive in brightly lit conditions *Page 139*

Confirmation Bias Preferring information that confirms preexisting positions or beliefs, while ignoring or discounting contradictory evidence *Page 294*

Conflict Forced choice between two or more incompatible goals or impulses *Page 102*

Conformity Changing behavior because of real or imagined group pressure *Page 590*

Conscious In Freudian terms, thoughts or motives that a person is currently aware of or is remembering *Page 466*

Consciousness An organism's awareness of its own self and surroundings *Page 170*

Conservation Understanding that certain physical characteristics (such as volume) remain unchanged, even when their outward appearance changes *Page 344*

Consolidation Process by which neural changes associated with recent learning become durable and stable *Page 264*

Constructive Process Organizing and shaping of information during processing, storage, and retrieval of memories *Page 249*

Continuous Reinforcement Every correct response is reinforced *Page 219*

Control Group Group receiving no treatment in an experiment *Page 25*

Controlled Processes Mental activities requiring focused attention that generally interfere with other ongoing activities *Page 171*

Conventional Level Kohlberg's second level of moral development, where moral judgments are based on compliance with the rules and values of society *Page 363*

Convergence Binocular depth cue in which the closer the object, the more the eyes converge, or turn inward *Page 155*

Convergent Thinking Narrowing down a list of alternatives to converge on a single correct answer (e.g., standard academic tests generally require convergent thinking) *Page 297*

Cooing Vowel-like sounds infants produce beginning around 2 to 3 months of age *Page 302*

Corpus Callosum [CORE-pus] [cah-LOH-suhm] Bundle of nerve fibers connecting the brain's left and right hemispheres *Page 79*

Correlation Coefficient A number that indicates the degree and direction of the relationship between two variables *Page 34*

Correlational Research Scientific study in which the researcher observes or measures (without directly manipulating) two or more variables to find the relationships between them *Page 34*

Creativity The ability to produce valued outcomes in a novel way *Page 297*

Critical Period A period of special sensitivity to specific types of learning that shapes the capacity for future development *Page 327*

Critical Thinking Process of objectively evaluating, comparing, analyzing, and synthesizing information *Page 5*

Cross-Sectional Method Measures individuals of various ages at one point in time and gives information about age differences *Page 328*

Crystallized Intelligence Knowledge and skills gained through experience and education that tend to increase over the life span *Page 307*

Debriefing Informing participants after the research about the purpose of the study, the nature of the anticipated results, and any deceptions used *Page 21*

Defense Mechanisms In Freudian theory, the ego's protective method of reducing anxiety by disorting reality *Page 468*

Defense Mechanisms Unconscious strategies used to distort reality and relieve anxiety and guilt *Page 120*

Deindividuation Reduced self-consciousness, inhibition, and personal responsibility that sometimes occurs in a group, particularly when the members feel anonymous *Page 598*

Delusions Mistaken beliefs based on a misrepresentations of reality *Page 519*

Dendrites Branching neuron structures that receive neural impulses from other neurons and convey impulses toward the cell body *Page 55*

Dependent Variable (DV) Experimental factor that is measured; it is affected by (or dependent on) the independent variable *Page 25*

Depressants Psychoactive drugs that act on the central nervous system to suppress or slow bodily processes and reduce overall responsiveness *Page 192*

Depth Perception The ability to perceive three-dimensional space and to accurately judge distance *Page 154*

Descriptive Research Research methods that observe and record behavior without producing causal explanations *Page 31*

Developmental Psychology Study of age-related changes in behavior and mental processes from conception to death *Page 326*

Diagnostic and Statistical Manual of Mental Disorders (DSM-IV-TR) Classification system developed by the American Psychiatric Association used to describe abnormal behaviors; the "IV-TR" indicates it is the text revision (TR) of the fourth major revision (IV). *Page 503*

Difference Threshold Minimal difference needed to notice a stimulus change; also called the "just noticeable difference" (JND) *Page 133*

Diffusion of Responsibility The dilution (or diffusion) of personal responsibility for acting by spreading it among all other group members *Page 606*

Discrimination Negative behaviors directed at members of a group *Page 581*

Discriminative Stimulus A cue that signals when a specific response will lead to the expected reinforcement *Page 226*

Disengagement Theory Successful aging is characterized by mutual withdrawal between the elderly and society *Page 379*

Dissociative Disorder Amnesia, fugue, or multiple personalities resulting from a splitting apart of experience from memory or consciousness *Page 526*

Dissociative Identity Disorder (DID) Presence of two or more distinct personality systems in the same individual at different times; previously known as multiple personality disorder *Page 527*

Distress Unpleasant, objectionable stress *Page 99*

Distributed Practice Practice (or study) sessions are interspersed with rest periods *Page 266*

Divergent Thinking Thinking that produces many alternatives or ideas; a major element of creativity (e.g., finding as many uses as possible for a paper clip) *Page 297*

Dopamine Hypothesis Theory that overactivity of dopamine neurons may contribute to some forms of schizophrenia *Page 521*

Double-Blind Study Procedure in which both the researcher and the participants are unaware (blind) of who is in the experimental or control group *Page 27*

Double Standard Beliefs, values, and norms that subtly encourage male sexuality and discourage female sexuality *Page 409*

Dream Analysis In psychoanalysis, interpreting the underlying true meaning of dreams to reveal unconscious processes *Page 538*

Drive-Reduction Theory Motivation begins with a physiological need (a lack or deficiency) that elicits a drive toward behavior that will satisfy the original need; once the need is met, a state of balance (homeostasis) is restored and motivation decreases *Page 423*

Drug Abuse Drug taking that causes emotional or physical harm to the drug user or others *Page 189*

Eclectic Approach Combining techniques from various theories to find the most appropriate treatment *Page 561*

www.wiley.com/college/huffman

Ego In Freud's theory, the rational part of the psyche that deals with reality by controlling the id, while also satisfying the superego; from the Latin term *ego*, meaning "I" *Page 467*

Egocentrism The inability to consider another's point of view, which Piaget considered a hallmark of the preoperational stage *Page 343*

Egoistic Model Helping that's motivated by anticipated gain—later reciprocation, increased self-esteem, or avoidance of distress and guilt *Page 605*

Elaborative Rehearsal Linking new information to previously stored material (also known as deeper levels of processing) *Page 259*

Electroconvulsive Therapy (ECT) Biomedical therapy based on passing electrical current through the brain; used almost exclusively to treat serious depression when drug therapy does not work *Page 557*

Embryonic Period Second stage of prenatal development, which begins after uterine implantation and lasts through the eighth week *Page 332*

Emotion A subjective feeling that includes arousal (heart pounding), cognitions (thoughts, values, and expectations), and expressions (frowns, smiles, and running) *Page 422*

Emotion-Focused Forms of Coping Coping strategies based on changing one's perceptions of stressful situations *Page 120*

Emotional Intelligence Goleman's term for the ability to know and manage one's emotions, empathize with others, and maintain satisfying relationships *Page 448*

Empathy In Rogerian terms, an insightful awareness and ability to share another's inner experience *Page 546*

Empathy–Altruism Hypothesis Helping because of empathy for someone in need *Page 605*

Encoding Translating information into neural codes (language) *Page 250*

Encoding Specificity Principle Retrieval of information is improved when conditions of recovery are similar to the conditions when information was encoded *Page 261*

Endocrine [EN-doh-krin] System Collection of glands located throughout the body that manufacture and secrete hormones into the bloodstream *Page 61*

Endorphins [en-DOR-fins] Chemical substances in the nervous system that are similar in structure and action to opiates and are involved in pain control, pleasure, and memory *Page 59*

Episodic Memory A part of explicit/ declarative memory that stores memories of personally experienced events; a mental diary of a person's life *Page 256*

Ethnocentrism Believing that one's culture is typical of all cultures; also, viewing one's own ethnic group (or culture) as central and "correct," and judging others according to this standard *Page 27*

Eustress Pleasant, desirable stress *Page 99*

Evolutionary/Circadian Theory As a part of circadian rhythms, sleep evolved to conserve energy and as protection from predators *Page 181*

Evolutionary Perspective Focuses on natural selection, adaptation, and evolution of behavior and mental processes *Page 13*

Evolutionary Psychology Branch of psychology that studies the ways in which natural selection and adaptation can explain behavior and mental processes. *Page 84*

Excitement Phase First stage of the sexual response cycle, characterized by increasing levels of arousal and increased engorgement of the genitals *Page 404*

Experiment Carefully controlled scientific procedure that involves manipulation of variables to determine cause and effect *Page 25*

Experimental Group Group receiving treatment in an experiment *Page 25*

Experimenter Bias Occurs when researcher influences research results in the expected direction *Page 27*

Explicit (Declarative) Memory Subsystem within long-term memory that consciously stores facts, information, and personal life experiences *Page 256*

External Locus of Control Believing that chance or outside forces beyond one's control determine one's fate *Page 122*

Extinction Gradual weakening or suppression of a previously conditioned response (CR) *Page 214*

Extrasensory Perception (ESP) Perceptual, or "psychic," abilities that supposedly go beyond the known senses (e.g., telepathy, clairvoyance, precognition, and psychokinesis) *Page 163*

Extrinsic Motivation Motivation based on obvious external rewards or threats of punishment *Page 444*

Facial-Feedback Hypothesis Movements of the facial muscles produce or intensify emotional reactions *Page 444*

Factor Analysis Statistical procedure for determining the most basic units or factors in a large array of data *Page 460*

Family Therapy Treatment to change maladaptive interaction patterns within a family *Page 548*

Farsightedness (Hyperopia) Visual acuity problem resulting from the cornea and lens focusing an image behind the retina. *Page 138*

Feature Detectors Specialized neurons that respond only to certain sensory information *Page 147*

Fetal Alcohol Syndrome (FAS) A combination of birth defects, including organ deformities and mental, motor, and/or growth retardation, that results from maternal alcohol abuse *Page 334*

Fetal Period The third, and final, stage of prenatal development (eight weeks to birth), characterized by rapid weight gain in the fetus and the fine detailing of body organs and systems *Page 332*

Five-Factor Model (FFM) Trait theory of personality that includes openness, conscientiousness, extroversion, agreeableness, and neuroticism *Page 460*

Fixed Interval (FI) Schedule Reinforcement occurs after a predetermined time has elapsed; the interval (time) is fixed *Page 220*

Fixed Ratio (FR) Schedule Reinforcement occurs after a predetermined set of responses; the ratio (number or amount) is fixed *Page 220*

Fluid Intelligence Aspects of innate intelligence, including reasoning abilities, memory, and speed of information processing, that are relatively independent of education and tend to decline as people age *Page 306*

Foot-in-the-Door Technique A first, small request is used as a setup for later, larger requests *Page 596*

Forebrain Collection of upper-level brain structures including the thalamus, hypothalamus, limbic system, and cerebral cortex *Page 70*

Formal Operational Stage Piaget's fourth stage (around age 11 and beyond), characterized by abstract and hypothetical thinking *Page 345*

Fovea A tiny pit in the center of the retina filled with cones and responsible for sharp vision *Page 139*

Free Association In psychoanalysis, reporting whatever comes to mind without monitoring its contents *Page 538*

Frequency How often a light or sound wave cycles (i.e., the number of complete wavelengths that pass a point in a given time) *Page 136*

Frequency Theory Explains how we hear lower-pitched sounds; hair cells in the basilar membrane bend and fire neural messages (action potentials) at the same rate as the sound frequency *Page 141*

Frontal Lobes Two lobes at the front of the brain governing motor control, speech production, and higher functions, such as thinking, personality, emotion, and memory *Page 74*

Frustration Unpleasant tension, anxiety, and heightened sympathetic activity resulting from a blocked goal *Page 102*

Frustration–Aggression Hypothesis Blocking of a desired goal (frustration) creates anger that may lead to aggression *Page 602*

Functional Fixedness Tendency to think of an object functioning only in its usual or customary way *Page 293*

Fundamental Attribution Error (FAE) Misjudging the causes of others' behavior as due to internal (dispositional) causes rather than external (situational) ones *Page 575*

Gate-Control Theory of Pain Theory that pain sensations are processed and altered by mechanisms within the spinal cord *Page 134*

Gender Psychological and sociocultural meanings added to biological maleness or femaleness *Page 392*

Gender Identity Self-identification as either a man or a woman *Page 392*

Gender Role Societal expectations for normal and appropriate male and female behavior *Page 393*

Gene A segment of DNA (deoxyribonucleic acid) that occupies a specific place on a particular chromosome and carries the code for hereditary transmission *Page 84*

General Adaptation Syndrome (GAS) Selye's three-phase (alarm, resistance, and exhaustion) reaction to severe stress *Page 105*

Generalized Anxiety Disorder Persistent, uncontrollable, and free-floating anxiety *Page 507*

Genuineness In Rogerian terms, authenticity or congruence; the awareness of one's true inner thoughts and feelings and being able to share them honestly with others *Page 545*

Germinal Period First stage of prenatal development, which begins with conception and ends with implantation in the uterus (the first two weeks) *Page 332*

Glial Cells Cells that provide structural, nutritional, and other support for the neurons, as well as communication within the nervous system; also called glia or neuroglia *Page 55*

Grammar Rules that specify how phonemes, morphemes, words, and phrases should be combined to express thoughts *Page 300*

Group Polarization Group's movement toward either riskier or more conservative behavior, depending on the members' initial dominant tendency *Page 599*

Group Therapy A number of people meet together to work toward therapeutic goals *Page 547*

Groupthink Faulty decision making that occurs when a highly cohesive group strives for agreement and avoids inconsistent information *Page 599*

Gustation Sense of taste *Page 143*

Habituation Tendency of the brain to ignore environmental factors that remain constant *Page 148*

Hallucinations Imaginary sensory perceptions that occur without external stimuli *Page 531*

Hallucinogens [hal-LOO-sin-oh-jenz] Drugs that produce sensory or perceptual distortions called hallucinations *Page 194*

Hardiness Resilient personality that includes a strong commitment to personal goals, control over life, and viewing change as a challenge rather than a threat *Page 108*

Hassles Small problems of daily living that accumulate and sometimes become a major source of stress *Page 101*

Health Psychology Studies how biological, psychological, and social factors affect health and illness *Page 112*

Heritability A measure of the degree to which a characteristic is related to genetic, inherited factors *Page 86*

Heuristics Strategies, or simple rules, used in problem solving and decision making that do not guarantee a solution but offer a likely shortcut to it *Page 291*

Hierarchy of Needs Maslow's theory that some motives (such as physiological and safety needs) must be met before going on to higher needs (such as belonging and self-actualization) *Page 427*

Higher-Order Conditioning A neutral stimulus (NS) becomes a conditioned stimulus (CS) through repeated pairings with a previously conditioned stimulus (CS) *Page 214*

Hindbrain Collection of brain structures including the medulla, pons, and cerebellum *Page 68*

HIV Positive Being infected by the human immunodeficiency virus (HIV) *Page 414*

Homeostasis A body's tendency to maintain a relatively stable state, such as a constant internal temperature *Page 424*

Hormones Chemicals manufactured by endocrine glands and circulated in the bloodstream to produce bodily changes or maintain normal bodily functions *Page 61*

HPA Axis The hypothalamus, pituitary gland, and adrenal cortex, which are activated by stress *Page 104*

Humanist Perspective Emphasizes free will, self-actualization, and human nature as naturally positive and growth-seeking *Page 12*

Humanistic Therapy Therapy to maximize personal growth through affective restructuring (emotional readjustment) *Page 545*

Hypnosis A trancelike state of heightened suggestibility, deep relaxation, and intense focus *Page 200*

Hypothalamus [hi-poh-THAL-uh-muss] Small brain structure beneath the thalamus responsible for emotions and drives (hunger, thirst, sex, and aggression), and regulating the body's internal environment *Page 71*

Hypothesis Specific prediction about how one variable relates to another *Page 19*

Id According to Freud, the source of instinctual energy, which works on the pleasure principle and is concerned with immediate gratification *Page 467*

Identity Crisis Erikson's term for an adolescent's search for self, which requires intense self-reflection and questioning *Page 370*

Illusion False or misleading perceptions *Page 146*

Implicit (Nondeclarative) Memory Subsystem within long-term memory that consists of unconscious procedural skills, simple classically conditioned responses, and priming *Page 257*

Imprinting An innate form of learning within a critical period that involves attachment to the first large moving object seen *Page 349*

Incentive Theory Motivation results from external stimuli that "pull" the organism in certain directions *Page 425*

Independent Variable (IV) Experimental factor manipulated to determine its causal effect on the dependent variable *Page 25*

Individualistic Cultures The needs and goals of the individual are emphasized over the needs and goals of the group. *Page 488*

Inferiority Complex Adler's idea that feelings of inferiority develop from early childhood experiences of helplessness and incompetence *Page 471*

Informational Social Influence Conforming because of a need for information and direction *Page 592*

Informed Consent Participant's agreement to take part in a study after being told what to expect *Page 21*

Ingroup Favoritism Viewing members of the ingroup more positively than members of an outgroup *Page 582*

Insanity Legal term applied when people cannot be held responsible for their actions, or are judged incompetent to manage their own affairs, because of mental illness. *Page 531*

Insight Sudden understanding of a problem that implies the solution. *Page 228*

Insomnia Persistent problems in falling asleep, staying asleep, or awakening too early *Page 185*

Instinctive Drift Conditioned responses shift (or drift) back toward innate response patterns *Page 235*

www.wiley.com/college/huffman

Instincts Fixed response patterns that are unlearned and found in almost all members of a species *Page 423*

Intelligence Global capacity to think rationally, act purposefully, and deal effectively with the environment *Page 306*

Interaction Process in which multiple factors mutually influence one another and the outcome—as in the interaction between heredity and environment *Page 7*

Internal Locus of Control Believing that one controls one's own fate *Page 122*

Interneurons Neurons within the central nervous system that internally communicate and intervene between the sensory and motor neurons *Page 66*

Interpersonal Attraction Positive feelings toward another *Page 583*

Interpretation A psychoanalyst's explanation of a patient's free associations, dreams, resistance, and transference; more generally, any statement by a therapist that presents a patient's problem in a new way *Page 568*

Intrinsic Motivation Motivation resulting from personal enjoyment of a task or activity *Page 444*

James–Lange Theory Emotions result from physiological arousal and behavioral expression ("I feel sad because I'm crying"); in this view, each emotion is physiologically distinct *Page 439*

Kinesthesia Sensory system for body posture and orientation *Page 145*

Language Form of communication using sounds and symbols combined according to specified rules *Page 299*

Language Acquisition Device (LAD) According to Chomsky, an innate mechanism that enables a child to analyze language and extract the basic rules of grammar *Page 303*

Latent Content The true, unconscious meaning of a dream, according to Freudian dream theory *Page 182*

Latent Learning Hidden learning that exists without behavioral signs *Page 229*

Lateralization Specialization of the left and right hemispheres of the brain for particular operations *Page 78*

Law of Effect Thorndike's rule that the probability of an action being repeated is strengthened when it is followed by a pleasant or satisfying consequence *Page 216*

Learned Helplessness Seligman's term for a state of helplessness or resignation in which human or nonhuman animals learn that escape from something painful is impossible and depression results. *Page 514*

Learning A relatively permanent change in behavior or mental processes resulting from practice or experience *Page 208*

Levels of Processing The degree or depth of mental processing that occurs when mate-

rial is initially encountered determines how well it's later remembered. *Page 251*

Limbic System Interconnected group of forebrain structures involved with emotions, drives, and memory *Page 71*

Lobotomy Outmoded medical procedure for mental disorders, which involved cutting nerve pathways between the frontal lobes and the thalamus and hypothalamus *Page 558*

Localization of Function Specialization of various parts of the brain for particular functions *Page 68*

Longitudinal Method Measures a single individual or group of individuals over an extended period and gives information about age changes *Page 328*

Long-Term Memory (LTM) Third stage of memory that stores information for long periods of time; its capacity is virtually limitless, and its duration is relatively permanent *Page 256*

Long-Term Potentiation (LTP) Long-lasting increase in neural excitability, which may be a biological mechanism for learning and memory. *Page 269*

Maintenance Rehearsal Repeating information over and over to maintain it in short-term memory (STM) *Page 254*

Major Depressive Disorder Long-lasting depressed mood that interferes with the ability to function, feel pleasure, or maintain interest in life *Page 512*

Manifest Content According to Freud, the surface content of a dream, which contains dream symbols that distort and disguise the dream's true meaning *Page 182*

Massed Practice Time spent learning is grouped (or massed) into long, unbroken intervals (also known as cramming) *Page 266*

Maturation Development governed by automatic, genetically predetermined signals *Page 327*

Medical Model Perspective that assumes diseases (including mental illness) have physical causes that can be diagnosed, treated, and possibly cured *Page 502*

Meditation A group of techniques designed to refocus attention, block out all distractions, and produce an alternate state of consciousness *Page 199*

Medulla [muh-DUL-uh] Hindbrain structure responsible for automatic body functions such as breathing and heartbeat *Page 68*

Memory An internal record or representation of some prior event or experience *Page 249*

Mental Image Mental representation of a previously stored sensory experience, including visual, auditory, olfactory, tactile, motor, or gustatory imagery (e.g., visualizing a train and hearing its horn) *Page 287*

Mental Set Persisting in using problem-solving strategies that have worked in the past rather than trying new ones *Page 293*

Meta-analysis Statistical procedure for combining and analyzing data from many studies *Page 20*

Midbrain Collection of brain structures in the middle of the brain responsible for coordinating movement patterns, sleep, and arousal *Page 70*

Minnesota Multiphasic Personality Inventory (MMPI) The most widely researched and clinically used self-report personality test (MMPI-2 is the revised version) *Page 483*

Misattribution of Arousal Physiologically aroused individuals make mistaken inferences about what is causing the arousal *Page 29*

Mnemonic [nih-MON-ik] Device Memory-improvement technique based on encoding items in a special way *Page 279*

Modeling Therapy Watching and imitating models that demonstrate desirable behaviors *Page 554*

Monocular Cues Visual input from a single eye alone that contributes to perception of depth or distance *Page 155*

Morality Principle The principle on which the superego may operate, which results in feelings of guilt if its rules are violated *Page 468*

Morpheme [MOR-feem] Smallest meaningful unit of language, formed from a combination of phonemes *Page 300*

Motivation Set of factors that activate, direct, and maintain behavior, usually toward a goal *Page 422*

Motor Neurons Transmit messages from the central nervous system to organs, muscles, and glands; also known as efferent neurons *Page 66*

Myelin [MY-uh-lin] Sheath Layer of fatty insulation wrapped around the axon of some neurons, which increases the rate at which nerve impulses travel along the axon *Page 56*

Narcolepsy [NAR-co-lep-see] Sudden and irresistible onsets of sleep during normal waking hours. (*narco* = "numbness" and *lepsy* = "seizure") *Page 186*

Natural Selection The driving mechanism behind evolution, which allows individuals with genetically influenced traits that are adaptive in a particular environment to stay alive and produce offspring *Page 88*

Naturalistic Observation Observation and recording of behavior in the participant's natural state or habitat *Page 31*

Nature–Nurture Controversy Ongoing dispute over the relative contributions of nature (heredity) and nurture (environment) *Page 7*

Nearsightedness (Myopia) Visual acuity problem resulting from cornea and lens focusing an image in front of the retina *Page 138*

Need Compatibility Attraction based on sharing similar needs *Page 587*

Need Complementarity Attraction toward those with qualities we admire but personally lack *Page 586*

Negative Punishment Taking away (or removing) a stimulus that weakens a response and makes it less likely to recur *Page 220*

Negative Reinforcement Taking away (or removing) a stimulus, which strengthens a response and makes it more likely to recur *Page 218*

Nerve Deafness Inner-ear deafness resulting from damage to the cochlea, hair cells, or auditory nerve *Page 141*

Neurogenesis [nue-roh-JEN-uh-sis] The division and differentiation of nonneuronal cells to produce neurons *Page 91*

Neuron Cell of the nervous system responsible for receiving and transmitting electrochemical information *Page 55*

Neuroplasticity The brain's lifelong ability to reorganize and change its structure and function *Page 90*

Neuroscience Interdisciplinary field studying how biological processes relate to behavioral and mental processes *Page 54*

Neuroscience/Biopsychology Perspective Emphasizes genetics and other biological processes in the brain and other parts of the nervous system *Page 13*

Neurosis Outmoded term for disorders characterized by unrealistic anxiety and other associated problems *Page 531*

Neurotransmitters Chemicals released by neurons that affect other neurons *Page 58*

Neutral Stimulus (NS) A stimulus that, before conditioning, does not naturally bring about the response of interest *Page 210*

Night Terrors Abrupt awakenings from NREM (non-rapid-eye-movement) sleep accompanied by intense physiological arousal and feelings of panic *Page 186*

Nightmares Anxiety-arousing dreams generally occurring near the end of the sleep cycle, during REM sleep *Page 186*

Non-Rapid-Eye-Movement (NREM) Sleep Stages 1 to 4 of sleep with Stage 1 as the lightest level and Stage 4 as the deepest level *Page 179*

Norm Cultural rule of behavior prescribing what is acceptable in a given situation *Page 591*

Normative Social Influence Conforming to group pressure out of a need for approval and acceptance *Page 591*

Obedience Following direct commands, usually from an authority figure *Page 592*

Object Permanence Piagetian term for an infant's understanding that objects (or people) continue to exist even when they cannot be seen, heard, or touched directly *Page 342*

Observational Learning Learning new behavior or information by watching others (also known as social learning or modeling) *Page 229*

Obsessive-Compulsive Disorder (OCD) Intrusive, repetitive fearful thoughts (obsessions), urges to perform repetitive, ritualistic behaviors (compulsions), or both *Page 508*

Occipital [ahk-SIP-ih-tal] Lobes Two lobes at the back of the brain responsible for vision and visual perception *Page 77*

Oedipus [ED-uh-puss] Complex Period of conflict during the phallic stage when children are supposedly attracted to the opposite-sex parent and hostile toward the same-sex parent *Page 470*

Olfaction Sense of smell *Page 142*

Operant Conditioning Learning in which voluntary responses are controlled by their consequences (also known as instrumental or Skinnerian conditioning) *Page 216*

Operational Definition A precise description of how the variables in a study will be observed and measured (For example, drug abuse might be operationally defined as "the number of missed work days due to excessive use of an addictive substance.") *Page 19*

Opiates Drugs derived from opium that function as an analgesic or pain reliever (The word *opium* comes from the Greek word meaning "juice.") *Page 193*

Opponent-Process Theory Hering's theory that color perception is based on three systems of color opposites—blue–yellow, red–green, and black–white *Page 158*

Orgasm Phase Third stage of the sexual response cycle, when pleasurable sensations peak and orgasm occurs *Page 404*

Outgroup Homogeneity Effect Judging members of an outgroup as more alike and less diverse than members of the ingroup *Page 582*

Overextension Overly broad use of a word to include objects that do not fit the word's meaning (e.g., calling all men "Daddy") *Page 302*

Overgeneralize Applying the basic rules of grammar even to cases that are exceptions to the rule (e.g., saying "mans" instead of "men") *Page 303*

Panic Disorder Sudden and inexplicable panic attacks; symptoms include difficulty breathing, heart palpitations, dizziness, trembling, terror, and feelings of impending doom *Page 507*

Parallel Distributed Processing (PDP) Memory results from weblike connections among interacting processing units operating simultaneously, rather than sequentially (also known as the connectionist model) *Page 251*

Parasympathetic Nervous System Subdivision of the autonomic nervous system (ANS) responsible for calming the body and conserving energy *Page 66*

Parietal [puh-RYE-uh-tuhl] Lobes Two lobes at the top of the brain where bodily sensations are interpreted *Page 76*

Partial (Intermittent) Reinforcement Some, but not all, correct responses are reinforced *Page 219*

Participant Bias Occurs when experimental conditions influence the participant's behavior or mental proccesses *Page 28*

Perception Process of selecting, organizing, and interpreting sensory information *Page 130*

Perceptual Constancy Tendency for the environment to be perceived as remaining the same even with changes in sensory input *Page 152*

Perceptual Set Readiness to perceive in a particular manner based on expectations *Page 159*

Performance Anxiety Fear of being judged in connection with sexual activity *Page 409*

Peripheral Nervous System (PNS) All nerves and neurons connecting the central nervous system to the rest of the body *Page 63*

Personality Unique and relatively stable pattern of thoughts, feelings, and actions *Page 459*

Personality Disorders Inflexible, maladaptive personality traits that cause significant impairment of social and occupational functioning *Page 528*

Pheromones [FARE-oh-mones] Airborne chemicals that affect behavior, including recognition of family members, aggression, territorial marking, and sexual mating *Page 143*

Phobia Intense, irrational fear and avoidance of a specific object or situation *Page 507*

Phoneme [FOE-neem] Smallest basic unit of speech or sound *Page 300*

Physical Dependence Bodily processes have been so modified by repeated use of a drug that continued use is required to prevent withdrawal symptoms *Page 189*

Place Theory Explains how we hear higher-pitched sounds; different high-pitched sounds bend the basilar membrane hair cells at different locations in the cochlea *Page 141*

Placebo (pluh-SEE-boh) Inactive substance or fake treatment used as a control technique, usually in drug research, or given

www.wiley.com/college/huffman

by a medical practitioner to a patient *Page 27*

Plateau Phase Second stage of the sexual response cycle, characterized by a leveling off in a state of high arousal *Page 404*

Pleasure Principle In Freud's theory, the principle on which the id operates—seeking immediate pleasure *Page 467*

Polygraph Instrument that measures heart rate, respiration rate, blood pressure, and skin conductivity to detect emotional arousal, which in turn supposedly reflects lying versus truthfulness *Page 447*

Pons Hindbrain structure involved in respiration, movement, waking, sleep, and dreaming *Page 69*

Positive Punishment Adding (or presenting) a stimulus that weakens a response and makes it less likely to recur *Page 220*

Positive Reinforcement Adding (or presenting) a stimulus, which strengthens a response and makes it more likely to recur *Page 218*

Postconventional Level Kohlberg's highest level of moral development, in which individuals develop personal standards for right and wrong, and define morality in terms of abstract principles and values that apply to all situations and societies *Page 365*

Posttraumatic Stress Disorder (PTSD) Anxiety disorder following exposure to a life-threatening or other extreme event that evoked great horror or helplessness; characterized by flashbacks, nightmares, and impaired functioning *Page 109*

Preconscious Freud's term for thoughts, motives, or memories that can voluntarily be brought to mind *Page 466*

Preconventional Level Kohlberg's first level of moral development, in which morality is based on rewards, punishment, and exchange of favors *Page 363*

Prejudice A learned, generally negative, attitude toward members of a group; it includes thoughts (stereotypes), feelings, and behavioral tendencies (possible discrimination) *Page 581*

Premack Principle Using a naturally occurring high-frequency response to reinforce and increase low-frequency responses *Page 219*

Preoperational Stage Piaget's second stage (roughly age 2 to 7), characterized by the ability to employ significant language and to think symbolically, but the child lacks operations (reversible mental processes), and thinking is egocentric and animistic *Page 343*

Primary Reinforcers Stimuli that increase the probability of a response because they satisfy a biological need, such as food, water, and sex *Page 218*

Priming Prior exposure to a stimulus (or prime) facilitates or inhibits the processing of new information, even when one has no conscious memory of the initial learning and storage *Page 257*

Proactive Interference Old information interferes with remembering new information; forward-acting interference *Page 264*

Problem-Focused Forms of Coping Coping strategies that use problem-solving strategies to decrease or eliminate the source of stress *Page 120*

Projective Tests Psychological tests using ambiguous stimuli, such as inkblots or drawings, which allow the test taker to project his or her unconscious onto the test material *Page 484*

Prototype A representation of the "best" or most typical example of a category (e.g., baseball is a prototype of the concept of sports) *Page 289*

Proximity Attraction based on geographic closeness *Page 586*

Psychiatry Branch of medicine dealing with the diagnosis, treatment, and prevention of mental disorders *Page 502*

Psychoactive Drugs Chemicals that change conscious awareness, mood, or perception *Page 188*

Psychoanalysis Freudian therapy designed to bring unconscious conflicts, which usually date back to early childhood experiences, into consciousness; also Freud's theoretical school of thought emphasizing unconscious processes *Page 538*

Psychoanalytic/Psychodynamic Perspective Focuses on unconscious processes and unresolved past conflicts *Page 11*

Psychodynamic Therapy A briefer, more directive, and more modern form of psychoanalysis that focuses on conscious processes and current problems *Page 540*

Psychological Dependence Desire or craving to achieve the effects produced by a drug *Page 189*

Psychology Scientific study of behavior and mental processes *Page 5*

Psychoneuroimmunology [sye-koh-NEW-roh-IM-you-NOLL-oh-gee] Interdisciplinary field that studies the effects of psychological factors on the immune system *Page 104*

Psychopharmacology The study of drug effects on mind and behavior *Page 555*

Psychophysics Study of the relation between attributes of the physical world and our psychological experience of them *Page 133*

Psychosexual Stages In Freudian theory, five developmental periods (oral, anal, phallic, latency, and genital) during which particular kinds of pleasures must be gratified if

personality development is to proceed normally *Page 469*

Psychosis Serious mental disorders characterized by extreme mental disruption and loss of contact with reality *Page 503*

Psychosocial Stages Erikson's theory that individuals pass through eight developmental stages, each involving a crisis that must be successfully resolved *Page 368*

Psychosurgery Operative procedures on the brain designed to relieve severe mental symptoms that have not responded to other forms of treatment *Page 558*

Psychotherapy Techniques employed to improve psychological functioning and promote adjustment to life *Page 537*

Puberty Biological changes during adolescence that lead to an adult-sized body and sexual maturity *Page 337*

Punishment Weakens a response and makes it less likely to recur *Page 216*

Random Assignment Using chance methods to assign participants to experimental or control conditions, thus minimizing the possibility of biases or preexisting differences in the groups *Page 28*

Rapid-Eye-Movement (REM) Sleep A stage of sleep marked by rapid eye movements, high-frequency brain waves, paralysis of large muscles, and dreaming *Page 178*

Rational-Emotive Behavior Therapy (REBT) Ellis's cognitive therapy to eliminate self-defeating beliefs through rational examination *Page 542*

Reality Principle According to Freud, the principle on which the conscious ego operates as it tries to meet the demands of the id and superego and the realities of the environment *Page 467*

Recall Retrieving a memory using a general cue *Page 260*

Reciprocal Determinism Bandura's belief that cognitions, behaviors, and the environment interact to produce personality *Page 478*

Recognition Retrieving a memory using a specific cue *Page 260*

Reference Groups People we conform to, or go along with, because we like and admire them and want to be like them *Page 592*

Reflex Innate, automatic response to a stimulus, such as the knee-jerk reflex *Page 64*

Refractory Period Phase following orgasm, during which further orgasm is considered physiologically impossible for men *Page 404*

Reinforcement Strengthens a response and makes it more likely to recur *Page 216*

Relearning Learning material a second time, which usually takes less time than original learning (also called the savings method) *Page 263*

Reliability A measure of the consistency and stability of test scores when the test is readministered *Page 311*

Repair/Restoration Theory Sleep serves a recuperative function, allowing organisms to repair or replenish key factors *Page 180*

Representativeness Heuristic Estimating the probability of something based on how well the circumstances match (or represent) our previous prototype *Page 295*

Repression Freud's first and most basic defense mechanism, which blocks unacceptable impulses from coming into awareness *Page 468*

Resiliency The ability to adapt effectively in the face of threats *Page 376*

Resistance In psychoanalysis, the person's inability or unwillingness to discuss or reveal certain memories, thoughts, motives, or experiences. *Page 539*

Resolution Phase Final stage of the sexual response cycle, when the body returns to its unaroused state *Page 404*

Reticular Formation (RF) Diffuse set of neurons that screens incoming information and controls arousal *Page 70*

Retina Light-sensitive inner surface of the back of the eye, which contains the receptor cells for vision (rods and cones) *Page 139*

Retinal Disparity Binocular cue to distance where the separation of the eyes causes different images to fall on each retina *Page 155*

Retrieval Recovering information from memory storage *Page 250*

Retrieval Cue A clue or prompt that helps stimulate recall or retrieval of a stored piece of information from long-term memory *Page 260*

Retroactive Interference New information interferes with remembering old information; backward-acting interference *Page 263*

Retrograde Amnesia Loss of memory for events before a brain injury; backward-acting amnesia *Page 272*

Rods Receptor cells in the retina that detect shades of gray and are responsible for peripheral vision and are most sensitive in dim light *Page 139*

Romantic Love Intense feeling of attraction to another within an erotic context and with future expectations *Page 588*

Rorschach [ROAR-shock] Inkblot Test A projective test that presents a set of 10 cards with symmetrical abstract patterns, known as inkblots, and asks respondents to describe what they "see" in the image; their response is thought to be a projection of unconscious processes *Page 485*

Saliency Bias Focusing on the most noticeable (salient) factors when explaining the causes of behavior *Page 576*

Sample Bias Occurs when research participants are not representative of the larger population *Page 28*

Savant Syndrome A condition in which a person with mental retardation exhibits exceptional skill or brilliance in some limited field. *Page 314*

Schachter's Two-Factor Theory Emotions result from physical arousal and cognitive labeling (or interpretation) of that arousal based on external cues *Page 442*

Schema Cognitive structures or patterns consisting of a number of organized ideas that grow and differentiate with experience *Page 341*

Schizophrenia [skit-so-FREE-nee-uh] Group of psychotic disorders involving major disturbances in perception, language, thought, emotion, and behavior; the individual withdraws from people and reality, often into a fantasy life of delusions and hallucinations *Page 517*

Secondary Reinforcers Stimuli that increase the probability of a response because of their learned value, such as money and material possessions *Page 218*

Selective Attention Filtering out and attending only to important sensory messages *Page 147*

Self-Actualization Maslow's term for the inborn drive to develop all one's talents and capabilities *Page 477*

Self-Concept Rogers's term for all the information and beliefs individuals have about their own nature, qualities, and behavior *Page 475*

Self-Efficacy Bandura's term for a person's learned expectation of success *Page 478*

Self-Help Group Leaderless or nonprofessionally guided groups in which members assist each other with a specific problem, as in Alcoholics Anonymous *Page 547*

Self-Serving Bias Taking credit for our successes and externalizing our failures *Page 576*

Self-Talk Internal dialogue; the things people say to themselves when they interpret events *Page 542*

Semantic Memory A part of explicit/declarative memory that stores general knowledge; a mental encyclopedia or dictionary *Page 256*

Semantics Meaning, or the study of meaning, derived from words and word combinations *Page 301*

Sensation Process of receiving, converting, and transmitting raw sensory information from the external and internal environments to the brain *Page 130*

Sensorimotor Stage Piaget's first stage (birth to approximately age 2 years), in which schemas are developed through sensory and motor activities *Page 342*

Sensory Adaptation Repeated or constant stimulation decreases the number of sensory messages sent to the brain, which causes decreased sensation *Page 134*

Sensory Memory First memory stage that holds sensory information; relatively large capacity, but duration is only a few seconds *Page 253*

Sensory Neurons Transmit messages from sense organs to the central nervous system; also known as afferent neurons *Page 66*

Sensory Reduction Filtering and analyzing incoming sensations before sending a neural message to the cortex *Page 132*

Serial Position Effect Information at the beginning and end of a list is remembered better than material in the middle *Page 266*

Sex Biological maleness and femaleness, including chromosomal sex; also, activities related to sexual behaviors, such as masturbation and intercourse *Page 392*

Sexual Dysfunction Impairment of the normal physiological processes of arousal and orgasm *Page 407*

Sexual Orientation Primary erotic attraction toward members of the same sex (homosexual, gay or lesbian), both sexes (bisexual), or other sex (heterosexual) *Page 393*

Sexual Prejudice Negative attitudes toward an individual because of her or his sexual orientation *Page 406*

Sexual Response Cycle Masters and Johnson's description of the four-stage bodily response to sexual arousal, which consists of excitement, plateau, orgasm, and resolution *Page 403*

Sexual Scripts Socially dictated descriptions of "appropriate" behaviors for sexual interactions *Page 410*

Shaping Reinforcement delivered for successive approximations of the desired response *Page 220*

Short-Term Memory (STM) Second memory stage that temporarily stores sensory information and decides whether to send it on to long-term memory (LTM); capacity is limited to five to nine items and duration is about 30 seconds *Page 253*

Sleep Apnea Repeated interruption of breathing during sleep because air passages to the lungs are physically blocked or the brain stops activating the diaphragm *Page 185*

Sleeper Effect Information from an unreliable source, which was initially discounted, later gains credibility because the source is forgotten *Page 266*

Social Psychology The study of how others influence our thoughts, feelings, and actions *Page 574*

www.wiley.com/college/huffman

Sociocultural Perspective Emphasizes social interaction and cultural determinants of behavior and mental processes *Page 13*

Socioemotional Selectivity Theory A natural decline in social contact occurs as older adults become more selective with their time *Page 379*

Somatic Nervous System (SNS) A subdivision of the peripheral nervous system (PNS) that connects to sensory receptors and controls skeletal muscles *Page 66*

Source Amnesia Forgetting the true source of a memory (also called source confusion or source misattribution) *Page 266*

Split Brain Surgical separation of the brain's two hemispheres used medically to treat severe epilepsy; split-brain patients provide data on the functions of the two hemispheres *Page 79*

Spontaneous Recovery Reappearance of a previously extinguished conditioned response (CR) *Page 214*

Standardization Establishment of the norms and uniform procedures for giving and scoring a test *Page 310*

Stem Cell Precursor (immature) cells that give birth to new specialized cells; a stem cell holds all the information it needs to make bone, blood, brain—any part of a human body—and can also copy itself to maintain a stock of stem cells *Page 91*

Stereotype A set of beliefs about the characteristics of people in a group that is generalized to all group members; also, the cognitive component of prejudice *Page 581*

Stereotype Threat Negative stereotypes about minority groups cause some members to doubt their abilities *Page 318*

Stimulants Drugs that act on the brain and nervous system to increase their overall activity and general responsiveness *Page 192*

Stimulus Discrimination Learned response to a specific stimulus but not to other, similar stimuli *Page 214*

Stimulus Generalization Learned response to stimuli that are like the original conditioned stimulus *Page 213*

Storage Retaining neurally coded information over time *Page 250*

Stress Nonspecific response of the body to any demand made on it; the arousal, both physical and mental, to situations or events that we perceive as threatening or challenging *Page 98*

Subliminal Pertaining to any stimulus presented below the threshold of conscious awareness *Page 162*

Substance-Related Disorders Abuse of, or dependence on, a mood- or behavior-altering drug *Page 525*

Superego In Freud's theory, the part of the personality that incorporates parental and societal standards for morality *Page 467*

Survey Research technique that questions a large sample of people to assess their behaviors and attitudes *Page 32*

Sympathetic Nervous System Subdivision of the autonomic nervous system (ANS) responsible for arousing the body and mobilizing its energy during times of stress; also called the "fight-or-flight" system *Page 66*

Synapse [SIN-aps] Junction between the axon tip of the sending neuron and the dendrite or cell body of the receiving neuron. During an action potential, chemicals called neurotransmitters are released and flow across the synaptic gap *Page 58*

Synesthesia A mixing of sensory experiences (e.g., "seeing" colors when a sound is heard) *Page 132*

Syntax Grammatical rules that specify how words and phrases should be arranged in a sentence to convey meaning *Page 300*

Systematic Desensitization A gradual process of extinguishing a learned fear (or phobia) by working through a hierarchy of fear-evoking stimuli while staying deeply relaxed *Page 551*

Taste Aversion A classically conditioned negative reaction to a particular taste that has been associated with nausea or other illness *Page 234*

Telegraphic Speech Two- or three-word sentences of young children that contain only the most necessary words *Page 302*

Temperament An individual's innate behavioral style and characteristic emotional response *Page 367*

Temporal Lobes Two lobes on each side of the brain above the ears involved in audition (hearing), language comprehension, memory, and some emotional control *Page 77*

Teratogen [Tuh-RAT-uh-jen] Environmental agent that causes damage during prenatal development; the term comes from the Greek word *teras*, meaning "malformation" *Page 334*

Thalamus [THAL-uh-muss] Forebrain structure at the top of the brainstem that relays sensory messages to the cerebral cortex *Page 71*

Thanatology [than-uh-TALL-uh-gee] The study of death and dying; the term comes from *thanatos*, the Greek name for a mythical personification of death, and was borrowed by Freud to represent the death instinct *Page 383*

Thematic Apperception Test (TAT) A projective test that shows a series of ambiguous black-and-white pictures and asks the test-taker to create a story related to each; the responses presumably reflect a projection of unconscious processes *Page 485*

Theory Interrelated set of concepts that explain a body of data *Page 21*

Tip-of-the-Tongue (TOT) Phenomenon Feeling that specific information is stored in long-term memory but of being temporarily unable to retrieve it *Page 265*

Tolerance Decreased sensitivity to a drug brought about by its continuous use *Page 190*

Top-Down Processing Information processing that starts "at the top," with the observer's thoughts, expectations, and knowledge, and works down *Page 160*

Trait Relatively stable personal characteristic that can be used to describe someone *Page 459*

Transduction Converting a stimulus to a receptor into neural impulses *Page 132*

Transference In psychoanalysis, the patient may displace (or transfer) unconscious feelings about a significant person in his or her life onto the therapist *Page 539*

Trichromatic Theory. Young's theory that color perception results from mixing three distinct color systems—red, green, and blue *Page 158*

Type A Personality Behavior characteristics including intense ambition, competition, exaggerated time urgency, and a cynical, hostile outlook *Page 107*

Type B Personality Behavior characteristics consistent with a calm, patient, relaxed attitude *Page 107*

Unconditional Positive Regard Rogers's term for love and acceptance with no contingencies attached *Page 476, 545*

Unconditioned Response (UCR) Unlearned reaction to an unconditioned stimulus (UCS) that occurs without previous conditioning *Page 210*

Unconditioned Stimulus (UCS) Stimulus that elicits an unconditioned response (UCR) without previous conditioning *Page 210*

Unconscious Freud's term for thoughts, motives, and memories blocked from normal awareness *Page 466*

Validity Ability of a test to measure what it was designed to measure *Page 311*

Variable Interval (VI) Schedule Reinforcement occurs unpredictably; the interval (time) varies *Page 220*

Variable Ratio (VR) Schedule Reinforcement occurs unpredictably; the ratio (number or amount) varies *Page 220*

Wavelength Distance between the crests (or peaks) of light or sound waves; the shorter the wavelength, the higher the frequency *Page 136*

Withdrawal Discomfort and distress, including physical pain and intense cravings, experienced after stopping the use of addictive drugs *Page 189*

REFERENCES

Aarons, L. (1976). Evoked sleep-talking. *Perceptual and Motor Skills, 31,* 27–40.

Aarre, T. F., Dahl, A. A., Johansen, J. B., Kjonniksen, I., & Neckelmann, D. (2003). Efficacy of repetitive transcranial magnetic stimulation in depression: A review of the evidence. *Nordic Journal of Psychiatry, 57(3),* 227–232.

Abadinsky, H. (2001). *Drugs: An introduction* (4th ed.). Stamford, CT: Thomson Learning.

Abbey, C., & Dallos, R. (2004). The experience of the impact of divorce on sibling relationships: A qualitative study. *Clinical Child Psychology & Psychiatry, 9(2),* 241–259.

Abbott, A. (2004). Striking back. *Nature, 429(6990),* 338–339.

Abel, S., Park, J., Tipene-Leach, D., Finau, S., & Lennan, M. (2001). Infant care practices in New Zealand: A cross-cultural qualitative study. *Social Science & Medicine, 53(9),* 1135–1148.

Aboud, F. E. (2003). The formation of ingroup favoritism and out-group prejudice in young children: Are they distinct attitudes? *Developmental Psychology, 39(1),* 48–60.

About James Randi. (2002). Detail biography. www.randi.org/jr/bio.html.

Abrams, L., White, K. K., & Eitel, S. L. (2003). Isolating phonological components that increase tip-of-the-tongue resolution. *Memory & Cognition, 31(8),* 1153–1162.

Abusharaf, R. (1998, March/April). Unmasking tradition. *The Sciences,* 22–27.

Achenbaum, W. A., & Bengtson, V. L. (1994). Re-engaging the disengagement theory of aging: On the history and assessment of theory development in gerontology. *Gerontologist, 34,* 756–763.

Acierno, R., Brady, K., Gray, M., Kilpatrick, D. G., Resnick, H., & Best, C. L. (2002). Psychopathology following interpersonal violence: A comparison of risk factors in older and younger adults. *Journal of Clinical Geropsychology, 8(1),* 13–23.

Acierno, R., Gray, M., Best, C., Resnick, H., Kilpatrick, D., Saunders, B., & Brady, K. (2001). Rape and physical violence: Comparison of assault characteristics in older and younger adults in the National Women's Study. *Journal of Traumatic Stress, 14(4),* 685–695.

Acklin, M. W. (1999). Behavioral science foundations of the Rorschach Test: Research and clinical applications. *Assessment, 6(4),* 319–326.

Adamopoulos, J., & Kashima, Y. (1999). *Social psychology and cultural context.* Thousand Oaks, CA: Sage.

Adelman, P. K., & Zajonc, R. B. (1989). Facial efference and the experience of emotion. In M. R. Rosenzweig & L. W. Porter (Eds.), *Annual review of psychology* (pp. 249–280). Palo Alto, CA: Annual Reviews Inc.

Adinoff, B. (2004). Neurobiologic processes in drug reward and addiction. *Harvard Review of Psychiatry, 12(6),* 305–320.

Adler, A. (1964). The individual psychology of Alfred Adler. In H. L. Ansbacher & R. R. Ansbacher (Eds.), *The individual psychology of Alfred Adler.* New York: Harper & Row.

Adler, A. (1998). *Understanding human nature.* Center City: MN: Hazelden Information Education.

Agar, M., & Reisinger, H. S. (2004). Ecstasy: Commodity or disease? *Journal of Psychoactive Drugs. 36(2),* 253–264.

Ahijevych, K., Yerardi, R., & Nedilsky, N. (2000). Descriptive outcomes of the American Lung Association of Ohio hypnotherapy smoking cessation program. *International Journal of Clinical & Experimental Hypnosis,48(4),* 374–387.

Ainsworth, M. D. S. (1967). *Infancy in Uganda: Infant care and the growth of love.* Baltimore: Johns Hopkins University Press.

Ainsworth, M. D. S., Blehar, M., Waters, E., & Wall, S. (1978). *Patterns of attachment: Observations in the strange situation and at home.* Hillsdale, NJ: Erlbaum.

Akan, G. E., & Grilo, C. M. (1995). Sociocultural influences on eating attitudes and behaviors, body image, and psychological functioning: A comparison of African American, Asian American, and Caucasian college women. *International Journal of Eating Disorders, 18,* 181–187.

Akirav, I., & Richter-Levin, G. (1999). Biphasic modulation of hippocampal plasticity by behavioral stress and basolateral amygdala stimulation in the rat. *Journal of Neuroscience, 19,* 10530–10535.

Al'absi, M., Hugdahl, K., & Lovallo, W. R. (2002). Adrenocortical stress responses and altered working memory performance. *Psychophysiology, 39(1),* 95–99.

Alan Guttmacher Institute. (2004). *U.S. teenage pregnancy statistics.* New York: Alan Guttmacher Institute.

Albadalejo, M. F., Arissó, P. N., R., De La Torre F. R., R. Jürschik, S. P., León, S. A.,

Peiró, A. M., Peiró, G. Y. A., Lozano, N. P., Agulló, M. S., & Morell, J. C. (2003). Estudios controlados en humanos de éxtasis. / Controlled trials of ecstasy administration in humans. *Adicciones, 15*(Suppl2), 121–154.

Albert, U., Maina, G., Ravizza, L., & Bogetto, F. (2002). An exploratory study on obsessive-compulsive disorder with and without a familial component: Are there any phenomenological differences? *Psychopathology, 35(1),* 8–16.

Alberti, R., & Emmons, M. (2001). *Your perfect right: Assertiveness and equality in your life and relationships* (8th ed.). Atascadero, CA, US: Impact Publishers Inc.

Alden, L. E., Mellings, T. M. B., & Laposa, J. M. (2004). Framing social information and generalized social phobia. *Behaviour Research & Therapy, 42(5),* 585–600.

Alden, L. E., & Wallace, S. T. (1995). Social phobia and social appraisal in successful and unsuccessful social interactions. *Behaviour Research and Therapy, 33(5),* 497–505.

Al-Issa, I. (2000). Culture and mental illness in Algeria. In I. Al-Issa (Ed.), *Al-Junun: Mental illness in the Islamic world* (pp. 101–119). Madison, CT: International Universities Press, Inc.

Allen, B. (2006). *Personality theories: Development, growth, and diversity* (5th ed.). Boston, MA: Allyn & Bacon/Longman.

Allen, P. L. (2000). *The wages of sin: Sex and disease, past and present.* Chicago: University of Chicago Press.

Allgeier, A. R., & Allgeier, E. R. (2000). *Sexual interactions* (6th ed.). Boston, MA: Houghton Mifflin.

Allik, J., & McCrae, R. R. (2004). Toward a geography of personality traits: Patterns of profiles across 36 cultures. *Journal of Cross-Cultural Psychology, 35(1),* 13–28.

Allison, D. B., Fontaine, K. R., Manson, J. E., Stevens, J., & Van Itallie, T. B. (1999). Annual deaths attributable to obesity in the United States. *Journal of the American Medical Association, 282,* 1530–1538.

Alloy, L. B., Abramson, L. Y., Whitehouse, W. G., Hogan, M. E., Tashman, N. A., Steinberg, D. L., Rose, D. T., & Donovan, P. (1999). Depressogenic cognitive styles: Predictive validity, information processing and personality characteristics, and developmental origins. *Behaviour Research and Therapy, 37,* 503–531.

Alloy, L. B., & Clements, C. M. (1998). Hopelessness theory of depression. *Cognitive Therapy and Research, 22,* 303–335.

Allport, G. W. (1937). *Personality: A psychological interpretation.* New York: Holt, Rinehart and Winston.

Allport, G. W., & Odbert, H. S. (1936). Trait-names: A psycho-lexical study. *Psychological Monographs: General and Applied, 47,* 1–21.

Almeida, O. P., Burton, E. J., Ferrier, N., McKeith, I. G., & O'Brien, J. T. (2003). Depression with late onset is associated with right frontal lobe atrophy. *Psychological Medicine, 33(4),* 675–681.

Altamura, A. C., Bassetti, R., Bocchio, L., Santini, A., & Mundo, E. (2003). Season of birth and inflammatory response system in schizophrenia. *Progress in Neuro-Psychopharmacology & Biological Psychiatry, 27(5),* 879–880.

Aluja-Fabregat, A., & Torrubia-Beltri, R. (1998). Viewing of mass media violence, perception of violence, personality and academic achievement. *Personality and Individual Differences, 25,* 973–989.

American Cancer Society (2004). *Women and smoking.* [On-line]. Available: http://www.cancer.org/docroot/PED/content/PED_10_2X_Women_and_Smoking.asp?sitearea=PED

American Cancer Society. (2000). *Pregnant women may have ample motivation to quit smoking, but few have access to smoking cessation programs tailored to their maternal condition.* [On-line]. Available: http://www2.cancer.org/zine/index.cfm?fn=001_11031998_0

American Heart Association. (2000). *Heart Patient Information.* [On-line]. Available: http://americanheart.org/Patient_Information/hindex.html

American Heart Association (2003). *Obesity and overweight.* [On-line]. Available: http://www.networkforgood.org/siteURL=http://www.americanheart.org/

American Heart Association (2004). *Heart disease and stroke statistics—2004 update.* [On-line]. Available: http://www.americanheart.org/presenter.jhtml?identifier=3000090

American Medical Association. (2003). *Alcohol and other drug abuse.* [On-line]. Available: http://www.ama-assn.org/ama/pub/category/3337.html.

American Psychiatric Association. (2000). *Diagnostic and statistical manual of mental disorders* (4th ed. TR). Washington, DC: American Psychiatric Press.

American Psychiatric Association. (2002). APA *Let's talk facts about posttraumatic stress disorder.* [On-line]. Available: http://www.psych.org/disasterpsych/fs/ptsd.cfm.

American Psychiatric Association Work Group on Alzheimer's Disease & Related Dementias. (1997). Practice guideline for the treatment of patients with Alzheimer's disease and other dementias of late life. *American Journal of Psychiatry, 154(5,* Suppl), 1–39.

American Psychological Association. (1984). *Behavioral research with animals.* Washington, DC: Author.

American Psychological Association. (1992). Ethical principles of psychologists and code of conduct. *American Psychologist, 47,* 1597–1611.

American Psychological Association. (2005). *APA online: Psychology matters. Putting the power of television to good use.* [On-line]. Available: http://www.psychologymatters.org/Bandura.html

Amidzic, O., Riehle, H. J., Fehr, T., Wienbruch, C., & Elbert, T. (2001). Pattern of focal outbursts in chess players. *Nature, 412(6847),* 603.

Amorim, K. S., & Rossetti-Ferreira, M. C. (2004). Ethnotheories and childrearing practices: Some constraints on their investigation. *Culture & Psychology, 10(3),* 337–351.

Anderson, A. K., & Phelps, E. A. (2000). Expression without recognition: Contributions of the human amygdala to emotional communication. *Psychological Science, 11(2),* 106–111.

Anderson, C. A. (2001). Heat and violence. *Current Directions in Psychological Science, 10(1),* 33–38.

Anderson, C. A. (2004). An update on the effects of playing violent video games. *Journal of Adolescence, 27(1),* 113–122.

Anderson, C. A., Anderson, K. B., Dorr, N., DeNeve, K. M., & Flanagan, M. (2000). Temperature and aggression. *Advances in Experimental Social Psychology, 32,* 63–133.

Anderson, C. A., Berkowitz, L., Donnerstein, E., Huesmann, L. R., Johnson, J. D., Linz, D., Malamuth, N. M., & Wartella, E. (2003). The influence of media violence on youth. *Psychological Science in the Public Interest, 4(3),* 81–110.

Anderson, C. A., & Bushman, B. J. (2001). Effects of violent video games on aggressive behavior, aggressive cognition, aggressive affect, physiological arousal, and prosocial behavior: A meta-analytic review of the scientific literature. *Psychological Science, 12(5),* 353–359.

Anderson, C. A., & Dill, K. E. (2000). Video games and aggressive thoughts, feelings, and behavior in the laboratory and in life. *Journal of Personality & Social Psychology, 78(4),* 772–790.

Anderson, C. A., & Hamilton, M. (2005). Gender role stereotyping of parents in children's picture books: The invisible father. *Sex Roles. 52(3–4),* 145–151.

Anderson, M. C. (2001). Active forgetting: Evidence for functional inhibition as a source of memory failure. *Journal of Aggression, Maltreatment & Trauma, 4(2),* 185–210.

Anderson, M. C., Bjork, R. A. & Bjork, E. L. (1994). Remembering can cause forgetting: Retrieval dynamics in long-term memory. *Journal of Experimental Psychology: Learning, Memory, and Cognition, 20,* 1063–1087.

Anderson, M. C., Ochsner, K. N., Kuhl, B., Cooper, J., Robertson, E., Gabrieli, S. W., Glover, G. H., & Gabrieli, J. D. E. (2004). Neural systems underlying the suppression of unwanted memories. *Science, 303(5655),* 232–235.

Andrade, T. G. C. S., & Graeff, F. G. (2001). Effect of electrolytic and neurotoxic lesions of the median raphe nucleus on anxiety and stress. *Pharmacology, Biochemistry & Behavior, 70(1),* 1–14.

Andreasen, J. (2000). Meditation meets behavioural medicine: The story of experimental research on meditation. *Journal of Consciousness Studies, 7(11–12),* 17–73.

Anetzberger, G. J. (2001). Elder abuse identification and referral: The importance of screening tools and referral protocols. *Journal of Elder Abuse & Neglect, 13(2),* 3–22.

Angenendt, A. (2003). Safety and security from the air traffic control services' point of view. *Human Factors & Aerospace Safety, 3(3),* 207–209.

Angst, J., Gamma, A., Gastpar, M., Lepine, J. P., Mendlewicz, J., & Tylee, A. (2002). Gender differences in depression: Epidemiological findings from the European DEPRES I and II studies. *European Archives of Psychiatry & Clinical Neuroscience, 252(5),* 201–209.

Archbold, R., & Harmon, M. (2001). *International success: Acceptance.* Online: The Five O'Clock Club. [On-line]. Available: http://www.fiveoclockclub.com/articles/

Ardelt, M. (2000). Still stable after all these years? Personality stability theory revisited. *Social Psychology Quarterly, 63(4),* 392–405.

Aries, P. (1981). *The hour of our death.* (H. Weaver, Trans.). New York: Knopf.

Ariznavarreta, C., Cardinali, D. P., Villanua, M. A., Granados, B., Martin, M., Chiesa, J. J., Golombek, D. A., & Tresguerres, J. A. F. (2002). Circadian rhythms in airline pilots submitted to long-haul transmeridian flights. *Aviation, Space, & Environmental Medicine, 73(5),* 445–455.

Aronson, J., Fried, C. B., & Good, C. (2002). Reducing the effects of stereotype threat on African American college students shaping theories of intelligence. *Journal of*

Experimental Social Psychology, 38(2), 113–125.

Asch, S. E. (1951). Effects of group pressure upon the modification and distortion of judgment. In H. Guetzkow (Ed.), *Groups, leadership, and men.* Pittsburgh: Carnegie Press.

Ashby, F. G., & Maddox, W. T. (2005). Human category learning. *Annual Review of Psychology, 56,* 149–178.

Astin, J. A. (2004). Mind-body therapies for the management of pain. *Clinical Journal of Pain, 20*(1), 27–32.

Atchley, P., & Kramer, A. F. (2000). Age related changes in the control of attention in depth. *Psychology & Aging, 15*(1), 78–87.

Atchley, R. C. (1997). *Social forces and aging* (8th ed.). Belmont, CA: Wadsworth.

Atkins, C. K., Panicker, S., & Cunningham, C. L. (2005). *Laboratory animals in research and teaching: Ethics, care, and methods.* Washington, DC: American Psychological Association.

Atkinson, R. C., & Shiffrin, R. M. (1968). Human memory: A proposed system and its control processes. In K. W. Spence & J. T. Spence (Eds.), *The psychology of learning and motivation* (Vol. 2). New York: Academic Press.

Aubert, A., & Dantzer, R. (2005). The taste of sickness: Lipopolysaccharide-induced finickiness in rats. *Physiology & Behavior, 84*(3), 437–444.

Austin, J. H. (2001). *Zen and the brain: Toward an understanding of meditation and consciousness.* Cambridge, MA: First MIT Press.

Axtell, R. E. (1998). *Gestures: The do's and taboos of body language around the world, revised and expanded ed.* New York: Wiley.

Ayoko, O. B., & Härtel, C. E. J. (2003). The role of space as both a conflict trigger and a conflict control mechanism in culturally heterogeneous workgroups. *Applied Psychology: An International Review, 52*(3), 383–412.

Bachevalier, J., & Vargha-Khadem, F. (2005). The primate hippocampus: Ontogeny, early insult and memory. *Current Opinion in Neurobiology, 15*(2), 168–174.

Bachman, G., & Zakahi, W. R. (2000). Adult attachment and strategic relational communication: Love schemas and affinity-seeking. *Communication Reports, 13*(1), 11–19.

Badawy, A. B. (2003). Alcohol and violence and the possible role of serotonin. *Criminal Behaviour & Mental Health, 13*(1), 31–44.

Baddeley, A. D. (1992). Working memory. *Science, 255,* 556–559.

Baddeley, A. D. (1998). Recent developments in working memory. *Current Opinion in Neurobiology, 8,* 234–238.

Baddeley, A. D. (2000). Short-term and working memory. In E. Tulving, F. I. M. Craik, et al. (Eds.), *The Oxford handbook of memory.* New York: Oxford University Press.

Badr, L. K., & Abdallah, B. (2001). Physical attractiveness of premature infants affects outcome at discharge from the NICU. *Infant Behavior & Development, 24*(1), 129–133.

Baer, J. (1994). Divergent thinking is not a general trait: A multi-domain training experiment. *Creativity Research Journal, 7,* 35–36.

Bagby, R. M., Rogers, R., & Buis, T. (1994). Detecting malingered and defensive responding on the MMPI–2 in a forensic inpatient sample. *Journal of Personality Assessment, 62,* 191–203.

Bagermihl, B. (1999). *Biological exuberance: Animal homosexuality and natural diversity.* New York: St Martins Press.

Bailer, U., de Zwaan, M., Leisch, F., Strnad, A., Lennkh-Wolfsberg, C., El-Giamal, N., Hornik, K., & Kasper, S. (2004). Guided self-help versus cognitive-behavioral group therapy in the treatment of bulimia nervosa. *International Journal of Eating Disorders, 35*(4), 522–537.

Bailey, J. M., Dunne, M. P., & Martin, N. G. (2000). Genetic and environmental influences on sexual orientation and its correlates in an Australian twin sample. *Journal of Personality & Social Psychology, 78*(3), 524–536.

Bailey, K. R., & Mair, R. G. (2005). Lesions of specific and nonspecific thalamic nuclei affect prefrontal cortex-dependent spects of spatial working memory. *Behavioral Neuroscience, 119*(2), 410–419.

Baillargeon, R. (2000). Reply to Bogartz, Shinskey, and Schilling; Schilling; and Cashon and Cohen. *Infancy, 1,* 447–462.

Baker, R. A. (1996). *Hidden memories.* New York: Prometheus Books.

Baker, R. A. (1998). A view of hypnosis. *Harvard Mental Health Letter, 14,* 5–6.

Baldessarini, R. J., & Hennen, J. (2004). Genetics of suicide: An overview. *Harvard Review of Psychiatry, 12*(1), 1–13.

Baldwin, N. (2001). *Edison: Inventing the century.* Chicago: University of Chicago Press.

Baldwin, S., & Oxlad, M. (2000). *Electroshock and minors: A fifty year review.* New York: Greenwood Publishing Group.

Balfour, D. J. K. (2004). The neurobiology of tobacco dependence: A preclinical perspective on the role of the dopamine projections to the nucleus. *Nicotine & Tobacco Research, 6*(6), 899–912.

Ballesteros, S., & Manuel Reales, J. (2004). Intact haptic priming in normal aging and Alzheimer's disease: Evidence for dissociable memory systems. *Neuropsychologia, 42*(8), 1063–1070.

Bancroft, J. (2002). The medicalization of female sexual dysfunction: The need for caution. *Archives of Sexual Behavior, 31*(5), 451–455.

Bandstra, E. S., Morrow, C. E., Vogel, A. L., Fifer, R. C., Ofir, A. Y., Dausa, A. T., Xue, L., & Anthony, J. C. (2002). Longitudinal influence of prenatal cocaine exposure on child language functioning. *Neurotoxicology & Teratology, 24*(3), 297–308.

Bandura, A. (1969). *Principles of behavior modification.* New York: Holt, Rinehart and Winston.

Bandura, A. (1986). *Social foundations of thought and action: A social cognitive theory.* Englewood Cliffs, NJ: Prentice Hall.

Bandura, A. (1989). Social cognitive theory. In R. Vasta (Ed.), *Annals of child development* (Vol. 6). Greenwich, CT: JAI Press.

Bandura, A. (1991). Social cognitive theory of moral thought and action. In W. M. Kurtines & J. L. Gewirtz (Eds.), *Handbook of moral behavior and development: Vol. 1. Theory.* Hillsdale, NJ: Erlbaum.

Bandura, A. (1997). *Self-efficacy: The exercise of control.* New York: Freeman.

Bandura, A. (1999). Social cognitive theory of personality. In L. A Pervin, & O. P. John (Eds.), *Handbook of personality: Theory and Research.* New York: Guilford Press.

Bandura, A. (2000). Exercise of human agency through collective efficacy. *Current Directions in Psychological Science, 9*(3), 75–83.

Bandura, A. (2003). On the psychosocial impact and mechanisms of spiritual modeling: Comment. *International Journal for the Psychology of Religion, 13*(3), 167–173.

Bandura, A., Blanchard, E. B., & Ritter, B. J. (1969). The relative efficacy of desensitization and modeling therapeutic approaches for inducing behavioral, affective, and attitudinal changes. *Journal of Personality and Social Psychology, 13,* 173–199.

Bandura, A., & Locke, E. A. (2003). Negative self-efficacy and goal effects revisited. *Journal of Applied Psychology, 88*(1), 87–99.

Bandura, A., Ross, D., & Ross, S. (1961). Transmission of aggression through imitation of aggressive models. *Journal of Abnormal & Social Psychology, 63,* 575–582.

Bandura, A., & Walters, R. H. (1963). *Social learning and personality development.* New York: Holt, Rinehart and Winston.

Banks, A., & Gartrell, N. K. (1995). Hormones and sexual orientation: A questionable link. *Journal of Homosexuality, 28*(3–4), 247–268.

Banks, M. S., & Salapatek, P. (1983). Infant visual perception. In M. M. Haith & J. J. Campos (Eds.), *Handbook of child psychology.* New York: Wiley.

Barber, N. (2000a). On the relationship between country sex ratios and teen pregnancy rates: A replication. *Cross-Cultural Research: The Journal of Comparative Social Science, 34,* 26–37.

Barber, T. X. (2000b). A deeper understanding of hypnosis: Its secrets, its nature, its essence. *American Journal of Clinical Hypnosis, 42*(3–4), 208–272.

Barch, D. M. (2005). The cognitive neuroscience of schizophrenia. *Annual Review of Clinical Psychology, 1,* 321–353.

Bard, C. (1934). On emotional expression after decortication with some remarks on certain theoretical views. *Psychological Review, 41,* 309–329.

Barinaga, M. (1999). Learning visualized, on the double. *Science, 286,* 1661.

Barker, P. (2000). *Basic family therapy.* Malden, MA: Blackwell Science, Inc.

Barley, N. (1997). *Grave matters: A lively history of death around the world.* Austin, TX: Henry Holt & Company.

Barlow, D. H. (1999). *Anxiety and its disorders: The nature and treatment of anxiety and panic* (2nd ed.). New York: Guilford.

Barlow, D. H., Esler, J. L., & Vitali, A. E. (1998). Psychosocial treatments for panic disorders, phobias, and generalized anxiety disorder. In P. E. Nathan, J. M. Gorman, et al. (Eds.), *A guide to treatments that work* (pp. 288–318). New York: Oxford University Press.

Barnet, B., Duggan, A. K., & Devoe, M. (2003). Reduced low birth weight for teenagers receiving prenatal care at a school-based health center: Effect of access and comprehensive care. *Journal of Adolescent Health. 33*(5), 349–358.

Barnouw, V. (1985). *Culture and personality* (4th ed.). Homewood, IL: Dorsey Press.

Baron, R. (2000). *Social psychology* (7th ed.). Boston: Allyn & Bacon.

Baron, R. (2000). *The handbook of emotional intelligence.* New York: Jossey-Bass.

Baron, R. A., & Byrne, D. (2003). *Social psychology (10th ed.).* Boston, MA: Allyn & Bacon.

Bar-On, R., & Parker, J. D. A. (Eds.). (2000). *The handbook of emotional intelligence: Theory, development, assessment, and application at home, school, and in the workplace.* San Francisco, CA: Jossey-Bass.

Barry, D. T. (2002). An ethnic identity scale for East Asian immigrants. *Journal of Immigrant Health, 4*(2), 87–94.

Barry, D. T., Grilo, C. M., & Masheb, R. M. (2002). Gender differences in patients with binge eating disorder. *International Journal of Eating Disorders, 31(1),* 63–70.

Bartholow, B. D., & Anderson, C. A. (2002). Effects of violent video games on aggressive behavior: Potential sex differences. *Journal of Experimental Social Psychology, 38*(3), 283–290.

Barton, J. J. S., Press, D. Z., Keenan, J. P., & O'Connor, M. (2002). Lesions of the fusiform face area impair perception of facial configuration in prosopagnosia. *Neurology, 58*(1), 71–78.

Batel, P. (2000). Addiction and schizophrenia. *European Psychiatry, 15,* 115–122.

Bates, P., & Rutherford, J. (2003). Problem substance use and schizophrenia. *British Journal of Psychiatry, 182*(5), 455.

Batson, C. D. (1991). *The altruism question: Toward a social-psychological answer.* Hillsdale, NJ: Erlbaum.

Batson, C. D. (1998). Altruism and prosocial behavior. In D. T. Gilbert, S. T. Fiske, and G. Lindzey (Eds.), *The handbook of social psychology, Vol. 2* (4th ed.) (pp. 282–316). Boston, MA: McGraw-Hill.

Batson, C. D., & Ahmad, N. (2001). Empathy-induced altruism in a prisoner's dilemma II: What if the target of empathy has defected? *European Journal of Social Psychology, 31*(1), 25–36.

Baumrind, D. (1980). New directions in socialization research. *American Psychologist, 35,* 639–652.

Baumrind, D. (1995). *Child maltreatment and optimal caregiving in social contexts.* New York: Garland.

Beach, F. A. (1977). *Human sexuality in four perspectives.* Baltimore: The Johns Hopkins University Press.

Bearer, C. F., Stoler, J. M., Cook, J. D., & Carpenter, S. J. (2004–2005). Biomarkers of alcohol use in pregnancy. *Alcohol Research & Health, 28*(1), 38–43.

Beauregard, M., Levesque, J., & Bourgouin, P. (2001). Neural correlates of conscious self-regulation of emotion. *Journal of Neuroscience, 21*(18), 6993–7000.

Beck, A. T. (1976). *Cognitive therapy and the emotional disorders.* New York: International Universities Press.

Beck, A. T. (2000). *Prisoners of hate.* New York: Harperperennial.

Beck, A., & Rector, N. A. (2005). Cognitive approaches to schizophrenia: Theory and therapy. *Annual Review of Clinical Psychology, 1,* 577–606.

Becker, H., & Kunstmann, W. (2001). The homeless mentally ill in Germany. *International Journal of Mental Health, 30*(3), 57–73.

Beckerman, S., Hardy, S. B., Baker, R. R., Crocker, W. H., Valentine, P., & Hawkes, K. (1999). Partible paternity: Matings with multiple men leading to multiple fathers per child. *Meeting of the American Association for the Advancement of Science.* January, Anaheim, CA.

Becvar, D., & Becvar, R. (2006). *Family therapy: A systemic integration* (6th ed.). Boston, MA: Allyn & Bacon/Longman.

Begg, I. M., Needham, D. R., & Bookbinder, M. (1993). Do backward messages unconsciously affect listeners? No. *Canadian Journal of Experimental Psychology, 47,* 1–14.

Begic, D., & Jokic-Begic, N. (2002). Violent behaviour and post-traumatic stress disorder. *Current Opinion in Psychiatry, 15*(6), 623–626.

Begley, S. (2000, January 1). Rewiring your gray matter. *Newsweek,* pp. 63, 65.

Beilin, H. (1992). Piaget's enduring contribution to developmental psychology. *Developmental Psychology, 28,* 191–204.

Belsky, J., & Cassidy, J. (1994). Attachment: Theory and evidence. In M. Rutter & D. Hay (Eds.), *Development through life: A handbook for clinicians* (pp. 373–402). Oxford, England: Blackwell.

Bem, S. L. (1974). The measurement of psychological androgyny. *Journal of Consulting and Clinical Psychology, 42*(2), 155–162.

Bem, S. L. (1981). Gender schema theory: A cognitive account of sex typing. *Psychological Review, 88,* 354–364.

Bem, S. L. (1993). *The lenses of gender: Transforming the debate on sexual inequality.* New Haven, CT: Yale University Press.

Benazzi, F. (2004). Testing early-onset chronic atypical depression subtype. *Neuropsychopharmacology, 29*(2), 440–441.

Bender, L. (Producer), & Van Sant, G. (Director). (1997). *Good Will Hunting [Motion Picture].* United States: Miramax. [On-line]. Available: http://www.amazon.com/exec/obidos/tg/detail/-/0788814664/qid= 1124997431/sr=1–2/ref=sr_1_2/002–381996 8–8449638?v=glance&s=dvd

Benjamin, L. T. (2005). A history of clinical psychology as a profession in America (and a glimpse at its future). *Annual Review of Clinical Psychology, 1,* 1–30.

Benjamin, L. T., Cavell, T. A., & Shallenberger, W. R. (1984). Staying with initial answers on objective tests: Is it a myth? *Teaching of Psychology, 11,* 133–141.

Benloucif, S., Orbeta, L., Ortiz, R., Janssen, I., Finkel, S., Bleiberg, J., & Zee, P. C. (2004). Morning or evening activity improves neuropsychological performance and subjective sleep quality in older adults. *Sleep: Journal of Sleep & Sleep Disorders Research, 27*(8), 1542–1551.

Bennett, J. B. (1988). Power and influence as distinct personality traits: Development and validation of a psychometric measure.

Journal of Research in Personality, 22, 361–394.

Bennett, M., Barrett, M., Karakozov, R., Kipiani, G., Lyons, E., Pavlenko, V., & Riazanova, T. (2004). Young children's evaluations of the ingroup and of outgroups: A multi-national study. *Social Development, 13*(1), 124–141.

Bennett, M. E., McCrady, B. S., Frankenstein, W., Lisa, A., et al. (1993). Identifying young adult substance abusers: The Rutgers Collegiate Substance Abuse Screening Test. *Journal of Studies on Alcohol, 54*(5), 522–527.

Benson, H. (1977). Systematic hypertension and the relaxation response. *New England Journal of Medicine, 296,* 1152–1156.

Beraki, S., Aronsson, F., Karlsson, H., Ögren, S. O., & Kristensson, K. (2005). Influenza A virus infection causes alterations in expression of synaptic regulatory genes combined with changes in cognitive and emotional behaviors in mice. *Molecular Psychiatry, 10*(3), 299–308.

Berman, M. E., Tracy, J. I., & Coccaro, E. F. (1997). The serotonin hypothesis of aggression revisited. *Clinical Psychology Review, 17*(6), 651–665.

Bermond, B., Fasotti, L., Nieuwenhuyse, B., & Schuerman, J. (1991). Spinal cord lesions, peripheral feedback, and intensities of emotional feelings. *Cognition and Emotion, 5,* 201–220.

Bernard, L. L. (1924). *Instinct.* New York: Holt.

Bernardi, L., Sleight, P., Bandinelli, G., Cencetti, S., Fattorini, L., Wdowczyc-Szulc, J., & Lagi, A. (2001). Effect of rosary prayer and yoga mantras on autonomic cardiovascular rhythms: Comparative study. *BMJ: British Medical Journal, 323*(7327), 1446–1449.

Bernhardt, T., Seidler, A., & Froelich, L. (2002). Der Einfluss von psychosozialen Faktoren auf das Demenzerkrankungsrisiko. Psychosocial risk factors and dementia—A review. *Fortschritte der Neurologie, Psychiatrie, 70*(6), 283–288.

Bernheim, K. F., & Lewine, R. R. J. (1979). *Schizophrenia: Symptoms, causes, and treatments.* New York: Norton.

Berreman, G. (1971). *Anthropology today.* Del Mar, CA: CRM Books.

Berrettini, W. H. (2000a). Genetics of psychiatric disease. *Annual Review of Medicine, 51,* 465–479.

Berrettini, W. H. (2000b). Susceptibility loci for bipolar disorder: Overlap with inherited vulnerability to schizophrenia. *Biological Psychiatry, 47*(3), 245–251.

Berry, J. W., Poortinga, Y. A., Segall, M. H., & Dasen, P. R. (1992). *Cross-cultural psy-chology: Research and applications.* New York: Cambridge University Press.

Berry, J. W., Poortinga, Y. H., Segall, M. H., & Dasen, P. R. (2002). *Cross-cultural psychology: Research and applications* (2nd ed.). New York: Cambridge University Press.

Berthoud, H. (2002). Multiple neural systems controlling food intake and body weight. *Neuroscience & Biobehavioral Reviews, 26*(4), 393–428.

Bertram, K., & Widener, A. (1998). Repressed memories: The real story. *Professional Psychology: Research & Practice, 29,* 482–487.

Besançon, F. (2004). Warning signs for suicide: Everyone's business. *Suicide & Life-Threatening Behavior, 34*(2), 197–198.

Best, J. B. (1999). *Cognitive psychology,* (5th ed.) Belmont, CA: Wadsworth.

Beutler, L. E., Brown, M. T., Crothers, L., Booker, K., et al. (1996). The dilemma of factitious demographic distinctions in psychological research. *Journal of Consulting and Clinical Psychology, 64,* 892–902.

Beutler, L. E., Shurkin, J. N., Bongar, B. M., & Gray, J. (2000). *A consumers guide to psychotherapy.* Oxford: Oxford University Press.

Beyth-Marom, Shlomith, D., Gombo, R., & Shaked, M. (1985). *An elementary approach to thinking under uncertainty.* Hillsdale, NJ: Erlbaum.

Bhatt, S., Gregg, T. R., & Siegel, A. (2003). NK-sub-1 receptors in the medial hypothalamus potentiate defensive rage behavior elicited from the midbrain periaqueductal gray matter of the cat. *Brain Research, 966*(1), 54–64.

Bhattacharya, S. K., & Muruganandam, A. V. (2003). Adaptogenic activity of Withania somnifera: An experimental study using a rat model of chronic stress. *Pharmacology, Biochemistry & Behavior, 75*(3), 547–555.

Bhugra, D. (2000). Disturbances in objects of desire: Cross-cultural issues. *Sexual & Relationship Therapy, 15*(1), 67–78.

Biehl, M., Matsumoto, D., Ekman, P., Hearn, V., Heider, K., Kudoh, T., & Ton, V. (1997). Matsumoto and Ekman's Japanese and Caucasian facial expressions of emotion (JACFEE): Reliability data and cross–national differences. *Journal of Nonverbal Behavior, 21,* 3–21.

Bink, M. L., & Marsh, R. L. (2000). Cognitive regularities in creative activity. *Review of General Psychology, 4*(1), 59–78.

Birkenhäger, T. K., Renes, J., & Pluijms, E. M. (2004). One-year follow-up after successful ECT: A naturalistic study in depressed inpatients. *Journal of Clinical Psychiatry, 65*(1), 87–91.

Bishop, C. A. (1974). *The northern Objibwa and the fur trade.* Toronto: Holt, Rinehart, and Winston.

Bjorkqvist, K. (1994). Sex differences in physical, verbal, and indirect aggression: A review of recent research. *Sex Roles, 30,* 177–188.

Bjornæs, H., Stabell, K. E., Roste, G. K., & Bakke, S. J. (2005). Changes in verbal and nonverbal memory following anterior temporal lobe surgery for refractory seizures: Effects of sex and laterality. *Epilepsy & Behavior, 6*(1), 71–84.

Black, J. S. (2005). Integrating medical and psychological treatment for sexual problems: The psyche and the soma. *Sexual & Relationship Therapy, 20*(1), 105–113.

Blaine, B., & McElroy, J. (2002). Selling stereotypes: Weight loss infomercials, sexism, and weightism. *Sex Roles, 46*(9–10), 351–357.

Blair, H. T., Huynh, V. K., Vaz, V. T., Van, J., Patel, R. R., Hiteshi, A. K., Lee, J. E., & Tarpley, J. W. (2005). Unilateral storage of fear memories by the amygdala. *Journal of Neuroscience, 25*(16), 4198–4205.

Blair, R. J. R. (2004). The roles of orbital frontal cortex in the modulation of antisocial behavior. *Brain & Cognition, 55*(1), 198–208.

Blakemore, C., & Cooper, G. F. (1970). Development of the brain depends on the visual environment. *Nature, 228,* 477–478.

Blakemore, S-J. (2003). Deluding the motor system. *Consciousness & Cognition: An International Journal, 12*(4), 647–655.

Blanco, C., Schneier, F. R., Schmidt, A., Blanco-Jerez, C. R., Marshall, R. D., Sanchez-Lacay, A., & Liebowitz, M. R. (2003). Pharmacological treatment of social anxiety disorder: A meta-analysis. *Depression & Anxiety,18*(1), 29–40.

Blanton, C. K. (2000). "They cannot master abstractions, but they can often be made efficient workers": Race and class in the intelligence testing of Mexican Americans and African Americans in Texas during the 1920s. *Social Science Quarterly, 81*(4), 1014–1026.

Blass, T. (1991). Understanding behavior in the Milgram obedience experiment: The role of personality, situations, and their interactions. *Journal of Personality & Social Psychology, 60*(3), 398–413.

Blass, T. (2000). Stanley Milgram. In A. E. Kazdin (Ed.), *Encyclopedia of psychology,* Vol. 5 (pp. 248–250). Washington, DC: American Psychological Association.

Blass, T., & Schmitt, C. (2001). The nature of perceived authority in the Milgram paradigm: Two replications. *Current Psychology: Developmental, Learning, Personality, Social, 20*(2), 115–121.

Bleckley, M. K., Durso, F. T., Crutchfield, J. M., Engle, R. W., & Khanna, M. M. (2003). Individual differences in working memory capacity predict visual attention allocation. *Psychonomic Bulletin & Review, 10*(4), 884–889.

Block, R. I., O'Leary, D. S., Hichwa, R. D., Augustinack, J. C., Ponto, L. L. B., Ghoneim, M. M., Arndt, S., Hurtig, R. R., Watkins, G. L., Hall, J. A., Nathan, P. E., & Andreasen, N. C. (2002). Effects of frequent marijuana use on memory-related regional cerebral blood flow. *Pharmacology, Biochemistry & Behavior, 72*(1–2), 237–250.

Blonna, R., & Levitan, J. (2000). *Healthy sexuality.* Englewood, CO: Morton.

Bloom, F. E., & Lazerson, A. (1988). Brain, mind, and behavior (2nd ed.). New York: W. H. Freeman.

Blum, K., Braverman, E. R., Holder, J. M., Lubar, J. F., Monastra, V. J., Miller, D., Lubar, J. O., Chen, T. J. H., & Comings, D. E. (2000). Reward deficiency syndrome: A biogenetic model for the diagnosis and treatment of impulsive, addictive, and compulsive behaviors. *Journal of Psychoactive Drugs, 32*(Suppl), 1–68.

Boake, C. (2002). From the Binet-Simon to the Wechsler-Bellevue: Tracing the history of intelligence testing. *Journal of Clinical & Experimental Neuropsychology, 24(3),* 383–405.

Bobak, M., McKee, M., Rose, R., & Marmot, M. (1999). Alcohol consumption in a national sample of the Russian population. *Addiction, 94*(6), 857–866.

Bock, G. R., & Goode, J. A. (Eds.) (1996). *Genetics of criminal and antisocial behavior.* Chichester, England: Wiley.

Boden, M. A. (2000). State of the art: Computer models of creativity. *Psychologist, 13*(2), 72–76.

Bohus, M., Haaf, B., Simms, T., Limberger, M. F., Schmahl, C., Unckel, C., Lieb, K., & Linehan, M. M. (2004). Effectiveness of inpatient dialectical behavioral therapy for borderline personality disorder: A controlled trial. *Behaviour Research & Therapy, 42*(5), 487–499.

Bois, J. E., Sarrazin, P. G., Brustad, R. J., Trouilloud, D. O., & Cury, F. (2002). Mothers' expectancies and young adolescents' perceived physical competence: A yearlong study. *Journal of Early Adolescence, 22(4),* 384–406.

Bolles, R. C. (1970). Species–specific defense reactions and avoidance learning. *Psychological Review, 77,* 32–48.

Bolles, R. C. (1975). *Theory of motivation* (2nd ed.). New York: Harper & Row.

Bonanno, G. A., Papa, A. Lalande, K. Zhang, N., & Noll, J. G. (2005). Grief processing and deliberate grief avoidance: A prospective comparison of bereaved spouses and parents in the United States and the People's Republic of China. *Journal of Consulting & Clinical Psychology, 73*(1), 86–98.

Bonavia, M. T., & Pardo, I. Q. (1999). Par-Creencias directivas y participacion de los empleados. Management culture and employee involvement. *Revista de Psicologia del Trabajo y de las Organizaciones, 15*(3), 367–383.

Bond, F. W., & Bunce, D. (2000). Mediators of change in emotion-focused and problem-focused worksite stress management intervention. *Journal of Occupational Health Psychology, 5,* 153–163.

Bond, M. H., & Smith, P. B. (1996). Cross-cultural social and organizational psychology. *Annual Review of Psychology, 47,* 205–235.

Bonnel, A., Mottron, L., Peretz, I., Trudel, M., Gallun, E., & Bonnel, A-M. (2003). Enhanced pitch sensitivity in individuals with autism: A signal detection analysis. *Cognitive Neuroscience, 5*(2), 226–235.

Bonson, K. R., Grant, S. J., Contoreggi, C. S., Links, J. M., Metcalfe, J., Weyl, H. L., Kurian, V., Ernst, M., & London, E. D. (2002). Neural systems and cue-induced cocaine craving. *Neuropsychopharmacology, 26*(3), 376–386.

Book, A. S., Starzyk, K. B., & Qunisey, V. L. (2002). The relationship between testosterone and aggression: A meta-analysis. *Aggression & Violent Behavior, 6(6),* 579–599.

Boonstra, H. (2002, February). *The Guttmacher report on public policy.* [On-line]. Available: http://www.guttmacher.org/pubs/ib_1–02.html.

Borbely, A. A. (1982). Circadian and sleep-dependent processes in sleep regulation. In J. Aschoff, S. Daan, & G. A. Groos (Eds.), *Vertebrate circadian rhythms* (pp. 237–242). Berlin: Springer/Verlag.

Bouchard, T. J. (2004). Genetic influence on human psychological traits: A survey. *Current Directions in Psychological Science, 13*(4), 148–151.

Bouchard, T. J., & McGue, M. (1981). Familial studies of intelligence: A review. *Science, 212*(4498), 1055–1059.

Bouchard, T. J., Jr. (1994). Genes, environment, and personality. *Science, 264,* 1700–1701.

Bouchard, T. J., Jr. (1997). The genetics of personality. In K. Blum & E. P. Noble (Eds.), *Handbook of psychiatric genetics.* Boca Raton, FL: CRC Press.

Bouchard, T. J., Jr. (1999). The search for intelligence. *Science, 284,* 922–923.

Bouchard, T. J., Jr., & Hur, Y. (1998). Genetic and environmental influences on the continuous scales of the Myers-Briggs Type Indicator: An analysis based on twins reared apart. *Journal of Personality, 66,* 135–149.

Bouchard, T. J., Jr., Mcgue, M., Hur, Y., & Horn, J. M. (1998). A genetic and environmental analysis of the California Psychological Inventory using adult twins reared apart and together. *European Journal of Personality, 12,* 307–320.

Boucher, L., & Dienes, Z. (2003). Two ways of learning associations. *Cognitive Science, 27*(6), 807–842.

Bourgeois-Bougrine, S., Carbon, P., Gounelle, C., Mollard, R., & Coblentz, A. (2003). Perceived fatigue for short- and long-haul flights: A survey of 739 airline pilots. *Aviation, Space, and Environmental Medicine, 74*(10), 1072–1077.

Bourne, L. E., Dominowski, R. L., & Loftus, E. F. (1979). *Cognitive processes.* Englewood Cliffs, NJ: Prentice Hall.

Bouton, M. E. (1994). Context, ambiguity, and classical conditioning. *Current Directions in Psychological Science, 2,* 49–53.

Bouton, M. E., Mineka, S., & Barlow, D. H. (2001). A modern learning theory perspective on the etiology of panic disorder. *Psychological Review, 108*(1), 4–32.

Bovbjerg, D. H. (2003). Circadian disruption and cancer: Sleep and immune regulation. *Brain, Behavior & Immunity, 17*(Suppl1), 48–S50.

Bower, B. (2000). Cooperative strangers turn a mutual profit. *Science News, 157,* 231.

Bower, H. (2001). The gender identity disorder in the DSM-IV classification: A critical evaluation. *Australian & New Zealand Journal of Psychiatry, 35*(1), 1–8.

Bowers, K. S., & Woody, E. Z. (1996). Hypnotic amnesia and the paradox of intentional forgetting. *Journal of Abnormal Psychology, 105,* 381–390.

Bowker, A., & Gray, M. (2004). An Introduction to the supervision of the cybersex offender. *Federal Probation, 68*(3), 3–8.

Bowlby, J. (1969). *Attachment and loss, Vol. I: Attachment.* New York: Basic Books.

Bowlby, J. (1973). *Attachment and loss, Vol. II: Separation and anxiety.* New York: Basic Books.

Bowlby, J. (1979). *The making and breaking of affectional bonds.* London, England: Tavistock.

Bowlby, J. (1982). Attachment and loss: Retrospect and prospect. *American Journal of Orthopsychiatry, 52,* 664–678.

Bowlby, J. (1989). *Secure attachment.* New York: Basic Books.

Bowlby, J. (2000). *Attachment.* New York: Basic Books.

Bowler, D. F. (2001). "It's all in your mind": The final common pathway. *Work: Journal of Prevention, Assessment & Rehabilitation, 17(3)*, 167–174.

Bowling, A. C., & Mackenzie, B. D. (1996). The relationship between speed of information processing and cognitive ability. *Personality & Individual Differences, 20(6)*, 775–800.

Boyle, S. H., Williams, R. B., Mark, D. B., Brummett, B. H., Siegler, I. C., Helms, M. J., & Barefoot, J. C. (2004). Hostility as a predictor of survival in patients with coronary artery disease. *Psychosomatic Medicine, 66(5)*, 629–632.

Bragdon, A. D., & Gamon, D. (1999). *Building left-brain power: Left-brain conditioning exercises and tips to strengthen language, math, and uniquely human skills.* Thousand Oaks, CA: Brainwaves Books.

Brandon, T. H., Collins, B. N., Juliano, L. M., & Lazev, A. B. (2000). Preventing relapse among former smokers: A comparison of minimal interventions through telephone and mail. *Journal of Consulting and Clinical Psychology, 68(1)*, 103–113.

Brandon, T. H., Meade, C. D., Herzog, T. A., Chirikos, T. N., Webb, M. S., & Cantor, A. B. (2004). Efficacy and cost-effectiveness of a minimal intervention to prevent smoking relapse: Dismantling the effects of amount of content versus contact. *Journal of Consulting & Clinical Psychology, 72(5)*, 797–808.

Brannon, L. (2005). *Gender: Psychological perspectives.* Boston, MA: Pearson.

Braver, S. L., Griffin, W. A., & Cookston, J. T. (2005). Prevention programs for divorced nonresident fathers. *Family Court Review, 43(1)*, 81–96.

Brawman-Mintzer, O., & Lydiard, R. B. (1996). Generalized anxiety disorder: Issues in epidemiology. *Journal of Clinical Psychiatry, 57*, 3–8.

Brawman-Mintzer, O., & Lydiard, R. B. (1997). Biological basis of generalized anxiety disorder. *Journal of Clinical Psychiatry, 58*, 16–25.

Breger, L. (2000). *Freud: Darkness in the midst of vision.* New York: Wiley.

Breggin, P. R. (2004). *Psychiatric drug facts.* [On-line]. Available: http://www.breggin.com/

Breland, K., & Breland, M. (1961). The misbehavior of organisms. *American Psychologist, 16*, 681–684.

Bremner, J. D., Vythilingam, M., Vermetten, E., Anderson, G., Newcomer, J. W. & Charney, D. S. (2004). Effects of Glucocorticoids on declarative memory function in major depression. *Biological Psychiatry, 55(8)*, 811–815.

Brendgen, M., Vitaro, F., & Bukowski, W. M. (2000). Deviant friends and early adolescents' emotional and behavioral adjustment. *Journal of Research on Adolescence, 10(2)*, 173–189.

Brewer, J. B., Zhao, Z., Desmond, J. E., Glover, G. H., & Gabrieli, J. D. (1998). Making memories: Brain activity that predicts how well visual experience will be remembered. *Science, 281*, 1185–1187.

Brewer, M. B. (1996). When contact is not enough: Social identity and intergroup cooperation. *International Journal of Intercultural Relations, 20(3–4)*, 291–303.

Brewer, W. F., & Pani, J. R. (1996). Reports of mental imagery in retrieval from long-term memory. *Consciousness & Cognition: An International Journal, 5*, 265–287.

Brim, O. (1999). *The MacArthur Foundation study of midlife development.* Vero Beach, FL: MacArthur Foundation.

Briñol, P., Petty, R. E., & Tormala, Z. L. (2004). Self-validation of cognitive responses to advertisements. *Journal of Consumer Research, 30(4)*, 559–573.

Brislin, R. W. (1993). *Understanding culture's influence on behavior.* Orlando, FL: Harcourt Brace Jovanovich.

Brislin, R. W. (1997) (2nd ed.). *Understanding culture's influence on behavior.* San Diego: Harcourt Brace.

Brislin, R. W. (2000). *Understanding culture's influence on behavior.* Ft. Worth, TX: Harcourt.

Brislin, R. W., Cushner, K., Cherrie, C., & Yong, M. (1986). *Intercultural interactions: A practical guide.* Newbury Park, CA: Sage.

Brkich, M., Jeffs, D., & Carless, S. A. (2002). A global self-report measure of person-job fit. *European Journal of Psychological Assessment, 18(1)*, 43–51.

Brody, A., Olmstead, R. E., London, E. D., Farahi, J., Meyer, J. H., Grossman, P., Lee, G. S., Huang, J., Hahn, E. L., & Mandelkern, M. A. (2004). Smoking-induced ventral striatum dopamine release. *American Journal of Psychiatry, 161(7)*, 1211–1218.

Brody, N. (1992). *Intelligence* (2nd ed.). San Diego, CA: Academic Press.

Broman-Fulks, J. J., Berman, M. E., Rabian, B. A., & Webster, M. J. (2004). Effects of aerobic exercise on anxiety sensitivity. *Behaviour Research & Therapy, 42(2)*, 125–136.

Brooks, D. J. (2004). Safety and tolerability of COMT inhibitors. *Neurology, 62(1,Suppl1)*, S39–S46.

Brown, D. (2001). (Mis)representations of the long-term effects of childhood sexual abuse in the courts. *Journal of Child Sexual Abuse, 9(3–4)*, 79–108.

Brown, D., Scheflin, A. W., & Hammond, D. C. (1997). *Memory, trauma treatment and the law.* New York: Norton.

Brown, E., Deffenbacher, K., & Sturgill, K. (1977). Memory for faces and the circumstances of encounter. *Journal of Applied Psychology, 62*, 311–318.

Brown, J. D., & Rogers, R. J. (1991). Self-serving attributions: The role of physiological arousal. *Personality and Social Psychology Bulletin, 17*, 501–506.

Brown, K., & Bradley, L. J. (2002). Reducing the stigma of mental illness. *Journal of Mental Health Counseling, 24(1)*, 81–87.

Brown, K. T., Brown, T. N., Jackson, J., Sellers, R. M., & Manuel, W. J. (2003). Teammates on and off the field? White student athletes. *Journal of Applied Social Psychology, 33(7)*, 1379–1403.

Brown, R., & Kulik, J. (1977). Flashbulb memories. *Cognition, 5*, 73–99.

Brown, R., & McNeill, D. (1966). The "tip of the tongue" phenomenon. *Journal of Verbal Learning and Verbal Behavior, 5*, 325–337.

Brown, R. P., & Josephs, R. A. (1999). A burden of proof: Stereotype relevance and gender differences in math performance. *Journal of Personality & Social Psychology, 76(2)*, 246–257.

Browne, K. O. (2001). Cultural formulation of psychiatric diagnoses. *Culture, Medicine & Psychiatry, 25(4)*, 411–425.

Bruck, C. S., & Allen, T. D. (2003). The relationship between big five personality traits, negative affectivity, type A behavior, and work-family conflict. *Journal of Vocational Behavior, 63(3)*, 457–472.

Bruggeman, E. L., & Hart, K. J. (1996). Cheating, lying, and moral reasoning by religious and secular high school students. *Journal of Educational Research, 89*, 340–344.

Brummett, B. H., Babyak, M. A., Mark, D. B., Clapp-Channing, N. E., Siegler, I. C., & Barefoot, J. C. (2004). Prospective study of perceived stress in cardiac patients. *Annals of Behavioral Medicine, 27(1)*, 22–30.

Brym, R. J., & Lie, J. (2003). *Sociology: Your compass for a new world.* Belmont, CA: Thomson Learning, Inc.

Buchanan, T. W., & Lovallo, W. R. (2001). Enhanced memory for emotional material following stress-level cortisol treatment in humans. *Psychoneuroendocrinology, 26(3)*, 307–317.

Buck, R. (1984). *The communication of emotion.* New York: Guilford Press.

Buddie, A. M, & Parks, K. A. (2003). The role of the bar context and social behaviors on women's risk for aggression. *Journal of Interpersonal Violence, 18(12)*, 1378–1393.

Bugental, B. B., & Goodnow, J. J. (1998). Socialization process. In W. Damon & N. Eisenberg (Eds.), *Handbook of child psychology* (5th ed.). New York: John Wiley & Sons.

EFERENCES

B., & **Johnston, C.** (2000). '...ild cognitions in the context '...nual Review of Psychology, 51,

..., C. M., Sullivan, P. F., & Kendler, K. S. (2002). Medical and psychiatric morbidity in obese women with and without binge eating. *International Journal of Eating Disorders, 32(1)*, 72–78.

Bull, L. (2003). What can be done to prevent smoking in pregnancy? A literature review. *Early Child Development & Care, 173(6)*, 661–667.

Buller, D. B., Burgoon, M., Hall, J. R., Levine, N., Taylor, A. M., Beach, B., Buller, M. K., & Melcher, C. (2000). Long-term effects of language intensity in preventive messages on planned family solar protection. *Health Communication, 12(3)*, 261–275.

Bullough, B., & Bullough, V. (1997). Are transvestites necessarily heterosexual? *Archives of Sexual Behavior, 26*, 1–12.

Burgdorf, J., Knutson, B., & Panksepp, J. (2000). Anticipation of rewarding electrical brain stimulation evokes ultrasonic vocalization in rats. *Behavioural Neuroscience, 114(2)*, 320–327.

Burger, J. M., & Guadagno, R. E. (2003). Self-concept clarity and the foot-in-the-door procedure. *Basic & Applied Social Psychology, 25(1)*, 79–86.

Burka, J. B., & Yuen, L. M. (2004). *Procrastination.* Cambridge, MA: DaCapo Press.

Burns, N. R., Nettelbeck, T., & Cooper, C. J. (2000). Event-related potential correlates of some human cognitive ability constructs. *Personality & Individual Differences, 29(1)*, 157–168.

Burns, R. A., Johnson, K. S., Harris, B. A., Kinney, B. A., & Wright, S. E. (2004). Functional cues for position learning effects in animals. *Psychological Record, 54(2)*, 233–254.

Burns, R. G., & Katovich, M. A. (2003). Examining road rage/aggressive driving: Media depiction and prevention suggestions. *Environment & Behavior, 35(5)*, 621–636.

Burton, L. A., Rabin, L., Vardy, S. B., Frohlich, J., Wyatt, G., Dimitri, D., Constante, S, & Guterman, E. (2004). Gender differences in implicit and explicit memory for affective passages. *Brain & Cognition, 54(3)*, 218–224.

Bushman, B. J. (2002). Does venting anger feed or extinguish the flame? Catharsis, rumination, distraction, anger and aggressive responding. *Personality & Social Psychology Bulletin, 28(6)*, 724–731.

Bushman, B. J., Baumeister, R. F., & Stack, A. D. (1999). Catharsis, aggression, and persuasive influence: Self-fulfilling or self-defeating prophecies? *Journal of Personality and Social Psychology, 76*, 367–376.

Buss, D. M. (1989). Sex differences in human mate preferences: Evolutionary hypotheses tested in 37 cultures. *Behavioral and Brain Sciences, 12*, 1–49.

Buss, D. M. (1999). *Evolutionary Psychology: The new science of the mind.* Boston: Allyn & Bacon.

Buss, D. M. (2003a). *Evolutionary psychology: The new science of the mind (2nd ed.).* Boston: Allyn & Bacon.

Buss, D. M. (2003b). *The evolution of desire: Strategies of human mating.* New York: Basic Books.

Buss, D. M. (2005). *The handbook of evolutionary psychology.* Hoboken, NJ: Wiley.

Buss, D. M. and 40 colleagues. (1990). International preferences in selecting mates: A study of 37 cultures. *Journal of Cross-Cultural Psychology, 21*, 5–47.

Butcher, J. N. (2000). Revising psychological tests: Lessons learned from the revision of the MMPI. *Psychological Assessment, 12(3)*, 263–271.

Butcher, J. N. (2005). *A beginner's guide to the MMPI-2 (2nd ed.).* Washington, DC: American Psychological Association.

Butcher, J. N., & Rouse, S. V. (1996). Personality: Individual differences and clinical assessment. *Annual Review of Psychology, 47*, 87–111.

Butler, K. Joel, J. C., & Jeffries, M. (2000). *Clinical handbook of psychotropic drugs.* New York: Wiley.

Butler, R. A. (1954, February). Curiosity in monkeys. *Scientific American, 190*, 70–75.

Butterweck, V. (2003). Mechanism of action of St John's Wort in depression: What is known? *CNS Drugs, 17(8)*, 539–562.

Buunk, B. P., Dijkstra, P., Fetchenhauer, D., & Kenrick, D. (2002). Age and gender differences in mate selection criteria for various involvement levels. *Personal Relationships, 9(3)*, 271–278.

Byrne, D. (1971). *The attraction paradigm.* New York: Academic Press.

Cacioppo, J. T., Petty, R. E., Feinstein, J. A., & Jarvis, W. B. G. (1996). Dispositional differences in cognitive motivation: The life and times of individuals varying in need for cognition. *Psychological Bulletin, 119(2)*, 197–253.

Cadoret, R. J., Leve, L. D., & Devor, E. (1997). Genetics of aggressive and violent behavior. *Psychiatric Clinics of North America, 20*, 301–322.

Cairns, D., & Pasino, J. A. (1977). Comparison of verbal reinforcement and feedback in the operant treatment of disability due to chronic back pain. *Behavior Therapy, 8(4)*, 621–630.

Camarena, B., Aguilar, A., Loyzaga, C., & Nicolini, H. (2004a). A family-based association study of the 5–HT-1DB receptor gene in obsessive-compulsive disorder. *International Journal of Neuropsychopharmacology, 7(1)*, 49–53.

Camarena, B., Santiago, H., Aguilar, A., Ruvinskis, E., González-Barranco, J., & Nicolini, H. (2004b). Family-based association study between the monoamine oxidase A gene and obesity: Implications for psycho pharma cogenetic studies. *Neuropsychobiology, 49(3)*, 126–129.

Camodeca, M., Goossens, F. A., Meerum T. M., & Schuengel, C. (2002). Bullying and victimization among school-age children: Stability and links to proactive and reactive aggression. *Social Development, 11(3)*, 332–345.

Campbell, L., Simpson, J. A. , Kashy, D. A., & Fletcher, G. J. O. (2001). Ideal standards, the self, and flexibility of ideals in close relationships. *Personality & Social Psychology Bulletin, 27(4)*, 447–462.

Cannon, A. (2002, January 14). One life, in ashes. *U.S. News & World Report*, p. 23.

Cannon, T. D., Kaprio, J., Lonnqvist, J., Huttunen, M., & Koskenvuo, M. (1998). The genetic epidemiology of schizophrenia in a Finnish twin cohort. *Archives of General Psychiatry, 55*, 67–74.

Cannon, T. D., van Erp, T. G. M., Rosso, I. M., Huttunen, M., Loenqvist, J., Pirkola, T., Salonen, O., Valanne, L., Poutanen, V., & Standertskjoeld-Nordenstam, C. (2002). Fetal hypoxia and structural brain abnormalities in schizophrenic patients, their siblings, and controls. *Archives of General Psychiatry, 59(1)*, 35–41.

Cannon, W. B. (1927). The James-Lange theory of emotions: A critical examination and an alternative theory. *American Journal of Psychology, 39*, 106–124.

Cannon, W. B., Lewis, J. T., & Britton, S. W. (1927). The dispensability of the sympathetic division of the autonomic nervous system. *Boston Medical Surgery Journal, 197*, 514.

Cannon, W. B., & Washburn, A. (1912). An explanation of hunger. *American Journal of Physiology, 29*, 441–454.

Cantor, J. M., Blanchard, R., Paterson, A. D., & Bogaert, A. F. (2002). How many gay men owe their sexual orientation to fraternal birth order? *Archives of Sexual Behavior, 31(1)*, 63–71.

Carducci, B. J. (1998). *The psychology of personality: Viewpoints, research, and applications.* Pacific Grove, CA: Brooks/Cole.

Careers in Health Psychology. (2004). [Online]. Available: http://www.healthpsych.com/#Health Psychology

Carlson, N. R. (1998). *Physiology of behavior* (6th ed.). Boston: Allyn and Bacon.

Carmaciu, C. D., Anderson, C. S., & Markar, H. R. (2001). Secondary koro with unusual features in a Briton. *Transcultural Psychiatry, 38*(4), 528–533.

Carnagey, N. L., & Anderson, C. A. (2004). Violent video game exposure and aggression: A literature review. *Minerva Psichiatrica, 45*(1), 1–18.

Carnes, P. J. (2001). Cybersex, courtship, and escalating arousal: Factors in addictive sexual desire. *Sexual Addiction & Compulsivity, 8*(1), 45–78.

Carney, S., Cowen, P., Geddes, J., Goodwin, G., Rogers, R., Dearness, K., Tomlin, A., Eastaugh, J., Freemantle, N., Lester, H., Harvey, A., & Scott, A. (2003). Efficacy and safety of electroconvulsive therapy in depressive disorders: A systematic review and meta-analysis. *Lancet, 361*(9360), 799–808.

Carpenter, S., & Radhakrishnan, P. (2002). The relation between allocentrism and perceptions of ingroups. *Personality & Social Psychology Bulletin, 28*(11), 1528–1537.

Carr, J. L., & VanDeusen, & K. M. (2004). Risk factors for male sexual aggression on college campuses. *Journal of Family Violence, 19*(5), 279–289.

Carskadon, M. A., & Dement, W. C. (2002). *Adolescent sleep patterns.* New York: Cambridge University Press.

Carstensen, L. L. (1995). Evidence for a life-span theory of socioemotional selectivity. *Current Directions in Psychological Science, 4*(5), 151–156.

Carstensen, L. L., Fung, H. H., & Charles, S. (2003). Socioemotional selectivity theory and the regulation of emotion in the second half of life. *Motivation & Emotion, 27*(2), 103–123.

Carton, J. S. (1996). The differential effects of tangible rewards and praise on intrinsic motivation: A comparison of cognitive evaluation theory and operant theory. *Behavior Analyst, 19*, 237–255.

Caspi, A. (2000). The child is father of the man: Personality continuities from childhood to adulthood. *Journal of Personality and Social Psychology, 78*(1), 158–172.

Caspi, A., Roberts, B. W., & Shiner, R. L. (2005). Personality development: Stability and change. *Annual Review of Psychology, 56*, 453–484.

Casti, J. L. (2000). *Paradigms regained: A further exploration of the mysteries of modern science.* New York:Morrow.

Castillo, R. J. (2003). Trance, functional psychosis, and culture. *Psychiatry: Interpersonal & Biological Processes, 66*(1), 9–21.

Cattell, R. B. (1950). *Personality: A systematic, theoretical, and factual study.* New York: McGraw-Hill.

Cattell, R. B. (1963). Theory of fluid and crystallized intelligence: A critical experiment. *Journal of Educational Psychology, 54*, 1–22.

Cattell, R. B. (1965). *The scientific analysis of personality.* Baltimore: Penguin.

Cattell, R. B. (1971). *Abilities: Their structure, growth, and action.* Boston, MA: Houghton Mifflin.

Cattell, R. B. (1990). Advances in Cattellian personality theory. In L. A. Pervin (Ed.), *Handbook of personality: Theory and research.* New York: Guilford Press.

Cavacuiti, C. A. (2004). You, me, and drugs—A love triangle: Important considerations when both members of a couple are abusing substances. *Substance Use & Misuse, 39*(4), 645–656.

CBS News/60 Minutes. (2003). *Mind of the suicide bomber.* [On-line]. Available: http://www.cbsnews.com/

Centers for Disease Control (CDC). (2002). *The burden of chronic diseases as causes of death.* [On-line]. Available: http://www.cdc.gov/nccdphp/statbook/pdf/section1.pdf

Centers for Disease Control (CDC). (2003). *The Tobacco Atlas: Deaths.* [On-line]. Available: http://www.5.who.”int/tobacco/repository/stp84/36%209%20Deaths.pdf

Centers for Disease Control (CDC) (2004a). *Health risk factors: Physical activity.* [On-line]. Available: http://www.cdc.gov/nchs/data/hus/hus03cht.pdf

Centers for Disease Control (CDC) (2004b). *Health risk factors: Smoking.* [On-line]. Available: http://www.cdc.gov/nchs/data/hus/hus03cht.pdf

Centers for Disease Control (CDC). (2005). *Tracking the Hidden Epidemics: Trends in STDs in the United States, 2005.* [On-line]. Available: http://www.cdc.gov/nchstp/dstd/Stats_Trends/Trends2005.pdf

Centers for Disease Control and Prevention. (2005). *Division of HIV/AIDS prevention.* [On-line]. Available: http://www.cdc.gov/hiv/pubs/facts.htm.

Centers for Disease Control and Prevention. (2005). *Calculate your BMI.* [On-line]. Available: http://www.cdc.gov/nccdphp/dnpa/bmi/index.htm.

Centers for Disease Control and Prevention. (2005). *CDC's national leadership role in addressing obesity.* [On-line]. Available: http://www.cdc.gov/doc.do?id=0900f3ec803207fd&print=on.

Centers for Disease Control and Prevention. (2005). *Overweight and obesity: Defining overweight and obesity.* [On-line]. Available: http://cdc.gov/nccdphp/dnpa/obes defining.htm

Cervone, D. (2005). Personality architecture: Within-person structures and processes. *Annual Review of Psychology, 56*, 423–452.

Cervone, D., & Shoda, Y. (1999). Beyond traits in the study of personality coherence. *Current Directions in Psychological Science, 8*(1), 27–32.

Cesario, J., & Crawford, I. (2002). The effect of homosexuality on perceptions of persuasiveness and trustworthiness. *Journal of Homosexuality, 43*(2), 93–110.

Cesaro, P, & Ollat, H. (1997). Pain and its treatments. *European Neurology, 38*, 209–215.

Ceschi, G., & Scherer, K. R. (2001). Controler l'expression faciale et changer l'emotion : Une approche developpementale. The role of facial expression in emotion: A developmental perspective. *Enfance, 53*(3), 257–269.

Chabrol, H., Montovany, A., Ducongé, E., Kallmeyer, A., Mullet, E., & Leichsenring, F. (2004). Factor structure of the borderline personality inventory in adolescents. *European Journal of Psychological Assessment, 20*(1), 59–65.

Chaikin, N. D., & Prout, M. F. (2004). Treating complex trauma in women within community mental health. *American Journal of Orthopsychiatry, 74*(2), 160–173.

Challem, J., Berkson, B., Smith, M. D., & Berkson, B. (2000). *Syndrome X: The complete program to prevent and reverse insulin resistance.* New York: Wiley.

Chaney, J. M., Mullins, L. L., Wagner, J. L., Hommel, K. A., Page, M. C., Doppler, & Matthew J. (2004). A longitudinal examination of causal attributions and depression symptomatology in rheumatoid arthritis. *Rehabilitation Psychology, 49*(2), 126–133.

Chang, G., Orav, J., McNamara, T. K., Tong, M-Y., & Antin, J. H. (2005). Psychosocial function after hematopoietic stem cell transplantation. *Psychosomatics: Journal of Consultation Liaison Psychiatry, 46*(1), 34–40.

Chang, R. C., Stout, S., & Miller, R. R. (2004). Comparing excitatory backward and forward conditioning. *Quarterly Journal of Experimental Psychology: Comparative & Physiological Psychology, 57B*(1), 1–23.

Chapelot, D., Marmonier, C., Aubert, R., Gausseres, N., & Louis-Sylvestre, J. (2004). A role for glucose and insulin preprandial profiles to differentiate meals and snacks. *Physiology & Behavior, 80*(5), 721–731.

Charland, W. A. (1992, January). Nightshift narcosis. *The Rotarion, 160*, 16–19.

Charney, D. S. (2003). Neuroanatomical circuits modulating fear and anxiety behaviors.

inavica, 108(Suppl417),

, S., & Burger, J. ulation backfires: , and requester on . technique. *Journal of* *ychology, 29,* 211–221.

, M. M. (2000). Leadership research . theory: A functional integration. *Group Dynamics, 4,* 27–43.

Chen, F., & Kenrick, D. T. (2002). Repulsion or attraction? Group membership and assumed attitude similarity. *Journal of Personality & Social Psychology, 83(1),* 111–125.

Cherney, I. D. (2005). Children's and adults' recall of sex-stereotyped toy pictures: Effects of presentation and memory task. *Infant & Child Development, 14*(1), 11–27.

Cheung, C., & Rudowicz, E. (2003). Underachievement and attributions among students attending schools stratified by student ability. *Social Psychology of Education, 6*(4), 303–323.

Cheung, M. S., Gilbert, P., & Irons, C. (2004). An exploration of shame, social rank, and rumination in relation to depression. *Personality & Individual Differences, 36*(5), 1143–1153.

Chi, I., & Chou, K. (1999). Financial strain and depressive symptoms among Hong Kong Chinese elderly: A longitudinal study. *Journal of Gerontological Social Work, 32,* 41–60.

Chipman, K., Hampson, E., & Kimura, D. (2002). A sex difference in reliance on vision during manual sequencing tasks. *Neuropsychologia, 40(7),* 910–916.

Cho, K. (2001). Chronic "jet lag" produces temporal lobe atrophy and spatial cognitive deficits. *Nature Neuroscience, 4(6),* 567–568.

Choi, I., & Nisbett, R. E. (2000). Cultural psychology of surprise: Holistic theories and recognition of contradiction. *Journal of Personality & Social Psychology, 79*(6), 890–905.

Choi, N. (2004). Sex role group differences in specific, academic, and general self-efficacy. *Journal of Psychology: Interdisciplinary & Applied, 138*(2), 149–159.

Chomsky, N. (1968). *Language and mind.* New York: Harcourt, Brace, World.

Chomsky, N. (1980). *Rules and representations.* New York: Columbia University Press.

Chrisler, J. C. (2003). Ageism: The equal opportunity oppression. *Psychology of Women Quarterly, 27*(2), 187–188.

Christ, G. H., Siegel, K., & Christ, A. E. (2002). Adolescent grief: "It never really hit me...until it actually happened." *JAMA: Journal of the American Medical Association, 288(10),* 1269–1278.

Christensen, D. (2000). Is snoring a dizzease? Nighttime snoring may serve as a

wake-up call for future illness. *Science News, 157,* 172–173.

Christian, K. M., & Thompson, R. F. (2005). Long-term storage of an associative memory trace in the cerebellum. *Behavioral Neuroscience, 119*(2), 526–537.

Chuang, D. (1998). Cited in J. Travis, Stimulating clue hints how lithium works. *Science News, 153,* 165.

Chuang, Y. (2002). Sex differences in mate selection preference and sexual strategy: Tests for evolutionary hypotheses. *Chinese Journal of Psychology, 44(1),* 75–93.

Cialdini, R. A. (2001a). *Influence: Science and practice* (4th ed.). Boston, MA: Allyn & Bacon.

Cialdini, R. A. (2001b). The science of persuasion. *Scientific American, 284*(2), 76–81.

Cicchetti, D., & Toth, S. L. (2005). Child maltreatment. *Annual Review of Clinical Psychology, 1,* 409–438.

Cillessen A. H. N., & Mayeux L. (2004). From censure to reinforcement: Developmental changes in the association between aggression and social status. *Child Development, 75,* 147–163.

Clark, K. B., & Clark, M. P. (1939). The development of consciousness of self and the emergence of racial identification in Negro preschool children. *Journal of Social Psychology, 10,* 591–599.

Clarke-Stewart, K. A., Fitzpatrick, M. J., Allhusen, V. D., & Goldberg, W. A. (2000). Measuring difficult temperament the easy way. *Journal of Developmental and Behavioral Pediatrics, 21*(3), 207–220.

Clarke-Stewart, K. A., Vandell, D. L., McCartney, K., Owen, M. T., & Booth, C. (2000). Effects of parental separation and divorce on very young children. *Journal of Family Psychology, 14*(2), 304–326.

Clifford, J. S., Boufal, M. M., & Kurtz, J. E. (2004). Personality traits and critical thinking: Skills in college students empirical tests of a two-factor theory. *Assessment, 11*(2), 169–176.

Clinton, S. M., & Meador-Woodruff, J H. (2004). Thalamic dysfunction in schizophrenia: Neurochemical, neuropathological, and in vivo imaging abnormalities. *Schizophrenia Research. 69*(2–3), 237–253.

Cloud, J. (2001, February 26). New sparks over electroshock. *Time,* 60–62.

Cohen, A. (1997, September 8). Battle of the binge. *Time,* pp. 54–56.

Cohen, D., Mason, K., & Farley, T. A. (2004). Beer consumption and premature mortality in Louisiana: An ecologic analysis. *Journal of Studies on Alcohol, 65*(3), 398–403.

Cohen, R. A., Brumm, V., Zawacki, T. M., Paul, R., Sweet, L., & Rosenbaum, A. (2003). Impulsivity and verbal deficits asso-

ciated with domestic violence. *Journal of the International Neuropsychological Society, 9*(5), 760–770.

Cohen, R. A., Paul, R., Zawacki, T. M., Moser, D. J., Sweet, L., & Wilkinson, H. (2001). Emotional and personality changes following cingulotomy. *Emotion, 1(1),* 38–50.

Cohen, S., Hamrick, N., Rodriguez, M. S., Feldman, P. J., Rabin, B. S., & Manuck, S. B. (2002). Reactivity and vulnerability to stress-associated risk for upper respiratory illness. *Psychosomatic Medicine, 64(2),* 302–310.

Cohen, S., & Williamson, G. M. (1991). Stress and infectious disease in humans. *Psychological Bulletin, 109,* 5–24.

Colapinto, J. (2000). *As nature made him: The boy that was raised as a girl.* New York: HarperCollins.

Colapinto, J. (2004, June 3). *What were the real reasons behind David Reimer's suicide?* [On-line]. Available: http://slate.msn.com/id/2101678/.

Cole, D. L. (1982). Psychology as a liberating art. *Teaching of Psychology, 9,* 23–26.

Cole, E., & Brown, R. S. (2002). Psychological needs of post-war children in Kosovo: A preliminary analysis. *School Psychology International, 23*(2), 131–147

Cole, M., Gray, J., Glick, J. A., & Sharp, D. W. (1971). *The cultural context of learning and thinking.* New York: Basic Books.

Coley, R. L., & Chase-Lansdale, P. L. (1998). Adolescent pregnancy and parenthood: Recent evidence and future directions. *American Psychologist, 53*(2), 152–166.

Collocan, L. K., Tuma, F. K.., & Fleischman, A. R. (2004). Research with victims of disaster: Institutional review board considerations. *IRB: Ethics & Human Research, 26*(4), 9–11.

Compton, W. M., Grant, B. F., Colliver, J. D., Glantz, M. D., & Stinson, F. S. (2004). Prevalence of marijuana use disorders in the United States: (1991)–(1992) and (2001)-(2002). *JAMA: Journal of the American Medical Association, 291*(17), 2114–2121.

Conger, J. A. (1999). Charismatic and transformational leadership in organizations: An insider's perspective on these developing streams of research. *Leadership Quarterly, 10*(2), 145–179.

Connolly, S. (2000). *LSD (just the facts).* Baltimore: Heinemann Library.

Connor, J., Norton, R., Ameratunga, S., Robinson, E., Civil, I., Dunn, R., Bailey, J., & Jackson, R. (2002). Driver sleepiness and risk of serious injury to car occupants: Population based case control study. *BMJ: British Medical Journal, 324(7346),* 1125–1128.

Connor, K. M., & Davidson, J. R. T. (2002). A placebo-controlled study of Kava kava in generalized anxiety disorder. *International Clinical Psychopharmacology, 17(4),* 185–188.

Contrada, R. J., Ashmore, R. D., Gary, M. L., Coups, E., Egeth, J. D., Sewell, A., Ewell, K., Goyal, T. M., & Chasse, V. (2000). Ethnicity-related sources of stress and their effects on well-being. *Current Directions in Psychological Science, 9(4),* 136–139.

Conway, M. A., & Pleydell-Pearce, C. W. (2000). The construction of autobiographical memories in the self-memory system. *Psychological Review, 107,* 261–288.

Conyers, J. E. (2002). Racial inequality: Emphasis on explanations. *Western Journal of Black Studies, 26(4),* 249–254.

Cook, A. S., & Dworkin, D. S. (1992). *Helping the bereaved: Therapeutic interventions for children, adolescents, and adults.* New York: Basic Books.

Cook, M., & Mineka, S. (1989). Observational conditioning of fear to fear-relevant versus fear-irrelevant stimuli in rhesus monkeys. *Journal of Abnormal Psychology, 98,* 448–459.

Cook, P. F. (2000). Effects of counselors' etiology attributions on college students' procrastination. *Journal of Counseling Psychology, 47(3),* 352–361.

Coolen, L. M., Allard, J., Truitt, W. A., & McKenna, K. E. (2004). Central regulation of ejaculation. *Physiology & Behavior, 83(2),* 203–215.

Coombs, R. H. (2004). *Handbook of addictive disorders.* Hoboken, NJ: Wiley.

Cooper, E. E. (2000). Spatial-temporal intelligence: Original thinking processes of gifted inventors. *Journal for the Education of the Gifted, 24(2),* 170–193.

Cooper, M. L., Shaver, P. R., & Collins, N. L. (1998). Attachment styles, emotion regulation, and adjustment in adolescence. *Journal of Personality and Social Psychology, 74(5),* 1380–1397.

Cooper, R. (2004). What is wrong with the DSM? *History of Psychiatry, 15(57,Pt1),* 5–25.

Cooper, W. E. Jr., Pérez-Mellado, V., Vitt, L. J., & Budzinsky, B. (2002). Behavioral responses to plant toxins in two omnivorous lizard species. *Physiology & Behavior, 76(2),* 297–303.

Corcoran, C., Walker, E., Huot, R., Mittal, V., Tessner, K., Kestler, L., & Malaspina, D. (2003). The stress cascade and schizophrenia: Etiology and onset. *Schizophrenia Bulletin, 29(4),* 671–692.

Coren, S. (1996). *Sleep thieves: An eye-opening exploration into the science and mysteries of sleep.* New York: Freeman.

Corey, G. (2001a). *Case approach to counseling and psychotherapy.* Belmont, CA: Wadsworth.

Corey, G. (2001b). *The art of integrative counseling.* Belmont, CA: Wadsworth.

Corey, G. (2005). *Theory and practice of counseling and psychotherapy (7th ed.).* Belmont, CA: Wadsworth.

Corkin, S. (2002). What's new with the amnesic patient H.M.? *Nature Reviews Neuroscience, 3,* 153–160.

Costa, J. L., Brennen, M. B., & Hochgeschwender, U. (2002). The human genetics of eating disorders: Lessons from the leptin/melanocortin system. *Child & Adolescent Psychiatric Clinics of North America, 11(2),* 387–397.

Coulson, S., & Wu, Y. C. (2005). Right hemisphere activation of joke-related information: An event-related brain potential study. *Journal of Cognitive Neuroscience, 17(3),* 494–506.

Courage, M. L., & Adams, R. J. (1990). Visual acuity assessment from birth to three years using the acuity card procedures: Cross-sectional and longitudinal samples. *Optometry and Vision Science, 67,* 713–718.

Courtenay, W. H. (2000). Engendering health: A social constructionist examination of men's health beliefs and behaviors. *Psychology of Men and Masculinity, 1(1),* 4–15.

Covington, M. V., & Mueller, K. J. (2001). Intrinsic versus extrinsic motivation: An approach/avoidance reformulation. *Educational Psychology Review, 13(2),* 157–176.

Cowan, R. L. (2001). Patient's page: Ecstasy. *Journal of the Gay & Lesbian Medical Assn, 5(1),* 25–26.

Cowen, P. J. (2002). Cortisol, serotonin and depression: All stressed out? *British Journal of Psychiatry, 180(2),* 99–100.

Coyne, S. M., Archer, J., & Eslea, M. (2004). Cruel intentions on television and in real life: Can viewing indirect aggression increase viewers' subsequent indirect aggression? *Journal of Experimental Child Psychology, 88(3),* 234–253.

Craig, A. D., & Bushnell, M. C. (1994). The thermal grill illusion: Unmasking the burn of cold pain. *Science, 265,* 252–255.

Craik, F. I. M., & Lockhart, R. S. (1972). Levels of processing: A framework for memory research. *Journal of Verbal Learning and Verbal Behavior, 11,* 671–684.

Crair, M. C., Gillespie, D. C., & Stryker, M. P. (1998). The role of visual experience in the development of columns in cat visual cortex. *Science, 279,* 566–570.

Crandall, C. S., & Martinez, R. (1996). Culture, ideology, and antifat attitudes. *Personality and Social Psychology Bulletin, 22,* 1165–1176.

Craske, B. (1977). Perception of impossible limb positions induced by tendon vibration. *Science, 196(4285),* 71–73.

Craske, M. C. (2000). *Mastery of your anxiety and panic: Therapist guide (3rd ed.).* New York: Academic Press.

Craske, M. C., & Waters, A. M. (2005). Panic disorder, phobias, and generalized anxiety disorder. *Annual Review of Clinical Psychology, 1,* 197–225.

Craske, M. G. (1999). *Anxiety disorders: Psychological approaches to theory and treatment.* Boulder, CO: Westview.

Crews, F. (1997). The verdict on Freud. *Psychological Science, 7(2),* 63–68.

Crews, F. T., Collins, M. A., Dlugos, C., Littleton, J., Wilkins, L., Neafsey, E. J., Pentney, R., Snell, L. D., Tabakoff, B., Zou, J., & Noronha, A. (2004). Alcohol-induced neurodegeneration: When, where and why? *Alcoholism: Clinical & Experimental Research, 28(2),* 350–364.

Cristofalo, V. J. (1996). Ten years later: What have we learned about human aging from studies of cell cultures? *Gerontologist, 36,* 737–741.

Cronbach, L. (1990). *Essentials of psychological testing.* New York: Harper & Row.

Crone, C. C., & Gabriel, G. (2002). Herbal and nonherbal supplements in medical-psychiatric patient populations. *Psychiatric Clinics of North America, 25(1),* 211–230.

Crooks, R., & Baur, K. (2005). *Our sexuality (9th ed.).* Pacific Grove: Brooks/Cole.

Crosby, B. (2003). Case studies in rational emotive behavior therapy with children and adolescents. *Journal of Cognitive Psychotherapy, 17(3),* 289–291.

Crow, T. J. (2004). Cerebral asymmetry and the lateralization of language: Core deficits in schizophrenia as pointers to the gene. *Current Opinion in Psychiatry, 17(2),* 97–106.

Crowder, R. G. (1976). *Principles of learning and memory.* Hillsdale, NJ: Erlbaum.

Crowley, A. E., & Hoyer, W. D. (1994). An integrative framework for understanding two-sided persuasion. *Journal of Consumer Research, 20(4),* 561–574.

Csernansky, J. G., Schindler, M. K., Splinter, N. R., Wang, L., Gado, M., Selemon, L. D., Rastogi-Cruz, D., Posener, J. A., Thompson, P. A., & Miller, M. I. (2004). Abnormalities of thalamic volume and shape in schizophrenia. *American Journal of Psychiatry, 161(5),* 896–902.

Cubitt, S., & Burt, C. (2002). Leadership style, loneliness and occupational stress in New Zealand primary school principals. *New Zealand Journal of Educational Studies, 37(2),* 159–169.

Cullen, D., & Gotell, L. (2002). From orgasms to organizations: Maslow, women's sexuality and the gendered foundations of the needs hierarchy. *Gender, Work & Organization, 9*(5), 537–555.

Cummings, E., & Henry, W. E. (1961). *Growing old: The process of disengagement.* New York: Basic Books.

Cunningham, M. R., Roberts, A. R., Barbee, A. P. Druen, P. B., & Wu, C. (1995). "Their ideas of beauty are on the whole, the same as ours": Consistency and variability in the cross-cultural perception of female physical attractiveness. *Journal of Personality and Social Psychology, 68,* 261–279.

Currie, S., & Wang, J. (2004). Chronic back pain and major depression in the general Canadian population. *Pain, 107*(1–2), 54–60.

Curtiss, S. (1977). *Genie: A psycholinguistic study of a modern-day "wild child."* New York: Academic Press.

D'Alessio, D., & Allen, M. (2002). Selective exposure and dissonance after decisions. *Psychological Reports, 91*(2), 527–532.

Dabbs, J. M., & Dabbs, M. G. (2000). *Heroes, rogues, and lovers: Testosterone and behavior.* New York: McGraw-Hill.

Dackis, C. A., & O'Brien, C. P. (2001). Cocaine dependence: A disease of the brain's reward centers. *Journal of Substance Abuse Treatment, 21*(3), 111–117.

Dadds, M. R., Bovbjerg, D. H., Redd, W. H., & Cutmore, T. R. H. (1997). Imagery in human classical conditioning. *Psychological Bulletin, 122,* 89–103.

Dade, L. A., Zatorre, R. J., & Jones-Gotman, M. (2002). Olfactory learning: Convergent findings from lesion and brain imaging studies in humans. *Brain, 125,* 86–101.

Dalenberg, C. J. (2000). *Countertransference and the treatment of trauma.* Washington, DC: American Psychological Association.

Dalton, P. (2002). Olfaction. In H. Pashler & S. Yantis (Eds.), *Steven's handbook of experimental psychology: Vol. 1. Sensation and perception* (3rd ed.d.). New York: Wiley.

Damak, S., Rong, M., Yasumatsu, K., Kokrashvili, Z., Varadarajan, V., Zou, S., Jiang, P., Ninomiya, Y., & Margolskee, R. F. (2003). Detection of sweet and umami taste in the absence of taste receptor T1r3. *Science, 301*(5634), 850–851.

Damasio, A. R. (1994). *Descartes' error.* New York: Putnam's Sons.

Damasio, A. R. (1999). *The feeling of what happens: Body and emotion in the making of consciousness.* New York: Harcourt Brace.

Dana, R. H. (1998). Cultural identity assessment of culturally diverse groups. *Journal of Personality Assessment, 70*(1), 1–16.

Darwin, C. (1859). *On the origin of species.* London: Murray.

Davalos, D. B., Compagnon, N., Heinlein, S., & Ross, R. G. (2004). Neuropsychological deficits in children associated with increased familial risk for schizophrenia. *Schizophrenia Research, 67*(2–3), 123–130.

David, D., & Brown, R. J. (2002). Suggestibility and negative priming: Two replication studies. *International Journal of Clinical & Experimental Hypnosis, 50*(3), 215–228.

David, D., Schnur, J. E., & Belloiu, A. (2002). Another search for the "hot" cognitions: Appraisal, irrational beliefs, attributions, and their relation to emotion. *Journal of Rational-Emotive & Cognitive Behavior Therapy, 20*(2), 93–132.

David, D., Woodward, C., Esquenazi, J., & Mellman, T. A. (2004). Comparison of comorbid physical illnesses among veterans with PTSD and veterans with alcohol dependence. *Psychiatric Services, 55*(1), 82–85.

Davidson, J. R., Waisberg, J. L., Brundage, M. D., & Maclean, A. W. (2001). Nonpharmacologic group treatment of insomnia: A preliminary study with cancer survivors. *Psycho-Oncology,10*(5), 389–397.

Davidson, R. J., Putnam, K. M., & Larson, C. L. (2000). Dysfunction in the neural circuitry of emotion regulation—a possible prelude to violence. *Science, 289*(5479), 591–594.

Davies, I. (1998). A study of colour grouping in three languages: A test of the linguistic relativity hypothesis. *British Journal of Psychology, 89,* 433–452.

Davies, J. M. (1996). Dissociation, repression and reality testing in the countertransference: the controversey over memory and false memory in the psychoanalytic treatment of adult survivors of childhood sexual abuse. *Psychoanalytic Dialogues, 6,* 189–218.

Davis, C., Dionne, M., & Shuster, B. (2001). Physical and psychological correlates of appearance orientation. *Personality & Individual Differences, 30*(1), 21–30.

Davison, G. C., Neale, J. M., & Kring, A. M. (2004). *Abnormal psychology* (9th. ed.). New Jersey: Wiley.

Davison, K. P., Pennebaker, J. W., & Dickerson, S. S. (2000). Who talks? The social psychology of illness support groups. *American Psychologist, 55*(2), 205–217.

Dawson, K. A. (2004). Temporal organization of the brain: Neurocognitive mechanisms and clinical implications. *Brain & Cognition, 54*(1), 75–94.

de Charms, R., & Moeller, G. H. (1962). Values expressed in American children's readers: 1800–1950. *Journal of Abnormal and Social Psychology, 64*(2), 136–142.

De Coteau, T. J., Hope, D. A., & Anderson, J. (2003). Anxiety, stress, and health in northern plains Native Americans. *Behavior Therapy, 34*(3), 365–380.

De Cremer, D., & van Knippenberg, D. (2002). How do leaders promote cooperation? The effects of charisma and procedural fairness. *Journal of Applied Psychology, 87*(5), 858–866.

De Rosnay, M., & Harris, P. L. (2002). Individual differences in children's understanding of emotion: The roles of attachment and language. *Attachment & Human Development, 4*(1), 39–54.

Deary, I. J., Bell, P. J., Bell, A. J., Campbell, M. L., & Fazal, N. D. (2004). Sensory discrimination and intelligence: Testing Spearman's other hypothesis. *American Journal of Psychology, 117*(1), 1–18.

Deary, I. J., & Stough, C. (1996). Intelligence and inspection time: Achievements, prospects, and problems. *American Psychologist, 51,* 599–608.

Deary, I. J., & Stough, C. (1997). Looking down on human intelligence. *American Psychologist, 52,* 1148–1149.

Deason, R. G., & Marsolek, C. J. (2005). A critical boundary to the left-hemisphere advantage in visual-word processing. *Brain & Language, 92*(3), 251–261.

Debaere, F., Wenderoth, N., Sunaert, S., Van Hecke, P., & Swinnen, S. P. (2004). Changes in brain activation during the acquisition of a new bimanual coordination task. *Neuropsychologia, 42*(7), 855–867.

DeCasper, A. J., & Fifer, W. D. (1980). Of human bonding: Newborns prefer their mother's voices. *Science, 208,* 1174–1176.

Deci, E. L. (1995). *Why we do what we do: The dynamics of personal autonomy.* New York: Putnam's Sons.

Deci, E. L., Koestner, R., & Ryan, R. M. (1999). A meta-analytic review of experiments examining the effects of extrinsic rewards on intrinsic motivation. *Psychological Bulletin,125*(6), 627–668.

Deckers, L. (2005). *Motivation: Biological, psychological, and environmental* (2nd ed.). Boston, MA: Allyn & Bacon/Longman.

DeClue, G. (2003). The polygraph and lie detection. *Journal of Psychiatry & Law, 31*(3), 361–368.

Delahanty, D. L., Liegey Dougall, A., Hayward, M., Forlenza, M., Hawk, L. W. & Baum, A. (2000). Gender differences in cardiovascular and natural killer cell reactivity to acute stress following a hassling task. *International Journal of Behavioral Medicine, 7,* 19–27.

Delamater, A. R., LoLordo, V. M., & Sosa, W. (2003). Outcome-specific conditioned inhibition in Pavlovian backward conditioning. *Learning & Behavior, 31*(4), 393–402.

Delgado, J. M. R. (1960). Emotional behavior in animals and humans. *Psychiatric Research Report, 12,* 259–271.

Delgado, P. L. (2004). How antidepressants help depression: Mechanisms of action and clinical response. *Journal of Clinical Psychiatry, 65,* 25–30.

Delgado-Gaitan, C. (1994). Socializing young children in Mexican-American families: An intergenerational perspective. In P. M. Greenfield & R. R. Cocking (Eds.), *Cross-cultural roots of minority child development* (pp. 55–86). Hillsdale, NJ: Erlbaum.

DeLisi, L. E., Sakuma, M., Maurizio, A. M., Relja, M., & Hoff, A. L. (2004). Cerebral ventricular change over the first 10 years after the onset of schizophrenia. *Psychiatry Research: Neuroimaging, 130*(1), 57–70.

Delville, Y., Mansour, K. M., & Ferris. C. F. (1996). Testosterone facilitates aggression by modulating vasopressin receptors in the hypothalamus. *Physiology and Behavior, 60,* 25–29.

Dement, W. C. (1992, March). The sleep-watchers. *Stanford,* pp. 55–59.

Dement, W. C., & Vaughan, C. (1999). *The promise of sleep.* New York: Delacorte Press.

Dement, W. C., & Wolpert, E. (1958). The relation of eye movements, bodily motility, and external stimuli to dream content. *Journal of Experimental Psychology, 53,* 543–553.

Demo, D. H. (1992). Parent–child relations: Assessing recent changes. *Journal of Marriage and the Family, 54,* 104–117.

den Boer, J. A. (2000). Social anxiety disorder/social phobia: Epidemiology, diagnosis, neurobiology, and treatment. *Comprehensive Psychiatry, 41*(6), 405–415.

Denmark, F. L., Rabinowitz, V. C., & Sechzer, J. A. (2005). *Engendering psychology: Women and gender revisited* (2nd ed.). Boston, MA: Allyn and Bacon.

Dennis, W., & Dennis, M. G. (1940). Cradles and cradling customs of the Pueblo Indians. *American Anthropologist, 42,* 107–115.

Depue, R. A., & Collins, P. F. (1999). Neurobiology of the structure of personality: Dopamine, facilitation of incentive motivation, and extraversion. *Behavioral & Brain Sciences, 22*(3), 491–569.

Der-Karabetian, A., Stephenson, K., & Poggi, T. (1996). Environmental risk perception, activism and world-mindedness among samples of British and U. S. college students. *Perceptual and Motor Skills, 83*(2), 451–462.

Dervin, D. (2002). From American Taliban to Taliban America: The role of the dele-gate, the rule of group-fantasy post-9/11. *Journal of Psychohistory, 30*(2), 155–163.

DeStefano, D., & LeFevre, J. (2004). The role of working memory in mental arithmetic. *European Journal of Cognitive Psychology, 16*(3), 353–386.

DeValois, R. L. (1965). Behavioral and electrophysiological studies of primate vision. In W. D. Neff (Ed.), *Contributions to sensory physiology* (Vol. 1). New York: Academic Press.

Devlin, M. J., Yanovski, S. Z., & Wilson, G. T. (2000). Obesity: What mental health professionals need to know. *American Journal of Psychiatry, 157*(6), 854–866.

Devos-Comby, L., & Salovey, P. (2002). Applying persuasion strategies to alter HIV-relevant thoughts and behavior. *Review of General Psychology, 6*(3), 287–304.

Diamond, L. M. (2004). Emerging perspectives on distinctions between romantic love and sexual desire. *Current Directions in Psychological Science, 13*(3), 116–119.

Diamond, M., & Sigmundson, H. K. (1997). Sex reassignment at birth: Long-term review and clinical implications. *Archives of Pediatrics and Adolescent Medicine, 151,* 298–304.

Dickens, W. T., & Flynn, J. R. (2001). Heritability estimates versus large environmental effects: The IQ paradox resolved. *Psychological Review, 108*(2), 346–369.

Dickinson, D. J., O'Connell, D. Q., & Dunn, J. S. (1996). Distributed study, cognitive study strategies and aptitude on student learning. *Psychology: A Journal of Human Behavior, 33*(3), 31–39.

Diehm, R., & Armatas, C. (2004). Surfing: An avenue for socially acceptable risk-taking, satisfying needs for sensation seeking and experience seeking. *Personality & Individual Differences, 36*(3), 663–677.

Diener, E., & Diener, C. (1996). Most people are happy. *Psychological Science, 7,* 181–185.

Diener, E., Lucas, R. E., Oishi, S., & Suh, E. M. (2002). Looking up and down: Weighting good and bad information in life satisfaction judgments. *Personality & Social Psychology Bulletin, 28*(4), 437–445.

Diener, M. L., Mengelsdorf, S. C., McHale, J. L., & Frosch, C. A. (2002). Infants' behavioral strategies for emotion regulation with fathers and mothers: Associations with emotional expressions and attachment quality. *Infancy, 3*(2), 153–174.

Dieter, J. N. I., Field, T., Hernandez-Reif, M., Emory, E. K., & Redzepi, M. (2003). Stable preterm infants gain more weight and sleep less after five days of massage therapy. *Journal of Pediatric Psychology, 28*(6), 403–411.

Dietz, T. L. (1998). An examination of violence and gender role portrayals in video games. *Sex Roles, 38,* 425–442.

DiLauro, M. D. (2004). Psychosocial factors associated with types of child maltreatment. *Child Welfare, 83*(1), 69–99.

Dimberg, U., & Thunberg, M. (1998). Rapid facial reactions to emotion facial expressions. *Scandinavian Journal of Psychology, 39*(1), 39–46.

Dimberg, U., Thunberg, M., & Elmehed, K. (2000). Unconscious facial reactions to emotional facial expressions. *Psychological Science, 11*(1), 86–89.

Dinnel, D. L., Kleinknecht, R. A., & Tanaka-Matsumi, J. (2002). A cross-cultural comparison of social phobia symptoms. *Journal of Psychopathology & Behavioral Assessment, 24*(2), 75–84.

Dobbin, A., Faulkner, S., Heaney, D., Selvaraj. S., & Gruzelier, J. (2004). Impact on health status of a hypnosis clinic in general practice. *Contemporary Hypnosis, 21*(4), 153–160.

Dodd, M. D., & MacLeod, C. M. (2004). False recognition without intentional learning. *Psychonomic Bulletin & Review, 11*(1), 137–142.

Dodge, B., Sandfort, T. G. M., Yarber, W. L., & de Wit, J. (2005). Sexual health among male college students in the United States and the Netherlands. *American Journal of Health Behavior, 29*(2), 172–182.

Doghramji, K. (2000, December). Sleepless in America: Diagnosing and treating insomnia. [On-line serial]. Available: http://psychiatry.medscape.com/Medscape/psychiatry/ClinicalMgmt/CM.v02/public/index-CM.v02.html

Dollard, J., Doob, L., Miller, N., Mowrer, O. H., & Sears, R. R. (1939). *Frustration and aggression.* New Haven, CT: Yale University Press.

Dols, M., Willems, B., van den Hout, M., & Bittoun, R. (2000). Smokers can learn to influence their urge to smoke. *Addictive Behaviors, 25*(1), 103–108.

Domhoff, G. W. (1996). *Finding meaning in dreams: A quantitative approach.* New York: Plenum.

Domhoff, G. W. (1999). New directions in the study of dream content using the Hall and Van de Castle coding system. *Dreaming, 9,* 115–137.

Domhoff, G. W. (2001). A new neurocognitive theory of dreams. *Dreaming, 11*(1), 13–33.

Domhoff, G. W. (2003). *The scientific study of dreams: Neural networks, cognitive development, and content analysis.* Washington, DC: American Psychological Association.

Domhoff, G. W. (2004). Why did empirical dream researchers reject Freud? A critique of historical claims by Mark Solms. *Dreaming, 14*(1), 3–17.

Domhoff, G. W. (2005). A reply to Hobson (2005). *Dreaming, 15*(1), 30–32.

Domino, G., & Morales, A. (2000). Reliability and validity of the D-48 with Mexican American college students. *Hispanic Journal of Behavioral Sciences, 22*(3), 382–389.

Domjan, M. (2005). Pavlovian conditioning: A functional perspective. *Annual Review of Psychology, 56,* 179–206.

Donahey, K. & Miller, S. (2001). Applying a common factors perspective to sex therapy. *Journal of Sex Education and Therapy, 25,* 221–230.

Dondi, M., Simion, F., & Caltran, G. (1999). Can newborns discriminate between their own cry and the cry of another newborn infant? *Developmental Psychology, 35,* 418–426.

Donini, L. M., Savina, C., & Cannella, C. (2003). Eating habits and appetite control in the elderly: The anorexia of aging. *International Psychogeriatrics, 15*(1), 73–87.

Donovan, J. J., & Radosevich, D. J. (1999). A meta-analytic review of the distribution of practice effect: Now you see it, now you don't. *Journal of Applied Psychology, 84,* 795–805.

Dorfman, A. (2002, May). Send in the roborats. *Time,* p. 61.

Dorian, L., & Garfinkel, P. E. (2002). Culture and body image in Western culture. *Eating & Weight Disorders, 7*(1), 1–19.

Dornin, R. (2004). Law center: Jury recommends death for Peterson. [On-line]. Available: http://www.cnn.com/2004/LAW/12/13/peterson.case/

Dougherty, D. D., Baer, L., Cosgrove, G. R., Cassem, E. H., Price, B. H., Nierenberg, A. A., Jenike, M. A., & Rauch, S. L. (2002). Prospective long-term follow-up of 44 patients who received cingulotomy for treatment-refractory obsessive-compulsive disorder. *American Journal of Psychiatry, 159*(2), 269–275.

Dovidio, J. F., Brigham, J. C., Johnson, B. T., & Gaertner, S. L. (1995). Stereotyping, prejudice, and discrimination: Another look. In N. Macrae, M. Hewstone, & C. Stangor (Eds.), *Foundations of stereotypes and stereotyping.* New York: Guilford.

Dowd, E. T. (2004). Cognition and the cognitive revolution in psychotherapy: Promises and advances. *Journal of Clinical Psychology, 60*(4), 415–428.

Doweiko, H. E. (1999). *Concepts of chemical dependency.* Pacific Grove, CA: Brooks/Cole.

Doyère, V., Schafe, G. E., Sigurdsson, T., & LeDoux, J. E. (2003). Long-term potentia-tion in freely moving rats reveals asymmetries in thalamic and cortical inputs to the lateral amygdala. *European Journal of Neuroscience, 17*(12), 2703–2715.

Doyle, A., & Pollack, M. H. (2004). Long-term management of panic disorder. *Journal of Clinical Psychiatry. 65*(Suppl5), 24–28.

Draguns, J., & Tanaka-Matsumi, J. (2003). Assessment of psychopathology across and within cultures: Issues and findings. *Behaviour Research & Therapy, 41*(7), 755–776.

Drescher, J. (2003). Gold or lead? Introductory remarks on conversions. *Journal of Gay & Lesbian Psychotherapy, 7*(3), 1–13.

Dresser, N. (1996). *Multicultural manners: New rules of etiquette for a changing society.* New York: Wiley.

Driscoll, R., Davis, K. E., & Lipetz, M. E. (1972). Parental interference and romantic love: The Romeo and Juliet effect. *Journal of Personality and Social Psychology, 24,* 1–10.

Druckman, D., & Bjork, R. A. (Eds.) (1994). *Learning, remembering, believing: Enhancing human performance.* Washington, DC: National Academy Press.

Druckman, D., & Swets, J. A. (1988). *Enhancing human performance: Issues, theories, and techniques.* Washington, DC: National Academy Press.

Drummey, A. B., & Newcombe, N. S. (2002). Developmental changes in source memory. *Developmental Science, 5*(4), 502–513.

Dryer, D. C., & Horowitz, L. M. (1997). When do opposites attract? Interpersonal complementarity versus similarity. *Journal of Personality and Social Psychology, 72,* 592–603.

DuBrin, A. J. (2001). *Leadership: Research findings, practice, and skills (3rd ed.).* New York: Houghton-Mifflin.

Duckworth, K., & Borus, J. F. (1999). Population-based psychiatry in the public sector and managed care. In A. M. Nicholi (Ed.), *The Harvard guide to psychiatry.* Cambridge, MA: Harvard University Press.

Duncan, J. (2005). Frontal lobe function and general intelligence: Why it matters. *Cortex. 41*(2), 215–217.

Duncan, J., & Owen, A. M. (2000). Common regions of the human frontal lobe recruited by diverse cognitive demands. *Trends in Neurosciences, 23*(10), 475–483.

Duncker, K. (1945). On problem-solving. *Psychological Monographs, 58,* 361–362.

Dunn, D. M., & Goodnight, L. J. (2003). *Communication: Embracing differences.* Boston, MA: Allyn & Bacon.

Dunn, M. (2000). *Good death guide: Everything you wanted to know but were afraid to ask.* New York: How to Books.

Durand, M. V., & Barlow, D. H. (2003). *Essentials of abnormal psychology (3rd ed.).* Belmont Park, CA: Thompson Learning.

Durham, M. D., & Dane, F. C. (1999). Juror knowledge of eyewitness behavior: Evidence for the necessity of expert testimony. *Journal of Social Behavior & Personality, 14,* 299–308.

Durkin, K., & Judge, J. (2001). Effects of language and social behaviour on children's reactions to foreign people in television. *British Journal of Developmental Psychology, 19*(4), 597–612.

Dutton, D. G., & Aron, A. P. (1974). Some evidence for heightened sexual attraction under conditions of high anxiety. *Journal of Personality & Social Psychology, 30*(4), 510–517.

Dworkin, A. (1974). *Woman hating.* New York: E. P. Dutton.

Eagly, A. H., & Wood, W. (1999). The origins of sex differences in human behavior: Evolved dispositions versus social roles. *American Psychologist, 54,* 408–423.

Eby, L. T., Cader, J., & Noble, C. L. (2003). Why do high self-monitors emerge as leaders in small groups? A comparative analysis of the behaviors of high versus low self-monitors. *Journal of Applied Social Psychology, 33*(7), 1457–1479.

Eccles, J. S., Buchanan, C. M., Flanagan, C., Fuligni, A., Midgley, C., & Yee, D. (1999). Control versus autonomy during early adolescence. In L. E. Berk (Ed.), *Landscapes of development* (pp. 393–406). Belmont, CA: Wadsworth.

Eckstein, D., & Goldman, A. (2001). The Couples' Gender-Based Communication Questionnaire (CGCQ). *Family Journal-Counseling & Therapy for Couples & Families, 9*(1), 62–74.

Edery-Halpern, G., & Nachson, I. (2004). Distinctiveness in flashbulb memory: Comparative analysis of five terrorist attacks. *Memory, 12*(2), 147–157.

Edwards, B. (1999). *The new drawing on the right side of the brain.* Baltimore: J P Tarcher.

Ehrenreich, B. (2004). *All together now.* [Online]. Available: http://www.nytimes.com/2004/07/15/opinion/15EHRE.html?ex=1090888763&ei=1&en=3b4b6318aa24f4cc

Eibl-Eibesfeldt, I. (1980). Strategies of social interaction. In R. Plutchik & H. Kelerman (Eds.), *Emotion: Theory, research, and experience.* New York: Academic Press.

Eisen, S. A., Chantarujikapong, Sta, Xian, H., Lyons, M. J., Toomey, R., True, W. R., Scherrer, J. F., Goldberg, J., & Tsuang, M. T. (2002). Does marijuana use have residual adverse effects on self-reported health measures, sociodemographics and quality of life?

A monozygotic co-twin control study in men. *Addiction, 97(9),* 1137–1144.

Eisenberger, R., & Armeli, S. (1997). Can salient reward increase creative performance without reducing intrinsic creative interest? *Journal of Personality and Social Psychology, 72,* 652–663.

Eisenberger, R., & Rhoades, L. (2002). Incremental effects of reward on creativity. *Journal of Personality & Social Psychology, 81(4),* 728–741.

Ekman, P. (1993). Facial expression and emotion. *American Psychologist, 48,* 384–392.

Ekman, P. (2004). *Emotions revealed: Recognizing faces and feelings to improve communication and emotional life.* Thousand Oaks, CA: Owl Books.

Ekman, P., & Friesen, W. V. (1971). Constants across cultures in the face and emotion. *Journal of Personality and Social Psychology, 17,* 124–129.

Ekman, P., Friesen, W. V., & Bear, J. (1984, May). The international language of gestures. *Psychology Today,* 66–69.

Ekman, P., & Keltner, D. (1997). Universal facial expressions of emotion: An old controversy and new findings. In U. C. Segerstrale & P. Molnar (Eds.), *Nonverbal communication: Where nature meets culture.* Mahwah, NJ: Erlbaum.

Elder, G. (1998). The life course as developmental theory. *Current Directions in Psychological Science, 69,* 1–12.

Elkin, A., Kalidindi, S., & McGuffin, P. (2004). Have schizophrenia genes been found? *Current Opinion in Psychiatry, 17(2),* 107–113.

Elkind, D. (1967). Egocentrism in adolescence. *Child Development, 38,* 1025–1034.

Elkind, D. (1981). *The hurried child.* Reading, MA: Addison-Wesley.

Elkind, D. (2000). A quixotic approach to issues in early childhood education. *Human Development, 43(4–5),* 279–283.

Elkins, R. L. (1991). An appraisal of chemical aversion (emetic therapy) approaches to alcoholism treatment. *Behaviour Research & Therapy, 29(5),* 387–413.

Ellis, A. (1961). *A guide to rational living.* Englewood Cliffs, NJ: Prentice-Hall.

Ellis, A. (1996). *Better, deeper, and more enduring brief therapy.* New York: Institute for Rational Emotive Therapy.

Ellis, A. (1997). Using Rational Emotive Behavior Therapy techniques to cope with disability. *Professional Psychology: Research and Practice, 28,* 17–22.

Ellis, A. (2003a). Early theories and practices of rational emotive behavior therapy and how they have been augmented and revised during the last three decades. *Journal of Rational-Emotive & Cognitive Behavior Therapy, 21(3–4),* 219–243.

Ellis, A. (2003b). Similarities and differences between rational emotive behavior therapy and cognitive therapy. *Journal of Cognitive Psychotherapy, 17(3),* 225–240.

Ellis, A. (2004). Why rational emotive behavior therapy is the most comprehensive and effective form of behavior therapy. *Journal of Rational-Emotive & Cognitive Behavior Therapy, 22(2),* 85–92.

Ellis, R. T., & Granger, J. M. (2002). African American adults' perceptions of the effects of parental loss during adolescence. *Child & Adolescent Social Work Journal, 19(4),* 271–284.

Emery, R. E. (1999). *Marriage, divorce, and children's adjustment* (2nd ed). Thousand Oaks, CA: Sage.

Emery, R. E., & Laumann-Billings, L. (1998). An overview of the nature, causes, and consequences of abusive family relationships: Toward differentiating maltreatment and violence. *American Psychologist, 53(2),* 121–135.

Endersbe, J. (2000). *Teen pregnancy: Tough choices.* New York: Life Matters.

Engel, J. M., Jensen, M. P., & Schwartz, L. (2004). Outcome of biofeedback-assisted relaxation for pain in adults with cerebral palsy: *Preliminary findings. Applied Psychophysiology & Biofeedback, 29(2),* 135–140.

Ennis, N. E., Hobfoll, S. E., & Schroeder, K. E. E. (2000). Money doesn't talk, it swears: How economic stress and resistance resources impact inner-city women's depressive mood. *American Journal of Community Psychology, 28,* 149–173.

Erdelyi, M. H., & Applebaum, A. G. (1973). Cognitive masking: The disruptive effect of an emotional stimulus upon the perception of contiguous neutral items. *Bulletin of the Psychonomic Society, 1,* 59–61.

Eriksen, J., Jensen, M. K., Sjogren, P., Ekholm, O., & Rasmussen, N. K. (2003). Epidemiology of chronic non-malignant pain in Denmark. *Pain, 106(3),* 221–228.

Erikson, E. (1950). *Childhood and society.* New York: W. W. Norton.

Erlacher, D., & Schredl, M. (2004). Dreams reflecting waking sport activities: A comparison of sport and psychology students. *International Journal of Sport Psychology, 35(4),* 301–308.

Eslinger, P. J., & Tranel, D. (2005). Integrative study of cognitive, social, and emotional processes in clinical neuroscience. *Cognitive & Behavioral Neurology. 18(1),* 1–4.

Espin, O. M. (1993). Feminist theory: Not for or by white women only. *Counseling Psychologist, 21,* 103–108.

Esses, V. M., Dovidio, J. F., Jackson, L. M., & Armstrong, T. L. (2001). The immigration dilemma: The role of perceived group competition, ethnic prejudice, and national identity. *Journal of Social Issues, 57(3),* 389–412.

Esterson, A. (2002). The myth of Freud's ostracism by the medical community in 1896–1905: Jeffrey Masson's assault on truth. *History of Psychology, 5(2),* 115–134.

Etcoff, N. (1999). *Survival of the prettiest: The science of beauty.* New York: Doubleday.

Ethical Principles of Psychologists and Code of Conduct. (1992). *American Psychologist, 47,* 1597–1611.

European School Survey Project on Alcohol and Other Drugs (ESPAD) (2001). Substance abuse increasing among European adolescents. *Reuters Medical News for the Professional* [On-line]. Available: psychiatry.medscape.com/reuters/prof/2001/02/02.21

Evans, J. S. B. T. (2003). In two minds: Dual-process accounts of reasoning. *Trends in Cognitive Sciences, 7(10),* 454–459.

Everett, C., & Everett, S. V. (1994). *Healthy divorce.* San Francisco: Jossey-Bass.

Ewart, C. K., & Fitzgerald, S. T. (1994). Changing behaviour and promoting well-being after heart attack: A social action theory approach. *Irish Journal of Psychology, 15(1),* 219–241.

Eysenck, H. J. (1967). *The biological basis of personality.* Springfield, IL: Charles C Thomas.

Eysenck, H. J. (1982). *Personality, genetics, and behavior: Selected papers.* New York: Prager.

Eysenck, H. J. (1990). Biological dimensions of personality. In L. A. Pervin (Ed.), *Handbook of personality: Theory and research.* New York: Guilford Press.

Eysenck, H. J. (1991). *Smoking, personality, and stress: Psychosocial factors in the prevention of cancer and coronary heart disease.* New York: Springer-Verlag.

Facon, B., & Facon-Bollengier, T. (1999). Chronological age and crystallized intelligence of people with intellectual disability. *Journal of Intellectual Disability Research, 43(6),* 489–496.

Faddiman, A. (1997). *The spirit catches you and you fall down.* New York: Straus & Giroux.

Faigman, D. L., Kaye, D., Saks, M. J., & Sanders, J. (1997). *Modern scientific evidence: The law and science of expert testimony.* St. Paul, MN: West.

Famous people and schizophrenia. (2004). [On-line]. Available: http://www.schizophrenia.com/family/Famous.html

Famous people with mental illness. (2004). [On-line]. Available: http://www.quia.com/fc/263.html

Fanselow, M. S., & Poulos, A. M. (2005). The neuroscience of mammalian associative learning. *Annual Review of Psychology, 56,* 207–234.

Fantz, R. L. (1956). A method for studying early visual development. *Perceptual and Motor Skills, 6,* 13–15.

Fantz, R. L. (1963). Pattern vision in newborn infants. *Science, 140,* 296–297.

Fanz, E. A., Waldie, K. E., & Smith, M. J. (2000). The effect of callostomy on novel versus familiar bimanual actions: A neural dissociation between controlled and automatic processes. *Psychological Science, 11*(1), 82–85.

Farber P. L. (2000) *Finding order in nature: The naturalist tradition from Linnaeus to E. O. Wilson.* Baltimore: Johns Hopkins University Press.

Farrington, D. P. (2000). Psychosocial predictors of adult antisocial personality and adult convictions. *Behavioral Sciences & the Law, 18*(5), 605–622.

Fein, S. & Spencer, S. J. (1997). Prejudice as self-image maintenance: Affirming the self through derogating others. *Journal of Personality and Social Psychology, 73*(1), 31–44.

Feiring, C., Deblinger, E., Hoch-Espada, A., & Haworht T. (2002). Romantic relationship aggression and attitudes in high school students: The role of gender, grade, and attachment and emotional styles. *Journal of Youth & Adolescence, 31*(5), 373–385.

Feldman, R. S. (1982). *Development of nonverbal behavior in children.* Seacaucus, NJ: Springer-Verlag.

Fenton, G. W. (1998). Neurosurgery for mental disorder. *Irish Journal of Psychological Medicine, 15,* 45–48.

Fernandez, G., et al. (1999). Real-time tracking of memory formation in the human rhinal cortex and hippocampus. *Science, 285,* 1582–1585.

Fernández, M. I., Bowen, G. S., Varga, L. M., Collazo, J. B., Hernandez, N., Perrino, T., & Rebbein, A. (2005). High rates of club drug use and risky sexual practices among Hispanic men who have sex with men in Miami, Florida. *Substance Use & Misuse, 40*(9–10), 1347–1362.

Fernández-Dols, J-M., Carrera, P., & Russell, J. A. (2002). Are facial displays social? Situational influences in the attribution of emotion to facial expressions. *Spanish Journal of Psychology, 5*(2), 119–124.

Festinger, L. A. (1957). *A theory of cognitive dissonance.* Palo Alto, CA: Stanford University Press.

Festinger, L. A., & Carlsmith, L. M. (1959). Cognitive consequences of forced compliance. *Journal of Abnormal and Social Psychology, 58,* 203–210.

Fiedler, F. E. (1981. Leadership effectiveness. *American Behavioral Scientist, 24,* 619–632.

Field, C. A., Caetano, R., & Nelson, S. (2004). Alcohol and violence related cognitive risk factors associated with the perpetration of intimate partner violence. *Journal of Family Violence, 19*(4), 249–253.

Field, C. E., Nash, H. M., Handwerk, M. L., & Friman, P. C. (2004). A modification of the token economy for nonresponsive youth in family-style residential care. *Behavior Modification, 28*(3), 438–457.

Field, K. M., Woodson, R., Greenberg, R., & Cohen, D. (1982). Discrimination and imitation of facial expressions by neonates. *Science, 218,* 179–181.

Field, T., & Hernandez-Reif, M. (2001). Sleep problems in infants decrease following massage therapy. *Early Child Development & Care, 168,* 95–104.

Filcheck, H. A., McNeil, C. B., Greco, L. A., & Bernard, R. S. (2004). Using a whole-class token economy and coaching of teacher skills in a preschool classroom to manage disruptive behavior. *Psychology in the Schools, 41*(3), 351–361.

Finch, E., & Munro, V. E. (2005). Juror stereotypes and blame attribution in rape cases involving intoxicants: The findings of a pilot study. *British Journal of Criminology, 45*(1), 25–38.

Fink, B., Manning, J. T., Neave, N., & Grammer, K. (2004). Second to fourth digit ratio and facial asymmetry. *Evolution & Human Behavior, 25*(2), 125–132.

Fink, B., & Penton-Voak, I. (2002). Evolutionary psychology of facial attractiveness. *Current Directions in Psychological Science, 11*(5),154–158.

Fink, M. (1999). *Electroshock: Restoring the mind.* London: Oxford University Press.

First, M., & Tasman, A. (2004). *DSM-IV-TR mental disorders: Diagnosis, etiology, and treatment.* Hoboken, NJ: Wiley.

First, M. B., Pincus, H. A., & Frances, A. (1999). Another perspective on "Putting DSM-IV in perspective." *American Journal of Psychiatry, 156*(3), 499–500.

Fisher, G., & Harrison, T. (2005). *Substance abuse: Information for school counselors, social workers, therapists, and counselors* (3rd ed.). Boston, MA: Allyn & Bacon/Longman.

Fisher, S., & Greenberg, R. P. (1996). *Freud scientifically reappraised: Testing the theories and therapy.* New York: Wiley.

Fiske, S. T. (1998). Stereotyping, prejudice, and discrimination. In D. T. Gilbert, S. T. Fiske, and G. Lindzey (Eds.), *The handbook of social psychology,* Vol. 2 (4th ed.) (pp. 357–411). Boston, MA: McGraw-Hill.

Fiske, S. T. (2002). What we know about bias and intergroup conflict, the problem of the century. *Current Directions in Psychological Science, 11*(4), 123–128.

Fitzgerald, P. B., Brown, T. L., Marston, N. A. U., Daskalakis, Z. J., de Castella, A., & Kulkarni, J. (2003). Transcranial magnetic stimulation in the treatment of depression: A double-blind, placebo-controlled trial. *Archives of General Psychiatry, 60*(10), 1002–1008.

Flaskerud, J. H. (2000). Ethnicity, culture, and neuropsychiatry. *Issues in Mental Health Nursing, 21*(1), 5–29.

Flavell, J. H., Miller, P. H., & Miller, S. A. (2002). *Cognitive development* (4th ed.). Upper Saddle River, NJ: Prentice-Hall.

Flegal, K. M., Graubard, B. I., Williamson, D. F., & Gail, M. H. (2005). Excess deaths associated with underweight, overweight, and obesity. *Journal of the American Medical Association, 293,* 1861–1867.

Fletcher, G. J. O., & Simpson, J. A. (2000). Ideal standards in close relationships: Their structure and functions. *Current Directions in Psychological Science, 9*(3), 102–105.

Flora, M. E. (2000). *Meditation: Key to spiritual awakening.* New York: CDM Publications.

Flynn, J. R. (1987). Massive IQ gains in 14 nations: What IQ tests really measure. *Psychological Bulletin, 101,* 171–191.

Flynn, J. R. (2000). IQ gains and fluid g. *American Psychologist, 55*(5), 543.

Flynn, J. R. (2003). Movies about intelligence: The limitations of g. *Current Directions in Psychological Science,12*(3), 95–99.

Folk, C. L., & Remington, R. W. (1998). Selectivity in distraction by irrelevant featural singletons: Evidence for two forms of attentional capture. *Journal of Experimental Psychology: Human Perception and Performance, 24,* 1–12.

Fone, B. R. S. (2000). *Homophobia: A history.* New York: Metropolitan Books.

Fontaine, K. R., Redden, D. T., Wang, C., Westfall, A. O., & Allison, D. B. (2003). Years of life lost due to obesity. *Journal of the American Medical Association, 289,* 187–193.

Ford, T. E., Ferguson, M. A., Brooks, J. L., & Hagadone, K. M. (2004). Coping sense of humor reduces effects of stereotype threat on women's math performance. *Personality & Social Psychology Bulletin, 30*(5), 643–653.

Fortin, N. J., Agster, K. L.. & Eichenbaum, H. B. (2002). Critical role of the hippocampus in memory for sequences of events. *Nature Neuroscience, 5*(5), 458–462.

Foster, C. A., Witcher, B. S., Campbell, W. K., & Green, J. D. (1998). Arousal and attraction: Evidence for automatic and controlled processes. *Journal of Personality and Social Psychology, 74*, 86–101.

Foulkes, D. (1982). *Children's dreams.* New York: Wiley.

Foulkes, D. (1993). Children's dreaming. In D. Foulkes & C. Cavallero (Eds.), *Dreaming as cognition,* pp. 114–132. New York: Harvester Wheatsheaf.

Fouts, R. (2000, July). One-on-one with our closest cousins: "My best friend is a chimp." *Psychology Today, 33*, 34–36.

Fowler, J. S., Volkow, N. D., Wang, G. J., Pappas, N., Logan, J., MacGregor, R., Alexoff, D., Shea, C., Shyler, D., Wolf, A. P., Warner, D., Zazulkova, I., & Cilento, R. (1996). Inhibition of monoamine oxidase B in the brains of smokers. *Nature, 379*, 733–736.

Fowler, R. D. (1986, May). Howard Hughes: A psychological autopsy. *Psychology Today,* pp. 22–33.

Fox, N. A., Henderson, H. A., Marshall, P. J., Nichols, K. E., & Ghera, M. M. (2005). Behavioral inhibition: Linking biology and behavior within a developmental framework. *Annual Review of Psychology, 56,* 235–262.

Fraley, R. C., & Shaver, P. R. (1997). Adult attachment and the suppression of unwanted thoughts. *Journal of Personality and Social Psychology, 73,* 1080–1091.

Frances, A., & First, M. B. (1998). *Your mental health: A layman's guide to the psychiatrist's bible.* New York: Scribners.

Frank, M. J. (2005). Dynamic dopamine modulation in the basal ganglia: A neurocomputational account of cognitive deficits in medicated and nonmedicated Parkinsonism. *Journal of Cognitive Neuroscience, 17(1),* 51–72.

Frankenburg, W., Dodds, J., Archer, P., Shapiro, H., & Bresnick, B. (1992). The Denver II: A major revision and restandardization of the Denver Developmental Screening Test. *Pediatrics, 89,* 91–97.

Franklin, T. R., Acton, P. D., Maldjian, J. A., Gray, J. D., Croft, J. R., Dackis, C. A., O'Brien, C. P., & Childress, A. R. (2002). Decreased gray matter concentration in the insular, orbitofrontal, cingulate, and temporal cortices of cocaine patients. *Biological Psychiatry, 51(2),* 134–142.

Frayser, S. (1985). *Varieties of sexual experience: An anthropological perspective on human sexuality.* New Haven, CT: Human Relations Area Files Press.

Fredricks, J. A., & Eccles, J. S. (2005). Family socialization, gender, and sport motivation and involvement. *Journal of Sport & Exercise Psychology, 27(1),* 3–31.

French, J. R. P. Jr., & Raven, B. (1959). The bases of social power. In D. Cartwright (Ed.), *Studies in social power* (pp. 150–167). Ann Arbor, MI: Institute for Social Research.

Freud, S. (1953). The interpretation of dreams. In J. Stratchey (Ed. and Trans.), *The standard edition of the complete psychological works of Sigmund Freud* (Vols. 4 and 5). London: Hogarth Press. (Original work published 1900).

Frick, Willard B. (2000). Remembering Maslow: Reflections on a 1968 interview. *Journal of Humanistic Psychology, 40(2),* 128–147.

Friedman, H., & Schustack, M. (2006). *Personality: Classic theories and modern research* (3rd ed.). Boston, MA: Allyn & Bacon/Longman.

Friedman, J. (2002). Diabetes: Fat in all the wrong places. *Nature, 415,* 268–269.

Friedman, M., & Rosenman, R. H. (1959). Association of specific overt behavior patterns with blood and cardiovascular findings: Blood cholesterol level, blood clotting time, incidence of arcus senilis and clinical coronary artery disease. *Journal of the American Medical Association, 169,* 1286–1296.

Friedman, M., Thoresen, C. E., Gill, J. J., Ulmer, D., Powell, L. H., Price, V. A., Brown, B., Thompson, L., Rabin, D. D., Breall, W. S., Bourg, E., Levy, R., & Dixon, T. (1986). Alteration of Type A behavior and its effect on cardiac recurrences in past myocardial infarction patients: Summary results of the Recurrent Coronary Prevention Project. *American Heart Journal, 112,* 653–665.

Friston, K. J. (2005). Models of brain function in neuroimaging. *Annual Review of Psychology, 56,* 57–87.

Fry, C. L. (1985). Culture, behavior, and aging in the comparative perspective. In J. E. Birren, K. W. Schaie, et al. (Eds.), *Handbook of the psychology of aging* (2nd ed.), pp, 216–244. New York: Van Nostrand Reinhold Co.

Fukutake, T., Akada, K., Ito, S., Okuda, T., & Ueki, Y. (2002). Severe personality changes after unilateral left paramedian thalamic infarct. *European Neurology, 47(3),* 156–160.

Funder, D. C. (2000). Personality. *Annual Review of Psychology, 52,* 197–221.

Funder, D. C. (2001). The really, really fundamental attribution error. *Psychological Inquiry, 12(1),* 21–23.

Furman, E. (1990, November). Plant a potato learn about life (and death). *Young Children, 46(1),* 15–20.

Gaab, J., Rohleder, N., Nater, U. M., & Ehlert, U. (2005). Psychological determinants of the cortisol stress response: The role of anticipatory cognitive appraisal. *Psychoneuroendocrinology, 30(6),* Jul 2005, 599–610.

Gabbard, G. O., Gunderson, J. G., & Fonagy, P. (2002). The place of psychoanalytic treatments within psychiatry. *Archives of General Psychiatry, 59(6),* 505–510.

Gabry, K. E., Chrousos, G. P., Rice, K. C., Mostafa, R. M., Sternberg, E., Negrao, A. B., Webster, E. L., McCann, S. M., & Gold, P. W. (2002). Marked suppression of gastric ulcerogenesis and intestinal responses to stress by a novel class of drugs. *Molecular Psychiatry, 7(5),* 474–483.

Gaertner, S. L., Dovidio, J. F., Rust, M. C., Nier, J. A., Banker, B. S., Ward, C. M., Mottola, G. R., & Houlette, M. (1999). Reducing intergroup bias: Elements of intergroup cooperation. *Journal of Personality and Social Psychology, 76(3),* 388–402.

Gaetz, M., Weinberg, H. Rzempoluck, E., & Jantzen, K. J. (1998). Neural network classifications and correlational analysis of EEG and MEG activity accompanying spontaneous reversals of the Necker Cube. *Cognitive Brain Research, 6,* 335–346.

Gage, F. H. (2000). Mammalian neural stem cells. *Science, 287,* 1433–1438.

Gagnon, J. H. (1990). The explicit and implicit use of the scripting perspective in sex research. *Annual Review of Sex Research, 1,* 1–43.

Galaburda, A. M., & Duchaine, B. C. (2003). Developmental disorders of vision. *Neurologic Clinics, 21(3),* 687–707.

Galinsky, A. D., & Moskowitz, G. B. (2000). Perspective-taking: Decreasing stereotype expression, stereotype accessibility, and in-group favoritism. *Journal of Personality & Social Psychology, 78(4),* 708–724.

Galinsky, A., D., & Ku, G. (2004). The effects of perspective-taking on prejudice: The moderating role of self-evaluation. *Personality & Social Psychology Bulletin, 30(5),* 594–604.

Gallagher, A. M., De Lisi, R., Holst, P. C., McGillicuddy-De Lisi, A. V., Morely, M., & Cahalan, C. (2000). Gender differences in advanced mathematical problem solving. *Journal of Experimental Child Psychology, 75(3),* 165–190.

Galloway, J. L. (1999, March 8). Into the heart of darkness. *U. S. News and World Report,* pp. 25–32.

Galvan, J., Unikel, C., Rodriguez, E., Ortiz, A., Soriano, A., & Flores, J. C. (2000). General perspective of flunitracepam (Rohypnol) abuse in a sample of drug users of Mexico City. *Salud Mental, 23(1),* 1–7.

Gangestad, S. W., & Thornhill, R. (2003). Facial masculinity and fluctuating asymmetry. *Evolution & Human Behavior, 24*(4), 231–241.

Gannon, N., & Ranzijn, R. (2005). Does emotional intelligence predict unique variance in life satisfaction beyond IQ and personality? *Personality & Individual Differences, 38*(6), 1353–1364.

Garbarino, S., Beelke, M., Costa, G., Violani, C., Lucidi, F., & Ferrillo, F. (2002). Brain function and effects of shift work: Implications for clinical neuropharmacology. *Neuropsychobiology, 45*(1), 50–56.

Garcia, G. M., & Stafford, M. E. (2000). Prediction of reading by Ga and Gc specific cognitive abilities for low-SES White and Hispanic English-speaking children. *Psychology in the Schools, 37*(3), 227–235.

Garcia, J. (2003). Psychology is not an enclave. In R. Sternberg (Ed.), *Psychologists defying the crowd: Stories of those who battled the establishment and won* (pp. 67–77). Washington, DC, US: American Psychological Association.

Garcia, J., Brett, L. P., & Rusiniak, K. W. (1989). Limits of Darwinian conditioning. In S. B. Klein & R. R. Mowrer (Eds.), *Contemporary learning theories: Instrumental conditioning theory and the impact of biological constraints on learning* (pp. 181–203). Hillsdale, NJ, England: Lawrence Erlbaum Associates.

Garcia, J., Ervin, F. R., & Koelling, R. A. (1966). Learning with prolonged delay of reinforcement. *Psychonomic Science, 5*(3), 121–122.

Garcia, J., & Koelling, R. S. (1966). Relation of cue to consequence in avoidance learning. *Psychonomic Science, 4*, 123–124.

Garcia, S. D., & Khersonsky, D. (1997). "They are a lovely couple": Further examination of perceptions of couple attractiveness. *Journal of Social Behavior and Personality, 12*, 367–380.

Gardiner, H., & Kosmitzki, G. (2005). *Lives across cultures: Cross-cultural human development* (3 ed.). Boston, MA: Allyn & Bacon/Longman.

Gardner, B. T., & Gardner, R. A. (1971). Two-way communication with an infant chimpanzee. In A. M. Schrier & F. Stollnitz (Eds.), *Behavior of nonhuman primates* (Vol. 4). New York: Academic Press.

Gardner, H. (1983). *Frames of mind.* New York: Basic Books.

Gardner, H. (1998). A multiplicity of intelligences. *Scientific American Presents Exploring Intelligence, 9*, 18–23.

Gardner, H. (1999, February). Who owns intelligence? *Atlantic Monthly*, pp. 67–76.

Gardner, R. A., & Gardner, B. T. (1969). Teaching sign language to a chimpanzee. *Science, 165*, 664–672.

Garnefski, N. (2000). *Journal of the American Academy of Child and Adolescent Psychiatry, 39*, 1175–1181.

Garnefski, N., Teerds, J., Kraaij, V., Legerstee, J., & van den Kommer, T. (2004). Cognitive emotion regulation strategies and Depressive symptoms: differences between males and females. *Personality & Individual Differences, 36*(2), 267–276.

Gaser, C., Nenadic, I., Buchsbaum, B. R., Hazeltt, E. A., & Buchsbaum, M. S. (2004). Ventricular enlargement in schizophrenia related to volume reduction of the thalamus, striatum, and superior temporal cortex. *American Journal of Psychiatry, 161*(1), 154–156.

Gattuso, S., & Shadbolt, A. (2002). Attitudes toward aging among Pacific Islander health students in Fiji. *Educational Gerontology, 28*(2), 99–106.

Gawronski, B. (2003). On difficult questions and evident answers: Dispositional inference from role-constrained behavior. *Personality & Social Psychology Bulletin, 29*(11), 1459–1475.

Gay, M-C., Philippot, P., & Luminet, O. (2002). Differential effectiveness of psychological interventions for reducing osteoarthritis pain: A comparison of Erickson hypnosis and Jacobson relaxation. *European Journal of Pain, 6*, 1–16.

Gay, P. (1983). *The bourgeois experience: Victoria to Freud. Vol. 1: Education of the senses.* New York: Oxford University Press.

Gay, P. (1999, March 29). Psychoanalyst Sigmund Freud. *Time*, 65–69.

Gay, P. (2000). *Freud for historians.* Boston, MA: Replica Books.

Gazzaniga, M. S. (1970). *The bisected brain.* New York: Appleton-Century-Crofts.

Gazzaniga, M. S. (1995). On neural circuits and cognition. *Neural Computation, 7*(1), 1–12.

Gazzaniga, M. S. (2000). *The mind's past.* University California Press.

Geary, D. C. (2005). The motivation to control and the origin of mind: Exploring the life-mind joint point in the tree of knowledge system. *Journal of Clinical Psychology, 61*(1), 21–46.

Gemignani, A., Santarcangelo, E., Sebastiani, L., Marchese, C., Mammoliti, R., Simoni, A., & Ghelarducci, B. (2000). Changes in autonomic and EEG patterns induced by hypnotic imagination of aversive stimuli in man. *Brain Research Bulletin, 53*(1), 105–111.

Gerra, G., Angioni, L., Zaimovic, A., Moi, G., Bussandri, M., Bertacca, S., Santoro, G., Gardini, S., Caccavari, R., & Nicoli, M. A. (2004). Substance use among high-school students: Relationships with temperament, personality traits, and parental care perception. *Substance Use & Misuse, 39*(2), 345–367.

Gershon, E. S., & Rieder, R. O. (1993). Major disorders of mind and brain. *Mind and brain: Readings from Scientific American Magazine* (pp. 91–100). New York, NY: Freeman.

Geschwind, N. (1979). Specialization of the human brain. *Scientific American, 241*, 180–199.

Getting the facts: When someone has schizophrenia. (2004). [On-line]. Available: http://www.mhsource.com/schizophrenia/schizknow.html

Giacobbi, P. Jr., Foore, B., & Weinberg, R. S. (2004). Broken clubs and expletives: The sources of stress and coping responses of skilled and moderately skilled golfers. *Journal of Applied Sport Psychology, 16*(2), 166–182.

Gianakos, I. (2000). Gender roles and coping with work stress. *Sex Roles, 42*, 1059–1079.

Gibbs, N. (1995, October 2). The EQ factor. *Time*, pp. 60–68.

Gibson, E. J., & Walk, R. D. (1960). The visual cliff. *Scientific American, 202*(2), 67–71.

Gifford, R., & Hine, D. W. (1997). "I'm cooperative, but you're greedy": Some cognitive tendencies in a commons dilemma. *Canadian Journal of Behavioural Science, 29*(4), 257–265.

Gilbert, T. (2003). Managing passive-aggressive behavior of children and youth at school and home: The angry smile. *Education & Treatment of Children, 26*(3), 305–306.

Giles, B. (2004). *Thinking about storytelling and narrative journalism. Neiman Reports*, p. 3. [On-line]. Available: http://www.nieman.harvard.edu/reports/04–1NRSpring/3V58N1.pdf.

Giles, J. W., & Heyman, G. D. (2005). Young children's beliefs about the relationship between gender and aggressive behavior. *Child Development, 76*(1), 107–121.

Gilligan, C. (1977). In a different voice: Women's conception of morality. *Harvard Educational Review, 47*(4), 481–517.

Gilligan, C. (1990). Teaching Shakespeare's sister. In C. Gilligan, N. Lyons, & T. Hanmer (Eds.), *Mapping the moral domain* (pp. 73–86). Cambridge, MA: Harvard University Press.

Gilligan, C. (1993). Adolescent development reconsidered. In A. Garrod (Ed.), *Approaches to moral development: New research and emerging themes.* New York: Teachers College Press.

Gilligan, J. (2000). *Violence: Reflections on a Western epidemic.* London: Jessica Kingsley.

Gilmour, D. R., & Walkey, F. H. (1981). Identifying violent offenders using a video measure of interpersonal distance. *Journal of Consulting and Clinical Psychology, 49,* 287–291.

Gilovich, T., Griffin, D., & Kahneman, D. (2002). *Heuristics and biases: The psychology of intuitive judgment.* New York, NY: Cambridge University Press.

Girandola, F. (2002). Sequential requests and organ donation. *Journal of Social Psychology, 142*(2), 171–178.

Gitau, R., Modi, N., Gianakoulopoulos, X., Bond, C., Glover, V., & Stevenson, J. (2002). Acute effects of maternal skin-to-skin contact and massage on saliva cortisol in preterm babies. *Journal of Reproductive & Infant Psychology, 20*(2), 83–88.

Glick, N. D. (2002). The relationship between cross cultural experience and training, and leader effectiveness in the US Foreign Service. *International Journal of Cross Cultural Management, 2*(3), 339–356.

Glimcher, P. W. (2005). Indeterminacy in brain and behavior. *Annual Review of Psychology, 56,* 25–56.

Godden, D. R., & Baddeley, A. D. (1975). Context-dependent memory in two natural environments: On land and underwater. *British Journal of Psychology, 66,* 325–331.

Goebel, M. U., & Mills, P. J. (2000). Acute psychological stress and exercise and changes in peripheral leukocyte adhesion molecule expression and density. *Psychosomatic Medicine, 62*(5), 664–670.

Goerke, M., Möller, J., Schulz-Hardt, S., Napiersky, U., & Frey, D. (2004). "It's not my fault-but only I can change it": Counterfactual and prefactual thoughts of managers. *Journal of Applied Psychology, 89*(2), 279–292.

Gogtay, N., Sporn, A., Clasen, L. S., Nugent, T. F. III, Greenstein, D., Nicolson, R., Giedd, J. N., Lenane, M., Gochman, P., Evans, A., & Rapoport, J. L. (2004). Comparison of progressive cortical gray matter loss in childhood-onset schizophrenia with that in childhood-onset atypical psychoses. *Archives of General Psychiatry, 61*(1), 17–22.

Goldberg, S. (2000). *Attachment and development.* New York: Edward Arnold.

Goldstein, B. (1976). *Introduction to human sexuality.* New York: McGraw-Hill.

Goleman, D. (1980, February). 1,528 little geniuses and how they grew. *Psychology Today,* pp. 28–53.

Goleman, D. (1995a). *Emotional intelligence: Why it can matter more than IQ.* New York: Bantam.

Goleman, D. (1995b, December 5). Making room on the couch for culture. *New York Times,* C1–C3, C4.

Goleman, D. (2000). *Working with emotional intelligence.* New York: Bantam Doubleday.

Gollan, T. H., & Acenas, L. R. (2004). What Is a TOT? Cognate and translation effects on tip-of-the-tongue states in Spanish-English and Tagalog-English bilinguals. *Journal of Experimental Psychology: Learning, Memory, & Cognition, 30*(1), 246–269.

Golob, E. J., & Starr, A. (2004). Serial position effects in auditory event-related potentials during working memory retrieval. *Journal of Cognitive Neuroscience, 16*(1), 40–52.

Golub, A., Johnson, B. D., Sifaneck, S. J., Chesluk, B., & Parker, H. (2001). Is the U.S. experiencing an incipient epidemic of hallucinogen use? *Substance Use & Misuse, 36*(12), 1699–1729.

Gómez-Gil, E., Gastó, C., Carretero, M., Díaz-Ricart, M., Salamero, M., Navinés, R., & Escolar, G. (2004). Decrease of the platelet 5–HT-sub(2A) receptor function long-term imipramine treatment in endogenous depression. *Human Psychopharmacology: Clinical & Experimental, 19*(4), 251–258.

Gonzales, P. M., Blanton, H., & Williams, K. J. (2002). The effects of stereotype threat and double-minority status on the test performance of Latino women. *Personality & Social Psychology Bulletin, 28*(5), 659–670.

Gonzalez, A. R., Holbein, M. F. D., & Quilter, S. (2002). High school students' goal orientations and their relationship to perceived parenting styles. *Contemporary Educational Psychology, 27*(3), 450–470.

Goodall, J. (1971). *Tiwi wives.* Seattle, WA: University of Washington Press.

Goodall, J. (1990). *Through a window: My thirty years with the chimpanzees of Gombe.* Boston: Houghton-Mifflin.

Goode, E. E., Schrof, J. M., & Burke, S. (1991, June 24). Where emotions come from. *U. S. News and World Report,* pp. 54–60.

Goodman, G. S., Ghetti, S., Quas, J. A., Edelstein, R. S., Alexander, K. W., Redlich, A. D., Cordon, I. M., & Jones, D. P. H. (2003). A prospective study of memory for child sexual abuse: New findings relevant to the repressed-memory controversy. *Psychological Science, 14,* in press.

Goodman, M., & Yehuda, R. (2002). The relationship between psychological trauma and borderline personality disorder. *Psychiatric Annals, 32*(6), 337–345.

Goodwin, C. J. (2005). *A history of modern psychology (2nd ed.).* Hoboken, NJ: Wiley.

Goodwin, D. K. (2005, July 5). The master of the game. *Time,* pp. 48–50, 53–54.

Goodwin, D. W. (2000). *Alcoholism: The facts.* London: Oxford University Press.

Goodwin, F. K., Simon, G., Revicki, D., Hunkeler, E., Fireman, B., & Lee, E. (2004). "Pharmacotherapy and risk of suicidal behaviors among patients with bipolar disorder": Reply. *JAMA: Journal of the American Medical Association, 291*(8), 940.

Goodwin, R. D., Fergusson, D. M., & Horwood, L. J. (2004). Association between anxiety disorders and substance use disorders among young persons: Results of a 21–year longitudinal study. *Journal of Psychiatric Research, 38*(3), 295–304.

Gordon, R. A. (2000). *Eating disorders: Anatomy of a social epidemic* (2nd ed.). Malden, MA: Blackwell Publishers.

Gordon, T. (1975). *Parent effectiveness training.* New York: Plume.

Gordon, W. C. (1989). *Learning and memory.* Pacific Grove, CA: Brooks/Cole.

Gorman, C. (2001, February 5). Repairing the damage. *Time,* 53–58.

Gorman, J. (2000). Neuroanatomical hypothesis of panic disorder revised. *American Journal of Psychiatry, 57,* 493–505.

Gorman, J. M. (2005). In the wake of trauma. *CNS Spectrums, 10*(2), 81–85.

Gosling, S. D., & John, O. P. (1999). Personality dimensions in nonhuman animals: A cross-species review. *Current Directions in Psychological Science, 8*(3), 69–75.

Gosling, S. D., Kwan, V. S. Y., & John, O. P. (2004). A dog's got personality: A cross-species comparative approach to personality judgments in dogs and humans. *Journal of Personality and Social Psychology, 85*(6), 1161–1169.

Goswami, S., Mattoo, S. K., Basu, D., & Singh, G. (2004). Substance-abusing schizophrenics: Do they self-medicate? *American Journal on Addictions, 13*(2), 139–150.

Gotlieb, I. H., & Abramson, L. Y. (1999). Attributional theories of emotion. In T. Dalgleish & M. Power (Eds.), *Handbook of cognition and emotion.* New York: Wiley.

Gottesman, I. I. (1991). *Schizophrenia genesis: The origins of madness.* New York: Freeman.

Gottesman, I. I., & Hanson, D. R. (2005). Human development: Biological and genetic processes. *Annual Review of Psychology, 56,* 263–286.

Gottlieb, G. (2000). Environmental and behavioral influences on gene activity. *Current Directions in Psychological Science, 9*(3), 93–97.

Gottman, J. M., Coan, J., Carrere, S., & Swanson, C. (1998). Predicting happiness and stability from newlywed interactions. *Journal of Marriage and the Family, 60,* 42–48.

Gottman, J. M., & Levenson, R. W. (2002). A two-factor model for predicting when a couple will divorce: Exploratory analyses using 14–year longitudinal data. *Family Process, 41(1),* 83–96.

Gottman, J. M., & Notarius, C. I. (2000). Decade review: Observing marital interaction. *Journal of Marriage & the Family, 62(4),* 927–947.

Gould, R. L. (1975, August). Adult life stages: Growth toward self-tolerance. *Psychology Today,* pp. 74–78.

Goveas, J. S., Csernansky, J. G., & Coccaro, E. F. (2004). Platelet serotonin content correlates inversely with life history of aggression in personality-disordered subjects. *Psychiatry Research, 126(1),* 23–32.

Gracely, R. H., Farrell, M. J., & Grant, M. A. (2002). Temperature and pain perception. In H. Pashler & S. Yantis (Eds.), *Steven's handbook of experimental psychology: Vol. 1. Sensation and perception* (3rd ed.d.). New York: Wiley.

Graham, G. H., Unruh, J., & Jennings, P. (1991). The impact of nonverbal communications in organizations: A survey of perceptions. *The Journal of Business Communication, 60,* 43–45.

Graham, J. R. (1991). Comments on Duckworth's review of the Minnesota Multiphasic Personality Inventory-2. *Journal of Counseling and Development, 69,* 570–571.

Grant, S., et al. (1996). Activation of memory circuits during the cue-elicited cocaine craving. *Proceedings of the National Academy of Sciences, 93,* 12–40.

Graw, P., Krauchi, K., Knoblauch, V., Wirz-Justice, A., & Cajochen, C. (2004). Circadian and wake-dependent modulation of fastest and slowest reaction times during the psychomotor vigilance task. *Physiology & Behavior, 80(5),* 695–701.

Gray, J. D., & Silver, R. C. (1990). Opposite sides of the same coin: Former spouses' divergent perspectives in coping with their divorce. *Journal of Personality & Social Psychology, 59(6),* 1180–1191.

Greeff, A. P., & Malherbe, H. L. (2001). Intimacy and marital satisfaction in spouses. *Journal of Sex & Marital Therapy, 27(3),* 247–257.

Greeff, A. P., & Van Der Merwe, S. (2004). Variables associated with resilience in divorced families. *Social Indicators Research, 68(1),* 59–75.

Green, A. I. (2000). What is the relationship between schizophrenia and substance abuse? *Harvard Mental Health Letter, 17(4),* 8.

Green, A. I., Tohen, M. F., Hamer, R. M., Strakowski, S. M., Lieberman, J. A., Glick, I., Clark, W. S., & HGDH Research Group. (2004). First episode schizophrenia-related psychosis and substance use disorders: Acute response to olanzapine and haloperidol. *Schizophrenia Research, 66(2–3),* 125–135.

Green, J. W. (1999). *Cultural awareness in the human services: A multi-ethnic approach.* Needham Heights, MA: Allyn & Bacon.

Greenberg, D. L. (2004). President Bush's false "flashbulb" memory of 9/11/01. *Applied Cognitive Psychology, 18(3),* 363–370.

Greenberg, J., Pyszcynski, T., Solomon, S., Pinel, E., et al. (1993). Effects of self-esteem on vulnerability-denying defensive distortions: Further evidence of an anxiety-buffering function of self-esteem. *Journal of Experimental Social Psychology, 29(3),* 229–251.

Greene, K., Kremar, M., Walters, L. H., Rubin, D. L., Hale, J., & Hale, L. (2000). Targeting adolescent risk-taking behaviors: The contributions of egocentrism and sensation-seeking. *Journal of Adolescence, 23,* 439–461.

Greenfield, P. M. (1984). A theory of the teacher in the learning activities of everyday life. In B. Rogoff & J. Lave (Eds.), *Everyday cognition* (pp. 117–138). Cambridge, MA: Harvard University Press.

Greenfield, P. M. (1994). *Cross-cultural roots of minority child development.* Hillsdale, NJ: Erlbaum.

Greenfield, P. M. (1997). You can't take it with you: Why ability assessments don't cross cultures. *American Psychologist, 52,* 1115–1124.

Greenfield, P. M. (2004). *Weaving generations together: Evolving creativity in the Maya of Chiapas.* Santa Fe, NM: School of American Research Press.

Gregersen, E. (1996). *The world of human sexuality: Behaviors, customs, and beliefs.* New York: Irvington.

Gregory, R. L. (1969). Apparatus for investigating visual perception. *American Psychologist, 24(3),* 219–225.

Grigorenko, E. L., Jarvin, L., & Sternberg, R. J. (2002). School-based tests of the triarchic theory of intelligence: Three settings, three samples, three syllabi. *Contemporary Educational Psychology, 27(2),* 167–208.

Grilly, D. (2006). *Drugs and human behavior* (5th ed.). Boston, MA: Allyn & Bacon/Longman.

Grondin, S., Ouellet, B., & Roussel, M. (2004). Benefits and limits of explicit counting for discriminating temporal intervals. *Canadian Journal of Experimental Psychology, 58(1),* 1–12.

Grossmann, K., Grossmann, K. E., Fremmer-Bombik, E., Kindler, H., Scheuerer-Englisch, H., & Zimmermann, P. (2002). The uniqueness of the child-father attachment relationship: Fathers' sensitive and challenging play as a pivotal variable in a 16–year longitudinal study. *Social Development, 11(3),* 307–331.

Grove, W. M., Barden, R. C., Garb, H. N., & Lilienfeld, S. O. (2002). Failure of Rorschach-Comprehensive-System-based testimony to be admissible under the Daubert-Joiner-Kumho standard. *Psychology, Public Policy, & Law, 8(2),* 216–234.

Gruber, U., Fegg, M., Buchmann, M., Kolb, H-J., & Hiddemann, W. (2003). The long-term psychosocial effects of haematopoetic stem cell transplantation. *European Journal of Cancer Care, 12(3),* 249–256.

Grych, J. H. (2005). Interparental conflict as a risk factor for child maladjustment: Implications for the development of prevention programs. *Family Court Review, 43(1),* 97–108.

Guarnaccia, P. J., & Rogler, L. H. (1999). Research on culture-bound syndromes: New directions. *American Journal of Psychiatry, 156(9),* 1322–1327.

Guastello, D. D., & Guastello, S. J. (2003). Androgyny, gender role behavior, and emotional intelligence among college students and their parents. *Sex Roles, 49(11–12),* 663–673.

Guastello, S. J., Guastello, D. D., & Craft, L. L. (1989). Assessment of the Barnum effect in computer-based test interpretations. *Journal of Psychology, 123,* 477–484.

Guéguen, N. (2003). Fund-raising on the web: The effect of an electronic door-in-the-face technique on compliance to a request. *CyberPsychology & Behavior, 6(2),* 189–193.

Guidelines for the treatment of animals in behavioural research and teaching. (2002). *Animal Behaviour, 63(1),* 195–199.

Guidelines for the treatment of animals in behavioural research and training. (2003). *Animal Behaviour, 65(1),* 249–255.

Guidelines for the treatment of animals in behavioural research and teaching. (2005). *Animal Behaviour, 69(1),* i–vi.

Guilarte, T. R., Toscano, C. D., McGlothan, J. L., & Weaver, S. A. (2003). Environmental enrichment reverses cognitive and molecular deficits induced developmental lead exposure. *Annals of Neurology, 53(1),* 50–56.

Guilford, J. P. (1967). *The nature of human intelligence.* New York: McGraw-Hill.

Guinard, J., et al. (1996). Does consumption of beer, alcohol, and bitter substances affect bitterness perception? *Physiology & Behavior, 49,* 625–631.

Guinote, A., & Fiske, S. T. (2003). Being in the outgroup territory increases stereotypic perceptions of outgroups: Situational sources of category activation. *Group Processes & Intergroup Relations, 6*(4), 323–331.

Gunzerath, L., Faden, V., Zakhari, S., & Warren, K. (2004). National institute on alcohol abuse and alcoholism report on moderate drinking. *Alcoholism: Clinical & Experimental Research, 28*(6), 829–847.

Gustavson, C. R., & Garcia, J. (1974, August). Pulling a gag on the wily coyote. *Psychology Today,* pp. 68–72.

Gustavson, C. R., Kelly, D. J., Sweeney, M., & Garcia, J. (1976). Prey-lithium aversions: I. Coyotes and wolves. *Behavioral Biology, 17,* 61–72.

Guthrie, E., Margison, F., Mackay, H., Chew-Graham, C., Moorey, J., & Sibbald, B. (2004). Effectiveness of psychodynamic interpersonal therapy training for primary care counselors. *Psychotherapy Research, 14*(2), 161–175.

Guthrie, R. V. (1998). *Even the rat was white.* Boston: Allyn & Bacon.

Haier, R. J., Chueh, D., Touchette, P., Lott, I., Buchsbaum, M. S., MacMillan, D., Sandman, C., LaCasse, L., & Sosa, E. (1995). Brain size and cerebral glucose metabolic rate in non-specific mental retardation and Down Syndrome. *Intelligence, 20,* 191–210.

Haith, M. M., & Benson, J. B. (1998). Infant cognition. In W. Damon & R. M. Lerner (Eds.), *Handbook of child psychology* (Vol. 1). New York: John Wiley & Sons.

Halaris, A. (2003). Sexual dysfunction: A neglected area of knowledge. *CNS Spectrums, 8*(3), 2003,178.

Hall, C. S., & Van de Castle, R. L. (1996). *The content analysis of dreams.* New York: Appleton-Century-Crofts.

Hall, E. T. (1960). The silent language in overseas business. *Harvard Business Review, 38,* 87–96.

Hall, E. T. (1966). *The hidden dimension.* New York: Doubleday.

Haller, S., Radue, E. W., Erb, M., Grodd, W. & Kircher, T. (2005). Overt sentence production in event-related fMRI. *Neuropsychologia, 43*(5), 807–814.

Halperin, J. M., Schulz, K. P., McKay, K. E., Sharma, V., & Newcorn, J. H. (2003). Familial correlates of central serotonin function in children with disruptive behavior disorders. *Psychiatry Research, 119*(3), 205–216.

Halpern, D. F. (1997). Sex differences in intelligence: Implications for education. *American Psychologist, 52,* 1091–1102.

Halpern, D. F. (1998). Teaching critical thinking for transfer across domains. *American Psychologist, 53,* 449–455.

Halpern, D. F. (2000). *Sex differences in cognitive abilities.* Hillsdale, NJ: Erlbaum.

Ham, B. D. (2004). The effects of divorce and remarriage on the academic achievement of high school seniors. *Journal of Divorce & Remarriage, 42*(1–2),159–178.

Hamer, D. H., & Copeland, P. (1999). *Living with our genes: Why they matter more than you think.*

Hamid, P. N., & Chan, W. T. (1998). Locus of control and occupational stress in Chinese professionals. *Psychological Reports, 82,* 75–79.

Hamilton, V. L. (1978). Obedience and responsibility: A jury simulation. *Journal of Personality and Social Psychology, 36,* 126–146.

Hamm, J. P., Johnson, B. W., & Corballis, M. C. (2004). One good turn deserves another: An event-related brain potential study of rotated mirror-normal letter discriminations. *Neuropsychologia, 42*(6), 810–820.

Hammack, P. L. (2003). The question of cognitive therapy in a postmodern world. *Ethical Human Sciences & Services, 5*(3), 209–224.

Hammen, C. (2005). Stress and depression. *Annual Review of Clinical Psychology, 1,* 293–319.

Hammond, D. C. (2005). Neurofeedback with anxiety and affective disorders. *Child & Adolescent Psychiatric Clinics of North America, 14*(1), 105–123.

Haney, C., Banks, C., & Zimbardo, P. (1978). Interpersonal dynamics in a simulated prison. *International Journal of Criminology and Penology, 1,* 69–97.

Hanley, S. J., & Abell, S. C. (2002). Maslow and relatedness: Creating an interpersonal model of self-actualization. *Journal of Humanistic Psychology, 42*(4), 37–56.

Hanna, S. M., & Brown, J. H. (1999). *The practice of family therapy: Key elements across models* (2nd ed.). Belmont, CA: Brooks/Cole.

Hansell, J. H., & Damour, L. K. (2005). *Abnormal psychology.* Hoboken, NJ: Wiley.

Hanson, G., Venturelli, P. J., & Fleckenstein, A. E. (2002). *Drugs and society* (7th ed.). New York: Jones & Bartlett.

Harandi, A. A., Esfandani, A., & Shakibaei, F. (2004). The effect of hypnotherapy on procedural pain and state anxiety related to physiotherapy in women hospitalized in a burn unit. *Contemporary Hypnosis, 21*(1), 28–34.

Hardy, J. B., & Zabin, L. S. (1991). *Adolescent pregnancy in an urban environment: Issues, programs, and evaluation.* Baltimore: Urban and Schwarzenberg.

Hardy, Q. (1993, June, 16). Death at the club is par for the course in golf-crazed Japan. *Wall Street Journal,* A1, A8.

Hare, R. D. (1993). *Without conscience: The disturbing world of the psychopaths among us.* New York: Pocket Books.

Harker, L., & Keltner, D. (2001). Expressions of positive emotion in women's college yearbook pictures and their relationship to personality and life outcomes across adulthood. *Journal of Personality & Social Psychology. Jan80*(1), 112–124.

Harkness, S., & Super, C. M. (1996). *Parents' cultural belief systems: Their origins, expressions, and consequences.* New York: Guilford Press.

Harlow, H. F., & Harlow, M. K. (1966). Learning to love. *American Scientist, 54,* 244–272.

Harlow, H. F., Harlow, M. K., & Meyer, D. R. (1950). Learning motivated by a manipulation drive. *Journal of Experimental Psychology, 40,* 228–234.

Harlow, H. F., & Zimmerman, R. R. (1959). Affectional responses in the infant monkey. *Science, 130,* 421–432.

Harlow, J. (1868). Recovery from the passage of an iron bar through the head. *Publications of the Massachusetts Medical Society, 2,* 237–246.

Harmer, C. J., Shelley, N. C., Cowen, P. J., & Goodwin, G. M. (2004). Increased positive versus negative affective perception and memory in healthy volunteers following selective serotonin and nor e pinephrine reuptake inhibition. *American Journal of Psychiatry, 161*(7), 1256–1263.

Harper, F. D., Harper, J. A., & Stills, A. B. (2003). Counseling children in crisis based on Maslow's hierarchy of basic needs. *International Journal for the Advancement of Counselling, 25*(1), 10–25.

Harrigan, J. A., Lucic, K. S., Kay, D., McLaney, A., et al. (1991). Effect of expresser role and type of self-touching on observers' perceptions. *Journal of Applied Social Psychology, 21*(7), 585–609.

Harris, A. C. (1996). African American and Anglo American gender identities: An empirical study. *Journal of Black Psychology, 22,* 182–194.

Harrison, E. (2005). *How meditation heals: Scientific evidence and practical applications* (2nd ed.). Berkeley, CA: Ulysses Press.

Harrison, L., & Gardiner, E. (1999). Do the rich really die young? Alcohol-related mortality and social class in Great Britain, 1988–94. *Addiction, 94*(12), 1871–1880.

Harvey, A. G., & McGuire, B.E. (2000). Suppressing and attending to pain-related thoughts in chronic pain patients. *Behaviour Research & Therapy, 38*(11), 1117–1124.

Harvey, M. G., & Miceli, N. (1999). Antisocial behavior and the continuing tragedy of the commons. *Journal of Applied Social Psychology, 29*, 109–138.

Hatfield, E., & Rapson, R. L. (1996). *Love and Sex: Cross-cultural perspectives.* Needham Heights, MA: Allyn & Bacon.

Hätinen, M., Kinnunen, U., Pekkonen, M., & Aro, A. (2004). Burnout patterns in rehabilitation: Short-term changes in job conditions, personal resources, and health. *Journal of Occupational Health Psychology, 9*(3), 220–237.

Haugen, R., Ommundsen, Y., & Lund, T. (2004). The concept of expectancy: A central factor in various personality dispositions. *Educational Psychology, 24*(1), Feb 2004, 43–55.

Hawkins, R. S., & Hart, A. D. (2003). The use of thermal biofeedback in the treatment of pain associated with endometriosis: Preliminary findings. *Applied Psychophysiology & Biofeedback, 28*(4), 279–289.

Hawkley, L. C., & Cacioppo, J. T. (2004). Stress and the aging immune system. *Brain, Behavior & Immunity, 18*(2), 114–119.

Hay, D. F. (1994). Prosocial development. *Journal of Child Psychology and Psychiatry, 35*, 29–71.

Hayflick, L. (1977). The cellular basis for biological aging. In C. E. Finch & L. Hayflick (Eds.), *Handbook of the biology of aging* (pp. 159–186). New York: Van Nostrand Reinhold.

Hayflick, L. (1996). *How and why we age.* New York: Ballantine Books.

Hayne, H., Boniface, J., & Barr, R. (2000). The development of declarative memory in human infants: Age-related changes in deferred imitation. *Behavioral Neuroscience, 114*(1), 77–83.

Hays, W. S. T. (2003). Human pheromones: Have they been demonstrated? *Behavioral Ecology & Sociobiology, 54*(2), 89–97.

Hazan, C., & Shaver, P. (1987). Romantic love conceptualized as an attachment process. *Journal of Personality and Social Psychology, 52*, 511–524.

Hazan, C., & Shaver, P. R. (1994). Attachment as an organizational framework for research on close relationships. *Psychological Inquiry, 5*, 1–22.

Healy, A. F., & McNamara, D. S. (1996). Verbal learning and memory: Does the modal model still work? *Annual Review of Psychology, 47*, 143–172.

Heath, A. C., Madden, P. A. F., Bucholz, K. K., Nelson, E. C., Todorov, A., Price, R. K., Whitfield, J. B., Martin, N. G., Plomin, R. (Ed.), DeFries, J. C. (Ed.), et al. (2003). Genetic and environmental risks of dependence on alcohol, tobacco, and other drugs. *Behavioral genetics in the postgenomic era.* (pp.

309–334). Washington, DC, US: American Psychological Association.

Heaton, T. B. (2002). Factors contributing to increasing marital stability in the US. *Journal of Family Issues, 23*(3), 392–409.

Hébert, S., Racette, A., Gagnon, L., & Peretz, I. (2003). Revisiting the dissociation between singing and speaking in expressive aphasia. *Brain, 126*(8), 1838–1850.

Heckers, S., Weiss, A. P., Alpert, N. M., & Schacter, D. L. (2002). Hippocampal and brain stem activation during word retrieval after repeated and semantic encoding.

Hedges, D., & Burchfield, C. (2006). *Mind, brain, and drug: An introduction to psychopharmacology.* Boston, MA: Allyn & Bacon/Longman.

Heffelfinger, A. K., & Newcomer, J. W. (2001). Glucocorticoid effects on memory function over the human life span. *Development & Psychopathology, 13*(3), 491–513.

Hehir, T. (2002). Eliminating ableism in education. *Harvard Educational Review, 72*(1), 1–32.

Heider, F. (1958). *The psychology of interpersonal relations.* New York: Wiley.

Heimann, M., & Meltzoff, A. N. (1996). Deferred imitation in 9– and 14–month-old infants. *British Journal of Developmental Psychology, 14*, 55–64.

Heine, S. J., & Renshaw, K. (2002).Interjudge agreement, self-enhancement, and liking: Cross-cultural divergences. *Personality & Social Psychology Bulletin, 28*(5), 578–587.

Hejmadi, S., Davidson, R. J., & Rozin, P. (2000). Exploring Hindu Indian emotion expressions: Evidence for accurate recognition by Americans and Indians. *Psychological Science, 11*, 183–187.

Helgeland, M. I., & Torgersen, S. (2004). Developmental antecedents of borderline personality disorder. *Comprehensive Psychiatry, 45*(2), 138–147

Helms, J. E., & Cook, D. A. (1999). *Using race and culture in counseling and psychotherapy: Theory and process.* Boston: Allyn & Bacon.

Henderlong, J., & Lepper, M. R. (2002). The effects of praise on children's intrinsic motivation: A review and synthesis. *Psychological Bulletin, 128*, 774–795.

Henke, P. G. (1992). Stomach pathology and the amygdala. In J. P. Aggleton (Ed), *The amygdala: Neurobiological aspects of emotion, memory, and mental dysfunction* (pp. 323–338). New York: Wiley.

Hennessey, B. A., & Amabile, T. M. (1998). Reward, intrinsic motivation, and creativity. *American Psychologist, 53*, 674–675.

Henning, K., & Feder, L. (2004). A comparison of men and women arrested for domestic violence: Who presents the greater

threat? *Journal of Family Violence, 19*(2), 69–80.

Henrich, J., & Boyd, R. (1998). The evolution of conformist transmission and the emergence of between group differences. *Evolution and Human Behavior, 19*, 215–241.

Henslin, J. M. (2003). *Sociology: A down-to-earth approach.* Boston: Allyn & Bacon.

Herdt, G. H. (1981). *Guardians of the flutes: Idioms of masculinity.* New York: McGraw-Hill.

Herek, G. (2000). The psychology of prejudice. *Current Directions in Psychological Science, 9*(1), 19–22.

Hergovich, A., & Olbrich, A. (2003). The impact of the Northern Ireland conflict on social identity, groupthink and integrative complexity in Great Britain. *Review of Psychology, 10*(2), 95–106.

Heriot, S. A., & Pritchard, M. (2004). "Reciprocal inhibition as the main basis of psychotherapeutic effects" by Joseph Wolpe (1954). *Clinical Child Psychology & Psychiatry, 9*(2), 297–307.

Herman, B. H., & O'Brien, C. P. (1997). Clinical medications development for opiate addiction: Focus on nonopiods and opiod antagonists for the amelioration of opiate withdrawal symptoms and relapse prevention. *Seminars in Neuroscience, 9*, 158.

Herman, L. M., Richards, D. G., & Woltz, J. P. (1984). Comprehension of sentences by bottlenosed dolphins. *Cognition, 16*, 129–139.

Herrera, E. A., Johnston, C. A., & Steele, R. G. (2004). A comparison of cognitive and behavioral treatments for pediatric obesity. *Children's Health Care, 33*(2), 151–167.

Herrnstein, R. J., & Murray, C. (1994). *The bell curve: Intelligence and class structure in American life.* New York: Free Press.

Hervé, H., Mitchell, D., Cooper, B. S., Spidel, A., & Hare, R. D. (2004). Psychopathy and unlawful confinement: An examination of perpetrator and event characteristics. *Canadian Journal of Behavioural Science, 36*(2), 137–145.

Herz, R. S., & Inzlicht, M. (2002). Sex differences in response to physical and social factors involved in human mate selection: The importance of smell for women. *Evolution & Human Behavior, 23*(5), 359–364.

Hetherington, E. M., & Stanley-Hagan, M. (2002). Diversity among stepfamilies. In D. H. Demo, K. R. Allen, et al. (Eds.), *Handbook of family diversity*(pp. 173–196). New York: Oxford University Press.

Hewitt, J. K. (1997). The genetics of obesity: What have genetic studies told us about the environment? *Behavior Genetics, 27*, 353–358.

Hewlett, B. S. (1992). Introduction. In B. S. Hewlett (Ed.), *Father-child relations: Cultural and biosocial contexts.* New York: Aldine de Gruyter.

Heyder, K. Suchan, B., & Daum, I. (2004). Cortico-subcortical contributions to executive control. *Acta Psychologica, 115*(2–3), 271–289.

Higgins, L. T. (2004). Cultural effects on the expression of some fears by Chinese and British female students. *Journal of Genetic Psychology, 165*(1), 37–49.

Higgins, N. C., & Bhatt, G. (2001). Culture moderates the self-serving bias: Etic and emic features of causal attributions in India and in Canada. *Social Behavior & Personality, 29*(1), 49–61.

Hilgard, E. R. (1978). Hypnosis and consciousness. *Human Nature, 1,* 42–51.

Hilgard, E. R. (1986). *Divided consciousness: Multiple controls in human thought and action* (expanded ed.). New York: Wiley-Interscience.

Hilgard, E. R. (1992). Divided consciousness and dissociation. *Consciousness and Cognition, 1,* 16–31.

Hill, E. L. (2004). Evaluating the theory of executive dysfunction in autism. *Developmental Review, 24*(2), 189–233.

Hiller, J. (2004). Speculations on the links between feelings, emotions and sexual behaviour: Are vasopressin and oxytocin involved? Sexual & Relationship Therapy, 19(4), 393–429.

Hilsenroth, K. J., Ackerman, S. J., Blagys, M. D., Baity, M. R., & Mooney, M. A. (2003). Short-term psychodynamic psychotherapy for depression: An examination of statistical, clinically significant, and technique-specific change. *Journal of Nervous & Mental Disease, 191*(6), 2003, 349–357.

Hinton, E. C., Parkinson, J. A., Holland, A. J., Arana, F. S., Roberts, A. C., & Owen, A. M. (2004). Neural contributions to the motivational control of appetite in humans. *European Journal of Neuroscience, 20*(5), 1411–1418.

Hirao-Try, Y. (2003). Hypertension and women: Gender specific differences. *Clinical Excellence for Nurse Practitioners, 7*(1–2), 4–8.

Hirosumi, J., Tuncman, G., Chang, L., Gorgun, C. Z., Uysal, K. T., Maeda, K., Karin, M., & Hotamisligil, G. S. (2002). Obesity is closely associated with insulin resistance and establishes the leading risk factor for type 2 diabetes mellitus, yet the molecular mechanisms. *Nature, 420,* 333–336.

Hirshkowitz, M., Moore, C. A., & Minhoto, G. (1997). The basics of sleep. In M. R. Pressman & W. C. Orr (Eds.), *Understanding sleep: The evaluation and treatment of sleep disorders.* Washington, DC: American Psychological Association.

Hittner, J. B., & Daniels, J.R. (2002). Gender-role orientation, creative accomplishments and cognitive styles. *Journal of Creative Behavior, 36*(1), 62–75.

Ho, P. S. Y., & Tsang, A. K. T. (2002). The things girls shouldn't see: Relocating the penis in sex education in Hong Kong. *Sex Education, 2*(1), 61–73.

Hobson, J. A. (1988). *The dreaming brain.* New York: Basic Books.

Hobson, J. A. (1999). *Dreaming as delirium: How the brain goes out of its mind.* Cambridge, MA: MIT Press.

Hobson, J. A. (2002). *Dreaming: An introduction to the science of sleep.* New York: Oxford University Press.

Hobson, J. A. (2005). In bed with Mark Solms? What a nightmare! A reply to Domhoff. *Dreaming, 15*(1), 21–29.

Hobson, J. A., & McCarley, R. W. (1977). The brain as a dream state generator: An activation-synthesis hypothesis of the dream process. *American Journal of Psychiatry, 134,* 1335–1348.

Hobson, J. A., & Silvestri, L. (1999). Parasomnias. *The Harvard Mental Health Letter, 15*(8), 3–5.

Hock, R. (2001). *Forty studies that changed psychology: Explorations into the history of psychological research* (4th ed). Englewood Cliffs, NJ: Prentice Hall.

Hoek, H. W., van Harten, P. N., Hermans, K. M. E., Katzman, M. A., Matroos, G. E., & Susser, E. S. (2005). The incidence of anorexia nervosa on Curacao. *American Journal of Psychiatry, 162,* 748–752.

Hoek, H. W., Van Harten, P. N., Van Hoeken, D., & Susser, E. (1998). Lack of relation between culture and anorexia nervosa: Results of an incidence study on Curacao. *New England Journal of Medicine, 338,* 1231–1232.

Hoffman, M. L. (1993). Empathy, social cognition, and moral education. In A. Garrod (Ed.), *Approaches to moral development: New research and emerging themes.* New York: Teachers College Press.

Hoffman, M. L. (2000). *Empathy and moral development: Implications for caring and justice.* New York: Cambridge University Press.

Hoffman, P. (1997). The endorphin hypothesis. In W. P. Morgan, et al., (Eds.), *Physical activity and mental health. Series in health psychology and behavioral medicine* (pp. 163–177). Washington, DC: Taylor & Francis.

Hofman, A. (1968). Psychotomimetic agents. In A. Burger (Ed.), *Drugs affecting the central nervous system* (Vol. 2). New York: Dekker.

Hogan, T.P. (2003). *Psychological testing: A practical introduction.* New York: Wiley.

Holden, C. (1980). Identical twins reared apart. *Science, 207,* 1323–1325.

Holland, J. L. (1985). *Making vocational choices: A theory of vocational personalites and work environments (2nd ed).* Englewood Cliffs, NJ: Prentice Hall.

Holland, J. L. (1994). *Self-directed search form R.* Lutz, Fl: Psychological Assessment Resources.

Holmes, T. H., & Rahe, R. H. (1967). The social readjustment rating scale. *Journal of Psychosomatic Research, 11,* 213–218.

Holt, N. L., & Dunn, J. G. H. (2004). Longitudinal idiographic analyses of appraisal and coping responses in sport. *Psychology of Sport & Exercise, 5*(2), 213–222.

Holtzworth-Munroe, A. (2000). A typology of men who are violent toward their female partners: Making sense of the heterogeneity in husband violence. *Current Directions in Psychological Science, 9*(4), 140–143.

Holtzworth-Munroe, A., Meehan, J. C., Herron, K., Rehman, U., & Stuart, G. L. (2003). Do subtypes of maritally violent men continue to differ over time? *Journal of Consulting & Clinical Psychology, 71*(4), 728–740.

Hong, S. (2000). Exercise and psychoneuroimmunology. *International Journal of Sport Psychology, 31*(2), 204–227.

Honts, C. R., & Kircher, J. C. (1994). Mental and physical countermeasures reduce the accuracy of polygraph tests. *Journal of Applied Psychology, 79*(2), 252–259.

Hooley, J. M., & Hiller, J. B. (2000). Personality and expressed emotion. *Journal of Abnormal Psychology, 109,* 40–44.

Hooley, J. M., & Hiller, J. B. (2001). Family relationships and major mental disorder: Risk factors and preventive strategies. In B. R. Sarason & S. Duck (Eds.), *Personal relationships: implications for clinical and community psychology.* New York: Wiley.

Hopkins, C. D., Tanner, J. F. Jr., & Raymond, M. A. (2004). Risk avoidance versus risk reduction: A framework and segmentation profile for understanding adolescent sexual activity. *Health Marketing Quarterly, 21*(3), 79–105.

Horenczyk, G., & Tatar, M. (2002). Teachers' attitudes toward multiculturalism and their perceptions of the school organizational culture. *Teaching & Teacher Education, 18*(4), 435–445.

Horiuchi, Y., Nakayama, K., Ishiguro, H., Ohtsuki, T., Detera-Wadleigh, S. D., Toyota, T., Yamada, K., Nankai, M., Shibuya, H., Yoshikawa, T., & Arinami, T. (2004). Possible association between a haplotype of the GABA-A receptor alpha 1 subunit gene

(GABRA1) and mood disorders. *Biological Psychiatry, 55*(1), 40–45.

Horney, K. (1939). *New ways in psychoanalysis.* New York: International Universities Press.

Horney, K. (1945). *Our inner conflicts: A constructive theory of neurosis.* New York: Norton.

Horning, L. E., & Rouse, K. A. G. (2002). Resilience in preschoolers and toddlers from low-income families. *Early Childhood Education Journal, 29*(3), 155–159.

Horton, S. L. (2002). Conceptualizing transition: The role of metaphor in describing the experience of change at midlife. *Journal of Adult Development, 9*(4), 277–290.

House, R. J., Spangler, W. D., & Woycke, J. (1991). Personality and charisma in the U.S. presidency: A psychological theory of leader effectiveness. *Administrative Science Quarterly, 36*(3), 364–396.

Hovland, C. I. (1937). The generalization of conditioned responses: II. The sensory generalization of conditioned responses with varying intensities of tone. *Journal of Genetic Psychology, 51,* 279–291.

Howe, M. L., & O'Sullivan, J. T. (1997). What children's memories tell us about recalling our childhoods: A review of storage and retrieval processes in the development of long-term retention. *Developmental Review, 17,* 148–204.

Hrebickva, M., Cermak, I., & Osecka, L. (2000). Development of personality structure from adolescence to old age: Preliminary findings. *Studia Psychologica, 42*(3), 163–166.

Huang, L. N., & Ying, Y. (1989). Japanese children and adolescents. In J. T. Gibbs & Ln N. Huang (Eds.), *Children of color.* San Francisco: Jossey-Bass.

Huang, M., & Hauser, R. M. (1998). Trends in Black–White test-score differentials: II. The WORDSUM Vocabulary Test. In U. Neisser (Ed.), *The rising curve: Long-term gains in IQ and related measures* (pp. 303–334). Washington, DC: American Psychological Association.

Hubel, D. H., & Wiesel, T. N. (1965). Receptive fields and the functional architecture in two nonstriate visual areas (18 and 19) of the cat. *Journal of Neurophysiology, 28,* 229–289.

Hubel, D. H., & Wiesel, T. N. (1979). Brain mechanisms of vision. *Scientific American, 241,* 150–162.

Huettel, S. A., Mack, P. B., & McCarthy, G. (2002). Perceiving patterns in random series: Dynamic processing of sequence in prefrontal cortex. *Nature Neuroscience, 5*(5), 485–490.

Huffman, C. J., Matthews, T. D., & Gagne, P. E. (2001). The role of part-set cuing in the recall of chess positions: Influence of chunking in memory. *North American Journal of Psychology, 3*(3), 535–542.

Hull, C. (1952). *A behavior system.* New Haven, CT: Yale University Press.

Hulshoff Pol, H. E., Brans, R. G. H., van Haren, N. E. M., Schnack, H. G., Langen, M., Baare, W. F. C., van Oel, C. J., & Kahn, R. S. (2004). Gray and white matter volume abnormalities in monozygotic and same-gender dizygotic twins discordant for schizophrenia. *Biological Psychiatry, 55*(2), 126–130.

Hunkeler, N. et al. (2000). Efficacy of nurse telehealth care and peer support in augmenting treatment of depression in primary care. *Archives of Family Medicine, 9,* 700–708.

Hunt, M. (1993). *The story of psychology.* New York: Doubleday.

Hvas, L. (2001). Positive aspects of menopause: A qualitative study. *Maturitas, 39*(1), 11–17.

Hyde, J. S., & DeLamater, J. D. (2006). *Understanding human sexuality* (9th ed.). New York: McGraw-Hill.

Hyman, R. (1981). Cold reading: How to convince strangers that you know all about them. In K. Fraizer (Ed.), *Paranormal borderlands of science* (pp. 232–244). Buffalo, NY: Prometheus.

Hyman, R. (1996). The evidence for psychic functioning: Claims vs. reality. *Skeptical Inquirer, 20,* 24–26.

Hypericum Depression Trial Study Group (2002). Effect of Hypericum performatum (St John's wort) in major depressive disorder: A randomized controlled trial. *JAMA: Journal of the American Medical Association, 287*(14), 1807–1814.

Iacono, W. G., & Lykken, D. T. (1997). The validity of the lie detector: Two surveys of scientific opinion. *Journal of Applied Psychology, 82*(3), 426–433.

Ibanez, A., Blanco C., & Saiz-Ruiz, J. (2002). Neurobiology and genetics of pathological gambling. *Psychiatric Annals, 32*(3), 181–185.

Ice, G. H., Katz-Stein, A., Himes, J., & Kane, R. L. (2004). Diurnal cycles of salivary cortisol in older adults. *Psychoneuroendocrinology, 29*(3), 355–370.

Igartua, J. José, Cheng, L. & Lopes, O. (2003). To think or not to think: Two pathways towards persuasion by short films on AIDS prevention. *Journal of Health Communication, 8*(6), 513–528.

Ikemoto, K. (2004). Significance of human striatal D-neurons: Implications in neuropsychiatric functions. *Neuropsychopharmacology, 29*(4), 429–434.

Ingram, K. M., Jones, D. A., & Smith, N. (2001). Grant Adjustment among people who have experienced AIDS-related multiple loss: The role of unsupportive social interactions, social support, and coping. *Omega: Journal of Death & Dying, 43*(4), 287–309.

Iori, R. (1988, June, 10). The good, the bad, and the useless. *Wall Street Journal,* 18R.

Irwin, M., Mascovich, A., Gillin, J. C., Willoughby, R., et al. (1994). Partial sleep deprivation reduced natural killer cell activity in humans. *Psychosomatic Medicine, 56*(6), 493–498.

Israel, P. (1998). *Edison: A life of invention.* New York: Wiley.

Itakura, S. (1992). Symbolic association between individuals and objects by a chimpanzee as an initiation of ownership. *Psychological Reports, 70,* 539–544.

Ivanenko, A., Crabtree, V. M., Tauman, R., & Gozal, D. (2003). Melatonin in children and adolescents with insomnia: A retrospective study. *Clinical Pediatrics, 42*(1), 51–58.

Ivanovic, D. M., Leiva, B. P., Pérez, H. T., Olivares, M. G., Díaz, N. S., Urrutia, M. S. C., Almagià, A. F., Toro, T. D., Miller, P. T., Bosch, E. O., & Larraín, C. G. (2004). Head size and intelligence, learning, nutritional status and brain development Head, IQ, learning, nutrition and brain. *Neuropsychologia, 42*(8), 1118–1131.

Iversen, L. (2003). Cannabis and the brain. *Brain, 126*(6), 1252–1270.

Iyer, P. (2001). *The global soul: Jet lag, shopping malls, and the search for home.* London: Vintage Books.

Jackendoff, R. (2003). Foundations of language-brain, meaning, grammar, evolution. *Applied Cognitive Psychology, 17*(1), 121–122.

Jacks, J. Z., & Devine, P. G. (2000). Attitude importance, forwarning of message content, and resistance to persuasion. *Basic & Applied Social Psychology, 22*(1), 19–29.

Jackson, C. J., Furnham, A., Forder, L., & Cotter, T. (2000). The structure of the Eysenck Personality Profiler. *British Journal of Psychology, 91,* 233–239.

Jacob, S., McClintock, M. K., Zelano, B., & Ober, C. (2002). Paternally inherited HLA alleles are associated with women's choice of male odor. *Nature Genetics,* DOI: 10.1038/ng830.

Jacobi, C., Hayward, C., de Zwaan, M., Kraemer, H. C., & Agras, W. S. (2004). Coming to terms with risk factors for eating disorders: Application of risk terminology and suggestions for a general taxonomy. *Psychological Bulletin, 130*(1), 19–65.

Jacobsen, T., & Hofmann, V. (1997). Children's attachment representations: Longitudinal relations to school behavior and academic competency in middle childhood and adolescence. *Developmental Psychology, 33,* 703–710.

Jacoby, L. L., Levy, B. A., & Steinbach, K. (1992). Episodic transfer and automaticity: Integration of data-driven and conceptually-driven processing in rereading. *Journal of Experimental Psychology: Learning, Memory, & Cognition, 18*(1), 15–24.

Jaffee, S., & Hyde, J. S. (2000). Gender differences in moral orientation: A meta-analysis. *Psychological Bulletin, 126*(5), 703–726.

James, J. W., & Friedman, R. (1998). *The grief recovery handbook: The action program for moving beyond death, divorce, and other losses.* New York: HarperCollins.

James, W. (1890). *The principles of psychology* (Vol. 2). New York: Holt.

Jang, K. L., McCrae, R. R., Angleitner, A., Riemann, R., & Livesley, W. J. (1998). Heritability of facet-level traits in a cross-culture twin sample: Support for a hierarchical model of personality. *Journal of Personality and Social Psychology, 74*(6), 1556–1565.

Jang, K. L., Stein, M. B., Taylor, S., Asmundson, G. J. G., & Livesley, W. J. (2003). Exposure to traumatic events and experiences: Aetiological relationships with personality function. *Psychiatry Research, 120*(1), 61–69.

Janis, I. L. (1972). *Victims of groupthink: A psychological study of foreign-policy decisions and fiascoes.* Boston: Houghton Mifflin.

Janis, I. L. (1989). *Crucial decisions: Leadership in policymaking and crisis management.* New York: Free Press.

Jankowiak, W. (1997). *Romantic passion: A universal experience.* New York: Columbia University Press.

Jankowiak, W., & Fischer, E. (1992). Cross-cultural perspective on romantic love. *Ethnology, 31,* 149–155.

Jansen, A. S. P., Nguyen, X. V., Karpitsky, V., Mettenleiter, T. C., & Loewy, A. D. (1995). Central command neurons of the sympathetic nervous system: Basis of the fight-or-flight response. *Science, 270,* 644–646.

Jaroff, L. (2001, March 5). Talking to the dead. *Time,* 52.

Jausovec, N., & Jausovec, K. (2000). Correlations between ERP parameters and intelligence: A reconsideration. *Biological Psychology, 55*(2), 137–154.

Javo, C., Ronning, J. A., & Heyerdahl, S. (2004). Child-rearing in an indigenous Sami population in Norway: A cross-cultural comparison of parental attitudes and expectations. *Scandinavian Journal of Psychology 45*(1), 67–78.

Javo, C., Ronning, J. A., Heyerdahl, S., & Rudmin, F. W. (2004). Parenting correlates of child behavior problems in a multiethnic community sample of preschool children in northern Norway. *European Child & Adolescent Psychiatry, 13*(1), 8–18.

Jellison, W. A., McConnell, A. R., & Gabriel, S. (2004). Implicit and explicit measures of sexual orientation attitudes: Ingroup preferences and related behaviors and beliefs among gay and straight men. *Personality & Social Psychology Bulletin, 30*(5), 629–642.

Jennings, L., & Skovholt, T. M. (1999). The cognitive, emotional, and relational characteristics of master therapists. *Journal of Counseling Psychology, 46*(1), 3–11.

Jensen, A. R., Nyborg, H., & Nyborg, H. (2003). *The scientific study of general intelligence.* New York: Elsevier Science.

Jiang, R., Wang, Y., & Gu, B. (2002). EEG biofeedback on cognitive function of children with ADHD. *Chinese Mental Health Journal, 16*(6), 407–410.

Jiang, Y., Olson, I. R., & Chun, M. M. (2000). Organization of visual short-term memory. *Journal of Experimental Psychology: Learning, memory, and cognition, 26,* 683–702.

Jog, M. S., Kubota, Y., Connolly, C. I., Hillegaart, V., & Graybiel, A. M. (1999). Building neural representations of habits, *Science, 286,* 1745–1749.

John, U., & Hanke, M. (2003). Tobacco- and alcohol-attributable mortality and years of potential life lost in Germany. *European Journal of Public Health, 13*(3), 275–277.

Johnson, K. P. (2002). The sleepy teenager. *Harvard Mental Health Letter, 18*(5), 6–8.

Johnson, M. D., & Ojemann, G. A. (2000). The role of the human thalamus in language and memory: Evidence from electrophysiological studies. *Brain & Cognition, 42,* 218–230.

Johnson, T. J., & Cropsey, K. L. (2000). Sensation seeking and drinking game participation in heavy-drinking college students. *Addictive Behaviors, 25*(1), 109–116.

Johnson, W., Bouchard, T. J. Jr., Krueger, R. F., McGue, M., & Gottesman, I. I. (2004). Just one g: Consistent results from three test batteries. *Intelligence, 32*(1), 95–107.

Johnson, W., Bouchard, T., J. Jr., Segal, N. L., & Samuels, J. (2005). General intelligence and reading performance in adults: Is the genetic factor structure the same as for children? *Personality & Individual Differences, 38*(6), 1413–1428.

Johnson, W., McGue, M., Krueger, R. F., & Bouchard, T. J. Jr. (2004). Marriage and personality: A genetic analysis. *Journal of Personality & Social Psychology. 86*(2), 285–294.

Johnston, J. J. (1978). Answer-changing behavior and grades. *Teaching of Psychology, 5*(1), 44–45.

Johnstone, L. (1999). Adverse psychological effects of ECT. *Journal of Mental Health (UK), 8*(1), 69–85.

Joiner, T. E. Jr., Brown, J. S., & Wingate, L. R. (2005). The psychology and neurobiology of suicidal behavior. *Annual Review of Psychology, 56,* 287–314.

Jolliffe, C. D., & Nicholas, M. K. (2004). Verbally reinforcing pain reports: An experimental test of the operant conditioning of chronic pain. *Pain, 107,* 167–175.

Jones, D. G., Anderson, E. R., & Galvin, K. A. (2003). Spinal cord regeneration: Moving tentatively towards new perspectives. *NeuroRehabilitation, 18*(4), 339–351.

Jorge, R. E., Robinson, R. G., Tateno, A., Narushima, K., Acion, L., Moser, D., & Arndt, S., Chemerinski, E. (2004). Repetitive transcranial magnetic stimulation as treatment of poststroke depression: A preliminary study. *Biological Psychiatry, 55*(4), 398–405.

Joseph, R. (2000). The evolution of sex differences in language, sexuality, and visual-spatial skills. *Archives of Sexual Behavior, 29*(1), 35–66.

Josephs, R. A., Newman, M. L., Brown, R. P., & Beer, J. M. (2003). Status, testosterone, and human intellectual performance: Stereotype threat as status concern. *Psychological Science, 14*(2),158–163.

Jouvet, M. (1999). Sleep and serotonin: An unfinished story. *Neuropsychopharmacology, 21*(Suppl, 2), 24S–27S.

Joy, M. (2003). Toward a non-speciesist psychoethic. *Society & Animals, 11*(1), 103–104.

Judge, T. A., & Bono, J. E. (2000). Five-factor model of personality and transformational leadership. *Journal of Applied Psychology, 85*(5), 751–765.

Judge, T. A., Bono, J. E., Ilies, R., & Gerhardt, M. W. (2002). Personality and leadership: A qualitative and quantitative review. *Journal of Applied Psychology, 87*(4), 765–780.

Julien, R. M. (2001). *A primer of drug action: A concise, nontechnical guide to the actions, uses, and side effects of psychoactive drugs.* New York: Freeman.

Jung, C. (1969). The concept of the collective unconscious. In *Collected works* (Vol. 9, Part 1). Princeton, NJ: Princeton University Press. (Original work published 1936).

Jung, C. G. (1946). *Psychological types.* New York: Harcourt Brace.

Jung, C. G. (1959). The archetypes and the collective unconscious. In H. Read, M. Fordham, & G. Adler (Eds.), *The collected*

works of C. G. Jung, Vol. 9. New York: Pantheon.

Jurado, M. A., Junque, C., Vallejo, J., Salgado, P., & Grafman, J. (2002). Obsessive-compulsive disorder (OCD) patients are impaired in remembering temporal order and in judging their own performance. *Journal of Clinical & Experimental Neuropsychology, 24(3)*, 261–269.

Kagan, J. (1998). Biology and the child. In W. Damon & R. M. Lerner (Eds.), *Handbook of child psychology* (Vol. 1). New York: John Wiley & Sons.

Kahneman, D. (2003). Experiences of collaborative research. *American Psychologist, 58(9)*, 723–730.

Kane, T. A., Loxton, N. J., Staiger, P. K., & Dawe, S. (2004). Does the tendency to act impulsively underlie binge eating and alcohol use problems? An empirical investigation. *Personality & Individual Differences, 36(1)*, 83–94.

Kanner, A. D., Coyne, J. C., Schaefer, C., & Lazarus, R. S. (1981). Comparison of two modes of stress management: Daily hassles and uplifts versus major life events. *Journal of Behavioral Medicine, 4*, 1–39.

Kapner, D. A. (2004). Infofacts resources: Alcohol and other drugs on campus. [Online]. Available: http://www.edc.org/hec/pubs/factsheets/scope.html

Kapur, S., Sridhar, N., & Remington, G. (2004). The newer antipsychotics: Underlying mechanisms and the new clinical realities. *Current Opinion in Psychiatry, 17(2)*, 115–121.

Karama, S., Lecours, A. R., Leroux, J., Bourgouin, P., Beaudoin, G., Joubert, S., & Beauregard, M. (2002). Areas of brain activation in males and females during viewing of erotic film excerpts. *Human Brain Mapping, 16(1)*, 1–13.

Karmiloff, K, & Karmiloff-Smith, A. (2002). *Pathways to language: From fetus to adolescent.* Cambridge, MA: Harvard University Press.

Kasser, T., & Sharma, Y. S. (1999). Reproductive freedom, educational equality, and females' preference for resource-acquisition characteristics in mates. *Psychological Science, 10(4)*, 374–377.

Kastenbaum, R. (1999). Dying and bereavement. In J. C. Cavanaugh & S. K. Whitbourne (Eds.), *Gerontology: An interdisciplinary perspective.* New York: Oxford University Press.

Katz, G., Knobler, H. Y., Laibel, Z., Strauss, Z., & Durst, R. (2002). Time zone change and major psychiatric morbidity: The results of a 6–year study in Jerusalem. *Comprehensive Psychiatry, 43(1)*, 37–40.

Katz, M., Marsella, A., Dube, K., Olatawura, M., et al. (1988). On the expression of psychosis in different cultures: Schizophrenia in an Indian and in a Nigerian community. *Culture, Medicine, and Psychiatry, 12*, 331–355.

Kauffmann, C. D., Cheema, M. A., & Miller, B. E. (2004). Slow right prefrontal transcranial magnetic stimulation as a treatment for medication-resistant depression: A double-blind, placebo-controlled study. *Depression & Anxiety, 19(1)*, 59–62.

Kaufman, J. C. (2002). Dissecting the golden goose: Components of studying creative writers. *Creativity Research Journal, 14(1)*, 27–40.

Kaufman, K. R., & Kaufman, N. D. (2005). Childhood mourning: Prospective case analysis of multiple losses. *Death Studies, 29(3)*, 237–249.

Kaukiainen, A., Bjoerkqvist, K., Lagerspetz, K., Oesterman, K., Salmivalli, C. et al. (1999). The relationship between social intelligence, empathy, and three types of aggression. *Aggressive Behavior, 25*, 81–89.

Kaul, R. E. (2002). A social worker's account of 31 days responding to the Pentagon disaster: Crisis intervention training and self-care practices. *Brief Treatment & Crisis Intervention, 2(1)*, 33–37.

Kavanau, J. L. (2000). Sleep, memory maintenance, and mental disorders. *Journal of Neuropsychiatry & Clinical Neurosciences, 12(2)*, 199–208.

Kawakami, K., Dovidio, J. F., Moll, J., Hermsen, S., & Russin, A. (2000). Just say no (to stereotyping): Effects of training in the negation of stereotypic associations on stereotype activation. *Journal of Personality & Social Psychology, 78(5)*, 871–888.

Kaya, N., & Erkip, F. (1999). Invasion of personal space under the condition of short-term crowding: A case study on an automatic teller machine. *Journal of Environmental Psychology, 19(2)*, 183–189.

Kaye, W. H., Devlin, B., Barbarich, N., Bulik, C. M., Thornton, L., Bacanu, S., Fichter, M. M., Halmi, K. A., Kaplan, A. S., Strober, M., Woodside, D. B., Bergen, A. W., Crow, S., Mitchell, J., Rotondo, A., Mauri, M., Cassano, G., Keel, P., Plotnicov, K., Pollice, C., Klump, K. L., Lilenfeld, L. R., Ganjei, J. K., Quadflieg, N., & Berrettini, W. H. (2004). Genetic analysis of bulimia nervosa: Methods and sample description. *International Journal of Eating Disorders, 35(4)*, 556–570.

Kazdin, A. E. (1994). Methodology, design, and evaluation in psychotherapy research. In A. E. Bergin & S. L. Garfield (Eds.), *Handbook of psychotherapy and behavior change* (4th ed.). New York: Wiley.

Keating, C. R. (1994). World without words: Messages from face and body. In W. J. Lonner & R. Malpass (Eds.), *Psychology and culture* (pp. 175–182). Boston: Allyn & Bacon.

Keats, D. M. (1982). Cultural bases of concepts of intelligence: A Chinese versus Australian comparison. In P. Sukontasarp, N. Yongsiri, P. Intasuwan, N. Jotiban, & C. Suvannathat (Eds.), *Proceedings of the Second Asian Workshop on Child and Adolescent Development* (pp. 67–75). Bangkok: Burapasilpa Press.

Keefe, F. J., Abernethy, A. P., & Campbell, L. C. (2005). Psychological approaches to understanding and treating disease-related pain. *Annual Review of Psychology, 56*, 601–630.

Keillor, J. M., Barrett, A. M., Crucian, G. P., Kortenkamp, S., & Heilman, K. M. (2002). Emotional experience and perception in the absence of facial feedback. *Journal of the International Neuropsychological Society, 8*, 130–135.

Keller, H. (1962). Quoted in R. Harrity & R. G. Martin, *The three lives of Helen Keller* (p. 23). Garden City, NY: Doubleday.

Keller, H., Yovsi, R. D., & Voelker, S. (2002). The role of motor stimulation in parental ethnotheories: The case of Cameroonian Nso and German women. *Journal of Cross-Cultural Psychology, 33(4)*, 398–414.

Kellogg, W. N., & Kellogg, L. A. (1933). *The ape and the child.* New York: McGraw-Hill.

Keltner, D., Kring, A. M., & Bonanno, G. A. (1999). Fleeting signs of the course of life: Facial expression and personal adjustment. *Current Directions in Psychological Science, 8(1)*, 18–22.

Kempermann, G. (2002). Why new neurons? Possible functions for adult hippocampal neurogenesis. *Journal of Neuroscience, 22*, 635–638.

Kemps, E., Tiggemann, M., Woods, D., & Soekov, B. (2004). Reduction of food cravings through concurrent visuospatial processing. *International Journal of Eating Disorders, 36(1)*, 31–40.

Kendler, K. S., Gallagher, T. J., Abelson, J. M., & Kessler, R. C. (1996). Lifetime prevalence, demographic risk factors, and diagnostic validity of nonaffective psychosis as assessed in a U. S. community sample. *Archives of General Psychiatry, 53*, 1022–1031.

Kendler, K. S., Jacobson, K. C., Myers, J., & Prescott, C. A. (2002). Sex differences in genetic and environmental risk factors for irrational fears and phobias. *Psychological Medicine, 32(2)*, 209–217.

Kenealy, P. M. (1997). Mood-state-dependent retrieval: The effects of induced mood on memory reconsidered. *Quarterly Journal*

of Experimental Psychology: Human Experimental Psychology, 50A, 290–317.

Kessler, R. C., McGonagle, K. A., Zhao, S., Nelson, C. B., Hughes, M., Eshleman, S., Wittchen, H., & Kendler, K. S. (1994). Lifetime and 12–month prevalence of DSM-III-R psychiatric disorders in the United States. *Archives of General Psychiatry, 51,* 8–19.

Kets, D. V., & Manfred, F. R. (2000). A journey into the "wild East": Leadership style and organizational practices in Russia. *Organizational Dynamics, 28*(4), 67–81.

Khachaturian, A. S., Corcoran, C. D., Mayer, L. S., Zandi, P. P., Breitner, J. C. S., & Cache County Study Investigators, UT, US. (2004). Apolipoprotein E ε4 count affects age at onset of Alzheimer disease, but not lifetime susceptibility: The Cache County Study. *Archives of General Psychiatry, 61*(5), 518–524.

Khandai, P. (2004). Managing stress. *Social Science International, 20*(1), 100–106.

Kicklighter, K. (2000). *Psychotherapy has gone online—and critics say that's depressing.* [Online]. Available: http://www.metanoia.org/imhs/atlanta.htm

Kieffer, K. M., Schinka, J. A., & Curtiss, G. (2004). Person-environment congruence and personality domains in the prediction of job performance and work quality. *Journal of Counseling.Psychology, 51*(2), 168–177.

Kiehl, K. A., Smith, A. M., Mendrek, A., Forster, B. B., Hare, R.D., & Liddle, P. F. (2004). Temporal lobe abnormalities in semantic processing of criminal psychopaths as revealed by functional magnetic resonance imaging. *Psychiatry Research: Neuroimaging, 130*(1), 27–42.

Kiessling, J., Pichora-Fuller, M. K., Gatehouse, S., Stephen, D., Arlinger, S., Chisolm, T., Davis, A. C., Erber, N. P., Hickson, L., Holmes, A., Rosenhall, U., & von Wedel, H. (2003). Candidature for and delivery of audiological services: Special needs of older people. *International Journal of Audiology, 42*(Suppl2), 2S92–2S101.

Kiester, E. (1984, July). The playing fields of the mind. *Psychology Today,* 18–24..

Kihlstrom, J. F. (1997). Memory, abuse, and science. *American Psychologist, 52,* 994–995.

Kihlstrom, J. F. (2004). An unbalanced balancing act: Blocked, recovered, and false memories in the laboratory and clinic. *Clinical Psychology: Science & Practice, 11*(1), 34–41.

Kihlstrom, J. F. (2005). Dissociative disorders. *Annual Review of Clinical Psychology, 1,* 227–253.

Kikusui, T., Aoyagi, A., & Kaneko, T. (2000). Spatial working memory is independent of hippocampal CA1 long-term potentiation in rats. *Behavioral Neuroscience, 114,* 700–706.

Killen, M., & Hart, D. (1999). *Morality in everyday life: Developmental perspectives.* New York: Cambridge University Press.

Kim, D-H., Moon, Y-S., Kim, H-S., Jung, J-S, Park, H-M., Suh, H-W., Kim, Y-H., & Song, D-K. (2005). Effect of Zen meditation on serum nitric oxide activity and lipid peroxidation. *Progress in Neuropsychopharmacology & Biological Psychiatry, 29*(2), 327–331.

Kim, J., & Hatfield, E. (2004). Love types and subjective well-being: A cross cultural study. *Social Behavior & Personality, 32*(2), 173–182.

Kim, J-H., Auerbach, J. M., Rodriquez-Gomez, J. A., Velasco, I., Gavin, D., Lumelsky, N., Lee, S-H., Nguyen, J., Sanchez-Pernaute, R., Bankiewicz, K., & McKay, R. (2002). Dopamine neurons derived from embryonic stem cells function in an animal model of Parkinson's disease. *Nature, 418,* 50–56.

Kim, S. U. (2004). Human neural stem cells genetically modified for brain repair in neurological disorders. *Neuropathology, 24*(3), 159–171.

Kimmel, M. S. (2000). *The gendered society.* London: Oxford University Press.

King, N. J., Clowes-Hollins, V., & Ollendick, T. H. (1997). The etiology of childhood dog phobia. *Behaviour Research and Therapy, 35,* 77.

Kingree, J. B., Braithwaite, R., & Woodring, T. (2000). Unprotected sex as a function of alcohol and marijuana use among adolescent detainees. *Journal of Adolescent Health, 27*(3), 179–185.

Kinsbourne, M. (1972). Behavioral analysis of the repetition deficit in conduction aphasia. *Neurology, 22*(11), 1126–1132.

Kirk, K. M., Bailey, J. M., Dunne, M. P., & Martin, N. G. (2000). Measurement models for sexual orientation in a community twin sample. *Behavior Genetics, 30*(4), 345–356.

Kirkman, C. A. (2002). Non-incarcerated psychopaths: Why we need to know more about the psychopaths who live amongst us. *Journal of Psychiatric & Mental Health Nursing, 9*(2), 155–160.

Kirkpatrick, S. A., & Locke, E. A. (1996). Direct and indirect effects of three core charismatic leadership components on performance and attitudes. *Journal of Applied Psychology, 81*(1), 36–51.

Kirsch, I., & Braffman, W. (2001). Imaginative suggestibility and hypnotizability. *Current Directions in Psychological Science, 10*(2), 57–61.

Kirsch, I., & Lynn, S. J. (1995). The altered state of hypnosis. *American Psychologist, 50,* 846–858.

Kirschenbaum, H. & Jourdan, A. (2005). The current status of Carl Rogers and the person-centered approach. *Psychotherapy: Theory, Research Practice, Training, 42*(1), 37–51.

Kirschner, S. M., Litwack, T. R., & Galperin, G. J. (2004). The defense of extreme emotional disturbance: A qualitative analysis of cases in New York county. *Psychology, Public Policy, & Law, 10*(1–2), 102–133.

Kisilevsky, B. S., Hains, S. M. J., Lee, K., Xie, X., Huang, H., Ye, H., Zhang, K., & Wang, Z. (2003). Effects of experience on fetal voice recognition. *Psychological Science, 14*(3), 220–224.

Klatzky, R. L. (1984). *Memory and awareness.* New York: Freeman.

Kleinman, A., & Cohen, A. (1997, March). Psychiatry's global challenge. *Scientific American,* 86–89.

Kline, K. N., & Mattson, M. (2000). Breast self-examination pamphlets: A content analysis grounded in fear appeal research. *Health Communication, 12*(1), 1–21.

Klohnen, E. C., & Bera, S. (1998). Behavioral and experiential patterns of avoidantly and securely attached women across adulthood: A 31–year longitudinal perspective. *Journal of Personality and Social Psychology, 74*(1), 211–223.

Knecht, S., Floeel, A., Draeger, B., Breitenstein, C., Sommer, J., Henningsen, H., Ringelstein, E. B., & Pascual-Leone, A. (2002). Degree of language lateralization determines susceptibility to unilateral brain lesions. *Nature Neuroscience, 5*(7), 695–699.

Kniffin, K. M., & Wilson, D. S. (2004). The effect of nonphysical traits on the perception of physical attractiveness: Three naturalistic studies. *Evolution & Human Behavior, 25*(2), 88–101.

Knoblauch, K., Vital-Durand, F., & Barbur, J. L. (2000). Variation of chromatic sensitivity across the life span. *Vision Research, 41*(1), 23–36.

Kobasa, S. (1979). Stressful life events, personality, and health: An inquiry into hardiness. *Journal of Personality and Social Psychology, 37,* 1–11.

Koenig, S. (2000). The inmates and the asylum: How Hollywood depicts mental hospitals.

Koerner, A. F., & Fitzpatrick, M. A. (2002). Nonverbal communication and marital adjustment and satisfaction: The role of decoding relationship relevant and relationship irrelevant affect. *Communication Monographs, 69*(1), 33–51.

Kohlberg, L. (1964). Development of moral character and moral behavior. In L. W. Hoffman & M. L. Hoffman (Eds.), *Review of child development research* (Vol. 1). New York: Sage.

Kohlberg, L. (1966). A cognitive-developmental analysis of children's sex-role concepts and attitudes. In E. E. Maccoby (Ed.), *The development of sex differences.* Stanford, CA: Stanford University Press.

Kohlberg, L. (1969). Stage and sequence: The cognitive-developmental approach to socialization. In D. A. Goslin (Ed.), *Handbook of socialization theory and research.* Chicago: Rand McNally.

Kohlberg, L. (1981). *The meaning and measurement of moral development.* Worcester, MA: Clark University Press.

Kohlberg, L. (1984). *The psychology of moral development: Essays on moral development* (Vol. II). San Francisco: Harper & Row.

Köhler, W. (1925). *The mentality of apes.* New York: Harcourt, Brace.

Kohn, A. (2000). *Punished by rewards: The trouble with gold stars, incentive plans, A's, and other bribes.* New York: Houghton Mifflin.

Kolata, G. (2005, April 20). *Some extra heft may be helpful, new study says. New York Times.* [On-line]. Available: http://query.nytimes.com/gst/health/article-page.html?res=9E07E6DA1631F933A15757C0A9639C8B63

Komiya, N., Good, G. E., & Sherrod, N. B. (2000). Emotional openness as a predictor of college students' attitudes toward seeking psychological help. *Journal of Counseling Psychology, 47*(1), 138–143.

Koob, G. F., & Nestler, E. J. (1997). Neurobiology of drug addiction. *Journal of Neuropsychiatry and Clinical Neuroscience, 9*(3), 482–497.

Koop, C. E., Richmond, J., & Steinfeld, J. (2004). America's choice: Reducing tobacco addiction and disease. *American Journal of Public Health, 94*(2), 174–176.

Kopelman, M. D., Reed, L. J., Marsden, P., Mayes, A. R., Jaldow, E., Laing, H., & Isaac, C. (2002). Amnesic syndrome and severe ataxia following the recreational use of 3,4–methylene-dioxymethamphetamine (MDMA, "ecstasy") and other substances. *Neurocase, 7*(5), 423–432.

Koppel, J. (2000). *Good/Grief.* New York: Harperennial.

Korkman, M., Kettunen, S., & Autti-Rämö, I. (2003). Neurocognitive impairment in early adolescence following prenatal alcohol exposure of varying duration. *Child Neuropsychology, 9*(2), 117–128.

Kornstein, S. G. (2002). Chronic depression in women. *Journal of Clinical Psychiatry, 63*(7), 602–609.

Koulack, D. (1997). Recognition memory, circadian rhythms, and sleep. *Perceptual & Motor Skills, 85,* 99–104.

Kozel, F. A., Padgett, T. M., & George, M. S. (2004). A replication study of the neural correlates of deception. *Behavioral Neuroscience, 118*(4), 852–856.

Kraaij, V., Arensman, E., & Spinhoven, P. (2002). Negative life events and depression in elderly persons: A meta-analysis. *Journals of Gerontology: Series B: Psychological Sciences & Social Sciences, 57B*(1), 87–94.

Kramer, A. F., Hahn, S., Irwin, D. E., & Theeuwes, J. (2000). Age differences in the control of looking behavior. *Psychological Science, 11*(3), 210–217.

Krantz, D. S., & McCeney, M. K. (2002). Effects of psychological and social factors on organic disease: A critical assessment of research on coronary heart disease. *Annual Review of Psychology, (1),* 341–369.

Kranz, K., & Daniluk, J. C. (2002). Gone but not forgotten: The meaning and experience of mother-loss for midlife daughters. *Women & Therapy, 25*(1), 1–18.

Krings, F. (2004). Automatic and controlled influences of associations with age on memory. *Swiss Journal of Psychology, 63*(4), 247–259.

Krishna, G. (1999). *The dawn of a new science.* Los Angeles: Institute for Consciousness Research.

Kronenberger, W. G., Mathews, V. P., Dunn, D. W., Wang, Y., Wood, E. A., Larsen, J. J., Rembusch, M. E., Lowe, M. J., Giauque, A. L., & Lurito, J. T. (2005). Media violence exposure in aggressive and control adolescents: Differences in self- and parent-reported exposure to violence on television and in video games. *Aggressive Behavior, 31*(3), 201–216.

Kryger, M. H., Walld, R., & Manfreda, J. (2002). Diagnoses received by narcolepsy patients in the year prior to diagnosis by a sleep specialist. *Sleep: Journal of Sleep & Sleep Disorders Research, 25*(1), 36–41.

Kübler-Ross, E. (1975). *Questions and answers on death and dying.* Oxford, England: Macmillan

Kübler-Ross, E. (1983). *On children and death.* New York: Macmillan.

Kübler-Ross, E. (1997). *Death: The final stage of growth.* New York: Simon & Schuster.

Kübler-Ross, E. (1999). *On death and dying.* New York: Simon & Schuster.

Kudo, E., & Numazaki, M. (2003). Explicit and direct self-serving bias in Japan. Reexamination of self-serving bias for success and failure. *Journal of Cross-Cultural Psychology, 34*(5), 511–521.

Kuebli, J. (1999). Young children's understanding of everyday emotions. In L. E.

Berk, *Landscapes of development* (pp. 123–136). Belmont, CA: Wadsworth.

Kuhn, C., Swartzwelder, S., & Wilson, W. (2003). *Buzzed: The straight facts about the most used and abused drugs from alcohol to ecstasy* (2nd ed.). New York: W.W. Norton & Company.

Kulik, L. (2005). Intrafamiliar congruence in gender role attitudes and ethnic stereotypes: The Israeli case. *Journal of Comparative Family Studies, 36*(2), 289–303.

Kumkale, G. T., & Albarracín, D. (2004). The sleeper effect in persuasion: A meta-analytic review. *Psychological Bulletin, 130*(1), 143–172.

Kumpfer, K. L., Alvarado, R., & Whiteside, H. O. (2003). Family-based interventions for substance use and misuse prevention. *Substance Use & Misuse, 38*(11–13), 1759–1787.

Kunz, D., & Hermann, W. M. (2000). Sleep-wake cycle, sleep-related disturbances, and sleep disorders: A chronobiological approach. *Comparative Psychology, 41,* 104–105.

Kuriansky, J. (1998). *The complete idiot's guide to a healthy relationship.* New York: Alpha Books.

Kuritzky, L., & Weaver, A. (2003). Advances in rheumatology: Coxibs and beyond. *Journal of Pain & Symptom Management, 25,* S6–S20.

Labiano, L. M., & Brusasca, C. (2002). Tratamientos psicologicos en la hipertension arterial. / Psychological treatments in arterial hypertension. *Interdisciplinaria, 19*(1), 85–97.

Lachman, M. E. (2004). Development in midlife. *Annual Review of Psychology, 55,* 305–331.

Lackner, J. R., & DiZio, P. (2005). Vestibular, proprioceptive, and haptic contributions to spatial orientation. *Annual Review of Psychology, 56,* 115–147.

Laine, T., Pekka, J., Ahonen, A., Raesaenen, P., & Tiihonen, J. (2001). Dopamine transporter density and novelty seeking among alcoholics. *Journal of Addictive Diseases, 20*(4), 91–96.

Lakein, A. (1998). *Give me a moment and I'll change your life: Tools for moment management.* New York: Andrews McMeel Publishing.

Lalovic, A., Sequeira, A., DeGuzman, R., Chawky, N., Lesage, A , Seguin, M., & Turecki, G. (2004). Investigation of completed suicide and genes involved in cholesterol metabolism. *Journal of Affective Disorders, 79*(1–3), 25–32.

Lamb, H. R. (2000). Deinstitutionalization and public policy. In R. W. Menninger & J.C. Nemiah (Eds.), *American psychiatry after World War II.* Washington, DC: American Psychiatric Press.

Lamberg, L. (1998). Gay is okay with APA-Forum honors landmark 1973 events. *Journal of the American Medical Association, 280,* 497–499.

Lambert, M. J. (2004). *Bergin and Garfield's handbook of psychotherapy and behavior change* (5th ed.). Hoboken, NJ: Wiley.

Lambert, S., Sampaio, E., Mauss, Y., & Scheiber, C. (2004). Blindness and brain plasticity: Contribution of mental imagery? An fMRI study. *Cognitive Brain Research, 20*(1), 1–11.

Landay, J. S., & Kuhnehenn, J. (2004, July 10). Probe blasts CIA on Iraq data. *The Philadelphia Inquirer,* p. AO1.

Landeira-Fernandez, J. (2004). Analysis of the cold-water restraint procedure in gastric ulceration and body temperature. *Physiology & Behavior, 82*(5), 827–833.

Landen, M., Walinder, J., & Lundstrom, B. (1998). Clinical characteristics of a total cohort of female and male applicants for sex reassignment: A descriptive study. *Acta Psychiatrica Scandinavia, 97,* 189–194.

Landry, D. W. (1997). Immunotherapy for cocaine addiction. *Scientific American, 276,* 42–45.

Landry, M.J. (2002). MDMA: A review of epidemiologic data. *Journal of Psychoactive Drugs, 34(2),* 163–169.

Lane, R. D., Reiman, E. M., Ahern, G. L., & Schwartz, G. E. (1997). Neuroanatomical correlates of happiness, sadness, and disgust. *American Journal of Psychiatry, 154,* 926–933.

Lang, F. R., & Carstensen, L. L. (2002). Time counts: Future time perspective, goals, and social relationships. *Psychology & Aging, 17(1),* 125–139.

Langenecker, S. A., Bieliauskas, L. A., Rapport, L. J., Zubieta, J-K., Wilde, E. A., & Berent, S. (2005). Face emotion perception and executive functioning deficits in depression. *Journal of Clinical & Experimental Neuropsychology, 27*(3), 320–333.

Langer, T. (1962). A twenty-two item screening score of psychiatric symptoms indicating impairment. *Journal of Health and Human Behavior, 3,* 269–276.

Langlois, J. H., Kalakanis, L., Rubenstein, A. J., Larson, A., Hallam, M., & Smoot, M. (2000). Maxims or myths of beauty? A meta-analytic and theoretical review. *Psychological Bulletin, 126*(3), 390–423.

LaPointe, L. L. (Ed) (2005). Feral children. *Journal of Medical Speech-Language Pathology, 13*(1), vii–ix.

Lariviere, N., Gelinas, I., Mazer, B., Tallant, B., & Paquette, I. (2002). Discharging older adults with a severe and chronic mental illness in the community. *Canadian Journal of Occupational Therapy, 69(2),* 71–83.

Larzelere, R. E., & Johnson, B. (1999). Evaluations of the effects of Sweden's spanking ban on physical child abuse rates: A literature review. *Psychological Reports, 85*(2), 381–392.

Lashley, K. (1929). *Brain mechanisms and intelligence.* Chicago: University of Chicago Press.

Lashley, K. (1950). In search of the engram. *Symposia of the Society of Experimental Biology, 4,* 454–482.

Latane, B., & Darley, J. M. (1970). *The unresponsive bystander: Why doesn't he help?* New York: Appleton-Century-Crofts.

Lauc, G., Zvonar, K., Vuksic-Mihaljevic, Z., & Flögel, M. (2004). Post-awakening changes in salivary cortisol in veterans with and without PTSD. *Stress & Health: Journal of the International Society for the Investigation of Stress, 20*(2), 99–102.

Laumann, E., Gagnon, J., Michael, R., & Michaels, S. (1994). *The social organization of sexuality: Sexual practices in the United States.* Chicago: University of Chicago Press.

Lawrence, S. A. (2002). Behavioral interventions to increase physical activity. *Journal of Human Behavior in the Social Environment, 6(1),* 25–44.

Lawrence, S. A., Wodarski, L. A., & Wodarski, J. (2002). Behavioral medicine paradigm: Behavioral interventions for chronic pain and headache. *Journal of Human Behavior in the Social Environment, 5(2),* 1–14.

Lazarus, A. A. (1971). *Behavior therapy and beyond.* New York: McGraw-Hill.

Lazarus, R. S. (1999). *Stress and emotion: A new synthesis.* New York: Springer.

Lazarus, R. S., & Folkman, S. (1984). *Stress appraisal and coping.* New York: Springer.

Lazev, A. B., Herzog, T. A., & Brandon, T. H. (1999). Classical conditioning of environmental cues to cigarette smoking. *Experimental & Clinical Psychopharmacology, 7*(1), 56–63.

Leaper, C. (2000). Gender, affiliation, assertion, and the interactive context of parent–child play. *Developmental Psychology, 36*(3), 381–393.

Lecrubier, Y., Clerc, G., Didi, R., & Kieser, M. (2002). Efficacy of St. John's wort extract WS 5570 in major depression: A double-blind, placebo-controlled trial. *American Journal of Psychiatry, 159(8),* 1361–1366.

LeDoux, J. (1996a). *The emotional brain: The mysterious underpinnings of emotional life.* New York: Simon & Schuster.

LeDoux, J. (2002). *Synaptic self: How our brains become who we are.* New York: Viking.

LeDoux, J. E. (1996b). Sensory systems and emotion: A model of affective processing. *Integrative Psychiatry, 4,* 237–243.

Lee, D. (1950). The conception of the self among the Wintu Indians. In D. Lee (Ed.), *Freedom and culture.* Englewood Cliffs, NJ: Prentice-Hall.

Lee, J., Pomeroy, E. C., Yoo, S-K., & Rheinboldt, K. T. (2005). Attitudes toward rape: A comparison between Asian and Caucasian college students. *Violence Against Women, 11*(2), 177–196.

Lee, K. T., Mattson, S. N., & Riley, E. P. (2004). Classifying children with heavy prenatal alcohol exposure using measures of attention. *Journal of the International Neuropsychological Society, 10*(2), 271–277.

Lee, W-Y. (2002). One therapist, four cultures: Working with families in Greater China. *Journal of Family Therapy, 24*(3), 258–275.

Leeper, R. W. (1935). A study of a neglected portion of the field of learning: The development of sensory organization. *Journal of Genetic Psychology, 46,* 41–75.

Lefley, H. P. (2000). Cultural perspectives on families, mental illness, and the law. *International Journal of Law and Psychiatry, 23,* 229–243.

Leichtman, M. D., & Ceci, S. J. (1995). The effects of stereotypes and suggestions on preschoolers' reports. *Developmental Psychology, 31,* 568–578.

Lengua, L. J., Wolchik, S. A., Sandler, I. N., & West, S. G. (2000). The additive and interactive effects of parenting and temperament in predicting problems of children of divorce. *Journal of Clinical Child Psychology, 29*(2), 232–244.

Lensvelt-Mulders, G., & Hettema, J. (2001). Analysis of genetic influences on the consistency and variability of the Big Five across different stressful situations. *European Journal of Personality, 15*(5), 355–371.

Leonard, B. E. (2003). *Fundamentals of psychopharmacology* (3rd ed.). New York: Wiley.

Lepper, M. R., Greene, D., & Nisbett, R. E. (1973). Undermining children's intrinsic interest with extrinsic rewards: A test of the overjustification hypothesis. *Journal of Personality and Social Psychology, 28,* 129–137.

Lerner, J. S., Gonzalez, R. M., Small, D. A., & Fischhoff, B. (2003). Effects of fear and anger on perceived risks of terrorism: A national field experiment. *Psychological Science, 14,* 144–150.

Lerner, R. M., & Galambos, N. L. (1998). Adolescent development: Challenges and opportunities for research, programs, and policies. *Annual Review of Psychology, 49,* 413–446.

Leslie, M. (2000). *The vexing legacy of Lewis Terman. Stanford Magazine.* [On-line]. Available: http://www.stanfordalumni.org/jg/

mig/news_magazine/magazine/julaug00/index.html

Lettvin, J. Y., Maturana, H. R., McCulloch, W. S., & Pitts, W. H. (1959). What the frog's eye tells the frog's brain. *Proceedings of the Institute of Radio Engineers, 47,* 1940–1951.

LeVay, S. (2003). Queer science: The use and abuse of research into homosexuality. *Archives of Sexual Behavior, 32*(2),187–189.

Levenson, R. W. (1992). Autonomic nervous system differences among emotions. *Psychological Science, 3,* 23–27.

Leveton, D. (2002, August 23). "O'Keeffe, Georgia," World Book Online Americas Edition. [On-line]. Available: http://www.worldbookonline.com/ar?/na/ar/co/ar400900.htm.

Levine, J. R. (2001). *Why do fools fall in love: Experiencing the magic, mystery, and meaning of successful relationships.* New York: Jossey-Bass.

Levinson, D. J. (1977). The mid-life transition, *Psychiatry, 40,* 99–112.

Levinson, D. J. (1996). *The seasons of a woman's life.* New York: Knopf.

Levinthal, C. (2002). *Drugs, behavior, and modern society* (3rd ed.). Boston, MA: Allyn & Bacon.

Levinthal, C. (2006). *Drugs, society, and criminal justice.* Boston, MA: Allyn & Bacon/Longman.

Lewald, J. (2004). Gender-specific hemispheric asymmetry in auditory space perception. *Cognitive Brain Research, 19*(1), 92–99.

Lewig, K. A., & Dollard, M. F. (2003). Emotional dissonance, emotional exhaustion and job satisfaction in call centre workers. *European Journal of Work & Organizational Psychology, 12*(4), 366–392.

Lewis, S. (1963). *Dear Shari.* New York: Stein & Day.

Li, N. P., Bailey, J. M., Kenrick, D. T., & Linsenmeier, J. A. W. (2002). The necessities and luxuries of mate preferences: Testing the tradeoffs. *Journal of Personality & Social Psychology, 82*(6), 947–955.

Li, S., Lindenberger, U., Hommel, B., Aschersleben, G., Prinz, W., & Baltes, P. B. (2004). Transformations in the couplings among intellectual abilities and constituent cognitive processes across the life span. *Psychological Science,15*(3), 155–163.

Lieberman, P. (1998). *Eve spoke: Human language and human evolution.* New York: W.W. Norton and Company.

Life behind the legend: Lincoln's journey from the frontier to Ford's theatre. (2005, July 4). *Time,* pp. 43–44.

Liggett, D. R. (2000). Enhancing imagery through hypnosis: A performance aid for athletes. *American Journal of Clinical Hypnosis, 43*(2), 149–157.

Lilienfeld, L. R., Kaye, W. H., Greeno, C. G., Merikangas, K. R., Plotnicov, K., et al. (1999). Psychiatric disorders in women with bulimia nervosa and their first-degree relatives: Effects of comorbid substance dependence. *International Journal of Eating Disorders, 22,* 253–264.

Lillard, A. (1998). Ethnopsychologies: Cultural variations in theories of mind. *Psychological Bulletin, 123,* 3–32.

Lindahl, K., & Obstbaum, K. (2004). Entering the canon: A tribute to Chess and Thomas. *PsycCRITIQUES.* [np].

Linden, E. (1993). Can animals think? *Time,* pp. 54–61.

Lindholm, E., Aberg, K., Ekholm, B., Pettersson, U., Adolfsson, R., & Jazin, E. E. (2004). Reconstruction of ancestral haplotypes in a 12–generation schizophrenia pedigree. *Psychiatric Genetics, 14*(1), 1–8.

Lindsay, D. S., Allen, B. P., Chan, J. C. K., & Dahl, L. C. (2004). Eyewitness suggestibility and source similarity: Intrusions of details from one event into memory reports of another event. *Journal of Memory & Language, 50*(1), 96–111.

Links, P. S., Heslegrave, R., & van Reekum, R. (1998). Prospective follow-up of borderline personality disorder: Prognosis, prediction outcome, and Axis II comorbidity. *Canadian Journal of Psychiatry, 43,* 265–270.

Linzer, M., Gerrity, M., Douglas, J. A., McMurray, J. E., Williams, E. S., Konrad, T. R., & Society of General Medicine Career Satisfaction Study Group (2002). Physician stress: Results from the physician worklife study. Stress & Health: *Journal of the International Society for the Investigation of Stress, 18(1),* 37–42.

Lipowski, Z. J. (1986). Psychosomatic medicine: Past and present: I. Historical background. *Canadian Journal of Psychiatry, 31*(1), 2–7.

Lippa, R. A. (2002). *Gender, nature, and nurture.* Hillsdale, NJ: Lawrence Erlbaum Assoc.

Lipsanen, T., Korkeila, J., Peltola, P., Järvinen, J., Langen, K., & Lauerma, H. (2004). Dissociative disorders among psychiatric patients: Comparison with a nonclinical sample. *European Psychiatry, 19*(1), 53–55.

Lissek, S., & Powers, A. S. (2003). Sensation seeking and startle modulation by physically threatening images. *Biological Psychology, 63*(2), 179–197.

Liu, H., Mantyh, P, & Basbaum, A. I. (1997). NMDA-receptor regulation of substance P release from primary afferent nociceptors. *Nature, 386,* 721–724.

Liu, J. H., & Latane, B. (1998). Extremitization of attitudes: Does thought- and discussion-induced polarization cumulate? *Basic and Applied Social Psychology, 20,* 103–110.

Livingston, J. A. (1999). Something old and something new: Love, creativity, and the enduring relationship. *Bulletin of the Menninger Clinic, 63,* 40–52.

Lizarraga, M. L. S., & Ganuza, J. M. G. (2003). Improvement of mental rotation in girls and boys. *Sex Roles, 49*(5–6), 277–286.

Loftus, E. (1982). Memory and its distortions. In A. G. Kraut (Ed.), *The G. Stanley Hall Lecture Series* (Vol. 2, pp. 123–154). Washington, DC: American Psychological Association.

Loftus, E. (1993). Psychologists in the eyewitness world. *American Psychologist, 48,* 550–552.

Loftus, E., & Ketcham, K. (1994). *The myth of repressed memories: False memories and allegations of sexual abuse.* New York: St. Martin's Press.

Loftus, E. (1997). Memory for a past that never was. *Current Directions in Psychological Science, 6*(3), 60–65.

Loftus, E. (2000). Remembering what never happened. In E. Tulving, et al. (Eds.), *Memory, consciousness, and the brain: The Tallinn Conference,* pp. 106–118. Philadelphia, PA: Psychology Press/Taylor & Francis.

Loftus, E. (2001). Imagining the past. *Psychologist, 14*(11), 584–587.

Loftus, E. (2002, May/June). My story: Dear Mother. *Psychology Today,* pp. 67–70.

Loftus, E., & Polage, D. C. (1999). Repressed memories: When are they real? When are they false? *Psychiatric Clinics of North America, 22,* 61–70.

London, L. H., Tierney, G., Buhin, L., Greco, D. M., & Cooper, C. J. (2002). Kids' college: Enhancing children's appreciation and acceptance of cultural diversity. *Journal of Prevention & Intervention in the Community, 24*(2), 63–78

Loo, R., & Thorpe, K. (1998). Attitudes toward women's roles in society. *Sex Roles, 39,* 903–912.

Lopez, F., & Hsu, P-C. (2002). Further validation of a measure of parent-adult attachment style. *Measurement & Evaluation in Counseling & Development, 34*(4), 223–237.

Lopez, J. C. (2002). Brain repair: A spinal scaffold. *Nature Reviews Neuroscience, 3,* 256.

López, M., & Cantora, R. (2003). Associative interference with taste aversions after contextual discrimination learning. *Learning & Motivation, 34*(4), 372–388.

Lopez, S. R., & Guarnaccia, P. J. J. (2000). Cultural psychopathology: Uncovering the social world of mental illness. *Annual Review of Psychology, 51,* 571–598.

Lorenz, K. Z. (1937). The companion in the bird's world. *Auk, 54,* 245–273.

Lorenz, K. Z. (1981). *The foundations of ethology.* New York: Springer-Verlag.

Lott, D. A. (2000). *The new flirting game.* London: Sage.

Lu, L., Kao, S-F., Cooper, C. L., & Spector, P. E. (2000). Managerial stress, locus of control, and job strain in Taiwan and UK: A comparative study. *International Journal of Stress Management, 7(3),* 209–226.

Lu, Z. L., Williamson, S. J., & Kaufman, L. (1992). Behavioral lifetime of human auditory sensory memory predicted by physiological measures. *Science, 258,* 1668–1670.

Lubinski, D., & Benbow, C. P. (2000). States of excellence. *American Psychologist, 55(1),* 137–150.

Lubinski, D., & Dawis, R. V. (1992). Aptitudes, skills, and proficiencies. In M. D. Dunnette & L. M. Hough (Eds.), *The handbook of industrial/organizational psychology* (pp. 1–59). Palo Alto, CA: Consulting Psychologists Press.

Lucio-Gomez, E., Ampudia-Rueda, A., Duran-Patino, C., Gallegos-Mejia, L., & Leon-Guzman, I. (1999). La nueva version del Inventario Multifasico de la Personalidad de Minnesota para adolescentes Mexicanos. /The new version of the Minnesota Multiphasic Personality Inventory for Mexican adolescents. *Revista Mexicana de Psicologia, 16(2),* 217–226.

Luecken, L. J., & Lemery, K. S. (2004). Early caregiving and physiological stress responses. *Clinical Psychology Review, 24(2),* 171–191.

Luecken, L. J., Tartaro, J., & Appelhans, B. (2004). Strategic coping responses and attentional biases. *Cognitive Therapy & Research, 28(1),* 23–37.

Luria, A. R. (1968). *The mind of a mnemonist: A little book about a vast memory.* New York: Basic Books.

Luria, A. R. (1976). *Cognitive development: Its cultural and social foundations.* Cambridge, MA: Harvard University Press.

Lykken, D. T. (1984). Polygraphic interrogation. *Nature, 307,* 681–684.

Lykken, D. T. (1998). *A tremor in the blood: Uses and abuses of the lie detector.* New York: Plenum Press.

Lynam, D. R., & Gudonis, L. (2005). The development of psychopathy. *Annual Review of Clinical Psychology, 1,* 381–407.

Lynch, P. E. (2003). An interview with Richard C. Pillard, MD. *Journal of Gay & Lesbian Psychotherapy, 7(4),* 63–70.

Lynn, R. (1995). Cross-cultural differences in intelligence and personality. In D. H. Saklofske & M. Zeidner (Eds.), *International handbook of personality and intelligence.* New York: Plenum.

Lynn, R. (2002). Racial and ethnic differences in psychopathic personality. *Personality & Individual Differences, 32(2),* 273–316.

Lynn, S. J., Vanderhoff, H., Shindler, K., & Stafford, J. (2002). Defining hypnosis as a trance vs. cooperation: Hypnotic inductions, suggestibility, and performance standards. *American Journal of Clinical Hypnosis, 44(3–4),* 231–240.

Lyoo, I. K., Kim, M. J., Stoll, A. L., Demopulos, C. M., Parow, A. M., Dager, S. R., Friedman, S. D., Dunner, D. L., & Renshaw, P. F. (2004). Frontal lobe gray matter density decreases in Bipolar I Disorder. *Biological Psychiatry, 55(6),* 648–651.

Lytle, M. E., Bilt, J. V., Pandav, R. S., Dodge, H. H., & Ganguli, M. (2004). Exercise level and cognitive decline: The MoVIES project. *Alzheimer Disease & Associated Disorders, 18(2),* 57–64.

Maas, J. B. (1999). *Power sleep.* New York: HarperPerennial.

Maccoby, E. E. (2000). Parenting and its effects on children: On reading and misreading behavior genetics. *Annual Review of Psychology, 51,* 1–27.

Mackay, J. (2001). Global sex: Sexuality and sexual practices around the world. *Sexual & Relationship Therapy, 16(1),* 71–82.

Mackey, R. A., & O'Brien, B. A. (1998). Marital conflict management: Gender and ethnic differences. *Social Work, 43(2),* 128–141.

MacKinnon, D. F., Jamison, K. R., & DePaulo, J. R. (1997). Genetics of manic-depressive illness. *Annual Review of Neuroscience, 10,* 355–373.

MacLaren, V. V. (2001). A qualitative review of the Guilty Knowledge Test. *Journal of Applied Psychology, 86(4),* 674–683.

Macmillan, M. B. (2000). *An odd kind of fame: Stories of Phineas Gage.* Cambridge, MA: MIT Press.

Macmillan, M. B. (2001). The reliability and validity of Freud's methods of free association and interpretation. *Psychological Inquiry, 12(3),* 167–175.

Maddi, S. R. (2004). Hardiness: An operationalization of existential courage. *Journal of Humanistic Psychology, 44(3),* 279–298.

Maehr, M. L., & Urdan, T. C. (2000). *Advances in motivation and achievement: The role of context.* Greewich, CT: JAI Press.

Magid, K., & McKelvey, C. A. (1987). *High risk: Children without a conscience.* New York: Bantam.

Maguen, S., Armistead, L., & Kalichman, S. (2000). Predictors of HIV antibody testing among gay, lesbian, and bisexual youth. *Journal of Adolescent Health, 26,* 252–257.

Magura, S., Laudet, A. B., Mahmood, D., Rosenblum, A., Vogel, H. S., & Knight, E. L. (2003). Role of self-help processes in achieving abstinence among dually diagnosed persons. *Addictive Behaviors, 28(3),* 399–413.

Mah, K., & Binik, Y. M. (2005). Are orgasms in the mind or the body? Psychosocial versus physiological correlates of orgasmic pleasure and satisfaction. *Journal of Sex & Marital Therapy, 31(3),* 187–200.

Maier, S. E., & West, J. R. (2001). Drinking patterns and alcohol-related birth defects. *Alcohol Research & Health, 25(3),* 168–174.

Major, B., & O'Brien, L. T. (2005). The social psychology of stigma. *Annual Review of Psychology, 56,* 393–421.

Major, B., Spencer, S., Schmader, T., Wolfe, C., & Crocker, J. (1998). Coping with negative stereotypes about intellectual performance: The role of psychological disengagement. *Personality & Social Psychology Bulletin, 24(1),* 34–50.

Manly, J. J., Byrd, D., Touradji, P., Sanchez, D., & Stern, Y. (2004). Literacy and cognitive change among ethnically diverse elders. *International Journal of Psychology, 39(1),* 47–60.

Manoach, D. S., Gollub, R. L., Benson, E. S., Searl, M., Goff, D. C., Halpern, E., Saper, C., & Rauch, S. L. (2000). Schizophenia subjects show aberrant fMRI activation of dorsolateral prefrontal cortex and basal ganglia during working memory performance. *Biological Psychiatry, 48,* 99–109.

Maquet, P., Peigneux, P., Laureys, S., Boly, M., Dang-Vu, T., Desseilles, M., & Cleeremans, A. (2003). Memory processing during human sleep as assessed functional neuroimaging. *Revue Neurologique, 159(11),* 6S27–6S29.

Marcia, J. E. (2002). Identity and psychosocial development in adulthood. *Identity, 2(1),* 7–28.

Markon, K. E., Krueger, R. F., Bouchard, T. J., & Gottesman, I. I. (2002). Normal and abnormal personality traits: Evidence for genetic and environmental relationships in the Minnesota Study of Twins Reared Apart. *Journal of Personality, 70(5),* 661–693.

Markovitz, P. J. (2004). Recent trends in the pharmacotherapy of personality disorders. *Journal of Personality Disorders, 18(1),* 99–101.

Markowitz, J. C. (2003). Interpersonal psychotherapy for chronic depression. *Journal of Clinical Psychology, 59(8),* 847–858.

Marks, D. F. (1990). Comprehensive commentary, insightful criticism. *Skeptical Inquirer, 14,* 413–418.

Markus, H. R., & Kitayama, S. (1998). The cultural psychology of personality. *Journal of Cross-Cultural Psychology, 29,* 63–87.

Markus, H. R., & Kitayama, S. (2003). Culture, self, and the reality of the social. *Psychological Inquiry, 14*(3–4), 277–283.

Marshall, D. S. (1971). Sexual behavior in Mangaia. In D. S. Marshall & R. C. Suggs (Eds.), *Human sexual behavior* (pp. 103–162). Englewood Cliffs, NJ: Prentice Hall.

Martin, C. L., & Ruble, D. (2004). Children's search for gender cues: Cognitive perspectives on gender development. *Current Directions in Psychological Science, 13*(2), 67–70.

Martin, J. L. R., Barbanoj, M. J., Schlaepfer, T. E., Thompson, E., Perez, V., & Kulisevsky, J. (2003). Repetitive transcranial magnetic stimulation for the treatment of depression: Systematic review and meta-analysis. *British Journal of Psychiatry, 182*(6), 480–491.

Martin, S. E., Snyder, L. B., Hamilton, M., Fleming-Milici, F., Slater, M. D., Stacy, A., Chen, M., & Grube, J. W. (2002). Alcohol advertising and youth. *Alcoholism: Clinical & Experimental Research, 26*(6), 900–906.

Martindale, J. L., & Palmes, G. K. (2005). Troubled children and youth: Turning problems into opportunities. *Journal of the American Academy of Child & Adolescent Psychiatry, 44*(5), 503–504.

Martins, S. S., Mazzotti, G., & Chilcoat, H. D. (2005). Trends in ecstasy use in the United States from 1995 to 2001: Comparison with marijuana users and association with other drug use. *Experimental and Clinical Psychopharmacology, 13*(3), 244–252.

Maslow, A. H. (1954). *Motivation and personality.* New York: Harper & Row.

Maslow, A. H. (1970). *Motivation and personality* (2nd ed.). New York: Harper & Row.

Maslow, A. H. (1999). *Toward a psychology of being* (3rd ed.). New York: Wiley.

Mason, P. T., & Kreger, R. (1998). *Stop walking on eggshells: Taking your life back when someone you care about has borderline personality disorder.* New York: New Harbinger Publishers.

Mast, M. (2002). Dominance as expresses and inferred through speaking time: A meta-analysis. *Human Communication Research, 28*(3), 420–450.

Masten, A. S. (1998). Resilience comes of age: Reflections on the past and outlook for the next generation of research. In M. D. Glantz, J. Johnson, & L. Huffman (Eds.), *Resilience and development: Positive life adaptations.* New York: Plenum.

Masten, A. S. (2001). Ordinary magic: Resilience processes in development. *American Psychologist, 56,* 227–238.

Masten A. S., & Coatsworth, J. D. (1998). The development of competence in favorable and unfavorable environments. *American Psychologist, 53*(2), 205–220.

Masters, W. H., & Johnson, V. E. (1961). Orgasm, anatomy of the female. In A. Ellis & A. Abarbonel (Eds.). *Encyclopedia of Sexual Behavior,* Vol. 2. New York: Hawthorn.

Masters, W. H., & Johnson, V. E. (1966). *Human sexual response.* Boston: Little, Brown.

Masters, W. H., & Johnson, V. E. (1970). *Human sexual inadequacy.* Boston: Little, Brown.

Mathews, A., & MacLeod, C. (2005). Cognitive vulnerability to emotional disorders. *Annual Review of Clinical Psychology, 1,* 167–195.

Matlin, M. W. (2003). From menarche to menopause: Misconceptions about women's reproductive lives. *Psychology Science, 45*(Suppl2), 106–122.

Matlin, M. W. (2005). *Cognition* (6th ed.). Hoboken, NJ: Wiley.

Matlin, M. W., & Foley, H. J. (1997). *Sensation and perception* (4th ed.). Boston: Allyn and Bacon.

Matsumoto, D. (1992). More evidence for the universality of a contempt expression. *Motivation and Emotion, 16,* 363–368.

Matsumoto, D. (2000). *Culture and psychology: People around the world.* Belmont, CA: Wadsworth.

Matsumoto, D., & Juang, L. (2004). *Culture and psychology* (3rd ed.). Belmont, CA: Wadsworth.

Matsumoto, D., & Kupperbusch, C. (2001). Idiocentric and allocentric differences in emotional expression, experience, and the coherence between expression and experience. *Asian Journal of Social Psychology, 4*(2), 113–131.

Matusov, E., & Hayes, R. (2000). Sociocultural critique of Piaget and Vygotsky. *New Ideas in Psychology, 18*(2–3), 215–239.

Matuszek, P. A. C. (2000). A biofeedback-enhanced stress management program for the fire service. *Dissertation Abstracts International: Section B: The Sciences & Engineering, 60*(7–B), 3212.

May, P. A., & Gossage, J. P. (2001). Estimating the prevalence of fetal alcohol syndrome: A summary. *Alcohol Research & Health, 25*(3), 159–167.

Mayers, A. G., Baldwin, D. S., Dyson, R., Middleton, R. W., & Mustapha, A. (2003). Use of St John's wort (Hypericum perforatum L) in members of a depression self-help organization: A 12–week open prospective pilot study using the HADS scale. *Primary Care Psychiatry, 9*(1), 15–20.

Maynard, A. E., & Greenfield, P. M. (2003). Implicit cognitive development in cultural tools and children: Lessons from Maya Mexico. *Cognitive Development, 18*(4), 489–510.

Mazur, A., & Booth, A. (1998). Testosterone and dominance in men. *Behavioral and Brain Sciences, 21,* 353–363.

McAllister-Williams, R. H., & Rugg, M. D. (2002). Effects of repeated cortisol administration on brain potential correlates of episodic memory retrieval. *Psychopharmacology, 160*(1), 74–83.

McCabe, D. L. (2001). *Student cheating in American high schools. Center for Academic Integrity.* [On-line]. Available: http://www.academicintegrity.org.

McCabe, M. P., & Ricciardelli, L. A. (2003). Body image and strategies to lose weight and increase muscle among boys and girls. *Health Psychology, 22*(1), 39–46.

McCarley, J. S., Kramer, A. F., Colcombe, A. M., & Scialfa, C. T. (2004). Priming of pop-out in visual search: A comparison of young and old adults. *Aging, Neuropsychology, & Cognition, 11*(1), 80–88.

McCarthy, M. M., Auger, A. P., & Perrot-Sinal, T. S. (2002). Getting excited about GABA and sex differences in the brain. *Trends in Neurosciences, 25*(6), 307–312.

McCartt, A. T., Rohrbaugh, J. W., Hammer, M. C., & Fuller, S. Z. (2000). Factors associated with falling asleep at the wheel among long-distance truck drivers. *Accident Analysis and Prevention, 32*(4), 493–504.

McClelland, D. C. (1958). Risk-taking in children with high and low need for achievement. In J. W. Atkinson (Ed.), *Motives in fantasy, action, and society.* Princeton, NJ: Van Nostrand.

McClelland, D. C. (1987). Characteristics of successful entrepreneurs. *Journal of Creative Behavior, 3,* 219–233.

McClelland, D. C. (1993). Intelligence is not the best predictor of job performance. *Current Directions in Psychological Science, 2,* 5–6.

McClelland, J. L. (1995). Constructive memory and memory distortions: A parallel-distributed processing approach. In D. L. Schachter (Ed.), *Memory distortions: How minds, brains, and societies reconstruct the past* (pp. 69–90). Cambridge: Harvard University Press.

McConkey, K. M. (1995). Hypnosis, memory, and the ethics of uncertainty. *Australian Psychologist, 30,* 1–10.

McCormack, L., & Mellor, D. (2002). The role of personality in leadership: An application of the Five-Factor Model in the Australian military. *Military Psychology, 14*(3), 179–197.

McCrae, R. R. (2001). Facts and interpretations of personality trait stability: A reply to Quackenbush. *Theory & Psychology, 11(6)*, 837–844.

McCrae, R. R. (2004). Human nature and culture: A trait perspective. *Journal of Research in Personality, 38*(1), 3–14.

McCrae, R. R., & Costa, P. T. Jr. (1990). *Personality in adulthood*. New York: Guilford Press.

McCrae, R. R., & Costa, P. T. Jr. (1999). A five-factor theory of personality. In L. A. Pervin, & O. P. John (Eds.), *Handbook of personality: Theory and research*. New York: Guilford Press.

McCrae, R. R., & Costa, P. T. Jr., de Lirna, M. P., Simoes, A., Ostendorf, F., Angleitner, A., Marusic, I., Bratko, D., Caprara, G. V., Barbaranelli, C., Chae, J. H., & Piedmont, R. L. (1999). Age differences in personality across the adult life span: Parallels in five cultures. *Developmental Psychology, 35*, 466–477.

McCrae, R. R., Costa, P. T. Jr., Hrebícková, M., Urbánek, T., Martin, T. A., Oryol, V. E., Rukavishnikov, A. A., & Senin, I. G. (2004a). Age differences in personality traits across cultures: Self-report and observer perspectives. *European Journal of Personality, 18*(2), 143–157.

McCrae, R. R., Costa, P. T. Jr., Martin, T. A., Oryol, V. E., Rukavishnikov, A. A., Senin, I. G., Hrebícková, M., & Urbánek, T. (2004b). Consensual validation of personality traits across cultures. *Journal of Research in Personality, 38*(2), 179–201.

McCrae, R. R., Costa, P. T., Jr., Ostendorf, F., Angleitner, A., Hrebickova, M., Avia, M. D., Sanz, J., Sanchez-Bernardos, M. L., Kusdil, M. E., Woodfield, R., Saunders, P. R., & Smith, P. B. (2000). Nature over nurture: Temperament, personality, and life span development. *Journal of Personality & Social Psychology, 78*(1), 173–186.

McDonald, J. W., Liu, X. Z., Qu, Y., Liu, S., Mickey, S. K., Turetsky, D., Gottlieb, D. I., & Choi, D. W. (1999). Transplanted embryonic stem cells survive, differentiate, and promote recovery in injured rat spinal cord. *Nature & Medicine, 5*, 1410–1412.

McDonald, M. (2001, January 8). Psst! Want a hot tip? Try a crystal ball. *U.S. News & World Report*, 34.

McDougall, W. (1908). *Social psychology*. New York: Putnam's Sons.

McGaugh, J. L., & Roozendaal, B. (2002). Role of adrenal stress hormones in forming lasting memories in the brain. *Current Opinion in Neurobiology, 12(2)*, 205–210.

McGhie, A., & Chapman, H. (1961). Disorders of attention and perception in early schizophrenia. *British Journal of Medical Psychology, 34*, 103–116.

McGrath, M.G., & Casey, E. (2002). Forensic psychiatry and the Internet: Practical perspectives on sexual predators and obsessional harassers in cyberspace. *Journal of the American Academy of Psychiatry & the Law, 30(1)*, 81–94.

McGrath, P. (2002). Qualitative findings on the experience of end-of-life care for hematological malignancies. *American Journal of Hospice & Palliative Care, 19(2)*, 103–111.

McGregor, D. (1960). *The human side of enterprise*. New York: McGraw-Hill.

McGue, M., Bouchard, T. J., Iacono, W. G., & Lykken, D. T. (1993). Behavioral genetics of cognitive ability: A life-span perspective. In R. Plomin & G. McClearn (Eds.), *Nature, nurture, and psychology*. Washington, DC: American Psychological Association.

McKay, D., Gavigan, C. A., & Kulchycky, S. (2004). Social skills and sex-role functioning in borderline personality disorder: Relationship to self-mutilating behavior. *Cognitive Behaviour Therapy, 33*(1), 27–35.

McKay, M., Davis, M, & Fanning, P. (1997). *Thoughts & feelings: Taking control of your moods and your life*. Oakland, CA: New Harbinger Publications, Inc.

McKee, P., & Barber, C. E. (2001). Plato's theory of aging. *Journal of Aging & Identity, 6(2)*, 93–104.

McKellar, P. (1972). Imagery from the standpoint of introspection. In P. W. Sheehan (Ed.), *The function and nature of imagery*. New York: Academic Press.

McKelvie, S. J., & Drumheller, A. (2001). The availability heuristic with famous names: A replication. *Perceptual & Motor Skills, 92*(2), 507–516.

McKim, W. A. (2002). *Drugs and behavior: An introduction to behavioral pharmacology* (5th ed). Englewood Cliffs, NJ: Prentice Hall.

McLoyd, V. C. (1998). Socio-economic disadvantage and child development. *American Psychologist, 53*, 185–204.

McMahon, J. A. (2002). An explanation for normal and anomalous drawing ability and some implications for research on perception and imagery. *Visual Arts Research, 28*(1,Issue55), 38–52.

McNally, R. J. (2004). The science and folklore of traumatic amnesia. *Clinical Psychology: Science & Practice, 11*(1), 29–33.

McPherson, M. B., Kearney, P., & Plax, T. G. (2003). The dark side of instruction: Teacher anger as classroom norm violations. *Journal of Applied Communication Research, 31*(1), 76–90.

Medina, J. J. (1996). *The clock of ages: Why we age*. Cambridge, MA: Cambridge University Press.

Meeus, W., & Raaijmakers, Q. (1989). Autoritätsgehorsam in Experimenten des Milgram-Typs: Eine Forschungsübersicht. / Obedience to authority in Milgram-type studies: A research review. *Zeitschrift für Sozialpsychologie, 20*(2), 70–85.

Mehrabian, A. (1968). A relationship of attitude to seated posture orientation and distance. *Journal of Personality and Social Psychology, 10*, 26–30.

Mehrabian, A. (1971). *Nonverbal communication*. Nebraska Symposium on Motivation, 107–161.

Meltzer, L. (2004). Resilience and learning disabilities: Research on internal and external protective dynamics. *Learning Disabilities Research & Practice,19*(1), 1–2.

Meltzoff, A. N., & Moore, M. K. (1977). Imitation of facial and manual gestures by human neonates. *Science, 198*, 75–78.

Meltzoff, A. N., & Moore, M. K. (1985). Cognitive foundations and social functions of imitation and intermodal representation in infancy. In J. Mehler & R. Fox (Eds.), *Neonate cognition: Beyond the blooming buzzing confusion*. Hillsdale, NJ: Erlbaum.

Meltzoff, A. N., & Moore, M. K. (1994). Imitation, memory, and the representation of persons. *Infant Behavior and Development, 17*, 83–99.

Melzack, R. (1999). Pain and stress: A new perspective. In R. J. Gatchel & D. C. Turk (Eds.), *Psychosocial factors in pain: Critical perspectives*. New York: Guilford Press.

Melzack, R., & Wall, P. D. (1965). Pain mechanisms: A new theory. *Science, 150*, 971–979.

Mendrek, A., Kiehl, K. A., Smith, A. M., Irwin, D., Forster, B. B., & Liddle, P. F. (2005). Dysfunction of a distributed neural circuitry in schizophrenia patients during a working-memory performance. *Psychological Medicine, 35*(2), 187–196.

Meston, C. M., & Frohlich, P. F. (2003). Love at first fright: Partner salience moderates roller-coaster-induced excitation transfer. *Archives of Sexual Behavior, 32*(6), 537–544.

Metcalf, P., & Huntington, R. (1991). *Celebrations of death: The anthropology of mortuary ritual* (2nd ed.). Cambridge, England: Cambridge University Press.

Meyer, I. H. (2003). Prejudice, social stress, and mental health in lesbian, gay, and bisexual populations: Conceptual issues and research evidence. *Psychological Bulletin, 129*(5), 674–697.

Meyer, R. G., & Salmon, P. (1988). *Abnormal psychology* (2nd ed.). Boston: Allyn & Bacon.

Michael, R., Gagnon, J., Laumann, E., & Kolata, G. (1994). *Sex in America*. Boston: Little, Brown.

Migueles, M, & Garcia-Bajos, E. (1999). Recall, recognition, and confidence patterns in eyewitness testimony. *Applied Cognitive Psychology, 13*, 257–268.

Miles, D. R., & Carey, G. (1997). Genetic and environmental architecture on human aggression. *Journal of Personality and Social Psychology, 72*, 207–217.

Milgram, S. (1963). Behavioral study of obedience. *Journal of Abnormal and Social Psychology, 67*, 371–378.

Milgram, S. (1974). *Obedience to authority: An experimental view*. New York: Harper & Row.

Millar, M. (2002). Effects of a guilt induction and guilt reduction on door in the face. *Communication Research, 29*(6), 666–680.

Miller, B., Wood, B., Balkansky, A., Mercader, J., & Panger, M. (2006). *Anthropology*. Boston, MA: Allyn & Bacon/Longman.

Miller, G. (2004). Brain cells may pay the price for a bad night's sleep. *Science, 306*(5699), 1126.

Miller, G. A. (1956). The magical number seven, plus or minus two: Some limits on our capacity for processing information. *Psychological Review, 63*, 81–97.

Miller, J. G., & Bersoff, D. M. (1998). The role of liking in perceptions of the moral responsibility to help: A cultural perspective. *Journal of Experimental Social Psychology, 34*, 443–469.

Miller, L. C., & Fishkin, S. A. (1997). On the dynamics of human bonding and reproductive success: Seeking windows on the adapted-for-human-environmental interface. In J. A. Simpson & D. T. Kenrick (Eds.). *Evolutionary social psychology* (pp. 197–236). Mahwah, NJ: Erlbaum.

Miller, M., & Kantrowitz, B. (1999, January 25). Unmasking Sybil: A reexamination of the most famous psychiatric patient in history. *Newsweek*, pp. 11–16.

Millon, T. (2004). *Masters of the mind: Exploring the story of mental illness from ancient times to the new millennium*. Hoboken, NJ: Wiley.

Mills, T. C., Paul, J., Stall, R., Pollack, L., Canchola, J., Chang, Y. J., Moskowitz, J. T., & Catania, J. A. (2004). Distress and depression in men who have sex with men: The urban men's health study. *American Journal of Psychiatry, 161*(2), 278–285.

Milton, J., & Wiseman, R. (1999). Does psi exist? Lack of replication of an anomalous process of information transfer. *Psychological Bulletin, 125*, 387–391.

Milton, J., & Wiseman, R. (2001). Does psi exist? Reply to Storm and Ertel 2000. *Psychological Bulletin, 127*(3), 434–438.

Mineka, S., & Oehman, A. (2002). Phobias and preparedness: The selective, automatic, and encapsulated nature of fear. *Biological Psychiatry, 51*(9), 927–937.

Mingo, C., Herman, C. J., & Jasperse, M. (2000). Women's stories: Ethnic variations in women's attitudes and experiences of menopause, hysterectomy, and hormone replacement therapy. *Journal of Women's Health and Gender Based Medicine, 9*, S27–S38.

Miracle, T. S., Miracle, A. W., & Baumeister, R. F. (2003). *Human sexuality: Meeting your basic needs*. Upper Saddle River, NJ: Pearson Education, Inc.

Miracle, T. S., Miracle, A. W., & Baumeister, R. F. (2006). *Human sexuality: Meeting your basic needs (2nd ed.)*. Upper Saddle River, NJ: Pearson Education, Inc.

Mischel, W., & Shoda, Y. (1999). Integrating dispositions and processing dynamics within a unified theory of personality: The cognitive-affective personality system. In L. A. Pervin, & O. P. John (Eds.), *Handbook of personality: Theory and research*. New York: Guilford Press.

Mita, T. H., Dermer, M., & Knight, J. (1977). Reversed facial images and the mere-exposure hypothesis. *Journal of Personality & Social Psychology, 35*(8), 597–601.

Mitchell, E., Sachs, A., & Tu, J. I-Chin (1997, September 29). Teaching feelings 101. *Time*, p. 62.

Mitchell, R. (2003). Ideological reflections on the DSM-IV-R (or pay no attention to that man behind the curtain, Dorothy!). *Child & Youth Care Forum, 32*(5), 281–298.

Mitchell, S. A. (2002). Psychodynamics, homosexuality, and the question of pathology. *Studies in Gender & Sexuality, 3*(1), 3–21.

Mitchell, T. W., Mufson, E. J., Schneider, J. A., Cochran, E. J., Nissanov, J., Han, L., Bienias, J. L., Lee, V. M., Trojanowski, J. Q., Bennett, D. A., & Arnold, S. E. (2002). Parahippocampal tau pathology in healthy aging, mild cognitive impairment, and early Alzhiemer's disease. *Annals of Neurology, 51*(2), 182–189

Mittag, O., & Maurischat, C. (2004). Die Cook-Medley Hostility Scale (Ho-Skala) im Vergleich zu den Inhaltsskalen "Zynismus", "Ärger" sowie "Typ A" aus dem MMPI-2: Zur zukünftigen Operationalisierung von Feindseligkeit. / A comparison of the Cook-Medley Hostility Scale (Ho-scale) and the content scales "cynicism," "anger," and "type A" out of the MMPI-2: On the future assessment of hostility. *Zeitschrift für Medizinische Psychologie, 13*(1), 7–12.

Moffitt, T. E., Caspi, A., Harrington, H., & Milne, B. J. (2002). Males on the life-course-persistent and adolescence-limited antisocial pathways: Follow-up at age 26 years. *Development & Psychopathology, 14*(1), 179–207.

Mokdad, A. H., Ford, E. S., Bowman, B. A., Dietz, W. H., Frank, V., Bales, V. S., & Marks, J. S. (2003). Prevalence of obesity, diabetes, and obesity-related health risk factors. *Journal of the American Medical Association, 289*, 76–79.

Mokdad, A. H., Marks, J. S., Stroup, D. F., & Gerberding, L. (2004). Actual causes of death in the United States, 2000. *JAMA: Journal of the American Medical Association, 291*(10), 1238–1245.

Molsberger, A. F., Mau, J., Pawelec, D. B., & Winkler, J. (2002). Does acupuncture improve the orthopedic management of chronic low back pain: A randomized, blinded, controlled trial with 3 months follow up. *Pain, 99*(3), 579–587.

Moneta, G. B., & Siu, C. M. Y. (2002). Trait intrinsic and extrinsic motivations, academic performance, and creativity in Hong Kong college students. *Journal of College Student Development, 43*(5), 664–683.

Money, J. (1985a). Sexual reformation and counter-reformation in law and medicine. *Medicine and Law, 4*, 479–488.

Money, J., & Ehrhardt, A. A. (1972). *Man and woman, boy and girl*. Baltimore: The Johns Hopkins University Press.

Money, J., Prakasam, K. S., & Joshi, V. N. (1991). Semen-conservation doctrine from ancient Ayurvedic to modern sexological theory. *American Journal of Psychotherapy, 45*, 9–13.

Mong, J. A., & Pfaff, D. W. (2003). Hormonal and genetic influences underlying arousal as it drives sex and aggression in animal and human brains. *Neurobiology of Aging, 24*(Suppl1), S83–S88.

Monin, B. (2003). The warm glow heuristic: When liking leads to familiarity. *Journal of Personality & Social Psychology, 85*(6), 1035–1048.

Montaldo, C. (2005). Judge Delucchi upholds Peterson's death sentence. [Online]. Available: http://crime.about.com/b/a/154141.htm

Monte, C. F., & Sollod, R.N., (2003). *Beneath the mask: An introduction to theories of personality*. Hoboken, NJ: Wiley.

Monteleone, P., Martiadis, V., Fabrazzo, M., Serritella, C., & Maj, M. (2003). Ghrelin and leptin responses to food ingestion in bulimia nervosa: Implications for binge-eating and compensatory behaviours. *Psychological Medicine, 33*(8), 1387–1394.

Montes, L. G. A., Uribe, M. P. O., Sotres, J. C., & Martin, G. H. (2003). Treatment of primary insomnia with melatonin: A double-blind, placebo controlled, crossover study. *Journal of Psychiatry & Neuroscience, 28*(3), 191–196.

Montgomery, G. H., Weltz, C. R., Seltz, M., & Bovbjerg, D. H. (2002). Brief presurgery hypnosis reduces distress and pain in excisional breast biopsy patients. *International Journal of Clinical & Experimental Hypnosis, 50(1),* 17–32.

Montuori, A., & Fahim, U. (2004). Cross-cultural encounter as an opportunity for personal growth. *Journal of Humanistic Psychology. 44*(2), 243–265.

Moore, M. M. (1998). The science of sexual signaling. In G. C. Brannigan, E. R. Allgeier, & A. R. Allgeier (Eds.), *The sex scientists* (pp. 61–75). New York: Longman.

Moore, R. Y. (1997). Circadian rhythms: Basic neurobiology and clinical applications. *Annual Review of Medicine, 48,* 253–266.

Moore, S., Grunberg, L., & Greenberg, E. (2004). Repeated downsizing contact: The effects of similar and dissimilar layoff experiences on work and well-being outcomes. *Journal of Occupational Health Psychology, 9*(3), 247–257.

Morelli, G. A., Oppenheim, D., Rogoff, B., & Goldsmith, D. (1992). Cultural variations in infant sleeping arrangements: Questions of independence. *Developmental Psychology, 28,* 604–613.

Moretti, R., Torre, P., Antonello, R. M., & Cazzato, G. (2001). Fronto-temporal dementia versus Alzheimer disease. *Archives of Gerontology & Geriatrics, 7,* 273–278.

Morgan, M. J., McFie, L., Fleetwood, L. H., & Robinson, J. A. (2002). Ecstasy (MDMA): Are the psychological problems associated with its use reversed by prolonged abstinence? *Psychopharmacology, 159(3),* 294–303.

Morris, J. S., Frith, C. D., Perrett, D. L., Rowland, D., Young, A. W., Calder, A. J., & Dolan, R. J. (1996). A differential neural response in the human amygdala to fearful and happy expressions. *Nature, 383,* 812–815.

Morris, R. (1994). *New worlds from fragments.* Boulder, CO: Westview.

Morrison, C., & Westman, A. S. (2001). Women report being more likely than men to model their relationships after what they have seen on TV. *Psychological Reports, 89*(2), 252–254.

Morrison, M. F., & Tweedy, K. (2000). Effects of estrogen on mood and cognition in aging women. *Psychiatric Annals, 30*(2), 113–119.

Moss, D. (2004). Biofeedback. *Applied Psychophysiology & Biofeedback, 29*(1), 75–78.

Mueller, C. M., & Dweck, C. S. (1998). Praise for intelligence can undermine children's motivation and performance. *Journal of Personality & Social Psychology, 75,* 33–52.

Mueser, K. T., Salyers, M. P., Rosenberg, S. D., Goodman, L. A., Essock, S. M., Osher, F. C., Swartz, M. S., Butterfield, M. I., & 5 Site Health and Risk Study Research Committee. (2004). Interpersonal trauma and posttraumatic stress disorder in patients with severe mental illness: Demographic, clinical, and health correlates. *Schizophrenia Bulletin, 30*(1), 45–57.

Mulac, A., Bradac, J. J., & Gibbons, P. (2001). Empirical support for the gender-as-culture hypothesis: An intercultural analysis of male/female language differences. *Human Communication Research, 27*(1), 121–152.

Mulilis, J-P., Duval, T. S., & Rombach, D. (2001). Personal responsibility for tornado preparedness: Commitment or choice? *Journal of Applied Social Psychology, 31,* 1659–1688.

Murakami, K., & Hayashi, T. (2002). Interaction between mind-heart and gene. *Journal of International Society of Life Information Science, 20(1),* 122–126.

Muris, P., Merckelbach, H., Gadet, B., & Moulaert, V. (2000). Fears, worries, and scary dreams in 4- to 12-year-old children: Their content, developmental pattern, and origins. *Journal of Clinical Child Psychology, 29*(1), 43–52.

Murray, B. (1995, October). Americans dream about food, Brazilians dream about sex. *APA Monitor,* p. 30.

Murray, H. A. (1938). *Explorations in personality.* New York: Oxford University Press.

Myers, L. B., & Vetere, A. (2002). Adult romantic attachment styles and health-related measures. *Psychology, Health & Medicine, 7(2),* 175–180.

Myerson, J., Rank, M. R., Raines, F. Q., & Schnitzler, M. A. (1998). Race and general cognitive ability: The myth of diminishing returns to education. *Psychological Science, 9,* 139–142.

Naglieri, J. A., & Ronning, M. E. (2000). Comparison of White, African American, Hispanic, and Asian children on the Naglieri Nonverbal Ability Test. *Psychological Assessment, 12*(3), 328–334.

Nahas, G. G., Frick, H. C., Lattimer, J. K., Latour, C., & Harvey, D. (2002). Pharmacokinetics of THC in brain and testis, male gametotoxicity and premature apoptosis of spermatozoa. *Human Psychopharmacology: Clinical & Experimental., 17*(2), 103–113.

Nakajima, S., & Masaki, T. (2004). Taste aversion learning induced forced swimming in rats. *Physiology & Behavior, 80*(5), 623–628.

Napolitane, C. (1997). *Living and loving after divorce.* New York: Signet.

Nathan, R., Rollinson, L., Harvey, K., & Hill, J. (2003). The Liverpool violence assessment: An investigator-based measure of serious violence. *Criminal Behaviour & Mental Health, 13*(2), 106–120.

National Center for Health Statistics. (2004). *New report examines Americans' health behaviors.* [On-line]. Available: http://www.cdc.gov/nchs/pressroom/04facts/healthbehaviors.htm

National Institute of Mental Health. (1999). *Facts about anxiety disorders.* [On-line]. Available: http://www.nimh.nih.gov/anxiety/adfacts.cfm

National Institute on Drug Abuse (2002). *Club drugs: Community drug alert bulletin.* [On-line]. Available: http://www.drugabuse.gov/ClubAlert/Clubdrugalert.html.

National Institute on Drug Abuse. (2005). *NIDA infofacts: Club drugs.* [On-line]. Available: http://www.nida.nih.gov/infofacts/Clubdrugs.html.

National Research Council. (2002). *The polygraph and lie detection.* Retrieved April 13, 2004 from the National Academies Web site. [On-line]. Available: http://www.nap.edu/books/0309084369/html/

National Sleep Foundation (2001). *Less fun, less sleep, more work: An American portrait.* [On-line]. Available: http://www.sleepfoundation.org/PressArchivs/lessfun_lesssleep.html.

National Sleep Foundation. (2004). *Myths and facts about sleep.* [On-line]. Available: http://www.sleepfoundation. org/

Nayda, R. (2002). Influences on registered nurses' decision-making in cases of suspected child abuse. *Child Abuse Review, 11(3),* 168–178.

Neale, J. M., Oltmanns, T. F., & Winters, K. C. (1983). Recent developments in the assessment and conceptualization of schizophrenia. *Behavioral Assessment, 5,* 33–54.

Neese, R. M. (2000). Is depression an adaptation? *Archives of General Psychiatry, 57,* 14–20.

Negrotti, A., Secchi, C., & Gentilucci, M. (2005). Effects of disease progression and L-dopa therapy on the control of reaching-grasping in Parkinson's disease. *Neuropsychologia, 43*(3), 450–459.

Neher, A. (1991). Maslow's theory of motivation: A critique. *Journal of Humanistic Psychology, 31,* 89–112.

Neisser, U. (1967). *Cognitive psychology.* New York: Appleton-Century-Crofts.

Neisser, U. (1998). Introduction: Rising test scores and what they mean. In U. Neisser (Ed.), *The rising curve: Long-term gains in IQ and related measures.* Washington, DC: American Psychological Association.

Nelson, G. (2006). *The psychology of prejudice* (2nd ed.). Boston, MA: Allyn & Bacon/Longman.

Nelson, G., Chandrashekar, J., Hoon, M. A., Feng, L., Zhao, G., Ryba, N. J. P., & Zuker, C. S. (2002). An amino-acid taste receptor. *Nature, 416,* 199–202.

Nelson, R. J., & Chiavegatto, S. (2001). Molecular basis of aggression. *Trends in Neurosciences, 24(12),* 713–719.

Neria, Y., Bromet, E. J., Sievers, S., Lavelle, J., & Fochtmann, L. J. (2002). Trauma exposure and posttraumatic stress disorder in psychosis: Findings from a first-admission cohort. *Journal of Consulting & Clinical Psychology, 70(1),* 246–251.

Neto, F., & Furnham, A. (2005). Gender-role portrayals in children's television advertisements. *International Journal of Adolescence & Youth, 12(1–2),* 69–90.

Neubauer, A. C. (2000). Physiological approaches to human intelligence: A review. *Psychologische Beitrage, 42(2),* 161–173.

Neubauer, A. C., Grabner, R. H., Freudenthaler, H. H., Beckmann, J. F., & Guthke, J. (2004). Intelligence and individual differences in becoming neurally efficient. *Acta Psychologica, 116(1),* 55–74.

Neugarten, B. L., Havighurst, R. J., & Tobin, S. S. (1968). The measurement of life satisfaction. *Journal of Gerontology,16,*134–143.

Neumann, K., Preibisch, C., Euler, H. A., von Gudenberg, A. W., Lanfermann, H., Gall, V., & Giraud, A-L. (2005). Cortical plasticity associated with stuttering therapy. *Journal of Fluency Disorders, 30(1),* 23–39.

Neumark-Sztainer, D., Wall, M. M., Story, M., & Perry, C. L. (2003). Correlates of unhealthy weight-control behaviors among adolescents: *Implications for prevention programs. Health Psychology, 22(1),* 88–98.

Neuringer, A., Deiss, C., & Olson, G. (2000). Reinforced variability and operant learning. *Journal of Experimental Psychology: Animal Behavior Processes, 26(1),* 98–111.

Newman, L. S., Duff, K., & Baumeister, R. (1997). A new look at defensive projection: Thought suppression, accessibility, and biased person perception. *Journal of Personality and Social Psychology, 72,* 980–1001.

Newman, R. (2001). Professional point: Not a question of "for" or "against." *APA Monitor on Psychology, 32.* [On-line]. Available: http://www.apa.org/monitor/mar01/pp.html

Newton-John, T. O., Spence, S. H., & Schotte, D. (1995). Cognitive-behavioral therapy versus EMG biofeedback in the treatment of chronic low back pain. *Behaviour Research & Therapy, 33,* 691–697.

Nicholls, M. E. R., Searle, D. A., & Bradshaw, J. L. (2004). Read my lips: Asymmetries in the visual expression and perception of speech revealed through the McGurk Effect. *Psychological Science, 15(2),* 138–141.

Nickerson, R. (1998). Confirmation bias: A ubiquitous phenomenon in many guises. *Review of General Psychology, 2,* 175–220.

Nickerson, R. S., & Adams, M. J. (1979). Long-term memory for a common object. *Cognitive Psychology, 11,* 287–307.

Nisbett, R. E., Peng, K., Choi, L., & Norenzayan, A. (2000). Culture and systems of thought: Holistic vs. analytic cognition. *Psychological Review, 21,* 34–45.

Nishimoto, R. (1988). A cross-cultural analysis of psychiatric symptom expression using Langer's twenty-two item index. *Journal of Sociology and Social Welfare, 15,* 45–62.

Noble, E. P. (2000). Addiction and its reward process through polymorphisms of the D-sub-2 dopamine receptor gene: A review. *European Psychiatry, 15(2),* 79–89.

Noël, M., Désert, M., Aubrun, A., & Seron, X. (2001). Involvement of short-term memory in complex mental calculation. *Memory & Cognition, 29(1),* 34–42.

Nolen-Hoeksema, S., Larson, J., & Grayson, C. (2000). Explaining the gender difference in depressive symptoms. *Journal of Personality and Social Psychology, 77,* 1061–1072.

Nordhus, I. H., & Pallesen, S. (2003). Psychological treatment of late-life anxiety: An empirical review. *Journal of Consulting & Clinical Psychology, 71(4),* 643–651.

Norenzayan, A., & Nisbett, R. E. (2000). Culture and causal cognition. *Current Directions in Psychological Science, 9(4),* 132–135.

Núñez, J. P., & de Vicente, F. (2004). Unconscious learning. Conditioning to subliminal visual stimuli. *Spanish Journal of Psychology, 7(1),* 13–28.

O'Connor, D. B., Archer, J., Hair, W. M., & Wu, F. C. W. (2002). Exogenous testosterone, aggression, and mood in eugonadal and hypogonadal men. *Physiology & Behavior, 75(4),* 557–566.

O'Flynn, D. (2001). Approaching employment. Mental health, work projects and the Care Programme Approach. *Psychiatric Bulletin, 25(5),* 169–171.

O'Keefe, D. J., & Hale, S. L. (2001). An odds-ratio-based meta-analysis of research on the door-in-the-face influence strategy. *Communication Reports, 14(1),* 31–38.

O'Leary, D. S., Block, R. I., Flaum, M., Schultz, S. K., Ponto, L. L. Boles, Watkins, G. L., Hurtig, R. R., Andreasen, N. C., & Hichwa, R. D. (2000). Acute marijuana effects on rCBF and cognition: A PET study. *Neuroreport: For Rapid Communication of Neuroscience Research, 11(17),* 3835–3841.

O'Sullivan, M. (2003). The fundamental attribution error in detecting deception: The boy-who-cried-wolf effect. *Personality & Social Psychology Bulletin, 29(10),* 1316–1327.

Oakes, M. A., & Hyman, I. E., Jr. (2001). The role of the self in false memory creation. *Journal of Aggression, Maltreatment & Trauma, 4(2),* 87–103.

Obeso, J. A., Rodriguez-Oroz, M., Marin, C., Alonso, F., Zamarbide, I., Lanciego, J. L., & Rodriguez-Diaz, M. (2004). The origin of motor fluctuations in Parkinson's disease: Importance of dopaminergic innervation and basal ganglia circuits. *Neurology, 62(1,Suppl1),* S17–S30.

Oeztuerk, L., Tufan, Y., & Gueler, F. (2002). Self-reported traffic accidents and sleepiness in a professional group of Turkish drivers. *Sleep & Hypnosis, 4(3),* 106–110.

Ogilvie, R. D., Wilkinson, R. T., & Allison, S. (1989). The detection of sleep onset: Behavioral, physiological, and subjective convergence. *Sleep, 12(5),* 458–474.

Ohayon, M. M. (1997). Prevalence of DSM-IV diagnostic criteria of insomnia: Distinguishing insomnia related to mental disorders from sleep disorders. *Journal of Psychiatric Research, 31,* 333–346.

Ohayon, M. M., & Schatzberg, A. F. (2002). Prevalence of depressive episodes with psychotic features in the general population. *American Journal of Psychiatry,159(11),*1855–1861.

Olds, J., & Milner, P. M. (1954). Positive reinforcement produced by electrical stimulation of septal area and other regions of rat brains. *Journal of Comparative and Physiological Psychology, 47,* 419–427.

Olfson, M., Marcus, S., Pincus, H. A., Zito, J. M., Thompson, J. W., & Zarin, D. A. (1998). Antidepressant prescribing practices of outpatient psychiatrists. *Archives of General Psychiatry, 55,* 310, 316.

Oliver, M. B., & Fonash, D. (2002). Race and crime in the news: Whites' identification and misidentification of violent and nonviolent criminal suspects. *Media Psychology, 4(2),* 137–156.

Oliver, R. J. (2002). Tobacco abuse in pregnancy. *Journal of Prenatal Psychology & Health, 17(2),* 153–166.

Olson, J. M., & Zanna, M. P. (1993). Attitudes and attitude change. *Annual Review of Psychology, 44,* 117–154.

Olson, R. K. (2004). SSSR, environment, and genes. *Scientific Studies of Reading, 8(2),* 111–124.

Oppenheimer, D. M. (2004). Spontaneous discounting of availability in frequency judgment tasks. *Psychological Science, 15(2),* 100–105.

Orpinas, P. (1999). *Who is violent?: Factors associated with aggressive behavior in Latin America and Spain.* [On-line]. Available: http://www.paho.org/English/DD/PUB/Vol-5-4&5-Orpinas.htm

Orubuloye, I., Caldwell, J., & Caldwell, P. (1997). Perceived male sexual needs and male sexual behavior in southwest Nigeria. *Social Science and Medicine, 44,* 1195–1207.

Oshima, K. (2000). Ethnic jokes and social function in Hawaii. *Humor: International Journal of Humor Research, 13(1),* 41–57.

Ostrov, J. M., & Keating, C. F. (2004). Gender differences in preschool aggression during free play and structured interactions: An observational study. *Social Development, 13(2),* 255–277.

Overmier, J. B., & Murison, R. (2000). Anxiety and helplessness in the face of stress predisposes, precipitates, and sustains gastric ulceration. *Behavioural Brain Research, 110(1–2),* 161–174.

Owens, M. J. (2004). Selectivity of antidepressants: From the monoamine hypothesis of depression to the SSRI revolution and beyond. *Journal of Clinical Psychiatry, 65,* 5–10.

Oxley, N. L., & Dzindolet, M. T., & Miller, J. L. (2002). Sex differences in communication with close friends: Testing Tannen's claims. *Psychological Reports, 91(2),* 537–544.

Ozinga, J. A. (2000). *Altruism.* New York: Praeger Pub.

Paice, E., Rutter, H., Wetherell, M., Winder, B., & McManus, I. C. (2002). Stressful incidents, stress and coping strategies in the pre-registration house officer year. *Medical Education, 36(1),* 56–65.

Palfai, T. P., Monti, P. M., Ostafin, B., & Hutchinson, K. (2000). Effects of nicotine deprivation on alcohol-related information processing and drinking behavior. *Journal of Abnormal Psychology, 109,* 96–105.

Palmer, S., & Ellis, A. (1995). Stress counseling and stress management: The rational emotive behavior approach. Dr. Stephen Palmer interviews Dr. Albert Ellis. *The Rational Emotive Behaviour Therapist, 3(2),* 82–86.

Panksepp, J. (2005). Affective consciousness: Core emotional feelings in animals and humans. *Consciousness & Cognition: An International Journal, 14(1),* 30–80.

Papalia, D. E., Olds, S. W., & Feldman, R. D. (2001). *A child's world: Infancy through adolescence* (9th ed.). New York, NY: McGraw-Hill.

Pappas, N. T., McKenry, P. C., & Catlett, B. S. (2004). Athlete aggression on the rink and off the ice: Athlete violence and aggression in hockey and interpersonal relationships. *Men & Masculinities, 6(3),* 291–312.

Paquet, F., Soucy, J. P., Stip, E., Lévesque, M., Elie, A., & Bédard, M. A. (2004). Comparison between olanzapine and haloperidol on procedural learning and the relationship with striatal D-sub-2 receptor occupancy in schizophrenia. *Journal of Neuropsychiatry & Clinical Neurosciences, 16(1),* 47–56.

Paquier, P. F., & Mariën, P. (2005). A synthesis of the role of the cerebellum in cognition. *Aphasiology, 19(1),* 3–19.

Paris, J. (2000). Childhood precursors of personality disorder. *Psychiatric Clinics of North America, 23,* 77–88.

Paris, J. (2004). Half in love with easeful death: The meaning of chronic suicidality in borderline personality disorder. *Harvard Review of Psychiatry, 12(1),* 42–48.

Parke, R. D., & Buriel, R. (1998). Socialization in the family: Ethnic and ecological perspectives. In W. Damon (Ed.), *Handbook of child psychology (Vol. 3).* New York: Wiley.

Parker, G. B., & Brotchie, H. L. (2004). From diathesis to dimorphism: The biology of gender differences in depression. *Journal of Nervous & Mental Disease, 192(3),* 210–216.

Parker, R. N. & Auerhahn, K. (1998). Alcohol, drugs, and violence. *Annual Review of Sociology, 24,* 291–311.

Parker-Oliver, D. (2002). Redefining hope for the terminally ill. *American Journal of Hospice & Palliative Care, 19(2),* 115–120.

Parkes, C. M. (1972). *Bereavement: Studies of grief in adult life.* New York: International Universities Press.

Parkes, C. M. (1991). Attachment, bonding, and psychiatric problems after bereavement in adult life. In C. M. Parkes, J. Stevenson-Hinde, & P. Marris (Eds.), *Attachment across the life cycle.* London: Tavistock/Routledge.

Parrott, A., Morinan, A., Moss, M., & Scholey, A. (2004). *Understanding drugs and behavior.* Hoboken, NJ: Wiley.

Pasley, K., Kerpelman, J., & Guilbert, D. E. (2001). Gendered conflict, identity disruption, and marital instability: Expanding Gottman's model. *Journal of Social & Personal Relationships, 18(1),* 5–27.

Pasternak, T. & Greenlee, M. W. (2005). Working memory in primate sensory systems. *Nature Reviews Neuroscience, 6(2),* 97–107.

Patterson, F., & Linden, E. (1981). *The education of Koko.* New York: Holt, Rinehart and Winston.

Patterson, J. M., Holm, K. E., & Gurney, J. G. (2004). The impact of childhood cancer on the family: A qualitative analysis of strains, resources, and coping behaviors. *Psycho-Oncology, 13(6),* 390–407.

Patterson, P. (2002). Penny's journal: Koko wants to have a baby. Available: http://www.koko.org/world/"journal.phtml?offset=5

Paul, D. B., & Blumenthal, A. L. (1989). On the trail of little Albert. *The Psychological Record, 39,* 547–553.

Pearlman, C. (2002). Electroconvulsive therapy in clinical psychopharmacology. *Journal of Clinical Psychopharmacology, 22(4),* 345–346.

Pedro-Carroll, J. L. (2005). Fostering resilience in the aftermath of divorce: The role of evidence-based programs for children. *Family Court Review, 43(1),* 52–64.

Peiró, J., & Meliá, J. (2003). Formal and informal interpersonal power in organisations: Testing a bifactorial model of power in role-sets. *Applied Psychology: An International Review, 52(1),* 14–35.

Pelletier, J. G., & Paré, D. (2004). Role of amygdala oscillations in the consolidation of emotional memories. *Biological Psychiatry, 55(6),* 559–562.

Peltzer, K. (2003). Magical thinking and paranormal beliefs among secondary and university students in South Africa. *Personality & Individual Differences, 35(6),* 1419–1426.

Penner, L. A., Dovidio, J. F., Piliavin, J. A., & Schroeder, D. A. (2005). Prosocial behavior: Multilevel perspectives. *Annual Review of Psychology, 56,* 365–392.

Penzien, D. B., Rains, J., C., & Andrasik, F. (2002). Behavioral management of recurrent headache: Three decades of experience and empiricism. *Applied Psychophysiology & Biofeedback, 27(2),* 163–181.

Peppard, P. E., Young, T., Palta, M., & Skatrud, J. (2000). Prospective study of the association between sleep-disordered breathing and hypertension. *New England Journal of Medicine, 342(19),* 1378–1384.

Peretti, P. O., & Abplanalp, R. R. Jr. (2004). Chemistry in the college dating process: Structure and function. *Social Behavior & Personality, 32(2),* 147–154.

Perez, R. L. (2000). Fiesta as tradition, fiesta as change: Ritual, alcohol, and violence in a Mexican community. *Addiction, 95(3),* 365–373.

Perry, C. (1997). Admissability and per se exclusion of hypnotically elicited recall in American courts of law. *International Journal of Clinical and Experimental Hypnosis, 45,* 266–279.

Perry, C., Orne, M. T., London, R. W., & Orne, E. C. (1996). Rethinking per se exclusions of hypnotically elicited recall as legal testimony. *International Journal of Clinical & Experimental Hypnosis, 44*(1), 66–81.

Pert, C. B., & Snyder, S. H. (1973). The opiate receptor: Demonstration in nervous tissue. *Science, 179,* 1011–1014.

Peterson, C., & Vaidya, R. S. (2001). Explanatory style, expectations, and depressive symptoms. *Personality & Individual Differences, 31*(7), 1217–1223.

Peterson, Z. D., & Muehlenhard, C. L. (2004). Was it rape? The fFunction of women's rape myth acceptance and definitions of sex in labeling their own experiences. *Sex Roles, 51*(3–4), 129–144.

Petronis, A. (2000). The genes for major psychosis: Aberrant sequence or regulation? *Neuropsychopharmacology, 23,* 1–12.

Pettigrew, T. F. (1998). Reactions towards the new minorities of Western Europe. *Annual Review of Sociology, 24,* 77–103.

Petty, R. E., Wegener, D. T., & Fabrigar, L. R. (1997). Attitudes and attitude change. *Annual Review of Psychology, 48,* 609–647.

Petty, R. E., Wegener, D. T., & White, P. H. (1998). Flexible correction processes in social judgment: Implications for persuasion. *Social Cognition, 16*(1), 93–113.

Petty, R. E., Wheeler, S. C., & Bizer, G. Y. (2000). Attitude functions and persuasion: An elaboration likelihood approach to matched versus mismatched messages. In G. R. Maio & J. M. Olson (Eds.), *Why we evaluate: Functions of attitudes* (pp. 133–162). Mahwah, NJ: Erlbuam.

Pfaffmann, C. (1982). Taste: A model of incentive motivation. In D. W. Pfaff (Ed.), *The physiological mechanisms of motivation.* New York: Springer-Verlag.

Pfeffer, C. R., Jiang, H., Kakuma, T., Hwang, J., & Metsch, M. (2002). Group intervention for children bereaved by the suicide of a relative. *Journal of the American Academy of Child & Adolescent Psychiatry, 41*(5), 505–513.

Pham, T.M., Winblad, B., Granholm, A-C., & Mohammed, A. H. (2002). Environmental influences on brain neurotrophins in rats. *Pharmacology, Biochemistry & Behavior, 73(1),* 167–175.

Phelps, J. A., Davis, J. O., & Schartz, K. M. (1997). Nature, nurture, and twin research strategies. *Current Directions in Psychological Science, 6,* 117–120.

Philipsen, M. I. (2003). Race, the college classroom, and service learning: A practitioner's tale. *Journal of Negro Education, 72*(2), 230–240.

Philliber, S., Brooks, L., Lehrer, L. P., Oakley, M., & Waggoner, S. (2003). Outcomes of teen parenting programs in New Mexico. *Adolescence, 38*(151), 535–553.

Phillips, M. D., Lowe, M. J., Lurito, J. T., Dzemidzic, M., & Mathews, V. P. (2001). Temporal lobe activation demonstrates sex-based differences during passive listening. *Radiology, 220*(1), 202–207.

Phillips, S. T., & Ziller, R. C. (1997). Toward a theory and measure of the nature of nonprejudice. *Journal of Personality and Social Psychology, 72,* 420–434.

Pich, E. M., Pagliusi, S. R., Tessari, M., Talabot-Ayer, D., Van Huijsduijnen, R. H., & Chiamulera, C. (1997). Common neural substrates for the addictive properties of nicotine and cocaine. *Science, 275,* 83–86.

Pickering, A., Farmer, A., & McGuffin, P. (2004). The role of personality in childhood sexual abuse. *Personality & Individual Differences, 36*(6), 1295–1303.

Pierce, J. D. Jr., Cohen, A. B., & Ulrich, P. M. (2004). Responsivity to two odorants, androstenone and amyl acetate, and the affective impact of odors on interpersonal relationships. *Journal of Comparative Psychology, 118*(1), 14–19.

Pietromonaco, P. R., & Carnelley, K. B. (1994). Gender and working models of attachment: Consequences for perception of self and romantic relationships. *Personal Relationships, 1,* 3–26.

Pillard, R. C., & Bailey, M. J. (1995). A biological perspective on sexual orientation. *The Psychiatric Clinics of North America, 18,* 71–84.

Pinker, S. (2002). *The blank slate: The modern denial of human nature.* New York: Viking.

Pissiota, A., Frans, Ö., Michelgård, Å., Appel, L., Långström, B., Flaten, M. A., & Fredrikson, M. (2003). Amygdala and anterior cingulate cortex activation during affective startle modulation: A PET study of fear. *European Journal of Neuroscience, 18*(5), 1325–1331.

Plomin, R. (1990). The role of inheritance in behavior. *Science, 248,* 183–188.

Plomin, R. (1997, May). Cited in B. Azar, Nature, nurture: Not mutually exclusive. *APA Monitor,* p. 32.

Plomin, R. (1999). Genetics and general cognitive ability. *Nature, 402,* C25–C29.

Plomin, R., & Crabbe, J. (2000). DNA. *Psychological Bulletin, 126,* 806–828.

Plomin, R., & DeFries, J. C. (1998). *The genetics of cognitive abilities and disabilities.* New York: Freeman.

Plous, S. (1991). An attitude survey of animal rights activists. *Psychological Science, 2,* 194–196.

Plous, S. (1998). Signs of change within the animal rights movement: Results from a follow-up survey of activists. *Journal of Comparative Psychology, 112*(1), 48–54.

Plummer, D. C. (2001). The quest for modern manhood: Masculine stereotypes, peer culture and the social significance of homophobia. *Journal of Adolescence, 24*(1), 15–23.

Plutchik, R. (1984). Emotions: A general psychoevolutionary theory. In K. R. Scherer, & P. Ekman (Eds), *Approaches to emotion.* Hillsdale, NJ: Erlbaum.

Plutchik, R. (1994). *The psychology and biology of emotion.* New York: HarperCollins.

Plutchik, R. (2000). *Emotions in the practice of psychotherapy: Clinical implications of affect theories.* Washington, DC: American Psychological Association.

Pomponio, A. T. (2001). *Psychological consequences of terror.* New York: Wiley.

Pontius, A. A. (2005). Fastest fight/flight reaction via amygdalar visual pathway implicates simple face drawing as its marker: Neuroscientific data consistent with neuropsychological findings. *Aggression & Violent Behavior, 10*(3), 363–373.

Poppe, E. (2001). Effects of changes in GNP and perceived group characteristics on national and ethnic stereotypes in central and Eastern Europe. *Journal of Applied Social Psychology, 31*(8), 1689–1708.

Population Communications International. (2005). *What is PCI?* [On-line]. Available: http://population.org/index.shtml

Pornpitakpan, C. (2004). The persuasiveness of source credibility: A critical review of five decades' evidence. *Journal of Applied Social Psychology, 34*(2), 243–281.

Porter, J. F., Spates, C. R., & Smitham, S. (2004). Behavioral activation group therapy in public mental health settings: A pilot investigation. *Professional Psychology: Research & Practice, 35*(3), 297–301.

Porzelius, L. K., Dinsmore, B. D., & Staffelbach, D. (2001). Eating disorders. In M. Hersen & V. B. Van Hasselt (Eds.), *Advanced abnormal psychology (2nd ed.).* Netherlands: Klewer Academic Publishers.

Posthuma, D., de Geus, E. J. C., & & Boomsma, D. I. (2001). Perceptual speed and IQ are associated through common genetic factors. *Behavior Genetics, 31*(6), 593–602.

Posthuma, D., de Geus, E. J. C., Baare, W. E. C., Hulshoff Pol, H. E., Kahn, R. S., & Boomsma, D. I. (2002). The association between brain volume and intelligence is of genetic origin. *Nature Neuroscience, 5(2),* 83–84.

Posthuma, D., Neale, M. C., Boomsma, D. I., & de Geus, E. J. C. (2001). Are smarter brains running faster? Heritability of alpha peak frequency, IQ, and their interrelation. *Behavior Genetics, 31*(6), 567–579.

Powell, D. H. (1998). *The nine myths of aging: Maximizing the quality of later life.* San Francisco: Freeman.

Powell, G. N., Butterfield, D. A., & Parent, J. D. (2002). Gender and managerial stereotypes: Have the times changed? *Journal of Management, 28(2)*, 177–193.

Powell-Hopson, D., & Hopson, D. S. (1988). Implications of doll color preferences among Black preschool children and White preschool children. *Journal of Black Psychology, 14,* 57–63.

Powlishta, K. K. (1999). Gender segregation among children: Understanding the "cootie phenomenon." In L. E. Berk, (Ed.), *Landscapes of development* (pp. 281–294). Belmont, CA: Wadsworth.

Pratt, M. W., Skoe, E. E., & Arnold, M. (2004). Care reasoning development and family socialisation patterns in later adolescence: A longitudinal analysis. *International Journal of Behavioral Development, 28(2),* 139–147.

Premack, D. (1976). Language and intelligence in ape and man. *American Scientist, 64(6),* 674–683.

Pressman, J. D. (1998). *Last resort psychosurgery and the limits of medicine.* Cambridge, MA: Cambridge University Press.

Preuss, U. W., Zetzsche, T., Jäger, M., Groll, C., Frodl, T., Bottlender, R., Leinsinger, G., Hegerl, U., Hahn, K., Möller, H. J., & Meisenzahl, E. M. (2005). Thalamic volume in first-episode and chronic schizophrenic subjects: A volumetric MRI study. *Schizophrenia Research, 73(1),* 91–101.

Price, W. F., & Crapo, R. H. (2002). *Cross-cultural perspectives in introductory psychology* (4th ed.). Belmont, CA: Wadsworth.

Priebe, S., Hoffmann, K., Isermann, M., & Kaiser, W. (2002). Do long-term hospitalised patients benefit from discharge into the community? *Social Psychiatry & Psychiatric Epidemiology, 37(8),* 387–392.

Priest, R. F., & Sawyer, J. (1967). Proximity and peership: Bases of balance in interpersonal attraction. *American Journal of Sociology, 72,* 633–649.

Priester, J. R., & Petty, R. E. (2003). The influence of spokesperson trustworthiness on message elaboration, attitude strength, and advertising effectiveness. *Journal of Consumer Psychology, 13(4),* 2003, 408–421.

Primavera, L. H., & Herron, W. G. (1996). The effect of viewing television violence on aggression. *International Journal of Instructional Media, 23,* 91–104.

Pring, L., & Hermelin, B. (2002). Numbers and letters: Exploring an autistic savant's unpractised ability. *Neurocase, 8(4),* 330–337.

Prinstein, M. J., & Aikins, J. W. (2004). Cognitive moderators of the longitudinal association between peer rejection and adolescent depressive symptoms. *Journal of Abnormal Child Psychology, 32(2),* 147–158.

Prkachin, K. M., & Silverman, B. E. (2002). Hostility and facial expression in young men and women: Is social regulation more important than negative affect? *Health Psychology, 21(1),* 33–39.

Prudic, J., Olfson, M., Marcus, S. C., Fuller, R. B., & Sackeim, H. A. (2004). Effectiveness of electroconvulsive therapy in community settings. *Biological Psychiatry, 55(3),* 301–312.

Pulido, R., & Marco, A. (2000). El efecto Barnum en estudiantes universitarios y profesionales de la psicologia en Mexico. /The Barnum effect in university students and psychology professionals in Mexico. *Revista Intercontinental de Psicoanalisis Contemporaneo, 2(2),* 59–66.

Pullum, G. K. (1991). *The great Eskimo vocabulary hoax and other irreverent essays on the study of language.* Chicago: University of Chicago Press.

Purdy, J. E., Markham, M. R., Schwartz, B. L., & Gordon, W. C. (2001). *Learning and memory* (2nd ed.). Belmont, CA: Wadsworth.

Purnell, M. T., Feyer, A. M., & Herbison, G. P. (2002). The impact of a nap opportunity during the night shift on the performance and alertness of 12-hour shift workers. *Journal of Sleep Research, 11(3),* 219–227.

Putnam, F. W. (1992). Altered states: Peeling away the layers of multiple personality. *Science, 32(6),* 30–36.

Quaiser-Pohl, C., & Lehmann, W. (2002). Girls' spatial abilities: Charting the contributions of experiences and attitudes in different academic groups. *British Journal of Educational Psychology, 72(2),* 245–260.

Quinn, J., Barrowclough, C., & Tarrier, N. (2003). The Family Questionnaire (FQ): A scale for measuring symptom appraisal in relatives of schizophrenic patients. *Acta Psychiatrica Scandinavica, 108(4),* 290–296.

Raesaenen, P. M., Tiihonen, J., Isohanni, M., Rantakallio, P., Lehtonen, J., & Moring, J. (1998). Schizophrenia, alcohol abuse, and violent behavior: A 26–year follow up study of an unselected birth cohort. *Schizophrenia Bulletin, 24,* 437–441.

Raesaenen, S., Pakaslahti, A., Syvaelahti, E., Jones, P. B., & Isohanni, M. (2000). Sex differences in schizophrenia: A review. *Nordic Journal of Psychiatry, 54,* 37–45.

Rahman, Q., & Wilson, G. D. (2003). Born gay? The psychobiology of human sexual orientation. *Personality & Individual Differences. 34(8),* 1337–1382.

Raine, A., Lencz, T., Bihrle, S., LaCasse, L., & Colletti, P. (2000). Reduced prefrontal gray matter volume and reduced autonomic activity in antisocial personality disorder. *Archives of General Psychiatry, 57,* 119–127.

Raine, A., Meloy, J. R., Bihrle, S., Stoddard, J., LaCasse, L., & Buchsbaum, M. S. (1998). Reduced prefrontal and increased subcortical brain functioning assessed using positron emission tomography in predatory and affective murderers. *Behavioral Sciences & the Law, 16(3),* 319–332.

Raloff, J. (1999). Common pollutants undermine masculinity. *Science News, 155,* 213.

Ramirez, G., Zemba, D., & Geiselman, R. E. (1996). Judges' cautionary instructions on eyewitness testimony. *American Journal of Forensic Psychology, 14,* 31–66.

Ramirez, J. M. (2003). Hormones and aggression in childhood and adolescence. *Aggression & Violent Behavior, 8(6),* 621–644.

Randi, J. (1997). *An encyclopedia of claims, frauds, and hoaxes of the occult and supernatural: James Randi's decidedly skeptical definitions of alternate realities.* New York: St Martin's Press.

Rathus, S. A. (1973). A 30–item schedule for assessing assertive behavior. *Behavior Therapy, 4,* 398–406.

Rathus, S. A., & Nevid, J. S. (2002). *Psychology and the challenges of life: Adjustment in the new millennium* (8th ed.). New York: Wiley.

Rauhut, A. S., Thomas, B. L., & Ayres, J. J. B. (2001). Treatments that weaken Pavlovian conditioned fear and thwart its renewal in rats: Implications for treating human phobias. *Journal of Experimental Psychology: Animal Behavior Processes, 27(2),* 99–114.

Ray, W. J. (2003). *Methods: Toward a science of behavior and experience.* (7th ed.). Wadsworth: Belmont, CA.

Realmuto, G. M., August, G. J., & Egan, E. A. (2004). Testing the goodness-of-fit of a multifaceted preventive intervention for children at risk for conduct disorder. *Canadian Journal of Psychiatry, 49(11),* 743–752.

Rechtschaffen, A., & Bergmann, B. M. (1995). Sleep deprivation in the rat by the disk-over-water method. *Behavioural Brain Research, 69,* 55–63.

Rechtschaffen, A., Bergmann, B. M., Everson, C. A., Kushida, C. A., & Gilliland, M. A. (2002). Sleep deprivation in the rat: X. Integration and discussion of the findings. *Sleep: Journal of Sleep & Sleep Disorders Research, 25(1),* 68–87.

Reed, L. J., Lasserson, D., Marsden, P., Bright, P., Stanhope, N., & Kopelman, M. D. (2005). Correlations of regional cerebral metabolism with memory performance and executive function in patients with herpes encephalitis or frontal lobe lesions. *Neuropsychology, 19*(5), 555–565.

Reeder, C., Newton, E., Frangou, S., & Wykes, T. (2004). Which executive skills should we target to affect social functioning and symptom change? A study of a cognitive remediation therapy program. *Schizophrenia Bulletin, 30*(1), 87–100.

Reeve, J. (2005). *Understanding motivation and emotion* (4th ed.). Hoboken, NJ: Wiley.

Regier, D. A., Narrow, W. E., Rae, D. S., Mander-scheid, R. W., Locke, B. Z., & Goodwin, F. K. (1993). The de facto US mental and addictive disorders service system. *Archives of General Psychiatry, 50*, 85–93.

Reich, D. A. (2004). What you expect is not always what you get: The roles of extremity, optimism, and pessimism in the behavioral confirmation process. *Journal of Experimental Social Psychology, 40*(2), 199–215.

Reifman, A. (2000). Revisiting the Bell Curve. *Psychology, 11*, 21–29.

Reilly, P. (2005). Teaching law students how to feel: Using negotiations training to increase motional intelligence. *Negotiation Journal, 21*(2), 301–314.

Reiner, W. G., & Gearhart, J. P. (2004). Discordant sexual identity in some genetic males with cloacal exstrophy assigned to female sex at birth. *New England Journal of Medicine, 350*(4), 333–341.

Reis, C., Ahmed, A. T., Amowitz, L. L., Kushner, A. L., Elahi, M., & Iacopino, V. (2004). Physician participation in human rights abuses in southern Iraq. *JAMA: Journal of the American Medical Association, 291*(12), 1480–1486.

Reneman, L., Booij, J., de Bruin, K., Reitsma, J. R., de Wolff, F. A., Gunning, W. B., den Heeten, G. J., & van den Brink, W. (2001). Effects of dose, sex, and long-term abstention from use on toxic effects of MDMA (Ecstasy) on brain serotonin neurons. *Lancet, 358*(9296), 1864–1869.

Renzetti, C., Curran, D., & Kennedy-Bergen, R. (2006). *Understanding diversity.* Boston, MA: Allyn & Bacon/Longman.

Resing, W. C., & Nijland, M. I. (2002). Worden kinderen intelligenter? Een kwart eeuw onderzoek met de Leidse Diagnostische Test. /Are children becoming more intelligent? Twenty-five years' research using the Leiden Diagnostic Test. *Kind en Adolescent, 23(1),* 42–49.

Ressler, K., & Davis, M. (2003). Genetics of childhood disorders: L. Learning and memory, part 3: Fear conditioning. *Journal of the American Academy of Child & Adolescent Psychiatry, 42*(5), 612–615.

Rest, J. R., Turiel E., & Kohlberg L. (1969). Relations between level of moral judgment and preference and comprehension of the moral judgments of others. *Journal of Personality, 37*, 225–252.

Rest, J., Narvaez, D., Bebeau, M., & Thoma, S. (1999). A neo-Kohlbergian approach: The DIT and schema theory. *Educational Psychology Review, 11*(4), 291–324.

Reston, J. (1981). *Our father who art in hell.* New York: Times Books.

Reuter, M., Stark, R., Hennig, J., Walter, B., Kirsch, P., Schienle, A., & Vaitl, D. (2004). Personality and emotion: Test of Gray's personality theory by means of an fMRI study. *Behavioral Neuroscience, 118*(3), 462–469.

Rhodes, G., Halberstadt, J., & Brajkovich, G. (2001). Generalization of mere exposure effects to averaged composite faces. *Social Cognition, 19*(1), 57–70.

Rice, M. E. (1997). Violent offender research and implications for the criminal justice system. *American Psychologist, 52*, 414–423.

Rice, T. W. (2003). Believe it or not: Religious and other paranormal beliefs in the United States. *Journal for the Scientific Study of Religion, 42*(1), 95–106.

Richardson, G. A., Ryan, C., Willford, J., Day, N. L., & Goldschmidt, L. (2002). Prenatal alcohol and marijuana exposure: Effects on neuropsychological outcomes at 10 years. *Neurotoxicology & Teratology, 24(3),* 311–320.

Ridley, R. M., Baker, H. F., Cummings, R. M., Green, M. E., & Leow-Dyke, A. (2005). Mild topographical memory impairment following crossed unilateral lesions of the mediodorsal thalamic nucleus and the inferotemporal cortex. *Behavioral Neuroscience, 119*(2), 518–525.

Riemann, D., & Voderholzer, U. (2003). Primary insomnia: a risk factor to develop depression? *Journal of Affective Disorders, 76*(1–3), 255–259.

Riggio, H. R. (2004). Parental marital conflict and divorce, parent-child relationships, social support, and relationship anxiety in young adulthood. *Personal Relationships, 11*(1), 99–114.

Ripley, A. (June 31, 2004). Redefining torture. *Time, 163,* p. 29.

Robbins, S. P. (1996). *Organizational behavior: Concepts, controversies, and applications.* Englewood Cliffs, NJ: Prentice Hall.

Robert-McComb, J. J. (2001). Eating disorders. In J. J. Robert-McComb (Ed), *Eating disorders in women and children: Prevention, stress management, and treatment* (pp. 3–37). Boca Raton, FL: CRC Press.

Roberts, W. W., & Nagel, J. (1996). First-order projections activated by stimulation of hypothalamic sites eliciting attack and flight in rats. *Behavioral Neuroscience, 110,* 509–527.

Robertson, D. A., Gernsbacher, M. A., Guidotti, S. J., Robertson, R. R. W., Irwin, W., Mock, B. J., & Campana, M. E. (2000). Functional neuroanatomy of the cognitive process of mapping during discourse comprehension. *Psychological Science, 11*(3), 255–260.

Robie, C., Born, M., & Schmit, M. J. (2001). Personal and situational determinants of personality responses: A partial reanalysis and reinterpretation of the Schmit et al. (1995) data. *Journal of Business & Psychology, 16(1),* 101–117.

Roelcke, V. (1997). Biologizing social facts: An early 20th century debate on Kraepelin's concepts of culture, neurasthenia, and degeneration. *Culture, Medicine, and Psychiatry, 21,* 383–403.

Rogers, C. R. (1961). *On becoming a person.* Boston: Houghton Mifflin.

Rogers, C. R. (1980). A way of being. Boston: Houghton Mifflin.

Rogers, T. T., Lambon Ralph, M. A., Garrard, P., Bozeat, S., McClelland, J. L., Hodges, J. R., & Patterson, K. (2004). Structure and deterioration of semantic memory: A neuropsychological and computational investigation. *Psychological Review, 111*(1), 205–235.

Rogosch, F. A., & Cicchetti, D. (2004). Child maltreatment and emergent personality organization: Perspectives from the five-factor model. *Journal of Abnormal Child Psychology, 32*(2), 123–145.

Rohner, R. (1986). *The warmth dimension.* Newbury Park, CA: Sage.

Rohner, R. P., & Britner, P. A. (2002). Worldwide mental health correlates of parental acceptance-rejection: Review of cross-cultural and intracultural evidence. *Cross-Cultural Research: The Journal of Comparative Social Science, 36*(1), 15–47.

Rohner, R. P., & Veneziano, R. A. (2001). The importance of father love: History and contemporary evidence. *Review of General Psychology, 5*(4), 382–405.

Roiser, J. P., Cook, L. J., Cooper, J. D., Rubinsztein, D. C., & Sahakian, B. J. (2005). Association of a functional polymorphism in the serotonin transporter gene with abnormal emotional processing in ecstasy users. *American Journal of Psychiatry, 162*(3), 609–612.

Roller, C. G. (2004). Sex addiction and women: A nursing issue. *Journal of Addictions Nursing, 15*(2), 2004, 53–61.

Rolnick, A., & Lubow, R. E. (1991). Why is the driver rarely motion sick? The role of controllability in motion sickness. *Ergonomics, 34*(7), 867–879.

Romo, R., Brody, C. D., Hernandez, A., & Lemus, L. (1999). Neuronal correlates of parametric working memory in the prefrontal cortex. *Nature, 399,* 470–473.

Rönnberg, J., Rudner, M., & Ingvar, M. (2004). Neural correlates of working memory for sign language. *Cognitive Brain Research, 20*(2), 165–182.

Rook, K. S. (2000). The evolution of social relationships in later adulthood. In S. H. Qualls & N. Abeles (Eds.), *Psychology and the aging revolution.* Washington, DC: American Psychological Association.

Roques, P. Lambin, M., Jeunier, B., & Strayer, F. (1997). Multivariate analysis of personal space in a primary school classroom. *Enfance, 4,* 451–468.

Rosch, E. (1978). Principles of organization. In E. Rosch & H. L. Lloyd (Eds.), *Cognition and categorization.* Hillsdale, NJ: Erlbaum.

Rosch, E. H. (1973). Natural categories. *Cognitive Psychology, 4,* 328–350.

Rose, C. R., & Konnerth, A. (2002). Exciting glial oscillations. *Nature Neuroscience, 4,* 773–774.

Rosen, R. C. (2002). Sexual function assessment and the role of vasoactive drugs in female sexual dysfunction. *Archives of Sexual Behavior, 31*(5), 439–443.

Rosenberg, M. (2003). Recognizing gay, lesbian, and transgender teens in a child and adolescent psychiatry practice. *Journal of the American Academy of Child & Adolescent Psychiatry, 42*(12), 1517–1521.

Rosen-Grandon, J. R., Myers, J. E., & Hattie, J. A. (2004). The relationship between marital characteristics, marital interaction processes, and marital satisfaction. *Journal of Counseling & Development, 82*(1), 58–68.

Rosenhan, D. (1973). On being sane in insane places. *Science, 197,* 250–258.

Rosenthal, R. (1965). *Clever Hans: A case study of scientific method, Introduction to Clever Hans.* New York: Holt, Rinehart & Winston.

Rosenzweig, E. S., Barnes, C. A., & McNaughton, B. L. (2002). Making room for new memories. *Nature Neuroscience, 5*(1), 6–8.

Rosenzweig, M. R., & Bennett, E. L. (1996). Psychobiology of plasticity: Effects of training and experience on brain and behavior. *Behavioural Brain Research, 78*(1), 57–65.

Rosenzweig, M. R., Bennet, E. L., & Diamond, M. C. (1972). Brain changes in response to experience. *Scientific American, 226,* 22–29.

Ross, B. M., & Millson, C. (1970). Repeated memory of oral prose in Ghana and New York. *International Journal of Psychology, 5,* 173–181.

Ross, H., Smith, J., Spielmacher, C., & Recchia, H. (2004). Shading the truth: Self-serving biases in children's reports of sibling conflicts. *Merrill-Palmer Quarterly, 50*(1), 61–85.

Rossano, M. J. (2003). *Evolutionary psychology: The science of human behavior and evolution.* Hoboken, NJ: Wiley.

Roth, M. D., Whittaker, K., Salehi, K., Tashkin, D. P., & Baldwin, G. C. (2004). Mechanisms for impaired effector function in alveolar macrophages from marijuana and cocaine smokers. *Journal of Neuroimmunology, 147*(1–2), 82–86.

Rothrauff, T., Middlemiss, W., & Jacobson, L. (2004). Comparison of American and Austrian infants' and toddlers' sleep habits: A retrospective, exploratory study. *North American Journal of Psychology, 6*(1), 125–144.

Rotter, J. B. (1954). *Social learning and clinical psychology.* Englewood Cliffs, NJ: Prentice Hall.

Rotter, J. B. (1990). Internal versus external control of reinforcement: A case history of a variable. *American Psychologist, 45,* 489–493.

Rowe, R., Maughan, B., Worthman, C. M., Costello, E. J., & Angold, A. (2004). Testosterone, antisocial behavior, and social dominance in boys: Pubertal development and biosocial interaction. *Biological Psychiatry, 55*(5), 546–552.

Roy, T. S., Seidler, F. J., & Slotkin, T. A. (2002). Prenatal nicotine exposure evokes alterations of cell structure in hippocampus and somatosensory cortex. *Journal of Pharmacology & Experimental Therapeutics, 300*(1), 124–133.

Royce, R., Sena, A., Cates, W., & Cohen, M. (1997). Sexual transmission of HIV. *New England Journal of Medicine, 336,* 1072–1078.

Rozencwajg, P., Cherfi, M., Ferrandez, A. M., Lautrey, J., Lemoine, C., & Loarer, E. (2005). Age related differences in the strategies used by middle aged adults to solve a block design task. *International Journal of Aging & Human Development, 60*(2), 159–182.

Rubin, L. B. (1992). The empty nest. In J. M. Henslin (Ed.), *Marriage and family in a changing society* (4th ed., pp. 261–270). New York: Free Press.

Rubin, Z. (1970). Measurement of romantic love. *Journal of Personality and Social Psychology, 16,* 265–273.

Ruby, N. F., Dark, J., Burns, D. E., Heller, H. C., & Zucker, I. (2002). The suprachiasmatic nucleus is essential for circadian body temperature rhythms in hibernating ground squirrels. *Journal of Neuroscience, 22*(1), 357–364.

Ruiter, R. A. C., Kok, G., Verplanken, B., & van Eersel, G. (2003). Strengthening the persuasive impact of fear appeals: The role of action framing. *Journal of Social Psychology, 143*(3), 397–400.

Ruiter, R. A. C., Verplanken, B., De Cremer, D., & Kok, G. (2004). Danger and fear control in response to fear appeals: The role of need for cognition. *Basic & Applied Social Psychology, 26*(1), 13–24.

Rumbaugh, D. M., et al. (1974). Lana (chimpanzee) learning language: A progress report. *Brain & Language, 1*(2), 205–212.

Rumpel, S., LeDoux, J., Zador, A., & Malinow, R. (2005). Postsynaptic receptor trafficking underlying a form of associative learning. *Science, 308*(5718), 83–88.

Ruschena, E., Prior, M., Sanson, A., & Smart, D. (2005). A longitudinal study of adolescent adjustment following family transitions. *Journal of Child Psychology & Psychiatry, 46*(4), 353–363.

Rushton, J. P. (2001). Black-White differences on the g-factor in South Africa: A "Jensen Effect" on the Wechsler Intelligence Scale for Children—Revised. *Personality & Individual Differences, 31*(8), 1227–1232.

Rushton, J. P. (2003a). The battlegrounds of bioscience: Cross-examining the experts on evolutionary psychology, race, intelligence, & genetics, population, environment, & cloning. *Intelligence, 31*(6), 607–608.

Rushton, J. P. (2003b). Race, brain size, and IQ: The case for consilience. *Behavioral & Brain Sciences, 26*(5), 648–649.

Rushton, J. P., & Ankney, C. D. (2000). Size matters: A review and new analyses of racial differences in cranial capacity and intelligence that refute Kamin and Omari. *Personality & Individual Differences, 29*(4), 591–620.

Rushton, J. P., & Jensen, A. R. (2005). Wanted: More race realism, less moralistic fallacy. *Psychology, Public Policy, and Law, 11*(2), 328–336.

Rutler, M. L. (1997). Nature–nurture integration: The example of antisocial behavior. *American Psychologist, 52,* 390–398.

Ruzovsky, F. A. (1984). *Consent to treatment: A practical guide.* Boston: Little, Brown.

Ryback, D., Ikemi, A., & Miki, Y. (2001). Japanese psychology in crisis: Thinking inside the (empty) box. *Journal of Humanistic Psychology, 41*(4), 124–136.

Rybacki, J. J., & Long, J. W. (1999). *The essential guide to prescription drugs 1999*. New York: HarperPerennial.

Rymer, R. (1993). *Genie: An abused child's first flight from silence*. New York: Harper-Collins.

Saab, C. Y., & Willis, W. D. (2003). The cerebellum: Organization, functions and its role in nociception. *Brain Research Reviews, 42*(1), 85–95.

Saadeh, W., Rizzo, C. P., & Roberts, D. G. (2002). Spanking. *Clinical Pediatrics, 41*(2), 87–88.

Sabbagh, M. A. (2004). Understanding orbitofrontal contributions to theory-of-mind reasoning: Implications for autism. *Brain & Cognition, 55*(1), 209–219.

Sabini, J., & Silver, M. (1993). Critical thinking and obedience to authority. In J. Chaffee (Ed.), *Critical thinking* (2nd ed.) (pp. 367–376). Palo Alto, CA: Houghton Mifflin.

Safarik, M. E., Jarvis, J. P., & Nussbaum, K. E. (2002). Sexual homicide of elderly females: Linking offender characteristics to victim and crime scene attributes. *Journal of Interpersonal Violence, 17*(5), 500–525.

Salmivalli, C., & Kaukiainen, A. (2004). "Female aggression" revisited: Variable- and person-centered approaches to studying gender differences in different types of aggression. *Aggressive Behavior, 30*(2),158–163.

Saltus, R. (2000, June 22). Brain cells are coaxed into repair duty. *Boston Globe*, A18.

Salyers, M.P., & Mueser, K.T. (2001). Schizophrenia. In M. Hersen & V.B. Van Hasselt (Eds.), *Advanced abnormal psychology* (2nd ed.). New York: Klewer Academic/Plenum.

Sampselle, C. M., Harris, V. Harlow, S. D., & Sowers, M. F. (2002). Midlife development and menopause in African American and Caucasian women. *Health Care for Women International, 23*(4), 351–363.

Sanderson, C. A. (2004). *Health psychology*. Hoboken, NJ: Wiley.

Sangha, S., McComb, C., Scheibenstock, A., Johannes, C., & Lukowiak, K. (2002). The effects of continuous versus partial reinforcement schedules on associative learning, memory, and extinction in Lymnaea stagnalis. *Journal of Experimental Biology, 205*, 1171–1178.

Sangwan, S. (2001). Ecological factors as related to I.Q. of children. *Psycho-Lingua, 31*(2), 89–92.

Sansone, R. A., Levengood, J. V., & Sellbom, M. (2004). Psychological aspects of fibromyalgia research vs. clinician impressions. *Journal of Psychosomatic Research, 56*(2), 185–188.

Sapolsky, R. M. (2004). *Why zebras don't get ulcers*. Thousand Oaks, CA: Owl Books.

Sarafino, E. P. (2000). *Behavior modification: Understanding principles of behavior change*. Springfield, MA: Mayfield.

Sarafino, E. P. (2005). *Health psychology: Biopsychosocial interactions* (5th ed.). Hoboken, NJ: Wiley.

Sarkar, P., Rathee, S. P., & Neera, N. (1999). Comparative efficacy of pharmacotherapy and biofeedback among cases of generalized anxiety disorder. *Journal of Projective Psychology & Mental Health, 6*, 69–77.

Sarnthein, J., Morel, A., von Stein, A., & Jeanmonod, D. (2005). Thalamocortical theta coherence in neurological patients at rest and during a working memory task. *International Journal of Psychophysiology, 57*(2), 87–96.

Satterfield, J. M., Folkman, S., & Acree, M. (2002). Explanatory style predicts depressive symptoms following AIDS-related bereavement. *Cognitive Therapy & Research, 26*(3), 393–403.

Saudino, K. J. (1997). Moving beyond the heritability question: New directions in behavioral genetic studies of personality. *Current Directions in Psychological Science, 6*, 86–90.

Savage-Rumbaugh, E. S. (1990). Language acquisition in a nonhuman species: Implications for the innateness debate. *Developmental Psychobiology, 23*, 599–620.

Sawa, A., & Kamiya, A. (2003). Elucidating the pathogenesis of schizophrenia: DISC-l gene may predispose to neurodevelopmental changes underlying schizophrenia. *BMJ: British Medical Journal, 327*(7416), 632–633.

Sawaya, A. L., Fuss, P. J., Dallal, G. E., Tsay, R., McCrory, M. A., Young, V., & Roberts, S. B. (2001). Meal palatability, substrate oxidation and blood glucose in young and older men. *Physiology & Behavior, 72*(1–2), 5–12.

Saxe, L., & Ben-Shakhar, G. (1999). Admissibility of polygraph tests: The application of scientific standards post-Daubert. *Psychology, Public Policy, & Law, 5*(1), 203–223.

Scarr, S. (1992). Developmental theories for the 1990s: Development and individual differences. *Child Development, 63*, 1–19.

Schachter, S., & Singer, J. E. (1962). Cognitive, social, and physiological determinants of emotional state. *Psychological Review, 69*, 379–399.

Schafe, G. E., & LeDoux, J. E. (2002). Emotional plasticity. In H. Pashler & R. Gallistel (Eds.), *Steven's handbook of experimental psychology* (3rd ed.), *Vol. 3: Learning, motivation, and emotion*. New York: John Wiley & Sons, Inc.

Schafe, G. E., Fitts, D. A., Thiele, T. E., LeDoux, J. E., & Bernstein, I. L. (2000). The induction of c-Fos in the NTS after taste aversion learning is not correlated with measures of conditioned fear. *Behavioral Neuroscience, 114*(1), 99–106.

Schaie, K. W. (1993). The Seattle longitudinal studies of intelligence. *Current Directions in Psychological Science, 2*, 171–175.

Schaie, K. W. (1994). The life course of adult intellectual development. *American Psychologist, 49*, 304–313.

Scherer, K. R., & Wallbott, H. G. (1994). Evidence for universal and cultural variation of differential emotion response patterning. *Journal of Personality and Social Psychology, 66*(2), 310–328.

Schermerhorn, J. R., Hunt, J. G., & Osborn, R. N. (2000). *Organizational behavior* (7th ed.). New York, Wiley.

Schermerhorn, J. R., Hunt, J. G., & Osborn, R. N. (2003). *Organizational behavior* (8th ed.). New York, Wiley.

Schiffer, F, Zaidel, E, Bogen, J, & Chasan-Taber, S. (1998). Different psychological status in the two hemispheres of two split-brain patients. *Neuropsychiatry, Neuropsychology, & Behavioral Neurology, 11*, 151–156.

Schlegel, A., & Barry, H. (1991). *Adolescence: An anthropological inquiry*. New York, NY: Free Press.

Schmahl, C. G., Vermetten, E., Elzinga, B. M., & Bremner, J. D. (2004). A positron emission tomography study of memories of childhood abuse in borderline personality disorder. *Biological Psychiatry, 55*(7), 759–765.

Schmidt, L. A. (1999). Frontal brain electrical activity in shyness and sociability. *Psychological Science, 10*(4), 316–320.

Schmidt, U. (2004). Undue influence of weight on self-evaluation: A population-based twin study of gender differences. *International Journal of Eating Disorders, 35*(2), 133–135.

Schmidt-Hieber, C., Jonas, P., & Bischofberger, J. (2004). Enhanced synaptic plasticity in newly generated granule cells of the adult hippocampus. *Nature, 149*, 184–17.

Schneider, D. M., & Sharp, L. (1969). *The dream life of a primitive people: The dreams of the Yir Yoront of Australia*. Ann Arbor, MI: University of Michigan.

Schneider, J. P. (2000). A qualitative study of cybersex participants: Gender differences, recovery issues, and implications for therapists. *Sexual Addiction & Compulsivity, 7*(4), 249–278.

Schneiderman, N., Ironson, & Siegel, S. D. (2005). Stress and health: Psychological, behavioral, and biological determinants. *Annual Review of Clinical Psychology, 1*, 607–628.

Schnurr, P.P., & Green, B. L. (2004). *Trauma and health: Physical health consequences of exposure to extreme stress.* Washington, DC: American Psychological Association.

Schofield, W. (1964). *Psychotherapy: The purchase of friendship.* Englewood Cliffs, NJ: Prentice Hall.

Schredl, M., Ciric, P., Bishop, A., Gölitz, E., & Buschtöns, D. (2003). Content analysis of German students' dreams: Comparison to American findings. *Dreaming, 13*(4), 237–243.

Schredl, M., Ciric, P., Götz, S., & Wittmann, L. (2004). Typical dreams: Stability and gender differences. *Journal of Psychology: Interdisciplinary & Applied, 138*(6), 485–494.

Schwartz, J., & Broder, J. M. (2003, February 13). *Engineer warned of dire effects of lift-off damage.* [On-line]. Available: http://www.nytimes.com/2003/02/13/national/national-special/13SHUT.html?th

Schwartz, M. W., & Morton, G. J. (2002). Obesity: Keeping hunger at bay. *Nature, 418*, 595–597.

Schwartz, R. C., & Smith, S. D. (2004). Suicidality and psychosis: The predictive potential of symptomatology and insight into illness. *Journal of Psychiatric Research, 38*(2), 185–191.

Schwartz, R. H. (2002). Marijuana: A decade and a half later, still a crude drug with underappreciated toxicity. *Journal of the American Academy of Child & Adolescent Psychiatry, 41*(10), 1215.

Scribner, S. (1979). Modes of thinking and ways of speaking: Culture and logic reconsidered. In I. O. Freedle (Ed.), *New directions in discourse processing* (pp. 223–243). Norwood, NJ: Able.

Scully, J. A., Tosi, H., & Banning, K. (2000). Life event checklists: Revisiting the Social Readjustment Rating Scale after 30 years. *Educational & Psychological Measurement, 60*(6), 864–876.

Seager, S. B. (1998). *Street crazy: The tragedy of the homeless mentally ill.* New York: Westcom Press.

Sebre, S., Sprugevica, I., Novotni, A., Bonevski, D., Pakalniskiene, V., Popescu, D., Turchina, T., Friedrich, W., & Lewis, O. (2004). Cross-cultural comparisons of child-reported emotional and physical abuse: Rates, risk factors and psychosocial symptoms. *Child Abuse & Neglect, 28*(1), 113–127.

Secker, D. L., Kazantzis, N., Pachana, N. A., & Kazantzis, N. (2004). Cognitive behavior therapy for older adults: Practical guidelines for adapting therapy structure. *Journal of Rational-Emotive & Cognitive Behavior Therapy, 22*(2), 93–109.

Segal, N. L., & Bouchard, T. J. (2000). *Entwined lives: Twins and what they tell us about human behavior.* New York: Plumsock.

Segall, M. H., Dasen, P. R., Berry, J. W., & Portinga, Y. H. (1990). *Human behavior in global perspective: An introduction to cross-cultural psychology.* Elmsford, NY: Pergamon Press.

Segerstrale, U. (2000). *Defenders of the truth: The battle for science in the sociobiology debate and beyond.* London: Oxford University Press.

Segerstrom, S. C. (2003). Individual differences, immunity, and cancer: Lessons from personality psychology. *Brain, Behavior & Immunity, 17*(Suppl1), S92–S97.

Segerstrom, S., C., & Miller, G. E. (2004). Psychological stress and the human immune system: A meta-analytic study of 30 years of inquiry. *Psychological Bulletin, 130*(4), 601–630.

Seligman, M. E. P. (1975) *Helplessness: On depression, development, and death.* San Francisco: Freeman.

Seligman, M. E. P. (1994). *What you can change and what you can't.* New York: Alfred A. Knopf.

Seligman, M. E. P. (1995). The effectiveness of psychotherapy: The Consumer Reports study. *American Psychologist, 50*, 965–974.

Selye, H. (1936). A syndrome produced by diverse nocuous agents. *Nature, 138*, 32.

Selye, H. (1974). *Stress without distress.* New York: Harper & Row.

Senior, C., Ward, J., & David, A. S. (2002). Representational momentum and the brain: An investigation into the functional necessity of V5/MT. *Visual Cognition, 9*, 81–92.

Sequeira, A., Mamdani, F., Lalovic, A., Anguelova, M., Lesage, A., Seguin, M., Chawky, N., Desautels, A., & Turecki, G. (2004). Alpha 2A adrenergic receptor gene and suicide. *Psychiatry Research, 125*(2), 87–93.

Shadish, W. R., & Baldwin, S. A. (2003). Meta-analysis of MFT interventions. *Journal of Marital & Family Therapy, 29*(4), 547–570.

Shahin, A., Bosnyak, D. J., Trainor, L. J., & Roberts, L. E. (2003). Enhancement of neuroplastic P2 and N1c auditory evoked potentials in musicians. *Journal of Neuroscience, 23*(13), 5545–5552.

Shapiro, K. J. (1997). The separate world of animal research. *American Psychologist, 52*(11), 1250.

Shaver, P. R., & Mikulincer, M. (2005). Attachment theory and research: Resurrection of the psychodynamic approach to personality. *Journal of Research in Personality, 39*(1), 22–45.

Shea, S. C. (1988). *Psychiatric interviewing: the art of understanding.* Philadelphia, PA: Saunders.

Sheehy, G. (1976). *Passages: Predictable crises of adult life.* New York: Dutton.

Sheldon, J. P., & Parent, S. L. (2002). Clergy's attitudes and attributions of blame toward female rape victims. *Violence Against Women, 8*(2), 233–256.

Shen, B-J., McCreary, C. P., & Myers, H. F. (2004). Independent and mediated contributions of personality, coping, social support, and depressive symptoms to physical functioning outcome among patients in cardiac rehabilitation. *Journal of Behavioral Medicine, 27*(1), 39–62.

Sher, K. J., Grekin, E. R., & Williams, N. A. (2005). The development of alcohol use disorders. *Annual Review of Clinical Psychology, 1*, 493–523.

Sher, L. (2000). Psychological factors, immunity, and heart disease. *Psychosomatics, 41*, 372–373.

Sherif, M. (1966). *In common predicament: Social psychology of intergroup conflict and cooperation.* Boston: Houghton Mifflin.

Sherif, M. (1998). Experiments in group conflict. In J. M. Jenkins, K. Oatley et al.(Eds.), *Human emotions: A reader* (pp. 245–252). Malden, MA: Blackwell Publishers Inc.

Sherwin, C. M., Christiansen, S. B., Duncan, I. J., Erhard, H. W., Lay, D. C., Jr., Mench, J. A., O'Connor, C. E., & Petherick, J. C. (2003). Guidelines for the ethical use of animals in applied ethology studies. *Applied Animal Behaviour Science, 81*(3), 291–305.

Shi, Y., Devadas, S., Greeneltch, K. M., Yin, D., Mufson, R. A., & Zhou, J. (2003). Stressed to death: Implication of lymphocyte apoptosis for psychoneuroimmunology. *Brain, Behavior & Immunity. 7*(Suppl1), S18–S26.

Shimizu-Albergine, M., Ippolito, D. L., & Beavo, J. A. (2001). Downregulation of fasting-induced cAMP response element-mediated gene induction by leptin in neuropeptide Y neurons of the arcuate nucleus. *Journal of Neuroscience, 21*(4), 1238–1246.

Shiraev, E., & Levy, D. (2004). *Introduction to cross-cultural psychology: Critical thinking and contemporary applications* (2nd ed.). Boston: Allyn & Bacon/Longman.

Shriver, T. P., & Weissberg, R. P. (2005, August 16). *No emotion left behind. New York Times.* [On-line]. Available: http://www.casel.org/downloads/NYToped.doc.

Shukla, P. V. (2001). Management people for higher performance in under-developed region. *Psycho-Lingua, 31*(1), 25–32.

Sias, P. M., Heath, R. G., Perry, T., Silva, D., Fix, B., & Metts, S. (Ed.). (2004). Narratives of workplace friendship deterioration. *Journal of Social & Personal Relationships, 21(3),* 321–340.

Siegel, J. M. (2000, January). Narcolepsy. *Scientific American,* pp. 76–81.

Silke, A. (2003). Deindividuation, anonymity, and violence: Findings from Northern Ireland. *Journal of Social Psychology, 143(4),* 493–499.

Silverman, I., & Phillips, K. (1998). The evolutionary psychology of spatial sex differences. In C. Crawford, & D. L Krebs (Eds.), *Handbook of evolutionary psychology: Ideas, issues, and applications.* Mahwah, NJ: Erlbaum.

Silvester, J., Anderson-Gough, F. M., Anderson, N. R., & Mohamed, A. R. (2002). Locus of control, attributions and impression management in the selection interview. *Journal of Occupational & Organizational Psychology, 75(1),* 59–76.

Simcock, G., & Hayne, H. (2002). Breaking the barrier? Children fail to translate their preverbal memories into language. *Psychological Science, 13(3),* 225–231.

Simon, C. W., & Emmons, W. H. (1956). Responses to material presented during various stages of sleep. *Journal of Experimental Psychology, 51,* 89–97.

Singelis, T. M., Triandis, H. C., Bhawuk, D. S., & Gelfand, M. (1995). Horizontal and vertical dimensions of individualism and collectivism: A theoretical and measurement refinement. *Cross-Cultural Research, 29,* 240–275.

Singer, M. I., Slovak, K., Frierson, T., & York, P. (1998). Viewing preferences, symptoms of psychological trauma, and violent behaviors among children who watch television. *Journal of the American Academy of Child and Adolescent Psychiatry, 37,* 1041–1048.

Sinha, R., Talih, M., Malison, R., Cooney, N., Anderson, G. M., & Kreek, M. J. (2003). Hypothalamic-pituitary-adrenal axis and sympatho-adreno-medullary responses during stress-induced and drug cue-induced cocaine craving states. *Psychopharmacology, 170(1),* 62–72.

Siqueland, L., Crits-Christoph, P., Gallop, R., Barber, J. P., Griffin, M. L., Thase, M. E., Daley, D., Frank, A., Gastfriend, D. R., Blaine, J., Connolly, M. B., & Gladis, M. (2002). Retention in psychosocial treatment of cocaine dependence: Predictors and impact on outcome. *American Journal on Addictions, 11(1),* 24–40.

Sirin, S. R., & Rogers-Sirin, L. (2004). Exploring school engagement of middle-class African American adolescents. *Youth & Society, 35(3),* 323–340.

Skinner, B. F. (1948). Superstition in the pigeon. *Journal of Experimental Psychology, 38,* 168–172.

Skinner, B. F. (1948/1976). *Walden Two.* New York: Macmillan.

Skinner, B. F. (1953). *Science and human behavior.* New York: Macmillan.

Skinner, B. F. (1961). Diagramming schedules of reinforcement. *Journal of the Experimental Analysis of Behavior,1,* 67–68.

Skinner, B. F. (1992). "Superstition" in the pigeon. *Journal of Experimental Psychology: General, 121(3),* 273–274.

Skrandies, W., Reik, P., & Kunze, C. (1999). Topography of evoked brain activity during mental arithmetic and language tasks: Sex differences. *Neuropsychologia, 37(4),* 424–430.

Slater, M. D., Henry, K. L, Swaim, R. C., & Anderson, L. L. (2003). Violent media content and aggressiveness in adolescents: A downward spiral model. *Communication Research, 30(6),* 713–736.

Sloan, L., Edmond, T., Rubin, A., & Doughty, M. (1998). Social workers' knowledge of and experience with sexual exploitation by psychotherapists. *Journal of the National Association of Social Workers, 43,* 43–53.

Sluzenski, J., Newcombe, N., & Ottinger, W. (2004). Changes in reality monitoring and episodic memory in early childhood. *Developmental Science, 7(2),* 225–245.

Smart, D. W., & Smart, J. F. (1997). DSM-IV and culturally sensitive diagnosis: Some observations for counselors. *Journal of Counseling and Development, 75,* 392–398.

Smart, R., & Peterson, C. (1997). Super's career stages and the decision to change careers. *Journal of Vocational Behavior, 51,* 358–374.

Smith, A. (1982). *Powers of mind.* New York: Summit.

Smith, C., & Smith, D. (2003). Ingestion of ethanol just prior to sleep onset impairs memory for procedural but not declarative tasks. *Sleep: Journal of Sleep & Sleep Disorders Research, 26(2),* 185–191.

Smith, D. (2002). The theory heard 'round the world. *Monitor on Psychology,* p. 30–32.

Smith, E. E. (1995). Concepts and categorization. In E. E. Smith, D. N. Osherson, et al. (Eds.), *Thinking: An invitation to cognitive science,* Vol. 3 (2nd ed.), (pp. 3–33). Cambridge: MIT Press.

Smith, L. J., Nowakowski, S., Soeffing, J. P., Orff, H. J., & Perlis, M. L. (2003). The measurement of sleep. In L. Michael & K. L. Lichstein (Eds.), *Treating sleep disorders: Principles and practice of behavioral sleep medicine.* New York: John Wiley & Sons, Inc.

Smith, T. W., Orleans, C. T., & Jenkins, C. D. (2004). Prevention and health promotion: Decades of progress, new challenges, and an emerging agenda. *Health Psychology, 23(2),* 126–131.

Smits, M. G., van Stel, H. F., van der Heijden, K., Meijer, A. M., Coenen, A. M. L., & Kerkhof, G. A. (2003). Melatonin improves health status and sleep in children with idiopathic chronic sleep-onset insomnia: A randomized placebo-controlled trial. *Journal of the American Academy of Child & Adolescent Psychiatry, 42(11),* 1286–1293.

Snarey, J. R. (1985). Cross-cultural universality of social-moral development: A critical review of Kohlbergian research. *Psychological Bulletin, 97,* 202–233.

Snarey, J. R. (1995). In communitarian voice: The sociological expansion of Kohlbergian theory, research, and practice. In W. M. Kurtines & J. L. Gerwirtz (Eds.), *Moral development: An introduction* (pp. 109–134). Boston: Allyn & Bacon.

Snowden, L. R., & Yamada, A-M. (2005). Cultural differences in access to care. *Annual Review of Clinical Psychology, 1,* 143–166.

Snyder, C. R. (2003). "Me conform? No way": Classroom demonstrations for sensitizing students to their conformity. *Teaching of Psychology, 30(1),* 59–61.

Sokol, R. J. Jr., Delaney-Black, V., & Nordstrom, B. (2003). Fetal alcohol spectrum disorder. *JAMA: Journal of the American Medical Association, 290(22),* 2996–2999.

Solan, H. A., & Mozlin, R. (2001). Children in poverty: Impact on health, visual development, and school failure. *Issues in Interdisciplinary Care, 3(4),* 271–288.

Solms, M. (1997). *The neuropsychology of dreams.* Mahwah, NJ: Lawrence Erlbaum.

Solso, R., Maclin, M., & Maclin, O. (2005). *Cognitive psychology* (7th ed.). Boston, MA: Allyn & Bacon/Longman.

Sommer, R. (1969). *Personal space.* Englewood Cliffs, NJ: Prentice Hall.

Son, L. K., & Metcalfe, J. (2000). Metacognitive and control strategies in study-time allocation. *Journal of Experimental Psychology: Learning, Memory, & Cognition, 26(1),* 204–221.

Song, H-J, Stevens, C. F., & Gage, F. H. (2002). Neural stem cells from adult hippocampus develop essential properties of functional CNS neurons. *Nature Neuroscience, 5,* 438–445.

Sotres-Bayon, F., & Pellicer, F. (2000). The role of the dopaminergic mesolimbic system in the affective component of chronic pain. *Salud Mental, 23(1),* 23–29.

Souchek, A. W. (1986). A comparison of dynamic stereoscopic acuities in both the primary and secondary positions of gaze. *Perception Research Proceedings, 8*(2), 23–28.

Soussignan, R. (2002). Duchenne smile, emotional experience, and autonomic reactivity: A test of the facial feedback hypothesis. *Emotion, 2(1),* 52–74.

Southwick, S. M., Vythilingam, M., & Charney, D. S. (2005). The psychobiology of depression and resilience to stress: Implications for prevention and treatment. *Annual Review of Clinical Psychology, 1,* 255–291.

Spangenberg, H. H., & Theron, C. C. (2002). Development of a uniquely South African leadership questionnaire. *South African Journal of Psychology, 32*(2), 9–25.

Spearman, C. (1923). *The nature of "intelligence" and the principles of cognition.* London: Macmillan.

Spector, P. E. (2003). *Industrial organizational psychology: Research and practice* (3rd ed.). New York: Wiley.

Spence, S. A. (2003). Detecting lies and deceit: The psychology of lying and the implications for professional practice. *Cognitive Neuropsychiatry, 8*(1), 76–77.

Spencer, P., & Vanden-Boom, E. (1999). Year after the death of Michigan State U. student, family advocates sensible drinking. Lansing, MI: University Wire.

Sperling, G. (1960). The information available in brief visual presentations. *Psychological Monographs, 74* (Whole No. 498).

Spiegel, D. (1999). An altered state. *Mind/Body Health Newsletter, 8*(1), 3–5.

Spiegel, D., & Maldonado, J. R. (1999). Dissociative disorders. In R. E. Hales, S. C. Yudofsky, & J. C. Talbott (Eds.), *American psychiatric press textbook of psychiatry.* Washington, DC: American Psychiatric Press.

Spinelli, S. N., Reid, H. M., & Norvilitis, J. M. (2002). Belief in and experience with the paranormal: Relations between personality boundaries, executive functioning, gender role, and academic variables. *Imagination, Cognition & Personality, 21*(4), 333–346

Spinweber, C. L. (1993). Randy Gardner. In M. A. Carskadon (Ed.), *Encyclopedia of sleep and dreaming.* New York: Macmillan.

Spitz, R. A., & Wolf, K. M. (1946). The smiling response: A contribution to the ontogenesis of social relations. *Genetic Psychology Monographs, 34,* 57–123.

Spokane, A. R., Meir, E. I., & Catalano, M. (2000). Person-environment congruence and Holland's theory: A review and reconsideration. *Journal of Vocational Behavior, 57*(2), 137–187.

Sprecher, S., & Regan, P. C. (2002). Liking some things (in some people) more than others: Partner preferences in romantic relationships and friendships. *Journal of Social & Personal Relationships, 19(4),* 463–481.

Springer, J. D. (2005). Measuring the Machiavellian mind. *PsycCRITIQUES, 50* (15), [np].

Springer, S. P., & Deutsch, G. (1998). *Left brain, right brain.* New York: Freeman.

Squier, L. H., & Domhoff, G. W. (1998). The presentation of dreaming and dreams in introductory psychology textbooks: A critical examination. *Dreaming, 10,* 21–26.

Squire, L. R., Schmolck, H., & Buffalo, E. A. (2001). Memory distortions develop over time: A reply to Horn. *Psychological Science, 121(2),* 182.

Stafford, J., & Lynn, S. J. (2002). Cultural scripts, memories of childhood abuse, and multiple identities: A study of role-played enactments. *International Journal of Clinical & Experimental Hypnosis, 50*(1), 67–85.

Stams, G-J. J. M., Juffer, F., van IJzendoorn, M. H. (2002). Maternal sensitivity, infant attachment, and temperament in early childhood predict adjustment in middle childhood: The case of adopted children and their biologically unrelated parents. *Developmental Psychology, 38*(5), 806–821.

Stanton, M. D. (2004). Getting reluctant substance abusers to engage in treatment/ self-help: A review of outcomes and clinical options. *Journal of Marital & Family Therapy, 30*(2), 165–182.

Starkman, N. & Rajani, N. (2002). The case for comprehensive sex education. *AIDS Patient Care & STD's, 16*(7), 313–318.

Steadman, H. J. (1993). *Reforming the insanity defense: An evaluation of pre- and post-Hinckley reforms.* New York: Guilford.

Steele, C. M. (2003). Through the back door to theory. *Psychological Inquiry, 14*(3–4), 314–317.

Steele, C. M., & Aronson, J. (1995). Stereotype threat and the intellectual test performance of African Americans. *Journal of Personality and Social Psychology, 69,* 797–811.

Steele, J., James, J. B., & Barnett, R. C. (2002). Learning in a man's world: Examining the perceptions of undergraduate women in male-dominated academic areas. *Psychology of Women Quarterly, 26(1),* 46–50.

Steffens, D. C., McQuoid, D. R., Welsh-Bohmer, K. A., & Krishnan, K. R. R. (2003). Left orbital frontal cortex volume and performance on the Benton Visual Retention Test in older depressives and controls. *Neuropsychopharmacology, 28*(12), 2179–2183.

Steiger, H., Israël, M., Gauvin, L., Kin, N. M. K. N. Y., & Young, S. N. (2003). Implications of compulsive and impulsive traits for serotonin status in women with bulimia nervosa. *Psychiatry Research, 120*(3), 219–229.

Steinhart, P. (1986, March). Personal boundaries. *Audubon,* pp. 8–11.

Steinmetz, J. E. (1999). The localization of a simple type of learning and memory: The cerebellum and classical eyeblink conditioning. *Contemporary Psychology, 7,* 72–77.

Stella, N., Schweitzer, P., & Piomelli, D. (1997). A second endogenous cannabinoid that modulates long-term potentiation. *Nature, 382,* 677–678.

Stelmack, R. M., Knott, V., & Beauchamp, C. M. (2003). Intelligence and neural transmission time: A brain stem auditory evoked potential analysis. *Personality & Individual Differences, 34*(1), 97–107.

Sternberg, R. J. (1985). *Beyond IQ: A triarchic theory of human intelligence.* New York: Cambridge University Press.

Sternberg, R. J. (1998). Principles of teaching for successful intelligence. *Educational Psychologist, 33,* 65–72.

Sternberg, R. J. (1999). The theory of successful intelligence. *Review of General Psychology, 3,* 292–316.

Sternberg, R. J. (2004). Four alternative futures for education in the United States: It's our choice. *School Psychology Review, 33*(1), 67–77.

Sternberg, R. J. (2005). The importance of converging operations in the study of human intelligence. *Cortex. 41*(2), 243–244.

Sternberg, R. J., & Hedlund, J. (2002). Practical intelligence, g, and work psychology. *Human Performance, 15(1–2),* 143–160.

Sternberg, R. J., & Kaufman, J. C. (1998). Human abilities. *Annual Review of Psychology, 49,* 479–502.

Sternberg, R. J., & Lubart, T. I. (1992). Buy low and sell high: An investment approach to creativity. *Current Directions in Psychological Science, 1*(1), 1–5.

Sternberg, R. J., & Lubart, T. I. (1996). Investing in creativity. *American Psychologist, 51*(7), 677–688.

Stetter, F., & Kupper, S. (2002). Autogenic training: A meta-analysis of clinical outcome studies. *Applied Psychophysiology & Biofeedback, 27(1),* 45–98.

Stewart, J. (2003). The mommy track: The consequences of gender ideology and aspirations on age at first motherhood. *Journal of Sociology & Social Welfare, 30*(2), 3–30.

Stockhorst, U., Spennes-Saleh, S., Koerholz, D., Goebel, U., Schneider, M. E., Steingrueber, H-J., & Klosterhalfen, S. (2000). Anticipatory symptoms and anticipatory immune responses in pediatric cancer patients receiving chemotherapy: Features of a classically conditioned response? *Brain, Behavior & Immunity, 14*(3), 198–218.

Stompe, T. G., Ortwein-Swoboda, K., Ritter, K., & Schanda, H. (2003). Old wine in new bottles? Stability and plasticity of the contents of schizophrenic delusions. *Psychopathology, 36*(1), 6–12.

Stoner, J. A. (1961). A comparison of individual and group decisions involving risk. *Unpublished master's thesis,* School of Industrial Management, MIT, Cambridge, MA.

Stormshak, E. A., Bierman, K. L., McMahon, R. J., & Lengua, L. J., Conduct Problems Prevention Research Group. (2000). Parenting practices and child disruptive behavior problems in early elementary school. *Journal of Clinical Child Psychology, 29*(1), 17–29.

Storosum, J. G., Elferink, A. J. A., van Zwieten, B. J., van den Brink, W., & Huyser, J. (2004). Natural course and placebo response in short-term, placebo-controlled studies in major depression: A meta-analysis of published and non-published studies. *Pharmacopsychiatry, 37*(1), 32–36.

Strack, F., Martin, L. L., & Stepper, S. (1988). Inhibiting and facilitating conditions of the human smile: A nonobstrusive test of the facial feedback hypothesis. *Journal of Personality and Social Psychology, 54,* 768–777.

Strange, J. M., & Mumford, M. D. (2002). The origins of vision: Charismatic versus ideological leadership. *Leadership Quarterly, 13*(4), 343–377.

Stratton, G. M. (1897). Vision without inversion of the retinal image. *Psychological Review, 4*(4), 341–360.

Streri, A., Gentaz, E., Spelke, E., & Van de Walle, G. (2004). Infants' haptic perception of object unity in rotating displays. *Quarterly Journal of Experimental Psychology: Human Experimental Psychology, 57A*(3), 523–538.

Stroebe, M., Schut, H., & Stroebe, W. (2005). Attachment in coping with bereavement: A theoretical integration. *Review of General Psychology, 9*(1), 48–66.

Subramanian, S., & Vollmer, R. R. (2002). Sympathetic activation fenfluramine depletes brown adipose tissue norepinephrine content in rats. *Pharmacology, Biochemistry & Behavior, 73*(3), 639–646.

Sue, D.W., & Sue, D. (2002). *Counseling the culturally diverse: Theory and practice.* New York: Wiley.

Suhr, J. A. (2002). Malingering, coaching, and the serial position effect. *Archives of Clinical Neuropsychology, 17*(1), 69–77.

Sullivan, M. J. L., Tripp, D. A., & Santor, D. (1998). Gender differences in pain and pain behavior: The role of catastrophizing. Paper presented at the annual meeting of the American Psychological Association, San Francisco.

Sullivan, P. F., Kendler, K. S., & Neale, M. C. (2003). Schizophrenia as a complex trait: Evidence from a meta-analysis of studies. *Archives of General Psychiatry, 60*(12), 1187–1192.

Suomi, S. J. (1991). Adolescent depression and depressive symptoms: Insights from longitudinal studies with rhesus monkeys. *Journal of Youth & Adolescence, 20,* 273–287.

Surawy, C., Roberts, J., & Silver, A. (2005). The effect of mindfulness training on mood and measures of fatigue, activity, and quality of life in patients with chronic fatigue syndrome on a hospital waiting list: A series of exploratory studies. *Behavioural & Cognitive Psychotherapy. 33*(1), 103–109.

Suzuki, L., & Aronson, J. (2005). The cultural malleability of intelligence and its impact on the racial/ethnic hierarchy. *Psychology, Public Policy, and Law, 11*(2), 320–327.

Suzuki, W. A., & Amaral, D. G. (2004). Functional neuroanatomy of the medial temporal lobe memory system. *Cortex, 40*(1), 220–222.

Swaab, D. F., Chung, W. C. J., Kruijver, F. P. M., Hofman, M. A., & Hestiantoro, A. (2003). Sex differences in the hypothalamus in the different stages of human life. *Neurobiology of Aging, 24*(Suppl1), S1–S16.

Swanson, J. W., Swartz, M. S., & Elbogen, E. B. (2004). Effectiveness of atypical antipsychotic medications in reducing violent behavior among persons with schizophrenia in community-based treatment. *Schizophrenia Bulletin, 30*(1), 3–20.

Swartz, K. L. & Margolis, S. (2004). *De pression and anxiety. Johns Hopkins White Papers.* Baltimore: Johns Hopkins Medical Institutions.

Sylvester, A. P., Mulsant, B. H., Chengappa, K. N. R., Sandman, A. R., & Haskett, R. F. (2000). Use of electroconvulsive therapy in a state hospital: A 10–year review. *Journal of Clinical Psychiatry, 61,* 534–544.

Szasz, T. (1960). The myth of mental illness. *American Psychologist, 15,* 113–118.

Szasz, T. (2000). Second commentary on "Aristotle's function argument." *Philosophy, Psychiatry, & Psychology, 7,* 3–16.

Szasz, T. (2004). The psychiatric protection order for the "battered mental patient." *British Medical Journal, 327*(7429), 1449–1451.

Tait, R. J., & Hulse, G. K. (2003). A systematic review of the effectiveness of brief interventions with substance using adolescents by type of drug. *Drug & Alcohol Review, 22*(3), 337–346.

Takeshita, T., & Morimoto, K. (1999). Self-reported alcohol-associated symptoms and drinking behavior in three ALDH2 genotypes among Japanese university students. *Alcoholism: Clinical & Experimental Research, 23*(6), 1065–1069.

Talbot, N. L., Duberstein, P. R., King, D. A., Cox, C., & Giles, D. E. (2000). Personality traits of women with a history of childhood sexual abuse. *Comprehensive Psychiatry, 41,* 130–136.

Talwar, S. K., Xu, S., Hawley, E. S., Weiss, S. A., Moxon, K. A., & Chapin, J. K. (2002). Rat navigation guided by remote control. *Nature, 417*(6884), 37–38.

Tanaka, T., Yoshida, M., Yokoo, H., Tomita, M., & Tanaka, M. (1998). Expression of aggression attenuates both stress-induced gastric ulcer formation and increases in noradrenaline release in the rat amygdala assessed intracerebral microdialysis. *Pharmacology, Biochemistry & Behavior, 59*(1), 27–31.

Tanda, G., & Goldberg, S. R. (2003). Cannabinoids: Reward, dependence, and underlying neurochemical mechanisms-a review of recent preclinical data. *Psychopharmacology, 169*(2), 115–134.

Tang, Y.-P., Wang, H., Feng, R., Kyin, M., & Tsien, J. Z. (2001). Differential effects of enrichment on learning and memory function in NR2B transgenic mice. *Neuropharmacology, 41*(6), 779–790.

Tannen, D. (1990). Gender differences in topical coherence: Creating involvement in best friends' talk. *Discourse Processes, 13*(1), 73–90.

Tanner-Halverson, P., Burden, T., & Sabers, D. (1993). WISC-III normative data for Tohono O'odham Native-American children. In B. A. Bracken & R. S. McCallum (Eds.), *Journal of Psychoeducational Assessment Monograph Series, Advances in Psychoeducational Assessment: Wechsler Intelligence Scale for Children–Third Edition* (pp. 125–133). Germantown, TN: Psychoeducational Corporation.

Taraban, R., Maki, W. S., & Rynearson, K. (1999). Measuring study time distributions: Implications for designing computer-based courses. *Behavior Research Methods, Instruments & Computers, 31,* 263–269.

Tarsy, D., Baldessarini, R. J., & Tarazi, F. I. (2002). Effects of newer antipsychotics on extrapyramidal function. *CNS Drugs, 16*(1), 23–45.

Task Force of the National Advisory Council on Alcohol Abuse and Alcoholism, National Institute on Alcohol Abuse and Alcoholism. *A Call to Action: Changing the Culture of Drinking at U.S. Colleges* (Washington, D.C.: National Institutes of Health, 2002). Retrieved from www.collegedrinkingprevention.gov/.

Tatrow, K., Blanchard, E. B., & Silverman, D. J. (2003). Posttraumatic headache: An exploratory treatment study. *Applied Psychophysiology & Biofeedback, 28*(4), 267–279.

Taub, E. (2004). Harnessing brain plasticity through behavioral techniques to produce new treatments in neurorehabilitation. *American Psychologist, 59*(8), 692–704.

Taub, E. et al. (2004). Efficacy of constraint-induced movement therapy for children with cerebral palsy with asymmetric motor impairment. *Pediatrics, 113,* 305–309.

Taub, E., Gitendra, U., & Thomas, E. (2002). New treatments in neurorehabilitation founded on basic research. *Nature Reviews Neuroscience, 3,* 228–236.

Taub, E., & Morris, D. (2002). Constraint-induced movement therapy to enhance recovery after stroke. *Current Artherosclerosis Reports, 3,* 279–86.

Taylor, D. J., Lichstein, K. L., & Durrence, H. H. (2003). Insomnia as a health risk factor. *Behavioral Sleep Medicine, 1*(4), 227–247.

Taylor, E. (1999). William James and Sigmund Freud: "The future of psychology belongs to your work." *Psychological Science, 10*(6), 465–469.

Taylor, R. C., Harris, N. A., Singleton, E. G., Moolchan, E. T., & Heishman, S. J. (2000). Tobacco craving: Intensity-related effects of imagery scripts in drug abusers. *Experimental and Clinical Psychopharmacology, 8*(1), 75–87.

Taylor, S. E., & Armor, D. A. (1996). Positive illusions and coping with adversity. *Journal of Personality, 64,* 873–898.

Tebartz van Elst, L, Hesslinger, B., Thiel, T., Geiger, E., Haegele, K., Lemieux, L., Lieb, K., Bohus, M., Hennig, J., & Ebert, D. (2003). Frontolimbic brain abnormalities in patients with borderline personality disorder: A volumetric magnetic resonance imaging study. *Biological Psychiatry, 54*(2), 163–171.

Tedlock, B. (1992). Zuni and Quiche dream sharing and interpreting. In B. Tedlock (Ed.), *Dreaming: Anthropological and psychological interpretations.* Santa Fe, NM: School of American Research Press.

Teesson, M., Hodder, T., & Buhrich, N. (2004). Psychiatric disorders in homeless men and women in inner Sydney. *Australian & New Zealand Journal of Psychiatry, 38*(3),162–168.

Tein, J-Y, Sandler, I. N., & Zautra, A. J. (2000). Stressful life events, psychological distress, coping, and parenting of divorced mothers longitudinal study. *Journal of Family Psychology, 14*(1), 27–42.

Tellegen, A. (1985). Structures of mood and personality and their relevance to assessing anxiety with an emphasis on self-report. In A. H. Tuma & J. D. Maser (Eds.), *Anxiety*

and the anxiety disorders (pp. 681–706). Hillsdale, NJ: Erlbaum.

Templer, D. I., Torneo, M. E., Arikawa, H., & Williams, R. (2003). Asian-Black differences in aptitude and difficulty of chosen academic disciplines. *Personality & Individual Differences, 35*(1), 237–241.

Terman, L. M. (1916). The measurement of intelligence. Boston: Houghton Mifflin.

Terman, L. M. (1954). Scientists and nonscientists in a group of 800 gifted men. *Psychological Monographs, 68*(7), 1–44.

Ternov, N., Kvorning, G., Lars, Åberg, A., Algotsson, L., & Åkeson, J. (2001). Acupuncture for lower back and pelvic pain in late pregnancy: A retrospective report on 167 consecutive cases. *Pain Medicine, 2*(3), 204–207.

Terrace, H. S. (1979, November). How Nim Chimpsky changed my mind. *Psychology Today,* pp. 65–76.

Terry, S. W. (2003). *Learning and memory: Basic principles, processes, and procedures* (2nd ed.). Boston, MA: Allyn & Bacon.

Tett, R. P., & Murphy, P. J. (2002). Personality and situations in co-worker preference: Similarity and complementarity in worker compatibility. *Journal of Business & Psychology, 17*(2), 223–243.

Teusch, L., Boehme, H., Finke, J., & Gastpar, K. (2001). Effects of client-centered psychotherapy for personality disorders alone and in combination with psychopharmacological treatment. *Psychotherapy & Psychosomatics, 70*(6), 328–336.

Thapar, A., Fowler, T., Rice, F., Scourfield, J., van den Bree, M., Thomas, H., Harold, G., & Hay, D. (2003). Maternal smoking during pregnancy and attention deficit hyperactivity disorder symptoms in offspring. *American Journal of Psychiatry, 160*(11), 1985–1989.

The Center for Academic Integrity (2001). *CAI Research.* [On-line]. Available: http://ethics.acusd.edu/video/cai/2001/McCabe/index_files/frame.html

Theoharides, T. C., & Cochrane, D. E. (2004). Critical role of mast cells in inflammatory diseases and the effect of acute stress. *Journal of Neuroimmunology, 146*(1–2), 1–12.

Thogersen, J. (2004). A cognitive dissonance interpretation of consistencies and inconsistencies in environmentally responsible behavior. *Journal of Environmental Psychology, 24*(1), 93–103.

Thomas, A., & Chess, S. (1977). *Temperament and development.* New York: Brunner/Mazel.

Thomas, A., & Chess, S. (1987). Roundtable: What is temperament: Four approaches. *Child Development, 58,* 505–529.

Thomas, A., & Chess, S. (1991). Temperament in adolescence and its functional significance. In R. M. Lerner, A. C. Petersen, & J. Brooks-Gunn (Eds.), *Encyclopedia of adolescence* (Vol. 2). New York: Garland.

Thomas, B. L., & Ayres, J. J. B. (2004). Use of the ABA fear renewal paradigm to assess the effects of extinction with co-present fear inhibitors or excitors: Implications for theories of extinction and for treating human fears and phobias. *Learning & Motivation, 35*(1), 22–52.

Thompson, D. (1997, March 24). A boy without a penis. *Time,* 83.

Thompson, R. F. (2005). In search of memory traces. *Annual Review of Clinical Psychology, 56,* 1–23.

Thorndike, E. L. (1898). Animal intelligence. *Psychological Review Monograph, 2*(8).

Thorndike, E. L. (1911). *Animal intelligence.* New York: Macmilan.

Thornhill, R., Gangestad, S. W., Miller, R., Scheyd, G., McCollough, J. K., & Franklin, M. (2003). Major histocompatibility complex genes, symmetry, and body scent attractiveness in men and women. *Behavioral Ecology, 14*(5), 668–678.

Thurstone, L. L. (1938). *Primary mental abilities.* Chicago: University of Chicago Press.

Tice, D. M., & Baumeister, R. F. (1997). Longitudinal study of procrastination, performance, stress, and health: The costs and benefits of dawdling. *Psychological Science, 8,* 454–458.

Tietzel, A. J., & Lack, L. C. (2001). The short-term benefits of brief and long naps following nocturnal sleep restriction. *Sleep: Journal of Sleep Research & Sleep Medicine, 24*(3), 293–300.

Tiihonen, J., Isohanni, M., Rasanen, P., Koiranen, M., & Moring, J. (1997). Specific major mental disorders and criminality: A 26–year prospective study of the 1966 northern Finland birth cohort. *American Journal of Psychiatry, 154,* 840–845.

Tirodkar, M. A., & Jain, A. (2003). Food messages on African American television shows. *American Journal of Public Health, 93*(3), 439–441.

Tjosvold, D., & De Dreu, C. (1997). Managing conflict in Dutch organizations: A test of the relevance of Deutsch's cooperation theory. *Journal of Applied Social Psychology, 27*(24), 2213–2227.

Todorov, A., & Bargh, J. A. (2002). Automatic sources of aggression. *Aggression & Violent Behavior, 7*(1), 53–68.

Tolman, E. C., & Honzik, C. H. (1930). Introduction and removal of reward and maze performance in rats. *University of California Publications in Psychology, 4,* 257–275.

Torrance, E. P. (2004). Great expectations: Creative achievements of the sociometric stars in a 30-year study. *Journal of Secondary Gifted Education, 16*(1), 5–13.

Torrey, E. F. (1998). *Out of the shadows: Confronting America's mental illness crisis.* New York: Wiley.

Torrey, E. F., & Yolken, R. H. (1998). Is household crowding a risk factor for schizophrenia and bipolar disorder? *Schizophrenia Bulletin, 24,* 321–324.

Torrey, E. F., & Yolken, R. H. (2000). Familial and genetic mechanisms in schizophrenia. *Brain Research Reviews, 31,* 113–117.

Trainor, B. C., Bird, I. M., & Marler, C. A. (2004). Opposing hormonal mechanisms of aggression revealed through short-lived testosterone manipulations and multiple winning experiences. *Hormones & Behavior, 45*(2), 115–121.

Trappey, C. (1996). A meta-analysis of consumer choice and subliminal advertising. *Psychology and Marketing, 13,* 517–530.

Triandis, H. C. (2001). Individualism-collectivism and personality. *Journal of Personality, 69*(6), 907–924.

Troll, S. J., Miller, J., & Atchley, R. C. (1979). *Families in later life.* Belmont, CA: Wadsworth.

Trotter, R. J. (1987, January). The play's the thing. *Psychology Today,* pp. 27–34.

Trudeau, K. J., Danoff-Burg, S., Svenson, T. A., & Paget, S. A. (2003). Agency and communion in people with rheumatoid arthritis. *Sex Roles, 49*(7–8), 303–311.

Trull, T., Sher, K. J., Minks-Brown, C., Durbin, J., & Burr, R. (2000). Borderline personality disorder and substance use disorders: A review and integration. *Clinical Psychology Review, 20,* 235–253.

Trull, T. T., & Durrett, C. A. (2005). Categorical and dimensional models of personality disorder. *Annual Review of Clinical Psychology, 1,* 355–380.

Trump, K. S. (2000). *Classroom killers? Hallway hostages? How schools can prevent and manage school crises.* Thousand Oaks, CA: Sage.

Tseng, W. (2004). Culture and psychotherapy: Asian perspectives. *Journal of Mental Health (UK). 13*(2), 151–161.

Tsien, J. Z. (2000, April). Building a brainier mouse. *Scientific American,* pp. 62–68.

Tu, G-C., & Israel, Y. (1995). Alcohol consumption by Orientals in North America is predicted largely by a single gene. *Behavior Genetics, 25*(1), 59–65.

Tulving, E. (2000). Concepts of memory. In E. Tulving & F. I. M. Craik (Eds.), *The Oxford handbook of memory.* New York: Oxford University Press.

Tulving, E., & Thompson, D. M. (1973). Encoding specificity and retrieval processes in episodic memory. *Psychological Review, 80,* 352–373.

Turkington, D., Dudley, R., Warman, D. M., & Beck, A. T. (2004). Cognitive-behavioral therapy for schizophrenia: A review. *Journal of Psychiatric Practice, 10*(1), 5–16.

Turnbull, C. M. (1961). Some observations regarding the experiences and behavior of the Bamputi pygmies. *American Journal of Psychology, 74,* 304–308.

Turner, M. E., & Horvitz, T. (2001). The dilemma of threat: Group effectiveness and ineffectiveness under adversity. In M. E. Turner (Ed.), *Groups at work: Theory and research.* Mahwah, NJ: Lawrence Erlbaum Associates.

Turnipseed, D. L. (2003). Hardy personality: A potential link with organizational citizenship behavior. *Psychological Reports, 93*(2), 529–543.

Tusing, K. J., & Dillard, J. P. (2000). The psychological reality of the door-in-the-face: It's helping, not bargaining. *Journal of Language & Social Psychology, 19*(1), 5–25.

Tversky, A., & Kahneman, D. (1974). Judgment under uncertainty: Heuristics and biases. *Science, 185,* 1124–1131.

Tversky, A., Kahneman, D. (1993). Probabilistic reasoning. In A. I. Goldman (Ed.), *Readings in philosophy and cognitive science.* Cambridge, MA: The MIT Press.

Twenge, J. M., Baumeister, R. F., Tice, D. M., & Stucke, T. S. (2001). If you can't join them, beat them: Effects of social exclusion on aggressive behavior. *Journal of Personality & Social Psychology, 81*(6), 1058–1069.

Uehara, I. (2000). Differences in episodic memory between four- and five-year-olds: False information versus real experiences. *Psychological Reports, 86*(3,Pt1), 745–755.

Uhlmann, E., & Swanson, J. (2004). Exposure to violent video games increases automatic aggressiveness. *Journal of Adolescence, 27*(1), 41–52.

Ulrich, R. E., Stachnik, T. J., & Stainton, N. R. (1963). Student acceptance of generalized personality interpretations. *Psychological Reports, 13,* 831–834.

Underwood, J., & Pezdek, K. (1998). Memory suggestibility as an example of the sleeper effect. *Psychonomic Bulletin & Review, 5,* 449–453.

Unger, J. B., Chou, C-P., Palmer, P. H., Ritt-Olson, A., Gallaher, P., Cen, S., Lichtman, K., Azen, S., & Johnson, C. A. (2004). Project FLAVOR: 1–Year outcomes of a multicultural, school-based smoking prevention curriculum for adolescents. *American Journal of Public Health, 94*(2), 263–265.

Unsworth, G., & Ward, T. (2001). Video games and aggressive behaviour. *Australian Psychologist, 36*(3), 184–192.

Urakubo, A., Jarskog, L. F., Lieberman, J. A., & Gilmore, J. H. (2001). Prenatal exposure to maternal infection alters cytokine expression in the placenta, amniotic fluid, and fetal brain. *Schizophrenia Research, 47*(1), 27–36.

USA Today. (2005, June 2) *CDC retreats from recent obesity study.* [On-line]. Available: http://www.usatoday.com/news/health/2005-06-02-obesity-confusion_x.htm

Valdez, P., Ramírez, C., & García, A. (2003). Adjustment of the sleep-wake cycle to small (1–2 h) changes in schedule. *Biological Rhythm Research, 34*(2), 145–155.

Valenstein, E. S. (1998). *Blaming the brain: The truth about drugs and mental health.* New York: Free Press.

Valsiner, J. (2000). *Culture and human development.* Thousand Oaks, CA: Sage.

Van de Carr, F. R., & Lehrer, M. (1997). *While you are expecting: Your own prenatal classroom.* New York: Humanics Publishing.

Van de Castle, R. L. (1995). *Our dreaming mind.* New York: Ballantine Books.

Van Hulle, C. A., Goldsmith, H. H., & Lemery, K. S. (2004). Genetic, environmental, and gender effects on individual differences in toddler expressive language. *Journal of Speech, Language, & Hearing Research, 47*(4), 904–912.

van IJzendoorn, M. H., & De Wolff, M. S. (1997). In search of the absent father: Meta-analyses of infant-father attachment: A rejoinder to our discussants. *Child Development, 68,* 604–609.

Van Overwalle, F., & Jordens, K. (2002). An adaptive connectionist model of cognitive dissonance.

van Schaick, K., & Stolberg, A. L. (2001). The impact of paternal involvement and parental divorce on young adults' intimate relationships. *Journal of Divorce & Remarriage, 36*(1–2), 99–122.

Van Vugt, M., & De Cremer, D. (1999). Leadership in social dilemmas: The effects of group identification on collective actions to provide public goods. *Journal of Personality & Social Psychology, 76*(4), 587–599.

Van Vugt, M., Jepson, S. F., Hart, C. M., & De Cremer, D. (2004). Autocratic leadership in social dilemmas: A threat to group stability. *Journal of Experimental Social Psychology, 40*(1), 1–13.

Van Wel, F., Linnsen, H., & Abma, R. (2000). The parental bond and the well-being of adolescents and young adults. *Journal of Youth & Adolescence, 29,* 307–318.

Vance, J. E., Fernandez, G., & Biber, M. (1998). Educational progress in a population of youth with aggression and emotional disturbance: The role of risk and protective factors. *Journal of Emotional and Behavioral Disorders, 6,* 214–221.

Vandenberghe, C., Stordeur, S., & D'hoore, W. (2002). Transactional and transformational leadership in nursing: Structural validity and substantive relationships. *European Journal of Psychological Assessment, 18(1),* 16–29.

Vanderwerker, L. C., & Prigerson, H. G. (2004). Social support and technological connectedness as protective factors in bereavement. *Journal of Loss & Trauma, 9(1),* 45–57.

Vaughan, P. (2004). *Telling stories, saving lives. Population Communications International (PCI).* [On-line]. Available: http://population.org/entsummit/transcript04_vaughan.shtm.

Vaughn, D. (1996). *The Challenger launch decision: Risky technology, culture, and deviance at NASA.* Chicago: University of Chicago Press.

Venkatesh, V., Morris, M. G., Sykes, T. A., & Ackerman, P. L. (2004). Individual reactions to new technologies in the workplace: The role of gender as a psychological construct. *Journal of Applied Social Psychology, 34(3),* 445–467.

Ventner, C. et al., (2001). The sequence of the human genome. *Science, 291,* 1304–1323.

Verplanken, B., & Holland, R. W. (2002). Motivated decision making: Effects of activation and self-centrality of values on choices and behavior. *Journal of Personality & Social Psychology, 82(3),* 434–447.

Verschuere, B., Crombez, G., & Koster, E. H. W. (2004). Orienting to guilty knowledge. *Cognition & Emotion, 18(2),* 265–279.

Vertosick, F. T. (2000). *Why we hurt: The natural history of pain.* New York: Harcourt, Inc.

Vickers, J. C., et al. (2000). The cause of neuronal degeneration in Alzheimer's disease. *Progress in Neurobiology, 60,* 139–165.

Vidmar, N. (1997). Generic prejudice and the presumption of guilt in sex abuse trials. *Law and Human Behavior, 21(1),* 5–25.

Villarreal, D. M., Do, V., Haddad, E., & Derrick, B. E. (2002). MDA receptor antagonists sustain LTP and spatial memory: Active processes mediate LTP decay. *Nature Neuroscience, 5(1),* 48–52.

Vitaterna, M. H., Takahashi, J. S., & Turek, F. W. (2001). Overview of circadian rhythms. *Alcohol Research & Health, 25(2),* 85–93.

Vocks, S., Ockenfels, M., Jürgensen, R., Mussgay, L., & Rüddel, H. (2004). Blood pressure reactivity can be reduced by a cognitive behavioral stress management program. *International Journal of Behavioral Medicine, 11(2),* 63–70.

Volavka, J. (2002). Risk for individuals with schizophrenia who are living in the community. *Psychiatric Services, 53(4),* 484–485.

Von Bergen, C. W., Soper, B., & Foster, T. (2002). Unintended negative effects of diversity management. *Public Personnel Management, 31(2),* 239–251.

Voyer, D., Voyer, S., & Bryden, M. (1995). Magnitude of sex differences in spatial abilities: A meta-analysis and consideration of critical variables. *Psychological Bulletin, 117,* 250–270.

Vroomen, J., & de Gelder, B. (2004). Temporal ventriloquism: Sound modulates the flash-lag effect. *Journal of Experimental Psychology: Human Perception & Performance, 30(3),* 513–518.

Wada, K., Suzuki, H., Taira,T., Akiyama, K., & Kuroda, S. (2004). Successful use of intravenous clomipramine in depressive-catatonic state associated with corticosteroid treatment. *International Journal of Psychiatry in Clinical Practice, 8(2),*131–133.

Wadden, T. A., Brownell, K. D., & Foster, G. D. (2002). Obesity: Responding to the global epidemic. *Journal of Consulting & Clinical Psychology, 70(3),* 510–525.

Wagner, U., Hallschmid, M., Verleger, R., & Born, J. (2003). Signs of REM sleep dependent enhancement of implicit face memory: A repetition priming study. *Biological Psychology, 62(3),* 197–210.

Wahl, H., Becker, S., Burmedi, D., & Schilling, O. (2004). The role of primary and secondary control in adaptation to age-related vision loss: A study of older adults with macular degeneration. *Psychology & Aging, 19(1),* 235–239.

Wahlgren, K., & Lester, D. (2003). The big four: Personality in dogs. *Psychological Reports, 92(3),* 828.

Wakfield, M., Flay, B., Nichter, M., & Giovino, G. (2003). Role of the media in influencing trajectories of youth smoking. *Addiction, 98*(Suppl1), 79–103.

Wakimoto, S., & Fujihara, T. (2004). The correlation between intimacy and objective similarity in interpersonal relationships. *Social Behavior & Personality, 32(1),* 95–102.

Walinder, J., & Rutz, W. (2002). Male depression and suicide. *International Clinical Psychopharmacology, 16(Suppl2),* S21–S24.

Walker, E., Kestler, L., Bollini, A., & Hochman, K. M. Schizophrenia: Etiology and course. (2004). *Annual Review of Psychology, 55,* 401–430.

Walker, I., & Crogan, M. (1998). Academic performance, prejudice, and the jigsaw classroom: New pieces to the puzzle. *Journal of Community and Applied Social Psychology, 8,* 381–393.

Walker, J. (2004). *The death of David Reimer: A tale of sex, science, and abuse.* [On-line]. Available: http://www.reason.com/links/links052404.shtml

Wallace, A. F. C. (1958). Dreams and wishes of the soul: A type of psychoanalytic theory among the seventeenth century Iroquois. *American Anthropologist, 60,* 234–248.

Wallace, D. C. (1997, August). Mitochondrial DNA in aging and disease. *Scientific American,* 40–47.

Waller, M. R., & McLanahan, S. S. (2005). "His" and "her" marriage expectations: Determinants and consequences. *Journal of Marriage & Family, 67(1),* 53–67.

Waller, N. G., & Ross, C. A. (1997). The prevalence and biometric structure of pathological dissociation in the general population: Taxometric and behavior genetics findings. *Journal of Abnormal Psychology, 106,* 499–510.

Walsh, J. K., & Lindblom, S. S. (1997). Psychophysiology of sleep deprivation and disruption. In M. R. Pressman, W. C. Orr, et al. (Eds.), *Understanding sleep: The evaluation and treatment of sleep disorders. Application and practice in health psychology* (pp. 73–110). Washington, DC: American Psychological Association.

Waples, K. A., & Gales, N. J. (2001). Evaluating and minimising social stress in the care of captive bottlenose dolphins (Tursiops aduncus). *Zoo Biology, 21(1),* 5–26.

Ward, I. (2000). *Introducing psychoanalysis.* Thousand Oaks, CA: Totem Books.

Wark, G. R., & Krebs, D. L. (1996). Gender and dilemma differences in real-life moral judgment. *Developmental Psychology, 32,* 220–230.

Warner, M. (2004, May 11). *Heart of darkness. PBS Online NewsHour.* [On-line]. Available: http://www.pbs.org/newshour/bb/middle_east/jan-june04/prisoners_5-11.html

Warr, P., Butcher, V., & Robertson, I. (2004). Activity and psychological well-being in older people. *Aging & Mental Health, 8(2),* 172–183.

Wartik, N. (1996). Learning to mourn. *American Health, 15(4),* 76–79, 96.

Wason, P. C. (1968). Reasoning about a rule. *Quarterly Journal of Experimental Psychology, 20(3),* 273–281.

Wasserman, D., & Wachbroit, R. S. (2000). *Genetics and criminal behavior.* Cambridge, MA: Cambridge University Press.

Watkins, L. M., & Johnston, L. (2000). Screening job applicants: The impact of physical attractiveness and application quality. *International Journal of Selection & Assessment, 8(2),* 76–84.

Watkins, L. R., & Maier, S. F. (2000). The pain of being sick: Implications of immune-to-brain communication for understanding pain. *Annual Review of Psychology, 51,* 29–57.

Watson, J. (1913). Psychology as the behaviorist views it. *Psychological Review, 20,* 158–177.

Watson, J. B., Mednick, S. A., Huttunen, M., & Wang, X. (1999). Prenatal teratogens and the development of adult mental illness. *Development & Psychopathology, 11*(3), 457–466.

Watson, J. B., & Rayner, R. (1920). Conditioned emotional reactions. *Journal of Experimental Psychology, 3,* 1–14.

Watson, J. B., & Rayner, R. (2000). Conditioned emotional reactions. *American Psychologist, 55*(3), 313–317.

Wax, M. L. (2004). Dream sharing as social practice. *Dreaming, 14*(2–3), 83–93.

Waye, K. P., Bengtsson, J., Rylander, R., Hucklebridge, F., Evans, P., & Clow, A. (2002). Low frequency noise enhances cortisol among noise sensitive subjects during work performance. *Life Sciences, 70*(7), 745–758.

Waynforth, D. (2001). Mate choice trade-offs and women's preference for physically attractive men. *Human Nature, 12*(3), 207–219.

Weaver, C. A., & Kelemen, W. L. (1997). Judgments of learning at delays: Shifts in response patterns or increased metamemory accuracy? *Psychological Science, 8,* 318–321.

Wechsler, D. (1944). *The measurement of adult intelligence* (3rd ed.). Baltimore: Williams & Wilkins.

Wechsler, D. (1977). *Manual for the Wechsler Intelligence Scale for Children* (Rev.). New York: Psychological Corporation.

Wechsler, H., Lee, J. E., Kuo, M., Seibring, M., Nelson, T. F., & Lee, H. (2002). Trends in college binge drinking during a period of increased prevention efforts: Findings from 4 Harvard School of Public Health College Alcohol Study Surveys, 1993–2001. *Journal of American College Health, 50,* 203–217.

Wehrle, T., Kaiser, S., Schmidt, S., & Scherer, K. R. (2000). Studying the dynamics of emotional expression using synthesized facial muscle movements. *Journal of Personality and Social Psychology, 78*(1), 105–119.

Weinberger, J., & Westen, D. (2001). Science and psychodynamics: From arguments about Freud to data. *Psychological Inquiry, 12*(3), 129–132.

Weiner, B. (1972). *Theories of motivation.* Chicago: Rand-McNally.

Weiner, B. (1982). The emotional consequences of causal attributions. In M. S.

Clark & S. T. Fiske (Eds.), *Affect and cognition.* Hillsdale, NJ: Erlbaum.

Weinstock, H., Berman, S., & Cates, W. (2004). Sexually transmitted diseases among American youth: Incidence and prevalence estimates, 2000. *Perspectives on Sexual and Reproductive Health, 36,* 6–10.

Weissman, M. M., Markowitz, J. C., & Klerman, G. L. (2003). Comprehensive guide to interpersonal psychotherapy. *American Journal of Psychiatry, 160*(2), 398–400.

Weisz, J. R., Doss, A. J., & Hawley, K. M. (2005). Youth psychotherapy outcome research: A review and critique of the evidence base. *Annual Review of Psychology, 56,* 337–363.

Weitlauf, J. C., Cervone, D., Smith, R. E., & Wright, P. M. (2001). Assessing generalization in perceived self-efficacy: Multidomain and global assessments of the effects of self-defense training for women. *Personality & Social Psychology Bulletin, 27*(12), 1683–1691.

Wells, A., & Carter, K. (2001). Further tests of a cognitive model of generalized anxiety disorder: Metacognitions and worry in GAD, panic disorder, social phobia, depression, and nonpatients. *Behavior Therapy, 32*(1), 85–102.

Werner, J. S., & Wooten, B. R. (1979). Human infant color vision and color perception. *Infant Behavior and Development, 2*(3), 241–273.

Werth, J. L. Jr., Wright, K. S., Archambault, R. J., & Bardash, R. (2003). When does the "duty to protect" apply with a client who has anorexia nervosa? *Counseling Psychologist. 31*(4), 427–450.

Westen, D. (1998). Unconscious thought, feeling, and motivation: The end of a century-long debate. In R. F. Bornstein & J. M. Masling (Eds.), *Empirical perspectives on the psychoanalytic unconscious.* Washington, DC: American Psychological Association.

Westen, D. (2000). Psychoanalysis: Theories. In A. E. Kazdin (Ed.), *Encyclopedia of psychology, Vol. 6* (pp. 344–349). Washington, DC: American Psychological Association.

Whitbourne, S. K. (2005). *Adult development and aging: Biopsychosocial perspectives.* Hoboken, NJ: Wiley.

White, J. R., & Freeman, A. S. (2000). *Cognitive-behavioral group therapy for specific problems and populations.* Washington, DC: American Psychological Association.

White, L. K., & Rogers, S. J. (1997). Strong support but uneasy relationships: Coresidence and adult children's relationships with their parents. *Journal of Marriage and the Family, 59,* 62–76.

White, T., Andreasen, N. C., & Nopoulos, P. (2002). Brain volumes and surface mor-

phology in monozygotic twins. *Cerebral Cortex, 12*(5), 486–493.

Whitney, D. K., Kusznir, A., & Dixie, A. (2002). Women with depression: The importance of social, psychological and occupational factors in illness and recovery. *Journal of Occupational Science, 9*(1), 20–27.

Whorf, B. L. (1956). Science and linguistics. In J. B. Carroll (Ed.), *Language, thought and reality.* Cambridge, MA: MIT Press.

Whyte, M. K., (1992, March-April). Choosing mates—the American way. *Society,* pp. 71–77.

Wickelgren, I. (1998). Teaching the brain to take drugs. *Science, 280,* 2045–2047.

Wickelgren, I. (2002). *Animal studies raise hopes for spinal cord repair.* [On-line]. Available: http://www.sciencemag.org/cgi/content/full/297/5579/178

Wicker, B., Perrett, D. I., Baron-Cohen, S., & Marety, J. (2003). Being the target of another's emotion: A PET study. *Neuropsychologia, 41*(2), 139–146.

Widiger, T. A., & Sankis, L. M. (2000). Adult psychopathology. *Annual Review of Psychology, 51,* 377–404.

Wieseler-Frank, J., Maier, S. F., & Watkins, L. R. (2005). Immune-to-brain communication dynamically modulates pain: Physiological and pathological consequences. *Brain, Behavior, & Immunity, 19*(2), 104–111.

Wigfield, A., & Eccles, J. S. (2000). Expectancy-value of achievement motivation. *Contemporary Educational Psychology, 25*(1), 68–81.

Wild, B., Rodden, F. A., Grodd, W., & Ruch, W. (2003). Neural correlates of laughter and humour. *Brain, 126*(10), 2121–2138.

Wilfley, D. E., Welch, R. R., Stein, R., Spurrell, E., Cohen, L. R., Saelens, B. E., Dounchis, J. Z., Frank, M. A., Wiseman, C. V., & Matt, G. E. (2002). A randomized comparison of group cognitive-behavioral therapy and group interpersonal psychotherapy for the treatment of overweight individuals with binge-eating disorder. *Archives of General Psychiatry, 59*(8), 713–721.

Williams, A. L., Haber, D., Weaver, G. D., & Freeman, J. L. (1998). Altruistic activity: Does it make a difference in the senior center? *Activities, Adaptation and Aging, 22*(4), 31–39.

Williams, G., Cai, X. J., Elliott, J. C., & Harrold, J. A. (2004). Anabolic neuropeptides. *Physiology & Behavior, 81*(2), 211–222.

Williams, J. E., & Best, D. L. (1990). *Sex and psyche: Gender and self viewed cross-culturally.* Newbury Park, CA: Sage.

Williams, S. S. (2001). Sexual lying among college students in close and casual relationships. *Journal of Applied Social Psychology*, *31*(11), 2322–2338.

Williams, W. M., & Ceci, S. J. (1997). Are Americans becoming more or less alike? Trends in race, class, and ability differences in intelligence. *American Psychologist, 52,* 1126–1235.

Williamson, M. (1997). Circumcision anesthesia: A study of nursing implication for dorsal penile nerve block. *Pediatric Nursing, 23,* 59–63.

Willingham, D.B. (2001). *Cognition: The thinking animal.* Upper Saddle River, NJ: Prentice Hall.

Willis, J. et al. (2002). Forced use treatment of childhood hemiparesis. *Pediatrics, 110,* 94–101.

Wilson, A. E., Smith, M. D., Ross, H. S., & Ross, M. (2004). Young children's personal accounts of their sibling disputes. *Merrill-Palmer Quarterly, 50*(1), 39–60.

Wilson, C. (1967). Existential psychology: A novelist's approach. In J. F. T. Bugental (Ed.), *Challenges of humanistic psychology.* New York: McGraw-Hill.

Wilson, E. O. (1975). *Sociobiology: The new synthesis.* Cambridge, MA: Harvard University Press.

Wilson, E. O. (1978). *On human nature.* Cambridge, MA: Harvard University Press.

Wilson, R. S., Gilley, D. W., Bennett, D. A., Beckett, L. A., & Evans, D. A. (2000). Person-specific paths of cognitive decline in Alzheimer's disease and their relation to age. *Psychology & Aging, 15*(1), 18–28.

Wilson, T. G. (2005). Psychological treatment of eating disorders. *Annual Review of Clinical Psychology, 1,* 439–465.

Winerman, L. (2005). *A joint call for increased attention to behavior change in health care. Monitor on Psychology, 36*(5). [On-line]. Available: http://www.apa.org/monitor/may05/attention.html

Winterich, J. A. (2003). Sex, menopause, and culture: Sexual orientation and the meaning of menopause for women's sex lives. *Gender & Society, 17*(4), 627–642.

Witelson, S. F., Kigar, D. L., & Harvey, T. (1999). The exceptional brain of Albert Einstein. *The Lancet, 353,* 2149–2153.

Witt, S. D. (1997). Parental influences on children's socialization to gender roles. *Adolescence, 32,* 253–259.

Wixted, J. T. (2004). The psychology and neuroscience of forgetting. *Annual Review of Psychology, 55,* 235–269.

Wixted, J. T. (2005). A theory about why we forget what we once knew. *Current Directions in Psychological Science, 14*(1), 6–9.

Wolf, O. T., & Kirschbaum, C. (2003). Gedächtnisleistung im Alter: Welche Rolle Spielen die Steroidhormone? / Memory in aging: What role do steroid hormones play? *Psychologische Rundschau, 54*(3), 150–156.

Wolff, P. (1969). The natural history of crying and vocalization in early infancy. In B. M. Foss (Ed.), *Determinants of infant behavior* (Vol. IV). London: Methuen.

Wolpe, J., & Plaud, J. J. (1997). Pavlov's contributions to behavior therapy. *American Psychologist, 52*(9), 966–972.

Wood, D., Bruner, J. S., & Ross, G. (1976). The role of tutoring in problem solving. *Journal of Child Psychology & Psychiatry & Allied Disciplines, 17*(2), 89–100.

Wood, J. M., Lilienfeld, S. O., Nezworski, M. T., & Garb, H. N. (2001). Coming to grips with negative evidence for the comprehensive system for the Rorschach: A comment on Gacono, Loving, and Bodholdt, Ganellen, and Bornstein. *Journal of Personality Assessment, 77*(1), 48–70.

Wood, W., Christensen, P. N., Hebl, M. R., & Rothgerber, H. (1997). Conformity to sex-typed norms, affect, and the self-concept. *Journal of Personality & Social Psychology, 73*(3), 523–535.

Woods, S. C., Schwartz, M. W., Baskin, D. G., & Seeley, R. J. (2000). Food intake and the regulation of body weight. *Annual Review of Psychology, 51,* 255–277.

World Health Organization. (2000). *Epidemiology of Mental Disorders and Psychosocial Problems.* [On-line]. Available: http://www.who.int/dsa/cat98/men8.htm

World Health Organization. (2004). *Health hazards of tobacco: Some facts.* [On-line]. Available: http://www.who.int/archives/ntday/ntday96/pk96_3.htm

World Health Organization. (2004). *Tobacco free initiative.* [On-line]. Available: http://www.who.int/tobacco/about/en/

Wright, J. H., & Beck, A. T. (1999). Cognitive therapies. In R. E. Hales, S. C. Yudofsky, & J. A. Talbott (Eds.), *American Psychiatric Press textbook of psychiatry.* Washington, DC: American Psychiatric Press.

Wright, K. (2003). Relationships with death: The terminally ill talk about dying. *Journal of Marital & Family Therapy, 29*(4), 439–454.

Wright, T. A., Cropanzano, R., Denney, P. J., & Moline, G. L. (2002). When a happy worker is a productive worker: A preliminary examination of three models. *Canadian Journal of Behavioural Science, 34*(3), 146–150.

Wright, W. (1998). *Born that way: Genes, behavior, personality.* New York: Knopf.

Wu, W., Yamaura, T., Murakami, K., Murata, J., Matsumoto, K., Watanabe, H., & Saiki, I. (2000). Social isolation stress enhanced liver metastasis of murine colon 26–L5 carcinoma cells by suppressing immune responses in mice. *Life Sciences, 66*(19),1827–1838.

Wüst, S., Entringer, S., Federenko, I. S., Schlotz, W., & Hellhammer, D. H. (2003). Birth weight is associated with salivary cortisol responses to psychosocial stress in adult life. *Psychoneuroendocrinology. 30*(6), 591–598.

Wyatt, J. K., & Bootzin, R. R. (1994). Cognitive processing and sleep: Implications for enhancing job performance. *Human Performance, 7,* 119–139.

Yacoubian, G. S. Jr., Green, M. K., & Peters, R. J. (2003). Identifying the prevalence and correlates of ecstasy and other club drug (EOCD) use among high school seniors. *Journal of Ethnicity in Substance Abuse, 2*(2), 53–66.

Yamada, H. (1997). *Different games, different rules: Why Americans and Japanese misunderstand each other.* London: Oxford University Press.

Yarmey, A. D. (2004). Eyewitness recall and photo identification: A field experiment. *Psychology, Crime & Law, 10*(1), 53–68.

Yee, A. H., Fairchild, H. H., Weizmann, F., & Wyatt, G. E. (1993). Addressing psychology's problem with race. *American Psychologist, 48,* 1132–1140.

Yeh, S. J., & Lo, S. K. (2004). Living alone, social support, and feeling lonely among the elderly. *Social Behavior & Personality, 32*(2), 129–138.

Yesavage, J. A., Friedman, L., Kraemer, H., Tinklenberg, J. R., Salehi, A., Noda, A., Taylor, J. L., O'Hara, R., & Murphy, G. (2004). Sleep/wake disruption in Alzheimer's disease: APOE status and longitudinal course. *Journal of Geriatric Psychiatry & Neurology, 17*(1), 20–24.

Young, T. (1802). Color vision. *Philosophical Transactions of the Royal Society,* p. 12.

Young, T., Skatrud, J., & Peppard, P. E. (2004). Risk factors for obstructive sleep apnea in adults. *JAMA: Journal of the American Medical Association, 291*(16), 2013–2016.

Young, T., Turner, J., Denny, G., & Young, M. (2004). Examining external and internal poverty as antecedents of teen pregnancy. *American Journal of Health Behavior, 28*(4), 361–373.

Zaccaro, S. J., Foti, R. J., & Kenny, D. A. (1991). Self-monitoring and trait-based variance in leadership: An investigation of leader flexibility across multiple group situations. *Journal of Applied Psychology, 76*(2), 308–315.

Zagnoni, P. G., & Albano, C. (2002). Psychostimulants and epilepsy. *Epilepsia, 43,* 28–31.

Zahn-Waxler, C., Friedman, R. J., Cole, P. M., Mizuta, I., & Himura, N. (1996).

Japanese and United States preschool children's responses to conflict and distress. *Child Development, 67,* 2462–2477.

Zajonc, R. B. (1968). The attitudinal effects of mere exposure. *Journal of Personality and Social Psychology, 9,* 1–27.

Zajonc, R. B. (1998). Emotions. In D. T. Gilbert, S. T. Fiske, & G. Lindzey (Eds.), *The handbook of social psychology,* Vol. 2 (4th ed.) (pp. 591–632). Boston, MA: McGraw-Hill.

Zeanah, C. H. (2000). Disturbances of attachment in young children adopted from institutions. *Journal of Developmental & Behavioral Pediatrics, 21*(3), 230–236.

Zebrowitz, L. A., Hall, J. A., Murphy, N. A., & Rhodes, G. (2002). Looking smart and looking good: Facial cues to intelligence and their origins. *Personality & Social Psychology Bulletin, 28(2),* 238–249.

Zhukov, D. A., & Vinogradova, K. P. (2002). Learned helplessness or learned inactivity after inescapable stress? Interpretation depends on coping styles. *Integrative Physiological & Behavioral Science, 37(1),* 35–43.

Ziegler, J. M., Gustavson, C. R., Holzer, G. A., & Gruber, D. (1983). Anthelmintic-based taste aversions in wolves (Canis lupus). *Applied Animal Ethology, 3–sup-4,* 373–377.

Zimbardo, P. G. (1970). The human choice: Individuation, reason, and order versus deindividuation, impulse, and chaos. In W. J. Arnold & D. Levine (Eds.), *Nebraska symposium on motivation.* Lincoln: University of Nebraska Press.

Zimbardo, P. G. (1993). Stanford prison experiment: A 20-year retrospective. *Invited presentation at the meeting of the Western Psychological Association,* Phoenix, AZ.

Zimbardo, P. G., Ebbeson, E. B., & Maslach, C. (1977). *Influencing attitudes and changing behavior.* Reading, MA: Addison-Wesley.

Zucker, K. J. (2005). Gender identity disorder in children and adolescents. *Annual Review of Clinical Psychology, 1,* 467–492.

Zuckerman, L., &, Weiner, I. (2005). Maternal immune activation leads to behavioral and pharmacological changes in the adult offspring. *Journal of Psychiatric Research, 39*(3), 311–323.

Zuckerman, M. (1979). *Sensation seeking: Beyond the optimal level of arousal.* Hillsdale, NJ: Erlbaum.

Zuckerman, M. (1994). *Behavioral expressions and biosocial bases of sensation seeking.* New York: Cambridge University Press.

Zuckerman, M. (2004). The shaping of personality: Genes, environments, and chance encounters. *Journal of Personality Assessment, 82*(1), 11–22.

TEXT AND ILLUSTRATION CREDITS

Chapter 1 Figure 1.1: From Caccioppo, Petty, and Jarvis; *Dispositional Differences in Cognitive Motivation*, Psychological Bulletin, 119(2), pg. 197–253, © 1996 American Psychological Association. Table 1.4: From Plous, S., *An attitude survey of animal rights activists*, American Psychological Society (1991). Copyright © 1991 American Psychological Society. Reprinted by permission of the American Psychological Society and S. Plous.

Chapter 2 Figures 2.21 and 2.22: From Kimura, D.; *Sex Differences in the Brain*, Scientific American, Sept. 1992, pg. 120 © 1992 Jared Schneidman Designs.

Chapter 3 Figure 3.2: From Selye; *Stress Without Distress*, © 1974 Harper & Row Publishers. Critical Thinking/Active Learning Exercise (pg. 104): Robbins, S. P., *Organizational behavior: Concepts, controversies, and applications* ©1996 Prentice-Hall, Englewood Cliffs, NJ reprinted with permission. Table 3.1: From Holmes & Rahe, *The social readjustment rating scale*, © 1967 Journal of Psychosomatic Research, 11 pg. 213–218. Figure 3.5: Smoking shortens your life. Source: World Health Organization, 2004. http://www.who.int/topics/smoking/en. Table 3.2: From Pomponio, © 2002 John Wiley & Sons.

Chapter 4 Figure 4.17: From Luria, A. R., *Cognitive development: Its cultural and social foundations*, Harvard University Press (1976). Reprinted by permission of Harvard University Press. Copyright © 1976 by the President and Fellows of Harvard College. Figure 4.27: From Erdelyi, M.H. & Applebaum, A.G., *Cognitive Masking*, © 1973 Bulletin of the Psychonomic Society I, pg. 59–61.

Chapter 5 Figure 5.3: From Julien; *A Primer of Drug Action*, © 2000 W.H. Freeman. Figure 5.4: From William, Karacan, and Hursch; *Electroencephalogy of Human Sleep*, © 1974 John Wiley & Sons. Prose: From Benson, Herbert, "Systematic hypertension and the relaxation response". *New England Journal of Medicine*, 296, 1977. Reprinted with permission.

Chapter 7 Figure 7.8: From Bahrick, Bahrick, and Wittlinger; *Those Unforgettable High School Days*, Reprinted with permission from Psychology Today Magazine, © 1978 Sussex Publishers, Inc. Figure 7.11: From Murdock, Jr.; *The Serial Effect of Free Recall*, the Journal of Experimental Psychology, 64(5) pg. 482–488, Figure 1 pg. 483, © 1962 American Psychological Association.

Chapter 8 Try This Yourself pg. 281: From Shepard and Metzler; *Mental Rotation of Three-Dimensional Objects*, © 1971 American Association for the Advancement of Science. Figure 8.8: From Gardner; The Atlantic Monthly, Feb. 1999 pp. 67–76, © 1999 Howard Gardner. Table 8.6: From Sternberg; *Beyond IQ*, © 1985 Cambridge University Press. Figure 8.9: From Sternberg; *The Theory of Successful Intelligence*, Review of General Psychology, 3, pg. 292–316, © 1999 American Psychological Association.

Chapter 9 Figure 9.2: From Schaie; *The life course of Adult Intellectual Abilities*, American Psychologist, 49, pg. 304–313, © 1994 The American Psychological Association. Reprinted with permission. Table 9.5: From Clarke-Stewart and Friedman; *Child Development*, © 1985 John Wiley & Sons. Reprinted with permission. Figure 9.7: From Frankenburg & Dodds, *Denver II Training Manual* © 1991 Denver Developmental Materials. Figure 9.9: "Milestones in motor development." Source: WK Frankenburg, J Dobbs, P Archer, H Shapiro and B Bresnick, *The Denver II: a major revision and restandardization of theDenver Developmental Screening Test*. Pediatrics, Jan 1992; 89:91–97. Figure 9.10: From Tanner, J. M., Whitehouse, R. N., and Takaislu, M., "Male/female growth spurt." *Archives of Diseases in Childhood*, 41, 454–471, 1966. Reprinted with permission. Application: From Schaie, K. W. The life course of adult intellectual abilities. *American Psychologist*, 49, 304–313, 1994. Copyright © 1994 by the American Psychological Association. Reprinted with permission. Figure 9.13: From Chart of elderly achievers. In *The brain: A user's manual*. Copyright © 1982 by Diagram Visual Information.

Chapter 10 Achievement 10.1: Adapted from *Handbook of socialization theory and research* (1969) D. A. Goslin (ed.). Reprinted by permission of Houghton Mifflin. Table 10.1: Kohlberg's Stages of Moral Development. Source: Adapted from Kohlberg, L. "Stage and Sequence: The Cognitive Development Approach to Socialization." In D. A. Goslin, *The Handbook of Socialization Theory and Research*. Chicago: Rand McNally, 1969, p. 376 (Table 6.2). Table 10.2: From Papalia, Olds & Feldman; *Human Development* 8e, © 2001 McGraw-Hill. Reprinted with permission. Figure 10.2: From Brown, Adams, and Kellam, *Research in community and mental health* (1981). Reprinted with permission. Figure 10.3: From Cartensen et al.; *The Social Context of Emotion*, Annual Review of Geriatrics & Gerontology, 17, pg. 331, © 1997

Springer Publishing Company, Inc., New York 10012. Used by permission. Table 10.3: Are you in the right job? Source: Reproduced by special permission of the Publisher, Psychological Assessment Resources, Inc. from *Making Vocational Choices*, 3rd ed., by John L. Holland, PhD. Copyright 1973, 1985, 1992, 1997 by PAR, Inc. Further reproduction is prohibited without permission from PAR, Inc.

Chapter 11 Figure 11.2: From Miracle, Miracle, & Baumeister; *Human Sexuality: Meeting Your Basic Needs*, Study Guide Figure 10.4, pg. 302, Reprinted by Permission of Pearson Education, Inc. © 2003 Pearson Education. Figure 11.5: From Hebb, D. O., *Organization of behavior*, John Wiley and Sons, Inc. Copyright © 1949. Reprinted by permission of D. O. Hebb and J. Nichols Hebb Paul, sole executor and daughter. Figure 11.7: From Hat- field, Elaine and Rapson, Richard L, *Love, sex, and intimacy*. Copyright © 1993 by Elaine Hat- field and Richard L. Rapson. Reprinted by permission of Addison-Wesley Educational Publishers Inc. Figure 11.9: From Strong, DeVault, and Sayad, *Core concepts in human sexuality*. Mountain View, California: Mayfield. Reprinted by permission. Try This Yourself: From Hyde, Janis S., *Half the human experience: The psychology of women (fifth edition)*. Copyright © 1995 by D. C. Heath & Company, Lexington, Mass. Reprinted by permission of Houghton-Mifflin Co. Table 11.4: From Laumann et al.; *The Social Organization of Sexuality*, © 1994 University of Chicago Press.

Chapter 12 Table 12.1: From Diagnostic and Statistical Manual of Mental Disorders; fourth edition text revision, Washington DC, © 2000 American Psychiatric Association. Figure 12.4: From Murray, H. H. *Thematic Apperception Test (TAT) card*. Harvard University Press. Printed with permission. Figure 12.5: From Lepper, Greene, and Nisbett; *Undermining Children's Intrinsic Interest In Extrinsic Rewards*, Journal of Personality and Social Psychology, 8e, pg. 129–137, © 1973 American Psychological Association. Figure 12.8: From Maslow; "*A Theory of Motivation*," in Motivation and Personality, 3e © 1997. Reprinted by permission of Pearson Education, Inc., Upper Saddle River, NJ. Figure 12.15: From Plutchik; *Emotion: A Psychoevolutionary Synthesis*, © 1980 Published by Allyn and Bacon, Boston, MA. Copyright © 1980 by Pearson Education. Adapted by permission of the publisher. Try This Yourself, pg. 416–417: From Zuckerman; "*The Search for High Sensation*", Psychology

NAME INDEX

SUBJECT INDEX

Ablation for brain research, 37
Abnormal behavior, 498
  culture and, 498–500, 501
  identification of, 498–499
Absolute threshold, 133
Abu Ghraib prison scandal, 574, 575, 594, 598
Academic cheating, morality and, 366–367
Acceptance stage of dying, 383
Accidents, circadian rhythm disruptions and, 174–175
Accommodation, 341
  depth perception and, 156–157
  of eye, 138
Acetylcholine (ACh), 61
  actions of, 59
  nicotine and, 113
Achievement motivation, 434–435
Achievement tests, 484
Acquired immunodeficiency syndrome (AIDS), 414–415
ACSs. See Alternate states of consciousness (ASCs)
Action potentials, 56, 57
Activation-synthesis hypothesis of dreams, 182
Active learning, 227
Active listening in client-centered therapy, 546
Active reading, 43–45
Activity theory of aging, 379
Acupuncture, 134
AD. See Alzheimer's disease (AD)
Adaptation
  of body senses, 134
  of brain, 233
  diseases of, 105
  perceptual, 158–159
  sensory, 134–135
Addiction, 189. See also Alcoholism
  neurotransmitters and, 198
Adiponectin, hunger and, 430
Adolescence
  definition of, 337
  physical development in, 337–340
  pregnancy in, 375–376
Adolescent egocentrism, 343, 346
Adoption studies, 86
Adrenal cortex, stress and, 104
Adrenaline. See Epinephrine; Norepinephrine [noradrenaline] (NE)

Adrenal medulla, stress and, 103
Adulthood, 372–381
  families and, 374–377
  late, physical development in, 339–340
  marriage and, 372–374
  middle, physical development during, 338–339
  work and retirement and, 377–381
Adults Molested as Children (AMAC), 375, 547
Advertising, classical conditioning in, 236
Affect, flattened, in schizophrenia, 519
Affective component of attitudes, 577, 581
Affective disorders. See Mood disorders
African Americans
  aging and, 380
  androgyny among, 398
  eating disorders among, 433
  intelligence of, 317, 318, 319
  prejudice against, 208
  in psychology, 14
  Rosa Parks's disobedience and, 609–610
Aftereffects, color, 158, 159
2-AG, 195
Ageism, 339, 383
  cultural differences in, 379–380
Aggression, 601–604. See also Violence
  alcohol and, 115
  biological factors in, 601–602
  brain and, 71
  cognitive-social learning and, 241–252
  controlling or eliminating, 603
  displaced, prejudice as, 582–583
  gender differences in, 397
  psychological perspectives on, 13
  psychosocial factors in, 602–603
  punishment and, 223
Aging, theories of, 340, 379
Agonist drugs, 61, 196–197
Agoraphobia, 507–508
  treatment of, 553
Agreeableness as personality dimension, 460
AIDS (acquired immunodeficiency syndrome), 414–415

Alarm reaction, 105
Alcohol, 115–117, 188, 189
  binge drinking and, 115, 116–117
  cerebellar depression by, 70
  dependence on, signs of, 116
  effects of, 115
  maternal use of, prenatal development and, 334
  mixing with barbiturates, 191, 192
  sexual effects of, 411
Alcohol-dependence diseases, 498
Alcoholics Anonymous, 548
Alcoholism
  classical conditioning for treatment of, 237
  maternal, prenatal development and, 334
  treatment of, 552
Algorithms, 291
All-or-none law, 57
All-or-nothing thinking in depression, 544
Alpha waves, 177
Alternate states of consciousness (ASCs), 171. See also Psychoactive drugs; Sleep
  hypnosis and, 200–202
  medication and, 199–200
Alternative therapies, 563
Altruism, 604–606
Alzheimer's disease (AD), 339
  genetics of, 86
  memory in, 273
AMAC (Adults Molested as Children), 375, 547
Ambien, 185
American Psychological Association (APA)
  ethical guidelines of, 21, 23
  first woman president of, 14
Ames room illusion, 153
Amnesia. See also Forgetting
  anterograde, 272
  dissociative, 526
  retrograde, 272
  source, 267, 275
Amphetamines
  schizophrenia and, 521
  sexual effects of, 411
Amplitude
  of light waves, 136
  of sound waves, 140
Amygdala, 69, 71
  dreams and, 182
  emotion and, 437

fear and, 34
  memory and, 269, 271
Anal-expulsive personality, 470
Anal-retentive personality, 470
Anal stage, 470
Analytical intelligence, 308
Analytical psychology, 472
Androgyny, 397–398
Anger, epidemic of, in America, 603–604
Anger stage of dying, 383
Angina, 107
Anima/animus, 472
Animals
  attachment research using, 350
  language in, 286, 303–305
  personality in, 463–464
  respecting rights of, 21–22
Animism in preoperational stage, 344
Anonymity, deindividuation and, 599
Anorexia nervosa, 432–434
ANS. See Autonomic nervous system (ANS)
Antabuse, 552
Antagonist drugs, 61, 197
Anterograde amnesia, 272
Antianxiety drugs, 555, 556
Antidepressant drugs, 60, 514, 556–557
Antipsychotic drugs, 555–556
Antismoking laws, 113
Antisocial personality disorder, 528–529
Anxiety
  about death, 384
  basic, 473
  castration, 470
  performance, 409
  in posttraumatic stress disorder, 109
  test, 425, 552
Anxiety disorders, 506–611
Anxious/ambivalent children, 351
APA. See American Psychological Association (APA)
Aphasia
  Broca's, 75
  Wernicke's, 77
Aplysia, memory in, 269
Applied research, 17
Approach-approach conflict, 102
Approach-avoidance conflict, 102–103
Archetypes, 472

HISTORY OF PSYCHOLOGY TIMELINE FROM 1859 TO 1992

▶ 1859
Charles Darwin
Publishes *On the Origin of Species*, in which he outlines his highly influential theory of evolution through natural selection.

▶ 1879
Wilhelm Wundt
Creates the first psychology laboratory at the University of Leipzig in Germany, publishes the first psychology text, *Principles of Physiological Psychology*, and is considered the founder of experimental psychology.

▶ 1882
G. Stanley Hall
Receives first American Ph.D. in psychology, establishes what some consider the first American Psychology lab at Johns Hopkins University, and later founds the American Psychological Association.

▶ 1890
William James
Writes *The Principles of Psychology*, in which he promotes his psychological ideas that are later grouped together under the term functionalism.

▶ 1900
Sigmund Freud
Publishes *Interpretation of Dreams* and presents his ideas on psychoanalysis, which later became a very influential form of psychotherapy and theory of personality.

▶ 1905
Alfred Binet
Develops the first intelligence test in France. Lewis Terman later published the Stanford-Binet Intelligence Scale, which becomes the world's foremost intelligence test.

▶ 1906
Ivan Pavlov
Publishes his learning research on the salivation response in dogs, which later became known as classical conditioning.

▶ 1913
John Watson
Publishes his article "*Psychology as the Behaviorist Views It*," in which he describes the science of behaviorism.

▶ 1925
Wolfgang Kohler
Publishes *The Mentality of Apes*, in which he describes his theory of insight learning and becomes a major proponent of the Gestalt school of psychology.

▶ 1929
Edwin G. Boring
Publishes influential *A History of Experimental Psychology*.

▶ 1932
Jean Piaget
Publishes *The Moral Judgement of the Child* and later becomes a very important figure in child development and cognitive psychology.

▶ 1937
Gordon Allport
Publishes *Personality: A Psychological Interpretation*, and is considered the father of modern personality theory.

▶ 1954
Abraham Maslow
Helps found the school of humanistic psychology and later develops an influential theory of motivation.

▶ 1954
Kenneth B. Clark
Research with his wife Mamie is cited by the U.S. Supreme Court in a decision to overturn racial discrimination in schools. He later becomes the first African American president of the American Psychological Association.

▶ 1957
Leon Festinger
Develops what many consider the most important and comprehensive theory in social psychology—the theory of cognitive dissonance.

▶ 1958
Herbert Simon
Presents his views on information processing theory and later receives the Nobel Prize for his research on cognition.

▶ 1965
Stanley Milgram
Conducts highly controversial study of obedience and disobedience to authority, which many consider the most famous single study in psychology.

▶ 1970
Mary Ainsworth
Demonstrates the importance of attachment in the social development of children.

▶ 1980
David Hubel & Torsten Wiesel
Win the Nobel Prize for their work identifying cortical cells that respond to specific events in the visual field.

▶ 1987
Anne Anastasi
Author of the classic text on psychological testing, as well as numerous articles on psychological testing and assessment and is awarded the National Medal of Science.